The cmdty Yearbook 2024

cmdty by Barchart

www.barchart.com/cmdty

cmdty Editorial Board

President	Editor	Contributing Author
Eero A. Pikat	Christopher J. Lown	Richard W. Asplund

Barchart.com
222 South Riverside Plaza, Suite 810
Chicago, Illinois 60606
Phone: 877.247.4394
Fax: 312.939.4135
Website: www.barchart.com/cmdty
Email: commodities@barchart.com

Table of Contents

barchart

Barchart OnDemand
Market Data APIs

Our flexible cloud-based APIs make getting powerful data into your applications, workflows and products simple.

Power your business with Barchart OnDemand

Construct dynamic apps and tools

Integrate market data into your website

Simplify your current data strategy

Power charts with real-time or historical data

Get to market faster with built-in scale

Scale Your Business

Data is served through AWS ensuring reliability, redundancy, and built-in security that scales dynamically as your business grows

Always Compatible

Barchart OnDemand works with any operating system or programming language allowing you to start building in minutes

Reliable Performance

We embrace the cloud but also maintain physical data centers allowing us to cater to low latency requirements and provide a true physical back-up

Data Coverage

- Exchange Price Data
- Index Price Data
- Commodities
- Technical Data

- OTC & Cash Markets
- Economic Data
- News
- Weather

- Equities
- ETFs & Mutual Funds
- Forex
- Corporate Actions

Barchart Solutions
solutions@barchart.com
312.566.9235

Commodity Indexes

The Refinitiv/Core Commodity CRB® Index in 2023 traded sideways in a choppy range, consolidating below the 12-year high posted in June 2022. The Index closed 2023 down -5.0%, reversing a small portion of the sharp gains seen in the previous two years of +38.5% in 2021 and +19.5% in 2022.

Commodity prices in 2023 fell back as the US Federal Reserve, from early-2022 through mid-2023, raised the mid-point of its federal funds target range by a total of 5.25 percentage points to 5.375%. That interest rate hike reduced liquidity in the financial system and undercut US economic growth, putting downward pressure on commodity prices. Previously, commodity prices rallied sharply in the aftermath of the Covid pandemic that began in 2020 due to massive government monetary and fiscal stimulus measures, a booming global economy, and supply disruptions for many commodity markets.

Two of the six commodity sub-sectors closed higher in 2023, while four sub-sectors closed lower. The ranked returns in 2023 were as follows: Softs +32.9%, Precious Metals +2.1%, Industrials -0.4%, Livestock -5.2%, Grains -22.0%, and Energy -23.3%.

Energy

The Energy sub-sector includes Crude Oil, Heating Oil, and Natural Gas. The Energy sub-sector in 2023 fell by -23.3%, falling back after strong gains of +54.5% in 2021 and +20.3% in 2022. On a nearest-futures basis, crude oil in 2023 fell by -10.7%, gasoline fell by -14.5%, heating oil fell by -24.1%, and natural gas fell by -43.8%. Crude oil and petroleum products fell in 2023 as rising interest rates undercut global economic growth and energy demand. Natural gas prices fell as mild winter weather reduced heating demand.

Grains

The Grains and Oilseeds sub-sector includes Corn, Soybeans, and Wheat. The Grains and Oilseeds sub-sector in 2023 fell by -22.0%, falling back after five consecutive years of gains. On a nearest-futures basis, soybeans in 2023 fell by -14.9%, corn fell by -30.5%, and wheat fell by -20.7%.

Industrials

The Industrials sub-sector includes Copper and Cotton. The Industrials sub-sector in 2023 fell slightly by -0.4%, stabilizing after the sharp -20.3% decline seen in 2022. Copper in 2023 rose by +2.1%, reversing part of the -14.6% decline seen in 2022. Cotton in 2023 fell by -2.8%, adding to the -26.0% decline seen in 2022.

Livestock

The Livestock sub-sector includes Live Cattle and Lean Hogs. The Livestock sub-sector in 2023 closed lower by an average of -5.2%, reversing part of the +19.5% gain in 2021 and the +9.6% gain in 2022. On a nearest-futures basis, live cattle futures in 2023 closed up +12.2%, adding to the gains of +23.0% in 2021 and +11.5% in 2022. Lean hog futures in 2023 fell by -22.5%, reversing the gains of +15.9% in 2021 and +7.6% in 2022.

Precious Metals

The Precious Metals sub-sector includes Gold, Platinum, and Silver. The Precious Metals sub-sector in 2023 closed mildly higher by +2.1%, adding to the +4.7% gain seen in 2022. In 2023, gold rose by +13.4%, silver rose by +0.2%, and platinum fell by -7.3%.

Softs

The Softs sub-sector includes Cocoa, Coffee, Orange Juice, and Sugar #11. The Softs sub-sector in 2023 rallied by +32.9%, the fifth consecutive annual gain. In 2023, coffee closed up +12.6%, sugar closed up +2.7%, orange juice closed up +55.1%, and cocoa closed up +61.4%.

Unweighted Index of 23 Commodities: Hides, tallow, copper scrap, lead scrap, steel scrap, zinc, tin, burlap, cotton, print cloth, wool tops, rosin, rubber, hogs, steers, lard, butter, soybean oil, cocoa, corn, Kansas City wheat, Minneapolis wheat, and sugar.   Shaded areas indicate US recessions.

Unweighted Index of 23 Commodities.   Shaded areas indicate US recessions.

cmdty BLS Commodity Price Index   (1967=100)

Year	Jan.	Feb.	Mar.	Apr.	May	June	July	Aug.	Sept.	Oct.	Nov.	Dec.	Average
2014	457.25	465.09	487.18	497.58	500.90	495.60	491.20	484.78	479.78	465.82	455.62	445.75	477.21
2015	429.10	420.06	416.96	415.41	425.99	424.32	416.08	408.18	405.50	397.38	385.58	379.17	410.31
2016	377.44	385.09	396.03	410.34	413.55	416.74	411.76	409.65	402.79	401.09	411.91	424.17	405.05
2017	431.01	433.68	433.15	423.76	431.69	440.28	444.10	439.00	430.79	428.83	430.05	430.49	433.07
2018	438.94	441.96	442.40	441.42	444.86	445.13	434.09	417.91	412.39	416.93	415.79	413.91	430.48
2019	412.09	413.25	419.52	424.52	414.57	412.09	405.07	395.48	385.93	390.23	389.27	395.16	404.77
2020	406.45	401.38	394.37	347.43	362.02	364.77	368.33	383.96	402.56	410.48	419.93	435.95	391.47
2021	454.27	473.30	498.71	518.14	540.48	555.37	558.51	561.32	554.25	564.60	569.46	570.96	534.95
2022	583.18	598.12	627.49	637.85	633.50	618.54	579.83	587.38	567.58	557.75	560.41	557.79	592.45
2023	556.85	553.19	545.83	548.51	543.38	548.86	559.19	553.94	552.24	545.50	532.89	516.25	546.39

Average.   *Source: cmdty by Barchart*

CMDTY INDEXES

cmdty BLS Metals Price Index
Quarterly Cash as of 03/28/2024

QUARTERLY CASH
As of 03/28/2024
Chart High 1430.67 on 04/04/2022
Chart Low 66.00 on 06/21/1949

Unweighted Index of 5 Commodities: Copper scrap, lead scrap, steel scrap, tin, and zinc.   Shaded areas indicate US recessions.

cmdty BLS Metals Price Index
Weekly Cash as of 03/28/2024

WEEKLY CASH
As of 03/28/2024
Chart High 1430.67 on 04/04/2022
Chart Low 539.33 on 12/17/2015

Unweighted Index of 5 Commodities.   Shaded areas indicate US recessions.

cmdty BLS Metal Price Index   (1967=100)

Year	Jan.	Feb.	Mar.	Apr.	May	June	July	Aug.	Sept.	Oct.	Nov.	Dec.	Average
2014	925.99	920.45	900.88	905.67	908.51	897.46	921.84	922.59	903.65	876.01	856.97	836.99	898.08
2015	808.63	753.27	725.64	726.61	741.70	717.50	693.73	662.74	649.72	619.91	560.90	546.74	683.92
2016	549.39	582.24	628.81	662.38	675.30	676.25	698.07	709.14	710.14	705.02	762.46	807.03	680.52
2017	834.55	840.10	854.85	833.46	828.55	825.47	849.85	882.09	891.55	884.15	871.25	885.11	856.75
2018	938.18	960.91	957.84	970.72	955.27	954.43	896.38	848.71	816.40	837.13	842.37	840.64	901.58
2019	833.16	861.27	882.86	872.14	822.84	783.29	756.30	737.84	731.65	718.48	729.26	749.17	789.86
2020	766.00	732.19	688.18	636.00	651.04	680.58	713.15	739.13	775.25	780.54	806.50	886.86	737.95
2021	960.01	1,010.63	1,057.85	1,074.57	1,141.44	1,155.92	1,170.18	1,172.74	1,163.57	1,216.13	1,243.58	1,258.00	1,135.39
2022	1,266.43	1,279.96	1,365.47	1,398.48	1,262.43	1,197.29	1,046.36	1,061.52	981.39	946.24	960.10	1,010.85	1,148.04
2023	1,093.05	1,088.15	1,066.84	1,064.21	1,013.75	1,000.06	1,009.25	994.81	996.72	977.52	990.51	1,012.48	1,025.61

Average.   *Source: cmdty by Barchart*

cmdty BLS Textiles Price Index
Quarterly Cash as of 03/28/2024

QUARTERLY CASH
As of 03/28/2024
Chart High 390.65 on 05/04/2022
Chart Low 92.40 on 03/09/1971

Unweighted Index of 4 Commodities: Burlap, cotton, print cloth, and wool tops.   Shaded areas indicate US recessions.

cmdty BLS Textiles Price Index
Weekly Cash as of 03/28/2024

WEEKLY CASH
As of 03/28/2024
Chart High 390.65 on 05/04/2022
Chart Low 255.07 on 11/17/2014

Unweighted Index of 4 Commodities.   Shaded areas indicate US recessions.

cmdty BLS Textiles Price Index   (1967=100)

Year	Jan.	Feb.	Mar.	Apr.	May	June	July	Aug.	Sept.	Oct.	Nov.	Dec.	Average
2014	278.29	278.84	283.25	283.66	283.35	277.98	268.12	262.53	262.02	259.07	257.53	258.34	271.08
2015	257.16	260.85	261.80	265.21	265.95	267.24	267.42	267.46	263.78	266.74	268.72	271.68	265.33
2016	275.67	273.67	268.32	271.13	270.18	270.66	274.89	272.29	271.23	279.05	286.95	287.39	275.12
2017	292.60	296.28	299.77	300.52	299.68	293.69	290.06	292.93	295.83	293.56	295.50	301.02	295.95
2018	308.00	305.82	307.44	304.71	305.47	306.44	305.15	303.14	299.06	295.34	291.57	291.47	301.97
2019	288.81	288.83	292.65	293.47	284.62	281.83	275.44	268.15	269.65	271.96	273.52	277.23	280.51
2020	283.37	282.02	270.53	266.59	271.63	277.34	282.17	284.87	285.48	291.03	295.42	300.70	282.60
2021	308.57	317.15	319.60	320.76	323.43	326.35	331.00	334.13	337.65	351.79	359.31	353.65	331.95
2022	362.31	367.39	371.60	379.59	384.06	374.64	352.60	358.12	344.57	325.61	325.75	323.76	355.83
2023	324.20	321.22	317.78	322.68	321.81	319.73	320.06	321.00	320.12	319.75	314.67	316.76	319.98

Average.   *Source: cmdty by Barchart*

CMDTY INDEXES

cmdty BLS Industrials Price Index
Quarterly Cash as of 03/28/2024

QUARTERLY CASH
As of 03/28/2024
Chart High 689.01 on 04/04/2022
Chart Low 86.30 on 06/28/1949

Unweighted Index of 13 Commodities: Hides, tallow, copper scrap, lead scrap, steel scrap, zinc, tin, burlap, cotton, print cloth, wool tops, rosin, and rubber.   Shaded areas indicate US recessions.

cmdty BLS Industrials Price Index
Weekly Cash as of 03/28/2024

WEEKLY CASH
As of 03/28/2024
Chart High 689.01 on 04/04/2022
Chart Low 397.92 on 11/23/2015

Unweighted Index of 13 Commodities.   Shaded areas indicate US recessions.

cmdty BLS Industrials Price Index   (1967=100)

Year	Jan.	Feb.	Mar.	Apr.	May	June	July	Aug.	Sept.	Oct.	Nov.	Dec.	Average
2014	528.48	527.92	535.44	541.50	542.77	534.33	532.02	529.81	520.65	506.18	504.60	497.80	525.13
2015	485.52	474.22	470.13	467.83	471.58	466.96	451.80	443.96	439.86	424.27	403.04	401.58	450.06
2016	409.74	421.84	436.56	450.36	452.52	451.96	457.45	456.93	456.68	460.60	484.07	494.37	452.76
2017	503.07	506.20	510.83	505.47	504.70	502.57	504.42	511.92	513.67	502.70	499.14	506.88	505.96
2018	522.93	524.51	525.49	524.02	519.13	522.01	509.95	496.98	483.37	483.58	484.68	485.14	506.82
2019	479.23	482.58	490.35	490.65	471.54	458.61	449.63	445.49	442.17	438.31	438.36	446.51	461.12
2020	461.10	457.03	434.96	413.57	418.55	418.45	426.77	444.66	457.42	465.93	475.68	502.37	448.04
2021	527.24	546.05	563.14	569.68	586.71	605.53	613.90	619.74	618.97	640.13	648.37	640.69	598.35
2022	645.69	648.80	671.38	682.65	661.92	642.27	599.13	607.90	580.53	560.64	563.83	570.90	619.64
2023	579.04	570.02	559.85	560.22	552.43	550.14	556.95	556.21	556.78	546.73	540.06	540.80	555.77

Average.   *Source: cmdty by Barchart*

Unweighted Index of 10 Commodities: Hogs, steers, lard, butter, soybean oil, cocoa, corn, Kansas City wheat, Minneapolis wheat, and sugar.   Shaded areas indicate US recessions.

Unweighted Index of 10 Commodities.   Shaded areas indicate US recessions.

cmdty BLS Foodstuffs Price Index   (1967=100)

Year	Jan.	Feb.	Mar.	Apr.	May	June	July	Aug.	Sept.	Oct.	Nov.	Dec.	Average
2014	370.69	387.03	424.76	440.01	445.70	444.24	437.38	426.08	426.02	412.87	392.84	379.75	415.61
2015	358.69	352.29	350.34	349.61	367.54	369.24	369.14	361.25	360.32	361.29	361.42	348.87	359.17
2016	334.98	337.31	343.78	358.46	362.83	370.40	353.47	349.64	335.73	328.19	326.03	339.73	345.05
2017	344.49	346.60	341.09	328.23	344.21	363.46	369.20	351.43	333.86	340.67	346.50	339.79	345.79
2018	340.59	344.84	344.76	344.32	355.67	353.36	343.73	325.14	327.65	336.27	332.96	328.82	339.84
2019	331.10	330.08	334.65	344.14	343.99	352.85	348.13	332.80	316.85	329.71	327.67	330.97	335.25
2020	338.49	332.49	320.43	284.57	293.39	298.94	297.53	310.40	334.49	341.57	350.47	354.96	321.48
2021	366.06	384.70	418.16	451.53	479.68	489.80	486.85	486.15	472.21	470.62	471.75	483.05	455.05
2022	503.07	531.47	568.68	577.88	594.19	585.39	552.61	558.94	548.99	553.22	555.09	538.98	555.71
2023	525.93	529.38	525.80	531.63	530.19	546.62	562.02	550.27	545.33	543.33	522.31	482.59	532.95

Average.   *Source: cmdty by Barchart*

CMDTY INDEXES

cmdty BLS Fats and Oils Price Index
Quarterly Cash as of 03/28/2024

QUARTERLY CASH
As of 03/28/2024
Chart High 868.33 on 05/19/2022
Chart Low 88.00 on 10/08/1968

Unweighted Index of 4 Commodities: Butter, cottonseed oil, lard, and tallow.   Shaded areas indicate US recessions.

cmdty BLS Fats and Oils Price Index
Weekly Cash as of 03/28/2024

WEEKLY CASH
As of 03/28/2024
Chart High 868.33 on 05/19/2022
Chart Low 307.93 on 04/15/2020

Unweighted Index of 4 Commodities.   Shaded areas indicate US recessions.

cmdty BLS Fats and Oils Price Index   (1967=100)

Year	Jan.	Feb.	Mar.	Apr.	May	June	July	Aug.	Sept.	Oct.	Nov.	Dec.	Average
2014	383.34	388.71	444.35	482.96	511.46	492.95	483.40	482.99	488.24	444.49	416.67	383.76	450.28
2015	345.69	348.02	348.93	342.31	357.64	363.99	355.78	368.38	378.59	356.58	362.48	345.06	356.12
2016	325.81	337.32	352.31	387.99	386.67	491.94	378.62	384.16	381.65	376.69	394.32	405.54	383.59
2017	390.86	379.46	372.45	367.41	387.20	417.41	431.12	432.99	422.43	398.69	392.43	390.23	398.56
2018	372.28	362.23	365.82	365.04	364.99	368.91	368.71	370.93	360.64	360.00	365.24	363.08	365.66
2019	362.32	366.62	364.16	366.46	368.12	377.58	378.90	379.58	366.11	360.90	350.84	358.63	366.69
2020	372.49	371.78	349.23	315.98	339.57	347.49	342.96	368.86	380.44	377.46	385.37	413.22	363.74
2021	424.74	446.78	523.90	574.71	609.44	641.69	641.84	655.41	659.00	678.44	681.08	662.18	599.93
2022	732.60	760.02	803.67	818.63	855.02	848.92	811.05	828.36	826.21	831.71	833.34	776.71	810.52
2023	743.85	714.86	685.35	669.81	665.61	681.32	746.28	765.69	790.39	767.97	686.14	603.96	710.10

Average.   *Source: cmdty by Barchart*

cmdty BLS Livestock Price Index
Quarterly Cash as of 03/28/2024

QUARTERLY CASH
As of 03/28/2024
Chart High 738.33 on 08/22/2022
Chart Low 87.80 on 08/06/1968

Unweighted Index of 5 Commodities: Hides, hogs, lard, steers, and tallow.   Shaded areas indicate US recessions.

cmdty BLS Livestock Price Index
Weekly Cash as of 03/28/2024

WEEKLY CASH
As of 03/28/2024
Chart High 738.33 on 08/22/2022
Chart Low 301.48 on 07/01/2020

Unweighted Index of 5 Commodities.   Shaded areas indicate US recessions.

cmdty BLS Livestock Price Index   (1967=100)

Year	Jan.	Feb.	Mar.	Apr.	May	June	July	Aug.	Sept.	Oct.	Nov.	Dec.	Average
2014	543.02	557.63	645.13	685.62	689.00	676.46	683.71	661.15	656.18	639.12	613.66	573.26	635.33
2015	523.85	500.96	503.91	491.27	517.22	513.03	484.28	490.90	477.86	452.68	419.99	404.96	481.74
2016	410.40	432.01	453.40	479.17	491.47	491.94	473.49	461.17	443.34	423.46	428.92	449.89	453.22
2017	459.17	470.78	466.97	452.02	478.49	506.82	500.73	478.13	439.94	438.59	442.67	443.87	464.85
2018	450.12	447.67	433.39	415.52	427.78	447.09	441.73	396.16	401.17	409.82	406.81	396.83	422.84
2019	399.14	388.75	407.21	437.39	426.55	409.36	408.37	410.57	370.18	379.01	360.20	373.81	397.55
2020	400.48	404.58	394.37	347.43	351.93	319.36	318.49	358.55	396.49	419.00	418.06	427.44	379.68
2021	442.88	470.67	524.44	573.09	592.29	659.71	658.18	665.79	643.40	625.72	608.99	605.67	589.24
2022	618.76	657.61	690.72	687.49	708.61	711.95	718.04	728.27	691.62	690.80	685.48	669.79	688.26
2023	628.96	619.57	613.19	601.86	620.15	645.18	671.23	665.41	661.38	635.63	596.40	514.25	622.77

Average.   *Source: cmdty by Barchart*

CMDTY INDEXES

S&P Goldman Sachs Commodity Index
Quarterly Cash as of 03/28/2024

QUARTERLY CASH
As of 03/28/2024
Chart High 893.86 on 07/03/2008
Chart Low 98.92 on 05/26/1970

Standard & Poor's GSCI is a registered trademark of Standard & Poor's Financial Services LLC ("S&P"), a subsidiary of The McGraw-Hill Companies, Inc.
Currently the S&P GSCI includes 24 commodity nearby futures contracts.   Shaded areas indicate US recessions.

S&P Goldman Sachs Commodity Index
Weekly Cash as of 03/28/2024

WEEKLY CASH
As of 03/28/2024
Chart High 853.27 on 03/08/2022
Chart Low 217.95 on 04/21/2020

Standard & Poor's GSCI is a registered trademark of Standard & Poor's Financial Services LLC ("S&P"), a subsidiary of The McGraw-Hill Companies, Inc.
Currently the S&P GSCI includes 24 commodity nearby futures contracts.   Shaded areas indicate US recessions.

S&P GSCI Index   (12/31/1969=100)

Year	Jan.	Feb.	Mar.	Apr.	May	June	July	Aug.	Sept.	Oct.	Nov.	Dec.	Average
2014	617.20	640.25	645.88	653.19	652.42	657.64	636.14	609.55	588.76	548.78	521.86	449.57	601.77
2015	388.27	412.87	403.39	423.64	443.38	436.70	402.75	360.85	362.48	364.45	345.91	315.98	388.39
2016	289.97	293.46	324.99	337.79	361.37	377.36	354.83	353.51	353.18	372.96	359.92	391.89	347.60
2017	396.61	402.05	385.28	390.60	381.04	364.63	374.75	380.46	394.88	401.99	425.01	425.39	393.56
2018	452.52	444.49	446.07	463.57	484.33	472.75	465.94	459.42	470.55	479.81	428.86	396.52	455.40
2019	401.35	417.75	430.35	449.24	434.87	412.23	421.95	398.31	410.88	405.91	417.71	428.12	419.06
2020	420.61	386.88	297.14	258.35	284.90	320.86	338.20	353.55	348.00	354.70	368.28	396.92	344.03
2021	428.99	464.45	478.68	485.80	516.16	528.92	530.65	520.37	538.90	583.89	573.46	545.64	516.33
2022	596.98	645.02	746.61	740.08	764.01	773.66	677.38	668.93	631.62	638.30	632.79	594.99	675.86
2023	598.91	585.60	565.51	582.25	544.06	542.98	566.92	585.07	611.28	587.89	563.07	537.70	572.60

Average.   *Source: CME Group; Chicago Mercantile Ezchange*

Bloomberg Commodity Index
Quarterly Cash as of 03/28/2024

QUARTERLY CASH
As of 03/28/2024
Chart High 238.521 on 07/03/2008
Chart Low 11.490 on 08/19/1940

Bloomberg and Bloomberg Indices are trademarks or service marks of Bloomberg Finance L.P.   12/31/1990=100   Shaded areas indicate US recessions.

Bloomberg Commodity Index
Weekly Cash as of 03/28/2024

WEEKLY CASH
As of 03/28/2024
Chart High 143.670 on 02/01/2013
Chart Low 58.870 on 04/22/2020

Bloomberg and Bloomberg Indices are trademarks or service marks of Bloomberg Finance L.P.   12/31/1990=100   Shaded areas indicate US recessions.

Bloomberg Commodity Index   (12/31/1990=100)

Year	Jan.	Feb.	Mar.	Apr.	May	June	July	Aug.	Sept.	Oct.	Nov.	Dec.	Average
2014	125.24	130.97	134.71	136.56	135.81	134.75	130.44	126.39	121.57	117.97	116.95	109.39	126.73
2015	102.09	102.74	99.64	100.95	103.32	100.92	96.70	89.46	88.43	88.72	83.31	78.74	94.58
2016	75.41	75.36	79.16	81.15	84.40	88.25	85.82	84.51	84.08	85.97	83.99	87.30	82.95
2017	87.80	88.15	85.30	84.99	83.53	81.21	83.04	83.40	85.03	85.16	86.78	85.14	84.96
2018	89.02	88.02	87.59	88.72	90.37	88.31	84.53	83.90	83.50	85.94	83.10	80.58	86.13
2019	79.75	80.90	81.35	81.88	79.22	78.20	79.38	76.81	78.81	78.54	79.05	79.49	79.45
2020	79.01	74.65	65.70	61.54	62.23	64.17	67.10	71.48	71.66	72.55	73.68	75.75	69.96
2021	80.12	84.29	84.74	86.53	92.29	93.34	94.57	94.54	97.88	103.57	102.23	97.27	92.61
2022	103.83	111.11	125.48	128.54	130.12	128.91	116.02	121.45	116.22	113.81	115.71	112.65	118.65
2023	110.74	107.42	104.43	106.33	101.31	101.58	104.77	105.20	106.47	104.23	102.78	98.81	104.50

Average.   Bloomberg and Bloomberg Indices are trademarks or service marks of Bloomberg Finance L.P.   Formerly the Dow Jones-UBS Commodity Index.   *Source: CME Group; Chicago Board of Trade*

The US economy remained generally strong in 2023 despite the sharp increase in interest rates by the US Federal Reserve through mid-2023. However, the US macroeconomic situation has not yet returned to normal following the massive pandemic disruptions.

Due to the Covid pandemic, which began in early 2020, the Fed was forced to slash interest rates to near-zero in 2020, and the US government pumped a massive $5 trillion of stimulus into the economy to soften the blow from the widespread pandemic shutdowns. US real GDP growth plunged by -5.3% (quarter-on-quarter annualized) in Q1-2020 and -28.0% in Q2-2020 due to the pandemic shutdowns. However, US GDP rebounded sharply by +34.8% in Q3-2020 as the government's massive stimulus programs took effect.

The massive stimulus provided by the US government resulted in a serious inflation outbreak that forced the Fed to raise interest rates beginning in early 2022. The US CPI (consumer price index) soared to a 4-decade high of +9.1% yr/yr in June 2022, and the core CPI (ex food and energy) peaked at +6.6% yr/yr in September 2022.

The inflation surge was caused by the booming global economy, high commodity and raw material costs, supply chain disruptions that sparked shortages in many industries, and excess liquidity in the financial system.

The Fed responded to the inflation surge by progressively raising the mid-point of its federal funds target range from the 0.125% level that prevailed during the pandemic to a peak of 5.375% by June 2023. That overall 5.25 percentage point rate hike, in the space of just 1-1/2 years, was the Fed's largest rate hike cycle since 1980, when inflation had spiked up to +14.8%.

The US economy saw a small technical recession in Q1-Q2 2022 but then showed positive quarterly GDP growth through the remainder of 2022 and 2023, despite the Fed's steady series of rate hikes that lasted into mid-2023.

The Fed's rate-hike regime caused a big problem in March 2023 with the failure of California-based Silicon Valley Bank, one of the 20 largest US banks. That failure sparked a run on other regional US banks and also brought down NY-based Signature Bank and San Francisco-based First Republic Bank.

S&P 500 Index

The run on Silicon Valley Bank was caused by the fact that its balance sheet had a big hole after it had loaded up on Treasury notes and bonds during the pandemic that lost value when the Fed raised interest rates sharply beginning in 2022. The markets were worried that other large financial institutions might be in a similar predicament.

The US government managed to halt the run on regional banks with an unlimited extension of its deposit insurance program to guarantee against any losses by individuals or businesses in their checking and savings deposits at banks. Yet the US banking system remained under a separate threat from exposure to more than $1 trillion in office building debt, some of which will likely fall into default over the next several years.

In some better news, the US inflation figures by mid-2023 eased, and the Fed was able to halt its rate-hike regime. By the end of 2023, the US CPI had eased to +3.4% yr/yr, and the core CPI had eased to +3.9% yr/yr.

Those inflation figures were still well above the Fed's inflation target rate of +2%. However, the decline in the CPI figures was enough for the Fed to halt its rate-hike regime to see if inflation would continue to fall back towards its +2% target.

The markets currently expect the Fed to cut interest rates by three-quarters of a percentage point in 2024 due to expectations of fading inflation and weak GDP growth. The Fed believes the longer-run neutral rate for the federal funds rate is 2.5%, as seen in the FOMC's "Summary of

US Real GDP 2000-2023 (annual)

10-year T-Note Yield

Refinitiv/Core Commodity CRB® Index (CRY)

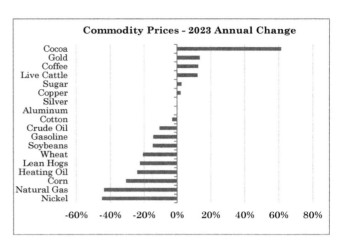

Commodity Prices - 2023 Annual Change

Economic Projections." That implies that the Fed expects to cut the funds rate by a total of nearly three percentage points over the next several years to the neutral level of 2.5% from the current mid-point target of 5.375%.

The markets currently expect US GDP growth to be tepid in 2024 and 2025 due to the current high level of interest rates. The current consensus is for US GDP growth rates of +2.1% in 2024 and +1.7% in 2025, which would be below the 2023 GDP growth of +2.5% and the post-war average of +3.3%.

The 10-year T-note yield in the latter half of 2023 surged to a 16-year high of 5.02% in October 2023 but then eased to close 2023 at 3.88%, virtually unchanged from the previous year's close. The 10-year T-note yield spiked higher in mid-2023 due to the Fed's hawkish policy and concern about inflation. However, the 10-year T-note yield fell back in late 2023 as inflation eased and the markets looked forward to interest rate cuts in 2024.

The dollar index surged to a 21-year high in September 2022 but then fell back and traded in a choppy range during 2023, finally closing the year mildly lower by -2.2% yr/yr. The dollar index surged during 2022 as the Fed raised interest rates much faster than other major central banks, thus boosting the dollar's interest rate differentials. However, the dollar index then fell back during 2023 as the Fed completed its rate-hike cycle in mid-2023, and the markets pivoted towards expecting Fed rate cuts in 2024.

The US stock market rallied during 2023 and closed

the year up +24.2% yr/yr, overcoming nearly all of the losses seen in 2022. The stock market rallied as the Fed completed its interest rate hike cycle and the markets looked forward to interest rate cuts in 2024. The markets were also pleased that the US economy held up better than expected in 2023.

The tech-heavy Nasdaq 100 index showed an even bigger rally and closed the year up +53.8%. Tech stocks were driven higher by a frenzy over artificial intelligence and improved profitability as many tech companies implemented cost-cutting measures.

Commodity prices in 2023 traded mostly sideways on consolidation after the sharp post-pandemic rally that was driven by the massive stimulus by the US government. The Refinitiv/CoreCommodity CRB Index® in 2023 closed the year down -5.0% yr/yr, giving back a small part of the sharp rallies of +19.5% seen in 2022 and +38.5% in 2021.

Gold prices rallied in late 2023 and closed the year up +13.% yr/yr as the dollar weakened and the markets looked towards interest rate cuts in 2024.

Crude oil prices showed strength in mid-2023 but fell later in the year to close down -10.7% yr/yr. Crude oil prices in 2023 remained supported by production cuts by the OPEC+ cartel. However, oil prices faded in late 2023 as the markets anticipated weak demand and a world oil surplus. Also, OPEC+ in 2023 did not cut production by as much as they claimed they would in their agreements.

Dollar Index

WTI Crude Oil Nearest-Futures Price

Conversion Factors

Commonly Used Agricultural Weights and Measurements

Bushel Weights:
Corn, Sorghum and Rye = 56 lbs.
Wheat and Soybeans = 60 lbs.
Canola = 50 lbs.
Barley Grain = 48 lbs.
Barley Malt = 34 lbs.
Oats = 32 lbs.

Bushels to tonnes:
Corn, Sorghum and Rye = bushels x 0.0254
Wheat and Soybeans = bushels x 0.027216
Barley Grain = bushels x 0.021772
Oats = bushels x 0.014515

1 tonne (metric ton) equals:
2204.622 lbs.
1,000 kilograms
22.046 hundredweight
10 quintals

Ethanol
1 bushel Corn = 2.75 gallons Ethanol = 18 lbs Dried Distillers Grain
1 tonne Corn = 101.0 gallons Ethanol = 661 lbs Dried Distillers Grain
1 tonne Sugar = 149.3 gallons Ethanol

1 tonne (metric ton) equals:
39.3679 bushels of Corn, Sorghum or Rye
36.7437 bushels of Wheat or Soybeans
22.046 hundredweight
45.9296 bushels of Barley Grain
68.8944 bushels of Oats
4.5929 Cotton bales (the statistical bale used by the USDA and ICAC contains a net weight of 480 pounds of lint)

Area Measurements:
1 acre = 43,560 square feet = 0.040694 hectare
1 hectare = 2.4710 acres = 10,000 square meters
640 acres = 1 square mile = 259 hectares

Yields:
Rye, Corn: bushels per acre x 0.6277 = quintals per hectare
Wheat: bushels per acre x 0.6725 = quintals per hectare
Barley Grain: bushels per acre x 0.538 = quintals per hectare
Oats: bushels per acre x 0.3587 = quintals per hectare

Commonly Used Weights

The troy, avoirdupois and apothecaries' grains are identical in U.S. and British weight systems, equal to 0.0648 gram in the metric system. One avoirdupois ounce equals 437.5 grains. The troy and apothecaries' ounces equal 480 grains, and their pounds contain 12 ounces.

Troy weights and conversions:
24 grains = 1 pennyweigh
20 pennyweights = 1 ounce
12 ounces = 1 pound
1 troy ounce = 31.103 grams
1 troy ounce = 0.0311033 kilogram
1 troy pound = 0.37224 kilogram
1 kilogram = 32.1507 troy ounces
1 tonne = 32,151 troy ounces

Avoirdupois weights and conversions:
27 11/32 grains = 1 dram
16 drams = 1 ounce
16 ounces = 1 lb.
1 lb. = 7,000 grains
14 lbs. = 1 stone (British)
100 lbs. = 1 hundredweight (U.S.)
112 lbs. = 8 stone = 1 hundredweight (British)
2,000 lbs. = 1 short ton (U.S. ton)
2,240 lbs. = 1 long ton (British ton)
160 stone = 1 long ton
20 hundredweight = 1 ton
1 lb. = 0.4536 kilogram
1 hundredweight (cwt.) = 45.359 kilograms
1 short ton = 907.18 kilograms
1 long ton = 1,016.05 kilograms

Metric weights and conversions:
1,000 grams = 1 kilogram
100 kilograms = 1 quintal
1 tonne = 1,000 kilograms = 10 quintals
1 kilogram = 2.204622 lbs.
1 quintal = 220.462 lbs.
1 tonne = 2204.6 lbs.
1 tonne = 1.102 short tons
1 tonne = 0.9842 long ton

U.S. dry volumes and conversions:
1 pint = 33.6 cubic inches = 0.5506 liter
2 pints = 1 quart = 1.1012 liters
8 quarts = 1 peck = 8.8098 liters
4 pecks = 1 bushel = 35.2391 liters
1 cubic foot = 28.3169 liters

U.S. liquid volumes and conversions:
1 ounce = 1.8047 cubic inches = 29.6 milliliters
1 cup = 8 ounces = 0.24 liter = 237 milliliters
1 pint = 16 ounces = 0.48 liter = 473 milliliters
1 quart = 2 pints = 0.946 liter = 946 milliliters
1 gallon = 4 quarts = 231 cubic inches = 3.785 liters
1 milliliter = 0.033815 fluid ounce
1 liter = 1.0567 quarts = 1,000 milliliters
1 liter = 33.815 fluid ounces
1 imperial gallon = 277.42 cubic inches = 1.2 U.S. gallons = 4.546 liters

Energy Conversion Factors

U.S. Crude Oil (average gravity)
1 U.S. barrel = 42 U.S. gallons
1 short ton = 6.65 barrels
1 tonne = 7.33 barrels

Barrels per tonne for various origins

Abu Dhabi	7.624
Algeria	7.661
Angola	7.206
Australia	7.775
Bahrain	7.335
Brunei	7.334
Canada	7.428
Dubai	7.295
Ecuador	7.580
Gabon	7.245
Indonesia	7.348
Iran	7.370
Iraq	7.453
Kuwait	7.261
Libya	7.615
Mexico	7.104
Neutral Zone	6.825
Nigeria	7.410
Norway	7.444
Oman	7.390
Qatar	7.573
Romania	7.453
Saudi Arabia	7.338
Trinidad	6.989
Tunisia	7.709
United Arab Emirates	7.522
United Kingdom	7.279
United States	7.418
Former Soviet Union	7.350
Venezuela	7.005
Zaire	7.206

Barrels per tonne of refined products:

aviation gasoline	8.90
motor gasoline	8.50
kerosene	7.75
jet fuel	8.00
distillate, including diesel	7.46
(continued above)	

residual fuel oil	6.45
lubricating oil	7.00
grease	6.30
white spirits	8.50
paraffin oil	7.14
paraffin wax	7.87
petrolatum	7.87
asphalt and road oil	6.06
petroleum coke	5.50
bitumen	6.06
LPG	11.6

Approximate heat content of refined products:
(Million Btu per barrel, 1 British thermal unit is the amount of heat required to raise the temperature of 1 pound of water 1 degree F.)

Petroleum Product	Heat Content
asphalt	6.636
aviation gasoline	5.048
butane	4.326
distillate fuel oil	5.825
ethane	3.082
isobutane	3.974
jet fuel, kerosene	5.670
jet fuel, naptha	5.355
kerosene	5.670
lubricants	6.065
motor gasoline	5.253
natural gasoline	4.620
pentanes plus	4.620

Petrochemical feedstocks:

naptha less than 401*F	5.248
other oils equal to or greater than 401*F	5.825
still gas	6.000
petroleum coke	6.024
plant condensate	5.418
propane	3.836
residual fuel oil	6.287
special napthas	5.248
unfinished oils	5.825
unfractionated steam	5.418
waxes	5.537

Source: U.S. Department of Energy

Natural Gas Conversions

Although there are approximately 1,031 Btu in a cubic foot of gas, for most applications, the following conversions are sufficient:

Cubic Feet			MMBtu		
1,000	(one thousand cubic feet)	=	1 Mcf	=	1
1,000,000	(one million cubic feet)	=	1 MMcf	=	1,000
10,000,000	(ten million cubic feet)	=	10 MMcf	=	10,000
1,000,000,000	(one billion cubic feet)	=	1 Bcf	=	1,000,000
1,000,000,000,000	(one trillion cubic feet)	=	1 Tcf	=	1,000,000,000

Acknowledgments

The editors wish to thank the following for source material:

Agricultural Marketing Service (AMS)

Agricultural Research Service (ARS)

American Bureau of Metal Statistics, Inc. (ABMS)

American Metal Market (AMM)

Bureau of the Census

Bureau of Economic Analysis (BEA)

Bureau of Labor Statistics (BLS)

Chicago Board of Trade (CBT)

Chicago Mercantile Exchange (CME / IMM / IOM)

Commodity Credit Corporation (CCC)

Commodity Futures Trading Commision (CFTC)

Economic Research Service (ERS)

Farm Service Agency (FSA)

Federal Reserve Bank of St. Louis

Food and Agriculture Organization of the United Nations (FAO)

Foreign Agricultural Service (FAS)

Futures Industry Association (FIA)

ICE Futures U.S, Canada, Europe (ICE)

International Cotton Advisory Committee (ICAC)

International Cocoa Organization (ICCO)

Minneapolis Grain Exchange (MGEX)

National Agricultural Statistics Service (NASS)

New York Mercantile Exchange (NYMEX)

Oil World

The Organisation for Economic Co-Operation and Development (OECD)

The Silver Institute

United Nations (UN)

United States Department of Agriculture (USDA)

Wall Street Journal (WSJ)

Aluminum

Aluminum (atomic symbol Al) is a silvery, lightweight metal that is the most abundant metallic element in the earth's crust. Aluminum was first isolated in 1825 by a Danish chemist, Hans Christian Oersted, using a chemical process involving a potassium amalgam. A German chemist, Friedrich Woehler, improved Oersted's process by using metallic potassium in 1827. He was the first to show aluminum's lightness. In France, Henri Sainte-Claire Deville isolated the metal by reducing aluminum chloride with sodium and established a large-scale experimental plant in 1854. He displayed pure aluminum at the Paris Exposition of 1855. In 1886, Charles Martin Hall in the U.S. and Paul L.T. Heroult in France simultaneously discovered the first practical method for producing aluminum through electrolytic reduction, which is still the primary method of aluminum production today.

By volume, aluminum weighs less than a third as much as steel. This high strength-to-weight ratio makes aluminum a good choice for the construction of aircraft, railroad cars, and automobiles. Aluminum is used in cooking utensils and the pistons of internal-combustion engines because of its high heat conductivity. Aluminum foil, siding, and storm windows make excellent insulators. Because it absorbs relatively few neutrons, aluminum is used in low-temperature nuclear reactors. Aluminum is also useful in boat hulls and various marine devices due to its resistance to corrosion in saltwater.

Futures and options on Primary Aluminum and Aluminum Alloy are traded on the London Metal Exchange (LME). Aluminum futures are traded on the Multi Commodity Exchange of India, and the Shanghai Futures Exchange (SHFE). The London Metals Exchange aluminum futures contracts are priced in terms of dollars.

Supply – World production of aluminum in 2023 rose by +2.3% yr/yr to a new record high of 70 million metric tons. The world's largest producers of aluminum in 2023 were China with 58.6% of world production, Russia with 5.4%, Canada with 4.3%, and Australia with 2.1%. US production of primary aluminum in 2023 fell by -1.6% yr/yr to 610,000 metric tons.

Demand – US consumption of aluminum in 2023 fell by -16.0% yr/yr to 4.000 million metric tons.

Trade – US aluminum exports in 2023 rose by +8.6% yr/yr to 3.300 million metric tons, below the 2012 record high of 3.480 million metric tons. US imports of aluminum in 2023 fell by -12.1% yr/yr to 5.540 million metric tons. The US was a net importer of aluminum in 2023 and relied on imports for 44.0% of its consumption.

World Production of Primary Aluminum   In Thousands of Metric Tons

Year	Australia	Brazil	Canada	China	France	Germany	Norway	Russia	Spain	United Kingdom	United States	Vene-zuela	World Total
2014	1,704	962	2,858	28,300	360	531	1,250	3,300	350	42	1,710	138	54,100
2015	1,646	772	2,880	31,400	420	541	1,225	3,529	350	47	1,590	119	57,800
2016	1,635	793	3,209	32,698	425	547	1,247	3,561	350	48	818	147	59,400
2017	1,487	802	3,212	32,273	430	550	1,253	3,583	350	47	741	144	59,400
2018	1,574	659	2,923	35,802	390	529	1,295	3,627	350	44	891	86	63,300
2019	1,570	650	2,854	35,044	390	508	1,300	3,637	220	39	1,093	8	62,600
2020	1,585	685	3,119	37,080	396	529	1,330	3,639	200	36	1,012	20	65,000
2021	1,565	772	3,137	38,900	400	500	1,400	3,640	200	40	889	20	67,500
2022[1]	1,510	811	2,770	40,200			1,400	3,720			861		68,400
2023[2]	1,500	1,100	3,000	41,000			1,300	3,800			750		70,000

[1] Preliminary.   [2] Estimate.   *Source: U.S. Geological Survey (USGS)*

Production of Primary Aluminum (Domestic and Foreign Ores) in the U.S.   In Thousands of Metric Tons

Year	Jan.	Feb.	Mar.	Apr.	May	June	July	Aug.	Sept.	Oct.	Nov.	Dec.	Total
2014	153	139	153	143	147	140	143	143	136	137	134	141	1,710
2015	142	130	143	138	142	133	134	135	128	128	121	113	1,587
2016	106	96	77	63	64	62	64	62	61	62	61	63	841
2017	62	56	63	60	64	61	63	63	60	63	61	64	741
2018	66	61	71	71	73	63	68	76	76	84	88	95	892
2019	95	87	93	92	94	91	92	90	87	91	89	91	1,092
2020	92	88	95	92	96	89	82	80	72	75	74	77	1,012
2021	78	69	75	72	75	72	73	73	72	76	75	79	889
2022	82	75	84	82	84	78	64	61	61	64	62	64	861
2023[1]	64	59	65	63	65	62	64	62	60	61	61	64	750

[1] Preliminary.   *Source: U.S. Geological Survey (USGS)*

ALUMINUM

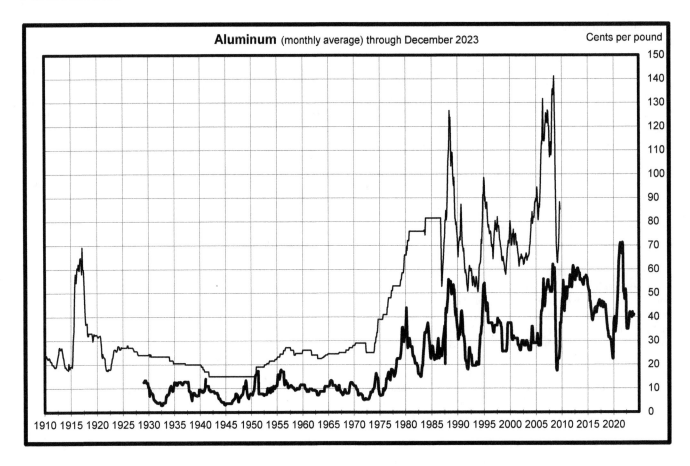

Aluminum (monthly average) through December 2023 — Cents per pound

Salient Statistics of Aluminum in the United States   In Thousands of Metric Tons

Year	Net Import Reliance as a % of Apparent Consump	Production Primary	Production Secondary	Primary Shipments	Recovery from Scrap Old	Recovery from Scrap New	Apparent Consumption	Plate, Sheet, Foil	Rolled Structural Shapes³	Extruded Shapes⁴	All	Permanent Mold	Die	Sand	Total All Net Shipments
2014	33	1,710	3,640	9,960	1,690	1,870	5,070	5,020	887	2,100	8,007	563	1,330	214	2,120	10,127
2015	41	1,587	3,380	10,400	1,560	2,000	5,300	5,220	629	2,460	8,309	526	1,470	295	2,300	10,609
2016	53	818	3,580	10,600	1,570	2,010	5,090	5,330	626	2,490	8,446	505	1,550	284	2,350	10,796
2017	59	741	3,630	11,000	1,590	2,050	5,680	5,580	708	2,580	8,868	645	1,400	237	2,290	11,158
2018	50	891	3,710	11,200	1,570	2,140	4,900	5,760	669	2,710	9,139	517	1,410	272	2,220	11,359
2019	47	1,090	3,470	11,200	1,540	1,920	4,980	5,840	659	2,600	9,099	494	1,300	352	2,150	11,249
2020	38	1,010	3,050	9,810	1,420	1,630	3,930	5,230	646	2,280	8,156	432	1,130	208	1,790	9,946
2021	40	889	3,300	10,900	1,520	1,780	4,020	5,830	704	2,650	9,184	444	1,070	245	1,780	10,964
2022	52	861	3,340		1,450	1,890	4,760									
2023¹	44	750			1,500	1,800	4,000									

Net Shipments⁵ by Producers — Wrought Products — Castings

¹ Preliminary.   ² To domestic industry.   ³ Also rod, bar & wire.   ⁴ Also rod, bar, tube, blooms & tubing.   ⁵ Consists of total shipments less shipments to other mills for further fabrication.   *Source: U.S. Geological Survey (USGS)*

Supply and Distribution of Aluminum in the United States   In Thousands of Metric Tons

Year	Apparent Consumption	Production Primary	Production From Old Scrap	Imports	Exports	Inventories Private	Inventories Government³	Year	Apparent Consumption	Production Primary	Production From Old Scrap	Imports	Exports	Inventories Private	Inventories Government³
2012	3,950	2,070	1,630	4,349	3,480	1,140	----	2018	4,900	891	1,570	6,245	3,070	1,570	----
2013	4,520	1,946	1,630	4,725	3,390	1,130	----	2019	4,980	1,090	1,540	5,876	2,970	1,600	----
2014	5,070	1,710	1,690	4,849	3,240	1,280	----	2020	3,930	1,010	1,420	4,802	2,746	1,490	----
2015	5,300	1,587	1,560	5,081	3,010	1,350	----	2021	4,020	889	1,520	5,500	3,000	1,870	----
2016	5,090	818	1,570	6,019	2,820	1,400	----	2022¹	4,760	861	1,450	6,300	3,040	2,050	----
2017	5,680	741	1,590	6,920	2,900	1,470	----	2023²	4,000	750	1,500	5,540	3,300	1,800	----

¹ Preliminary.   ² Estimate.   ³ National Defense Stockpile.   *Source: U.S. Geological Survey (USGS)*

Aluminum Products Distribution of End-Use Shipments in the United States   In Thousands of Metric Tons

Year	Containers & Packaging	Building & Construction	Trans-portation	Electrical	Consumer Durables	Machinery & Equipment	Other Markets	Total to Domestic Users	Exports	Total
2012	2,110	1,180	3,220	861	672	696	343	9,080	1,690	10,800
2013	2,090	1,310	3,430	867	700	726	332	9,450	1,720	11,200
2014	2,090	1,390	3,810	807	748	768	343	9,960	1,620	11,600
2015	2,140	1,420	4,180	800	741	768	327	10,400	1,620	12,000
2016	2,160	1,470	4,220	836	794	784	318	10,600	1,410	12,000
2017	2,130	1,530	4,370	919	860	841	333	11,000	1,340	12,300
2018	2,170	1,570	4,520	880	860	852	356	11,200	1,550	12,800
2019	2,220	1,530	4,540	871	832	837	347	11,200	1,300	12,500
2020	2,250	1,450	3,450	876	725	753	312	9,810	1,250	11,100
2021[1]	2,430	1,570	3,860	964	874	896	347	10,900	982	11,900

[1] Preliminary.   Source: U.S. Geological Survey (USGS)

Salient Statistics of Recycling Aluminum in the United States

Year	Percent Recycled	New Scrap[1]	Old Scrap[2]	Recycled Metal[3]	Apparent Supply	New Scrap[1]	Old Scrap[2]	Recycled Metal[3]	Apparent Supply
		In Metric Tons				Value in Thousands of Dollars			
2012	1,750,000	1,620,000	3,380,000	5,880,000	57.0	3,900,000	3,620,000	7,510,000	13,100,000
2013	1,790,000	1,630,000	3,410,000	6,310,000	54.0	3,710,000	3,380,000	7,090,000	13,100,000
2014	1,930,000	1,700,000	3,640,000	7,010,000	52.0	4,450,000	3,920,000	8,380,000	16,200,000
2015	1,910,000	1,470,000	3,380,000	7,120,000	47.0	3,710,000	2,850,000	6,560,000	13,900,000
2016	2,010,000	1,570,000	3,580,000	7,100,000	50.0	3,560,000	2,790,000	6,350,000	12,600,000
2017	2,050,000	1,590,000	3,630,000	7,730,000	47.0	4,430,000	3,440,000	7,870,000	16,700,000
2018	2,140,000	1,570,000	3,710,000	7,040,000	53.0	5,410,000	3,970,000	9,280,000	17,800,000
2019	1,920,000	1,540,000	3,470,000	6,910,000	50.0	4,220,000	3,380,000	7,600,000	15,200,000
2020	1,630,000	1,420,000	3,050,000	5,560,000	55.0	3,230,000	2,800,000	6,030,000	11,000,000
2021	1,780,000	1,520,000	3,300,000	5,860,000	56.0	5,440,000	4,630,000	10,100,000	17,900,000

[1] Scrap that results from the manufacturing process.   [2] Scrap that results from consumer products.   [3] Metal recovered from new plus old scrap.
Source: U.S. Geological Survey (USGS)

Producer Prices for Aluminum Used Beverage Can Scrap   In Cents Per Pound

Year	Jan.	Feb.	Mar.	Apr.	May	June	July	Aug.	Sept.	Oct.	Nov.	Dec.	Average
2014	73.24	76.75	77.52	82.43	79.62	80.41	83.80	85.33	85.93	85.92	91.17	88.64	82.56
2015	83.85	81.13	75.14	71.00	61.70	56.09	57.86	58.00	60.24	59.30	56.84	59.89	65.09
2016	60.63	61.60	59.87	60.71	59.90	60.36	61.30	61.52	60.02	63.00	67.15	67.81	61.99
2017	70.30	72.37	73.35	71.55	68.27	67.23	67.05	70.98	73.12	74.09	72.88	69.95	70.93
2018	75.57	75.66	75.59	81.81	84.41	85.29	77.40	73.37	65.87	63.50	59.35	58.12	73.00
2019	54.98	57.58	59.60	59.48	57.00	54.12	54.00	53.18	51.50	51.59	53.24	53.12	54.95
2020	53.40	51.66	50.02	40.79	39.80	44.77	47.45	48.40	50.93	52.18	56.55	62.82	49.90
2021	65.00	67.50	73.00	75.50	74.13	70.88	71.40	77.63	83.30	87.50	84.00	85.70	76.30
2022	99.38	111.63	129.30	122.38	106.25	93.70	76.88	77.50	72.80	73.00	72.38	79.30	92.88
2023	83.25	88.50	83.30	77.25	73.13	69.20	68.00	67.80	67.75	68.00	69.50	70.38	73.84

Source: American Metal Market (AMM)

Average Price of Cast Aluminum Scrap (Crank Cases) in Chicago[1]   In Cents Per Pound

Year	Jan.	Feb.	Mar.	Apr.	May	June	July	Aug.	Sept.	Oct.	Nov.	Dec.	Average
2014	54.50	53.50	53.50	55.00	56.50	56.50	56.50	56.55	57.40	56.50	56.50	55.45	55.70
2015	53.40	52.50	51.32	50.50	51.00	46.50	46.41	43.88	42.45	41.41	38.97	38.64	46.42
2016	39.97	40.50	41.50	41.50	43.45	43.05	44.05	43.46	41.93	43.50	44.50	44.50	42.66
2017	45.60	45.97	46.93	47.00	45.95	44.95	44.50	44.65	46.50	46.50	45.95	44.00	45.71
2018	45.40	46.03	44.50	44.02	45.05	44.98	41.93	39.93	37.45	36.50	34.50	34.00	41.19
2019	31.50	31.50	31.50	31.50	30.50	30.50	29.91	27.41	25.50	22.93	22.50	22.50	28.15
2020	37.07	39.24	39.95	34.17	33.80	35.77	37.20	39.60	43.60	47.00	51.76	57.50	41.39
2021	63.00	65.50	68.50	70.50	71.00	68.75	67.40	66.63	67.60	71.25	70.00	50.50	68.34
2022	51.50	50.00	47.50	50.00	51.50	49.00	39.50	35.00	35.00	35.00	35.00	36.50	42.96
2023	38.00	41.50	42.00	41.00	40.50	40.50	40.00	40.00	42.00	40.50	40.50	41.00	40.63

[1] Dealer buying prices.   Source: American Metal Market (AMM)

ALUMINUM

Aluminum Exports of Crude Metal and Alloys from the United States   In Thousands of Metric Tons

Year	Jan.	Feb.	Mar.	Apr.	May	June	July	Aug.	Sept.	Oct.	Nov.	Dec.	Total
2014	31.1	25.6	30.5	30.7	33.0	31.0	28.7	31.5	30.0	33.7	26.9	28.2	360.9
2015	26.5	26.0	25.2	25.0	26.9	29.5	26.7	27.2	25.2	26.1	22.9	22.8	310.0
2016	25.7	24.5	25.3	22.1	22.7	18.7	19.4	20.1	23.6	21.7	21.2	17.1	262.1
2017	24.9	20.5	23.7	22.3	22.4	24.5	22.8	27.7	21.0	23.9	22.5	18.9	275.1
2018	25.6	28.4	23.6	25.5	25.3	22.8	24.9	27.5	23.0	25.5	22.2	18.1	292.4
2019	22.2	18.6	20.9	21.8	20.9	19.0	18.3	19.2	17.4	18.6	18.4	17.5	232.8
2020	16.6	19.0	20.3	10.0	9.1	15.9	14.6	14.8	16.8	15.5	15.3	14.4	182.2
2021	15.7	15.3	19.5	17.7	16.1	18.3	14.8	14.2	13.0	13.7	14.4	12.6	185.3
2022	17.3	17.8	19.2	19.1	26.2	22.8	23.0	24.6	25.5	31.0	27.8	23.6	277.9
2023[1]	29.1	29.3	35.2	32.7	36.6	39.5	39.9	43.5	40.3	41.7	45.2	47.3	460.3

[1] Preliminary.   *Source: U.S. Geological Survey (USGS)*

Aluminum General Imports of Crude Metal and Alloys into the United States   In Thousands of Metric Tons

Year	Jan.	Feb.	Mar.	Apr.	May	June	July	Aug.	Sept.	Oct.	Nov.	Dec.	Total
2014	253.0	221.0	439.0	291.0	290.0	294.0	237.0	270.0	253.0	271.0	213.0	270.0	3,302.0
2015	273.0	245.0	312.0	322.0	299.0	301.0	301.0	251.0	283.0	270.0	267.0	259.0	3,383.0
2016	362.0	270.0	385.0	350.0	336.0	401.0	346.0	345.0	349.0	316.0	392.0	381.0	4,233.0
2017	459.0	394.0	476.0	434.0	411.0	410.0	411.0	379.0	338.0	358.0	358.0	400.0	4,828.0
2018	333.0	374.0	555.0	381.0	349.0	297.0	332.0	292.0	313.0	306.0	294.0	306.0	4,132.0
2019	298.0	284.0	312.0	314.0	287.0	315.0	91.2	73.8	53.9	65.1	302.0	317.0	2,713.0
2020	347.0	208.0	246.0	338.0	316.0	262.0	253.0	270.0	214.0	231.0	241.0	229.0	3,155.0
2021	250.0	243.0	308.0	324.0	313.0	294.0	299.0	319.0	285.0	339.0	338.0	316.0	3,628.0
2022	343.0	262.0	341.0	331.0	404.0	460.0	345.0	360.0	317.0	322.0	279.0	388.0	4,152.0
2023[1]	307.0	238.0	316.0	375.0	407.0	345.0	331.0	283.0	309.0	313.0	277.0	311.0	3,812.0

[1] Preliminary.   *Source: U.S. Geological Survey (USGS)*

Average Price of Aluminum (Cash) in London   In U.S. Dollars per Metric Ton

Year	Jan.	Feb.	Mar.	Apr.	May	June	July	Aug.	Sept.	Oct.	Nov.	Dec.	Average
2014	1,727.4	1,695.2	1,705.4	1,810.7	1,751.1	1,839.0	1,948.3	2,030.5	1,990.4	1,946.2	2,055.6	1,909.5	1,867.4
2015	1,814.7	1,817.8	1,773.9	1,819.2	1,804.0	1,687.7	1,639.5	1,548.1	1,589.6	1,516.5	1,467.9	1,497.2	1,664.7
2016	1,481.1	1,531.3	1,531.0	1,571.2	1,550.6	1,593.5	1,629.1	1,639.3	1,592.4	1,665.9	1,737.1	1,727.7	1,604.2
2017	1,791.2	1,860.8	1,901.5	1,921.2	1,913.0	1,885.3	1,903.0	2,030.3	2,096.5	2,131.5	2,097.4	2,080.5	1,967.7
2018	2,209.7	2,182.4	2,070.8	2,254.7	2,299.7	2,237.6	2,082.2	2,051.5	2,026.5	2,029.9	1,938.5	1,920.4	2,108.7
2019	1,853.7	1,863.0	1,871.2	1,845.5	1,781.3	1,756.0	1,797.0	1,740.7	1,753.5	1,726.0	1,774.8	1,771.4	1,794.5
2020	1,773.1	1,688.1	1,610.9	1,459.9	1,466.4	1,568.6	1,643.8	1,737.3	1,743.8	1,806.1	1,935.3	2,014.7	1,704.0
2021	2,004.0	2,078.6	2,190.5	2,319.4	2,433.5	2,446.7	2,497.6	2,603.0	2,834.6	2,934.4	2,636.5	2,695.5	2,472.8
2022	3,006.0	3,245.8	3,498.4	3,244.4	2,837.8	2,563.4	2,408.4	2,430.8	2,224.1	2,255.5	2,350.7	2,401.7	2,705.6
2023	2,501.8	2,416.2	2,296.4	2,343.2	2,268.6	2,184.8	2,159.7	2,136.6	2,184.7	2,194.4	2,202.3	2,182.4	2,255.9

Contract Size = 25 Metric Tons   *Source: London Metal Exchange (LME)*

Average Price of Aluminum (3-Month) in London   In U.S. Dollars per Metric Ton

Year	Jan.	Feb.	Mar.	Apr.	May	June	July	Aug.	Sept.	Oct.	Nov.	Dec.	Average
2014	1,771.7	1,738.5	1,748.5	1,848.0	1,792.4	1,873.3	1,968.9	2,040.1	2,022.0	1,962.2	2,043.7	1,927.5	1,894.7
2015	1,827.3	1,835.0	1,781.7	1,809.7	1,836.8	1,726.6	1,680.2	1,576.4	1,605.3	1,541.0	1,482.0	1,497.9	1,683.3
2016	1,481.5	1,525.0	1,537.7	1,581.1	1,564.5	1,602.1	1,641.0	1,651.6	1,606.4	1,671.3	1,735.3	1,720.4	1,609.8
2017	1,786.8	1,870.7	1,912.3	1,933.4	1,917.1	1,892.1	1,921.1	2,036.7	2,122.6	2,150.6	2,114.8	2,096.7	1,979.6
2018	2,217.8	2,171.0	2,088.9	2,251.8	2,298.7	2,233.9	2,065.6	2,074.9	2,058.1	2,040.8	1,950.8	1,922.8	2,114.6
2019	1,867.4	1,888.2	1,895.1	1,865.0	1,809.6	1,782.9	1,819.4	1,770.2	1,779.4	1,733.7	1,767.6	1,781.9	1,813.3
2020	1,792.8	1,713.2	1,633.6	1,497.1	1,498.3	1,590.6	1,677.4	1,774.5	1,781.3	1,822.6	1,948.7	2,026.6	1,729.7
2021	2,005.1	2,084.8	2,211.3	2,328.9	2,454.3	2,455.7	2,509.9	2,595.0	2,849.6	2,951.1	2,639.6	2,695.4	2,481.7
2022	3,002.5	3,215.8	3,509.7	3,263.4	2,864.6	2,585.8	2,414.4	2,423.9	2,235.9	2,261.2	2,373.0	2,434.7	2,715.4
2023	2,533.6	2,454.7	2,343.0	2,367.3	2,267.0	2,221.5	2,203.5	2,183.3	2,225.4	2,219.3	2,231.8	2,226.7	2,289.7

Contract Size = 25 Metric Tons   *Source: London Metal Exchange (LME)*

Antimony

Antimony (atomic symbol Sb) is a lustrous, extremely brittle and hard crystalline semi-metal that is silvery-white in its most common allotropic form. Antimony is a poor conductor of heat and electricity. In nature, antimony has a strong affinity for sulfur and such metals as lead, silver, and copper. Antimony is primarily a byproduct of the mining, smelting, and refining of lead, silver, and copper ores. There is no longer any mine production of antimony in the U.S.

The most common use of antimony is in antimony trioxide, a chemical that is used as a flame retardant in textiles, plastics, adhesives, and building materials. Antimony trioxide is also used in battery components, ceramics, bearings, chemicals, glass, and ammunition.

Prices – Antimony prices in 2023 fell by -8.3% yr/yr to 546.55 cents per pound, remaining below the record high of 671.10 posted in 2011.

Supply – World mine production of antimony in 2023 fell by -0.1% yr/yr to 83,000 metric tons. China accounted for 48.2% of world antimony production in 2023. After China, the only significant antimony producers were Tajikistan with 25.3%, and Türkiye with 7.2%. US secondary production of antimony in 2023 fell by -2.4% yr/yr to 4,000 metric tons.

Demand – US industrial consumption of antimony in 2020 fell by -5.3% yr/yr to 5,500 metric tons, the lowest since the data series began in 1943. Regarding consumption of antimony in the US in 2020, 36.2% was used for metal products, 40.4% was used for flame-retardants, and 23.5% was used for non-metal products.

Trade – The gross weight of US imports of antimony oxide in 2023 fell by -17.2% yr/yr to 14,000 metric tons. US exports of antimony oxide in 2023 fell by -25.6% yr/yr to 1,800 metric tons.

World Mine Production of Antimony (Content of Ore)   In Metric Tons

Year	Australia	Bolivia	Canada	China	Kyrgyzstan	Russia	South Africa	Tajikistan	Türkiye	World Total
2018	2,173	3,110	----	95,300	----	30,000	----	15,240	1,840	153,000
2019	2,032	3,000	----	60,200	----	30,000	----	14,000	1,970	120,000
2020	3,903	2,600	2	61,000	----	25,000	----	13,000	1,330	111,000
2021	4,000	2,600	2	61,000	----	20,000	----	1,800	1,300	112,000
2022[1]	2,290	3,000	2	40,000	----	4,300	----	21,000	5,800	83,100
2023[2]	2,300	3,000	2	40,000	----	4,300	----	21,000	6,000	83,000

[1] Preliminary.   [2] Estimate.   [3] Less than 1/2 unit.   *Source: U.S. Geological Survey (USGS)*

Salient Statistics of Antimony in the United States   In Metric Tons

Year	Avg. Price Cents/lb. C.i.F. U.S. Ports	Production[3] Primary[2] Mine	Production[3] Primary[2] Smelter	Production[3] Secondary (Alloys)[2]	Imports for Consumption Ore Gross Weight	Imports for Consumption Ore Antimony Content	Imports for Consumption Oxide (Gross Weight)	Exports (Oxide)	Industry Stocks, December 31[3] Metallic	Industry Stocks, December 31[3] Oxide	Industry Stocks, December 31[3] Sulfide	Industry Stocks, December 31[3] Other	Industry Stocks, December 31[3] Total
2019	390.00	----	W	4,140	----	121	17,200	1,570			----		
2020	267.00	----	W	3,520	----	105	15,000	1,230			----		
2021	531.00	----	W	4,050	----	31	19,100	1,530			----		
2022[1]	618.00	----	W	4,100	----	29	16,900	2,420			----		
2023[2]	560.00	----	W	4,000	----	8	14,000	1,800			----		

[1] Preliminary.   [2] Estimate.   [3] Antimony content.   [4] Including primary antimony residues & slag.   W = Withheld proprietary data.
Source: U.S. Geological Survey (USGS)

Industrial Consumption of Primary Antimony in the United States   In Metric Tons (Antimony Content)

Year	Metal Products Ammunition	Metal Products Antimonial Lead[3]	Metal Products Sheet & Pipe[4]	Metal Products Bearing Metal & Bearings	Metal Products Solder	Metal Products Products	Flame Retardents Plastics	Flame Retardents Total	Non-Metal Products Ceramics & Glass	Non-Metal Products Pigments	Non-Metal Products Plastics	Non-Metal Products Total	Grand Total
2016	W	W	W	9	15	2,840	2,290	2,790	W	703	W	2,770	8,400
2017	W	W	W	8	14	2,410	2,420	2,810	W	W	W	1,330	6,550
2018	W	W	W	8	13	2,380	2,030	2,470	W	W	W	1,330	6,260
2019	W	W	W	7	17	2,100	1,900	2,430	W	W	W	1,290	5,810
2020[1]	W	W	W	7	19	1,990	1,740	2,220	W	W	W	1,290	5,500

[1] Preliminary.   [2] Estimated coverage based on 77% of the industry.   W = Withheld proprietary data.   *Source: U.S. Geological Survey (USGS)*

Average Price of Antimony[1] in the United States   In Cents Per Pound

Year	Jan.	Feb.	Mar.	Apr.	May	June	July	Aug.	Sept.	Oct.	Nov.	Dec.	Average
2019	360.51	358.34	345.38	325.66	317.62	294.82	276.95	272.52	269.13	282.44	283.66	275.56	305.22
2020	267.17	283.95	288.74	267.92	257.79	247.65	240.97	248.91	263.84	271.59	284.21	299.81	268.55
2021	351.73	415.61	524.16	486.10	451.19	458.07	489.00	543.32	568.13	602.02	596.48	601.02	507.24
2022	605.84	612.50	666.41	675.68	620.92	606.66	626.22	598.14	579.90	552.25	515.15	490.77	595.87
2023	564.12	593.36	568.58	536.54	551.12	553.56	527.87	535.24	549.99	533.93	518.74	525.54	546.55

[1] Prices are for antimony metal (99.65%) merchants, minimum 18-ton containers, c.i.f. U.S. Ports.   *Source: American Metal Market (AMM)*

Apples

The apple tree is the common name of trees from the rose family, Rosaceae, and the fruit that comes from them. The apple tree is a deciduous plant and grows mainly in the temperate areas of the world. The apple tree is believed to have originated in the Caspian and Black Sea area. Apples were the favorite fruit of the ancient Greeks and Romans. The early settlers brought apple seeds with them and introduced them to America. John Champman, also known as Johnny Appleseed, was responsible for the extensive planting of apple trees in the Midwestern United States.

Futures on apples are traded in the Zhengzhou Commodity Exchange.

Prices – The average monthly price of apples received by growers in the US in 2023 rose by +6.7% yr/yr to 81.75 cents per pound.

Supply – World apple production in the 2023-24 marketing year rose by +0.2% yr/yr to 83.109 million metric tons. The world's largest apple producers in 2022/23 were China (with 54.1% of world production), the European Union (14.7%), Turkey (5.8%), and the US (5.2%). US apple production in 2023/24 rose by +5.2% to 4.456 million metric tons, well above the 3-decade low of 3.798 million metric tons posted in 2002-03.

World Production of Apples, Fresh (Dessert & Cooking)   In Thousands of Metric Tons

Crop Year	Argentina	Brazil	Chile	China	European Union	India	Japan	Russia	South Africa	Türkiye	Ukraine	United States	World Total
2016-17	560	1,308	1,310	40,393	12,479	2,258	735	1,509	902	2,926	1,076	5,010	76,698
2017-18	560	1,203	1,330	41,390	9,798	1,920	756	1,360	836	3,032	1,462	5,085	75,192
2018-19	550	1,223	1,210	33,000	14,810	2,371	702	1,611	894	3,600	1,154	4,479	71,849
2019-20	600	983	1,124	42,425	11,480	2,370	763	1,779	991	3,620	1,115	4,852	78,665
2020-21	550	1,297	1,099	44,066	11,935	2,300	733	1,540	1,164	4,300	1,279	4,505	81,247
2021-22	427	1,297	1,040	45,973	12,266	2,300	733	1,641	1,250	4,493	1,279	4,375	83,436
2022-23[1]	464	1,297	920	44,500	12,683	2,400	733	1,742	1,150	4,968	1,279	4,300	82,934
2023-24[2]	487	1,297	907	45,000	12,208	2,410	733	1,844	1,230	4,850	1,279	4,356	83,109

[1] Preliminary.   [2] Estimate.   *Source: Foreign Agricultural Service, U.S. Department of Agriculture (FAS-USDA)*

Salient Statistics of Apples[2] in the United States

	-- Production --		- Growers Prices -		----------- Utilization of Quantities Sold ------------						Avg. Farm Price Cents/ lb.	----- Foreign Trade[4] -----				Fresh Per Capita Consumption Lbs.
			Fresh Cents/ lb.	Processing $/ton	--------------- Processed[5] ---------------							--- Domestic ---				
Year	Total	Utilized			Fresh	Canned	Dried	Frozen	Juice & Cider	Other[3]		Farm Value Million $	Exports Fresh	Imports Dried[5]	Fresh & Dried[5]	
			------------------------------ Millions of Pounds ------------------------------									----- Metric Tons -----			
2015	10,103	10,023	44.1	201.0	6,928	1,110	179	188	1,329	187	33.6	3,350.1	747.3	28.0	233.6	17.5
2016	11,495	11,046	40.5	214.0	7,745	1,211	339	138	1,342	137	31.6	3,492.6	867.5	----	171.0	19.2
2017	11,554	11,210	40.7	248.0	7,816	1,162	370	123	1,395	180	32.1	3,601.4	1,007.3	----	134.3	18.1
2018	10,240	9,874	38.7	207.0	6,827	----	----	----	----	----	29.9	2,954.2	742.3	----	146.4	16.8
2019	11,086	10,696	32.7	200.0	7,456	----	----	----	----	----	25.8	2,762.3	861.4	----	107.8	17.6
2020	10,285	9,932	38.4	203.0	6,827	----	----	----	----	----	29.6	2,936.6	775.4	----	108.9	16.2
2021	9,933	9,645	37.0	268.0	6,651	----	----	----	----	----	29.6	2,859.2	721.1	----	105.6	15.9
2022[1]	9,765	9,479	41.6	251.0	6,416	----	----	----	----	----	32.2	3,054.4	611.3	----	99.7	15.8

[1] Preliminary.   [2] Commercial crop.   [3] Mostly crushed for vinegar, jam, etc.   [4] Year beginning July.   [5] Fresh weight basis.
Source: Economic Research Service, U.S. Department of Agriculture (ERS-USDA)

Price of Apples Received by Growers (for Fresh Use) in the United States   In Cents Per Pound

Year	Jan.	Feb.	Mar.	Apr.	May	June	July	Aug.	Sept.	Oct.	Nov.	Dec.	Average
2016	44.7	44.7	45.9	45.1	39.1	38.0	40.6	46.1	53.0	45.2	39.9	39.6	43.5
2017	39.7	36.9	35.8	35.3	36.0	36.3	37.0	42.6	59.1	45.9	39.9	39.7	40.4
2018	37.5	35.0	33.6	32.7	29.6	28.6	31.1	29.6	45.2	39.6	38.7	40.1	35.1
2019	39.7	37.9	37.7	38.1	38.3	37.2	38.8	40.2	48.9	39.1	33.3	33.6	38.6
2020	31.3	58.3	57.7	57.7	57.9	58.6	60.0	64.2	70.7	69.1	69.7	70.2	60.5
2021	72.3	73.7	73.5	73.7	72.1	71.8	73.5	76.1	81.4	72.6	71.5	71.6	73.7
2022	74.6	75.9	76.1	74.6	73.7	72.0	69.0	71.5	78.4	81.0	84.1	88.9	76.7
2023[1]	92.2	91.5	88.2	83.4	82.6	83.8	86.3	84.4	82.2	74.2	68.3	63.9	81.8

[1] Preliminary.   NQ = No quote.   *Source: Economic Research Service, U.S. Department of Agriculture (ERS-USDA)*

Arsenic

Arsenic (atomic symbol As) is a silver-gray, extremely poisonous, semi-metallic element. Arsenic, which is odorless and flavorless, has been known since ancient times, but it wasn't until the Middle Ages that its poisonous characteristics first became known. Metallic arsenic was first produced in the 17th century by heating arsenic with potash and soap. Arsenic is rarely found in nature in its elemental form and is typically recovered as a by-product of ore processing. Recently, small doses of arsenic have been found to put some types of cancer into remission. It can also help thin blood. Homoeopathists have successfully used undetectable amounts of arsenic to cure stomach cramps.

The U.S. does not produce any arsenic and instead imports all its consumption needs for arsenic metals and compounds. More than 95 percent of the arsenic consumed in the U.S. is in compound form, mostly as arsenic trioxide, which in turn is converted into arsenic acid. Production of chromated copper arsenate, a wood preservative, accounts for about 90% of the domestic consumption of arsenic trioxide. Three companies in the U.S. manufacture chromate copper arsenate. Another company used arsenic acid to produce an arsenical herbicide. Arsenic metal is used to produce nonferrous alloys, primarily for lead-acid batteries.

One area where there is increased consumption of arsenic is in the semiconductor industry. Very high-purity arsenic is used in the production of gallium arsenide. High-speed and high-frequency integrated circuits that use gallium arsenide have better signal reception and lower power consumption. An estimated 30 metric tons per year of high-purity arsenic is used in the production of semiconductor materials.

In the early 2000s, as much as 88% of U.S. arsenic production was used for wood preservative treatments, so the demand for arsenic was closely tied to new home construction, home renovation, and deck construction. However, the total demand for arsenic in 2004 dropped by 69% from 2003. Due to arsenic's toxicity and tighter environmental regulation, only 65% of that much smaller amount was used for wood preservative treatments.

Supply – World production of white arsenic (arsenic trioxide) in 2023 fell by -0.2% yr/yr to 60,000 metric tons. The world's largest producer in 2023 was Peru with 45.0% of world production, followed by China with 40.0% of world production, Morocco with 13.3%, Belgium with 1.7%, and Russia with 0.3%. The US supply of arsenic in 2023 fell by -39.6% yr/yr to 6,410 metric tons.

Demand – US demand for arsenic in 2023 fell by -39.6% to 6,400 metric tons. Arsenic is mainly used in wood preservatives, with smaller usage levels in non-ferrous alloys, electrical, and glass.

Trade – US imports of trioxide arsenic in 2022 rose by +72.6% yr/yr to 10,600 metric tons. US exports of trioxide arsenic in 2023 fell by -81.7% yr/yr to 15 metric tons, far below the record high of 3,270 metric tons in 2005.

World Production of White Arsenic (Arsenic Trioxide)   In Metric Tons

Year	Belgium	Bolivia	Chile	China	Japan	Mexico	Morocco	Namibia	Peru	Russia	World Total
2016	1,000	38	----	25,000	45	----	7,600	1,900	33,000	1,500	70,100
2017	1,000	20	----	24,000	45	----	6,879	700	32,000	1,500	66,500
2018	1,000	238	----	24,000	45	----	5,578	----	29,000	----	59,900
2019	1,000	126	----	24,000	45	----	5,055	----	35,000	2,226	67,500
2020	1,000	50	----	24,000	40	----	7,694	----	27,000	500	60,300
2021	1,000	100	----	24,000	40	----	6,883	----	27,000	800	59,800
2022[1]	1,000	40	----	24,000	40	----	7,500	----	27,000	500	60,100
2023[2]	1,000	----	----	24,000	40	----	8,000	----	27,000	200	60,000

[1] Preliminary. [2] Estimate. [3] Output of Tsumeb Corp. Ltd. only. [4] Includes low-grade dusts that were exported to the U.S. for further refining.
Source: U.S. Geological Survey (USGS)

Salient Statistics of Arsenic in the United States   (In Metric Tons -- Arsenic Content)

| | Supply | | | | Distribution | | Estimated Demand Pattern | | | | | | Average Price | | | |
| | Imports | | Industry | | | Industry | Agricultural | | Wood | Non-Ferrous | | | Trioxide | Metal | | |
Year	Metal	Compounds	Stocks Jan. 1	Total	Apparent Demand	Stocks Dec. 31	Chemicals	Glass	Preservatives	Alloys & Electric	Other	Total	Mexican Cents/Pound	Chinese	Imports Trioxide[3]	Exports
2016	793	5,320	----	6,113	6,120	----	----	----	----	----	----	6,120	----	2	7,000	1,760
2017	942	5,980	----	6,922	6,920	----	----	----	----	----	----	6,920	----	2	7,900	698
2018	929	5,540	----	6,469	6,470	----	----	----	----	----	----	6,470	----	1	7,320	107
2019	391	7,090	----	7,481	7,480	----	----	----	----	----	----	7,480	----	2	9,130	56
2020	522	7,750	----	8,272	8,270	----	----	----	----	----	----	8,270	----	2	10,000	29
2021	835	4,760	----	5,595	5,600	----	----	----	----	----	----	5,600	----	1	6,140	31
2022[1]	858	9,750	----	10,608	10,600	----	----	----	----	----	----	10,600	----		10,600	82
2023[2]	710	5,700	----	6,410	6,400	----	----	----	----	----	----	6,400	----			15

[1] Preliminary.   [2] Estimate.   [3] For Consumption.   *Source: U.S. Geological Survey (USGS)*

Barley

Barley is the common name for the genus of cereal grass and is native to Asia and Ethiopia. Barley is an ancient crop and was grown by the Egyptians, Greek, Romans, and Chinese. Barley is now the world's fourth-largest grain crop, after wheat, rice, and corn. Barley is planted in the spring in most of Europe, Canada and the United States. The U.S. barley crop year begins June 1. It is planted in the autumn in parts of California, Arizona, and along the Mediterranean Sea. Barley is hardy and drought resistant and can be grown on marginal cropland. Salt-resistant strains are being developed for use in coastal regions. Barley grain, along with hay, straw, and several by-products are used for animal feed. Barley is used for malt beverages and for cooking. Barley, like other cereals, contains a large proportion of carbohydrate (67%) and protein (12.8%).

Barley futures are traded on ASX 24 exchange and National Commodity & Derivatives Exchange (NCDEX).

Prices – The monthly average price for all barley received by US farmers in the 2022/23 marketing year rose by +35.0% yr/yr to $7.29 per bushel.

Supply – World barley production in the 2023/24 marketing year is forecasted to fall by -5.8% yr/yr to 142.871 million metric tons. The world's largest barley crop of 179.038 million metric tons occurred in 1990/91. The world's largest barley producers in 2023/24 are expected to be the European Union with 33.2% of world production, Russia with 14.3%, Australia with 7.0%, Canada with 6.2%, Turkey with 5.6%, and Ukraine with 4.4%.

US barley production in the 2023/24 marketing year is expected to rise by +5.7% yr/yr to 185.036 million bushels, which would be far below the record US barley crop of 608.532 million bushels seen in 1986/87. US farmers are expected to harvest +4.5% yr/yr more acres in 2023/24 to 2.555 million acres. Ending stocks for the 2023/24 marketing year are expected to rise by +16.8% to 76.856 million bushels.

Demand – US total barley disappearance in 2023/24 is expected to rise by +11.4% yr/yr to 188.000 million bushels. About 65.2% of barley is used for food and alcoholic beverages, 32.4% for animal feed and residual, and 2.3% for seed.

Trade – World exports of barley in 2023/24 are expected to fall by -9.7% yr/yr to 27.588 million metric tons. The largest world exporters of barley in 2023/24 are expected to be the European Union with 22.5% of world exports, Russia with 21.0%, Australia with 18.8%, and Argentina with 11.6%. The largest importers of barley in 2023/24 are expected to be China with 29.4% of world imports and Saudi Arabia with 14.1% of the world's imports.

World Production of Barley   In Thousands of Metric Tons

Crop Year	Argentina	Australia	Canada	Ethiopia	European Union	Iran	Kazakhstan	Morocco	Russia	Türkiye	Ukraine	United States	World Total
2014-15	2,900	8,646	7,117	1,953	60,609	1,000	2,412	1,638	20,026	4,000	9,450	3,953	141,648
2015-16	4,940	8,993	8,257	2,047	62,095	1,550	2,675	3,397	17,083	7,400	8,751	4,750	149,528
2016-17	3,300	13,506	8,839	2,221	53,211	1,550	3,231	620	17,547	4,750	9,874	4,353	147,208
2017-18	3,740	9,254	7,891	1,960	51,482	975	3,305	2,466	20,211	6,400	8,695	3,119	143,318
2018-19	4,635	8,819	8,380	1,749	49,470	780	3,971	2,919	16,737	7,000	7,604	3,293	139,539
2019-20	3,615	10,127	10,383	2,378	55,180	1,600	3,830	1,161	19,939	7,900	9,528	3,754	159,283
2020-21	4,035	14,649	10,741	2,261	54,235	1,550	3,659	950	20,629	8,100	7,947	3,717	161,450
2021-22	5,300	14,337	6,984	2,350	52,009	700	2,367	2,780	17,505	4,500	9,923	2,626	145,368
2022-23[1]	4,620	14,137	9,987	2,184	51,692	680	3,287	700	21,500	7,400	6,100	3,787	151,623
2023-24[2]	5,000	10,000	8,896	2,400	47,500	800	2,700	1,350	20,500	8,000	6,350	4,029	142,871

[1] Preliminary.   [2] Estimate.   *Source: Foreign Agricultural Service, U.S. Department of Agriculture (FAS-USDA)*

World Consumption of Barley   In Thousands of Metric Tons

Crop Year	Australia	Belarus	Canada	China	European Union	Iran	Morocco	Russia	Saudi Arabia	Türkiye	Ukraine	United States	World Total
2014-15	3,000	2,000	6,471	11,400	51,000	4,600	2,650	14,100	8,525	5,350	5,500	4,235	143,319
2015-16	3,300	1,850	7,040	7,500	51,400	5,200	3,200	13,700	10,225	6,900	4,300	4,408	145,382
2016-17	3,500	1,400	6,680	9,200	47,800	5,200	2,400	14,700	9,825	5,500	4,900	4,375	148,448
2017-18	3,700	1,450	6,805	9,300	46,900	6,000	2,800	14,500	8,525	6,700	4,500	3,466	146,735
2018-19	5,000	1,150	6,508	7,000	45,600	6,200	2,900	12,200	7,025	7,500	4,200	3,476	140,069
2019-20	6,000	1,300	8,108	8,000	49,500	6,400	2,500	15,400	7,025	8,500	4,600	3,822	157,146
2020-21	6,500	1,450	7,747	13,000	48,250	6,900	1,470	14,400	7,025	8,990	4,100	3,860	162,434
2021-22	6,000	1,050	5,399	11,400	45,450	4,700	3,120	14,300	4,225	7,400	4,100	3,532	145,805
2022-23[1]	6,000	1,150	6,698	10,600	46,700	5,600	1,590	16,700	4,325	8,900	3,400	3,630	150,256
2023-24[2]	6,500	1,150	6,400	10,050	43,600	5,200	2,300	15,100	3,925	8,500	3,750	4,029	144,664

[1] Preliminary.   [2] Estimate.   *Source: Foreign Agricultural Service, U.S. Department of Agriculture (FAS-USDA)*

World Exports of Barley   In Thousands of Metric Tons

Crop Year	Argentina	Australia	Canada	Ethiopia	European Union	Iran	Kazakhstan	Morocco	Russia	Türkiye	Ukraine	United States	World Total
2014-15	1,552	5,219	1,517	9,547	431	483	5,348	21	9	4,456	311	43	29,030
2015-16	3,077	5,745	1,195	10,834	81	804	4,241	54	3	4,412	235	42	30,823
2016-17	2,556	9,190	1,546	5,672	1	682	2,951	26	129	5,354	95	114	29,492
2017-18	2,399	5,662	2,021	5,934	1	1,347	5,884	53	147	4,289	111	7	29,099
2018-19	3,237	3,687	2,296	4,898	6	1,820	4,661	68	148	3,561	107	62	25,541
2019-20	2,421	3,324	2,244	7,767	1	1,366	4,470	52	2	4,984	125	45	28,952
2020-21	2,336	8,342	3,534	7,399	2	1,085	6,259	117	60	4,187	300	241	36,281
2021-22	3,831	8,007	1,981	7,331	2	427	3,300	120	173	5,705	160	262	32,342
2022-23[1]	2,857	7,768	3,149	6,673	7	1,113	4,500	102	225	2,712	46	139	30,561
2023-24[2]	3,200	5,200	2,600	6,200	5	850	5,800	150	250	2,100	65	75	27,588

[1] Preliminary.   [2] Estimate.   *Source: Foreign Agricultural Service, U.S. Department of Agriculture (FAS-USDA)*

World Imports of Barley   In Thousands of Metric Tons

Crop Year	Algeria	Brazil	China	Iran	Japan	Jordan	Kuwait	Libya	Saudi Arabia	Tunisia	United Arab Emirates	United States	World Total
2014-15	876	484	9,859	2,200	1,097	891	412	1,001	8,200	483	393	513	29,925
2015-16	837	547	5,869	1,700	1,155	796	511	1,324	11,200	561	668	405	28,638
2016-17	635	691	8,104	1,200	1,197	838	569	1,084	8,100	584	501	210	28,764
2017-18	528	547	8,144	3,200	1,253	907	521	438	8,000	604	263	199	30,243
2018-19	325	656	5,181	3,100	1,158	1,017	434	884	6,500	558	352	128	24,770
2019-20	560	664	5,969	2,900	1,253	389	500	895	6,700	613	434	154	28,646
2020-21	834	501	12,049	3,500	1,132	548	507	1,043	7,000	995	453	142	36,076
2021-22	772	637	8,282	1,600	1,184	1,278	551	535	4,200	909	337	320	30,087
2022-23[1]	93	628	8,582	2,600	1,227	1,119	410	1,400	4,300	665	260	513	31,240
2023-24[2]	700	500	8,100	2,200	1,250	1,000	450	500	3,900	800	350	305	27,591

[1] Preliminary.   [2] Estimate.   *Source: Foreign Agricultural Service, U.S. Department of Agriculture (FAS-USDA)*

World Ending Stocks of Barley   In Thousands of Metric Tons

Crop Year	Algeria	Australia	Canada	China	European Union	Iran	Morocco	Russia/3	Saudi Arabia	Türkiye	Ukraine	United States	World Total
2014-15	1,304	1,120	1,260	302	5,771	1,058	375	1,510	3,076	364	1,565	1,711	23,750
2015-16	1,291	1,068	1,443	82	5,924	758	1,394	729	4,065	905	1,609	2,223	25,711
2016-17	876	1,884	2,120	178	5,557	482	82	839	2,353	282	1,237	2,316	23,743
2017-18	522	1,776	1,244	107	5,592	782	158	750	1,841	724	1,149	2,057	21,470
2018-19	804	1,908	863	309	5,457	482	381	640	1,327	465	1,008	1,895	20,169
2019-20	662	2,711	957	289	5,205	582	98	743	1,016	766	953	1,856	22,000
2020-21	359	2,518	711	1,374	5,011	782	34	757	1,002	522	661	1,555	20,811
2021-22	131	2,848	543	256	5,232	382	609	712	991	316	780	809	18,119
2022-23[1]	174	3,217	709	238	5,539	382	65	1,062	980	732	770	1,433	20,165
2023-24[2]	149	1,517	635	288	5,039	382	115	712	967	482	1,272	1,673	18,375

[1] Preliminary.   [2] Estimate.   *Source: Foreign Agricultural Service, U.S. Department of Agriculture (FAS-USDA)*

Barley Acreage and Prices in the United States

Crop Year Beginning June 1	Acreage 1,000 Acres Planted	Acreage 1,000 Acres Harvested for Gain	Yield Per Harvested Acre -- Bushels --	Seasonal Prices — Received by Farmers[3] All	Seasonal Prices — Received by Farmers[3] Feed[4]	Seasonal Prices — Received by Farmers[3] Malting[4]	Portland No. 2 Western	Government Price Support Operations — National Average Loan Rate	Government Price Support Operations — Target Price	Government Price Support Operations — Put Under Support (mil. Bu.)	Percent of Production
2014-15	3,031	2,497	72.7	5.22	3.20	5.77	----	1.95	4.95	3.9	2.1
2015-16	3,623	3,158	69.1	5.46	3.11	5.78	----	1.95	4.95	8.3	3.8
2016-17	3,059	2,565	77.9	4.97	2.73	5.26	----	1.95	4.95	9.3	4.6
2017-18	2,486	1,962	73.0	4.47	3.00	4.67	----	1.95	4.95	4.5	3.1
2018-19	2,548	1,982	77.5	4.64	3.25	4.80	----	1.95	4.95	5.1	3.3
2019-20	2,772	2,221	77.7	4.69	3.37	4.85	----	2.50	4.95	6.1	3.6
2020-21	2,726	2,214	77.2	4.77	3.42	4.94	----	2.50			
2021-22	2,707	1,994	60.5	5.40	5.39	5.40	----	2.50			
2022-23[1]	2,927	2,425	71.7	7.29	6.23	7.41	----	2.50			
2023-24[2]	3,101	2,555	72.4	7.32	5.25	7.68	----				

[1] Preliminary.   [2] Estimate.   [3] Excludes support payments.   *Source: Economic Research Service, U.S. Department of Agriculture (ERS-USDA)*

BARLEY

Salient Statistics of Barley in the United States   In Millions of Bushels

Crop Year Beginning June 1	Beginning Stocks	Pro- duction	Imports	Total Supply	Food & Alcohol Beverage	Seed	Feed & Residual	Total	Exports	Total Disap- pearance	Gov't Owned	Privately Owned	Total Stocks
2014-15	82.3	181.5	23.6	287.4	154.3	5.9	34.4	194.5	14.3	208.8	----	78.6	78.6
2015-16	78.6	218.2	18.6	315.3	153.1	5.2	44.2	202.4	10.8	213.2	----	102.1	102.1
2016-17	102.1	199.9	9.6	311.7	151.6	4.2	45.2	200.9	4.4	205.3	----	106.4	106.4
2017-18	106.4	143.3	9.1	258.8	147.5	4.3	7.4	159.2	5.1	164.3	----	94.5	94.5
2018-19	94.5	153.5	5.9	253.9	143.7	4.7	14.0	162.4	4.9	167.4	----	86.5	86.5
2019-20	86.5	172.5	7.1	266.1	137.2	4.6	38.4	180.1	5.7	185.9	----	80.3	80.3
2020-21	85.3	170.8	6.5	262.5	142.1	4.6	30.6	177.3	13.8	191.1	----	71.4	71.4
2021-22	71.4	120.1	14.7	206.7	134.6	4.9	22.7	162.2	7.3	169.6	----	37.2	37.2
2022-23[1]	37.2	175.0	23.5	234.6	126.8	4.3	35.6	166.7	2.1	168.8	----	65.8	65.8
2023-24[2]	65.8	185.0	14.0	264.9	120.7	4.3	60.0	185.0	3.0	188.0	----	76.9	76.9

[1] Preliminary.   [2] Estimate.   [3] Uncommitted inventory.   [4] Includes quantity under loan & farmer-owned reserve.   [5] Included in Food & Alcohol.
Source: Economic Research Service, U.S. Department of Agriculture (ERS-USDA)

Stocks of Barley in the United States   In Thousands of Bushels

Year	On Farms Mar. 1	June 1	Sept. 1	Dec. 1	Off Farms Mar. 1	June 1	Sept. 1	Dec. 1	Total Stocks Mar. 1	June 1	Sept. 1	Dec. 1
2014	43,830	19,110	97,820	74,510	77,734	63,145	81,997	81,625	121,564	82,255	179,817	156,135
2015	41,990	20,940	135,840	96,670	76,247	57,639	83,132	83,738	118,237	78,579	218,972	180,408
2016	57,910	27,740	130,600	99,100	79,832	74,370	99,737	93,408	137,742	102,110	230,337	192,508
2017	56,490	27,050	90,400	74,340	88,211	79,314	89,283	84,528	144,701	106,364	179,683	158,868
2018	48,540	26,420	91,350	72,070	81,491	68,061	83,456	80,561	130,031	94,481	174,806	152,631
2019	46,180	22,870	116,720	87,630	75,216	63,653	73,112	69,756	121,396	86,523	189,832	157,386
2020	51,580	25,100	108,980	85,190	63,760	55,153	70,484	63,437	115,340	80,253	179,464	148,627
2021	55,850	21,390	77,680	43,120	64,628	50,028	57,716	54,103	120,478	71,418	135,396	97,223
2022	25,250	9,760	121,370	86,790	47,591	32,397	44,234	51,681	72,841	37,157	165,604	138,471
2023[1]	36,680	19,110	124,150	85,910	52,042	46,710	55,640	56,261	88,722	65,820	179,790	142,171

[1] Preliminary.   *Source: National Agricultural Statistics Service, U.S. Department of Agriculture (NASS-USDA)*

Production of Barley in the United States, by State   In Thousands of Bushels

Crop Year	Arizona	California	Colorado	Idaho	Minn- esota	Montana	North Dakota	Oregon	Penn- sylvania	Virginia	Wash- ington	Wyoming	Total
2014	4,000	1,825	6,696	51,700	3,120	44,660	35,845	1,900	3,550	2,212	6,300	7,276	181,542
2015	1,920	1,595	8,190	56,260	9,240	44,720	67,200	1,924	2,600	1,200	5,040	8,170	218,187
2016	2,048	4,500	9,675	62,060	5,214	46,800	42,880	2,144	2,850	804	7,161	7,872	199,914
2017	2,227	1,450	8,976	48,450	5,168	28,815	26,000	2,356	3,150	803	4,505	6,426	143,258
2018	1,100	1,794	7,685	53,530	5,092	33,600	28,490	1,378	2,079	630	4,891	5,100	153,527
2019	1,890	3,102	7,176	55,120	3,685	44,840	32,040	2,730	1,750	455	5,880	7,062	172,499
2020	976	1,551	6,815	55,000	2,350	49,770	28,980	2,160	2,280	441	6,390	6,432	170,813
2021	2,000	819	5,217	44,500	1,870	24,700	21,930	672	2,240	525	2,660	6,552	120,090
2022	2,128	1,045	4,440	59,940	3,960	24,850	48,180	1,045	1,340	602	5,040	5,487	175,023
2023[1]	1,980	1,425	6,681	60,480	3,996	49,735	40,470	792	2,268	498	4,452	6,032	185,036

[1] Preliminary.   *Source: National Agricultural Statistics Service, U.S. Department of Agriculture (NASS-USDA)*

Average Price Received by Farmers for All Barley in the United States   In Dollars Per Bushel

Crop Year	June	July	Aug.	Sept.	Oct.	Nov.	Dec.	Jan.	Feb.	Mar.	Apr.	May	Average
2014-15	6.01	5.62	5.60	5.31	5.24	5.09	5.16	4.86	5.22	4.87	4.94	4.75	5.22
2015-16	5.04	5.19	5.59	5.49	5.54	5.55	5.88	5.47	5.51	5.43	5.29	5.59	5.46
2016-17	5.39	5.00	4.89	4.54	4.85	4.97	5.12	4.91	5.08	4.97	4.87	5.05	4.97
2017-18	4.47	4.54	4.52	4.32	4.44	4.60	4.38	4.45	4.58	4.46	4.44	4.45	4.47
2018-19	4.62	4.52	4.54	4.49	4.25	4.78	4.64	4.57	4.65	4.88	4.80	4.90	4.64
2019-20	4.81	4.69	4.74	4.56	4.58	4.74	4.51	4.67	4.68	4.89	4.64	4.76	4.69
2020-21	4.57	4.66	4.60	4.76	4.74	4.78	4.79	4.67	4.97	4.90	4.83	4.92	4.77
2021-22	4.86	5.02	5.04	5.11	5.38	5.22	5.41	5.59	5.43	5.69	6.00	6.07	5.40
2022-23	6.44	6.60	7.47	7.51	7.52	7.36	7.48	7.28	7.65	7.48	7.16	7.56	7.29
2023-24[1]	7.39	7.08	7.52	7.45	7.16	7.77	6.68	7.53					7.32

[1] Preliminary.   *Source: National Agricultural Statistical Service, U.S. Department of Agriculture (NASS-USDA)*

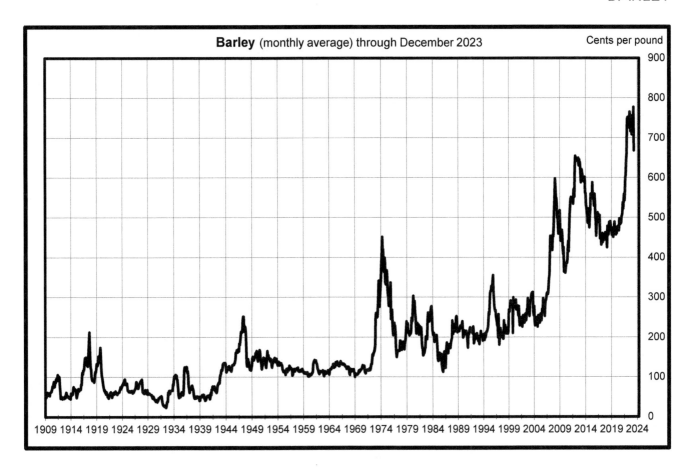

Barley (monthly average) through December 2023 — Cents per pound

Average Price Received by Farmers for Feed Barley in the United States   In Dollars Per Bushel

Crop Year	June	July	Aug.	Sept.	Oct.	Nov.	Dec.	Jan.	Feb.	Mar.	Apr.	May	Average
2014-15	4.32	3.85	3.31	2.97	3.13	2.84	2.99	2.99	2.94	3.08	3.05	2.90	3.20
2015-16	3.55	2.97	3.00	3.24	2.97	3.03	3.11	3.14	3.07	2.79	2.82	3.67	3.11
2016-17	3.38	3.18	2.75	2.39	2.52	2.49	2.87	2.61	2.75	2.50	2.64	2.69	2.73
2017-18	3.47	3.04	2.97	2.62	3.07	2.80	2.85	3.01	2.83	2.90	3.08	3.33	3.00
2018-19	3.79	3.41	3.12	3.07	2.97	3.23	3.06	3.11	3.23	3.23	3.39	3.44	3.25
2019-20	4.32	3.89	3.43	3.18	3.10	2.81	3.32	3.27	3.16	3.55	3.16	3.20	3.37
2020-21	3.25	3.37	3.04	3.11	3.28	3.32	3.01	3.20	3.50	3.82	3.91	4.21	3.42
2021-22	4.33	3.98	4.62	4.98	5.37	5.56	5.51	5.76	6.05	6.12	6.34	6.08	5.39
2022-23	6.72	6.69	5.96	5.65	5.70	6.14	6.08	6.29	6.64	6.13	6.39	6.41	6.23
2023-24[1]	5.43	6.07	5.60	5.23	4.79	5.18	4.62	5.05					5.25

[1] Preliminary.   *Source: National Agricultural Statistical Service, U.S. Department of Agriculture (NASS-USDA)*

Average Price Received by Farmers for Malting Barley in the United States   In Dollars Per Bushel

Crop Year	June	July	Aug.	Sept.	Oct.	Nov.	Dec.	Jan.	Feb.	Mar.	Apr.	May	Average
2014-15	6.30	5.90	6.11	5.91	5.76	5.69	5.63	5.47	5.67	5.39	5.75	5.62	5.77
2015-16	5.68	5.73	5.91	5.74	5.78	5.80	5.99	5.68	5.70	5.64	5.71	6.03	5.78
2016-17	5.70	5.33	5.31	5.13	5.17	5.21	5.32	5.19	5.20	5.13	5.13	5.27	5.26
2017-18	4.66	4.78	4.70	4.64	4.64	4.81	4.51	4.60	4.77	4.60	4.73	4.58	4.67
2018-19	4.88	4.79	4.68	4.72	4.42	4.85	4.78	4.71	4.75	5.02	4.92	5.03	4.80
2019-20	4.88	4.83	4.89	4.78	4.77	4.84	4.81	4.82	4.78	5.07	4.74	4.98	4.85
2020-21	4.95	4.92	4.77	4.92	4.98	5.00	4.86	4.82	5.02	5.04	5.04	5.00	4.94
2021-22	4.99	5.18	5.10	5.16	5.38	5.17	5.39	5.54	5.33	5.59	5.90	6.07	5.40
2022-23	6.41	6.59	7.59	7.70	7.68	7.50	7.62	7.41	7.77	7.63	7.24	7.74	7.41
2023-24[1]	7.84	7.28	7.79	7.66	7.65	8.10	7.23	7.88					7.68

[1] Preliminary.   *Source: National Agricultural Statistical Service, U.S. Department of Agriculture (NASS-USDA)*

BARLEY

Weekly Outstanding Export Sales and Cumulative Exports of U.S. Barley   In Thousands of Metric Tons

Marketing Year 2022/2023 Week Ending	Weekly Exports	Accumulated Exports	Net Sales	Outstanding Sales	Marketing Year 2023/2024 Week Ending	Weekly Exports	Accumulated Exports	Net Sales	Outstanding Sales
Jun 02, 2022				13,768	Jun 01, 2023			3,283	9,323
Jun 09, 2022	964	964		12,804	Jun 08, 2023			7,000	16,323
Jun 16, 2022	473	1,437	1,600	13,931	Jun 15, 2023				16,323
Jun 23, 2022	728	2,165	-1,688	11,515	Jun 22, 2023				16,323
Jun 30, 2022	32	2,197	1,830	13,313	Jun 29, 2023				16,323
Jul 07, 2022	513	2,710		12,800	Jul 06, 2023				16,323
Jul 14, 2022		2,710		12,800	Jul 13, 2023				16,323
Jul 21, 2022		2,710		12,800	Jul 20, 2023				16,323
Jul 28, 2022	42	2,752		12,758	Jul 27, 2023				16,323
Aug 04, 2022	1,015	3,767		11,743	Aug 03, 2023			-265	16,058
Aug 11, 2022		3,767		11,743	Aug 10, 2023				16,058
Aug 18, 2022		3,767		11,743	Aug 17, 2023				16,058
Aug 25, 2022	154	3,921		11,589	Aug 24, 2023				16,058
Sep 01, 2022		3,921		11,589	Aug 31, 2023	22	22		16,036
Sep 08, 2022		3,921		11,589	Sep 07, 2023		22		16,036
Sep 15, 2022		3,921		11,589	Sep 14, 2023	66	88		15,970
Sep 22, 2022		3,921		11,589	Sep 21, 2023	53	141	76	15,993
Sep 29, 2022		3,921		11,589	Sep 28, 2023		141		15,993
Oct 06, 2022		3,921		11,589	Oct 05, 2023	88	229	1	15,906
Oct 13, 2022		3,921		11,589	Oct 12, 2023		229		15,906
Oct 20, 2022		3,921		11,589	Oct 19, 2023		229		15,906
Oct 27, 2022		3,921	-1,516	10,073	Oct 26, 2023		229		15,906
Nov 03, 2022		3,921		10,073	Nov 02, 2023		229		15,906
Nov 10, 2022		3,921		10,073	Nov 09, 2023		229		15,906
Nov 17, 2022	331	4,252	-2,364	7,378	Nov 16, 2023		229		15,906
Nov 24, 2022	770	5,022		6,608	Nov 23, 2023	44	273		15,862
Dec 01, 2022	514	5,536		6,094	Nov 30, 2023		273	460	16,322
Dec 08, 2022		5,536		6,094	Dec 07, 2023		273		16,322
Dec 15, 2022	921	6,457		5,173	Dec 14, 2023	22	295		16,300
Dec 22, 2022		6,457		5,173	Dec 21, 2023	200	495	5	16,105
Dec 29, 2022		6,457		5,173	Dec 28, 2023	525	1,020		15,580
Jan 05, 2023	288	6,745		4,885	Jan 04, 2024	2,189	3,209	2	13,393
Jan 12, 2023		6,745		4,885	Jan 11, 2024	755	3,964		12,638
Jan 19, 2023	445	7,190		4,440	Jan 18, 2024		3,964		12,638
Jan 26, 2023		7,190		4,440	Jan 25, 2024		3,964		12,638
Feb 02, 2023		7,190		4,440	Feb 01, 2024		3,964		12,638
Feb 09, 2023		7,190		4,440	Feb 08, 2024	200	4,164		12,438
Feb 16, 2023	771	7,961	264	3,933	Feb 15, 2024	91	4,255		12,347
Feb 23, 2023		7,961		3,933	Feb 22, 2024		4,255		12,347
Mar 02, 2023		7,961		3,933	Feb 29, 2024		4,255		12,347
Mar 09, 2023		7,961		3,933	Mar 07, 2024	251	4,506		12,096
Mar 16, 2023		7,961		3,933	Mar 14, 2024		4,506		12,096
Mar 23, 2023	214	8,175	-396	3,323	Mar 21, 2024				
Mar 30, 2023		8,175		3,323	Mar 28, 2024				
Apr 06, 2023		8,175		3,323	Apr 04, 2024				
Apr 13, 2023		8,175		3,323	Apr 11, 2024				
Apr 20, 2023		8,175	522	3,845	Apr 18, 2024				
Apr 27, 2023	304	8,479		3,541	Apr 25, 2024				
May 04, 2023		8,479		3,541	May 02, 2024				
May 11, 2023		8,479		3,541	May 09, 2024				
May 18, 2023		8,479		3,541	May 16, 2024				
May 25, 2023	218	8,697		3,323	May 23, 2024				
Jun 01, 2023	40	8,737		3,283	May 30, 2024				

Source: Foreign Agricultural Service, U.S. Department of Agriculture (FAS-USDA)

Bauxite

Bauxite is a naturally occurring, heterogeneous material comprised of one or more aluminum hydroxide minerals plus various mixtures of silica, iron oxide, titanium, alumina-silicates, and other impurities in trace amounts. Bauxite is an important ore of aluminum and forms by the rapid weathering of granite rocks in warm, humid climates. It is easily purified and can be converted directly into either alum or metallic aluminum. It is a soft mineral with hardness varying from 1 to 3, and specific gravity from 2 to 2.55. Bauxite is dull in appearance and may vary in color from white to brown. It usually occurs in aggregates in pea-sized lumps.

Bauxite is the only raw material used in the production of alumina on a commercial scale in the United States. Bauxite is classified according to the intended commercial application, such as abrasive, cement, chemical, metallurgical, and refractory. Of all the bauxite mined, about 95 percent is converted to alumina to produce aluminum metal with some smaller amounts going to nonmetal uses as various forms of specialty alumina. Small amounts are used in non-metallurgical bauxite applications. Bauxite is also used to produce aluminum chemicals and is used in the steel industry.

Supply – World production of bauxite in 2023 remained unchanged yr/yr at 400.000 million metric tons. The world's largest producer of bauxite in 2023 was Australia, with 24.5% of the world's production, followed by Guinea with 24.3%, China with 23.3%, Brazil with 8.7%, India with 5.8%, and both Russia and Jamica with 1.5%.

Demand – US consumption of bauxite in 2023 fell by -17.1% yr/yr to 1.800 million metric tons, below the record high of 15.962 million metric tons seen in 1980.

Trade – The US relies on imports for almost 100% of its bauxite consumption needs. Domestic ore, which provides less than 1 percent of the US requirement for bauxite, is mined by one company from surface mines in the states of Alabama and Georgia. US imports of bauxite in 2023 fell by -14.6% yr/yr to 3.100 million metric tons, the lowest since 1951. US exports of bauxite in 2020 remain unchanged yr/yr at 3.00 million metric tons.

World Production of Bauxite   In Thousands of Metric Tons

Year	Australia	Brazil	China	Greece	Guinea	Guyana[3]	Hungary	India	Jamaica[3]	Russia[3]	Sierra Leone	Suriname	World Total
2016	83,517	39,244	68,620	1,880	31,500	1,480	17	23,886	8,540	5,431	1,369	----	286,000
2017	89,421	38,072	68,390	1,927	46,160	1,482	4	22,803	8,245	5,523	1,788	----	307,000
2018	95,948	32,377	77,170	1,559	57,000	1,924	5	23,229	10,058	5,651	1,938	----	340,000
2019	105,544	31,938	105,000	1,492	67,000	1,900	----	22,321	9,022	5,574	1,884	----	387,000
2020	104,328	31,000	92,700	1,500	86,000	900	----	20,200	7,546	5,570	1,342	----	391,000
2021	103,000	33,000	90,000		86,000		----	17,400	5,950	5,680		----	384,000
2022[1]	102,000	30,000	90,000		100,000		----	24,000	4,370	5,780		----	400,000
2023[2]	98,000	31,000	93,000		97,000		----	23,000	6,000	5,800		----	400,000

[1] Preliminary.   [2] Estimate.   [3] Dry Bauxite equivalent of ore processed.   *Source: U.S. Geological Survey (USGS)*

Salient Statistics of Bauxite in the United States   In Thousands of Metric Tons

Year	Net Import Reliance as a % of Apparent Consump	Average Price F.O.B. Mine $ per Ton	Consumtion by Industry Total	Alumina	Abrasive	Chemical	Refractoty	Dry Equivalent Imports[4]	Exports[3]	Consumption	Stocks, December 31 Producers & Consumers	Gov't Owned	Total
2016	>75	----	5,360	5,080	----	----	----	4,930	5	6,630	W	----	W
2017	>75	----	4,330	2,340	----	----	----	4,350	5	4,330	W	----	W
2018	>75	----	4,460	2,800	----	----	----	3,980	4	4,460	W	----	W
2019	>75	----	3,680	3,130	----	----	----	4,620	3	3,680	W	----	W
2020	>75	----	3,330	2,530	----	----	----	3,760	3	3,330	W	----	W
2021	>75	----	2,790	2,410	----	----	----	3,880			W	----	W
2022[1]	>75	----	2,170	2,620	----	----	----	3,630			W	----	W
2023[2]	>75	----	1,800	1,900	----	----	----	3,100			W	----	W

[1] Preliminary.   [2] Estimate.   [3] Including concentrates.   [4] For consumption.   W = Withheld.   *Source: U.S. Geological Survey (USGS)*

World Production of Alumina   In Thousands of Metric Tons

Year	Australia	Brazil	China	Germany	India	Ireland	Jamaica	Kazakhstan	Russia	Suriname	Ukraine	United States	World Total
2016	20,681	10,886	61,034	1,900	6,028	1,967	1,865	1,500	2,682	----	1,510	2,360	121,000
2017	20,486	11,061	69,017	1,900	6,055	1,937	1,782	1,509	2,822	----	1,676	1,430	129,000
2018	20,062	8,258	72,531	1,900	6,430	1,874	2,484	1,481	2,763	----	1,715	1,570	131,000
2019	20,192	8,700	72,474	1,900	6,690	1,893	2,173	1,500	2,755	----	1,690	1,410	133,000
2020	20,800	10,300	73,100	1,900	6,560	1,880	1,620	1,400	2,870	----	1,730	1,340	136,000
2021	20,400	12,000	75,200	900	7,000	1,880	1,160	1,400	3,050	----	1,770	1,180	139,000
2022[1]	19,500	10,000	81,900	1,000	7,500	1,630	634	1,340	3,080	----	300	920	140,000
2023[2]	19,000	10,000	82,000	720	7,300	1,200	1,500	1,300	2,400	----	----	780	140,000

[1] Preliminary.   [2] Estimate.   *Source: U.S. Geological Survey (USGS)*

Bismuth

Bismuth (symbol Bi) is a rare metallic element with a pinkish tinge. Bismuth has been known since ancient times, but it was confused with lead, tin, and zinc until the middle of the 18th century. Among the elements in the earth's crust, bismuth is ranked about 73rd in natural abundance. This makes bismuth about as rare as silver. Most industrial bismuth is obtained as a by-product of ore extraction.

Bismuth is useful for castings because of the unusual way that it expands after solidifying. Some of bismuth's alloys have unusually low melting points. Bismuth is one of the most difficult of all substances to magnetize. It tends to turn at right angles to a magnetic field. Because of this property, it is used in instruments for measuring the strength of magnetic fields.

Bismuth finds a wide variety of uses such as pharmaceutical compounds, ceramic glazes, crystal ware, and chemicals and pigments. Bismuth is found in household pharmaceuticals and is used to treat stomach ulcers. Bismuth is opaque to X-rays and can be used in fluoroscopy. Bismuth has also found new use as a nontoxic substitute for lead in various applications such as brass plumbing fixtures, crystal ware, lubricating greases, pigments, and solders. There has been environmental interest in the use of bismuth as a replacement for lead used in shot for waterfowl hunting and in fishing sinkers. Another use has been for galvanizing to improve drainage characteristics of galvanizing alloys. Zinc-bismuth alloys have the same drainage properties as zinc-lead without being as hazardous.

Prices – The average price of bismuth (99.99% pure) in the US in 2023 rose by +5.1% yr/yr to $4.10 per pound, well below the 2007 record high of $14.07 per pound.

Supply – World refinery production of bismuth in 2023 rose by +5.3% to 20,000 metric tons. China had 80.0% of production, Japan had 2.5%, and Kazakhstan had 0.8%. The US does not have any significant domestic refinery production of bismuth.

Demand – US consumption of bismuth in 2022 rose by +21.3% yr/yr to 724 metric tons. In 2021, the consumption uses of bismuth were 64.3% for chemicals and 10.9% for fusible alloys.

Trade – US imports of bismuth in 2023 fell by -41.7% yr/yr to 1.800 million metric tons. US exports of bismuth and alloys in 2023 rose by +3.6% yr/yr to 520 metric tons, well below the 2010 record high of 1,040 metric tons.

World Production of Bismuth   In Metric Tons (Mine Output=Metal Content)

| | Mine Output, Metal Content | | | | | | Refined Metal | | | | | |
Year	Bolivia	Canada	China	Mexico	Russia	World Total	Belgium	China	Japan	Kazak-hastan[3]	Mexico	Peru	World Total
2017	----	----	----	----	----	----	----	14,813	525	270	513	----	19,800
2018	----	----	----	----	----	----	----	15,537	571	280	3	----	20,700
2019	----	----	----	----	----	----	----	15,450	570	230	3	----	19,200
2020	----	----	----	----	----	----	----	15,500	570	230	----	----	18,900
2021	----	----	----	----	----	----	----	16,000	500	200	----	----	20,000
2022[1]	----	----	----	----	----	----	----	15,500	490	190	----	----	19,000
2023[2]	----	----	----	----	----	----	----	16,000	500	160	----	----	20,000

[1] Preliminary.   [2] Estimate.   [3] Less than 1/2 unit..   *Source U.S. Geological Survey (USGS)*

Salient Statistics of Bismuth in the United States   In Metric Tons

| | Bismuth Consumed, By Uses | | | | | | | Imports from | | | | |
| | Metal-lurgical Additives | Other Alloys & Uses | Fusible Alloys | Chem-icals[3] | Total Con-sumption | Consumer Stocks Dec. 31 | Exports of Metal & Alloys | Metallic Bismuth from | | | | Dealer Price $ Per Pound |
Year								Belgium	Mexico	Preu	Total	
2017	W	W	99	439	694	489	392	141.0	176.0	----	2,820	4.94
2018	W	W	96	314	570	346	653	143.0	205.0	----	2,510	4.61
2019	W	W	118	305	548	443	636	116.0	195.0	----	2,340	3.18
2020	W	W	84	305	513	271	699	24.2	3.3	----	1,650	2.72
2021	W	W	65	384	597	297	1,010	10.8	7.4	----	1,980	3.74
2022[1]	W	W	182	W	724	356	502	71.7	14.2	----	3,090	3.90
2023[2]				W		340	520			----	1,800	4.10

[1] Preliminary.   [2] Estimate.   [3] Includes pharmaceuticals.   *Source: U.S. Geological Survey (USGS)*

Average Price of Bismuth (99.99%) in the United States   In Dollars Per Pound

Year	Jan.	Feb.	Mar.	Apr.	May	June	July	Aug.	Sept.	Oct.	Nov.	Dec.	Average
2017	4.72	4.63	4.70	4.84	4.93	4.87	4.85	4.87	5.17	5.20	5.20	5.25	4.94
2018	5.22	5.21	5.28	5.22	5.04	4.68	4.55	4.35	4.27	4.17	3.80	3.69	4.62
2019	3.68	3.94	3.68	3.57	3.42	3.19	2.92	2.84	2.74	2.75	2.81	2.66	3.18
2020	2.58	2.58	2.63	2.57	2.59	2.60	2.61	2.67	2.91	2.98	2.98	2.98	2.72
2021	3.00	3.16	3.59	3.83	3.85	3.87	3.79	3.84	3.87	3.94	4.06	4.08	3.74
2022	4.00	3.97	4.01	3.91	3.88	3.84	3.83	3.85	3.76	3.93	3.98	3.87	3.90
2023	3.81	3.86	4.10	4.36	4.38	4.20	3.91	4.02	4.16	4.18	4.00	3.92	4.08

Source: American Metal Market (AMM)

Broilers

Broiler chickens are raised for meat rather than for eggs. The broiler industry was started in the late 1950s when chickens were selectively bred for meat production. Broiler chickens are housed in massive flocks, mainly between 20,000 and 50,000 birds, with some flocks reaching over 100,000 birds. Broiler chicken farmers usually rear five or six batches of chickens per year.

After just six or seven weeks, broiler chickens are slaughtered (a chicken's natural lifespan is around seven years). Chickens marketed as pouissons, or spring chickens, are slaughtered after four weeks. A few are kept longer than seven weeks to be sold as the larger roasting chickens.

Prices – The average monthly price received by farmers for broilers (live weight) in 2023 fell by -14.5% yr/yr to 72.8 cents per pound. The average monthly price of wholesale broilers (ready-to-cook) in 2023 fell by -11.5% to 134.48 cents per pound, below the 2022 record high of 140.53 cents per pound.

Supply – Total production of broilers in 2023 remained unchanged yr/yr at 46.209 billion pounds. The number of broilers raised for commercial production in 2023 was down -0.5% yr/yr to 9.379 billion birds, below from 2022's record high. The average live weight per bird rose by +0.9% to 6.54 pounds, which was a new record high and far heavier than the average bird weight of 3.62 pounds seen in 1970, attesting to the increased efficiency of the industry.

Demand – US per capita consumption of broilers in 2023 rose by +0.3% to 99.2 pounds (ready-to-cook) per-person per-year, up from 2022's record high. US consumption of chicken has more than doubled in the past four decades, up from 47.0 pounds in 1980, as consumers have increased their consumption of chicken because of the focus on low-carb diets and because chicken is a leaner and healthier meat than either beef or pork.

Broiler Supply and Prices in the United States

Years and Quarters	---- Federally Inspected Slaughter ---- Number (Million)	Average Weight (Pounds)	Liveweight Pounds (Mil. Lbs.)	Certified RTC[3] Weight (Mil. Lbs.)	Total Production RTC[3] (Mil. Lbs.)	Per Capita Consumption RTC[3] Basis (Mil. Lbs.)	Prices Farm	Georgia Dock[4]
							---- Cents per Pound ----	
2018	8,984	6.25	56,185	42,328	43,905	92.4	56.83	----
2019	9,135	6.31	57,641	43,426	43,905	95.1	48.18	----
2020	9,139	6.43	58,599	44,163	44,583	95.8	36.42	----
2021	9,151	6.45	59,019	44,540	44,899	96.5	56.02	----
2022	9,331	6.47	60,370	45,588	46,206	98.9	85.13	----
2023[1]	9,353	6.54	61,203	46,248	46,209	99.2	72.68	----
I	2,351	6.50	15,294	11,549	11,549	24.8	72.77	----
II	2,346	6.51	15,280	11,545	11,545	24.7	84.37	----
III	2,346	6.51	15,280	11,545	11,665	25.2	65.70	----
IV	2,310	6.64	15,349	11,610	11,450	24.5	67.87	----

[1] Preliminary. [2] Estimate. [3] Total production equals federal inspected slaughter plus other slaughter minus cut-up & further processing condemnation. [4] Ready-to-cook basis. *Source: Economic Research Service, U.S. Department of Agriculture (ERS-USDA)*

Salient Statistics of Broilers in the United States

Year	Commercial Production Number (Mil. Lbs.)	Commercial Production Liveweight (Mil. Lbs.)	Average Liveweight Per Bird (Mil. Lbs.)	Average Price (cents Lb.)	Value of Production (Mil. $)	Total Chickens[3] Supply and Distribution — Production Federally Inspected (In Millions of Pounds)	Other Chickens	Total	Storage Stocks January 1	Exports	Broiler Feed Ratio (pounds)	Consumption Total (Mil. Lbs.)	Per Capita[4] (Pounds)
2017	8,916	55,313	6.20	54.6	30,232	41,661		41,661	786	6,910	5.4	34,895	
2018	9,032	56,518	6.26	56.8	31,750	42,583		42,583					
2019	9,221	58,266	6.32	48.2	28,314	43,889		43,889					
2020	9,230	59,146	6.41	36.4	21,267	44,582		44,582					
2021	9,209	59,473	6.46	56.0	31,520	44,890		44,890					
2022[1]	9,430	61,181	6.49	85.1	50,446	46,206		46,206					
2023[2]	9,380	61,371	6.54	72.7		46,383		46,383					

[1] Preliminary. [2] Estimate. [3] Ready-to-cook. [4] Retail weight basis. Source: Economic Research Service, U.S. Department of Agriculture (ERS-USDA)

Average Wholesale Broiler[2] Prices RTC (Ready-to-Cook)   In Cents Per Pound

Year	Jan.	Feb.	Mar.	Apr.	May	June	July	Aug.	Sept.	Oct.	Nov.	Dec.	Average
2015	99.62	92.56	98.88	104.79	106.71	101.17	91.01	82.61	77.40	74.09	75.37	82.05	90.52
2016	87.90	81.52	84.46	88.41	93.72	96.93	88.62	79.71	76.68	70.73	79.28	84.04	84.33
2017	85.58	85.07	94.49	96.91	108.97	109.02	103.80	92.47	88.38	84.84	86.06	87.33	93.58
2018	94.00	91.08	101.97	108.73	117.59	118.92	110.60	87.33	83.13	83.56	86.91	89.75	97.80
2019	98.90	89.78	93.33	97.61	100.89	94.63	88.24	80.88	76.92	78.86	78.30	84.63	88.58
2020	90.56	80.64	79.35	53.52	73.75	73.60	70.41	66.08	63.58	67.70	76.80	82.47	73.21
2021	82.29	82.97	86.68	101.50	105.41	106.39	105.75	104.80	105.75	102.95	105.47	124.40	101.20
2022	131.40	125.79	148.04	166.89	169.67	165.83	153.31	130.40	124.70	121.94	124.66	123.69	140.53
2023[1]	121.84	121.68	130.05	140.15	142.43	135.21	118.48	111.24	116.02	113.30	115.58	126.59	124.38

[1] Preliminary. [2] 12-city composite wholesale price. *Source: Economic Research Service, U.S. Department of Agriculture (ERS-USDA)*

BROILERS

Certified Federally Inspected Chicken Slaughter in the United States   In Thousand Head

Year	Jan.	Feb.	Mar.	Apr.	May	June	July	Aug.	Sept.	Oct.	Nov.	Dec.	Total
2014	704,432	664,590	689,189	711,014	712,142	712,605	743,158	709,909	731,821	770,431	644,637	728,499	8,545,000
2015	724,764	654,077	741,648	725,427	704,517	747,484	762,580	740,789	748,689	743,126	674,127	720,679	8,688,700
2016	699,346	699,896	760,432	707,069	745,305	754,657	708,391	793,503	745,766	731,963	712,780	709,319	8,768,427
2017	749,302	679,696	771,634	690,347	782,516	763,000	725,770	809,566	728,356	782,869	728,303	704,485	8,915,844
2018	772,266	693,759	742,817	731,026	794,062	744,471	775,038	823,156	719,006	817,500	729,068	689,771	9,031,940
2019	788,098	697,844	730,928	758,037	803,158	738,489	814,385	804,355	766,832	849,010	712,323	757,769	9,221,228
2020	820,185	716,853	810,686	752,639	732,106	773,413	786,204	771,711	790,691	787,752	719,240	768,071	9,229,551
2021	745,452	676,811	832,145	762,423	738,961	804,545	769,481	799,282	794,794	771,627	749,916	763,139	9,208,576
2022	755,990	714,577	824,227	738,353	780,516	809,283	758,278	862,696	806,793	809,586	793,686	776,509	9,430,494
2023[1]	804,096	731,001	816,086	723,997	820,608	801,062	760,330	851,241	761,055	824,609	761,801	723,689	9,379,575

[1] Preliminary.   *Source: National Agricultural Statistics Service (NASS)*

Average Live Weight of Chickens Slaughtered in the United States   In Pounds

Year	Jan.	Feb.	Mar.	Apr.	May	June	July	Aug.	Sept.	Oct.	Nov.	Dec.	Average
2014	6.00	6.01	5.98	5.99	5.97	5.99	5.95	5.98	5.99	6.07	6.07	6.10	6.01
2015	6.12	6.09	6.07	6.12	6.11	6.09	6.05	6.12	6.18	6.19	6.17	6.14	6.12
2016	6.19	6.17	6.16	6.19	6.17	6.14	6.09	6.09	6.15	6.20	6.21	6.20	6.16
2017	6.20	6.16	6.16	6.18	6.18	6.16	6.14	6.18	6.25	6.29	6.27	6.27	6.20
2018	6.26	6.23	6.24	6.27	6.25	6.22	6.21	6.28	6.30	6.32	6.29	6.22	6.26
2019	6.25	6.21	6.20	6.29	6.33	6.32	6.32	6.34	6.38	6.41	6.38	6.39	6.32
2020	6.41	6.33	6.32	6.45	6.48	6.48	6.33	6.42	6.50	6.48	6.40	6.41	6.42
2021	6.43	6.39	6.39	6.44	6.46	6.47	6.46	6.47	6.55	6.56	6.48	6.40	6.46
2022	6.47	6.45	6.42	6.40	6.42	6.44	6.43	6.47	6.56	6.64	6.57	6.56	6.49
2023[1]	6.54	6.49	6.48	6.49	6.52	6.53	6.47	6.46	6.61	6.70	6.61	6.61	6.54

[1] Preliminary.   *Source: National Agricultural Statistics Service (NASS)*

Live Weight of Chickens Slaughtered in the United States   In Millions of Pounds

Year	Jan.	Feb.	Mar.	Apr.	May	June	July	Aug.	Sept.	Oct.	Nov.	Dec.	Total
2014	4,226.5	3,992.5	4,120.1	4,260.1	4,254.3	4,266.0	4,418.5	4,244.3	4,385.4	4,680.1	3,911.1	4,445.7	51,378.7
2015	4,433.9	3,982.6	4,501.6	4,436.6	4,303.9	4,551.0	4,609.9	4,533.9	4,623.3	4,600.6	4,159.2	4,428.1	53,376.2
2016	4,330.5	4,321.1	4,683.2	4,379.8	4,602.0	4,632.7	4,313.7	4,829.1	4,584.4	4,536.0	4,429.1	4,395.6	54,037.1
2017	4,644.2	4,185.8	4,756.9	4,267.0	4,838.3	4,702.1	4,456.9	4,999.9	4,554.7	4,920.9	4,568.1	4,418.2	55,313.2
2018	4,832.5	4,322.8	4,633.5	4,586.6	4,964.0	4,629.8	4,813.7	5,168.3	4,532.2	5,164.3	4,583.2	4,287.6	56,518.5
2019	4,929.0	4,331.4	4,529.2	4,766.2	5,080.0	4,666.0	5,146.8	5,101.5	4,889.0	5,439.3	4,544.5	4,842.7	58,265.7
2020	5,254.1	4,539.9	5,124.8	4,785.5	4,725.2	5,012.0	4,973.3	4,955.1	5,141.0	5,102.7	4,605.5	4,926.7	59,145.7
2021	4,790.0	4,322.9	5,315.0	4,907.0	4,776.2	5,208.1	4,971.0	5,170.9	5,203.5	5,061.3	4,859.4	4,887.8	59,472.9
2022	4,893.4	4,611.1	5,293.5	4,722.8	5,007.4	5,211.4	4,872.6	5,584.7	5,295.6	5,379.0	5,215.9	5,094.0	61,181.3
2023[1]	5,259.8	4,745.1	5,289.4	4,697.2	5,350.2	5,232.8	4,915.8	5,498.1	5,033.6	5,526.2	5,037.6	4,784.8	61,370.6

[1] Preliminary.   *Source: National Agricultural Statistics Service (NASS)*

Total Chilled and Frozen Pounds Certified[2] in the United States   In Millions of Pounds

Year	Jan.	Feb.	Mar.	Apr.	May	June	July	Aug.	Sept.	Oct.	Nov.	Dec.	Total
2014	3,175.9	3,008.8	3,098.6	3,210.9	3,201.2	3,205.6	3,331.1	3,197.6	3,306.6	3,525.2	2,939.9	3,348.5	38,549.8
2015	3,328.8	3,000.7	3,387.9	3,345.7	3,246.1	3,428.4	3,469.0	3,417.4	3,486.3	3,465.4	3,135.4	3,334.5	40,045.7
2016	3,256.8	3,256.5	3,525.9	3,302.1	3,466.4	3,484.8	3,246.2	3,633.1	3,454.8	3,417.1	3,337.0	3,311.5	40,691.9
2017	3,496.9	3,153.9	3,582.2	3,216.3	3,647.9	3,542.5	3,357.6	3,763.0	3,429.9	3,709.0	3,437.3	3,324.8	41,661.3
2018	3,639.0	3,256.7	3,489.7	3,456.2	3,738.0	3,490.9	3,629.5	3,892.3	3,417.8	3,893.4	3,450.7	3,228.7	42,583.0
2019	3,711.3	3,263.1	3,409.8	3,587.4	3,827.9	3,518.1	3,874.9	3,841.6	3,680.5	4,100.1	3,427.1	3,647.4	43,889.2
2020	3,957.1	3,418.5	3,861.2	3,600.3	3,559.4	3,780.0	3,745.8	3,733.9	3,878.4	3,848.9	3,478.0	3,720.1	44,581.6
2021	3,613.0	3,271.7	4,008.8	3,696.4	3,611.5	3,923.6	3,750.3	3,902.0	3,928.5	3,827.8	3,665.3	3,690.8	44,889.5
2022	3,690.3	3,484.5	3,995.0	3,564.9	3,778.9	3,934.9	3,684.8	4,211.0	4,000.5	4,068.5	3,940.9	3,851.6	46,205.8
2023[1]	3,971.9	3,585.0	3,992.2	3,545.0	4,043.4	3,956.3	3,717.2	4,156.7	3,805.5	4,177.3	3,817.3	3,615.0	46,382.6

[1] Preliminary.   [2] Ready-to-cook weights.   *Source: National Agricultural Statistics Service (NASS)*

Average Price Received by Farmers for Broilers (Liveweight)   In U.S. Cents per Pound

Year	Jan.	Feb.	Mar.	Apr.	May	June	July	Aug.	Sept.	Oct.	Nov.	Dec.	Average
2014	58.0	55.0	65.0	68.0	73.0	70.0	66.0	60.0	66.0	65.0	63.0	58.0	63.9
2015	60.0	54.0	59.0	64.0	65.0	62.0	51.0	47.0	43.0	41.0	42.0	47.0	52.9
2016	51.0	46.0	48.0	51.0	56.0	86.5	51.0	44.0	42.0	37.0	44.0	48.0	50.4
2017	49.0	48.0	55.0	57.0	66.0	66.0	62.0	54.0	51.0	48.0	49.0	50.0	54.6
2018	53.0	52.0	59.0	65.0	72.0	73.0	67.0	49.0	46.0	46.0	49.0	51.0	56.8
2019	56.0	49.0	51.0	55.0	57.0	54.0	48.7	42.1	39.1	41.0	40.3	44.9	48.2
2020	49.4	41.9	43.0	22.6	34.5	36.6	34.5	30.9	29.2	31.5	39.1	43.8	36.4
2021	43.2	43.8	43.1	54.8	59.3	60.0	59.3	58.7	59.5	57.8	59.2	73.5	56.0
2022	79.0	74.7	88.5	103.7	106.9	104.5	96.3	78.0	73.3	71.1	72.9	72.6	85.1
2023[1]	70.5	70.8	77.0	84.6	86.4	82.1	68.5	62.2	66.4	64.9	66.5	72.2	72.7

[1] Preliminary.   Source: Economic Research Service, U.S. Department of Agriculture (ERS-USDA)

Average Wholesale Price of Broilers (Breast, boneless)   In U.S. Cents per Pound

Year	Jan.	Feb.	Mar.	Apr.	May	June	July	Aug.	Sept.	Oct.	Nov.	Dec.	Average
2014	125.77	126.49	145.25	171.76	184.99	198.77	197.87	183.78	187.48	170.11	143.92	132.86	164.09
2015	135.47	139.97	140.74	153.47	163.91	146.67	137.30	140.20	130.32	110.48	105.98	103.33	133.99
2016	107.12	108.40	108.79	116.62	123.79	115.07	129.21	142.84	133.84	116.06	99.01	98.16	116.58
2017	101.00	108.90	125.94	129.90	151.42	163.80	156.62	145.98	133.97	112.69	103.93	103.52	128.14
2018	106.20	105.20	123.32	136.36	127.05	117.65	127.09	112.51	95.41	91.25	85.30	88.72	109.67
2019	100.86	107.06	113.96	127.65	120.11	115.97	110.99	105.06	93.37	86.91	88.86	98.00	105.73
2020	92.18	88.69	112.78	91.12	137.50	124.01	114.82	115.20	98.94	89.21	89.61	94.15	104.02
2021	108.84	132.75	141.28	171.92	212.97	203.54	182.75	188.22	208.42	186.50	182.55	200.58	176.69
2022	230.98	264.45	277.55	301.94	352.06	332.13	282.36	227.75	185.42	118.07	98.16	95.77	230.55
2023[1]	100.68	122.81	136.57	131.28	137.00	130.47	116.07	140.69	165.20	145.09	109.61	98.76	127.85

[1] Preliminary.   Source: Economic Research Service, U.S. Department of Agriculture (ERS-USDA)

Average Wholesale Price of Broilers (Breast, with ribs)   In U.S. Cents per Pound

Year	Jan.	Feb.	Mar.	Apr.	May	June	July	Aug.	Sept.	Oct.	Nov.	Dec.	Average
2014	109.57	103.23	103.27	115.54	127.95	135.96	134.97	130.79	129.09	129.51	119.74	119.52	121.60
2015	118.30	117.58	117.01	118.87	119.00	122.59	117.76	103.97	97.40	90.27	92.00	92.60	108.95
2016	97.38	101.37	102.38	104.93	112.84	114.15	108.53	101.41	103.81	102.72	100.76	103.25	104.46
2017	100.81	101.66	110.51	121.96	134.85	144.42	143.53	131.87	120.05	103.34	103.21	102.51	118.23
2018	114.34	117.06	121.50	131.82	132.40	136.01	131.90	119.48	110.71	104.91	109.29	111.90	120.11
2019	119.97	122.42	120.11	119.81	118.40	116.42	118.68	114.13	103.35	100.33	104.20	103.78	113.47
2020	104.40	99.49	109.63	92.34	98.84	104.10	106.44	105.38	97.83	102.77	104.43	106.38	102.67
2021	107.56	108.29	112.97	120.92	124.60	124.60	118.25	117.16	117.40	117.07	118.32	128.77	117.99
2022	133.08	135.61	154.45	173.80	203.64	211.55	210.71	201.21	163.63	144.79	114.68	114.01	163.43
2023[1]	120.00	134.38	136.86	139.67	144.17	140.74	142.12	141.87	141.87	134.57	129.65	130.35	136.35

[1] Preliminary.   Source: Economic Research Service, U.S. Department of Agriculture (ERS-USDA)

Average Wholesale Price of Broilers (Legs, whole)   In U.S. Cents per Pound

Year	Jan.	Feb.	Mar.	Apr.	May	June	July	Aug.	Sept.	Oct.	Nov.	Dec.	Average
2014	59.54	59.04	61.56	66.97	68.62	67.86	65.94	57.58	54.78	55.48	56.61	54.57	60.71
2015	51.17	44.64	44.83	48.08	41.35	37.95	35.24	36.62	36.15	32.13	32.40	30.76	39.28
2016	33.41	36.40	38.49	40.85	41.07	48.14	41.94	44.04	47.45	44.16	39.51	39.18	41.22
2017	39.31	40.51	44.61	50.24	51.86	53.12	52.53	52.53	48.50	41.93	44.80	42.63	46.88
2018	46.50	49.13	50.64	50.78	50.87	48.56	46.07	45.66	41.30	41.41	42.12	41.68	46.23
2019	51.52	50.32	59.34	59.38	59.50	62.03	61.34	61.66	60.83	58.85	56.26	64.53	58.80
2020	64.93	63.61	64.75	54.83	48.61	44.29	39.80	39.88	43.72	38.46	42.08	47.88	49.40
2021	39.25	44.83	49.36	58.70	61.98	59.85	60.00	60.10	61.49	56.35	54.34	52.06	54.86
2022	51.58	50.69	51.94	56.57	67.91	86.39	82.81	77.95	60.59	43.62	43.95	40.59	59.55
2023[1]	34.87	46.25	64.01	66.60	70.97	69.13	65.46	52.77	59.47	60.13	54.92	55.09	58.31

[1] Preliminary.   Source: Economic Research Service, U.S. Department of Agriculture (ERS-USDA)

Butter

Butter is a dairy product produced by churning the fat from milk, usually cow's milk, until it solidifies. In some parts of the world, butter is also made from the milk of goats, sheep, and even horses. Butter has been in use since at least 2,000 BC. Today butter is used principally as a food item, but in ancient times it was used more as an ointment, medicine, or illuminating oil. Butter was first churned in skin pouches thrown back and forth over the backs of trotting horses.

It takes about 10 quarts of milk to produce 1 pound of butter. The manufacture of butter is the third largest use of milk in the U.S. California is generally the largest producing state, followed closely by Wisconsin, with Washington as a distant third. Commercially finished butter is comprised of milk fat (80% to 85%), water (12% to 16%), and salt (about 2%). Although the price of butter is highly correlated with the price of milk, it also has its own supply and demand dynamics.

The consumption of butter has dropped in recent decades because pure butter has a high level of animal fat and cholesterol that have been linked to obesity and heart disease. The primary substitute for butter is margarine, which is produced from vegetable oil rather than milk fat. U.S. per capita consumption of margarine has risen from 2.6 pounds in 1930 to recent levels near 8.3 pounds, much higher than U.S. butter consumption.

Butter Futures and options are traded on the CME Group. The CME's butter futures contract calls for the delivery of 20,000 pounds of butter and is priced in cents per pound. Futures on butter are traded on the European Energy Exchange and the Singapore Exchange.

Prices – The average monthly price of butter at the CME in 2023 fell by -8.7% yr/yr to $2.61/pound, which was below the 2022 record annual average high of $2.87/pound.

Supply – World production of butter in 2024 is forecasted to rise by +1.6% yr/yr to 11.899 million metric tons, a new record high. The world's largest producers of butter for 2024 are forecasted to be India with 58.0% of the world production, the European Union with 17.5%, the US with 8.1%, New Zealand with 4.4%, and Russia with 2.4%. Production of creamery butter by US factories in 2023 rose by +1.7% yr/yr to 2.091 billion pounds.

Demand – Total commercial use of creamery butter in the US rose by +7.8% yr/yr to 2.158 million pounds in 2023. Cold storage stocks of creamery butter in the US on January 1, 2023, rose by +8.7% yr/yr to 216.295 million pounds.

Trade – World imports of butter in 2024 are expected to rise by +2.6% at 626,000 metric tons. US imports of butter in 2024 are expected to rise by +3.6% to 87,000 metric tons. World exports of butter in 2024 are expected to fall by -1.9% yr/yr to 1.033 million metric tons. US exports in 2024 are expected to rise by +7.0% yr/yr to 46,000 metric tons, far below the 1993 record high of 145,000 metric tons.

Supply and Distribution of Butter in the United States   In Millions of Pounds

Year	Production	Cold Storage Stocks[3] Jan. 1	Imports	Total Supply	Domestic Disappearance Total	Per Capita (Pounds)	Exports	Department of Agriculture Stocks[4] Jan. 1	Stocks[4] Dec 31	Removed by USDA Programs	Total Use	93 Score AA Wholesale Price $ per Pound
2015	1,849.5	104,728	83.775	2,039	1,834	5.6	51	----	----	----	1,885	2.0886
2016	1,839.4	155,082	103.616	2,097	1,872	5.7	60	----	----	----	1,931	2.0815
2017	1,847.5	166,043	90.389	2,103	1,872	5.7	64	----	----	----	1,936	2.3278
2018	1,891.0	168,787	130.071	2,266	1,980		108	----	----	----	2,088	2.2503
2019	1,977.0	179,333	145.504	2,319	2,072		57	----	----	----	2,130	2.2302
2020	2,145.9	189,655	154.322	2,489	2,156		60	----	----	----	2,216	1.5782
2021	2,071.7	273,805	152.117	2,489	2,163		128	----	----	----	2,291	1.7325
2022[1]	2,056.7	199,056	176.368	2,434	2,037		181	----	----	----	2,218	2.8665
2023[2]	2,111.0	216,295	185.186	2,507	2,213		95	----	----	----	2,308	2.6170

[1] Preliminary.   [2] Estimates.   [3] Includes butter-equivalent.   [4] Includes butteroil.   [5] Includes stocks held by USDA.
Source: Economic Research Service, U.S. Department of Agriculture (ERS-USDA)

Quarterly Commercial Disappearance of Creamery Butter in the United States   In Millions of Pounds

Year	First Quarter	Second Quarter	Third Quarter	Fourth Quarter	Total	Year	First Quarter	Second Quarter	Third Quarter	Fourth Quarter	Total
2012	402.5	403.6	435.6	491.3	1,733.0	2018	429.0	421.6	468.5	576.2	1,895.3
2013	412.3	372.2	434.2	517.8	1,736.5	2019	442.7	427.2	472.9	594.2	1,937.0
2014	380.9	433.5	433.6	508.5	1,756.4	2020	461.4	514.2	485.7	611.1	2,072.4
2015	417.3	403.2	468.4	509.5	1,798.4	2021	504.8	470.9	540.5	623.9	2,140.2
2016	447.6	406.3	457.7	546.4	1,857.9	2022	483.0	468.0	491.4	560.0	2,002.4
2017	412.9	428.8	463.5	550.5	1,855.8	2023[1]	507.2	524.7	537.7	588.8	2,158.4

[1] Preliminary.   *Source: Economic Research Service, U.S. Department of Agriculture (ERS-USDA)*

World Production of Butter[3]   In Thousands of Metric Tons

Year	Argentina	Australia	Brazil	Canada	European Union	India	Japan	Mexico	New Zealand	Russia	Ukraine	United States	World Total
2015	46	120	83	91	2,335	5,035	65	216	594	260	103	839	9,999
2016	37	110	82	93	2,021	5,200	66	217	570	246	103	834	9,938
2017	30	103	83	109	2,031	5,400	60	223	525	270	109	838	10,161
2018	33	93	85	116	2,069	5,600	60	228	550	256	106	893	10,452
2019	33	70	85	112	2,125	5,850	62	231	525	268	89	905	10,775
2020	34	75	82	118	2,173	6,100	72	233	500	282	89	973	11,153
2021	41	70	82	122	2,141	6,300	71	235	470	270	72	936	11,252
2022	40	55	81	120	2,090	6,500	75	236	500	275	60	934	11,403
2023[1]	39	50	81	125	2,100	6,750	70	245	510	280	57	955	11,712
2024[2]	40	45	82	130	2,080	6,900	75	250	525	285	55	965	11,899

[1] Preliminary.   [2] Forecast.   [3] Factory (including creameries and dairies) & farm.   NA = Not available.
Source: Foreign Agricultural Service, U.S. Department of Agriculture (FAS-USDA)

World Consumption of Butter   In Thousands of Metric Tons

Year	Argentina	Australia	Brazil	Canada	European Union	India	Japan	Mexico	Russia	Taiwan	Ukraine	United States	World Total
2015	37	94	84	106	2,150	5,032	77	249	350	25	97	832	9,373
2016	32	102	89	117	1,810	5,196	72	267	353	24	93	849	9,411
2017	28	115	88	121	1,862	5,387	72	264	357	24	82	849	9,701
2018	21	117	91	124	1,898	5,577	78	250	346	23	76	898	9,944
2019	19	104	89	141	1,900	5,803	83	277	384	24	80	940	10,315
2020	14	106	85	141	1,909	6,081	79	266	402	22	83	978	10,680
2021	10	95	88	147	1,927	6,289	81	256	393	24	72	981	10,895
2022	11	91	86	150	1,910	6,458	85	245	389	24	52	924	10,969
2023[1]	14	92	87	160	1,870	6,725	92	265	400	26	51	1,004	11,322
2024[2]	12	95	86	165	1,870	6,870	94	270	410	25	51	1,009	11,497

[1] Preliminary.   [2] Forecast.   *Source: Foreign Agricultural Service, U.S. Department of Agriculture (FAS-USDA)*

World Exports of Butter   In Thousands of Metric Tons

Year	Argentina	Australia	Brazil	Canada	European Union	India	Mexico	New Zealand	Russia	Ukraine	United Kingdom	United States	World Total
2015	9	35	1	1	183	9	10	552	3	11	----	23	908
2016	6	30	----	1	302	9	15	554	4	9	65	27	1,100
2017	4	16	----	1	255	15	8	476	3	28	56	29	966
2018	11	17	----	2	247	33	11	501	3	29	65	49	1,048
2019	15	18	1	2	302	47	13	509	2	16	73	26	1,094
2020	21	16	----	5	316	20	9	466	3	9	65	27	1,027
2021	31	22	1	1	265	11	2	439	3	9	55	58	977
2022	29	15	1	1	255	42	----	494	3	13	51	82	1,066
2023[1]	23	9	----	1	285	25	----	520	3	7	55	43	1,053
2024[2]	30	13	1	1	275	30	----	480	3	5	65	46	1,033

[1] Preliminary.   [2] Forecast.   *Source: Foreign Agricultural Service, U.S. Department of Agriculture (FAS-USDA)*

World Imports of Butter   In Thousands of Metric Tons

Year	Australia	Brazil	Canada	European Union	India	Japan	Mexico	New Zealand	Russia	Taiwan	Ukraine	United States	World Total
2015	22	2	17	27	6	16	43	1	90	25	1	38	363
2016	30	7	27	64	6	13	65	2	106	24	1	47	555
2017	35	5	22	62	2	8	49	1	99	24	1	41	525
2018	42	6	22	76	1	16	33	1	88	23	1	59	566
2019	40	5	25	77	----	25	59	1	117	24	4	66	608
2020	43	3	24	52	1	18	42	1	128	22	10	70	611
2021	37	7	28	51	----	12	23	1	122	24	10	69	578
2022	41	6	33	75	----	10	9	2	120	24	1	80	607
2023[1]	50	6	37	55	----	14	20	1	125	26	1	84	610
2024[2]	55	5	36	65	----	16	20	1	125	25	1	87	626

[1] Preliminary.   [2] Forecast.   *Source: Foreign Agricultural Service, U.S. Department of Agriculture (FAS-USDA)*

BUTTER

World Ending Stocks of Butter   In Thousands of Metric Tons

Year	Argentina	Australia	Canada	European Union	India	Japan	New Zealand	Russia	United States	World Total
2015	4	77	10	51	8	19	72	16	70	332
2016	3	85	12	25	9	26	62	11	75	314
2017	2	92	21	----	9	22	84	20	76	333
2018	3	93	33	----	----	20	105	15	81	359
2019	2	81	27	----	----	24	93	14	86	333
2020	1	77	23	----	----	35	98	19	124	390
2021	1	67	25	----	----	37	99	15	90	348
2022	1	57	27	----	----	37	75	18	98	323
2023[1]	3	56	28	----	----	29	34	20	90	270
2024[2]	1	48	28	----	----	26	48	17	87	265

[1] Preliminary.   [2] Forecast.   Source: Foreign Agricultural Service, U.S. Department of Agriculture (FAS-USDA)

Production of Creamery Butter in Factories in the United States   In Thousands of Pounds

Year	Jan.	Feb.	Mar.	Apr.	May	June	July	Aug.	Sept.	Oct.	Nov.	Dec.	Total
2014	184,030	166,097	166,626	167,730	166,285	140,391	137,788	129,092	131,802	151,201	144,518	169,755	1,855,315
2015	173,634	155,976	167,816	165,457	169,409	143,692	135,525	128,072	133,652	148,414	152,323	175,549	1,849,519
2016	170,746	168,272	174,916	171,210	166,178	147,705	135,169	123,523	135,283	139,858	143,086	163,453	1,839,399
2017	178,060	161,013	177,021	161,956	163,397	139,200	135,625	131,152	134,552	144,671	149,721	171,105	1,847,473
2018	182,143	167,669	181,847	175,216	170,122	142,122	134,564	133,571	135,041	148,896	149,428	170,388	1,891,007
2019	189,642	164,525	180,694	172,371	170,044	154,848	150,705	141,323	144,334	162,921	161,852	183,774	1,977,033
2020	204,948	194,756	200,052	227,212	172,353	149,145	152,958	150,931	150,721	161,991	172,909	207,926	2,145,902
2021	222,262	188,833	199,574	182,991	183,041	156,965	147,112	147,053	143,640	164,296	155,987	179,962	2,071,716
2022	194,034	183,462	202,211	181,303	179,812	158,979	151,755	142,959	140,552	162,114	171,461	188,022	2,056,664
2023[1]	201,347	187,200	204,964	196,909	194,581	162,129	159,267	139,969	142,737	162,325	165,844	193,767	2,111,039

[1] Preliminary.   Source: Economic Research Service, U.S. Department of Agriculture (ERS-USDA)

Cold Storage Holdings of Creamery Butter in the United States, on First of Month   In Millions of Pounds

Year	Jan.	Feb.	Mar.	Apr.	May	June	July	Aug.	Sept.	Oct.	Nov.	Dec.
2014	112,467	143,890	171,773	191,755	186,914	209,430	199,248	180,834	172,789	152,361	147,956	107,566
2015	104,728	148,885	179,003	184,373	232,372	265,198	256,000	254,347	212,189	187,528	178,834	132,740
2016	155,082	192,101	235,559	243,134	295,771	324,942	328,149	332,848	318,774	269,125	228,158	161,203
2017	166,043	221,556	269,857	272,500	292,284	313,593	310,158	307,359	280,194	255,839	217,918	159,258
2018	168,787	226,694	265,756	273,955	307,325	338,492	336,625	318,325	209,851	282,379	231,223	154,366
2019	179,333	211,168	243,511	269,697	290,820	313,822	326,297	329,595	304,368	290,649	234,507	180,637
2020	189,655	247,376	301,820	309,587	372,598	375,777	362,452	371,467	371,519	343,948	299,731	251,820
2021	273,805	331,912	354,595	355,784	390,145	413,926	414,654	396,474	362,708	324,395	278,772	210,473
2022	199,056	219,353	263,028	282,821	298,334	321,575	330,844	315,097	278,298	267,356	239,666	199,775
2023[1]	216,295	264,294	294,033	309,486	331,506	367,868	349,779	329,353	291,750	266,635	240,153	212,632

[1] Preliminary.   Source: Agricultural Statistics Board, U.S. Department of Agriculture (ASB-USDA)

Average Price of Butter at Chicago Mercantile Exchange   In Cents Per Pound

Year	Jan.	Feb.	Mar.	Apr.	May	June	July	Aug.	Sept.	Oct.	Nov.	Dec.	Average
2014	1.7756	1.8047	1.9145	1.9357	2.1713	2.2630	2.4624	2.5913	2.9740	2.3184	1.9968	1.7633	2.1643
2015	1.5714	1.7293	1.7166	1.7937	1.9309	1.9065	1.9056	2.1542	2.6690	2.4757	2.8779	2.3318	2.0886
2016	2.1214	2.0840	1.9605	2.0563	2.0554	2.2640	2.2731	2.1776	1.9950	1.8239	1.9899	2.1763	2.0815
2017	2.2393	2.1534	2.1392	2.0992	2.2684	2.5688	2.6195	2.6473	2.4370	2.3293	2.2244	2.2078	2.3278
2018	2.1587	2.1211	2.2011	2.3145	2.3751	2.3270	2.2361	2.3009	2.2545	2.2600	2.2480	2.2071	2.2503
2019	2.2481	2.2659	2.2773	2.2635	2.3366	2.3884	2.3897	2.2942	2.1690	2.1071	2.0495	1.9736	2.2302
2020	1.8813	1.7913	1.7235	1.1999	1.4710	1.8291	1.6925	1.5038	1.5163	1.4550	1.3941	1.4806	1.5782
2021	1.4548	1.3586	1.5898	1.7814	1.8107	1.7934	1.7401	1.6998	1.7725	1.7746	1.9503	2.0641	1.7325
2022	2.6130	2.6668	2.7260	2.7694	2.7360	2.9232	2.9461	2.9792	3.1156	3.1911	2.9560	2.7759	2.8665
2023	2.4599	2.4158	2.4258	2.4018	2.4483	2.4510	2.4825	2.6668	2.7532	3.2387	3.0293	2.6305	2.6170

Source: Economic Research Service, U.S. Department of Agriculture (ERS-USDA)

Cadmium

Cadmium (atomic symbol Cd) is a soft, bluish-white, metallic element that can easily be shaped and cut with a knife. Cadmium melts at 321 degrees Celsius and boils at 765 degrees Celsius. Cadmium burns brightly in air when heated, forming the oxide CdO. In 1871, the German chemist Friedrich Stromeyer discovered cadmium in incrustations in zinc furnaces.

Rare greenockite is the only mineral-bearing cadmium. Cadmium occurs most often in small quantities associated with zinc ores, such as sphalerite. Electrolysis or fractional distillation is used to separate the cadmium and zinc. About 80% of world cadmium output is a by-product of zinc refining. The remaining 20% comes from secondary sources and the recycling of cadmium products. Cadmium recycling is practical only from nickel-cadmium batteries and from some alloys and dust from electric-arc furnaces.

Cadmium is used primarily for metal plating and coating operations in transportation equipment, machinery, baking enamels, photography, and television phosphors. It is also used in solar modules, pigments and lasers, and in nickel-cadmium and solar batteries.

Supply – World cadmium production in 2023 rose by +1.8% yr/yr to 23,000 metric tons, below the 2018 record high of 26,800 metric tons. The largest producer was China, with 39.1% of total world production, followed by South Korea with 17.4%, and both Japan and Canada with 7.8%.

Trade – US imports in 2023 fell by -41.4% yr/yr to 82 metric tons. US exports of cadmium in 2023 rose by +37.7% yr/yr to 179 metric tons.

World Refinery Production of Cadmium   In Metric Tons

Year	Australia	Canada	China	Germany	India	Japan	Kazakh-stan	Korea, South	Mexico	Nether-lands	Russia	United States[3]	World Total
2015	380	1,159	8,162	400	130	1,959	1,475	5,600	1,283	1,100	1,200	W	25,100
2016	352	2,305	8,222	400	21	1,988	1,500	5,273	1,244	1,000	1,200	W	25,600
2017	388	1,802	8,411	500	61	2,142	1,500	4,960	1,142	890	1,200	470	25,500
2018	342	1,857	10,349	500	----	1,979	1,500	4,905	1,357	960	1,150	375	26,800
2019	174	1,803	10,000	500	----	1,783	1,500	4,400	1,395	860	1,000	207	25,200
2020	348	1,800	10,000	450	----	1,880	1,500	3,000	978	880	1,000	229	24,000
2021	402	1,800	10,000	417	----	1,900	1,200	4,000	859	854	1,000	241	24,700
2022[1]	328	1,800	8,700	320	----	1,800	1,000	4,000	1,170	574	1,000	212	22,600
2023[2]	380	1,800	9,000	----	----	1,800	1,000	4,000	1,100	750	1,000	220	23,000

[1] Preliminary.   [2] Estimate.   [3] Primary and secondary metal.   *Source: U.S. Geological Survey (USGS)*

Salient Statistics of Cadmium in the United States   In Metric Tons of Contained Cadmium

Year	Net import Reliance As a % of Apparent Consumption	Production (Metal)	Producer Shipments	Cadmium Sulfide Production	Production Other Compounds	Imports of Cadmium Metal[3]	Exports[4]	Apparent Consumption	Industry Stocks Dec. 31[5]	New York Dealer Price $ Per Lb.
2015	E	W	W	----	----	326	596	W	W	.67
2016	<25	W	W	----	----	292	540	W	W	.61
2017	<25	W	W	----	----	296	428	W	W	.79
2018	<75	W	W	----	----	294	139	W	W	1.31
2019	<75	W	W	----	----	492	122	W	W	1.21
2020	<75	W	W	----	----	375	486	W	W	1.04
2021	<50	W	W	----	----	242	268	W	W	1.16
2022[1]	<25	W	W	----	----	140	130	W	W	1.55
2023[2]	E	W	W	----	----	82	179	W	W	1.86

[1] Preliminary.   [2] Estimate.   [3] For consumption.   [4] Cadmium metal, alloys, dross, flue dust.   [5] Metallic, Compounds, Distributors.   [6] Sticks & Balls in 1 to 5 short ton lots of metal (99.95%).   E = Net exporter.   *Source: U.S. Geological Survey (USGS)*

Average Price of Cadmium (99.95%) in the United States   In Dollars Per Pound

Year	Jan.	Feb.	Mar.	Apr.	May	June	July	Aug.	Sept.	Oct.	Nov.	Dec.	Average
2015	79.90	73.82	64.61	54.91	50.25	44.66	41.97	39.16	35.50	36.11	39.33	42.83	50.25
2016	46.79	52.36	58.74	68.79	73.00	71.64	64.29	54.30	50.77	54.05	63.89	67.50	60.51
2017	67.50	70.75	74.20	77.90	78.35	74.32	70.69	70.50	71.64	90.86	104.55	102.14	79.45
2018	101.00	121.85	152.50	155.43	143.46	130.83	129.66	127.50	127.50	127.50	127.50	126.50	130.94
2019	125.30	135.88	138.00	137.66	131.11	123.10	113.22	109.09	108.57	110.00	108.10	116.38	121.37
2020	119.15	119.75	121.50	116.67	107.50	105.00	97.30	94.25	91.61	89.56	89.75	93.89	103.83
2021	96.22	110.38	24.56	129.50	129.50	116.17	104.94	96.25	104.28	118.33	130.25	131.90	107.69
2022	132.50	134.38	144.95	154.67	158.13	156.67	154.34	150.67	157.33	166.88	172.45	180.00	155.25
2023	180.32	191.26	212.90	233.93	208.61	161.94	147.50	155.00	173.28	201.88	179.17	169.44	184.60

Source: American Metal Market (AMM)

Canola (Rapeseed)

Canola is a genetic variation of rapeseed that was developed by Canadian plant breeders specifically for its nutritional qualities and its low level of saturated fat. The term *Canola* is a contraction of "Canadian oil." The history of canola oil begins with the rapeseed plant, a member of the mustard family. The rape plant is grown both as feed for livestock and birdfeed. For 4,000 years, the oil from the rapeseed was used in China and India for cooking and as lamp oil. During World War II, rapeseed oil was used as a marine and industrial lubricant. After the war, the market for rapeseed oil plummeted. Rapeseed growers needed other uses for their crops, and that stimulated the research that led to the development of canola. In 1974, Canadian plant breeders from the University of Manitoba produced canola by genetically altering rapeseed. Each canola plant produces yellow flowers, which then produce pods. The tiny round seeds within each pod are crushed to produce canola oil. Each canola seed contains approximately 40% oil. Canola oil is the world's third-largest source of vegetable oil, accounting for 13% of world vegetable oils, following soybean oil at 32%, and palm oil at 28%. The rest of the seed is processed into canola meal, which is used as high-protein livestock feed.

The climate in Canada is especially suitable for canola plant growth. Today, over 13 million acres of Canadian soil are dedicated to canola production. Canola oil is Canada's leading vegetable oil. Due to strong demand from the U.S. for canola oil, approximately 70% of Canada's canola oil is exported to the U.S. Canola oil is used as a salad oil, cooking oil, and for margarine as well as in the manufacture of inks, biodegradable greases, pharmaceuticals, fuel, soap, and cosmetics.

Canola futures and options are traded on the ICE Futures U.S. exchange. The futures contract calls for the delivery of 20 metric tons of canola and 5 contracts are together called a "1 board lot." The futures contract is priced in Canadian dollars per metric ton.

Prices – ICE canola prices on the nearest-futures chart (Barchart.com symbol code RS) in 2023 fell by -24.5% yr/yr to CD $648.40 per metric ton. The average monthly wholesale price of canola oil in the Midwest in 2023 fell by -23.2% yr/yr to 68.77 cents per pound. The average monthly wholesale price of canola meal (delivery Pacific Northwest) in the 2022/23 crop year fell by -1.8% to $431.33 per short ton.

Supply – World canola production in the 2023/24 marketing year is forecasted to fall by -1.9% yr/yr to 87.103 million metric tons, below the record high from 2022/2023. The world's largest canola producers in 2023/24 are expected to be the European Union with 23.0% of world production, Canada with 21.6%, China with 17.7%, and India with 13.4%. US production of canola in 2023/24 is expected to rise by +9.0% yr/yr to 1.895 million metric tons. US production of canola oil in 2023/24 is expected to rise by +0.5% to 820,000 metric tons. World production of canola meal in 2023/24 is expected to rise by +1.6% to 47.776 million metric tons.

Demand – World crush demand for canola in 2023/24 is expected to rise by +1.9% yr/yr to 82.123 million metric tons. World consumption of canola meal in 2023/24 is expected to rise by +0.4% yr/yr to 47.234 million metric tons. World consumption of canola oil in 2023/24 is expected to rise by +0.8% to 32.792 million metric tons.

Trade – World canola exports in 2023/24 are expected to fall by -16.8% to 17.143 million metric tons below the record high in 2022/23. World canola oil exports are expected to rise by +13.8% to 7.310 million metric tons. World canola meal exports are expected to fall by -2.7% yr/yr to 9.302 million metric tons. World canola imports in 2023/24 are expected to fall by -20.2% to 16.015 million metric tons, world canola oil imports are expected to rise by +1.7% to 7.077 million metric tons, and world canola meal imports are expected to fall by -3.2% to 9.031 million metric tons. Regarding US canola trade, US canola imports in 2023/24 are expected to fall by -31.7% to 394,000 metric tons, and US exports are expected to rise by +20.8% to 180,000 metric tons.

World Production of Canola (Rapeseed)   In Thousands of Metric Tons

Year	Australia	Bangla-desh	Belarus	Canada	China	European Union	India	Kazakh-stan	Pakistan	Russia	Ukraine	United States	World Total
2014-15	3,540	670	730	16,410	13,914	24,587	5,080	241	211	1,324	2,200	1,138	70,990
2015-16	2,775	700	382	18,377	13,859	21,997	5,920	138	200	1,001	1,744	1,305	69,403
2016-17	4,313	705	260	19,599	13,128	18,763	6,620	170	196	997	1,250	1,405	70,165
2017-18	3,893	610	603	21,458	13,274	20,017	7,100	279	261	1,497	2,217	1,394	75,797
2018-19	2,366	680	456	20,724	13,281	18,048	7,500	394	343	1,989	2,850	1,642	73,480
2019-20	2,299	750	578	19,912	13,485	15,252	7,400	241	561	2,040	3,465	1,551	70,321
2020-21	4,756	787	731	19,485	14,049	16,732	8,600	153	337	2,567	2,750	1,596	74,737
2021-22[1]	6,820	822	715	14,248	14,714	17,389	11,100	146	477	2,775	3,015	1,242	75,829
2022-23[2]	8,273	1,050	800	18,695	15,531	19,620	11,300	189	740	4,300	3,500	1,739	88,787
2023-24[3]	5,500	1,030	900	18,800	15,400	20,050	11,700	150	650	4,100	4,300	1,895	87,103

[1] Preliminary.   [2] Estimate.   [3] Forecast.   *Source: Economic Research Service, U.S. Department of Agriculture (ERS-USDA); The Oil World*

World Supply and Distribution of Canola   In Thousands of Metric Tons

Crop Year	Supply Production	Supply Imports	Supply Total	Disapearance Exports	Disapearance Crush	Disapearance Consumption	Ending Stocks
2014-15	70,990	14,316	93,106	15,105	67,562	70,630	7,371
2015-16	69,403	14,127	90,901	14,399	67,139	70,136	6,366
2016-17	70,165	15,795	92,383	16,145	67,935	70,930	5,308
2017-18	75,797	15,728	96,833	16,595	68,915	72,095	8,143
2018-19	73,480	14,636	96,259	14,678	68,673	71,837	9,744
2019-20	70,321	15,818	95,883	16,012	69,029	72,227	7,644
2020-21	74,737	16,657	99,038	18,138	71,913	74,535	6,365
2021-22[1]	75,829	13,840	96,034	15,344	72,233	76,207	4,483
2022-23[2]	88,787	20,059	113,329	20,615	80,568	84,866	7,848
2023-24[3]	87,103	16,015	110,966	17,143	82,123	86,482	7,341

Crop year beginning June 1.   [1] Preliminary.   [2] Estimate.   [3] Forecast.   *Source: Economic Research Service, U.S. Department of Agriculture (USDA)*

World Supply and Distribution of Canola Meal   In Thousands of Metric Tons

Crop Year	Supply Production	Supply Imports	Supply Total	Disapearance Exports	Disapearance Consumption	Ending Stocks
2014-15	38,985	6,008	45,896	6,068	38,858	970
2015-16	38,882	5,706	45,558	5,695	38,712	1,151
2016-17	39,102	6,187	46,619	6,255	38,962	1,402
2017-18	39,681	6,509	47,592	6,675	39,436	1,481
2018-19	39,559	7,173	48,213	7,217	39,749	1,247
2019-20	39,812	8,007	49,066	7,722	39,934	1,410
2020-21	41,521	8,370	51,301	8,225	41,855	1,221
2021-22[1]	42,149	7,669	51,039	7,647	41,897	1,495
2022-23[2]	47,021	9,327	57,843	9,565	47,041	1,237
2023-24[3]	47,776	9,031	58,044	9,302	47,234	1,508

Crop year beginning June 1.   [1] Preliminary.   [2] Estimate.   [3] Forecast.   *Source: Economic Research Service, U.S. Department of Agriculture (USDA)*

World Supply and Distribution of Canola Oil   In Thousands of Metric Tons

Crop Year	Supply Production	Supply Imports	Supply Total	Disapearance Exports	Disapearance Consumption	Ending Stocks
2014-15	27,621	3,954	37,854	4,066	27,105	6,683
2015-16	27,567	4,127	38,377	4,171	28,499	5,707
2016-17	27,813	4,556	38,028	4,638	29,140	4,250
2017-18	28,330	4,837	37,417	4,834	29,186	3,397
2018-19	28,019	5,180	36,596	5,263	28,332	3,001
2019-20	28,336	5,801	37,138	5,874	28,392	2,872
2020-21	29,355	6,327	38,554	6,419	28,673	3,462
2021-22[1]	29,240	5,129	37,831	5,289	29,939	2,603
2022-23[2]	32,636	6,956	42,195	6,423	32,538	3,234
2023-24[3]	33,292	7,077	43,603	7,310	32,792	3,501

Crop year beginning June 1.   [1] Preliminary.   [2] Estimate.   [3] Forecast.   *Source: Economic Research Service, U.S. Department of Agriculture (USDA)*

Salient Statistics of Canola in the United States   In Thousands of Metric Tons

Crop Year	Supply Beginning Stocks	Supply Imports	Supply Imports	Supply Total	Disapearance Exports	Disapearance Crush	Consumption
2014-15	129	1,138	777	2,044	160	1,737	2,044
2015-16	110	1,305	359	1,774	176	1,542	1,774
2016-17	161	1,405	697	2,263	118	2,003	2,263
2017-18	109	1,394	651	2,154	154	1,765	2,154
2018-19	88	1,642	564	2,294	181	1,723	2,294
2019-20	139	1,551	563	2,253	183	1,834	2,253
2020-21	219	1,596	440	2,255	156	2,080	2,255
2021-22[1]	214	1,242	503	1,959	129	1,659	1,959
2022-23[2]	110	1,739	577	2,426	149	1,930	2,426
2023-24[3]	222	1,895	394	2,511	180	2,027	2,511

Crop year beginning June 1.   [1] Preliminary.   [2] Estimate.   [3] Forecast.   *Source: Economic Research Service, U.S. Department of Agriculture (USDA)*

CANOLA

CANOLA - ICE-US
Weekly Nearest Futures as of 03/28/2024

WEEKLY NEAREST FUTURES
As of 03/28/2024

Chart High 1226.00 on 05/13/2022
Chart Low 388.00 on 09/22/2014

CAD / metric ton

Nearby Futures through Last Trading Day.

Volume of Trading of Canola Futures in Winnipeg   In 20 Metric Ton Units

Year	Jan.	Feb.	Mar.	Apr.	May	June	July	Aug.	Sept.	Oct.	Nov.	Dec.	Total
2014	536,669	570,465	454,015	552,959	369,170	424,087	331,748	298,308	486,457	615,158	346,000	568,886	5,553,922
2015	489,637	486,854	400,209	447,467	327,911	644,971	335,432	365,804	447,279	624,741	403,539	585,625	5,559,469
2016	408,059	641,600	441,094	619,493	518,643	644,052	358,823	385,481	407,031	702,156	490,671	627,053	6,244,156
2017	397,507	549,415	508,671	521,424	344,251	530,093	331,900	298,854	390,755	625,937	381,367	511,181	5,391,355
2018	349,016	530,467	351,802	541,694	324,795	561,388	269,381	251,140	260,732	537,386	333,575	516,654	4,828,030
2019	368,405	516,738	415,251	588,285	438,572	513,703	275,852	296,384	435,966	767,539	323,919	671,042	5,611,656
2020	496,090	575,177	481,171	426,406	297,740	508,999	409,940	425,008	661,995	702,630	505,482	729,352	6,219,990
2021	664,635	538,933	550,593	480,895	434,674	457,399	389,025	369,036	543,404	578,551	505,083	403,009	5,915,237
2022	483,771	457,952	391,689	383,358	333,590	535,822	344,636	514,163	684,010	728,966	696,913	546,626	6,101,496
2023	671,831	619,786	801,487	709,534	627,332	845,157	618,746	574,701	717,888	953,529	693,469	840,838	8,674,298

Contract size = 20 tonnes.   *Source: ICE Futures Canada (ICE)*

Average Open Interest of Canola Futures in Winnipeg   In 20 Metric Ton Units

Year	Jan.	Feb.	Mar.	Apr.	May	June	July	Aug.	Sept.	Oct.	Nov.	Dec.
2014	230,796	224,847	230,852	219,844	168,705	165,651	147,462	165,501	173,282	159,986	142,371	139,732
2015	170,492	217,729	205,075	168,204	151,739	189,500	180,410	173,734	172,828	186,334	174,098	187,855
2016	187,904	177,999	171,820	162,225	173,204	172,984	155,301	173,698	195,884	190,086	208,329	210,792
2017	181,938	181,007	185,572	185,411	178,603	159,381	117,599	128,345	180,168	173,585	192,341	171,325
2018	171,262	180,496	184,370	210,695	207,565	200,361	172,198	173,769	178,603	147,365	168,872	175,750
2019	179,931	175,601	186,451	182,587	181,226	149,724	145,360	160,362	191,328	189,443	178,886	185,330
2020	187,307	189,665	177,355	173,681	178,525	171,799	165,281	199,313	230,858	205,153	220,330	210,429
2021	208,767	214,023	215,803	200,943	189,813	197,136	205,549	215,315	210,134	205,707	194,497	184,288
2022	173,223	157,954	146,356	143,578	140,476	141,374	132,475	157,169	204,760	218,705	232,219	231,568
2023	224,486	258,866	299,065	270,150	258,066	232,173	215,427	260,833	297,481	293,853	270,368	254,512

Contract size = 20 tonnes.   *Source: ICE Futures Canada (ICE)*

Production of Canola in the United States, by States   In Thousands of Pounds

Year	Idaho	Kansas	Minnesota	Montana	North Dakota	Oklahoma	Oregon	Washington	Other	Total
2014	61,200	----	22,275	84,180	2,142,000	96,100	15,000	56,400	33,840	2,510,995
2015	37,800	----	40,420	93,940	2,492,000	131,100	3,240	37,400	42,570	2,878,470
2016	45,100	46,560	46,750	100,200	2,668,000	101,500	8,880	62,000	----	3,078,990
2017	37,910	62,040	71,760	117,820	2,496,000	168,000	11,160	90,720	----	3,055,410
2018	88,200	33,600	92,700	129,920	3,096,800	46,640	7,650	119,930	----	3,615,440
2019	----	20,710	110,095	200,100	2,898,000	29,610	----	142,350	----	3,400,865
2020	----	5,012	75,360	241,380	2,920,400	10,710	----	200,200	----	3,453,062
2021	----	7,800	104,550	144,900	2,304,800	15,500	----	137,500	----	2,715,050
2022	----	4,623	166,290	172,010	3,248,700	5,600	----	217,600	----	3,814,823
2023[1]	----	420	195,130	227,200	3,466,150	1,200	----	267,320	----	4,157,420

[1] Preliminary.   Source: Economic Research Service, U.S. Department of Agriculture (ERS-USDA)

Average Price Received by Farmers for Canola in the United States   In U.S. Dollars per cwt.

Year	Jan.	Feb.	Mar.	Apr.	May	June	July	Aug.	Sept.	Oct.	Nov.	Dec.	Average
2014	19.80	18.50	18.40	19.50	21.70	20.80	20.70	17.80	16.20	15.80	17.10	16.60	18.58
2015	17.80	17.20	16.60	16.30	16.70	17.80	18.10	15.60	15.10	14.80	15.10	14.90	16.33
2016	13.80	15.30	15.10	16.10	W	18.80	16.60	15.60	15.50	15.80	16.20	17.10	15.99
2017	17.30	17.40	17.60	18.00	16.80	17.40	17.80	17.70	17.30	16.60	17.20	16.70	17.32
2018	17.70	18.30	18.20	17.50	18.50	17.20	17.10	15.30	15.20	15.60	16.10	16.30	16.92
2019	16.70	16.20	15.80	15.80	15.20	14.90	14.80	14.50	14.20	14.20	14.30	14.70	15.11
2020	16.10	16.10	15.70	15.20	14.40	15.20	15.60	15.10	16.40	16.30	18.10	17.20	15.95
2021	18.80	20.40	22.00	23.80	26.10	26.00	27.70	30.90	28.70	29.60	31.70	32.50	26.52
2022	33.70	37.50	39.20	41.30	42.90	45.60	42.60	40.00	28.10	28.10	29.20	29.20	36.45
2023[1]	30.10	30.70	30.90	26.80	25.20	27.30	27.20	28.10	25.10	23.60	25.50	24.20	27.06

[1] Preliminary.   Source: Economic Research Service, U.S. Department of Agriculture (ERS-USDA)

Wholesale Price of Canola Oil in Midwest   In Cents Per Pound

Year	Jan.	Feb.	Mar.	Apr.	May	June	July	Aug.	Sept.	Oct.	Nov.	Dec.	Average
2014	39.75	42.56	45.75	47.63	47.50	46.00	43.63	40.10	38.94	39.45	38.94	39.25	42.46
2015	38.80	38.94	35.69	37.19	38.55	40.19	38.30	35.13	33.31	34.20	33.63	36.50	36.70
2016	34.06	34.63	35.55	36.80	35.06	35.10	33.55	36.94	37.25	38.94	39.25	40.20	36.44
2017	38.69	37.25	37.30	36.13	37.06	37.85	39.75	41.19	41.15	39.06	39.69	38.65	38.65
2018	38.31	37.44	37.10	37.31	38.25	37.75	38.69	38.75	38.19	38.94	37.45	36.75	37.91
2019	37.13	37.75	36.15	35.44	34.10	34.63	34.56	35.25	35.00	36.31	36.15	38.06	35.88
2020	37.90	35.50	32.88	32.38	32.40	36.63	40.50	47.81	47.94	44.35	49.50	51.65	40.79
2021	53.31	58.94	71.31	79.55	94.06	93.50	92.30	81.00	76.00	82.30	84.38	82.95	79.13
2022	88.56	85.88	92.00	103.15	108.69	102.25	87.90	91.31	76.85	80.13	84.38	74.05	89.59
2023[1]	71.19	68.25	64.60	62.63	62.13	71.85	83.00	81.69	73.75	65.19	61.63	59.45	68.78

[1] Preliminary.   Source: Economic Research Service, U.S. Department of Agriculture (ERS-USDA)

Average Wholesale Price of Canola Meal, 36% Pacific Northwest   In Dollars Per Short Ton

Crop Year	Oct.	Nov.	Dec.	Jan.	Feb.	Mar.	Apr.	May	June	July	Aug.	Sept.	Average
2014-15	301.75	356.31	349.31	311.56	296.21	279.54	261.35	274.60	305.85	328.03	285.83	264.01	301.20
2015-16	257.69	248.98	240.64	231.76	224.34	228.87	247.53	329.01	345.14	306.03	255.35	231.00	262.20
2016-17	225.05	234.78	243.30	267.41	276.90	276.33	270.66	279.64	281.66	307.73	289.45	262.33	267.94
2017-18	257.73	255.74	266.53	270.20	315.95	334.58	332.16	336.93	302.75	279.84	274.55	266.86	291.15
2018-19	279.40	279.16	291.42	----	----	----	----	259.55	278.76	265.45	----	253.03	272.40
2019-20	267.90	----	----	----	253.67	274.75	274.53	276.25	270.03	271.11	281.09	296.60	273.99
2020-21	327.24	333.89	338.55	387.53	376.08	365.14	377.58	391.45	345.90	326.68	329.45	322.96	351.87
2021-22	322.83	350.22	382.97	410.88	454.63	487.04	470.78	454.50	478.18	501.18	521.53	434.54	439.10
2022-23	409.18	403.00	437.10	474.03	501.03	466.60	434.75	407.03	405.06	432.10	412.90	393.26	431.34
2023-24[1]	407.10	441.77	395.05	349.30									398.31

[1] Preliminary.   Source: Economic Research Service, U.S. Department of Agriculture (ERS-USDA)

Cattle and Calves

The beef cycle begins with the cow-calf operation, which breeds the new calves. Most ranchers breed their herds of cows in summer, thus producing the new crop of calves in spring (the gestation period is about nine months). This allows the calves to be born during the milder weather of spring and provides the calves with ample forage through the summer and early autumn. The calves are weaned from the mother after 6-8 months, and most are then moved into the "stocker" operation. The calves usually spend 6-10 months in the stocker operation, growing to near full-sized by foraging for summer grass or winter wheat. When the cattle reach 600-800 pounds, they are typically sent to a feedlot and become "feeder cattle." In the feedlot, the cattle are fed with a special food mix to encourage rapid weight gain. The mix includes grain (corn, milo, or wheat), a protein supplement (soybean, cottonseed, or linseed meal), and roughage (alfalfa, silage, prairie hay, or an agricultural by-product such as sugar beet pulp). The animal is considered "finished" when it reaches full weight and is ready for slaughter, typically at around 1,200 pounds, which produces a dressed carcass of around 745 pounds. After reaching full weight, the cattle are sold for slaughter to a meatpacking plant.

Futures and options on live cattle and feeder cattle are traded at the CME Group. Both the live and feeder cattle futures contracts trade in terms of cents per pound.

Prices – CME live cattle futures prices (Barchart.com symbol LE) in early 2023 extended the 4-year rally that began in 2020. A shrinking US cattle herd underpinned live cattle prices as the USDA's biannual cattle inventory report, released in January 2023, showed the US cattle herd dropped to 89.27 million head, the smallest herd since 2014. Years-long drought in the US Plains withered pastures and reduced supplies of feeds, including hay and corn, forcing ranchers to liquidate herds to cut costs. In addition, beef cows, developed for breeding to raise calves, fell to the lowest number since 1962. Cattle prices continued higher into Q3 of 2023 and posted a record high of $1.875 a pound in September as the smaller US breeding herd kept cattle supplies tight. The shrinking US cattle herd reduced cattle slaughter rates and cut into beef supplies as US beef supplies in cold storage fell to an 8-year low in August of 395.4 million pounds. Cattle prices fell back from record highs into the year-end as higher cash cattle prices curbed cattle demand from beef processors. Also, an improvement in beef packer profit margins prompted cattle ranchers to send more cattle to slaughter as September cattle-on-feed placements rose +6.1% yr/yr to 2.206 million head, the most in 2 years. In addition, the number of cattle on feed increased, with cattle on feed in November climbing to a 1-1/2 year high of 11.943 million head. Cattle prices finished 2023 up +6.7% yr/yr at $1.6850 per pound.

Supply – The number of world cattle as of January 1, 2024, remained unchanged at 943.9 million head. As of January 1, 2024, the number of cattle on farms in India (the world's largest herd) rose by +0.1% to 307.635 million head, and on Brazilian farms (the world's second-largest herd) fell by -0.2% to 193.900 million head. As of January 1, 2024, the number of cattle and calves on US farms fell by -1.9% yr/yr to 87.157 million head. The USDA reported that US commercial production of beef in 2023 fell by -4.2% yr/yr to 25.810 billion pounds.

Demand – The federally-inspected slaughter of cattle in the US, a measure of cattle consumption, fell by -4.3% yr/yr to 32.232 million head in 2023, well above the 5-decade low of 28.296 million head in 2015.

Trade – US imports of live cattle in 2023 rose by +24.7% yr/yr to 2.030 million head. US imports of beef in 2024 rose by +1.0% to 3.690 billion pounds. US exports of beef in 2023 fell by -6.3% yr/yr to a record 2.845 billion pounds.

World Cattle and Buffalo Numbers as of January 1   In Thousands of Head

Year	Argentina	Australia	Brazil	Canada	China	European Union	India	Mexico	New Zealand	Russia	United States	Uruguay	World Total
2013	52,201	28,418	184,464	12,240	91,373	87,106	299,600	18,521	10,180	19,680	90,095	11,384	949,549
2014	52,396	29,291	184,988	12,050	89,858	87,619	300,200	17,760	10,183	19,273	88,243	11,903	946,084
2015	52,168	29,102	187,474	11,640	90,073	88,383	300,600	17,120	10,368	18,920	89,173	12,053	929,251
2016	53,118	27,413	190,062	11,610	90,558	79,303	301,000	16,615	10,033	18,528	91,888	12,016	929,707
2017	54,163	24,971	187,285	11,535	88,345	79,698	301,400	16,490	10,152	18,248	93,625	11,864	925,578
2018	54,793	26,176	186,245	11,670	90,386	79,010	301,900	16,584	10,146	18,195	94,298	11,744	929,055
2019	55,008	25,699	187,290	11,670	89,153	77,840	302,700	16,699	10,107	18,050	94,805	11,396	928,341
2020	54,461	23,655	190,026	11,540	91,383	77,161	303,200	16,900	10,151	18,022	93,793	11,436	929,581
2021	53,540	23,021	193,195	11,515	95,621	76,551	305,500	17,000	10,083	17,953	93,790	11,966	937,691
2022	53,400	23,944	193,780	11,515	98,172	75,705	306,700	17,314	10,150	17,798	92,077	11,646	940,365
2023[1]	54,100	25,800	194,365	11,295	102,160	74,808	307,400	17,850	9,965	17,435	89,274	11,795	944,244
2024[2]	52,200	27,160	193,900	10,995	105,500	74,550	307,635	17,950	9,775	17,160	87,800	11,695	943,908

[1] Preliminary.   [2] Forecast.   *Source: Foreign Agricultural Service, U.S. Department of Agriculture (FAS-USDA)*

Cattle Supply and Distribution in the United States   In Thousands of Head

Year	Cattle & Calves on Farms Jan. 1	Imports	Calves Born	Total Supply	Federally Inspected	Other[3]	All Commercial	Farm	Total Slaughter	Deaths on Farms	Exports	Total Disappearance
						Commercial						
2014	88,243	2,358	33,522	124,123	30,242	494	30,242	124	30,366	3,850	108	34,323
2015	89,173	1,985	34,087	125,244	28,742	462	28,742	116	28,858	3,880	73	32,811
2016	91,888	1,708	35,063	128,659	30,602	472	30,602	123	30,725	3,875	69	34,670
2017	96,325	1,806	35,758	133,889	32,208	494	32,208	116	32,323	3,928	195	36,446
2018	94,298	1,900	36,313	132,510	33,090	495	33,090	118	33,208	3,991	240	37,438
2019	94,805	2,043	35,592	132,439	33,648	489	33,648	123	33,770	4,156	306	38,232
2020	93,793	2,114	35,496	131,403	32,599		32,599	123	32,722	3,940	321	36,983
2021	93,790	1,776	35,166	130,731	33,568		33,568	118	33,687	3,913	511	38,111
2022[1]	92,077	1,628	34,440	128,144	34,029		34,029	119	34,147	3,804	422	38,373
2023[2]	88,841	2,031	33,593	124,465	32,518		32,518		32,518		350	32,868

[1] Preliminary.   [2] Estimate.   [3] Wholesale and retail.   *Source: Economic Research Service, U.S. Department of Agriculture (ERS-USDA)*

Beef Supply and Utilization in the United States

Years and Quarters	Beginning Stocks	Commercial	Total	Imports	Total Supply	Exports	Ending Stocks	Total Disappearance	Carcass Weight	Retail Weight Total
		Production						Total - Per Capita Disappearance -		
2020	----	27,174	27,174	3,339	30,513	2,951	----	----	----	58.1
I	----	6,931	6,931	774	7,705	769	----	----	----	14.6
II	----	6,059	6,059	848	6,907	605	----	----	----	13.5
III	----	7,115	7,115	1,025	8,140	759	----	----	----	15.5
IV	----	7,069	7,069	693	7,762	819	----	----	----	14.5
2021	----	27,948	27,948	3,346	31,294	3,441	----	----	----	58.9
I	----	6,900	6,900	696	7,596	798	----	----	----	14.5
II	----	6,963	6,963	865	7,828	875	----	----	----	14.9
III	----	6,979	6,979	923	7,902	912	----	----	----	14.6
IV	----	7,106	7,106	863	7,969	856	----	----	----	14.8
2022	----	28,291	28,291	3,390	31,681	3,544	----	----	----	59.1
I	----	7,023	7,023	985	8,008	843	----	----	----	15.0
II	----	7,072	7,072	859	7,931	944	----	----	----	14.7
III	----	7,144	7,144	797	7,941	912	----	----	----	14.7
IV	----	7,052	7,052	750	7,802	846	----	----	----	14.6
2023[1]	----	26,932	26,932	3,727	30,659	3,038	----	----	----	58.1
I	----	6,821	6,821	956	7,777	779	----	----	----	14.9
II	----	6,710	6,710	901	7,611	805	----	----	----	14.4
III	----	6,621	6,621	966	7,587	731	----	----	----	14.3
IV	----	6,780	6,780	904	7,684	723	----	----	----	14.3
2024[2]	----	25,810	25,810	4,175	29,985	2,785	----	----	----	57.8
I	----	6,600	6,600	1,200	7,800	720	----	----	----	14.8
II	----	6,685	6,685	1,000	7,685	740	----	----	----	14.6
III	----	6,535	6,535	1,025	7,560	670	----	----	----	14.3
IV	----	6,505	6,505	950	7,455	655	----	----	----	14.1

[1] Preliminary.   [2] Forecast.   *Source: Economic Research Service, U.S. Department of Agriculture (ERS-USDA)*

United States Cattle on Feed in 13 States   In Thousands of Head

Year	Number on Feed[3]	Placed on Feed	Marketings	Other Disappearance	Year	Number on Feed[3]	Placed on Feed	Marketings	Other Disappearance
2020	11,958	22,626	21,892	725	2022[1]	12,042	22,932	22,590	702
I	11,958	5,228	5,716	173	I	12,042	5,877	5,598	176
II	11,297	5,282	4,943	198	II	12,145	5,327	5,868	199
III	11,438	6,177	5,728	170	III	11,405	5,954	5,688	162
IV	11,717	5,939	5,505	184	IV	11,509	5,774	5,436	165
2021	11,967	23,294	22,522	697	2023[2]	11,727	22,631	21,669	714
I	11,967	5,713	5,609	174	I	11,727	5,666	5,557	174
II	11,897	5,404	5,827	179	II	11,612	5,391	5,605	194
III	11,295	5,999	5,572	172	III	11,204	5,822	5,269	177
IV	11,550	6,178	5,514	172	IV	11,580	5,752	5,238	169

[1] Preliminary.   [2] Estimate.   [3] Beginning of period.   *Source: Economic Research Service, U.S. Department of Agriculture (ERS-USDA)*

CATTLE AND CALVES

United States Cattle on Feed, 1000+ Capacity Feedlots, on First of Month   In Thousands of Head

Year	Jan.	Feb.	Mar.	Apr.	May	June	July	Aug.	Sept.	Oct.	Nov.	Dec.
2014	10,523	10,678	10,716	10,792	10,554	10,497	10,043	9,752	9,719	9,985	10,571	10,816
2015	10,626	10,713	10,688	10,797	10,640	10,571	10,236	10,002	9,986	10,228	10,809	10,800
2016	10,575	10,709	10,770	10,853	10,783	10,804	10,356	10,165	10,135	10,256	10,665	10,652
2017	10,605	10,782	10,772	10,919	10,998	11,096	10,821	10,604	10,504	10,813	11,332	11,516
2018	11,489	11,630	11,715	11,729	11,558	11,553	11,287	11,093	11,125	11,400	11,692	11,739
2019	11,680	11,676	11,785	11,953	11,807	11,728	11,480	11,112	10,982	11,288	11,816	12,031
2020	11,958	11,928	11,811	11,297	11,200	11,671	11,438	11,284	11,394	11,717	11,973	12,036
2021	11,967	12,106	12,000	11,897	11,731	11,704	11,295	11,074	11,234	11,550	11,948	11,985
2022	12,042	12,209	12,193	12,145	12,022	11,901	11,405	11,289	11,342	11,509	11,736	11,693
2023[1]	11,727	11,754	11,650	11,612	11,617	11,552	11,204	11,030	11,094	11,580	11,943	12,011

[1] Preliminary.   *Source: Economic Research Service, U.S. Department of Agriculture (ERS-USDA)*

United States Cattle Placed on Feed, 1000+ Capacity Feedlots   In Thousands of Head

Year	Jan.	Feb.	Mar.	Apr.	May	June	July	Aug.	Sept.	Oct.	Nov.	Dec.	Total
2014	2,014	1,658	1,801	1,623	1,909	1,468	1,559	1,725	2,014	2,368	1,794	1,537	21,470
2015	1,789	1,551	1,809	1,548	1,719	1,481	1,547	1,632	1,941	2,286	1,602	1,527	20,432
2016	1,779	1,710	1,892	1,664	1,889	1,525	1,572	1,879	1,895	2,171	1,843	1,785	21,604
2017	1,981	1,694	2,117	1,848	2,119	1,770	1,615	1,928	2,150	2,393	2,099	1,799	23,513
2018	2,068	1,817	1,921	1,695	2,124	1,798	1,742	2,070	2,051	2,248	1,996	1,757	23,287
2019	1,967	1,858	2,014	1,842	2,063	1,761	1,705	1,884	2,103	2,462	2,093	1,828	23,580
2020	1,955	1,716	1,557	1,432	2,052	1,798	1,893	2,057	2,227	2,192	1,903	1,844	22,626
2021	2,024	1,691	1,998	1,825	1,910	1,669	1,733	2,103	2,163	2,246	1,967	1,965	23,294
2022	2,004	1,868	2,005	1,824	1,869	1,634	1,764	2,110	2,080	2,085	1,905	1,784	22,932
2023[1]	1,936	1,738	1,992	1,758	1,955	1,678	1,613	2,003	2,206	2,181	1,873	1,698	22,631

[1] Preliminary.   *Source: Economic Research Service, U.S. Department of Agriculture (ERS-USDA)*

United States Cattle Marketings, 1000+ Capacity Feedlots[2]   In Thousands of Head

Year	Jan.	Feb.	Mar.	Apr.	May	June	July	Aug.	Sept.	Oct.	Nov.	Dec.	Total
2014	1,788	1,549	1,660	1,778	1,865	1,847	1,787	1,692	1,683	1,685	1,475	1,655	20,464
2015	1,625	1,516	1,631	1,639	1,711	1,747	1,725	1,588	1,642	1,630	1,532	1,674	19,660
2016	1,589	1,591	1,747	1,658	1,794	1,912	1,713	1,868	1,732	1,705	1,787	1,777	20,873
2017	1,751	1,648	1,914	1,703	1,951	1,989	1,784	1,979	1,783	1,801	1,844	1,752	21,899
2018	1,858	1,675	1,840	1,803	2,056	2,006	1,873	1,983	1,719	1,887	1,869	1,741	22,310
2019	1,910	1,683	1,777	1,928	2,070	1,943	2,002	1,953	1,738	1,875	1,813	1,834	22,526
2020	1,931	1,775	2,010	1,459	1,515	1,969	1,990	1,892	1,846	1,873	1,779	1,853	21,892
2021	1,829	1,739	2,041	1,936	1,870	2,021	1,899	1,884	1,789	1,791	1,869	1,854	22,522
2022	1,773	1,825	2,000	1,893	1,914	2,061	1,824	2,004	1,860	1,804	1,891	1,741	22,590
2023[1]	1,846	1,734	1,977	1,702	1,946	1,957	1,722	1,884	1,663	1,763	1,751	1,724	21,669

[1] Preliminary.   *Source: Economic Research Service, U.S. Department of Agriculture (ERS-USDA)*

Quarterly Trade of Live Cattle in the United States   In Head

	Imports					Exports				
Year	First Quarter	Second Quarter	Third Quarter	Fourth Quarter	Total	First Quarter	Second Quarter	Third Quarter	Fourth Quarter	Total
2014	599,440	562,937	415,409	780,581	2,358,367	27,541	25,988	25,813	28,342	107,684
2015	564,315	534,024	413,354	472,875	1,984,568	12,576	23,575	15,664	20,744	72,559
2016	490,504	459,089	288,205	470,251	1,708,049	13,498	11,733	10,219	34,035	69,485
2017	517,913	439,901	317,584	530,501	1,805,899	31,987	32,447	34,867	95,332	194,633
2018	467,307	497,270	364,205	570,731	1,899,513	37,834	47,737	62,942	90,987	239,500
2019	567,085	562,871	330,188	582,609	2,042,753	61,985	49,821	68,007	125,937	305,750
2020	530,203	584,788	432,959	566,261	2,114,211	69,291	52,041	77,718	122,092	321,142
2021	478,802	423,336	355,851	517,513	1,775,502	124,620	132,925	126,313	127,620	511,478
2022	470,555	384,719	298,059	474,830	1,628,163	91,421	78,388	102,434	150,102	422,345
2023[1]	497,499	455,063	418,990	659,034	2,030,586	95,350	71,639	86,823	96,133	349,945

[1] Preliminary.   *Source: Economic Research Service, U.S. Department of Agriculture (ERS-USDA)*

Federally Inspected Slaughter of Cattle in the United States   In Thousands of Head

Year	Jan.	Feb.	Mar.	Apr.	May	June	July	Aug.	Sept.	Oct.	Nov.	Dec.	Total
2014	2,634	2,204	2,413	2,556	2,597	2,568	2,562	2,463	2,490	2,591	2,210	2,398	29,684
2015	2,377	2,135	2,342	2,346	2,345	2,430	2,459	2,288	2,435	2,469	2,259	2,414	28,296
2016	2,320	2,252	2,493	2,373	2,479	2,670	2,443	2,711	2,578	2,592	2,632	2,572	30,115
2017	2,533	2,330	2,726	2,425	2,713	2,821	2,577	2,903	2,655	2,753	2,726	2,543	31,704
2018	2,714	2,378	2,661	2,599	2,868	2,842	2,729	2,937	2,577	2,908	2,762	2,544	32,518
2019	2,786	2,416	2,609	2,789	2,900	2,769	2,903	2,887	2,635	2,926	2,737	2,713	33,069
2020	2,854	2,539	2,875	2,189	2,223	2,820	2,866	2,751	2,756	2,889	2,657	2,734	32,152
2021	2,691	2,473	2,947	2,794	2,645	2,897	2,801	2,834	2,732	2,794	2,805	2,772	33,184
2022	2,649	2,634	2,955	2,759	2,760	2,985	2,731	3,019	2,840	2,842	2,855	2,638	33,667
2023[1]	2,773	2,500	2,884	2,493	2,787	2,844	2,554	2,841	2,560	2,768	2,681	2,549	32,233

[1] Preliminary.   Source: National Agricultural Statistics Service, U.S. Department of Agriculture (NASS-USDA)

Federally Inspected Slaughter of Calves and Vealers in the United States   In Thousands of Head

Year	Jan.	Feb.	Mar.	Apr.	May	June	July	Aug.	Sept.	Oct.	Nov.	Dec.	Total
2014	62.0	51.5	52.9	48.0	45.9	44.6	47.8	43.0	41.8	42.6	35.2	42.2	557.5
2015	39.3	36.1	39.2	34.7	32.7	34.5	36.0	33.9	36.8	39.6	38.2	44.5	445.5
2016	41.2	37.8	41.3	34.2	34.9	37.0	37.1	40.3	41.8	47.6	46.6	48.1	487.9
2017	45.9	39.6	44.3	38.4	38.5	39.6	38.3	45.4	42.9	43.2	41.7	45.6	503.4
2018	48.4	40.4	43.0	42.1	45.7	44.6	47.0	51.6	47.8	52.9	54.9	53.0	571.4
2019	53.0	47.9	45.1	42.1	45.5	43.7	53.0	50.2	48.4	54.6	45.8	49.1	578.4
2020	49.2	39.1	42.5	32.6	31.7	35.9	40.3	33.4	31.6	36.3	34.4	40.0	447.0
2021	31.8	32.5	31.0	26.8	24.8	31.2	32.9	34.3	33.5	34.6	32.5	38.1	384.0
2022	31.7	29.8	31.9	27.4	26.8	28.6	28.9	33.3	30.9	29.7	30.7	32.4	362.1
2023[1]	30.0	25.1	25.5	21.4	23.8	22.9	22.5	25.9	21.0	22.3	23.4	21.8	285.6

[1] Preliminary.   Source: Crop Reporting Board, U.S. Department of Agriculture (CRB-USDA)

Average Live Weight of Cattle Slaughtered Under Federal Inspection   In Pounds per Head

Year	Jan.	Feb.	Mar.	Apr.	May	June	July	Aug.	Sept.	Oct.	Nov.	Dec.	Average
2014	1,338	1,334	1,321	1,308	1,302	1,309	1,322	1,332	1,347	1,359	1,367	1,367	1,334
2015	1,362	1,359	1,351	1,341	1,335	1,335	1,348	1,365	1,386	1,394	1,396	1,391	1,364
2016	1,385	1,375	1,373	1,351	1,335	1,337	1,347	1,354	1,373	1,385	1,387	1,384	1,366
2017	1,374	1,363	1,352	1,327	1,309	1,323	1,335	1,347	1,362	1,364	1,376	1,382	1,351
2018	1,380	1,370	1,360	1,336	1,317	1,322	1,332	1,346	1,361	1,366	1,372	1,370	1,353
2019	1,366	1,354	1,341	1,330	1,317	1,315	1,328	1,340	1,354	1,363	1,378	1,376	1,347
2020	1,378	1,379	1,371	1,357	1,371	1,368	1,366	1,368	1,382	1,389	1,391	1,392	1,376
2021	1,403	1,394	1,376	1,369	1,363	1,349	1,351	1,356	1,368	1,379	1,386	1,395	1,374
2022	1,401	1,398	1,388	1,376	1,353	1,342	1,343	1,351	1,368	1,379	1,387	1,388	1,373
2023[1]	1,383	1,377	1,369	1,357	1,352	1,341	1,346	1,353	1,365	1,378	1,390	1,404	1,368

[1] Preliminary.   Source: National Agricultural Statistics Board, U.S. Department of Agriculture (NASS-USDA)

Beef Steer-Corn Price Ratio[1] in the United States

Year	Jan.	Feb.	Mar.	Apr.	May	June	July	Aug.	Sept.	Oct.	Nov.	Dec.	Average
2014	31.7	33.3	33.2	31.8	31.2	32.9	38.7	43.8	45.3	45.7	46.9	43.8	38.2
2015	43.5	42.5	42.5	43.7	44.2	43.5	39.5	40.5	38.0	35.1	36.5	33.7	40.3
2016	36.1	37.4	38.5	37.4	35.1	33.2	33.3	36.8	33.9	31.0	32.7	34.0	35.0
2017	35.0	35.2	36.4	37.9	40.0	38.8	34.7	35.2	32.7	34.0	38.4	37.2	36.3
2018	37.4	37.6	36.2	34.1	33.2	31.6	32.3	33.3	32.4	32.7	33.7	33.6	34.0
2019	34.8	35.0	35.7	36.3	33.6	28.9	27.2	28.5	27.4	28.3	31.3	32.3	31.6
2020	33.0	32.3	31.0	33.7	34.7	34.8	30.5	33.3	30.8	29.9	28.8	28.0	31.7
2021	26.4	24.2	23.7	22.8	20.5	20.5	20.4	19.8	23.2	25.1	25.1	25.8	23.1
2022	24.9	23.2	21.6	20.1	19.8	19.2	19.9	19.9	20.5	22.8	23.7	24.0	21.6
2023[1]	24.1	23.8	25.0	26.1	27.1	28.4	29.6	32.5	35.3	37.7	39.5	36.7	30.5

[1] Bushels of corn equal in value to 100 pounds of steers and heifers.   [2] Preliminary.   Source: Economic Research Service, U.S. Department of Agriculture

CATTLE AND CALVES

LIVE CATTLE
Quarterly Cash as of 03/28/2024

QUARTERLY CASH
As of 03/28/2024

Chart High 190.000 on 06/08/2023
Chart Low   9.080   on 02/29/1940

Cents / lb.

All grades, Chicago: to 12/1947; Good, Chicago: 01/1948 to 12/1964; Choice, Chicago: 01/1965 to 07/1971; Choice, Omaha: 08/1971 to 08/1987; Average, Texas-Oklahoma: 09/1987 to date.

Average Price Received by Farmers for Beef Cattle in the United States   In Dollars Per 100 Pounds

Year	Jan.	Feb.	Mar.	Apr.	May	June	July	Aug.	Sept.	Oct.	Nov.	Dec.	Average
2014	138.00	144.00	148.00	148.00	146.00	147.00	156.00	158.00	157.00	161.00	167.00	164.00	152.83
2015	164.00	159.00	160.00	162.00	160.00	155.00	149.00	148.00	139.00	128.00	129.00	122.00	147.92
2016	130.00	132.00	135.00	131.00	128.00	125.00	119.00	117.00	108.00	101.00	104.00	111.00	120.08
2017	117.00	119.00	125.00	128.00	136.00	132.00	120.00	114.00	105.00	109.00	119.00	118.00	120.17
2018	120.00	125.00	125.00	119.00	120.00	112.00	110.00	110.00	108.00	110.00	113.00	117.00	115.75
2019	121.00	123.00	126.00	125.00	120.00	114.00	112.00	111.00	103.00	107.00	113.00	118.00	116.08
2020	122.00	120.00	113.00	108.00	109.00	109.00	97.10	103.00	104.00	106.00	107.00	108.00	108.84
2021	110.00	112.00	113.00	118.00	118.00	121.00	122.00	123.00	124.00	123.00	129.00	137.00	120.83
2022	135.00	137.00	139.00	139.00	141.00	140.00	142.00	141.00	143.00	145.00	151.00	154.00	142.25
2023[1]	156.00	158.00	164.00	171.00	173.00	181.00	181.00	182.00	181.00	182.00	180.00	172.00	173.42

[1] Preliminary.   *Source: National Agricultural Statistics Service, U.S. Department of Agriculture (NASS-USDA)*

Average Price Received by Farmers for Calves in the United States   In Dollars Per 100 Pounds

Year	Jan.	Feb.	Mar.	Apr.	May	June	July	Aug.	Sept.	Oct.	Nov.	Dec.	Average
2014	208.00	209.00	216.00	222.00	229.00	249.00	257.00	271.00	279.00	307.00	305.00	303.00	254.58
2015	288.00	277.00	290.00	288.00	288.00	292.00	275.00	273.00	241.00	234.00	217.00	193.00	263.00
2016	196.00	201.00	199.00	183.00	173.00	168.00	145.00	158.00	142.00	134.00	144.00	148.00	165.92
2017	152.00	151.00	159.00	164.00	171.00	164.00	157.00	163.00	173.00	177.00	177.00	174.00	165.17
2018	174.00	180.00	175.00	170.00	165.00	158.00	153.00	160.00	169.00	174.00	169.00	166.00	167.75
2019	169.00	170.00	170.00	174.00	148.00	149.00	144.00	142.00	144.00	154.00	158.00	159.00	156.75
2020	168.00	168.00	160.00	151.00	151.00	149.00	149.00	153.00	155.00	156.00	162.00	165.00	157.25
2021	165.00	167.00	163.00	168.00	159.00	159.00	165.00	175.00	173.00	175.00	174.00	181.00	168.67
2022	185.00	194.00	187.00	186.00	183.00	184.00	186.00	197.00	195.00	200.00	203.00	206.00	192.17
2023[1]	209.00	217.00	230.00	244.00	251.00	260.00	262.00	272.00	279.00	297.00	290.00	280.00	257.58

[1] Preliminary.   *Source: National Agricultural Statistics Board, U.S. Department of Agriculture (NASS-USDA)*

CATTLE, LIVE - CME
Weekly Selected Futures as of 03/28/2024

WEEKLY SELECTED FUTURES
As of 03/28/2024
Chart High 190.275 on 03/14/2024
Chart Low 81.450 on 04/24/2020

Nearby Futures through Last Trading Day.

Volume of Trading of Live Cattle Futures Chicago   In Thousands of Contracts

Year	Jan.	Feb.	Mar.	Apr.	May	June	July	Aug.	Sept.	Oct.	Nov.	Dec.	Total
2014	1,381.4	970.0	1,270.2	847.7	1,139.3	1,126.6	1,503.5	1,023.5	1,303.4	1,061.5	962.5	1,009.6	13,599.3
2015	1,282.2	918.7	1,163.5	959.6	1,139.1	955.3	1,166.5	901.6	1,344.2	1,222.5	1,213.9	1,173.9	13,440.9
2016	1,127.6	956.2	1,187.4	1,010.7	1,234.8	852.5	1,070.5	990.9	1,335.8	1,028.2	1,257.5	1,070.7	13,122.8
2017	1,300.9	958.4	1,552.2	1,260.5	2,164.7	1,201.2	1,487.1	1,155.8	1,364.4	1,228.1	1,501.6	990.4	16,165.2
2018	1,493.4	1,078.6	1,621.7	1,294.7	1,680.4	1,170.3	1,476.9	1,205.5	1,433.2	1,397.4	1,466.9	1,121.1	16,440.1
2019	1,657.5	1,139.7	1,778.9	1,440.6	1,760.8	1,132.9	1,321.6	1,338.6	1,539.7	1,154.9	1,488.3	965.6	16,719.1
2020	1,607.7	1,452.6	2,194.9	1,204.7	1,499.0	997.6	1,373.3	1,120.5	1,331.4	1,239.8	1,211.4	905.9	16,138.8
2021	1,419.5	1,040.4	1,341.3	1,143.1	1,179.2	1,017.1	1,201.6	1,115.8	1,366.8	888.8	1,274.1	955.3	13,943.1
2022	1,420.9	1,112.8	1,539.4	1,014.1	1,300.6	1,091.1	1,146.4	1,035.0	1,329.6	1,051.5	1,213.9	895.7	14,150.8
2023	1,436.8	1,029.6	1,660.8	1,014.4	1,584.2	1,457.9	1,546.0	1,209.8	1,395.1	1,429.5	1,546.1	993.6	16,303.7

Contract size = 40,000 lbs.   Source: CME Group; Chicago Mercantile Exchange (CME)

Average Open Interest of Live Cattle Futures in Chicago   In Contracts

Year	Jan.	Feb.	Mar.	Apr.	May	June	July	Aug.	Sept.	Oct.	Nov.	Dec.
2014	354,327	371,310	369,611	352,639	345,372	352,223	343,096	313,046	315,722	313,134	317,289	286,556
2015	261,167	243,091	259,858	273,309	296,935	287,815	241,553	236,485	258,984	258,122	271,979	256,669
2016	274,078	272,513	291,131	282,634	271,110	247,299	248,641	247,108	262,608	268,144	278,901	294,562
2017	333,745	332,286	360,860	404,610	421,183	403,152	372,623	320,894	327,393	334,666	380,212	341,419
2018	353,135	370,641	362,617	348,766	356,141	329,947	317,434	301,001	314,505	335,731	342,814	347,681
2019	386,607	393,106	437,825	440,940	384,191	357,676	331,025	324,793	338,349	308,578	362,444	381,270
2020	384,707	341,499	305,367	266,157	264,856	271,676	273,740	291,037	294,504	279,047	275,585	284,898
2021	315,035	330,683	336,111	333,141	318,494	300,080	300,394	295,926	297,788	284,484	302,468	309,096
2022	330,015	352,569	320,520	307,172	303,632	283,487	265,660	266,581	293,460	271,432	289,848	302,343
2023	320,037	331,337	335,659	340,759	328,656	336,972	343,112	309,830	325,890	291,409	283,984	265,536

Contract size = 40,000 lbs.   Source: CME Group; Chicago Mercantile Exchange (CME)

FEEDER CATTLE
Quarterly Cash as of 03/28/2024

QUARTERLY CASH
As of 03/28/2024

Chart High 254.100 on 09/25/2023
Chart Low 24.750 on 01/31/1975

Oklahoma City: to date.

Average Slaughter Steer Price, Choice 2-4, Nebraska Direct (1100-1300 Lb.)   In Dollars Per 100 Pounds

Year	Jan.	Feb.	Mar.	Apr.	May	June	July	Aug.	Sept.	Oct.	Nov.	Dec.	Average
2014	143.33	146.45	151.93	149.01	146.19	149.55	158.57	158.35	159.86	164.91	170.04	163.09	155.11
2015	165.13	160.29	163.42	162.98	160.76	151.13	149.17	149.06	136.28	132.88	126.90	125.00	148.58
2016	133.15	133.85	137.83	129.52	129.90	122.95	117.10	116.91	106.22	101.76	106.23	115.24	120.70
2017	119.92	121.83	126.91	131.18	138.42	130.10	118.08	113.01	107.73	113.40	122.49	119.73	121.90
2018	124.35	127.93	124.97	121.11	116.14	110.10	112.39	109.98	110.69	111.53	115.28	120.34	117.07
2019	123.28	124.66	127.51	125.82	118.03	113.08	112.99	111.13	103.30	109.80	115.96	120.20	117.15
2020	123.86	117.31	111.06	105.18	103.14	99.98	97.72	105.51	103.28	106.36	109.39	110.00	107.73
2021	109.84	114.00	114.71	121.67	118.00	121.98	124.75	124.31	124.00	124.91	134.17	140.12	122.71
2022	NA	140.39	138.39	143.09	143.59	142.79	142.53	142.25	141.66	149.00	155.92	156.62	145.11
2023[1]	155.76	161.99	166.45	178.22	176.50	185.92	184.01	185.71	183.35	184.66	181.71	171.45	176.31

[1] Preliminary.   *Source: Economic Research Service, U.S. Department of Agriculture (ERS-USDA)*

Average Price of Feeder Steers in Oklahoma City   In Dollars Per 100 Pounds

Year	Jan.	Feb.	Mar.	Apr.	May	June	July	Aug.	Sept.	Oct.	Nov.	Dec.	Average
2014	170.98	170.61	174.43	178.55	185.49	201.90	216.19	221.28	228.15	239.59	240.37	233.67	205.10
2015	224.57	210.18	212.80	218.29	219.14	226.34	219.98	215.14	200.97	188.55	181.41	159.43	206.40
2016	162.19	158.82	160.13	154.07	146.07	144.74	142.23	146.88	136.34	124.66	126.85	131.41	144.53
2017	132.65	127.78	129.29	136.04	144.23	150.36	149.39	146.20	149.54	155.21	157.93	152.81	144.29
2018	149.61	147.91	141.90	136.73	136.14	140.75	147.25	150.14	153.97	156.14	149.97	146.09	146.38
2019	144.00	141.23	139.72	143.93	135.89	132.53	138.02	139.56	138.44	144.50	146.22	144.35	140.70
2020	145.17	140.57	128.37	118.95	123.91	128.99	135.40	142.24	141.42	139.14	137.16	138.37	134.97
2021	134.97	137.08	135.59	139.20	133.29	141.79	151.35	156.62	155.27	154.31	156.42	161.21	146.42
2022	161.24	161.34	155.01	155.61	154.93	160.89	170.18	178.63	179.03	174.49	176.09	178.75	167.18
2023	179.87	182.35	188.64	199.34	203.20	222.77	238.30	245.60	251.59	246.38	231.24	219.97	217.44

Source: Economic Research Service, U.S. Department of Agriculture (ERS-USDA)

CATTLE, FEEDER - CME
Weekly Nearest Futures as of 03/28/2024

WEEKLY NEAREST FUTURES
As of 03/28/2024
Chart High 267.500 on 09/16/2023
Chart Low 103.950 on 04/06/2020

Nearby Futures through Last Trading Day using Selected contract months: February, April, June, August, October and December.

Volume of Trading of Feeder Cattle Futures Chicago   In Contracts

Year	Jan.	Feb.	Mar.	Apr.	May	June	July	Aug.	Sept.	Oct.	Nov.	Dec.	Total
2014	145,259	146,539	162,287	146,874	133,506	158,374	225,649	223,720	202,774	225,198	128,870	216,672	2,115,722
2015	238,256	194,105	223,149	200,013	163,686	157,044	213,709	216,119	221,822	242,183	192,224	230,741	2,493,051
2016	188,497	201,016	245,203	234,293	182,499	153,988	191,531	248,780	248,507	251,274	191,263	201,104	2,537,955
2017	203,909	229,093	303,851	355,689	337,360	257,443	300,121	383,206	319,319	328,842	248,101	274,899	3,541,833
2018	253,040	289,662	339,715	339,742	269,509	244,093	338,063	372,382	293,434	331,588	226,165	231,572	3,528,965
2019	259,892	265,244	369,642	367,089	337,636	278,936	305,091	363,903	301,660	281,320	234,331	243,802	3,608,546
2020	306,940	345,608	382,220	227,965	181,226	179,978	310,756	363,903	267,000	297,802	211,790	245,495	3,320,683
2021	233,141	194,993	290,080	286,614	201,385	217,986	260,875	314,469	342,624	253,647	234,357	237,760	3,067,931
2022	240,504	275,227	294,599	281,093	218,127	253,220	296,538	318,085	338,797	306,717	278,749	254,055	3,355,711
2023	271,881	311,045	438,468	359,185	333,172	347,011	361,019	405,073	434,510	408,553	375,257	337,059	4,382,233

Contract size = 40,000 lbs.   *Source: CME Group; Chicago Mercantile Exchange (CME)*

Average Open Interest of Feeder Cattle Futures in Chicago   In Contracts

Year	Jan.	Feb.	Mar.	Apr.	May	June	July	Aug.	Sept.	Oct.	Nov.	Dec.
2014	50,558	48,154	49,331	44,614	45,889	48,933	49,843	44,856	44,339	45,027	45,056	42,924
2015	40,979	38,257	40,956	39,645	38,528	44,008	42,717	41,337	36,061	34,280	34,208	35,145
2016	36,524	39,140	41,160	41,481	41,159	40,322	43,402	43,468	42,550	43,049	43,052	44,837
2017	49,515	50,369	53,105	59,119	57,620	56,183	59,574	56,346	54,234	60,884	60,534	54,316
2018	52,654	56,500	53,852	49,675	45,338	44,834	50,036	50,612	52,540	54,729	48,850	49,150
2019	50,475	49,902	53,540	51,765	50,005	48,816	48,400	47,550	46,855	40,898	43,622	49,468
2020	53,349	56,346	41,760	32,784	29,922	33,428	40,400	44,587	42,971	43,704	37,461	42,381
2021	41,053	41,296	45,950	46,256	44,208	42,766	45,672	49,861	42,908	39,704	41,239	40,542
2022	44,876	47,112	43,989	42,282	44,958	44,609	39,808	43,167	43,734	48,734	47,473	45,983
2023	47,886	48,139	56,607	58,748	61,972	60,419	59,850	58,227	60,109	50,979	50,488	50,907

Contract size = 40,000 lbs.   *Source: CME Group; Chicago Mercantile Exchange (CME)*

CATTLE AND CALVES

Imports of Live Cattle to the United States   In Head

Year	Jan.	Feb.	Mar.	Apr.	May	June	July	Aug.	Sept.	Oct.	Nov.	Dec.	Total
2014	157,455	207,261	234,724	247,523	181,306	134,108	134,894	115,476	165,039	234,626	269,330	276,625	2,358,367
2015	135,659	194,466	234,190	207,189	162,677	164,158	147,554	119,789	146,011	167,165	150,282	155,428	1,984,568
2016	104,397	151,467	234,640	212,913	131,340	114,836	82,366	98,247	107,592	117,113	176,971	176,167	1,708,049
2017	132,418	168,473	217,022	153,851	158,767	127,283	118,288	98,361	100,935	139,922	206,296	184,283	1,805,899
2018	114,278	153,951	199,078	172,772	169,813	154,685	126,622	119,865	117,718	167,968	208,127	194,636	1,899,513
2019	142,628	189,372	235,085	222,429	190,006	150,436	121,463	98,408	110,317	165,526	204,458	212,625	2,042,753
2020	146,927	169,997	213,279	201,339	190,279	193,170	158,200	128,333	146,426	181,890	186,471	197,900	2,114,211
2021	133,149	155,017	190,636	179,484	121,792	122,060	113,284	121,055	121,512	148,223	183,674	185,616	1,775,502
2022	132,431	156,522	181,602	124,780	132,692	127,247	96,706	107,749	93,604	116,528	177,067	181,235	1,628,163
2023[1]	145,846	156,097	195,556	153,399	157,841	143,823	117,889	132,042	169,059	205,381	277,477	176,176	2,030,586

[1] Preliminary.   *Source: Economic Research Service, U.S. Department of Agriculture (ERS-USDA)*

Exports of Live Cattle to the United States   In Head

Year	Jan.	Feb.	Mar.	Apr.	May	June	July	Aug.	Sept.	Oct.	Nov.	Dec.	Total
2014	8,824	7,740	10,977	9,351	11,531	5,106	9,438	10,303	6,072	10,932	7,871	9,539	107,684
2015	3,280	5,139	4,157	7,543	10,196	5,836	7,338	5,265	3,061	4,382	8,119	8,243	72,559
2016	3,331	5,010	5,157	3,893	3,365	4,475	3,332	3,309	3,578	7,072	13,111	13,852	69,485
2017	13,085	8,319	10,583	12,477	7,745	12,225	7,199	11,583	16,085	34,433	36,655	24,244	194,633
2018	7,797	14,893	15,144	15,122	14,746	17,869	17,312	19,387	26,243	44,207	26,237	20,543	239,500
2019	22,983	19,572	19,430	17,229	16,696	15,896	16,713	20,589	30,705	55,073	43,253	27,611	305,750
2020	31,438	24,628	13,225	16,355	19,271	16,415	21,581	18,384	37,753	43,842	40,553	37,697	321,142
2021	36,994	39,725	47,901	41,022	40,044	51,859	46,895	36,215	43,203	57,483	39,223	30,914	511,478
2022	35,762	28,594	27,065	31,488	24,594	22,306	22,763	30,521	49,150	59,240	49,604	41,258	422,345
2023[1]	34,507	31,094	29,749	24,635	17,705	29,299	24,818	27,195	34,810	44,844	26,296	24,993	349,945

[1] Preliminary.   *Source: Economic Research Service, U.S. Department of Agriculture (ERS-USDA)*

Federally Inspected Slaughter of Bison in the United States   In Thousands of Head

Year	Jan.	Feb.	Mar.	Apr.	May	June	July	Aug.	Sept.	Oct.	Nov.	Dec.	Total
2014	4.8	3.9	4.7	4.2	4.6	4.5	4.4	3.9	4.1	4.4	3.8	4.4	51.7
2015	4.8	4.0	4.6	3.9	4.5	4.2	4.7	4.2	4.2	4.2	4.5	4.1	51.9
2016	4.2	4.3	4.9	4.3	4.8	4.9	4.3	4.4	4.1	4.1	4.5	3.9	52.7
2017	4.2	4.1	4.8	4.0	4.8	5.1	4.5	4.3	3.8	4.5	4.3	3.4	51.8
2018	3.8	3.7	4.6	4.2	4.7	5.0	4.6	4.4	3.5	4.4	4.4	3.7	51.0
2019	4.8	3.8	4.5	4.7	4.6	4.5	4.7	4.6	4.2	5.0	4.3	4.6	54.3
2020	4.9	4.4	5.8	5.4	5.7	5.2	5.6	5.0	4.8	5.5	5.0	5.4	62.7
2021	5.2	4.8	5.7	5.7	5.4	5.5	5.4	5.1	5.6	5.8	6.2	5.9	66.3
2022	6.1	5.9	6.3	5.4	5.9	6.4	5.6	6.4	5.5	6.0	6.3	6.4	72.2
2023[1]	6.6	6.0	7.4	5.8	6.5	6.4	5.7	6.2	5.6	6.3	6.6	6.2	75.3

[1] Preliminary.   *Source: Economic Research Service, U.S. Department of Agriculture (ERS-USDA)*

Other Slaughter of Bison in the United States   In Thousands of Head

Year	Jan.	Feb.	Mar.	Apr.	May	June	July	Aug.	Sept.	Oct.	Nov.	Dec.	Total
2014	0.9	0.8	0.9	0.7	0.6	0.6	0.7	0.7	0.6	0.8	0.7	0.7	8.6
2015	0.8	0.8	1.1	0.7	0.6	0.8	0.6	0.6	0.7	0.7	0.7	0.7	8.8
2016	0.7	0.7	0.9	0.7	0.7	0.8	0.6	0.6	0.6	0.7	0.6	0.5	8.1
2017	0.6	0.6	1.2	0.4	0.4	0.4	0.4	0.5	0.6	0.7	0.5	0.4	6.7
2018	0.5	0.4	1.0	0.4	0.4	0.3	0.3	0.5	0.4	0.5	0.5	0.6	5.8
2019	0.6	0.5	0.6	0.5	0.4	0.4	0.3	0.4	0.4	0.5	0.4	0.5	5.5
2020	0.6	0.5	0.6	0.2	0.2	0.1	0.1	0.2	0.2	0.3	0.3	0.3	3.6
2021	0.4	0.2	0.3	0.2	0.2	0.2	0.2	0.3	0.3	0.4	0.3	0.3	3.4
2022	0.4	0.3	0.3	0.1	0.2	0.3	0.2	0.2	0.2	0.3	0.2	0.3	3.0
2023[1]	0.3	0.3	0.3	0.2	0.2	0.3	0.3	0.2	0.2	0.3	0.3	0.3	3.2

[1] Preliminary.   *Source: Economic Research Service, U.S. Department of Agriculture (ERS-USDA)*

Cement

Cement is made in a wide variety of compositions and is used in many ways. The best-known cement is *Portland cement*, which is bound with sand and gravel to create concrete. Concrete is used to unite the surfaces of various materials and to coat surfaces to protect them from various chemicals. Portland cement is almost universally used for structural concrete. It is manufactured from lime-bearing materials, usually limestone, together with clays, blast-furnace slag containing alumina and silica or shale. The combination is usually approximately 60 percent lime, 19 percent silica, 8 percent alumina, 5 percent iron, 5 percent magnesia, and 3 percent sulfur trioxide. Gypsum is often added to slow the hardening process. In 1924, the name "Portland cement" was coined by Joseph Aspdin, a British cement maker, because of the resemblance between concrete made from his cement and Portland stone. The United States did not start producing Portland cement in any great quantity until the 20th century. Hydraulic cements are those that set and harden in water. Clinker cement is an intermediate product in cement manufacture. The production and consumption of cement is directly related to the level of activity in the construction industry.

Prices – The average value (F.O.B. mill) of Portland cement in 2023 rose by +7.1% to $150 per metric ton.

Supply – World production of hydraulic cement in 2023 remain unchanged yr/yr at 4.100 billion metric tons. The world's largest hydraulic cement producers were China with 51.2% of world production in 2022, India with 10.0%, the US with 2.2%, and Turkey with 1.9%.

US production of cement in 2023 fell by -2.2% yr/yr to 91.00 million metric tons, but still below the 2005 record high of 99.319 million metric tons. US shipments of cement from mills in the US in 2023 remained unchanged yr/yr at 110.000 million metric tons, below the 2005 record high of 128.000 million metric tons.

Demand – US consumption of cement in 2022 remained unchanged yr/yr at 120.000 million metric tons, well below the 2005 record high of 128.260 million metric tons.

Trade – The US relied on imports for 22.0% of its cement consumption in 2023. The two main suppliers of cement to the US were Canada and Mexico. US exports of cement in 2023 fell by -0.2% yr/yr to 900,000 metric tons.

World Production of Hydraulic Cement   In Thousands of Short Tons

Year	Brazil	China	France	Germany	India	Italy	Japan	Korea, South	Russia	Spain	Türkiye	United States	World Total
2016	57,557	2,410,000	15,900	32,737	284,000	19,300	53,255	56,747	54,935	15,000	75,403	85,153	4,140,000
2017	54,004	2,331,000	16,900	33,991	308,000	19,300	55,195	57,400	54,721	14,500	80,552	86,799	4,120,000
2018	53,553	2,236,000	16,500	33,633	310,000	19,300	55,307	52,093	53,678	16,215	72,544	87,021	4,060,000
2019	56,611	2,340,000	16,500	34,185	334,000	19,200	53,462	50,635	57,676	16,998	56,966	88,100	4,200,000
2020	61,052	2,377,000	16,700	35,485	290,000	20,400	50,905	47,518	56,165	15,600	72,299	89,800	4,210,000
2021	65,884	2,360,000	16,900	34,000	350,000	23,500	50,083	49,864	61,000	18,000	82,000	93,300	4,360,000
2022[1]	64,000	2,100,000			380,000		53,000	51,000	61,000		74,000	93,000	4,100,000
2023[2]	63,000	2,100,000			410,000		50,000	50,000	57,000		79,000	91,000	4,100,000

[1] Preliminary.   [2] Estimate.   *Source: U.S. Geological Survey (USGS)*

Salient Statistics of Cement in the United States

Year	Net Import Reliance as a % of Apparent Consump	Production Portland	Production Other[3]	Production Total	Capacity Used at Portland Mills %	Shipments From Mills Total (Mil. MT)	Shipments From Mills Value[4] (Mil. $)	Average Value (F.O.B. Mill) $ per MT	Stocks at Mills Dec. 31	Exports	Apparent Consumption	Imports for Consumption[5] by Country Canada	Japan	Mexico	Spain	Total
		1,000 Metric tons										1,000 Metric Tons				
2016	13	82,181	2,514	84,695	69.5	94,300	10,500	111.00	7,420	1,283	95,150	4,512	1	466	[389]	13,238
2017	13	83,963	2,393	86,356	69.8	96,900	11,300	117.00	7,870	1,035	97,160	4,352	1	686	601	13,497
2018	14	84,000	2,400	86,400	69.9	96,900	11,300	121.00	8,580	919	98,500	5,326	1	1,024	429	14,660
2019	15	85,800	1,800	87,600	69.9	102,823	11,900	124.00	7,990	1,024	102,000	5,252	1	1,324	242	15,833
2020	15	87,400	1,900	89,300	71.3	104,580	12,700	125.00	7,180	884	105,000	5,031	1	1,705	123	16,735
2021	19	89,000	2,000	91,000	72.5	108,969	12,900	127.00	6,280	940	111,000	5,258	6	1,762	288	21,500
2022[1]	22			93,000		110,000	13,600	140.00	8,000	902	120,000					
2023[2]	22			91,000		110,000		150.00	7,500	900	120,000					

[1] Preliminary.   [2] Estimate.   [3] Masonry, natural & pozzolan (slag-line).   [4] Value received F.O.B. mill, excluding cost of containers.   [5] Hydraulic & clinker cement for consumption.   [6] Less than 1/2 unit.   *Source: U.S. Geological Survey (USGS)*

Shipments of Finished Portland Cement from Mills in the United States   In Thousands of Metric Tons

Year	Jan.	Feb.	Mar.	Apr.	May	June	July	Aug.	Sept.	Oct.	Nov.	Dec.	Total
2017	4,869.2	5,398.2	6,687.5	6,673.6	7,738.1	8,236.3	7,507.0	8,497.2	7,606.4	8,222.6	7,253.1	5,515.0	84,204.1
2018	5,125.4	5,130.2	6,589.9	7,220.0	8,205.8	8,135.0	8,034.7	8,769.6	7,307.9	8,421.8	6,699.3	5,346.6	84,986.2
2019	5,565.0	5,013.8	6,386.3	7,550.0	7,941.0	7,791.7	8,653.3	8,910.4	8,162.9	8,656.2	6,830.7	5,809.9	87,271.3
2020	5,962.4	5,447.4	6,619.2	7,119.8	7,562.4	8,734.2	8,497.4	8,298.4	8,019.8	8,602.4	7,429.4	6,480.3	88,773.7
2021	5,728.0	4,791.9	7,555.3	8,239.3	7,755.9	8,568.3	8,154.1	8,562.8	8,296.0	8,299.4	8,036.2	6,936.1	90,923.3
2022	5,645.3	5,577.4	7,766.0	7,584.0	8,113.7	9,097.5	7,985.7	8,910.8	8,471.3	8,248.9	6,895.9	5,766.9	90,063.5
2023[1]	5,573.2	5,572.2	7,057.9	7,141.1	8,563.4	8,749.2	7,765.8	8,761.1	7,788.5	8,241.6	7,161.5	5,843.8	88,219.3

[1] Preliminary.   *Source: U.S. Geological Survey (USGS)*

Cheese

Since prehistoric times, humans have been making and eating cheese. Dating back as far as 6,000 BC, archaeologists have discovered that cheese had been made from cow and goat milk and stored in tall jars. The Romans turned cheese-making into a culinary art, mixing sheep and goat milk and adding herbs and spices for flavoring. By 300 AD, cheese was being exported regularly to countries along the Mediterranean coast.

Cheese is made from the milk of cows and other mammals such as sheep, goats, buffalo, reindeer, camels, yaks, and mares. More than 400 varieties of cheese exist. There are three basic steps common to all cheese making. First, proteins in milk are transformed into curds, or solid lumps. Second, the curds are separated from the milky liquid (or whey) and shaped or pressed into molds. Finally, the shaped curds are ripened using a variety of aging and curing techniques. Cheeses are usually grouped according to their moisture content into fresh, soft, semi-soft, hard, and very hard. Many classifications overlap due to texture changes with aging.

Cheese is a multi-billion-dollar a year industry in the U.S. Cheddar cheese is the most common natural cheese produced in the U.S., accounting for 35% of U.S. production. Cheeses originating in America include Colby, cream cheese, and Monterey Jack. Varieties other than American cheeses, mostly Italian, now have had a combined level of production that easily exceeds American cheeses.

Futures and options on cheese are traded on the CME Group. The CME's cheese futures contract calls for the delivery of 20,000 pounds of cheese and is priced in Dollars per pound.

Prices – The average monthly price of American Cheese at the CME Group in 2023 fell by -13.6% yr/yr to $1.8154 per pound, below the 2014 record high of $2.1094 cents per pound.

Supply – World production of cheese in 2024 is expected to rise by +1.0% yr/yr to 22.358 million metric tons, which would be a new record high. The European Union is expected to be the world's largest producer of cheese, with 46.6% of the total world production in 2024. US production was the next largest with 29.3% of the total. US production of all cheese in 2023 rose by +0.1% to 14.074 billion pounds, which was a new record high.

World Production of Cheese   In Thousands of Metric Tons

Year	Argentina	Australia	Brazil	Canada	European Union	Japan	Korea, South	Mexico	New Zealand	Russia	Ukraine	United States	World Total
2013	549	318	722	388	9,368	49	22	316	311	713	247	5,036	18,227
2014	562	328	736	396	9,560	46	24	343	325	760	203	5,222	18,738
2015	566	343	754	419	9,740	46	23	363	355	861	190	5,367	19,276
2016	552	344	745	445	9,640	47	25	375	360	865	186	5,525	19,835
2017	514	348	771	497	9,796	46	35	396	386	951	190	5,733	20,390
2018	444	366	760	510	9,872	45	37	419	370	970	192	5,914	20,656
2019	523	364	770	515	10,155	44	40	437	365	983	187	5,959	21,128
2020	488	379	790	523	10,362	48	45	446	350	1,059	180	6,005	21,525
2021	530	393	790	522	10,401	49	45	448	380	1,075	182	6,242	21,935
2022	535	400	745	517	10,340	48	47	455	375	1,085	150	6,379	21,983
2023[1]	520	425	770	522	10,390	47	45	465	400	1,100	135	6,400	22,146
2024[2]	480	445	780	530	10,420	50	47	474	400	1,115	132	6,545	22,358

[1] Preliminary.   [2] Forecast.   NA = Not available.   *Source: Foreign Agricultural Service, U.S. Department of Agriculture (FAS-USDA)*

Production of Cheese in the United States   In Millions of Pounds

	American			Swiss, Including				Crean & Lim- Neufchatel				Total of All	Cottage Cheese		
Year	Whole Milk	Part Skim	Total	Block	Munster	Brick	burger	Cheese	Italian Varieties	Blue Mond	All Other Varieties	Cheese[2]	Lowfat	Curd[3]	Cream-ed[4]
2014	4,588	----	4,588	297.8	163.7	2.9	[5]	851.7	4,950.2	[5]	154.2	11,512	364.6	381.1	303.1
2015	4,694	----	4,694	312.0	177.5	3.4	[5]	876.3	5,081.8	[5]	----	11,831	363.0	400.6	317.5
2016	4,769	----	4,769	312.0	181.4	2.8	[5]	909.0	5,304.4	[5]	----	12,182	367.8	406.4	329.4
2017	5,072	----	5,072	316.7	189.2	2.4	[5]	918.1	5,395.2	[5]	----	12,640	344.4	390.4	330.5
2018	5,254	----	5,254	332.3	191.2	2.3	[5]	914.8	5,556.9	[5]	----	13,025	342.1	402.4	352.8
2019	5,211	----	5,211	338.3	196.9	2.0	[5]	931.6	5,668.1	[5]	----	13,107	324.9	388.0	353.5
2020	5,337	----	5,337	324.9	188.5	1.6	[5]	1,002.0	5,624.3	[5]	----	13,238	308.4	378.8	361.8
2021	5,563	----	5,563	330.2	191.5	2.0	[5]	1,034.9	5,750.6	[5]	----	13,695	302.5	358.4	348.2
2022	5,635	----	5,635	350.9	191.6	1.5	[5]	1,120.4	5,930.9	[5]	----	14,070	294.3	372.2	344.0
2023[1]	5,711	----	5,711	335.5			[5]	1,124.2	5,862.4	[5]	----	14,094	331.8	396.9	378.1

[1] Preliminary.   [2] Excludes full-skim cheddar and cottage cheese.   [3] Includes cottage, pot, and baker's cheese with a butterfat content of less than 4%.
[4] Includes cheese with a butterfat content of 4 to 19 %.   [5] Included in All Other Varieties.   NA = Not available.
Source: Economic Research Service, U.S. Department of Agriculture ERS-USDA)

World Consumption of Cheese   In Thousands of Metric Tons

Year	Argentina	Australia	Brazil	Canada	European Union	Japan	Korea, South	Mexico	New Zealand	Russia	Ukraine	United States	World Total
2015	524	270	773	415	9,087	294	137	475	41	1,041	184	5,149	18,599
2016	508	275	785	458	8,616	304	136	496	42	1,069	187	5,379	19,252
2017	485	291	799	504	8,727	324	159	511	40	1,141	188	5,494	19,690
2018	380	293	785	536	8,790	329	155	526	38	1,200	198	5,675	19,958
2019	461	297	795	539	9,019	346	166	551	38	1,231	205	5,751	20,462
2020	420	305	817	555	9,183	335	188	549	38	1,338	222	5,745	20,768
2021	457	330	817	562	9,212	335	195	568	38	1,363	230	5,964	21,172
2022	435	330	774	559	9,191	326	197	597	39	1,390	175	6,055	21,139
2023[1]	440	365	808	566	9,200	297	195	633	40	1,430	157	6,106	21,364
2024[2]	395	380	823	581	9,230	314	195	644	40	1,480	151	6,231	21,619

[1] Preliminary.   [2] Forecast.   NA = Not available.   *Source: Foreign Agricultural Service, U.S. Department of Agriculture (FAS-USDA)*

World Exports of Cheese   In Thousands of Metric Tons

Year	Argentina	Australia	Brazil	Canada	European Union	Japan	Korea, South	Mexico	New Zealand	Russia	Ukraine	United States	World Total
2015	43	171	3	12	719	4	327	24	11	317	1,815	4,938	18,420
2016	53	167	3	13	1,231	5	355	25	8	287	2,515	5,367	19,276
2017	44	171	4	13	1,275	7	343	25	9	340	2,589	5,525	19,835
2018	61	172	4	10	1,279	16	322	24	8	348	2,643	5,733	20,390
2019	61	160	3	12	1,348	7	335	26	7	357	2,767	5,914	20,656
2020	70	153	4	11	1,402	11	323	30	6	355	2,833	5,959	21,128
2021	78	157	5	8	1,385	12	361	35	7	402	2,905	6,005	21,525
2022	82	145	4	8	1,336	14	340	40	9	451	2,918	6,217	22,051
2023[1]	82	130	3	9	1,355	12	391	45	9	433	2,958	6,350	22,167
2024[2]	87	160	2	10	1,380	15	370	50	10	466	3,049	6,425	22,353

[1] Preliminary.   [2] Forecast.   NA = Not available.   *Source: Foreign Agricultural Service, U.S. Department of Agriculture (FAS-USDA)*

World Imports of Cheese   In Thousands of Metric Tons

Year	Australia	Brazil	Canada	European Union	Japan	Korea, South	Mexico	Philip-pines	Russia	Taiwan	Ukraine	United States	World Total
2015	89	22	26	61	249	112	116	27	209	29	5	157	1,196
2016	99	43	27	195	258	110	126	30	223	32	7	165	1,909
2017	116	32	28	191	273	125	122	38	226	32	10	138	1,938
2018	98	29	31	197	286	124	123	38	250	32	14	138	1,998
2019	97	28	36	212	303	131	121	40	273	31	24	139	2,095
2020	98	31	41	223	292	148	114	41	311	34	47	128	2,139
2021	97	32	48	196	288	157	132	49	326	37	55	145	2,159
2022	96	33	52	187	274	154	156	50	345	35	34	143	2,136
2023[1]	110	41	54	165	250	142	180	46	375	33	31	134	2,192
2024[2]	100	45	56	190	265	145	185	50	375	36	29	144	2,263

[1] Preliminary.   [2] Forecast.   NA = Not available.   *Source: Foreign Agricultural Service, U.S. Department of Agriculture (FAS-USDA)*

World Ending Stocks of Cheese   In Thousands of Metric Tons

Year	Argentina	Australia	Canada	Japan	Korea, South	New Zealand	Russia	Ukraine	United States	World Total
2015	40	48	81	15	2	59	35	8	520	850
2016	34	49	82	15	1	32	29	6	544	827
2017	23	51	90	9	2	46	40	9	581	876
2018	30	50	85	10	8	68	36	9	610	929
2019	33	54	85	10	13	73	35	8	600	923
2020	32	73	83	14	17	72	37	7	633	986
2021	30	76	83	15	23	64	40	7	654	1,003
2022	53	97	85	10	26	70	40	7	670	1,065
2023[1]	54	137	86	9	16	54	40	7	665	1,081
2024[2]	54	142	81	9	11	59		7	657	1,034

[1] Preliminary.   [2] Forecast.   NA = Not available.   *Source: Foreign Agricultural Service, U.S. Department of Agriculture (FAS-USDA)*

CHEESE

Production of Cheese[2] in the United States   In Millions of Pounds

Year	Jan.	Feb.	Mar.	Apr.	May	June	July	Aug.	Sept.	Oct.	Nov.	Dec.	Total
2014	962.4	859.4	976.0	967.3	977.2	951.0	965.0	935.6	943.0	987.8	965.2	1,022.1	11,512.1
2015	994.1	896.7	1,013.0	977.3	988.2	976.1	1,002.0	979.0	965.5	1,018.0	986.4	1,035.1	11,831.4
2016	1,025.7	947.5	1,028.6	1,003.2	1,010.7	998.4	1,020.8	1,006.8	991.4	1,052.2	1,029.2	1,067.0	12,181.5
2017	1,060.9	958.4	1,069.8	1,057.1	1,074.7	1,044.0	1,052.0	1,045.3	1,026.8	1,082.4	1,065.7	1,102.8	12,640.0
2018	1,098.7	992.8	1,108.0	1,078.1	1,085.2	1,066.0	1,087.1	1,087.0	1,059.1	1,154.2	1,096.0	1,112.4	13,024.6
2019	1,098.4	991.3	1,122.4	1,085.0	1,105.9	1,067.7	1,087.6	1,113.6	1,080.5	1,138.2	1,093.4	1,122.5	13,106.7
2020	1,110.5	1,031.7	1,121.4	1,052.0	1,101.2	1,121.6	1,110.1	1,091.5	1,104.2	1,136.9	1,102.3	1,154.5	13,237.9
2021	1,135.6	1,043.5	1,183.4	1,154.6	1,163.2	1,126.8	1,145.7	1,148.8	1,134.4	1,152.1	1,130.4	1,176.5	13,694.9
2022	1,172.0	1,105.3	1,231.2	1,173.4	1,204.7	1,165.8	1,170.1	1,157.3	1,150.8	1,184.5	1,156.2	1,198.7	14,070.1
2023[1]	1,205.3	1,100.3	1,231.9	1,170.0	1,203.7	1,170.3	1,155.8	1,156.5	1,149.7	1,194.3	1,158.6	1,197.7	14,094.0

[1] Preliminary.   [2] Excludes cottage cheese.   *Source: National Agricultural Statistics Service, U.S. Department of Agriculture (NASS-USDA)*

Production of American Cheese[2] in the United States   In Thousands of Pounds

Year	Jan.	Feb.	Mar.	Apr.	May	June	July	Aug.	Sept.	Oct.	Nov.	Dec.	Total
2014	388,420	345,464	387,071	385,322	399,239	374,373	385,175	376,203	369,843	393,414	383,500	399,999	4,588,023
2015	402,222	357,376	395,823	396,691	407,667	390,447	397,235	394,943	379,550	392,592	380,004	399,921	4,694,471
2016	402,377	368,000	402,001	398,750	403,040	392,166	401,815	393,459	379,456	403,397	400,983	423,444	4,768,888
2017	434,638	390,324	429,569	434,669	443,095	419,273	414,508	414,292	403,555	430,496	413,725	443,985	5,072,129
2018	448,124	406,189	443,185	444,287	442,968	429,076	440,937	435,388	424,032	457,122	434,185	448,340	5,253,833
2019	439,283	391,027	442,723	430,539	443,683	427,638	434,449	452,030	415,687	445,601	432,438	456,378	5,211,476
2020	437,451	418,605	446,423	446,525	441,148	431,782	453,096	445,137	432,114	460,217	449,783	474,946	5,337,227
2021	474,315	426,094	480,500	478,196	481,545	457,394	467,274	462,477	454,668	460,680	449,639	469,770	5,562,552
2022	471,650	442,683	482,811	477,133	488,333	466,040	473,984	457,667	446,931	475,411	466,253	485,708	5,634,604
2023[1]	498,646	443,179	498,889	485,838	510,181	473,627	468,347	458,648	462,501	470,128	460,868	480,237	5,711,089

[1] Preliminary.   [2] Includes Cheddar, Colby, Monterey, and Jack.   *Source: National Agricultural Statistics Service, U.S. Department of Agriculture*

Production of Blue and Gorgonzola Cheese in the United States   In Thousands of Pounds

Year	Jan.	Feb.	Mar.	Apr.	May	June	July	Aug.	Sept.	Oct.	Nov.	Dec.	Total
2014	7,272	6,611	8,028	8,329	7,917	7,819	8,687	8,231	7,966	7,464	6,884	7,637	92,845
2015	7,402	7,730	8,198	7,777	7,929	7,933	7,930	7,729	8,208	7,751	7,843	8,059	94,489
2016	6,994	7,289	8,046	7,010	8,685	8,083	7,284	8,195	6,980	7,493	7,704	7,109	90,872
2017	7,620	7,060	7,182	7,876	8,607	7,942	7,845	7,840	6,904	7,899	7,532	7,009	91,316
2018	7,459	7,115	8,151	7,863	7,994	7,246	7,890	8,027	8,339	8,379	7,442	8,743	94,648
2019	7,522	6,482	7,977	7,588	8,331	8,758	7,914	8,387	8,099	9,270	7,668	6,648	94,644
2020	7,120	7,035	7,230	3,131	4,434	6,966	7,710	8,646	6,677	6,530	5,646	4,918	76,043
2021	5,345	6,795	7,782	7,393	8,207	7,751	6,742	7,314	7,494	8,896	7,913	7,556	89,188
2022	8,197	8,170	7,575	7,859	7,797	8,009	7,034	7,361	7,217	7,495	7,744	6,577	91,035
2023[1]	6,363	6,838	8,093	6,510	7,269	7,019	7,043	7,847	6,096	7,323	7,142	6,787	84,330

[1] Preliminary.   *Source: National Agricultural Statistics Service, U.S. Department of Agriculture (NASS-USDA)*

Production of Brick and Muenster Cheeses in the United States   In Thousands of Pounds

Year	Jan.	Feb.	Mar.	Apr.	May	June	July	Aug.	Sept.	Oct.	Nov.	Dec.	Total
2014	13,079	11,606	13,757	13,698	15,174	13,951	14,862	14,726	13,309	14,520	13,738	14,172	166,592
2015	15,384	13,060	14,748	14,919	16,314	14,151	17,246	14,663	13,301	16,667	16,051	14,485	180,989
2016	14,898	14,227	14,075	15,955	16,252	15,053	16,390	15,165	15,161	16,958	15,634	14,431	184,199
2017	15,104	13,208	15,947	16,755	16,496	15,581	18,274	16,667	15,147	17,595	16,248	14,568	191,591
2018	15,282	14,089	15,117	16,133	17,079	16,235	18,151	16,169	15,964	18,514	16,100	14,690	193,523
2019	18,222	14,853	14,806	16,927	18,167	16,749	17,710	15,723	15,664	19,217	15,745	15,123	198,906
2020	15,036	14,760	16,684	13,573	18,188	17,343	16,319	14,535	16,252	16,842	16,755	13,785	190,072
2021	16,076	15,557	17,561	15,481	17,421	17,509	16,321	14,383	14,620	16,082	16,266	16,264	193,541
2022	16,142	15,097	16,507	17,698	15,873	17,123	16,162	15,515	15,428	16,488	15,748	15,328	193,109
2023[1]	17,186	13,804	15,895	14,525	15,393	15,984	17,329	18,957	16,682	16,307	16,287	17,193	195,542

[1] Preliminary.   *Source: National Agricultural Statistics Service, U.S. Department of Agriculture (NASS-USDA)*

Production of Cream and Neufchatel Cheeses in the United States   In Thousands of Pounds

Year	Jan.	Feb.	Mar.	Apr.	May	June	July	Aug.	Sept.	Oct.	Nov.	Dec.	Total
2014	62,019	54,268	66,734	71,432	65,134	69,553	71,158	73,798	76,243	83,428	80,094	77,852	851,713
2015	64,490	59,747	71,231	61,357	61,071	68,551	74,875	82,070	83,438	96,108	81,217	72,131	876,286
2016	72,325	69,992	66,940	70,299	61,734	71,636	71,859	84,945	78,674	93,188	86,074	81,306	908,972
2017	73,848	64,164	63,346	69,644	70,934	69,356	78,631	86,692	89,137	84,929	83,126	84,264	918,071
2018	71,932	63,932	72,774	68,434	67,467	74,650	73,530	85,203	78,516	95,019	85,805	77,562	914,824
2019	72,842	60,192	79,212	70,516	72,309	71,339	79,986	85,171	86,328	89,440	85,127	79,176	931,638
2020	79,982	62,709	76,471	63,071	76,750	94,387	90,069	91,402	92,527	91,338	94,664	88,646	1,002,016
2021	78,479	72,787	82,298	81,648	93,185	86,574	82,130	94,946	92,398	86,516	90,978	92,979	1,034,918
2022	87,407	85,210	104,684	89,417	103,490	96,800	93,977	96,976	91,102	92,415	86,822	92,120	1,120,420
2023[1]	95,203	93,812	100,237	92,221	95,103	95,875	88,070	91,755	90,969	99,452	92,682	88,801	1,124,180

[1] Preliminary.   *Source: National Agricultural Statistics Service, U.S. Department of Agriculture (NASS-USDA)*

Production of Swiss Cheese in the United States   In Thousands of Pounds

Year	Jan.	Feb.	Mar.	Apr.	May	June	July	Aug.	Sept.	Oct.	Nov.	Dec.	Total
2014	26,055	23,148	25,699	25,550	26,690	25,092	25,734	22,695	22,599	23,350	23,763	27,427	297,802
2015	24,427	23,571	26,662	26,616	27,387	25,619	26,802	26,152	25,278	26,529	25,150	27,822	312,015
2016	27,434	24,429	26,020	24,257	26,336	27,140	27,001	25,403	25,034	26,017	25,883	27,023	311,977
2017	26,286	24,169	26,846	26,383	26,262	26,040	26,736	25,646	25,622	27,338	26,837	28,489	316,654
2018	28,183	26,350	28,685	26,828	28,816	27,763	28,195	27,884	26,414	27,390	27,888	27,907	332,303
2019	29,913	26,489	27,682	27,601	29,824	28,290	29,103	28,896	27,705	29,136	26,100	27,534	338,273
2020	28,525	26,640	27,396	25,754	24,242	26,314	26,340	28,424	27,438	28,070	27,985	27,793	324,921
2021	25,977	22,988	26,004	28,832	28,347	29,639	28,870	27,257	25,653	27,949	27,249	31,460	330,225
2022	31,137	28,209	31,558	30,394	30,632	28,961	28,618	27,873	26,537	26,958	29,491	30,520	350,888
2023[1]	30,061	24,660	27,163	28,254	31,283	29,009	28,993	27,645	26,641	26,139	26,550	29,146	335,544

[1] Preliminary.   *Source: National Agricultural Statistics Service, U.S. Department of Agriculture (NASS-USDA)*

Production of Cheddar Cheese in the United States   In Thousands of Pounds

Year	Jan.	Feb.	Mar.	Apr.	May	June	July	Aug.	Sept.	Oct.	Nov.	Dec.	Total
2014	283,595	254,140	283,494	290,713	293,923	274,257	274,163	265,918	262,230	277,835	266,025	290,745	3,317,038
2015	296,767	262,602	287,042	287,350	296,447	287,956	286,435	279,379	271,551	278,915	265,947	292,720	3,393,111
2016	297,480	258,530	286,426	300,166	293,238	280,220	284,607	281,932	271,561	284,058	286,571	309,709	3,434,498
2017	327,339	291,518	323,453	329,682	327,467	302,102	298,297	298,318	291,766	307,844	296,609	327,073	3,721,468
2018	331,985	301,256	320,257	319,153	318,665	312,869	325,217	311,974	297,632	323,213	314,170	326,117	3,802,508
2019	323,210	280,816	315,229	306,510	321,122	307,403	305,911	321,190	284,142	309,584	309,223	330,369	3,714,709
2020	319,240	302,408	314,114	330,119	315,704	302,960	322,775	323,153	303,253	325,354	321,553	349,162	3,829,795
2021	346,949	300,535	336,776	337,847	348,365	329,810	325,011	320,293	309,879	324,914	313,524	333,665	3,927,568
2022	332,479	308,061	333,498	327,173	339,704	341,624	340,236	318,114	305,153	340,233	323,788	343,228	3,953,291
2023[1]	353,921	317,059	348,055	345,668	356,583	338,004	323,377	313,182	311,284	328,858	314,280	331,032	3,981,303

[1] Preliminary.   *Source: National Agricultural Statistics Service, U.S. Department of Agriculture (NASS-USDA)*

Production of Feta Cheese in the United States   In Thousands of Pounds

Year	Jan.	Feb.	Mar.	Apr.	May	June	July	Aug.	Sept.	Oct.	Nov.	Dec.	Total
2014	7,957	8,142	9,201	9,681	9,672	9,743	10,214	8,459	8,842	8,610	7,209	7,892	105,622
2015	8,706	8,227	9,871	11,258	10,222	9,785	10,512	9,277	9,237	9,095	7,563	8,671	112,424
2016	11,927	9,183	11,212	11,113	10,959	10,234	10,185	11,071	10,518	11,504	10,506	8,437	126,849
2017	8,723	9,235	10,637	11,010	11,717	11,622	11,701	10,388	9,874	10,120	8,368	9,075	122,470
2018	9,667	9,692	11,187	12,036	12,706	11,959	12,603	10,564	10,018	12,507	8,411	8,473	129,823
2019	9,763	10,434	11,479	12,413	12,585	11,539	11,570	10,948	10,710	11,074	8,365	9,820	130,700
2020	10,193	9,400	12,930	7,473	10,090	11,372	14,479	13,765	13,477	12,583	8,274	8,938	132,974
2021	8,459	12,097	15,470	15,602	15,678	15,465	15,336	15,462	15,237	13,588	11,739	12,554	166,687
2022	9,606	11,942	12,109	12,432	12,046	12,206	11,191	12,522	15,544	14,549	9,758	9,821	143,726
2023[1]	10,057	10,059	13,909	12,883	12,561	13,517	12,763	13,645	12,447	15,118	10,810	9,765	147,534

[1] Preliminary.   *Source: National Agricultural Statistics Service, U.S. Department of Agriculture (NASS-USDA)*

CHEESE

Production of Gouda Cheese in the United States In Thousands of Pounds

Year	Jan.	Feb.	Mar.	Apr.	May	June	July	Aug.	Sept.	Oct.	Nov.	Dec.	Total
2014	5,735	5,391	4,941	3,638	5,334	7,578	7,089	5,692	2,258	2,436	3,038	2,781	55,911
2015	4,671	6,295	6,469	4,966	4,388	2,572	3,686	5,231	5,216	4,524	5,739	4,581	58,317
2016	4,327	4,737	5,689	3,761	6,356	2,031	4,045	5,592	5,988	6,732	5,412	3,931	58,601
2017	3,875	7,314	5,984	5,095	4,069	4,728	5,365	5,073	4,678	5,302	8,213	5,704	65,400
2018	5,121	3,457	5,924	4,513	6,123	6,243	5,509	7,001	4,871	6,132	6,369	3,989	65,252
2019	5,439	2,710	4,136	3,594	3,126	3,330	3,896	5,192	4,810	4,152	4,149	4,119	48,653
2020	4,559	4,927	4,242	3,231	2,703	3,674	3,918	2,939	2,838	3,810	4,058	3,864	44,763
2021	5,211	5,210	5,374	3,549	5,723	4,597	5,070	4,503	4,419	3,768	4,358	4,226	56,008
2022	5,957	5,340	6,990	5,339	5,624	5,910	4,176	4,261	4,007	3,486	5,146	4,984	61,220
2023[1]	4,747	5,486	5,687	5,549	4,323	4,871	6,047	5,774	4,572	3,816	5,801	5,686	62,359

[1] Preliminary.   *Source: National Agricultural Statistics Service, U.S. Department of Agriculture (NASS-USDA)*

Production of Hispanic Cheese in the United States In Thousands of Pounds

Year	Jan.	Feb.	Mar.	Apr.	May	June	July	Aug.	Sept.	Oct.	Nov.	Dec.	Total
2014	19,519	17,945	22,557	19,677	20,898	20,671	21,306	22,101	21,007	22,417	19,873	21,608	249,579
2015	20,976	19,761	23,127	20,881	21,019	20,869	20,587	20,796	22,084	21,595	21,152	21,444	254,291
2016	20,407	21,975	22,698	21,429	20,735	22,588	21,781	22,619	22,850	22,729	22,592	22,538	264,941
2017	22,079	21,700	25,936	23,715	24,637	24,228	22,886	24,544	22,428	26,827	24,423	23,118	286,521
2018	24,032	21,791	25,611	24,115	26,245	25,727	24,709	27,013	25,193	30,134	27,373	29,973	311,916
2019	23,433	27,287	28,755	27,877	29,824	25,877	26,805	27,679	28,068	30,543	27,890	26,441	330,479
2020	27,247	26,821	31,839	28,953	29,871	30,969	29,475	28,119	29,938	29,092	26,589	27,561	346,474
2021	27,384	28,250	32,336	27,579	27,919	29,352	30,462	28,675	30,327	31,735	28,114	28,693	350,826
2022	26,340	28,836	32,745	29,058	31,174	32,259	33,317	35,079	32,965	33,917	33,852	32,636	382,178
2023[1]	30,707	31,439	36,069	32,355	31,714	35,849	32,429	35,667	36,501	35,609	38,283	38,421	415,043

[1] Preliminary.   *Source: National Agricultural Statistics Service, U.S. Department of Agriculture (NASS-USDA)*

Production of Italian Cheese in the United States In Thousands of Pounds

Year	Jan.	Feb.	Mar.	Apr.	May	June	July	Aug.	Sept.	Oct.	Nov.	Dec.	Total
2014	420,216	374,469	426,306	417,452	415,297	410,340	409,723	392,972	406,080	417,600	413,496	446,284	4,950,235
2015	433,087	389,962	441,855	420,852	419,504	422,133	429,399	403,150	402,466	428,460	426,849	464,109	5,081,826
2016	451,589	415,039	458,663	438,996	443,594	436,333	447,386	426,222	431,888	449,808	439,889	464,948	5,304,355
2017	455,515	407,544	471,216	449,326	454,425	451,434	452,010	437,910	433,070	454,859	457,497	470,442	5,395,248
2018	473,913	428,100	483,095	460,768	460,817	450,929	462,769	453,431	450,964	483,852	469,207	479,005	5,556,850
2019	480,134	441,082	493,275	475,467	474,522	461,688	463,865	466,578	470,642	485,559	471,962	483,331	5,668,105
2020	485,398	448,190	485,546	447,648	482,323	485,761	454,998	445,538	469,823	473,294	454,904	490,878	5,624,301
2021	481,029	443,254	502,101	483,156	472,514	465,030	480,260	480,009	475,972	488,426	479,853	498,981	5,750,585
2022	503,643	466,287	519,279	491,105	496,930	485,592	488,763	486,732	496,490	499,233	488,746	508,061	5,930,861
2023[1]	499,904	458,867	512,918	479,150	482,542	480,836	482,907	483,985	479,742	506,674	485,901	508,944	5,862,370

[1] Preliminary.   *Source: National Agricultural Statistics Service, U.S. Department of Agriculture (NASS-USDA)*

Production of Mozzarella Cheese in the United States In Thousands of Pounds

Year	Jan.	Feb.	Mar.	Apr.	May	June	July	Aug.	Sept.	Oct.	Nov.	Dec.	Total
2014	333,319	300,506	335,385	332,466	331,181	328,829	327,914	311,973	319,861	326,866	326,093	350,532	3,924,925
2015	341,183	305,421	344,459	330,958	333,451	331,196	338,554	316,045	316,408	332,824	335,210	363,227	3,988,936
2016	353,001	323,713	358,081	340,584	345,063	339,993	350,089	328,118	334,808	346,013	338,728	359,555	4,117,746
2017	353,165	315,534	362,560	348,680	352,115	350,106	351,858	336,517	332,291	347,484	351,563	365,619	4,167,492
2018	365,563	328,591	372,712	358,320	359,072	355,249	367,437	357,346	358,579	381,217	370,269	377,006	4,351,361
2019	379,627	347,234	391,166	372,686	374,770	370,364	368,167	370,384	375,726	384,612	375,266	383,976	4,493,978
2020	381,983	353,200	386,397	353,043	379,446	389,307	364,832	355,527	371,610	371,411	358,817	382,737	4,448,310
2021	374,948	345,504	392,656	377,151	371,087	364,385	374,441	374,517	369,882	378,302	375,299	388,985	4,487,157
2022	394,810	359,283	408,184	386,577	377,519	386,708	392,366	383,858	385,587	390,597	384,171	399,393	4,649,053
2023[1]	393,111	361,531	401,721	380,896	379,497	380,049	382,947	382,496	379,942	399,380	379,783	403,231	4,624,584

[1] Preliminary.   *Source: National Agricultural Statistics Service, U.S. Department of Agriculture (NASS-USDA)*

CHEESE

Production of Parmesan Cheese in the United States In Thousands of Pounds

Year	Jan.	Feb.	Mar.	Apr.	May	June	July	Aug.	Sept.	Oct.	Nov.	Dec.	Total
2014	24,452	21,546	25,563	24,830	26,551	25,717	26,618	23,618	25,439	25,670	24,036	27,808	301,848
2015	30,754	27,711	30,742	28,762	28,369	29,611	29,656	25,168	23,607	27,644	25,501	31,478	339,003
2016	33,820	31,383	33,371	35,973	35,073	34,343	37,542	33,156	30,373	32,957	32,273	37,055	407,319
2017	38,697	32,553	39,191	38,242	38,033	38,418	39,411	36,612	34,641	37,766	37,886	39,190	450,640
2018	42,568	38,996	41,508	39,631	37,515	33,192	32,003	28,959	26,467	33,656	32,470	37,526	424,491
2019	37,840	35,654	37,118	38,548	38,170	32,682	33,174	32,410	30,153	32,349	30,314	33,962	412,374
2020	38,288	36,596	34,337	37,774	35,179	29,904	29,991	31,273	34,035	35,822	33,825	42,139	419,163
2021	40,967	37,301	41,629	40,900	40,065	39,627	41,960	37,738	38,861	40,503	39,024	44,605	483,180
2022	45,578	45,376	43,694	40,473	37,846	38,019	37,707	38,284	45,010	43,214	41,034	42,877	499,112
2023[1]	43,308	40,130	44,117	36,688	42,661	42,548	40,525	37,516	35,264	40,719	39,845	41,079	484,400

[1] Preliminary.   Source: National Agricultural Statistics Service, U.S. Department of Agriculture (NASS-USDA)

Production of Provolone Cheese in the United States In Thousands of Pounds

Year	Jan.	Feb.	Mar.	Apr.	May	June	July	Aug.	Sept.	Oct.	Nov.	Dec.	Total
2014	31,575	25,631	33,268	30,371	30,740	29,372	29,718	29,504	30,048	30,429	29,847	30,585	361,088
2015	30,169	28,261	31,522	31,975	31,620	31,796	32,427	32,387	32,591	32,875	31,175	32,518	379,316
2016	32,849	29,130	33,162	33,729	34,445	34,196	33,892	34,108	33,924	35,058	33,840	33,256	401,589
2017	31,434	28,740	34,517	32,669	32,456	34,090	34,139	34,184	33,438	34,101	32,535	31,489	393,792
2018	32,633	29,285	33,826	34,496	34,396	32,809	34,606	35,501	34,374	34,283	31,173	30,404	397,786
2019	30,472	29,682	30,873	33,053	32,436	31,166	33,498	33,216	33,468	34,272	30,150	30,084	382,370
2020	31,236	29,137	29,698	26,762	33,655	35,309	31,853	27,450	31,047	32,403	29,199	30,165	367,914
2021	31,245	28,052	30,776	32,804	32,232	31,032	34,310	34,156	31,888	31,708	29,589	27,563	375,355
2022	28,271	28,997	30,826	29,552	49,105	29,303	29,326	32,262	31,195	32,349	31,081	30,136	382,403
2023[1]	28,794	27,805	32,212	29,843	32,575	30,388	31,066	32,542	32,651	31,649	30,491	30,299	370,315

[1] Preliminary.   Source: National Agricultural Statistics Service, U.S. Department of Agriculture (NASS-USDA)

Production of Ricota Cheese in the United States In Thousands of Pounds

Year	Jan.	Feb.	Mar.	Apr.	May	June	July	Aug.	Sept.	Oct.	Nov.	Dec.	Total
2014	22,124	18,067	21,697	19,807	17,557	16,571	16,012	19,041	21,133	24,273	23,120	25,882	245,284
2015	20,273	17,646	23,689	17,440	15,215	17,914	17,789	19,500	20,722	24,234	24,100	24,942	243,464
2016	22,197	20,754	23,758	18,209	18,196	17,449	15,914	21,982	22,289	24,251	23,890	23,342	252,231
2017	21,050	19,046	23,083	18,102	19,000	17,300	15,963	20,568	21,857	24,226	23,327	22,390	245,912
2018	22,989	20,886	23,200	17,734	18,077	17,656	17,463	21,221	20,976	23,902	23,204	22,153	249,461
2019	21,577	18,614	22,352	19,824	18,244	16,645	17,800	19,418	20,130	23,459	23,973	22,905	244,941
2020	22,354	19,096	23,777	19,610	22,703	20,726	18,556	21,249	22,286	22,985	21,952	23,349	258,643
2021	22,547	21,646	24,556	19,813	16,005	16,478	16,188	20,747	22,070	23,161	22,621	22,492	248,324
2022	21,525	18,741	23,109	21,043	20,304	18,701	17,474	20,460	21,177	21,019	20,216	22,717	246,486
2023[1]	23,697	19,210	22,749	18,302	16,616	17,033	17,850	20,871	21,506	23,583	23,226	22,745	247,388

[1] Preliminary.   Source: National Agricultural Statistics Service, U.S. Department of Agriculture (NASS-USDA)

Production of Romano Cheese in the United States In Thousands of Pounds

Year	Jan.	Feb.	Mar.	Apr.	May	June	July	Aug.	Sept.	Oct.	Nov.	Dec.	Total
2014	3,270	3,003	3,785	3,822	3,666	3,889	4,003	3,184	3,470	4,198	4,011	4,720	45,021
2015	4,857	4,770	3,937	4,801	4,368	5,319	5,287	3,920	3,578	4,137	4,551	5,509	55,034
2016	3,626	4,341	4,428	4,971	4,407	4,462	4,452	3,918	4,017	4,844	4,565	4,417	52,448
2017	4,571	5,175	4,269	4,974	6,276	4,521	4,587	4,407	4,107	5,029	4,967	5,419	58,302
2018	4,611	4,653	5,432	4,678	5,086	5,195	5,176	4,223	3,840	4,537	5,104	5,523	58,058
2019	3,868	3,822	4,301	4,631	4,452	4,676	4,328	4,007	4,148	5,169	5,545	5,281	54,228
2020	4,728	4,265	4,598	5,307	4,768	4,420	4,413	3,926	3,976	3,950	4,458	5,707	54,516
2021	5,038	4,571	5,352	5,911	6,310	5,870	5,611	5,143	5,632	6,131	5,039	6,457	67,065
2022	5,507	6,586	4,630	5,393	4,087	4,770	4,470	4,718	5,284	4,123	4,407	4,355	58,330
2023[1]	3,839	3,611	4,721	3,934	3,998	4,023	3,993	3,512	3,839	4,027	5,395	4,388	49,280

[1] Preliminary.   Source: National Agricultural Statistics Service, U.S. Department of Agriculture (NASS-USDA)

41

CHEESE

Cold Storage of All Varieties of Cheese in the United States, on First of Month   In Thousands of Pounds

Year	Jan.	Feb.	Mar.	Apr.	May	June	July	Aug.	Sept.	Oct.	Nov.	Dec.
2014	1,009,381	1,015,053	1,010,132	1,018,290	1,037,586	1,065,540	1,055,442	1,054,892	1,041,408	1,013,782	995,666	1,017,192
2015	1,017,936	1,048,243	1,067,060	1,068,645	1,085,909	1,111,854	1,142,241	1,161,796	1,167,393	1,152,446	1,146,191	1,148,060
2016	1,146,086	1,178,194	1,182,308	1,191,394	1,209,222	1,249,382	1,250,328	1,275,546	1,241,119	1,235,452	1,222,315	1,182,646
2017	1,198,334	1,192,166	1,226,457	1,262,244	1,303,328	1,308,929	1,316,698	1,369,506	1,333,551	1,308,072	1,267,950	1,258,630
2018	1,280,484	1,278,637	1,317,731	1,324,728	1,345,280	1,384,940	1,388,638	1,412,980	1,360,489	1,379,703	1,375,149	1,352,739
2019	1,344,794	1,369,236	1,366,937	1,384,366	1,397,974	1,385,616	1,380,784	1,360,510	1,364,830	1,373,856	1,341,695	1,322,482
2020	1,322,014	1,353,618	1,362,091	1,374,507	1,478,640	1,454,505	1,415,905	1,391,664	1,377,907	1,355,799	1,341,428	1,348,101
2021	1,396,311	1,408,243	1,436,246	1,468,976	1,448,762	1,458,368	1,435,146	1,449,523	1,432,852	1,457,850	1,448,595	1,422,271
2022	1,441,631	1,445,090	1,466,985	1,465,825	1,480,872	1,512,915	1,506,266	1,521,797	1,481,468	1,469,792	1,448,071	1,430,970
2023[1]	1,445,133	1,446,501	1,437,447	1,460,381	1,468,499	1,497,820	1,510,341	1,492,832	1,495,372	1,483,634	1,458,691	1,436,634

Quantities are given in "net weight."   [1] Preliminary.   *Source: National Agricultural Statistics Service, U.S. Department of Agriculture (NASS-USDA)*

Cold Storage of Natural American Cheese in the United States, on First of Month   In Thousands of Pounds

Year	Jan.	Feb.	Mar.	Apr.	May	June	July	Aug.	Sept.	Oct.	Nov.	Dec.
2014	618,265	630,820	628,679	639,067	648,900	656,446	655,239	660,438	648,784	631,279	623,336	635,776
2015	627,769	636,019	645,670	634,270	644,113	669,464	685,745	698,029	709,029	698,875	696,781	699,794
2016	701,073	716,370	716,357	725,837	734,121	757,530	756,950	769,705	742,497	742,804	736,017	713,231
2017	726,403	722,449	744,640	772,702	804,645	816,266	810,234	831,538	800,994	780,466	740,404	733,378
2018	746,846	741,772	762,770	766,628	780,256	804,075	800,379	823,342	787,435	803,750	811,593	798,970
2019	800,336	803,578	783,210	784,761	782,769	786,579	784,362	773,183	767,366	774,761	743,621	740,367
2020	749,886	779,672	778,265	776,360	834,295	820,018	793,026	785,521	789,594	772,362	756,168	762,041
2021	801,720	809,110	817,169	834,403	826,740	827,995	809,825	817,589	827,067	844,115	843,347	834,775
2022	842,869	837,609	831,198	828,448	835,747	857,892	846,750	859,995	841,513	843,112	831,191	816,077
2023[1]	825,285	823,405	809,238	826,768	841,910	857,083	853,497	841,822	852,876	851,186	833,923	828,377

Quantities are given in "net weight."   [1] Preliminary.   *Source: National Agricultural Statistics Service, U.S. Department of Agriculture (NASS-USDA)*

Cold Storage of Swiss Cheese in the United States, on First of Month   In Thousands of Pounds

Year	Jan.	Feb.	Mar.	Apr.	May	June	July	Aug.	Sept.	Oct.	Nov.	Dec.
2014	24,688	25,421	26,942	27,425	28,316	30,538	27,972	24,593	27,085	25,684	25,600	24,419
2015	21,282	22,411	23,587	24,573	23,986	21,424	20,841	21,591	22,203	22,037	21,404	22,665
2016	24,587	24,100	24,703	24,629	24,592	24,967	24,492	25,702	26,019	26,055	24,428	24,749
2017	24,200	23,930	26,999	26,053	26,962	26,242	25,495	27,009	26,831	25,408	24,277	24,933
2018	26,367	28,733	27,884	29,080	29,193	31,424	31,312	32,189	31,211	30,848	30,775	29,866
2019	29,775	29,353	31,047	31,487	28,176	24,685	27,417	27,179	27,340	26,392	26,144	24,540
2020	24,178	22,902	24,089	23,272	25,694	24,548	24,005	20,537	20,602	20,762	20,149	20,063
2021	19,851	21,344	21,692	22,661	21,160	21,877	22,623	22,768	22,475	21,879	21,363	20,669
2022	21,928	23,530	25,206	23,199	23,975	25,840	24,570	22,506	21,140	23,115	21,947	22,397
2023[1]	24,218	23,334	23,929	21,605	21,584	24,329	22,643	22,771	22,594	21,828	20,826	20,936

Quantities are given in "net weight."   [1] Preliminary.   *Source: National Agricultural Statistics Service, U.S. Department of Agriculture (NASS-USDA)*

Cold Storage of Other Natural American Cheese in the United States, on First of Month   In Thousands of Lbs.

Year	Jan.	Feb.	Mar.	Apr.	May	June	July	Aug.	Sept.	Oct.	Nov.	Dec.
2014	366,428	358,812	354,511	351,798	360,370	378,556	372,231	369,861	365,539	356,819	346,730	356,997
2015	368,885	389,813	397,035	409,802	417,810	420,966	435,655	442,176	436,161	431,534	428,006	425,601
2016	420,426	437,724	441,248	440,928	450,509	466,885	468,886	480,139	472,603	466,593	461,870	444,666
2017	447,731	445,787	454,818	463,489	471,721	466,421	480,969	510,959	505,726	502,198	503,269	500,319
2018	507,271	508,132	527,077	529,020	535,831	549,441	556,947	557,449	541,843	545,105	532,781	523,903
2019	514,683	536,305	552,680	568,118	587,029	574,352	569,005	560,148	570,124	572,703	571,930	557,575
2020	547,950	551,044	559,737	574,875	618,651	609,939	598,874	585,606	567,711	562,675	565,111	565,997
2021	574,740	577,789	597,385	611,912	600,862	608,496	602,698	609,166	583,310	591,859	583,885	566,827
2022	576,834	583,951	610,581	614,178	621,150	629,183	634,946	639,296	618,815	603,565	594,933	592,496
2023[1]	595,630	599,762	604,280	612,008	605,005	616,408	634,201	628,239	619,902	610,620	603,942	587,321

Quantities are given in "net weight."   [1] Preliminary.   *Source: National Agricultural Statistics Service, U.S. Department of Agriculture (NASS-USDA)*

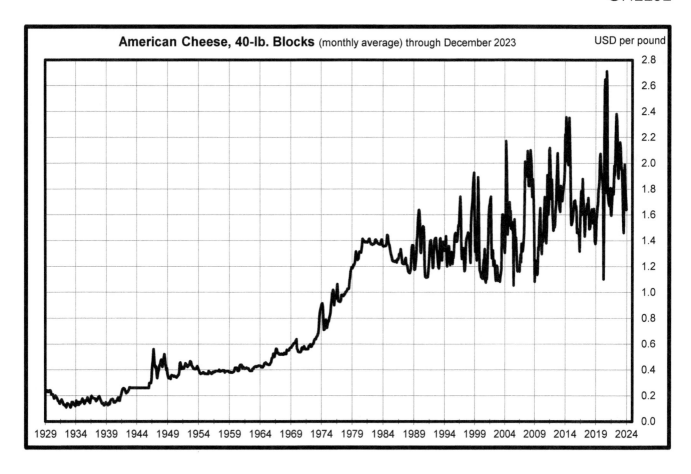

American Cheese, 40-lb. Blocks (monthly average) through December 2023 — USD per pound

Average Price of Cheese, 40-lb. Blocks, Chicago Mercantile Exchange   In U.S. Dollars Per Pound

Year	Jan.	Feb.	Mar.	Apr.	May	June	July	Aug.	Sept.	Oct.	Nov.	Dec.	Average
2014	2.2227	2.1945	2.3554	2.2439	2.0155	2.0237	1.9870	2.1820	2.3499	2.1932	1.9513	1.5938	2.1094
2015	1.5218	1.5382	1.5549	1.5890	1.6308	1.7052	1.6659	1.7111	1.6605	1.6674	1.6176	1.4616	1.6103
2016	1.4757	1.4744	1.4877	1.4194	1.3174	1.5005	1.6613	1.7826	1.6224	1.6035	1.8775	1.7335	1.5797
2017	1.6866	1.6199	1.4342	1.4976	1.6264	1.6022	1.6586	1.6852	1.6370	1.7305	1.6590	1.4900	1.6106
2018	1.4938	1.5157	1.5614	1.6062	1.6397	1.5617	1.5364	1.6341	1.6438	1.5874	1.3951	1.3764	1.5460
2019	1.4087	1.5589	1.5908	1.6619	1.6799	1.7906	1.8180	1.8791	2.0395	2.0703	1.9664	1.8764	1.7784
2020	1.9142	1.8343	1.7550	1.1019	1.6704	2.5620	2.6466	1.7730	2.3277	2.7103	2.5808	1.7708	2.0539
2021	1.7171	1.6870	1.6695	1.7918	1.8072	1.6058	1.5948	1.6902	1.7761	1.8070	1.7605	1.8633	1.7309
2022	1.9787	1.9091	2.0748	2.2759	2.3798	2.3214	2.1622	1.9484	1.8835	2.0453	2.0748	2.1594	2.1011
2023[1]	2.1147	1.9874	1.9503	1.9406	1.7277	1.5568	1.4614	1.8625	1.9895	1.8044	1.7511	1.6385	1.8154

[1] Preliminary.   *Source: Economic Research Service, U.S. Department of Agriculture (ERS-USDA)*

Average Price of American Cheese, Barrels, Chicago Mercantile Exchange   In U.S. Dollars Per Pound

Year	Jan.	Feb.	Mar.	Apr.	May	June	July	Aug.	Sept.	Oct.	Nov.	Dec.	Average
2014	2.1727	2.1757	2.2790	2.1842	1.9985	1.9856	1.9970	2.1961	2.3663	2.0782	1.9326	1.5305	2.0747
2015	1.4995	1.4849	1.5290	1.6135	1.6250	1.6690	1.6313	1.6689	1.5840	1.6072	1.5305	1.4638	1.5756
2016	1.4842	1.4573	1.4530	1.4231	1.3529	1.5301	1.7363	1.8110	1.5415	1.5295	1.7424	1.6132	1.5562
2017	1.5573	1.6230	1.4072	1.4307	1.4806	1.3972	1.4396	1.5993	1.5691	1.6970	1.6656	1.5426	1.5341
2018	1.3345	1.4096	1.5071	1.4721	1.5870	1.4145	1.3707	1.5835	1.4503	1.3152	1.3100	1.2829	1.4198
2019	1.2379	1.3867	1.4910	1.5925	1.6278	1.6258	1.7343	1.7081	1.7463	2.0224	2.2554	1.8410	1.6891
2020	1.5721	1.5470	1.4399	1.0690	1.5980	2.3376	2.4080	1.4937	1.6401	2.2213	2.2929	1.4944	1.7595
2021	1.5601	1.4841	1.5023	1.6011	1.8035	1.6506	1.5663	1.4371	1.4873	1.7011	1.7272	1.6263	1.5956
2022	1.7951	1.8746	2.0066	2.2759	2.4187	2.3472	2.2054	1.9698	1.9830	2.2210	2.0744	1.9293	2.0918
2023[1]	1.8226	1.6602	1.7188	1.7942	1.5715	1.5561	1.4789	1.7764	1.8616	1.6502	1.7034	1.5813	1.6813

[1] Preliminary.   *Source: Economic Research Service, U.S. Department of Agriculture (ERS-USDA)*

Chromium

Chromium (atomic symbol Cr) is a steel-gray, hard, and brittle, metallic element that can take on a high polish. Chromium and its compounds are toxic. Discovered in 1797 by Louis Vauquelin, chromium is named after the Greek word for color, *khroma*. Vauquelin also discovered that an emerald's green color is due to the presence of chromium. Many precious stones owe their color to the presence of chromium compounds.

Chromium is primarily found in chromite ore. The primary use of chromium is to form alloys with iron, nickel, or cobalt. Chromium improves hardness and resistance to corrosion and oxidation in iron, steel, and nonferrous alloys. It is a critical alloying ingredient in the production of stainless steel, making up 10% or more of the final composition. More than half of the chromium consumed is used in metallic products, and about one-third is used in refractories. Chromium is also used as a lustrous decorative plating agent, in pigments, leather processing, plating of metals, and catalysts.

Supply – World mine production of chromium in 2023 fell by -2.1% yr/yr to 41.000 million metric tons. The world's largest producers of chromium in 2023 were South Africa with 43.9% of world production, and both Türkiye and Kazakhstan with 14.6%. South Africa's production in 2023 fell by -5.8% yr/yr to 18.000 million metric tons, below the record high of 19.084 million metric tons in 2019.

Trade – The US relied on imports for 74% of its chromium consumption in 2023, well below the record high of 91% posted back in the 1970s. US chromium imports in 2021 rose by +21.8% yr/yr to 367,170 metric tons. US exports of chromium in 2021 rose by +36.7% yr/yr to 3,765 metric tons.

World Mine Production of Chromium   In Thousands of Metric Tons (Gross Weight)

Year	Albania	Brazil	Cuba	Finland	India	Iran	Kazakh-stan	Mada-gascar	Philip-pines	South Africa	Türkiye	Zim-babwe	World Total
2016	727	426	----	2,105	3,329	420	5,543	108	26	14,708	6,066	736	35,500
2017	808	450	----	1,954	3,478	292	6,313	208	21	18,680	7,850	1,674	43,000
2018	1,143	450	----	2,211	4,076	119	6,689	109	45	18,983	10,757	1,756	48,200
2019	1,288	199	----	2,415	4,139	122	7,019	76	32	19,084	8,666	1,550	46,400
2020	627	227	----	2,293	2,500	135	7,000	60	35	13,243	8,000	1,197	37,000
2021	650	200	----	2,274	4,250		6,500			18,600	6,960		42,200
2022[1]			----	2,000	4,000		6,000			19,100	5,410		41,900
2023[2]			----	2,000	4,200		6,000			18,000	6,000		41,000

[1] Preliminary.   [2] Estimate.   *Source: U.S. Geological Survey (USGS)*

World Production of Ferrochromium   In Thousands of Metric Tons (Gross Weight)

Year	Albania	Brazil	China	Finland	Germany	India	Kazakh-stan	Russia	South Africa	Sweden	Türkiye	Zim-babwe	World Total
2014	35	285	4,120	441	18	944	1,352	440	3,719	67	86	235	11,800
2015	44	173	3,940	457	17	944	1,414	363	3,685	90	83	116	11,400
2016	45	150	4,230	469	17	944	1,525	268	3,596	82	75	78	11,600
2017	51	172	4,940	416	29	944	1,640	436	3,485	92	84	143	12,600
2018	93	175	5,280	493	31	944	1,740	332	3,516	101	92	365	13,500
2019	66	137	6,030	505	26	930	1,858	384	3,248	118	82	312	14,000
2020[1]	54	254	5,700	498	11	826	1,841	343	2,404	87	94	134	12,500
2021[2]	110	214	5,900	515	12	1,090	1,705	350	3,700	115	101	307	14,500

[1] Preliminary.   [2] Estimate.   *Source: U.S. Geological Survey (USGS)*

Salient Statistics of Chromite in the United States   In Thousands of Metric Tons (Gross Weight)

Year	Net Import Reliance as a % of Appearent Consumpn	Production of Ferro-chromium	Exports	Imports for Con-sumption	Reexports	Consumption by -- Primary Consumer Group -- Total	Metal-lurgical & Chemical	Refractory	Government[5] Stocks, Dec. 31 Metal-lurgical & Chemical	Refractory	Total Stocks	South Africa[3]	Turkish[4]
2016	66	W	3	348	----	----	----	----	----	----	----	----	----
2017	71	W	7	399	----	----	----	----	----	----	----	----	----
2018	76	W	5	432	----	----	----	----	----	----	----	----	----
2019	74	W	3	365	----	----	----	----	----	----	----	----	----
2020	73	W	3	301	----	----	----	----	----	----	----	----	----
2021	80	W	4	367	----	----	----	----	----	----	----	----	----
2022[1]	84	W			----	----	----	----	----	----	----	----	----
2023[2]	74	W			----	----	----	----	----	----	----	----	----

[1] Preliminary.   [2] Estimate.   [3] Cr_2O_3 44% (Transvaal).   [4] 48% Cr_2O_3.   [5] Data through 1999 are for Consumer.   W = Withheld.
Source: U.S. Geological Survey (USGS)

Coal

Coal is a sedimentary rock composed primarily of carbon, hydrogen, and oxygen. Coal is a fossil fuel formed from ancient plants buried deep in the Earth's crust over 300 million years ago. Historians believe coal was first used commercially in China for smelting copper and for casting coins around 1,000 BC. Almost 92% of all coal consumed in the U.S. is burned by electric power plants, and coal accounts for about 55% of total electricity output. Coal is also used in the manufacture of steel. The steel industry first converts coal into coke, then combines the coke with iron ore and limestone, and finally heats the mixture to produce iron. Other industries use coal to make fertilizers, solvents, medicine, pesticides, and synthetic fuels.

There are four types of mined coal: anthracite (used in high-grade steel production), bituminous (used for electricity generation and for making coke), sub-bituminous, and lignite (both used primarily for electricity generation).

Futures and options on coal trade at the ICE Futures Europe, New York Mercantile Exchange, and Singapore Exchange. Futures are traded on CME Group, Dalian Commodity Exchange, and Zhengzhou Commodity Exchange. The CME's contract trades in units of 1,550 tons and is priced in terms of dollars and cents per ton.

Prices – In 2022, the average mine price rose by +49.4% to $54.46 per short ton.

Supply – US production of bituminous coal in 2023 fell by -2.1% yr/yr to 581.613 million tons.

Demand – US consumption of coal in 2022 fell by -5.5% to 515.533 million tons.

Trade – US exports of coal in 2023 rose by +16.1% yr/yr to 99.791 million tons. The major exporting destinations for the US are Europe and Asia. US imports in 2023 fell by -36.5% yr/yr to 4.010 million tons.

World Production of Primary Coal   In Thousands of Short Tons

Year	Australia	China	Colom-bia	Germany	India	Indonesia	Kazakh-stan	Poland	Russia	South Africa	Türkiye	United States	World Total
2013	516,068	4,380,935	94,247	210,493	621,072	522,904	131,808	156,875	385,818	282,162	72,877	984,842	9,002,208
2014	548,559	4,270,260	97,640	205,597	659,542	504,965	125,647	150,374	393,765	287,196	71,911	1,000,049	8,915,862
2015	574,181	4,129,849	94,300	203,612	696,349	508,789	118,299	149,147	409,701	282,334	64,390	896,941	8,706,618
2016	560,423	3,759,538	99,772	193,593	720,040	502,871	113,620	143,996	423,095	281,986	80,473	728,364	8,178,071
2017	557,423	3,884,055	99,813	193,039	739,669	508,438	111,782	139,597	449,579	283,431	81,679	774,609	8,416,439
2018	541,744	4,076,056	92,907	186,311	788,582	614,839	118,660	134,432	476,919	281,553	92,524	756,167	8,747,686
2019	564,027	4,239,848	92,972	144,749	805,053	679,199	115,216	123,406	481,701	284,234	95,999	706,307	8,901,840
2020	550,889	4,300,747	54,378	118,363	793,418	621,403	113,920	110,638	442,475	272,392	82,356	535,434	8,486,367
2021[1]	514,937	4,548,131	61,948	139,174	839,963	676,808	98,214	118,346	479,800	259,844	94,394	577,361	8,899,735
2022[2]	510,991	4,766,784	59,884	144,183	1,040,500	726,817	127,438	119,269	508,541	269,292	92,546	593,608	9,435,569

[1] Preliminary.   [2] Estimate.   NA = Not available.   *Source: United Nations*

World Imports of Primary Coal   In Thousands of Short Tons

Year	China	Germany	India	Italy	Japan	Korea, South	Nether-lands	Russia	Taiwan	Türkiye	United Kingdom	United States	World Total
2013	321,195	56,415	200,091	22,435	211,162	139,452	53,386	28,318	74,146	29,358	55,789	8,906	1,491,489
2014	267,667	63,239	247,369	21,570	207,700	144,440	59,917	27,693	73,959	32,868	46,545	11,350	1,509,819
2015	224,937	62,077	243,544	21,578	210,160	148,907	62,097	26,914	72,731	37,461	26,674	11,318	1,454,416
2016	281,695	60,802	217,086	19,041	209,162	148,170	57,458	24,433	72,343	40,050	9,363	9,846	1,464,977
2017	298,649	53,720	219,434	17,767	212,532	162,239	51,703	27,454	74,506	43,129	9,367	7,803	1,541,238
2018	310,120	49,852	247,125	16,324	208,700	163,935	48,835	27,801	73,318	42,295	11,116	5,954	1,598,989
2019	330,527	45,577	266,445	11,933	205,233	155,862	41,514	26,742	74,221	41,615	6,866	6,697	1,609,864
2020	335,177	33,000	238,732	8,608	191,439	136,127	23,469	26,399	69,735	44,364	4,995	5,137	1,488,000
2021[1]	356,794	42,753	210,811	8,714	201,137	138,468	33,896	27,246	74,297	40,253	5,079	5,389	1,533,775
2022[2]	345,489	46,778	234,147	13,536	209,407	133,348	27,371	25,423	70,157	40,600	7,008	6,313	1,528,234

[1] Preliminary.   [2] Estimate.   *Source: Energy Information Administration, U.S. Department of Energy (EIA-DOE)*

World Exports of Primary Coal   In Thousands of Short Tons

Year	Australia	Canada	China	Colombia	Indonesia	Kazakh-stan	Mongolia	Poland	Russia	South Africa	United States	Vietnam	World Total
2013	391,684	43,099	8,278	82,408	420,201	36,691	20,255	12,219	156,087	83,515	117,659	17,368	1,492,632
2014	426,338	37,821	6,327	96,035	421,052	31,400	21,262	10,241	167,419	83,555	97,257	10,262	1,509,257
2015	432,489	33,760	5,886	80,242	403,140	30,496	15,945	10,398	174,262	83,114	73,958	1,904	1,439,134
2016	429,130	33,602	9,689	91,881	406,630	27,733	29,097	10,340	187,614	83,935	60,271	1,252	1,470,586
2017	418,028	34,284	8,918	92,886	429,383	29,147	37,600	8,160	223,176	92,349	96,945	2,101	1,550,837
2018	421,021	35,647	5,445	92,366	449,757	28,356	39,950	5,781	233,963	88,521	116,244	1,922	1,590,590
2019	433,135	39,324	6,604	78,869	488,219	28,285	39,912	5,061	246,269	86,717	93,765	1,260	1,621,285
2020	409,335	34,875	3,487	74,775	451,520	27,260	31,611	5,193	244,312	82,573	69,067	982	1,486,412
2021[1]	403,224	34,910	3,540	61,289	478,029	26,280	24,977	7,177	260,738	71,755	85,115	1,070	1,523,096
2022[2]	401,299	31,826	4,381	62,335	516,741	41,107	21,460	6,072	242,608	83,103	85,956	1,124	1,561,117

[1] Preliminary.   [2] Estimate.   *Source: Energy Information Administration, U.S. Department of Energy (EIA-DOE)*

COAL

World Consumption of Primary Coal   In Thousands of Short Tons

Year	Australia	China	Germany	India	Japan	Kazakh-stan	Korea, South	Poland	Russia	South Africa	Türkiye	United States	World Total
2013	124,974	4,733,478	272,161	807,223	219,371	98,451	158,229	218,386	202,731	139,556	92,719	924,442	9,020,925
2014	119,086	4,585,493	264,633	895,227	215,079	91,383	151,044	210,323	201,737	144,083	106,463	917,731	8,910,462
2015	124,698	4,407,410	264,188	938,601	212,558	84,313	149,679	234,110	197,530	148,403	101,722	798,115	8,682,651
2016	126,265	4,286,002	255,911	936,107	212,493	82,075	148,848	227,095	199,817	148,576	116,878	731,071	8,455,765
2017	121,663	4,314,474	245,811	957,950	214,393	79,863	150,121	229,361	199,901	152,392	122,959	716,856	8,536,426
2018	116,348	4,381,153	238,344	1,034,586	208,504	83,703	146,983	243,703	189,076	153,102	134,169	688,105	8,668,311
2019	112,009	4,430,349	188,825	1,070,521	206,517	83,259	131,484	247,454	208,987	146,355	137,176	586,543	8,593,126
2020	106,909	4,456,931	152,854	1,031,109	203,062	82,186	120,794	231,471	207,376	138,065	113,735	476,693	8,271,548
2021[1]	109,921	4,675,321	181,467	1,049,853	201,875	83,303	128,278	273,031	189,300	139,458	120,818	548,847	8,698,185
2022[2]	116,523	5,311,746	195,816	1,273,287	206,881	90,674	134,175	291,357	192,244	133,767	130,490	515,555	9,632,382

[1] Preliminary.   [2] Estimate.   *Source: Energy Information Administration, U.S. Department of Energy (EIA-DOE)*

Production of Bituminous & Lignite Coal in the United States   In Thousands of Short Tons

Year	Alabama	Colorado	Illinois	Indiana	Kentucky	Montana	Ohio	Pennsyl-vania	Texas	West Virginia	Virginia	Wyoming	Total
2013	18,620	24,236	52,147	39,102	80,380	42,231	25,113	54,009	42,851	16,619	112,786	387,924	984,842
2014	16,363	24,007	57,969	39,267	77,335	44,562	22,252	60,910	43,654	15,059	112,187	395,665	1,000,049
2015	13,191	18,879	56,101	34,295	61,425	41,864	17,041	50,031	35,918	13,914	95,633	375,773	896,941
2016	9,643	12,634	43,422	28,767	42,868	32,336	12,564	45,720	39,001	12,910	79,757	297,218	728,364
2017	12,613	15,047	48,128	31,418	42,608	35,232	9,336	49,065	36,338	13,205	92,733	316,454	774,118
2018	14,783	14,026	49,482	34,598	39,740	38,610	8,993	49,968	24,823	13,012	95,510	304,188	756,167
2019	14,124	12,868	45,853	31,559	36,006	34,468	7,779	50,053	23,307	12,297	93,279	276,912	706,309
2020	12,151	10,035	31,578	19,942	24,217	26,422	3,587	36,305	19,682	9,685	67,278	218,556	535,434
2021[1]	9,444	11,875	36,848	19,470	26,426	28,580	2,759	42,422	17,250	10,902	78,620	238,773	575,320
2022[2]	10,408	12,782	38,346	23,512	28,457	28,233	2,492	39,807	17,084	10,995	83,487	244,860	592,067

[1] Preliminary.   [2] Estimate.   *Source: Energy Information Administration, U.S. Department of Energy (EIA-DOE)*

Production[2] of Bituminous Coal in the United States   In Thousands of Short Tons

Year	Jan.	Feb.	Mar.	Apr.	May	June	July	Aug.	Sept.	Oct.	Nov.	Dec.	Total
2014	82,835	75,177	86,794	82,835	83,645	78,929	84,275	87,167	83,410	85,286	81,587	86,163	998,102
2015	86,548	72,210	81,430	74,704	69,942	66,484	76,618	82,777	77,868	75,705	68,613	63,036	895,936
2016	60,413	57,181	55,186	48,089	52,983	59,356	61,667	68,118	64,947	68,578	67,006	63,176	726,700
2017	68,236	64,221	64,167	58,598	61,950	66,053	62,834	70,434	62,759	66,201	64,184	63,061	772,697
2018	61,827	60,129	65,351	57,892	61,048	61,408	62,817	69,160	62,289	66,355	62,690	63,305	754,271
2019	65,644	58,145	55,505	60,981	61,627	56,491	58,862	63,571	58,392	57,405	54,139	52,936	703,698
2020	55,667	47,425	46,106	39,347	37,263	39,608	43,217	47,523	45,141	44,988	44,345	44,804	535,434
2021	48,496	40,817	50,818	45,295	48,607	48,773	48,473	50,039	49,760	48,954	48,825	48,576	577,431
2022	49,887	47,875	51,548	46,387	49,553	48,670	49,301	53,601	51,574	51,332	48,754	45,673	594,155
2023[1]	51,010	45,713	51,984	46,969	48,223	47,146	46,520	50,543	48,542	49,074	48,951	46,940	581,614

[1] Preliminary.   [2] Includes small amount of lignite.   *Source: Energy Information Administration, U.S. Department of Energy (EIA-DOE)*

Production[2] of Pennsylvania Anthracite Coal   In Thousands of Short Tons

Year	Jan.	Feb.	Mar.	Apr.	May	June	July	Aug.	Sept.	Oct.	Nov.	Dec.	Total
2014	157	143	165	147	148	140	174	180	172	176	168	177	1,947
2015	170	142	160	182	171	162	204	220	207	192	174	160	2,145
2016	156	147	142	128	141	157	117	129	123	147	144	135	1,665
2017	178	168	168	156	165	176	133	149	133	167	162	159	1,912
2018	144	140	152	155	163	164	151	166	149	177	167	169	1,896
2019	192	170	162	232	235	215	207	224	205	269	253	248	2,611
2020	247	210	205	185	175	186	194	213	202	186	184	186	2,372
2021	177	149	186	150	161	162	166	171	170	207	206	205	2,111
2022	211	203	218	193	206	203	198	216	207	233	222	208	2,519
2023[1]	250	224	255	200	205	200	273	297	285				2,921

[1] Preliminary.   [2] Represents production in Pennsylvania only.   *Source: Energy Information Administration, U.S. Department of Energy (EIA-DOE)*

Salient Statistics of Coal in the United States   In Thousands of Short Tons

| | | | | Exports | | | | | Total Ending Stocks[2] | Losses & Unaccounted For[3] |
Year	Production	Imports	Consumption	Brazil	Canada	Europe	Asia	Total		
2013	984,842	8,906	924,442	8,610	7,110	60,755	27,245	117,659	200,335	1,451
2014	1,000,049	11,350	917,731	8,032	6,724	52,469	19,450	97,257	197,727	10,858
2015	896,941	11,318	798,115	6,339	5,958	37,894	17,544	73,958	238,431	5,331
2016	728,364	9,846	731,071	6,939	5,011	27,381	15,714	60,271	192,990	2,346
2017	774,609	7,803	716,856	7,563	5,286	39,561	32,841	96,945	166,956	5,029
2018	756,167	5,954	688,105	8,595	5,726	43,808	40,281	116,244	129,796	5,397
2019	706,309	6,697	586,543	7,591	5,118	33,370	33,148	93,765	165,260	5,238
2020	535,434	5,137	476,693	7,889	4,587	22,154	27,680	69,067	159,822	7,129
2021	577,431	5,388	545,679	6,252	4,587	22,341	42,175	85,115	115,356	4,154
2022[1]	594,155	6,313	515,534	6,503	4,257	33,049	32,255	85,956	112,025	9,296

[1] Preliminary.   [2] Producer & distributor and consumer stocks, excludes stocks held by retail dealers for consumption by the residential and commercial sector.   [3] Equals production plus imports minus the change in producer & distributor and consumer stocks minus consumption minus exports.
Source: Energy Information Administraion, U.S. Department of Energy (EIA-DOE)

Consumption and Stocks of Coal in the United States   In Thousands of Short Tons

| | Consumption | | | | | | | | Stocks, Dec. 31 | | | |
| | Electric Utilities | | | | Industrial | | Residential and | | Consumer | | | Producers and |
Year	Anthracite	Bituminous	Lignite	Total	Coke Plants	Other Industrial[2]	Commercial	Total	Electric Utilities	Coke Plants	Other Industrials	Distributors
2013	----	----	----	857,962	21,474	43,055	1,951	924,442	147,884	2,200	4,097	45,652
2014	----	----	----	851,602	21,297	42,946	1,887	917,731	151,792	2,640	4,196	38,894
2015	----	----	----	738,444	19,708	38,459	1,503	798,115	195,912	2,236	4,382	35,871
2016	----	----	----	678,554	16,485	34,849	1,183	731,071	162,476	1,675	3,637	25,309
2017	----	----	----	664,993	17,538	33,264	1,061	716,856	137,721	1,718	3,242	23,999
2018	----	----	----	637,217	18,337	31,580	972	688,105	102,793	1,807	3,258	21,692
2019	----	----	----	538,606	17,967	29,095	876	586,543	128,102	2,333	3,258	31,320
2020	----	----	----	435,827	14,414	25,660	793	476,693	131,431	1,654	2,848	23,640
2021	----	----	----	501,435	17,589	25,845	811	545,679	91,884	1,658	2,624	19,013
2022[1]	----	----	----	472,834	16,009	25,891	800	515,534	88,861	1,627	2,499	20,820

[1] Preliminary.   [2] Including transportation.   [3] Excludes stocks held at retail dealers for consumption by the residential and commercial sector.
Source: Energy Information Administration, U.S. Department of Energy (EIA-DOE)

Trends in Bituminous Coal, Lignite and Pennsylvania Anthracite in the United States   In Thousands of Short Tons

	Bituminous Coal and Lignite							Pennsylvania Anthracite					All Mines
	Production				Labor Productivity							Labor Productivity	Labor Productivity
	Under-			Miners[1]	Under-Ground	Surface	Average	Under-			Miners[1]	Short Tons	Short Tons
Year	Ground	Surface	Total	Employd	Short Tons Per Miner Per Hour			Ground	Surface	Total	Employed	Miner/Hr.	Miner/Hr.
2013	341,685	643,157	984,842	80,396	3.07	9.69	5.53	95	1,965	2,060	1,095	1.01	5.53
2014	354,704	645,345	1,000,049	74,931	3.35	10.42	5.95	93	1,740	1,833	956	.98	5.96
2015	306,821	590,119	896,941	65,971	3.45	10.95	6.28	86	1,867	1,953	1,005	.94	6.28
2016	252,106	476,258	728,364	51,795	3.83	10.73	6.61	91	1,409	1,500	952	.83	6.61
2017	273,129	501,480	774,609	53,051	3.77	10.92	6.55	79	1,788	1,867	914	1.07	6.55
2018	275,361	480,806	756,167	53,583	3.68	10.36	6.24	72	1,739	1,811	900	1.03	6.23
2019	267,373	438,936	706,309	52,804	3.60	9.88	5.95	63	2,522	2,585	916	1.43	5.94
2020	195,530	339,905	535,434	42,159	3.60	10.24	6.12	63	2,352	2,415	902	1.44	6.12
2021	220,597	356,834	577,431	39,518	4.03	11.38	6.71	54	2,043	2,097	810	1.29	6.71
2022	222,143	372,012	594,155	43,582	3.62	10.39	6.11	52	2,357	2,409	851	1.41	6.11

[1] Excludes miners employed at mines producing less than 10,000 tons.
Source: Energy Information Administration, U.S. Department of Energy (EIA-DOE)

Average Prices of Coal in the United States   In Dollars Per Short Ton

| | End-Use Sector | | | Exports | | | | End-Use Sector | | | Exports | | |
Year	Electric Utilities	Coke Plants	Other Industrial[2]	Imports[3]	Steam	Metal-lurgical	Total Average[3]	Year	Electric Utilities	Coke Plants	Other Industrial[2]	Imports[3]	Steam	Metal-lurgical	Total Average[3]
2013	----	156.99	69.32	83.35	69.23	115.50	95.06	2018	----	----	----	82.39	64.60	138.98	104.63
2014	----	----	----	80.96	67.05	99.49	87.08	2019	----	----	----	80.04	63.76	137.44	105.34
2015	----	----	----	71.61	56.44	89.31	76.89	2020	----	----	----	71.79	62.51	104.55	88.08
2016	----	----	----	65.75	48.58	71.13	73.66	2021	----	----	----	91.49	64.73	159.28	114.69
2017	----	----	----	79.53	58.29	134.55	102.09	2022[1]	----	----	----	118.04	110.97	280.47	203.77

[1] Preliminary.   [2] Manufacturing plants only.   [3] Based on the free alongside ship (F.A.S.) value.
Source: Energy Information Administration, U.S. Department of Energy (EIA-DOE)

COAL

Exports of Coal in the United States   In Thousands of Short Tons

Year	Jan.	Feb.	Mar.	Apr.	May	June	July	Aug.	Sept.	Oct.	Nov.	Dec.	Total
2014	8,152	8,972	10,460	7,952	8,182	8,540	7,119	7,637	7,966	7,738	7,557	6,981	97,257
2015	7,871	6,496	7,612	7,216	6,761	5,789	5,117	6,409	5,388	5,744	4,709	4,846	73,958
2016	4,433	4,511	5,208	4,583	4,209	5,432	3,276	5,003	4,273	4,863	6,554	7,926	60,271
2017	7,403	7,062	8,075	7,132	7,200	7,504	7,154	8,592	8,825	9,130	9,049	9,818	96,945
2018	8,659	8,983	9,886	11,032	9,400	10,107	9,924	9,995	9,683	10,768	8,920	8,888	116,244
2019	9,329	6,752	9,132	8,642	8,979	8,308	6,469	7,749	7,742	6,590	7,582	6,491	93,765
2020	6,230	6,611	7,070	5,551	4,714	4,583	5,344	4,545	5,371	4,921	7,034	7,093	69,067
2021	6,021	6,990	7,728	6,843	7,482	7,692	6,446	7,353	6,796	7,516	6,834	7,413	85,115
2022	5,518	7,305	7,578	7,803	7,538	8,092	6,289	7,545	7,280	6,782	7,286	6,940	85,956
2023[1]	7,140	7,995	9,485	7,408	8,692	8,003	7,141	8,999	8,747	9,453	8,252		99,618

[1] Preliminary.   *Source: Energy Information Administration, U.S. Department of Energy (EIA-DOE)*

Imports of Coal in the United States   In Thousands of Short Tons

Year	Jan.	Feb.	Mar.	Apr.	May	June	July	Aug.	Sept.	Oct.	Nov.	Dec.	Total
2014	1,065	582	803	930	1,280	1,365	928	1,076	1,148	584	1,005	586	11,350
2015	1,293	866	850	879	919	842	1,091	970	904	854	882	969	11,318
2016	693	819	1,186	740	910	641	990	943	800	768	706	652	9,850
2017	743	612	560	493	1,053	651	956	839	513	582	368	408	7,777
2018	500	349	518	494	544	509	692	484	263	304	400	898	5,954
2019	625	358	706	537	408	660	511	519	651	742	466	515	6,697
2020	535	343	461	365	535	227	530	314	501	264	639	423	5,137
2021	525	309	241	509	512	509	564	368	202	526	436	689	5,388
2022	503	289	530	684	325	627	660	779	531	404	689	292	6,313
2023[1]	479	260	281	426	305	282	326	355	314	413	335		4,121

[1] Preliminary.   *Source: Energy Information Administration, U.S. Department of Energy (EIA-DOE)*

Consumption of Coal in the United States   In Thousands of Short Tons

Year	Jan.	Feb.	Mar.	Apr.	May	June	July	Aug.	Sept.	Oct.	Nov.	Dec.	Total
2014	89,063	81,581	77,685	63,210	69,185	79,487	86,802	86,357	74,294	66,494	70,155	73,419	917,731
2015	76,895	72,318	63,560	53,207	61,923	73,845	81,449	78,574	69,369	58,405	53,640	54,930	798,115
2016	66,662	55,211	44,575	43,384	49,343	67,551	78,569	78,175	66,615	58,953	52,533	69,501	731,071
2017	68,006	52,381	53,325	48,565	55,202	63,099	74,214	70,229	59,039	54,436	55,357	63,003	716,856
2018	69,254	50,025	48,870	44,793	51,574	60,240	68,083	67,976	58,159	52,811	56,170	60,149	688,105
2019	60,199	49,200	48,348	37,282	44,060	48,267	59,802	56,311	51,113	41,518	45,869	44,575	586,543
2020	40,771	36,012	32,843	26,754	29,784	39,798	52,852	53,610	41,828	37,393	37,874	47,175	476,693
2021	49,010	51,521	38,331	33,634	39,282	51,590	60,022	59,904	47,960	39,435	36,623	38,368	545,679
2022	52,533	43,694	38,219	34,554	38,843	45,340	53,059	51,963	40,842	35,109	35,987	45,392	515,534
2023[1]	39,081	30,374	32,252	26,029	28,786	36,643	47,529	47,030	37,360	33,104			429,826

[1] Preliminary.   *Source: Energy Information Administration, U.S. Department of Energy (EIA-DOE)*

Stocks of Coal in the United States   In Thousands of Short Tons

Year	Jan.	Feb.	Mar.	Apr.	May	June	July	Aug.	Sept.	Oct.	Nov.	Dec.
2014	185,093	170,792	168,718	179,555	186,696	182,153	174,083	167,818	170,214	182,218	187,891	197,727
2015	200,117	195,189	200,119	213,690	219,265	212,713	204,074	200,714	205,997	219,276	232,337	238,431
2016	229,181	228,793	232,962	234,322	232,520	220,992	205,411	193,859	189,600	193,082	201,620	192,990
2017	186,622	190,868	191,964	194,162	192,045	186,694	176,606	170,839	168,490	170,338	172,472	166,956
2018	153,075	150,337	155,418	156,693	155,559	148,806	136,250	130,535	128,015	131,900	131,733	129,796
2019	125,763	127,331	126,150	136,039	145,314	146,872	141,511	142,445	144,192	154,104	158,921	165,334
2020	171,201	176,447	181,242	188,040	190,533	184,699	170,072	160,630	158,555	162,077	163,547	159,822
2021	150,115	134,839	136,555	142,475	144,939	135,727	121,063	106,398	101,149	105,479	112,730	115,356
2022	108,011	104,648	109,968	114,699	117,044	111,618	103,834	100,178	104,162	112,527	118,548	113,973
2023[1]	118,234	126,326	135,661	144,709	153,186	154,365	146,443	141,869	139,665	146,311	154,603	

[1] Preliminary.   *Source: Energy Information Administration, U.S. Department of Energy (EIA-DOE)*

Stocks of Coal, Producers and Distributors, in the United States   In Thousands of Short Tons

Year	Jan.	Feb.	Mar.	Apr.	May	June	July	Aug.	Sept.	Oct.	Nov.	Dec.
2014	44,951	44,804	44,728	44,813	43,871	42,682	41,939	39,892	38,828	38,266	38,159	38,894
2015	38,817	39,581	39,610	40,226	39,817	39,399	38,993	37,353	36,213	36,233	36,509	35,871
2016	35,236	35,258	35,207	35,011	34,053	32,932	31,393	29,126	27,282	26,425	25,645	25,309
2017	24,974	25,170	25,190	25,169	24,350	23,430	25,465	24,226	23,430	23,459	23,705	23,999
2018	24,769	24,938	24,736	23,417	22,841	22,997	21,025	21,806	22,537	21,878	22,419	21,692
2019	21,391	23,551	24,160	22,767	24,273	24,529	25,240	26,441	27,714	29,683	30,717	31,320
2020	31,382	31,803	30,829	31,168	31,522	29,510	27,716	27,138	25,537	25,025	24,152	23,640
2021	21,805	22,682	22,629	22,532	22,444	22,361	21,420	19,986	19,042	19,026	19,022	19,013
2022	19,114	19,360	19,674	19,801	20,200	20,597	20,439	20,315	20,445	20,846	21,029	20,820
2023[1]	21,446	22,453	22,390	22,292	22,196	22,092	21,051	19,536	18,506	18,488	18,465	

[1] Preliminary.   Source: Energy Information Administration, U.S. Department of Energy (EIA-DOE)

Stocks of Coal, Residential and Commercial, in the United States   In Thousands of Short Tons

Year	Jan.	Feb.	Mar.	Apr.	May	June	July	Aug.	Sept.	Oct.	Nov.	Dec.
2014	465	435	405	413	421	429	440	451	462	458	454	449
2015	429	408	388	387	386	386	388	390	392	393	394	394
2016	373	353	332	334	336	337	348	359	370	367	364	360
2017	352	343	335	333	331	329	332	335	337	328	319	310
2018	298	287	275	268	262	256	257	259	260	256	251	247
2019	238	229	221	214	208	201	212	222	232	237	242	246
2020	235	223	212	212	212	213	220	227	234	239	245	250
2021	243	236	229	223	217	210	207	204	201	193	184	176
2022	170	163	157	158	158	158	168	177	187	180	173	167
2023[1]	165	163	162	161	161	160	163	165	168	208	207	

[1] Preliminary.   Source: Energy Information Administration, U.S. Department of Energy (EIA-DOE)

Stocks of Coal, Coke Plants, in the United States   In Thousands of Short Tons

Year	Jan.	Feb.	Mar.	Apr.	May	June	July	Aug.	Sept.	Oct.	Nov.	Dec.
2014	2,064	1,927	1,791	1,840	1,888	1,937	2,060	2,184	2,307	2,418	2,529	2,640
2015	2,471	2,303	2,135	2,299	2,463	2,627	2,756	2,884	3,013	2,754	2,495	2,236
2016	2,129	2,022	1,914	1,877	1,839	1,802	1,755	1,707	1,660	1,665	1,670	1,675
2017	1,579	1,483	1,388	1,467	1,547	1,626	1,641	1,655	1,670	1,686	1,702	1,718
2018	1,648	1,578	1,508	1,544	1,580	1,616	1,681	1,746	1,811	1,809	1,808	1,807
2019	1,873	1,939	2,005	2,102	2,199	2,296	2,352	2,407	2,463	2,420	2,376	2,333
2020	2,271	2,210	2,148	2,106	2,064	2,022	2,007	1,991	1,975	1,868	1,761	1,654
2021	1,618	1,581	1,545	1,648	1,750	1,853	1,833	1,814	1,794	1,749	1,704	1,658
2022	1,636	1,613	1,590	1,600	1,610	1,620	1,629	1,638	1,646	1,640	1,633	1,627
2023[1]	1,635	1,643	1,650	1,662	1,673	1,684	1,674	1,664	1,655	1,722	1,701	

[1] Preliminary.   Source: Energy Information Administration, U.S. Department of Energy (EIA-DOE)

Stocks of Coal, Total End-Use Sectors, in the United States   In Thousands of Short Tons

Year	Jan.	Feb.	Mar.	Apr.	May	June	July	Aug.	Sept.	Oct.	Nov.	Dec.
2014	6,438	6,083	5,729	5,817	5,904	5,992	6,274	6,557	6,840	6,988	7,136	7,285
2015	6,911	6,536	6,162	6,400	6,639	6,877	7,143	7,410	7,676	7,455	7,233	7,012
2016	6,742	6,472	6,202	6,126	6,050	5,973	5,899	5,825	5,751	5,724	5,698	5,672
2017	5,434	5,196	4,959	5,056	5,153	5,250	5,330	5,409	5,489	5,416	5,343	5,270
2018	5,072	4,873	4,674	4,705	4,736	4,768	4,876	4,985	5,094	5,166	5,239	5,312
2019	5,227	5,142	5,058	5,199	5,341	5,483	5,609	5,736	5,863	5,855	5,846	5,838
2020	5,685	5,533	5,380	5,338	5,296	5,253	5,208	5,162	5,116	4,994	4,873	4,751
2021	4,605	4,459	4,312	4,438	4,563	4,688	4,669	4,650	4,631	4,574	4,516	4,459
2022	4,356	4,254	4,151	4,152	4,152	4,153	4,223	4,293	4,363	4,339	4,316	4,293
2023[1]	4,283	4,273	4,263	4,379	4,494	4,609	4,597	4,585	4,572	4,871	4,862	

[1] Preliminary.   Source: Energy Information Administration, U.S. Department of Energy (EIA-DOE)

COAL

Stocks of Coal, Electric Power Sector[2], in the United States — In Thousands of Short Tons

Year	Jan.	Feb.	Mar.	Apr.	May	June	July	Aug.	Sept.	Oct.	Nov.	Dec.
2014	133,705	119,904	118,260	128,925	136,921	133,479	125,870	121,369	124,546	136,964	142,595	151,548
2015	154,390	149,071	154,347	167,063	172,809	166,437	157,938	155,952	162,109	175,588	188,595	195,548
2016	187,203	187,064	191,553	193,185	192,417	182,086	168,119	158,908	156,567	160,932	170,277	162,009
2017	156,214	160,502	161,815	163,937	162,542	158,014	145,811	141,204	139,571	141,463	143,424	137,687
2018	123,235	120,526	126,008	128,571	127,982	121,041	110,348	103,744	100,384	104,855	104,075	102,793
2019	99,378	98,835	97,102	108,852	115,888	117,710	110,933	110,560	110,952	119,045	123,033	128,497
2020	134,134	139,112	145,034	151,534	153,716	149,935	137,149	128,330	127,902	132,058	134,522	131,431
2021	123,705	107,698	109,614	115,505	117,932	108,678	94,974	81,762	77,476	81,880	89,192	91,884
2022	84,541	81,034	86,143	90,746	92,692	86,869	79,172	75,570	79,354	87,342	93,203	88,861
2023[1]	92,505	99,600	109,007	118,038	126,496	127,663	120,795	117,748	116,587	122,952	131,277	

[1] Preliminary. [2] The electric power sector comprises electricity-only and combined-heat-and power (CHP) plants within the NAICS 22 category whose primary business is to sell electricity, or electricity and heat, to the public. *Source: Energy Information Administration, U.S. Department of Energy (EIA-DOE)*

Average Mine Prices of Coal in the United States — In Dollars Per Short Ton

	Average Mine Prices by Method			Average Mine Prices by Rank				Bituminous & Lignite FOB Mines[2]	Anthracite FOB Mines[2]	All Coal CIF[3] Electric Utility Plants
Year	Under-ground	Surface	Total	Lignite	Sub-bituminous	Bituminous	Anthracite[1]			
2013	60.98	24.50	37.24	19.96	14.86	60.61	87.82	60.61	87.82	45.03
2014	56.97	22.83	34.83	19.44	14.72	55.99	90.98	55.99	90.98	45.66
2015	52.20	21.47	31.83	22.36	14.63	51.57	97.91	51.57	97.91	42.58
2016	49.02	20.47	30.57	19.99	14.83	48.40	97.61	48.40	97.61	40.39
2017	56.99	20.95	33.72	19.51	14.29	55.60	93.17	55.60	93.17	33.72
2018	60.38	21.90	35.99	20.21	13.64	59.43	99.97	59.43	99.97	35.99
2019	58.68	22.47	36.07	19.86	14.01	58.93	102.22	58.93	102.22	38.53
2020	49.80	20.67	31.41	22.16	14.43	50.05	90.68	50.05	90.68	36.14
2021	60.49	21.32	36.45	20.10	14.18	61.68	107.08	61.68	107.08	37.32
2022	96.47	29.20	54.46	21.79	16.55	97.96	155.03	97.96	155.03	44.51

[1] Produced in Pennsylvania.   [2] FOB = free on board.   [3] CIF = cost, insurance and freight.   W = Withheld data.
Source: Energy Information Adminstration, U.S. Department of Energy (EIA-DOE)

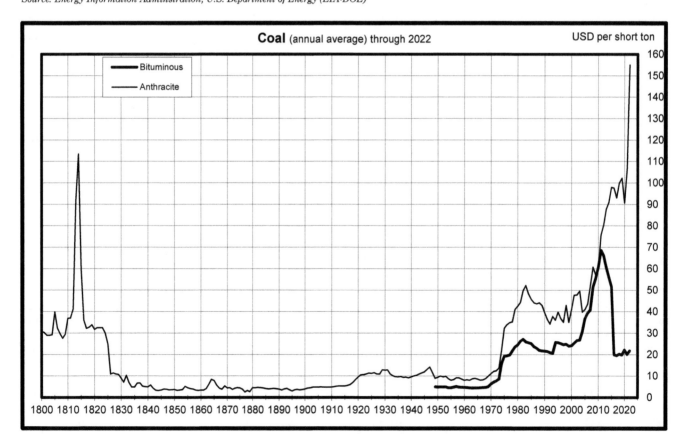

Coal (annual average) through 2022 — USD per short ton

Cobalt

Cobalt (atomic symbol Co) is a lustrous, silvery-white, magnetic, metallic element used chiefly for making alloys. Cobalt was known in ancient times and used by the Persians in 2250 BC to color glass. The name *cobalt* comes from the German word *kobalt* or *kobold*, meaning evil spirit. Miners gave cobalt its name because it was poisonous and troublesome since it polluted and degraded other mined elements, like nickel. In the 1730s, George Brandt first isolated metallic cobalt and was able to show that cobalt was the source of the blue color in glasses. In 1780, it was recognized as an element. Cobalt is generally not found in nature as a free metal and is instead found in ores. Cobalt is mainly produced as a by-product of nickel and copper mining.

Cobalt is used in a variety of applications: high-temperature steel alloys; fasteners in gas turbine engines; magnets and magnetic recording media; drying agents for paints and pigments; and steel-belted radial tires. Cobalt-60, an important radioactive tracer and cancer-treatment agent, is an artificially produced radioactive isotope of cobalt.

Prices – The price of cobalt in 2023 fell by -44.8% yr/yr to $17.00 per pound, well below the 2008 record high of $39.01 per pound.

Supply – World production of cobalt in 2023 rose by +16.8% yr/yr to 230,000 metric tons, a new record high. The world's largest cobalt mine producers in 2023 were the Congo with 73.9% of world production, Indonesia with 7.4%, and Russia with 3.8%.

The US does not target cobalt for mining or refining, although some cobalt is produced as a byproduct of other mining operations. Imports, stock releases, and secondary materials comprise the US cobalt supply. Secondary production includes extraction from superalloy scrap, cemented carbide scrap, and spent catalysts. In the US there are two domestic producers of extra-fine cobalt powder. US secondary production of cobalt in 2023 rose by +10.5% yr/yr to 2,100 metric tons.

Demand – US consumption of cobalt in 2023 fell by -9.7% yr/yr to 6,400 metric tons. In 2020, the largest use of cobalt by far was for superalloys, accounting for 35.6% of consumption. Other smaller-scaled applications for cobalt include cutting and wear-resistant materials at 7.4%.

Trade – US imports of cobalt in 2023 fell -8.6% to 9,600 metric tons, below the 2019 record high of 13,900. In 2023, the US relied on imports for 67% of its cobalt consumption, down from the 99% level seen in the early 1970s.

World Mine Production of Cobalt   In Metric Tons (Cobalt Content)

Year	Australia	Botswana	Brazil	Canada	China	Congo[3] (Kinshasa)	Cuba	Indonesia	Morocco	New Caledonia	Russia	Zambia	World Total
2014	6,201	196	3,828	3,907	2,800	65,000	3,300	1,300	1,400	4,040	6,300	2,300	115,000
2015	5,721	316	2,771	4,339	2,600	72,000	4,000	1,300	1,500	3,640	6,200	1,700	122,000
2016	5,140	248	852	4,126	2,300	68,000	3,900	1,200	1,600	3,390	8,600	600	115,000
2017	5,034	----	185	3,704	2,500	80,000	3,900	1,200	2,300	2,780	8,900	990	128,000
2018	4,878	----	----	3,279	2,000	104,000	3,500	1,200	2,300	2,100	8,700	835	149,000
2019	5,746	----	30	3,956	2,241	107,000	3,800	1,100	2,300	1,700	8,700	379	153,000
2020	5,632	----	160	3,693	2,200	98,000	3,800	1,100	2,300	2,200	9,000	316	142,000
2021	5,295	----		4,361	2,200	119,000	4,000	2,700	2,300		8,000		165,000
2022[1]	5,790	----		3,060	2,200	144,000	3,700	9,600	2,300		9,200		197,000
2023[2]	4,600	----		2,100		170,000	3,200	17,000			8,800		230,000

[1] Preliminary.   [2] Estimate.   [3] Formerly Zaire.   *Source: U.S. Geological Survey (USGS)*

Salient Statistics of Cobalt in the United States   In Metric Tons (Cobalt Content)

Year	Net Import Reliance As a % of Apparent Consump	Cobalt Secondary Production	Processor and Consumer Stocks Dec. 31	Imports for Consumption	Ground Coat Frit	Stainless & Heat Resisting	Catalysts	Superalloys	Tool Steel	Magnetic Alloys	Pigments	Drier in Paints, etc	Cutting & Wear-Resistant Material	Welding Materials	Total Apparent Uses	Price $ Per Pound[4]
								Consumption by End Uses								
2014	75	2,200	1,410	11,300	----	----	----	3,930	----	328	----	----	783	573	8,710	14.48
2015	73	2,750	1,070	11,400	----	----	----	3,960	----	----	----	----	726	----	10,300	13.44
2016	76	2,750	969	12,800	----	----	----	4,080	----	----	----	----	672	----	11,500	12.01
2017	69	2,750	1,020	11,900	----	----	----	4,240	----	----	----	----	753	----	8,950	26.97
2018	64	2,750	1,060	11,900	----	----	----	4,240	----	----	----	----	800	----	7,680	37.43
2019	78	2,750	1,090	13,900	----	----	----	4,220	----	----	----	----	799	----	12,500	16.95
2020	76	2,010	952	9,740	----	----	----	3,020	----	----	----	----	629	----	8,480	15.70
2021	73	1,800	1,010	9,790											6,650	24.21
2022[1]	73	1,900	1,000	10,500											7,090	30.78
2023[2]	67	2,100	1,000	9,600											6,400	17.00

[1] Preliminary.   [2] Estimate.   [3] Or related usage.   [4] Annual spot for cathodes.   W = Withheld.   *Source: U.S. Geological Survey (USGS)*

Cocoa

Cocoa is the common name for a powder derived from the fruit seeds of the cacao tree. The Spanish called cocoa "the food of the gods" when they found it in South America 500 years ago. Today, it remains a valued commodity. Dating back to the time of the Aztecs, cocoa was mainly used as a beverage. The processing of the cacao seeds, also known as cocoa beans, begins when the harvested fruit is fermented or cured into a pulpy state for three to nine days. The cocoa beans are then dried in the sun and cleaned in special machines before they are roasted to bring out the chocolate flavor. After roasting, they are put into a crushing machine and ground into cocoa powder. Cocoa has a high food value because it contains as much as 20 percent protein, 40 percent carbohydrate, and 40 percent fat. It is also mildly stimulating because of the presence of theobromine, an alkaloid that is closely related to caffeine. Roughly two-thirds of cocoa bean production is used to make chocolate and one-third to make cocoa powder.

Four major West African cocoa producers, the Ivory Coast, Ghana, Nigeria, and Cameroon, together account for about two-thirds of world cocoa production. Outside of West Africa, the major producers of cocoa are Indonesia, Brazil, Malaysia, Ecuador, and the Dominican Republic. Cocoa producers like Ghana and Indonesia have been making efforts to increase cocoa production while producers like Malaysia have been switching to other crops. Ghana has had an ongoing problem with black pod disease and the crop's smuggling into the neighboring Ivory Coast. Brazil was once one of the largest cocoa producers but has had problems with witches' broom disease. In West Africa, the main crop harvest starts in the September-October period and can be extended into the January-March period. Cocoa trees reach maturity in 5-6 years but can live to be 50 years old or more. The cocoa tree will produce thousands of flowers during a growing season, but only a few will develop into cocoa pods.

Cocoa futures and options are traded at the ICE Futures U.S. and ICE Futures Europe exchanges. The futures contracts call for the delivery of 10 metric tons of cocoa and the contract is priced in US dollars per metric ton.

Prices – ICE cocoa futures prices (Barchart.com

symbol CC) in 2023 were well supported and posted the low for the year in January at $2,507 per metric ton. Cocoa prices were supported by concern that an El Nino weather event would cause drought in West Africa and hamper global cocoa production. The unfavorable growing conditions and crop disease on West African farms throughout 2023 curbed cocoa production and fueled a scorching rally in cocoa prices. Continuous rain led to the spread of swollen shoot disease in the Ivory Coast, the world's largest cocoa producer, and undercut its cocoa output. Concern about lower cocoa production in Ghana, the world's second-largest producer, also supported cocoa prices. Ghana's cocoa regulator said in August that some of its cocoa farmers were unlikely to fulfill some of their cocoa contracts in 2023 for a second season. In December, the Ivory Coast's regulator halted forward sales for the 2023-24 Ivory Coast mid-crop so the nation's production forecast could be reviewed. The halt added to the tumult of the region's cocoa supplies, and the impact could multiply if the halt extends into the next season. Expectations of declining cocoa production stoked concern that current cocoa production cannot replenish supplies to avoid a global deficit. The International Cocoa Organization (ICCO) estimated end-of-season 2022/23 global cocoa stocks at 1.707 MMT and the cocoa stocks-to-grinding ratio at a 7-year low of 34.5%. ICCO also estimated the global cocoa deficit for 2022/23 at -99,000 MT. Cocoa prices rallied throughout 2023, posted a 46-year nearest-futures high of $4.478 per metric ton, and finished 2023 up sharply by +61.4% yr/yr at $4,196 per metric ton.

Supply – The world's production of cocoa beans in the 2022/23 crop year rose by +1.4% to 5.584 million metric tons. The world's largest cocoa producer by far is the Ivory Coast, with 38.0% of the world's production, followed by Ghana with 18.9%, and Indonesia with 11.4%. Closing stocks of cocoa in the 2022/23 crop year fell by -5.4% yr/yr to 1.744 million metric tons.

Demand – World seasonal grindings of cocoa in 2022/23 rose by +0.2% yr/yr to 5.002 million metric tons.

Trade – US imports of cocoa and cocoa products in 2023 fell by -11.6% yr/yr to 1.341 million metric tons.

World Supply and Demand Cocoa   In Thousands of Metric Tons

Crop Year Beginning Oct. 1	Stocks Oct. 1	Net World Production[4]	Total Availability	Seasonal Grindings	Closing Stocks	Stock Change	Stock/Consumption Ratio %
2013-14	1,552	4,370	5,922	4,335	1,543	-9	35.6
2014-15	1,543	4,252	5,795	4,152	1,600	57	38.5
2015-16	1,600	3,994	5,594	4,133	1,421	-179	34.4
2016-17	1,421	4,768	6,189	4,391	1,750	329	39.9
2017-18	1,750	4,647	6,397	4,576	1,775	25	38.8
2018-19	1,775	4,811	6,586	4,742	1,796	21	37.9
2019-20	1,796	4,752	6,548	4,685	1,815	19	38.7
2020-21[1]	1,815	5,245	7,060	4,949	2,059	244	41.6
2021-22[2]	2,059	4,826	6,885	4,994	1,843	-216	36.9
2022-23[3]	1,843	4,953	6,796	5,002	1,744	-99	34.9

[1] Preliminary.   [2] Estimate.   [3] Forecast.   [4] Obtained by adjusting the gross world crop for a one percent loss in weight.
Source: International Cocoa Organization (ICO

World Production of Cocoa Beans   In Metric Tons

Crop Year Beginning Oct. 1	Brazil	Cameroon	Colombia	Côte d'Ivoire	Dominican Republic	Ecuador	Ghana	Indonesia	Malaysia	Mexico	Nigeria	Papau New Guinea	World Total
2013-14	256,186	275,000	46,739	1,448,992	68,021	128,446	835,466	720,900	2,809	33,284	367,000	41,200	4,486,396
2014-15	273,793	269,228	47,732	1,637,778	69,913	156,216	858,720	728,400	2,665	26,969	329,870	45,369	4,742,041
2015-16	278,299	310,000	54,798	1,796,000	75,500	180,192	858,720	593,331	1,729	28,007	302,066	36,100	4,817,460
2016-17	213,871	344,752	56,785	1,634,000	81,246	177,551	858,720	656,817	1,723	26,863	298,029	38,000	4,777,750
2017-18	235,809	322,248	89,282	2,034,000	86,599	205,955	969,300	590,684	1,012	27,287	250,000	36,900	5,235,372
2018-19	239,318	317,530	97,978	2,113,189	85,991	235,182	904,700	767,280	826	28,399	270,000	33,300	5,506,006
2019-20	259,451	301,255	102,154	2,235,043	76,113	283,680	811,700	734,795	1,017	28,452	250,000	35,700	5,513,558
2020-21[1]	269,740	280,077	63,416	2,200,000	77,681	327,903	800,000	720,660	706	29,429	357,608	38,000	5,602,251
2021-22[2]	302,126	295,000	65,164	2,228,459	70,631	302,094	1,047,385	688,210	537	28,106	280,000	41,900	5,792,868
2022-23[3]	273,873	300,000	62,158	2,230,000	75,900	337,149	1,108,663	667,296	493	28,115	280,000	42,000	5,874,582

[1] Preliminary.   [2] Estimate.   [3] Forecast.   *Source: Food and Agricultural Organization of the United Nations (FAO)*

World Consumption of Cocoa[4]   In Thousands of Metric Tons

Crop Year Beginning Oct. 1	Canada	Côte d'Ivoire	Brazil	European Union	Ghana	Indonesia	Japan	Malaysia	Singapore	Türkiye	United States	Russia	World Total
2010-11	62	361	239	1,492	230	190	40	305	83	70	401	61	3,938
2011-12	60	431	243	1,383	212	270	40	297	83	75	387	63	3,972
2012-13	64	471	241	1,443	225	290	40	293	77	75	429	71	4,180
2013-14	67	519	240	1,461	234	340	44	259	79	88	446	62	4,335
2014-15	62	558	224	1,432	234	335	45	195	81	86	400	46	4,152
2015-16	62	492	225	1,483	202	382	47	194	81	84	398	49	4,127
2016-17	62	577	227	1,503	250	455	49	216	82	102	390	52	4,397
2017-18[1]	62	559	231	1,575	310	483	55	236	90	99	385	55	4,596
2018-19[2]	61	605	235	1,585	320	487	54	327	89	104	400	60	4,805
2019-20[3]	58	615	222	1,560	333	512	57	360	95	111	400	60	4,861

[1] Preliminary.   [2] Estimate.   [3] Forecast.   [4] Figures represent the "grindings" of cocoa beans in each country.
Source: International Cocoa Organization (ICO)

Imports of Cocoa Butter in Selected Countries   In Metric Tons

Year	Australia	Austria	Belgium	Canada	France	Germany	Italy	Japan	Netherlands	Sweden	Switzerland	United Kingdom	United States
2013	17,902	5,413	76,070	25,910	63,618	114,623	30,308	24,262	92,355	6,191	28,797	50,604	80,664
2014	17,624	5,045	79,684	26,256	67,811	134,808	28,365	27,353	79,957	6,402	28,768	47,082	97,776
2015	18,239	4,126	80,403	24,954	63,003	118,046	28,408	21,308	62,405	6,284	27,549	58,901	95,121
2016	17,221	4,947	92,337	26,222	64,442	133,378	28,154	23,585	77,256	6,247	27,546	52,872	82,675
2017	17,796	5,557	94,982	25,383	78,734	145,442	29,012	23,551	95,498	6,521	29,484	53,365	111,693
2018	18,550	4,577	103,143	24,493	75,186	151,175	32,288	26,741	94,243	6,391	29,016	52,596	109,143
2019	16,816	4,853	118,270	26,579	71,288	165,861	33,122	26,215	100,797	7,375	30,001	56,240	114,572
2020	19,736	6,004	114,785	28,255	77,832	152,100	36,851	21,576	86,003	8,120	25,950	56,367	98,227
2021	20,194	6,122	131,605	30,568	88,744	164,733	43,845	23,843	97,864	8,048	28,277	43,537	104,796
2022[1]	23,879	6,044	107,896	34,513	90,793	167,922	51,857	23,751	113,071	8,171	30,744	58,531	126,846

[1] Preliminary.   *Sources: Food and Agricultural Organization of the United Nations (FAO)*

Imports of Cocoa Liquor and Cocoa Powder in Selected Countries   In Metric Tons

	Cocoa Liquor						Cocoa Powder						
Year	France	Germany	Japan	Netherlands	United Kingdom	United States	Belgium	France	Germany	Italy	Japan	Netherlands	United States
2013	96,202	82,807	8,489	98,498	9,929	18,379	19,336	65,479	59,576	26,630	15,897	49,255	150,266
2014	93,549	79,662	9,832	112,929	9,223	22,304	18,833	59,356	69,838	28,444	17,705	56,878	154,294
2015	69,452	76,611	11,884	76,546	10,251	14,760	47,539	56,542	69,652	33,407	19,771	28,048	137,590
2016	73,165	75,047	12,198	79,736	15,897	32,561	46,881	46,516	69,627	33,500	19,768	30,216	180,582
2017	96,669	64,033	14,720	114,652	13,830	30,066	29,992	41,469	68,300	35,693	21,258	71,285	182,884
2018	86,061	63,112	15,851	120,019	13,324	35,068	23,502	46,315	70,963	37,269	19,976	79,249	156,978
2019	81,104	63,966	15,945	127,987	18,822	46,559	27,160	49,100	70,960	39,228	17,840	98,996	163,504
2020	110,347	75,194	12,373	130,759	14,288	77,944	25,972	50,395	187,478	40,161	21,244	80,228	177,571
2021	69,819	71,499	14,624	128,256	10,739	68,308							
2022[1]	70,244	72,648	15,486	107,316	16,744	72,992							

[1] Preliminary.   *Source: Food and Agricultural Organization of the United Nations (FAO)*

COCOA

Imports of Cocoa and Products in the United States   In Metric Tons

Year	Jan.	Feb.	Mar.	Apr.	May	June	July	Aug.	Sept.	Oct.	Nov.	Dec.	Total
2014	105,743	141,186	165,373	133,870	95,607	94,784	104,583	98,192	91,016	93,453	80,532	91,672	1,296,010
2015	109,669	121,573	132,182	138,943	115,781	124,700	107,942	88,465	101,383	105,487	87,698	105,521	1,339,343
2016	123,193	144,838	122,403	125,085	99,749	95,351	97,444	109,180	100,657	114,504	105,660	129,828	1,367,892
2017	143,196	143,358	175,485	162,652	129,538	111,460	108,712	100,961	90,012	95,449	95,478	99,473	1,455,775
2018	149,657	134,349	134,869	129,987	111,950	93,772	104,645	111,269	92,118	105,331	99,051	108,658	1,375,657
2019	129,159	139,778	126,889	139,919	130,856	104,081	112,192	105,572	103,153	106,925	86,189	112,285	1,396,996
2020	122,994	144,552	152,889	128,688	105,708	111,954	106,218	99,647	111,169	104,048	95,729	109,582	1,393,178
2021	144,402	122,963	187,430	154,240	129,183	131,072	100,701	107,233	119,621	110,146	117,616	109,737	1,534,343
2022	125,413	96,994	138,493	147,052	146,602	152,770	120,292	130,113	123,600	124,929	117,729	93,514	1,517,499
2023[1]	139,334	120,940	140,305	144,454	112,438	99,874	101,867	104,086	96,710	99,820	91,150	90,136	1,341,113

[1] Preliminary.   Source: Foreign Agricultural Service, U.S. Department of Agriculture (FAS-USDA)

Visible Stocks of Cocoa in Port of Hampton Road Warehouses[1], at End of Month   In Thousands of Bags

Year	Jan.	Feb.	Mar.	Apr.	May	June	July	Aug.	Sept.	Oct.	Nov.	Dec.
2014	9.6	9.6	9.6	9.6	9.6	9.6	9.6	9.6	9.6	9.6	9.6	9.6
2015	9.6	9.6	9.6	9.6	9.6	7.2	7.2	7.2	7.2	7.2	7.2	7.2
2016	7.2	7.2	7.2	7.2	7.2	7.2	7.2	7.2	7.2	7.2	7.2	7.2
2017	7.2	6.5	6.5	6.5	6.5	6.5	6.5	6.5	6.5	6.5	2.7	2.7
2018	2.4	2.4	2.0	2.0	1.9	1.9	1.4	1.4	----	----	----	----
2019	----	----	----	----	----	----	----	----	----	----	----	----
2020	----	----	----	----	----	----	----	----	----	----	----	----
2021	----	----	----	----	----	----	----	53.9	67.2	88.4	110.7	89.5
2022	87.5	87.4	87.4	88.1	88.4	93.3	94.4	106.7	113.2	119.2	116.5	110.1
2023	111.8	107.7	96.6	99.4	99.4	99.4	99.4	98.9	89.3	88.5	87.6	85.5

[1] Licensed warehouses approved by ICE.   Source: ICE Futures U.S. (ICE)

Visible Stocks of Cocoa in Philadelphia (Del. River) Warehouses[1], at End of Month   In Thousands of Bags

Year	Jan.	Feb.	Mar.	Apr.	May	June	July	Aug.	Sept.	Oct.	Nov.	Dec.
2014	3,215.1	3,687.7	4,395.1	4,862.6	4,647.1	4,354.2	4,167.4	3,909.4	3,569.5	3,168.6	2,816.0	2,494.7
2015	2,640.6	2,953.7	3,044.0	3,700.4	3,780.4	4,166.1	4,013.1	3,788.7	3,568.2	3,286.3	3,146.1	2,956.1
2016	3,186.6	3,464.0	3,960.3	3,809.4	3,690.7	3,441.0	3,155.1	2,908.5	2,606.9	2,546.0	2,479.5	2,493.6
2017	2,961.9	3,695.8	4,460.4	5,117.8	5,394.3	5,245.8	4,992.7	4,669.1	4,318.8	3,834.3	3,462.8	3,147.5
2018	3,746.2	4,259.6	4,501.8	5,054.0	4,870.3	4,579.7	4,386.0	4,215.1	3,955.9	3,633.1	3,269.1	3,236.1
2019	3,344.6	3,701.7	3,901.5	4,104.4	4,281.1	4,171.4	3,958.4	3,706.2	3,461.9	3,112.4	2,808.2	2,550.9
2020	2,797.9	3,406.5	3,637.2	3,906.0	3,904.8	3,823.1	3,731.8	3,496.9	3,380.1	3,218.4	2,885.5	2,831.3
2021	3,030.6	3,514.0	4,141.7	4,430.4	5,153.9	5,467.4	5,379.2	5,186.7	5,103.7	4,952.8	4,697.6	4,307.3
2022	4,214.9	4,347.0	4,321.0	4,606.8	4,846.7	5,113.6	5,104.5	5,278.5	5,226.8	5,114.3	5,075.8	4,709.7
2023	4,522.3	4,679.3	4,925.5	5,062.8	5,330.3	5,170.5	4,996.9	4,799.3	4,592.4	4,282.5	4,007.7	3,844.1

[1] Licensed warehouses approved by ICE.   Source: ICE Futures U.S. (ICE)

Visible Stocks of Cocoa in New York Warehouses[1], at End of Month   In Thousands of Bags

Year	Jan.	Feb.	Mar.	Apr.	May	June	July	Aug.	Sept.	Oct.	Nov.	Dec.
2014	391.0	386.7	364.5	482.6	619.3	566.5	505.4	435.9	419.3	380.9	317.1	308.3
2015	276.6	266.0	245.3	260.4	286.9	366.0	342.2	314.5	284.7	277.7	278.0	287.8
2016	283.3	353.2	412.3	388.1	317.4	302.9	299.7	311.3	312.4	289.8	250.2	274.9
2017	336.9	318.2	344.6	388.7	424.8	399.4	367.4	331.1	291.6	252.7	244.0	232.2
2018	271.1	281.8	288.4	315.4	278.3	264.7	265.4	240.5	224.6	206.8	197.7	230.7
2019	223.0	245.5	305.6	327.8	351.3	335.2	326.5	296.8	288.6	246.5	198.2	175.7
2020	250.2	310.0	336.6	375.0	358.1	323.2	305.2	289.6	266.7	237.2	224.5	228.8
2021	221.7	237.4	332.7	381.9	394.5	392.2	348.0	304.0	288.5	283.0	283.7	279.0
2022	265.9	271.1	313.6	331.3	348.0	342.5	338.2	342.2	323.2	313.6	316.0	322.4
2023	308.5	297.4	289.4	299.4	274.9	272.0	274.6	270.4	285.5	274.2	266.4	238.0

[1] Licensed warehouses approved by ICE.   Source: ICE Futures U.S. (ICE)

COCOA
Quarterly Cash as of 03/28/2024

QUARTERLY CASH
As of 03/28/2024
Chart High 9897.0 on 03/27/2024
Chart Low 93.0 on 08/30/1940
USD/metric ton

USD/metric ton

Exchange Standard: to 10/1946; ACCRA: 11/1946 to 09/1980; Ivory Coast: 10/1980 to date.

Average Cash Price of Cocoa, Ivory Coast in New York   In Dollars Per Metric Ton

Year	Jan.	Feb.	Mar.	Apr.	May	June	July	Aug.	Sept.	Oct.	Nov.	Dec.	Average
2014	3,068	3,281	3,325	3,340	3,287	3,476	3,494	3,591	3,523	3,455	3,176	3,191	3,351
2015	3,170	3,181	3,181	3,129	3,331	3,493	3,590	3,424	3,546	3,434	3,630	3,632	3,395
2016	3,297	3,124	3,327	3,333	3,412	3,439	3,482	3,434	3,288	3,070	2,800	2,620	3,219
2017	2,493	2,379	2,381	2,214	2,200	2,235	2,195	2,256	2,231	2,354	2,411	2,190	2,295
2018	2,148	2,362	2,701	2,974	2,952	2,800	2,748	2,573	2,626	2,511	2,569	2,530	2,625
2019	2,304	2,251	2,205	2,380	2,369	2,483	2,458	2,199	2,370	2,471	2,610	2,531	2,386
2020	2,669	2,870	2,433	2,326	2,400	2,404	2,211	2,508	2,607	2,421	2,624	2,581	2,505
2021	2,524	2,571	2,521	2,400	2,444	2,358	2,345	2,530	2,626	2,633	2,453	2,482	2,491
2022	2,540	2,639	2,591	2,560	2,485	2,396	2,334	2,369	2,339	2,338	2,450	2,539	2,465
2023	2,612	2,650	2,792	3,037	2,982	3,157	3,403	3,419	3,599	3,604	4,075	4,297	3,302

Source: Economic Research Service, U.S. Department of Agriculture (ERS-USDA)

Total Visible Stocks of Cocoa in Warehouses[1], at End of Month   In Thousands of Bags

Year	Jan.	Feb.	Mar.	Apr.	May	June	July	Aug.	Sept.	Oct.	Nov.	Dec.
2014	3,648.9	4,117.1	4,800.1	5,384.4	5,305.6	4,960.0	4,711.8	4,384.1	4,027.5	3,588.3	3,171.9	2,824.9
2015	2,939.1	3,241.1	3,310.7	3,978.6	4,085.2	4,546.7	4,369.9	4,117.8	3,867.5	3,578.7	3,438.3	3,255.3
2016	3,481.4	3,828.6	4,384.0	4,209.0	4,019.5	3,755.4	3,465.7	3,230.7	2,930.3	2,846.7	2,740.7	2,779.4
2017	3,309.3	4,023.4	4,814.4	5,515.9	5,828.5	5,654.6	5,369.5	5,009.6	4,617.9	4,096.9	3,714.4	3,386.7
2018	4,025.4	4,549.1	4,793.7	5,372.4	5,151.2	4,847.1	4,653.5	4,457.3	4,180.9	3,840.3	3,467.2	3,467.2
2019	3,568.1	3,947.6	4,207.5	4,432.2	4,632.3	4,506.6	4,284.9	4,003.0	3,750.5	3,358.8	3,006.4	2,726.6
2020	3,048.2	3,716.5	3,973.8	4,280.9	4,262.9	4,146.3	4,037.0	3,786.5	3,646.7	3,455.6	3,110.0	3,060.1
2021	3,252.3	3,751.4	4,474.4	4,812.3	5,548.4	5,859.6	5,727.1	5,544.6	5,459.4	5,324.2	5,092.0	4,675.8
2022	4,568.3	4,705.5	4,722.0	5,026.2	5,283.1	5,549.5	5,537.1	5,727.4	5,663.2	5,547.0	5,508.3	5,142.2
2023	4,942.6	5,084.3	5,311.4	5,461.6	5,704.5	5,541.9	5,370.9	5,168.6	4,967.2	4,645.1	4,361.7	4,167.6

[1] Licensed warehouses approved by ICE.   *Source: ICE Futures U.S. (ICE)*

COCOA

COCOA - ICE-US
Weekly Nearest Futures as of 03/28/2024

WEEKLY NEAREST FUTURES
As of 03/28/2024

Chart High 10080.0 on 03/26/2024
Chart Low 1769.0 on 06/22/2017

Nearby Futures through Last Trading Day.

Volume of Trading of Cocoa Futures in New York   In Thousands of Contracts

Year	Jan.	Feb.	Mar.	Apr.	May	June	July	Aug.	Sept.	Oct.	Nov.	Dec.	Total
2014	571.9	588.5	453.2	593.1	454.4	625.4	552.0	541.1	478.5	617.5	508.5	331.8	6,315.8
2015	586.6	679.4	694.1	739.8	520.0	710.6	531.4	801.8	602.1	770.4	775.6	501.3	7,913.0
2016	940.4	950.7	667.6	927.4	857.7	778.3	712.6	988.0	730.5	856.4	829.0	623.5	9,862.2
2017	797.5	929.4	906.3	974.0	927.0	1,095.5	790.4	1,116.9	660.7	1,066.3	1,049.7	747.9	11,061.6
2018	973.4	1,122.9	1,135.9	1,266.5	972.5	1,176.0	884.3	1,090.3	707.9	1,021.6	1,077.3	607.0	12,035.6
2019	959.8	1,002.6	902.9	1,276.7	972.2	973.9	855.8	1,253.7	1,031.8	1,059.9	1,171.3	789.2	12,249.9
2020	1,103.1	1,164.8	1,236.8	704.7	636.7	846.5	698.2	916.9	661.5	791.5	996.2	595.1	10,352.1
2021	697.1	910.7	893.6	955.7	841.4	937.1	863.8	1,177.2	744.9	955.2	1,140.5	713.4	10,830.5
2022	993.8	1,065.9	1,000.7	939.4	1,007.5	1,156.5	952.1	1,416.4	939.0	1,128.8	1,333.1	732.0	12,665.3
2023	949.6	1,223.4	1,394.6	1,188.5	915.8	1,498.4	861.6	1,546.1	843.5	952.6	1,280.7	808.2	13,463.1

Source: ICE Futures U.S. (ICE)

Average Open Interest of Cocoa Futures in New York   In Contracts

Year	Jan.	Feb.	Mar.	Apr.	May	June	July	Aug.	Sept.	Oct.	Nov.	Dec.
2014	210,130	216,867	215,297	206,091	204,253	216,264	214,879	213,149	208,448	199,236	177,425	186,443
2015	200,884	193,672	211,199	199,675	208,637	215,736	219,497	182,777	200,200	216,932	232,054	234,884
2016	227,549	234,056	238,732	234,122	242,073	198,093	215,818	206,006	210,888	251,984	244,643	254,911
2017	275,443	265,621	285,852	284,418	296,408	257,541	273,750	244,093	258,013	253,440	241,566	251,261
2018	275,944	263,249	296,500	289,878	304,760	266,004	247,961	240,819	242,329	264,377	241,641	235,570
2019	251,715	236,101	255,428	244,996	251,723	265,064	281,033	265,389	284,179	304,661	316,902	314,178
2020	311,242	347,493	278,299	215,335	224,401	219,668	224,055	209,904	219,811	211,501	192,405	214,734
2021	225,150	215,702	200,366	195,012	203,638	220,400	256,845	232,266	233,303	250,609	239,954	237,002
2022	240,988	253,691	243,660	241,588	285,017	303,130	310,780	301,967	303,177	307,044	274,001	266,888
2023	295,816	295,448	355,401	344,845	331,787	340,399	353,054	291,663	294,656	294,794	295,894	294,015

Source: ICE Futures U.S. (ICE)

Coconut Oil and Copra

Coconut oil and copra come from the fruit of the coconut palm tree, which originated in Southeast Asia. Coconut oil has been used for thousands of years as cooking oil and is still a staple in the diets of many people living in tropical areas. Until shortages of imported oil developed during WWII, Americans also used coconut oil for cooking.

Copra is the meaty inner lining of the coconut. It is an oil-rich pulp with a light, slightly sweet, nutty flavor. Copra is used mainly as a source of coconut oil and is also used shredded for baking. High-quality copra contains about 65% to 72% oil, and oil made from the copra is called crude coconut oil. Crude coconut oil is processed from copra by expeller press and solvent extraction. It is not considered fit for human consumption until it has been refined, which consists of neutralizing, bleaching, and deodorizing it at high heat with a vacuum. The remaining oil cake obtained as a by-product is used for livestock feed.

Premium grade coconut oil, also called virgin coconut oil, is the oil made from the first pressing without the addition of any chemicals. Premium grade coconut oil is more expensive than refined or crude oil because the producers use only selected raw materials, and there is a lower production yield due to only one pressing.

Coconut oil accounts for approximately 20% of all vegetable oils used worldwide. Coconut oil is used in margarines, vegetable shortening, salad oils, confections, and sports drinks to boost energy and enhance athletic performance. It is also used in the manufacture of soaps, detergents, shampoos, cosmetics, candles, glycerin, and synthetic rubber. Coconut oil is very healthy, unless it is hydrogenated, and is easily digested.

Supply – World production of copra in 2023 fell by -8.0% to 4.751 million metric tons and remained below the record high of 5.662 million metric tons posted in 2001. The world's largest producers of copra in 2022 were the Philippines with 34.3% of world production, Indonesia with 29.7%, India with 13.3%, and Mexico with 5.1%. World production of coconut oil in the 2022/23 marketing year fell by -6.3% yr/yr to 2.956 million metric tons.

Demand – Virtually all the world's production of copra goes for crushing into coconut meal and oil. World consumption of coconut oil in 2022/23 fell by -3.2% yr/yr to 3.015 million metric tons.

Trade – Copra is generally crushed in the country of origin, meaning that less than 4% of copra itself is exported; the rest is exported in the form of coconut oil. World exports of coconut oil in 2022/23 fell by -9.9% yr/yr to 2.069 million metric tons.

World Production of Copra   In Thousands of Metric Tons

Year	India	Indonesia	Ivory Coast	Malaysia	Mexico	Mozam-bique	Papua New Guinea	Philip-pines	Sri Lanka	Thailand	Vanuatu	Vietnam	World Total
2014	670	1,530	27	62	203	52	72	1,740	80	49	25	57	4,881
2015	620	1,540	28	64	209	54	95	1,680	83	49	18	57	4,812
2016	580	1,290	26	58	221	50	97	1,280	95	46	28	55	4,141
2017	420	1,180	28	67	231	52	114	1,370	90	46	27	56	4,001
2018	530	1,460	30	65	237	52	118	1,670	91	48	21	57	4,704
2019	580	1,320	30	78	236	53	85	1,820	107	50	21	60	4,756
2020	560	1,240	30	80	237	46	98	1,460	88	46	20	65	4,285
2021[1]	610	1,330	28	85	239	46	94	1,530	96	48	19	66	4,513
2022[2]	620	1,450	24	86	240	45	104	2,020	115	48	22	67	5,165
2023[3]	630	1,410	25	89	243	45	105	1,630	110	49	21	68	4,751

[1] Preliminary.   [2] Estimate.   [3] Forecast.   *Source: The Oil World*

World Supply and Distribution of Coconut Oil   In Thousands of Metric Tons

	Production				Consumption								Ending Stocks		
Crop Year	India	Indo-nesia	Malay-sia	Philip-pines	World Total	World Exports	World Imports	European Union	India	Indo-nesia	Philip-pines	United States	World Total	Philip-pines	United States	World Total
2013-14	391	933	51	1,153	3,050	1,866	1,859	646	392	176	364	518	3,119	68	65	359
2014-15	377	937	51	1,093	2,968	1,964	1,953	537	389	161	233	531	2,893	69	61	424
2015-16	346	805	45	888	2,594	1,671	1,684	501	340	166	198	469	2,685	74	66	345
2016-17	270	691	45	953	2,481	1,698	1,673	457	262	181	119	439	2,464	58	52	338
2017-18	304	845	41	1,030	2,754	1,791	1,791	550	298	195	133	429	2,658	100	47	434
2018-19	344	802	43	1,226	2,958	2,171	2,111	613	340	228	87	439	2,819	65	41	512
2019-20	342	745	50	1,037	2,719	1,979	1,961	590	339	204	66	446	2,747	40	57	466
2020-21[1]	359	766	53	913	2,648	1,834	1,916	553	349	216	70	427	2,831	59	51	364
2021-22[2]	362	845	55	1,316	3,154	2,297	2,355	646	340	219	63	464	3,117	55	97	460
2022-23[3]	366	878	57	1,074	2,957	2,070	2,046	599	345	214	88	470	3,016	42	60	377

[1] Preliminary.   [2] Estimate.   [3] Forecast.   *Source: The Oil World*

COCONUT OIL AND COPRA

Supply and Distribution of Coconut Oil in the United States   In Millions of Pounds

Crop Year	Copra Tonne --- $ U.S. ---	Coconut Oil, CIF	Imports For Consumption	Stocks Oct. 1	Total Supply	Exports	Total Domestic	Edible Products	Inedible Products	Total	Oct.-Dec.	Jan.-Mar.	April-June	July-Sept.
2013-14	854	1,278	1,173	143	1,316	64	1,142	----	----	----	----	----	----	----
2014-15	749	1,128	1,261	134	1,395	99	1,171	----	----	----	----	----	----	----
2015-16	907	1,360	1,157	146	1,302	111	1,034	----	----	----	----	----	----	----
2016-17	1,076	1,620	1,036	115	1,151	98	968	----	----	----	----	----	----	----
2017-18	784	1,175	988	104	1,091	54	945	----	----	----	----	----	----	----
2018-19	483	724	996	90	1,086	42	967	----	----	----	----	----	----	----
2019-20	602	899	1,060	126	1,186	41	984	----	----	----	----	----	----	----
2020-21	993	1,483	981	113	1,094	52	942	----	----	----	----	----	----	----
2021-22[1]	1,197	1,800	1,179	214	1,393	57	1,022	----	----	----	----	----	----	----
2022-23[2]	745	1,117	1,003	132	1,135	49	1,036	----	----	----	----	----	----	----

[1] Preliminary.   [2] Forecast.   *Source: Bureau of Census, U.S. Department of Commerce*

Average Price of Coconut Oil (Crude) Tank Cars in New York   In Cents Per Pound

Year	Jan.	Feb.	Mar.	Apr.	May	June	July	Aug.	Sept.	Oct.	Nov.	Dec.	Average
2013	39.38	41.25	39.30	38.00	38.20	40.75	41.50	41.50	46.00	45.00	59.30	61.00	44.26
2014	59.70	63.00	65.38	62.75	65.70	65.31	62.88	56.60	55.31	53.75	55.69	56.50	60.21
2015	56.30	54.94	52.94	49.50	52.25	53.19	52.30	51.56	50.75	51.05	50.31	52.20	52.27
2016	53.69	54.44	67.75	76.90	68.38	69.35	70.85	72.06	74.30	70.00	73.50	78.20	69.12
2017	83.63	90.00	73.90	82.81	84.00	83.60	81.00	85.88	86.63	68.50	72.25	72.10	80.36
2018	68.75	66.00	55.90	58.75	52.50	46.20	45.00	45.00	44.50	43.00	39.00	37.50	50.18
2019	39.00	37.25	35.30	33.50	33.00	32.00	32.00	33.20	34.50	34.00	35.60	44.50	35.32
2020	32.88	32.38	32.40	36.63	40.50	47.81	47.94	37.87	44.35	49.50	51.65	53.31	42.27
2021	68.75	66.00	52.13	72.60	78.00	80.00	80.00	80.00	80.00	85.00	92.50	87.00	76.83
2022[1]	89.50	98.50	112.50	112.80	102.50	88.00	88.00	88.00	73.60	66.25	65.00	65.00	87.47

[1] Preliminary.   *Source: Economic Research Service, U.S. Department of Agriculture (ERS-USDA)*

Consumption of Coconut Oil in End Products (Edible and Inedible) in the United States   In Millions of Pounds

Year	Jan.	Feb.	Mar.	Apr.	May	June	July	Aug.	Sept.	Oct.	Nov.	Dec.	Total
2002	55.4	41.3	50.8	59.3	53.9	46.4	50.7	51.8	45.9	54.3	56.1	49.4	615.4
2003	51.2	49.3	56.8	50.6	52.3	46.7	48.9	49.6	50.3	47.8	41.8	38.5	583.7
2004	50.0	51.7	58.5	54.6	48.5	55.6	52.9	55.1	48.9	48.2	64.3	51.7	640.0
2005	46.7	52.0	47.9	48.8	51.4	55.5	47.2	58.1	49.2	52.8	53.4	58.1	621.1
2006	70.4	62.7	50.4	47.5	50.7	51.6	43.1	51.6	43.8	49.6	44.4	40.8	606.4
2007	49.8	48.5	47.0	51.2	53.7	60.3	60.3	74.2	67.5	71.8	71.3	62.7	718.3
2008	63.6	72.1	64.8	74.4	69.7	70.4	65.8	67.6	65.8	63.0	63.6	53.6	794.5
2009	67.9	62.8	60.2	66.9	66.9	27.6	36.5	28.1	29.4	32.8	32.1	30.6	541.8
2010	41.0	36.6	45.3	34.9	39.8	38.6	37.2	40.4	32.1	41.4	39.9	70.8	498.0
2011[1]	34.6	37.0	40.6	38.0	39.0	37.0	26.7	NA	NA	NA	NA	NA	433.5

[1] Preliminary.   *Source: Bureau of Census, U.S. Department of Commerce*

Stocks of Coconut Oil (Crude and Refined) in the United States, on First of Month   In Millions of Pounds

Year	Jan.	Feb.	Mar.	Apr.	May	June	July	Aug.	Sept.	Oct.	Nov.	Dec.
2002	245.9	238.8	249.6	251.3	233.5	231.6	303.3	301.6	245.8	226.5	273.8	264.1
2003	195.2	194.0	214.3	224.9	223.7	187.8	162.2	202.9	195.6	218.9	184.6	186.1
2004	167.2	160.3	192.6	181.7	131.4	108.7	90.6	132.8	149.2	131.3	147.7	182.5
2005	225.9	163.7	188.4	191.0	170.6	187.7	263.5	250.4	253.7	242.1	252.3	273.3
2006	268.3	236.9	224.5	227.3	260.2	229.1	213.8	214.4	204.7	224.5	179.2	180.2
2007	214.4	228.5	261.5	223.1	191.8	157.9	171.2	154.4	127.7	128.4	142.5	212.6
2008	205.6	192.9	180.9	191.9	223.9	203.9	187.8	181.5	180.4	182.2	163.3	174.6
2009	164.1	183.7	215.6	167.2	143.9	138.0	134.8	133.2	102.3	182.3	159.0	154.7
2010	220.2	204.5	172.1	144.6	119.3	120.3	172.2	179.3	197.1	185.8	166.7	167.2
2011[1]	181.5	150.2	162.7	154.6	150.0	157.6	158.4	190.9	NA	NA	NA	NA

[1] Preliminary.   *Source: Bureau of Census, U.S. Department of Commerce*

Coffee

Coffee is one of the world's most important cash commodities. Coffee is the common name for any type of tree in the genus madder family. Coffee is a tropical evergreen shrub that has the potential to grow 100 feet tall. The coffee tree grows in tropical regions between the Tropics of Cancer and Capricorn in areas with abundant rainfall, year-round warm temperatures averaging about 70 degrees Fahrenheit, and no frost. In the U.S., the only places that produce any significant amount of coffee are Puerto Rico and Hawaii. The coffee plant will produce its first full crop of beans at about five years old and then be productive for about 15 years. The average coffee tree produces enough beans to make about 1 to 1 ½ pound of roasted coffee per year. It takes approximately 4,000 handpicked green coffee beans to make a pound of coffee. Wine was the first drink made from the coffee tree using coffee cherries, honey, and water. In the 17th century, the first coffee house, also known as a "penny university" because of the price per cup, opened in London. The London Stock Exchange grew from one of these first coffee houses.

Coffee is generally classified into two types of beans: arabica and robusta. The most widely produced coffee is arabica, which makes up about 70 percent of total production. It grows mainly at high altitudes of 600 to 2,000 meters, with Brazil and Colombia being the largest producers. Arabic coffee is traded at the ICE Futures U.S. Exchange. The stronger of the two types is robusta. It is grown at lower altitudes, with the largest producers being Indonesia, West Africa, Brazil, and Vietnam. Robusta coffee is traded on the ICE Futures Europe Exchange.

Ninety percent of the world coffee trade is in green (unroasted) coffee beans. Seasonal factors have a significant influence on the price of coffee. There is no extreme peak in world production at any one time of the year, although coffee consumption declines by 12 percent or more below the year's average in the warm summer months. Therefore, coffee imports and roasts both tend to decline in spring and summer and pick up again in fall and winter.

Meager prices for coffee can create serious long-term problems for coffee producers. When prices fall below production costs, there is little economic incentive to produce coffee, and coffee trees may be neglected or completely abandoned. When prices are low, producers cannot afford to hire the labor needed to maintain the trees and pick the crop at harvest. The result is that trees yield less due to reduced use of fertilizer and fewer employed coffee workers. One effect is a decline in the quality of the coffee that is produced. Higher quality Arabica coffee is often produced at higher altitudes, which entails higher costs. It is this coffee that is often abandoned. Although the pressure on producers can be severe, the market eventually comes back into balance as supply declines in response to low prices.

Coffee prices are subject to upward spikes in June, July, and August due to possible freeze scares in Brazil during the winter months in the Southern Hemisphere. The Brazilian coffee crop is harvested starting in May and extending for several weeks into the winter months in Brazil. A major freeze in Brazil occurs roughly every five years on average.

Coffee futures and options are traded at the ICE Futures U.S. and ICE Futures Europe exchanges, and the B3 Exchange (formerly BM&F/BOVESPA). Coffee futures are traded on the JSE Securities Exchange (JSE).

Prices – ICE Arabica coffee futures prices (Barchart. com symbol KC) began 2023 on a weak note and fell to a 2-1/2 year low in January of 142.05 cents per pound. Coffee prices were under pressure from the outlook for a bumper crop in Brazil after Conab, Brazil's crop forecasting agency, projected in Janu-ary that Brazil's 2023 coffee production would climb +7.9% yr/yr to 54.9 mil-lion bags. A rebound in coffee supplies also weighed on prices after ICE-monitored arabica coffee inventories climbed to a 1-1/2 year high in February. Coffee prices recovered into April and posted a 1-1/4 year high of 207.45 cents per pound. Concern about a global coffee deficit boosted coffee prices after the International Coffee Organization (ICO) projected in April that the global 2022/23 coffee deficit would widen to 7.3 million bags from 7.1 million bags in 2021/22. The El Nino weather event that began in June 2023 was bullish for coffee prices. An El Nino pattern typically brings heavy rain to Brazil and drought to India, negatively impacting coffee crop production. Strength in the Brazilian real also underpinned coffee prices in mid-2023 after the real climbed to a 1-1/2 year high against the dollar in July. The stronger real discourages export selling from Brazil's coffee producers. However, coffee prices then ratcheted lower into October as favorable weather boosted Brazil's coffee crop. ICO projected that 2023/24 global coffee production would climb +5.8% y/y to 178 million bags due to an exceptional off-biennial crop year. Coffee prices then reversed and pushed higher into year-end as supplies tightened. In November, ICE-monitored arabica coffee inventories fell to a 24-year low of 224,066 bags. Coffee prices finished 2023 up +12.5% yr/yr at 188.30 cents per pound.

Supply – World coffee production in the 2023/24 marketing year (July-June) is expected to rise by +4.2% yr/yr to 171.425 million bags (1 bag equals 60 kilo-grams or 132.3 pounds). Coffee ending stocks in the 2023/24 marketing year are expected to fall by -4.0% yr/yr to 26.529 million bags. Brazil is the world's largest coffee producer by far with 38.7% of the world's supply, followed by Vietnam with 16.0%.

Demand – World consumption of green coffee in 2023/24 is expected to rise by +0.3% yr/yr to 169.500 million bags.

Trade – World coffee exports in 2023/24 are forecasted to rise by +5.8% yr/yr to 142.226 million bags, below the 2020/21 record high of 144.386 million bags. The world's largest exporters of coffee in 2023/24 are expected to be Brazil with 30.8% of world exports, Vietnam with 17.6%, and Columbia with 8.4%. US coffee imports in 2023 rose by +41.7% yr/yr to 40.311 million bags, a new record high. The key countries from which the US imported coffee in 2023 were Brazil, accounting for 15.0% of total US imports, Columbia for 10.9%, Mexico for 3.7%, and Guatemala for 3.2%.

COFFEE

World Supply and Distribution of Coffee for Producing Countries   In Thousands of 60 Kilogram Bags

Crop Year	Beginning Stocks	Production	Imports	Total Supply	Total Exports	Bean Exports	Rst/Grn Exports	Soluble Exports	Domestic Use	Ending Stocks
2014-15	41,184	153,796	119,330	314,310	123,630	103,721	3,523	16,386	147,548	43,132
2015-16	43,132	152,404	126,429	321,965	133,140	112,322	3,817	17,001	153,874	34,951
2016-17	34,951	161,129	129,128	325,208	132,946	112,675	4,087	16,184	155,809	36,453
2017-18	36,453	159,839	130,480	326,772	133,599	112,919	4,155	16,525	161,182	31,991
2018-19	31,991	175,956	138,503	346,450	142,890	121,273	4,390	17,227	166,437	37,123
2019-20	37,123	169,080	131,190	337,393	138,506	116,320	4,967	17,219	162,661	36,226
2020-21	36,226	176,584	132,128	344,938	144,386	121,142	5,502	17,742	162,430	38,122
2021-22[1]	38,122	165,089	140,692	343,903	143,171	118,952	5,713	18,506	167,921	32,811
2022-23[2]	32,811	164,532	133,783	331,126	134,487	111,566	5,656	17,265	169,011	27,628
2023-24[3]	27,628	171,425	139,202	338,255	142,226	119,925	5,211	17,090	169,500	26,529

[1] Preliminary.   [2] Estimate.   [3] Forecast.   132.276 Lbs. Per Bag   *Source: Foreign Agricultural Service, U.S. Department of Agriculture (FAS-USDA)*

World Production of Green Coffee   In Thousands of 60 Kilogram Bags

Crop Year	Brazil	Colombia	Costa Rica	Cote d'Ivoire	El Salvador	Ethiopia	Guatemala	India	Indonesia	Mexico	Uganda	Vietnam	World Total
2014-15	54,300	13,300	1,400	1,400	700	6,475	3,185	5,440	10,470	3,180	3,500	27,400	153,796
2015-16	49,400	14,000	1,625	1,600	560	6,510	3,295	5,800	12,100	2,300	3,550	28,930	152,404
2016-17	56,100	14,600	1,300	1,090	600	6,943	3,570	5,200	10,600	3,300	4,875	26,700	161,129
2017-18	52,100	13,825	1,525	1,250	660	7,055	3,780	5,266	10,400	4,000	4,600	29,300	159,839
2018-19	66,500	13,870	1,250	2,000	654	7,350	3,770	5,325	10,600	3,550	4,650	30,400	175,956
2019-20	60,500	14,100	1,466	1,775	510	7,475	3,645	4,967	10,700	3,700	5,475	31,300	169,080
2020-21	69,900	13,400	1,472	910	540	7,600	3,930	5,567	10,700	3,530	6,630	29,000	176,584
2021-22[1]	58,100	11,800	1,215	1,110	600	8,150	3,540	5,700	10,580	3,740	6,050	31,580	165,089
2022-23[2]	62,600	10,700	1,425	1,050	550	7,300	3,270	5,867	11,850	3,545	6,565	27,200	164,532
2023-24[3]	66,300	11,500	1,440	1,350	670	8,350	3,435	5,950	9,700	4,090	6,850	27,500	171,425

[1] Preliminary.   [2] Estimate.   [3] Forecast.   132.276 Lbs. Per Bag   *Source: Foreign Agricultural Service, U.S. Department of Agriculture (FAS-USDA)*

World Exportable[4] Production of Green Coffee   In Thousands of 60 Kilogram Bags

Crop Year	Brazil	Colombia	Cote d'Ivoire	Ethiopia	Guatemala	Honduras	India	Indonesia	Mexico	Peru	Uganda	Vietnam	World Total
2014-15	36,573	12,420	1,350	3,500	3,070	4,760	4,894	8,720	2,560	2,750	3,350	21,567	123,630
2015-16	35,543	12,390	1,540	3,405	3,044	5,000	5,693	9,896	2,340	3,300	3,300	29,065	133,140
2016-17	33,081	13,755	990	3,853	3,330	7,175	6,158	8,174	2,865	4,025	4,600	26,450	132,946
2017-18	30,454	12,725	1,170	3,893	3,465	7,225	6,148	8,010	3,220	4,185	4,300	29,907	133,599
2018-19	41,426	13,615	1,965	4,174	3,604	6,910	5,778	6,150	2,896	4,293	4,450	28,318	142,890
2019-20	40,256	13,005	1,715	4,135	3,220	4,900	5,185	7,152	2,986	3,720	5,350	27,326	138,506
2020-21	45,675	12,755	865	4,675	3,691	6,010	5,794	7,872	3,007	3,326	6,514	25,300	144,386
2021-22[1]	39,685	12,365	1,060	4,831	3,354	4,650	7,258	7,428	2,933	4,065	5,850	29,010	143,171
2022-23[2]	36,145	10,700	1,000	3,910	3,004	5,350	6,306	8,792	2,530	3,300	6,250	27,740	134,487
2023-24[3]	43,850	12,000	1,300	4,820	3,169	6,200	6,336	6,050	3,025	4,060	6,515	25,000	142,226

[1] Preliminary.   [2] Estimate.   [3] Forecast.   [4] Marketing year begins in October in some countries and April or July in others. Exportable production represents total harvested production minus estimated domestic consumption.   132.276 Lbs. Per Bag
Source: Foreign Agricultural Service, U.S. Department of Agriculture (FAS-USDA)

Coffee Imports in the United States   In Thousands of 60 Kilogram Bags

Year	Brazil	Colombia	Costa Rica	Republic	Ecuador	El Salvador	Ethiopia	Guatemala	Indonesia	Mexico	Peru	Venezuela	World Total
2014	7,326	4,611	671	23	71	205	293	1,390	1,117	1,393	873		26,221
2015	7,817	5,376	586	4	54	287	366	1,190	1,218	1,230	776		26,415
2016	6,704	5,253	648	4	52	217	292	1,011	1,212	1,030	1,112		27,502
2017	6,218	5,767	492	9	41	273	439	1,282	1,247	1,305	1,065		27,918
2018	6,347	5,701	603	7	4	248	425	1,380	969	1,366	1,052	71	27,217
2019	7,974	5,964	511	16	3	273	430	1,404	1,039	1,306	1,051	52	29,216
2020	7,839	5,063	584	10	12	200	409	1,185	930	1,290	958	0	26,543
2021	8,037	5,096	483	21	5	242	494	1,490	890	1,445	672	30	27,381
2022	8,229	5,228	506	84	19	253	483	1,474	1,141	1,714	1,046	72	28,443
2023[1]	6,030	4,386	521	41	13	221	361	1,278	724	1,494	897	7	40,311

[1] Preliminary.   132.276 Lbs. Per Bag   *Source: Bureau of Census, U.S. Department of Commerce*

COFFEE
Quarterly Cash as of 03/28/2024

QUARTERLY CASH
As of 03/28/2024

Chart High   359.00   on 05/29/1997
Chart Low   5.57   on 08/30/1940

Cents / lb.

Santos #4, NY: to 07/1975; Brazilian, NY: 07/1975 to date.

Monthly Coffee Imports in the United States   In Thousands of 60 Kilogram Bags (132.276 Lbs. Per Bag)

Year	Jan.	Feb.	Mar.	Apr.	May	June	July	Aug.	Sept.	Oct.	Nov.	Dec.	Total
2014	1,919	1,895	2,407	2,489	2,545	2,468	2,356	2,357	2,174	2,019	1,640	1,943	26,213
2015	1,780	1,708	2,430	2,255	2,489	2,407	2,338	2,265	2,269	2,120	2,154	2,194	26,410
2016	2,135	2,166	2,293	2,305	2,551	2,408	2,316	2,333	2,382	2,014	2,419	2,179	27,503
2017	2,349	2,362	2,681	2,280	2,476	2,532	2,350	2,437	2,109	2,119	1,992	2,235	27,921
2018	2,090	2,220	2,420	2,382	2,542	2,225	2,274	2,186	2,013	2,260	2,266	2,349	27,225
2019	2,472	2,216	2,495	2,519	2,942	2,640	2,625	2,628	2,299	2,128	1,988	2,259	29,211
2020	2,293	1,901	2,384	2,417	2,547	2,674	2,173	1,913	1,915	2,073	1,991	2,261	26,543
2021	2,006	2,096	2,253	2,269	2,612	2,464	2,492	2,663	2,021	2,435	1,877	2,209	27,398
2022	2,429	2,055	2,545	2,792	2,226	2,552	2,770	2,369	2,228	2,429	1,893	2,159	28,447
2023[1]	2,142	2,000	2,315	2,112	2,207	2,308	2,266	2,036	1,787	1,758	1,793	1,615	24,338

[1] Preliminary.   Source: Bureau of the Census, U.S. Department of Commerce

Average Price of Brazilian[1] Coffee in New York   In Cents Per Pound

Year	Jan.	Feb.	Mar.	Apr.	May	June	July	Aug.	Sept.	Oct.	Nov.	Dec.	Average
2014	107.49	142.75	174.89	182.89	170.89	154.02	154.00	171.99	168.11	181.58	169.10	157.87	161.30
2015	151.21	143.32	127.81	129.02	123.49	124.97	119.77	121.21	113.14	118.43	122.95	123.73	126.59
2016	121.21	122.24	130.38	128.10	129.05	138.38	144.76	141.41	149.80	153.15	157.72	137.14	137.78
2017	145.70	137.68	134.07	130.39	125.40	122.39	127.26	128.24	124.46	120.01	117.26	114.00	127.24
2018	115.60	114.19	112.99	112.56	113.34	110.44	107.20	102.41	98.17	111.21	109.59	100.61	109.03
2019	101.56	100.67	97.50	94.42	93.33	99.97	103.01	96.07	97.74	97.35	107.23	117.37	100.52
2020	106.89	102.00	109.05	108.91	104.45	99.05	103.66	114.78	116.25	105.85	109.70	114.74	107.94
2021	115.73	119.35	120.36	122.03	134.77	141.03	152.24	160.14	170.02	181.57	195.17	203.06	151.29
2022	204.29	210.89	194.78	198.43	193.71	202.46	190.82	200.11	199.63	178.54	156.66	157.19	190.63
2023	156.95	174.77	170.03	178.57	175.48	171.25	158.88	154.53	153.13	151.94	161.53	175.29	165.20

[1] And other Arabicas.   Source: Foreign Agricultural Service, U.S. Department of Agriculture (FAS-USDA)

COFFEE

Average Monthly Retail[1] Price of Coffee in the United States · In Cents Per Pound

Year	Jan.	Feb.	Mar.	Apr.	May	June	July	Aug.	Sept.	Oct.	Nov.	Dec.	Average
2016	4.498	4.447	4.405	4.428	4.443	4.481	4.428	4.316	4.372	4.309	4.306	4.281	4.393
2017	4.468	4.583	4.650	4.622	4.597	4.545	4.335	4.373	4.323	4.327	4.324	4.285	4.453
2018	4.291	4.267	4.343	4.313	4.294	----	----	----	4.306	----	----	----	4.302
2019	----	----	----	----	----	----	----	----	----	4.174	4.197	4.053	4.141
2020	4.174	4.250	4.334	4.396	4.466	4.517	4.536	4.504	4.487	4.522	4.485	4.520	4.433
2021	4.591	4.673	4.671	4.752	4.566	4.605	4.562	4.726	4.733	4.800	4.816	4.965	4.705
2022	5.135	5.247	5.410	5.529	5.835	5.793	6.112	6.235	6.170	6.408	6.356	6.465	5.891
2023	6.358	6.351	6.184	6.040	6.094	6.091	6.141	6.091	6.085	6.178	6.169	6.092	6.156

[1] Roasted in 13.1 to 20 ounce cans. *Source: Foreign Agricultural Service, U.S. Department of Agriculture (FAS-USDA)*

Average Price of Colombian Mild Arabicas[1] in the United States · In Cents Per Pound

Year	Jan.	Feb.	Mar.	Apr.	May	June	July	Aug.	Sept.	Oct.	Nov.	Dec.	Average
2016	135.21	137.17	145.20	143.66	144.49	156.86	164.46	160.78	168.85	172.28	177.85	156.64	155.29
2017	164.96	163.67	158.40	154.97	151.41	146.12	152.51	155.15	151.47	144.26	144.09	141.62	152.39
2018	143.77	141.50	139.45	139.29	140.26	138.55	133.92	129.99	125.74	140.83	139.27	127.86	136.70
2019	129.28	127.93	125.23	124.42	124.40	133.49	137.63	129.20	131.90	132.09	146.12	161.50	133.60
2020	147.52	146.43	158.99	161.92	154.96	147.16	153.38	167.22	168.36	154.28	161.21	170.44	157.66
2021	173.42	176.96	177.49	181.70	198.99	206.53	218.66	225.40	240.38	258.87	279.56	290.57	219.04
2022	294.93	306.36	285.81	292.76	286.44	301.57	286.07	295.66	294.09	261.95	223.22	224.12	279.42
2023	218.91	238.39	225.23	234.85	226.93	211.85	190.58	187.55	184.98	185.97	195.85	210.18	209.27

[1] ICO monthly and composite indicator prices on the New York Market, 1979 ICA Agreement basis. *Source: Foreign Agricultural Service, U.S. Department of Agriculture (FAS-USDA)*

Average Price of Other Mild Arabicas[1] in the United States · In Cents Per Pound

Year	Jan.	Feb.	Mar.	Apr.	May	June	July	Aug.	Sept.	Oct.	Nov.	Dec.	Average
2016	145.03	147.70	157.50	154.22	155.19	165.45	171.76	167.54	176.30	178.96	184.12	161.78	163.80
2017	168.61	166.35	160.15	155.40	150.00	143.22	149.66	149.88	146.56	140.71	140.90	137.42	150.74
2018	138.81	136.28	135.03	134.34	135.61	134.03	130.60	125.21	121.18	137.34	137.11	127.10	132.72
2019	128.46	128.45	123.89	121.13	120.55	129.73	135.47	126.23	128.89	126.99	140.98	157.11	130.66
2020	142.19	135.50	148.33	154.52	149.84	141.52	146.78	163.25	166.56	152.06	150.73	157.81	150.76
2021	160.69	166.43	167.05	168.65	186.46	192.45	204.29	216.24	225.54	241.06	258.95	267.71	204.63
2022	271.08	279.83	258.49	265.40	260.42	273.69	255.91	268.43	267.49	240.08	213.85	210.24	255.41
2023	206.76	229.73	222.36	229.56	220.12	207.39	193.49	186.73	183.52	183.95	197.18	210.32	205.93

[1] ICO monthly and composite indicator prices on the New York Market, 1979 ICA Agreement basis. *Source: Foreign Agricultural Service, U.S. Department of Agriculture (FAS-USDA)*

Average Price of Robustas 1976[1] in the United States · In Cents Per Pound

Year	Jan.	Feb.	Mar.	Apr.	May	June	July	Aug.	Sept.	Oct.	Nov.	Dec.	Average
2016	74.71	74.04	75.60	80.18	83.93	85.94	90.82	91.79	96.88	103.65	103.72	101.85	88.59
2017	108.32	106.49	106.73	103.58	98.36	101.95	104.94	104.52	99.18	98.39	91.33	87.59	100.95
2018	88.65	89.24	88.18	88.31	88.74	86.07	84.42	80.74	76.70	85.32	83.52	77.57	84.79
2019	78.24	78.65	76.96	73.28	71.12	74.02	73.93	70.78	70.64	68.63	73.28	73.22	73.56
2020	70.55	68.07	67.46	63.97	64.53	64.62	67.69	72.68	72.77	68.36	72.38	72.04	68.76
2021	70.71	73.37	73.86	74.47	79.68	84.85	94.37	95.18	104.60	105.24	109.40	112.76	89.87
2022	109.71	109.44	103.82	103.96	103.10	103.81	100.44	109.65	111.36	103.01	92.59	93.76	103.72
2023	95.98	103.93	106.49	115.70	122.55	132.13	127.58	124.62	123.89	118.83	122.63	135.09	119.12

[1] ICO monthly and composite indicator prices on the New York Market, 1979 ICA Agreement basis. *Source: Foreign Agricultural Service, U.S. Department of Agriculture (FAS-USDA)*

Average Price of Composite 1979[1] in the United States · In Cents Per Pound

Year	Jan.	Feb.	Mar.	Apr.	May	June	July	Aug.	Sept.	Oct.	Nov.	Dec.	Average
2016	110.89	111.75	117.83	117.93	119.91	127.05	132.98	131.00	138.22	142.68	145.82	131.70	127.31
2017	139.07	145.50	139.67	136.09	131.21	123.71	129.19	131.93	129.67	124.55	124.28	121.47	131.36
2018	123.67	120.83	119.80	118.76	119.57	115.10	110.54	104.46	99.87	115.59	113.27	102.10	113.63
2019	102.94	100.06	95.81	92.47	91.95	100.69	105.43	95.85	98.73	98.10	109.94	126.36	101.53
2020	110.73	102.62	112.87	111.22	101.69	92.56	97.96	111.79	113.81	100.37	106.41	114.96	106.42
2021	116.69	120.06	122.16	124.18	140.85	148.12	160.62	174.89	183.72	199.98	218.90	230.26	161.70
2022	233.80	245.05	222.03	226.23	217.84	230.40	214.80	221.91	219.59	192.27	166.54	169.00	213.29
2023	170.03	195.18	187.02	195.26	186.80	176.48	159.50	154.66	154.19	155.52	169.25	184.73	174.05

[1] ICO monthly and composite indicator prices on the New York Market, 1979 ICA Agreement basis. *Source: Foreign Agricultural Service, U.S. Department of Agriculture (FAS-USDA)*

COFFEE 'C' - ICE-US
Weekly Nearest Futures as of 03/28/2024

WEEKLY NEAREST FUTURES
As of 03/28/2024

Chart High 260.45   on 02/10/2022
Chart Low   86.35   on 04/17/2019

Nearby Futures through Last Trading Day.

Volume of Trading of Coffee "C" Futures in New York   In Thousands of Contracts

Year	Jan.	Feb.	Mar.	Apr.	May	June	July	Aug.	Sept.	Oct.	Nov.	Dec.	Total
2014	567.6	1,140.9	597.0	736.5	458.7	596.7	404.4	619.6	395.0	583.3	610.8	341.8	7,052.2
2015	586.6	795.0	615.1	786.6	596.2	847.1	541.0	964.6	490.3	633.1	864.1	388.4	8,108.1
2016	665.2	983.2	863.9	1,009.1	777.4	1,181.7	554.0	908.3	600.7	695.4	1,092.8	524.6	9,856.3
2017	621.0	824.7	618.4	1,018.5	642.1	1,079.2	637.4	983.2	599.2	701.7	1,135.5	573.0	9,434.1
2018	931.7	1,202.8	818.5	1,357.2	937.4	1,313.8	939.8	1,698.4	734.9	1,493.0	1,342.6	617.5	13,387.7
2019	954.9	1,329.5	980.4	1,766.3	1,246.7	1,552.9	1,096.3	1,277.2	751.0	1,133.9	1,715.1	1,216.9	15,020.9
2020	1,060.2	1,556.0	1,401.1	884.6	716.1	1,157.4	916.7	1,259.8	1,001.2	829.1	1,139.7	635.7	12,557.5
2021	789.1	1,169.0	967.0	1,164.0	821.5	1,182.8	1,171.2	1,202.8	663.3	830.3	1,367.5	635.6	11,964.1
2022	850.1	1,080.8	864.4	891.5	722.2	933.4	677.3	965.0	569.7	983.0	907.8	546.9	9,991.9
2023	1,021.8	1,053.3	858.7	1,010.4	785.5	1,061.2	680.9	1,039.7	697.7	1,027.8	1,138.9	821.3	11,197.1

Contract size = 37,500 lbs.   *Source: ICE Futures U.S. (ICE)*

Average Open Interest of Coffee "C" Futures in New York   In Contracts

Year	Jan.	Feb.	Mar.	Apr.	May	June	July	Aug.	Sept.	Oct.	Nov.	Dec.
2014	146,800	162,005	169,201	160,266	162,103	163,163	161,218	156,931	154,752	168,847	156,410	155,382
2015	166,609	172,443	195,176	190,207	190,814	183,516	186,782	178,827	187,577	188,355	188,664	169,129
2016	193,283	190,752	194,420	190,067	190,161	182,825	182,322	175,300	180,542	194,806	205,128	187,602
2017	184,650	177,790	184,499	200,509	210,358	220,709	222,738	197,922	197,826	225,779	216,415	211,636
2018	232,027	234,405	257,968	267,133	256,291	272,561	306,898	319,784	326,360	303,193	252,010	262,406
2019	289,302	298,522	330,681	339,589	340,252	289,964	266,503	269,809	265,338	297,591	288,911	280,314
2020	288,410	297,314	257,518	231,067	243,733	269,731	270,527	263,448	271,972	275,901	269,054	258,135
2021	268,082	267,944	279,077	280,999	288,427	280,142	286,325	288,914	289,185	305,743	292,093	261,912
2022	268,965	263,173	227,846	214,353	209,923	205,870	197,482	197,924	192,472	198,120	203,558	193,893
2023	218,135	207,232	199,730	193,929	196,506	187,673	194,755	191,019	198,300	209,518	194,478	214,856

Contract size = 37,500 lbs.   *Source: ICE Futures U.S. (ICE)*

Coke

Coke is the hard and porous residue left after certain types of bituminous coals are heated to high temperatures (up to 2,000 degrees Fahrenheit) for about 17 hours. It is blackish-gray and has a metallic luster. The residue is mostly carbon. Coke is used as a reducing agent in the smelting of pig iron and the production of steel. Petroleum coke is made from the heavy tar-like residue of the petroleum refining process. It is used primarily to generate electricity.

Futures on coke are traded on the Dalian Commodity Exchange.

Supply – Production of petroleum coke in the US in 2023 fell by -2.5% yr/yr to 287.160 million barrels and remained below the US production record of 369.305 million barrels posted back in 1957. US stocks of coke at coke plants (Dec 31) in 2022 fell by -14.5% yr/yr to 301,000 tons.

Trade – US coke exports in 2022 rose by +11.9% yr/yr to 2.331 million short tons, and 45.0% of that went to Canada. US coke imports in 2022 fell by -42.5% yr/yr to 67,393 short tons. About 16.5% of US imports were from Canada.

Salient Statistics of Coke in the United States — In Thousands of Short Tons

Year	Total Production	Coke Total	Breeze Total	Consumption[2]	Producer and Distributor Stocks: Dec. 31	Exports	Imports
2016	12,416	11,855	561	11,212	579	1,000	229
2017	13,554	12,948	606	11,815	558	1,209	58
2018	14,507	13,806	701	12,976	354	1,151	117
2019	13,523	12,870	653	11,932	440	967	116
2020	10,860	10,353	507	9,791	481	684	162
2021	13,155	12,545	610	10,708	352	2,083	117
2022[1]	11,868	11,394	474	9,181	301	2,332	67

[1] Preliminary. [2] Equal to production plus imports minus the change in producer and distributor stocks minus exports.
W = Withheld. *Source: Energy Information Administration, U.S. Department of Energy (EIA-DOE)*

Production of Petroleum Coke in the United States — In Thousands of Barrels

Year	Jan.	Feb.	Mar.	Apr.	May	June	July	Aug.	Sept.	Oct.	Nov.	Dec.	Total
2017	28,715	24,498	26,747	27,709	29,018	28,113	29,113	28,358	24,187	26,703	27,286	28,556	329,003
2018	27,460	24,563	27,740	27,003	28,074	27,423	28,199	29,609	26,529	26,862	26,718	29,164	329,344
2019	26,971	22,775	25,638	24,593	24,422	25,582	28,008	27,677	24,694	24,956	26,196	28,599	310,111
2020	28,158	25,862	25,247	21,759	22,173	22,165	24,200	23,099	21,900	22,324	21,675	22,150	280,712
2021	22,350	17,560	21,734	22,152	24,707	25,056	24,927	25,168	23,212	23,057	23,614	25,621	279,158
2022	23,942	21,800	24,420	24,415	25,237	25,633	25,768	25,447	24,271	24,394	24,940	24,214	294,481
2023[1]	18,674	21,701	23,978	23,732	24,772	25,096	26,230	25,713	24,904	23,811	24,619		287,160

[1] Preliminary. *Source: Energy Information Administration, U.S. Department of Energy (EIA-DOE)*

Coke and Breeze Production at Coke Plants in the United States — In Thousands of Short Tons

Year	Middle Atlantic	East North Central	East South Central	Other	U.S. Total	Coke Total	Breeze Total
2016	3,560	6,645	1,231	980	12,416	11,855	561
2017	4,066	7,181	1,238	1,069	13,554	12,948	606
2018	4,353	7,810	1,301	1,043	14,508	13,806	701
2019	4,017	7,278	1,376	852	13,523	12,870	653
2020	2,730	6,225	1,219	687	10,860	10,353	507
2021	4,013	7,262	1,235	645	13,155	12,545	610
2022[1]	3,934	6,651	737	547	1,868	11,394	474

[1] Preliminary. W = Withheld. *Source: Energy Information Administration, U.S. Department of Energy (EIA-DOE)*

Coal Carbonized and Coke and Breeze Stocks at Coke Plants in the United States — In Thousands of Short Tons

	Coal Carbonized at Coke Plants By Census Division					Stocks at Coke Plants, Dec. 31 By Census Division						
Year	Middle Atlantic	East North Central	East South Central	Other	Total	Middle Atlantic	East North Central	East South Central	Other	Total	Coke Total	Breeze Total
2016	4,694	8,947	1,253	1,591	16,485	304	1,024	203	144	1,675	----	----
2017	5,347	9,295	1,308	1,588	17,538	355	1,042	145	176	1,718	----	----
2018	5,731	9,694	1,242	1,670	18,337	444	1,015	197	151	1,807	----	----
2019	5,505	9,772	978	1,712	17,967	446	1,371	286	230	2,333	----	----
2020	3,667	8,441	770	1,536	14,414	364	929	194	167	1,654	----	----
2021	5,292	9,847	752	1,698	17,589	442	886	98	232	1,658	----	----
2022[1]	5,427	9,033	566	983	16,009	496	932	128	71	1,627	----	----

[1] Preliminary. W = Withheld. *Source: Energy Information Administration, U.S. Department of Energy (EIA-DOE)*

Copper

The word *copper* comes from the name of the Mediterranean island Cyprus that was a primary source of the metal. Dating back more than 10,000 years, copper is the oldest metal used by humans. From the Pyramid of Cheops in Egypt, archeologists recovered a portion of a water plumbing system that had copper tubing in serviceable condition after more than 5,000 years.

Copper is one of the most widely used industrial metals because it is an excellent conductor of electricity, has strong corrosion-resistance properties, and is very ductile. It is also used to produce the alloys of brass (a copper-zinc alloy) and bronze (a copper-tin alloy), both of which are far harder and stronger than pure copper. Electrical uses of copper account for about 75% of total copper usage, and building construction is the single largest market (the average U.S. home contains 400 pounds of copper). Copper is biostatic, meaning that bacteria will not grow on its surface, and it is therefore used in air-conditioning systems, food processing surfaces, and doorknobs to prevent the spread of disease.

Copper futures and options are traded on the CME Group and the London Metal Exchange (LME). Copper futures are traded on the Shanghai Futures Exchange. The CME copper futures contract calls for the delivery of 25,000 pounds of Grade 1 electrolyte copper and is priced in terms of cents per pound.

Prices – CME copper futures prices (Barchart.com symbol HG) rallied to a 1-1/2 year high of $4.3145 per pound in January 2023. Protests at copper mines in Peru, the world's second-largest producer, threatened 2% of global copper production and boosted prices. Copper prices were also supported by hopes for increased copper demand from China as it reopened its economy from the pandemic. However, copper prices fell back into mid-2023 as China's recovery was weaker than expected due to the country's ongoing property crisis. Copper prices perked up into July after the dollar index tumbled to a 1-1/2 year low. Prices then reversed and fell to a 1-year low in October of $3.53 per pound. The tepid global recovery curbed copper demand and boosted supplies as LME copper inventories rose to a 2-year high in October. Also, the International Copper Study Group (ICSG) projected a global 2024 copper surplus of 467,000 MT, a 10-year high. Copper prices recovered into year-end on speculation the US Federal Reserve had finished with its cycle of interest rate hikes. Copper prices finished 2023 up +1% yr/yr at $3.8805 per pound.

Supply – World production of copper in 2023 rose by +0.5% yr/yr to a record 22.000 million metric tons. The largest producer of copper was Chile, with 22.7% of the world's production, followed by Peru with 11.8%, China with 7.7%, the US with 5.0%, and Russia with 4.1%. US production of total new copper in 2023 fell by -6.8% yr/yr to 850,000 metric tons, far below the record US production level of 2.140 million metric tons seen in 1998.

Demand – US consumption of refined copper in 2023 fell by -1.2% yr/yr to 1.700 million metric tons. The primary users of copper in the US are wire rod mills, followed by brass mills.

Trade – US exports of refined copper in 2022 fell by -41.5% yr/yr to 27,810 metric tons. US imports of copper in 2022 fell by -20.3% yr/yr to 732,400 metric tons, below the record high of 1.070 million metric tons in 2006.

World Mine Production of Copper (Content of Ore) In Thousands of Metric Tons

Year	Australia	Canada[3]	Chile	China	Indonesia	Mexico	Peru	Poland	Russia	South Africa	United States[3]	Zambia	World Total[2]
2014	970.0	673.0	5,749.6	1780	374.4	515.0	1,379.6	421.7	742	87.6	1,357	708.0	18,410
2015	971.0	697.0	5,764.0	1710	574.5	594.0	1,700.8	425.9	732	77.4	1,383	712.0	19,130
2016	948.0	695.5	5,552.6	1900	710.8	794.0	2,353.9	424.3	702	65.3	1,430	791.3	20,500
2017	856.0	597.2	5,503.5	1706	600.2	742.2	2,445.6	419.3	761	65.5	1,260	829.7	20,100
2018	920.0	542.9	5,831.6	1625	608.1	696.6	2,437.0	401.3	871	46.9	1,220	887.3	20,600
2019	934.0	572.7	5,787.4	1684	350.8	713.7	2,455.4	398.9	812	52.5	1,260	799.9	20,400
2020	885.0	584.6	5,733.1	1723	505.4	732.9	2,154.0	392.7	811	29.1	1,200	852.7	20,600
2021	813.0	550.0	5,620.0	1910	731.0	734.0	2,300.0	391.0	940		1,230	842.0	21,200
2022[1]	819.0	520.0	5,330.0	1940	941.0	754.0	2,450.0	393.0	936		1,230	797.0	21,900
2023[2]	810.0	480.0	5,000.0	1700	840.0	750.0	2,600.0	400.0	910		1,100	760.0	22,000

[1] Preliminary. [2] Estimate. [3] Recoverable.   *Source: U.S. Geological Survey (USGS)*

Commodity Exchange Warehouse Stocks of Copper, on First of Month In Short Tons

Year	Jan. 1	Feb. 1	Mar. 1	Apr. 1	May 1	June 1	July 1	Aug. 1	Sept. 1	Oct. 1	Nov. 1	Dec. 1
2014	13,033	19,224	13,589	19,967	18,292	16,378	19,653	23,912	27,984	34,162	29,759	28,137
2015	26,157	21,289	18,034	26,864	23,316	22,518	30,120	37,283	36,860	40,153	53,517	72,749
2016	69,753	65,615	67,502	71,991	65,495	61,044	62,445	65,416	67,282	70,575	71,961	78,310
2017	88,902	102,072	125,849	144,120	155,295	157,922	163,072	171,314	181,926	196,210	206,099	209,143
2018	210,972	221,036	230,376	233,927	248,744	231,364	223,981	200,039	189,050	172,440	157,434	135,536
2019	110,086	85,970	57,629	42,692	34,300	31,637	33,886	40,110	43,829	39,719	36,285	40,097
2020	37,550	31,415	28,617	32,253	42,268	60,505	62,206	89,049	85,425	79,843	79,945	81,592
2021	77,599	74,238	69,556	71,435	66,536	60,708	49,345	45,885	50,811	56,467	57,235	58,671
2022	69,667	81,066	70,886	74,733	83,504	79,652	74,345	60,740	51,077	44,951	36,971	36,847
2023	35,091	28,543	17,072	16,543	27,647	27,702	33,929	43,460	32,404	25,340	21,921	19,655

Source: CME Group; Commodity Exchange (COMEX)

COPPER

Salient Statistics of Copper in the United States   In Thousands of Metric Tons

Year	New Copper Produced - From Domestic Ores - Mines	Smelters	Refin-eries	From Foreign Ores	Total New	Secon-dary Re-covery	Imports[5] Unmanu-factured	Refined	Exports Ore, Concen-trate[6]	Refined[7]	COMEX	Primary Producers (Refined)	Blister & Material in Solution	Apparent Consumption Refined Copper (Reported)	Primary & Old Copper[8]
2014	1,360	522	535	----	1,050	173	----	620	410	127	24	190	10	1,760	1,780
2015	1,380	527	503	----	1,090	166	----	687	392	86	63	209	14	1,810	1,820
2016	1,430	563	561	----	1,180	149	----	708	331	134	81	223	14	1,800	1,880
2017	1,260	470	482	----	1,040	146	----	813	237	94	191	265	13	1,800	1,860
2018	1,220	536	538	----	1,070	149	----	778	253	190	100	244	9	1,820	1,820
2019	1,260	464	457	----	985	166	----	663	356	125	34	110	16	1,810	1,820
2020	1,200	315	315	----	874	161	----	676	383	41	70	118	9	1,680	1,660
2021	1,230			----	922	157	----	919	344	48		117		1,750	1,950
2022[1]	1,230			----	912	150	----	732	353	28		83		1,720	1,800
2023[2]	1,100			----	850	150	----	890	350	30		100		1,700	1,800

[1] Preliminary.   [2] Estimate.   [3] Also from matte, etc., refinery reports.   [4] From old scrap only.   [5] For consumption.   [6] Blister (copper content).
[7] Ingots, bars, etc.   [8] Old scrap only.   W = Withheld.   *Source: U.S. Geological Survey (USGS)*

Consumption of Refined Copper[3] in the United States   In Thousands of Metric Tons

Year	By-Products Cathodes	Wire Bars	Ingots and Ingot Bars	Cakes & Slabs	Billets	Other[4]	By Class of Consumer Wire Rod Mills	Brass Mills	Chemical Plants	Ingot Makers	Foundries	Miscel-laneous[5]	Total Con-sumption
2011	1,580.0	W	2.5	43.8	W	136.0	1,270.0	430.0	1.5	5.0	17.7	37.5	1,760.0
2012	1,610.0	W	2.3	42.8	W	102.0	1,280.0	424.0	0.3	4.5	19.9	34.3	1,760.0
2013	1,680.0	W	2.1	43.5	W	103.0	1,310.0	457.0	0.2	4.5	18.5	36.2	1,830.0
2014	1,620.0	----	2.9	43.7	----	92.5	1,270.0	424.0	0.2	W	27.9	26.1	1,760.0
2015	1,670.0	----	3.0	42.3	----	99.4	1,320.0	422.0	6.6	W	32.8	26.0	1,810.0
2016	1,660.0	----	3.1	43.7	----	91.6	1,320.0	421.0	0.2	4.6	30.3	25.7	1,800.0
2017	1,660.0	----	4.8	43.9	----	91.4	1,320.0	420.0	0.2	4.6	32.1	25.6	1,800.0
2018	1,650.0	----	4.3	43.8	----	113.0	1,330.0	419.0	0.2	4.6	34.0	26.6	1,820.0
2019[1]	1,650.0	----	3.9	43.9	----	111.0	1,330.0	413.0	0.2	8.7	30.7	23.9	1,810.0
2020[2]	1,620.0	----	3.7	43.7	----	111.0	1,300.0	414.0	0.2	8.9	29.7	23.3	1,770.0

[1] Preliminary.   [2] Estimate.   [3] Primary & secondary.   [4] Includes Wirebars and Billets.   [5] Includes iron and steel plants, primary smelters producing alloys other than copper, consumers of copper powder and copper shot, and other manufacturers.   W = Withheld.
Source: U.S. Geological Survey (USGS)

Salient Statistics of Recycling Copper in the United States

Year	New Scrap[1]	Old Scrap[2]	Recycled Metal[3]	Apparent Supply	Percent Recycled	New Scrap[1]	Old Scrap[2]	Recycled Metal[3]	Apparent Supply
	In Metric Tons					Value in Thousands of Dollars			
2012	642,000	164,000	807,000	2,400,000	34.0	5,200,000	1,330,000	6,530,000	19,400,000
2013	630,000	166,000	797,000	2,390,000	33.0	4,720,000	1,250,000	5,970,000	17,900,000
2014	672,000	173,000	845,000	2,450,000	35.0	4,710,000	1,210,000	5,930,000	17,200,000
2015	640,000	166,000	806,000	2,480,000	33.0	3,610,000	940,000	4,550,000	14,000,000
2016	690,000	149,000	838,000	2,570,000	33.0	3,420,000	737,000	4,160,000	12,800,000
2017	702,000	146,000	847,000	2,560,000	33.0	4,410,000	918,000	5,330,000	16,100,000
2018	712,000	141,000	853,000	2,530,000	34.0	4,690,000	926,000	5,620,000	16,700,000
2019	700,000	166,000	866,000	2,520,000	34.0	4,320,000	1,020,000	5,340,000	15,500,000
2020	697,000	161,000	858,000	2,360,000	36.0	4,410,000	1,010,000	5,420,000	14,900,000
2021	683,000	157,000	840,000	2,630,000	32.0	6,510,000	1,490,000	8,000,000	25,100,000

[1] Scrap that results from the manufacturing process.   [2] Scrap that results from consumer products.   [3] Metal recovered from new plus old scrap.
Source: U.S. Geological Survey (USGS)

Copper Refined from Scrap in the United States   In Metric Tons

Year	Jan.	Feb.	Mar.	Apr.	May	June	July	Aug.	Sept.	Oct.	Nov.	Dec.	Total
2014	3,860	3,870	3,750	3,960	3,810	3,900	3,930	3,430	4,210	3,900	3,800	3,600	46,000
2015	4,030	3,810	4,150	4,180	4,360	3,310	3,570	3,890	4,200	5,010	4,250	4,050	48,800
2016	4,250	7,190	4,900	3,200	3,180	3,260	3,280	3,300	3,810	3,410	3,220	3,330	46,330
2017	3,240	4,090	3,240	3,230	3,380	3,280	3,220	3,340	3,310	3,280	3,240	3,250	40,100
2018	3,220	3,260	3,220	3,260	3,330	3,400	3,390	3,220	3,810	4,180	3,370	3,520	41,180
2019	3,770	3,330	3,950	3,600	3,470	3,480	3,860	5,860	3,360	3,220	3,240	3,240	44,380
2020	3,260	3,220	3,220	4,530	4,380	3,620	3,720	3,380	3,490	3,220	3,290	3,300	42,630
2021	3,220	4,060	3,460	5,190	4,560	5,060	3,340	3,750	4,590	3,540	3,990	4,060	48,820
2022	3,990	3,280	3,490	3,250	3,220	3,370	3,250	3,260	3,220	3,220	3,280	3,240	40,070
2023[1]	3,220	3,230	3,220	3,220	3,260	3,230	3,270	3,220	3,300	3,250	3,220	3,240	38,880

[1] Preliminary.   *Source: U.S. Geological Survey (USGS)*

Imports of Refined Copper into the United States   In Metric Tons

Year	Jan.	Feb.	Mar.	Apr.	May	June	July	Aug.	Sept.	Oct.	Nov.	Dec.	Total
2014	42,900	36,200	45,100	56,200	54,100	53,000	62,900	46,700	59,900	58,600	46,000	58,500	620,000
2015	70,900	50,300	68,700	60,500	56,100	64,500	78,500	47,400	47,800	51,700	44,200	45,400	686,000
2016	57,700	57,700	52,000	53,600	51,800	55,100	61,100	60,200	55,200	64,500	67,100	72,000	708,000
2017	72,600	59,600	84,800	51,900	63,500	66,100	72,500	55,200	86,800	76,500	65,200	58,400	813,100
2018	88,300	77,000	72,900	61,800	64,600	66,200	59,500	59,700	67,300	64,700	51,000	44,500	777,500
2019	57,300	37,800	40,500	65,400	52,400	55,200	68,200	50,600	60,700	69,300	49,000	59,500	665,900
2020	62,300	34,400	70,500	74,300	66,200	63,300	37,300	59,800	39,900	57,300	53,300	57,400	676,000
2021	42,400	73,000	99,700	85,200	66,600	69,600	57,100	105,000	90,700	92,300	60,000	77,300	918,900
2022	140,000	34,300	48,700	64,800	74,300	75,900	80,900	36,400	50,700	49,700	37,900	38,800	732,400
2023[1]	39,000	48,700	126,000	97,900	86,700	92,800	60,300	54,300	59,700	48,800	30,000	26,800	771,000

[1] Preliminary.   Source: U.S. Geological Survey (USGS)

Exports of Refined Copper from the United States   In Metric Tons

Year	Jan.	Feb.	Mar.	Apr.	May	June	July	Aug.	Sept.	Oct.	Nov.	Dec.	Total
2014	9,420	9,000	8,630	5,470	7,670	6,270	10,200	8,360	11,000	11,100	17,300	22,900	127,000
2015	5,860	8,490	10,100	6,620	7,190	9,400	5,870	6,430	4,490	6,110	8,690	7,270	86,500
2016	6,390	16,800	24,800	9,650	22,000	5,600	6,510	6,420	6,630	7,750	13,100	8,040	133,690
2017	12,300	9,100	9,760	12,200	9,230	6,140	7,140	6,680	7,190	5,210	4,400	4,810	94,160
2018	9,550	7,270	12,100	13,700	13,800	11,200	11,300	15,700	15,600	31,000	36,200	12,400	189,820
2019	12,600	13,100	10,200	13,500	11,000	13,800	9,810	6,960	8,410	8,530	9,510	7,830	125,250
2020	4,170	2,470	4,000	1,580	540	1,220	5,300	6,470	4,570	2,930	3,090	5,150	41,490
2021	4,350	2,970	3,360	5,280	5,580	6,880	5,270	1,830	2,300	3,490	2,630	3,630	47,570
2022	2,530	3,110	2,590	2,820	2,890	1,720	1,900	3,060	2,470	1,190	1,430	2,100	27,810
2023[1]	1,190	2,000	1,290	2,020	1,910	1,770	4,700	3,580	3,650	3,910	4,870	3,540	34,430

[1] Preliminary.   Source: U.S. Geological Survey (USGS)

Production of Refined Copper in the United States   In Metric Tons

Year	Jan.	Feb.	Mar.	Apr.	May	June	July	Aug.	Sept.	Oct.	Nov.	Dec.	Total
2014	96,600	87,300	88,400	95,500	99,600	98,400	103,000	101,000	91,600	80,900	70,000	82,300	1,090,000
2015	83,700	85,500	93,900	90,700	86,700	91,000	94,400	93,000	97,600	104,000	107,000	113,000	1,140,000
2016	110,000	99,200	110,000	100,000	103,000	97,500	100,000	101,000	103,000	105,000	98,500	94,100	1,221,300
2017	101,000	93,900	105,000	91,000	84,800	83,000	90,600	99,400	95,700	82,400	70,900	81,200	1,078,900
2018	92,800	92,300	98,000	85,200	90,900	88,000	95,300	97,100	87,000	93,400	96,400	94,700	1,111,100
2019	83,200	68,100	76,400	83,000	86,500	90,000	96,500	94,100	97,000	95,500	W	W	1,030,000
2020	77,900	74,800	78,100	69,100	72,600	71,900	78,400	77,500	74,200	70,900	80,400	81,700	907,500
2021	85,400	82,900	85,000	74,200	74,000	76,700	80,400	84,900	83,500	83,900	79,700	80,800	971,400
2022	84,400	78,600	87,000	78,200	82,300	79,900	81,200	80,400	80,400	81,100	77,200	80,000	970,700
2023[1]	81,400	73,700	79,200	69,600	68,700	72,200	75,400	72,100	70,200	75,200	69,700	73,300	880,700

Recoverable Copper Content.   [1] Preliminary.   Source: U.S. Geological Survey (USGS)

Mine Production of Recoverable Copper in the United States   In Thousands of Metric Tons

Year	Recoverable Copper			Contained Copper		
	Arizona	Others[2]	Total	Electrowon	Concentrates[3]	Total
2014	893.0	464.0	1,360.0	514.0	871.0	1,380.0
2015	985.0	419.0	1,410.0	588.0	851.0	1,440.0
2016	968.5	461.2	1,431.0	614.5	848.9	1,464.0
2017	867.7	391.1	1,257.5	557.5	729.6	1,287.0
2018	801.2	420.8	1,223.1	532.0	715.7	1,247.3
2019	860.8	398.5	1,256.6	527.6	757.7	1,285.9
2020	880.4	317.8	1,198.7	559.1	664.8	1,224.3
2021	872.2	359.9	1,227.8	563.1	692.6	1,254.9
2022	854.5	379.0	1,235.9	555.5	704.1	1,259.8
2023[1]	792.8	320.3	1,112.8	514.8	621.4	1,135.8

[1] Preliminary.   [2] Includes production from Alaska, Idaho, Missouri, Montana, Nevada, New Mexico, and Utah.   [3] Includes copper content of precipitates and other metal concentrates.   Source: U.S. Geological Survey (USGS)

COPPER

Production of Recoverable Copper in Arizona   In Thousands of Metric Tons

Year	Jan.	Feb.	Mar.	Apr.	May	June	July	Aug.	Sept.	Oct.	Nov.	Dec.	Total
2014	69.7	66.6	75.1	70.3	68.6	73.1	75.8	76.2	73.3	82.3	72.1	85.6	893.0
2015	78.4	70.5	80.5	75.9	76.5	77.2	81.3	84.1	83.9	89.3	85.7	90.3	985.0
2016	84.5	79.4	81.6	81.2	83.5	79.8	80.2	86.4	80.1	81.0	74.2	76.6	968.5
2017	71.0	64.2	77.5	72.5	75.1	71.9	73.5	71.2	75.0	66.9	72.8	76.1	867.7
2018	68.8	61.5	68.2	65.4	69.3	70.6	66.8	69.1	63.0	64.0	65.2	69.3	801.2
2019	67.9	63.6	74.0	69.7	71.5	73.4	79.2	77.3	74.0	72.3	66.0	71.9	860.8
2020	70.8	65.4	67.6	76.4	75.5	77.8	79.5	78.9	72.6	71.0	69.9	75.0	880.4
2021	71.6	70.6	76.2	66.9	68.4	74.2	68.2	76.0	78.4	73.1	73.5	75.1	872.2
2022	72.2	65.5	73.1	72.2	77.9	73.9	73.3	69.6	69.7	68.9	66.8	71.4	854.5
2023[1]	67.4	62.0	67.8	67.3	66.0	70.2	69.0	66.7	64.6	63.1	63.0	65.7	792.8

[1] Preliminary.   *Source: U.S. Geological Survey (USGS)*

Production of Recoverable Copper in the United States   In Thousands of Metric Tons

Year	Jan.	Feb.	Mar.	Apr.	May	June	July	Aug.	Sept.	Oct.	Nov.	Dec.	Total
2014	115.0	105.0	119.0	113.0	113.0	111.0	116.0	113.0	116.0	112.0	99.3	121.0	1,360.0
2015	111.0	105.0	121.0	111.0	109.0	109.0	121.0	119.0	117.0	124.0	122.0	126.0	1,410.0
2016	122.0	118.0	122.0	121.0	123.0	117.0	115.0	127.0	117.0	125.0	112.0	112.0	1,431.0
2017	110.0	98.7	114.0	109.0	107.0	109.0	104.0	102.0	99.5	99.3	104.0	101.0	1,257.5
2018	102.0	89.2	96.0	100.0	99.1	113.0	105.0	108.0	99.8	101.0	103.0	107.0	1,223.1
2019	97.8	97.1	108.0	101.0	105.0	106.0	117.0	114.0	112.0	101.0	95.7	102.0	1,256.6
2020	99.6	94.0	96.0	101.0	102.0	105.0	106.0	105.0	97.9	96.5	95.7	100.0	1,198.7
2021	96.7	96.4	104.0	95.5	99.0	103.0	99.2	108.0	107.0	106.0	106.0	107.0	1,227.8
2022	106.0	97.6	105.0	103.0	108.0	103.0	107.0	102.0	102.0	100.0	99.3	103.0	1,235.9
2023[1]	92.4	85.2	91.9	90.3	90.9	93.8	100.0	96.3	92.7	91.7	91.0	96.6	1,112.8

[1] Preliminary.   *Source: U.S. Geological Survey (USGS)*

Production of Contained (Electrowon) Copper in the United States   In Thousands of Metric Tons

Year	Jan.	Feb.	Mar.	Apr.	May	June	July	Aug.	Sept.	Oct.	Nov.	Dec.	Total
2014	42.9	38.5	41.3	41.1	41.4	41.6	43.0	43.0	43.3	47.3	42.9	47.2	514.0
2015	44.5	40.5	46.6	45.4	46.0	45.9	48.3	52.4	54.5	55.3	53.8	55.7	588.0
2016	54.5	48.5	51.4	49.7	51.7	50.7	54.0	52.7	51.4	53.3	48.7	47.9	614.5
2017	46.8	41.6	49.0	45.6	48.6	46.6	44.9	46.9	46.7	46.6	46.6	47.6	557.5
2018	46.8	40.5	44.3	43.2	46.0	44.9	46.0	45.4	43.0	43.1	43.0	45.8	532.0
2019	42.4	39.8	44.6	41.3	44.7	45.9	47.6	46.5	44.7	45.8	41.1	43.2	527.6
2020	44.6	41.0	44.9	44.6	48.2	48.3	49.6	49.1	45.7	47.6	47.1	48.4	559.1
2021	47.1	43.9	46.5	44.0	44.4	46.6	47.2	51.3	49.0	50.4	45.8	46.9	563.1
2022	45.4	40.3	48.5	44.9	49.1	46.5	47.5	46.7	46.7	48.5	44.5	46.9	555.5
2023[1]	45.5	37.8	43.3	43.4	42.4	46.0	47.7	44.5	42.5	43.0	37.6	41.1	514.8

[1] Preliminary.   *Source: U.S. Geological Survey (USGS)*

Production of contained Copper (Concentrates[2]) in the United States   In Thousands of Metric Tons

Year	Jan.	Feb.	Mar.	Apr.	May	June	July	Aug.	Sept.	Oct.	Nov.	Dec.	Total
2014	74.5	69.4	80.2	74.8	74.0	71.8	75.5	73.0	74.8	69.2	58.6	76.3	871.0
2015	69.0	67.0	77.4	68.1	65.9	65.2	76.1	69.8	67.4	71.3	70.9	73.1	851.0
2016	70.4	72.8	73.0	73.9	74.0	69.0	63.7	76.9	67.6	74.9	66.1	66.6	848.9
2017	66.9	59.4	67.9	66.0	60.9	64.7	61.6	57.0	55.0	54.8	59.7	55.7	729.6
2018	56.9	50.7	53.7	58.8	55.2	70.1	61.4	64.6	59.1	59.8	62.4	63.0	715.7
2019	57.6	59.5	65.7	62.3	62.8	62.1	72.3	70.5	69.8	57.0	56.7	61.4	757.7
2020	57.2	55.1	53.1	58.8	55.7	58.6	58.9	57.9	54.3	50.8	50.6	53.8	664.8
2021	51.7	54.7	59.9	53.6	56.8	59.0	54.1	58.8	60.8	57.9	62.3	63.0	692.6
2022	62.8	59.4	58.4	59.9	60.9	58.2	61.3	57.4	57.4	53.8	56.8	57.8	704.1
2023[1]	48.8	49.4	50.5	48.8	50.5	49.8	54.8	53.8	52.0	50.6	55.5	56.9	621.4

[1] Preliminary.   [2] Includes copper content of precipitates and other metal concentrates.   *Source: U.S. Geological Survey (USGS)*

Production of Contained Copper in the United States   In Thousands of Metric Tons

Year	Jan.	Feb.	Mar.	Apr.	May	June	July	Aug.	Sept.	Oct.	Nov.	Dec.	Total
2014	117.0	108.0	121.0	116.0	115.0	113.0	118.0	116.0	118.0	116.0	102.0	123.0	1,380.0
2015	113.0	108.0	124.0	114.0	112.0	111.0	124.0	122.0	122.0	127.0	125.0	129.0	1,440.0
2016	125.0	121.0	124.0	124.0	126.0	120.0	118.0	130.0	118.0	128.0	115.0	115.0	1,464.0
2017	114.0	101.0	117.0	112.0	109.0	111.0	107.0	104.0	102.0	101.0	106.0	103.0	1,287.0
2018	104.0	91.3	98.0	102.0	101.0	115.0	107.0	110.0	102.0	103.0	105.0	109.0	1,247.3
2019	99.9	99.2	110.0	104.0	108.0	108.0	120.0	117.0	114.0	103.0	97.8	105.0	1,285.9
2020	102.0	96.1	98.0	103.0	104.0	107.0	109.0	107.0	100.0	98.5	97.7	102.0	1,224.3
2021	98.8	98.5	106.0	97.6	101.0	106.0	101.0	110.0	110.0	108.0	108.0	110.0	1,254.9
2022	108.0	99.8	107.0	105.0	110.0	105.0	109.0	104.0	104.0	102.0	101.0	105.0	1,259.8
2023[1]	94.3	87.2	93.9	92.3	92.9	95.7	102.0	98.3	94.5	93.6	93.1	98.0	1,135.8

[1] Preliminary.   Source: U.S. Geological Survey (USGS)

Production of Copper at Smelters in the United States   In Thousands of Metric Tons

Year	Jan.	Feb.	Mar.	Apr.	May	June	July	Aug.	Sept.	Oct.	Nov.	Dec.	Total
2014	47.4	47.6	51.3	48.1	53.4	49.7	57.3	54.4	34.7	21.0	17.0	40.2	522.0
2015	47.8	42.8	45.7	34.9	40.7	42.6	41.8	40.3	39.6	48.7	46.5	55.1	527.0
2016	45.6	46.1	41.4	47.3	51.9	45.4	33.1	47.7	54.0	51.9	43.3	55.0	562.7
2017	48.9	47.8	52.2	40.7	20.1	37.1	45.8	47.2	49.0	29.3	14.5	37.8	470.4
2018	53.9	42.2	41.5	44.8	39.0	45.7	47.5	46.1	40.8	48.2	45.3	40.6	535.6
2019	34.7	17.7	37.0	32.9	54.1	51.8	34.5	49.2	43.2	43.8	W	W	464.0
2020	30.0	30.0	30.0	20.0	20.0	20.0	25.0	25.0	25.0	30.0	30.0	30.0	315.0
2021	35.0	35.0	35.0	25.0	25.0	25.0	30.0	30.0	30.0	30.0	30.0	30.0	360.0
2022	35.0	35.0	35.0	30.0	30.0	30.0	35.0	35.0	35.0	29.4	29.4	25.0	383.8
2023[1]	40.0	40.0	40.0	28.0	28.0	28.0	22.0	22.0	22.0	36.0	36.0	36.0	378.0

[1] Preliminary.   Source: U.S. Geological Survey (USGS)

Production of Copper at Brass Mills in the United States   In Thousands of Metric Tons

Year	Jan.	Feb.	Mar.	Apr.	May	June	July	Aug.	Sept.	Oct.	Nov.	Dec.	Total
2014	78.0	85.0	82.6	80.5	81.4	79.7	76.7	79.1	79.5	78.4	79.1	77.2	954.0
2015	77.8	78.9	76.9	74.3	73.8	75.0	72.7	74.1	74.6	74.2	72.5	72.7	891.0
2016	73.6	73.6	75.0	73.5	72.3	72.3	72.8	74.4	72.5	74.8	72.7	72.3	879.8
2017	73.5	72.8	74.2	72.2	74.7	73.3	73.0	75.0	74.0	74.1	72.5	72.1	881.4
2018	73.6	72.7	74.3	73.6	73.6	73.9	73.4	73.8	73.5	74.3	73.5	73.8	884.0
2019	74.2	73.5	74.2	73.7	73.8	73.6	70.3	73.8	73.2	73.9	73.2	72.7	880.1
2020	73.7	73.9	74.5	72.5	73.4	73.7	73.5	73.7	73.8	74.4	73.6	73.7	884.4
2021	73.9	74.1	74.7	75.0	73.2	74.2	74.6	76.0	74.0	74.6	74.5	74.4	893.2
2022	74.3	76.0	76.9	76.3	74.2	74.8	74.6	75.3	79.9	75.4	74.9	74.8	907.4
2023[1]	76.4	75.3	77.0	73.5	72.9	73.1	73.7	74.8	74.1	74.7	71.2	73.5	890.2

[1] Preliminary.   Source: U.S. Geological Survey (USGS)

Production of Copper at Wire-rod Mills in the United States   In Thousands of Metric Tons

Year	Jan.	Feb.	Mar.	Apr.	May	June	July	Aug.	Sept.	Oct.	Nov.	Dec.	Total
2014	115.0	104.0	102.0	110.0	111.0	110.0	115.0	113.0	104.0	118.0	99.9	78.8	1,280.0
2015	118.0	105.0	118.0	114.0	116.0	116.0	112.0	109.0	108.0	114.0	95.9	92.2	1,320.0
2016	112.0	109.0	117.0	109.0	110.0	115.0	98.5	118.0	107.0	115.0	112.0	94.3	1,316.8
2017	114.0	105.0	117.0	112.0	112.0	115.0	97.2	119.0	115.0	117.0	106.0	92.5	1,321.7
2018	114.0	107.0	115.0	103.0	115.0	118.0	99.3	124.0	110.0	114.0	113.0	97.7	1,330.0
2019	113.0	103.0	117.0	104.0	116.0	109.0	110.0	112.0	113.0	112.0	101.0	93.5	1,303.5
2020	110.0	110.0	108.0	94.6	95.3	89.4	108.0	104.0	105.0	108.0	106.0	101.0	1,239.3
2021	104.0	102.0	125.0	115.0	120.0	119.0	112.0	117.0	118.0	115.0	115.0	86.1	1,348.1
2022	117.0	103.0	118.0	117.0	112.0	111.0	117.0	112.0	116.0	115.0	94.8	82.2	1,315.0
2023[1]	95.6	98.5	108.0	97.5	100.0	85.2	101.0	103.0	103.0	100.0	93.5	84.7	1,170.0

[1] Preliminary.   Source: U.S. Geological Survey (USGS)

COPPER

Shipments of Copper at Brass Mills in the United States   In Thousands of Metric Tons

Year	Jan.	Feb.	Mar.	Apr.	May	June	July	Aug.	Sept.	Oct.	Nov.	Dec.	Total
2014	78.6	84.9	81.9	80.2	80.6	80.3	76.8	79.1	79.8	78.9	78.0	77.8	954.0
2015	77.7	78.2	76.9	74.7	73.7	74.9	72.9	74.2	74.9	73.5	72.8	73.1	891.0
2016	73.4	73.9	74.2	73.3	73.7	71.2	72.7	73.8	73.5	75.1	72.8	72.1	879.7
2017	72.9	73.1	74.4	72.8	74.5	73.0	73.2	74.2	73.6	74.1	72.8	72.0	880.6
2018	73.5	73.4	74.0	73.6	74.0	73.8	73.7	74.2	73.3	73.9	73.4	73.0	883.8
2019	73.8	73.6	73.8	73.9	74.1	73.5	70.9	73.7	73.3	74.0	73.0	72.2	879.8
2020	74.2	73.6	74.1	73.5	73.4	73.6	73.3	73.6	73.7	74.0	73.8	74.5	885.3
2021	74.0	73.8	74.5	75.3	73.3	74.0	74.8	74.5	74.3	74.4	74.3	74.2	891.4
2022	74.3	75.8	77.0	76.1	74.3	74.9	74.8	75.2	79.4	75.1	74.8	74.3	906.0
2023[1]	75.4	74.5	75.0	74.7	74.0	73.0	73.2	74.9	73.9	74.3	71.8	72.7	887.4

[1] Preliminary.   *Source: U.S. Geological Survey (USGS)*

Shipments of Copper at Wire-rod Mills in the United States   In Thousands of Metric Tons

Year	Jan.	Feb.	Mar.	Apr.	May	June	July	Aug.	Sept.	Oct.	Nov.	Dec.	Total
2014	113.0	106.0	102.0	112.0	110.0	107.0	112.0	112.0	108.0	115.0	95.3	91.7	1,280.0
2015	109.0	109.0	120.0	113.0	114.0	113.0	110.0	111.0	106.0	114.0	100.0	92.2	1,310.0
2016	110.0	108.0	113.0	108.0	111.0	113.0	99.9	121.0	112.0	111.0	109.0	97.7	1,313.6
2017	117.0	98.0	120.0	104.0	117.0	117.0	97.4	125.0	109.0	118.0	108.0	89.8	1,320.2
2018	114.0	107.0	117.0	111.0	113.0	114.0	102.0	120.0	111.0	120.0	108.0	92.1	1,329.1
2019	116.0	110.0	112.0	111.0	112.0	116.0	113.0	116.0	110.0	114.0	100.0	94.1	1,324.1
2020	106.0	106.0	112.0	96.2	91.4	96.1	104.0	111.0	107.0	110.0	106.0	97.8	1,243.5
2021	106.0	103.0	123.0	117.0	117.0	119.0	114.0	113.0	120.0	110.0	110.0	95.1	1,347.1
2022	114.0	107.0	116.0	112.0	116.0	115.0	114.0	115.0	119.0	114.0	94.7	79.7	1,316.4
2023[1]	95.6	102.0	105.0	91.7	101.0	93.5	97.0	101.0	101.0	108.0	94.6	79.6	1,170.0

[1] Preliminary.   *Source: U.S. Geological Survey (USGS)*

Consumption of Refined Copper at Brass Mills in the United States   In Thousands of Metric Tons

Year	Jan.	Feb.	Mar.	Apr.	May	June	July	Aug.	Sept.	Oct.	Nov.	Dec.	Total
2014	39.0	36.5	38.8	38.6	35.4	37.4	35.4	35.2	35.2	34.4	35.9	35.1	424.0
2015	35.5	35.3	35.7	36.2	35.1	34.8	33.8	35.2	35.5	34.9	35.3	35.0	422.0
2016	34.8	35.7	35.4	34.9	34.4	35.5	35.5	35.6	35.4	35.4	34.4	33.8	420.8
2017	34.6	34.8	35.3	34.2	35.3	34.7	35.0	35.3	35.2	35.4	34.7	34.9	419.4
2018	34.6	35.1	34.9	35.1	34.9	34.9	34.8	35.1	35.1	34.9	34.7	34.6	418.7
2019	34.9	34.8	34.9	34.9	35.4	34.2	34.1	34.0	34.1	34.2	34.1	33.1	412.7
2020	34.5	33.6	33.6	34.5	34.1	34.7	34.3	34.7	34.6	34.6	34.6	34.8	412.6
2021	34.7	34.9	35.3	34.3	34.1	34.2	34.4	34.5	34.7	34.7	34.3	34.7	414.8
2022	34.9	34.8	36.6	34.6	34.9	34.8	34.9	35.0	34.9	35.0	35.0	35.2	420.6
2023[1]	34.7	36.2	34.1	35.8	35.9	35.2	35.5	35.2	35.0	36.5	31.8	33.3	419.2

[1] Preliminary.   *Source: U.S. Geological Survey (USGS)*

Consumption of Refined Copper at Wire-rod Mills in the United States   In Thousands of Metric Tons

Year	Jan.	Feb.	Mar.	Apr.	May	June	July	Aug.	Sept.	Oct.	Nov.	Dec.	Total
2014	115.0	104.0	102.0	111.0	107.0	111.0	115.0	113.0	103.0	114.0	98.8	78.5	1,270.0
2015	118.0	105.0	118.0	113.0	116.0	116.0	112.0	109.0	108.0	113.0	97.5	95.8	1,320.0
2016	110.0	107.0	116.0	107.0	108.0	115.0	98.3	119.0	107.0	116.0	116.0	93.2	1,312.5
2017	113.0	114.0	116.0	112.0	113.0	114.0	96.3	106.0	115.0	118.0	106.0	91.8	1,315.1
2018	114.0	107.0	115.0	105.0	115.0	106.0	104.0	121.0	122.0	112.0	113.0	98.0	1,332.0
2019	116.0	106.0	123.0	119.0	114.0	110.0	107.0	116.0	110.0	118.0	112.0	104.0	1,355.0
2020	120.0	117.0	104.0	107.0	102.0	95.3	107.0	103.0	105.0	106.0	105.0	99.9	1,271.2
2021	93.4	96.1	119.0	108.0	119.0	112.0	108.0	113.0	112.0	109.0	110.0	81.8	1,281.3
2022	111.0	101.0	114.0	113.0	109.0	107.0	112.0	106.0	101.0	105.0	83.7	88.7	1,251.4
2023[1]	91.1	91.2	104.0	92.4	96.6	86.4	94.4	99.8	96.0	90.3	86.9	84.3	1,113.4

[1] Preliminary.   *Source: U.S. Geological Survey (USGS)*

Consumption of Refined Copper at Other Plants[2] in the United States   In Thousands of Metric Tons

Year	Jan.	Feb.	Mar.	Apr.	May	June	July	Aug.	Sept.	Oct.	Nov.	Dec.	Total
2014	4.9	5.0	5.0	5.0	5.0	5.0	5.0	5.0	5.0	5.0	5.0	5.0	59.4
2015	4.7	4.7	4.7	4.7	4.7	4.7	4.7	4.7	4.7	4.7	4.7	4.7	56.2
2016	5.8	5.8	5.8	5.8	5.8	5.8	5.8	5.8	5.8	5.8	5.8	5.8	69.8
2017	5.6	5.6	5.6	5.6	5.6	5.6	5.6	5.1	5.1	5.1	5.1	5.1	64.7
2018	5.2	5.2	5.2	5.2	5.2	5.2	5.2	5.2	5.2	5.2	5.2	5.2	62.0
2019	5.5	5.5	5.5	5.5	5.5	5.5	5.5	5.5	5.5	5.5	5.5	5.5	65.4
2020	5.5	5.5	5.5	5.5	5.5	5.5	5.5	5.5	5.5	5.5	5.5	5.5	65.4
2021	5.2	5.2	5.2	5.2	5.2	5.2	5.2	5.2	5.2	5.2	5.2	5.2	62.2
2022	3.6	3.6	3.6	3.6	3.6	3.6	3.6	3.6	3.6	3.6	3.6	3.6	43.1
2023[1]	3.6	3.6	3.6	3.6	3.6	3.6	3.6	3.6	3.6	3.6	3.6	3.6	43.1

[1] Preliminary.   [2] Monthly estimates based on reported and annual data, comprising stocks at ingot makers, chemical plants, foundries, and miscellaneous manufacturers.   *Source: U.S. Geological Survey (USGS)*

Consumption of Refined Copper in the United States   In Thousands of Metric Tons

Year	Jan.	Feb.	Mar.	Apr.	May	June	July	Aug.	Sept.	Oct.	Nov.	Dec.	Total
2014	159.0	146.0	146.0	155.0	147.0	153.0	156.0	154.0	143.0	153.0	140.0	119.0	1,760.0
2015	158.0	145.0	158.0	154.0	155.0	155.0	150.0	149.0	148.0	152.0	137.0	135.0	1,800.0
2016	150.0	149.0	157.0	148.0	149.0	156.0	140.0	160.0	148.0	157.0	156.0	133.0	1,803.0
2017	153.0	154.0	157.0	152.0	154.0	155.0	137.0	147.0	156.0	159.0	145.0	132.0	1,801.0
2018	154.0	147.0	155.0	145.0	155.0	146.0	144.0	161.0	163.0	152.0	153.0	138.0	1,813.0
2019	156.0	146.0	163.0	159.0	154.0	150.0	147.0	155.0	150.0	158.0	151.0	142.0	1,831.0
2020	160.0	156.0	143.0	146.0	142.0	135.0	147.0	143.0	145.0	147.0	145.0	140.0	1,749.0
2021	134.0	136.0	159.0	147.0	158.0	151.0	147.0	153.0	152.0	148.0	150.0	122.0	1,757.0
2022	149.0	140.0	154.0	152.0	147.0	146.0	151.0	145.0	140.0	144.0	122.0	127.0	1,717.0
2023[1]	129.0	131.0	142.0	132.0	136.0	125.0	133.0	139.0	135.0	130.0	122.0	121.0	1,575.0

[1] Preliminary.   *Source: U.S. Geological Survey (USGS)*

Copper Stocks in the United States at Yearend   In Metric Tons

Year	Crude Copper[2]	Refined Copper Refineries[3]	Wire-rod Mills[3]	Brass Mills[3]	Other[4]	Comex	LME[5]	Total Refined
2014	9.9	9.5	42.0	6.4	4.4	24.2	102.0	189.0
2015	13.9	12.0	36.2	7.6	7.6	63.3	83.8	210.0
2016	14.4	4.2	26.7	7.4	5.7	80.1	98.9	223.0
2017	12.6	5.8	27.8	7.9	5.5	192.0	27.1	265.0
2018	9.2	3.9	21.8	8.2	5.4	99.6	104.0	243.0
2019	16.4	7.0	20.0	7.5	7.1	34.1	35.0	111.0
2020	9.4	3.9	10.7	7.9	7.1	70.2	18.3	118.0
2021	16.1	5.4	11.5	9.1	6.9	63.8	20.2	117.0
2022	13.3	9.1	18.0	11.0	6.2	31.7	6.9	82.8
2023[1]	10.5	6.8	16.9	9.7	6.2	17.2	70.1	127.0

[1] Preliminary.   [2] Copper content of blister and anode.   [3] Stocks of refined copper as reported; no estimates are made for nonrespondents.   [4] Monthly estimates based on reported and 2011 annual data, comprising stocks at ingot makers, chemical plants, foundries, and miscellaneous manufacturers. [5] London Metal Exchange Ltd., U.S. warehouses.   *Source: U.S. Geological Survey (USGS)*

Stocks of Crude Copper[2] in the United States, at End of Month   In Thousands of Metric Tons

Year	Jan.	Feb.	Mar.	Apr.	May	June	July	Aug.	Sept.	Oct.	Nov.	Dec.
2014	13.4	13.8	18.4	15.1	22.2	14.7	10.3	15.9	15.7	11.3	9.7	9.9
2015	14.2	11.3	11.3	11.3	16.6	15.4	13.2	14.3	21.2	17.9	13.5	13.9
2016	13.7	14.5	13.6	12.4	16.1	19.5	13.5	12.5	12.6	14.7	13.8	14.4
2017	11.7	13.2	13.5	26.1	11.0	11.0	11.0	7.4	12.1	13.6	16.7	12.6
2018	15.0	14.6	9.0	9.9	8.1	14.3	9.7	9.0	9.1	8.9	7.4	9.2
2019	9.6	10.2	15.0	8.9	9.2	13.6	15.5	14.5	8.3	25.4	10.2	16.4
2020	9.6	17.9	7.9	7.4	11.9	11.0	11.3	15.7	13.5	15.2	12.5	9.4
2021	17.5	23.8	15.3	12.4	13.1	10.3	12.3	12.0	10.2	15.7	15.9	16.1
2022	11.8	13.3	12.2	16.1	11.5	13.1	12.9	14.2	14.9	18.5	14.6	13.3
2023[1]	13.6	13.0	14.3	35.1	39.9	34.5	20.4	17.7	15.0	14.3	10.5	10.5

[1] Preliminary.   [2] Copper content of blister and anode.   *Source: U.S. Geological Survey (USGS)*

COPPER

Stocks of Refined Copper at Refineries[2] in the United States, at End of Month   In Thousands of Metric Tons

Year	Jan.	Feb.	Mar.	Apr.	May	June	July	Aug.	Sept.	Oct.	Nov.	Dec.
2014	6.7	7.7	9.2	8.7	8.8	6.8	6.5	9.0	7.1	5.3	6.9	9.5
2015	6.7	8.3	6.6	6.7	5.7	5.5	6.3	8.7	6.6	9.3	8.1	12.0
2016	13.8	8.8	7.9	3.2	4.0	2.8	3.0	5.7	4.2	3.2	4.3	4.2
2017	9.3	8.0	3.9	6.0	5.3	4.7	5.8	5.6	8.7	5.6	4.7	5.8
2018	6.2	7.7	4.8	4.5	5.0	3.6	5.0	4.6	3.1	4.3	5.6	3.9
2019	2.7	2.8	3.0	6.6	3.6	5.0	4.4	5.1	7.2	10.6	6.7	7.0
2020	7.2	7.8	2.8	10.3	3.6	2.1	3.1	4.5	3.7	3.5	3.4	3.9
2021	3.8	5.3	3.4	3.3	2.9	3.2	4.4	3.6	5.4	6.4	5.3	5.4
2022	5.0	4.9	3.7	5.0	3.1	5.8	4.0	4.8	5.6	4.3	3.5	9.1
2023[1]	9.6	6.0	9.2	12.0	10.1	9.1	5.2	6.6	2.2	2.2	3.1	6.8

[1] Preliminary.   [2] As reported; no estimates are made for nonrespondents.   *Source: U.S. Geological Survey (USGS)*

Stocks of Refined Copper at Wire Rod Mills[2] in the United States, at End of Month   In Thousands of Metric Tons

Year	Jan.	Feb.	Mar.	Apr.	May	June	July	Aug.	Sept.	Oct.	Nov.	Dec.
2014	40.8	43.0	45.4	46.3	43.8	36.1	42.7	34.1	36.7	35.7	32.6	42.0
2015	41.2	40.6	38.9	44.7	35.6	36.0	40.5	41.8	43.3	35.6	34.0	36.2
2016	34.6	33.4	28.7	41.6	40.1	24.6	34.1	28.0	30.0	32.0	29.7	26.7
2017	30.3	27.7	34.4	27.9	24.4	22.7	21.5	25.7	24.6	27.4	32.9	27.8
2018	25.5	19.4	19.9	15.0	16.8	16.1	28.7	22.6	18.5	19.9	19.2	21.8
2019	19.7	32.3	24.8	28.1	23.2	20.7	25.0	15.4	16.2	17.5	18.2	20.0
2020	24.8	21.9	28.6	19.9	21.2	17.2	21.2	15.9	14.5	15.3	16.2	10.7
2021	9.2	11.9	13.2	12.8	12.4	19.3	14.0	14.2	13.7	17.2	16.3	11.5
2022	10.9	13.7	15.4	10.6	12.0	11.7	13.1	13.1	15.5	19.2	21.5	18.0
2023[1]	22.1	22.2	22.2	19.0	15.4	19.0	16.5	14.7	16.8	20.1	15.1	16.9

[1] Preliminary.   [2] As reported; no estimates are made for nonrespondents.   *Source: U.S. Geological Survey (USGS)*

Stocks of Refined Copper at Brass Mills[2] in the United States, at End of Month   In Thousands of Metric Tons

Year	Jan.	Feb.	Mar.	Apr.	May	June	July	Aug.	Sept.	Oct.	Nov.	Dec.
2014	6.3	5.9	6.1	6.5	8.3	6.7	6.0	6.3	6.2	6.7	6.0	6.4
2015	6.3	6.6	7.3	6.9	7.6	7.8	7.6	7.6	7.3	7.7	7.4	7.6
2016	8.3	7.8	7.5	8.0	8.7	7.7	7.9	7.9	7.7	7.3	7.1	7.4
2017	7.4	7.3	7.1	8.0	7.4	7.4	7.9	7.7	7.4	7.7	8.2	7.9
2018	8.0	7.9	8.0	7.9	8.2	8.0	8.2	7.9	7.7	7.5	7.7	8.2
2019	8.4	8.3	8.4	8.4	7.3	7.1	7.1	6.9	6.8	6.7	6.6	7.5
2020	7.3	7.3	7.3	7.2	7.7	7.9	7.8	8.2	8.2	8.2	8.1	7.9
2021	8.0	8.6	8.6	7.6	7.9	8.0	8.2	8.3	8.7	8.6	9.1	9.1
2022	9.5	9.9	8.2	8.6	8.3	8.3	8.6	9.0	9.8	10.4	10.8	11.0
2023[1]	10.9	9.4	11.4	11.2	11.7	10.7	10.8	11.1	11.7	10.5	9.5	9.7

[1] Preliminary.   [2] As reported; no estimates are made for nonrespondents.   *Source: U.S. Geological Survey (USGS)*

Total Stocks of Refined Copper in the United States, at End of Month   In Thousands of Metric Tons

Year	Jan.	Feb.	Mar.	Apr.	May	June	July	Aug.	Sept.	Oct.	Nov.	Dec.
2014	246.0	239.0	258.0	246.0	222.0	201.0	198.0	202.0	215.0	210.0	193.0	189.0
2015	182.0	186.0	195.0	197.0	178.0	171.0	166.0	185.0	187.0	190.0	198.0	210.0
2016	220.0	215.0	187.0	172.0	163.0	134.0	149.0	152.0	177.0	192.0	210.0	223.0
2017	241.0	242.0	248.0	243.0	218.0	219.0	222.0	246.0	256.0	268.0	266.0	265.0
2018	286.0	283.0	297.0	315.0	323.0	344.0	357.0	347.0	316.0	283.0	258.0	243.0
2019	229.0	191.0	135.0	128.0	117.0	107.0	117.0	118.0	120.0	117.0	121.0	111.0
2020	93.3	107.0	114.0	120.0	139.0	158.0	165.0	153.0	159.0	140.0	130.0	118.0
2021	111.0	109.0	109.0	101.0	86.6	83.5	76.2	79.5	86.0	91.5	105.0	117.0
2022	132.0	131.0	132.0	133.0	126.0	124.0	125.0	116.0	114.0	106.0	95.1	82.8
2023[1]	77.3	60.5	65.7	73.8	74.4	104.0	101.0	105.0	126.0	142.0	143.0	127.0

[1] Preliminary.   *Source: U.S. Geological Survey (USGS)*

QUARTERLY CASH
As of 03/28/2024
Chart High 492.90 on 03/04/2022
Chart Low 10.69 on 07/31/1940

COPPER
Quarterly Cash as of 03/28/2024

Producer Cathode: to 04/1995; NYMEX Spot: 05/1995 to date.

Producers' Price of Electrolytic (Wirebar) Copper, Delivered to U.S. Destinations   In Cents Per Pound

Year	Jan.	Feb.	Mar.	Apr.	May	June	July	Aug.	Sept.	Oct.	Nov.	Dec.	Average
2014	342.10	334.93	315.05	313.99	320.45	317.04	329.34	322.01	315.28	309.62	308.64	296.45	318.74
2015	271.73	268.95	277.04	281.50	295.59	273.57	254.27	239.79	243.31	243.04	222.34	214.01	257.10
2016	206.43	213.16	228.88	224.08	217.34	216.02	226.98	220.02	219.50	219.55	251.14	262.05	225.43
2017	267.08	274.55	269.56	264.04	260.33	265.44	278.13	301.13	303.66	314.81	314.38	315.32	285.70
2018	324.91	322.49	312.22	314.51	312.31	318.18	286.26	276.64	276.71	283.18	282.25	279.59	299.10
2019	275.49	292.82	297.25	299.38	281.88	275.57	276.24	264.69	267.12	268.29	272.78	284.49	279.67
2020	282.85	266.00	243.96	237.63	245.55	266.32	293.10	298.73	309.80	313.31	326.70	360.80	287.06
2021	369.82	393.69	416.35	432.58	47.62	448.00	443.73	437.72	435.04	453.61	445.52	441.72	397.12
2022	452.50	459.21	477.43	474.26	435.55	424.11	351.49	373.18	359.52	358.77	378.94	392.65	411.47
2023	423.30	419.82	416.11	411.64	385.16	389.81	393.57	386.24	382.04	268.10	379.45	393.15	387.37

Source: American Metal Market (AMM)

Dealers' Buying Price of No. 2 Heavy Copper Scrap in Chicago   In Cents Per Pound

Year	Jan.	Feb.	Mar.	Apr.	May	June	July	Aug.	Sept.	Oct.	Nov.	Dec.	Average
2011	285.00	292.50	299.13	295.00	290.72	295.23	315.00	311.41	293.69	241.55	261.50	256.97	286.48
2012	262.50	287.75	292.50	283.93	280.00	259.64	262.50	262.50	275.39	282.50	270.25	281.39	275.07
2013	287.74	292.24	287.02	272.50	263.18	269.00	255.23	260.55	265.00	274.63	272.76	277.76	273.13
2014	287.02	277.50	266.55	262.73	270.36	269.07	270.64	268.26	262.64	257.24	255.50	240.31	265.65
2015	220.60	205.08	215.50	218.86	232.50	219.77	212.86	195.79	195.12	193.91	184.97	165.64	205.05
2016	160.61	158.50	168.02	169.50	170.26	166.27	173.15	172.20	169.21	170.40	182.00	198.45	171.55
2017	194.80	202.97	199.67	195.50	193.23	191.95	195.50	205.93	213.85	218.95	222.00	220.00	204.53
2018	229.79	231.50	227.50	223.02	222.59	228.17	212.93	201.80	192.45	201.50	199.00	201.50	214.31
2019	196.50	205.87	214.50	218.50	210.32	195.00	193.32	188.68	177.50	177.50	179.50	179.12	194.69
2020	----	----	----	----	----	----	----	----	----	----	----	----	----

Source: American Metal Market (AMM)

COPPER

COPPER, HIGH GRADE - COMEX
Weekly Selected Futures as of 03/28/2024

WEEKLY SELECTED FUTURES
As of 03/28/2024
Chart High 501.00 on 03/07/2022
Chart Low 193.55 on 01/19/2016

Nearby Futures through Last Trading Day using selected contract months: March, May, July, September and December.

Volume of Trading of Copper Futures in Chicago   In Thousands of Contracts

Year	Jan.	Feb.	Mar.	Apr.	May	June	July	Aug.	Sept.	Oct.	Nov.	Dec.	Total
2014	1,049.9	1,236.2	1,401.8	1,422.9	933.0	1,434.3	1,081.3	1,276.8	1,089.7	1,269.0	1,459.4	927.7	14,582.2
2015	1,376.3	1,513.4	1,327.0	1,570.8	1,078.6	1,638.6	1,410.3	1,753.1	1,197.7	1,227.4	1,843.6	1,049.2	16,986.1
2016	1,324.0	1,754.8	1,611.4	2,018.8	1,522.9	2,148.7	1,510.2	1,876.0	1,294.0	1,498.6	3,531.3	1,433.8	21,524.5
2017	1,697.3	2,348.1	1,823.1	2,266.8	1,867.4	2,297.6	1,740.5	2,945.0	2,309.5	2,410.7	2,992.4	2,353.2	27,051.5
2018	2,761.2	3,000.6	2,510.6	3,091.0	2,562.9	3,619.8	2,833.2	3,402.4	2,349.7	2,625.9	2,546.7	1,406.1	32,710.1
2019	2,015.9	2,441.6	1,748.1	2,243.5	2,082.2	2,257.1	1,875.7	2,397.1	1,491.4	1,674.0	2,116.7	1,665.7	24,008.9
2020	2,072.0	2,823.8	2,324.8	1,761.1	1,252.2	2,228.5	1,944.9	2,322.5	1,984.5	1,837.2	2,214.5	1,551.7	24,317.8
2021	1,846.8	2,943.2	2,332.5	2,419.1	2,192.6	2,583.1	1,822.8	2,108.9	1,409.3	1,786.1	1,977.8	1,162.3	24,584.5
2022	1,678.1	2,021.7	1,610.7	1,731.5	1,354.8	2,021.0	1,658.9	2,117.6	1,735.8	1,820.5	2,498.1	1,285.3	21,534.1
2023	1,986.1	2,527.7	2,233.8	2,154.5	1,928.2	2,434.0	1,763.3	2,539.8	1,618.6	2,003.5	2,648.6	1,826.5	25,664.7

Source: CME Group; Commodity Exchange (COMEX)

Average Open Interest of Copper Futures in Chicago   In Contracts

Year	Jan.	Feb.	Mar.	Apr.	May	June	July	Aug.	Sept.	Oct.	Nov.	Dec.
2014	160,638	155,280	153,880	153,104	148,544	148,751	171,388	153,255	146,669	170,902	167,274	155,661
2015	175,389	178,359	165,403	163,159	173,340	174,453	165,716	180,019	153,941	160,277	181,603	175,301
2016	192,827	185,631	174,735	192,037	197,457	211,980	174,617	187,041	193,526	198,811	230,065	233,247
2017	253,784	288,886	266,753	273,442	249,694	258,588	280,781	328,948	300,294	297,370	283,754	254,501
2018	287,421	266,506	275,877	253,876	256,236	273,982	294,730	270,229	234,947	241,389	235,321	214,508
2019	259,860	249,458	255,711	252,487	260,544	273,779	263,606	283,002	239,479	252,253	230,046	244,905
2020	269,401	265,190	211,541	182,166	169,597	186,131	220,836	229,403	240,197	238,695	231,769	245,818
2021	255,134	264,271	239,741	247,277	246,376	220,526	203,022	202,183	188,780	208,237	205,020	175,321
2022	198,849	205,541	197,709	203,487	186,330	188,062	178,699	178,405	164,430	173,241	165,627	158,649
2023	198,433	216,036	207,588	207,017	207,667	210,359	214,489	216,387	202,834	216,204	199,882	183,286

Source: CME Group; Commodity Exchange (COMEX)

Corn

Corn is a member of the grass family of plants and is a native grain of the American continents. Fossils of corn pollen that are over 80,000 years old have been found in lake sediment under Mexico City. Archaeological discoveries show that cultivated corn existed in the southwestern U.S. for at least 3,000 years, indicating that the indigenous people of the region cultivated corn as a food crop long before the Europeans reached the New World. Corn is a hardy plant that grows in many different areas of the world. It can grow at altitudes as low as sea level and as high as 12,000 feet in the South American Andes Mountains. Corn can also grow in tropical climates that receive up to 400 inches of rainfall per year, or in areas that receive only 12 inches of rainfall per year. Corn is used primarily as livestock feed in the United States and the rest of the world. Other uses for corn are alcohol additives for gasoline, adhesives, corn oil for cooking and margarine, sweeteners, and as food for humans. Corn is the largest crop in the U.S., both in terms of dollar value and the number of acres planted.

The largest futures market for corn is at the CME Group. Corn futures also trade at the B3 exchange, the Dalian Commodity Exchange, the Euronext Derivatives Market, the JSE Securities Exchange, the MATba ROFEX exchange, and the Osaka Exchange. The CME futures contract calls for the delivery of 5000 bushels of No. 2 yellow corn at par contract price, No. 1 yellow at 1-1/2 cents per bushel over the contract price, or No. 3 yellow at 1-1/2 cents per bushel below the contract price.

Prices – CME corn futures prices (Barchart.com symbol code ZC) in 2023 posted their high for the year in January at $6.8875 per bushel. Corn prices then traded sideways to slightly lower as concern eased about global corn supplies after an extension of the Black Sea grain export deal with Russia kept Ukrainian grain supplies flowing. Also, the prospects for record-high corn production weighed on prices after the USDA, in its May WASDE report, projected global 2023/24 corn production would climb +6.0% yr/yr to a record 1,219 MMT. Corn prices jumped more than $1 a bushel into June as drought conditions intensified in the US Midwest and stressed corn plants. The condition of the US corn crop deteriorated and fell to 50% in good-to-excellent condition in June, the lowest rating in 10 years. Corn prices then fell back as much-needed rain arrived in the central US, easing drought concerns and improving the condition of the corn crop. Also, the outlook for a bumper US corn crop undercut corn prices as the USDA in its July WASDE report projected US 2023/24 corn production would climb +11.6% yr/yr to a record 15.32 million bushels. In addition, US corn supplies were abundant as the USDA estimated US 2023/24 corn ending stocks would surge +61% yr/yr to a 7-year high of 2.263 million bushels. Corn prices ratcheted lower for the remainder of 2023 and posted a 3-year low of $4.47 per

bushel in November. A record US corn harvest kept the pressure on corn prices after the USDA in its November WASDE report estimated US corn production at a record 15.234 million bushels. Global corn supplies were robust as the USDA projected record global 2023/24 corn production of 1,221 MMT and global corn ending stocks at a 4-year high of 315 MMT. Corn production in Brazil also ramped up as Brazil in 2023 surpassed the US as the world's biggest corn exporter. The USDA estimated Brazil's share of global corn exports in 2023 rose to 32%, better than 23% for the US. Exports of US corn have been declining in recent years as the federal government has been incentivizing the use of domestic grown corn for ethanol, with about 40% of US corn going to supply domestic mills producing ethanol. Corn prices recovered slightly into year-end and finished 2023 down -30.5% yr/yr at $4.7125 a bushel.

Supply – World production of corn in the 2023/24 marketing year is expected to rise by +6.9% yr/yr to 1.235 billion metric tons. The world's largest corn producers are expected to be the US with 31.5% of world production, China with 23.4%, and Brazil with 10.3%. The world area harvested with corn in 2021/22 fell by -0.6% yr/yr to 342.0 million hectares. World ending stocks of corn and coarse grains in 2023/24 are expected to rise by +1.5% yr/yr to 339.5 million metric tons.

US corn production for the 2023/24 marketing year (Sep-Aug) is forecasted to rise by +11.1% yr/yr to 15.234 billion bushels. US farmers are forecasted to harvest 87.096 million acres of corn for grain usage in 2023/24, which is up by +10.0% yr/yr. The US corn yield in 2023/24 is forecasted to rise +0.3% yr/yr to 173.8 bushels per acre. US 2022/23 ending stocks decreased by -1.2% yr/yr to 1.360 billion bushels. The largest corn-producing states in the US in 2023 were Iowa with 16.5% of US production, Illinois with 14.7%, Nebraska with 10.9%, Minnesota with 9.7%, and Indiana with 7.1%.

Demand – World consumption of course grains in the 2023/24 crop year is expected to rise by +2.7% yr/yr to a record high of 1.492 billion metric tons. The largest category of usage in 2022/23, aside from animal feed, was for ethanol production (alcohol fuel) with 5.275 billion bushels, which is 78.6% of total non-feed usage. That was dowb by -1.0% yr/yr. After ethanol, the largest non-feed usage categories are high fructose corn syrup (HFCS) with 6.2% of US usage, glucose and dextrose sugars with 5.5%, corn starch with 3.6%, cereal and other corn products with 3.2%, and alcoholic beverages with 2.4%.

Trade – US exports of corn in 2023/24 are expected to rise by +26.4% yr/yr to 53.342 million metric tons. Brazil's corn exports in 2023/24 are expected to fall by -5.3% yr/yr to 54.000 million metric tons. Argentina's corn exports are expected to rise +78.3% yr/yr to 41.000 million metric tons.

CORN

World Production of Corn or Maize   In Thousands of Metric Tons

Crop Year Beginning Oct. 1	Argentina	Brazil	Canada	China	European Union	India	Indonesia	Mexico	Russia	South Africa	Ukraine	United States	World Total
2014-15	29,750	85,000	11,606	249,764	75,734	24,173	9,000	25,480	11,325	10,629	28,450	361,136	1,058,217
2015-16	29,500	67,000	13,680	264,992	58,748	22,567	10,500	25,971	13,168	8,214	23,333	345,506	1,015,916
2016-17	41,000	98,500	13,889	263,613	61,909	25,900	10,900	27,575	15,305	17,551	27,969	384,778	1,128,230
2017-18	32,000	82,000	14,096	259,071	62,021	28,753	11,900	27,569	13,201	13,104	24,115	371,096	1,081,608
2018-19	51,000	101,000	13,885	257,174	64,351	27,715	12,000	27,671	11,415	11,824	35,805	363,787	1,128,163
2019-20	51,000	102,000	13,404	260,779	66,742	28,766	12,000	26,658	14,275	15,844	35,887	344,651	1,121,873
2020-21	52,000	87,000	13,563	260,670	67,440	31,647	12,600	27,346	13,872	16,951	30,297	357,819	1,128,685
2021-22[1]	49,500	116,000	14,611	272,552	71,549	33,730	12,700	26,762	15,225	16,137	42,126	381,469	1,215,898
2022-23[2]	34,000	137,000	14,539	277,200	52,403	38,085	12,900	28,077	15,832	17,100	27,000	346,739	1,155,631
2023-24[3]	55,000	127,000	15,076	288,842	60,100	35,000	12,900	25,500	17,000	16,800	30,500	389,694	1,235,730

[1] Preliminary.   [2] Estimate.   [3] Forecast.   *Source: Foreign Agricultural Service, U.S. Department of Agriculture (FAS-USDA)*

World Supply and Demand of Coarse Grains   In Millions of Metric Tons/Hectares

Crop Year Beginning Oct. 1	Area Harvested	Yield	Production	World Trade	Total Consumption	Ending Stocks	Stocks as % of Consumption[3]
2014-15	332.6	4.00	1,346.4	174.3	1,281.3	315.2	24.6
2015-16	325.9	4.00	1,304.3	185.8	1,271.5	348.0	27.4
2016-17	338.6	4.20	1,418.9	184.8	1,380.7	386.3	28.0
2017-18	329.8	4.10	1,361.0	191.7	1,374.6	372.7	27.1
2018-19	331.3	4.20	1,401.3	207.0	1,421.9	352.2	24.8
2019-20	333.8	4.30	1,418.7	214.8	1,431.4	339.5	23.7
2020-21	343.6	4.20	1,441.4	235.1	1,458.0	323.0	22.2
2021-22	343.5	4.40	1,500.7	237.0	1,486.0	337.8	22.7
2022-23[1]	334.4	4.30	1,446.0	221.1	1,453.5	330.3	22.7
2023-24[2]	339.5	4.50	1,513.8	238.3	1,492.4	351.7	23.6

[1] Preliminary.   [2] Estimate.   [3] Represents the ratio of marketing year ending stocks to total consumption.   *Source: Foreign Agricultural Service, U.S. Department of Agriculture (FAS-USDA)*

Acreage and Supply of Corn in the United States   In Millions of Bushels

Crop Year Beginning Sept. 1	Planted	Harvested For Grain	Harvested For Silage	Yield Per Harvested Acre Bushels	Carry-over, Sept. 1 On Farms	Carry-over, Sept. 1 Off Farms	Supply Beginning Stocks	Supply Production	Supply Imports	Supply Total Supply
	In Thousands of Acres									
2014-15	90,597	83,136	6,371	171.0	462	770	1,232	14,216	32	15,479
2015-16	88,019	80,753	6,237	168.4	593	1,138	1,731	13,602	68	15,401
2016-17	94,004	86,748	6,186	174.6	627	1,110	1,737	15,148	57	16,942
2017-18	90,167	82,733	6,434	176.6	787	1,506	2,293	14,609	36	16,939
2018-19	88,871	81,276	5,061	176.4	620	1,520	2,140	14,340	28	16,509
2019-20	89,745	81,337	6,615	167.5	814	1,407	2,221	13,620	42	15,883
2020-21	90,652	82,313	6,711	171.4	751	1,169	2,004	14,111	24	16,115
2021-22	92,901	84,988	6,451	176.7	395	840	1,235	15,018	24	16,277
2022-23[1]	88,162	78,705	6,851	173.4	510	867	1,377	13,651	39	15,066
2023-24[2]	94,641	86,513	6,471	177.3	604	756	1,377	15,342	25	16,727

[1] Preliminary.   [2] Estimate.   *Source: Economic Research Service, U.S. Department of Agriculture (ERS-USDA)*

Production of Corn (For Grain) in the United States, by State   In Millions of Bushels

Year	Illinois	Indiana	Iowa	Kansas	Michigan	Minnesota	Missouri	Nebraska	Ohio	South Dakota	Texas	Wisconsin	US Total
2014	2,350.0	1,084.8	2,367.4	566.2	355.8	1,177.8	628.7	1,602.1	610.7	787.4	294.5	485.2	14,215.5
2015	2,012.5	822.0	2,505.6	580.2	335.3	1,428.8	437.4	1,692.8	498.8	799.8	266.0	492.0	13,602.0
2016	2,255.7	946.3	2,740.5	698.6	320.3	1,544.0	570.5	1,699.9	524.7	825.9	323.9	573.2	15,148.0
2017	2,201.0	936.0	2,605.8	686.4	300.5	1,480.2	552.5	1,683.3	557.6	736.6	313.6	509.8	14,609.4
2018	2,268.0	967.7	2,499.0	642.4	289.2	1,357.7	466.2	1,785.6	617.1	777.6	189.0	545.2	14,340.4
2019	1,846.2	814.6	2,583.9	800.7	236.7	1,254.3	463.5	1,785.4	421.5	557.3	286.0	443.2	13,619.9
2020	2,120.1	981.8	2,283.3	766.5	304.5	1,434.4	560.9	1,780.2	564.3	720.9	231.7	506.9	14,111.4
2021	2,191.7	1,027.7	2,539.8	750.6	346.3	1,387.7	545.4	1,854.6	644.6	734.3	236.8	540.0	15,017.8
2022	2,268.4	974.7	2,470.0	510.6	334.3	1,460.6	500.7	1,455.3	594.7	661.3	153.0	538.2	13,650.5
2023[1]	2,276.3	1,077.9	2,522.6	612.9	346.1	1,513.3	561.5	1,729.0	673.2	854.2	256.2	552.6	15,341.6

[1] Preliminary.   *Source: National Agricultural Statistics Service, U.S. Department of Agriculture (NASS-USDA)*

Quarterly Supply and Disappearance of Corn in the United States   In Millions of Bushels

Crop Year Beginning Sept. 1	Beginning Stocks	Pro-duction	Imports	Total Supply	Food & Alcohol	Seed	Feed & Residual	Total	Exports	Total Disap-pearance	Total Ending Stocks
2019-20	2,221	13,620	41.9	15,883	6,256	29.8	5,900	12,186	1,777	13,963	1,919.5
Sept.-Nov.	2,221	13,620	17.9	15,859	1,628	----	2,632	4,260	271	4,531	11,327.3
Dec.-Feb.	11,327	----	8.9	11,336	1,713	----	1,318	3,031	353	3,385	7,951.6
Mar.-May	7,952	----	9.5	7,961	1,333	27.8	995	2,356	602	2,958	5,003.0
June-Aug.	5,003	----	5.6	5,009	1,582	2.1	955	2,539	550	3,089	1,919.5
2020-21	2,004	14,087	24.2	16,115	6,436	30.6	5,667	12,134	2,747	14,881	1,234.5
Sept.-Nov.	2,004	14,087	5.8	16,097	1,612	----	2,219	3,831	449	4,280	11,817.0
Dec.-Feb.	11,817	----	5.4	11,822	1,509	----	1,832	3,341	674	4,016	7,806.8
Mar.-May	7,807	----	7.1	7,814	1,645	29.4	1,000	2,674	1,029	3,703	4,111.2
June-Aug.	4,111	----	6.0	4,117	1,670	1.2	617	2,288	595	2,883	1,234.5
2021-22	1,235	15,018	24.2	16,277	6,728	29.1	5,671	12,427	2,472	14,900	1,376.9
Sept.-Nov.	1,235	15,018	6.7	16,259	1,689	----	2,508	4,197	431	4,628	11,631.2
Dec.-Feb.	11,631	----	7.1	11,638	1,682	----	1,534	3,217	664	3,881	7,757.0
Mar.-May	7,757	----	4.7	7,762	1,683	25.6	851	2,559	854	3,413	4,349.0
June-Aug.	4,349	----	5.8	4,355	1,673	3.5	778	2,454	524	2,978	1,376.9
2022-23[1]	1,377	13,651	38.7	15,066	6,527	31.4	5,486	12,045	1,661	13,706	1,360.2
Sept.-Nov.	1,377	13,651	5.9	15,033	1,627	----	2,310	3,937	283	4,220	10,813.2
Dec.-Feb.	10,813	----	6.2	10,819	1,588	----	1,436	3,024	399	3,423	7,396.4
Mar.-May	7,396	----	9.7	7,406	1,635	29.6	1,005	2,669	634	3,303	4,103.3
June-Aug.	4,103	----	16.9	4,120	1,677	1.9	736	2,415	345	2,760	1,360.2
2023-24[2]	1,360	15,342	25.0	16,727	6,759	31.0	5,675	12,465	2,100	14,565	2,161.8
Sept.-Nov.	1,360	15,342	9.2	16,711	1,685	----	2,480	4,165	377	4,542	12,168.9

[1] Preliminary.   [2] Estimate.   *Source: Economic Research Service, U.S. Department of Agriculture (ERS-USDA)*

Corn Production Estimates and Cash Price in the United States

Crop Year Beginning Sept. 1	Aug. 1	Sept. 1	Oct. 1	Nov. 1	Final	St. Louis No. 2 Yellow	Omaha No. 2 Yellow	Gulf Ports No. 2 Yellow	Kansas City No. 2 White	Chicago No. 2 Yellow	Average Farm Price[2]	Value of Pro-duction (Mil. $)
			In Thousands of Bushels					Dollars Per Bushel				
2014-15	14,031,915	14,395,350	14,474,920	14,407,420	14,215,532	3.82	3.60	4.35	3.75	3.76	3.69	52,952
2015-16	13,686,063	13,584,945	13,554,923	13,653,507	13,601,964	3.80	3.49	4.18	3.75	3.75	3.61	49,339
2016-17	15,153,472	15,092,908	15,057,404	15,225,586	15,148,038	3.64	3.28	3.95	3.62	3.55	3.37	51,304
2017-18	14,152,966	14,184,466	14,280,112	14,577,502	14,609,407	3.63	3.46	4.07	3.71	3.55	3.40	49,568
2018-19	14,586,485	14,826,690	14,777,826	14,625,974	14,340,369	3.85	3.68	4.29	3.98	3.79	3.65	52,102
2019-20	13,900,651	13,799,151	13,779,335	13,661,005	13,619,928	3.74	3.26	3.93	3.65	3.65	3.52	48,941
2020-21	15,278,202	14,899,557	14,721,705	14,506,795	14,111,449	5.66	5.31	6.07	5.55	5.51	4.86	64,314
2021-22	14,750,368	14,996,417	15,018,542	15,062,002	15,017,788	6.84	6.74	7.62	7.48	6.78	6.30	90,616
2022-23	14,358,679	13,943,913	13,895,176	13,929,921	13,650,531	6.57	6.69	7.28	6.76	6.50	6.54	91,730
2023-24[1]	15,110,787	15,133,911	15,064,420	15,234,285	15,341,595	4.78	4.76	5.40		4.83	4.87	

[1] Preliminary.   [2] Season-average price based on monthly prices weigthed by monthly marketings.
Source: Economic Research Service, U.S. Department of Agriculture (ERS-USDA)

Distribution of Corn in the United States   In Millions of Bushels

Crop Year Beginning Sept. 1	HFCS	Glucose & Dextrose	Starch	Fuel	Bev-rage[3]	Seed	Cereal & Other Products	Total	Livestock Feed[4]	Exports (Including Grain Equiv. of Products)	Domestic Disap-pearance	Total Utilization
2014-15	478	298	246	5,200	142	29.3	201	6,595	5,287	1,866.9	11,883	13,750
2015-16	472	337	238	5,224	143	30.6	203	6,647	5,118	1,898.6	11,765	13,664
2016-17	467	371	235	5,432	146	29.3	204	6,885	5,470	2,294.0	12,355	14,649
2017-18	459	371	236	5,605	149	29.6	207	7,057	5,305	2,437.1	12,361	14,798
2018-19	441	355	231	5,378	150	29.1	209	6,793	5,392	2,068.3	12,185	14,253
2019-20	418	356	232	4,857	173	29.9	220	6,286	5,778	1,778.5	12,064	13,843
2020-21	421	365	252	5,028	157	30.6	214	6,466	5,667	2,746.9	12,134	14,881
2021-22	415	371	246	5,320	161	29.1	214	6,757	5,671	2,472.4	12,427	14,900
2022-23[1]	409	343	219	5,176	162	31.4	217	6,558	5,487	1,661.2	12,045	13,706
2023-24[2]	410	350	230	5,375	165	31.0	219	6,780	5,675	2,100.0	12,455	14,555

[1] Preliminary.   [2] Estimate.   [3] Also includes nonfuel industrial alcohol.   [4] Feed and waste (residual, mostly feed).
Source: Economic Research Service, U.S. Department of Agriculture (ERS-USDA)

CORN

#3 yellow, Chicago: to 12/1939; #2 yellow, Chicago: 01/1940 to date.

Average Cash Price of Corn, No. 2 Yellow in Central Illinois   In Dollars Per Bushel

Crop Year	Sept.	Oct.	Nov.	Dec.	Jan.	Feb.	Mar.	Apr.	May	June	July	Aug.	Average
2014-15	3.16	3.09	3.45	3.75	3.67	3.65	3.66	3.59	3.49	3.52	3.85	3.51	3.53
2015-16	3.55	3.67	3.62	3.62	3.55	3.56	3.54	3.61	3.74	3.91	3.28	3.09	3.56
2016-17	3.09	3.27	3.28	3.34	3.45	3.51	3.40	3.41	3.47	3.49	3.51	3.27	3.37
2017-18	3.15	3.15	3.14	3.21	3.29	3.45	3.52	3.54	3.73	3.38	3.22	3.24	3.34
2018-19	3.12	3.28	3.36	3.53	3.53	3.50	3.43	3.37	3.59	4.21	4.29	3.95	3.60
2019-20	3.55	3.79	3.66	3.73	3.82	3.75	3.51	3.06	2.99	3.13	3.21	3.84	3.50
2020-21	3.62	3.97	4.22	4.45	5.23	5.56	5.56	6.27	7.08	6.81	6.49	6.43	5.47
2021-22	5.35	5.37	5.80	6.03	6.16	6.54	7.46	7.93	8.04	7.95	7.09	6.87	6.72
2022-23	6.98	6.79	6.71	6.64	6.78	6.82	6.49	6.66	6.25	6.41	5.78	5.25	6.46
2023-24[1]	4.75	4.75	4.62	4.62	4.46	4.22							4.57

[1] Preliminary.   *Source: Economic Research Service, U.S. Department of Agriculture (ERS-USDA)*

Average Cash Price of Corn, No. 2 Yellow at Gulf Ports[2]   In Dollars Per Bushel

Crop Year	Sept.	Oct.	Nov.	Dec.	Jan.	Feb.	Mar.	Apr.	May	June	July	Aug.	Average
2014-15	4.14	4.15	4.54	4.55	4.44	4.41	4.43	4.38	4.23	4.24	4.56	4.14	4.35
2015-16	4.22	4.36	4.22	4.17	4.09	4.06	4.05	4.17	4.30	4.62	4.11	3.82	4.18
2016-17	3.78	3.88	3.83	3.88	4.07	4.14	4.04	3.98	4.03	4.01	4.00	3.77	3.95
2017-18	3.74	3.77	3.78	3.79	3.96	4.15	4.36	4.46	4.55	4.19	3.98	4.13	4.07
2018-19	3.93	4.07	4.09	4.25	4.24	4.31	4.23	4.11	4.36	4.96	4.81	4.14	4.29
2019-20	4.00	4.25	4.23	4.24	4.36	4.29	4.12	3.73	2.66	3.76	3.88	3.65	3.93
2020-21	4.23	4.74	4.85	5.06	5.89	6.24	6.24	6.82	7.73	7.43	7.07	6.53	6.07
2021-22	----	6.09	6.32	6.72	7.04	7.44	8.54	8.85	8.76	8.53	8.20	7.36	7.62
2022-23	7.94	8.73	8.15	7.68	7.69	7.58	7.18	7.40	6.81	6.78	6.16	5.27	7.28
2023-24[1]	5.68	5.52	5.25	5.13	4.99	4.80							5.23

[1] Preliminary.   [2] Barge delivered to Louisiana Gulf.   *Source: Economic Research Service, U.S. Department of Agriculture (ERS-USDA)*

Weekly Outstanding Export Sales and Cumulative Exports of U.S. Corn   In Thousands of Metric Tons

Marketing Year 2022/2023 Week Ending	Weekly Exports	Accumu-lated Exports	Net Sales	Out-standing Sales	Marketing Year 2023/2024 Week Ending	Weekly Exports	Accumu-lated Exports	Net Sales	Out-standing Sales
Sep 01, 2022	36,819	36,819	1,853,836	11,681,340	Sep 07, 2023	726,028	726,028	753,298	10,433,897
Sep 08, 2022	426,802	463,621	583,110	11,837,648	Sep 14, 2023	602,519	1,328,547	566,857	10,398,235
Sep 15, 2022	563,029	1,026,650	182,339	11,456,958	Sep 21, 2023	729,976	2,058,523	841,783	10,510,042
Sep 22, 2022	574,680	1,601,330	512,045	11,394,323	Sep 28, 2023	612,369	2,670,892	1,815,964	11,713,637
Sep 29, 2022	645,508	2,246,838	227,045	10,975,860	Oct 05, 2023	812,877	3,483,769	910,411	11,811,171
Oct 06, 2022	419,590	2,666,428	197,191	10,753,461	Oct 12, 2023	516,294	4,000,063	881,345	12,176,222
Oct 13, 2022	407,161	3,073,589	408,310	10,754,610	Oct 19, 2023	483,692	4,483,755	1,351,088	13,043,618
Oct 20, 2022	618,958	3,692,547	263,999	10,399,651	Oct 26, 2023	505,885	4,989,640	748,070	13,285,803
Oct 27, 2022	450,158	4,142,705	372,220	10,321,713	Nov 02, 2023	824,884	5,814,524	1,015,320	13,476,239
Nov 03, 2022	259,441	4,402,146	265,335	10,327,607	Nov 09, 2023	683,062	6,497,586	1,807,524	14,600,701
Nov 10, 2022	564,394	4,966,540	1,169,693	10,932,906	Nov 16, 2023	623,813	7,121,399	1,432,407	15,409,295
Nov 17, 2022	462,286	5,428,826	1,850,271	12,320,891	Nov 23, 2023	499,858	7,621,257	1,927,760	16,837,197
Nov 24, 2022	344,485	5,773,311	602,656	12,579,062	Nov 30, 2023	1,086,074	8,707,331	1,288,887	17,040,010
Dec 01, 2022	900,068	6,673,379	691,556	12,370,550	Dec 07, 2023	850,964	9,558,295	1,418,637	17,607,683
Dec 08, 2022	590,514	7,263,893	958,920	12,738,956	Dec 14, 2023	870,882	10,429,177	1,013,095	17,749,896
Dec 15, 2022	958,747	8,222,640	636,811	12,417,020	Dec 21, 2023	1,279,454	11,708,631	1,242,116	17,712,558
Dec 22, 2022	1,012,459	9,235,099	781,583	12,186,144	Dec 28, 2023	681,465	12,390,096	367,484	17,398,577
Dec 29, 2022	761,797	9,996,896	319,242	11,743,589	Jan 04, 2024	1,037,102	13,427,198	487,609	16,849,084
Jan 05, 2023	387,077	10,383,973	255,687	11,612,199	Jan 11, 2024	1,000,420	14,427,618	1,251,109	17,099,773
Jan 12, 2023	715,740	11,099,713	1,132,142	12,028,601	Jan 18, 2024	931,753	15,359,371	954,796	17,122,816
Jan 19, 2023	912,584	12,012,297	910,400	12,026,417	Jan 25, 2024	911,350	16,270,721	1,206,718	17,418,184
Jan 26, 2023	598,291	12,610,588	1,593,223	13,021,349	Feb 01, 2024	782,753	17,053,474	1,219,325	17,854,756
Feb 02, 2023	394,890	13,005,478	1,160,280	13,786,739	Feb 08, 2024	903,258	17,956,732	1,306,889	18,258,387
Feb 09, 2023	670,541	13,676,019	1,024,499	14,140,697	Feb 15, 2024	1,024,525	18,981,257	820,419	18,054,281
Feb 16, 2023	687,399	14,363,418	823,177	14,276,475	Feb 22, 2024	1,216,166	20,197,423	1,082,328	17,920,443
Feb 23, 2023	666,416	15,029,834	598,109	14,208,168	Feb 29, 2024	1,159,489	21,356,912	1,109,591	17,870,545
Mar 02, 2023	1,052,015	16,081,849	1,412,074	14,568,227	Mar 07, 2024	1,258,584	22,615,496	1,283,415	17,895,376
Mar 09, 2023	1,112,432	17,193,281	1,183,747	14,639,542	Mar 14, 2024	1,528,506	24,144,002	1,185,807	17,552,677
Mar 16, 2023	1,381,336	18,574,617	3,095,895	16,354,101	Mar 21, 2024				
Mar 23, 2023	668,188	19,242,805	1,036,432	16,722,345	Mar 28, 2024				
Mar 30, 2023	1,136,820	20,379,625	1,246,607	16,832,132	Apr 04, 2024				
Apr 06, 2023	916,951	21,296,576	527,719	16,442,900	Apr 11, 2024				
Apr 13, 2023	1,298,544	22,595,120	312,442	15,456,798	Apr 18, 2024				
Apr 20, 2023	1,076,270	23,671,390	399,972	14,780,500	Apr 25, 2024				
Apr 27, 2023	1,699,186	25,370,576	-315,639	12,765,675	May 02, 2024				
May 04, 2023	1,146,083	26,516,659	257,279	11,876,871	May 09, 2024				
May 11, 2023	1,086,516	27,603,175	-338,974	10,451,381	May 16, 2024				
May 18, 2023	1,502,794	29,105,969	-75,153	8,873,434	May 23, 2024				
May 25, 2023	1,434,779	30,540,748	186,695	7,625,350	May 30, 2024				
Jun 01, 2023	1,244,740	31,785,488	172,709	6,553,319	Jun 06, 2024				
Jun 08, 2023	1,192,627	32,978,115	273,255	5,633,947	Jun 13, 2024				
Jun 15, 2023	668,316	33,646,431	35,988	5,001,619	Jun 20, 2024				
Jun 22, 2023	605,304	34,251,735	140,387	4,536,702	Jun 27, 2024				
Jun 29, 2023	707,456	34,959,191	251,693	4,080,939	Jul 04, 2024				
Jul 06, 2023	492,711	35,451,902	468,432	4,056,660	Jul 11, 2024				
Jul 13, 2023	383,830	35,835,732	236,809	3,909,639	Jul 18, 2024				
Jul 20, 2023	409,142	36,244,874	311,929	3,812,426	Jul 25, 2024				
Jul 27, 2023	626,168	36,871,042	107,521	3,293,779	Aug 01, 2024				
Aug 03, 2023	478,426	37,349,468	150,434	2,965,787	Aug 08, 2024				
Aug 10, 2023	444,842	37,794,310	233,471	2,754,416	Aug 15, 2024				
Aug 17, 2023	496,472	38,290,782	-22,726	2,235,218	Aug 22, 2024				
Aug 24, 2023	663,383	38,954,165	71,737	1,643,572	Aug 29, 2024				
Aug 31, 2023	514,958	39,469,123	-15,236	1,113,378	Aug 31, 2023				

Source: Foreign Agricultural Service, U.S. Department of Agriculture (FAS-USDA)

CORN

Average Price Received by Farmers for Corn in the United States   In Dollars Per Bushel

Crop Year	Sept.	Oct.	Nov.	Dec.	Jan.	Feb.	Mar.	Apr.	May	June	July	Aug.	Average
2014-15	3.49	3.57	3.60	3.79	3.82	3.79	3.81	3.75	3.64	3.59	3.80	3.68	3.69
2015-16	3.68	3.67	3.59	3.65	3.66	3.58	3.56	3.56	3.68	3.82	3.60	3.21	3.61
2016-17	3.22	3.29	3.24	3.32	3.40	3.44	3.49	3.43	3.45	3.43	3.49	3.27	3.37
2017-18	3.27	3.26	3.15	3.23	3.29	3.38	3.51	3.58	3.68	3.58	3.47	3.36	3.40
2018-19	3.40	3.42	3.41	3.54	3.56	3.60	3.61	3.53	3.63	3.98	4.16	3.93	3.65
2019-20	3.80	3.85	3.68	3.71	3.79	3.78	3.68	3.29	3.20	3.16	3.21	3.12	3.52
2020-21	3.41	3.61	3.79	3.97	4.24	4.75	4.89	5.31	5.91	6.00	6.12	6.32	4.86
2021-22	5.47	5.02	5.26	5.47	5.58	6.09	6.56	7.07	7.26	7.38	7.25	7.24	6.30
2022-23	7.09	6.49	6.49	6.58	6.63	6.80	6.67	6.70	6.54	6.49	6.22	5.73	6.54
2023-24[1]	5.21	4.93	4.66	4.80	4.74	4.36							4.78

[1] Preliminary.   *Source: Economic Research Service, U.S. Department of Agriculture (ERS-USDA)*

Corn Price Support Data in the United States

Crop Year Beginning Sept. 1	National Average Loan Rate[3]	Target Price	Placed Under Loan	% of Production	Acquired by CCC	Owned by CCC Aug. 31	CCC Inventory As of Dec. 31 — CCC Owned	Under CCC Loan	Quantity Pledged (Thousands of Bushels)	Face Amount (Thousands of Dollars)
	--- Dollars Per Bushel -----		------------------------------ Millions of Bushels ----------------------------							
2012-13	1.95	2.63	368	3.4	0	0	0	----	367,998	675,046
2013-14	1.95	2.63	460	3.3	0	0	0	----	460,885	823,153
2014-15	1.95	3.70	574	4.0	0	0	0	----	7,822	16,432
2015-16	1.95	3.70	746	5.5	0	0	0	----	44,185	110,902
2016-17	1.95	3.70	880	5.8	0	0	0	----	59,619	116,982
2017-18	1.95	3.70	980	6.7	0	0	0	----	885,563	1,689,795
2018-19	1.95	3.70	919	6.4	0	0	0	----	78,890	152,614
2019-20	2.20	3.70	805	5.9	0	0	0	----	66,091	130,973
2020-21[2]	2.20									
2021-22[2]	2.20									

[1] Preliminary.   [2] Estimate.   [3] Findley or announced loan rate.   NA = Not available.
Source: National Agricultural Statistics Service, U.S. Department of Agriculture (NASS-USDA)

U.S. Exports[1] of Corn (Including Seed), By Country of Destination   In Thousands of Metric Tons

Crop Year Beginning Oct. 1	Algeria	Canada	Egypt	Israel	Japan	Mexico	Korea, South	Russia	Saudi Arabia	Spain	Taiwan	Vene-zuela	Total
2013-14	76	604	2,940	469	12,379	5,312	10,895	----	1,030	693	1,772	1,058	50,599
2014-15	239	1,444	1,127	26	11,832	3,645	11,220	1	1,184	66	1,830	806	46,758
2015-16	663	926	792	388	11,187	3,881	13,535	----	1,522	66	2,302	1,078	50,989
2016-17	91	650	258	107	12,579	4,762	14,297	----	2,029	205	2,663	384	55,561
2017-18	48	1,724	1,640	757	13,811	6,047	15,498	----	1,577	1,167	2,766	440	63,569
2018-19	----	2,395	225	134	12,558	3,292	15,688	----	770	1	1,721	95	49,223
2019-20	43	1,712	49	497	10,086	2,894	14,506	----	850	0	779	469	46,970
2020-21	181	1,736	506	542	11,053	3,319	15,658	0	717	0	1,655	413	68,225
2021-22	----	6,013	22	225	11,097	1,371	16,788	----	763	498	801	480	62,827
2022-23[2]	----	1,986	0	27	6,868	826	16,474	----	553	58	713	243	42,724

[1] Excludes exports of corn by-products.   [2] Preliminary.   *Source: Foreign Agricultural Service, U.S. Department of Agriculture (FAS-USDA)*

Stocks of Corn (Shelled and Ear) in the United States   In Millions of Bushels

Year	On Farms Mar. 1	June 1	Sept. 1	Dec. 1	Off Farms Mar. 1	June 1	Sept. 1	Dec. 1	Total Stocks Mar. 1	June 1	Sept. 1	Dec. 1
2014	3,860,500	1,863,200	462,000	7,087,000	3,147,623	1,988,516	769,904	4,124,380	7,008,123	3,851,716	1,231,904	11,211,380
2015	4,380,000	2,275,000	593,000	6,829,000	3,369,806	2,177,988	1,138,164	4,406,178	7,749,806	4,452,988	1,731,164	11,234,178
2016	4,335,000	2,471,400	627,400	7,611,000	3,487,233	2,239,679	1,109,658	4,774,776	7,822,233	4,711,079	1,737,058	12,385,776
2017	4,908,000	2,841,400	787,000	7,739,000	3,713,992	2,387,682	1,506,303	4,827,501	8,621,992	5,229,082	2,293,303	12,566,501
2018	5,002,000	2,750,100	620,000	7,451,000	3,890,126	2,554,704	1,520,335	4,485,798	8,892,126	5,304,804	2,140,335	11,936,798
2019	5,131,000	2,949,600	814,100	7,103,000	3,482,206	2,252,636	1,406,649	4,224,338	8,613,206	5,202,236	2,220,749	11,327,338
2020	4,454,000	2,867,000	750,800	7,046,000	3,497,576	2,135,987	1,168,662	4,247,750	7,951,576	5,002,987	1,919,462	11,293,750
2021	4,036,500	1,743,600	394,900	7,234,000	3,659,648	2,367,581	839,612	4,407,181	7,696,148	4,111,181	1,234,512	11,641,181
2022	4,079,000	2,120,700	509,500	6,740,000	3,678,036	2,228,268	867,390	4,073,207	7,758,036	4,348,968	1,376,890	10,821,207
2023[1]	4,105,000	2,216,800	604,400	7,830,000	3,291,403	1,886,509	755,801	4,341,163	7,396,403	4,103,309	1,360,201	12,171,163

[1] Preliminary.   *Source: National Agricultural Statistics Service, U.S. Department of Agriculture (NASS-USDA)*

CORN - CBOT
Weekly Selected Futures as of 03/28/2024

WEEKLY SELECTED FUTURES
As of 03/28/2024
Chart High 827.00 on 04/29/2022
Chart Low 300.25 on 04/29/2020

Nearby Futures through Last Trading Day using selected contract months: March, May, July, September and December.

Volume of Trading of Corn Futures in Chicago   In Thousands of Contracts

Year	Jan.	Feb.	Mar.	Apr.	May	June	July	Aug.	Sept.	Oct.	Nov.	Dec.	Total
2014	5,790.8	7,614.4	5,772.2	6,996.2	4,613.5	6,677.8	4,938.4	5,781.3	3,784.4	5,875.4	7,439.7	4,153.1	69,437.3
2015	5,468.9	6,810.9	6,111.2	7,860.2	5,957.5	10,795.4	8,553.2	7,835.9	4,880.3	5,708.6	8,736.5	4,375.5	83,094.3
2016	5,878.1	7,858.5	6,061.1	11,510.4	6,909.2	11,322.0	6,258.8	7,704.5	4,498.0	5,321.4	8,319.7	3,983.4	85,625.2
2017	5,911.2	8,379.3	6,001.8	8,751.1	6,167.8	11,804.7	8,516.1	9,294.9	4,606.4	5,878.6	10,685.8	3,879.2	89,876.8
2018	6,474.5	10,818.8	8,754.6	10,249.8	8,164.3	11,485.8	6,613.3	8,637.0	5,584.7	6,586.2	9,690.5	4,327.7	97,387.2
2019	6,008.6	10,270.7	7,945.3	10,348.0	13,559.8	13,195.1	8,041.4	10,317.4	5,322.1	6,103.5	8,302.7	3,774.4	103,189.1
2020	6,270.8	8,339.9	7,778.8	8,115.2	4,561.6	10,234.8	7,114.3	9,064.2	5,978.7	8,256.3	8,792.8	5,245.7	89,753.1
2021	8,734.6	8,568.1	6,261.9	10,045.0	7,913.4	10,020.6	5,491.8	7,366.9	4,903.3	4,961.3	8,162.8	4,472.6	86,902.0
2022	6,340.1	9,255.5	7,185.7	7,292.9	5,420.9	8,335.2	5,943.2	7,017.8	4,738.7	5,015.7	7,303.6	4,031.5	77,880.8
2023	5,681.3	7,239.0	7,314.0	7,307.7	7,579.5	10,968.6	6,916.4	7,373.4	4,325.1	5,623.3	8,839.2	3,943.0	83,110.5

Contract size = 5,000 bu.   *Source: CME Group; Chicago Board of Trade (CBT)*

Average Open Interest of Corn Futures in Chicago   In Thousands of Contracts

Year	Jan.	Feb.	Mar.	Apr.	May	June	July	Aug.	Sept.	Oct.	Nov.	Dec.
2014	1,284.5	1,343.4	1,318.8	1,396.1	1,338.9	1,370.7	1,332.4	1,316.6	1,254.5	1,289.5	1,298.1	1,216.6
2015	1,291.3	1,332.4	1,296.8	1,360.9	1,370.6	1,428.7	1,350.7	1,346.0	1,253.1	1,309.6	1,365.9	1,291.4
2016	1,374.6	1,372.9	1,349.8	1,432.1	1,364.2	1,438.5	1,297.8	1,353.5	1,303.9	1,322.3	1,345.3	1,227.3
2017	1,306.7	1,431.1	1,403.8	1,443.3	1,364.3	1,406.1	1,377.3	1,412.7	1,378.6	1,496.8	1,641.6	1,522.8
2018	1,623.6	1,670.6	1,821.7	1,837.2	1,852.3	1,950.0	1,850.8	1,729.7	1,693.3	1,659.4	1,702.9	1,574.6
2019	1,646.1	1,720.2	1,769.3	1,774.3	1,688.8	1,789.0	1,781.6	1,732.2	1,612.6	1,597.3	1,589.0	1,471.0
2020	1,530.9	1,576.5	1,435.7	1,441.2	1,428.9	1,564.1	1,531.9	1,525.6	1,458.9	1,601.4	1,733.7	1,684.7
2021	1,884.2	1,940.5	1,774.0	1,769.6	1,706.6	1,671.3	1,486.5	1,436.3	1,383.0	1,416.8	1,550.9	1,469.5
2022	1,517.3	1,567.6	1,505.9	1,569.4	1,531.1	1,488.7	1,321.3	1,315.2	1,317.5	1,419.8	1,403.2	1,208.5
2023	1,249.3	1,323.7	1,324.6	1,300.5	1,283.2	1,285.6	1,277.1	1,278.7	1,289.5	1,378.0	1,404.3	1,264.7

Contract size = 5,000 bu.   *Source: CME Group; Chicago Board of Trade (CBT)*

Corn Oil

Corn oil is a bland, odorless oil produced by refining the crude corn oil that is mechanically extracted from the germ of the plant seed. High-oil corn, the most common type of corn used to make corn oil, typically has an oil content of 7% or higher compared to about 4% for normal corn. Corn oil is widely used as cooking oil, for making margarine and mayonnaise, and for making inedible products such as soap, paints, inks, varnishes, and cosmetics. For humans, studies have shown that no vegetable oil is more effective than corn oil in lowering blood cholesterol levels.

Prices –The average monthly price of corn oil (wet mill price in Chicago) in the 2022/23 marketing year (Oct-Sep) fell by -3.5% to 62.00 cents per pound.

Supply – US corn oil production in 2022/23 marketing year rose by +0.2% yr/yr to 6.100 billion pounds. US stocks in the 2022/23 marketing year (beginning Oct 1) fell by -4.9% to 148 million pounds.

Demand – US usage (domestic disappearance) in 2022/23 remain unchanged yr/yr at 5.978 billion pounds.

Exports – US corn oil exports in 2021/22 rose by +17.9% to 320 million pounds. US corn oil imports in 2022/23 rose by +28.6% to 200 million pounds.

Supply and Disappearance of Corn Oil in the United States   In Millions of Pounds

		Supply			Baking and Frying Fats	Salad and Cooking Oil	Marg- arine	Total Edible Products	Domestic Disap- pearance	Exports	Total Disap- pearance
Crop Year	Stocks Oct. 1	Pro- duction	Imports	Total Supply							
2013-14	165	3,890	42.0	4,097	----	----	----	----	2,928	1,004	3,932
2014-15	165	4,740	39.0	4,944	----	----	----	----	3,870	909	4,779
2015-16	165	5,300	83.0	5,548	----	----	----	----	4,289	1,094	5,383
2016-17	165	5,850	74.0	6,089	----	----	----	----	4,841	1,120	5,961
2017-18	127	6,066	63.0	6,256	----	----	----	----	5,423	728	6,152
2018-19	104	5,765	65.0	5,934	----	----	----	----	5,279	573	5,852
2019-20	82	5,394	54.2	5,530	----	----	----	----	4,946	482	5,428
2020-21	102	5,724	51.3	5,877	----	----	----	----	5,297	424	5,721
2021-22[1]	156	6,088	155.5	6,400	----	----	----	----	5,980	271	6,251
2022-23[2]	148	6,100	200.0	6,448	----	----	----	----	5,978	320	6,298

[1] Preliminary.   [2] Estimate.   W = Withheld.   *Source: Economic Research Service, U.S. Department of Agriculture (ERS-USDA)*

Production[2] of Crude Corn Oil in the United States   In Millions of Pounds

Crop Year	Oct.	Nov.	Dec.	Jan.	Feb.	Mar.	Apr.	May	June	July	Aug.	Sept.	Total
2004-05	208.8	187.1	191.0	205.2	182.5	206.6	217.2	188.2	211.5	206.7	198.5	189.0	2,392
2005-06	207.5	199.9	200.3	209.2	184.8	217.6	191.7	218.7	206.7	215.3	222.0	209.0	2,483
2006-07	228.7	216.0	226.1	224.7	187.9	216.4	194.1	214.4	212.7	219.8	209.5	209.4	2,560
2007-08	213.5	213.0	214.0	205.4	193.7	222.5	190.7	220.9	193.7	214.9	217.3	207.3	2,507
2008-09	206.3	210.6	198.7	200.3	199.8	218.8	189.4	202.5	189.0	186.0	201.4	215.8	2,419
2009-10	212.9	205.2	203.2	197.9	188.1	212.4	214.7	205.4	214.7	216.8	213.6	200.1	2,485
2010-11[1]	205.1	211.2	198.9	220.9	199.4	218.1	203.1	215.0	216.3	205.7			2,512

[1] Preliminary.   [2] Not seasonally adjusted.   *Source: Bureau of the Census, U.S. Department of Commerce*

Average Corn Oil Price, Wet Mill in Chicago   In Cents Per Pound

Crop Year	Oct.	Nov.	Dec.	Jan.	Feb.	Mar.	Apr.	May	June	July	Aug.	Sept.	Average
2014-15	34.50	33.96	33.68	34.86	36.13	37.73	39.27	39.50	40.34	41.49	40.75	37.55	37.48
2015-16	36.60	36.43	38.25	39.93	40.29	41.05	42.12	40.33	39.94	38.86	39.06	38.11	39.25
2016-17	36.22	36.83	38.12	37.89	38.11	37.90	37.63	37.71	38.00	37.53	36.75	36.48	37.43
2017-18	34.96	34.46	33.96	30.68	29.72	29.66	29.50	29.65	29.54	28.76	26.80	26.46	30.35
2018-19	27.18	26.37	26.46	26.21	25.65	26.72	27.94	27.76	27.38	26.75	27.31	27.48	26.93
2019-20	28.30	30.36	31.25	33.30	36.00	36.94	44.88	47.64	51.34	45.45	44.75	43.38	39.47
2020-21	42.44	42.53	41.73	43.34	44.95	52.05	59.81	68.25	67.60	66.10	64.16	53.19	53.85
2021-22	57.07	57.92	56.09	54.09	59.29	67.19	71.55	77.80	76.38	62.25	65.44	66.26	64.28
2022-23	65.41	69.67	60.00	61.00	NA	NA	NA	52.00	NA	NA	NA	NA	61.62
2023-24[1]	NA	NA	NA	NA									

[1] Preliminary.   *Source: Economic Research Service, U.S. Department of Agriculture (ERS-USDA)*

Cotton

Cotton is a natural vegetable fiber that comes from small trees and shrubs of a genus belonging to the mallow family, one of which is the common American Upland cotton plant. Cotton has been used in India for at least the last 5,000 years and probably much longer, and was also used by the ancient Chinese, Egyptians, and North and South Americans. Cotton was one of the earliest crops grown by European settlers in the U.S.

Cotton requires a long growing season, plenty of sunshine and water during the growing season, and then dry weather for harvesting. In the United States, the Cotton Belt stretches from northern Florida to North Carolina and westward to California. In the U.S., planting time varies from the beginning of February in Southern Texas to the beginning of June in the northern sections of the Cotton Belt. The flower bud of the plant blossoms and develops into an oval boll that splits open at maturity. At maturity, cotton is most vulnerable to damage from wind and rain. Approximately 95% of the cotton in the U.S. is now harvested mechanically with spindle-type pickers or strippers and then sent off to cotton gins for processing. There it is dried, cleaned, separated, and packed into bales.

Cotton is used in a wide range of products, from clothing to home furnishings to medical products. The value of cotton is determined by the staple, grade, and character of each bale. Staple refers to short, medium, long, or extra-long fiber length, with medium staple accounting for about 70% of all U.S. cotton. Grade refers to the color, brightness, and amount of foreign matter and is established by the U.S. Department of Agriculture. Character refers to the fiber's diameter, strength, body, maturity (ratio of mature to immature fibers), uniformity, and smoothness. Cotton is the fifth leading cash crop in the U.S. and is one of the nation's principal agricultural exports. The weight of cotton is typically measured in terms of a "bale," which equals 480 pounds.

Cotton futures and options are traded at the ICE Futures U.S exchange. Cotton futures are also traded on the B3 exchange and the Multi Commodity Exchange of India, and the Zhengzhou Commodity Exchange. Cotton yarn futures are traded on the Zhengzhou Commodity Exchange. The ICE Futures U.S. exchange's futures contract calls for the delivery of 50,000 pounds net weight (approximately 100 bales) of No. 2 cotton with a quality rating of Strict Low Middling and a staple length of 1-and-2/32 inch. Delivery points include Texas (Galveston and Houston), New Orleans, Memphis, and Greenville/Spartanburg in South Carolina.

Prices – ICE cotton futures prices (Barchart.com symbol CT) moved slightly lower in the first half of 2023. Weak global cotton consumption weighed on prices after the USDA, in its March WASDE report, forecasted that global 2022/23 cotton consumption would fall -5% yr/yr to a 3-year low of 110 million bales. The decline in consumption pushed global cotton ending stocks up to a 3-year high of 91.15 million bales. Weak cotton consumption in Turkey, the world's fifth-biggest cotton importer, weighed on prices after an earthquake shuttered 80% of the country's cotton yarn capacity. The March USDA planting intentions report

was bearish for cotton as the USDA estimated US 2023 cotton acreage of 11.3 million acres, above expectations of 11 million acres. Cotton prices recovered into mid-2023 as demand improved after the USDA, in the May WASDE report estimated global 2023/24 cotton consumption of 116.23 million bales, above expectations of 114.79 million bales. Cotton prices posted their high for 2023 in September of 90.75 cents a pound. An El Nino weather event in 2023 was bullish for cotton prices since an El Nino pattern typically brings drought to India, the world's second-biggest cotton producer. In the September WASDE report, the USDA cut its 2023/24 global cotton production estimate to 112.30 million bales, below expectations of 113.50 million bales. However, cotton prices turned lower late in the year and posted the low for 2023 of 74.77 cents a pound in November. Improved growing conditions in the US boosted the US cotton crop as the USDA, in its November WASDE report, projected US cotton production at 13.09 bales, higher than expectations of 12.73 million bales. Also, in December, Cotlook raised its global 2023/24 cotton surplus estimate to 559,000 MT from a November estimate of 188,000 MT. Cotton prices finished 2023 down -2.8% yr/yr at 81.00 cents a pound.

Supply – World cotton production in 2023/24 is forecasted to decrease by -2.9% yr/yr to 113.179 million bales (480 pounds per bale), below the 2011/12 record high of 127.244 million bales. The world's largest cotton producers are forecasted to be China with 24.3% of world production in 2024/25, India with 22.1%, Brazil with 12.9%, the US with 11.0%, and Pakistan with 5.9%. World ending stocks in 2023/24 are forecasted to rise by +1.4% yr/yr to 84.382 million bales, below the 2014/15 record high of 105.293.

The US cotton crop in 2023/24 is forecasted to fall by -14.1% yr/yr to 12.434 million bales, below the 2005/06 record high of 23.890 million bales. US farmers are forecasted to harvest 8.020 million acres of cotton in 2023/24, up by +9.8% yr/yr. The US cotton yield in 2023/24 is forecasted to fall by -19.5% yr/yr to 765 pounds per acre, below the 2022/23 record high of 950 pounds per acre. The leading US producing states for cotton in 2023 were Texas with 24.5% of US production, Georgia with 18.4%, Arkansas with 11.0%, Missouri with 7.1%, Mississippi with 6.7%, North Carolina with 5.8%, and Alabama with 5.6%.

Demand – World cotton consumption in 2023/24 is forecasted to rise by +1.1% yr/yr to 112.425 million bales. The largest consumers of cotton in 2023/24 are expected to be China with 32.5% of the world total, India with 21.1%, and Pakistan with 8.7%. The US consumption of cotton by mills in 2023/24 is expected to fall by -7.3% yr/yr to 1.900 million bales.

Trade – World exports of cotton in 2023/24 are expected to rise by +16.5% yr/yr to 43.052 million bales, below the record high of 48.999 million bales posted in 2020/21. Major world cotton importers for 2023/24 are expected to be China with 26.7% of total world imports, Bangladesh with 18.6%, Vietnam with 15.6%, Turkey with 9.5%, and Pakistan with 8.8%.

COTTON

Supply and Distribution of All Cotton in the United States   In Thousands of 480-Pound Bales

Crop Year Beginning Aug. 1	Planted --- Acre --- Harvested --- 1,000 Acres ---		Yield Lbs./Acre	Beginning Stocks[3]	Pro-duction[4]	Supply Imports	Total	Mill Use	Exports	Total	Unac-counted	Ending Stocks	Farm Price[5]	"A" Index Price[6]	Value of Pro-duction Million USD
2014-15	11,037	9,347	838	2,350	16,319	12	18,681	3,575	11,246	18,681	-210	3,650	65.7	----	5,147.2
2015-16	8,581	8,075	766	3,650	12,888	33	16,571	3,450	9,153	16,571	-168	3,800	64.5	----	3,989.0
2016-17	10,074	9,508	867	3,800	17,170	7	20,977	3,250	14,917	20,977	-60	2,750	70.5	----	5,813.8
2017-18	12,718	11,100	905	2,750	20,923	3	23,676	3,225	16,281	23,676	-30	4,200	71.9	----	7,222.5
2018-19	14,100	9,991	882	4,200	18,367	3	22,570	2,975	14,833	22,570	-88	4,850	72.3	----	6,375.2
2019-20	13,736	11,613	810	4,850	19,913	3	24,766	2,150	15,512	24,766	-146	7,250	61.4	----	5,865.1
2020-21	12,092	8,275	847	7,250	14,608	2	21,860	2,400	16,352	21,860	-42	3,150	68.3	----	4,828.8
2021-22	11,207	10,263	820	3,150	17,523	5	20,678	2,550	14,481	20,678	-403	4,050	94.7	----	7,963.0
2022-23[1]	13,749	7,290	953	4,050	14,468	2	18,520	2,050	12,766	18,520	-546	4,250	89.1	----	6,186.0
2023-24[2]	10,230	7,065	845	4,250	12,434	5	16,689	1,900	12,100	16,689	-211	2,900	77.7	----	4,635.2

[1] Preliminary.   [2] Estimate.   [3] Excludes preseason ginnings (adjusted to 480-lb. bale net weight basis).   [4] Includes preseason ginnings.   [5] Marketing year average price.   [6] Average of 5 cheapest types of SLM 1 3/32" staple length cotton offered on the European market.
Source: Economic Research Service, U.S. Department of Agriculture (ERS-USDA)

World Production of All Cotton   In Thousands of 480-Pound Bales

Crop Year Beginning Aug. 1	Australia	Brazil	Burkina	China	Greece	India	Mexico	Pakistan	Türkiye	Turkmen-istan	United States	Uzbek-istan	World Total
2014-15	2,300	7,960	1,350	30,000	1,286	29,500	1,319	10,600	3,200	1,525	16,319	3,900	120,006
2015-16	2,850	7,180	1,100	22,000	1,010	25,900	943	7,000	2,650	1,450	12,888	3,800	97,604
2016-17	4,050	5,920	1,310	22,750	1,033	27,000	765	7,700	3,200	1,325	17,170	4,410	106,287
2017-18	4,800	7,020	1,200	27,500	1,222	29,000	1,560	8,200	4,000	1,340	20,923	4,360	122,154
2018-19	2,200	9,220	850	28,000	1,410	26,000	1,735	7,600	3,750	910	18,367	2,770	114,532
2019-20	625	13,000	880	27,450	1,675	28,500	1,570	6,200	3,450	920	19,913	2,440	119,102
2020-21	2,800	13,780	950	29,600	1,400	27,500	1,020	4,500	2,900	920	14,608	3,180	113,995
2021-22	5,850	10,820	960	26,800	1,400	24,300	1,220	6,000	3,800	900	17,523	2,865	114,463
2022-23[1]	5,800	11,720	775	30,700	1,450	26,300	1,580	3,900	4,900	900	14,468	3,300	116,561
2023-24[2]	5,100	14,560	700	27,500	950	25,000	925	6,700	3,200	900	12,434	2,900	113,179

[1] Preliminary.   [2] Estimate.   *Source: Foreign Agricultural Service, U.S. Department of Agriculture (FAS-USDA)*

World Consumption of Cotton   In Thousands of 480-Pound Bales

Crop Year Beginning Aug. 1	Bangla-desh	Brazil	China	India	Indonesia	Mexico	Pakistan	Thailand	Türkiye	United States	Uzbek-istan	Vietnam	World Total
2014-15	5,800	3,400	34,500	24,500	3,250	1,950	10,700	1,475	6,500	3,575	1,750	4,100	112,422
2015-16	6,300	3,100	36,000	24,750	3,000	1,850	10,300	1,325	6,700	3,450	1,800	4,500	113,324
2016-17	6,800	3,200	38,500	24,350	3,300	1,800	10,400	1,250	6,650	3,250	2,100	5,400	116,771
2017-18	7,500	3,400	41,000	24,750	3,500	1,950	10,900	1,175	7,300	3,225	2,400	6,600	123,248
2018-19	7,200	3,400	39,500	24,300	3,150	2,000	10,700	1,100	6,900	2,975	2,050	7,000	119,564
2019-20	7,100	2,700	34,250	20,500	2,400	1,500	9,500	800	7,150	2,150	2,375	6,600	104,971
2020-21	8,700	3,100	41,250	26,000	2,450	1,725	10,900	625	8,350	2,400	3,250	7,300	124,151
2021-22	8,800	3,300	33,750	25,000	2,600	1,900	10,700	735	8,600	2,550	3,250	6,700	116,097
2022-23[1]	7,700	3,200	37,500	23,500	1,750	1,750	8,700	675	7,500	2,050	2,625	6,450	111,161
2023-24[2]	7,800	3,300	36,500	23,700	1,900	1,550	9,800	625	7,400	1,900	3,000	6,700	112,425

[1] Preliminary.   [2] Estimate.   *Source: Foreign Agricultural Service, U.S. Department of Agriculture (FAS-USDA)*

World Ending Stocks of Cotton   In Thousands of 480-Pound Bales

Crop Year Beginning Aug. 1	Argen-tina	Australia	Bangla-desh	Brazil	China	India	Mexico	Pakistan	Türkiye	Turkmen-istan	United States	Uzbek-istan	World Total
2014-15	862	1,748	1,396	3,696	66,420	10,586	703	2,950	1,671	1,279	3,650	1,298	105,293
2015-16	825	1,835	1,590	3,553	56,698	7,044	640	2,700	1,652	829	3,800	1,098	90,214
2016-17	729	2,259	1,715	3,673	45,927	7,880	455	2,325	1,594	654	2,750	1,658	79,451
2017-18	1,000	3,284	1,950	3,201	37,999	8,625	640	2,865	2,200	669	4,200	2,631	78,308
2018-19	962	1,922	1,888	3,020	35,914	8,604	704	2,555	1,944	629	4,850	2,645	74,189
2019-20	1,375	1,198	2,630	4,388	36,094	15,684	704	3,200	2,466	694	7,250	2,269	88,003
2020-21	1,490	2,507	2,477	4,066	37,294	11,839	439	2,175	1,758	714	3,150	1,774	77,631
2021-22	1,482	4,960	2,278	3,883	38,064	8,396	315	1,925	1,915	664	4,050	1,390	76,365
2022-23[1]	2,071	4,772	1,731	5,755	37,402	11,824	427	1,525	2,629	714	4,250	2,065	83,215
2023-24[2]	2,246	4,312	1,586	5,535	39,812	12,824	302	2,150	1,479	714	2,900	2,015	84,382

[1] Preliminary.   [2] Estimate.   *Source: Foreign Agricultural Service, U.S. Department of Agriculture (FAS-USDA)*

World Exports of Cotton   In Thousands of 480-Pound Bales

Crop Year Beginning Aug. 1	Australia	Benin	Brazil	Burkina	Cote d'Ivoire	Greece	India	Malaysia	Mali	Turkmen-istan	United States	Uzbek-istan	World Total
2014-15	2,404	750	3,910	1,340	860	1,165	4,199	81	850	1,500	11,246	2,600	36,221
2015-16	2,828	650	4,314	1,077	780	959	5,764	142	1,000	1,250	9,153	2,200	34,886
2016-17	3,731	825	2,789	1,154	625	1,017	4,550	111	1,100	850	14,917	1,750	38,114
2017-18	3,915	1,070	4,174	1,218	620	1,076	5,182	152	1,300	625	16,281	987	41,606
2018-19	3,632	1,390	6,018	796	895	1,355	3,521	313	1,350	200	14,833	711	41,638
2019-20	1,359	970	8,937	950	643	1,467	3,200	220	1,175	130	15,512	456	41,207
2020-21	1,581	1,570	11,014	1,067	1,176	1,630	6,189	255	700	100	16,352	450	48,999
2021-22	3,577	1,700	7,727	900	1,343	1,428	3,743	10	1,300	200	14,481	53	43,192
2022-23[1]	6,168	1,000	6,656	750	479	1,331	1,099	26	750	125	12,766	25	36,962
2023-24[2]	5,750	1,100	11,500	675	675	975	1,600	75	1,125	150	12,100	25	43,052

[1] Preliminary.   [2] Estimate.   Source: Foreign Agricultural Service, U.S. Department of Agriculture (FAS-USDA)

World Imports of Cotton   In Thousands of 480-Pound Bales

Crop Year Beginning Aug. 1	Bangla-desh	China	India	Indonesia	Korea, South	Malaysia	Mexico	Pakistan	Taiwan	Thailand	Türkiye	Vietnam	World Total
2014-15	5,750	8,284	1,226	3,345	1,321	280	830	950	873	1,475	4,074	4,275	36,513
2015-16	6,375	4,406	1,072	2,941	1,175	443	975	3,300	707	1,275	4,486	4,600	35,616
2016-17	6,800	5,040	2,736	3,391	1,025	392	1,000	2,450	644	1,226	3,851	5,508	37,771
2017-18	7,600	5,708	1,677	3,517	904	739	925	3,400	632	1,149	4,391	6,986	41,362
2018-19	7,000	9,628	1,800	3,051	781	744	850	2,850	592	1,075	3,607	6,931	42,388
2019-20	7,700	7,137	2,280	2,512	571	704	590	4,000	398	700	4,672	6,481	40,724
2020-21	8,400	12,860	844	2,307	556	629	928	5,400	260	598	5,327	7,288	48,641
2021-22	8,450	7,840	1,000	2,577	558	444	959	4,500	242	750	5,524	6,631	42,962
2022-23[1]	7,000	6,232	1,727	1,664	440	687	689	4,500	245	662	4,189	6,471	37,691
2023-24[2]	7,500	11,500	1,300	2,000	400	600	750	3,800	260	625	4,100	6,700	43,054

[1] Preliminary.   [2] Estimate.   Source: Foreign Agricultural Service, U.S. Department of Agriculture (FAS-USDA)

Average Spot Cotton, 1-3/32", Price (SLM) at Designated U.S. Markets[2]   In Cents Per Pound (Net Weight)

Crop Year	Aug.	Sept.	Oct.	Nov.	Dec.	Jan.	Feb.	Mar.	Apr.	May	June	July	Average
2014-15	68.94	68.70	67.32	63.40	63.13	62.12	66.02	64.89	67.33	67.30	67.09	66.60	66.07
2015-16	66.09	63.93	65.06	65.17	66.47	64.76	62.05	59.91	63.51	64.42	66.74	73.12	65.10
2016-17	72.48	71.58	71.93	73.41	73.31	75.24	75.92	77.10	76.91	78.55	72.72	69.05	74.02
2017-18	70.52	71.93	69.47	71.10	76.32	80.83	78.44	82.77	82.52	85.57	88.85	87.33	78.80
2018-19	84.10	80.10	77.12	77.06	76.07	72.23	70.61	73.25	75.65	67.58	64.71	61.60	73.34
2019-20	57.69	60.54	64.25	64.46	65.87	69.08	65.86	55.84	52.25	56.02	59.48	61.94	61.11
2020-21	62.08	62.94	67.40	69.92	74.03	80.38	86.37	84.08	83.41	84.38	85.40	88.54	77.41
2021-22	93.22	95.24	109.10	116.37	108.45	119.11	123.19	126.11	137.34	143.34	130.18	107.55	117.43
2022-23	119.51	103.61	85.12	86.28	85.49	86.36	85.09	81.59	82.18	82.25	80.32	81.90	88.31
2023-24[1]	84.20	85.30	83.26	77.52	79.75								82.01

[1] Preliminary.   Source: Agricultural Marketing Service, U.S. Department of Agriculture (AMS-USDA)

Average Producer Price Index of Gray Cotton Broadwovens   Index 1982 = 100

Year	Jan.	Feb.	Mar.	Apr.	May	June	July	Aug.	Sept.	Oct.	Nov.	Dec.	Average
2009	111.0	111.0	111.0	107.2	107.2	107.2	107.2	107.5	107.5	107.5	108.9	108.9	108.5
2010	109.8	113.7	113.7	113.7	114.9	116.6	119.0	118.8	118.8	118.8	119.1	119.1	116.3
2011	144.8	145.4	147.0	153.5	154.3	154.3	162.1	162.0	161.3	148.5	148.5	141.1	151.9
2012	139.1	139.2	139.2	135.0	135.0	135.2	126.1	126.1	126.1	124.7	123.6	122.7	131.0
2013	122.6	122.3	123.3	126.9	126.4	126.4	126.4	126.4	126.4	127.7	127.7	127.7	125.9
2014	124.5	124.5	121.8	124.7	124.7	124.7	124.8	124.8	124.8	123.3	123.3	123.3	124.1
2015	118.2	121.2	121.2	121.5	121.5	121.5	123.7	123.7	123.7	123.5	123.5	123.5	122.2
2016	122.6	122.6	122.6	121.9	121.9	121.9	122.6	122.6	122.6	123.6	123.6	123.6	122.7
2017	125.2	125.3	125.3	129.2	129.2	129.2	128.5	128.5	128.5	126.4	126.4	126.4	127.3
2018[1]	127.3	127.3	127.3	133.1	133.1	133.1	133.1	----	----	----	----	----	130.6

[1] Preliminary.   Source: Bureau of Labor Statistics (0337-01), U.S. Department of Commerce

COTTON

COTTON
Quarterly Cash as of 03/28/2024

QUARTERLY CASH
As of 03/28/2024
Chart High 209.60 on 03/07/2011
Chart Low   9.21   on 05/31/1940

Cents / lb.

1-1/16" 7-Market Average

Average Price of SLM 1-1/16", Cotton/5 at Designated U.S. Markets   In Cents Per Pound (Net Weight)

Crop Year	Aug.	Sept.	Oct.	Nov.	Dec.	Jan.	Feb.	Mar.	Apr.	May	June	July	Average
2014-15	64.99	64.83	63.51	59.64	59.38	58.19	61.74	60.65	63.08	63.06	62.86	62.36	62.02
2015-16	61.85	59.70	60.83	60.99	62.32	60.69	58.06	55.96	59.65	60.36	62.78	69.25	61.04
2016-17	68.57	67.65	68.04	69.42	69.69	71.81	73.02	74.33	74.13	75.75	69.85	66.24	70.71
2017-18	67.71	69.12	66.67	68.09	73.13	77.58	75.24	79.57	79.34	82.40	85.54	83.95	75.70
2018-19	80.75	76.72	73.90	73.72	72.66	68.72	67.17	69.78	72.27	64.05	61.19	58.08	69.92
2019-20	54.17	57.01	60.63	60.89	62.39	65.60	62.38	52.35	48.73	52.40	56.00	58.46	57.58
2020-21	58.60	59.46	63.87	66.30	70.37	76.69	82.79	80.56	79.89	80.86	81.88	85.03	73.86
2021-22	89.70	91.67	105.50	112.87	105.14	115.90	120.09	123.02	134.25	140.06	127.09	104.26	114.13
2022-23	116.41	100.51	81.99	82.99	82.35	83.24	82.07	78.57	79.16	79.22	77.27	78.86	85.22
2023-24[1]	81.08	82.03	79.99	74.22	76.22	78.80	88.11						80.06

[1] Preliminary.   [2] Grade 41, leaf 4, staple 34, mike 35-36 and 43-49 , strength 23.5-26.4.   *Source: Agricultural Marketing Service, U.S. Department of Agriculture (AMS-USDA)*

Average Price[1] Received by Farmers for Upland Cotton in the United States   In Cents Per Pound

Crop Year	Aug.	Sept.	Oct.	Nov.	Dec.	Jan.	Feb.	Mar.	Apr.	May	June	July	Average
2014-15	70.5	68.9	64.5	62.7	60.8	59.1	57.8	61.3	62.6	65.9	66.8	69.3	64.2
2015-16	58.0	60.3	57.9	60.0	61.3	60.3	59.8	58.2	58.7	63.2	67.0	74.5	61.6
2016-17	67.1	67.0	66.0	67.2	67.9	67.0	68.8	69.2	69.3	69.9	70.4	73.0	68.6
2017-18	64.7	64.1	66.5	67.3	68.6	68.9	68.1	68.3	67.7	69.6	75.7	76.4	68.8
2018-19	69.7	70.8	72.1	72.9	72.6	65.4	67.6	68.9	70.5	69.6	68.2	74.7	70.3
2019-20	56.2	59.4	59.0	59.7	61.6	59.7	60.6	57.6	55.0	54.9	56.5	60.3	58.4
2020-21	57.1	59.3	60.1	63.4	65.7	69.3	72.8	70.0	71.1	71.2	72.9	74.5	67.3
2021-22	78.3	76.4	84.3	85.9	87.7	96.3	98.6	104.0	99.4	95.9	98.3	98.2	91.9
2022-23	94.6	85.9	86.4	80.1	84.6	81.4	80.3	80.3	76.0	85.3	75.0	96.0	83.8
2023-24[2]	76.4	76.3	75.1	72.4	73.2	76.4	77.6						75.3

[1] Weighted average by sales.   [2] Preliminary.   *Source: Agricultural Marketing Service, U.S. Department of Agriculture (AMS-USDA)*

Purchases Reported by Exchanges in Designated U.S. Spot Markets[1]   In Running Bales

Crop Year Beginning Aug. 1	Aug.	Sept.	Oct.	Nov.	Dec.	Jan.	Feb.	Mar.	Apr.	May	June	July	Market Total
2014-15	21,486	35,934	141,203	200,756	593,113	425,345	404,710	121,097	117,746	26,509	19,259	20,128	2,127,286
2015-16	18,634	24,429	56,127	220,807	424,830	297,380	196,419	128,004	61,364	28,446	16,622	56,367	1,529,429
2016-17	9,555	26,482	54,441	251,092	253,534	549,344	214,644	159,483	38,442	8,097	2,411	3,121	1,570,646
2017-18	16,659	20,322	57,282	341,259	429,829	427,512	255,750	152,678	156,773	152,630	35,949	13,783	2,060,426
2018-19	11,511	5,796	18,533	79,339	122,132	226,334	204,858	331,767	115,807	74,715	64,716	27,775	1,283,283
2019-20	35,241	71,105	103,590	199,665	455,781	350,099	108,467	49,111	77,192	46,280	47,722	----	1,544,253
2020-21	111,277	70,474	120,167	192,423	419,707	229,316	109,048	64,204	36,866	13,682	15,765	13,755	1,396,684
2021-22	9,723	47,215	94,933	232,941	383,757	482,976	186,439	129,568	52,864	10,303	5,870	2,114	1,638,703
2022-23	7,158	19,108	10,473	31,153	130,230	158,189	92,994	83,345	70,904	100,500	35,177	40,420	779,651
2023-24	43,795	45,497	33,771	77,536	234,689	260,935	83,974						780,197

[1] Seven markets.   *Source: Agricultural Marketing Service, U.S. Department of Agriculture (AMS-USDA)*

Production of All Cotton in the United States   In Thousands of 480-Pound Bales

Year	Alabama	Arizona	Arkansas	California	Georgia	Louisiana	Mississippi	Missouri	North Carolina	South Carolina	Tennessee	Texas	Total
2014	653	520	787	714	2,570	404	1,078	570	995	528	494	6,203	16,319
2015	554	308	471	526	2,255	189	672	400	527	155	305	5,748	12,888
2016	706	395	840	747	2,180	268	1,081	566	343	250	575	8,133	17,170
2017	808	515	1,074	865	2,225	404	1,351	750	741	471	732	9,296	20,923
2018	888	466	1,133	914	1,955	420	1,462	921	702	420	770	6,884	18,367
2019	1,028	393	1,506	821	2,740	582	1,621	915	1,040	497	960	6,337	19,913
2020	734	316	1,277	615	2,180	339	1,180	684	522	299	611	4,613	14,608
2021	690	334	1,235	374	2,210	219	893	814	773	425	583	7,726	17,523
2022[1]	833	308	1,548	445	2,650	358	1,186	878	1,005	505	713	3,104	14,468
2023[2]	715	277	1,410	274	2,250	210	890	920	730	395	670	2,825	12,434

[1] Preliminary.   [2] Forecast.   *Source: Agricultural Statistics Board, U.S. Department of Agriculture (ASB-USDA)*

Cotton Production and Yield Estimates in the United States

Year	Forecasts of Production (1,000 Bales of 480 Lbs.[1])						Actual Crop	Forecasts of Yield (Lbs. Per Harvested Acre)						Actual Yield
	Aug. 1	Sept. 1	Oct. 1	Nov. 1	Dec. 1	Jan. 1		Aug. 1	Sept. 1	Oct. 1	Nov. 1	Dec. 1	Jan. 1	
2014	17,502	16,538	16,255	16,397	15,923	----	16,319	820	803	790	797	773	----	838
2015	13,082	13,428	13,338	13,281	13,031	----	12,888	795	789	784	782	768	----	766
2016	15,879	16,142	16,034	16,162	16,524	----	17,170	800	802	797	803	821	----	867
2017	20,545	21,758	21,115	21,377	21,440	----	20,923	892	908	889	900	902	----	905
2018	19,235	19,682	19,763	18,408	18,588	----	18,367	911	895	901	852	860	----	882
2019	22,516	21,862	21,705	20,817	20,206	----	19,913	855	839	833	799	775	----	810
2020	18,080	17,064	17,045	17,092	15,949	----	14,608	938	910	909	911	850	----	847
2021	17,264	18,509	18,004	18,198	18,284	----	17,523	800	895	871	880	885	----	820
2022	12,570	13,832	13,812	14,031	14,242	----	14,468	846	843	842	855	868	----	953
2023	13,992	13,132	12,817	13,090	12,776	----	12,434	779	786	767	783	765	----	845

[1] Net weight bales.   *Source: Agricultural Statistics Board, U.S. Department of Agriculture (ASB-USDA)*

Supply and Distribution of Upland Cotton in the United States   In Thousands of 480-Pound Bales

Crop Year Beginning Aug. 1	Area			Supply				Disappearance				Farm Price[5] Cents/ Lb.
	Planted	Harvested	Yield	Beginning Stocks[3]	Pro-duction	Imports	Total Supply	Mill Use	Exports	Total	Ending Stocks	
	1,000 Acres		Lbs./Acre									
2014-15	10,845	9,157	826	2,225	15,753	9	17,987	3,550	10,836	14,386	3,391	64.2
2015-16	8,422	7,903	756	3,391	12,455	30	15,876	3,425	8,619	12,044	3,664	61.6
2016-17	9,878	9,320	855	3,664	16,601	5	20,270	3,221	14,309	17,530	2,680	68.6
2017-18	12,465	10,850	895	2,680	20,223	1	22,904	3,198	15,651	18,849	4,085	68.8
2018-19	13,850	9,742	865	4,085	17,566		21,651	2,953	14,169	17,122	4,617	70.3
2019-20	13,507	11,274	819	4,617	19,227		23,844	2,135	15,011	17,146	6,844	58.4
2020-21	11,890	8,081	835	6,844	14,061		20,905	2,385	15,574	17,959	2,988	67.3
2021-22	11,089	10,149	813	2,988	17,191	1	20,180	2,538	14,160	16,698	3,726	91.9
2022-23[1]	13,579	7,132	942	3,726	13,998		17,724	2,042	12,483	14,525	3,529	83.8
2023-24[2]	10,978	8,518	773	3,529	13,724		17,253	2,140	12,175	14,315	2,991	

[1] Preliminary.   [2] Estimate.   [3] Excludes preseason ginnings (adjusted to 480-lb. bale net weight basis).   [4] Includes preseason ginnings.
[5] Marketing year average price.   *Source: Economic Research Service, U.S. Department of Agriculture (ERS-USDA)*

COTTON

COTTON #2 - ICE-US
Weekly Selected Futures as of 03/28/2024

WEEKLY SELECTED FUTURES
As of 03/28/2024
Chart High 158.02 on 05/04/2022
Chart Low 48.35 on 04/01/2020

Cents / lb.

Nearby Futures through Last Trading Day using selected contract months: March, May, July, October and December.

Volume of Trading of Cotton #2 Futures in New York   In Contracts

Year	Jan.	Feb.	Mar.	Apr.	May	June	July	Aug.	Sept.	Oct.	Nov.	Dec.	Total
2014	544,180	602,542	446,810	568,063	399,736	611,785	362,461	338,548	460,119	477,742	625,593	350,304	5,787,883
2015	474,061	764,365	532,511	774,667	504,552	748,679	391,137	541,234	378,522	492,136	718,549	405,429	6,725,842
2016	556,311	939,909	544,144	920,712	567,195	802,595	582,169	538,811	437,283	528,534	876,713	408,670	7,703,046
2017	621,642	919,593	648,217	805,263	728,004	731,750	367,996	499,490	527,357	539,450	954,722	564,023	7,907,507
2018	908,692	1,040,986	697,571	967,537	865,014	966,955	395,024	544,209	451,364	641,924	889,009	507,810	8,876,095
2019	607,201	901,354	685,982	877,964	771,698	778,893	467,666	555,618	498,553	771,503	953,641	591,376	8,461,449
2020	803,523	1,108,447	999,072	819,599	497,631	678,605	409,570	476,008	508,333	701,383	828,278	493,784	8,324,233
2021	678,039	1,073,253	765,629	821,506	529,388	726,755	464,057	549,246	699,970	837,650	889,742	466,475	8,501,710
2022	604,075	750,095	699,484	770,233	569,484	787,118	505,337	586,289	608,181	747,084	892,753	470,840	7,990,973
2023	661,831	850,348	764,720	771,306	832,841	791,064	627,727	577,490	628,091	860,774	991,380	532,960	8,890,532

Contract size = 50,000 lbs.   Source: ICE Futures U.S. (ICE)

Average Open Interest of Cotton #2 Futures in New York   In Contracts

Year	Jan.	Feb.	Mar.	Apr.	May	June	July	Aug.	Sept.	Oct.	Nov.	Dec.
2014	180,149	171,213	178,245	178,514	190,808	169,165	152,321	167,437	181,359	190,436	181,192	175,349
2015	197,949	192,586	182,898	180,941	191,700	175,835	177,911	185,267	180,786	192,945	184,447	188,025
2016	188,149	196,230	211,958	203,691	191,903	197,043	216,925	236,332	238,644	251,736	250,363	248,786
2017	263,192	275,644	277,202	252,849	254,360	219,791	213,858	221,829	238,371	230,544	232,469	262,608
2018	301,515	271,212	272,354	270,033	290,493	289,963	257,708	260,562	253,033	259,661	241,659	217,465
2019	228,469	234,159	223,225	218,548	217,558	192,072	190,297	213,722	231,086	238,617	224,486	205,207
2020	251,311	219,080	204,701	183,388	179,296	172,208	173,848	194,284	218,706	237,465	229,699	220,397
2021	246,900	248,748	232,954	221,735	224,032	218,868	233,682	262,436	273,079	287,023	271,733	235,083
2022	248,960	251,289	229,142	215,618	205,319	196,138	178,838	197,036	214,220	237,548	214,383	195,515
2023	204,313	196,925	192,733	176,489	184,338	178,784	183,870	208,582	232,958	246,587	211,576	196,462

Contract size = 50,000 lbs.   Source: ICE Futures U.S. (ICE)

Average Spot Prices of U.S. Cotton,[2] Base Quality (SLM) at Designated Markets   In Cents Per Pound

Crop Year Beginning Aug. 1	Dallas (EastTex.-Okl.)	Fresno (San Joaquin Valley)	Greenville (South-east)	Greenwood (South Delta)	Lubbock (West Texas)	Memphis (North Delta)	Phoenix Desert (Southwest)	Average
2013-14	79.27	78.88	82.74	81.85	79.14	81.85	78.23	80.28
2014-15	60.75	62.32	63.55	62.64	60.71	62.64	61.57	62.02
2015-16	59.29	60.88	63.32	62.44	59.16	62.44	59.73	61.04
2016-17	70.25	69.62	72.91	71.81	70.06	71.81	68.51	70.71
2017-18	74.38	74.55	78.79	77.59	73.14	77.60	73.52	76.01
2018-19	68.59	69.92	71.52	68.67	68.04	71.52	68.54	72.55
2019-20	57.06	55.16	60.53	59.40	56.90	59.47	54.66	57.58
2020-21	66.91	72.67	76.20	74.47	72.20	75.62	71.34	75.11
2021-22	112.24	114.13	117.19	112.20	110.66	117.19	111.16	118.25
2022-23[1]	88.39	89.94	92.20	88.46	87.37	92.20	87.77	93.18

[1] Preliminary.   [2] Prices are for mixed lots, net weight, uncompressed in warehouse.
Source: Agricultural Marketing Service, U.S. Department of Agriculture (AMS-USDA)

Cotton Ginnings[1] in the United States To: In Thousands of Running Bales

Crop Year	Aug. 1	Sept. 1	Sept. 15	Oct. 1	Oct. 15	Nov. 1	Nov. 15	Dec. 1	Dec. 15	Jan. 1	Jan. 15	Feb. 1	Mar. 1	Total Crop
2014-15	1	367	696	1,154	2,108	4,807	7,530	10,246	12,601	14,214	15,030	15,538	----	15,876
2015-16	----	105	293	635	1,448	3,704	5,738	7,955	9,830	11,092	11,737	12,251	12,517	12,529
2016-17	35	438	701	1,167	2,308	5,016	7,584	10,296	12,261	13,858	14,840	15,881	16,559	16,710
2017-18	107	571	789	1,249	2,298	4,915	7,878	11,287	13,963	16,120	17,398	18,654	19,557	20,441
2018-19	20	489	745	1,287	2,421	4,878	7,083	10,265	12,275	NA	NA	16,651	17,473	17,909
2019-20	4	359	622	1,283	2,840	6,250	9,304	12,924	15,598	17,472	18,278	18,925	19,303	19,409
2020-21	4	288	587	915	1,661	3,987	6,535	9,570	11,538	12,966	13,417	13,955	14,153	14,255
2021-22	W	200	W	741	1,108	3,543	6,278	9,804	12,451	14,632	15,542	16,552	17,013	17,108
2022-23	31	506	694	1,084	1,969	4,246	6,585	9,271	11,227	12,783	13,490	13,879	14,313	14,116
2023-24[2]	21	484	687	958	1,734	3,656	5,787	8,481	10,210	11,187	11,558	11,750		

[1] Excluding linters.   [2] Preliminary.   W = Withheld.   *Source: National Agricultural Statistics Service, U.S. Department of Agriculture (NASS-USDA)*

Exports of All Cotton[2] from the United States   In Thousands of Running Bales

Crop Year	Aug.	Sept.	Oct.	Nov.	Dec.	Jan.	Feb.	Mar.	Apr.	May	June	July	Total
2014-15	499	380	354	572	1,024	1,126	1,430	1,596	1,418	1,369	945	769	11,482
2015-16	560	404	370	396	643	776	918	1,083	1,083	1,077	1,042	909	9,261
2016-17	966	799	569	828	1,291	1,580	1,734	1,936	1,634	1,592	1,209	1,175	15,313
2017-18	933	577	447	727	1,399	1,647	1,980	2,329	2,198	1,989	1,428	1,088	16,741
2018-19	815	715	609	681	976	1,225	1,484	2,110	1,758	1,831	1,687	1,430	15,320
2019-20	1,034	910	732	841	1,320	1,699	1,969	2,003	1,254	1,238	1,464	1,629	16,093
2020-21	1,424	924	1,195	1,329	1,425	1,614	1,571	1,637	1,585	1,637	1,208	1,102	16,650
2021-22	974	572	452	450	842	1,406	1,632	1,946	1,887	1,890	1,697	1,405	15,153
2022-23	1,231	704	547	760	675	981	1,375	1,577	1,551	1,485	1,126	981	12,991
2023-24[1]	1,039	654	390	558	1,106								8,991

[1] Preliminary.   *Source: Foreign Agricultural Service, U.S. Department of Agriculture (FAS-USDA)*

U.S. Exports of American Cotton to Countries of Destination   In Thousands of 480-Pound Bales

Crop Year Beginning Aug. 1	Canada	China	Hong Kong	Indo-nesia	Italy	Japan	Korea, South	Mexico	Philip-pines	Taiwan	Thailand	United Kingdom	Total
2013-14	2	2,646	13	701	9	115	461	1,009	39	299	457	0	10,418
2014-15	2	2,709	16	978	22	114	670	950	42	349	466	7	11,460
2015-16	1	842	0	690	9	124	476	994	34	330	379	0	9,260
2016-17	1	2,310	1	1,476	9	121	598	1,007	65	422	577	1	15,314
2017-18	1	2,626	2	1,587	14	122	606	949	57	466	666	1	16,714
2018-19	1	1,637	7	1,037	9	101	450	794	46	431	563	1	15,449
2019-20	0	2,980	16	861	16	126	402	522	9	275	409	0	15,918
2020-21	1	5,233	33	686	9	104	340	820	16	171	311	0	16,612
2021-22[1]	1	4,859	27	417	8	107	238	923	7	106	238	0	14,871
2022-23[2]	1	3,343	144	392	6	94	152	613	6	192	181	0	13,056

[1] Preliminary.   [2] Estimate.   *Source: Foreign Agricultural Service, U.S. Department of Agriculture (FAS-USDA)*

COTTON

Cotton[1] Government Loan Program in the United States

Crop Year Beginning Aug. 1	Support Price	Target Price	Put Under Support	% of Pro- duction	Acquired	Owned July 31	Crop Year Beginning Aug. 1	Support Price	Target Price	Put Under Support	% of Pro- duction	Acquired	Owned July 31
	--- Cents Per Lb. ---		Ths Bales		----- Ths. Bales -----			--- Cents Per Lb. ---		Ths Bales		----- Ths. Bales -----	
2011-12	52.00	71.3	7,268	49.3	1	0	2016-17	52.00	NA	9,373	56.4	0	0
2012-13	52.00	71.3	8,330	50.4	0	0	2017-18	49.49	NA	9,597	46.7	0	0
2013-14	52.00	71.3	3,981	32.4	0	0	2018-19	52.00	36.7	8,250	47.0	73	0
2014-15	52.00	NA	7,625	48.4	0	0	2019-20	52.00	36.7	11,787	61.3	0	0
2015-16	52.00	NA	6,758	54.3	0	0	2020-21[1]	52.00	36.7	8,326	59.2	0	0

[1] Upland. [2] Preliminary. NA = Not applicable. *Source: Economic Research Service, U.S. Department of Agriculture (ERS-USDA)*

Weekly Outstanding Export Sales and Cumulative Exports of U.S. Cotton   In Running Bales

Marketing Year 2022/2023 Week Ending	Weekly Exports	Accumu- lated Exports	Net Sales	Out- standing Sales	Marketing Year 2023/2024 Week Ending	Weekly Exports	Accumu- lated Exports	Net Sales	Out- standing Sales
Aug 04, 2022	181,259	181,259	2,490,143	7,136,910	Aug 03, 2023	128,995	128,995	2,430,238	4,811,200
Aug 11, 2022	267,374	448,633	49,522	6,919,058	Aug 10, 2023	202,297	331,292	186,276	4,795,179
Aug 18, 2022		448,633		6,919,058	Aug 17, 2023	204,200	535,492	38,893	4,629,872
Aug 25, 2022	580,671	1,029,304	258,126	6,596,513	Aug 24, 2023	214,068	749,560	61,438	4,477,242
Sep 01, 2022	235,392	1,264,696	230,655	6,591,776	Aug 31, 2023	175,351	924,911	85,093	4,386,984
Sep 08, 2022	141,000	1,405,696	100,261	6,551,037	Sep 07, 2023	118,175	1,043,086	67,429	4,336,238
Sep 15, 2022	232,316	1,638,012	32,432	6,351,153	Sep 14, 2023	150,687	1,193,773	105,767	4,291,318
Sep 22, 2022	187,858	1,825,870	30,222	6,193,517	Sep 21, 2023	159,388	1,353,161	55,323	4,187,253
Sep 29, 2022	209,649	2,035,519	121,209	6,105,077	Sep 28, 2023	149,616	1,502,777	239,975	4,277,612
Oct 06, 2022	168,057	2,203,576	144,820	6,081,840	Oct 05, 2023	103,989	1,606,766	43,399	4,217,022
Oct 13, 2022	165,741	2,369,317	84,471	6,000,570	Oct 12, 2023	109,892	1,716,658	71,311	4,178,441
Oct 20, 2022	177,579	2,546,896	68,437	5,891,428	Oct 19, 2023	98,007	1,814,665	186,061	4,266,495
Oct 27, 2022	118,961	2,665,857	191,755	5,964,222	Oct 26, 2023	132,173	1,946,838	457,129	4,591,451
Nov 03, 2022	108,121	2,773,978	145,795	6,001,896	Nov 02, 2023	90,645	2,037,483	395,170	4,895,976
Nov 10, 2022	182,951	2,956,929	25,059	5,844,004	Nov 09, 2023	112,891	2,150,374	328,347	5,111,432
Nov 17, 2022	143,698	3,100,627	-116,428	5,583,878	Nov 16, 2023	77,869	2,228,243	322,212	5,355,775
Nov 24, 2022	139,458	3,240,085	16,494	5,460,914	Nov 23, 2023	88,846	2,317,089	217,662	5,484,591
Dec 01, 2022	141,145	3,381,230	32,640	5,352,409	Nov 30, 2023	139,156	2,456,245	116,429	5,461,864
Dec 08, 2022	141,851	3,523,081	18,647	5,229,205	Dec 07, 2023	148,741	2,604,986	57,765	5,370,888
Dec 15, 2022	110,440	3,633,521	-87,805	5,030,960	Dec 14, 2023	222,322	2,827,308	146,671	5,295,237
Dec 22, 2022	140,310	3,773,831	82,254	4,972,904	Dec 21, 2023	230,981	3,058,289	369,857	5,434,113
Dec 29, 2022	93,622	3,867,453	39,615	4,918,897	Dec 28, 2023	213,246	3,271,535	131,063	5,351,930
Jan 05, 2023	150,500	4,017,953	72,610	4,841,007	Jan 04, 2024	228,062	3,499,597	262,478	5,386,346
Jan 12, 2023	183,105	4,201,058	209,435	4,867,337	Jan 11, 2024	257,695	3,757,292	420,047	5,548,698
Jan 19, 2023	175,793	4,376,851	213,680	4,905,224	Jan 18, 2024	142,242	3,899,534	207,044	5,613,500
Jan 26, 2023	212,244	4,589,095	171,160	4,864,140	Jan 25, 2024	396,711	4,296,245	349,365	5,566,154
Feb 02, 2023	210,127	4,799,222	262,788	4,916,801	Feb 01, 2024	248,512	4,544,757	284,057	5,601,699
Feb 09, 2023	186,392	4,985,614	216,915	4,947,324	Feb 08, 2024	276,057	4,820,814	160,465	5,486,107
Feb 16, 2023	193,571	5,179,185	425,322	5,179,075	Feb 15, 2024	255,484	5,076,298	130,468	5,361,091
Feb 23, 2023	207,748	5,386,933	170,583	5,141,910	Feb 22, 2024	267,115	5,343,413	39,966	5,133,942
Mar 02, 2023	287,452	5,674,385	114,525	4,968,983	Feb 29, 2024	330,790	5,674,203	52,012	4,855,164
Mar 09, 2023	273,922	5,948,307	225,535	4,920,596	Mar 07, 2024	293,282	5,967,485	85,845	4,647,727
Mar 16, 2023	272,519	6,220,826	310,236	4,958,313	Mar 14, 2024	397,297	6,364,782	92,620	4,343,050
Mar 23, 2023	340,964	6,561,790	281,281	4,898,630	Mar 21, 2024				
Mar 30, 2023	250,100	6,811,890	160,457	4,808,987	Mar 28, 2024				
Apr 06, 2023	334,569	7,146,459	143,203	4,617,621	Apr 04, 2024				
Apr 13, 2023	289,787	7,436,246	62,080	4,389,914	Apr 11, 2024				
Apr 20, 2023	398,414	7,834,660	194,936	4,186,436	Apr 18, 2024				
Apr 27, 2023	413,954	8,248,614	231,274	4,003,756	Apr 25, 2024				
May 04, 2023	331,020	8,579,634	246,817	3,919,553	May 02, 2024				
May 11, 2023	332,691	8,912,325	132,443	3,719,305	May 09, 2024				
May 18, 2023	268,748	9,181,073	131,245	3,581,802	May 16, 2024				
May 25, 2023	282,951	9,464,024	267,767	3,566,618	May 23, 2024				
Jun 01, 2023	316,953	9,780,977	480,399	3,730,064	May 30, 2024				
Jun 08, 2023	244,792	10,025,769	98,915	3,584,187	Jun 06, 2024				
Jun 15, 2023	236,768	10,262,537	42,721	3,390,140	Jun 13, 2024				
Jun 22, 2023	225,173	10,487,710	125,556	3,290,523	Jun 20, 2024				
Jun 29, 2023	260,106	10,747,816	109,209	3,139,626	Jun 27, 2024				
Jul 06, 2023	208,329	10,956,145	23,066	2,954,363	Jul 04, 2024				
Jul 13, 2023	233,063	11,189,208	67,050	2,788,350	Jul 11, 2024				
Jul 20, 2023	197,841	11,387,049	-18,665	2,571,844	Jul 18, 2024				
Jul 27, 2023	194,637	11,581,686	-9,912	2,367,295	Jul 25, 2024				
Aug 03, 2023	195,799	11,777,485	-18,973	2,152,523					

Source: Foreign Agricultural Service, U.S. Department of Agriculture (FAS-USDA)

Cottonseed and Products

Cottonseed is crushed to produce both oil and meal. Cottonseed oil is typically used for cooking oil, and cottonseed meal is fed to livestock. Before the cottonseed is crushed for oil and meal, it is de-linted of its linters. Linters are used for padding in furniture, absorbent cotton swabs, and for the manufacture of many cellulose products. The sediment left by cottonseed oil refining, called "foots," provides fatty acids for industrial products. The value of cottonseeds represents a substantial 18% of a cotton producer's income.

Prices – The average monthly price of cottonseed oil in 2023 fell by -12.7% yr/yr to 96.65 cents per pound. The average monthly price of cottonseed meal in 2023 fell by -5.2% yr/yr to $363.298 per short ton.

Supply – World production of cottonseed in the 2023/24 marketing year is forecasted to fall by -2.6% to 41.455 million metric tons, below the 2011/12 record high of 47.862. The world's largest cottonseed producers in 2023/24 are expected to be the China with 26.0% of world production, Brazil with 11.7%, and the US with 8.3%. US production of cottonseed in the 2023/24 marketing year is expected to fall by -14.2% yr/yr to 3.788 million tons. US production of cottonseed oil in 2023/24 is expected remain unchanged at 365 million pounds, far below the high of 957 million pounds posted in 2004-05.

Demand – US cottonseed crushed (consumed) in the US in the 2023/24 marketing year is expected to fall by -2.9% to 1.350 million tons, which is far below the levels of over 4 million tons seen in the 1970s.

Trade – US exports of cottonseed in 2023/24 are expected to rise by +21.2 % to 225 million tons. US imports of cottonseed in 2023/24 are expected to fall by -50.6% to 50 short tons.

World Production of Cottonseed   In Thousands of Metric Ton

Crop Year Beginning Oct. 1	Argentina	Australia	Brazil	Burkina	Burma	China	European Union	India	Mali	Pakistan	Türkiye	United States	World Total
2015-16	323	881	2,383	304	451	8,600	409	10,996	276	3,032	870	3,668	36,380
2016-17	297	1,250	1,965	362	358	8,800	413	11,463	351	3,336	1,050	4,871	39,154
2017-18	407	1,442	2,330	332	253	10,800	489	12,312	396	3,552	1,300	5,826	44,700
2018-19	407	661	3,061	235	196	10,973	557	11,038	359	3,292	1,224	5,108	41,957
2019-20	510	187	4,316	243	142	10,758	642	12,100	382	2,686	1,126	5,393	43,445
2020-21	510	841	4,575	262	124	11,600	542	11,675	84	1,949	947	4,053	42,050
2021-22	536	1,757	3,592	265	129	10,503	534	10,316	404	2,599	1,241	4,829	41,513
2022-23[1]	431	1,742	3,891	214	114	12,031	525	11,166	208	1,689	1,600	4,005	42,566
2023-24[2]	629	1,442	4,834	212	194	10,777	338	10,614	367	2,902	1,045	3,436	41,455

[1] Preliminary.   [2] Estimate.   *Source: The Oil World*

Salient Statistics of Cottonseed in the United States   In Thousands of Short Tons

Crop Year Beginning Aug. 1	Supply				Disappearance				Farm Price USD/Ton	Value of Production Mil. USD	Oil (Million Pounds)	Meal (1,000 Short Tons)
	Stocks	Production	Imports	Total Supply	Crush	Exports	Other	Total				
2015-16	437	4,043	16	4,496	1,500	136	2,469	4,105	227.0	933	465	705
2016-17	391	5,369	51	5,811	1,769	342	3,300	5,411	195.0	1,056	542	805
2017-18	400	6,422	0	6,822	1,854	478	4,040	6,372	142.0	912	561	845
2018-19	451	5,631	1	6,083	1,760	387	3,458	5,606	155.0	878	456	748
2019-20	477	5,945	1	6,423	1,712	341	3,914	5,967	161.0	968	481	780
2020-21	456	4,468	1	4,925	1,563	280	2,687	4,529	194.0	875	400	649
2021-22	395	5,323	25	5,743	1,557	293	3,498	5,348	243.0	1,302	430	695
2022-23[1]	395	4,415	101	4,912	1,390	186	2,951	4,526	306.0	1,356	365	590
2023-24[2]	385	3,788	50	4,223	1,350	225	2,305	3,880	230.0	871	365	595

[1] Preliminary.   [2] Estimate.   *Source: Economic Research Service, U.S. Department of Agriculture (ERS-USDA)*

Average Wholesale Price of Cottonseed Meal (41% Solvent)[2] in Memphis   In Dollars Per Short Ton

Year	Jan.	Feb.	Mar.	Apr.	May	June	July	Aug.	Sept.	Oct.	Nov.	Dec.	Average
2015	313.75	302.50	310.50	288.13	274.38	281.00	299.38	295.63	293.50	292.50	291.88	267.50	292.55
2016	248.75	238.13	216.50	207.50	242.50	284.00	280.00	280.00	285.00	241.88	221.00	217.50	246.90
2017	223.50	221.88	210.63	195.00	179.50	179.38	200.84	198.50	213.75	229.00	228.75	232.50	209.44
2018	259.00	303.13	323.13	263.13	262.50	257.50	253.13	260.00	258.75	249.00	240.00	243.75	264.42
2019	247.50	235.00	226.25	216.50	215.00	215.63	218.00	221.25	215.83	213.13	233.75	250.83	225.72
2020	239.38	250.63	259.00	281.88	251.88	245.50	245.00	245.00	248.50	301.88	365.63	435.83	280.84
2021	443.75	460.00	456.00	415.00	360.63	337.50	321.88	303.00	305.00	298.75	304.50	311.25	359.77
2022	318.13	333.75	345.63	355.00	388.75	383.75	369.50	405.00	450.00	451.88	405.00	390.63	383.08
2023[1]	386.25	392.50	386.25	364.38	370.63	362.50	347.50	348.33	343.75	348.75	350.00	358.75	363.30

[1] Preliminary.   *Source: Economic Research Service, U.S. Department of Agriculture (ERS-USDA)*

COTTONSEED AND PRODUCTS

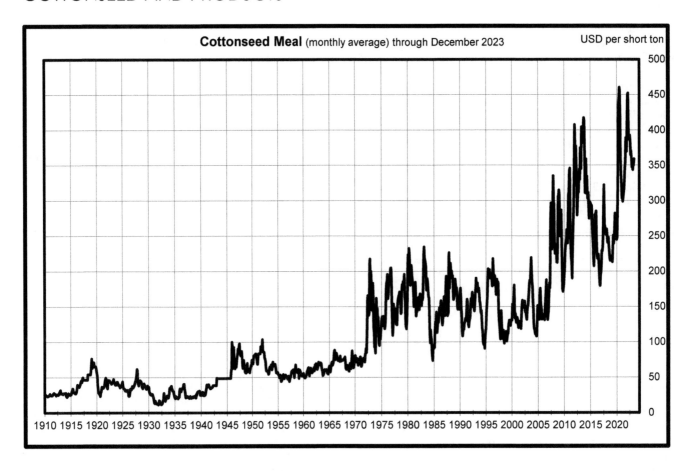

Cottonseed Meal (monthly average) through December 2023 — USD per short ton

Supply and Distribution of Cottonseed Oil in the United States   In Millions of Pounds

Crop Year Beginning Oct. 1	Supply				Disappearance			Per Capita Consumption of Salad & Cooking Oils --- In Lbs. ---	Utilization Food Uses			Prices	
	Stocks	Pro-duction	Imports	Total Supply	Domestic	Exports	Total		Short-ening	Salad & Cooking Oils	Total	U.S.[3] (Crude)	Rott[4] (Cif)
												--- $/Metric Ton ---	
2014-15	90	610	17.0	717	541	119	659	----	----	----	----	1,008	----
2015-16	58	465	7.0	530	433	55	488	----	----	----	----	1,011	----
2016-17	42	542	0	583	435	104	539	----	----	----	----	902	----
2017-18	44	561	0	605	461	112	573	----	----	----	----	703	----
2018-19	32	456	0	488	370	83	453	----	----	----	----	775	----
2019-20	35	481	0	517	388	84	472	----	----	----	----	886	----
2020-21	45	400	21.0	466	355	63	418	----	----	----	----	1,784	----
2021-22	48	430	24.9	503	326	128	453	----	----	----	----	2,362	----
2022-23[1]	50	365	16.0	431	310	71	381	----	----	----	----	2,260	----
2023-24[2]	50	365	20.0	435	315	70	385	----	----	----	----	1,918	----

[1] Preliminary.   [2] Estimate.   [3] Valley Points FOB; Tank Cars.   [4] Rotterdam; US, PBSY, fob gulf.   W = Withheld.
Source: Economic Research Service, U.S. Department of Agriculture (ERS-USDA)

Exports of Cottonseed Oil (Crude and Refined) from the United States   In Thousands of Pounds

Year	Jan.	Feb.	Mar.	Apr.	May	June	July	Aug.	Sept.	Oct.	Nov.	Dec.	Total
2014	13,667	19,061	18,084	20,029	8,709	7,165	2,999	5,895	12,687	12,384	11,780	14,205	146,664
2015	19,843	8,117	10,559	11,852	6,246	6,162	4,005	8,573	4,379	8,700	4,634	6,080	99,149
2016	5,390	1,338	3,211	5,406	4,703	3,031	2,271	5,894	4,168	6,622	15,929	10,107	68,070
2017	10,899	8,438	9,269	8,538	6,577	5,865	5,385	11,003	5,265	7,084	8,038	6,769	93,130
2018	16,387	9,282	10,793	6,797	7,626	6,980	18,567	8,421	4,152	13,262	13,725	4,527	120,518
2019	10,254	5,764	12,006	4,045	3,495	8,860	3,112	3,251	9,663	6,932	13,835	6,506	87,723
2020	7,387	4,120	6,094	14,813	4,922	5,424	4,624	3,120	5,917	6,340	5,883	4,765	73,409
2021	3,449	3,859	9,344	6,803	7,021	6,188	3,219	2,520	2,709	9,822	12,986	9,135	77,055
2022	12,105	11,748	7,332	10,476	6,901	18,294	10,869	8,983	9,146	7,125	5,920	4,634	113,533
2023[1]	6,555	7,897	17,105	7,534	6,631	2,858	1,125	1,617	1,698	3,067	1,032	1,192	58,313

[1] Preliminary.   *Source: Economic Research Service, U.S. Department of Agriculture (ERS-USDA)*

Cottonseed Oil (monthly average) through December 2023 — Cents per pound

Average Price of Crude Cottonseed Oil, PBSY, Greenwood, MS.[1] in Tank Cars   In Cents Per Pound

Year	Jan.	Feb.	Mar.	Apr.	May	June	July	Aug.	Sept.	Oct.	Nov.	Dec.	Average
2014	47.10	57.81	69.94	75.00	84.25	83.31	73.15	61.25	49.63	41.45	40.75	40.31	60.33
2015	44.95	48.81	46.06	48.19	48.90	49.94	49.15	46.25	44.13	44.25	45.19	48.35	47.01
2016	47.31	46.06	46.20	47.35	46.06	45.55	44.75	45.25	44.15	44.88	45.81	46.40	45.81
2017	44.56	41.50	39.45	37.56	38.63	38.60	38.88	36.38	38.45	37.06	37.00	34.25	38.53
2018	32.75	31.44	31.35	31.19	31.25	29.90	28.75	28.60	28.88	30.56	31.45	32.06	30.68
2019	33.94	36.44	35.70	37.13	35.65	36.69	37.50	36.45	38.07	37.94	38.40	40.25	37.01
2020	40.10	38.50	36.19	37.31	37.20	36.75	43.00	46.81	49.69	48.35	54.44	59.20	43.96
2021	63.19	73.63	86.94	92.65	102.19	100.69	99.90	96.50	93.63	98.50	96.75	93.30	91.49
2022	97.94	101.38	114.88	120.05	119.56	115.75	100.80	113.75	113.20	110.19	116.69	105.10	110.77
2023[1]	102.19	100.00	96.55	92.56	91.75	97.85	107.75	108.19	101.50	92.00	86.38	83.10	96.65

[1] Preliminary.   Source: Economic Research Service, U.S. Department of Agriculture (ERS-USDA)

Exports of Cottonseed Oil to Important Countries from the United States   In Metric Tons

Year	Canada	Dominican Republic	Egypt	Guate-mala	Japan	Mexico	Nether-lands	El Salvador	Korea, South	Türkiye	Venez-uela	Total
2014	11,934.5	----	----	----	2,118.0	----	36,433.4	925.6	----	315.9	----	66,688.9
2015	12,316.0	----	----	134.2	913.4	529.0	24,767.3	466.8	----	67.5	----	44,990.0
2016	3,473.7	----	----	311.2	473.6	512.3	19,599.3	.8	----	.6	----	30,837.0
2017	5,141.1	----	----	206.7	591.0	----	22,013.1	2.3	----	29.1	----	41,770.0
2018	6,303.6	----	3,149.7	----	1,100.6	42.7	17,088.9	----	----	20.3	----	47,319.2
2019	3,990.3	----	----	----	1,242.1	109.6	21,069.1	----	----	9.4	----	37,747.7
2020	5,096.9	2.4	----	----	1,800.4	68.6	18,882.9	----	----	9.4	----	33,348.1
2021	4,652.6	1.4	----	----	1,178.0	1,632.6	22,968.7	----	----	16.2	----	35,263.2
2022	8,626.0	.2	65.7	----	199.1	4.6	22,102.0	4,537.4	----	19.1	----	51,646.2
2023[1]	708.4	5.2	----	----	----	334.9	20,419.6	----	----	----	----	25,909.7

[1] Preliminary.   Source: Foreign Agricultural Service, U.S. Department of Agriculture (FAS-USDA)

Currencies

A "currency" rate involves the price of the base currency (e.g., the dollar) quoted in terms of another currency (e.g., the yen), or in terms of a basket of currencies (e.g., the dollar index). The world's major currencies have traded in a floating exchange rate regime ever since the Bretton-Woods international payments system broke down in 1971 when President Nixon broke the dollar's peg to gold. The two key factors affecting a currency's value are central bank monetary policy and the trade balance. An easy monetary policy (low interest rates) is bearish for a currency because the central bank is aggressively pumping new currency reserves into the marketplace and because foreign investors are not attracted to the low interest rate returns available in the country. By contrast, a tight monetary policy (high interest rates) is bullish for a currency because of the tight supply of new currency reserves and attractive interest rate returns for foreign investors.

The other key factor driving currency values is the nation's current account balance. A current account *surplus* is bullish for a currency due to the net inflow of the currency, while a current account *deficit* is bearish for a currency due to the net outflow of the currency. Currency values are also affected by economic growth and investment opportunities in the country. A country with a strong economy and lucrative investment opportunities will typically have a strong currency because global companies and investors want to buy into that country's investment opportunities. Futures on major currencies and on cross-currency rates are traded primarily at the CME Group.

Dollar – The dollar index (Barchart.com symbol DXY00) traded sideways in the first half of 2023 and was supported by the Federal Reserve's hike in its federal funds rate target range by +25 bp at the February, March, and May policy meetings. Sticky US price pressures and a strong labor market kept the Fed hawkish, with the January CPI rising by +6.4% yr/yr, well above the Fed's 2% inflation target, and the April unemployment rate falling to match a 54-year low of 3.4%. In addition, a crisis in US regional banks boosted safe-haven demand for the dollar after Silicon Valley Bank collapsed in March, the biggest US bank failure since 2008. However, the dollar weakened in June and July, posting a 1-3/4 year low. At its June meeting, the FOMC kept its federal funds rate target range unchanged at 5.00%-5.25%. Inflation pressures abated and weighed on the dollar after June CPI eased to +3.0% yr/yr, the smallest increase in 3 years. The Fed then paused its rate hike cycle after raising the fed funds target range to the cycle high of 5.25%-5.50% at the July FOMC meeting. However, the 10-year T-note yield rose to a 16-year high of 5.019% in October, pushing the dollar index up to 1-year high of 107.348. The dollar index retreated into year-end after the FOMC at its December meeting signaled a pivot to rate cuts in 2024. The dollar index finished 2023 down -1.9% yr/yr at 101.333.

Euro – EUR/USD (Barchart.com symbol ^EURUSD) ratcheted higher into mid-2023 and posted a 2-year high of 1.1275 in July. The European Central Bank (ECB) in 2023 raised its deposit rate by a total of 200 basis points to a record high of 4.00% in September, 2023. Sticky price pressures kept the ECB hawkish into Q3 of 2023 as the Eurozone CPI in September eased to only 4.3% yr/yr, more than double the ECB's 2% price target. However, the euro fell to a 1-year low in October as high interest rates hurt the Eurozone economy. Eurozone manufacturing activity in July contracted by the most in 3-1/2 years, and Eurozone real GDP in Q3-2023 fell to zero growth year-on-year from +0.6% yr/yr in Q2. The euro recovered into year-end after ECB President Lagarde at the October ECB meeting said talks of ECB rate cuts "are totally premature." The 10-year German bund yield climbed to a 12-year high of 3.03% in October, boosting the euro. EUR/USD finished 2023 up +3.1% yr/yr at $1.1038 per euro.

Yen – USD/JPY (Barchart.com symbol ^USDJPY) posted a 1-1/2 year low of 127.23 yen per dollar in January. The yen had support in early 2023 on speculation the Bank of Japan (BOJ) was close to exiting its negative rate policy. The BOJ, at its July policy meeting, widened its yield-curve-control and raised the upper limit of its 10-year JGB yield target to 1.0% from 0.5%, which was bullish for the yen. However, the yen weakened and fell to a 1-year low against the dollar in November as the BOJ continued its large-scale bond buying program and maintained its negative interest rate target at -0.1%. Weakness in Japan's economy dampened expectations that the BOJ would end its bond buying and negative interest rates after Japan's Q3 GDP fell -3.3% (yr/yr annualized), the steepest pace of contraction in 3 years. The yen then strengthened into year-end on weakness in the dollar when the Federal Reserve in December signaled a pivot toward cutting interest rates. USD/JPY finished 2023 up +7.6% yr/yr at 141.03 yen per dollar.

BRITISH POUND - CME
Weekly Selected Futures as of 03/28/2024

WEEKLY SELECTED FUTURES
As of 03/28/2024

Chart High 1.7184 on 07/15/2014
Chart Low 1.0379 on 09/26/2022

Nearby Futures through Last Trading Day.

U.S. Dollars per British Pound

Year	Jan.	Feb.	Mar.	Apr.	May	June	July	Aug.	Sept.	Oct.	Nov.	Dec.	Average
2014	1.6468	1.6566	1.6617	1.6747	1.6841	1.6916	1.7075	1.6700	1.6303	1.6077	1.5773	1.5631	1.6476
2015	1.5139	1.5334	1.4969	1.4960	1.5454	1.5586	1.5558	1.5581	1.5334	1.5335	1.5193	1.4984	1.5286
2016	1.4387	1.4309	1.4256	1.4315	1.4523	1.4210	1.3145	1.3103	1.3148	1.2336	1.2441	1.2471	1.3554
2017	1.2351	1.2487	1.2348	1.2643	1.2923	1.2812	1.2999	1.2956	1.3317	1.3202	1.3232	1.3405	1.2890
2018	1.3828	1.3962	1.3976	1.4070	1.3462	1.3285	1.3169	1.2879	1.3057	1.3011	1.2896	1.2663	1.3355
2019	1.2907	1.3012	1.3174	1.3028	1.2839	1.2674	1.2462	1.2150	1.2353	1.2656	1.2881	1.3103	1.2770
2020	1.3074	1.2951	1.2355	1.2415	1.2291	1.2525	1.2684	1.3134	1.2953	1.2973	1.3214	1.3446	1.2835
2021	1.3640	1.3864	1.3856	1.3839	1.4085	1.4015	1.3808	1.3795	1.3721	1.3685	1.3446	1.3310	1.3755
2022	1.3551	1.3532	1.3162	1.2922	1.2450	1.2312	1.1997	1.1968	1.1320	1.1306	1.1753	1.2175	1.2371
2023	1.2237	1.2079	1.2144	1.2452	1.2479	1.2637	1.2887	1.2704	1.2385	1.2174	1.2432	1.2661	1.2439

Average.   *Source: FOREX*

Volume of Trading of British Pound Futures in Chicago   In Thousands of Contracts

Year	Jan.	Feb.	Mar.	Apr.	May	June	July	Aug.	Sept.	Oct.	Nov.	Dec.	Total
2014	2,123.0	2,139.8	2,315.4	1,415.6	1,592.2	2,547.6	1,728.8	1,781.2	3,181.2	2,283.2	1,740.6	1,988.2	24,837.0
2015	2,024.6	1,677.7	2,854.7	1,918.6	2,234.4	2,374.3	1,744.8	2,048.9	2,139.5	1,635.5	1,506.4	1,985.3	24,144.7
2016	1,919.1	2,025.0	2,574.4	1,967.0	1,953.3	4,034.0	2,337.1	1,855.1	2,559.9	2,714.9	2,678.6	2,507.8	29,126.0
2017	2,491.4	1,975.1	3,110.3	2,009.6	2,313.0	3,147.8	1,991.9	2,124.7	3,406.7	2,570.9	2,940.8	3,085.7	31,167.9
2018	2,930.4	2,739.3	3,020.1	2,256.6	2,838.9	3,023.7	2,501.4	2,318.6	2,974.4	2,407.6	2,873.0	2,555.1	32,439.0
2019	2,387.4	2,153.5	3,367.7	1,911.6	2,340.7	2,398.6	2,081.9	2,341.3	3,177.6	3,406.7	1,731.0	3,243.9	30,542.3
2020	1,979.5	2,268.4	3,581.3	1,329.0	1,635.6	2,592.6	2,052.1	1,964.1	2,959.7	2,410.4	1,893.8	3,325.5	27,991.8
2021	1,686.4	1,783.0	2,325.1	1,627.1	1,787.1	2,546.7	2,098.4	1,589.3	2,416.0	1,856.3	2,050.7	2,479.9	24,246.0
2022	1,941.3	2,139.9	2,951.2	1,995.0	2,190.9	2,949.1	2,279.8	2,427.1	4,450.5	3,109.1	2,388.5	2,410.4	31,232.7
2023	1,719.8	1,826.5	3,130.0	1,624.8	2,053.1	2,826.7	2,037.2	2,100.0	2,762.6	2,175.3	2,275.9	2,287.0	26,818.9

Contract size = 62,500 GBP.   *Source: CME Group; Chicago Mercantile Exchange (CME)*

Average Open Interest of British Pound Futures in Chicago   In Contracts

Year	Jan.	Feb.	Mar.	Apr.	May	June	July	Aug.	Sept.	Oct.	Nov.	Dec.
2014	207,609	232,142	231,703	226,479	236,374	262,034	246,579	231,599	184,224	135,955	160,534	165,669
2015	178,585	173,893	187,709	180,094	179,361	174,693	167,418	168,889	163,232	155,414	169,080	191,263
2016	252,441	261,454	274,786	240,358	242,020	225,029	231,642	245,379	247,713	259,915	250,809	229,322
2017	223,750	212,997	257,227	252,578	258,691	226,183	199,970	215,422	220,244	182,430	180,126	203,247
2018	220,399	202,010	190,552	186,782	193,666	210,213	186,764	243,357	252,436	216,670	227,938	229,210
2019	210,633	197,522	170,408	150,947	179,450	216,885	249,765	278,217	256,642	234,991	214,554	228,383
2020	200,192	213,507	194,982	157,693	175,157	183,015	177,970	180,039	169,698	150,271	140,788	150,321
2021	149,906	170,763	156,694	153,697	167,714	171,653	179,481	185,703	171,516	166,856	200,514	222,783
2022	189,408	194,150	217,780	262,657	259,413	243,631	231,360	236,695	278,958	254,622	232,233	214,788
2023	199,394	208,683	205,973	228,783	239,898	241,921	239,687	220,514	224,403	231,732	214,959	203,802

Contract size = 62,500 GBP.   *Source: CME Group; Chicago Mercantile Exchange (CME)*

CURRENCIES

CANADIAN DOLLAR - CME
Weekly Selected Futures as of 03/28/2024

WEEKLY SELECTED FUTURES
As of 03/28/2024
Chart High .93990 on 07/03/2014
Chart Low .68090 on 01/20/2016

Nearby Futures through Last Trading Day.

Canadian Dollars per U.S. Dollar

Year	Jan.	Feb.	Mar.	Apr.	May	June	July	Aug.	Sept.	Oct.	Nov.	Dec.	Average
2014	1.0947	1.1054	1.1106	1.0992	1.0890	1.0825	1.0734	1.0922	1.1007	1.1214	1.1332	1.1542	1.1047
2015	1.2128	1.2500	1.2610	1.2338	1.2183	1.2354	1.2851	1.3144	1.3270	1.3071	1.3275	1.3710	1.2786
2016	1.4229	1.3790	1.3212	1.2814	1.2949	1.2890	1.3037	1.3000	1.3091	1.3247	1.3446	1.3351	1.3255
2017	1.3206	1.3110	1.3382	1.3435	1.3597	1.3293	1.2698	1.2608	1.2295	1.2599	1.2766	1.2767	1.2980
2018	1.2432	1.2586	1.2930	1.2729	1.2867	1.3129	1.3133	1.3036	1.3033	1.3014	1.3205	1.3447	1.2962
2019	1.3296	1.3207	1.3370	1.3377	1.3459	1.3281	1.3100	1.3269	1.3242	1.3189	1.3236	1.3165	1.3266
2020	1.3084	1.3284	1.3943	1.4047	1.3969	1.3548	1.3501	1.3229	1.3221	1.3209	1.3064	1.2806	1.3409
2021	1.2716	1.2694	1.2570	1.2491	1.2119	1.2223	1.2512	1.2593	1.2668	1.2433	1.2562	1.2785	1.2530
2022	1.2623	1.2713	1.2649	1.2625	1.2838	1.2809	1.2920	1.2914	1.3325	1.3686	1.3433	1.3592	1.3011
2023	1.3424	1.3451	1.3682	1.3481	1.3518	1.3286	1.3217	1.3481	1.3543	1.3712	1.3708	1.3413	1.3493

Average.   *Source: FOREX*

Volume of Trading of Canadian Dollar Futures in Chicago   In Thousands of Contracts

Year	Jan.	Feb.	Mar.	Apr.	May	June	July	Aug.	Sept.	Oct.	Nov.	Dec.	Total
2014	1,495.5	1,064.6	1,572.7	903.8	917.2	1,253.6	1,064.6	1,057.9	1,612.2	1,569.7	1,191.6	1,393.1	15,096.5
2015	1,371.7	1,298.8	1,881.8	1,394.8	1,170.1	1,595.7	1,447.1	1,477.1	1,710.6	1,283.7	1,040.4	1,630.2	17,301.9
2016	1,794.8	1,487.2	1,748.1	1,481.8	1,476.4	1,665.3	1,240.5	1,408.3	1,860.5	1,507.1	1,614.2	1,413.1	18,697.3
2017	1,405.8	1,093.9	1,726.1	1,277.3	1,559.2	2,136.4	1,641.9	1,517.9	2,143.3	1,559.1	1,420.4	1,741.3	19,222.5
2018	1,721.5	1,622.3	2,110.0	1,530.7	1,964.4	2,133.5	1,410.3	1,639.3	1,688.7	1,667.5	1,544.8	1,986.5	21,019.4
2019	1,526.4	1,255.7	1,866.9	1,538.3	1,735.1	1,939.3	1,391.6	1,651.6	1,931.9	1,886.1	1,347.5	1,936.1	20,006.5
2020	1,518.8	1,768.0	2,724.2	1,230.4	1,118.7	1,770.0	1,364.4	1,277.8	1,893.1	1,527.5	1,378.3	1,895.2	19,466.4
2021	1,389.7	1,451.9	2,136.3	1,502.6	1,427.4	1,991.3	1,686.4	1,503.3	2,055.5	1,495.8	1,566.5	1,895.8	20,102.5
2022	1,558.1	1,501.2	2,109.0	1,465.5	1,725.8	2,323.4	1,883.5	1,777.9	2,686.5	2,044.4	1,791.4	1,899.1	22,765.8
2023	1,402.4	1,533.3	2,602.4	1,351.5	1,596.5	2,011.4	1,288.5	1,603.6	2,321.6	1,942.5	1,622.4	2,046.0	21,322.1

Contract size = 100,000 CAD.   *Source: CME Group; Chicago Mercantile Exchange (CME)*

Average Open Interest of Canadian Dollar Futures in Chicago   In Contracts

Year	Jan.	Feb.	Mar.	Apr.	May	June	July	Aug.	Sept.	Oct.	Nov.	Dec.
2014	159,815	152,844	144,262	119,310	123,899	117,918	125,230	111,259	91,900	100,526	106,812	106,069
2015	108,171	115,078	124,649	120,477	120,938	101,560	143,112	167,447	148,706	121,352	137,170	164,083
2016	165,688	157,798	129,610	111,929	124,671	127,872	117,139	122,876	115,488	105,483	122,002	102,506
2017	98,335	125,839	131,989	145,292	209,032	184,268	169,578	192,761	210,929	173,057	147,137	136,029
2018	158,422	156,598	142,004	125,633	132,447	160,264	154,993	145,448	136,094	119,192	130,139	163,042
2019	158,349	145,288	150,911	150,358	146,396	148,551	175,565	162,610	152,850	156,993	180,311	171,026
2020	189,278	169,358	149,473	118,708	124,870	115,870	135,503	135,224	126,834	119,361	135,770	159,984
2021	160,854	161,399	168,574	173,283	207,298	213,318	189,760	172,322	138,642	142,214	152,038	149,566
2022	142,071	143,762	136,806	155,457	146,940	149,879	141,970	148,925	148,272	143,086	141,720	152,318
2023	136,448	151,714	190,614	157,858	165,788	163,684	150,169	159,554	199,376	187,917	205,039	193,541

Contract size = 100,000 CAD.   *Source: CME Group; Chicago Mercantile Exchange (CME)*

EURO FX - CME
Weekly Selected Futures as of 03/28/2024

WEEKLY SELECTED FUTURES
As of 03/28/2024

Chart High 1.3993 on 05/08/2014
Chart Low .9592 on 09/28/2022

Nearby Futures through Last Trading Day.

Euro per U.S. Dollar

Year	Jan.	Feb.	Mar.	Apr.	May	June	July	Aug.	Sept.	Oct.	Nov.	Dec.	Average
2014	1.3616	1.3669	1.3827	1.3811	1.3733	1.3600	1.3538	1.3315	1.2895	1.2680	1.2474	1.2307	1.3289
2015	1.1605	1.1352	1.0830	1.0817	1.1157	1.1237	1.0997	1.1144	1.1236	1.1218	1.0728	1.0896	1.1101
2016	1.0868	1.1106	1.1143	1.1339	1.1298	1.1241	1.1065	1.1205	1.1214	1.1023	1.0786	1.0538	1.1069
2017	1.0630	1.0640	1.0688	1.0718	1.1057	1.1238	1.1531	1.1820	1.1906	1.1757	1.1745	1.1835	1.1297
2018	1.2202	1.2345	1.2339	1.2274	1.1814	1.1675	1.1686	1.1548	1.1661	1.1483	1.1363	1.1377	1.1814
2019	1.1419	1.1346	1.1300	1.1232	1.1184	1.1295	1.1212	1.1122	1.1006	1.1056	1.1046	1.1113	1.1194
2020	1.1098	1.0904	1.1060	1.0869	1.0904	1.1257	1.1473	1.1829	1.1785	1.1765	1.1836	1.2170	1.1413
2021	1.2170	1.2094	1.1899	1.1970	1.2147	1.2039	1.1823	1.1766	1.1764	1.1598	1.1407	1.1305	1.1832
2022	1.1316	1.1342	1.1014	1.0796	1.0579	1.0559	1.0179	1.0120	0.9896	0.9841	1.0210	1.0588	1.0537
2023	1.0779	1.0703	1.0713	1.0966	1.0863	1.0846	1.1058	1.0907	1.0672	1.0564	1.0818	1.0914	1.0817

Average.   *Source: FOREX*

Volume of Trading of Euro FX Futures in Chicago   In Thousands of Contracts

Year	Jan.	Feb.	Mar.	Apr.	May	June	July	Aug.	Sept.	Oct.	Nov.	Dec.	Total
2014	4,422.1	3,733.1	4,781.4	3,046.6	3,338.3	4,261.9	3,048.4	3,507.4	6,106.3	5,900.3	4,564.9	5,497.7	52,208.3
2015	5,560.3	3,639.7	7,724.4	5,745.4	5,549.4	6,980.8	4,666.0	5,245.6	5,468.3	4,455.2	4,243.0	6,077.9	65,356.1
2016	4,077.1	4,559.6	5,453.9	3,688.1	3,192.6	4,996.0	2,734.2	2,994.6	4,677.7	3,357.0	4,596.8	5,128.3	49,455.9
2017	4,328.4	3,667.0	5,810.9	3,353.5	4,129.2	5,345.8	4,449.8	4,681.0	5,929.7	4,704.7	4,593.7	5,462.1	56,455.8
2018	6,129.6	4,985.2	6,336.2	4,410.2	7,312.1	7,459.5	4,527.2	6,009.6	6,216.1	5,419.0	4,626.7	5,353.7	68,785.1
2019	4,149.7	3,318.9	5,517.7	3,915.4	3,879.5	5,625.9	3,785.7	3,989.0	5,715.2	3,891.3	2,976.1	5,725.8	52,490.1
2020	3,592.5	4,460.3	7,943.4	2,910.0	3,047.6	5,615.9	4,709.7	4,291.7	5,891.3	3,726.3	3,359.6	5,870.9	55,419.2
2021	3,372.8	3,372.8	5,965.5	3,365.9	3,288.3	5,478.9	3,533.3	2,905.4	5,100.2	3,409.1	3,940.8	5,123.8	48,856.6
2022	3,431.2	3,985.7	6,936.4	3,582.5	4,072.3	6,099.8	4,798.2	5,018.3	8,107.4	4,652.7	4,687.2	6,132.8	61,504.4
2023	3,944.4	3,994.6	7,331.6	3,402.9	4,472.8	6,041.4	3,963.3	4,167.1	6,078.7	4,663.4	4,407.5	5,904.3	58,372.1

Contract size = 125,000 EUR.   *Source: CME Group; Chicago Mercantile Exchange (CME)*

Average Open Interest of Euro FX Futures in Chicago   In Contracts

Year	Jan.	Feb.	Mar.	Apr.	May	June	July	Aug.	Sept.	Oct.	Nov.	Dec.
2014	251,507	285,722	289,786	266,980	270,902	302,019	322,167	390,128	429,750	434,763	467,267	427,194
2015	430,963	443,172	477,046	453,055	436,488	388,813	358,550	366,585	340,638	357,347	432,251	432,591
2016	402,675	425,594	367,707	340,746	352,037	344,370	380,293	367,126	350,287	403,624	430,112	425,424
2017	413,834	410,809	414,949	414,920	429,990	435,606	439,731	464,075	459,095	444,328	467,275	505,655
2018	587,907	576,878	540,887	501,746	521,277	539,601	491,694	522,487	503,058	486,553	526,379	541,129
2019	523,488	531,388	513,724	501,896	518,852	525,286	536,433	541,997	533,735	522,478	573,113	576,176
2020	575,652	614,696	620,821	546,543	550,837	592,110	630,078	705,319	684,320	643,667	637,589	676,072
2021	676,833	681,580	678,964	657,266	708,387	724,854	686,851	694,731	680,222	686,614	697,867	686,236
2022	686,407	698,994	694,818	678,280	703,595	696,563	683,016	702,536	702,466	649,608	680,220	742,950
2023	758,604	788,946	769,098	764,302	786,713	765,836	756,915	755,706	733,405	696,021	707,166	747,272

Contract size = 125,000 EUR.   *Source: CME Group; Chicago Mercantile Exchange (CME)*

CURRENCIES

JAPANESE YEN - CME
Weekly Selected Futures as of 03/28/2024

WEEKLY SELECTED FUTURES
As of 03/28/2024
Chart High 1.01310 on 06/24/2016
Chart Low   .66110 on 11/14/2023

Nearby Futures through Last Trading Day.

Japanese Yen per U.S. Dollar

Year	Jan.	Feb.	Mar.	Apr.	May	June	July	Aug.	Sept.	Oct.	Nov.	Dec.	Average
2014	103.80	102.12	102.34	102.51	101.83	102.07	101.75	102.97	107.37	108.03	116.37	119.42	105.88
2015	118.27	118.75	120.36	119.52	120.85	123.67	123.31	123.04	120.08	120.15	122.63	121.63	121.02
2016	118.20	114.63	112.94	109.58	109.00	105.46	104.08	101.31	101.84	103.85	108.63	116.12	108.80
2017	114.94	112.98	112.90	110.05	112.23	110.96	112.37	109.85	110.81	112.93	112.82	112.92	112.14
2018	110.89	107.87	106.09	107.62	109.69	110.13	111.48	111.04	112.04	112.77	113.35	112.25	110.43
2019	108.95	110.46	111.14	111.69	109.98	108.06	108.24	106.21	107.50	108.16	108.90	109.09	109.03
2020	109.30	110.03	107.67	107.77	107.19	107.60	106.72	106.04	105.60	105.20	104.40	103.75	106.77
2021	103.74	105.34	108.71	109.02	109.13	110.14	110.21	109.82	110.15	113.16	114.04	113.89	109.78
2022	114.84	115.18	118.66	126.37	128.74	134.09	136.59	135.36	143.18	147.09	142.04	134.90	131.42
2023	130.37	133.13	133.68	133.50	137.25	141.45	141.03	144.89	147.89	149.60	149.81	143.81	140.53

Average.   *Source: FOREX*

Volume of Trading of Japanese Yen Futures in Chicago   In Thousands of Contracts

Year	Jan.	Feb.	Mar.	Apr.	May	June	July	Aug.	Sept.	Oct.	Nov.	Dec.	Total
2014	3,335.1	2,865.2	3,324.4	2,335.1	2,285.1	2,615.9	2,143.3	2,335.6	3,904.6	4,728.3	3,791.3	4,655.9	38,319.8
2015	4,041.9	2,593.2	3,160.9	2,462.5	2,548.1	3,539.0	2,236.0	3,410.2	3,926.7	2,985.0	2,201.2	3,075.8	36,180.5
2016	3,637.8	3,997.1	3,022.3	2,736.8	2,141.9	3,547.6	2,632.9	2,225.8	3,262.3	2,343.2	3,889.4	3,151.8	36,588.8
2017	3,844.0	2,739.9	4,044.3	2,989.3	3,355.7	3,767.5	2,819.8	3,398.4	4,610.2	3,425.4	3,496.3	3,132.6	41,623.4
2018	3,479.6	3,457.9	3,574.2	2,600.7	3,248.2	3,097.7	2,775.9	2,522.3	2,585.9	3,624.0	2,707.5	3,305.4	36,979.3
2019	2,676.8	2,013.3	2,896.6	2,126.6	3,223.0	3,162.4	2,168.4	3,377.7	2,995.4	2,562.4	2,303.3	3,067.8	32,573.8
2020	2,894.9	3,621.5	4,886.9	1,517.2	1,465.3	2,354.0	1,858.3	1,849.7	2,070.0	1,762.1	2,067.2	2,597.3	28,944.4
2021	1,721.2	1,889.3	2,806.3	2,207.4	1,961.2	2,507.8	2,028.8	1,958.9	2,825.5	2,332.1	2,485.0	2,377.6	27,101.0
2022	2,172.2	2,145.8	3,417.4	2,869.2	2,959.4	3,975.5	3,080.9	3,671.9	5,025.5	3,665.6	3,038.4	3,543.0	39,564.9
2023	2,963.0	2,654.9	4,642.6	2,805.7	3,721.5	4,454.5	4,121.0	3,121.2	3,879.9	3,676.3	3,930.0	4,281.4	44,252.0

Contract size = 12,500,000 JPY.   *Source: CME Group; Chicago Mercantile Exchange (CME)*

Average Open Interest of Japanese Yen Futures in Chicago   In Contracts

Year	Jan.	Feb.	Mar.	Apr.	May	June	July	Aug.	Sept.	Oct.	Nov.	Dec.
2014	217,565	201,386	190,296	174,544	163,960	170,679	163,460	202,088	234,084	205,740	233,431	252,694
2015	218,141	204,791	206,382	190,770	217,291	275,725	249,546	259,312	213,125	181,162	237,763	217,541
2016	243,541	246,520	196,787	171,510	161,320	155,959	156,403	163,674	156,868	157,987	177,739	247,079
2017	206,164	203,979	208,760	199,364	209,490	199,979	238,520	221,773	210,652	262,262	270,180	240,954
2018	242,152	261,583	232,642	151,792	163,587	159,871	195,077	189,113	204,846	225,418	222,065	225,312
2019	218,956	188,471	182,210	186,856	183,500	150,681	136,179	154,403	149,503	155,896	185,665	189,780
2020	185,583	207,128	148,638	127,937	154,095	145,299	146,576	150,267	155,711	170,881	179,877	203,787
2021	195,954	186,577	177,791	160,902	155,987	176,021	200,529	195,981	204,572	247,775	243,804	196,904
2022	212,141	198,166	226,901	245,026	243,487	235,455	227,188	234,905	266,006	260,853	239,717	201,962
2023	175,290	178,973	185,325	179,358	210,599	252,728	239,048	241,511	274,068	267,469	265,567	228,160

Contract size = 12,500,000 JPY.   *Source: CME Group; Chicago Mercantile Exchange (CME)*

SWISS FRANC - CME
Weekly Selected Futures as of 03/28/2024

WEEKLY SELECTED FUTURES
As of 03/28/2024
Chart High 1.22820 on 01/16/2015
Chart Low .96690 on 12/15/2016

Nearby Futures through Last Trading Day.

Swiss Francs per U.S. Dollar

Year	Jan.	Feb.	Mar.	Apr.	May	June	July	Aug.	Sept.	Oct.	Nov.	Dec.	Average
2014	0.9039	0.8934	0.8805	0.8830	0.8888	0.8955	0.8977	0.9100	0.9367	0.9526	0.9641	0.9769	0.9152
2015	0.9412	0.9361	0.9796	0.9602	0.9325	0.9309	0.9544	0.9685	0.9723	0.9697	1.0099	0.9938	0.9624
2016	1.0070	0.9916	0.9809	0.9642	0.9792	0.9691	0.9820	0.9716	0.9737	0.9872	0.9969	1.0201	0.9853
2017	1.0079	1.0017	1.0022	1.0007	0.9863	0.9678	0.9602	0.9653	0.9626	0.9820	0.9913	0.9869	0.9846
2018	0.9605	0.9346	0.9478	0.9686	0.9972	0.9901	0.9945	0.9879	0.9682	0.9940	1.0009	0.9922	0.9780
2019	0.9895	1.0018	1.0003	1.0087	1.0105	0.9878	0.9878	0.9788	0.9906	0.9929	0.9931	0.9819	0.9936
2020	0.9693	0.9763	0.9578	0.9700	0.9692	0.9517	0.9334	0.9101	0.9150	0.9123	0.9107	0.8880	0.9387
2021	0.8865	0.8976	0.9296	0.9214	0.9023	0.9080	0.9170	0.9144	0.9227	0.9227	0.9216	0.9200	0.9136
2022	0.9189	0.9220	0.9291	0.9456	0.9789	0.9697	0.9687	0.9570	0.9728	0.9951	0.9636	0.9321	0.9545
2023	0.9241	0.9258	0.9256	0.8983	0.8975	0.9001	0.8734	0.8786	0.8995	0.9037	0.8908	0.8645	0.8985

Average.   *Source: FOREX*

Volume of Trading of Swiss Franc Futures in Chicago   In Thousands of Contracts

Year	Jan.	Feb.	Mar.	Apr.	May	June	July	Aug.	Sept.	Oct.	Nov.	Dec.	Total
2014	714.1	552.0	819.7	535.8	607.3	792.8	721.4	758.5	1,121.3	1,026.6	834.4	1,154.9	9,638.9
2015	752.0	244.8	537.2	472.1	421.0	513.2	379.8	433.0	433.6	381.7	458.4	607.8	5,634.4
2016	406.6	559.6	531.2	399.3	393.9	650.6	328.1	418.4	596.9	454.4	604.0	625.8	5,968.8
2017	474.3	372.0	598.5	391.8	645.0	638.1	603.4	687.9	772.9	551.5	527.2	715.5	6,978.1
2018	712.9	521.6	651.2	504.3	626.3	699.4	502.7	633.4	709.1	564.5	483.6	653.0	7,262.1
2019	470.9	340.4	688.3	514.3	526.3	809.6	463.6	623.8	725.4	645.6	532.9	805.3	7,146.4
2020	574.8	644.6	1,190.5	379.1	399.9	578.0	517.6	510.5	646.6	408.3	436.8	619.2	6,906.0
2021	384.6	475.1	645.8	397.5	410.5	600.0	473.1	437.5	634.7	466.6	543.4	516.1	5,984.8
2022	432.9	409.2	647.0	381.5	529.1	743.0	550.1	545.0	783.5	458.6	452.5	460.0	6,392.4
2023	391.1	342.9	615.4	394.1	429.5	546.9	424.2	372.2	570.9	498.4	432.9	692.7	5,711.3

Contract size = 125,000 CHF.   *Source: CME Group; Chicago Mercantile Exchange (CME)*

Average Open Interest of Swiss Franc Futures in Chicago   In Contracts

Year	Jan.	Feb.	Mar.	Apr.	May	June	July	Aug.	Sept.	Oct.	Nov.	Dec.
2014	42,329	48,122	56,682	47,081	49,564	42,368	38,273	52,798	61,701	58,348	60,929	63,108
2015	54,230	35,769	42,525	32,785	32,615	26,518	26,717	40,075	40,143	37,866	64,828	62,677
2016	50,939	51,074	43,286	40,453	46,929	48,028	42,074	42,193	43,527	58,626	57,887	63,292
2017	48,235	47,924	48,104	45,251	49,672	45,409	40,566	40,367	41,027	56,027	80,732	88,812
2018	72,099	71,614	56,365	60,123	100,513	102,678	91,755	89,149	66,738	65,735	78,129	79,614
2019	64,926	72,668	80,612	83,816	92,633	66,089	52,993	55,459	60,491	64,391	70,885	68,183
2020	50,882	53,178	41,286	33,135	39,248	41,089	49,709	55,420	53,401	48,887	51,484	53,062
2021	49,008	50,264	46,672	41,958	42,158	43,685	44,316	44,076	51,682	55,297	50,744	43,939
2022	42,130	44,359	46,913	43,812	51,052	44,171	41,654	43,057	45,804	45,032	45,045	38,765
2023	39,536	40,620	40,322	43,566	40,915	43,106	43,379	50,481	59,445	58,423	55,478	34,784

Contract size = 125,000 CHF.   *Source: CME Group; Chicago Mercantile Exchange (CME)*

CURRENCIES

United States Merchandise Trade Balance[2]   In Millions of Dollars

Year	Jan.	Feb.	Mar.	Apr.	May	June	July	Aug.	Sept.	Oct.	Nov.	Dec.	Total
2014	-37,433	-40,119	-42,940	-43,735	-39,575	-38,895	-38,935	-36,935	-41,672	-41,067	-39,808	-42,838	-483,952
2015	-38,865	-33,903	-48,732	-39,836	-38,502	-42,425	-40,340	-44,205	-41,641	-40,873	-40,451	-41,003	-490,776
2016	-40,044	-43,306	-36,801	-38,048	-39,032	-41,719	-39,931	-40,146	-37,004	-38,555	-43,896	-40,976	-479,458
2017	-43,556	-39,785	-41,124	-44,227	-43,985	-42,579	-43,854	-41,391	-41,593	-42,848	-45,463	-46,535	-516,940
2018	-47,072	-48,793	-43,508	-46,129	-41,421	-44,811	-49,673	-49,558	-50,563	-52,453	-49,401	-55,212	-578,594
2019	-49,146	-47,264	-48,467	-49,433	-50,303	-48,518	-48,289	-48,565	-44,542	-41,804	-38,956	-44,107	-559,394
2020	-43,950	-40,611	-43,967	-52,981	-54,700	-49,121	-59,470	-62,219	-58,182	-61,489	-64,414	-61,776	-652,880
2021	-62,331	-64,872	-65,941	-65,898	-66,379	-70,831	-69,338	-71,816	-76,771	-67,360	-79,379	-80,656	-841,572
2022	-86,503	-86,960	-102,536	-86,016	-84,075	-80,851	-71,672	-67,315	-71,726	-78,329	-63,818	-71,386	-951,187
2023[1]	-70,229	-70,072	-59,855	-72,348	-66,325	-63,484	-64,415	-58,077	-60,603	-63,935	-61,883	-62,201	-773,427

[1] Preliminary.   [2] Not seasonally adjusted.   *Source: Bureau of Economic Analysis, U.S. Department of Commerce (BEA)*

Index of Real Trade-Weighted Dollar Exchange Rates for Total Agriculture[3] (U.S. Markets)   (2000 = 100)

Year	Jan.	Feb.	Mar.	Apr.	May	June	July	Aug.	Sept.	Oct.	Nov.	Dec.
2015	95.5	96.9	98.6	98.0	97.8	99.0	100.5	102.5	103.1	101.8	102.6	103.5
2016	105.6	104.7	102.6	101.2	102.4	102.9	103.0	102.2	103.0	103.7	106.2	107.8
2017	107.9	106.4	106.0	105.2	105.3	104.0	102.5	101.6	101.1	102.6	102.7	102.2
2018	100.5	100.0	100.5	100.4	103.1	104.7	104.8	105.1	105.5	105.8	106.5	106.2
2019	104.8	104.7	105.3	105.6	106.7	106.2	105.5	107.0	107.3	106.8	106.3	105.6
2020	105.0	106.1	109.9	111.9	111.1	108.9	108.8	107.8	107.2	106.3	104.6	102.9
2021	102.4	103.0	104.5	104.6	104.2	105.2	106.6	106.9	106.9	107.7	108.5	109.5
2022	109.1	109.4	110.8	111.5	114.4	115.6	117.4	116.7	119.5	121.5	119.1	116.5
2023[1]	114.7	115.3	115.9	115.1	115.8	116.2	115.4	117.0	118.1	117.8	117.3	117.0
2024[2]	116.8	116.5	116.6	116.8	116.9	117.0	117.0	116.9	116.8	116.7	116.7	116.7

[1] Preliminary.   [2] Forecast.   [3] Real indexes adjust nominal exchange rates for differences in rates of inflation, to avoid the distortion caused by high-inflation countries. A higher value means the dollar has appreciated. Federal Reserve Board Index of trade-weighted value of the U.S. dollar against 10 major currencies. Weights are based on relative importance in world financial markets.
Source: Bureau of Economic Analysis, U.S. Department of Commerce (BEA)

Index of Real Trade-Weighted Dollar Exchange Rates for Total Agriculture[3] (U.S. Competitors)   (2000 = 100)

Year	Jan.	Feb.	Mar.	Apr.	May	June	July	Aug.	Sept.	Oct.	Nov.	Dec.
2015	94.3	96.2	99.5	99.0	97.7	98.6	100.2	101.5	102.8	101.8	103.7	103.9
2016	106.3	104.8	103.1	101.0	101.5	101.7	101.8	100.8	101.4	102.1	104.2	105.6
2017	105.2	104.0	103.7	103.0	101.9	101.0	99.3	97.9	97.4	98.6	98.9	98.0
2018	96.2	95.9	96.4	96.9	100.8	102.4	102.6	104.0	105.1	104.9	104.9	104.7
2019	104.0	104.0	105.0	105.5	106.7	105.4	104.8	107.2	108.2	107.8	107.6	106.4
2020	106.5	108.4	111.1	113.2	112.8	109.4	108.9	107.6	107.7	107.8	106.3	103.6
2021	103.6	104.1	106.0	105.5	104.9	105.7	107.6	107.9	107.6	108.8	109.9	111.1
2022	110.6	110.1	111.7	111.8	114.8	115.8	118.9	118.0	120.2	121.6	118.7	115.3
2023[1]	114.1	114.5	115.0	113.1	113.8	114.2	113.0	115.2	117.1	116.5	115.9	115.6
2024[2]	115.3	114.9	115.0	115.5	115.7	115.8	115.8	115.8	115.7	115.6	115.6	115.7

[1] Preliminary.   [2] Forecast.   [3] Real indexes adjust nominal exchange rates for differences in rates of inflation, to avoid the distortion caused by high-inflation countries. A higher value means the dollar has appreciated. Federal Reserve Board Index of trade-weighted value of the U.S. dollar against 10 major currencies. Weights are based on relative importance in world financial markets.
Source: Bureau of Economic Analysis, U.S. Department of Commerce (BEA)

Merchandise Trade and Current Account Balances[3]   In Billions of Dollars

Year	Merchanise Trade Balance					Current Account Balance				
	Canada	Germany	Japan	Switzerland	United Kingdom	Canada	Germany	Japan	Switzerland	United Kingdom
2011	-49.7	229.4	128.3	54.5	-51.5	-40.7	195.3	146.5	40.7	-84.4
2012	-65.7	252.1	62.5	71.2	-101.3	-58.2	185.7	221.3	86.1	-83.0
2013	-59.4	245.9	46.4	79.7	-142.3	-49.7	226.3	128.1	54.5	-51.5
2014	-43.1	282.4	36.8	60.2	-149.3	-65.7	250.5	62.5	71.3	-101.3
2015	-55.3	289.1	136.9	76.5	-142.1	-59.4	254.7	46.3	79.7	-142.3
2016	-49.0	292.0	193.6	63.2	-139.7	-43.1	292.9	36.6	60.2	-149.3
2017	-46.5	297.7	204.4	45.2	-88.1	-56.1	302.5	136.4	75.6	-142.1
2018	-45.4	297.7	175.6	72.5	-108.5	-49.4	296.2	189.2	66.1	-139.7
2019[1]	-48.9	286.2	150.5	65.9	-157.7	-48.9	297.1	196.6	64.4	-98.6
2020[2]	-47.1	281.2	162.6	65.9	-145.7	-52.8	311.0	163.6	78.6	-94.4

[1] Estimate.   [2] Projection.   [3] Not seasonally adjusted.   *Source: Organization for Economic Cooperation and Development (OECD)*

EURO / SWISS FRANC
Weekly Cash as of 03/28/2024

WEEKLY CASH
As of 03/28/2024

Chart High 1.2647 on 05/22/2013
Chart Low .8597 on 01/15/2015

EURO / BRITISH POUND
Weekly Cash as of 03/28/2024

WEEKLY CASH
As of 03/28/2024

Chart High .94972 on 03/19/2020
Chart Low .69371 on 07/17/2015

BRITISH POUND / JAPANESE YEN
Weekly Cash as of 03/28/2024

WEEKLY CASH
As of 03/28/2024

Chart High 195.897 on 06/24/2015
Chart Low 124.162 on 03/18/2020

Forex.

EURO / JAPANESE YEN
Weekly Cash as of 03/28/2024

WEEKLY CASH
As of 03/28/2024

Chart High 165.36 on 03/20/2024
Chart Low 109.56 on 06/24/2016

Forex.

Diamonds

The diamond, which is the mineral form of carbon, is the hardest, strongest natural material known on earth. The name *diamond* is derived from *adamas*, the ancient Greek term meaning "invincible." Diamonds form deep within the Earth's crust and are typically billions of years old. Diamonds have also have been found in and near meteorites and their craters. Diamonds are considered precious gemstones but lower grade diamonds are used for industrial applications such as drilling, cutting, grinding and polishing.

Supply – World production of natural gem diamonds in 2023 fell by -1.6% yr/yr to 74.0 million carats, well below the 2008 record high of 114.0 million carats (one carat equals 1/5 gram or 200 milligrams). The world's largest producers of natural gem diamonds are Russia with 32.4% of world production in 2023, Botswana with 23.0%, Angola with 10.7%, and South Africa with 5.1%. World production of natural industrial diamonds in 2023 remained unchanged yr/yr at 45.000 million carats. The main producers of natural industrial diamonds in 2023 were Russia with 40.0% of world production, Congo with 17.8%, Botswana with 15.6%, and South Africa with 13.3%.

Trade – The US in 2023 imported 400,000 carats of natural diamonds and relied on imports for 56% of its consumption.

World Production of Natural Gem Diamonds   In Thousands of Carats

Year	Angola	Australia	Botswana	Brazil, unspec-ified	Central African Republic	China, unspec-ified	Congo (Kinshasa)	Ghana, unspec-ified	Namibia	Russia	Sierra Leone	South Africa	World Total
2018	7,570	281	17,200	251	11	99	3,030	59	2,397	24,200	593	3,960	85,200
2019	8,230	260	16,600	166	21	51	3,830	38	2,018	25,400	649	2,870	80,700
2020	6,960	219	11,900	125	45	21	2,550	26	1,550	17,500	513	3,390	58,900
2021	7,850	220	16,000	143	73		2,820		1,760	21,900	671	3,890	73,900
2022[1]	7,890		17,100	158	73		1,980		2,050	23,500	551	3,860	75,200
2023[2]	7,900		17,000	160			2,000		2,000	24,000	550	3,800	74,000

[1] Preliminary.   [2] Estimate.   [3] Less than 1/2 unit.   *Source: U.S. Geological Survey (USGS)*

World Production of Natural Industrial Diamonds[4]   In Thousands of Carats

Year	Angola	Australia	Botswana	Brazil	Central African Republic	China	Congo (Kinshasa)	Ghana	Russia	Sierra Leone	South Africa	Vene-zuela	World Total
2018	841	13,800	7,300	----	3	----	12,100	----	19,000	148	5,950	----	62,200
2019	915	12,700	7,090	----	6	----	11,300	----	19,900	162	4,310	----	58,500
2020	773	10,700	5,080	----	11	----	10,200	----	13,700	128	5,090	----	48,200
2021	1,000	8,000	7,000	----		----	11,000	----	17,000		6,000	----	45,000
2022[1]	1,000		7,000	----		----	8,000	----	18,000		6,000	----	45,000
2023[2]	1,000		7,000	----		----	8,000	----	18,000		6,000	----	45,000

[1] Preliminary.   [2] Estimate.   [3] Formerly Zaire.   *Source: U.S. Geological Survey (USGS)*

U.S. Exports of Industrial Diamonds   In Thousands of Carats

Year	Belgium	France	Hong Kong	India	Israel	Mexico	Singa-pore	Switzer-land	Thailand	United Arab Emirates	United Kingdom	Other	World Total
2015	187.0	67.1	1,660.0	672.0	243.0	316.0	6.8	12.3	146.0	391.0	6.7	6.2	4,020.0
2016	564.0	9.4	1,170.0	669.0	184.0	331.0	5.1	44.2	148.0	408.0	49.7	6.3	3,790.0
2017	85.7	0.9	1,420.0	561.0	61.0	609.0	1.1	22.8	96.4	97.3	6.4	9.0	3,130.0
2018	14.1	22.4	761.0	620.0	54.8	253.0	6.7	5.9	56.5	183.0	21.9	12.9	2,220.0
2019[1]	25.4	1.4	593.0	291.0	34.9	286.0	2.4	4.8	536.0	80.7	4.8	22.4	2,000.0
2020[2]	4.9	0.7	233.0	316.0	28.8	298.0	0.2	4.3	40.2	112.0	19.5	32.2	1,180.0

[1] Preliminary.   [2] Estimate.   *Source: U.S. Geological Survey (USGS)*

Salient Statistics of Industrial Diamonds in the United States   In Millions of Carats

	Bort, Grit & Powder & Dust Natural and Synthetic							Stones (Natural)					Net Import Reliance
	--- Production ---												
Year	Manu-factured Diamond	Secon-dary	Imports for Con-sumption	Exports & Reexports	In Manu-factured Products	Gov't Sales	Apparent Con-sumption	Price Value of Imports $/Carat	Secon dary Pro-duction	Imports for Con-sumption	Exports & Reexports	Gov't Sales	Apparent Con-sumption	Price Value of Imports $/Carat	% of Con-sumption
---	---	---	---	---	---	---	---	---	---	---	---	---	---	---	---
2018	----	32.0	574.0	39.0	----	----	652.0	.12	----	2.5	----	----	----	2.96	67
2019	----	35.6	306.0	114.0	----	----	342.0	.14	----	1.1	----	----	----	5.82	56
2020	----	35.0	190.0	90.7	----	----	264.0	.19	----	.5	----	----	----	8.41	38
2021	----	1.2	261.0	99.1	----	----	295.0	.18	----	.3	----	----	----	13.00	55
2022[1]	----	14.4	303.0	94.0	----	----	373.0	.19	----	.8	----	----	----	8.40	56
2023[2]	----	14.0	280.0	72.0	----	----	370.0	.16	----	.4	----	----	----	14.00	56

[1] Preliminary.   [2] Estimate.   [3] Less than 1/2 unit.   *Source: U.S. Geological Survey (USGS)*

Eggs

Eggs provide a low-priced protein source worldwide. Each commercial chicken lays between 265-280 eggs per year. In the United States, the grade and size of eggs are regulated under the federal Egg Products Inspection Act (1970). The grades of eggs are AA, A, and B, and must have sound, whole shells and must be clean. The difference among the grades of eggs is internal and mostly reflects the freshness of the egg. Table eggs vary in color and can be determined by the color of the chicken's earlobe. For example, chickens with white earlobes lay white eggs and chickens with reddish-brown earlobes lay brown eggs. In the U.S., egg size is determined by the weight of a dozen eggs, not individual eggs, and range from Peewee to Jumbo. Store-bought eggs in the shell stay fresh for 3 to 5 weeks in a home refrigerator, according to the USDA.

Eggs are primarily used as a source of food, although eggs are also widely used for medical purposes. Fertile eggs, as a source of purified proteins, are used to produce many vaccines. Flu vaccines are produced by growing single strains of the flu virus in eggs, which are then extracted to make the vaccine. Eggs are also used in biotechnology to create new drugs. The hen's genetic make-up can be altered so that the whites of the eggs are rich in tailored proteins that form the basis of medicines to fight cancer and other diseases. The U.S. biotech company Viragen and the Roslin Institute in Edinburgh have produced eggs with 100 mg or more of the easily extracted proteins used in new drugs to treat various illnesses, including ovarian and breast cancers.

Futures on eggs are traded on the Dalian Commodity Exchange.

Prices – The average monthly price of all eggs received by farmers in the US in 2023 fell by -26.9% yr/yr to 174.8 cents per dozen, falling below the posted record in 2022.

Supply – World egg production in 2022 rose by +0.3% at 1.662 billion eggs. The world's largest egg producers were China with 35.8% of world production, the US with 6.6%, Mexico and Brazil with 3.5%, Russia with 2.8%, Japan with 2.6%, France with 0.9%, and Germany and Spain with 0.8%. US egg production in 2023 rose by +1.3% to 110.249 billion eggs, below the 2019 record high of 113.370. The average number of hens and pullets on US farms in 2022 fell by -3.1% yr/yr to 379.304 million, below the 2019 record high of 399.500.

Demand – US consumption of eggs in 2020 rose by +1.0% yr/yr to 8.085 billion dozen eggs, a new record high. US per capita egg consumption in 2023 rose by +3.9% yr/yr to 287.4 eggs per year per person. Per capita egg consumption reached a high of 277.2 eggs in 1970, fell sharply in the 1990s to a low of 174.9 in 1995, and then began rebounding to current levels.

Trade – US imports of eggs in 2020 fell by -0.6% yr/yr to 18.0 million dozen eggs. US exports of eggs in 2020 fell by -0.6% yr/yr to 280.0 million dozen eggs, down from the 2014 record high of 393.844 million dozen.

World Production of Eggs   In Millions of Eggs

Year	Brazil	China	France	Germany	Italy	Japan	Mexico	Russia	Spain	Ukraine	United Kingdom	United States	World Total
2014	44,811	459,063	15,935	12,685	12,749	41,699	48,438	41,313	12,498	19,391	11,653	100,879	1,275,706
2015	45,219	465,424	16,319	11,807	13,093	42,015	50,048	42,093	12,780	16,615	11,966	97,208	1,297,144
2016	46,115	465,802	13,605	11,979	13,300	42,704	51,324	43,043	13,183	14,799	12,370	102,112	1,318,728
2017	50,574	538,822	14,631	12,087	12,994	43,353	52,287	44,290	13,503	15,351	12,886	107,242	1,496,306
2018	53,163	544,305	15,351	12,326	13,150	43,796	54,187	44,398	13,186	15,971	13,303	110,074	1,523,269
2019	55,265	576,786	14,251	12,512	12,810	43,996	55,656	44,492	12,872	16,511	13,541	113,206	1,582,441
2020	57,204	604,681	15,121	12,937	12,372	43,881	56,905	44,503	13,648	16,006	13,266	111,734	1,647,971
2021[1]	57,862	594,654	15,609	13,044		42,904	57,489	44,578	13,342	13,931	13,800	111,395	1,647,465
2022[2]	58,639	592,217	15,364	13,225		43,279	58,526	45,717	13,477	11,803	10,854	109,514	1,652,288

[1] Preliminary.   [2] Forecast.   [3] Selected countries.   *Source: Food and Agricultural Organization of the United Nations (FAO)*

Salient Statistics of Eggs in the United States

	--- Hens & Pullets ---		Rate of Lay	----- Eggs -----							----- Consumption -----	
	On Farm Dec. 1[3]	Average Number During Year	Per Layer During Year[4]	Total Produced	Price in cents Per Dozen	Value of Production[5]	Total Egg Production	Imports[6]	Exports[6]	Used for Hatching	Total	Per Capita Eggs[6]
Year	----- Thousands -----		(Number)	----- Millions -----		Million USD	--------------- Million Dozen ---------------					Number
2015	346,343	352,411	276	97,208	164.6	13,608	8,101	123.3	313.6	995.6	6,781	256.3
2016	377,371	365,997	279	102,112	76.6	6,514	8,579	129.5	302.8	1,009.6	7,327	272.0
2017	382,266	378,787	281	105,841	86.3	7,597	8,879	34.2	354.9	1,035.2	7,589	280.3
2018	396,870	394,361	279	109,633	115.2	10,586	9,173	17.8	333.1	1,057.5	7,751	287.5
2019	403,273	399,500	283	113,370	79.9	7,335	9,434	18.1	281.8	1,179.3	8,009	291.6
2020	391,010	391,772	285	111,337	91.4	8,665	9,298	18.0	280.0	1,221.3	8,085	292.8
2021	393,078	391,242	285	110,953	99.3	8,713	9,283					
2022[1]	377,606	379,900	289	108,982	239.2	19,352	9,162					
2023[2]	388,700	382,338	286	109,708	174.8		9,127					

[1] Preliminary.   [2] Forecast.   [3] All layers of laying age.   [4] Number of eggs produced during the year divided by the average number of all layers of laying age on hand during the year.   [5] Value of sales plus value of eggs consumed in households of producers. 6/ Shell-egg equivalent of eggs and egg products.
Source: National Agricultural Statistics Service, U.S. Department of Agriculture (NASS-USDA)

EGGS

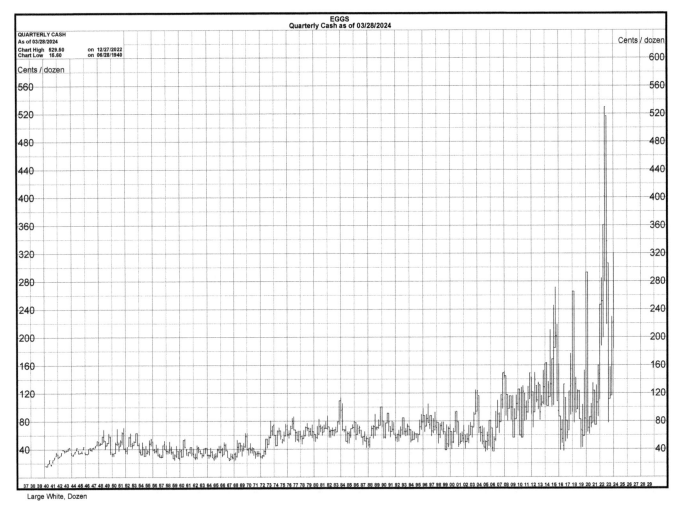

Large White, Dozen

Average Price Received by Farmers for All Eggs in the United States   In Cents Per Dozen

Year	Jan.	Feb.	Mar.	Apr.	May	June	July	Aug.	Sept.	Oct.	Nov.	Dec.	Average
2014	112.0	140.0	124.0	127.0	117.0	109.0	124.0	108.0	105.0	114.0	152.0	177.0	125.8
2015	125.0	129.0	154.0	108.0	173.0	200.0	190.0	239.0	190.0	143.0	200.0	124.0	164.6
2016	118.0	108.0	96.7	67.6	54.7	53.7	64.8	65.1	60.1	51.0	58.8	121.0	76.6
2017	79.5	62.3	78.3	63.3	61.9	63.5	82.3	74.9	109.0	90.1	138.0	133.0	86.3
2018	115.0	126.0	201.0	120.0	85.1	103.0	109.0	109.0	93.1	91.2	113.0	117.0	115.2
2019	101.0	92.3	86.6	63.3	47.5	71.4	51.1	89.1	68.0	66.3	129.0	93.1	79.9
2020	75.3	89.3	172.0	104.0	77.4	71.9	76.2	77.6	83.2	99.4	96.8	73.4	91.4
2021	93.5	99.4	115.0	85.9	83.1	81.1	86.9	108.0	103.0	90.3	109.0	136.0	99.3
2022	147.0	143.0	159.0	230.0	201.0	203.0	264.0	194.0	265.0	281.0	334.0	449.0	239.2
2023[1]	300.0	261.0	280.0	157.0	108.0	128.0	122.0	135.0	122.0	120.0	178.0	187.0	174.8

[1] Preliminary.   *Source: Economic Research Service, U.S. Department of Agriculture (ERS-USDA)*

Average Wholesale Price of Shell Eggs (Large) Delivered, Chicago   In Cents Per Dozen

Year	Jan.	Feb.	Mar.	Apr.	May	June	July	Aug.	Sept.	Oct.	Nov.	Dec.	Average
2014	113.10	135.97	133.93	145.98	116.21	115.83	122.16	116.02	111.93	117.11	143.18	194.45	130.49
2015	111.10	133.50	149.18	113.10	136.20	223.82	206.55	260.40	217.02	161.95	192.55	157.14	171.88
2016	106.71	131.80	93.05	62.93	55.45	46.18	69.70	57.24	64.74	44.07	58.07	94.31	73.69
2017	78.47	65.84	63.76	68.39	55.77	60.32	74.45	80.85	104.85	110.00	130.74	169.80	88.60
2018	116.40	150.24	205.07	177.93	90.95	88.93	129.55	105.22	93.45	99.54	115.26	120.80	124.45
2019	104.98	103.45	83.98	67.73	45.27	56.25	51.68	67.50	84.25	59.91	120.10	119.50	80.38
2020	70.29	96.50	151.59	200.77	83.70	69.14	73.00	66.93	81.21	100.41	101.10	78.73	97.78
2021	85.39	119.55	125.67	92.86	76.75	75.32	89.60	106.50	120.55	96.45	102.55	147.68	103.24
2022	128.95	164.13	155.85	260.31	238.74	205.98	306.00	236.28	266.93	332.40	368.52	474.21	261.53
2023[1]	408.55	248.71	297.72	205.24	87.18	111.76	111.50	123.15	138.55	116.50	184.93	190.50	185.36

[1] Preliminary.   *Source: National Agricultural Statistics Service, U.S. Department of Agriculture (NASS-USDA)*

Total Egg Production in the United States   In Millions of Eggs

Year	Jan.	Feb.	Mar.	Apr.	May	June	July	Aug.	Sept.	Oct.	Nov.	Dec.	Total
2014	8,490	7,636	8,522	8,298	8,523	8,242	8,597	8,591	8,289	8,632	8,521	8,845	101,186
2015	8,656	7,730	8,688	8,352	8,141	7,577	7,850	7,878	7,647	7,970	7,875	8,261	97,208
2016	8,308	7,948	8,622	8,333	8,643	8,349	8,672	8,751	8,507	8,851	8,707	9,100	102,112
2017	9,053	8,124	9,007	8,687	8,918	8,636	8,953	8,922	8,578	8,920	8,791	9,252	105,841
2018	9,132	8,278	9,243	8,932	9,252	8,966	9,239	9,305	9,052	9,370	9,171	9,693	109,633
2019	9,658	8,689	9,675	9,378	9,618	9,215	9,454	9,491	9,223	9,664	9,497	9,809	113,370
2020	9,690	8,946	9,539	9,096	9,121	8,832	9,317	9,353	9,057	9,505	9,327	9,554	111,337
2021	9,482	8,542	9,461	9,121	9,284	8,922	9,242	9,285	9,066	9,469	9,301	9,778	110,953
2022	9,677	8,684	9,471	8,895	9,028	8,697	9,056	9,158	8,899	9,225	8,947	9,245	108,982
2023[1]	9,048	8,210	9,233	9,014	9,295	8,951	9,282	9,337	9,118	9,543	9,251	9,428	109,708

[1] Preliminary.   Source: National Agricultural Statistics Service, U.S. Department of Agriculture (NASS-USDA)

Per Capita Disappearance of Eggs[4] in the United States   In Number of Eggs

Year	First Quarter	Second Quarter	Third Quarter	Fourth Quarter	Total	Year	First Quarter	Second Quarter	Third Quarter	Fourth Quarter	Total
2013	64.2	63.3	64.5	66.0	258.0	2019	72.7	72.6	72.3	74.0	291.6
2014	65.6	66.2	67.2	68.5	267.5	2020	72.1	69.3	71.1	72.8	285.5
2015	65.7	62.9	61.9	65.7	256.3	2021	69.8	68.7	69.3	72.6	280.4
2016	67.4	66.4	67.4	70.8	272.0	2022[1]	71.3	68.2	69.4	70.2	279.0
2017	69.0	69.3	70.3	71.2	280.3	2023[2]	67.5	69.5	71.4	72.4	280.8
2018	69.6	70.9	72.7	74.3	287.5	2024[3]	69.3	70.1	71.5	72.8	283.7

[1] Preliminary.   [2] Estimate.   [3] Forecast.   Source: Economic Research Service, U.S. Department of Agriculture (ERS-USDA)

Egg-Feed Ratio[1] in the United States

Year	Jan.	Feb.	Mar.	Apr.	May	June	July	Aug.	Sept.	Oct.	Nov.	Dec.	Average
2014	8.0	10.9	8.9	8.9	7.9	7.3	9.6	8.6	9.0	10.5	15.1	17.7	10.2
2015	11.4	12.2	15.3	9.6	18.2	21.8	19.5	26.5	20.7	14.7	22.9	12.2	17.1
2016	11.4	10.2	8.8	4.6	2.7	2.5	4.0	4.4	3.9	2.6	3.7	12.1	5.9
2017	6.7	4.3	6.4	4.4	4.2	4.5	6.9	6.1	10.9	8.3	15.3	14.4	7.7
2018	11.6	12.8	22.2	11.3	6.8	9.3	10.5	11.0	8.7	8.5	11.7	11.8	11.4
2019	9.5	8.4	7.6	4.6	2.3	5.1	2.5	7.6	5.0	4.7	13.0	8.3	6.6
2020	5.6	7.4	18.7	10.1	6.3	5.5	6.1	6.3	6.6	8.5	7.7	4.6	7.8
2021	6.6	6.3	7.5	4.4	3.7	3.6	4.1	5.8	6.2	5.4	7.0	9.3	5.8
2022	9.8	8.5	9.2	13.8	11.4	11.4	16.1	11.2	17.0	19.7	23.6	32.2	15.3
2023[1]	19.6	16.0	17.7	8.2	5.0	6.7	6.6	8.1	7.6	7.8	13.8	14.4	11.0

[1] Pounds of laying feed equivalent in value to one dozen eggs.   [2] Preliminary.   Source: Economic Research Service, U.S. Department of Agriculture (ERS-USDA)

Hens and Pullets of Laying Age (Layers) in the United States, on First of Month   In Thousands

Year	Jan. 1	Feb. 1	Mar. 1	Apr. 1	May 1	June 1	July 1	Aug. 1	Sept. 1	Oct. 1	Nov. 1	Dec. 1
2014	363,828	362,628	363,000	364,610	364,840	363,604	363,572	365,799	365,748	366,306	366,329	370,637
2015	368,380	364,996	365,857	366,022	357,858	332,788	332,422	334,040	334,912	338,273	340,554	346,343
2016	356,109	359,429	366,253	366,749	366,217	365,830	364,432	364,935	368,128	370,254	371,438	377,371
2017	377,198	376,955	375,688	376,790	374,671	372,584	372,241	372,995	374,769	376,694	379,323	382,266
2018	382,305	388,227	392,297	392,843	391,760	371,749	391,377	389,840	391,569	391,885	393,060	396,870
2019	403,274	402,220	404,853	406,457	402,890	397,289	392,406	392,182	394,418	396,565	400,204	403,273
2020	403,751	399,049	394,752	396,432	389,069	384,983	381,290	380,700	383,643	385,628	387,664	391,010
2021	392,205	394,810	394,342	392,330	387,478	382,924	383,120	384,082	385,268	388,051	391,369	393,078
2022	397,208	392,677	392,528	376,017	368,400	367,631	367,171	372,619	375,180	377,071	378,040	377,606
2023[1]	375,420	375,915	381,767	384,380	388,010	387,065	383,974	383,372	385,489	389,201	391,051	388,700

[1] Preliminary.   Source: National Agricultural Statistics Service, U.S. Department of Agriculture (NASS-USDA)

EGGS

Eggs Laid Per Hundred Layers in the United States — In Number of Eggs

Year	Jan.	Feb.	Mar.	Apr.	May	June	July	Aug.	Sept.	Oct.	Nov.	Dec.	Average
2014	2,337	2,105	2,342	2,275	2,340	2,267	2,357	2,349	2,265	2,356	2,312	2,388	2,308
2015	2,349	2,103	2,360	2,292	2,339	2,258	2,334	2,332	2,247	2,319	2,261	2,335	2,294
2016	2,322	2,190	2,352	2,274	2,361	2,287	2,378	2,387	2,304	2,386	2,328	2,411	2,332
2017	2,400	2,159	2,394	2,312	2,387	2,319	2,403	2,386	2,283	2,360	2,308	2,381	2,341
2018	2,351	2,121	2,354	2,277	2,362	2,290	2,365	2,381	2,311	2,387	2,322	2,406	2,327
2019	2,398	2,153	2,385	2,317	2,404	2,334	2,410	2,413	2,332	2,426	2,364	2,427	2,364
2020	2,414	2,254	2,411	2,316	2,357	2,305	2,445	2,447	2,355	2,458	2,396	2,438	2,383
2021	2,410	2,165	2,405	2,339	2,410	2,329	2,409	2,413	2,345	2,430	2,371	2,465	2,374
2022	2,450	2,212	2,465	2,390	2,453	2,367	2,448	2,449	2,366	2,443	2,368	2,438	2,404
2023[1]	2,408	2,167	2,407	2,338	2,418	2,347	2,440	2,446	2,369	2,459	2,386	2,464	2,387

[1] Preliminary.   *Source: National Agricultural Statistics Service, U.S. Department of Agriculture (NASS-USDA)*

Egg-Type Chicks Hatched by Commercial Hatcheries in the United States — In Thousands

Year	Jan.	Feb.	Mar.	Apr.	May	June	July	Aug.	Sept.	Oct.	Nov.	Dec.	Total
2014	44,345	41,269	44,801	46,384	49,684	44,271	42,489	39,731	43,671	44,665	36,544	42,991	520,845
2015	43,868	43,774	50,187	50,193	48,315	47,212	42,790	47,131	49,391	50,194	45,848	46,679	565,582
2016	47,775	54,289	57,055	51,266	57,306	57,562	41,609	43,258	44,892	43,344	41,648	45,731	585,735
2017	45,367	48,127	55,919	52,762	53,506	49,722	41,862	45,861	42,725	51,495	48,363	46,697	582,406
2018	51,900	50,148	58,147	58,986	59,756	53,019	50,806	53,207	49,610	54,960	47,043	46,370	633,952
2019	56,219	52,182	55,658	60,668	60,816	51,858	50,919	46,246	50,386	50,266	48,113	46,114	629,445
2020	52,727	48,148	56,212	61,015	52,790	55,537	46,140	50,007	49,989	50,597	48,042	51,765	622,969
2021	50,982	52,273	62,319	59,877	57,332	53,799	50,284	49,005	49,236	45,629	45,718	48,209	624,663
2022	49,048	51,796	60,099	50,636	57,802	56,816	49,915	55,991	53,242	50,330	46,679	48,438	630,792
2023[1]	50,748	52,009	58,971	55,713	58,888	58,209	50,433	52,677	51,036	51,082	48,468	48,415	636,649

[1] Preliminary.   *Source: National Agricultural Statistics Service, U.S. Department of Agriculture (NASS-USDA)*

Cold Storage Holdings of Frozen Eggs in the United States, on First of Month — In Thousands of Pounds[2]

Year	Jan.	Feb.	Mar.	Apr.	May	June	July	Aug.	Sept.	Oct.	Nov.	Dec.
2014	30,350	34,687	34,631	29,044	27,430	28,300	30,142	31,453	29,820	31,126	31,960	30,349
2015	30,718	34,670	35,648	31,978	31,260	28,216	26,890	27,408	30,572	32,324	37,486	36,013
2016	40,896	42,158	37,400	31,741	33,670	35,961	37,960	37,209	31,725	33,084	34,344	36,490
2017	35,652	36,913	41,071	41,911	41,176	39,033	41,712	40,193	35,166	33,934	32,928	27,911
2018	30,162	31,041	32,308	28,175	27,763	30,236	30,705	29,791	31,990	28,935	30,267	29,603
2019	29,376	32,257	34,492	37,561	36,093	35,413	37,369	36,266	36,362	36,299	33,680	35,236
2020	40,771	38,272	38,423	39,586	44,175	37,985	39,293	39,036	39,254	37,878	34,887	32,436
2021	31,696	32,006	29,581	26,739	24,164	26,172	25,342	26,859	26,769	25,183	26,391	23,067
2022	24,726	26,085	27,978	24,328	22,433	21,937	23,686	22,989	25,685	26,645	24,195	23,798
2023[1]	24,243	28,826	25,532	24,362	24,942	30,472	27,345	29,396	32,212	30,181	31,462	29,355

[1] Preliminary.   [2] Converted on basis 39.5 pounds frozen eggs equals 1 case.   *Source: National Agricultural Statistics Service, U.S. Department of Agriculture (NASS-USDA)*

Electric Power Production by Electric Utilities in the United States — In Millions of Kilowatt Hours

Year	Jan.	Feb.	Mar.	Apr.	May	June	July	Aug.	Sept.	Oct.	Nov.	Dec.	Total
2014	222,165	191,345	193,194	170,329	191,866	212,311	227,343	225,392	194,390	176,990	180,869	196,279	2,382,473
2015	208,073	194,871	184,609	165,379	184,165	208,270	229,212	223,696	196,273	172,561	165,247	182,965	2,315,323
2016	203,384	179,182	171,452	162,936	179,569	213,557	234,890	232,277	195,105	171,134	164,301	197,136	2,304,923
2017	199,391	164,437	179,245	164,153	183,781	205,299	233,807	220,364	185,458	174,251	168,569	195,521	2,274,276
2018	214,525	171,847	175,132	165,093	189,538	212,232	235,229	228,767	198,116	177,541	178,265	190,963	2,337,248
2019	202,052	174,633	177,458	159,490	185,133	198,468	229,082	224,601	197,147	168,516	168,594	180,830	2,266,004
2020	185,460	172,751	166,102	147,107	164,989	192,144	227,824	222,608	181,674	165,437	157,891	186,330	2,170,317
2021	191,445	180,728	163,643	151,506	170,419	207,176	226,361	227,827	185,991	164,951	162,702	177,439	2,210,188
2022	202,990	170,198	165,124	150,540	176,816	206,025	231,356	223,901	185,223	159,472	164,538	193,428	2,229,611
2023[1]	184,544	156,023	167,130	149,410	172,502	190,133	229,891	231,175	187,477	167,834	161,079		2,178,761

[1] Preliminary.   *Source: Energy Information Administration, U.S. Department of Energy (EIA-DOE)*

Electric Power

The modern electric utility industry began in the 1800s. In 1807, Humphry Davy constructed a practical battery and demonstrated both incandescent and arc light. In 1831, Michael Faraday built the first electric generator proving that rotary mechanical power could be converted into electric power. In 1879, Thomas Edison perfected a practical incandescent light bulb. The electric utility industry evolved from gas and electric carbon-arc commercial and street lighting systems. In 1882, in New York City, Thomas Edison's Pearl Street electricity generating station established the industry by displaying the four key elements of a modern electric utility system: reliable central generation, efficient distribution, successful end-use, and a competitive price.

Electricity is measured in units called watts and watt-hours. Electricity must be used when it is generated and cannot be stored to any significant degree. That means the power utilities must match the level of electricity generation to the level of demand to avoid wasteful over-production. The power industry has been deregulated to some degree in the past decade, and now major utility companies sell power back and forth across major national grids to meet supply and demand needs. The rapid changes in the supply-demand situation mean that the cost of electricity can be very volatile.

Electricity futures and options are traded on the ASX 24 exchange. Electricity futures are traded on Borsa Istanbul, Borsa Italiana (IDEM), ICE Futures Europe, Nasdaq Commodities, New York Mercantile Exchange, Singapore Exchange, and Tokyo Commodity Exchange.

Supply – US electricity production in 2023 fell by -2.3% yr/yr to 2.178 trillion kilowatt-hours. That was still well below the record high of 3.212 trillion kilowatt-hours in 1998 and indicates how electricity production has been reduced mainly by more efficient production and distribution systems, and to some extent by conservation of electricity by both business and residential consumers. US electricity generation in 2023 required the use of 13.274 billion cubic feet of natural gas (up +7.2% yr/yr), 387 million tons of coal (down -18.0% yr/yr), and 30 million barrels of petroleum (down -31.0% yr/yr).

In terms of kilowatt-hours, natural gas is the most widely used source of electricity production in the US, accounting for 37.4% of electricity production in 2022, followed by coal (19.5%), nuclear (18.2%), hydro (6.0%), and fuel oil (0.5%). Alternative sources of fuel for electricity generation that are gaining favor include solar, wind, geothermal, and biomass.

Demand – Residential use of electricity accounts for the largest single category of electricity demand with usage of 1.509 trillion kilowatt-hours in 2022, accounting for 38.4% of overall usage. Business users in total use more electricity than residential users, with commercial businesses accounting for 35.4% of usage and industrial businesses accounting for 26.0% of usage.

World Net Generation of Electricity   In Billions of Kilowatt Hours

Year	Brazil	Canada	China	France	Germany	India	Japan	Korea, South	Russia	Spain	United Kingdom	United States	World Total
2012	547.2	612.2	4,740.3	543.1	591.4	1,099.3	1,043.6	510.2	1,014.0	282.4	344.7	4,054.3	21,745.3
2013	563.5	637.7	5,171.5	552.4	601.5	1,164.9	1,027.4	515.9	1,003.6	270.5	339.3	4,074.1	22,439.7
2014	581.9	636.0	5,400.1	542.4	592.1	1,269.7	1,027.2	523.0	1,007.4	264.3	321.3	4,104.8	22,848.8
2015	571.6	638.9	5,584.8	550.2	611.5	1,334.3	1,003.0	523.5	1,010.0	266.1	328.1	4,092.9	23,292.9
2016	571.4	644.8	5,904.6	536.0	616.1	1,411.8	1,002.3	535.1	1,033.2	260.5	326.0	4,096.4	23,971.0
2017	581.1	644.6	6,389.8	533.0	620.1	1,490.1	1,005.9	539.8	1,036.3	262.3	324.6	4,059.4	24,690.7
2018	594.2	635.8	6,800.8	552.9	607.6	1,586.9	1,008.9	561.1	1,046.8	261.9	320.1	4,210.5	25,517.6
2019	618.7	627.8	7,152.5	543.8	577.6	1,615.9	989.0	553.3	1,062.9	261.9	313.5	4,165.5	25,887.4
2020[1]	614.4	624.0	7,455.5	506.0	545.4	1,581.3	960.8	550.3	1,044.3	251.2	303.5	4,051.3	25,884.2
2021[2]	662.6	625.9	8,151.5	530.4	557.1	1,702.1	954.9	587.3	1,109.7	259.4	288.6	4,164.6	27,295.2

[1] Preliminary.   [2] Estimate.   NA = Not avaliable.   *Source: Energy Information Administration, U.S. Department of Energy (EIA-DOE)*

World Consumption of Electricity   In Billions of Kilowatt Hours

Year	Brazil	Canada	China	France	Germany	India	Italy	Japan	Korea, South	Russia	United Kingdom	United States	World Total
2012	493.1	539.2	4,439.9	460.7	546.3	891.7	309.5	1,000.3	492.9	890.8	328.3	3,838.8	19,923.5
2013	508.8	560.7	4,846.2	465.2	544.8	946.3	299.8	979.9	497.6	882.9	327.2	3,876.5	20,578.4
2014	522.5	559.3	5,078.7	440.7	534.1	1,041.9	294.0	983.9	504.7	892.8	314.4	3,914.5	20,986.5
2015	512.9	543.4	5,273.5	450.0	537.6	1,093.5	300.1	962.4	505.5	891.8	320.6	3,914.3	21,405.4
2016	513.9	548.5	5,585.6	457.0	539.8	1,161.5	298.3	956.7	516.6	911.4	317.5	3,921.1	22,027.5
2017	519.9	547.0	6,057.2	454.2	540.6	1,228.6	304.7	965.2	521.0	920.4	312.5	3,888.3	22,721.7
2018	531.2	554.1	6,450.4	451.3	532.2	1,312.6	306.3	963.9	542.9	931.1	313.6	4,032.6	23,536.4
2019	538.0	547.3	6,802.7	448.0	517.5	1,342.1	284.0	944.9	534.3	945.4	309.3	3,989.4	23,921.4
2020[1]	533.4	533.5	7,115.1	425.1	499.2	1,328.7	287.3	914.5	531.7	940.0	295.1	3,897.9	23,965.6
2021[2]	577.3	554.7	7,805.7	447.4	511.7	1,442.8	299.9	913.1	567.7	996.4	287.3	3,979.3	25,342.8

[1] Preliminary.   [2] Estimate.   NA = Not avaliable.   *Source: Energy Information Administration, U.S. Department of Energy (EIA-DOE)*

ELECTRIC POWER

World Installed Capacity of Electricity   In Billions of Kilowatt Hours

Year	Brazil	Canada	China	France	Germany	India	Italy	Japan	Russia	Spain	United Kingdom	United States	World Total
2012	130.8	135.4	1,155.0	131.7	185.5	263.5	127.5	296.4	231.3	106.1	98.7	1,063.0	5,585.2
2013	138.2	135.3	1,267.2	131.2	192.9	285.3	127.5	304.1	238.9	107.0	96.6	1,060.1	5,820.3
2014	146.2	138.5	1,379.7	131.3	205.3	314.4	124.8	274.7	259.5	107.0	100.2	1,075.7	6,051.4
2015	154.1	146.0	1,518.6	133.5	211.3	346.9	120.0	285.0	257.5	107.5	100.5	1,073.8	6,313.6
2016	164.5	148.6	1,660.1	134.6	216.5	370.6	117.3	298.2	265.0	106.7	102.3	1,087.1	6,622.8
2017	172.2	149.5	1,790.8	134.6	222.7	393.5	117.4	308.9	267.2	104.9	108.3	1,100.5	6,888.7
2018	178.7	150.5	1,912.0	136.9	236.2	428.3	118.4	318.6	268.0	104.7	113.0	1,114.3	7,174.7
2019	187.6	151.6	2,023.6	138.1	239.3	442.6	120.0	323.3	273.0	110.7	109.6	1,122.3	7,406.9
2020[1]	195.0	152.4	2,224.8	138.3	243.8	453.5	119.4	328.3	276.5	109.9	109.2	1,143.3	7,735.2
2021[2]	205.0	153.6	2,355.6	142.2	250.4	469.5	120.9	334.6	282.6	114.0	108.7	1,176.7	8,013.0

[1] Preliminary.   [2] Estimate.   NA = Not avaliable.   *Source: Energy Information Administration, U.S. Department of Energy (EIA-DOE)*

Electricity in the United States   In Billions of Kilowatt Hours

	Net Generation				Trade				End Use		
Year	Electric Power Sector[2]	Commercial Sector[3]	Industrial Sector[4]	Total	Imports[5]	Exports[5]	Net Imports[5]	T&D Losses[6] and Unaccounted for[7]	Retail Sales[8]	Direct Use[9]	Total
2014	3,937.0	12.5	144.1	4,093.6	66.5	13.3	53.2	243.5	3,764.7	138.6	3,903.3
2015	3,919.3	12.6	145.7	4,077.6	75.8	9.1	66.7	244.1	3,759.0	141.2	3,900.2
2016	3,918.1	12.7	145.9	4,076.7	72.7	6.2	66.5	240.9	3,762.5	139.8	3,902.3
2017	3,877.5	13.1	143.8	4,034.3	65.7	9.4	56.3	226.1	3,723.4	141.1	3,864.5
2018	4,018.2	13.3	146.8	4,178.3	58.3	13.8	44.5	219.6	3,860.1	143.9	4,003.1
2019	3,965.6	13.7	148.5	4,127.9	59.1	20.0	39.0	212.5	3,811.2	143.3	3,954.4
2020	3,853.7	13.0	143.1	4,009.8	61.4	14.1	47.3	200.7	3,717.7	138.7	3,856.4
2021	3,957.2	12.8	139.8	4,109.7	53.2	13.9	39.3	204.2	3,805.9	138.9	3,944.8
2022	4,073.9	16.7	140.0	4,230.7	57.0	15.8	41.2	205.0	3,927.2	139.7	4,066.9
2023[1]	4,023.0	16.6	138.1	4,177.7	40.5	16.9	23.7	204.7	3,858.8	137.9	3,996.7

[1] Preliminary.   [2] Electricity-only and combined-heat-and-power (CHP) plants within the NAICS 22 category whose primary business is to sell electricity, or electricity and heat, to the public.   [3] Commercial combined-heat-and-power (CHP) and commercial electricity-only plants.   [4] Industrial combined-heat-and-power (CHP) and industrial electricity-only plants.   [5] Electricity transmitted across U.S. borders. Net imports equal imports minus exports.   [6] Transmission and distribution losses.   [7] Data collection frame differences and nonsampling error.   [8] Electricity retail sales to ultimate customers by electric utilities and other energy service providers.   [9] Use of electricity that is 1) self-generated, 2) produced by either the same entity that consumes the power or an affiliate, and 3) used in direct support of a service or industrial process located within the same facility or group of facilities that house the generating equipment. Direct use is exclusive of station use.   *Source: U.S. Geological Survey (USGS)*

Electricity Net Generation in the United States by Sector   In Millions of Kilowatt Hours

	Fossil Fuels						Renewable Energy						
Year	Coal[2]	Petroleum[3]	Natural Gas[4]	Other Gases[5]	Nuclear electric power	Hydroelectric Pumped Storage[6]	Conventional Hydroelectric Power	Biomass: Wood[7]	Biomass: Waste[8]	Geothermal	Solar/PV[9]	Wind	Total
2010	1,847,290	37,061	987,697	11,313	806,968	-5,501	260,203	37,172	18,917	15,219	1,212	94,652	4,125,060
2011	1,733,430	30,182	1,013,689	11,566	790,204	-6,421	319,355	37,449	19,222	15,316	1,818	120,177	4,100,141
2012	1,514,043	23,190	1,225,894	11,898	769,331	-4,950	276,240	37,799	19,823	15,562	4,327	140,822	4,047,765
2013	1,581,115	27,164	1,124,836	12,853	789,016	-4,681	268,565	40,028	20,830	15,775	9,036	167,840	4,065,964
2014	1,581,710	30,232	1,126,609	12,022	797,166	-6,174	259,367	42,340	21,650	15,877	17,691	181,655	4,093,606
2015	1,352,398	28,249	1,333,482	13,117	797,178	-5,091	249,080	41,929	21,703	15,918	24,893	190,719	4,077,601
2016	1,239,149	24,205	1,378,307	12,807	805,694	-6,686	267,812	40,947	21,813	15,826	36,054	226,993	4,076,827
2017	1,205,835	21,390	1,296,415	12,469	804,950	-6,495	300,333	41,152	21,610	15,927	53,286	254,303	4,034,268
2018	1,145,962	25,226	1,468,727	13,463	807,084	-5,905	292,524	41,005	17,410	15,967	63,825	272,650	4,170,912
2019[1]	966,148	18,567	1,581,815	13,634	809,409	-5,261	273,707	39,851	18,561	16,011	72,234	300,071	4,118,051

[1] Preliminary.   [2] Anthracite, bituminous coal, subbituminous coal, lignite, waste coal, and coal synfuel.   [3] Distillate fuel oil, residual fuel oil, petroleum coke, jet fuel, kerosene, other petroleum, waste oil, and propane.   [4] Natural gas, plus a small amount of supplemental gaseous fuels.   [5] Blast furnace gas, and other manufactured and waste gases derived from fossil fuels.   [6] Pumped storage facility production minus energy used for pumping.   [7] Wood and wood-derived fuels.   [8] Municipal solid waste from biogenic sources, landfill gas, sludge waste, agricultural byproducts, and other biomass.   [9] Solar thermal and photovoltaic (PV) energy.   *Source: U.S. Geological Survey (USGS)*

Total Electricity Net Generation in the United States   In Billions of Kilowatt Hours

Year	Jan.	Feb.	Mar.	Apr.	May	June	July	Aug.	Sept.	Oct.	Nov.	Dec.	Total
2014	377.3	324.3	331.8	297.6	324.7	357.8	385.8	384.3	339.9	314.5	317.5	338.0	4,093.6
2015	360.5	334.5	324.2	294.1	322.1	362.4	400.4	392.1	350.1	312.1	300.7	324.4	4,077.6
2016	352.7	313.7	304.4	292.9	316.8	367.8	411.9	409.7	351.5	312.9	297.1	345.3	4,076.7
2017	343.2	289.7	317.9	294.3	322.5	357.9	404.4	384.3	335.9	320.4	310.3	353.5	4,034.3
2018	373.2	306.9	321.5	300.8	338.9	371.9	411.3	408.0	356.3	324.9	322.4	342.1	4,178.3
2019	359.5	315.0	326.7	296.7	330.4	353.0	410.0	401.4	360.5	320.4	315.8	338.4	4,127.9
2020	342.0	319.7	309.9	279.8	304.8	352.0	409.9	398.5	333.5	313.7	301.4	344.5	4,009.8
2021	349.2	323.9	311.4	293.3	320.2	373.9	405.6	412.9	347.7	320.2	314.3	337.1	4,109.7
2022	373.8	324.3	324.5	304.0	342.2	379.1	423.0	412.1	351.7	313.9	321.8	360.3	4,230.7
2023[1]	347.8	309.1	329.8	299.7	327.5	356.7	425.6	423.9	358.1	329.4	321.8		4,177.7

[1] Preliminary.   Source: Energy Information Administration, U.S. Department of Energy (EIA-DOE)

Imports[2] of Electricity in the United States   In Billions of Kilowatt Hours

Year	Jan.	Feb.	Mar.	Apr.	May	June	July	Aug.	Sept.	Oct.	Nov.	Dec.	Total
2014	5.5	4.4	5.6	4.8	5.4	5.5	6.3	6.7	6.0	5.4	5.6	5.4	66.5
2015	6.0	5.6	6.6	6.5	6.6	6.7	6.9	7.2	6.6	5.3	5.8	5.9	75.8
2016	6.5	5.4	5.8	4.7	5.6	6.7	7.7	7.3	5.3	5.8	6.4	5.4	72.7
2017	7.0	5.7	6.0	5.6	5.1	6.0	5.9	6.5	5.2	4.0	3.9	4.8	65.7
2018	5.2	4.8	5.6	4.5	5.2	5.5	5.4	6.1	4.3	3.7	3.8	4.1	58.3
2019	4.8	4.6	5.0	4.4	4.7	5.2	5.6	5.9	5.3	3.7	4.8	5.2	59.1
2020	4.6	4.5	5.1	4.7	5.2	5.2	6.6	6.8	4.7	4.7	4.2	5.1	61.4
2021	5.1	4.0	4.6	4.4	4.7	5.2	5.5	4.6	3.9	4.2	3.0	4.0	53.2
2022	4.5	3.4	3.7	3.9	4.4	5.5	6.7	7.2	5.2	4.1	3.5	4.9	57.0
2023[1]	4.5	3.5	3.9	3.6	3.9	3.1	3.2	3.0	2.4	2.9	3.2		40.5

[1] Preliminary.   [2] Electricity transmitted across U.S. borders. Net imports equal imports minus exports.   Source: Energy Information Administration, U.S. Department of Energy (EIA-DOE)

Exports[2] of Electricity in the United States   In Billions of Kilowatt Hours

Year	Jan.	Feb.	Mar.	Apr.	May	June	July	Aug.	Sept.	Oct.	Nov.	Dec.	Total
2014	1.3	1.3	1.9	1.3	0.8	1.0	1.0	0.9	0.8	1.0	0.9	1.1	13.3
2015	0.8	1.4	0.9	0.6	0.6	0.6	0.6	0.7	0.7	0.7	0.7	0.8	9.1
2016	0.4	0.6	0.7	0.5	0.4	0.6	0.6	0.6	0.6	0.4	0.4	0.6	6.2
2017	0.5	0.7	1.0	1.1	0.8	0.8	0.7	0.8	0.7	0.7	0.8	0.7	9.4
2018	1.1	1.3	1.2	1.6	1.1	1.2	0.9	1.1	1.1	0.9	1.3	0.9	13.8
2019	1.5	1.4	2.5	2.0	1.7	1.5	2.0	1.8	1.8	1.5	1.2	1.2	20.0
2020	1.4	1.7	1.3	1.5	1.5	1.3	1.2	0.9	1.0	0.8	0.8	0.8	14.1
2021	0.9	1.1	0.7	1.1	1.0	0.8	1.1	1.3	1.2	1.3	1.8	1.6	13.9
2022	1.5	1.5	1.7	1.4	1.6	1.1	1.3	1.3	1.4	1.3	0.9	0.9	15.8
2023[1]	1.2	1.6	1.3	1.7	1.3	1.4	2.0	1.6	2.3	0.6	0.7		16.9

[1] Preliminary.   [2] Electricity transmitted across U.S. borders. Net imports equal imports minus exports.   Source: Energy Information Administration, U.S. Department of Energy (EIA-DOE)

Total End Use of Electricity in the United States   In Billions of Kilowatt Hours

Year	Jan.	Feb.	Mar.	Apr.	May	June	July	Aug.	Sept.	Oct.	Nov.	Dec.	Total
2014	353.3	319.6	313.8	286.7	302.6	334.2	363.9	364.3	338.5	307.9	296.7	321.8	3,903.3
2015	341.9	317.5	316.5	286.1	299.3	338.3	375.9	374.7	345.0	307.6	287.6	309.8	3,900.2
2016	332.8	307.9	297.4	280.4	296.1	341.6	384.7	393.9	348.4	308.0	288.6	322.4	3,902.3
2017	330.3	286.7	303.1	284.0	303.3	340.6	380.4	372.8	332.9	310.9	294.8	324.7	3,864.5
2018	356.9	303.8	308.5	289.5	315.0	350.1	388.0	394.2	349.3	321.0	302.5	324.6	4,003.1
2019	341.1	306.7	313.6	284.8	308.2	333.2	388.9	385.4	352.5	320.0	297.5	322.4	3,954.4
2020	328.2	306.4	301.8	273.1	285.6	331.4	391.6	381.0	333.7	307.9	288.2	327.5	3,856.4
2021	334.0	309.8	306.3	283.3	301.1	350.2	386.6	393.6	347.8	313.6	298.8	319.5	3,944.8
2022	351.1	316.7	315.9	295.8	321.2	358.8	401.8	402.2	351.9	308.4	303.8	339.5	4,066.9
2023[1]	333.9	301.6	317.4	290.3	308.8	339.5	397.0	402.4	354.5	316.2	302.3		3,996.7

[1] Preliminary.   Source: Energy Information Administration, U.S. Department of Energy (EIA-DOE)

Ethanol

World Production of Fuel Ethanol   In Thousands of Barrels per Day

Year	Australia	Brazil	Canada	China	Colombia	France	Germany	India	Jamaica	Spain	Thailand	United States	World Total
2013	84.5	6,727.9	473.3	809.8	107.1	298.3	198.6	105.4	----	114.2	262.2	13,292.7	24,391.4
2014	71.8	7,061.3	484.4	814.5	112.1	314.4	220.0	96.6	----	121.1	292.0	14,312.8	25,739.8
2015	69.0	7,525.8	474.7	804.2	125.9	313.8	213.4	189.1	----	123.5	324.0	14,807.2	26,830.5
2016	62.5	7,059.9	470.7	699.4	119.8	298.7	216.5	306.4	26.1	82.2	352.2	15,413.2	27,083.4
2017	52.7	6,977.7	479.2	839.3	108.5	294.1	198.6	186.3	----	104.5	403.2	15,936.3	27,620.9
2018	75.3	8,060.0	460.0	810.0	129.6	329.0	195.8	450.0	----	130.4	390.0	16,060.8	29,499.9
2019	65.9	8,860.0	497.0	1,020.0	124.1	307.4	165.7	500.0	----	135.5	430.0	15,776.4	29,400.0
2020		8,100.0	429.0	940.0				520.0	----		390.0	13,941.0	26,480.0
2021[1]		7,320.0	434.0	900.0				870.0	----		350.0	15,015.7	27,250.0
2022[2]		7,400.0	447.0	920.0				1,230.0	----		370.0	15,360.7	28,220.0

[1] Preliminary.   [2] Estimate.   *Source: Renewable Fuels Association*

Salient Statistics of Ethanol in the United States

Year	Ethanol Plants	Ethanol Production Capacity (mgy)	Plants Under Con-struction	Capacity Under Construction (mgy)	Farmer Owned Plants	Farmer Owned Capacity (mgy)	Percent of Total Capacity Farmer	Farmer Owned UC Plants	Farmers Owned UC Capacity	Percent of Total UC Capacity	States with Ethanol Plants
2014	210	14,879.5	7	167.0	----	----	----	----	----	----	28
2015	213	15,077.0	3	100.0	----	----	----	----	----	----	29
2016	214	15,594.0	3	162.0	----	----	----	----	----	----	28
2017	213	15,998.0	3	91.0	----	----	----	----	----	----	28
2018	211	16,241.0	7	465.0	----	----	----	----	----	----	28
2019	205	16,924.0	4	183.0	----	----	----	----	----	----	26
2020	210	16,501.0	9	350.0	----	----	----	----	----	----	27
2021	208	17,436.0	1	16.0	----	----	----	----	----	----	27
2022[1]	208	17,655.0	5	160.0	----	----	----	----	----	----	27
2023[2]	199	17,946.0	4	114.0	----	----	----	----	----	----	27

[1] Preliminary.   [2] Estimate.   *Source: Renewable Fuels Association*

Production of Fuel Ethanol in the United States   In Thousands of Barrels

Year	Jan.	Feb.	Mar.	Apr.	May	June	July	Aug.	Sept.	Oct.	Nov.	Dec.	Total
2014	28,194	25,269	28,120	27,733	28,888	28,629	29,413	28,665	27,807	28,644	28,588	30,831	340,781
2015	29,770	26,814	29,485	27,910	29,666	29,684	30,249	29,762	28,571	29,886	29,675	31,081	352,553
2016	30,452	28,810	30,957	28,208	30,346	30,443	31,469	31,856	30,048	31,006	30,706	32,680	366,981
2017	32,887	29,307	32,393	29,639	31,863	30,794	31,384	32,672	30,701	32,212	32,631	32,952	379,435
2018	32,428	29,519	32,216	30,532	32,215	31,924	33,496	33,773	30,667	32,380	31,514	31,736	382,400
2019	31,601	28,576	30,895	30,951	32,443	31,895	32,541	31,921	29,232	30,941	31,358	33,275	375,629
2020	33,346	30,511	29,409	17,003	21,157	25,959	28,708	28,420	27,779	29,614	29,915	30,108	331,928
2021	28,809	22,895	29,327	28,213	31,224	30,641	31,449	29,087	28,080	32,276	32,383	33,132	357,517
2022	32,191	28,304	31,581	28,956	31,256	31,288	31,498	30,520	27,072	31,440	31,580	30,046	365,731
2023[1]	31,189	28,089	30,753	29,236	31,016	31,146	32,024	31,137	30,290	31,870	31,609		369,121

[1] Preliminary.   *Source: Energy Information Administration, U.S. Department of Energy (EIA-DOE)*

Stocks of Fuel Ethanol in the United States   In Thousands of Barrels

Year	Jan.	Feb.	Mar.	Apr.	May	June	July	Aug.	Sept.	Oct.	Nov.	Dec.
2014	17,153	16,865	17,310	17,610	18,330	18,785	18,696	18,218	18,724	17,341	17,035	18,739
2015	20,647	21,057	20,878	20,854	20,154	20,128	19,701	19,390	18,944	18,984	20,099	21,596
2016	23,347	23,171	22,730	21,336	20,962	21,284	21,381	21,198	20,713	20,113	19,463	19,758
2017	22,679	23,195	23,981	23,671	22,855	21,770	21,167	21,186	21,507	21,663	23,203	23,043
2018	24,342	24,722	23,084	23,379	22,654	21,877	22,668	22,824	24,412	23,698	23,618	23,418
2019	25,115	24,506	23,396	23,331	22,843	22,583	22,892	22,727	23,012	21,784	21,646	22,352
2020	23,884	24,582	27,505	26,124	22,190	19,472	19,784	20,142	20,008	21,738	23,502	24,663
2021	26,117	24,712	22,869	22,368	22,057	21,980	22,656	21,135	20,235	20,067	20,503	22,036
2022	25,874	26,521	26,700	24,284	23,426	23,384	24,197	23,509	21,540	21,708	23,575	24,245
2023[1]	25,383	26,299	24,951	24,085	23,110	22,299	23,101	21,815	22,174	21,309	21,885	

[1] Preliminary.   *Source: Energy Information Administration, U.S. Department of Energy (EIA-DOE)*

ETHANOL
Quarterly Cash as of 03/28/2024

QUARTERLY CASH
As of 03/28/2024
Chart High 3.976 on 07/05/2006
Chart Low .735 on 04/03/2020

Iowa

Average Price of Ethanol in the United States[1]   In Dollars per Gallon

Year	Jan.	Feb.	Mar.	Apr.	May	June	July	Aug.	Sept.	Oct.	Nov.	Dec.	Average
2017	1.400	1.381	1.378	1.541	1.446	1.505	1.472	1.487	1.510	1.407	1.357	1.267	1.429
2018	1.270	1.338	1.408	1.430	1.397	1.403	1.406	1.341	1.223	1.196	1.230	1.156	1.317
2019	1.172	1.209	1.309	1.305	1.253	1.449	1.477	1.360	1.302	1.482	1.434	1.360	1.343
2020	1.245	1.238	1.079	0.774	0.997	1.188	1.284	1.182	1.303	1.370	1.387	1.211	1.188
2021	1.392	1.542	1.729	1.977	2.439	2.315	2.183	2.152	2.290	2.397	3.112	3.067	2.216
2022	2.225	2.027	2.351	2.500	2.711	2.700	2.504	2.483	2.456	2.336	2.468	2.119	2.407
2023	2.145	2.069	2.097	2.317	2.326	2.401	2.380	2.180	2.217	2.208	1.914	1.697	2.163

[1] Northeast and Northwest Iowa.   *Source: Agricultural Marketing Service, U.S. Department of Agriculture (AMS-USDA)*

Average Price of Corn Gluten Feed, 21% protein, Midwest   In Dollars per Ton

Crop Year	Oct.	Nov.	Dec.	Jan.	Feb.	Mar.	Apr.	May	June	July	Aug.	Sept.	Average
2017-18	80.70	93.00	96.25	98.80	106.25	105.15	113.38	138.20	117.63	111.30	106.75	110.13	106.46
2018-19	108.70	114.25	114.67	109.00	103.25	95.50	90.80	89.40	104.38	102.00	100.38	91.25	101.97
2019-20	96.10	110.00	125.13	141.80	112.11	104.80	111.63	104.38	102.80	100.00	96.25	100.00	108.75
2020-21	120.63	137.50	147.50	160.00	174.38	178.70	173.75	195.63	172.50	135.25	139.60	148.38	156.99
2021-22	156.88	174.00	183.34	191.25	195.75	217.79	226.35	224.37	216.25	189.38	201.00	226.15	200.21
2022-23	208.88	205.94	206.25	211.05	209.17	203.65	186.33	167.13	161.98	158.00	154.17	157.83	185.87
2023-24[1]	159.35	165.28	171.53	164.53									165.17

[1] Preliminary.   *Source: Agricultural Marketing Service, U.S. Department of Agriculture (AMS-USDA)*

Average Price of Corn Gluten Meal, 60% protein, Midwest   In Dollars per Ton

Crop Year	Oct.	Nov.	Dec.	Jan.	Feb.	Mar.	Apr.	May	June	July	Aug.	Sept.	Average
2017-18	469.30	487.24	482.88	477.60	483.13	524.75	515.00	500.00	455.00	430.00	435.00	444.00	475.32
2018-19	435.00	470.00	478.00	450.00	426.00	406.00	384.00	359.00	356.00	357.00	366.00	360.00	403.92
2019-20	373.00	385.50	395.00	423.13	456.25	464.50	493.75	453.75	383.40	397.50	405.63	405.50	419.74
2020-21	435.00	516.88	550.50	594.38	631.63	633.00	611.25	588.75	539.00	495.00	504.00	518.13	551.46
2021-22	530.00	562.50	591.67	610.00	614.07	659.84	681.64	642.70	627.29	642.03	657.86	652.08	622.64
2022-23	653.13	652.98	674.53	665.90	663.75	631.21	589.04	548.82	508.93	529.86	546.42	556.64	601.77
2023-24[1]	558.22	576.67	531.22	456.43									530.64

[1] Preliminary.   *Source: Agricultural Marketing Service, U.S. Department of Agriculture (AMS-USDA)*

ETHANOL

World Production of Biodiesel   In Thousands of Barrels per Day

Year	Argentina	Austria	Belgium	Brazil	China	France	Germany	Indo-nesia	Italy	Spain	Thailand	United States	World Total
2011	47.6	5.4	7.5	46.1	12.7	35.6	58.3	31.2	11.7	13.3	10.9	63.1	430.2
2012	48.3	3.4	6.1	46.8	16.0	39.8	52.0	39.1	6.4	9.1	15.7	64.6	456.8
2013	39.1	3.3	5.9	50.9	18.6	39.1	54.9	50.8	10.1	13.3	18.6	88.4	522.1
2014	50.6	4.8	8.2	59.6	19.5	37.7	61.7	60.3	10.4	22.3	20.2	83.4	580.1
2015	35.5	6.2	4.5	69.1	13.6	40.6	56.1	20.7	10.4	20.5	21.5	82.4	522.0
2016	52.0	5.4	4.3	65.5	15.7	36.6	56.7	60.3	10.3	25.1	21.4	102.3	596.1
2017	56.2	4.5	5.3	73.9	18.0	35.5	57.6	48.3	12.4	32.5	24.6	103.8	638.8
2018	47.5	4.7	4.6	93.2	16.9	40.5	60.1	96.4	13.5	31.7	27.0	141.0	751.0
2019[1]	42.0	5.3	4.6	102.0	21.9	37.4	64.4	132.6	15.6	36.6	31.8	145.9	843.9
2020[2]	22.6	4.0	3.9	111.9	32.4	36.4	58.0	146.4	22.5	34.0	31.7	154.9	850.3

[1] Preliminary.   [2] Estimate.   *Source: Renewable Fuels Association*

Production of Biodiesel in the United States   In Thousands of Barrels (mbbl)

Year	Jan.	Feb.	Mar.	Apr.	May	June	July	Aug.	Sept.	Oct.	Nov.	Dec.	Average
2015	1,727	1,851	2,326	2,568	2,784	2,901	2,883	2,933	2,479	2,535	2,521	2,573	30,080
2016	2,490	2,504	2,861	2,856	3,222	3,205	3,331	3,385	3,206	3,433	3,408	3,425	37,327
2017	2,208	2,238	2,761	3,020	3,242	3,344	3,560	3,559	3,507	3,515	3,523	3,515	37,993
2018	2,945	2,996	3,493	3,344	3,538	3,718	3,892	4,028	3,850	4,039	3,783	3,991	43,616
2019	3,427	3,108	3,353	3,623	3,675	3,370	3,776	3,712	3,377	3,436	3,034	3,163	41,054
2020	3,196	3,139	3,594	3,422	3,630	3,590	3,849	3,872	3,790	3,743	3,621	3,761	43,207
2021	3,352	2,578	3,585	3,430	3,537	3,415	3,552	3,560	3,185	3,473	3,360	3,661	40,686
2022	2,857	2,707	3,161	3,018	3,242	3,265	3,490	3,519	3,350	3,464	3,384	3,164	38,620
2023[1]	3,242	2,840	3,325	3,164	3,722	3,636	3,612	3,458	3,438	3,495	3,231		40,540

[1] Preliminary.   *Source: Energy Information Administration, U.S. Department of Energy (EIA-DOE)*

Stocks of Biodiesel in the United States   In Thousands of Barrels (Mbbl)

Year	Jan.	Feb.	Mar.	Apr.	May	June	July	Aug.	Sept.	Oct.	Nov.	Dec.
2016	4,222	4,133	4,167	4,358	4,091	4,726	4,443	4,265	4,227	4,690	5,314	6,398
2017	6,397	6,475	6,189	5,706	4,909	5,052	5,405	5,356	4,849	4,485	4,233	4,268
2018	4,565	4,934	4,925	4,716	4,275	3,850	3,742	3,425	3,371	3,647	4,039	4,662
2019	5,354	5,502	5,389	5,330	4,815	4,408	4,088	3,860	3,706	3,738	3,887	3,907
2020	4,273	4,220	4,429	4,411	4,513	4,318	3,879	3,563	3,221	3,418	3,741	3,665
2021	4,580	4,189	4,284	4,183	3,805	3,748	3,697	3,369	3,230	3,340	3,747	4,187
2022	4,544	4,457	4,692	4,212	3,839	3,404	3,240	2,894	2,826	2,903	3,232	3,608
2023[1]	4,297	4,861	5,055	4,847	4,413	3,978	3,719	3,589	3,576	3,514	3,675	

[1] Preliminary.   *Source: Energy Information Administration, U.S. Department of Energy (EIA-DOE)*

Imports of Biodiesel in the United States   In Thousands of Barrels (mbbl)

Year	Jan.	Feb.	Mar.	Apr.	May	June	July	Aug.	Sept.	Oct.	Nov.	Dec.	Total
2016	248	287	565	969	1,117	1,630	1,681	1,873	1,835	1,822	2,184	2,668	16,879
2017	241	549	650	681	948	1,736	1,670	1,582	205	386	222	504	9,374
2018	246	146	457	308	325	296	157	281	277	468	416	536	3,913
2019	308	267	509	410	281	310	333	140	280	314	417	433	4,002
2020	336	302	333	611	475	446	346	234	360	420	448	373	4,684
2021	228	263	361	500	316	446	357	287	418	473	660	696	5,005
2022	388	121	636	672	315	346	284	371	405	658	903	851	5,950
2023[1]	930	952	916	1,000	832	1,016	725	991	1,280	1,017	1,239		11,889

[1] Preliminary.   *Source: Energy Information Administration, U.S. Department of Energy (EIA-DOE)*

Exports of Biodiesel in the United States   In Thousands of Barrels (mbbl)

Year	Jan.	Feb.	Mar.	Apr.	May	June	July	Aug.	Sept.	Oct.	Nov.	Dec.	Total
2016	42	49	234	246	335	220	250	235	150	114	143	80	2,098
2017	42	59	136	283	239	226	453	387	100	217	49	35	2,228
2018	102	103	255	217	382	275	259	263	190	188	156	61	2,453
2019	72	92	240	370	419	300	392	290	238	158	56	83	2,710
2020	31	89	228	526	496	523	376	512	426	113	73	64	3,458
2021	166	122	267	494	564	658	489	549	474	213	166	291	4,452
2022	209	124	171	632	699	589	625	831	641	468	221	462	5,671
2023[1]	92	132	261	1,044	757	839	691	553	410	451	361		6,097

[1] Preliminary.   *Source: Energy Information Administration, U.S. Department of Energy (EIA-DOE)*

Fertilizer

A fertilizer is a natural or a synthetic chemical substance, or a mixture of both, that enriches the soil to promote plant growth. The three primary nutrients that fertilizers provide are nitrogen, potassium, and phosphorus. In ancient times, and still today, many commonly used fertilizers contain one or more of the three primary ingredients: manure (containing nitrogen), bones (containing small amounts of nitrogen and large quantities of phosphorus), and potash (containing potassium).

At least fourteen different nutrients have been found essential for crops. These include three organic nutrients (carbon, hydrogen, and oxygen, which are taken directly from air and water), three primary chemical nutrients (nitrogen, phosphorus, and potassium), and three secondary chemical nutrients (magnesium, calcium, and sulfur). The others are micronutrients or trace elements and include iron, manganese, copper, zinc, boron, and molybdenum.

Prices – The average price of ammonia (Gulf Coast delivery), a key source of ingredients for fertilizers, rose by -55.1% yr/yr in 2023 to $480 per metric ton, remaining below the 2022 record high of $1,070 per metric ton. The average price of potash in the US in 2022 rose by +69.2% yr/yr to $1,100.00 per metric ton, reaching a new record high.

Supply – World production of ammonia (as contained in nitrogen) in 2023 rose by +3.4% at 150.000 million metric tons, remaining the record high. The world's largest producers of ammonia in 2023 were China with 28.7% of world production, Russia the US and India with 9.3%.

World production of phosphate rock, basic slag, and guano in 2023 fell by -3.5% yr/yr to 220.000 million metric tons. The world's largest producers of phosphate rock in 2023 were China with 40.9% of world production, Morocco with 15.9%, the US with 9.1%, and Russia with 6.4%. US production in 2023 rose by +1.0% yr/yr to 20.000 million metric tons.

World production of marketable potash in 2023 fell by 4.6% yr/yr to 39.000 million metric tons. The world's largest producers of potash in 2023 were Canada with 33.3% of world production, Russia with 16.7%, China with 15.4%, and Belarus with 9.7%. US production of potash in fell by -7.0% to 400,000 metric tons.

Demand – US consumption of phosphate rock in 2023 rose by +7.6% to 24.000 million metric tons. US consumption of potash in 2023 rose by +3.9% yr/yr to 5.3 million metric tons. US consumption of nitrogen in 2021 fell by -1.5% to 9.680 million metric tons.

Trade – US imports of nitrogen in 2023 fell by -6.7% yr/yr to 1.800 million metric tons, and the US relied on imports for 6% of its consumption. US imports of phosphate rock in 2023 rose by +4.0% yr/yr to 2.600 million metric tons. US imports of potash in 2023 rose by +1.2% to 5.000 million metric tons, much higher than the low of 2.220 million metric tons in 2009. Imports accounted for 91% of US consumption.

World Production of Ammonia   In Thousands of Metric Tons of Contained Nitrogen

Year	Canada	China	France	Germany	India	Indo-nesia	Japan	Mexico	Nether-lands	Poland	Russia	United States	Total
2014	3,716	46,850	760	2,540	10,780	5,000	787	714	2,200	2,200	12,030	9,330	140,000
2015	4,004	47,603	1,040	2,370	11,309	5,000	790	473	2,300	2,200	12,455	9,590	142,000
2016	4,133	46,922	1,010	2,500	11,574	4,700	725	438	2,300	2,237	13,300	10,200	144,000
2017	3,745	40,656	750	2,580	11,405	4,900	717	411	2,300	2,367	14,056	11,600	141,000
2018	3,832	37,907	914	2,580	11,900	5,400	673	124	2,200	2,172	14,859	13,100	142,000
2019	3,909	38,922	884	2,415	12,200	6,100	694	----	2,200	2,101	15,802	13,500	145,000
2020	3,895	42,063	822	2,333	12,200	5,900	643	112	2,100	2,262	16,126	14,000	150,000
2021	3,760	42,000	880	2,290	12,100	6,000	691	201	2,000	2,100	16,300	12,700	150,000
2022[1]	3,410	43,000		1,460	13,700	6,000			2,000	1,820	14,000	13,800	145,000
2023[2]	3,400	43,000		1,500	14,000	6,000			2,000	1,800	14,000	14,000	150,000

[1] Preliminary.   [2] Estimate.   *Source: U.S. Geological Survey (USGS)*

Salient Statistics of Nitrogen[3] (Ammonia) in the United States   In Thousands of Metric Tons

Year	Net Import Reliance As a % of Apparent Consumption	Production[3] (Fixed) Fertilizer	Non-fertilizer	Total	Imprts[4] (Fixed)	Exports	Nitrogen[5] Compounds Pro-duced	Con-sumption	Stocks, Dec. 31 - Am-monia	Fixed Nitrogen Com-pounds	Ammonia Con-sumption (Apparent)	Urea FOB Gulf[6] Coast	Urea FOB Corn Belt	Ammonium Nitrate: FOB Corn Belt	Ammonia FOB Gulf Coast
2014	30	8,210	1,120	9,330	4,150	111	8,391	11,400	280	280	13,300	322-333	360-385	570-640	531
2015	30	8,440	1,150	9,590	4,320	93	8,266	12,000	420	420	13,700	225-230	265-295	445-470	481
2016	26	8,930	1,220	10,200	3,840	183	8,918	11,700	400	400	13,800	232-242	255-275	290-405	267
2017	18	10,200	1,390	11,600	3,090	612	9,666	11,900	320	480	14,100	243-260	270-280	260-270	247
2018	14	11,600	1,540	13,100	2,530	224	10,087	10,600	490	450	15,300	261	310	265	281
2019	11	11,900	1,570	13,500	2,020	338	10,260	10,600	420	570	15,200	217	255	245	232
2020	11	12,300	1,630	14,000	1,990	369	10,522	9,830	310	420	15,700	----	----	----	213
2021	13	11,200	1,480	12,700	2,080	231	9,597	9,680	270	570	14,600	----	----	----	578
2022[1]	7			13,800	1,930	700			440		14,800	----	----	----	1,070
2023[2]	6			14,000	1,800	1,000			420		15,000	----	----	----	480

[1] Preliminary.   [2] Estimate.   [3] Anhydrous ammonia, synthetic.   [4] For consumption.   [5] Major downstream nitrogen compounds.   [6] Granular.
Source: U.S. Geological Survey (USGS)

FERTILIZER

World Production of Phosphate Rock, Basic Slag & Guano   In Thousands of Metric Tons (Gross Weight)

Year	Brazil	China	Egypt	Israel	Jordan	Morocco	Russia	Senegal	Syria	Togo	Tunisia	United States	World Total
2014	6,513	120,000	5,378	3,357	7,144	27,390	10,800	1,285	1,234	1,098	3,784	25,300	237,000
2015	5,800	142,000	5,303	3,849	8,336	26,264	11,600	2,100	538	1,150	3,240	27,400	263,000
2016	5,850	144,400	4,300	3,946	7,991	26,900	12,300	1,610	30	850	3,664	27,100	265,000
2017	5,200	123,100	4,800	3,332	8,688	32,800	13,200	1,385	30	733	4,422	27,900	252,000
2018	5,740	96,310	5,000	3,550	8,022	34,400	13,600	1,649	350	1,030	2,800	25,800	224,000
2019	3,049	93,320	5,000	2,807	9,223	35,200	13,800	3,421	350	723	3,878	23,300	224,000
2020	5,223	90,900	4,800	3,090	8,938	37,400	13,800	2,013	420	1,360	3,144	23,500	221,000
2021	6,000	104,107	5,000	2,431	10,015	38,100	14,000	2,500	1,100	1,500	3,726	21,600	238,000
2022[1]	6,200	93,000	5,000	2,170	11,300	39,000	14,000	2,600	1,100	1,500	3,560	19,800	228,000
2023[2]	5,300	90,000	4,800	2,500	12,000	35,000	14,000	2,500	800	1,500	3,600	20,000	220,000

[1] Preliminary.   [2] Estimate.   *Source: U.S. Geological Survey (USGS)*

Salient Statistics of Phosphate Rock in the United States   In Thousands of Metric Tons

Year	Mine Production	Marketable Production	Value Million Dollars	Imports for Consumption	Exports	Apparent Consumption	Producer Stocks, Dec. 31	Avg. Price FOB Mine $/Metric Ton	Avg. Price of Florida & N. Carolina - $/Met. Ton - FOB Mine (-60% to +74%) - Domestic	Export	Average
2014	112,000	25,300	1,990	2,380	----	29,100	5,880	78.59	----	----	----
2015	127,000	27,400	1,980	1,960	----	28,100	6,730	72.41	----	----	----
2016	130,000	27,100	2,090	1,590	----	28,200	7,450	76.90	----	----	----
2017	123,000	27,900	2,060	2,470	----	28,800	8,440	73.67	----	----	----
2018	115,000	25,800	1,830	2,770	----	26,000	10,600	70.77	----	----	----
2019	105,000	23,300	1,580	2,140	----	25,500	9,830	67.90	----	----	----
2020	102,000	23,500	1,780	2,520	----	25,100	11,000	75.50	----	----	----
2021	91,000	21,600	1,800	2,460	----	24,400	10,700	82.40	----	----	----
2022[1]	84,900	19,800	1,960	2,500	----	22,300	10,600	98.00	----	----	----
2023[2]		20,000		2,600	----	24,000	10,000	100.00	----	----	----

[1] Preliminary.   [2] Estimate.   *Source: U.S. Geological Survey (USGS)*

World Production of Marketable Potash   In Thousands of Metric Tons (K_2O Equivalent)

Year	Belarus	Brazil	Canada	Chile	China	Germany	Israel	Jordan	Russia	Spain	United Kingdom	United States	World Total
2014	6,340	311	10,818	1,200	6,110	3,130	2,213	1,255	7,439	685	610	850	41,300
2015	6,468	304	11,462	1,200	5,710	3,110	1,540	1,413	6,954	668	384	740	40,400
2016	6,180	316	10,790	1,200	5,780	2,751	2,068	1,202	6,588	667	287	510	38,700
2017	7,102	306	12,563	1,100	5,510	2,964	1,900	1,392	7,320	789	200	480	42,100
2018	7,346	201	14,024	950	5,450	2,754	2,200	1,486	7,168	604	175	520	43,500
2019	7,348	249	12,770	660	5,900	2,615	2,034	1,516	7,340	520	89	510	42,100
2020	7,562	255	13,784	921	5,570	2,874	2,416	1,598	8,114	352	99	460	44,700
2021	8,000	270	14,239	858	6,000	2,793	2,379	1,563	9,101	376	110	480	47,000
2022[1]	4,000	200	14,593	600	6,000	2,700	2,447	1,637	6,800	420	133	430	40,900
2023[2]	3,800	200	13,000	600	6,000	2,600	2,400	1,800	6,500	250		400	39,000

[1] Preliminary.   [2] Estimate.   *Source: U.S. Geological Survey (USGS)*

Salient Statistics of Potash in the United States   In Thousands of Metric Tons (K_2O Equivalent)

Year	Net Import Reliance As a % of Apparent Consump	Production	Sales by Producers	Value Million Dollars	Imports for Consumption	Exports	Apparent Consumption	Producer Stocks Dec. 31	Dollars per Ton Avg Value of Product	Avg Value of K_2O Equiv	Avg. Price[3] (Metric Ton)
2014	85	850	930	680.0	4,970	100	5,800	----	345.00	735.00	555.00
2015	89	740	620	550.0	5,190	106	5,700	----	360.00	880.00	570.00
2016	88	510	600	410.0	4,550	96	5,100	----	290.00	680.00	460.00
2017	92	480	490	380.0	5,860	128	6,200	----	285.00	775.00	440.00
2018	92	520	520	390.0	5,710	105	6,100	----	275.00	755.00	490.00
2019	91	510	480	390.0	5,150	145	5,500	----	290.00	820.00	530.00
2020	92	460	500	420.0	5,370	147	5,700	----	305.00	850.00	510.00
2021	93	480	490	550.0	6,480	112	6,900	----	425.00	1,120.00	650.00
2022[1]	92	430	400	710.0	4,940	267	5,100	----	620.00	1,790.00	1,100.00
2023[2]	91	400	470		5,000	160	5,300	----		1,210.00	

[1] Preliminary.   [2] Estimate.   [3] Unit of K_2O, standard 60% muriate F.O.B. mine.   *Source: U.S. Geological Survey (USGS)*

114

Fish

Fish are the primary source of protein for a large portion of the world's population. The worldwide yearly harvest of all sea fish (including aquaculture) is between 85 and 130 million metric tons. There are approximately 20,000 species of fish, of which 9,000 are regularly caught. Only 22 fish species are harvested in large amounts. Ground-fish, which are fish that live near or on the ocean floor, account for about 10% of the world's fishery harvest and include cod, haddock, pollock, flounder, halibut, and sole. Large pelagic fish such as tuna, swordfish, marlin, and mahi-mahi, account for about 5% of world harvest. The fish eaten most often in the United States is canned tuna.

Rising global demand for fish has increased the pressure to harvest more fish to the point where all 17 of the world's major fishing areas have either reached or exceeded their limits. Atlantic stocks of cod, haddock, and blue-fin tuna are all depleted, while in the Pacific, anchovies, salmon, and halibut are all over-fished. Aquaculture, or fish farming, reduces pressure on wild stocks and now accounts for nearly 20% of world harvest.

Supply – The US total of fishery products in 2020 (latest data) fell by -2.1% to 21.342 billion pounds, which is down from the 2017 record high of 22.266. The US total domestic catch in 2020 fell by -10.5% to 8.378 billion pounds, and that comprised 39.3% of total US supply. Of the US total domestic catch in 2020, 69.0% of the catch was finfish for human consumption, 19.6% of the catch was a variety of fish for industrial use, and 11.0% was shellfish for human consumption.

The principal species of US fishery landings in 2019 were Pollock with 3.359 billion pounds, Menhaden with 1.507 billion pounds, Pacific Salmon with 838.0 million pounds, Flounder with 551.7 million pounds, and Sea Herring with 82.8 million pounds.

About 30% of the fish harvested in the world are processed directly into fishmeal and fish oil. Fishmeal is used primarily in animal feed. Fish oil is used in both animal feed and human food products. World fishmeal production in the 2022/23 marketing year fell by -4.4% to 5.164 million metric tons. Peru, the European Union, and Thailand are the world's largest producers of fish meal. World production of fish oil in the 2023/23 marketing year fell by -2.9% to 0.993 million metric tons. Chile, Japan, and China are the world's largest producers of fish oil.

World Production of Fish Meal   In Thousands of Metric Tons

Year	Chile	Denmark	European Union	Iceland	Japan	Norway	Peru	Russia	South Africa	Spain	Thailand	United States	World Total
2013-14	395.9	161.8	392.3	82.0	201.0	132.7	1,070.9	75.3	74.8	30.1	460.0	227.0	4,738.5
2014-15	338.8	192.0	427.1	152.0	198.0	174.1	671.2	87.8	72.2	30.4	430.0	279.1	4,482.3
2015-16	236.9	175.0	377.4	90.0	194.8	139.0	558.7	93.4	85.1	30.0	400.0	252.5	4,265.3
2016-17	313.2	222.1	428.4	117.0	192.0	156.8	1,087.0	98.8	80.3	31.0	366.0	251.3	5,001.3
2017-18	335.0	192.6	410.2	133.2	189.9	145.2	1,008.0	104.6	71.8	35.0	375.0	280.2	5,049.1
2018-19	364.2	174.6	397.8	93.0	185.0	142.1	1,006.5	126.9	59.1	33.0	387.0	252.7	5,176.2
2019-20	340.9	172.2	407.4	78.1	183.0	173.1	807.9	123.3	80.0	34.0	398.0	221.7	4,880.5
2020-21[1]	362.1	162.9	403.4	75.9	188.2	131.2	1,267.4	135.0	67.0	35.0	380.0	195.1	5,368.2
2021-22[2]	341.9	135.0	380.5	174.7	190.0	111.1	1,126.2	154.0	70.0	40.0	388.0	21.4	5,402.0
2022-23[3]	365.0	148.0	381.9	145.0	185.0	171.0	740.8	170.0	70.0	36.0	400.0	195.0	5,164.6

[1] Preliminary.   [2] Estimate.   [3] Forecast.   *Source: The Oil World*

World Production of Fish Oil   In Thousands of Metric Tons

Year	Canada	Chile	China	Denmark	Iceland	Japan	Norway	Peru	Africa	Russia	United States	World Total	Fish Oil CIF[4] $ Per Tonne
2013-14	6.0	137.9	20.0	50.1	44.3	60.0	53.2	174.4	4.8	8.6	60.8	969.4	1,791
2014-15	6.1	110.3	24.0	50.1	48.2	62.6	58.8	85.7	7.3	8.6	64.8	871.2	1,909
2015-16	6.1	87.9	44.3	53.7	29.2	61.8	56.8	77.0	7.6	21.0	80.7	858.1	1,713
2016-17	6.0	111.9	43.5	55.7	36.3	62.1	56.0	165.7	7.3	7.5	52.0	954.0	1,445
2017-18	6.0	136.2	55.8	49.7	44.3	71.0	46.8	178.4	6.4	14.1	76.8	1,044.3	1,683
2018-19	6.0	135.7	68.5	51.1	27.4	71.2	41.1	168.9	3.9	16.0	67.9	1,055.2	1,645
2019-20	5.8	125.8	66.2	48.0	27.2	66.3	52.2	110.1	7.6	21.3	60.1	973.7	1,969
2020-21[1]	6.0	156.8	61.0	49.8	24.4	66.0	39.2	218.0	5.6	14.6	50.6	1,084.0	1,905
2021-22[2]	5.0	129.2	62.0	43.5	76.1	67.4	45.6	137.2	10.0	20.1	51.7	1,022.9	2,828
2022-23[3]	5.4	150.0	65.0	45.0	49.0	66.3	61.0	45.0	9.0	16.7	56.0	993.4	3,647

[1] Preliminary.   [2] Estimate.   [3] Forecast.   [4] Any origin, N.W. Europe.   *Source: The Oil World*

FISH

Catfish Inventory of Total Foodsize Fish in the United States on January 1   In Thousands of Fish

Year	Alabama	Arkansas	California	Mississippi	North Carolina	Texas	Other[2]	Total
2015	40,700	9,020	2,670	85,620	3,940	6,360	1,810	150,120
2016	39,500	7,340	2,520	89,410	2,965	7,070	1,745	150,550
2017	40,010	6,400	2,240	73,150	2,440	6,560	1,290	132,090
2018	39,750	10,320	2,665	98,490	1,680	7,580	1,175	161,660
2019	51,090	10,620	2,450	83,970	2,700	6,960	1,945	159,735
2020	49,780	7,030	W	90,760	W	7,185	3,265	158,020
2021	46,490	10,190	W	89,900	W	7,250	2,785	156,615
2022	49,760	9,670	W	86,790	W	7,345	4,290	157,855
2023	45,120	9,340	W	91,710	W	7,355	3,495	157,020
2024[1]	39,160	8,780		81,490		7,315	5,514	215,183

[1] Preliminary.   [2] Other States include State estimates not shown and States suppressed due to disclosure.
Source: National Agricultural Statistics Service, U.S. Department of Agriculture (NASS-USDA)

Catfish Inventory of Total Stockers in the United States on January 1   In Thousands of Fish

Year	Alabama	Arkansas	California	Mississippi	North Carolina	Texas	Other[2]	Total
2015	34,500	44,430	W	147,800	14,160	380	7,520	248,790
2016	48,400	33,300	W	109,200	6,180	W	8,810	205,890
2017	85,400	30,280	W	179,600	W	W	13,660	308,940
2018	122,500	28,690	1,230	212,100	14,070	470	3,010	382,070
2019	85,800	36,650	840	170,400	1,910	1,340	4,120	301,060
2020	58,700	30,590	1,310	193,000	W	W	4,910	288,510
2021	63,100	W	W	209,400	W	W	40,555	313,055
2022	74,300	W	W	205,400	W	W	47,830	327,530
2023	97,200	W	W	198,000	W	W	50,150	345,350
2024[1]	44,400	W	W	127,100	W	W	52,945	224,445

[1] Preliminary.   [2] Other States include State estimates not shown and States suppressed due to disclosure.
Source: National Agricultural Statistics Service, U.S. Department of Agriculture (NASS-USDA)

Catfish Sales of Foodsize Fish in the United States   In Thousands of Fish

Year	Alabama	Arkansas	California	Mississippi	North Carolina	Texas	Other[2]	Total
2014	63,400	9,980	1,340	97,900	1,990	7,050	2,940	184,600
2015	63,000	9,560	1,050	110,000	2,120	7,880	1,900	195,510
2016	62,300	10,300	1,150	105,000	1,930	8,020	1,880	190,580
2017	66,300	11,100	910	112,000	1,380	6,740	1,400	199,830
2018	63,600	10,900	1,600	121,000	1,400	8,520	1,780	208,800
2019	60,300	10,700	1,210	113,000	W	W	11,235	196,445
2020	55,300	9,960	W	128,000	W	8,100	3,025	204,385
2021	47,700	10,400	W	121,000	W	8,950	3,250	191,300
2022	46,600	10,400	W	137,000	W	9,440	2,555	205,995
2023[1]	52,400	10,600	W	128,000	W	11,000	2,580	204,580

[1] Preliminary.   [2] Other States include State estimates not shown and States suppressed due to disclosure.
Source: National Agricultural Statistics Service, U.S. Department of Agriculture (NASS-USDA)

Catfish Sales of Foodsize Fish in the United States   In Thousands of Pounds (Live Weight)

Year	Alabama	Arkansas	California	Mississippi	North Carolina	Texas	Other[2]	Total
2014	105,300	17,200	2,550	161,500	3,400	14,300	3,248	307,498
2015	107,500	14,500	2,200	171,700	3,250	15,600	2,694	317,444
2016	109,000	16,300	1,640	172,000	3,500	15,400	2,334	320,174
2017	112,900	16,800	1,580	180,500	2,600	14,000	2,048	330,428
2018	104,600	18,300	2,850	192,000	2,500	20,200	3,151	343,601
2019	102,500	18,600	2,400	203,500	W	W	20,990	347,990
2020	94,000	15,700	W	192,100	W	17,000	5,328	324,128
2021	90,600	17,300	W	194,300	W	17,400	5,823	325,423
2022	83,900	18,000	W	203,400	W	18,500	5,096	328,896
2023[1]	96,200	16,600	W	188,200	W	21,600	5,205	327,805

[1] Preliminary.   [2] Other States include State estimates not shown and States suppressed due to disclosure.
Source: National Agricultural Statistics Service, U.S. Department of Agriculture (NASS-USDA)

Value of Trout Sold and Distributed and Trout Egg Sales in the United States

Year	Value of Fish Sold (excl. Eggs)	Value of Fish Sold (incl. Eggs)	Value of Distributed Fish (excl. Eggs)	Value of Distributed Fish (incl. Eggs)	Total United States: Number of Eggs (1,000)	Total United States: Average Price (US Dollars per 1,000 Eggs)	Total United States: Total Sales (1,000 US Dollars)
2013	97,414	106,053	110,075	NA	480	4,380	41,170
2014	103,216	111,990	112,239	NA	410	4,150	48,285
2015	104,393	113,099	119,181	NA	440	4,460	45,350
2016	104,983	113,904	129,526	NA	W	6,035	46,305
2017	109,368	118,212	132,247	NA	390	5,965	40,965
2018	101,294	111,879	128,623	NA	370	6,975	35,935
2019	108,469	118,528	136,793	NA	340	9,960	32,390
2020	96,244	104,284	135,325	NA	310	22,975	25,855
2021	98,838	110,997	138,716	NA	270	5,145	26,480
2022[1]	102,920	115,978	139,197	NA	250	4,515	27,205

[1] Preliminary.   Source: National Agricultural Statistics Service, U.S. Department of Agriculture (NASS-USDA)

Trout Sales by Size Category in the United States

	Fish 12" or longer : Live Weight					Fish 6" - 12" : Live Weight					Fish 1" - 6" : Live Weight				
Year	(1,000)	1,000 Pounds	(Lbs)	1,000 US Dollars	USD per Pound	(1,000)	1,000 Pounds	(Lbs)	1,000 US Dollars	USD per Pound	(1,000)	1,000 Pounds	(Lbs)	1,000 US Dollars	USD per Pound
2013	41,170	56,666	1.4	91,174	1.61	3,755	1,375	0.4	5,213	3.79	6,490	171	26.3	1,027	158
2014	48,285	60,733	1.3	95,741	1.58	5,165	1,781	0.3	5,858	3.29	8,350	206	24.7	1,617	194
2015	45,340	57,947	1.3	96,437	1.66	4,900	1,833	0.4	6,422	3.50	8,470	224	26.4	1,534	181
2016	46,305	59,099	1.3	97,076	1.64	5,940	1,699	0.3	6,616	3.89	5,875	135	23.0	1,291	220
2017	40,965	53,887	1.3	102,737	1.91	6,430	1,887	0.3	7,452	3.95	6,470	135	20.9	1,269	196
2018	35,935	47,548	1.3	91,759	1.93	8,050	2,190	0.3	8,152	3.72	6,715	154	22.9	1,383	206
2019	31,865	50,958	1.6	98,514	1.93	9,100	2,179	0.2	8,644	3.97	5,740	167	29.1	1,311	228
2020	25,855	44,513	1.7	88,565	1.99	6,775	1,833	0.3	6,668	3.64	4,785	107	22.4	1,011	211
2021	26,480	44,931	1.7	91,564	2.04	4,860	1,388	0.3	6,062	4.37	5,020	112	22.3	1,212	241
2022[1]	27,205	43,255	1.6	94,749	2.19	5,005	1,571	0.3	6,891	4.39	5,210	137	26.3	1,280	246

[1] Preliminary.   Source: National Agricultural Statistics Service, U.S. Department of Agriculture (NASS-USDA)

Trout Sales of Fish 12" or longer (Foodsize) in the United States   In Thousands of Fish

Year	California	Colorado	Georgia	Idaho	Michigan	North Carolina	Pennsylvania	Virginia	Washington	West Virginia	Wisconsin	Other[2]	Total
2013	W	250	145	30,100	145	3,310	870	430	W	440	480	4,380	41,170
2014	1,310	210	W	36,100	105	3,310	880	480	W	420	410	4,150	48,285
2015	1,350	310	W	32,700	W	3,220	910	590	W	550	440	4,460	45,350
2016	W	380	W	33,000	W	3,960	980	460	W	630	W	6,035	46,305
2017	W	640	W	27,700	W	3,500	970	500	W	590	390	5,965	40,965
2018	W	430	W	22,200	W	3,640	1,210	460	W	450	370	6,975	35,935
2019	W	W	W	19,900	W	W	1,090	440	W	400	340	9,960	32,390
2020	W	680	W	W	W	W	990	450	W	350	310	22,975	25,855
2021	W	610	W	15,400	W	3,100	1,280	510	W	W	270	5,145	26,480
2022[1]	W	570	W	17,100	W	2,910	1,090	550	W	W	250	4,515	27,205

[1] Preliminary.   [2] Other States include State estimates not shown and States suppressed due to disclosure.   W = Withheld.
Source: National Agricultural Statistics Service, U.S. Department of Agriculture (NASS-USDA)

Trout Sales of Fish 12" or longer (Foodsize) in the United States   In Thousands of Pounds (Live Weight)

Year	California	Colorado	Georgia	Idaho	Michigan	North Carolina	Pennsylvania	Virginia	Washington	West Virginia	Wisconsin	Other[2]	Total
2013	W	441	163	35,700	167	3,700	1,050	498	W	551	447	13,178	56,666
2014	1,550	404	W	42,200	119	4,050	1,030	489	W	518	403	9,121	60,733
2015	1,600	405	W	39,100	W	3,700	1,050	567	W	464	414	9,767	57,947
2016	W	441	W	39,700	W	4,400	1,090	427	W	569	W	11,598	59,087
2017	W	634	W	33,600	W	4,150	1,070	524	W	515	378	12,168	53,887
2018	W	591	W	27,000	W	4,000	1,200	512	W	435	357	13,261	47,548
2019	W	W	W	25,000	W	W	1,200	540	W	410	314	16,006	43,758
2020	W	814	W	W	W	W	1,160	683	W	343	291	41,222	44,513
2021	W	712	W	21,700	W	3,450	1,370	653	W	W	272	16,598	44,931
2022[1]	W	664	W	24,300	W	3,250	1,350	637	W	W	257	12,553	43,255

[1] Preliminary.   [2] Other States include State estimates not shown and States suppressed due to disclosure.   W = Withheld.
Source: National Agricultural Statistics Service, U.S. Department of Agriculture (NASS-USDA)

Flaxseed and Linseed Oil

Flaxseed, also called linseed, is an ancient crop that was cultivated by the Babylonians around 3,000 BC. Flaxseed is used for fiber in textiles and to produce oil. Flaxseeds contain approximately 35% oil, of which 60% is omega-3 fatty acid. Flaxseed or linseed oil is obtained through either the expeller extraction or solvent extraction method. Manufacturers filter the processed oil to remove some impurities and then sell it as unrefined. Unrefined oil retains its full flavor, aroma, color, and naturally occurring nutrients. Flaxseed oil is used for cooking and as a dietary supplement as well as for animal feed. Industrial linseed oil is not for internal consumption due to possible poisonous additives and is used for making putty, sealants, linoleum, wood preservation, varnishes, and oil paints.

Prices – The average monthly price received by US farmers for flaxseed in the 2022/23 marketing year fell by -35.2% yr/yr to $17.01 per bushel.

Supply – World production of flaxseed in the 2022/23 marketing year rose by +15.0% yr/yr to 3.496 million metric tons, becoming a new record high. The world's largest producer of flaxseed in 2022/23 was Russia at 61.6% of total world production, Canada with 13.5%, China with 8.3%, and India with 4.0%. US production of flaxseed in 2023 fell by -30.9% to 2.961 million bushels, far below the record level of 10.095 million bushels in 2015. North Dakota is by far the largest producing state for flaxseed and accounted for 73.0% of flaxseed production in 2023, followed by Montana with 27.0%.

World production of linseed oil in 2022/23 rose by +5.5% yr/yr to 839,500 metric tons. The world's largest producers of linseed oil were China with 34.0% of world production in 2022/23, Russia with 18.2%, Belgium with 13.0%, and the US with 8.9%. US production of linseed oil in 2022/23 rose by +6.7% yr/yr at 74.5 million pounds.

Demand – US distribution of flaxseed in 2022/23 rose by +11.9% yr/yr to 11.479 million bushels. The breakdown of usage was 85.8% for crushing into meal and oil, 8.2% for residual, 3.5% for exports, and 2.5% for seed.

Trade – US exports of flaxseed in 2022/23 fell by -16.3% yr/yr to 400,000 bushels. US imports of flaxseed in 2022/23 rose by +0.1% yr/yr to 6.687 million bushels.

World Production of Flaxseed   In Thousands of Metric Tons

Crop Year	Argentina	Australia	Bangladesh	Canada	China	Egypt	France	Hungary	India	Romania	United States	Former USSR	World Total
2013-14	20	6	6	731	399	2	16	1	140	4	85	618	2,255
2014-15	17	6	9	840	350	5	23	1	155	3	162	688	2,457
2015-16	20	6	5	943	330	5	48	1	125	4	256	873	2,835
2016-17	17	6	5	591	365	8	42	1	184	3	221	1,139	2,815
2017-18	14	6	4	555	362	8	55	2	174	4	98	1,350	2,848
2018-19	20	6	5	492	366	9	46	1	99	3	113	1,518	2,889
2019-20	10	6	4	486	360	8	46	2	16	6	162	1,689	3,113
2020-21[1]	20	6	3	578	340	8	59	1	140	2	145	1,707	3,218
2021-22[2]	12	7	4	337	340	9	73	2	135	3	69	1,827	3,040
2022-23[3]	29	7	4	473	290	9	60	2	140	4	109	2,152	3,496

[1] Preliminary.　[2] Estimate.　[3] Forecast.　*Source: The Oil World*

Supply and Distribution of Flaxseed in the United States   In Thousands of Bushels

Crop Year Beginning June 1	Planted	Harvested	Yield Per Acre (Bushels)	Beginning Stocks	Production	Imports	Total Supply	Seed	Crush	Exports	Residual	Total
	---- 1,000 Acres ----			----------- Supply -----------				----------- Distribution -----------				
2014-15	311	302	21.1	763	6,368	7,464	14,595	375	11,850	528	1,034	13,787
2015-16	463	456	22.1	808	10,095	4,436	15,339	303	10,700	870	553	12,425
2016-17	374	366	23.7	2,914	8,656	3,086	14,656	245	10,500	1,332	410	12,486
2017-18	303	272	14.1	2,170	3,842	5,451	11,463	168	9,000	480	186	9,834
2018-19	208	198	22.6	1,629	4,466	5,503	11,598	303	9,150	262	321	10,036
2019-20	374	284	19.8	1,562	5,625	4,382	11,569	247	8,950	875	234	10,306
2020-21	305	296	19.3	1,263	5,706	4,068	11,037	263	8,000	1,188	243	9,694
2021-22[1]	325	280	9.9	1,343	2,768	6,684	10,745	213	9,300	478	266	10,257
2022-23[2]	263	242	17.7	488	4,282	6,687	11,479	284	9,850	400	946	11,479
2023-24[3]	178	160	18.5		2,961							

[1] Preliminary.　[2] Estimate.　[3] Forecast.　NA = not avaliable.　*Source: Economic Research Service, U.S. Department of Agriculture (ERS-USDA)*

Supply and Distribution of Linseed Meal in the United States   In Millions of Pounds

Crop Year Beginning June 1	Stocks June 1	Production	Imports	Total Supply	Domestic Disappearance	Exports	Total Disappearance	Ending Stocks	Average Price at Minneapolis (34% Protein) Cents/Lb.
2014-15	5	213	3	221	212	4	216	5	263.90
2015-16	5	193	7	205	196	4	200	5	234.78
2016-17	5	189	6	200	190	5	195	5	313.17
2017-18	5	162	7	174	166	3	169	5	236.92
2018-19	5	165	8	177	170	2	172	5	236.37
2019-20	5	161	4	170	164	1	165	5	241.57
2020-21	5	144	4	153	145	2	148	5	277.36
2021-22	5	167	4	177	170	2	172	5	311.36
2022-23[1]	5	158	3	166	159	2	161	5	364.29
2023-24[2]	5	150	5	160	153	2	155	5	325.00

[1] Preliminary.   [2] Forecast.   Source: Economic Research Service, U.S. Department of Agriculture (ERS-USDA)

Supply and Distribution of Linseed Oil in the United States   In Millions of Pounds

Crop Year Beginning June 1	Stocks June 1	Production	Total Supply	Exports	Domestic Disappearance	Total Disappearance	Average Price at Minneapolis Cents/Lb.
2014-15	35	231	270	183	52	235	NA
2015-16	35	209	248	196	17	213	NA
2016-17	35	205	244	194	15	209	NA
2017-18	35	176	215	166	14	180	NA
2018-19	35	178	219	173	11	184	NA
2019-20	35	175	213	173	5	178	NA
2020-21	35	156	195	142	18	160	NA
2021-22	35	181	224	178	11	189	NA
2022-23[1]	35	171	219	176	8	184	NA
2023-24[2]	35	162	210	166	10	176	NA

[1] Preliminary.   [2] Forecast.   Source: Economic Research Service, U.S. Department of Agriculture (ERS-USDA)

World Production and Price of Linseed Oil   In Thousands of Metric Tons

Crop Year	Argentina	Bangladesh	Belgium	China	Egypt	Germany	India	Japan	United Kingdom	United States	Former USSR	World Total	Rotterdam Ex-Tank USD $/Tonne
2013-14	----	----	112.0	186.6	2.9	48.7	35.3	1.5	6.7	81.6	19.4	601.1	1,191
2014-15	----	----	123.2	216.7	3.3	49.4	38.6	2.6	6.1	108.7	40.2	696.7	1,162
2015-16	----	----	131.8	225.7	4.5	49.4	34.3	----	6.9	97.8	73.3	764.9	825
2016-17	----	----	125.4	210.7	5.2	52.6	46.8	----	8.5	89.0	91.5	821.2	828
2017-18	----	----	127.6	207.7	6.6	51.9	47.0	----	8.9	78.4	111.8	783.8	837
2018-19	----	----	127.6	216.7	6.6	57.6	39.6	----	10.2	82.3	143.4	807.8	835
2019-20	----	----	120.0	221.2	5.2	49.1	40.6	----	7.1	81.6	149.8	795.1	977
2020-21	----	----	122.5	235.6	5.1	47.6	36.2	----	8.8	70.6	153.6	803.5	1,738
2021-22[1]	----	----	114.2	254.2	4.7	36.7	33.9	----	14.3	69.8	137.0	796.1	1,956
2022-23[2]	----	----	108.8	285.2	4.7	31.3	35.3	----	11.6	74.5	152.6	839.5	1,238

[1] Preliminary.   [2] Forecast.   Source: The Oil World

Production of Flaxseed in the United States, by States   In Thousands of Bushels

Year	Minnesota	Montana	North Dakota	South Dakota	Total
2014	48	425	5,805	90	6,368
2015	42	450	9,315	288	10,095
2016	----	616	7,896	144	8,656
2017	----	342	3,435	65	3,842
2018	----	629	3,792	45	4,466
2019	----	1,335	4,290	----	5,625
2020	----	1,632	4,074	----	5,706
2021	----	545	2,223	----	2,768
2022	----	880	3,402	----	4,282
2023[1]	----	798	2,163	----	2,961

[1] Preliminary.   Source: National Agricultural Statistics Service, U.S. Department of Agriculture (NASS-USDA)

FLAXSEED AND LINSEED OIL

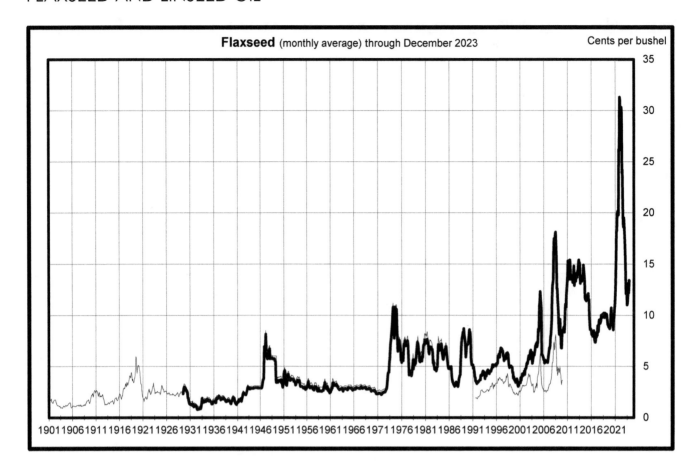

Flaxseed (monthly average) through December 2023   Cents per bushel

Average Price Received by Farmers for Flaxseed in the United States   In Dollars Per Bushel

Crop Year	July	Aug.	Sept.	Oct.	Nov.	Dec.	Jan.	Feb.	Mar.	Apr.	May	June	Average
2014-15	14.00	13.30	11.70	11.50	11.60	11.40	11.70	11.50	11.50	12.00	12.10	11.40	11.98
2015-16	11.50	10.00	9.07	8.57	8.71	8.62	8.46	8.10	8.37	8.10	7.93	8.44	8.82
2016-17	8.48	8.25	7.61	7.37	7.36	7.59	8.26	7.86	8.34	8.03	8.96	8.52	8.05
2017-18	8.40	9.30	9.55	9.23	9.21	9.36	9.40	10.00	9.76	9.92	10.10	10.00	9.52
2018-19	9.96	10.20	9.79	9.79	10.20	9.87	9.85	9.79	10.10	9.93	9.54	9.08	9.84
2019-20	9.10	8.84	8.84	9.01	8.70	8.91	8.97	10.40	10.70	9.31	9.57	10.00	9.36
2020-21	9.64	8.56	9.64	9.76	10.70	10.90	12.00	13.20	15.70	18.10	18.30	19.90	13.03
2021-22	20.10	20.20	19.80	26.20	26.10	31.30	31.00	27.50	28.90	30.20	29.70	23.90	26.24
2022-23	21.60	20.80	18.90	18.60	19.50	18.30	17.70	15.40	14.80	12.10	12.50	13.10	16.94
2023-24[1]	11.00	11.20	12.00	13.00	12.20	13.40	12.10	12.30					12.15

[1] Preliminary.   *Source: National Agricultural Statistics Service, U.S. Department of Agriculture (NASS-USDA)*

Average Price of Linseed Meal (34% protein) at Minneapolis   In Dollars Per Ton

Crop Year	July	Aug.	Sept.	Oct.	Nov.	Dec.	Jan.	Feb.	Mar.	Apr.	May	June	Average
2014-15	295.00	252.50	302.50	214.38	283.75	287.50	250.00	230.63	230.50	239.38	256.88	258.00	258.42
2015-16	284.38	287.50	256.00	215.00	209.80	200.00	195.00	197.50	195.00	218.13	301.50	375.63	244.62
2016-17	364.38	335.00	316.25	305.63	296.00	290.00	297.00	299.38	297.50	291.25	290.00	282.63	305.42
2017-18	250.63	253.00	236.88	214.00	205.00	209.17	215.50	233.13	237.50	238.13	267.50	271.25	235.97
2018-19	278.00	265.63	235.00	196.50	209.38	225.83	219.00	225.00	235.63	241.50	233.75	228.88	232.84
2019-20	232.50	235.00	226.25	226.50	226.88	231.67	248.13	262.50	263.00	260.00	257.50	245.63	242.96
2020-21	250.00	251.75	227.00	239.38	253.75	275.00	313.13	296.25	322.00	318.75	335.63	293.50	281.35
2021-22	262.50	287.50	260.00	265.63	252.00	309.17	326.25	350.00	392.50	386.00	351.25	322.50	313.77
2022-23	351.50	347.50	NA	NA	357.50	368.50	397.50	412.50	380.40	352.50	352.50	354.00	367.44
2023-24[1]	335.00	321.25	318.00	325.00	348.33	365.00	365.00						339.65

[1] Preliminary.   *Source: Economic Research Service, U.S. Department of Agriculture (ERS-USDA)*

Fruits

A fruit is any seed-bearing structure produced from a flowering plant. A widely used classification system divides fruit into fleshy or dry types. Fleshy fruits are juicy and include peaches, mangos, apples, and blueberries. Dry fruits include tree nuts such as almonds, walnuts, and pecans. Some foods that are commonly called vegetables, such as tomatoes, squash, peppers, and eggplant, are technically fruits because they develop from the ovary of a flower.

Worldwide, over 430 million tons of fruit are produced each year and are grown everywhere except the Arctic and the Antarctic. The tropics, because of their abundant moisture and warm temperatures, produce the most diverse and abundant fruits. Mexico and Chile produce more than half of all the fresh and frozen fruit imported into the U.S. In the U.S., the top three fruits produced are oranges, grapes, and apples. Virtually all U.S. production of almonds, pistachios, and walnuts occurs in California, which leads the U.S. in tree nut production.

Prices – In 2022 the fresh fruit component of the US Consumer Price Index (CPI) rose by +7.9% yr/yr to 406.3,

and the processed fruit component rose by +13.3% yr/yr to 188.5. In 2022, banana prices rose by +6.2% to $0.63 per pound, lemons rose by +7.3% to $2.12 per pound, and navel oranges rose by +15.4% to $1.57 per pound.

Supply – US commercial production of selected fruits in 2022 fell by -7.3% to 20.526 million short tons. By weight, grapes accounted for 28.9% of that US fruit production figure, followed by apples at 23.8%, and oranges at 16.7%. The value of US fruit production in 2022 fell by -11.0 yr/yr to $26.616 billion.

Demand – US per capita fresh fruit consumption in 2022 fell by -1.1% to 116.210 pounds per year, down from the 2020 record high of 118.040. The highest per capita consumption categories for non-citrus fruits in 2021 were bananas (26.620 pounds) and apples (15.770 pounds). Per capita consumption of citrus fruits were oranges (7.678 pounds), tangerines and tangelos (6.155 pounds), lemons (4.733 pounds), limes (4.590 pounds), and grapefruit (1.130 pounds). The value of utilized non-citrus fruit production in 2022 rose by +1.7% to $17.153 billion.

Commercial Production for Selected Fruits in the United States   In Thousands of Short Tons

Year	Apples	Cherries[2]	Cran-berries	Grapes	Grape-fruit	Lemons	Nect-arines	Oranges	Peach-es	Pears	Pine-apple[3]	Prunes & Plums	Straw-berries	Tang-elos	Tang-erines	Total All Fruits
2016	5,748	515	481	7,697	803	904	151	6,088	792	739	----	265	1,480	18	935	26,930
2017	5,777	568	420	7,384	698	882	142	5,088	701	737	----	443	1,360	7	1,029	25,586
2018	5,120	493	446	7,596	509	888	121	3,875	652	806	----	380	1,305	7	804	23,304
2019	5,543	483	396	6,961	604	1,002	126	5,427	681	715	----	362	1,141	7	1,107	24,835
2020	5,143	395	390	6,040	570	1,084	123	5,254	653	656	----	271	1,334	7	944	23,200
2021	4,966	467	350	6,035	438	886	117	4,388	691	653	----	334	1,335	7	1,194	22,154
2022[1]	4,883	354	403	5,923	374	1,058	109	3,426	626	644	----	308	1,391	7	736	20,527

[1] Preliminary.   [2] Sweet and tart.   [3] Utilized production.   *Source: Economic Research Service, U.S. Department of Agriculture (ERS-USDA)*

Utilized Production for Selected Fruits in the United States   In Thousands of Short Tons

Year	Citrus[2]	Noncitrus	Tree nuts[3]	Total	Citrus[2]	Noncitrus	Tree nuts[3]	Total
	----------------------- Utilized Production -----------------------				----------------------- Value of Production -----------------------			
	----------------------- In Thousands of Short Tons -----------------------				----------------------- In Thousands of Dollars -----------------------			
2016	8,748	18,598	3,110	30,456	3,435,675	17,571,574	8,690,836	29,698,085
2017	7,697	18,313	2,985	28,995	3,532,125	18,032,949	9,023,875	30,588,949
2018	6,076	17,487	3,227	26,789	3,330,152	16,184,328	9,690,038	29,204,518
2019	8,140	17,020	3,328	28,487	3,399,879	15,531,610	10,095,499	29,026,988
2020	7,852	15,666	4,132	27,649	3,396,467	15,060,995	9,434,960	27,892,422
2021	6,906	15,626	3,969	26,501	3,355,041	16,871,239	9,685,466	29,911,746
2022[1]	5,594	15,265	3,477	24,335	2,978,567	17,153,327	6,484,454	26,616,348

[1] Preliminary.   [2] Year harvest was completed.   [3] Tree nuts on an in-shell equivalent.
Source: Economic Research Service, U.S. Department of Agriculture (ERS-USDA)

Annual Average Retail Prices for Selected Fruits in the United States   In Dollars Per Pound

Year	Red Delicious Apples	Bananas	Anjou Pears	Thompson Seedless Grapes	Lemons	Grapefruit	Oranges Navel	Valencias
2016	1.442	.573	1.674	2.758	2.037	.970	1.246	NA
2017	1.294	.563	1.603	2.641	2.007	1.279	1.341	NA
2018	NA	.574	1.579	2.584	2.249	1.346	1.413	NA
2019	NA	.574	1.603	2.445	2.129	1.345	1.367	NA
2020	NA	.578	NA	2.283	1.935	1.248	1.245	NA
2021	NA	.600	NA	2.460	1.983	NA	1.362	NA
2022[1]	NA	.637	NA	NA	2.128	NA	1.572	NA

[1] Estimate.   *Source: Economic Research Service, U.S. Department of Agriculture (ERS-USDA)*

FRUITS

Utilization of Noncitrus Fruit Production, and Value in the United States   1,000 Short Tons (Fresh Equivalent)

Year	Utilized Production	Fresh	Canned	Dried	Juice	Frozen	Wine	Other Processed	Value of Utilized Production $1,000
					Processed				
2013	19,433	7,824	1,396	2,321	1,636	896	5,068	406	16,220,440
2014	19,151	8,291	1,221	2,194	1,638	897	4,526	459	16,410,049
2015	18,334	7,695	1,258	2,323	1,397	877	4,255	530	16,602,493
2016	18,598	7,916	1,232	1,858	1,547	898	4,668	479	17,571,574
2017	18,313	7,909	1,186	1,778	1,498	746	4,663	534	18,032,949
2018	17,487	5	5	5	5	5	5	5	16,184,328
2019	17,020	5	5	5	5	5	5	5	15,531,610
2020	15,666	5	5	5	5	5	5	5	15,060,995
2021	15,626	5	5	5	5	5	5	5	16,871,239
2022[1]	15,265	5	5	5	5	5	5	5	17,153,327

[1] Preliminary.   *Source: Economic Research Service, U.S. Department of Agriculture (ERS-USDA)*

Average Price Indexes for Fruits in the United States

Year	Index of all Fruit & Nut Prices Received by Growers (1990-92=100)	Fresh Fruit	Dried Fruit	Canned Fruits and Juices	Frozen Fruits and Juices	Fresh Fruit	Processed Fruit
		Producer Price Index 1982 = 100				Consumer Price Index 1982-84 = 100	
2013	119.1	121.2	----	206.4	170.3	343.2	154.5
2014	136.3	124.5	----	208.7	172.7	359.7	154.0
2015	138.6	124.2	----	217.1	176.8	352.0	157.5
2016	137.8	138.7	----	223.2	177.0	359.8	158.2
2017	129.6	147.9	----	229.4	180.4	361.4	156.5
2018	128.1	145.1	----	227.3	180.8	365.2	154.9
2019	119.3	136.3	----	223.0	179.5	360.1	158.2
2020	137.2	139.1	----	225.8	178.6	357.1	162.8
2021	134.6	146.4	----	232.7	180.2	376.5	166.4
2022[1]	155.1	172.8	----	259.1	190.4	406.3	188.5

[1] Estimate.   NA = Not availavle.   *Source: Economic Research Service, U.S. Department of Agriculture (ERS-USDA)*

Fresh Fruit: Per Capita Consumption[1] in the United States   In Pounds

Year	Oranges	Tangerines & Tangelos	Lemons	Limes	Grape-fruit	U.S. Total	Apples	Apricots	Avoc-ados	Bananas	Blue-berries	Cherries	Cran-berries
		Cutrus Fruit							Noncitrus Fruit				
2013	10.39	4.49	3.48	2.96	2.64	23.97	17.43	.11	6.11	27.99	1.41	.99	.08
2014	9.38	5.00	3.43	3.07	2.40	23.28	18.71	.12	6.98	27.86	1.51	1.17	.07
2015	8.67	5.22	3.60	3.02	2.24	22.75	17.48	.08	7.19	27.93	1.60	1.15	.12
2016	9.18	5.29	4.13	3.48	1.97	24.05	19.15	.13	6.86	27.44	1.78	1.17	.12
2017	8.03	5.86	4.25	3.75	1.92	23.81	18.06	.09	8.02	28.61	1.74	1.47	.09
2018	8.20	5.92	4.22	4.06	1.56	23.96	16.80	.12	8.47	28.30	2.00	1.29	.07
2019	8.46	6.80	4.87	4.10	1.43	25.67	17.59	.13	8.13	27.39	2.33	1.24	.07
2020	9.42	6.73	4.90	4.27	1.68	27.00	16.17	.08	9.22	27.09	2.33	1.23	.07
2021	8.17	6.97	4.92	4.66	1.47	26.20	15.91	.09	8.36	26.86	2.53	1.44	.05
2022[1]	7.68	6.15	4.73	4.59	1.13	24.29	15.77	.07	9.22	26.62	2.77	.99	.07

[1] Preliminary.   [2] All data on calendar-year basis except for citrus fruits; apples, August; grapes and pears, July; grapefruit, September; lemons, August of prior year; all other citrus, November.   *Source: Economic Research Service, U.S. Department of Agriculture (ERS-USDA)*

Fresh Fruit: Per Capita Consumption[1] in the United States   In Pounds

Year	Grapes	Kiwifruit	Mangos	& Peaches	Pears	Pineapples	Papaya	Prunes	Straw-berries	Total Noncitrus	Total Fruit
			Noncitrus Fruit Continued								
2013	7.76	.46	2.87	3.02	2.84	6.74	1.12	.54	5.63	85.47	109.44
2014	7.67	.56	2.52	3.15	2.85	7.19	1.14	.53	5.69	88.46	111.74
2015	7.87	.63	2.60	2.91	2.67	6.98	1.33	.56	5.46	87.45	110.21
2016	8.09	.58	2.96	2.73	2.76	7.28	1.43	.66	5.75	89.68	113.73
2017	8.23	.61	3.22	2.66	2.69	7.76	1.36	.68	5.94	92.09	115.90
2018	8.06	.62	3.17	2.20	2.92	7.81	1.26	.60	6.32	90.84	114.79
2019	8.38	.64	3.25	2.08	2.72	7.64	1.27	.57	6.00	90.32	115.99
2020	8.15	.73	3.61	2.36	2.83	7.26	1.26	.58	7.10	91.04	118.04
2021	8.49	.75	3.66	2.36	2.80	7.87	1.34	.51	7.32	91.26	117.46
2022[1]	8.64	.67	3.76	1.94	2.64	8.15	1.41	.54	7.62	91.93	116.21

[1] Preliminary.   [2] All data on calendar-year basis except for citrus fruits; apples, August; grapes and pears, July; grapefruit, September; lemons, August of prior year; all other citrus, November.   *Source: Economic Research Service, U.S. Department of Agriculture (ERS-USDA)*

Average Price Received by Growers for Grapefruit in the United States   In Dollars Per Box

Year	Jan.	Feb.	Mar.	Apr.	May	June	July	Aug.	Sept.	Oct.	Nov.	Dec.	Average
2014	7.30	5.78	5.60	5.34	7.89	7.69	7.19	8.05	13.40	12.33	9.82	8.92	8.28
2015	7.03	4.83	5.34	5.33	5.47	12.21	9.33	5.63	7.79	13.21	13.36	11.43	8.41
2016	10.70	9.13	8.86	12.77	14.81	13.82	15.26	14.08	W	19.08	13.14	12.14	13.07
2017	11.25	11.57	11.95	13.62	16.44	15.18	14.10	W	14.66	20.91	19.88	16.13	15.06
2018	15.88	15.80	16.04	18.21	17.02	14.71	13.34	9.57	15.16	20.61	20.89	18.68	16.33
2019	15.99	14.61	11.44	13.51	13.94	11.95	11.34	5.81	8.08	11.09	15.86	12.81	12.20
2020	10.23	8.95	9.56	11.03	12.00	13.80	16.13	16.56	14.55	24.09	21.30	15.95	14.51
2021	17.88	11.06	13.64	23.74	26.86	24.85	22.98	23.21	26.59	25.64	21.03	17.41	21.24
2022	15.71	13.12	11.55	16.38	7.10	19.04	13.17	11.99	13.17	14.58	27.42	22.66	15.49
2023[1]	20.98	17.55	17.14	15.97	17.30	14.04	11.96	8.87	12.05	19.60	28.22	30.21	17.82

On-tree equivalent.   [1]Preliminary.   *Source: National Agricultural Statistics Service, U.S. Department of Agriculture (NASS-USDA)*

Average Price Received by Growers for Lemons in the United States   In Dollars Per Box

Year	Jan.	Feb.	Mar.	Apr.	May	June	July	Aug.	Sept.	Oct.	Nov.	Dec.	Average
2014	21.17	21.69	21.31	22.39	24.54	29.91	40.05	33.68	37.40	38.47	29.54	21.15	28.44
2015	18.53	13.44	16.14	21.65	31.76	38.51	37.34	29.40	31.71	36.54	30.18	24.42	27.47
2016	23.05	22.04	24.29	25.09	31.67	29.95	26.47	29.54	31.84	31.49	27.88	23.13	27.20
2017	23.44	25.12	24.65	27.10	31.30	40.90	41.85	29.79	29.58	25.49	28.32	30.84	29.87
2018	30.17	23.65	20.72	18.20	21.73	29.14	40.34	53.01	49.63	41.29	31.76	26.23	32.16
2019	22.58	15.76	15.54	13.38	16.25	19.43	22.12	27.97	29.34	30.34	29.70	22.43	22.07
2020	16.14	14.35	10.25	10.72	14.38	19.50	21.01	21.50	21.85	24.41	25.52	23.23	18.57
2021	21.99	18.96	20.46	20.10	25.82	29.83	31.28	27.67	24.90	25.79	22.24	19.95	24.08
2022	18.29	13.00	14.12	12.35	11.84	11.60	9.06	15.30	17.12	24.51	22.36	17.55	15.59
2023[1]	15.97	10.30	14.65	11.91	11.97	13.23	21.07	26.81	35.13	34.99	28.51	22.31	20.57

On-tree equivalent.   [1]Preliminary.   *Source: National Agricultural Statistics Service, U.S. Department of Agriculture (NASS-USDA)*

Average Price Received by Growers for Grapes in the United States   In Dollars Per Box

Year	Jan.	Feb.	Mar.	Apr.	May	June	July	Aug.	Sept.	Oct.	Nov.	Dec.	Average
2014	NQ	NQ	NQ	NQ	NQ	1,870	1,550	1,360	1,350	1,530	1,660	1,680	1,571
2015	NQ	NQ	NQ	NQ	2,330	1,690	1,340	1,470	1,490	1,590	1,810	2,070	1,724
2016	NQ	NQ	NQ	NQ	NQ	NQ	1,480	1,330	1,360	1,460	1,520	2,310	1,577
2017	NQ	NQ	NQ	NQ	NQ	NQ	1,590	1,500	1,500	1,460	1,540	1,660	1,542
2018	NQ	NQ	NQ	NQ	NQ	2,550	1,600	1,310	1,210	1,080	1,030	1,140	1,417
2019	NQ	NQ	NQ	NQ	NQ	1,620	1,400	1,260	1,310	1,300	1,500	2,090	1,497
2020	NQ	NQ	NQ	NQ	NQ	2,630	2,280	2,150	2,040	2,010	2,020	2,100	2,176
2021	2,280	NQ	NQ	NQ	NQ	3,010	2,410	2,180	2,060	2,030	2,100	2,440	2,314
2022	3,290	NQ	NQ	NQ	NQ	3,110	2,470	2,240	2,280	2,270	2,270	2,310	2,530
2023[1]	NQ	NQ	NQ	NQ	NQ	3,030	2,730	2,880	3,260	3,350	3,450	3,690	3,199

Fresh.   [1]Preliminary.   NQ = No quote.   *Source: National Agricultural Statistics Service, U.S. Department of Agriculture (NASS-USDA)*

Average Price Received by Growers for Peaches in the United States   In Dollars Per Box

Year	Jan.	Feb.	Mar.	Apr.	May	June	July	Aug.	Sept.	Oct.	Nov.	Dec.	Average
2014	NQ	NQ	NQ	NQ	NQ	1,270	1,180	1,070	954	NQ	NQ	NQ	1,119
2015	NQ	NQ	NQ	NQ	1,480	1,110	937	1,030	835	NQ	NQ	NQ	1,078
2016	NQ	NQ	NQ	NQ	1,220	993	1,230	1,320	1,080	NQ	NQ	NQ	1,169
2017	NQ	NQ	NQ	NQ	NQ	1,530	1,710	1,400	1,310	NQ	NQ	NQ	1,488
2018	NQ	NQ	NQ	NQ	NQ	1,130	1,140	1,110	918	NQ	NQ	NQ	1,075
2019	NQ	NQ	NQ	NQ	1,720	1,180	1,090	1,150	941	NQ	NQ	NQ	1,216
2020	NQ	NQ	NQ	NQ	1,500	1,190	1,310	1,680	1,810	NQ	NQ	NQ	1,498
2021	NQ	NQ	NQ	NQ	1,560	1,270	1,210	1,220	1,310	NQ	NQ	NQ	1,314
2022	NQ	NQ	NQ	NQ	2,260	1,800	1,880	1,820	2,050	NQ	NQ	NQ	1,962
2023[1]	NQ	NQ	NQ	NQ	2,970	2,560	2,420	2,590	2,650	2,320	NQ	NQ	2,585

Fresh.   [1]Preliminary.   NQ = No quote.   *Source: National Agricultural Statistics Service, U.S. Department of Agriculture (NASS-USDA)*

FRUITS

Average Price Received by Growers for Pears in the United States   In Dollars Per Box

Year	Jan.	Feb.	Mar.	Apr.	May	June	July	Aug.	Sept.	Oct.	Nov.	Dec.	Average
2014	NQ	NQ	NQ	592	686	893	695	531	631	696	692	702	680
2015	725	729	652	610	619	633	635	706	690	747	778	813	695
2016	844	785	749	793	914	1,050	810	810	816	829	787	756	829
2017	782	806	722	668	694	734	631	764	829	848	832	888	767
2018	879	857	779	678	680	798	788	688	660	663	616	614	725
2019	574	561	539	545	620	731	781	696	722	693	678	721	655
2020	733	1,200	1,170	1,050	1,040	1,050	1,340	1,590	1,390	1,400	1,340	1,310	1,218
2021	1,290	1,290	1,280	1,300	1,310	1,330	1,430	1,420	1,340	1,300	1,230	1,220	1,312
2022	1,230	1,240	1,230	1,200	1,200	1,210	1,450	1,830	1,700	1,220	1,260	1,380	1,346
2023[1]	1,420	1,510	1,490	1,170	1,160	1,380	1,480	1,660	1,380	1,310	1,340	1,270	1,381

Fresh.   [1]Preliminary.   NA = Not available.   *Source: National Agricultural Statistics Service, U.S. Department of Agriculture (NASS-USDA)*

Average Price Received by Growers for Strawberries in the United States   In Dollars Per Box

Year	Jan.	Feb.	Mar.	Apr.	May	June	July	Aug.	Sept.	Oct.	Nov.	Dec.	Average
2014	NA	NA	NA	87.60	96.10	91.80	89.30	92.70	133.00	112.00	152.00	209.00	118.17
2015	135.00	101.00	63.60	76.80	72.60	61.50	60.20	86.70	71.30	100.00	190.00	193.00	100.98
2016	195.00	167.00	81.00	84.30	68.60	60.50	59.40	69.40	50.90	71.00	167.00	154.00	102.34
2017	147.00	128.00	94.90	66.60	53.20	59.20	74.10	84.70	109.00	98.00	164.00	182.00	105.06
2018	169.00	125.00	118.00	105.00	55.30	52.70	66.60	50.50	84.00	67.30	99.00	W	90.22
2019	222.00	126.00	114.00	79.20	61.80	80.30	79.20	83.30	104.00	100.00	115.00	W	105.89
2020	264.00	257.00	189.00	123.00	107.00	108.00	199.00	145.00	171.00	208.00	231.00	186.00	182.33
2021	245.00	207.00	143.00	216.00	145.00	131.00	130.00	175.00	142.00	151.00	301.00	247.00	186.08
2022	231.00	192.00	125.00	145.00	129.00	90.60	124.00	204.00	149.00	258.00	349.00	296.00	191.05
2023[1]	299.00	181.00	170.00	192.00	114.00	120.00	149.00	188.00	118.00	139.00	257.00	289.00	184.67

Fresh.   [1]Preliminary.   NA = Not available..   *Source: National Agricultural Statistics Service, U.S. Department of Agriculture (NASS-USDA)*

Cold Storage Stocks of Frozen Apples in the United States, on First of Month   In Thousands of Pounds

Year	Jan.	Feb.	Mar.	Apr.	May	June	July	Aug.	Sept.	Oct.	Nov.	Dec.
2014	49,831	56,312	60,384	61,220	60,693	58,666	56,046	55,517	52,050	49,676	53,072	52,828
2015	55,400	55,350	53,314	52,079	50,761	49,547	46,985	42,987	36,586	31,854	35,761	38,917
2016	37,596	38,707	37,994	37,761	39,147	38,682	39,040	36,171	32,361	29,104	28,198	32,407
2017	34,929	37,963	36,919	38,679	44,495	40,049	37,418	34,995	34,475	29,471	26,836	29,408
2018	32,007	34,420	35,915	36,968	35,087	32,441	33,715	30,609	24,822	22,366	21,602	23,141
2019	28,276	31,782	35,345	35,219	35,149	28,196	28,122	26,479	22,539	20,286	20,326	21,713
2020	27,323	28,963	29,614	28,680	29,494	30,574	29,982	29,829	28,310	27,780	26,264	29,653
2021	33,235	32,850	30,537	29,992	25,603	23,500	26,084	25,158	21,353	17,710	19,046	20,453
2022	20,665	23,963	22,821	26,350	30,272	31,508	29,414	23,681	19,781	21,064	40,670	41,875
2023[1]	51,885	50,189	30,587	29,356	29,406	32,045	29,611	29,784	25,596	24,031	22,935	26,232

[1] Preliminary.   *Source: Economic Research Service, U.S. Department of Agriculture (ERS-USDA)*

Cold Storage Stocks of Frozen Apricots in the United States, on First of Month   In Thousands of Pounds

Year	Jan.	Feb.	Mar.	Apr.	May	June	July	Aug.	Sept.	Oct.	Nov.	Dec.
2014	3,895	3,532	3,406	3,380	2,384	1,974	12,488	9,847	7,852	7,533	6,471	6,191
2015	5,941	5,246	4,720	4,162	4,051	3,390	11,760	11,058	10,059	7,931	6,128	5,640
2016	4,921	4,319	3,804	3,434	2,968	3,301	11,086	16,226	13,454	11,690	9,998	8,958
2017	8,456	6,506	4,103	3,163	2,848	2,279	11,696	11,048	8,512	7,335	6,098	5,506
2018	4,873	4,295	3,616	2,974	2,275	1,664	8,301	9,538	8,843	8,148	7,549	6,640
2019	6,458	4,762	4,248	3,432	2,770	2,082	3,760	3,819	3,528	3,237	6,689	6,054
2020	5,294	4,224	3,436	3,101	2,340	2,461	8,706	6,774	6,871	4,703	3,751	3,156
2021	2,602	2,073	2,278	1,841	1,830	1,443	6,381	10,289	10,314	9,807	8,991	7,777
2022	6,244	6,133	4,982	2,943	2,603	3,151	9,042	9,014	8,292	7,249	6,412	6,768
2023[1]	5,700	4,966	4,265	4,088	3,009	2,754	7,308	11,078	10,663	10,114	8,902	7,967

[1] Preliminary.   *Source: Economic Research Service, U.S. Department of Agriculture (ERS-USDA)*

Cold Storage Stocks of Frozen Blackberries[2] in the United States, on First of Month   In Thousands of Pounds

Year	Jan.	Feb.	Mar.	Apr.	May	June	July	Aug.	Sept.	Oct.	Nov.	Dec.
2014	30,066	28,823	27,183	22,994	21,110	21,107	22,053	42,581	40,339	37,494	34,756	32,368
2015	30,925	28,843	25,499	23,071	20,892	19,931	25,158	34,001	35,240	33,078	30,553	28,366
2016	26,594	24,457	23,752	23,008	20,296	19,131	36,373	43,885	43,330	38,711	36,110	33,134
2017	31,753	29,540	26,983	24,151	23,147	20,956	22,085	36,913	34,707	31,603	28,024	26,682
2018	24,449	21,402	18,205	16,182	14,751	12,534	14,481	38,714	33,447	32,294	30,098	27,069
2019	24,639	22,803	20,594	19,569	17,377	14,258	12,664	32,157	31,509	29,664	27,854	23,989
2020	21,741	18,410	16,608	13,943	14,291	12,998	14,030	34,685	33,928	28,560	23,801	23,249
2021	18,802	15,385	12,277	12,942	12,042	10,396	11,473	22,348	22,785	18,133	16,886	14,743
2022	14,265	13,502	11,730	10,976	10,444	10,772	11,038	28,752	31,034	30,863	28,106	26,116
2023[1]	26,644	25,937	27,288	27,160	25,942	24,416	23,730	34,219	32,924	31,253	27,484	25,352

[1] Preliminary.   [2] Includes IQF, Pails and Tubs, Barrels (400lbs net), and Concentrate.   *Source: Economic Research Service, U.S. Department of Agriculture (ERS-USDA)*

Cold Storage Stocks of Frozen Blueberries in the United States, on First of Month   In Thousands of Pounds

Year	Jan.	Feb.	Mar.	Apr.	May	June	July	Aug.	Sept.	Oct.	Nov.	Dec.
2014	201,834	172,718	150,626	130,825	117,065	98,716	102,012	171,661	269,537	265,303	240,830	229,225
2015	208,324	187,523	166,469	152,745	133,836	119,276	132,732	236,349	273,614	280,085	259,198	245,754
2016	224,696	211,459	191,351	164,927	154,142	145,414	157,928	260,675	315,436	332,379	308,554	294,135
2017	268,895	241,947	223,211	195,417	184,367	157,140	147,915	197,723	276,632	266,423	256,727	230,843
2018	222,060	192,354	162,564	134,469	116,387	96,891	99,912	175,163	244,902	247,396	228,308	199,883
2019	182,857	178,750	148,696	129,739	112,147	92,992	93,422	174,711	280,464	290,020	278,570	262,652
2020	246,625	240,304	215,903	196,198	175,610	166,842	176,415	233,701	319,296	316,717	291,261	261,142
2021	237,064	209,994	188,111	148,965	119,167	102,080	104,582	208,514	285,462	276,908	259,259	233,268
2022	218,041	192,947	173,490	153,110	130,925	116,789	117,311	154,555	271,594	280,829	258,648	243,184
2023[1]	235,329	219,495	205,619	193,371	178,480	166,823	173,717	246,414	333,928	325,820	302,451	287,217

[1] Preliminary.   *Source: Economic Research Service, U.S. Department of Agriculture (ERS-USDA)*

Cold Storage Stocks of Frozen Cherries[2] in the United States, on First of Month   In Thousands of Pounds

Year	Jan.	Feb.	Mar.	Apr.	May	June	July	Aug.	Sept.	Oct.	Nov.	Dec.
2014	18,051	14,477	14,136	13,065	12,245	10,659	9,448	13,469	27,390	23,525	23,173	22,722
2015	22,226	21,326	20,155	19,275	17,411	17,140	18,134	23,994	25,401	22,830	19,672	19,929
2016	18,076	17,920	16,287	16,745	15,021	14,314	14,104	22,800	26,433	25,383	24,069	21,616
2017	20,350	20,042	20,301	18,044	16,530	13,998	10,511	16,605	20,305	20,977	20,736	19,546
2018	17,801	16,935	14,840	14,400	13,710	12,447	10,877	16,941	22,197	20,896	16,924	14,646
2019	15,147	13,640	12,387	12,370	12,942	11,538	10,117	14,008	18,525	17,361	15,943	14,067
2020	12,628	11,118	9,362	8,144	7,415	7,503	9,028	16,644	20,662	18,230	16,890	16,058
2021	14,858	13,778	14,067	14,454	14,005	12,067	14,098	22,567	21,620	21,423	20,932	20,522
2022	19,114	18,020	18,029	16,980	16,273	15,167	14,937	24,646	22,898	22,964	22,375	21,646
2023[1]	20,485	18,528	18,379	17,621	16,738	16,338	16,137	20,984	20,319	19,439	18,016	16,207

[1] Preliminary.   [2] Tart (ripe tart pitted).   *Source: Economic Research Service, U.S. Department of Agriculture (ERS-USDA)*

Cold Storage Stocks of Frozen Peaches in the United States, on First of Month   In Thousands of Pounds

Year	Jan.	Feb.	Mar.	Apr.	May	June	July	Aug.	Sept.	Oct.	Nov.	Dec.
2014	61,092	53,367	47,862	39,621	32,936	25,714	19,497	34,001	54,810	63,033	57,543	52,384
2015	47,465	44,353	38,646	35,803	30,722	27,566	26,877	41,488	63,360	78,572	75,817	75,253
2016	74,308	68,463	62,266	54,489	52,746	49,601	48,346	62,290	83,003	93,794	91,530	88,731
2017	81,881	74,285	69,924	64,477	58,878	53,696	53,066	62,003	83,564	87,901	85,238	84,813
2018	76,686	68,986	60,036	54,899	46,756	40,717	35,517	37,622	47,951	69,188	69,577	64,956
2019	62,532	58,556	54,491	52,611	43,830	41,729	38,043	39,840	47,955	65,860	66,485	57,342
2020	52,109	45,926	43,092	38,683	33,640	32,659	28,069	35,796	48,826	52,050	47,520	43,389
2021	39,210	29,907	28,627	23,547	19,724	17,035	16,723	24,463	38,672	56,519	57,220	52,804
2022	49,403	44,159	38,984	35,308	32,763	28,322	24,391	28,957	37,567	43,208	46,194	43,028
2023[1]	42,736	39,569	35,693	30,815	28,254	22,324	17,780	18,939	25,651	29,227	28,498	24,153

[1] Preliminary.   *Source: Economic Research Service, U.S. Department of Agriculture (ERS-USDA)*

FRUITS

Cold Storage Stocks of Frozen Raspberries[2] in the United States, on First of Month   In Thousands of Pounds

Year	Jan.	Feb.	Mar.	Apr.	May	June	July	Aug.	Sept.	Oct.	Nov.	Dec.
2014	62,102	52,730	45,071	38,418	33,673	31,353	30,226	87,492	81,541	74,858	67,095	62,337
2015	57,298	52,133	47,260	42,776	37,243	32,411	40,185	76,637	70,585	69,798	63,343	61,126
2016	57,362	50,125	46,477	41,902	40,581	38,234	65,383	101,557	93,436	86,090	81,042	76,043
2017	68,388	61,275	54,772	48,895	44,148	39,664	33,818	83,871	93,184	87,305	80,655	79,382
2018	75,614	67,234	64,955	58,003	56,206	50,897	48,562	113,457	110,369	103,199	95,384	87,801
2019	84,774	71,910	59,437	50,300	46,125	43,751	39,598	87,779	89,143	84,398	76,399	67,766
2020	62,654	55,069	42,564	36,988	33,813	30,417	25,831	76,936	84,212	74,463	63,080	59,280
2021	54,226	47,047	41,682	33,213	31,662	27,841	25,527	68,382	70,932	60,564	54,230	50,201
2022	49,810	43,428	39,235	35,197	30,782	25,545	24,862	70,932	74,671	69,846	63,105	56,650
2023[1]	55,044	52,077	44,515	34,969	30,683	25,734	24,637	76,566	76,468	69,162	61,225	57,331

[1] Preliminary .   [2] Red: Includes IQF, Pails and Tubs, Barrels (400 lbs net), and Concentrate.   *Source: Economic Research Service, U.S. Department of Agriculture (ERS-USDA)*

Cold Storage Stocks of Frozen Strawberries[2] in the United States, on First of Month   In Thousands of Pounds

Year	Jan.	Feb.	Mar.	Apr.	May	June	July	Aug.	Sept.	Oct.	Nov.	Dec.
2014	279,977	240,382	215,168	211,064	233,147	257,783	357,526	362,127	330,666	294,969	270,553	236,828
2015	206,841	175,520	163,599	186,817	199,290	238,106	341,295	360,045	328,775	314,350	278,860	253,146
2016	235,852	208,274	190,132	203,784	225,525	264,440	390,681	396,716	377,156	376,035	367,939	331,389
2017	304,827	289,622	274,147	255,978	266,206	312,244	357,628	411,241	402,915	363,542	333,050	309,351
2018	281,076	253,019	216,083	195,880	186,979	249,528	377,233	373,196	350,619	328,177	286,210	253,178
2019	227,433	193,851	172,444	157,833	182,594	228,838	269,490	277,960	275,315	250,277	211,085	188,847
2020	157,388	129,425	115,173	127,571	159,405	231,699	265,090	268,538	263,164	216,688	186,749	157,224
2021	150,715	136,961	132,102	125,174	125,115	193,297	261,584	305,177	283,250	249,126	231,367	205,936
2022	195,102	175,389	161,781	153,891	181,596	236,226	317,880	321,727	292,450	269,496	249,652	230,173
2023[1]	211,256	184,738	177,634	177,417	170,849	201,416	254,993	258,463	251,098	234,888	210,851	183,473

[1] Preliminary.   [2] Includes IQF and Poly, Pails and Tubs, Barrels and Drums, and Juice Stock.   *Source: Economic Research Service, U.S. Department of Agriculture (ERS-USDA)*

Cold Storage Stocks of Other Frozen Fruit in the United States, on First of Month   In Thousands of Pounds

Year	Jan.	Feb.	Mar.	Apr.	May	June	July	Aug.	Sept.	Oct.	Nov.	Dec.
2014	575,025	528,790	475,527	440,532	389,071	341,283	305,249	286,727	264,490	293,231	542,534	576,843
2015	535,775	482,436	434,463	385,477	348,811	321,532	297,358	309,251	309,356	377,612	659,912	665,020
2016	587,967	603,399	557,741	521,065	525,633	489,438	473,450	483,812	464,629	514,081	853,189	872,413
2017	808,397	764,821	738,926	665,196	604,047	543,809	491,595	502,270	493,106	515,569	700,422	709,259
2018	666,624	595,561	554,544	487,759	462,212	399,596	404,649	395,232	361,493	398,684	741,609	710,973
2019	654,518	598,220	547,960	501,052	457,599	399,196	357,543	335,751	318,388	332,966	668,223	645,653
2020	592,537	514,997	447,440	401,446	371,327	324,116	284,967	250,533	259,942	326,544	538,236	506,235
2021	445,109	399,775	372,138	345,953	316,800	281,912	267,014	263,298	260,666	311,788	418,656	378,251
2022	368,941	358,995	330,581	294,262	303,704	293,360	264,472	260,484	247,890	331,532	434,105	522,731
2023[1]	485,376	415,959	379,615	340,446	300,491	291,258	273,622	250,331	235,917	367,894	699,731	671,870

[1] Preliminary.   *Source: Economic Research Service, U.S. Department of Agriculture (ERS-USDA)*

Cold Storage Stocks of Total Frozen Fruit in the United States, on First of Month   In Millions of Pounds

Year	Jan.	Feb.	Mar.	Apr.	May	June	July	Aug.	Sept.	Oct.	Nov.	Dec.
2014	1,405.6	1,261.1	1,140.4	1,052.0	981.1	912.1	972.2	1,176.0	1,317.9	1,286.1	1,461.4	1,426.8
2015	1,315.4	1,191.8	1,084.2	1,016.4	949.2	921.6	1,028.1	1,294.3	1,322.6	1,385.6	1,580.9	1,535.4
2016	1,398.6	1,349.4	1,240.4	1,165.4	1,163.7	1,141.0	1,309.2	1,611.2	1,658.5	1,707.9	1,993.9	1,934.0
2017	1,788.9	1,673.4	1,585.8	1,439.9	1,360.5	1,291.0	1,262.8	1,530.3	1,633.1	1,585.8	1,707.8	1,650.3
2018	1,547.8	1,390.3	1,256.2	1,119.0	1,041.0	992.9	1,117.5	1,379.1	1,417.4	1,425.1	1,677.2	1,556.3
2019	1,449.4	1,320.6	1,195.1	1,095.5	1,039.6	974.6	953.7	1,128.3	1,267.9	1,266.4	1,535.3	1,446.4
2020	1,325.1	1,183.9	1,046.0	973.1	935.1	938.6	933.0	1,079.0	1,194.9	1,189.5	1,315.0	1,216.9
2021	1,091.8	976.3	900.6	809.0	726.5	719.6	777.8	1,059.5	1,118.6	1,117.9	1,176.5	1,072.3
2022	1,017.8	945.0	862.4	784.2	789.8	802.2	849.4	1,040.3	1,140.6	1,209.3	1,267.8	1,302.8
2023[1]	1,240.4	1,108.4	1,012.8	940.2	862.5	858.1	889.3	1,052.7	1,113.4	1,227.8	1,483.8	1,395.0

[1] Preliminary.   *Source: Economic Research Service, U.S. Department of Agriculture (ERS-USDA)*

Gas

Natural gas is a fossil fuel that is colorless, shapeless, and odorless in its pure form. It is a mixture of hydrocarbon gases formed primarily of methane, but it can also include ethane, propane, butane, and pentane. Natural gas is combustible, clean-burning, and gives off a great deal of energy. Around 500 BC, the Chinese discovered that the energy in natural gas could be harnessed. They passed it through crude bamboo-shoot pipes and then burned it to boil sea water to create potable fresh water. Around 1785, Britain became the first country to commercially use natural gas produced from coal for streetlights and indoor lights. In 1821, William Hart dug the first well specifically intended to obtain natural gas, and he is generally regarded as the "father of natural gas" in America. There is a vast amount of natural gas estimated to still be in the ground in the U.S. Natural gas as a source of energy is significantly less expensive than electricity per Btu.

Natural gas futures and options are traded at the CME Group. The CME natural gas futures contract calls for the delivery of natural gas representing 10,000 million British thermal units (mmBtu) at the Henry Hub in Louisiana, which is the nexus of 16 intra-state and inter-state pipelines. The contract is priced in terms of U.S. Dollars per mmBtu. CME also has basic swap futures contracts available for 30 different natural gas pricing locations versus the benchmark Henry Hub location. Natural gas futures are also traded at ICE Futures Europe Exchange.

Prices – CME natural gas futures (Barchart.com symbol code NG) on the nearest-futures chart closed 2023 down by -43.8% at 2.514 per mmBtu.

Supply – US recovery of natural gas in 2022 fell by -5.1% to 43.802 trillion cubic feet. The top US producing states for natural gas in 2023 were Texas with 27.9% of US production, Pennsylvania with 18.5%, Louisiana with 10.4%, New Mexico with 7.7%, Oklahoma with 6.8%, Colorado with 4.4%, and Wyoming with 2.3%. In 2019 the world's largest natural gas producers were the US with 3,003,354 Terajoules and Russia with 2,051,081 Terajoules of production.

Demand – US total delivered consumption of natural gas in 2022 rose by +5.8% yr/yr to 49.900 trillion cubic feet, of which about 41.6% was delivered to electrical utility plants, 29.0% to industrial establishments, 17.1% to residences, and 12.1% to commercial establishments.

Trade – US imports of natural gas (consumed) in 2022 rose by +7.7% yr/yr to 3.042 trillion cubic feet, down from the 2007 record high of 4.608 trillion cubic feet. US exports of natural gas in 2022 rose by +3.8% yr/yr to 6.904 trillion cubic feet for a new record high.

World Dry Natural Gas Production   In Billion Cubic Feet

Year	Algeria	Canada	China	Indonesia	Iran	Nether-lands	Norway	Qatar	Russia	Saudi Arabia	United States	Uzbek-istan	World Total
2006	3,079	6,548	2,067	2,199	3,836	2,732	3,094	1,790	21,736	2,594	18,504	2,216	101,621
2007	2,996	6,416	2,446	2,422	3,952	2,687	3,168	2,232	21,595	2,628	19,266	2,302	104,141
2008	3,055	6,046	2,685	2,472	4,107	2,957	3,503	2,719	21,515	2,841	20,159	2,387	107,858
2009	2,876	5,634	2,975	2,557	4,986	2,786	3,664	3,154	18,890	2,770	20,624	2,169	105,418
2010	2,988	5,390	3,334	2,917	5,161	3,131	3,756	4,121	20,915	2,969	21,316	2,123	112,438
2011	2,923	5,218	3,629	2,693	5,361	2,851	3,576	5,130	22,202	3,127	22,902	2,226	116,690
2012	3,053	5,070	3,666	2,619	5,640	2,843	4,052	5,546	21,764	3,439	24,033	2,222	119,302
2013	2,813	5,129	3,986	2,606	5,696	3,053	3,841	5,800	22,139	3,462	24,334	2,106	120,879
2014[1]	2,942	5,349	4,360	2,594	6,162	2,482	3,843	5,650	21,225	3,547	25,890	2,180	122,305
2015[2]	2,933	5,295	4,487	2,571	6,526	1,935	4,139	5,794	21,141	3,614	27,059	1,967	124,090

[1] Preliminary.   [2] Estimate.   Source: Energy Information Administration, U.S. Department of Energy (EIA-DOE)

Marketed Production of Natural Gas in the United States, by States   In Million Cubic Feet

Year	Alaska	Arkansas	California	Colorado	Kansas	Louisiana	New Mexico	Oklahoma	Pennsyl-vania	Texas	Wyoming	Total
2014	345,310	1,122,733	238,988	1,643,487	286,480	1,960,813	1,229,519	2,331,086	4,257,693	7,985,019	1,794,413	27,497,754
2015	343,625	1,010,382	236,648	1,688,733	284,184	1,805,197	1,245,145	2,499,599	4,812,983	7,890,459	1,808,519	28,772,044
2016	332,749	823,196	205,025	1,685,755	244,795	1,784,396	1,229,647	2,468,312	5,210,209	7,225,472	1,662,909	28,400,049
2017	344,385	694,676	212,458	1,706,364	219,639	2,139,830	1,299,732	2,513,897	5,453,638	7,223,841	1,590,059	29,237,825
2018	341,315	589,985	202,617	1,847,402	201,391	2,832,404	1,493,082	2,875,787	6,264,832	8,041,010	1,637,517	33,008,867
2019	329,361	524,757	196,823	1,986,916	183,087	3,212,318	1,769,086	3,036,052	6,896,792	9,378,489	1,488,854	36,446,918
2020	339,337	481,205	155,979	1,996,740	163,362	3,205,574	1,965,533	2,673,207	7,168,902	9,813,035	1,206,122	36,520,826
2021	354,660	448,283	136,034	1,890,260	152,986	3,443,767	2,237,165	2,555,430	7,647,068	9,949,156	1,109,416	37,337,860
2022	373,141	416,196	136,220	1,833,019	147,846	4,064,791	2,687,231	2,764,019	7,511,179	10,828,515	1,032,634	39,428,350
2023[1]	368,027	393,193	129,808	1,823,967	133,869	4,306,772	3,165,181	2,816,636	7,619,991	11,536,695	950,243	41,296,084

[1] Preliminary.   Source: Energy Information Administration, U.S. Department of Energy (EIA-DOE)

GAS

World Production of Natural Gas Plant Liquids Thousand Barrels per Day

Year	Algeria	Canada	Mexico	Saudi Arabia	Russia	United States	Persian Gulf[2]	OAPEC[3]	OPEC-12[4]	OPEC-11[4]	World
2006	270	685	338	472	1,860	1,739	2,722	2,554	3,292	3,270	8,178
2007	260	726	328	486	1,940	1,783	2,813	2,582	3,407	3,383	8,394
2008	250	677	318	500	2,080	1,784	2,985	2,592	3,550	3,540	8,514
2009	325	640	326	539	1,980	1,910	2,922	2,744	3,562	3,552	8,641
2010	340	597	332	574	1,920	2,074	2,935	2,972	3,592	3,582	8,901
2011	322	591	334	611	1,920	2,216	3,102	2,958	3,637	3,627	9,130
2012	342	611	318	647	1,920	2,408	3,152	3,164	3,786	3,776	9,502
2013	300	639	320	684	1,920	2,606	3,141		3,685	3,673	9,636
2014[1]	300	665	320	720	1,800	2,964	3,117		3,644	3,629	10,013

Average. [1] Preliminary. [2] Bahrain, Iran, Iraq, Kuwait, Qatar, Saudi Arabia, and the United Arab Emirates. [3] Organization of Arab Petroleum Exporting Countriess: Algeria, Iraq, Kuwait, Libya, Qatar, Saudi Arabia, and the United Arab Emirates. [4] OPEC-12: Organization of the Petroleum Exporting Countries: Algeria, Angola, Indonesia, Iran, Iraq, Kuwait, Libya, Nigeria, Qatar, Saudi Arabia, the United Arab Emirates, and Venezuela. OPEC-11 does not include Angola. *Source: Energy Information Administration, U.S. Department of Energy (EIA-DOE)*

Recoverable Reserves and Deliveries of Natural Gas in the United States In Billions of Cubic Feet

Year	Gross With-drawals	Recoverable Reserves of Natural Gas Dec. 31[2]	Residential	Commercial	Electric Utility Plants[3]	Industrial	Total	Lease & Plant Fuel	Used as Pipeline Fuel	Heating Value BTU per Cubic Foot
2014	31,405	368,704	5,087	3,466	8,146	7,646	24,381	1,512	700	1,032
2015	32,915	307,730	4,613	3,202	9,613	7,522	24,989	1,576	678	1,037
2016	32,592	322,234	4,347	3,110	9,985	7,729	25,212	1,545	687	1,037
2017	33,292	438,460	4,413	3,165	9,266	7,943	24,835	1,583	722	1,036
2018	37,326	474,821	4,998	3,514	10,589	8,417	27,568	1,694	877	1,036
2019	40,780	465,405	5,019	3,515	11,288	8,417	28,291	1,823	1,018	1,038
2020	40,614	445,299	4,674	3,170	11,616	8,151	27,660	1,805	1,007	1,037
2021	41,666	589,236	4,716	3,298	11,271	8,295	27,634	1,901	1,130	1,037
2022[1]	43,370		4,990	3,525	12,118	8,455	29,140	1,983	1,190	1,036

[1] Preliminary. [2] Estimated proved recoverable reserves of dry natural gas. [3] Figures include gas other than natural (impossible to segregate); therefore, shown separately from other consumption. *Source: Energy Information Administration, U.S. Department of Energy (EIA-DOE)*

Salient Statistics of Natural Gas in the United States

	Supply						Disposition				Average Price Delivered to Customers						
Year	Marketed Production	Extraction Loss	Dry Production	Storage With-drawals	Imports (Con-sumed)	Total Supply	Con-sump-tion	Exports	Added to Storage	Total Dis-position	Well-head Price	Imports	Exports	Resi-dential	Com-mercial	Indus-trial	Electric Utilities
	In Billions of Cubic Feet										Dollars Per Thousand Cubic Feet						
2014	27,498	1,608	25,890	3,586	2,695	33,779	26,593	1,514	3,839	31,946	----	5.30	5.51	10.97	8.90	5.62	5.19
2015	28,772	1,707	27,065	3,100	2,718	34,590	27,244	1,784	3,638	32,666	----	2.99	3.07	10.38	7.91	3.93	3.38
2016	28,400	1,808	26,592	3,325	3,006	34,731	27,444	2,335	2,977	32,756	----	2.24	2.79	10.05	7.28	3.51	2.99
2017	29,204	1,897	27,306	3,590	3,033	35,827	27,146	3,154	3,337	33,636	----	2.60	3.54	10.91	7.88	4.08	3.51
2018	33,009	2,235	30,774	3,999	2,889	39,897	30,149	3,608	3,676	37,433	----	2.69	3.89	10.50	7.79	4.19	3.68
2019	36,447	2,548	33,899	3,653	2,742	42,841	31,143	4,658	4,153	39,953	----	2.55	3.64	10.51	7.61	3.90	2.99
2020	36,202	2,710	33,493	3,412	2,551	42,166	30,513	5,285	3,590	39,388	----	2.07	3.70	10.78	7.49	3.32	2.49
2021[1]	37,328	2,811	34,518	3,761	2,808	43,897	30,625	6,653	3,678	40,955	----			12.18	8.79	5.50	5.17
2022[2]	38,924	3,120	35,804	4,172	3,023	46,119	32,318	6,892	3,897	43,108	----			14.80	11.34	7.90	7.52

[1] Preliminary. [2] Estimate. *Source: Energy Information Administration, U.S. Department of Energy (EIA-DOE)*

Average Price of Natural Gas at Henry Hub In Dollars Per MMBtu

Year	Jan.	Feb.	Mar.	Apr.	May	June	July	Aug.	Sept.	Oct.	Nov.	Dec.	Average
2014	4.71	6.00	4.90	4.66	4.58	4.59	4.05	3.91	3.92	3.78	4.12	3.48	4.39
2015	3.00	2.88	2.83	2.61	2.85	2.78	2.84	2.77	2.66	2.34	2.09	1.94	2.63
2016	2.29	1.98	1.73	1.92	1.93	2.59	2.82	2.82	3.00	2.98	2.54	3.59	2.52
2017	3.28	2.86	2.88	3.11	3.15	2.98	2.98	2.90	2.98	2.88	3.01	2.82	2.99
2018	3.91	2.67	2.69	2.80	2.80	2.96	2.83	2.96	3.00	3.26	4.12	3.97	3.16
2019	3.11	2.69	2.89	2.65	2.64	2.40	2.36	2.22	2.56	2.33	2.65	2.22	2.56
2020	2.02	1.90	1.79	1.77	1.75	1.65	1.76	2.30	1.92	2.39	2.61	2.58	2.04
2021	2.71	5.35	2.62	2.66	2.91	3.26	3.84	4.07	5.16	5.51	5.05	3.79	3.91
2022	4.38	4.69	4.90	6.60	8.15	7.70	7.29	8.81	7.88	5.69	5.45	5.53	6.42
2023	3.30	2.38	2.31	2.16	2.15	2.18	2.56	2.58	2.64	3.00	2.71	2.52	2.54

Source: Energy Information Administration, U.S. Department of Energy (EIA-DOE)

NATURAL GAS - NYMEX
Weekly Nearest Futures as of 03/28/2024

WEEKLY NEAREST FUTURES
As of 03/28/2024
Chart High 10.028 on 08/23/2022
Chart Low 1.432 on 06/26/2020

Nearby Futures through Last Trading Day.

Volume of Trading of Natural Gas Futures in New York   In Thousands of Contracts

Year	Jan.	Feb.	Mar.	Apr.	May	June	July	Aug.	Sept.	Oct.	Nov.	Dec.	Total
2014	8,872.0	8,301.5	4,804.4	5,114.8	5,031.3	5,425.1	5,022.7	5,374.9	5,623.7	6,087.8	7,980.1	6,568.4	74,206.6
2015	7,617.0	7,014.7	6,255.0	6,141.5	6,663.2	7,705.9	6,403.9	6,458.0	5,714.9	7,578.3	6,236.2	7,984.0	81,772.5
2016	6,472.9	7,003.9	7,649.5	8,350.1	7,090.1	8,875.2	6,769.1	8,506.9	7,646.7	10,240.1	9,073.3	9,802.9	97,480.6
2017	8,858.6	8,635.1	9,138.2	7,911.2	9,389.8	9,195.0	7,515.3	8,159.4	8,498.8	10,583.3	10,006.5	10,500.6	108,391.8
2018	14,188.6	8,454.1	7,287.5	8,409.2	8,241.5	8,010.4	7,091.6	8,462.0	9,776.6	12,263.9	14,219.3	7,851.3	114,256.1
2019	9,169.8	7,329.3	6,074.7	6,944.0	7,049.8	8,344.2	9,037.2	9,283.3	9,893.3	10,971.2	9,960.5	9,337.3	103,394.5
2020	11,404.6	12,025.5	12,118.2	11,076.8	9,852.9	9,631.0	8,484.7	9,607.2	9,345.8	9,313.3	8,484.7	9,454.9	120,799.5
2021	7,930.8	10,928.2	6,723.9	6,860.4	6,018.5	9,016.1	7,187.7	8,269.1	10,407.5	9,021.2	7,555.3	7,670.1	97,588.8
2022	8,112.7	8,646.7	7,002.2	8,928.4	6,647.4	8,045.0	5,825.1	5,827.7	6,109.8	6,409.6	6,955.9	7,340.9	85,851.4
2023	7,813.5	9,420.1	8,774.5	8,063.9	8,562.1	9,069.1	6,476.2	8,657.8	7,282.0	9,252.0	8,711.5	9,895.6	101,978.4

Contract size = 10,000 MMBtu.   *Source: CME Group; New York Mercantile Exchange (NYMEX)*

Average Open Interest of Natural Gas Futures in New York   In Thousands of Contracts

Year	Jan.	Feb.	Mar.	Apr.	May	June	July	Aug.	Sept.	Oct.	Nov.	Dec.
2014	1,278.0	1,246.6	1,160.8	1,104.7	1,021.9	1,032.9	1,017.1	962.3	970.3	914.8	952.5	939.1
2015	991.0	1,004.6	979.6	1,016.3	1,015.3	1,038.6	1,001.3	957.0	918.7	977.8	1,011.8	1,007.1
2016	912.6	995.9	1,076.7	1,117.9	1,081.1	1,061.2	1,014.6	1,057.1	1,059.3	1,142.7	1,169.7	1,220.4
2017	1,195.9	1,247.4	1,364.8	1,432.0	1,537.9	1,421.3	1,337.6	1,324.8	1,317.7	1,374.0	1,377.5	1,505.8
2018	1,426.6	1,365.8	1,392.4	1,463.5	1,484.9	1,512.8	1,507.3	1,583.4	1,642.3	1,621.5	1,409.2	1,258.8
2019	1,313.6	1,253.7	1,180.5	1,226.5	1,290.5	1,317.6	1,314.3	1,337.1	1,214.9	1,235.8	1,185.8	1,297.0
2020	1,442.7	1,460.9	1,332.2	1,227.5	1,246.1	1,303.0	1,295.0	1,255.1	1,254.9	1,221.3	1,220.2	1,191.7
2021	1,138.8	1,180.2	1,206.4	1,187.5	1,201.0	1,304.0	1,449.0	1,423.5	1,413.8	1,321.4	1,294.4	1,164.5
2022	1,146.1	1,122.8	1,094.4	1,154.1	1,116.2	1,054.3	971.2	978.9	964.9	971.5	984.1	1,004.2
2023	1,089.4	1,232.6	1,266.3	1,327.1	1,354.2	1,315.3	1,220.3	1,175.4	1,162.9	1,182.3	1,283.5	1,376.9

Contract size = 10,000 MMBtu.   *Source: CME Group; New York Mercantile Exchange (NYMEX)*

Gasoline

Gasoline is a complex mixture of hundreds of lighter liquid hydrocarbons and is used chiefly as a fuel for internal-combustion engines. Petroleum crude, or crude oil, is still the most economical source of gasoline with refineries turning more than half of every barrel of crude oil into gasoline. The three main steps to all refining operations are the separation process (separating crude oil into various chemical components), conversion process (breaking the chemicals down into molecules called hydrocarbons), and treatment process (transforming and combining hydrocarbon molecules and other additives). Another process, called *hydro treating*, removes a significant amount of sulfur from finished gasoline, as is currently required by the state of California.

Octane is a measure of a gasoline's ability to resist pinging or knocking noise from an engine. Most gasoline stations offer three octane grades of unleaded fuel—regular at 87 (R+M)/2, mid-grade at 89 (R+M)/2, and premium at 93 (R+M)/2. Additional refining steps are needed to increase the octane, which increases the retail price. This does not make the gasoline any cleaner or better but yields a different blend of hydrocarbons that burn more slowly.

In an attempt to improve air quality and reduce harmful emissions from internal combustion engines, Congress in 1990 amended the Clean Air Act to mandate the addition of ethanol to gasoline. Some 2 billion gallons of ethanol are now added to gasoline each year in the U.S. The most common blend is E10, which contains 10% ethanol and 90% gasoline. Auto manufacturers have approved that mixture for use in all U.S. vehicles. Ethanol is an alcohol-based fuel produced by fermenting and distilling crops such as corn, barley, wheat, and sugar.

RBOB gasoline futures and options trade at the CME Group. The CME's gasoline futures contract calls for the delivery of 1,000 barrels (42,000 gallons) of RBOB gasoline in the New York harbor and is priced in terms of U.S. Dollars and cents per gallon.

Prices – CME gasoline futures prices (Barchart.com symbol code RB) moved mildly higher in early 2023 but then fell back and closed the year down -15.0% at $2.1063 per gallon. The average monthly retail price of regular unleaded gasoline in 2023 fell by -10.6% yr/yr to $3.66 per gallon. The average monthly retail price of unleaded premium motor gasoline in the US in 2023 fell by -8.1% to $4.47 per gallon.

Supply – US production of finished motor gasoline in 2023 rose by +0.8% yr/yr to 9.643 million barrels per day. Gasoline stocks in December of 2023 were up by +5.2% to 18.142 million barrels.

Demand – US consumption of finished motor gasoline in 2023 rose by +1.3% yr/yr to 8.926 million barrels per day, below the 2018 record high of 9.325 million barrels per day.

World Production of Motor Gasoline   In Thousands of Barrels Per Day

Year	Brazil	Canada	China	France	Germany	India	Italy	Japan	Mexico	Russia	United Kingdom	United States	World Total
2008	364.0	703.8	1,483.0	386.8	584.7	374.0	460.4	974.1	430.0	832.0	471.0	8,548.0	21,425.0
2009	374.0	717.8	1,711.0	365.8	559.9	527.0	434.0	980.0	454.5	837.0	472.3	8,786.0	22,247.9
2010	399.0	719.0	1,720.0	317.0	499.0	605.0	438.0	1,012.0	408.0	840.0	460.0	9,059.0	22,306.5
2011	425.0	670.4	1,850.0	303.5	499.3	627.0	405.3	943.4	387.2	857.0	453.3	9,058.0	22,288.5
2012	462.0	687.4	2,098.0	276.0	478.7	704.0	395.7	919.9	404.5	893.0	396.5	8,926.0	22,451.4
2013	491.0	675.3	2,298.0	250.7	473.4	708.0	357.8	934.0	422.8	920.0	406.8	9,234.0	22,882.9
2014	533.7	672.0	2,577.5	265.4	465.1	755.4	343.5	920.5	407.2	909.9	363.7	9,571.0	23,605.1
2015[1]		810.9		164.2	421.9		183.9	893.4	766.9		294.3	9,178.4	
2016[2]		847.5		169.3	420.9		181.2	896.8	795.9		289.8		
2017[2]		778.4		166.9	396.4		159.3	803.1	700.9		262.6		

[1] Preliminary.   [2] Estimate.   *Source: Energy Information Administration, U.S. Department of Energy (EIA-DOE)*

World Imports of Motor Gasoline   In Thousands of Barrels Per Day

Year	Australia	Canada	Indo-nesia	Iran	Malaysia	Mexico	Nether-lands	Nigeria	Saudi Arabia	Singa-pore	United Kingdom	United States	World Total
2004	59.6	65.0	99.7	142.6	54.7	161.7	181.3	136.9	----	161.6	50.2	496.4	2,891.4
2005	57.5	81.7	125.2	156.0	66.3	214.2	212.2	128.1	41.1	166.6	55.1	602.7	3,242.9
2006	56.1	98.8	128.9	172.9	76.3	245.5	242.4	126.4	79.2	172.4	87.8	475.2	3,212.4
2007	46.8	75.3	145.3	119.8	73.3	284.7	170.7	135.4	75.2	200.0	75.6	412.6	3,040.0
2008	70.7	94.2	94.8	130.0	78.1	307.1	225.2	107.4	108.0	230.3	53.7	301.6	3,030.0
2009	77.1	89.1	199.3	132.5	74.0	307.6	234.1	140.0	102.9	20.2	77.8	223.4	2,943.9
2010	47.3	79.9	219.0	93.9	97.1	354.4	217.2	162.7	86.2	324.9	85.3	134.3	3,366.9
2011	57.2	90.4	268.8	31.1	104.6	386.8	240.5	142.0	51.9	323.3	88.0	104.8	3,508.0
2012[1]	57.3	62.2	307.9	9.6	134.9	374.9	276.2	137.3	92.2	305.7	111.5	44.1	3,628.2
2013[2]	63.6	54.7				319.4	225.1				108.7	45.0	

[1] Preliminary.   [2] Estimate.   *Source: Energy Information Administration, U.S. Department of Energy (EIA-DOE)*

World Exports of Motor Gasoline   In Thousands of Barrels Per Day

Year	Canada	France	Germany	India	Italy	Nether-lands	Russia	Singa-pore	United Kingdom	United States	Vene-zuela	Virgin Islands	World Total
2004	156.2	161.7	121.5	67.5	127.6	340.4	98.3	240.4	169.3	124.3	178.0	158.9	3,358.6
2005	161.4	179.1	132.1	53.1	161.3	376.4	138.4	332.0	152.5	135.5	172.0	159.3	3,655.9
2006	138.8	160.0	128.6	86.4	161.3	400.4	147.4	330.2	161.5	141.8	132.0	131.6	3,669.6
2007	147.4	147.0	125.4	105.3	208.7	297.6	140.4	376.5	169.7	127.0	115.1	140.1	3,562.2
2008	129.3	182.6	132.2	126.8	196.6	357.1	104.3	428.7	162.6	171.7	117.0	131.9	3,635.9
2009	136.5	148.4	125.5	228.1	166.8	376.0	105.2	216.8	177.2	195.4	127.5	115.8	3,564.1
2010	149.7	133.2	112.1	318.9	192.7	382.9	69.2	525.4	208.4	295.8	9.5	107.9	3,887.4
2011	130.7	118.5	109.6	329.1	187.2	348.7	90.3	535.7	214.3	478.8	27.9	102.3	4,052.4
2012[1]	138.4	107.9	114.9	336.8	201.8	448.9	74.9	530.9	196.5	408.9	8.7	18.0	4,020.3
2013[2]	143.2	85.8	115.4		180.4	409.3			238.5	373.0			

[1] Preliminary.   [2] Estimate.   *Source: Energy Information Administration, U.S. Department of Energy (EIA-DOE)*

Production of Finished Motor Gasoline in the United States   In Thousands of Barrels Per Day

Year	Jan.	Feb.	Mar.	Apr.	May	June	July	Aug.	Sept.	Oct.	Nov.	Dec.	Average
2014	8,849	9,111	9,368	9,652	9,834	9,809	9,983	9,741	9,404	9,552	9,607	9,898	9,567
2015	9,260	9,504	9,524	9,720	9,771	9,846	9,989	9,998	9,878	9,935	9,799	9,806	9,752
2016	9,378	9,834	9,932	9,876	10,058	10,280	10,224	10,293	10,020	10,059	9,969	10,013	9,995
2017	9,281	9,507	9,802	9,855	10,126	10,270	10,164	10,176	9,778	10,129	10,220	10,104	9,951
2018	9,529	9,797	10,053	9,974	10,138	10,314	10,174	10,243	9,927	10,301	10,240	10,020	10,059
2019	9,747	9,744	10,060	10,020	10,229	10,236	10,240	10,437	9,916	10,259	10,229	9,992	10,092
2020	9,626	9,742	8,576	6,365	7,476	8,748	9,026	9,312	9,090	9,252	8,883	8,809	8,742
2021	8,523	8,395	9,286	9,644	9,874	9,961	9,934	9,866	9,686	9,698	9,731	9,666	9,522
2022	8,758	9,373	9,525	9,547	9,825	9,834	9,580	9,872	9,760	9,654	9,682	9,415	9,569
2023[1]	8,934	9,306	9,600	9,681	9,869	9,944	9,826	9,907	9,691	9,728	9,703	9,536	9,644

[1] Preliminary.   *Source: Energy Information Administration, U.S. Department of Energy (EIA-DOE)*

Disposition of Finished Motor Gasoline, Total Product Supplied in the United States   In Thousand Barrels per Day

Year	Jan.	Feb.	Mar.	Apr.	May	June	July	Aug.	Sept.	Oct.	Nov.	Dec.	Average
2014	8,273	8,647	8,697	8,955	9,023	9,039	9,249	9,311	8,822	9,148	8,921	8,941	8,919
2015	8,639	8,829	9,057	9,189	9,262	9,417	9,470	9,460	9,289	9,245	9,112	9,148	9,176
2016	8,653	9,221	9,373	9,176	9,417	9,608	9,578	9,687	9,484	9,093	9,233	9,283	9,317
2017	8,507	9,008	9,325	9,295	9,550	9,772	9,595	9,752	9,378	9,357	9,110	9,247	9,325
2018	8,788	8,796	9,465	9,206	9,515	9,797	9,640	9,778	9,153	9,294	9,290	9,179	9,325
2019	8,778	9,072	9,184	9,411	9,497	9,703	9,533	9,834	9,198	9,308	9,209	8,971	9,308
2020	8,724	9,050	7,779	5,866	7,198	8,292	8,460	8,524	8,541	8,316	8,001	7,855	8,051
2021	7,723	7,824	8,553	8,839	9,081	9,362	9,297	9,182	8,932	9,027	9,021	8,879	8,810
2022	8,062	8,650	9,005	8,799	9,119	9,075	8,812	9,115	8,847	8,807	8,827	8,596	8,809
2023[1]	8,282	8,715	9,007	8,996	9,105	9,279	9,013	9,299	8,832	9,094	8,845	8,649	8,926

[1] Preliminary.   *Source: Energy Information Administration, U.S. Department of Energy (EIA-DOE)*

Stocks of Finished Gasoline[2] on Hand in the United States, at End of Month   In Thousands of Barrels

Year	Jan.	Feb.	Mar.	Apr.	May	June	July	Aug.	Sept.	Oct.	Nov.	Dec.
2014	39,790	37,687	34,274	30,710	31,057	28,854	28,320	27,514	28,773	27,432	29,532	30,615
2015	29,923	30,558	26,891	25,898	26,580	25,678	24,418	26,048	29,028	27,638	27,805	28,453
2016	26,800	27,218	26,468	25,039	23,708	24,874	24,773	25,641	25,088	25,892	26,525	28,610
2017	28,496	25,727	21,728	21,828	21,983	22,480	23,157	24,584	21,765	23,154	23,595	24,641
2018	24,969	24,769	22,863	22,583	23,776	24,550	24,229	23,227	24,748	24,888	24,107	25,769
2019	28,705	23,864	20,865	20,866	22,169	21,491	21,916	23,084	23,007	23,330	24,834	26,129
2020	28,537	26,397	22,585	22,889	24,069	23,495	24,293	25,151	22,543	25,205	25,039	25,398
2021	22,939	20,896	20,259	21,280	20,361	18,600	17,887	18,165	18,506	18,286	18,045	17,743
2022	18,089	18,572	17,260	17,830	17,283	17,136	16,768	17,035	17,623	16,510	16,545	17,238
2023[1]	16,700	17,173	14,707	15,699	17,018	17,574	15,174	15,513	15,338	16,030	17,292	18,142

[1] Preliminary.   [2] Includes oxygenated and other finished.   *Source: Energy Information Administration, U.S. Department of Energy (EIA-DOE)*

GASOLINE

RBOB GASOLINE
Quarterly Cash as of 03/28/2024

QUARTERLY CASH
As of 03/28/2024
Chart High 4.9680 on 10/03/2022
Chart Low .2907 on 12/04/1998

USD / Gallon

Unleaded: to 12/2006; RBOB: 01/1997 to date.

Average Spot Price of Unleaded Gasoline in New York   In Dollars Per Gallon

Year	Jan.	Feb.	Mar.	Apr.	May	June	July	Aug.	Sept.	Oct.	Nov.	Dec.	Average
2014	2.6720	2.7950	2.7530	2.8960	2.8620	2.8960	2.8020	2.7050	2.7210	2.3980	2.1650	1.6830	2.6100
2015	1.3640	1.6070	1.6440	1.7930	1.9380	2.0050	1.8600	1.6200	1.4600	1.3970	1.3770	1.2760	1.6120
2016	1.1210	1.0580	1.2010	1.4480	1.5660	1.5060	1.3540	1.3790	1.4380	1.5220	1.4620	1.6340	1.3908
2017	1.6200	1.5470	1.4920	1.6110	1.5400	1.4450	1.5620	1.6880	1.8670	1.7150	1.8300	1.7570	1.6395
2018	1.8990	1.8170	1.8340	1.9950	2.1290	2.0300	2.0740	2.0770	2.0930	2.0280	1.6250	1.4490	1.9208
2019	1.4250	1.5680	1.8120	2.0420	1.9160	1.7400	1.8900	1.6940	1.7260	1.7280	1.7240	1.7130	1.7482
2020	1.6580	1.5800	0.8910	0.5930	0.8760	1.1210	1.2200	1.2480	1.2270	1.2010	1.1900	1.3590	1.1803
2021	1.5630	1.7610	1.9860	1.9880	2.1160	2.1670	2.2570	2.2350	2.2840	2.5000	2.3900	2.2030	2.1208
2022	2.4490	2.7390	3.1840	3.1930	3.8280	4.0820	3.4840	3.0270	2.6420	3.0130	2.8520	2.3660	3.0716
2023	2.5930	2.5320	2.5150	2.7650	2.5700	2.6590	2.7000	2.8740	2.8940	2.5240	2.3060	2.2260	2.5965

Source: Energy Information Administration, U.S. Department of Energy (EIA-DOE)

Average Refiner Price of Finished Motor Gasoline to End Users[2] in the United States   In Dollars Per Gallon

Year	Jan.	Feb.	Mar.	Apr.	May	June	July	Aug.	Sept.	Oct.	Nov.	Dec.	Average
2013	2.850	3.221	3.233	3.102	3.188	3.184	3.146	3.097	3.059	2.893	2.759	2.759	3.041
2014	2.816	2.913	3.104	3.214	3.245	3.265	3.128	3.016	2.936	2.670	2.406	2.013	2.894
2015	1.673	1.858	2.054	2.058	2.322	2.374	2.338	2.218	1.920	1.849	1.711	1.604	1.998
2016	1.505	1.332	1.552	1.725	1.869	1.961	1.804	1.754	1.788	1.819	1.759	1.849	1.726
2017	1.900	1.862	1.904	1.997	1.963	1.906	1.871	1.952	2.154	2.042	2.122	2.034	1.976
2018	2.108	2.127	2.160	2.315	2.494	2.469	2.442	2.421	2.428	2.441	2.205	1.973	2.299
2019	1.854	1.949	2.137	2.487	2.520	2.366	2.375	2.252	2.242	2.289	2.229	2.182	2.240
2020	2.150	2.060	1.862	1.490	1.598	1.768	1.806	1.814	1.804	1.773	1.736	1.828	1.807
2021	1.986	2.201	2.442	2.493	2.683	3.000	3.105	3.146	3.143	3.201	3.318	3.283	2.833
2022[1]	3.145	3.313	3.991										3.483

[1] Preliminary.   [2] Excludes aviation and taxes.   *Source: Energy Information Administration, U.S. Department of Energy (EIA-DOE)*

BLENDSTOCK GASOLINE (RBOB) - NYMEX
Weekly Nearest Futures as of 03/28/2024

WEEKLY NEAREST FUTURES
As of 03/28/2024
Chart High 4.3260 on 06/06/2022
Chart Low .3760 on 03/23/2020

Nearby Futures through Last Trading Day.

Volume of Trading of Gasoline, RBOB[1] Futures in New York   In Thousands of Contracts

Year	Jan.	Feb.	Mar.	Apr.	May	June	July	Aug.	Sept.	Oct.	Nov.	Dec.	Total
2014	2,470.9	2,417.0	2,562.7	3,316.9	3,240.6	2,679.3	3,001.7	2,894.1	3,173.3	3,170.5	2,713.5	2,781.4	34,421.9
2015	3,070.7	3,387.9	3,396.1	3,449.5	3,113.9	3,869.0	3,621.4	3,736.9	2,961.2	3,158.0	3,171.9	3,365.6	40,302.1
2016	3,362.4	3,841.7	3,723.6	3,546.6	3,874.1	4,362.3	3,427.0	4,134.4	4,677.2	3,413.1	3,844.7	3,221.5	45,428.7
2017	3,748.5	4,433.7	4,380.3	3,721.6	4,343.5	4,454.4	4,065.8	5,803.7	4,139.1	3,734.5	3,717.3	3,368.5	49,910.9
2018	4,290.5	3,815.0	3,992.9	4,067.4	4,569.1	4,175.0	3,959.4	4,858.9	3,901.0	4,626.3	3,953.8	3,404.7	49,613.9
2019	3,927.9	3,660.4	5,049.3	5,243.9	4,833.5	4,270.2	4,235.3	3,663.8	4,111.6	3,832.5	3,585.7	3,437.8	49,851.8
2020	4,556.7	4,861.5	5,625.8	3,936.0	3,244.3	3,495.7	3,338.0	3,613.2	3,361.7	3,635.1	3,386.0	3,438.6	46,492.5
2021	3,772.1	4,165.3	4,517.7	3,733.2	3,951.0	3,883.5	3,567.4	4,801.2	4,001.5	3,996.1	4,136.0	3,312.9	47,838.0
2022	3,747.8	4,413.8	4,222.9	3,152.3	3,992.0	3,718.9	2,960.3	3,246.7	2,801.7	3,049.6	2,890.2	2,796.1	40,992.4
2023	3,176.1	3,105.8	3,693.7	3,439.3	4,012.5	4,385.8	3,744.3	4,362.6	3,683.4	3,329.3	3,038.7	2,858.1	42,829.6

Contract size = 42,000 US gallons.   *Source: CME Group; New York Mercantile Exchange (NYMEX)*

Average Open Interest of Gasoline, RBOB[1] Futures in New York   In Contracts

Year	Jan.	Feb.	Mar.	Apr.	May	June	July	Aug.	Sept.	Oct.	Nov.	Dec.
2014	252,519	274,087	283,756	310,549	332,460	314,754	307,808	274,978	283,206	310,119	334,015	349,589
2015	366,741	362,191	372,013	383,705	383,960	372,487	367,208	378,562	371,326	345,971	360,109	365,200
2016	379,473	406,615	420,305	392,100	405,314	401,323	389,932	406,922	395,691	408,750	380,734	390,804
2017	425,330	421,979	398,661	406,054	403,723	402,039	392,477	408,427	415,138	403,480	429,908	400,346
2018	437,285	434,342	424,422	450,029	479,806	461,515	441,321	459,928	438,527	406,263	406,427	406,667
2019	419,362	415,527	410,706	432,882	408,391	373,707	393,550	403,171	378,190	366,086	398,540	378,433
2020	408,399	391,038	368,635	378,558	373,104	361,741	346,636	355,345	362,771	366,985	397,811	417,834
2021	418,253	416,260	402,728	376,515	390,452	419,925	362,481	352,072	333,672	325,172	315,505	297,385
2022	347,487	385,832	302,944	299,953	308,214	302,167	267,906	257,653	246,989	248,498	251,950	255,689
2023	283,980	323,965	309,082	311,034	307,764	333,650	352,732	370,222	370,512	320,612	331,097	340,176

Contract size = 42,000 US gallons.   *Source: CME Group; New York Mercantile Exchange (NYMEX)*

GASOLINE

Average Retail Price of Unleaded Premium Motor Gasoline[2] in the United States   In Dollars per Gallon

Year	Jan.	Feb.	Mar.	Apr.	May	June	July	Aug.	Sept.	Oct.	Nov.	Dec.	Average
2014	3.651	3.694	3.858	3.986	4.020	4.027	3.976	3.835	3.758	3.547	3.262	2.940	3.713
2015	2.497	2.621	2.867	2.868	3.166	3.218	3.252	3.120	2.860	2.749	2.640	2.532	2.866
2016	2.455	2.248	2.411	2.585	2.710	2.807	2.702	2.629	2.682	2.719	2.675	2.698	2.610
2017	2.815	2.793	2.827	2.909	2.894	2.859	2.800	2.883	3.120	2.996	3.056	2.985	2.911
2018	3.042	3.091	3.101	3.258	3.423	3.440	3.399	3.384	3.400	3.431	3.251	3.015	3.270
2019	2.874	2.901	3.079	3.382	3.471	3.328	3.327	3.222	3.214	3.297	3.254	3.190	3.212
2020	3.157	3.071	2.893	2.527	2.490	2.673	2.783	2.795	2.810	2.782	2.727	2.778	2.791
2021	2.921	3.073	3.386	3.455	3.596	3.802	3.897	3.938	3.945	4.040	4.148	4.100	3.692
2022	4.102	4.244	5.015	5.037	5.318	5.774	5.459	4.916	4.732	4.914	4.679	4.167	4.863
2023[1]	4.192	4.287	4.339	4.485	4.468	4.497	4.526	4.740	4.844	4.701	4.385	4.162	4.469

[1] Preliminary.   [2] Including taxes.   *Source: Energy Information Administration, U.S. Department of Energy (EIA-DOE)*

Average Retail Price of Unleaded Regular Motor Gasoline[2] in the United States   In Dollars per Gallon

Year	Jan.	Feb.	Mar.	Apr.	May	June	July	Aug.	Sept.	Oct.	Nov.	Dec.	Average
2014	3.320	3.364	3.532	3.659	3.691	3.695	3.633	3.481	3.403	3.182	2.887	2.560	3.367
2015	2.110	2.249	2.483	2.485	2.775	2.832	2.832	2.679	2.394	2.289	2.185	2.060	2.448
2016	1.967	1.767	1.958	2.134	2.264	2.363	2.225	2.155	2.208	2.243	2.187	2.230	2.142
2017	2.351	2.299	2.323	2.418	2.386	2.337	2.281	2.374	2.630	2.484	2.548	2.459	2.408
2018	2.539	2.575	2.572	2.737	2.907	2.914	2.873	2.862	2.873	2.887	2.671	2.414	2.735
2019	2.289	2.353	2.564	2.835	2.901	2.752	2.776	2.655	2.630	2.673	2.620	2.587	2.636
2020	2.567	2.465	2.267	1.876	1.879	2.076	2.176	2.177	2.193	2.159	2.090	2.168	2.174
2021	2.326	2.496	2.791	2.839	2.972	3.154	3.233	3.255	3.265	3.385	3.482	3.408	3.051
2022	3.413	3.592	4.312	4.271	4.604	5.058	4.667	4.101	3.881	4.016	3.853	3.356	4.094
2023[1]	3.452	3.514	3.551	3.735	3.685	3.712	3.732	3.955	3.988	3.782	3.500	3.289	3.658

[1] Preliminary.   [2] Including taxes.   *Source: Energy Information Administration, U.S. Department of Energy (EIA-DOE)*

Average Retail Price of All-Types[2] Motor Gasoline[3] in the United States   In Dollars per Gallon

Year	Jan.	Feb.	Mar.	Apr.	May	June	July	Aug.	Sept.	Oct.	Nov.	Dec.	Average
2014	3.378	3.422	3.590	3.717	3.745	3.750	3.690	3.540	3.463	3.241	2.945	2.618	3.425
2015	2.170	2.308	2.544	2.545	2.832	2.889	2.893	2.745	2.463	2.357	2.249	2.125	2.510
2016	2.034	1.833	2.021	2.196	2.324	2.422	2.287	2.218	2.269	2.304	2.246	2.289	2.204
2017	2.409	2.360	2.386	2.479	2.448	2.400	2.344	2.436	2.688	2.545	2.608	2.521	2.469
2018	2.596	2.632	2.631	2.795	2.963	2.970	2.930	2.919	2.930	2.945	2.733	2.479	2.794
2019	2.352	2.412	2.620	2.894	2.963	2.814	2.836	2.716	2.694	2.741	2.687	2.652	2.698
2020	2.631	2.530	2.334	1.946	1.946	2.141	2.243	2.245	2.260	2.228	2.159	2.235	2.242
2021	2.391	2.559	2.856	2.907	3.041	3.245	3.326	3.351	3.361	3.477	3.576	3.505	3.133
2022	3.500	3.675	4.401	4.369	4.695	5.149	4.768	4.205	3.990	4.130	3.958	3.459	4.192
2023[1]	3.555	3.622	3.660	3.839	3.794	3.821	3.842	4.064	4.107	3.910	3.623	3.411	3.771

[1] Preliminary.   [2] Also includes types of motor oil not shown separately.   [3] Including taxes.   *Source: Energy Information Administration, U.S. Department of Energy (EIA-DOE)*

Average Refiner Price of Finished Aviation Gasoline to End Users[2] in the United States   In Dollars per Gallon

Year	Jan.	Feb.	Mar.	Apr.	May	June	July	Aug.	Sept.	Oct.	Nov.	Dec.	Average
2013	W	4.060	4.022	3.860	3.900	4.191	4.224	4.298	3.982	3.653	3.673	3.678	3.932
2014	W	4.142	W	W	W	W	W	W	W	W	W	W	3.986
2015	W	W	W	W	W	W	W	W	W	W	W	W	W
2016	W	W	W	W	W	W	W	W	W	W	W	W	W
2017	W	W	W	W	W	W	W	W	W	W	W	W	W
2018	W	W	W	W	W	W	W	W	W	W	W	W	W
2019	W	W	W	W	W	W	W	W	W	W	W	W	W
2020	W	W	W	W	W	W	2.761	2.805	2.613	2.495	2.485	2.674	2.639
2021	2.829	3.148	3.364	3.363	3.447	3.492	W	W	W	3.783	3.778	W	3.401
2022[1]	3.689	W	4.581										4.135

[1] Preliminary.   [2] Excluding taxes.   NA = Not available.   W = Withheld proprietary data.   *Source: Energy Information Administration, U.S. Department Energy (EIA-DOE)*

Gold

Gold is a dense, bright yellow metallic element with a high luster. Gold is an inactive substance and is unaffected by air, heat, moisture, and most solvents. Gold has been coveted for centuries for its unique blend of rarity, beauty, and near indestructibility. The Egyptians mined gold before 2,000 BC. King Croesus of Lydia created the first known, pure gold coin in the sixth century BC.

Gold is found in nature in quartz veins and secondary alluvial deposits as a free metal. Gold is produced from mines on every continent apart from Antarctica, where mining is forbidden. Because gold is virtually indestructible, much of the gold that has ever been mined still exists in one form or another. The largest producer of gold in the U.S. by far is the state of Nevada, with Alaska and California running a distant second and third.

Gold is a vital industrial commodity. Pure gold is one of the most malleable and ductile of all the metals. It is a good conductor of heat and electricity. The prime industrial use of gold is in electronics. Another important sector is dental gold, where it has been used for almost 3,000 years. Other applications for gold include decorative gold leaf, reflective glass, and jewelry.

In 1792, the United States first assigned a formal monetary role for gold when Congress put the nation's currency on a bimetallic standard, backing it with gold and silver. Under the gold standard, the U.S. government was willing to exchange its paper currency for a set amount of gold, meaning its currency was backed by gold. However, President Nixon in 1971 severed the convertibility between the U.S. dollar and gold, which led to the breakdown of the Bretton Woods international payments system. Since then, the prices of gold and paper currencies have floated freely. U.S. and other central banks now hold physical gold reserves primarily as a store of wealth.

Gold futures and options are traded at the CME Group. Gold futures are traded at the Bolsa de Mercadorias and Futuros (BM&F) and at the Tokyo Commodity Exchange (TOCOM), and the Korea Futures Exchange (KFE). The CME gold futures contract calls for the delivery of 100 troy ounces of gold (0.995 fineness), and the contract trades in terms of dollars and cents per troy ounce.

Prices – CME gold futures prices (Barchart.com symbol GC) in early 2023 were under pressure and posted a 1-year low in February of $1,807.80 per troy ounce. Gold prices fell as US economic reports the first two months of 2023 were stronger than expected, which bolstered expectations for additional Fed rate hikes. Gold prices recovered into May after the collapse of some US regional banks and turmoil at Credit Suisse Group AG sparked some safe-haven buying of gold. Dollar weakness in mid-2023 also supported gold after the dollar index fell to a 1-1/2 year low in July. Gold prices ratcheted lower into October as T-note yields rose to a 16-year high after the Fed signaled monetary policy could remain tighter for longer. The outlook for tighter Fed policy sparked a mass exodus of investors from gold as holdings in gold ETFs fell to a 4-year low in October. Gold prices then rallied into year-end and posted a record high of $2,130.2 per ounce in December. Gold rallied after Fed Chair Powell signaled in December that the Fed was done with its tightening cycle and would pivot toward cutting interest rates in 2024. Gold prices finished 2023 up +13.3% yr/yr at $2,062.40 per troy ounce.

Supply – World mine production of gold in 2023 fell by -2.0% yr/yr to 3.000 million kilograms, below the 2018 record high of 3.310 million kilograms (1 kilogram equals 32.1507 troy ounces). The world's largest producers of gold in 2023 were China with 12.3% of world production, followed by both Australia and Russia with 10.3%, Canada with 6.7%, the U.S with 5.7%, Indonesia with 3.7%, both South Africa and Uzbekistan with 3.3%, and both Peru and Ghana with 3.0%.

US gold mine production in 2023 fell by -1.7% yr/yr to 170,000 kilograms. Canada's gold mine production in 2023 fell by -2.8% yr/yr at 200,000 kilograms, down from the 2021 record high of 223,000 kilograms.

US refinery production of gold from domestic and foreign ore sources in 2023 fell by -11.6% yr/yr to 160,000 kilograms. In addition, US refinery production of gold from secondary scrap sources in 2023 fell by -2.8% yr/yr to 90,000 kilograms.

Demand – US consumption of gold in 2023 fell by -2.7% yr/yr to 250,000 kilograms.

Trade – US exports of gold (excluding coinage) in 2023 fell by -40.5% yr/yr to 250,000 kilograms, well below the 2012 record high of 699,000 kilograms. US imports of gold for consumption in 2023 rose by +44.9% yr/yr to 200,000 kilograms.

World Mine Production of Gold   In Kilograms (1 Kilogram = 32.1507 Troy Ounces)

Year	Australia	Brazil	Canada	China	Ghana	Indonesia	Papua New Guinea	Peru	Russia	South Africa	United States	Uzbek-istan	World Total
2015	275,160	84,814	160,751	450,000	125,325	92,171	60,046	146,822	248,945	144,504	214,000	100,000	3,110,000
2016	290,800	77,845	161,497	453,500	124,196	80,868	62,293	152,990	253,579	142,202	232,000	89,000	3,180,000
2017	294,171	79,717	172,877	426,142	133,352	101,000	65,246	151,964	270,300	137,290	237,000	89,900	3,260,000
2018	313,028	85,301	191,882	401,119	148,336	132,734	64,532	140,211	277,139	117,144	226,000	92,716	3,310,000
2019	326,304	89,988	190,651	380,230	141,982	108,977	73,900	128,413	304,697	105,185	201,000	100,900	3,260,000
2020	327,952	79,619	178,055	365,340	125,552	65,900	53,000	87,457	308,560	95,786	193,000	104,600	3,050,000
2021	307,170	60,669	222,524	328,980	87,649	79,280	45,000	97,339	313,830	107,890	187,000	103,600	3,120,000
2022[1]	313,872	61,000	205,831	372,048	88,000	105,460	45,000	96,740	310,000	88,883	173,000	104,000	3,060,000
2023[2]	310,000	60,000	200,000	370,000	90,000	110,000		90,000	310,000	100,000	170,000	100,000	3,000,000

[1] Preliminary.   [2] Estimate.   *Source: U.S. Geological Survey (USGS)*

GOLD

GOLD
Quarterly Cash as of 03/28/2024

QUARTERLY CASH
As of 03/28/2024
Chart High 2231.01 on 03/28/2024
Chart Low 34.25 on 07/31/1941

USD / troy oz.

U.S. Gov't price control: to 12/1940; Black Market: 01/1941 to 02/1968; Handy and Harman: 03/1968 to 06/1990; Composite: 07/1990 to date.

Salient Statistics of Gold in the United States   In Kilograms (1 Kilogram = 32.1507 Troy Ounces)

			- Refinery Production -				-------- Stocks, Dec. 31 ---------				---------- Consumption ----------			
	Mine		Domestic		Exports,	Imports	Treasury			Official				
	Pro-	Value	& Foreign	Secondary	Excluding	for Con-	Depart-	Futures		World		Indus-	Jewelry	
Year	duction	Million $	Ores	(Old Scrap)	Coinage	sumption	ment[3]	Exchange	Industry	Reserves[4]	Dental	trial[5]	& Arts	Total
2014	210,000	8,570.0	253,000	135,000	492,000	308,000	8,140,000	325,000	7,540	32,000	----	----	----	152,000
2015	214,000	8,000.0	244,000	238,000	478,000	265,000	8,140,000	198,000	7,250	32,700	----	----	----	165,000
2016	222,000	9,350.0	242,000	220,000	393,000	374,000	8,140,000	285,000	4,030	33,300	----	----	----	210,000
2017	237,000	9,600.0	207,000	119,000	461,000	255,000	8,130,000	284,000	1,680	34,000	----	----	----	159,000
2018	225,600	9,220.0	205,000	93,500	474,000	213,000	8,130,000	262,000	3,380	34,200	----	----	----	154,000
2019	200,400	9,010.0	205,000	116,000	360,000	199,000	8,130,000	271,000	3,380	34,800	----	----	----	151,000
2020	192,400	11,000.0	181,000	91,800	297,000	545,000	8,130,000	1,190,000	3,670	35,300	----	----	----	187,000
2021	187,500	10,900.0	181,000	92,300	386,000	192,000	8,130,000	1,050,000	3,680	35,500	----	----	----	265,000
2022[1]	172,600	10,000.0	181,000	92,600	420,000	138,000	8,130,000	721,000	3,700	35,500	----	----	----	257,000
2023[2]	168,000		160,000	90,000	250,000	200,000	8,130,000				----	----	----	250,000

[1] Preliminary.   [2] Estimate.   [3] Includes gold in Exchange Stabilization Fund.   [4] Held by market economy country central banks and governments and international monetary orgainzations.   [5] Including space and defense.   NA = Not available.   *Source: U.S. Geological Survey (USGS)*

Monthly Average Gold Price (Handy & Harman) in New York   In Dollars Per Troy Ounce

Year	Jan.	Feb.	Mar.	Apr.	May	June	July	Aug.	Sept.	Oct.	Nov.	Dec.	Average
2013	1,670.17	1,628.47	1,592.85	1,490.22	1,415.91	1,342.36	1,288.31	1,349.30	1,346.63	1,316.19	1,276.94	1,220.65	1,411.50
2014	1,244.53	1,300.60	1,336.08	1,298.45	1,288.74	1,279.10	1,310.59	1,295.13	1,236.14	1,222.49	1,175.33	1,200.62	1,265.65
2015	1,250.75	1,227.08	1,178.63	1,198.93	1,198.63	1,181.50	1,128.31	1,117.93	1,124.88	1,159.25	1,086.44	1,068.25	1,160.05
2016	1,097.81	1,199.50	1,245.14	1,242.26	1,260.95	1,276.40	1,336.66	1,340.17	1,326.01	1,266.57	1,238.35	1,150.13	1,248.33
2017	1,192.10	1,234.20	1,231.09	1,266.88	1,246.04	1,260.26	1,236.84	1,283.04	1,314.07	1,279.51	1,281.90	1,264.44	1,257.53
2018	1,331.30	1,330.73	1,324.66	1,334.76	1,303.45	1,281.57	1,237.71	1,201.71	1,198.39	1,215.37	1,220.65	1,250.94	1,269.27
2019	1,291.75	1,320.06	1,300.90	1,285.91	1,283.70	1,359.04	1,412.89	1,500.41	1,510.58	1,494.81	1,470.50	1,481.23	1,392.65
2020	1,561.07	1,600.37	1,593.48	1,682.71	1,717.63	1,734.11	1,855.45	1,972.67	1,926.24	1,903.27	1,875.95	----	1,765.72
2021	1,868.77	1,807.69	1,718.23	1,760.04	1,850.26	1,834.57	1,807.84	1,785.74	1,775.14	1,776.85	1,822.81	1,790.43	1,799.86
2022	1,816.15	1,859.15	1,951.27	1,935.05	1,848.28	1,837.05	1,736.74	1,763.25	1,681.16	1,666.04			1,809.41

Source: U.S. Geological Survey (USGS)

GOLD - COMEX
Weekly Selected Futures as of 03/28/2024

WEEKLY SELECTED FUTURES
As of 03/28/2024

Chart High 2234.10   on 03/28/2024
Chart Low   1046.20   on 12/03/2015

USD / troy oz.

Nearby Futures through Last Trading Day using selected contract months: February, April, June, August, October and December.

Volume of Trading of Gold Futures in Chicago   In Thousands of Contracts

Year	Jan.	Feb.	Mar.	Apr.	May	June	July	Aug.	Sept.	Oct.	Nov.	Dec.	Total
2014	3,754.8	2,607.5	4,200.3	2,692.9	3,631.1	2,508.1	3,848.3	2,381.8	3,205.8	3,703.7	4,676.7	3,307.7	40,518.8
2015	4,507.9	2,558.8	4,403.4	3,057.0	3,721.5	2,856.0	4,554.8	3,431.6	2,917.1	3,070.1	4,034.0	2,735.2	41,847.3
2016	4,102.0	4,369.5	5,720.2	3,902.5	5,880.1	4,936.3	5,798.5	4,387.9	4,022.6	3,815.0	7,108.7	3,521.6	57,564.8
2017	5,978.9	4,392.4	6,119.4	4,612.2	6,367.4	4,906.6	5,957.0	6,808.8	7,184.1	6,665.5	8,623.3	5,186.6	72,802.2
2018	9,161.9	6,078.6	8,036.1	6,655.1	8,676.6	5,739.0	7,231.2	6,274.2	5,495.6	6,470.2	6,351.2	4,132.0	80,301.6
2019	6,245.8	4,010.5	6,711.5	5,096.3	7,142.7	7,308.6	9,490.3	9,582.3	8,582.9	8,016.2	8,927.4	5,394.2	86,508.7
2020	9,827.2	7,936.4	10,356.4	4,285.5	5,155.4	4,427.6	7,278.5	7,735.9	6,265.9	4,645.3	6,177.1	4,035.4	78,126.5
2021	6,164.8	4,569.4	6,266.2	3,590.4	6,310.8	4,800.1	5,603.2	3,910.7	3,926.2	4,119.0	6,130.6	3,073.6	58,465.0
2022	5,860.3	4,161.2	6,310.9	3,375.2	4,936.5	3,574.9	5,400.9	3,437.7	4,530.2	3,997.9	5,419.1	3,254.8	54,259.7
2023	5,289.2	3,649.1	7,075.9	3,887.9	6,109.8	4,018.3	5,146.2	3,526.4	3,788.0	4,989.4	5,284.0	3,746.7	56,511.0

Contract size = 100 oz.   *Source: CME Group; Commodity Exchange (COMEX)*

Average Open Interest of Gold Futures in Chicago   In Contracts

Year	Jan.	Feb.	Mar.	Apr.	May	June	July	Aug.	Sept.	Oct.	Nov.	Dec.
2014	397,700	381,045	404,828	369,755	395,313	385,660	400,977	365,066	381,961	400,455	433,102	372,432
2015	415,408	399,097	415,894	397,632	411,656	417,416	451,224	430,894	416,389	448,795	425,138	398,843
2016	403,929	421,355	491,060	496,873	561,027	553,721	616,676	571,588	576,954	508,303	484,383	401,266
2017	444,716	423,037	436,599	458,759	447,814	462,182	468,238	490,304	562,694	524,694	530,233	460,378
2018	563,606	528,812	525,719	505,825	496,142	461,716	499,723	471,934	468,159	472,864	490,986	416,930
2019	489,807	488,012	503,968	439,367	485,122	530,157	602,830	604,243	628,729	626,969	697,262	720,262
2020	770,857	690,974	592,184	492,108	509,613	501,447	583,285	549,531	565,752	555,588	553,266	551,544
2021	549,566	500,908	472,695	466,965	505,511	474,172	489,673	490,011	500,431	494,196	567,607	504,782
2022	536,208	557,923	612,579	566,980	550,695	498,898	511,093	457,632	462,882	442,675	470,246	432,849
2023	482,310	434,292	463,520	477,348	495,318	435,275	475,345	434,704	437,729	448,809	489,687	486,178

Contract size = 100 oz.   *Source: CME Group; Commodity Exchange (COMEX)*

GOLD

Commodity Exchange Warehouse Stocks of Gold, on First of Month   In Thousands of Troy Ounces

Year	Jan. 1	Feb. 1	Mar. 1	Apr. 1	May 1	June 1	July 1	Aug. 1	Sept. 1	Oct. 1	Nov. 1	Dec. 1
2014	7,828.1	7,081.3	7,177.1	7,740.8	7,935.6	8,262.7	8,298.5	8,684.3	9,927.3	9,127.3	8,056.0	7,928.7
2015	7,932.1	7,983.9	8,321.5	8,010.7	7,718.4	7,871.5	8,043.6	7,572.3	7,221.1	6,852.5	6,700.8	6,377.6
2016	6,352.5	6,427.0	6,785.0	6,851.2	7,250.3	8,452.7	9,286.6	10,718.8	10,932.9	10,702.4	10,600.9	10,002.9
2017	9,158.9	8,986.3	8,942.2	8,956.9	8,931.0	8,750.3	8,616.7	8,660.6	8,693.6	8,761.4	8,707.2	8,914.8
2018	9,142.7	9,257.9	9,132.9	9,060.6	9,049.6	9,017.2	8,564.6	8,641.4	8,388.7	8,330.7	8,066.5	8,020.7
2019	8,434.3	8,439.1	8,162.5	8,034.0	7,782.0	7,677.3	7,696.7	7,783.6	8,057.1	8,188.4	8,284.4	8,828.0
2020	8,699.0	8,712.8	8,647.4	9,245.5	10,362.6	10,423.1	12,758.9	14,820.9	16,093.3	16,718.8	17,356.2	17,326.8
2021	18,911.1	19,181.4	19,326.8	17,968.1	17,570.5	18,343.0	18,460.2	19,129.3	18,429.8	18,031.2	17,574.3	18,131.4
2022	17,679.6	17,570.8	17,360.7	18,087.3	18,358.7	18,026.7	17,179.4	15,264.1	13,684.7	13,093.0	11,331.3	11,296.9
2023	11,342.4	11,020.4	10,889.8	12,097.4	12,356.0	11,640.7	11,808.0	12,102.3	10,854.4	10,460.4	10,066.3	10,163.1

Source: CME Group; Commodity Exchange (COMEX)

Central Gold Bank Reserves   In Millions of Troy Ounces

Year	Belgium	Canada	France	Ger-many	Italy	Japan	Nether-lands	Switzer-land	United Kingdom	United States	World Total
2012	7.3	0.1	78.3	109.0	78.8	24.6	19.7	33.4	10.0	261.5	1,017.5
2013	7.3	0.1	78.3	108.9	78.8	24.6	19.7	33.4	10.0	261.5	1,023.0
2014	7.3	0.1	78.3	108.8	78.8	24.6	19.7	33.4	10.0	261.5	1,028.7
2015	7.3	0.1	78.3	108.7	78.8	24.6	19.7	33.4	10.0	261.5	1,051.5
2016	7.3	----	78.3	108.6	78.8	24.6	19.7	33.4	10.0	261.5	1,080.1
2017	7.3	----	78.3	108.5	78.8	24.6	19.7	33.4	10.0	261.5	1,093.1
2018	7.3	----	78.3	108.3	78.8	24.6	19.7	33.4	10.0	261.5	1,100.6
2019	7.3	----	78.3	108.2	78.8	24.6	19.7	33.4	10.0	261.5	1,118.3
2020	7.3	----	78.3	108.1	78.8	24.6	19.7	33.4	10.0	261.5	1,134.0
2021[1]	7.3	----	78.3	108.0	78.8	27.2	19.7	33.4	10.0	261.5	1,142.5

[1] Preliminary.   [2] International Monetary Fund.   *Source: American Metal Market (AMM)*

Mine Production of Recoverable Gold in the United States   In Kilograms

Year	Alaska	California	Nevada	Washington	Other States[2]	Total
2014	31,400	W	151,000	W	27,800	210,000
2015	28,000	W	162,000	W	24,200	214,000
2016	27,600	W	165,000	W	30,000	222,000
2017	26,200	W	173,000	W	37,400	237,000
2018	20,640	W	173,100	W	31,640	225,600
2019	16,930	W	151,600	W	55,250	200,400
2020	20,240	W	144,200	W	28,810	192,400
2021	19,950	W	139,500	W	28,020	187,500
2022	22,170	W	125,270	W	25,190	172,600
2023[1]	21,470	W	124,160	W	22,300	168,000

[1] Preliminary.   W = Withheld proprietary data, included in "Other States."   [2] Includes Arizona, California, Colorado, Idaho, Montana, New Mexico, South Dakota, Utah, and Washington.   *Source: U.S. Geological Survey (USGS)*

U.S. Exports of Gold, Total   In Kilograms

Year	Australia	Canada	China	Germany	Hong Kong	India	Mexico	South Africa	Switzer-land	Thailand	United Arab Emirates	United Kingdom	Total
2011	18,200	1,460	5,150	1,440	111,000	15,500	5,160	11,900	105,000	21,200	10,300	161,000	474,000
2012	5,140	18,400	1,200	2,230	133,000	66,900	7,040	8,260	280,000	9,280	64,200	137,000	692,000
2013	5,200	18,900	14,400	941	217,000	32,500	947	19,600	284,000	27,000	34,300	29,000	691,000
2014	6,430	3,300	12,600	232	147,000	27,300	434	----	173,000	13,800	20,300	80,000	500,000
2015	336	2,650	5,730	694	120,000	60,500	2,910	----	167,000	6,490	17,900	96,200	478,000
2016	952	5,390	4,500	1,430	69,900	41,400	1,880	----	150,000	2,030	17,000	94,900	393,000
2017	2,550	2,030	17,700	2,040	99,600	53,100	898	7	148,000	13	14,700	116,000	461,000
2018	6	16,000	24,200	721	51,500	46,100	1,680	29	161,000	3,010	8,780	149,000	474,000
2019	5,170	9,110	32	1,300	309	33,800	1,050	5	47,900	29	5,720	237,000	360,000
2020	9,090	5,010	31	641	3,860	5,390	305	----	76,600	1,060	1,800	185,000	297,000

Source: U.S. Geological Survey (USGS)

Grain Sorghum

Grain sorghums include milo, kafir, durra, feterita, and kaoliang. Grain sorghums are tolerant of drought by going into dormancy during dry and hot conditions and then resuming growth as conditions improve. Grain sorghums are a staple food in China, India, and Africa, but in the U.S., they are mainly used as livestock feed. The two key U.S. producing states are Texas and Kansas, each with about one-third of total U.S. production. U.S. sorghum production has become more popular with the breeding of dwarf grain sorghum hybrids, which are only about 3 feet tall (versus up to 10 feet tall for wild sorghum) and are easier to harvest with a combine. The U.S. sorghum crop year begins September 1.

Prices – The monthly average price for sorghum grain received by US farmers in the 2022/23 marketing year rose by +1.2% yr/yr to $11.30 per hundred pounds. The value of US grain sorghum production in the 2022/23 marketing year fell by -53.0% to $1.253 billion.

Supply – World production of sorghum in the 2023/24 marketing year is expected to rise by +8.4% to 60.011 million metric tons, below the record high of 66.683 million metric tons posted in 2007/08. US grain sorghum production in 2023/24 is expected to rise by +71.4% yr/yr to 321.820 million bushels. Sorghum acreage harvested in 2023/24 is forecasted to rise by +37.0% to 6.260 million acres. The harvested yield in 2023/24 is expected to rise by +48.2% to 60.9 bushels per acre.

Demand – World utilization (consumption) of grain sorghum in the 2023/24 marketing year is expected to rise by +7.6% to 59.753 million metric tons. The biggest consumers will be China, utilizing 17.9% of the world supply, and Nigeria utilizing 11.1%.

Trade – World exports of sorghum in the 2023/24 marketing year are expected to rise by +39.4% to 8.930 million metric tons, falling below the 2014/15 record high of 12.162 million metric tons. US exports in 2023/24 are expected to rise by +110.8% yr/yr to 5.842 million metric tons, accounting for 65.4% of total world exports. The other major exporters are Argentina with 1.500 million metric tons and Australia, with 1.300 million metric tons of exports expected. World imports of sorghum in 2023/24 are expected to rise by +44.8% yr/yr to 8.813 million metric tons. The world's largest importer is China.

World Production of Grain Sorghum   In Thousands of Metric Tons

Crop Year	Argen-tina	Australia	Brazil	Burkina	China	Ethiopia	India	Mexico	Niger	Nigeria	Sudan	United States	World Total
2014-15	2,150	505	2,000	1,700	12,700	4,100	5,100	6,600	1,450	6,833	6,000	2,459	65,138
2015-16	2,400	905	1,150	1,465	10,500	4,700	4,600	6,300	2,000	6,905	3,100	6,130	62,957
2016-17	2,100	675	1,700	1,640	7,400	4,700	4,500	5,300	2,000	7,350	5,950	6,283	61,566
2017-18	1,300	800	2,100	1,400	6,900	5,000	4,600	4,700	1,850	6,950	4,400	4,119	56,746
2018-19	1,250	1,050	2,200	1,800	3,600	5,000	3,550	5,100	2,100	6,650	5,300	6,212	57,351
2019-20	1,200	280	2,400	1,870	6,800	5,300	4,500	5,000	2,000	6,650	4,350	4,365	57,387
2020-21	1,050	95	2,100	1,900	11,400	5,200	4,550	4,500	2,050	6,550	5,100	2,638	61,054
2021-22[1]	1,150	160	3,000	1,650	14,000	4,650	4,450	5,000	1,400	6,650	3,700	3,175	61,585
2022-23[2]	900	160	2,900	1,950	7,800	4,000	3,900	5,100	2,000	6,650	5,200	2,584	55,548
2023-24[3]	1,150	260	3,600	1,900	10,700	4,300	4,250	5,000	1,950	6,650	5,100	2,286	59,753

[1] Preliminary. [2] Estimate. [3] Forecast.   *Source: Foreign Agricultural Service, U.S. Department of Agriculture (FAS-USDA)*

Salient Statistics of Grain Sorghum in the United States

Crop Year Beginning Sept. 1	Acreage Planted[4] for All Purposes	Acreage Harvested	Production (1,000 Bushels)	Yield Per Harvested Acre (Bushels)	Price in Cents Per Bushel	Value of Production (Million $)	Acreage Harvested (1,000 Acres)	Production (1,000 Tons)	Yield Per Harvested Acre (Tons)	On Farms Dec. 1	Off Farms Dec. 1	On Farms June 1	Off Farms June 1
	-- 1,000 Acres --									----------- 1,000 Bushels -----------			
2018-19	5,690	5,061	364,986	72.1	326	1,180.8	264	3,326	12.6	44,200	214,580	9,470	107,962
2019-20	5,265	4,675	341,460	73.0	325	1,125.8	339	4,019	11.9	30,200	220,161	8,360	64,227
2020-21	5,880	5,095	372,960	73.2	310	1,767.8	239	3,125	13.1	21,300	198,386	2,050	38,929
2021-22[1]	7,305	6,490	447,810	69.0		2,666.2	331	5,083	15.4	29,450	260,226	3,530	104,270
2022-23[2]	6,325	4,570	187,785	41.1		1,246.9	525	5,662	10.8	17,800	142,271	6,375	46,576
2023-24[3]	7,195	6,115	317,745	52.0		1,561.0	384	4,981	13.0	33,000	157,087		

[1] Preliminary. [2] Estimate. [3] Forecast.   *Source: Foreign Agricultural Service, U.S. Department of Agriculture (FAS-USDA)*

Production of All Sorghum for Grain in the United States, by States   In Thousands of Bushels

Year	Arkansas	Colorado	Illinois	Kansas	Louisiana	Mississippi	Missouri	Nebraska	New Mexico	Oklahoma	South Dakota	Texas	Total
2018	770	17,225	1,776	233,200	504	270	2,100	15,980	1,786	12,000	16,000	62,100	364,986
2019	----	12,710	----	204,000	----	----	----	12,090	----	13,260	14,000	85,400	341,460
2020	----	5,100	----	238,000	----	----	----	13,650	----	13,050	11,360	94,500	372,960
2021	----	14,800	----	265,200	----	----	----	19,780	----	20,520	13,440	114,070	447,810
2022	----	7,600	----	105,300	----	----	----	6,875	----	5,760	11,900	50,350	187,785
2023[1]	----	14,720	----	169,000	----	----	----	16,425	----	16,450	25,200	75,950	317,745

[1] Preliminary.   *Source: National Agricultural Statistics Service, U.S. Department of Agriculture (NASS-USDA)*

Quarterly Supply and Disappearance of Grain Sorghum in the United States   In Millions of Bushels

Crop Year Beginning Sept. 1	Beginning Stocks	Pro- duction	Imports[3]	Total Supply	Food & Alcohol	Seed	Feed & Residual	Total	Exports[3]	Total Disap- pearance	Ending Stocks
2020-21	30.1	373.0	.0	403.1	5.9	.9	97.1	103.8	278.9	382.8	20.3
Sept.-Nov.	30.1	373.0	.0	403.1	2.3		118.8	121.1	62.3	183.4	219.7
Dec.-Feb.	219.7	----	.0	219.7	1.3		-7.6	-6.3	89.1	82.8	136.9
Mar.-May	136.9	----	.0	136.9	.6	.4	.5	1.5	94.4	95.9	41.0
June-Aug.	41.0	----	.0	41.0	1.8	.5	-14.7	-12.4	33.1	20.7	20.3
2021-22	20.3	447.8	.0	468.1	44.2	.9	80.0	125.0	295.8	420.9	47.3
Sept.-Nov.	20.3	447.8	.0	468.1	4.7		129.0	133.7	44.8	178.5	289.7
Dec.-Feb.	289.7	----	.0	289.7	7.8		-4.8	3.0	79.6	82.6	207.1
Mar.-May	207.1	----	.0	207.1	9.0	.4	-29.3	-19.9	119.1	99.3	107.8
June-Aug.	107.8	----	.0	107.8	22.7	.5	-14.9	8.3	52.3	60.5	47.3
2022-23[1]	47.3	187.8	.0	235.1	58.4	.9	42.4	101.8	109.1	210.8	24.2
Sept.-Nov.	47.3	187.8	.0	235.1	17.3		41.5	58.8	16.2	75.0	160.1
Dec.-Feb.	160.1	----	.0	160.1	14.1		20.8	34.9	16.4	51.3	108.8
Mar.-May	108.8	----	.0	108.8	13.0	.4	2.2	15.6	40.2	55.8	53.0
June-Aug.	53.0	----		53.0	13.9	.5	-22.0	-7.6	36.3	28.7	24.2
2023-24[2]	24.2	317.7	.1	342.0	44.1	.9	45.0	90.0	230.0	320.0	22.0
Sept.-Nov.	24.2	317.7	.0	342.0	9.0		100.9	109.9	43.7	153.6	188.3

[1] Preliminary.   [2] Estimate.   [3] Uncommitted inventory.   [4] Includes quantity under loan and farmer-owned reserve.   *Source: Economic Research Service, U.S. Department of Agriculture (ERS-USDA)*

Average Price of Sorghum Grain, No. 2, Yellow in Kansas City   In Dollars Per Hundred Pounds (Cwt.)

Crop Year	Sept.	Oct.	Nov.	Dec.	Jan.	Feb.	Mar.	Apr.	May	June	July	Aug.	Average
2016-17	4.94	5.18	5.09	5.28	5.48	5.67	5.50	5.61	5.94	5.88	5.66	5.32	5.46
2017-18	5.39	5.49	5.51	5.85	6.12	5.81	6.13	6.17	6.22	6.07	5.62	5.73	5.84
2018-19	5.41	5.50	5.64	5.98	5.92	5.97	6.00	5.81	6.32	7.29	7.10	6.18	6.09
2019-20	5.90	6.39	6.14	6.22	6.36	6.25	6.24	6.00	5.90	6.30	6.37	6.00	6.17
2020-21	7.82	8.97	9.75	10.24	11.78	12.39	11.76	10.68	11.81	11.46	10.54	10.31	10.63
2021-22	9.50	9.72	10.65	11.30	11.59	12.40	12.82	13.49	13.44	12.71	10.39	11.08	11.59
2022-23	12.61	13.19	13.11	12.51	12.52	12.57	11.96	12.11	11.16	11.08	9.25	8.62	11.72
2023-24[1]	8.89	9.44	9.17	9.21	8.74	8.10							8.93

[1] Preliminary.   *Source: Economic Research Service, U.S. Department of Agriculture (ERS-USDA)*

Exports of Grain Sorghum, by Country of Destination from the United States   In Metric Tons

Crop Year	Canada	Ecuador	Eritrea (Ethiopia)	Israel	Japan	Jordan	Mexico	South Africa	Spain	Sudan	Türkiye	World Total
2016-17	4,937	----	----	----	220,243	----	530,086	68,936	----	121,825	----	5,982,920
2017-18	5,306	----	30,047	----	300,353	----	72,470	42,266	168,572	135,904	----	4,806,201
2018-19	4,469	----	60,300	----	244,358	----	516,439	73,835	512,968	117,330	----	2,372,692
2019-20	6,069	----	33,000	----	224,737	----	555,619	26,699	----	254,140	----	5,385,597
2020-21	6,704	----	60,686	----	30,450	----	120,933	15,000	----	143,100	----	6,905,773
2021-22[1]	6,992	----	95,211	----	11,804	----	347,614	14,590	118,526	114,868	----	7,364,922
2022-23[2]	8,720	----	63,000	----	8,209	----	159,030	35,940	76	104,280	----	2,941,169

[1] Preliminary.   [2] Estimate.   *Source: Economic Research Service, U.S. Department of Agriculture (ERS-USDA)*

Grain Sorghum Price Support Program and Market Prices in the United States

Crop Year	Price Support Quantity	% of Pro- duction	Aquired by CCC	Owned by CCC at Year End	Basic Loan Rate	Target Price	Findley Loan Rate	Effective Base[3] (Million Acres)	Partici- pation Rate[4] % of Base	Kansas City	Texas High Plains	Los Angeles	Gulf Ports
	Million Cwt.				Dollars Per Bushel					No. 2 Yellow ($ Per Cwt.)			
2014-15	.4	.2	0	0	3.48	7.05	1.95	----	----	6.94	----	----	9.10
2015-16	1.4	.4	0	0	3.48	7.05	1.95	----	----	5.93	----	----	8.07
2016-17	1.9	.7	0	0	3.48	7.05	1.95	----	----	5.46	----	----	7.56
2017-18	1.3	.6	0	0	3.48	7.05	1.95	----	----	5.84	----	----	----
2018-19	1.2	.6	0	0	3.48	7.05	1.95	----	----	6.09	----	----	----
2019-20[1]	1.6	.8	0	0	3.93	7.05	2.20	----	----	6.17	----	----	----
2020-21[2]	1.7	.8	0	0	3.93	7.05	2.20	----	----	10.63	----	----	----

[1] Preliminary.   [2] Estimate.   [3] National effective crop acreage base as determined by ASCS.   [4] Percentage of effective base acres enrolled in acreage reduction programs.   5/ Beginning with the 1996-7 marketing year, target prices are no longer applicable.   *Source: Economic Research Service, U.S. Department of Agriculture (ERS-USDA)*

Hay

Hay is a catchall term for forage plants, typically grasses such as timothy and Sudan-grass, and legumes such as alfalfa and clover. Alfalfa and alfalfa mixtures account for nearly half of all hay production. Hay is generally used to make cured feed for livestock. Curing, which is the proper drying of hay, is necessary to prevent spoilage. Hay, when properly cured, contains about 20% moisture. If hay is dried excessively, however, there is a loss of protein, which makes it less effective as livestock feed. Hay is harvested in almost all the lower 48 states.

Prices – The average monthly price of hay received by US farmers in the 2022/23 marketing year (May through April) rose by +22.1% yr/yr to $234.83 per ton. The farm

production value of hay produced in 2021/22 rose by +9.8% to $19.277 million.

Supply – US hay production in 2022/23 rose by +8.1% yr/yr to 21.252 million tons. US farmers are expected to harvest 51.976 million acres of hay in 2023/24, up by +4.9%. The yield in 2023/24 is expected to rise by +3.5% at 2.36 tons per acre, below the 2004/05 record high of 2.55. US ending stocks (May 1) in 2023/24 are expected to fall by -14.6% to 14.333 million tons. The largest hay-producing states in the US for 2022 were Texas with 5.8% of US hay production, Missouri with 5.2%, Idaho with 4.7%, South Dakota with 4.0%, and California with 3.9%.

Salient Statistics of All Hay in the United States

Crop Year Beginning May 1	Acres Harvested (1,000 Acres)	Yield Per Acre (Tons)	Pro-duction	Carry-over May 1	Disap-pearance	Supply Per Animal Unit	Disap-pearance	Animal Units Fed[3] (Millions)	Farm Price ($ Per Ton)	Farm Pro-duction Value Million $	Alfalfa (Certified)	Timothy	Red Clover	Sudan-grass
			-------- Millions of Tons --------			------ In Tons ------					----------- Dollars Per Cwt. -----------			
2018-19	52,839	2.34	123.6	15.3	----	1.02	0.91	----	166.7	17,288				
2019-20	52,425	2.46	128.9	14.9	----	1.07	0.92	----	163.1	18,040				
2020-21	52,238	2.43	126.8	20.4	----	2.09	1.83	----	157.5	17,552				
2021-22	50,396	2.38	119.8	18.0	----	0.99	0.87	----	192.3	19,649				
2022-23[1]	48,711	2.29	111.8	16.8	----	0.95	----	----	234.7	21,523				
2023-24[2]	52,821	2.25	118.8	14.3	----		----	----	208.0	21,313				

[1] Preliminary. [2] Estimate. [3] Roughage-consuming animal units fed annually. NA = Not available.
Source: Economic Research Service, U.S. Department of Agriculture (ERS-USDA)

Production of All Hay in the United States, by States   In Thousands of Tons

Year	California	Idaho	Iowa	Minne-sota	Missouri	New York	North Dakota	Ohio	Okla-homa	South Dakota	Texas	Wisconsin	Total
2018	5,682	5,019	2,998	3,077	5,408	6,985	4,419	2,356	5,121	5,788	8,374	2,953	123,600
2019	5,795	5,111	3,116	2,966	7,367	6,085	4,116	2,137	5,935	7,003	9,216	2,784	128,864
2020	4,610	5,270	3,697	3,546	6,437	6,370	3,596	2,102	5,364	5,365	9,604	3,483	126,812
2021	5,152	4,552	4,076	2,342	6,563	6,371	2,054	2,392	4,910	3,105	10,530	3,552	119,764
2022	4,634	5,284	3,581	3,139	5,906	4,331	3,823	2,199	3,890	4,527	6,078	2,990	111,828
2023[1]	4,275	5,250	2,946	2,257	4,831	5,330	4,428	2,431	7,313	6,123	8,748	2,235	118,769

[1] Preliminary. *Source: Agricultural Statistics Board, U.S. Department of Agriculture (ASB-USDA)*

Hay Production and Farm Stocks in the United States   In Thousands of Short Tons

Year	Alfalfa & Mixtures	All Others	All Hay	Corn for Silage[1]	Sorghum Silage[1]	Farm Stocks May 1	Farm Stocks Dec. 1
2018	52,634	70,966	123,600	121,564	3,326	15,348	79,055
2019	54,875	73,989	128,864	132,807	4,019	14,906	84,488
2020	53,067	73,745	126,812	137,675	3,125	20,426	84,020
2021	49,892	69,872	119,764	129,537	5,083	18,006	79,016
2022	48,838	62,990	111,828	128,287	5,662	16,777	71,761
2023[2]	49,916	68,853	118,769	129,994	4,981	14,333	76,721

[1] Not included in all tame hay. [2] Preliminary. *Source: Agricultural Statistics Board, U.S. Department of Agriculture (ASB-USDA)*

Average Price Received by Farmers for All Hay (Baled) in the United States   In Dollars Per Ton

Crop Year	May	June	July	Aug.	Sept.	Oct.	Nov.	Dec.	Jan.	Feb.	Mar.	Apr.	Average
2018-19	167.0	160.0	161.0	163.0	164.0	163.0	162.0	166.0	167.0	170.0	173.0	184.0	166.7
2019-20	187.0	177.0	164.0	162.0	160.0	161.0	159.0	158.0	155.0	157.0	156.0	161.0	163.1
2020-21	164.0	162.0	156.0	157.0	151.0	155.0	153.0	152.0	152.0	158.0	163.0	167.0	157.5
2021-22	176.0	179.0	186.0	193.0	193.0	196.0	192.0	193.0	188.0	195.0	198.0	219.0	192.3
2022-23	210.0	212.0	240.0	248.0	248.0	248.0	238.0	235.0	228.0	229.0	231.0	249.0	234.7
2023-24[1]	247.0	234.0	221.0	209.0	204.0	201.0	195.0	191.0	189.0	189.0			208.0

[1] Preliminary. [2] Marketing year average. *Source: Economic Research Service, U.S. Department of Agriculture (ERS-USDA)*

Heating Oil

Heating oil is a heavy fuel oil that is refined from crude oil. Heating oil is also known as No. 2 fuel oil and accounts for about 25% of the yield from a barrel of crude oil. That is the second-largest "cut" after gasoline. The price to consumers of home heating oil is generally comprised of 42% for crude oil, 12% for refining costs, and 46% for marketing and distribution costs (Source: EIA's Petroleum Marketing Monthly). Generally, a $1 increase in the price of crude oil translates into a 2.5-cent per gallon rise in heating oil. Because of this, heating oil prices are highly correlated with crude oil prices, although heating oil prices are also subject to swift supply and demand shifts due to weather changes or refinery shutdowns.

The primary use of heating oil is for residential heating. In the U.S., approximately 8.1 million households use heating oil as their main heating fuel. Most of the demand for heating oil occurs from October through March. The Northeast region, which includes the New England and the Central Atlantic States, is most reliant on heating oil. This region consumes approximately 70% of U.S. heating oil. However, demand for heating oil has been dropping as households switch to a more convenient heating source like natural gas. In fact, demand for heating oil is down by about 10 billion gallons/year from its peak use in 1976 (Source: American Petroleum Institute).

Refineries produce approximately 85% of U.S. heating oil as part of the "distillate fuel oil" product family, which includes heating oil and diesel fuel. The remainder of U.S. heating oil is imported from Canada, the Virgin Islands, and Venezuela.

Recently, a team of Purdue University researchers developed a way to make home heating oil from a mixture of soybean oil and conventional fuel oil. The oil blend is made by replacing 20% of the fuel oil with soybean oil, potentially saving 1.3 billion gallons of fuel oil per year. This soybean heating oil can be used in conventional furnaces without altering existing equipment. The soybean heating oil is relatively easy to produce and creates no sulfur emissions.

The "crack-spread" is the processing margin earned when refiners buy crude oil and refine it into heating oil and gasoline. The crack-spread ratio commonly used in the industry is the 3-2-1, which involves buying one heating oil contract and two gasoline futures contracts, and then selling three crude oil contracts. If the crack spread is positive, it is profitable for refiners to buy crude oil and refine it into products. The CME Group has a crack-spread calculator on their web site at www.cmegroup.com.

Heating oil futures and options are traded at the CME Group. The CME's heating oil futures contract calls for the delivery of 1,000 barrels of fungible No. 2 heating oil in the New York harbor. Futures are also traded on ICE Futures Europe and the Multi Commodity Exchange of Index (MCX).

Prices – CME heating oil futures prices (Barchart.com symbol code HO) on the nearest-futures chart closed 2023 down -23.3% at $2.5289 per gallon.

Supply – US production of distillate fuel oil in 2023 fell by -2.4% yr/yr to 4.890 million barrels per day, below the 2018 record high of 5.164. Stocks of distillate fuel oil in December 2023 were up by +9.9% yr/yr at 130.713 million barrels. US production of residual fuel in 2023 fell by -2.7% yr/yr to an average of 265,032 barrels per day, which is about a fifth of the production level of over 1 million barrels per day produced in the 1970s. US stocks of residual fuel oil as of December 2023 were down by -21.5% to 24.129 million barrels, below the 2015 record high of 42.189 million barrels.

Demand – US usage of distillate fuel oil in 2023 fell by -2.5% yr/yr to 3.928 million barrels per day, below the 2007 record high of 4.198 million barrels a day.

Trade – US imports of distillate fuel oil in 2023 fell by -11.1% to an average of 168,238 barrels per day, below the 2006 record high of 365,000 barrels per day. US imports of residual fuel oil in 2023 fell by -45.7% yr/yr to 109,542 barrels per day, far less than the levels of over 1 million barrels per day seen back in the 1970s.

World Production of Distillate Fuel Oil — In Thousands of Barrels Per Day

Year	Brazil	Canada	China	France	Germany	India	Italy	Japan	Korea, South	Russia	Saudi Arabia	United States	World Total
2008	793.0	557.0	2,767.5	991.2	1,104.4	1,054.0	642.0	908.7	388.3	640.0	577.8	3,945.4	25,428.5
2009	758.0	516.7	2,777.0	985.1	1,062.7	1,182.0	617.1	820.8	385.9	570.0	605.0	3,631.1	24,914.9
2010	855.0	569.6	3,011.3	983.7	1,096.5	1,226.0	614.5	825.8	399.4	583.0	618.9	3,800.3	25,366.6
2011	927.0	601.8	3,195.3	962.2	1,049.0	1,298.0	608.9	807.6	393.3	641.0	651.0	3,898.9	25,981.4
2012	992.0	582.7	3,461.4	962.9	1,076.1	1,420.0	569.5	811.3	405.2	582.0	704.8	3,741.4	26,602.0
2013	996.0	592.3	3,503.2	970.8	1,125.3	1,385.0	550.6	796.4	423.7	596.0	729.6	3,827.5	26,848.6
2014	1,023.0	580.8	3,513.6	949.2	1,079.8	1,417.7	568.2	772.8	432.2	577.1	753.3	4,037.2	27,209.9
2015[1]		571.5		965.1	1,100.8		558.0	770.1	472.6			3,995.2	
2016[2]		541.1		953.5	1,114.9		548.9	774.8	501.0				
2017[2]		533.1		890.3	1,046.5		505.0	696.4	462.5				

[1] Preliminary.   [2] Estimate.   *Source: Energy Information Administration, U.S. Department of Energy (EIA-DOE)*

HEATING OIL

World Imports of Distillate Fuel Oil   In Thousands of Barrels Per Day

Year	Australia	Belgium	France	Germany	Indonesia	Nether-lands	Singa-pore	Spain	Turkey	United Kingdom	United States	Vietnam	World Total
2004	63.0	164.7	322.3	265.8	130.1	203.0	112.5	230.1	77.8	81.8	325.5	111.6	4,268.5
2005	81.7	198.1	380.7	277.6	170.2	196.2	78.9	263.4	84.7	98.6	328.8	120.4	4,499.6
2006	105.7	166.1	317.3	332.0	176.1	278.0	125.2	264.9	130.9	158.3	364.7	110.8	4,906.3
2007	105.2	148.9	271.6	187.8	229.7	188.4	127.0	286.6	162.3	159.0	304.1	132.5	5,090.9
2008	147.8	156.4	292.1	317.2	211.6	250.9	178.6	246.3	169.8	152.6	212.9	132.6	5,466.6
2009	144.0	124.6	380.2	297.0	146.7	333.5	155.0	234.1	186.2	127.5	225.1	132.9	5,485.7
2010	141.7	111.8	414.0	318.9	259.0	385.2	393.5	220.7	197.9	193.0	228.4	100.5	6,318.7
2011	176.6	161.7	408.0	278.9	244.3	375.1	383.0	174.1	207.5	191.4	178.7	108.5	6,444.8
2012[1]	202.0	128.3	469.9	276.1	290.2	384.2	279.2	136.4	226.1	218.6	126.2	113.6	6,523.9
2013[2]	226.8	246.5	478.1	322.7		378.6		95.2	245.5	217.2	154.7		

[1] Preliminary.   [2] Estimate.   *Source: Energy Information Administration, U.S. Department of Energy (EIA-DOE)*

World Exports of Distillate Fuel Oil   In Thousands of Barrels Per Day

Year	Belgium	Germany	India	Italy	Japan	Korea, South	Kuwait	Nether-lands	Russia	Singa-pore	Taiwan	United States	World Total
2004	167.0	166.1	148.5	187.3	29.4	185.8	225.3	411.2	614.3	294.0	119.9	109.6	4,692.3
2005	182.3	204.4	173.0	179.8	64.1	234.3	221.2	430.4	649.2	300.0	149.2	138.4	5,038.9
2006	162.1	223.0	238.0	160.2	70.5	250.6	185.5	495.9	752.6	341.3	150.0	215.1	5,394.9
2007	177.9	250.6	292.4	183.5	137.2	281.9	194.0	420.4	751.9	359.3	176.5	267.7	5,268.0
2008	171.7	203.2	300.2	170.2	220.5	357.6	190.2	464.7	767.8	406.8	181.1	528.3	5,830.8
2009	140.2	181.8	377.3	168.2	215.7	343.6	152.8	562.3	812.9	346.3	206.6	587.4	6,153.4
2010	142.4	138.8	376.5	189.1	197.4	358.0	143.8	636.1	851.0	540.0	177.2	656.0	6,209.9
2011	156.2	132.2	430.5	153.6	160.0	436.8	143.8	631.1	807.8	553.7	157.5	854.1	6,404.8
2012[1]	160.7	128.9	459.1	178.8	120.2	481.8	153.0	608.5	840.9	469.8	191.7	1,007.2	6,781.3
2013[2]	226.4	135.0		142.8	167.6	446.6		604.1				1,133.9	

[1] Preliminary.   [2] Estimate.   *Source: Energy Information Administration, U.S. Department of Energy (EIA-DOE)*

Production of Distillate Fuel Oil in the United States   In Thousands of Barrels Per Day

Year	Jan.	Feb.	Mar.	Apr.	May	June	July	Aug.	Sept.	Oct.	Nov.	Dec.	Average
2014	4,685.3	4,594.5	4,779.7	4,987.9	5,026.1	4,896.0	5,021.2	5,042.5	4,939.8	4,662.0	5,011.6	5,322.9	4,914.1
2015	4,835.2	4,752.4	4,893.7	4,991.4	4,982.8	5,031.8	5,101.2	5,106.6	5,060.8	4,816.5	5,169.0	5,042.1	4,982.0
2016	4,530.3	4,667.8	4,848.3	4,658.8	4,760.4	4,953.6	4,933.4	4,939.2	4,888.1	4,614.1	5,066.0	5,147.6	4,834.0
2017	4,785.5	4,656.6	4,792.5	5,018.9	5,215.5	5,283.8	5,161.9	5,044.1	4,559.7	4,972.0	5,362.1	5,407.9	5,021.7
2018	5,005.9	4,584.1	4,822.5	5,119.5	5,214.1	5,410.4	5,257.1	5,369.5	5,230.0	5,035.4	5,350.1	5,575.6	5,164.5
2019	5,249.5	4,904.7	4,968.4	5,059.2	5,211.7	5,350.7	5,245.8	5,266.5	5,035.0	4,793.9	5,231.1	5,309.4	5,135.5
2020	5,086.5	4,812.9	4,952.9	5,078.8	4,818.2	4,579.7	4,842.7	4,822.7	4,493.5	4,204.2	4,522.0	4,632.9	4,737.3
2021	4,560.2	3,782.0	4,519.3	4,595.9	4,745.0	4,980.5	4,855.9	4,741.6	4,555.2	4,727.3	4,950.2	4,926.2	4,661.6
2022	4,670.4	4,682.1	5,004.1	4,835.3	4,987.9	5,196.5	5,124.5	5,142.4	5,183.2	5,077.2	5,338.4	4,872.9	5,009.6
2023[1]	4,703.3	4,696.0	4,685.3	4,756.7	4,966.4	4,996.3	4,993.6	5,036.9	4,923.4	4,747.1	5,118.3	5,062.9	4,890.5

[1] Preliminary.   *Source: Energy Information Administration; U.S. Department of Energy (EIA-DOE)*

Stocks of Distillate Fuel in the United States, on First of Month   In Thousands of Barrels

Year	Jan.	Feb.	Mar.	Apr.	May	June	July	Aug.	Sept.	Oct.	Nov.	Dec.
2014	114,534	112,897	115,337	116,827	121,757	121,674	125,559	128,132	131,289	120,093	126,085	136,065
2015	131,992	123,137	128,294	129,022	134,028	139,437	142,144	152,145	148,846	143,317	156,666	160,741
2016	160,583	162,696	160,620	154,692	154,389	149,239	155,969	159,534	160,378	153,884	160,173	165,456
2017	168,937	162,241	151,080	154,640	153,793	151,608	151,068	147,820	137,461	129,885	132,700	145,574
2018	141,340	138,888	130,478	120,928	115,580	120,549	127,215	132,266	137,249	124,773	126,543	140,162
2019	140,129	136,323	132,172	128,274	129,865	131,094	137,674	135,636	131,838	120,073	126,221	140,083
2020	143,190	132,918	126,782	150,922	176,627	176,947	178,800	179,763	172,502	156,235	157,205	161,188
2021	164,058	144,012	146,079	137,218	139,600	140,133	142,139	137,625	132,095	132,811	131,692	130,039
2022	125,282	120,610	114,658	106,291	109,712	111,329	112,591	113,122	110,531	110,492	120,601	118,899
2023[1]	123,013	124,821	112,292	112,061	113,140	112,598	120,208	116,890	119,170	110,433	113,783	130,713

[1] Preliminary.   *Source: Energy Information Administration; U.S. Department of Energy (EIA-DOE)*

Imports of Distillate Fuel Oil in the United States   In Thousands of Barrels Per Day

Year	Jan.	Feb.	Mar.	Apr.	May	June	July	Aug.	Sept.	Oct.	Nov.	Dec.	Average
2014	283	337	324	181	198	121	129	143	126	120	136	245	195
2015	349	388	324	243	191	132	143	140	103	101	150	155	202
2016	172	231	150	177	123	88	123	164	150	75	145	167	147
2017	204	199	108	116	124	102	111	112	112	134	180	282	149
2018	290	284	157	91	122	90	144	175	172	161	227	190	175
2019	307	361	180	121	160	126	174	154	118	186	258	295	203
2020	220	157	171	231	190	154	116	145	180	280	305	464	218
2021	371	353	470	198	272	240	165	257	224	291	330	292	288
2022	242	399	189	129	180	117	170	176	127	106	228	211	189
2023[1]	274	300	155	156	168	138	120	133	119	106	129	221	168

[1] Preliminary.   Source: Energy Information Administration, U.S. Department of Energy (EIA-DOE)

Disposition of Distillate Fuel Oil, Total Product Supplied in the United States   In Thousands of Barrels Per Day

Year	Jan.	Feb.	Mar.	Apr.	May	June	July	Aug.	Sept.	Oct.	Nov.	Dec.	Average
2014	4,340.0	4,160.3	4,066.2	3,989.8	3,951.6	3,901.6	3,866.5	3,874.8	3,933.4	4,266.3	3,917.2	4,178.2	4,037.1
2015	4,185.7	4,559.2	4,078.1	4,027.4	3,777.5	3,896.8	3,901.2	3,914.7	4,063.0	4,014.1	3,740.2	3,831.1	3,999.1
2016	3,850.3	3,996.1	3,947.0	3,798.9	3,732.0	3,852.7	3,597.4	3,880.4	3,912.0	3,986.3	3,938.4	4,043.1	3,877.9
2017	3,735.6	3,934.8	4,126.6	3,762.8	3,955.0	3,963.6	3,641.8	4,003.5	3,921.2	4,011.2	4,157.4	3,975.3	3,932.4
2018	4,491.0	3,979.3	4,196.5	4,139.0	4,208.8	3,959.4	3,962.6	4,195.7	4,022.2	4,347.8	4,203.8	4,019.4	4,143.8
2019	4,327.5	4,307.3	4,184.1	4,119.6	4,109.7	3,993.2	3,911.2	4,029.5	3,920.6	4,224.2	4,201.5	3,927.1	4,104.6
2020	4,024.4	4,079.6	3,960.9	3,528.1	3,446.2	3,494.6	3,614.6	3,667.8	3,814.0	4,036.5	3,879.5	3,888.2	3,786.2
2021	3,936.5	3,968.4	4,077.1	4,048.4	3,900.2	3,945.7	3,674.6	3,984.4	4,032.0	3,967.4	4,190.4	3,950.1	3,972.9
2022	4,128.7	4,364.9	4,183.2	3,975.6	3,875.8	4,049.2	3,721.5	3,940.5	4,087.5	4,162.8	4,059.5	3,792.7	4,028.5
2023[1]	3,901.6	4,018.2	4,103.2	3,900.1	3,929.8	3,958.3	3,647.6	4,133.8	3,921.1	4,067.3	4,010.8	3,544.9	3,928.1

[1] Preliminary.   Source: Energy Information Administration, U.S. Department of Energy (EIA-DOE)

World Production of Residual Fuel Oil   In Thousands of Barrels Per Day

Year	Brazil	China	India	Iran	Italy	Japan	Korea, South	Mexico	Russia	Saudi Arabia	United States	Venezuela	World Total
2008	213.0	738.9	241.0	328.2	212.7	546.7	331.7	265.1	264.0	363.7	622.2	100.5	10,326.9
2009	160.0	684.5	295.0	359.9	180.1	411.4	320.5	246.0	324.0	275.5	511.1	105.0	10,106.0
2010	184.0	878.4	179.0	318.6	144.0	395.6	321.3	224.0	303.0	272.0	535.1	117.0	9,856.0
2011	161.0	609.1	185.0	379.2	115.9	446.6	277.7	242.6	423.0	316.9	461.1	123.1	9,534.6
2012	167.0	583.7	184.0	420.3	107.2	565.4	268.8	244.9	407.0	330.9	368.8	115.0	9,371.2
2013	114.0	580.3	155.0	357.6	82.6	475.1	256.8	226.9	350.0	370.2	318.6	109.1	9,044.0
2014	139.3	552.9	148.4	335.3	72.7	413.3	218.8	164.7	243.5	438.3	257.2	71.3	8,836.6
2015[1]					77.7	368.1	237.3	144.6			259.3		
2016[2]					64.4	340.2	277.0	133.0					
2017[2]					62.3	260.9	210.3	139.6					

[1] Preliminary.   [2] Estimate.   Source: Energy Information Administration, U.S. Department of Energy (EIA-DOE)

Supply and Disposition of Residual Fuel Oil in the United States

Year	Supply — Total Production	Supply — Imports	Disposition — Stock Change	Disposition — Exports	Disposition — Product Supplied	Ending Stocks (Million Barrels)	Average Sales to End Users[3] (USD per Gallon)
2014	435	173	----	----	257	34	2.33
2015	417	192	----	----	259	42	1.29
2016	418	205	----	----	326	41	0.95
2017	427	189	----	----	342	29	1.29
2018	425	211	----	----	318	28	1.66
2019	361	149	----	----	275	31	1.58
2020	188	166	----	----	208	30	1.25
2021	213	186	----	----	314	26	1.86
2022	251	202	----	----	329	31	
2023[1]	269	110	----	----	271	25	

In Thousands of Barrels Per Day

[1] Preliminary.   [2] Less than +500 barrels per day and greater than -500 barrels per day.   [3] Refiner price excluding taxes.
Source: Energy Information Administration, U.S. Department of Energy (EIA-DOE)

HEATING OIL

HEATING OIL
Quarterly Cash as of 03/28/2024

QUARTERLY CASH
As of 03/28/2024
Chart High 5.1520   on 05/16/2022
Chart Low   .1044   on 01/31/1967

USD / Gallon

#2 Fuel Oil

Production of Residual Fuel Oil in the United States   In Thousands of Barrels Per Day

Year	Jan.	Feb.	Mar.	Apr.	May	June	July	Aug.	Sept.	Oct.	Nov.	Dec.	Average
2013	395.4	504.1	569.4	508.2	488.1	469.0	481.4	416.9	433.8	420.3	466.2	454.8	467.3
2014	476.3	427.5	460.8	420.4	454.3	454.7	402.1	438.7	409.8	415.6	462.0	401.2	435.3
2015	376.7	419.5	478.3	466.8	435.5	413.3	426.1	403.7	414.1	419.3	376.5	376.4	417.2
2016	395.0	403.4	399.9	435.0	427.0	389.4	400.6	419.8	436.0	454.8	450.1	400.9	417.7
2017	485.2	482.5	405.7	416.6	407.7	406.3	390.5	452.5	459.2	442.2	407.8	372.5	427.4
2018	467.4	461.5	403.2	450.4	414.8	347.6	444.2	391.3	429.4	397.2	449.8	440.3	424.8
2019	397.8	309.0	357.4	389.0	363.5	429.9	389.9	409.5	382.8	340.0	313.6	249.1	361.0
2020	225.7	251.0	240.9	138.6	142.7	238.4	218.7	192.7	167.3	147.5	153.2	145.7	188.5
2021	178.9	187.7	223.8	187.1	209.5	229.3	245.2	231.1	184.9	222.3	246.4	210.4	213.0
2022[1]	262.7	218.3	300.6	226.7	242.2	204.0	217.7	274.2	295.7	253.2	228.4	258.5	248.5

[1] Preliminary.   *Source: Energy Information Administration, U.S. Department of Energy (EIA-DOE)*

Average Price of Heating Oil #2   In Dollars Per Gallon

Year	Jan.	Feb.	Mar.	Apr.	May	June	July	Aug.	Sept.	Oct.	Nov.	Dec.	Average
2014	3.0633	3.0656	2.9124	2.8878	2.8603	2.8822	2.7758	2.7535	2.6332	2.4237	2.2493	1.8555	2.6969
2015	1.6163	1.8727	1.6315	1.7404	1.8317	1.7680	1.5505	1.3875	1.4311	1.4042	1.3198	1.0392	1.5494
2016	0.9396	0.9721	1.1289	1.1877	1.3527	1.4162	1.2850	1.3251	1.3521	1.4877	1.3872	1.5521	1.2822
2017	1.5474	1.5622	1.4925	1.5202	1.4521	1.3320	1.4248	1.5412	1.7915	1.7111	1.8216	1.8619	1.5882
2018	2.0315	1.8541	1.8698	2.0372	2.1880	2.1132	2.1067	2.1246	2.2260	2.3158	2.0360	1.7877	2.0576
2019	1.8310	1.9278	1.9668	2.0359	2.0086	1.8197	1.8894	1.7950	1.9247	1.9204	1.9146	1.9638	1.9165
2020	1.8290	1.5891	1.1564	0.8580	0.8425	1.0732	1.1874	1.1799	1.0694	1.0992	1.1673	1.3366	1.1990
2021	1.4766	1.6696	1.7051	1.7044	1.8341	1.9064	1.9470	1.8852	2.0531	2.3966	2.2518	2.1183	1.9124
2022	2.4809	2.7368	3.6350	3.9523	4.4974	4.2464	3.5523	3.4370	3.2574	4.1585	3.8732	2.9370	3.5637
2023	3.0850	2.6448	2.5705	2.4235	2.1807	2.2776	2.4976	2.9389	3.1682	2.9994	2.8108	2.5395	2.6780

Source: Energy Information Administration, U.S. Department of Energy (EIA-DOE)

ULSD NY HARBOR - NYMEX
Weekly Nearest Futures as of 03/28/2024

WEEKLY NEAREST FUTURES
As of 03/28/2024
Chart High 5.8595 on 04/29/2022
Chart Low .5800 on 04/28/2020

Nearby Futures through Last Trading Day.

Volume of Trading of Heating Oil #2 Futures in New York   In Thousands of Contracts

Year	Jan.	Feb.	Mar.	Apr.	May	June	July	Aug.	Sept.	Oct.	Nov.	Dec.	Total
2014	3,400.6	2,893.3	2,533.8	2,209.6	2,253.3	2,483.3	2,857.3	2,719.9	2,875.9	3,409.5	3,126.2	3,183.6	33,946.4
2015	3,247.1	3,451.1	3,022.4	2,733.6	2,616.5	2,981.7	3,024.6	3,254.2	2,906.7	3,473.0	2,765.9	3,470.1	36,947.0
2016	3,341.1	3,201.8	2,861.8	3,286.1	3,452.2	3,431.1	3,052.5	3,455.0	3,288.4	3,183.1	3,518.7	3,317.7	39,389.3
2017	3,322.5	3,332.7	3,497.4	3,091.7	3,867.4	3,642.3	3,601.1	4,759.9	3,577.9	3,849.6	3,549.3	3,504.4	43,596.2
2018	4,542.6	3,826.2	3,715.8	4,066.3	4,334.6	3,738.0	3,326.2	3,566.0	3,440.1	3,966.1	4,516.8	3,239.0	46,277.9
2019	3,428.3	3,043.1	3,382.3	2,999.0	4,011.8	3,370.8	3,082.3	3,379.1	3,916.7	5,096.9	3,973.8	3,716.7	43,400.8
2020	5,655.2	4,206.4	5,101.5	3,880.6	3,347.1	2,772.6	2,454.6	2,927.0	3,547.1	3,714.6	3,420.4	2,975.9	44,003.2
2021	2,945.6	3,644.0	3,758.3	2,510.6	2,828.3	2,724.3	2,668.8	3,564.8	3,558.3	3,886.4	3,817.3	2,804.9	38,711.5
2022	4,437.3	4,231.2	3,562.7	2,470.0	2,949.7	3,135.6	2,894.3	3,300.6	3,517.0	3,543.6	2,672.8	2,922.2	39,637.1
2023	3,389.3	3,012.4	3,489.9	2,737.4	2,767.2	3,256.1	3,101.7	3,998.7	3,781.9	3,667.0	3,385.5	2,668.1	39,255.1

Contract size = 42,000 US gallons.   *Source: CME Group; New York Mercantile Exchange (NYMEX)*

Average Open Interest of Heating Oil #2 Futures in New York   In Contracts

Year	Jan.	Feb.	Mar.	Apr.	May	June	July	Aug.	Sept.	Oct.	Nov.	Dec.
2014	281,102	294,144	280,719	263,461	269,766	285,931	313,266	353,133	373,004	390,505	391,923	355,367
2015	375,870	384,974	375,278	361,933	360,017	362,447	388,442	425,342	399,488	382,414	367,273	348,763
2016	349,641	365,010	367,707	389,364	399,419	404,855	370,778	396,411	391,168	408,496	395,976	431,825
2017	422,678	424,439	413,555	428,260	418,050	405,141	411,503	404,442	444,276	442,998	445,430	443,590
2018	469,402	433,230	401,046	436,876	438,501	403,757	403,666	390,752	420,964	422,927	376,499	369,267
2019	367,498	415,805	401,238	397,296	399,818	407,129	412,377	439,510	415,640	443,137	436,588	427,092
2020	415,494	408,798	378,779	365,527	382,637	378,457	358,653	376,359	424,716	425,509	398,259	374,290
2021	376,292	417,912	43,047	400,920	417,322	435,112	409,357	395,072	427,718	429,260	382,227	301,670
2022	350,798	344,310	236,804	225,758	248,510	264,245	266,402	288,448	289,423	277,553	272,789	263,472
2023	267,281	264,717	265,274	267,635	299,026	309,753	325,117	327,861	328,568	325,275	305,864	305,164

Contract size = 42,000 US gallons.   *Source: CME Group; New York Mercantile Exchange (NYMEX)*

Hides and Leather

Hides and leather have been used since ancient times for boots, clothing, shields, armor, tents, bottles, buckets, and cups. Leather is produced through the tanning of hides, pelts, and skins of animals. The remains of leather have been found in the Middle East dating back at least 7,000 years.

Today, most leather is made of cowhide, but it is also made from the hides of lamb, deer, ostrich, snakes, crocodiles, and even stingray. Cattle hides are the most valuable byproduct of the meat-packing industry. U.S. exports of cowhides bring more than $1 billion in foreign trade, and U.S. finished leather production is worth about $4 billion.

Prices – The average monthly price of wholesale cattle hides (packer heavy native steers FOB Chicago) in 2023 fell by -22.4% yr/yr to 32.13 cents per pound.

Supply – World production of cattle and buffalo hides in 2022 rose by +1.9% yr/yr to 10.108 million metric tons. The world's largest producers of cattle and buffalo hides in 2022 were the US with 11.6% of world production, Brazil with 10.2%, and Argentina with 5.0%.

Trade – US net exports of cattle hides in 2023 fell by -15.9% to 18.895 million hides. The largest destinations for US exports in 2023 were China (which took 67.7% of US exports), Mexico (14.7%), and South Korea (6.6%).

World Production of Cattle and Buffalo Hides   In Metric Tons

Year	Argentina	Australia	Brazil	Canada	Colom-bia	France	Germany	Italy	Mexico	Russia	United Kingdom	United States	World Total
2013	456,260	273,651	967,500	86,016	103,097	134,647	132,717	110,719	224,172	194,845	78,426	1,075,452	9,037,807
2014	432,391	301,037	972,300	89,762	100,828	135,659	135,819	92,177	226,702	197,335	81,204	1,067,197	9,119,504
2015	440,962	308,750	942,500	85,474	102,866	139,222	134,599	102,425	228,946	196,767	81,944	986,842	9,129,205
2016	427,540	268,655	928,400	93,407	95,910	140,971	137,350	105,260	233,099	189,537	84,722	1,049,782	9,144,460
2017	459,963	239,959	955,000	101,054	91,676	137,767	135,154	98,315	239,078	187,211	83,796	1,089,581	9,339,483
2018	495,794	267,791	990,000	106,339	92,874	138,111	133,542	105,362	245,772	191,848	85,370	1,118,080	9,551,482
2019	507,083	282,090	1,020,000	109,954	92,709	----	----	----	251,577	193,879	84,630	1,129,828	9,874,865
2020	512,349	246,516	997,500	108,876	89,572	----	----	----	258,231	194,903	86,296	1,130,179	9,723,804
2021[1]	482,146	219,674	975,000	113,305	91,358	----	----	----	264,351	199,651	83,889	1,161,667	9,915,870
2022[2]	506,629	217,858	1,035,000	115,807	85,442	----	----	----	269,933	193,350	85,648	1,175,959	10,108,415

[1] Preliminary.   [2] Forecast.   *Source: Food and Agricultural Organization of the United Nations (FAO-UN)*

Exports of Bovine Hides and Skins from the United States   In Thousands of Hides

Year	Canada	China	Hong Kong	Italy	Japan	Korea, South	Mexico	Nether-lands	Taiwan	Thailand	Türkiye	Vietnam	World Total
2014	33	10,881	227	174	180	2,282	1,277	127	1,232	221	37	53	16,882
2015	57	9,835	36	172	153	2,307	1,275	163	620	281	65	147	15,260
2016	79	9,856	39	292	164	2,538	1,906	69	481	292	65	115	16,180
2017	----	10,540	29	192	152	2,540	1,541	33	557	881	101	51	17,095
2018	----	8,882	12	183	175	2,474	1,670	64	374	1,497	114	30	16,047
2019	----	8,809	14	60	182	2,685	2,023	72	385	923	42	63	15,664
2020	----	12,940	31	45	42	1,434	1,857	10	249	369	98	86	17,587
2021	----	17,666	6	67	128	2,328	3,579	19	418	640	35	61	25,728
2022	----	13,169	2	286	132	2,436	3,093	22	266	1,342	442	95	22,468
2023[1]	----	12,795	----	238	65	1,249	2,784	2	144	481	308	19	18,895

[1] Preliminary.   *Source: Foreign Agricultural Service, U.S. Department of Agriculture (FAS-USDA)*

Imports of Bovine Hides and Skins in the United States   In Thousands of Hides

Year	Australia	Belgium-Luxem-bourg	Brazil	Canada	China	Colombia	Italy	Mexico	New Zealand	Pakistan	Thailand	Türkiye	World Total
2014	72.2	24.4	7.1	1,181.0	92.9	0.6	5.0	638.2	6.8	0.5	6.9	0.8	2,077.4
2015	97.2	43.8	1.0	1,218.8	5.2	33.7	5.9	375.8	1.0	0.1	8.8	0.8	2,193.2
2016	0.0	139.4	8.2	794.2	8.5	107.1	11.9	69.4	1.9	1.1	20.3	0.7	2,336.2
2017	5.2	203.7	18.5	625.1	0.2	27.1	10.2	16.6	4.1	0.8	5.7	0.0	1,449.7
2018	3.4	196.5	19.6	653.7	4.9	13.7	10.6	9.2	16.5	1.2	4.7	0.0	1,404.5
2019	8.1	118.8	14.6	347.1	0.2	2.0	6.9	31.8	3.9	----	7.9	5.8	912.4
2020	1.4	30.2	45.3	267.2	1.2	6.8	21.1	333.4	4.6	----	15.9	0.9	785.8
2021	3.7	18.0	47.6	365.5	0.0	9.3	1.9	489.9	5.8	----	14.9	0.9	1,081.8
2022	----	11.8	33.4	149.7	15.9	3.6	4.9	21.7	1.3	----	14.4	0.3	302.2
2023[1]	----	----	26.2	163.7	0.0	5.8	7.1	22.1	23.5	----	36.9	----	306.1

[1] Preliminary.   *Source: Foreign Agricultural Service, U.S. Department of Agriculture (FAS-USDA)*

Heavy Native Steers

Wholesale Price of Hides (Packer Heavy Native Steers) F.O.B. Chicago   In Cents Per Pound

Year	Jan.	Feb.	Mar.	Apr.	May	June	July	Aug.	Sept.	Oct.	Nov.	Dec.	Average
2014	104.76	107.00	110.62	112.00	108.90	108.14	108.59	112.00	114.43	114.37	114.29	107.16	110.19
2015	104.20	103.24	103.68	98.57	95.90	94.00	73.86	71.86	75.90	73.64	68.95	71.64	86.29
2016	72.37	70.85	73.18	72.93	71.86	72.77	73.80	73.70	73.81	75.43	77.33	75.45	73.62
2017	75.15	75.61	77.04	74.79	68.50	67.64	63.90	61.74	61.17	60.80	61.19	64.15	67.64
2018	66.17	66.24	65.89	63.86	61.36	59.98	57.52	55.63	54.92	54.17	52.10	52.00	59.15
2019	47.71	43.42	45.00	45.00	38.86	34.00	33.00	36.86	38.00	38.74	38.90	37.95	39.79
2020	40.00	40.00	36.75	29.50	24.62	24.50	25.05	27.14	30.07	34.64	36.10	39.25	32.30
2021	39.50	39.50	39.50	39.50	40.95	54.36	55.00	55.00	55.00	55.00	55.00	55.00	48.61
2022	45.65	39.37	41.00	41.00	40.71	39.00	40.05	42.00	42.00	42.00	42.00	42.00	41.40
2023	33.50	32.00	32.00	32.00	32.00	32.00	32.00	32.00	32.00	32.00	32.00	32.00	32.13

Source: National Agricultural Statistics Service, U.S. Department of Agriculture (NASS-USDA)

Hogs

Hogs are generally bred twice a year in a continuous cycle designed to provide a steady flow of production. The gestation period for hogs is 3-1/2 months, and the average litter size is nine pigs. The pigs are weaned at 3-4 weeks of age. The pigs are then fed to maximize weight gain. The feed consists primarily of grains such as corn, barley, milo, oats, and wheat. Protein is added from oilseed meals. Hogs typically gain 3.1 pounds per pound of feed. The time from birth to slaughter is typically six months. Hogs are ready for slaughter at about 254 pounds, producing a dressed carcass weight of around 190 pounds and an average 88.6 pounds of lean meat. The lean meat consists of 21% ham, 20% loin, 14% belly, 3% spareribs, 7% Boston butt roast and blade steaks, and 10% picnic, with the remaining 25% going into jowl, lean trim, fat, miscellaneous cuts, and trimmings. Futures on lean hogs are traded at the CME Group. The futures contract is settled in cash based on the CME Lean Hog Index price, meaning that no physical delivery of hogs occurs. The CME Lean Hog Index is based on the 2-day average net price of slaughtered hogs at the average lean percentage level.

Prices – CME lean hog futures prices (Barchart.com symbol HE) in early 2023 traded sideways to lower and fell to a 2-year low of 71.50 cents per pound in April. Hog prices were under pressure as robust Chinese production of pork reduced China's demand for imported US pork. China's Q1 pork output rose +1.9% y/y to 15.9 million tons, the highest level in five years. Reduced US pork exports boosted domestic supplies as the USDA's June cold storage report showed stocks of pork in US cold storage as of May 1, 2023, rose +6.3% yr/yr to a 3-year high of 567.4 million pounds. Hog prices then trended higher and posted a 1-1/2 year high of 104.95 cents per pound in July. A drought in the Midwest boosted corn prices, which increased feed costs and squeezed profits for hog producers as operating margins for pork processors fell to a 1-1/2 year low in June. The shrinking profits forced them to reduce production as the Q2 USDA Hogs & Pigs Inventory report showed the US hog herd on June 1 fell to a 1-1/2 year low of 73.551 million hogs. US domestic pork demand also increased, prompting the USDA to raise its US 2023 pork consumption estimates in July. However, hog prices tumbled and sank to a 3-year low of 65.40 cents per pound in October. An increase in hog supplies weighed on prices after the Q3 USDA Hogs & Pigs Inventory report showed the US hog herd on September 1 unexpectedly rose +1.1% y/y to a 3-year high of 75.323 million hogs. Hog prices ended 2023 down sharply by -22.5% yr/yr at 67.975 cents per pound.

Supply – The number of hogs on world farms as of January 1, 2024, fell by -4.0% yr/yr to 746.961 million head. The number of hogs in the US as of January 1, 2024, remained unchanged yr/yr to 74.971 million head. The countries with the largest number of hogs as of January 1, 2024, were China with 56.7% of the world's hogs, the European Union with 17.9%, the US with 10.0%, and Brazil with 4.4%.

Demand – The federally-inspected hog slaughter in the US in 2022 rose by +2.1% yr/yr to 127.333 million head.

Salient Statistics of Pigs and Hogs in the United States

Year	Spring[3] Sows Farrowed --- 1,000 Head ---	Pig Crop	Pigs Per Litter	Fall[4] Sows Farrowed --- 1,000 Head ---	Pig Crop	Pigs Per Litter	Value of Hogs on Farms, Dec. 1 $ Per Head	Total Million $	Hog Marketings (1,000 Head)	Quantity Produced (Live Wt.) (Mil. Lbs.)	Value of Production (Million$)	Federally Inspected	Other	U.S. Total	Farm	U.S. Total
2014	5,573	53,821	9.66	5,985	61,035	10.20	144.0	9,732	149,097	32,126	24,184	106,123	753	106,876	82	106,958
2015	5,749	59,219	10.30	5,946	62,191	10.46	96.0	6,636	159,725	34,739	18,814	114,616	811	115,427	87	115,514
2016	5,896	61,236	10.39	6,103	64,703	10.60	92.0	6,578	165,539	35,899	17,363	117,388	831	118,219	84	118,303
2017	6,007	63,025	10.49	6,209	66,402	10.69	99.0	7,207	171,320	36,963	19,159	120,517	801	121,317	73	121,390
2018	6,041	64,053	10.60	6,377	68,515	10.74	98.0	7,299	180,251	38,498	18,770	123,696	738	124,435	76	124,511
2019	6,231	67,619	10.85	6,471	71,829	11.10			187,661	43,103	21,243	129,211	702	129,913	77	129,990
2020	6,329	69,637	11.00	6,425	71,044	11.06			180,247	41,920	19,196	130,782	780	131,562	76	131,638
2021	5,964	65,292	10.95	6,098	68,067	11.16			181,594	40,091	28,952	128,288	696	128,984	77	129,060
2022[1]	5,886	64,582	10.97	6,174	69,019	11.18			182,096	40,596	29,990	124,674	648	125,322	79	125,400
2023[2]	5,893	65,951	11.19	6,023	70,087	11.64						127,334	635	127,969		127,969

[1] Preliminary.   [2] Estimate.   [3] December-May.   [4] June-November.   *Source: Economic Research Service, U.S. Department of Agriculture (ERS-USDA)*

World Hog Numbers in Specified Countries as of January 1   In Thousands of Head

Year	Australia	Belarus	Brazil	Canada	China	European Union	Japan	Korea, South	Mexico	Russia	Ukraine	United States	World Total
2015	2,308	2,925	39,395	13,180	471,602	148,341	9,440	10,090	9,788	19,308	7,492	67,626	801,495
2016	2,272	----	39,422	13,630	458,029	144,294	9,313	10,187	10,043	21,239	7,240	69,019	789,110
2017	----	----	39,215	13,935	442,092	142,650	9,346	11,487	10,229	21,782	6,816	71,345	773,435
2018	----	----	38,829	14,245	441,589	145,544	9,280	11,273	10,410	22,945	6,236	73,145	778,209
2019	----	----	38,427	14,070	428,070	143,519	9,156	11,333	10,700	23,600	6,150	75,055	764,728
2020	----	----	37,850	14,065	310,410	143,146	9,090	11,280	11,050	25,048	5,842	77,323	649,845
2021	----	----	37,350	14,120	406,500	145,911	9,290	11,078	11,500	25,744	5,986	77,022	749,329
2022	----	----	35,688	14,170	449,220	141,681	8,949	11,217	11,775	26,200	5,718	74,606	784,324
2023[1]	----	----	34,250	13,920	452,560	134,410	8,956	11,124	12,250	26,000	5,140	74,956	778,216
2024[2]	----	----	32,900	13,037	423,600	133,875	9,040	11,028	12,560	27,000	4,900	74,971	746,961

[1] Preliminary.   [2] Forecast.   *Source: Foreign Agricultural Service, U.S. Department of Agriculture (FAS-USDA)*

Hogs and Pigs on Farms in the United States on December 1   In Thousands of Head

Year	Georgia	Illinois	Indiana	Iowa	Kansas	Minne-sota	Missouri	Neb-raska	North Carolina	Ohio	South Dakota	Wis-consin	Total
2014	155	4,700	3,700	21,300	1,840	8,100	2,850	3,200	8,800	2,230	1,270	310	67,776
2015	160	5,100	3,850	20,900	1,940	8,100	3,050	3,300	8,900	2,500	1,360	320	68,919
2016	65	5,100	4,100	22,200	1,910	8,500	3,100	3,400	9,300	2,700	1,450	335	71,545
2017	80	5,400	4,000	22,800	2,110	8,500	3,400	3,600	9,000	2,700	1,560	305	73,145
2018	72	5,400	4,250	23,600	2,050	9,100	3,650	3,550	9,200	2,550	1,750	320	75,070
2019	62	5,450	4,400	24,900	2,160	9,400	3,350	3,800	9,400	2,750	2,000	365	78,228
2020	38	5,450	4,450	24,600	2,060	9,400	3,750	3,800	9,800	2,700	2,030	370	77,312
2021	45	5,400	4,350	23,900	1,990	8,900	3,450	3,650	8,000	2,750	2,010	370	74,446
2022	40	5,500	4,450	24,100	1,910	9,000	3,350	3,600	8,300	2,750	2,110	345	74,956
2023[1]	42	5,500	4,500	24,900	1,980	9,100	3,150	3,800	7,800	2,600	2,310	360	74,971

[1] Preliminary.   Source: National Agricultural Statistics Service, U.S. Department of Agriculture (NASS-USDA)

Cold Storage Holdings of Frozen Pork[2] in the United States, on First of Month   In Thousands of Pounds

Year	Jan.	Feb.	Mar.	Apr.	May	June	July	Aug.	Sept.	Oct.	Nov.	Dec.
2014	554,328	618,746	654,712	575,539	583,891	575,818	537,447	533,259	543,666	550,622	533,076	492,752
2015	503,792	595,673	686,063	672,431	701,083	655,301	634,525	633,214	653,760	655,930	603,454	560,915
2016	545,696	625,246	628,948	613,803	637,320	616,124	586,479	598,592	608,955	642,303	599,010	518,813
2017	475,387	524,215	567,855	545,463	590,324	588,216	559,010	554,854	575,698	618,563	598,374	502,324
2018	490,047	580,714	609,813	611,013	634,722	623,725	561,879	552,029	581,513	589,403	570,917	507,688
2019	505,287	562,733	615,674	608,379	621,456	628,956	619,454	611,692	606,784	598,750	611,916	574,840
2020	580,464	625,588	648,975	616,946	611,222	467,927	460,173	460,635	465,465	465,619	447,115	419,772
2021	415,935	457,508	483,374	451,042	456,921	462,446	441,916	441,664	454,203	469,917	442,370	402,189
2022	396,461	434,415	478,315	485,999	533,396	546,071	539,100	526,496	542,602	537,036	509,688	451,598
2023[1]	456,379	519,145	521,606	533,893	567,433	531,757	486,811	470,764	469,243	461,656	437,901	415,662

[1] Preliminary.   [2] Excludes lard.   Source: Economic Research Service, U.S. Department of Agriculture (ERS-USDA)

Cold Storage Holdings of Frozen Pork Belly in the United States, on First of Month   In Thousands of Pounds

Year	Jan.	Feb.	Mar.	Apr.	May	June	July	Aug.	Sept.	Oct.	Nov.	Dec.
2014	80,367	87,171	87,675	79,721	83,579	85,888	83,936	64,644	45,562	34,311	29,006	35,894
2015	47,455	53,507	67,794	68,297	70,412	64,805	44,432	23,634	13,738	10,872	17,853	41,160
2016	53,392	60,698	61,433	65,028	72,592	77,683	62,921	50,733	32,053	25,084	20,386	18,526
2017	17,986	13,995	16,153	20,570	33,536	31,589	22,291	17,602	19,213	20,897	32,268	35,164
2018	39,620	43,810	49,012	59,202	64,563	61,234	53,279	38,556	34,805	30,354	26,690	36,859
2019	42,251	53,736	53,771	58,783	61,110	64,124	56,468	52,647	45,723	40,543	45,414	54,416
2020	66,647	70,872	74,270	78,157	80,728	60,322	53,840	42,374	31,053	24,846	19,025	23,292
2021	30,715	31,232	37,556	35,398	35,204	36,391	36,385	27,778	17,562	12,928	11,614	25,224
2022	38,069	44,707	50,115	56,836	58,331	56,728	53,183	42,842	35,684	36,513	40,247	54,429
2023[1]	63,015	69,991	71,011	76,986	81,247	82,531	69,954	51,169	36,804	29,639	28,061	48,323

[1] Preliminary.   Source: National Agricultural Statistics Service, U.S. Department of Agriculture (NASS-USDA)

Cold Storage Holdings of Pork Hams in the United States, on First of Month   In Thousands of Pounds

Year	Jan.	Feb.	Mar.	Apr.	May	June	July	Aug.	Sept.	Oct.	Nov.	Dec.
2014	76,773	106,183	117,464	89,452	81,785	109,999	126,493	148,905	179,483	194,077	162,035	96,397
2015	66,349	110,404	127,712	98,031	136,222	158,882	180,473	205,549	236,531	247,145	196,460	109,042
2016	67,813	111,142	115,780	96,511	130,217	144,060	166,451	188,441	226,070	248,972	191,430	106,101
2017	68,821	95,365	125,167	90,193	112,815	143,641	178,311	194,968	203,887	232,034	195,327	98,224
2018	81,082	118,407	122,743	96,339	112,145	139,295	148,657	167,563	204,763	214,628	176,109	96,375
2019	73,118	112,660	127,740	103,486	121,331	150,109	168,599	182,555	202,454	201,258	173,804	110,635
2020	85,995	114,618	114,534	88,308	113,328	107,550	122,993	136,621	143,909	145,994	123,324	74,862
2021	53,675	84,208	92,122	60,776	80,389	109,337	130,550	152,598	185,640	194,549	150,043	76,788
2022	61,354	74,775	84,212	74,118	98,038	126,491	139,283	151,634	163,992	159,489	121,624	55,284
2023[1]	53,414	78,594	85,278	84,554	117,508	137,159	136,836	137,646	154,286	149,592	113,570	57,290

[1] Preliminary.   Source: National Agricultural Statistics Service, U.S. Department of Agriculture (NASS-USDA)

HOGS

Top, Chicago: to 03/1968; Farrowing, Chicago: 04/1968 to 05/1970; Average, Omaha: 05/1970 to 10/1995; CME Lean Hog Index: 11/1995 to date.

Average Price of Hogs, National Base 51-52% lean   In Dollars Per Hundred Pounds (Cwt.)

Year	Jan.	Feb.	Mar.	Apr.	May	June	July	Aug.	Sept.	Oct.	Nov.	Dec.	Average
2014	58.36	63.88	83.82	89.09	81.76	85.35	95.17	80.39	74.36	75.24	63.76	61.24	76.03
2015	54.05	45.75	45.61	45.13	57.23	57.25	56.21	55.91	51.64	52.68	42.01	39.30	50.23
2016	40.34	46.61	46.95	47.96	54.75	58.42	56.28	48.12	43.36	37.07	34.45	39.45	46.15
2017	45.60	53.02	50.56	44.04	50.46	60.61	65.15	57.99	43.64	43.75	46.46	44.23	50.46
2018	50.40	51.49	45.46	39.88	46.86	56.99	55.38	37.88	38.43	47.54	42.19	38.58	45.92
2019	40.50	39.03	42.46	57.69	59.61	56.58	53.05	55.45	41.74	44.74	42.33	42.27	47.95
2020	43.43	40.56	43.56	36.09	46.53	34.25	34.20	38.87	48.41	55.92	50.34	46.00	43.18
2021	47.44	53.93	65.75	75.59	81.01	86.15	81.00	78.59	68.84	62.80	54.53	51.75	67.28
2022	56.02	67.01	73.61	73.47	74.08	79.19	83.99	85.62	71.00	67.78	63.72	58.96	71.20
2023[1]	53.82	54.28	56.38	51.68	55.35	63.06	73.92	71.51	62.38	58.08	56.19	48.72	58.78

[1] Preliminary.   *Source: Economic Research Service, U.S. Department of Agriculture (ERS-USDA)*

Average Price Received by Farmers for Hogs in the United States   In Cents Per Pound

Year	Jan.	Feb.	Mar.	Apr.	May	June	July	Aug.	Sept.	Oct.	Nov.	Dec.	Average
2014	61.2	65.5	81.9	88.8	82.8	84.8	93.3	83.2	75.7	77.0	66.7	64.3	77.1
2015	57.4	50.4	50.3	49.0	58.9	59.9	58.7	59.0	54.5	55.5	45.9	42.8	53.5
2016	43.6	49.6	50.0	51.0	57.2	60.6	59.4	52.6	47.8	41.7	39.0	43.1	49.6
2017	48.1	54.4	53.0	48.4	53.6	62.1	67.3	61.5	48.9	47.3	50.0	48.6	53.6
2018	52.5	54.6	50.0	45.3	51.5	59.1	58.6	44.3	43.2	50.3	46.2	43.4	49.9
2019	44.6	43.4	46.5	59.4	62.3	59.5	56.6	58.5	47.7	49.1	48.0	47.3	51.9
2020	47.8	45.5	47.7	42.3	51.0	41.3	39.9	42.9	49.7	56.3	51.9	49.1	47.1
2021	50.2	56.4	67.2	75.6	79.3	82.7	80.0	79.0	70.8	65.5	58.6	56.5	68.5
2022	58.8	68.6	75.1	76.2	75.9	78.7	83.0	85.8	73.8	70.5	66.7	62.5	73.0
2023[1]	58.5	59.6	61.7	57.0	58.8	64.6	74.3	73.7	64.9	60.4	57.5	53.3	62.0

[1] Preliminary.   *Source: Economic Research Service, U.S. Department of Agriculture (ERS-USDA)*

Quarterly Hogs and Pigs Report in the United States, 10 States In Thousands of Head

Year[2]	Inventory[3]	Breeding[3]	Market[3]	Farrowings	Pig Crop	Year[2]	Inventory[3]	Breeding[3]	Market[3]	Farrowings	Pig Crop
2014	64,775	5,757	59,018	11,558	114,856	2019	75,070	6,326	68,745	12,701	139,448
I	64,775	5,757	59,018	2,763	26,326	I	75,070	6,326	68,745	3,098	33,164
II	61,494	5,851	55,643	2,810	27,495	II	74,661	6,349	68,313	3,132	34,455
III	61,568	5,855	55,713	2,991	30,402	III	75,725	6,410	69,316	3,274	36,370
IV	65,979	5,920	60,059	2,994	30,633	IV	78,583	6,431	72,153	3,197	35,459
2015	67,776	5,939	61,838	11,695	121,411	2020	78,228	6,471	72,577	12,754	140,680
I	67,776	5,939	61,838	2,895	29,627	I	78,228	6,471	72,577	3,182	35,016
II	67,399	5,982	61,418	2,854	29,593	II	75,164	6,425	68,739	3,147	34,621
III	67,165	5,926	61,240	3,017	31,343	III	77,664	6,426	71,238	3,260	36,056
IV	69,185	5,986	63,200	2,929	30,848	IV	78,104	6,333	71,771	3,165	34,987
2016	68,919	6,002	62,917	11,998	125,939	2021	77,312	6,176	71,136	12,062	133,359
I	68,919	6,002	62,917	2,927	30,139	I	77,312	6,176	71,136	2,929	32,059
II	68,124	5,980	62,144	2,968	31,097	II	73,933	6,215	67,718	3,034	33,233
III	69,281	5,979	63,302	3,057	32,331	III	73,153	6,220	66,933	3,050	33,944
IV	71,786	6,016	65,770	3,046	32,372	IV	74,867	6,190	68,677	3,049	34,123
2017	71,545	6,110	65,435	12,217	129,429	2022	74,446	6,125	68,321	12,060	133,602
I	71,545	6,110	65,435	2,990	31,187	I	74,446	6,125	68,321	2,919	31,947
II	70,916	6,098	64,818	3,018	31,839	II	73,249	6,148	67,101	2,967	32,635
III	71,210	6,109	65,101	3,106	33,075	III	72,654	6,218	66,436	3,082	34,319
IV	73,309	6,117	67,192	3,103	33,328	IV	74,525	6,252	68,273	3,092	34,701
2018	73,145	6,179	66,966	12,418	132,568	2023[1]	74,956	6,204	68,752	11,916	136,038
I	73,145	6,179	66,966	2,977	31,497	I	74,956	6,204	68,752	2,952	32,537
II	72,055	6,210	65,845	3,064	32,556	II	74,136	6,146	67,990	2,941	33,414
III	72,231	6,320	65,911	3,172	34,019	III	73,551	6,206	67,345	3,040	35,295
IV	74,556	6,330	68,226	3,205	34,496	IV	76,133	6,179	69,954	2,983	34,792

[1] Preliminary. [2] Quarters are Dec. preceding year-Feb.(I), Mar.-May(II), June-Aug.(III) and Sept.-Nov.(IV).
[3] Beginning of period. *Source: National Agricultural Statistics Service, U.S. Department of Agriculture (NASS-USDA)*

Federally Inspected Hog Slaughter in the United States In Thousands of Head

Year	Jan.	Feb.	Mar.	Apr.	May	June	July	Aug.	Sept.	Oct.	Nov.	Dec.	Total
2014	9,726	8,609	8,614	8,794	8,561	8,040	8,394	8,199	8,762	9,880	8,754	9,788	106,123
2015	9,698	9,018	9,818	9,612	8,686	9,364	9,332	9,272	9,652	10,173	9,700	10,292	114,616
2016	9,682	9,364	10,015	9,303	9,114	9,505	8,696	10,308	10,096	10,369	10,539	10,398	117,388
2017	10,059	9,310	10,611	9,282	9,886	9,809	8,953	10,583	10,213	10,922	10,487	10,400	120,517
2018	10,653	9,578	10,661	9,939	10,163	9,553	9,532	11,081	9,583	11,571	10,982	10,403	123,696
2019	10,984	10,051	10,667	10,526	10,301	9,939	10,516	10,798	10,581	12,233	11,279	11,336	129,211
2020	11,760	10,670	11,883	9,353	8,524	11,104	11,155	11,047	10,957	11,949	10,961	11,419	130,782
2021	11,192	10,376	11,678	10,767	9,596	10,594	9,737	10,546	10,697	11,020	11,081	11,005	128,288
2022	10,362	9,897	11,197	10,032	9,986	10,451	9,264	10,922	10,597	10,857	10,863	10,247	124,674
2023[1]	11,080	9,931	11,415	9,724	10,533	10,375	9,564	11,057	10,431	11,367	11,083	10,776	127,334

[1] Preliminary. *Source: National Agricultural Statistics Service, U.S. Department of Agriculture (NASS-USDA)*

Average Live Weight of all Hogs Slaughtered Under Federal Inspection In Pounds Per Head

Year	Jan.	Feb.	Mar.	Apr.	May	June	July	Aug.	Sept.	Oct.	Nov.	Dec.	Average
2014	284	283	285	287	287	285	284	283	283	286	287	287	285
2015	287	285	285	285	284	282	280	278	280	284	286	285	283
2016	286	284	284	285	283	281	278	276	280	282	283	283	282
2017	285	284	284	285	282	279	277	278	282	283	286	286	283
2018	286	286	287	287	285	280	277	278	280	283	286	286	283
2019	288	287	287	287	287	285	280	279	282	285	288	288	285
2020	290	288	288	290	294	288	283	283	285	291	294	294	289
2021	295	291	291	290	288	284	281	280	283	288	291	292	288
2022	294	293	293	293	291	288	284	282	285	289	290	292	290
2023[1]	293	291	292	291	289	284	281	278	281	285	289	291	287

[1] Preliminary. *Source: National Agricultural Statistics Service, U.S. Department of Agriculture (NASS-USDA)*

HOGS

Nearby Futures through Last Trading Day.

Volume of Trading of Lean Hog Futures in Chicago   In Thousands of Contracts

Year	Jan.	Feb.	Mar.	Apr.	May	June	July	Aug.	Sept.	Oct.	Nov.	Dec.	Total
2014	940.1	880.1	1,402.3	760.6	893.0	937.5	1,046.6	818.8	1,000.4	674.1	708.0	595.5	10,656.9
2015	883.0	743.3	961.8	716.4	830.1	962.1	971.2	640.8	745.3	717.5	836.7	567.7	9,575.9
2016	665.2	645.4	797.0	589.4	726.5	937.8	826.5	645.5	849.8	762.7	915.4	833.8	9,195.0
2017	847.3	742.4	963.2	690.5	1,012.1	1,120.1	981.2	976.0	1,124.1	955.6	1,098.2	731.3	11,242.0
2018	992.4	936.4	1,149.9	962.6	1,236.1	1,312.5	1,250.9	1,308.4	1,241.2	1,140.7	1,267.2	753.3	13,551.7
2019	1,112.4	982.8	1,716.1	1,353.3	1,435.2	1,417.1	1,570.5	1,216.7	1,456.4	1,240.1	1,235.0	886.4	15,621.8
2020	1,351.2	977.4	1,381.6	1,197.2	995.6	1,046.9	1,050.0	750.5	1,236.2	873.0	854.0	682.8	12,396.4
2021	916.6	827.4	1,080.1	868.6	1,044.2	1,301.1	1,017.5	786.1	1,099.7	748.7	969.0	752.7	11,411.7
2022	1,115.2	926.7	1,062.2	734.8	1,034.8	979.8	970.8	875.3	1,051.7	897.4	948.7	800.9	11,398.3
2023	1,015.9	853.2	1,344.3	802.2	1,433.1	1,291.6	1,140.3	987.7	1,042.5	918.1	1,175.4	791.6	12,796.0

Contract size = 40,000 lbs.   *Source: Chicago Mercantile Exchange (CME)*

Average Open Interest of Lean Hog Futures in Chicago   In Contracts

Year	Jan.	Feb.	Mar.	Apr.	May	June	July	Aug.	Sept.	Oct.	Nov.	Dec.
2014	266,366	282,321	288,484	265,981	256,474	248,869	248,878	234,967	237,877	236,417	230,578	216,735
2015	208,643	192,716	208,128	216,998	219,669	221,626	210,767	196,682	196,033	198,965	204,049	173,053
2016	168,096	191,458	218,393	224,392	233,337	255,818	234,949	212,182	215,947	227,447	225,542	199,554
2017	210,582	227,286	214,122	207,945	223,068	251,117	272,856	258,984	256,269	253,357	260,573	239,469
2018	246,345	232,492	230,504	241,846	244,654	231,674	233,594	230,352	222,734	225,483	227,359	207,286
2019	211,589	236,596	270,420	296,832	311,184	303,772	284,851	265,214	264,332	277,164	293,006	287,240
2020	294,780	291,757	257,704	222,412	208,909	218,716	225,379	219,996	223,259	223,208	206,542	189,728
2021	209,599	245,463	271,935	289,151	289,477	289,656	266,321	269,392	249,579	243,855	231,422	215,756
2022	230,763	273,066	242,790	226,703	207,407	189,158	200,317	227,873	207,701	192,337	194,307	184,800
2023	199,815	214,144	220,756	225,393	232,080	203,924	200,841	206,636	199,691	190,223	191,442	186,326

Contract size = 40,000 lbs.   *Source: Chicago Mercantile Exchange (CME)*

PORK BELLIES
Quarterly Cash as of 03/28/2024

QUARTERLY CASH
As of 03/28/2024
Chart High 279.970 on 08/11/2021
Chart Low   16.000   on 11/30/1959

12-14 lb., Chicago: to 09/1975; 12-14 lb., Midwest: 10/1975 to date.

Average Price of Pork Bellies (12-14 lbs.), Central, U.S.   In Cents Per Pound

Year	Jan.	Feb.	Mar.	Apr.	May	June	July	Aug.	Sept.	Oct.	Nov.	Dec.	Average
2014	124.07	137.58	176.77	191.73	156.63	173.03	174.29	139.46	120.57	127.81	111.33	105.57	144.90
2015	122.30	102.97	81.14	75.33	82.51	108.15	NA	184.67	166.82	165.54	127.35	114.96	121.07
2016	128.18	NA	NA	134.91	119.13	130.09	146.67	115.14	96.21	127.29	120.69	121.10	123.94
2017	136.39	NA	158.66	136.79	139.18	176.76	216.28	170.18	116.74	107.75	135.04	142.64	148.76
2018	137.69	157.64	133.63	111.96	110.14	157.22	NA	106.71	109.96	NA	181.14	131.26	133.73
2019	146.10	121.61	142.66	160.07	138.55	123.36	122.41	NA	113.37	140.82	131.25	110.06	131.84
2020	108.16	88.40	91.46	51.13	101.79	104.92	107.72	113.28	NA	NA	NA	NA	95.86
2021	144.35	154.48	NA	NA	185.04	212.84	206.00	247.07	196.04	217.17	154.49	NA	190.83
2022	NA	204.40	214.90	222.72	NA	NA	NA	NA	160.24	148.98	142.43	115.99	172.81
2023[1]	113.19	109.88	112.66	93.53	97.17	110.19	180.51	219.91	145.55	150.12	123.11	109.39	130.43

[1] Preliminary.   *Source: Economic Research Service, U.S. Department of Agriculture (ERS-USDA)*

Average Price of Pork Loins (12-14 lbs.)[2], Central, U.S.   In Cents Per Pound

Year	Jan.	Feb.	Mar.	Apr.	May	June	July	Aug.	Sept.	Oct.	Nov.	Dec.	Average
2014	115.27	128.19	165.28	147.55	135.39	153.75	167.79	150.01	153.69	152.92	117.50	115.82	141.93
2015	108.25	99.88	100.25	101.55	124.08	112.35	111.13	107.61	102.46	103.50	88.44	85.76	103.77
2016	100.14	93.52	90.52	89.61	111.77	112.56	104.71	98.27	110.10	89.52	76.73	85.90	96.95
2017	91.73	90.66	99.36	88.58	106.12	118.21	118.69	100.58	94.97	89.85	85.62	82.96	97.28
2018	83.63	89.53	88.98	84.45	96.25	101.34	98.72	98.35	107.17	92.36	98.72	75.40	92.91
2019	79.70	75.19	82.42	88.03	101.05	103.19	98.04	92.14	85.29	88.61	86.24	86.68	88.88
2020	85.62	85.04	112.98	129.14	192.07	88.83	74.05	82.25	81.48	100.89	80.43	77.82	99.22
2021	88.61	90.84	103.36	108.46	126.13	124.34	112.00	114.47	110.03	103.68	82.19	72.22	103.03
2022	93.34	124.53	109.32	115.91	122.56	126.86	132.61	127.18	121.11	111.50	105.80	102.29	116.08
2023[1]	105.17	99.32	97.07	93.81	104.87	110.87	121.18	117.74	117.66	110.48	101.72	101.15	106.75

[1] Preliminary.   *Source: Economic Research Service, U.S. Department of Agriculture (ERS-USDA)*

HOGS

Average Retail Price of Bacon, Sliced   In U.S. Dollars per Pound

Year	Jan.	Feb.	Mar.	Apr.	May	June	July	Aug.	Sept.	Oct.	Nov.	Dec.	Average
2014	5.56	5.46	5.55	5.69	6.05	6.11	6.01	6.07	5.95	5.76	5.57	5.53	5.78
2015	5.59	5.47	5.37	5.21	4.94	5.06	5.18	5.41	5.48	5.38	5.11	5.10	5.42
2016	5.66	5.39	5.49	5.61	5.55	5.37	5.45	5.45	5.48	5.38	5.71	5.63	5.77
2017	5.18	5.33	5.75	5.78	5.70	5.67	5.82	6.24	6.37	6.07	5.71	5.50	5.77
2018	5.65	5.53	5.53	5.42	5.45	5.25	5.42	5.58	5.50	5.37	5.39	5.50	5.47
2019	5.52	5.50	5.61	5.55	5.81	5.88	5.70	5.58	5.58	5.65	5.51	5.47	5.61
2020	5.51	5.50	5.26	5.35	5.35	5.77	5.78	5.56	5.62	5.72	5.75	5.83	5.58
2021	5.83	5.78	5.85	6.22	6.35	6.67	6.86	7.10	7.22	7.32	7.27	7.21	6.64
2022	7.22	7.10	7.20	7.42	7.36	7.40	7.42	7.37	7.38	7.61	7.24	6.96	7.31
2023[1]	6.81	6.60	6.61	6.55	6.34	6.22	6.24	6.50	7.08	7.22	6.90	6.77	6.65

[1] Preliminary.   *Source: Economic Research Service, U.S. Department of Agriculture (ERS-USDA)*

Average Wholesale Price of Pork Hams (20-23 lb) Bl trmd. TS1   In U.S. Cents per Pound

Year	Jan.	Feb.	Mar.	Apr.	May	June	July	Aug.	Sept.	Oct.	Nov.	Dec.	Average
2014	75.35	83.70	99.82	103.06	105.67	123.85	143.57	118.74	119.35	121.85	103.13	85.94	107.00
2015	73.24	64.53	53.89	53.37	69.21	64.04	58.78	72.53	67.42	71.54	66.91	65.83	65.11
2016	58.79	60.71	55.25	64.45	67.08	75.28	79.41	70.85	71.60	55.07	67.25	75.05	66.73
2017	55.74	58.15	60.54	60.25	67.75	69.53	78.14	67.81	63.87	67.00	66.81	59.97	64.63
2018	64.21	60.28	55.33	54.87	53.34	61.67	55.57	57.35	57.37	53.69	55.57	52.32	56.80
2019	48.42	43.76	63.16	66.82	77.59	73.51	72.68	71.31	60.75	64.86	90.53	78.54	67.66
2020	71.83	60.93	53.37	38.41	41.42	34.77	46.11	44.96	62.63	66.68	71.22	63.62	54.66
2021	62.07	70.62	73.25	86.90	82.07	79.41	88.00	70.80	62.06	55.17	58.28	53.52	70.18
2022	47.86	51.73	62.73	72.56	83.99	94.77	111.68	103.44	103.65	108.85	100.42	84.82	85.54
2023[1]	72.75	74.37	79.40	66.99	82.02	85.02	102.15	93.69	91.30	83.20	84.76	80.69	83.03

[1] Preliminary.   *Source: Economic Research Service, U.S. Department of Agriculture (ERS-USDA)*

Average Wholesale Price of Pork Cutout Composite   In U.S. Dollars per Pound

Year	Jan.	Feb.	Mar.	Apr.	May	June	July	Aug.	Sept.	Oct.	Nov.	Dec.	Average
2014	86.84	95.80	122.60	122.73	113.87	125.07	133.58	113.66	110.82	111.71	94.59	89.90	110.10
2015	83.28	72.57	67.96	67.58	82.56	84.84	83.33	88.37	84.41	86.43	74.24	72.00	78.96
2016	73.26	76.03	76.16	79.52	85.62	87.96	87.77	76.29	72.79	73.06	73.80	78.07	78.36
2017	80.67	83.75	79.86	74.83	84.79	97.12	102.97	91.02	77.36	75.11	81.55	79.19	84.02
2018	80.90	78.22	72.89	68.01	73.87	83.34	81.13	68.35	74.98	78.60	81.13	71.62	76.09
2019	69.36	62.80	72.36	84.69	85.08	80.27	77.37	83.65	71.01	76.42	83.41	79.20	77.14
2020	74.72	64.92	72.75	65.80	105.78	68.47	67.87	72.14	84.82	94.09	81.18	75.21	77.31
2021	80.31	88.34	101.25	111.17	117.46	123.27	120.00	119.40	107.99	102.62	90.95	86.60	104.11
2022	90.56	105.56	105.73	106.56	104.43	109.49	120.60	116.99	102.86	101.15	93.43	87.24	103.72
2023[1]	81.03	82.28	83.74	77.97	82.63	92.69	112.17	105.91	98.28	90.44	86.68	83.56	89.78

[1] Preliminary.   *Source: Economic Research Service, U.S. Department of Agriculture (ERS-USDA)*

Hog-Corn Price Ratio[2] in the United States   In Bushels

Year	Jan.	Feb.	Mar.	Apr.	May	June	July	Aug.	Sept.	Oct.	Nov.	Dec.	Average
2014	13.8	15.1	18.1	18.9	17.6	18.8	23.0	22.9	21.7	21.6	18.5	17.0	18.9
2015	15.0	13.3	13.2	13.1	16.2	16.7	15.4	16.0	14.8	15.1	12.8	11.7	14.4
2016	11.9	13.9	14.0	14.3	15.5	15.9	16.5	16.4	14.8	12.7	12.0	13.0	14.2
2017	14.1	15.8	15.2	14.1	15.5	18.1	19.3	18.8	15.0	14.5	15.9	15.0	15.9
2018	16.0	16.2	14.2	12.7	14.0	16.5	16.9	13.2	12.7	14.7	13.5	12.3	14.4
2019	12.5	12.1	12.9	16.8	17.2	14.9	13.6	14.9	12.6	12.8	13.0	12.7	13.8
2020	12.6	12.0	13.0	12.9	15.9	13.1	12.4	13.8	14.6	15.6	13.7	12.4	13.5
2021	11.8	11.9	13.7	14.2	13.4	13.8	13.1	12.5	12.9	13.0	11.1	10.3	12.6
2022	10.5	11.3	11.4	10.8	10.5	10.7	11.4	11.9	10.4	10.9	10.3	9.5	10.8
2023[1]	8.8	8.8	9.3	8.5	9.0	10.0	11.9	12.9	12.5	12.3	12.3	11.1	10.6

[1] Preliminary.   [2] Bushels of corn equal in value to 100 pounds of hog, live weight.   *Source: Economic Research Service, U.S. Department of Agriculture (ERS-USDA)*

Honey

Honey is the thick, supersaturated sugar solution produced by bees to feed their larvae. It is composed of fructose, glucose, and water in varying proportions and also contains several enzymes and oils. The color of honey varies due to the source of nectar and the age of the honey. Light-colored honeys are usually of higher quality than darker honeys. The average honeybee colony can produce more than 700 pounds of honey per year, but only 10 percent is usually harvested by the beekeeper. The rest of the honey is consumed by the colony during the year. American per capita honey consumption is 1 pound per person per year. Honey is said to be humanity's oldest sweet and beeswax the first plastic.

Honey is used in many ways, including direct human consumption, baking, and medicine. Honey has several healing properties. Its high sugar content nourishes injured tissues, thus enhancing faster healing time. Honey's phytochemicals create a form of hydrogen peroxide that cleans out the wound, and the thick consistency protects the wound from contact with air. Honey has also proven superior to antibiotic ointments for reducing rates of infection in people with burns.

Prices – US average domestic honey prices in 2022 rose by +11.7% to a new record high of 296.0 cents per pound. The value of US honey production in 2022 rose by +10.5% to $370.980 million, becoming a new record.

Supply – World production of honey in 2022 rose by +2.5% to 1.830 million metric tons, below the 2017 record high of 1.878 million metric tons. The major producers of honey in 2022 were China with 25.9% of the world's total, Argentina with 3.8%, and Russia with 3.7%. US production of honey in 2022 fell by -1.1% to 125.331 million pounds, remaining well below the high of 220.339 million pounds posted in 2000. Honey yield per colony in 2022 remained unchanged yr/yr at 47.0 pounds per colony. The number of colonies in 2022 fell by -1.1% to 2.667 million.

Salient Statistics of Honey in the United States   In Millions of Pounds

Year	Number of Colonies (1,000)	Yield Per Colony (Pounds)	Stocks Jan. 1	Total U.S. Production	Imports for Consumption	Domestic Disappearance	Exports	Total Supply	Domestic Avg. Price All Honey (cents/lb.)	Value of Production ($1,000)	U.S. Production: Beeswax	Domestic Avg. Price: Beeswax (cents/lb.)
2014	2,740	65.1	41.2	178.3	365.5	----	10.9	584.9	217.3	387.4	----	----
2015	2,660	58.9	42.2	156.5	386.3	----	11.3	585.1	208.3	326.1	----	----
2016	2,775	58.3	41.3	161.9	367.0	----	11.1	570.2	211.9	343.0	----	----
2017	2,683	55.5	30.7	149.0	432.1	----	9.9	611.7	219.9	334.2	----	----
2018	2,828	54.5	29.3	154.0	442.4	----	9.7	625.7	221.0	340.4	----	----
2019	2,812	55.8	40.9	156.9		----			199.0	312.3	----	----
2020	2,706	54.5	39.7	147.6		----			210.0	309.9	----	----
2021	2,697	47.0	23.5	126.7		----			265.0	335.9	----	----
2022	2,667	47.0	23.2	125.3		----			301.0	377.2	----	----
2023[1]	2,509	55.2	44.0	138.6		----			252.0	349.2	----	----

[1] Preliminary.   Source: Economic Research Service, U.S. Department of Agriculture (ERS-USDA)

Average Price of Honey, by Color Class in the United States   In U.S. Dollars per Pound

	Co-op and Private					Retail					All				
Year	Water White, Extra White, White	Extra Light Amber	Light Amber, Amber, Dark Amber	All Other Honey, Area Specialties	All Honey	Water White, Extra White, White	Extra Light Amber	Light Amber, Amber, Dark Amber	All Other Honey, Area Specialties	All Honey	Water White, Extra White, White	Extra Light Amber	Light Amber, Amber, Dark Amber	All Other Honey, Area Specialties	All Honey
2014	2.046	2.096	2.088	2.554	2.071	3.285	3.922	4.171	5.352	4.054	2.062	2.183	2.342	3.182	2.173
2015	1.886	2.025	2.004	2.849	1.950	3.054	4.118	4.121	6.566	4.099	1.906	2.132	2.347	3.515	2.083
2016	1.891	1.908	1.948	2.457	1.920	4.638	4.337	4.529	7.816	4.745	1.955	2.008	2.330	3.852	2.119
2017	2.047	2.060	2.028	2.872	2.051	3.143	4.873	4.970	6.279	4.450	2.063	2.173	2.411	3.834	2.199
2018	1.980	2.010	2.100	2.640	2.030	3.630	3.440	4.890	7.170	7.380	2.010	2.120	2.510	3.620	2.210
2019	1.630	1.700	1.950	3.160	1.730	4.700	3.630	5.300	6.620	4.820	1.700	1.900	2.570	3.990	1.990
2020	1.730	1.810	2.000	2.390	1.840	4.180	4.670	5.510	7.230	5.230	1.810	1.930	2.530	3.000	2.100
2021	2.330	2.340	2.520	2.640	2.400	5.360	4.150	5.550	6.480	5.270	2.430	2.470	2.980	3.760	2.650
2022	2.700	2.660	2.870	3.410	2.770	5.570	5.620	6.090	7.910	6.020	2.810	2.780	3.230	4.160	3.010
2023[1]	1.990	2.170	2.630	3.080	2.230	5.870	5.780	6.780	8.510	6.550	2.090	2.330	3.200	4.300	2.520

[1] Preliminary.   Source: National Agricultural Statistics Service, U.S. Department of Agriculture (NASS-USDA)

HONEY

World Production of Honey — In Metric Tons

Year	Argentina	Australia	Brazil	Canada	China	Germany	Japan	Mexico	Russia	United States	World Total
2013	67,500	13,864	35,365	34,685	461,431	18,953	2,766	56,907	68,446	67,812	1,688,386
2014	76,000	13,094	38,481	38,847	474,786	20,195	2,839	60,624	74,868	80,862	1,760,925
2015	52,600	12,281	37,859	41,735	484,726	23,398	2,865	61,881	67,736	71,008	1,821,403
2016	68,123	13,080	39,677	42,900	562,875	21,600	2,754	55,358	69,764	73,429	1,862,706
2017	76,379	12,180	41,696	43,550	548,857	21,600	2,827	51,066	65,167	67,596	1,878,347
2018	79,468	12,419	42,268	43,089	457,182	----	2,826	64,253	65,006	69,857	1,839,333
2019	79,140	12,064	45,801	39,295	446,961	24,100	2,911	61,986	63,526	71,179	1,759,933
2020	72,183	11,802	52,493	37,723	466,487	29,200	2,929	54,165	66,368	66,948	1,783,647
2021	70,715	11,313	55,679	39,976	485,960	19,600	2,745	62,079	64,533	57,490	1,785,852
2022[1]	70,437	10,938	60,966	33,745	474,107	----	2,626	64,320	67,014	56,849	1,830,768

[1] Preliminary.   *Source: Food and Agricultural Organization of the United Nations (FAO)*

United States Imports of Honey — In Metric Tons

Year	Argentina	Brazil	Canada	India	Mexico	New Zealand	Taiwan	Thailand	Türkiye	Ukraine	Uruguay	Vietnam	World Total
2013	44,221	11,677	9,386	25,867	5,648	1,234	1,827	846	1,897	3,308	8,710	33,586	153,102
2014	36,888	19,249	5,612	20,290	7,254	1,625	2,524	3,458	2,581	8,876	5,362	47,107	165,777
2015	27,081	15,440	8,234	36,123	5,364	1,992	4,443	10,753	5,195	11,411	7,243	36,973	175,243
2016	34,708	19,062	13,510	29,364	4,557	1,840	1,580	4,238	1,852	11,086	1,767	38,494	166,442
2017	35,378	24,031	15,762	45,144	4,783	4,200	1,649	4,490	2,393	19,363	4,025	36,288	202,415
2018	36,219	23,604	15,221	44,200	3,303	1,671	1,680	4,639	2,248	8,324	1,326	39,156	186,935
2019	36,468	23,913	7,872	49,657	3,239	1,660	1,651	1,579	826	8,739	1,362	36,980	178,964
2020	39,805	34,198	4,143	37,578	3,465	1,898	831	1,039	1,062	11,084	4,063	50,669	196,507
2021	43,245	34,493	2,992	56,581	4,125	2,740	1,100	720	2,268	5,953	4,229	56,009	220,298
2022[1]	42,456	27,397	5,775	67,397	11,819	2,598	3,126	2,191	6,597	4,408	8,550	14,414	205,006

[1] Preliminary.   *Source: Foreign Agricultural Service, U.S. Department of Agriculture (FAS-USDA)*

Production of Honey in the United States — In Thousands of Pounds

Year	California	Florida	Georgia	Idaho	Louisiana	Michigan	Minnesota	Montana	North Dakota	South Dakota	Texas	Wisconsin	Total
2014	12,480	14,700	4,526	3,400	4,032	5,733	7,920	14,256	42,140	24,360	9,048	2,862	178,270
2015	8,250	11,880	2,760	2,848	4,356	5,220	8,296	12,118	36,260	19,140	8,316	3,484	156,544
2016	11,160	10,750	3,744	3,298	4,300	5,340	7,316	12,243	37,830	19,880	9,310	3,348	161,882
2017	13,735	8,815	3,168	4,180	3,483	3,915	7,812	10,440	33,670	14,535	7,920	2,968	148,980
2018	13,735	10,535	3,332	2,976	3,735	4,048	7,259	14,720	38,160	11,985	7,392	2,295	154,008
2019	16,080	9,225	3,366	2,944	3,888	4,700	6,962	14,878	33,800	19,440	7,560	2,162	156,922
2020	13,760	8,832	3,434	3,745	2,277	4,465	5,940	8,910	38,610	14,945	8,949	2,250	147,594
2021	9,570	8,492	3,264	3,000	2,146	5,100	7,125	6,669	28,325	12,250	7,672	1,974	126,744
2022	11,590	7,350	3,296	2,726	2,562	3,362	5,202	7,503	31,200	7,215	8,321	2,915	125,331
2023[1]	13,608	4,704	2,541	2,944	1,440	3,850	6,148	9,690	38,325	18,444	3,885	2,790	138,571

[1] Preliminary.   *Source: National Agricultural Statistics Service, U.S. Department of Agriculture (NASS-USDA)*

Honey Producing Colonies in the United States — In Thousands

Year	California	Florida	Georgia	Idaho	Louisiana	Michigan	Minnesota	Montana	North Dakota	South Dakota	Texas	Wisconsin	Total
2014	320	245	73	100	48	91	122	162	490	280	116	53	2,740
2015	275	220	69	89	44	90	122	146	490	290	126	52	2,660
2016	310	215	96	97	50	89	124	159	485	280	133	54	2,775
2017	335	205	99	95	43	87	126	145	455	255	120	53	2,683
2018	335	215	98	96	45	97	119	160	550	255	132	51	2,828
2019	335	205	102	92	54	94	118	173	520	270	126	46	2,812
2020	320	192	101	107	33	95	108	110	495	245	157	45	2,706
2021	290	193	96	100	37	101	125	117	515	250	137	42	2,697
2022	305	210	103	94	42	82	102	123	520	185	157	53	2,667
2023[1]	324	147	77	92	32	70	106	114	511	212	111	62	2,509

[1] Preliminary.   *Source: National Agricultural Statistics Service, U.S. Department of Agriculture (NASS-USDA)*

Hops

Hop Stocks[2] in the United States   In Thousands of Pounds

Year	March 1: Growers	March 1: Dealers/ Growers	March 1: Brewers	March 1: Total Stocks	September 1: Growers	September 1: Dealers/ Growers	September 1: Brewers	September 1: Total Stocks
2015	----	76,000	43,000	119,000	----	46,000	37,000	83,000
2016	----	88,000	40,000	128,000	----	49,000	36,000	85,000
2017	----	105,000	35,000	140,000	----	64,000	34,000	98,000
2018	----	132,000	37,000	169,000	----	74,000	39,000	113,000
2019	----	130,000	35,000	165,000	----	78,000	37,000	115,000
2020	----	145,000	35,000	180,000	----	94,000	36,000	130,000
2021	----	150,000	35,000	185,000	----	97,000	31,000	128,000
2022	----	160,000	33,000	193,000	----	109,000	28,000	137,000
2023	----	159,000	26,000	185,000	----	106,000	24,000	130,000
2024[1]	----	161,000	23,000	184,000	----			

[1] Preliminary.   [2] Includes equivalent pounds of dry hops held in form of extract or pellets.   *Source: National Agricultural Statistics Service (NASS), Agricultural Statistics Board, United States Department of Agriculture (USDA)*

Salient Statistics of Hops in the United States

Year	Area Harvested (Acres)	Yield (Pounds)	Production (1,000 Pounds)	Price per Unit (US Dollars per Pound)	Value of Production (1,000 US Dollars)
2014	38,011	1,868.000	70,996	$3.67	$260,627
2015	43,633	1,807.000	78,846	$4.38	$345,388
2016	50,857	1,713.000	87,140	$5.72	$498,420
2017	53,989	1,956.000	105,622	$5.60	$591,375
2018	55,035	1,943.000	106,907	$5.46	$583,444
2019	56,544	1,981.000	112,041	$5.68	$636,580
2020	58,641	1,770.000	103,810	$5.97	$619,424
2021	60,872	1,900.000	115,631	$5.72	$661,618
2022[1]	59,785	1,694.000	101,856	$6.10	$621,098
2023[2]	54,318	1,915.000	104,043	$5.40	$562,146

[1] Preliminary.   [2] Forecast.   *Source: National Agricultural Statistics Service (NASS), Agricultural Statistics Board, United States Department of Agriculture (USDA)*

Production of Hops in the United States, by States   In Thousands of Pounds

Year	California	Idaho	Oregon	Washington	Total
2014	----	6,914	8,221	55,861	70,996
2015	----	8,725	10,668	59,453	78,846
2016	----	9,298	12,395	65,447	87,140
2017	----	14,067	12,470	79,084	105,622
2018	----	16,243	12,936	77,728	106,907
2019	----	17,003	13,023	82,015	112,041
2020	----	17,190	12,469	74,152	103,810
2021	----	18,415	12,608	84,608	115,631
2022[1]	----	16,572	13,472	71,112	101,856
2023[2]	----	16,853	10,630	76,560	104,043

[1] Preliminary.   [2] Forecast.   *Source: National Agricultural Statistics Service (NASS), Agricultural Statistics Board, United States Department of Agriculture (USDA)*

Production of Hops in Washington, by Variety   In Thousands of Pounds

Year	Amarillo, VGXP01	Cascade	Centennial	Citra, HBC 394	Columbus/ Tomahawk	Mosaic, HBC 369	Pahto, HBC 682	Simcoe, YCR 14	Summit	Zeus	Total
2014	----	8,821.0	3,818.8	2,622.5	4,569.2	1,493.2	----	2,805.8	5,308.3	9,488.4	55,861.1
2015	W	9,553.3	4,317.3	3,597.2	4,223.4	3,111.6	----	4,489.5	3,189.6	8,426.3	59,453.3
2016	W	9,638.8	5,908.6	5,035.0	2,787.9	4,720.4	W	6,305.1	2,914.5	6,178.5	65,446.6
2017	3,347.0	10,547.8	7,450.6	6,493.8	4,389.7	4,578.0	W	6,725.4	3,342.3	6,836.8	79,083.8
2018	3,539.9	8,428.3	5,285.5	7,792.4	5,048.4	4,542.1	3,591.7	5,095.1	2,874.1	6,788.4	77,727.7
2019	3,107.8	7,138.6	5,516.4	9,569.3	6,002.6	5,810.8	5,057.4	6,020.2	1,946.8	6,843.4	82,014.9
2020	2,300.4	4,462.2	4,008.2	12,426.2	10,507.9	7,422.6	4,458.0	5,280.6	701.4	----	74,151.5
2021	2,213.1	5,045.1	3,135.1	13,850.3	12,013.1	8,926.9	5,206.8	5,221.1	590.4	----	84,608.2
2022	1,967.5	5,323.1	2,992.4	11,719.9	9,019.5	8,166.1	3,643.6	4,821.7	W	----	71,111.6
2023[1]	2,421.1	6,176.3	2,504.7	10,007.7	13,052.2	7,303.0	----	5,360.3	W	----	76,559.8

[1] Preliminary.   [2] Includes data withheld to avoid disclosure of individual operations and varieties not listed.   W = Withheld to avoid disclosing data for individual operations.   *Source: National Agricultural Statistics Service (NASS), Agricultural Statistics Board, United States Department of Agriculture (USDA)*

Interest Rates - U.S.

U.S. interest rates can be characterized in two main ways, by credit quality and by maturity. Credit quality refers to the level of risk associated with a particular borrower. U.S. Treasury securities, for example, carry the lowest risk. Maturity refers to the time at which the security matures and must be repaid. Treasury securities carry a full spectrum of maturities, from short-term cash management bills, to T-bills (4-weeks, 3-months, 6-months), T-notes (2-year, 3-year, 5-year, 7-year, and 10-year), and 30-year T-bonds. The most active futures markets are the 10-year T-note futures, 30-year T-bond futures, and Eurodollar futures, all of which are traded at the CME Group.

Prices – CME 10-year T-note futures prices (Barchart.com symbol ZN) posted their high for 2023 in March. T-note prices had support in early 2023 as the Federal Reserve signaled it was nearing the end of its aggressive interest rate hiking campaign. At the March 2023 Federal Open Market Committee (FOMC) meeting, the central bank raised its federal funds rate target range by +25 bp to 4.75%-5.00% but was less hawkish in its post-meeting language. The FOMC shifted to an outlook for "some additional" policy firming versus its previous outlook for "ongoing" rate increases. T-note prices also garnered some safe-haven demand after the collapse of Silicon Valley Bank in March 2023.

T-note prices traded sideways into May 2023 when the FOMC raised its federal funds rate target range by +25 bp to 5.00%-5.25%, but Fed Chair Powell suggested the FOMC might pause its tightening campaign in June to assess how the US economy was responding to tighter credit conditions resulting from higher interest rates and stress in the banking sector.

The FOMC at its June meeting left its funds rate target unchanged but implemented its final +25 bp rate hike to a 22-year high of 5.25-5.50% at its July meeting. Fed Chair Powell, at the July meeting, left open the possibility of further rate hikes by saying the Fed still had a long way to go to return inflation to its 2% goal. In fact, US consumer prices remained sticky as they rose to +3.7% yr/yr in August after falling to a 3-year low of 3.0% yr/yr in June.

After July, the FOMC left its funds rate target unchanged at 5.25%-5.50% for the rest of its meetings in 2023. However, at its September meeting, the FOMC's guidance remained hawkish as policymakers indicated they might tighten monetary policy further and scaled back estimates for interest rate cuts in 2024. T-note prices tumbled to a 16-year low in October, and the 10-year T-note yield jumped to a 16-year high of 5.02%.

T-note prices recovered moderately into year-end as the US unemployment rate in October remained at a 2-year high of 3.8%, and the US November CPI eased to +3.1% yr/yr from +3.7% yr/yr in September. At its December meeting, the FOMC's dot plot indicated that FOMC members expected no further interest-rate hikes and instead expected an overall interest rate cut of 0.75 percentage points in 2024. The FOMC, at its December policy meeting, also shifted its guidance to a more dovish tone, with officials noting they would monitor a range of data and developments to see if "any" additional policy firming was appropriate. The 10-year T-note yield finished 2023 little changed at 3.88%.

U.S. Producer Price Index[2] for All Commodities   1982 = 100

Year	Jan.	Feb.	Mar.	Apr.	May	June	July	Aug.	Sept.	Oct.	Nov.	Dec.	Average
2014	203.8	205.7	207.0	208.3	208.0	208.3	208.0	207.0	206.4	203.4	200.9	197.0	205.3
2015	192.0	191.1	191.5	190.9	193.4	194.8	193.9	191.9	189.1	187.5	185.7	183.5	190.4
2016	182.6	181.3	182.1	183.2	185.3	187.6	187.7	186.6	186.9	186.7	186.3	188.2	185.4
2017	190.7	191.6	191.5	193.0	192.8	193.6	193.5	193.8	194.8	194.9	195.9	196.3	193.5
2018	197.9	199.3	199.3	200.3	203.2	204.2	204.3	203.4	203.6	204.6	202.3	201.0	202.0
2019	199.1	199.2	200.8	202.1	201.7	200.3	200.7	199.2	198.4	198.6	199.0	199.0	199.8
2020	199.3	196.7	193.1	185.5	188.6	191.2	193.0	194.3	195.5	196.5	198.3	200.5	194.4
2021	204.8	210.6	215.0	217.9	224.9	228.9	231.9	233.4	235.7	240.5	243.3	241.3	227.3
2022	246.5	252.7	260.0	265.3	273.3	280.3	272.3	269.5	267.9	265.1	263.2	257.9	264.5
2023[1]	260.2	258.7	257.1	256.9	253.7	253.9	253.8	257.7	258.9	255.0	252.8	249.6	255.7

[1] Preliminary. [2] Not seasonally adjusted. *Source: Bureau of Labor Statistics, U.S. Department of Commerce (BLS)*

U.S. Consumer Price Index[2] for All Urban Consumers   1982-84 = 100

Year	Jan.	Feb.	Mar.	Apr.	May	June	July	Aug.	Sept.	Oct.	Nov.	Dec.	Average
2014	233.9	234.8	236.3	237.1	237.9	238.3	238.3	237.9	238.0	237.4	236.2	234.8	236.7
2015	233.7	234.7	236.1	236.6	237.8	238.6	238.7	238.3	237.9	237.8	237.3	236.5	237.0
2016	236.9	237.1	238.1	239.3	240.2	241.0	240.6	240.8	241.4	241.7	241.4	241.4	240.0
2017	242.8	243.6	243.8	244.5	244.7	245.0	244.8	245.5	246.8	246.7	246.7	246.5	245.1
2018	247.9	249.0	249.6	250.5	251.6	252.0	252.0	252.1	252.4	252.9	252.0	251.2	251.1
2019	251.7	252.8	254.2	255.5	256.1	256.1	256.6	256.6	256.8	257.3	257.2	257.0	255.7
2020	258.0	258.7	258.1	256.4	256.4	257.8	259.1	259.9	260.3	260.4	260.2	260.5	258.8
2021	261.6	263.0	264.9	267.1	269.2	271.7	273.0	273.6	274.3	276.6	277.9	278.8	271.0
2022	281.1	283.7	287.5	289.1	292.3	296.3	296.3	296.2	296.8	298.0	297.7	296.8	292.7
2023[1]	299.2	300.8	301.8	303.4	304.1	305.1	305.7	307.0	307.8	307.7	307.1	306.7	304.7

[1] Preliminary. [2] Not seasonally adjusted. *Source: Bureau of Labor Statistics, U.S. Department of Commerce (BLS)*

EURODOLLARS - CME
Weekly Selected Futures as of 06/20/2023

WEEKLY SELECTED FUTURES
As of 06/20/2023
Chart High 99.8860   on 09/07/2021
Chart Low   94.3500   on 05/25/2023

% Yield Basis
100 - Price

Points of 100%

Nearby Futures through Last Trading Day.   Shaded areas indicate US recessions.

Volume of Trading of 3-month Eurodollar Futures in Chicago   In Thousands of Contracts

Year	Jan.	Feb.	Mar.	Apr.	May	June	July	Aug.	Sept.	Oct.	Nov.	Dec.	Total
2014	54,761.3	38,750.1	57,945.4	46,118.3	54,063.9	55,196.8	57,448.5	47,862.5	67,835.8	86,823.2	34,561.1	63,066.5	664,433
2015	60,557.7	53,474.6	56,886.5	39,486.9	46,358.9	55,022.2	45,717.3	51,075.2	47,750.9	44,983.2	39,937.9	45,661.9	586,913
2016	60,730.2	58,698.8	53,857.5	41,209.6	46,085.8	56,564.7	49,539.9	49,707.1	49,586.2	42,365.9	84,793.1	61,808.7	654,947
2017	62,542.9	57,145.8	72,934.8	51,369.1	53,434.7	54,122.6	40,527.4	44,393.5	54,731.0	52,213.9	49,599.8	46,831.7	639,847
2018	69,710.4	90,635.0	87,329.3	54,086.4	68,834.0	53,227.4	38,782.1	43,758.4	55,084.0	72,841.9	58,947.3	71,972.4	765,209
2019	61,232.1	46,129.1	69,360.8	50,245.2	73,665.3	78,392.8	56,286.0	73,101.1	52,788.6	53,025.6	36,353.1	36,492.9	687,073
2020	43,767.3	70,530.7	109,077.1	40,101.1	34,866.2	34,777.6	22,937.0	28,911.5	27,773.7	26,825.1	39,452.2	30,893.0	509,913
2021	42,111.1	57,854.3	65,666.3	38,424.2	41,200.7	60,571.6	48,300.5	40,873.1	43,998.8	67,575.3	60,504.9	43,350.3	610,431
2022	53,318.5	56,591.2	59,306.5	34,998.7	31,282.7	35,267.2	25,660.9	27,238.2	27,324.1	17,791.1	15,161.9	10,087.1	394,028
2023	8,497.1	7,669.8	9,985.8	1,327.2	520.8	224.7	----	----	----	----	----	----	28,225

Contract size = $1,000,000.   *Source: CME Group; International Monetary Market (IOM), division of the Chicago Mercantile Exchange (CME)*

Average Open Interest of 3-month Eurodollar Futures in Chicago   In Thousands of Contracts

Year	Jan.	Feb.	Mar.	Apr.	May	June	July	Aug.	Sept.	Oct.	Nov.	Dec.
2014	10,142.7	10,022.8	10,453.9	10,875.2	11,635.9	11,593.8	12,101.1	12,734.0	13,139.9	11,819.9	11,685.4	10,902.1
2015	10,860.6	11,099.2	10,806.9	10,972.8	11,415.8	11,292.4	11,483.9	12,050.4	11,528.6	11,072.0	11,202.6	10,704.9
2016	10,869.1	10,865.4	10,132.9	10,143.2	10,621.0	10,281.7	10,434.1	10,977.1	11,138.0	11,410.5	12,131.6	12,064.2
2017	11,865.7	12,254.8	12,710.3	13,160.6	13,531.5	13,596.4	12,979.5	13,523.7	13,474.4	12,863.1	13,241.6	13,513.2
2018	14,034.4	15,871.7	17,114.1	16,815.8	16,141.1	14,660.5	14,124.0	14,084.0	14,114.7	14,373.2	14,151.3	13,543.0
2019	12,512.6	12,419.9	12,454.4	12,738.4	12,954.5	12,974.4	13,014.0	13,194.8	12,634.5	12,047.7	12,116.6	11,583.0
2020	11,060.8	11,742.0	11,096.0	10,613.3	10,799.8	10,252.2	9,703.1	9,768.4	9,420.7	9,336.8	9,801.5	9,439.9
2021	10,017.5	11,304.1	11,209.8	11,618.0	12,636.6	12,706.4	12,202.5	12,338.7	12,367.6	12,711.8	12,342.1	11,576.3
2022	11,231.7	11,141.0	10,948.3	10,778.6	10,444.7	9,791.9	9,503.1	9,617.2	8,891.8	8,116.1	7,675.2	6,691.9
2023	5,959.3	5,798.2	5,074.5	2,622.2	586.8	521.3	----	----	----	----	----	----

Contract size = $1,000,000.   *Source: CME Group; International Monetary Market (IOM), division of the Chicago Mercantile Exchange (CME)*

INTEREST RATES - U.S.

T-NOTE, 2-YEAR - CBOT
Weekly Nearest Futures as of 03/28/2024

WEEKLY NEAREST FUTURES
As of 03/28/2024

Chart High 110-66   on 02/18/2021
Chart Low 100-120 on 10/19/2023

% Yield Basis
6% 2-Yr

Points -128ths

Nearby Futures through Last Trading Day.   Shaded areas indicate US recessions.

Volume of Trading of 2-Year U.S. Treasury Note Futures in Chicago   In Thousands of Contracts

Year	Jan.	Feb.	Mar.	Apr.	May	June	July	Aug.	Sept.	Oct.	Nov.	Dec.	Total
2014	4,004.9	4,637.1	4,670.2	4,402.3	8,206.8	4,404.6	3,913.5	9,120.7	6,155.0	6,801.9	8,643.1	5,054.2	70,014
2015	5,113.2	11,269.7	6,108.6	4,349.9	10,776.5	6,555.7	4,983.7	10,933.2	5,556.6	4,681.9	7,946.4	4,765.3	83,041
2016	5,229.6	9,923.0	5,521.3	4,421.2	8,907.1	6,095.0	5,000.2	8,969.9	5,775.0	5,733.4	11,524.6	4,773.8	81,874
2017	5,753.0	10,850.4	6,893.6	5,031.7	11,816.4	6,878.7	4,794.3	11,174.2	6,379.3	6,749.4	14,716.4	6,212.1	97,249
2018	8,227.0	19,349.2	9,652.2	7,441.3	17,938.9	6,815.9	5,398.5	14,407.6	6,704.9	10,226.4	20,088.5	9,248.8	135,499
2019	10,151.3	20,428.2	10,462.9	9,357.5	25,719.8	12,310.8	11,126.1	25,807.0	11,851.2	13,137.1	22,728.1	9,543.9	182,624
2020	11,002.4	26,537.8	19,825.0	7,580.4	14,444.6	6,637.1	4,419.0	12,570.6	5,110.8	4,401.1	11,777.0	4,544.2	128,850
2021	5,906.0	15,733.1	8,958.7	5,667.9	13,870.4	7,288.9	6,380.9	12,767.6	5,826.1	10,052.8	16,059.2	6,986.2	115,498
2022	9,990.1	20,210.9	13,750.9	12,885.0	20,621.1	12,879.6	9,994.5	19,609.0	12,297.1	10,599.6	18,542.8	8,282.9	169,664
2023	9,847.2	20,504.9	19,821.4	10,275.8	24,411.8	12,352.2	11,048.1	25,015.9	10,965.6	14,852.7	30,755.5	13,909.4	203,761

Contract size = $200,000.   *Source: CME Group; Chicago Board of Trade (CBT)*

Average Open Interest of 2-Year U.S. Treasury Note Futures in Chicago   In Thousands of Contracts

Year	Jan.	Feb.	Mar.	Apr.	May	June	July	Aug.	Sept.	Oct.	Nov.	Dec.
2014	858.0	934.8	942.0	1,077.5	1,153.4	1,051.2	1,164.8	1,400.5	1,546.2	1,425.6	1,432.8	1,292.8
2015	1,269.4	1,462.5	1,346.2	1,378.7	1,363.1	1,183.6	1,274.7	1,356.3	1,143.8	1,117.1	1,091.9	989.4
2016	1,048.4	1,164.5	961.0	1,021.2	1,117.2	1,004.6	1,053.3	1,124.5	1,008.8	1,225.0	1,202.6	1,140.2
2017	1,215.9	1,444.9	1,412.6	1,378.3	1,392.5	1,350.8	1,354.0	1,488.8	1,527.0	1,667.8	1,837.2	1,765.6
2018	1,900.4	2,030.6	1,896.1	1,973.5	2,138.0	1,828.2	1,930.1	4,255.5	2,164.6	2,268.6	2,682.1	2,636.3
2019	2,681.8	3,159.8	3,027.8	3,614.3	4,089.5	3,615.8	3,634.0	3,849.5	3,557.2	3,872.6	3,972.1	3,581.8
2020	3,643.6	3,813.2	3,203.0	2,607.4	2,389.1	2,130.8	2,110.2	2,129.6	2,006.4	1,982.9	2,001.6	1,883.6
2021	2,018.0	2,297.2	2,344.3	2,291.7	2,310.7	2,107.0	2,011.4	1,986.9	1,899.5	1,935.1	2,024.3	1,927.3
2022	2,084.2	2,219.9	2,169.2	2,229.5	2,333.7	2,081.2	2,060.9	2,095.5	1,993.5	2,068.5	2,231.4	2,188.3
2023	2,350.5	2,668.0	2,415.9	2,574.2	3,074.8	3,467.5	3,663.0	3,803.9	3,754.4	4,083.7	4,190.2	3,905.5

Contract size = $200,000.   *Source: CME Group; Chicago Board of Trade (CBT)*

T-NOTE, 5-YEAR - CBOT
Weekly Nearest Futures as of 03/28/2024

Nearby Futures through Last Trading Day.   Shaded areas indicate US recessions.

Volume of Trading of 5-Year U.S. Treasury Note Futures in Chicago   In Thousands of Contracts

Year	Jan.	Feb.	Mar.	Apr.	May	June	July	Aug.	Sept.	Oct.	Nov.	Dec.	Total
2014	13,081.6	18,022.0	16,060.6	14,088.2	20,473.5	13,605.3	14,182.4	20,546.3	16,596.0	20,858.3	15,933.0	12,982.0	196,429
2015	14,739.3	20,925.8	14,020.7	11,619.5	20,929.9	15,289.6	12,668.2	22,856.6	12,974.5	12,321.4	20,512.7	11,849.6	190,708
2016	13,618.7	24,294.8	13,229.2	11,144.4	22,079.7	15,245.5	11,120.9	23,442.5	12,453.2	11,484.3	30,046.2	13,745.4	201,905
2017	15,623.7	26,990.8	17,509.9	13,761.0	26,563.2	16,462.0	12,784.2	24,543.1	14,990.7	14,944.5	27,741.3	14,526.8	226,441
2018	18,302.4	35,388.6	19,974.6	16,208.0	36,454.5	17,379.4	14,187.0	30,353.9	15,664.4	25,561.2	36,989.9	20,757.0	287,221
2019	21,297.1	31,298.5	20,637.9	16,018.8	39,172.1	21,319.0	18,801.4	40,355.5	19,616.5	18,960.9	31,401.5	15,520.5	294,400
2020	17,703.1	39,907.6	33,449.4	13,308.2	26,063.5	14,361.0	9,499.5	25,390.4	11,492.4	13,501.2	26,265.6	13,900.9	244,843
2021	17,300.4	37,059.2	25,189.4	15,676.2	30,367.2	19,107.2	17,387.0	28,580.7	18,279.8	21,639.7	35,103.7	16,170.3	281,861
2022	22,603.0	39,905.0	27,667.2	22,967.4	37,472.0	23,186.2	20,411.4	34,940.9	23,725.9	22,351.7	34,850.5	16,721.0	326,802
2023	20,261.5	39,614.6	37,369.3	19,421.0	45,565.8	23,675.2	22,611.8	49,038.5	22,041.5	29,373.5	57,553.8	22,876.9	389,404

Contract size = $100,000.   *Source: CME Group; Chicago Board of Trade (CBT)*

Average Open Interest of 5-Year U.S. Treasury Note Futures in Chicago   In Thousands of Contracts

Year	Jan.	Feb.	Mar.	Apr.	May	June	July	Aug.	Sept.	Oct.	Nov.	Dec.
2014	1,939.7	2,002.5	1,959.1	2,036.7	2,126.3	2,070.6	2,130.6	2,190.1	2,130.5	1,992.7	1,993.5	1,844.4
2015	1,837.5	1,983.8	1,992.9	2,016.3	2,038.9	2,096.2	2,200.8	2,398.5	2,352.1	2,422.1	2,469.2	2,371.4
2016	2,497.2	2,734.3	2,476.6	2,477.3	2,575.0	2,632.8	2,676.0	2,866.4	2,799.2	2,756.9	2,961.3	2,924.3
2017	3,019.1	3,313.3	3,035.8	3,103.9	3,261.9	3,144.0	1,350.8	3,000.0	3,144.0	2,998.1	3,293.4	3,051.2
2018	3,236.9	3,538.2	3,376.7	3,519.0	3,813.1	3,742.6	3,892.1	4,255.5	4,380.4	4,536.9	4,922.3	4,702.5
2019	4,539.9	4,511.1	4,256.0	4,485.2	4,870.6	4,535.7	4,475.3	4,567.4	4,129.1	4,360.5	4,613.6	4,248.8
2020	4,334.7	4,699.7	4,280.2	3,683.9	3,658.0	3,471.2	3,481.9	3,455.3	3,261.6	3,126.7	3,204.8	3,184.9
2021	3,274.8	3,582.7	3,520.7	3,426.9	3,539.8	3,506.4	3,473.4	3,506.7	3,540.8	3,604.1	3,673.3	3,625.6
2022	3,861.1	4,065.8	3,798.7	3,812.4	3,836.6	3,868.5	3,971.2	4,040.0	3,993.0	4,045.0	4,295.5	4,144.8
2023	4,168.4	4,293.0	4,329.8	4,501.8	5,014.5	4,941.9	5,307.6	5,652.6	5,480.0	5,672.1	6,067.9	5,749.2

Contract size = $100,000.   *Source: CME Group; Chicago Board of Trade (CBT)*

INTEREST RATES - U.S.

T-NOTE, 10-YEAR - CBOT
Weekly Nearest Futures as of 03/28/2024

WEEKLY NEAREST FUTURES
As of 03/28/2024
Chart High 140 47/64 on 03/09/2020
Chart Low 105 21/64 on 10/19/2023

Nearby Futures through Last Trading Day.   Shaded areas indicate US recessions.

Volume of Trading of 10-year U.S. Treasury Note Futures in Chicago   In Thousands of Contracts

Year	Jan.	Feb.	Mar.	Apr.	May	June	July	Aug.	Sept.	Oct.	Nov.	Dec.	Total
2014	23,218.1	29,772.2	27,675.3	25,202.1	34,569.3	24,098.5	23,402.1	34,087.3	28,122.5	39,126.2	28,205.8	23,005.8	340,485
2015	27,499.2	33,705.2	24,770.7	22,343.8	38,005.7	29,805.4	23,574.7	34,287.1	22,586.7	23,505.9	28,612.5	19,644.2	328,341
2016	27,310.1	41,327.8	24,480.8	22,290.2	32,571.1	28,364.5	23,198.0	34,699.7	24,140.8	22,878.3	46,296.5	23,204.4	350,762
2017	28,552.5	38,619.2	29,608.9	25,570.4	39,797.5	28,177.2	24,476.4	39,078.3	27,756.7	28,826.3	41,497.4	23,377.8	375,338
2018	32,939.1	51,555.5	33,837.1	27,450.9	53,075.1	31,980.5	25,504.3	44,233.8	27,721.0	48,099.0	49,321.5	32,001.5	457,719
2019	31,722.5	41,654.0	34,503.4	27,261.9	56,919.4	33,426.3	29,998.8	56,558.9	34,095.1	32,378.8	42,883.4	28,427.2	449,830
2020	37,977.1	64,744.5	49,588.5	22,902.6	35,352.9	25,639.6	17,848.0	36,685.9	21,867.6	27,856.3	41,447.0	24,080.3	405,990
2021	32,660.6	56,374.6	45,442.0	31,239.9	47,982.2	33,519.7	32,475.6	44,239.3	33,123.8	37,373.5	49,554.6	25,760.8	469,747
2022	36,353.2	53,719.1	41,450.8	33,977.3	47,749.8	33,701.4	29,789.4	43,518.4	35,985.6	34,806.2	45,668.7	25,482.9	462,203
2023	30,928.8	51,985.0	49,184.9	26,046.8	52,736.0	32,560.9	29,864.7	55,871.5	30,696.0	43,163.2	63,166.0	32,053.7	498,258

Contract size = $100,000.   *Source: CME Group; Chicago Board of Trade (CBT)*

Average Open Interest of 10-year U.S. Treasury Note Futures in Chicago   In Thousands of Contracts

Year	Jan.	Feb.	Mar.	Apr.	May	June	July	Aug.	Sept.	Oct.	Nov.	Dec.
2014	2,260.5	2,426.0	2,433.4	2,526.5	2,720.3	2,591.6	2,679.0	2,853.2	2,705.4	2,776.0	2,855.5	2,652.6
2015	2,684.1	2,610.3	2,690.8	2,822.7	2,884.8	2,730.7	2,751.9	2,941.1	2,729.8	2,776.5	2,680.6	2,594.4
2016	2,747.8	3,065.1	2,714.8	2,726.7	2,732.6	2,750.5	2,815.6	2,849.5	2,818.1	2,890.3	3,017.2	3,026.9
2017	3,130.7	3,343.9	3,139.4	3,137.3	3,365.2	3,179.9	3,162.4	3,384.4	3,277.1	3,132.4	3,399.8	3,271.5
2018	3,420.6	3,740.6	3,480.6	3,590.4	3,854.8	3,462.9	3,696.0	3,990.4	3,963.9	4,153.7	4,281.3	4,136.0
2019	4,067.1	4,130.2	3,880.5	3,966.4	4,183.5	3,887.9	3,816.5	3,989.9	3,589.1	3,683.7	3,935.0	3,663.1
2020	3,779.7	4,161.3	3,629.1	3,243.8	3,449.8	3,318.0	3,442.3	3,491.5	3,287.1	3,214.7	3,271.9	3,188.9
2021	3,378.4	3,672.0	3,780.1	3,939.2	4,309.2	4,336.3	4,153.2	4,094.4	3,964.1	4,051.7	3,960.1	3,809.5
2022	3,830.0	4,005.7	3,678.5	3,688.4	3,669.6	3,452.9	3,484.2	3,565.5	3,681.2	3,873.2	4,008.5	3,785.5
2023	4,043.3	4,272.5	4,215.1	4,326.7	4,657.2	4,633.5	4,776.5	4,874.2	4,720.1	4,705.3	4,767.3	4,530.8

Contract size = $100,000.   *Source: CME Group; Chicago Board of Trade (CBT)*

T-BOND - CBOT
Weekly Nearest Futures as of 03/28/2024

WEEKLY NEAREST FUTURES
As of 03/28/2024

Chart High 200 /64 on 03/20/2020
Chart Low 107 8/64 on 10/23/2023

% Yield Basis
6% 20-Yr

Nearby Futures through Last Trading Day.   Shaded areas indicate US recessions.

Volume of Trading of 30-year U.S. Treasury Bond Futures in Chicago   In Thousands of Contracts

Year	Jan.	Feb.	Mar.	Apr.	May	June	July	Aug.	Sept.	Oct.	Nov.	Dec.	Total
2014	5,871.1	8,211.2	6,867.7	6,259.9	9,648.8	7,044.9	6,719.0	9,948.4	7,678.1	10,370.2	7,827.0	6,742.1	93,188
2015	7,956.2	8,611.4	5,183.2	4,747.5	6,832.7	5,708.3	5,453.9	7,438.7	4,884.1	4,927.9	5,625.8	4,531.9	71,902
2016	5,569.8	8,184.8	5,000.5	4,428.4	6,276.8	5,736.6	4,734.9	6,655.2	5,245.9	5,042.9	8,707.2	4,620.4	70,203
2017	5,165.8	7,149.6	5,818.2	4,614.0	7,713.7	6,144.7	4,672.2	7,620.6	5,442.3	5,668.0	8,212.6	5,115.4	73,337
2018	6,648.4	10,573.9	6,380.0	5,517.2	10,025.2	6,048.6	5,244.4	8,677.5	5,961.9	10,301.0	10,299.4	6,984.4	92,662
2019	6,441.9	8,404.9	6,758.6	4,783.9	9,727.9	6,005.7	5,736.2	12,286.6	6,763.9	6,752.0	8,383.3	5,750.6	87,796
2020	7,429.5	12,839.9	10,085.2	4,285.4	7,990.3	5,747.3	5,080.8	10,012.5	6,187.7	7,678.1	11,469.9	6,877.9	95,685
2021	8,031.6	13,439.3	11,047.3	7,472.6	11,631.7	7,779.6	7,393.7	10,433.7	8,496.7	9,022.5	12,060.4	6,637.8	113,447
2022	7,760.3	11,073.9	8,272.6	6,804.5	11,066.6	7,396.9	6,272.4	9,453.5	7,202.5	6,959.0	9,508.4	5,574.4	97,345
2023	6,414.7	10,318.8	9,972.7	4,813.1	10,300.4	6,734.2	6,643.2	12,570.6	8,630.5	12,194.9	14,275.3	8,644.8	111,513

Contract size = $100,000.   Source: CME Group; Chicago Board of Trade (CBT)

Average Open Interest of 30-year U.S. Treasury Bond Futures in Chicago   In Contracts

Year	Jan.	Feb.	Mar.	Apr.	May	June	July	Aug.	Sept.	Oct.	Nov.	Dec.
2014	666,663	716,926	712,174	722,390	780,781	738,607	758,214	870,115	860,417	870,759	850,561	889,272
2015	829,094	640,877	414,934	437,101	478,017	484,216	500,019	533,913	505,812	501,845	491,806	519,574
2016	517,291	562,305	510,970	525,831	528,077	570,427	575,832	583,950	562,062	562,046	574,628	586,673
2017	616,403	637,810	646,801	644,707	706,590	737,002	729,176	873,263	730,878	740,311	798,709	772,841
2018	790,518	834,751	806,285	798,849	878,533	804,968	826,864	878,497	859,024	917,822	964,126	966,317
2019	954,146	1,007,000	967,026	947,620	1,001,286	958,051	929,612	994,150	974,482	987,321	1,022,854	1,010,372
2020	1,052,137	1,294,602	1,154,433	997,024	1,048,643	1,003,052	1,048,720	1,152,639	1,168,654	1,212,653	1,248,831	1,155,056
2021	1,163,969	1,209,695	1,204,552	1,179,879	1,220,707	1,190,103	1,194,247	1,229,063	1,221,810	1,199,351	1,217,755	1,213,951
2022	1,206,255	1,195,809	1,117,441	1,129,546	1,226,123	1,188,242	1,181,664	1,192,749	1,217,481	1,215,548	1,206,085	1,184,506
2023	1,216,702	1,235,176	1,212,928	1,186,639	1,230,982	1,238,191	1,253,161	1,364,543	1,366,239	1,389,017	1,356,557	1,342,911

Contract size = $100,000.   Source: CME Group; Chicago Board of Trade (CBT)

INTEREST RATES - U.S.

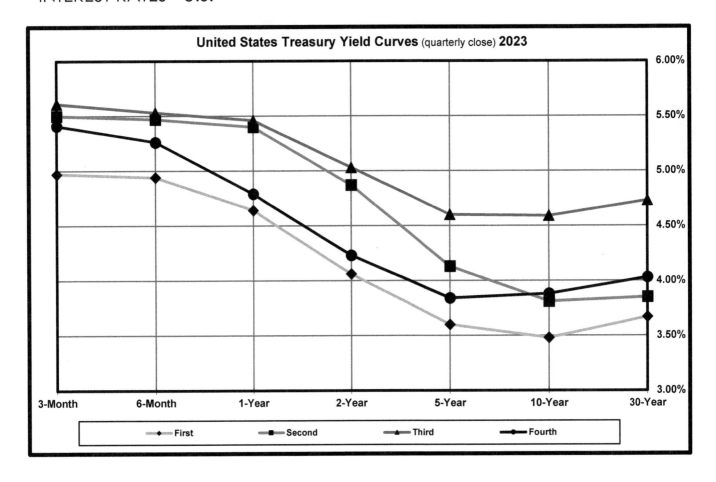

U.S. Federal Funds Rate   In Percent

Year	Jan.	Feb.	Mar.	Apr.	May	June	July	Aug.	Sept.	Oct.	Nov.	Dec.	Average
2014	0.07	0.07	0.08	0.09	0.09	0.10	0.09	0.09	0.09	0.09	0.09	0.12	0.09
2015	0.11	0.11	0.11	0.12	0.12	0.13	0.13	0.14	0.14	0.12	0.12	0.24	0.13
2016	0.34	0.38	0.36	0.37	0.37	0.38	0.39	0.40	0.40	0.40	0.41	0.54	0.40
2017	0.65	0.66	0.79	0.90	0.91	1.04	1.15	1.16	1.15	1.15	1.16	1.30	1.00
2018	1.41	1.42	1.51	1.69	1.70	1.82	1.91	1.91	1.95	2.19	2.20	2.27	1.83
2019	2.40	2.40	2.41	2.42	2.39	2.38	2.40	2.13	2.04	1.83	1.55	1.55	2.16
2020	1.55	1.58	0.65	0.05	0.05	0.08	0.09	0.10	0.09	0.09	0.09	0.09	0.38
2021	0.09	0.08	0.07	0.07	0.06	0.08	0.10	0.09	0.08	0.08	0.08	0.08	0.08
2022	0.08	0.08	0.20	0.33	0.77	1.21	1.68	2.33	2.56	3.08	3.78	4.10	1.68
2023	4.33	4.57	4.65	4.83	5.06	5.08	5.12	5.33	5.33	5.33	5.33	5.33	5.02

Source: Bureau of Economic Analysis, U.S. Department of Commerce (BEA)

U.S. Municipal Bond Yield[1]   In Percent

Year	Jan.	Feb.	Mar.	Apr.	May	June	July	Aug.	Sept.	Oct.	Nov.	Dec.	Average
2007	4.23	4.22	4.15	4.26	4.31	4.60	4.56	4.64	4.51	4.39	4.46	4.42	4.40
2008	4.27	4.64	4.93	4.70	4.58	4.69	4.68	4.69	4.86	5.50	5.23	5.56	4.86
2009	5.07	4.90	4.99	4.78	4.56	4.81	4.72	4.60	4.24	4.20	4.37	4.21	4.62
2010	4.33	4.36	4.36	4.41	4.29	4.36	4.32	4.03	3.87	3.87	4.40	4.92	4.29
2011	5.28	5.15	4.92	4.99	4.59	4.51	4.52	4.02	4.01	4.13	4.05	3.95	4.51
2012	3.68	3.66	3.91	3.95	3.77	3.94	3.78	3.74	3.73	3.65	3.46	3.48	3.73
2013	3.60	3.72	3.96	3.92	3.72	4.27	4.56	4.82	4.79	4.56	4.60	4.73	4.27
2014	4.59	4.44	4.46	4.35	4.29	4.35	4.33	4.23	4.13	3.96	3.96	3.70	4.23
2015	3.40	3.58	3.59	3.51	3.76	3.82	3.79	3.74	3.78	3.67	3.68	3.57	3.66
2016	3.41	3.30	3.38	3.30	3.29	3.13	2.83	2.85	2.93	3.20	Discontinued		3.16

[1] 20-bond average.   *Source: Bureau of Economic Analysis, U.S. Department of Commerce (BEA)*

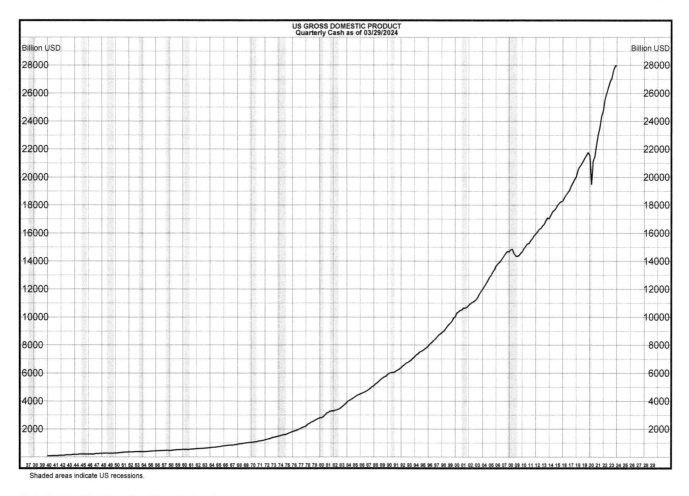

US GROSS DOMESTIC PRODUCT
Quarterly Cash as of 03/29/2024

Billion USD — Billion USD

Shaded areas indicate US recessions.

U.S. Industrial Production Index¹   1997 = 100

Year	Jan.	Feb.	Mar.	Apr.	May	June	July	Aug.	Sept.	Oct.	Nov.	Dec.	Average
2014	102.7	103.6	104.6	104.6	105.0	105.4	105.6	105.5	105.8	105.8	106.7	106.5	105.2
2015	106.0	105.4	105.1	104.5	104.1	103.7	104.3	104.2	103.8	103.4	102.7	102.1	104.1
2016	103.0	102.2	101.4	101.5	101.4	101.9	102.1	102.0	102.0	102.2	102.1	102.9	102.1
2017	103.0	102.6	103.3	104.3	104.4	104.6	104.5	104.0	104.1	105.6	106.2	106.5	104.4
2018	101.3	101.7	102.3	103.4	102.5	103.3	103.5	104.2	104.2	104.0	104.0	103.9	103.2
2019	103.3	102.8	102.9	102.4	102.6	102.6	102.2	102.9	102.6	101.8	102.1	101.8	102.5
2020	101.4	101.6	97.7	84.6	86.0	91.6	95.0	95.9	95.8	96.4	96.9	98.0	95.1
2021	98.8	95.4	98.1	98.3	99.2	99.5	100.1	100.1	99.1	100.3	101.2	100.9	99.2
2022	101.0	101.7	102.5	102.8	102.8	102.7	103.1	103.2	103.5	103.4	103.1	101.5	102.6
2023¹	102.5	102.6	102.7	103.2	102.9	102.3	103.2	103.2	103.3	102.5	102.4	102.5	102.8

¹ Total Index of the Federal Reserve Index of Quantity Output, seasonally adjusted.   ² Preliminary.   *Source: Bureau of Economic Analysis, U.S. Department of Commerce (BEA)*

U.S. Gross National Product, National Income, and Personal Income   In Billions of Constant Dollars¹

| | Gross Domestic Product | | | | | National Income | | | | | Personal Income | | | | |
Year	First Quarter	Second Quarter	Third Quarter	Fourth Quarter	Total	First Quarter	Second Quarter	Third Quarter	Fourth Quarter	Total	First Quarter	Second Quarter	Third Quarter	Fourth Quarter	Total
2014	17,144	17,463	17,743	17,853	17,551	14,826	15,141	15,412	15,533	15,228	14,625	14,875	15,100	15,307	14,977
2015	17,991	18,194	18,307	18,332	18,206	15,605	15,747	15,808	15,839	15,750	15,498	15,640	15,757	15,846	15,685
2016	18,425	18,612	18,776	18,968	18,695	15,905	15,911	16,056	16,261	16,033	15,919	16,002	16,152	16,315	16,097
2017	19,148	19,305	19,562	19,895	19,477	16,474	16,633	16,838	17,122	16,767	16,552	16,741	16,921	17,145	16,840
2018	20,156	20,470	20,687	20,819	20,533	17,364	17,530	17,793	17,960	17,662	17,355	17,551	17,801	18,029	17,684
2019	21,013	21,272	21,532	21,707	21,381	18,110	18,256	18,365	18,580	18,328	18,345	18,505	18,656	18,842	18,587
2020	21,538	19,637	21,362	21,705	21,060	18,611	16,507	17,773	18,688	17,895	19,034	20,479	20,019	19,797	19,832
2021	22,600	23,292	23,829	24,655	23,594	19,167	19,631	20,077	20,764	19,910	22,162	21,046	21,138	21,284	21,408
2022	25,029	25,544	25,995	26,408	25,744	21,150	21,638	21,973	21,954	21,678	21,411	21,660	22,019	22,274	21,841
2023¹	26,814	27,063	27,610	27,939	27,356	22,137	22,242	22,498		22,292	22,644	22,868	23,064	23,289	22,966

¹ Seasonally adjusted at annual rates.   ² Preliminary.   *Source: Bureau of Economic Analysis, U.S. Department of Commerce (BEA)*

INTEREST RATES - U.S.

U.S. Money Supply M1[2]   In Billions of Dollars

Year	Jan.	Feb.	Mar.	Apr.	May	June	July	Aug.	Sept.	Oct.	Nov.	Dec.	Average
2014	2,696.4	2,726.4	2,754.8	2,778.6	2,795.2	2,829.5	2,841.6	2,802.9	2,862.2	2,868.8	2,884.9	2,940.7	2,815.2
2015	2,941.0	3,007.1	2,999.6	3,000.9	2,986.6	3,020.0	3,039.7	3,028.5	3,044.2	3,018.6	3,081.7	3,094.9	3,021.9
2016	3,099.0	3,130.4	3,151.1	3,200.3	3,238.7	3,245.7	3,247.9	3,315.1	3,326.5	3,335.7	3,354.1	3,342.4	3,248.9
2017	3,390.9	3,404.7	3,445.5	3,454.2	3,517.3	3,525.9	3,550.9	3,580.7	3,574.2	3,606.7	3,630.6	3,612.0	3,524.5
2018	3,668.4	3,633.9	3,672.5	3,653.6	3,646.2	3,644.7	3,669.2	3,682.7	3,692.3	3,721.5	3,708.4	3,771.2	3,680.4
2019	3,772.9	3,783.4	3,746.4	3,770.6	3,775.4	3,813.4	3,844.8	3,844.0	3,887.7	3,926.1	3,955.6	4,011.2	3,844.3
2020	3,978.6	3,981.4	4,261.0	4,794.5	16,244.2	16,559.7	16,767.2	16,878.5	17,158.6	17,357.2	17,609.1	17,827.5	12,784.8
2021	18,099.3	18,362.7	18,634.8	18,933.6	19,266.7	19,358.9	19,534.4	19,733.7	19,865.8	20,034.8	20,250.0	20,494.7	19,380.8
2022	20,506.3	20,533.7	20,664.5	20,650.7	20,638.8	20,607.5	20,588.5	20,479.7	20,280.9	20,099.2	19,964.9	19,820.9	20,403.0
2023[1]	19,555.0	19,312.3	18,938.4	18,591.7	18,560.1	18,490.3	18,428.1	18,303.5	18,171.7	18,080.9	18,045.9	18,101.4	18,548.3

[1] Preliminary.   [2] M1 -- The sum of currency held outside the vaults of depository institutions, Federal Reserve Banks, and the U.S. Treasury; travelers checks; and demand and other checkable deposits issued by financial institutions (except demand deposits due to the Treasury and depository institutions), minus cash items in process of collection and Federal Reserve float. Seasonally adjusted.   *Source: Board of Governors of the Federal Reserve System*

U.S. Money Supply M2[2]   In Billions of Dollars

Year	Jan.	Feb.	Mar.	Apr.	May	June	July	Aug.	Sept.	Oct.	Nov.	Dec.	Average
2014	11,066.4	11,148.9	11,190.5	11,246.9	11,314.6	11,366.8	11,428.0	11,457.3	11,492.2	11,552.6	11,591.7	11,670.3	11,377.2
2015	11,733.4	11,852.6	11,869.0	11,916.4	11,947.8	11,993.3	12,045.5	12,097.0	12,154.0	12,187.9	12,277.7	12,336.1	12,034.2
2016	12,461.5	12,533.7	12,595.4	12,685.0	12,751.2	12,819.6	12,880.8	12,968.2	13,031.5	13,105.4	13,178.6	13,209.8	12,851.7
2017	13,282.5	13,340.2	13,405.5	13,470.3	13,520.9	13,550.8	13,616.1	13,671.0	13,716.9	13,779.0	13,809.5	13,852.0	13,584.6
2018	13,872.0	13,914.6	13,971.2	14,001.3	14,066.0	14,125.8	14,155.2	14,197.7	14,228.4	14,235.8	14,254.9	14,373.9	14,116.4
2019	14,443.3	14,486.2	14,533.5	14,568.9	14,668.4	14,787.0	14,857.9	14,935.2	15,026.6	15,153.1	15,251.3	15,325.8	14,836.4
2020	15,396.0	15,450.3	15,978.7	16,997.6	17,851.1	18,131.7	18,286.3	18,346.0	18,577.3	18,729.1	18,949.3	19,114.6	17,650.7
2021	19,357.5	19,600.6	19,840.8	20,116.8	20,431.1	20,506.7	20,663.1	20,847.8	20,964.3	21,115.6	21,315.7	21,549.3	20,525.8
2022	21,562.3	21,570.7	21,697.8	21,677.2	21,665.5	21,666.1	21,703.5	21,659.6	21,525.1	21,433.2	21,399.3	21,358.3	21,576.6
2023[1]	21,221.7	21,099.8	20,876.0	20,705.4	20,820.8	20,854.5	20,863.8	20,825.6	20,755.4	20,725.7	20,767.5	20,865.2	20,865.1

[1] Preliminary.   [2] M2 -- M1 plus savings deposits (including money market deposit accounts) and small-denomination (less than $100,000) time deposits issued by financial institutions; and shares in retail money market mutual funds (funds with initial investments of less than $50,000), net of retirement accounts. Seasonally adjusted.   *Source: Board of Governors of the Federal Reserve System*

Shaded areas indicate US recessions.

PRIME RATE AND DISCOUNT RATE
Quarterly Cash as of 03/28/2024

PRIME RATE = 8.50
% DISCOUNT RATE = 5.50

Shaded areas indicate US recessions.

US GROSS FEDERAL DEBT and SURPLUS OR DEFICIT
Quarterly Cash as of 03/29/2024

US GROSS FEDERAL DEBT = 32989.0
US FEDERAL SURPLUS OR DEFICIT = -1694

Billion USD

Shaded areas indicate US recessions.

INTEREST RATES - U.S.

Key Interest Rates
Weekly Cash as of 03/28/2024

PRIME RATE	= 8.50
T-BOND YIELD, 30-YEAR	= 4.340
DISCOUNT RATE	= 5.50
T-BILL RATE, 3-MONTH	= 5.2300

Points of 100%

Shaded areas indicate US recessions.

5-YEAR TREASURY NOTE YIELD
Quarterly Cash as of 03/28/2024

Shaded areas indicate US recessions.

Interest Rates - Worldwide

Interest rate futures contracts are widely traded throughout the world. The most popular futures contracts are generally 10-year government bonds and 3-month interest rate contracts. In Europe, futures on German interest rates are traded at the Eurex Exchange. Futures on UK interest rates are traded at the ICE Futures Europe exchange in London. Futures on Canadian interest rates are traded at the Montreal Exchange. Futures on Japanese interest rates are traded at the Singapore Exchange (SGX) and at the Tokyo Stock Exchange. A variety of other interest rate futures contracts are traded throughout the rest of the world.

Eurozone – The Eurex German 10-year Euro Bund futures contract (Barchart.com symbol GG) moved slightly higher during 2023 and closed the year up +4.29 points at 137.22. The Eurex French 10-year OAT bond futures contract (Barchart.com symbol FN) also moved slightly higher during 2023 and closed the year up +4.21 points at 131.51. The Eurex Italy Euro BTP 10-year bond futures contract (Barchart.com symbol II) moved higher during 2023 and closed the year up +10.23 points at 119.15.

European 10-year bond prices posted their highs for the year in January 2023 on hopes that the European Central Bank (ECB) might slow its pace of monetary tightening after media reports said the ECB was considering raising interest rates by only +25 bp at the March policy meeting after a +50 bp rate hike in February.

At its February meeting, the ECB raised the deposit facility rate by +50 bp to 2.50% and said, "Rates still have to rise significantly." That fueled a slide in 10-year bund prices to a 12-year low in March. The ECB, at its March meeting, raised its deposit facility rate again by +50 bp to 3.00% and said, "Inflation is projected to remain too high for too long."

Inflation in the Eurozone remained sticky, with the Eurozone CPI in April rising to +7.0% yr/yr from +6.9% yr/yr in March, well above the ECB's 2.0% target. Despite the inflation pressures, the ECB slowed its tightening pace and raised the deposit facility rate by only +25 bp at its May meeting and by another +25 bp in June to 3.50%. The ECB maintained a hawkish stance in June as ECB President Lagarde said the ECB still had ground to cover in raising rates and was "very likely" to raise rates again at its July meeting.

The ECB in July raised its deposit facility rate by +25 bp to 3.75% and then raised that rate by another +25 bp to 4.00% at its September meeting. The ECB in September maintained its hawkish guidance as ECB President Lagarde said the ECB would keep rates "at sufficiently restrictive levels" as "inflation is still seen as too high for too long." Bund prices sold off into October and posted a 12-year low. The 10-year bund yield rose to a 12-year high of 3.03%.

European bond prices recovered into year-end as inflation pressures eased, with the Eurozone November CPI falling to a 2-1/2 year low of 2.4% yr/yr. That allowed the ECB to put its rate hike regime on a permanent hold at its October and December policy meetings.

UK – The ICE UK 10-year gilt government bond futures contract (Barchart.com symbol G) traded sideways to lower for most of 2023, but then rebounded in Q4 and finished the year up slightly by +2.75 points. Gilt prices posted their high for 2023 in early February after the Bank of England (BOE), at its February policy meeting, raised its benchmark rate by +50 basis points to 4.00%, but BOE Governor Bailey said he was "seeing the first signs that inflation has turned a corner." Gilt prices then ratcheted lower into August when the 10-year gilt yield climbed to a 15-year high of 4.752%. The BOE remained hawkish as it raised rates into August and lifted the benchmark rate to 5.25%. The BOE then paused its rate hike campaign at its September policy meeting and kept the benchmark rate at 5.25% for the rest of the year as the economy cooled and inflation slowed. UK Q3 GDP in Q3 grew at a pace of only +0.2% y/y, the slowest since the pandemic. In November, the headline UK CPI eased to +3.9% yr/yr, and core CPI eased to a 2-year low of 5.1% yr/yr. The slowdown in the economy and inflation fueled a rally in gilts in Q4 on expectations the BOE was done raising rates and would soon pivot toward easing monetary policy.

Canada – The Montreal Exchange's Canadian 10-year government note futures contract (Barchart.com symbol CG) in 2023 rebounded from a 16-year low in October and closed the year slightly higher by +1.63 points. The Bank of Canada (BOC) raised its benchmark rate for an eighth consecutive meeting in January 2023 to 4.50% but declared a potential end to rate hikes. The BOC maintained a steady policy until June, when it unexpectedly raised the benchmark rate by +25 bp to 4.75%, saying the Canadian economy remained "clearly in excess demand." The BOC raised rates again at the July meeting by another +25 basis points to 5.00% and then held rates steady for the remainder of the year as inflation subsided, with Canada's June CPI falling to a 3-year low of 2.8% yr/yr. After falling to a 16-year nearest-futures low of 112.59 (CGZ23) in October, Canadian bond prices recovered into year-end as the economy slowed. At its December meeting, the BOC said the economy "was no longer" in excess demand, signaling a definitive end to the BOC's string of rate hikes.

Japan – The SGX Japan 10-year Japanese government bond (JGB) futures contract (Barchart.com symbol JX) began 2023 on a weak note and fell to a 10-year nearest-futures low in January. Japanese bond prices retreated due to soaring inflation pressures after Japan's January CPI jumped to a 42-year high of +4.3% yr/yr. Japanese bond prices then recovered to the high for 2023 in March as the failure of SVB Financial sparked banking turmoil in the US and fueled a global bond rally that eased the pressure on the Bank of Japan (BOJ) to raise interest rates. Japanese bond prices then ratcheted lower into October based on expectations that the BOJ would end its negative interest rate policy. The BOJ began preparing the markets for a normalization of monetary policy when it raised the upper limit for its 10-year JGB bond yield target range to 1.0% from 0.5% at its July meeting. The 10-year Japanese government bond futures price in October sank to a 10-year low after the BOJ raised its inflation forecast and removed the 1.0% upper limit for its 10-year bond yield target range at its October policy meeting. That action pushed the 10-year JGB bond yield up to a 10-year high of 0.974% in November. However, Japanese bond prices recovered into year-end after Japan's Q3 real GDP fell -3.2% (yr/yr annualized), the largest decline in 3-1/2 years. 10-year Japanese bond prices finished 2023 slightly higher by +1.06 points at 146.53.

INTEREST RATES - WORLDWIDE

GILT, LONG - ICE-LIFF
Weekly Nearest Futures as of 03/28/2024

WEEKLY NEAREST FUTURES
As of 03/28/2024

| Chart High | 140.32 | on 03/09/2020 |
| Chart Low | 90.38 | on 10/12/2022 |

Points- 100ths

% Yield Basis
6% 10-Yr

Nearby Futures through Last Trading Day.

STERLING, 3-MONTH - ICE-LIFF
Weekly Selected Futures as of 12/17/2021

WEEKLY SELECTED FUTURES
As of 12/17/2021

| Chart High | 100.0300 | on 01/06/2021 |
| Chart Low | 99.0450 | on 12/21/2018 |

Points of 100%

% Yield Basis
100 - Price

Nearby Futures through Last Trading Day.

JAPANESE GOVT BOND, 10-YEAR - JPX
Weekly Nearest Futures as of 03/29/2024

WEEKLY NEAREST FUTURES
As of 03/29/2024
Chart High 155.89   on 03/10/2020
Chart Low   143.44   on 11/01/2023

Points- 100ths

% Yield Basis
6% 10-Yr

Nearby Futures through Last Trading Day.

EUROYEN, 3-MONTH - TIFFE
Weekly Nearest Futures as of 03/29/2024

WEEKLY NEAREST FUTURES
As of 03/29/2024
Chart High 100.075   on 08/10/2021
Chart Low   99.780   on 01/14/2014

Points of 100%

% Yield Basis
100 - Price

Nearby Futures through Last Trading Day.

CANADIAN GOVT BOND, 10-YR - MNTRL
Weekly Nearest Futures as of 03/28/2024

WEEKLY NEAREST FUTURES
As of 03/28/2024

| Chart High | 155.220 | on 07/31/2020 |
| Chart Low | 112.590 | on 10/04/2023 |

Points- 100ths of pt

% Yield Basis
6% 10-Yr

Nearby Futures through Last Trading Day.

CAN. BANKERS' ACCEPTANCE, 3-MO - MNTRL
Weekly Selected Futures as of 03/28/2024

WEEKLY SELECTED FUTURES
As of 03/28/2024

| Chart High | 99.600 | on 01/18/2021 |
| Chart Low | 94.210 | on 09/21/2023 |

Points of 100%

% Yield Basis
100 - Price

Nearby Futures through Last Trading Day.

174

Australia -- Economic Statistics   Percentage Change from Previous Period

Year	Real GDP	Nominal GDP	Real Private Consump- tion	Real Public Consump- tion	Grossed Fixed Invest- ment	Real Total Domestic Demand	Real Exports of Goods & Services	Real Imports of Goods & Services	Consumer Prices[3]	Unem- ployment Rate
2015	2.3	1.6	2.4	4.1	-4.0	1.3	6.1	2.0	1.5	6.1
2016	2.7	3.8	2.6	5.4	-2.3	1.9	6.7	.4	1.3	5.7
2017	2.4	6.1	2.4	3.9	3.4	2.8	3.7	7.8	2.0	5.6
2018	2.8	5.1	2.4	4.1	2.5	3.0	5.1	4.5	1.9	5.3
2019	2.0	5.3	.8	6.4	-2.6	2.6	3.1	-1.8	1.6	5.2
2020	-2.2	-1.3	-5.8	7.3	-2.9	2.9	-9.5	-12.9	.9	6.5
2021	4.9	10.6	5.0	5.4	9.8		-2.1	6.5	2.8	5.1
2022[1]	4.0	11.1	7.0	5.4	8.3		2.7	12.2	6.5	3.7
2023[2]	1.9	4.8	2.0	1.2	2.4		5.0	3.7	4.5	3.5

[1] Estimate.   [2] Projection.   [3] National accounts implicit private consumption deflator.   *Source: Organization for Economic Co-operation and Development (OECD)*

Canada -- Economic Statistics   Percentage Change from Previous Period

Year	Real GDP	Nominal GDP	Real Private Consump- tion	Real Public Consump- tion	Grossed Fixed Invest- ment	Real Total Domestic Demand	Real Exports of Goods & Services	Real Imports of Goods & Services	Consumer Prices[3]	Unem- ployment Rate
2015	.7	-.2	2.3	1.4	-5.2	-.1	3.4	.8	1.1	6.9
2016	1.0	1.8	2.1	1.8	-4.7	.7	1.4	.1	1.4	7.0
2017	3.0	5.7	3.7	2.1	3.3	3.9	1.4	4.6	1.6	6.4
2018	2.8	4.4	2.6	3.2	2.5	1.7	3.8	3.3	2.2	5.9
2019	1.9	3.4	1.4	1.7	.0	.6	2.3	.4	2.0	5.7
2020	-5.2	-4.5	-6.1	.0	-2.8	1.7	-9.7	-10.8	.7	9.5
2021	4.5	13.0	4.9	5.8	7.1		1.4	7.7	3.4	7.4
2022[1]	3.2	11.8	5.4	1.6	.0		2.3	8.7	6.8	5.4
2023[2]	1.0	3.7	2.0	.7	.3		2.4	3.8	4.1	5.7

[1] Estimate.   [2] Projection.   [3] National accounts implicit private consumption deflator.   *Source: Organization for Economic Co-operation and Development (OECD)*

France -- Economic Statistics   Percentage Change from Previous Period

Year	Real GDP	Nominal GDP	Real Private Consump- tion	Real Public Consump- tion	Grossed Fixed Invest- ment	Real Total Domestic Demand	Real Exports of Goods & Services	Real Imports of Goods & Services	Consumer Prices[3]	Unem- ployment Rate
2015	1.1	2.2	1.4	1.0	.9	1.5	4.5	5.6	.1	10.4
2016	1.0	1.5	1.6	1.4	2.5	1.6	1.6	2.8	.3	10.1
2017	2.4	3.0	1.6	1.4	5.0	2.2	4.6	4.7	1.2	9.5
2018	1.8	2.8	1.0	.8	3.2	.9	4.5	3.1	2.1	9.1
2019	1.9	3.2	1.8	1.0	4.1	1.3	1.6	2.4	1.3	8.5
2020	-7.9	-5.3	-6.8	-4.0	-8.4	1.3	-17.0	-13.0	.5	8.1
2021	6.8	8.2	5.3	6.4	11.4		8.6	7.8	2.1	7.9
2022[1]	2.6	5.0	2.5	2.4	2.0		7.5	8.5	5.9	7.4
2023[2]	.6	4.0	.4	.5	1.1		2.8	3.0	5.7	7.7

[1] Estimate.   [2] Projection.   [3] National accounts implicit private consumption deflator.   *Source: Organization for Economic Co-operation and Development (OECD)*

Germany -- Economic Statistics   Percentage Change from Previous Period

Year	Real GDP	Nominal GDP	Real Private Consump- tion	Real Public Consump- tion	Grossed Fixed Invest- ment	Real Total Domestic Demand	Real Exports of Goods & Services	Real Imports of Goods & Services	Consumer Prices[3]	Unem- ployment Rate
2015	1.2	3.1	1.8	2.9	1.2	1.4	4.9	5.3	.7	4.4
2016	2.1	3.5	2.2	4.0	3.6	2.9	2.3	4.4	.4	3.9
2017	3.0	4.5	1.7	1.7	3.3	2.2	5.6	5.7	1.7	3.5
2018	1.0	3.0	1.5	.8	3.4	1.9	2.4	4.1	1.9	3.2
2019	1.1	3.2	1.7	2.6	2.0	1.6	1.3	2.9	1.4	3.0
2020	-4.1	-2.3	-5.9	4.0	-3.0	1.5	-10.1	-9.1	.4	3.7
2021	2.6	5.7	.4	3.8	1.0		9.5	8.9	3.2	3.6
2022[1]	1.8	7.6	4.5	3.8	.3		1.8	5.8	8.5	3.1
2023[2]	-.3	6.8	-.2	-.7	.4		1.7	2.1	8.0	3.5

[1] Estimate.   [2] Projection.   [3] National accounts implicit private consumption deflator.   *Source: Organization for Economic Co-operation and Development (OECD)*

INTEREST RATES - WORLDWIDE

Italy -- Economic Statistics   Percentage Change from Previous Period

Year	Real GDP	Nominal GDP	Real Private Consumption	Real Public Consumption	Grossed Fixed Investment	Real Total Domestic Demand	Real Exports of Goods & Services	Real Imports of Goods & Services	Consumer Prices[3]	Unemployment Rate
2015	.6	1.6	1.9	-.6	1.5	1.4	4.1	6.3	.1	12.0
2016	1.4	2.6	1.2	.7	4.2	1.6	2.0	4.2	-.1	11.7
2017	1.7	2.5	1.5	-.1	3.4	1.4	6.0	6.6	1.3	11.3
2018	.8	1.9	1.0	.1	2.8	.9	1.6	2.8	1.2	10.6
2019	.5	1.4	.2	-.6	1.2	-.2	1.8	-.5	.6	9.9
2020	-9.1	-7.6	-10.4	.0	-8.2	.6	-14.2	-12.7	-.1	9.3
2021	6.7	7.3	5.1	1.5	16.5		13.5	14.8	1.9	9.5
2022[1]	3.7	7.0	3.4	.0	8.7		10.4	12.9	8.1	8.1
2023[2]	.2	5.1	.2	-.7	.9		1.8	1.7	6.5	8.3

[1] Estimate.   [2] Projection.   [3] National accounts implicit private consumption deflator.   *Source: Organization for Economic Co-operation and Development (OECD)*

Japan -- Economic Statistics   Percentage Change from Previous Period

Year	Real GDP	Nominal GDP	Real Private Consumption	Real Public Consumption	Grossed Fixed Investment	Real Total Domestic Demand	Real Exports of Goods & Services	Real Imports of Goods & Services	Consumer Prices[3]	Unemployment Rate
2015	1.6	3.7	-.2	1.9	2.3	.8	3.2	.4	.8	3.4
2016	.8	1.2	-.4	1.6	1.2	.0	1.6	-1.2	-.1	3.1
2017	1.7	1.6	1.1	.1	1.6	1.4	6.6	3.3	.5	2.8
2018	.6	.6	.2	1.0	.6	.8	3.8	3.8	1.0	2.4
2019	-.4	.3	-.5	1.9	.5	1.0	-1.5	1.0	.5	2.4
2020	-4.6	-3.7	-5.2	2.3	-4.9	.2	-11.6	-6.7		2.8
2021	1.6	.8	1.3	2.1	-1.5		11.8	5.1	-.2	2.8
2022[1]	1.6	1.3	2.9	1.8	-1.0		4.6	7.4	2.3	2.6
2023[2]	1.8	3.0	1.4	.1	3.7		2.9	2.4	2.0	2.5

[1] Estimate.   [2] Projection.   [3] National accounts implicit private consumption deflator.   *Source: Organization for Economic Co-operation and Development (OECD)*

Switzerland -- Economic Statistics   Percentage Change from Previous Period

Year	Real GDP	Nominal GDP	Real Private Consumption	Real Public Consumption	Grossed Fixed Investment	Real Total Domestic Demand	Real Exports of Goods & Services	Real Imports of Goods & Services	Consumer Prices[3]	Unemployment Rate
2015	1.6	.3	2.5	.7	2.1	2.2	3.8	4.8	-1.1	4.8
2016	2.1	1.5	1.6	.3	2.6	.3	6.0	5.2	-.4	4.9
2017	1.4	1.1	1.2	1.0	3.5	1.5	-.2	-.3	.5	4.8
2018	2.9	3.7	.6	.8	.8	.2	3.3	.7	.9	4.7
2019	1.2	1.1	1.2	.8	.9	.9	-.6	.3	.4	4.4
2020	-2.5	-3.3	-4.2	3.5	-3.1	1.7	-5.5	-3.0	-.7	4.8
2021	4.2	5.3	1.7	3.5	4.1		12.2	4.9	.6	5.1
2022[1]	2.1	5.1	3.7	.9	.1		.4	2.1	2.9	4.4
2023[2]	.6	2.8	.7	-.2	.6		.7	2.0	2.5	4.6

[1] Estimate.   [2] Projection.   [3] National accounts implicit private consumption deflator.   *Source: Organization for Economic Co-operation and Development (OECD)*

United Kingdom -- Economic Statistics   Percentage Change from Previous Period

Year	Real GDP	Nominal GDP	Real Private Consumption	Real Public Consumption	Grossed Fixed Investment	Real Total Domestic Demand	Real Exports of Goods & Services	Real Imports of Goods & Services	Consumer Prices[3]	Unemployment Rate
2015	2.4	3.1	3.1	1.2	6.5	2.7	4.0	5.0	.1	5.4
2016	2.2	4.1	3.6	.8	4.9	2.4	3.2	4.0	.6	4.9
2017	2.4	4.3	1.9	.4	3.5	1.4	6.8	3.3	2.7	4.4
2018	1.7	3.5	2.5	.3	-.2	1.6	3.1	3.3	2.5	4.1
2019	1.6	3.8	1.1	4.1	1.9	3.6	1.7	2.6	1.8	3.8
2020	-11.0	-5.8	-13.2	-7.3	-10.5	.9	-12.1	-16.0	.9	4.6
2021	7.5	7.9	6.2	12.6	5.6		-.3	2.8	2.6	4.5
2022[1]	4.4	9.5	4.7	1.6	5.6		9.7	12.4	8.9	3.7
2023[2]	-.4	4.3	-1.1	2.3	1.0		5.5	-.5	6.6	4.3

[1] Estimate.   [2] Projection.   [3] National accounts implicit private consumption deflator.   *Source: Organization for Economic Co-operation and Development (OECD)*

Iron and Steel

Iron (atomic symbol Fe) is a soft, malleable, and ductile metallic element. Next to aluminum, iron is the most abundant of all metals. Pure iron melts at about 1535 degrees Celsius and boils at 2750 degrees Celsius. Archaeologists in Egypt discovered the earliest iron implements dating back to about 3000 BC, and iron ornaments were used even earlier.

Steel is an alloy of iron and carbon, often with an admixture of other elements. The physical properties of various types of steel and steel alloys depend primarily on the amount of carbon present and how it is distributed in the iron. Steel is marketed in a variety of sizes and shapes, such as rods, pipes, railroad rails, tees, channels, and I-beams. Steel mills roll and form heated ingots into the required shapes. The working of steel improves the quality of the steel by refining its crystalline structure and making the metal tougher. There are five classifications of steel: carbon steels, alloy steels, high-strength low-alloy steels, stainless steel, and tool steels.

Prices – In 2023, the average wholesale price for No. 1 heavy-melting steel scrap in Chicago fell by -9.6% yr/yr to $343.33 per metric ton.

Supply – World production of iron ore in 2022 fell by -3.0% yr/yr to 2.600 billion metric tons. The world's largest producers of iron ore are Australia with 33.8% of world production, Brazil with 15.8%, and China with 14.6%. The US accounted for only 1.8% of world iron ore production.

World production of raw steel (ingots and castings) in 2023 rose by +1.1 % yr/yr to 1.900 billion metric tons. The largest producers were China with 52.6% of world production, Japan with 4.6%, and the US with 4.2%. US production of steel ingots in 2023 fell by -0.6% yr/yr at 80.000 million metric tons. US production of pig iron (excluding ferro-alloys) in 2022 fell by -9.4% yr/yr to 21.200 million short tons.

Demand – US consumption of ferrous scrap and pig iron in 2021 rose by +2.3% yr/yr to 63.270 million metric tons. The largest consumers of ferrous scrap and pig iron were the manufacturers of steel ingots and castings, with 89.8% of consumption. Iron foundries and miscellaneous users accounted for 5.1% of consumption, and manufacturers of steel castings (scrap) accounted for 3.2% of consumption.

World Production of Raw Steel (Ingots and Castings) In Thousands of Metric Tons

Year	Brazil	Canada	China	France	Germany	Italy	Japan	Korea, South	Russia	Ukraine	United Kindom	United States	World Total
2014	33,912	12,730	822,300	16,143	42,943	23,714	110,666	71,542	70,548	27,373	12,120	88,200	1,670,000
2015	33,258	12,473	803,820	14,984	42,674	22,018	103,134	69,670	69,422	22,935	10,907	78,800	1,610,000
2016	31,642	12,646	807,610	14,413	42,081	23,373	104,775	68,575	70,808	24,197	7,635	78,500	1,630,000
2017	34,778	13,208	870,740	15,505	43,297	24,068	104,661	71,030	71,300	21,417	7,491	81,600	1,740,000
2018	35,407	13,443	920,027	15,387	42,435	24,496	104,319	72,463	71,682	21,101	7,268	86,600	1,820,000
2019	32,236	12,897	995,419	14,451	39,627	23,190	99,284	71,411	71,729	20,848	7,218	87,800	1,870,000
2020	31,415	10,986	1,064,767	11,596	35,658	20,379	83,186	67,098	71,621	20,616	7,086	72,700	1,880,000
2021	36,039	12,977	1,033,000	13,947	40,066	24,400	96,334	70,556	75,585	21,366	7,346	85,800	1,950,000
2022[1]	34,000	12,000	1,020,000		37,000	22,000	89,000	66,000	72,000	6,000		80,500	1,880,000
2023[2]	34,000	12,000	1,000,000		33,000	20,000	87,000	68,000	75,000	7,000		80,000	1,900,000

[1] Preliminary. [2] Estimate. *Source: U.S. Geological Survey (USGS)*

Average Wholesale Prices of Iron and Steel in the United States

	No. 1 Heavy Melting Steel Scrap		Sheet Bars			Pittsburg Prices					
	Pittsburg	Chicago	Hot Rolled	Hot Rolled	Cold Finished	Hot Rolled Strip	Carbon Steel Plates	Cold Rolled Strip	Galvanized Sheets	Rail Road Steel Scrap[2]	Used Steel Cans[3]
Year	----- $ Per Gross Ton -----		------------------ Cents Per Pound ------------------							---- $ Per Gross Ton ----	
2002	101.06	89.92	16.46	----	23.26	----	----	----	22.00	NA	66.71
2003	128.32	113.82	14.80	----	25.15	----	----	----	20.08	----	116.21
2004	221.05	220.13	30.84	----	38.67	----	----	----	36.69	----	192.80
2005	199.10	196.75	27.83	----	44.96	----	----	----	33.77	----	172.00
2006	222.39	225.21	29.78	----	44.02	----	----	----	38.09	----	212.63
2007	250.98	262.80	26.89	----	45.26	----	----	----	38.25	----	244.65
2008	365.62	357.88	44.56	----	61.67	----	----	----	54.91	----	314.63
2009	204.21	206.14	24.60	----	42.10	----	----	----	34.23	----	121.84
2010	339.54	334.48	31.65	----	50.82	----	----	----	41.72	----	296.91
2011[1]	408.64	417.00	38.02	----	63.63	----	----	----	48.45	----	391.50

[1] Preliminary. [2] Specialties scrap. [3] Consumer buying prices. NA = Not available. *Source: American Metal Market (AMM)*

IRON AND STEEL

Salient Statistics of Steel in the United States   In Thousands of Short Tons

Year	Pig Iron Production	Producer Price Index for Steel Mill Products (1982=100)	Raw Steel Production By Type of Furnace — Basic Oxygen	Open Hearth	Electric[2]	Stainless	Carbon	Alloy	Total	Net Shipments Steel Mill Products	Total Steel Products — Exports	Imports
2014	29,400	200.2	----	----	----	2,634	89,727	4,872	97,223	89,100	10,900	40,200
2015	25,400	177.1	----	----	----	2,590	81,129	3,230	86,861	78,500	9,050	35,200
2016	22,300	167.8	----	----	----	2,734	80,688	3,108	86,531	78,500	8,450	30,000
2017	22,400	187.4	----	----	----	3,031	83,444	3,494	89,948	82,500	9,550	34,600
2018	24,100	211.1	----	----	----	3,097	87,192	5,225	95,459	86,400	7,980	30,600
2019	22,300	204.0	----	----	----	2,855	88,735	5,159	96,782	87,300	6,700	25,300
2020	18,300	184.4	----	----	----	2,359	73,964	3,858	80,137	73,500	6,090	20,000
2021	22,200	350.9	----	----	----	2,612	86,751	5,159	94,577	85,900	7,500	28,500
2022	19,800	382.5	----	----	----							
2023[1]	21,000	325.0	----	----	----							

[1] Preliminary.   [2] Includes crucible steels.   *Sources: American Iron & Steel Institute (AISI); U.S. Geological Survey (USGS)*

Production of Steel Ingots, Rate of Capability Utilization[1] in the United States   In Percent

Year	Jan.	Feb.	Mar.	Apr.	May	June	July	Aug.	Sept.	Oct.	Nov.	Dec.	Average
2014	75.8	77.9	77.7	76.6	77.3	78.5	79.6	80.2	78.1	76.5	77.2	74.6	77.5
2015	76.4	72.1	67.7	69.8	72.1	74.4	73.2	72.2	70.5	68.1	62.7	62.1	70.1
2016	68.7	73.1	72.1	72.6	74.3	75.1	71.3	70.8	68.0	65.4	67.1	67.8	70.5
2017	73.3	75.9	73.6	73.6	73.7	74.9	74.3	75.8	73.4	73.2	73.3	71.9	73.9
2018	73.6	77.9	78.3	76.0	77.1	77.4	78.4	79.4	79.6	80.2	81.2	79.4	78.2
2019	80.4	82.4	82.2	81.3	80.8	80.1	79.4	79.1	77.4	78.0	78.8	78.5	79.9
2020	81.7	81.3	75.3	55.4	54.6	56.8	60.3	65.9	68.6	70.1	73.3	72.9	68.0
2021	76.6	76.8	78.0	80.8	81.0	83.0	84.4	84.8	83.3	83.2	82.7	80.1	81.2
2022	79.8	80.8	78.7	81.9	81.1	79.6	78.1	78.0	76.4	73.7	71.5	70.6	77.5
2023[1]	73.0	75.5	75.7	76.5	76.3	77.9	76.2	76.6	76.4	72.4	73.4	74.2	75.3

[1] Based on tonnage capability to produce raw steel for a full order book.   [2] Preliminary.   *Sources: American Iron and Steel Institute (AISI); U.S. Geological Survey (USGS)*

World Production of Pig Iron (Excludes Ferro-Alloys)   In Thousands of Metric Tons

Year	Belgium	Brazil	China	France	Germany	India	Italy	Japan	Russia	Ukraine	United Kingdom	United States	World Total
2014	4,388	27,016	713,740	10,866	27,379	55,166	6,371	83,872	51,460	24,801	9,705	29,400	1,260,000
2015	4,248	27,803	691,410	10,097	27,844	58,393	5,051	81,011	52,411	21,878	8,774	25,400	1,240,000
2016	4,869	26,129	702,270	9,724	27,269	63,714	6,048	80,186	51,874	23,560	6,142	22,300	1,250,000
2017	4,849	28,331	713,620	10,678	27,816	66,808	5,052	78,330	52,127	20,123	5,996	22,400	1,280,000
2018	4,754	28,655	779,880	10,530	27,271	72,610	4,836	77,328	51,797	20,531	5,590	24,100	1,370,000
2019	4,818	26,280	808,494	9,877	25,520	74,156	4,607	74,907	51,184	20,056	5,622	22,300	1,390,000
2020	3,647	24,628	888,976	7,696	22,470	67,782	3,405	61,600	52,003	20,226	5,235	18,300	1,420,000
2021	4,180	28,403	868,570	9,470	25,674	77,849	3,925	70,344	53,600	21,165	5,805	22,200	1,460,000
2022[1]		27,000	866,000		24,000	80,000	3,000	64,000	52,000	6,000		19,800	1,300,000
2023[2]		26,000	890,000		22,000	87,000	3,000	63,000	54,000	7,000		21,000	1,300,000

[1] Preliminary.   [2] Estimate.   *Source: U.S. Geological Survey (USGS)*

Production of Pig Iron (Excludes Ferro-Alloys) in the United States   In Thousands of Short Tons

Year	Jan.	Feb.	Mar.	Apr.	May	June	July	Aug.	Sept.	Oct.	Nov.	Dec.	Total
2014	2,430	2,450	2,820	2,580	2,710	2,760	2,930	2,920	2,740	2,690	2,740	2,860	32,630
2015	2,760	2,310	2,390	2,330	2,530	2,670	2,830	2,690	2,390	2,270	2,120	2,110	29,400
2016	2,200	2,260	2,380	2,150	1,910	2,280	2,220	1,860	1,770	1,610	1,660	1,810	24,110
2017	1,940	1,930	1,960	1,870	1,940	1,830	1,860	1,930	1,850	1,690	1,770	1,840	22,410
2018	1,920	1,790	1,970	1,930	2,070	2,060	2,100	2,030	2,010	2,060	2,030	2,100	24,070
2019	1,880	1,840	2,080	1,860	1,930	1,900	1,830	1,840	1,870	1,700	1,720	1,850	22,300
2020	1,680	1,920	1,910	1,110	949	1,170	1,310	1,520	1,610	1,700	1,700	1,660	18,239
2021	1,870	1,760	1,950	1,920	2,020	1,970	2,040	2,050	1,950	2,010	1,930	1,940	23,410
2022	1,920	1,750	1,890	1,910	1,960	1,860	1,900	1,700	1,610	1,620	1,520	1,560	21,200
2023[1]	1,680	1,610	1,800	1,720	1,800	1,780	1,810	1,820	1,760	1,740	1,700	1,790	21,010

[1] Preliminary.   *Source: American Iron and Steel Institute*

Salient Statistics of Ferrous Scrap and Pig Iron in the United States   In Thousands of Metric Tons

	Mfg. of Pig Iron & Steel ---- Ingots & Castings ----			Iron Foundries ------ & Misc. Users -------			Mfg. of Steel Castings	---------- All Uses ----------			Imports of Scrap[2]	Exports of Scrap[3]	Stocks, Dec. 31 Ferrous Scrap & Pig ---- Iron at Consumers -----		
Year	Scrap	Pig Iron	Total	Scrap	Pig Iron	Total	(Scrap)	Ferrous Scrap	Pig Iron	Grand Total					Total
2012	55,800	35,400	94,780	6,710	1,980	8,693	639	63,100	37,400	104,080	3,720	21,400	4,170	405	4,722
2013	52,100	31,800	88,390	5,660	2,260	7,923	1,180	59,000	34,100	97,590	3,930	18,500	3,970	427	4,504
2014	51,900	25,900	82,590	5,560	2,100	7,663	1,190	58,600	28,100	91,490	4,220	15,300	4,070	442	4,729
2015	46,100	22,200	72,430	4,420	632	5,055	1,970	52,500	22,900	79,530	3,510	12,800	4,200	672	5,088
2016	44,900	20,700	70,380	5,020	1,620	6,643	3,100	53,000	22,400	80,180	3,860	12,600	4,340	440	5,017
2017	45,600	19,800	67,290	4,130	634	4,767	409	50,200	20,500	72,590	4,630	15,000	4,530	453	5,248
2018	47,200	16,700	66,270	3,890	654	4,547	682	51,800	17,400	71,570	5,030	17,100	5,050	577	5,961
2019	46,700	16,100	65,290	2,490	482	2,975	436	50,100	16,600	69,200	4,270	17,600	3,950	496	4,670
2020	41,700	13,300	57,420	2,720	454	3,177	794	45,200	14,100	61,850	4,510	14,900	3,950	347	4,509
2021[1]	41,300	13,200	56,830	2,750	471	3,224	2,020	46,100	14,200	63,270	5,260	15,700	4,440	498	5,290

[1] Preliminary.   [2] Includes tinplate and terneplate.   [3] Excludes used rails for rerolling and other uses and ships, boats, and other vessels for scrapping.
Source: U.S. Geological Survey (USGS)

Consumption of Pig Iron in the United States, by Type of Furance or Equipment   In Thousands of Metric Tons

Year	Open Hearth	Electric	Cupola	Basic Oxygen Process	Air & Other Furnace	Direct Casting	Total
2012	----	5,790	57	31,500	10	36	37,400
2013	----	4,150	345	29,600	----	----	34,100
2014	----	4,230	148	23,800	----	----	28,100
2015	----	2,350	152	20,300	----	----	22,900
2016	----	3,620	155	18,600	----	----	22,400
2017	----	3,310	160	17,000	----	----	20,500
2018	----	2,790	182	14,400	----	----	17,400
2019	----	W	W	13,900	----	----	16,600
2020	----	2,290	137	11,700	----	----	14,100
2021[1]	----	2,400	146	11,700	----	----	14,200

[1] Preliminary.   W = Withheld.   *Source: U.S. Geological Survey (USGS)*

Volume of Trading of Hot Rolled Steel Futures in New York   In Contracts

Year	Jan.	Feb.	Mar.	Apr.	May	June	July	Aug.	Sept.	Oct.	Nov.	Dec.	Total
2014	3,953	2,376	6,002	4,292	4,220	1,082	3,543	905	4,863	5,777	7,661	3,556	48,230
2015	3,096	2,344	4,705	6,489	4,084	3,083	6,478	6,156	7,222	6,559	5,405	3,196	58,817
2016	3,058	7,225	4,165	8,576	2,303	4,454	3,415	5,006	4,506	5,836	2,623	2,717	53,884
2017	5,501	2,870	2,897	1,182	7,188	4,905	6,639	7,316	7,495	7,107	4,598	5,531	63,229
2018	10,435	9,072	9,655	12,074	9,487	5,226	10,861	17,235	6,668	9,665	11,986	7,205	119,569
2019	21,700	15,281	13,165	19,031	28,415	14,031	13,715	5,113	9,200	14,616	10,396	9,093	173,756
2020	15,359	11,979	30,709	14,865	17,503	18,463	10,608	21,175	20,827	22,823	19,194	16,901	220,406
2021	24,250	21,666	20,714	21,954	20,976	18,215	19,341	14,950	24,003	23,211	17,776	19,761	246,817
2022	28,166	20,424	38,809	20,984	17,278	21,505	16,521	22,324	21,551	22,649	21,823	21,531	273,565
2023	28,241	43,713	33,568	21,027	20,014	32,789	25,264	20,230	27,035	32,628	27,131	17,730	329,370

Contract size = 20 short tons.   *Source: CME Group; New York Mercantile Exchange (CME-NYMEX)*

Average Open Interest of Hot Rolled Steel Futures in New York   In Contracts

Year	Jan.	Feb.	Mar.	Apr.	May	June	July	Aug.	Sept.	Oct.	Nov.	Dec.
2014	10,308	10,308	9,720	9,537	10,242	10,769	11,092	11,507	12,037	15,739	19,703	22,501
2015	21,609	20,954	18,637	18,859	19,351	19,356	20,474	20,783	21,273	22,758	23,472	24,299
2016	23,157	24,528	24,610	22,721	21,525	20,796	19,304	18,927	17,829	18,390	16,825	14,694
2017	13,068	12,862	13,145	12,646	12,815	13,952	13,369	14,007	14,493	14,065	13,384	13,600
2018	12,892	12,056	13,044	14,466	14,375	13,879	13,800	16,712	15,926	16,338	17,185	16,261
2019	17,430	20,320	19,221	17,425	18,040	18,600	17,519	16,597	15,791	14,393	15,249	15,535
2020	17,062	18,409	22,053	23,953	23,226	22,892	23,499	24,443	23,059	21,712	21,311	22,280
2021	23,040	25,836	29,109	31,690	32,270	32,562	31,293	31,891	35,619	38,615	38,812	39,800
2022	40,401	37,781	31,833	28,285	26,844	26,565	24,287	23,518	21,424	22,290	23,740	23,486
2023	23,802	24,245	28,017	28,117	27,033	26,225	23,519	20,794	20,507	19,629	18,359	19,481

Contract size = 20 short tons.   *Source: CME Group; New York Mercantile Exchange (CME-NYMEX)*

No. 1 Heavy

Wholesale Price of No. 1 Heavy Melting Steel Scrap in Chicago   In Dollars Per Metric Ton

Year	Jan.	Feb.	Mar.	Apr.	May	June	July	Aug.	Sept.	Oct.	Nov.	Dec.	Average
2014	414.29	396.00	378.10	383.64	373.67	362.90	362.55	363.00	364.71	350.13	322.11	317.43	365.71
2015	323.60	250.00	225.91	225.00	229.00	246.36	242.27	222.86	211.43	171.36	136.32	130.00	217.84
2016	146.84	150.00	180.43	221.43	246.19	233.64	222.00	220.00	204.76	183.81	198.75	235.48	203.61
2017	274.75	261.58	283.91	266.00	260.00	255.91	255.00	263.26	265.00	240.45	235.00	259.00	259.99
2018	289.29	295.00	319.55	341.19	336.82	335.00	340.00	321.74	300.26	303.26	324.00	325.00	319.26
2019	302.14	295.00	311.19	294.76	266.82	236.00	222.27	236.36	216.00	181.09	190.79	219.29	247.64
2020	249.29	239.21	235.00	201.67	210.50	215.00	207.27	205.00	239.29	245.00	252.89	320.45	235.05
2021	425.00	375.00	425.00	405.00	425.00	475.00	475.00	455.00	430.00	430.00	480.00	480.00	440.00
2022	410.00	410.00	535.00	515.00	440.00	390.00	360.00	330.00	305.00	295.00	275.00	295.00	380.00
2023	335.00	355.00	390.00	370.00	340.00	310.00	310.00	330.00	330.00	330.00	340.00	380.00	343.33

Source: American Metal Market (AMM)

World Production of Iron Ore[3]   In Thousands of Metric Tons (Gross Weight)

Year	Australia	Brazil	Canada	China	India	Maur-itania	Russia	South Africa	Sweden	Ukraine	United States	Venezula	World Total
2013	609,730	386,270	42,063	417,287	140,416	11,975	102,157	71,645	25,300	70,400	52,800	11,198	2,190,000
2014	739,682	411,183	43,173	438,860	138,000	13,306	102,019	80,759	25,700	68,300	56,100	11,256	2,370,000
2015	809,882	430,838	46,220	396,899	142,399	11,607	101,049	72,806	24,500	66,900	46,100	11,716	2,370,000
2016	858,026	421,358	46,731	365,573	184,501	13,268	101,097	66,456	26,900	62,876	41,800	12,000	2,370,000
2017	885,357	453,704	50,300	345,472	201,815	11,714	95,042	74,857	31,764	60,574	47,900	4,005	2,440,000
2018	907,819	460,000	52,387	334,790	204,091	10,711	96,063	74,264	35,774	60,549	49,500	2,474	2,470,000
2019	918,731	404,900	58,472	351,000	238,144	12,200	97,531	72,430	35,700	63,205	46,900	1,096	2,450,000
2020	912,000	388,000	60,100	360,000	204,000	12,200	100,000	55,600	35,800	78,800	38,100	----	2,470,000
2021[1]	912,000	431,000	57,500	394,000	273,000	12,800	96,000	73,100	40,200	83,800	47,500	----	2,680,000
2022[2]	880,000	410,000	58,000	380,000	290,000	13,000	90,000	76,000	39,000	76,000	46,000	----	2,600,000

[1] Preliminary.   [2] Estimate.   [3] Iron ore, iron ore concentrates and iron ore agglomerates.   *Source: U.S. Geological Survey (USGS)*

Salient Statistics of Iron Ore[3] in the United States   In Thousands of Metric Tons

Year	Net Import Reliance As a % of Apparent Consump	Production Total	Production Lake Superior	Production Other Regions	Ship-ments	Value Million $ (at Mine)	Average Value $ at Mine Per Ton	Stock, Dec. 31 Mines	Stock, Dec. 31 Con-suming Plants	Stock, Dec. 31 Lake Erie Docks	Imports	Exports	Con-sumption	Total
2014	E	56,100	----	----	55,000	4,730.0	84.43	4,460	----	----	5,140	12,400	46,700	676.0
2015	E	46,100	----	----	43,500	3,750.0	81.19	4,760	----	----	4,550	7,500	42,100	455.0
2016	E	41,800	----	----	46,600	3,050.0	73.11	2,990	----	----	3,010	8,710	37,900	241.0
2017	E	47,900	----	----	46,900	3,760.0	78.54	3,930	----	----	3,720	10,600	40,100	357.0
2018	E	49,500	----	----	50,400	4,600.0	93.00	3,100	----	----	3,790	12,700	41,400	388.0
2019	E	46,900	----	----	47,000	4,370.0	92.94	3,470	----	----	3,980	11,400	39,100	499.0
2020	E	38,100	----	----	38,000	3,480.0	91.27	3,290	----	----	3,240	10,400	31,100	389.0
2021	E	47,500	----	----	43,400		141.75	3,170	----	----	3,740	14,300	36,800	
2022[1]	E	39,000	----	----	38,980		114.00	3,190	----	----	3,200	9,400	40,000	
2023[2]	E	45,420	----	----	45,130			3,480	----	----				

[1] Preliminary.   [2] Estimate.   [3] Usable iron ore exclusive of ore containing 5% or more manganese and includes byproduct ore.
NA = Not available.   *Source: U.S. Geological Survey (USGS)*

U.S. Imports (for Consumption) of Iron Ore[2]   In Thousands of Metric Tons

Year	Australia	Brazil	Canada	Chile	Mauritania	Peru	Sweden	Venezuela	Total
2011	----	562	3,910	165	----	14	81	279	5,270
2012	----	739	3,820	104	----	44	72	75	5,160
2013	----	630	2,090	152	----	12	49	----	3,250
2014	----	1,730	2,860	----	----	35	154	----	5,100
2015	----	2,050	2,040	1	----	22	85	25	4,550
2016	[3]	1,760	557	62	----	66	350	28	3,010
2017	24	2,040	793	283	----	31	363	----	3,710
2018	42	2,370	853	96	6	31	163	16	3,810
2019	42	2,190	838	117	----	----	122	----	5,100
2020[1]	24	1,510	775	81	----	----	463	----	

[1] Preliminary.   [2] Including agglomerates.   [3] Less than 1/2 unit.   *Source: U.S. Geological Survey (USGS)*

Iron Ore Stocks in the United States, at End of Month   In Thousands of Metric Tons

Year	Jan.	Feb.	Mar.	Apr.	May	June	July	Aug.	Sept.	Oct.	Nov.	Dec.
2014	6,530	9,240	12,400	13,600	12,500	11,300	9,770	8,190	7,320	6,600	6,290	5,430
2015	6,640	10,600	14,500	14,800	13,100	11,500	9,740	8,040	7,460	7,070	7,550	7,490
2016	8,940	11,800	13,600	12,100	11,000	10,200	9,470	8,300	7,630	7,170	6,500	6,050
2017	6,730	9,970	12,400	12,200	11,200	10,100	9,080	7,670	6,470	6,210	6,300	6,120
2018	8,290	12,000	14,700	14,300	13,000	12,200	10,900	9,520	8,270	7,480	4,120	3,100
2019	4,390	7,490	9,910	9,330	9,150	8,020	6,850	5,550	4,460	3,800	3,230	2,720
2020	4,790	8,100	10,700	9,430	6,900	4,980	3,760	4,410	4,470	4,150	3,770	3,530
2021	5,110	9,110	12,000	11,300	9,980	8,470	6,910	5,120	3,520	2,740	2,170	3,170
2022	6,280	7,800	7,640	5,410	4,350	4,930	3,820	3,460	2,670	25,350	2,860	3,190
2023[1]	4,810	7,790	9,930	9,370	8,250	7,060	5,850	5,170				

[1] Preliminary.   *Source: U.S. Geological Survey (USGS)*

Lard

Lard is the layer of fat found along the back and underneath the skin of a hog. The hog's fat is purified by washing it with water, melting it under constant heat, and straining it several times. Lard is an important byproduct of the meatpacking industry. It is valued highly as cooking oil because there is very little smoke when it is heated. However, demand for lard in cooking is declining because of the trend toward healthier eating. Lard is also used for medicinal purposes such as ointments, plasters, liniments, and occasionally as a laxative for children. Lard production is directly proportional to commercial hog production, meaning the largest producers of hogs are the largest producers of lard.

Supply – World production of lard in the 2022/23 marketing year rose by +0.1% yr/yr to 8.727 million metric tons, a new record high. The world's largest lard producers were China with 42.3% of world production, the US with 8.1%, Brazil with 7.4%, Germany and Spain with 5.1%, Russia with 4.9%, and Poland with 2.4%. US production of lard in 2021/22 fell by -2.6% yr/yr to 1.554 billion pounds.

Trade – US exports of lard in 2021/22 fell by -67.1% to 58.9 million pounds and accounted for only 3.8% of US production.

World Production of Lard — In Thousands of Metric Tons

Year	Brazil	Canada	China	France	Germany	Italy	Japan	Poland	Romania	Spain	United States	Ex-USSR	World Total
2013-14	443.5	131.3	3,745.1	132.1	558.0	186.3	51.0	231.5	70.5	310.7	594.3	514.5	8,434.5
2014-15	444.3	132.5	3,623.4	133.5	570.4	190.9	49.0	243.7	72.1	334.4	625.1	528.3	8,435.7
2015-16	470.8	136.9	3,599.9	135.6	566.1	198.4	51.0	252.6	68.7	356.0	639.9	557.1	8,567.3
2016-17	488.1	165.7	3,584.4	143.2	565.6	193.7	50.5	236.2	53.1	366.0	657.6	366.9	8,389.9
2017-18	505.1	164.7	3,678.6	148.9	547.1	193.4	51.2	248.6	52.0	393.5	674.3	380.6	8,584.0
2018-19	518.0	165.5	3,170.3	149.3	534.6	188.4	51.6	242.3	49.0	403.0	703.0	394.3	8,118.0
2019-20	570.8	171.2	2,601.5	150.1	526.6	167.9	52.0	233.9	46.5	426.7	730.8	419.1	7,661.6
2020-21[1]	598.1	170.8	3,432.4	150.0	511.9	173.7	53.0	240.0	46.9	450.0	724.0	422.9	8,581.2
2021-22[2]	615.9	167.2	3,649.8	147.5	469.8	167.6	51.6	221.7	40.7	448.4	705.2	423.2	8,714.9
2022-23[3]	644.7	163.9	3,689.4	142.7	443.7	159.2	51.8	211.6	39.4	441.4	703.9	429.2	8,727.5

[1] Preliminary. [2] Estimate. [3] Forecast. *Source: The Oil World*

Supply and Distribution of Lard in the United States — In Millions of Pounds

	Supply			Disappearance						
Year	Production	Stocks Oct. 1	Total Supply	Domestic	Baking or Frying Fats	Margarine[3]	Exports	Total Disappearance	Direct Use	Per Capita (Lbs.)
2012-13	1,319.9	20.0	1,339.9	816.4	W	W	64.8	881.2	NA	NA
2013-14	1,310.2	20.0	1,330.2	821.1	W	W	47.2	868.3	NA	NA
2014-15	1,378.1	20.0	1,398.1	896.9	W	W	43.6	940.5	NA	NA
2015-16	1,410.7	9.0	1,419.7	901.4	W	W	42.1	943.5	NA	NA
2016-17	1,449.7	8.0	1,457.7	934.9	W	W	37.9	972.8	NA	NA
2017-18	1,486.6	7.0	1,493.6	960.5	W	W	37.1	997.6	NA	NA
2018-19	1,549.8	11.0	1,560.8	1,005.6	W	W	49.6	1,055.3	NA	NA
2019-20	1,611.1	5.9	1,617.1	1,031.9	W	W	39.9	1,071.8	NA	NA
2020-21[1]	1,596.1	8.6	1,604.7	880.5	W	W	179.3	1,059.8	NA	NA
2021-22[2]	1,561.1	5.0	1,566.0	987.3	W	W	58.9	1,046.2	NA	NA

[1] Preliminary. [2] Forecast. [3] Includes edible tallow. W = Withheld.
Source: Economic Research Service, U.S. Department of Agriculture (ERS-USDA)

Average Wholesale Price of Lard--Loose, Tank Cars, in Chicago — In Cents Per Pound

Year	Jan.	Feb.	Mar.	Apr.	May	June	July	Aug.	Sept.	Oct.	Nov.	Dec.	Average
2014	33.00	38.00	40.67	53.00	NA	45.00	NA	46.50	50.67	48.00	42.81	35.91	43.36
2015	29.50	28.00	NA	26.64	28.00	NA	31.00	31.00	NA	34.23	35.50	28.80	30.30
2016	24.00	NA	29.00	33.00	NA	NA	NA	36.53	36.75	34.00	NA	31.00	32.04
2017	30.10	NA	NA	NA	NA	34.50	NA	NA	35.75	36.00	38.17	37.00	35.25
2018	32.08	32.20	NA	NA	NA	32.50	NA	32.38	32.93	33.00	34.33	31.00	32.55
2019	NA	NA	NA	NA	NA	NA	NA	NA	NA	NA	NA	NA	NA
2020	NA	NA	NA	32.00	35.50	36.50	NA	39.00	NA	NA	41.00	NA	36.80
2021	NA	NA	55.00	NA	58.00	68.00	NA	72.33	NA	NA	NA	NA	63.33
2022	NA	82.00	NA	NA	NA	NA	NA	NA	NA	88.00	NA	NA	85.00
2023	87.00	NA	NA	82.00	NA	80.00	NA	NA	NA	90.00	NA	65.00	80.80

Source: Economic Research Service, U.S. Department of Agriculture (ERS-USDA)

Lead

Lead (atomic symbol Pb) is a dense, toxic, bluish-gray metallic element, and is the heaviest stable element. Lead was one of the first known metals. The ancients used lead in face powders, rouges, mascaras, paints, condiments, wine preservatives, and water supply plumbing. The Romans were slowly poisoned by lead because of its diverse daily usage.

Lead is usually found in ore with zinc, silver, and most often copper. The most common lead ore is galena, containing 86.6% lead. Cerussite and angleside are other common varieties of lead. More than half of the lead currently used comes from recycling.

Lead is used in building construction, bullets and shot, tank and pipe lining, storage batteries, and electric cable sheathing. Lead is used extensively as a protective shielding for radioactive material (e.g., X-ray apparatus) because of its high density and nuclear properties. Lead is also part of solder, pewter, and fusible alloys.

Lead futures and options trade at the London Metal Exchange (LME). The LME lead futures contract calls for the delivery of 25 metric tons of at least 99.970% purity lead ingots (pigs). The contract is priced in U.S. dollars per metric ton. Lead first started trading on the LME in 1903.

Prices – The average price of pig lead among US producers in 2023 fell -2.6% yr/yr to $1.1500 per pound, below the record high of $1.2474 per pound in 2007.

Supply – World smelter production of lead (both primary and secondary) in 2020 fell by -4.2% yr/yr to 11.500 million metric tons, below the 12.000 million metric tons high in 2019.

The world's largest smelter producers of lead (both primary and secondary) in 2020 were China with 43.5% of world production, followed by the US with 8.7%, India with 7.1%, Mexico with 3.6%, South Korea with 3.2%, the United Kingdom with 3.1%, and Germany with 2.9%.

US mine production of recoverable lead in 2023 rose by +3.3% yr/yr to 272,850 metric tons. Missouri was responsible for 93.7% of US production in 2009, with the remainder produced mainly by Idaho and Montana. Lead recovered from scrap in the US (secondary production) fell by -5.1% yr/yr in 2022 to 951 million metric tons, below the 2008 record high of 1.220 million metric tons. The value of US secondary lead production in 2020 fell by -11.5% yr/yr to $2.080 billion, well below the 2007 record high of $3.220 billion.

Demand – US lead consumption in 2022 fell by -1.1% yr/yr to 1.577 million metric tons, below the 2017 record high of 1.760 million metric tons.

Trade – US imports of lead pigs and bars in 2020 fell by -22.9% yr/yr to 313,000 metric tons. US lead exports in 2019 were comprised of ore concentrate (259,000 metric tons), unwrought lead (25,500 metric tons), scrap (14,600 metric tons), and wrought lead (6,600 metric tons).

World Smelter (Primary and Secondary) Production of Lead   In Thousands of Metric Tons

Year	Australia[3]	Belgium[4]	Canada[3]	China[2]	France	Germany	Italy	Japan	Mexico[3]	Spain	United Kingdom[3]	United States	World Total
2011	213.0	282.6	4,600.0	429.0	419.0	149.5	218.0	416.9	317.7	177.0	269.0	1,248	10,300
2012	210.0	299.2	4,590.0	424.0	460.0	138.4	209.0	460.0	384.0	160.0	311.9	1,261	10,600
2013	232.5	281.8	4,940.0	400.0	463.0	180.0	208.1	427.7	371.0	157.0	329.2	1,274	10,800
2014	192.4	281.5	4,740.0	408.0	477.0	209.6	202.7	639.0	363.5	166.0	267.0	1,060	10,600
2015	227.3	268.9	4,422.0	378.0	501.0	209.9	194.7	641.0	493.8	165.0	307.0	1,050	10,500
2016	223.8	274.2	4,680.0	339.0	689.0	187.2	199.1	831.0	324.7	169.0	328.0	1,110	11,200
2017	211.3	275.1	4,726.0	354.0	812.1	173.7	199.4	803.3	322.5	188.0	387.0	1,140	11,600
2018	188.5	261.0	4,943.0	315.0	883.1	167.5	196.6	800.3	434.0	190.0	391.0	1,170	11,900
2019[1]	124.9	260.3	4,959.0	332.0	921.9	159.1	198.4	794.0	447.0	192.0	394.0	1,180	12,000
2020[2]	168.9	190.0	5,000.0	335.0	820.0	152.7	197.6	370.0	412.0	175.0	360.0	1,000	11,500

[1] Preliminary.   [2] Estimate.   [3] Refinded & bullion.   [4] Includes scrap.   *Source: U.S. Geological Survey (USGS)*

Consumption of Lead in the United States, by Products   In Metric Tons

Year	Ammunition: Shot and Bullets	Bearing Metals	Brass and Bronze	Cable Covering	Calking Lead	Casting Metals	Pipes, Traps & Bends[2]	Sheet Lead	Solder	Storage Batteries: Total	Other Metal Products[3]	Other Oxides[4]	Total U.S. Consumption
2011	75,100	1,150	1,620	W	W	16,000	6,110	7,170	6,170	1,250,000	23,100	9,760	1,410,000
2012	73,900	1,090	1,120	W	W	16,700	6,240	7,390	6,280	1,190,000	18,500	9,740	1,350,000
2013	84,800	1,110	1,420	W	W	20,400	7,030	4,870	8,200	1,200,000	177	9,740	1,390,000
2014	85,300	1,150	2,990	W	W	19,100	6,900	6,090	7,380	1,320,000	33,000	9,740	1,510,000
2015	78,400	1,090	1,580	W	W	14,200	7,060	9,020	6,490	1,770,000	31,100	11,500	1,960,000
2016	69,800	1,060	1,580	W	W	15,000	7,160	6,510	6,460	1,810,000	149	11,700	1,980,000
2017	67,000	1,010	1,600	W	W	12,700	6,560	5,110	6,590	1,940,000	W	11,100	2,110,000
2018	68,700	1,010	1,710	1,170	W	14,000	6,590	7,070	6,720	1,900,000	109	10,900	2,040,000
2019	71,700	2,280	1,590	1,920	W	13,200	1,940	7,440	6,740	1,720,000	31,000	10,100	1,880,000
2020[1]	63,000	2,950	1,010	1,920	W	13,200	1,940	6,640	6,710	1,700,000	30,900	10,100	1,850,000

[1] Preliminary.   [2] Including building.   [3] Including terne metal, type metal, and lead consumed in foil, collapsible tubes, annealing, plating, galvanizing and fishing weights.   [4] Includes paints, glass and ceramic products, and other pigments and chemicals.   W = Withheld.
Source: U.S. Geological Survey (USGS)

LEAD

Salient Statistics of Lead in the United States   In Thousands of Metric Tons

Year	Net Import Reliance as a % of Apparent Consump	Production of Refined Lead From Domestic Ores[3]	Foreighn Ores[3]	Total Primary	Total Value of Refined Million $	Secondary Lead Recovered As Soft Lead	In Anti-monial Lead	In Other Alloys	Total	Total Value of Secondary Million USD	Stocks, Dec. 31 Primary	Con-sumer[4]	Average Price - Cents Per Pound - New York	London
2014	35	----	W	----	----	786	224	8.8	1,060	2,640	W	56.4	----	95.04
2015	31	----	W	----	----	827	214	4.8	1,050	2,110	W	60.1	----	81.02
2016	33	----	W	----	----	882	225	5.7	1,110	2,320	W	60.3	----	84.84
2017	36	----	W	----	----	920	W	W	1,140	2,870	W	64.4	----	105.10
2018	30	----	W	----	----	957	W	W	1,170	2,850	W	66.8	----	101.76
2019	29	----	W	----	----	888	W	W	1,070	2,350	W	61.8	----	90.59
2020	25	----	W	----	----	876	W	W	1,030	2,080	W	54.0	----	82.74
2021	36	----	W	----	----				975		W		----	100.00
2022[1]	38	----	W	----	----				950		W		----	
2023[2]	35	----	W	----	----						W		----	

[1] Preliminary.   [2] Estimate.   [3] And base bullion.   [4] Also at secondary smelters.   W = Withheld.   E = Net exporter.

Source: U.S. Geological Survey (USGS)

U.S. Foreign Trade of Lead   In Thousands of Metric Tons

Year	Exports Ore Con-centrate	Un-wrought Lead[3]	Wrought Lead[4]	Scrap	Ash & Re-sidues[5]	Imports for Consumption Ores, Flue Dust or Fume & Mattes	Base Bullion	Pigs & Bars	Re-claimed Scrap, Etc.	Value Million $	General Import From: Ore, Flue, Dust & Matte Aus-tralia	Can-ada	Peru	Pigs & Bars Can-ada	Mexico	Peru
2011	223.0	40.1	7.0	31.1	----	----	0.4	313.0	2.4	718.4	----	----	----	250.0	56.0	0.1
2012	214.0	47.0	6.3	25.9	----	1.5	1.0	349.0	16.8	730.4	----	----	----	240.0	56.1	0.0
2013	215.0	41.6	6.6	34.9	----	0.0	1.9	500.0	15.6	1,060.4	----	----	----	257.0	111.0	39.6
2014	356.0	55.3	5.0	36.4	----	----	1.1	593.0	11.4	1,243.8	----	----	----	264.0	120.0	49.7
2015	350.0	50.1	2.9	29.1	----	----	0.3	417.0	3.5	771.2	----	----	----	162.0	105.0	----
2016	341.0	42.7	5.9	16.7	----	----	0.2	416.0	1.5	841.6	----	----	----	176.0	71.8	1.4
2017	269.0	23.9	7.6	22.7	----	----	----	538.0	4.2	1,239.9	----	----	----	160.0	103.0	3.9
2018	251.0	66.9	6.0	12.0	----	----	0.9	448.0	1.7	1,034.5	----	----	----	148.0	107.0	3.4
2019[1]	259.0	25.5	6.6	14.6	----	----	1.2	406.0	2.3	1,061.4	----	----	----	246.0	99.4	3.3
2020[2]	265.0	16.6	5.8	----	----	----	2.5	313.0	2.1	760.9	----	----	----	177.0	68.2	1.9

[1] Preliminary.   [2] Estimate.   [3] And lead alloys.   [4] Blocks, pigs, etc.   [5] Less than 1/2 unit.   Source: U.S. Geological Survey (USGS)

Annual Mine Production of Recoverable Lead in the United States   In Metric Tons

Year	Idaho	Missouri	Montana	Total
2014	----	----	----	367,000
2015	----	----	----	360,000
2016	----	----	----	336,000
2017	----	----	----	311,000
2018	----	----	----	271,000
2019	----	----	----	266,800
2020	----	----	----	291,200
2021	----	----	----	287,200
2022[1]	----	----	----	264,100
2023[2]	----	----	----	267,867

[1] Preliminary.   [2] Estimate.   W = Withheld, included in Total.   Source: U.S. Geological Survey (USGS)

Mine Production of Recoverable Lead in the United States   In Metric Tons

Year	Jan.	Feb.	Mar.	Apr.	May	June	July	Aug.	Sept.	Oct.	Nov.	Dec.	Total
2014	30,300	26,600	28,800	31,300	32,800	29,600	30,500	30,389	31,200	32,000	32,700	34,500	367,000
2015	28,200	30,100	35,700	32,100	31,300	28,900	31,200	31,500	26,100	27,100	27,200	27,400	360,000
2016	29,100	26,000	27,900	30,100	27,000	28,400	24,800	30,400	28,400	28,000	22,000	20,000	336,000
2017	25,400	25,500	31,300	27,900	24,400	25,300	23,100	25,400	21,000	24,900	27,500	21,900	311,000
2018	21,700	17,400	20,700	22,200	23,000	23,400	24,000	W	W	W	W	W	271,000
2019	22,800	19,800	18,100	24,600	26,700	23,800	22,100	24,700	24,000	17,200	21,300	21,700	266,800
2020	22,800	22,900	23,100	19,900	23,500	24,600	26,100	28,700	23,700	24,000	22,700	29,200	291,200
2021	25,600	22,000	25,000	24,000	23,800	25,800	23,500	25,700	23,700	26,400	18,000	23,700	287,200
2022	20,900	22,000	25,700	26,400	24,100	19,800	22,600	20,800	20,000	21,200	18,400	22,200	264,100
2023[1]	21,300	22,100	23,900	23,400	24,200	25,000	23,900	18,100	19,000				267,867

[1] Preliminary.   W = Withheld to avoid disclosing company proprietary data.   Source: U.S. Geological Survey (USGS)

LEAD
Quarterly Cash as of 03/28/2024

QUARTERLY CASH
As of 03/28/2024
Chart High 96.00 on 04/24/2018
Chart Low 10.20 on 03/20/1986

Average Price of Pig Lead, U.S. Primary Producers (Common Corroding)[1] In Cents Per Pound

Year	Jan.	Feb.	Mar.	Apr.	May	June	July	Aug.	Sept.	Oct.	Nov.	Dec.	Average
2014	110.40	108.69	106.23	107.71	107.99	108.35	112.31	114.44	108.97	105.16	104.11	100.29	107.89
2015	95.45	94.25	93.41	102.60	103.12	94.25	92.01	93.72	91.66	88.54	84.72	89.21	93.58
2016	86.75	92.12	93.74	90.37	89.89	89.70	95.09	95.44	100.00	103.71	109.36	111.81	96.50
2017	111.53	114.71	112.58	110.76	106.56	106.67	112.97	116.68	117.90	123.74	121.73	123.64	114.96
2018	127.40	126.93	118.69	116.99	116.98	120.64	109.97	103.62	101.77	99.98	97.87	99.13	111.66
2019	100.38	103.54	103.14	98.27	92.49	95.74	99.68	102.70	103.98	108.61	102.06	95.79	100.53
2020	96.89	94.35	88.10	83.78	81.89	87.40	91.00	96.85	94.32	90.19	96.04	101.42	91.85
2021	102.42	106.75	102.53	105.85	113.98	114.74	122.16	126.70	118.58	122.54	123.06	121.60	115.08
2022	124.99	123.13	126.01	128.25	116.93	113.87	109.63	115.93	106.92	112.09	117.00	121.44	118.02
2023	120.40	115.66	116.34	117.00	113.80	114.22	113.47	115.40	119.30	112.22	114.25	107.91	115.00

[1] New York Delivery.   *Source: American Metal Market*

Salient Statistics of Recycling Lead in the United States

Year	New Scrap[1]	Old Scrap[2]	Recycled Metal[3]	Apparent Supply	Percent Recycled	New Scrap[1]	Old Scrap[2]	Recycled Metal[3]	Apparent Supply
	---------------------- In Metric Tons ----------------------					----------------- Value in Thousands of Dollars -----------------			
2012	19,200	1,090,000	1,110,000	1,490,000	74.0	48,200	2,740,000	2,790,000	3,760,000
2013	19,200	1,140,000	1,160,000	1,440,000	80.0	46,600	3,760,000	3,800,000	3,870,000
2014	16,900	1,010,000	1,020,000	1,470,000	69.0	39,500	2,350,000	2,390,000	3,650,000
2015	16,900	989,000	1,010,000	1,410,000	71.0	34,000	1,990,000	2,020,000	2,830,000
2016	19,200	1,090,000	1,110,000	1,480,000	75.0	39,900	2,280,000	2,320,000	3,080,000
2017	20,000	1,120,000	1,140,000	1,650,000	69.0	50,600	2,820,000	2,870,000	4,170,000
2018	20,900	1,150,000	1,170,000	1,550,000	75.0	51,100	2,800,000	2,850,000	3,780,000
2019	20,100	1,160,000	1,180,000	1,560,000	76.0	44,300	2,550,000	2,590,000	3,430,000
2020	15,000	989,000	1,000,000	1,300,000	77.0	30,200	1,990,000	2,020,000	2,620,000
2021	14,500	1,040,000	1,060,000	1,520,000	69.0	36,100	2,600,000	2,640,000	3,800,000

[1] Scrap that results from the manufacturing process.   [2] Scrap that results from consumer products.   [3] Metal recovered from new plus old scrap.
Source: U.S. Geological Survey (USGS)

LEAD

Total[2] Lead Consumption in the United States   In Metric Tons

Year	Jan.	Feb.	Mar.	Apr.	May	June	July	Aug.	Sept.	Oct.	Nov.	Dec.	Total
2014	159,000	159,000	148,000	153,000	148,000	146,000	131,000	155,309	128,000	134,000	131,000	138,000	1,670,000
2015	132,000	121,000	135,000	151,000	130,000	135,000	128,000	125,000	121,000	145,000	134,000	129,000	1,590,000
2016	97,300	120,000	136,000	133,000	128,000	133,000	134,000	125,000	119,000	129,000	149,000	153,000	1,490,000
2017	146,000	157,000	167,000	156,000	171,000	125,000	147,000	128,000	147,000	130,000	129,000	120,000	1,760,000
2018	131,000	154,000	161,000	139,000	129,000	144,000	127,000	128,000	144,000	121,000	126,000	128,000	1,630,000
2019	139,000	130,000	133,000	149,000	124,000	133,000	127,000	154,000	142,000	134,000	125,000	140,000	1,630,000
2020	141,000	125,000	128,000	126,000	109,000	132,000	125,000	121,000	119,000	146,000	126,000	121,000	1,519,000
2021	132,000	129,000	135,000	151,000	132,000	142,000	116,000	142,000	135,000	131,000	114,000	136,000	1,595,000
2022	146,000	128,000	135,000	119,000	136,000	151,000	113,000	154,000	122,000	123,000	107,000	143,000	1,577,000
2023[1]	134,000	108,000	112,000	155,000	115,000	102,000	135,000	116,000	140,000				1,489,333

[1] Preliminary.   [1] Represents total consumption of primary & secondary lead as metal, in chemicals, or in alloys.   *Source: U.S. Geological Survey (USGS)*

Lead Recovered from Scrap in the United States   In Metric Tons (Lead Content)

Year	Jan.	Feb.	Mar.	Apr.	May	June	July	Aug.	Sept.	Oct.	Nov.	Dec.	Total
2014	92,700	91,100	97,300	96,300	94,500	94,500	96,900	93,796	94,800	94,400	88,600	94,800	1,130,000
2015	88,600	88,900	92,200	94,600	93,600	92,900	92,500	95,400	96,300	97,500	96,100	89,700	1,120,000
2016	94,300	90,800	92,300	93,500	91,900	86,500	83,900	92,600	86,700	106,000	102,000	102,000	1,000,000
2017	82,900	105,000	108,000	107,000	101,000	83,700	85,000	85,300	83,300	84,600	81,400	84,300	1,130,000
2018	95,100	90,300	96,300	97,300	91,400	92,400	97,000	96,600	92,900	94,600	93,600	96,000	1,140,000
2019	94,100	94,500	96,700	94,600	90,600	93,800	97,000	97,200	98,200	101,000	97,800	100,000	1,155,500
2020	101,000	99,500	95,900	86,100	82,600	98,100	99,700	98,100	95,800	97,800	98,700	98,400	1,151,700
2021	89,100	94,500	89,600	83,700	85,100	84,200	83,600	77,300	78,700	78,200	78,200	79,400	1,001,600
2022	75,500	76,100	81,200	82,700	80,900	78,600	79,500	79,800	79,600	80,100	78,600	78,400	951,000
2023[1]	78,400	78,600	78,600	80,900	80,900	78,000	77,900	76,300	74,900				939,333

[1] Preliminary.   *Source: U.S. Geological Survey (USGS)*

Total Stocks of Lead[1] in the United States at Refiners, at End of Month   In Metric Tons

Year	Jan.	Feb.	Mar.	Apr.	May	June	July	Aug.	Sept.	Oct.	Nov.	Dec.
2010	60,200	60,200	55,700	50,700	55,500	57,200	57,600	59,100	59,800	58,700	67,700	67,400
2011	67,100	53,000	53,200	61,100	62,600	61,500	62,800	60,500	58,800	56,300	53,500	54,800
2012	58,700	63,300	54,800	54,000	51,800	56,600	62,600	65,700	63,400	63,800	56,000	57,500
2013	69,900	76,200	83,100	94,300	98,000	93,400	83,600	81,400	77,400	69,300	65,100	69,400
2014	68,100	63,600	65,400	65,700	64,000	66,600	62,500	62,080	63,300	63,100	66,300	66,300
2015	64,900	63,800	63,600	64,100	62,700	62,400	60,800	66,900	69,500	68,600	67,900	64,500
2016	97,300	63,800	63,200	65,500	70,000	67,100	66,900	85,300	84,600	74,800	79,800	101,000
2017[1]	111,000	103,000	113,000	106,000	126,000	128,000	131,000	132,000	115,000	116,000	139,000	161,000
2018[1]	----	----	----	----	----	----	----	----	----	----	----	----
2019[1]	----	----	----	----	----	----	----	----	----	----	----	----

[1] Preliminary.   [2] Secondary smelters and consumers.   *Source: U.S. Geological Survey (USGS)*

Refiners Production[1] of Lead in the United States   In Metric Tons

Year	Jan.	Feb.	Mar.	Apr.	May	June	July	Aug.	Sept.	Oct.	Nov.	Dec.	Total
2001	NA	NA	NA	NA	NA	NA	NA	NA	NA	NA	NA	NA	290,000
2002	NA	NA	NA	NA	NA	NA	NA	NA	NA	NA	NA	NA	262,000
2003	NA	NA	NA	NA	NA	NA	NA	NA	NA	NA	NA	NA	245,000
2004	NA	NA	NA	NA	NA	NA	NA	NA	NA	NA	NA	NA	NA
2005	NA	NA	NA	NA	NA	NA	NA	NA	NA	NA	NA	NA	143,000
2006	NA	NA	NA	NA	NA	NA	NA	NA	NA	NA	NA	NA	143,000
2007	NA	NA	NA	NA	NA	NA	NA	NA	NA	NA	NA	NA	NA
2008	NA	NA	NA	NA	NA	NA	NA	NA	NA	NA	NA	NA	NA
2009	NA	NA	NA	NA	NA	NA	NA	NA	NA	NA	NA	NA	NA
2010[2]	NA	NA	NA	NA	NA	NA	NA	NA	NA	NA	NA	NA	NA

[1] Represents refined lead produced from domestic ores by primary smelters plus small amounts of secondary material passing through these smelters. Includes GSA metal purchased for remelt.   [2] Preliminary.   NA = Not available.   *Source: U.S. Geological Survey (USGS)*

Lithium

World Production of Lithium Minerals and Brine   In Metric Tons (gross weight)

Year	Argentina Subsurface Brine: Lithium Carbonate	Argentina Subsurface Brine: Lithium Chloride	Australia Spodumene	Brazil Concentrates (Spodumene)	Chile Subsurface Brine: Lithium Carbonate	Chile Subsurface Brine: Lithium Chloride	Chile Subsurface Brine: Lithium Hydroxide	China Lithium Carbonate equivalent[3]	Portugal Lepidolite	United States Lithium Carbonate	Zimbabwe Amblygonite, Eucryptite, Lepidolite, and Petalite
2013	9,248	5,156	405,119	7,982	52,358	4,091	4,197	19,068	19,940	4,600	50,000
2014	11,698	7,370	444,546	8,519	55,074	2,985	4,194	18,810	17,459	W	50,000
2015	21,111	5,848	439,514	5,781	50,418	2,069	3,888	20,470	17,120	W	50,000
2016	24,409	6,468	522,181	8,804	70,831	1,775	5,576	25,400	25,758	W	50,000
2017	26,559	4,501	1,706,618	10,547	73,563	2,535	5,280	37,300	52,741	W	40,000
2018	29,385	5,005	1,965,944	41,000	87,029	3,826	6,468	37,800	76,818	W	80,000
2019	29,994	4,284	1,587,980	38,500	100,787	1,886	9,934	57,500	59,912	W	60,400
2020[1]	26,911	4,836	1,427,380	57,500	114,260	----	9,030	70,600	23,185	W	20,859
2021[2]	28,520	3,723	1,985,670	6,000	150,348	----	12,129	75,000	60,000	W	35,500

[1] Preliminary.   [2] Estimate.   [3] Produced from subsurface brine and concentrates.   W = Withheld to avoid disclosing proprietary data.
Source: U.S. Geological Survey (USGS)

Salient U.S. Lithium Statistics   In Metric Tons (contained Lithium)

Year	Production[2]	Imports[3]	Exports[4]	Consumption: Estimated	Rest of World: Production[2]	Battery-grade Lithium Carbonate (USD per Metric ton)	Net Import Reliance as a % of Apparent Consumption	Employment, Mine and Mill (Number)
2015	W	2,750	1,789	2,000	32,200	6,500	>25	70
2016	W	3,140	1,520	3,000	40,200	8,650	>50	70
2017	W	3,330	1,960	3,000	76,400	15,000	>50	70
2018	W	3,420	1,660	3,000	91,800	16,000	>50	70
2019	W	2,620	1,660	2,000	83,800	12,100	>25	70
2020	W	2,460	1,170	2,000	82,700	8,600	>50	70
2021	W	2,640	1,870	2,000	107,000	12,600	>25	70
2022	W	3,270	2,440	3,000		68,100	>25	70
2023[1]	W	3,400	2,300			46,000	>25	70

[1] Preliminary.   [2] Mineral concentrate and carbonate.   [3] Compounds, concentrate, ores, and metal.   [4] Compounds.   W = Withheld to avoid disclosing proprietary data.   *Source: U.S. Geological Survey (USGS)*

U.S. Exports of Lithium Chemicals   In Metric Tons (gross weight)

Year	Lithium Carbonate	Lithium Carbonate (Li content)	Lithium Carbonate, U.S.P.	Lithium Carbonate, U.S.P. (Li content)	Lithium Hydroxide	Lithium Hydroxide (Li content)
2013	1,010	190	391	73	5,850	966
2014	904	170	77	14	7,590	1,240
2015	1,350	255	85	16	9,200	1,520
2016	1,040	195	108	20	7,910	1,300
2017	1,310	246	94	18	10,300	1,700
2018	1,320	249	141	27	8,400	1,390
2019	819	154	95	18	9,040	1,490
2020[1]	1,000	188	213	40	5,890	972
2021[2]	2,660	500	153	29	8,120	1,340

[1] Preliminary.   [2] Estimate.   [3] Less than 1/2 unit.   *Source: U.S. Geological Survey (USGS)*

U.S. Imports for Consumption of Lithium Chemicals   In Metric Tons (gross weight)

Year	Lithium Carbonate	Lithium Carbonate (Li content)	Lithium Carbonate, U.S.P.	Lithium Carbonate, U.S.P. (Li content)	Lithium Hydroxide	Lithium Hydroxide (Li content)
2013	10,500	1,980	45	8	1,340	221
2014	9,580	1,800	48	9	1,920	316
2015	12,900	2,420	31	6	1,960	324
2016	15,600	2,920	16	3	1,280	211
2017	16,100	3,030	----	----	1,830	302
2018	17,200	3,240	[3]	[3]	1,060	176
2019	12,800	2,410	[3]	[3]	1,240	206
2020[1]	11,700	2,190	[3]	[3]	1,600	265
2021[2]	12,300	2,310	[3]	[3]	1,980	329

[1] Preliminary.   [2] Estimate.   [3] Less than 1/2 unit.   *Source: U.S. Geological Survey (USGS)*

Lumber and Plywood

Humans have utilized lumber for construction for thousands of years, but due to the heaviness of timber and the manual methods of harvesting, large-scale lumbering didn't occur until the mechanical advances of the Industrial Revolution. Lumber is produced from both hardwood and softwood. Hardwood lumber comes from deciduous trees that have broad leaves. Most hardwood lumber is used for miscellaneous industrial applications, primarily wood pallets, and includes oak, gum, maple, and ash. Hardwood species with beautiful colors and patterns are used for such high-grade products as furniture, flooring, paneling, and cabinets and include black walnut, black cherry, and red oak. Wood from cone-bearing trees is called softwood, regardless of its actual hardness. Most lumber from the U.S. is softwood. Softwoods, such as southern yellow pine, Douglas fir, ponderosa pine, and true firs, are primarily used as structural lumber, such as 2x4s and 2x6s, poles, paper, and cardboard.

Plywood consists of several thin layers of veneer bonded together with adhesives. The veneer sheets are layered so that the grain of one sheet is perpendicular to that of the next, which makes plywood exceptionally strong for its weight. Most plywood has from three to nine layers of wood. Plywood manufacturers use both hard and softwoods, although hardwoods serve primarily for appearance and are not as strong as those made from softwoods. Plywood is used in construction, particularly for floors, roofs, walls, and doors. Homebuilding and remodeling account for two-thirds of U.S. lumber consumption. The price of lumber and plywood is highly correlated with the strength of the U.S. homebuilding market.

The forest and wood products industry is dominated by Weyerhaeuser Company (ticker symbol WY). Weyerhaeuser is a forest products conglomerate that engages not only in growing and harvesting timber but also in the production and distribution of forest products, real estate development, and construction of single-family homes. To maximize its long-term yield from its acreage, Weyerhaeuser engages in a number of forest management activities such as extensive planting, suppression of non-merchantable species, thinning, fertilization, and operational pruning.

Lumber futures and options are traded at the CME Group. The CME Group's lumber futures contract calls for the delivery of 27,500 board feet. The contract is priced in terms of dollars per thousand board feet.

Prices – CME lumber futures prices (Barchart.com symbol code LB) on the nearest-futures chart in 2023 closed the year up +9.5% at $543.50 per thousand feet.

Supply – The US leads the world in the production of industrial round wood. In 2022, US production was 382.544 million cubic meters (unchanged yr/yr), Russian production was 182.082 million cubic meters (-13.0% yr/yr), and Canadian production was 143.811 cubic meters (unchanged yr/yr).

The US also led the world in the production of plywood in 2022 with 9.254 million cubic meters of production (-4.6% yr/yr), followed by Russia with 3.241 million cubic meters (-28.8% yr/yr), and then Japan with 3.059 million cubic meters (-3.6% yr/yr).

Trade – World exports of plywood in 2022 fell by -6.0% yr/yr to 31.604 million cubic meters. The world's largest exporter of plywood is Russia, with a 6.7% share of world plywood exports in 2022, followed by Finland with 2.8%, the US with 2.4%, and Canada with 2.1%. In 2022, US exports rose by +1.6% yr/yr to 771.000 million cubic meters.

World exports of industrial roundwood in 2022 fell by -17.8% yr/yr to 108.561 million cubic meters. Germany was the world's largest exporter of roundwood in 2022 with a 9.1% share of world exports, followed by the Czech Republic with an 8.3% share, the US with a 6.8% share, Canada with a 3.5% share, and Russia with a 2.8% share. Russian exports of industrial roundwood in 2022 fell by -79.3% yr/yr to 3.075 million cubic meters. US exports of industrial roundwood in 2022 fell by -21.2% yr/yr to 7.420 million cubic meters.

SAAR: Seasonally Adjusted Annual Rate.   Shaded areas indicate US recessions.   January 2006: Housing Starts reach 30-year high of 2,273,000 units.

World Production of Industrial Roundwood by Selected Countries   In Thousands of Cubic Meters

Year	Austria	Canada	Czechia	Finland	France	Germany	Poland	Romania	Russia	Spain	Sweden	Türkiye	United States
2013	12,433	147,751	13,149	49,331	24,451	44,700	33,795	10,091	180,378	12,124	63,700	16,762	354,937
2014	12,030	148,825	13,365	49,202	25,750	45,386	35,677	10,471	188,300	12,686	67,400	18,535	356,812
2015	12,570	151,358	13,827	51,446	24,998	45,654	35,878	10,235	190,507	12,905	67,300	20,008	354,678
2016	12,173	154,694	15,273	54,327	25,086	44,016	37,106	9,953	198,194	13,325	67,900	20,389	374,476
2017	12,738	155,183	17,011	55,330	25,361	43,328	40,064	9,578	197,612	14,642	67,580	19,462	376,415
2018	13,949	155,629	21,443	60,530	25,721	52,874	41,353	10,436	219,569	15,457	67,712	22,466	392,510
2019	13,325	139,817	26,664	55,654	25,445	54,124	38,199	10,186	203,194	15,405	69,000	22,700	387,702
2020	11,462	141,068	26,621	51,191	24,064	58,436	35,859	11,629	203,194	13,881	69,000	23,306	369,175
2021[1]	13,521	143,811	25,146	57,803	26,189	59,379	38,587	11,335	209,290	14,100	71,400	31,136	382,420
2022[2]	13,934	143,811	20,705	56,251	26,189	56,534	38,235	10,903	182,082	14,366	71,200	29,881	382,544

[1] Preliminary.   [2] Estimate.   *Source: Food and Agriculture Organization of the United Nations (FAO)*

Imports of Industrial Roundwood by Selected Countries   In Thousands of Cubic Meters

Year	Austria	Belgium	Canada	Finland	France	Germany	Italy	Norway	Poland	Portugal	Spain	Sweden	United States
2013	8,214	4,507	4,872	6,694	1,244	8,442	2,691	661	2,270	2,320	2,047	7,532	926
2014	7,239	4,472	4,262	6,257	1,512	8,417	2,913	447	2,633	2,600	1,750	8,127	909
2015	7,849	4,021	4,616	5,709	1,349	8,745	2,665	378	2,535	2,014	751	6,941	1,191
2016	9,188	3,899	6,185	5,911	1,444	8,697	2,763	417	2,482	2,131	599	6,807	1,248
2017	8,825	3,373	4,293	4,830	1,222	8,783	2,846	513	1,682	2,042	584	6,673	1,154
2018	10,113	4,133	5,133	6,935	1,143	8,910	3,860	455	1,071	2,010	638	9,479	1,778
2019	10,586	4,253	4,744	6,234	1,263	7,318	3,374	402	1,607	2,051	667	8,804	942
2020	12,298	5,485	4,364	6,274	943	6,081	2,694	337	2,953	2,538	764	7,240	1,319
2021[1]	10,903	5,616	3,470	6,298	985	6,265	3,289	349	2,764	2,617	892	6,344	772
2022[2]	8,519	6,136	3,170	2,879	1,177	5,576	3,069	384	3,089	3,131	1,026	6,506	941

[1] Preliminary.   [2] Estimate.   *Source: Food and Agricultural Organization of the United Nations (FAO)*

Exports of Industrial Roundwood by Selected Countries   In Thousands of Cubic Meters

Year	Canada	Czechia	Estonia	France	Germany	Hungary	Latvia	Lithuania	Russia	Slovakia	Sweden	Switzerland	United States
2013	7,023	4,292	2,747	4,740	3,316	975	3,737	1,809	19,045	2,662	756	740	14,700
2014	6,696	4,931	2,758	4,398	3,387	871	3,836	1,716	20,909	2,932	630	764	13,962
2015	6,060	4,530	2,431	4,311	3,747	680	3,002	1,406	19,437	2,358	570	641	11,561
2016	8,172	5,225	2,548	4,000	3,947	683	2,871	1,473	20,046	2,157	573	559	12,047
2017	7,402	6,583	2,557	4,092	4,259	634	2,652	1,559	19,430	1,955	963	570	12,200
2018	8,494	8,309	2,927	4,066	5,364	547	2,652	2,028	19,197	2,042	755	753	12,270
2019	7,546	14,146	2,396	3,877	8,916	624	3,579	1,890	15,857	1,711	870	642	7,922
2020	5,994	18,163	1,583	3,583	13,051	728	2,930	1,774	15,471	2,219	1,071	642	7,355
2021[1]	4,220	12,605	1,734	4,123	11,953	838	3,065	1,517	14,886	2,015	1,315	453	9,415
2022[2]	3,750	9,046	1,652	4,180	9,849	728	3,602	1,517	3,075	1,863	2,196	453	7,420

[1] Preliminary.   [2] Estimate.   *Source: Food and Agricultural Organization of the United Nations (FAO)*

U.S. Housing Starts: Seasonally Adjusted Annual Rate   In Thousands

Year	Jan.	Feb.	Mar.	Apr.	May	June	July	Aug.	Sept.	Oct.	Nov.	Dec.	Average
2014	888	944	970	1,043	1,007	911	1,085	984	1,023	1,074	1,001	1,073	1,000
2015	1,085	886	960	1,190	1,079	1,205	1,146	1,130	1,224	1,058	1,172	1,146	1,107
2016	1,092	1,225	1,111	1,163	1,148	1,203	1,239	1,171	1,068	1,313	1,140	1,252	1,177
2017	1,193	1,281	1,190	1,145	1,160	1,247	1,202	1,159	1,175	1,248	1,278	1,182	1,205
2018	1,301	1,279	1,324	1,286	1,358	1,199	1,199	1,289	1,247	1,220	1,177	1,089	1,247
2019	1,232	1,129	1,200	1,280	1,308	1,235	1,232	1,370	1,297	1,328	1,343	1,538	1,291
2020	1,572	1,565	1,267	925	1,054	1,266	1,529	1,377	1,463	1,537	1,545	1,663	1,397
2021	1,602	1,422	1,700	1,484	1,600	1,661	1,593	1,576	1,560	1,572	1,712	1,787	1,606
2022	1,669	1,771	1,713	1,803	1,543	1,561	1,371	1,505	1,463	1,432	1,427	1,357	1,551
2023[1]	1,340	1,436	1,380	1,348	1,583	1,418	1,451	1,305	1,356	1,376	1,525	1,460	1,415

[1] Preliminary.   Total Privately owned.   *Source: Bureau of the Census, U.S. Department of Commerce*

LUMBER AND PLYWOOD

white-fir (2x4): to 12/1970; spruce-hem-fir (2x4): 01/1971 to 02/1980; spruce-pine-fir (2x4): 03/1980 to date.

Average Price of Lumber in the United States   In Dollars per Thousand Board Feet

Year	Jan.	Feb.	Mar.	Apr.	May	June	July	Aug.	Sept.	Oct.	Nov.	Dec.	Average
2010	238.50	287.00	281.50	312.00	272.50	207.50	203.40	219.75	231.75	245.80	275.33	283.80	254.90
2011	307.25	286.25	294.25	269.50	227.25	222.75	254.50	231.75	250.80	236.50	230.25	248.00	254.92
2012	253.50	262.67	280.75	281.25	305.50	300.00	294.25	310.20	292.33	298.00	339.50	370.00	299.00
2013	382.25	377.33	401.50	386.60	325.50	298.40	312.25	326.00	346.75	360.25	381.80	364.25	355.24
2014	373.20	364.00	362.75	339.00	342.00	323.75	351.50	361.00	355.25	347.00	333.75	337.75	349.25
2015	326.00	313.50	283.75	261.50	256.40	292.25	294.25	267.75	246.00	259.20	259.75	267.25	277.30
2016	258.75	251.50	292.00	298.60	317.50	319.50	323.40	326.00	313.60	318.75	306.25	319.60	303.79
2017	309.50	374.75	359.20	405.33	387.75	368.40	403.25	394.50	413.80	446.25	485.00	461.40	400.76
2018	492.50	523.25	524.20	551.75	621.33	617.80	564.25	468.20	413.75	316.33	338.00	320.25	479.30
2019	334.50	405.75	370.80	326.00	312.00	359.75	356.00	330.00	----	----	----	----	349.35

Source: National Agricultural Statistics Service, U.S. Department of Agriculture (NASS-USDA)

Average Price of Plywood in the United States   In Dollars per Thousand Board Feet

Year	Jan.	Feb.	Mar.	Apr.	May	June	July	Aug.	Sept.	Oct.	Nov.	Dec.	Average
2010	191.50	220.00	233.00	353.75	330.00	206.25	217.20	171.25	164.50	183.00	189.33	196.40	221.35
2011	210.75	196.75	189.25	178.25	167.25	180.25	171.25	192.25	188.60	190.75	185.00	192.00	186.86
2012	201.00	194.67	213.25	212.50	233.75	252.00	257.50	331.00	343.33	300.00	343.75	354.50	269.77
2013	401.50	412.67	430.00	410.00	354.33	279.25	256.25	254.40	244.75	263.00	244.00	227.75	314.83
2014	226.60	215.00	214.50	210.33	233.00	210.25	212.25	215.40	222.00	222.00	219.00	204.00	217.03
2015	200.80	194.25	183.50	177.50	194.00	207.25	194.00	200.50	218.33	239.20	257.00	233.50	208.32
2016	232.50	230.75	224.25	244.20	275.75	278.00	295.40	306.25	300.00	287.00	285.75	282.00	270.15
2017	278.50	291.25	307.00	327.00	329.75	330.40	378.00	412.00	432.20	454.25	396.25	304.00	353.38
2018	318.75	377.50	405.00	405.00	418.33	445.00	403.75	347.00	342.50	268.33	242.00	208.25	348.45
2019	209.50	214.50	212.00	188.75	189.00	184.25	211.75	218.00	----	----	----	----	203.47

Source: National Agricultural Statistics Service, U.S. Department of Agriculture (NASS-USDA)

LUMBER - CME
Weekly Nearest Futures as of 05/15/2023

WEEKLY NEAREST FUTURES
As of 05/15/2023
Chart High 1711.20 on 05/10/2021
Chart Low 214.40 on 09/28/2015

USD / 1000 board ft

USD / 1000 board ft

Nearby Futures through Last Trading Day.

Volume of Trading of Lumber[1] Futures in Chicago   In Contracts

Year	Jan.	Feb.	Mar.	Apr.	May	June	July	Aug.	Sept.	Oct.	Nov.	Dec.	Total
2014	13,001	14,025	12,632	14,563	13,365	17,276	10,119	14,977	11,766	16,481	8,959	13,333	160,497
2015	13,744	16,696	14,710	21,116	16,757	19,374	14,253	20,509	15,592	21,061	11,475	16,065	201,352
2016	13,340	14,415	16,933	15,931	12,953	16,806	10,911	19,397	13,373	16,510	13,574	12,839	176,982
2017	11,400	20,115	14,942	21,705	16,706	15,346	14,333	15,684	16,030	21,713	18,739	18,386	205,099
2018	15,690	21,225	15,354	22,545	22,211	23,128	15,731	19,983	14,424	20,532	14,222	11,541	216,586
2019	14,464	14,588	11,140	17,457	13,524	16,484	12,478	13,524	10,085	14,511	12,554	11,873	162,682
2020	11,487	20,021	14,549	9,142	7,448	11,808	15,612	24,128	10,932	9,071	7,691	14,136	156,025
2021	8,548	9,838	8,078	12,051	12,761	14,019	11,012	8,470	6,196	7,935	7,368	9,801	116,077
2022	8,334	10,138	7,808	7,007	6,534	9,110	6,392	11,962	10,315	12,521	8,364	13,115	111,600
2023	12,345	12,421	13,770	13,502	10,790	19,574	15,435	19,297	13,558	19,317	21,601	16,578	188,188

Contract size = 110,000 board feet.   [1]Data through March 1996, Lumber and Random Lumber; August 2022 through May 2023, Random Lumber and Physical Lumber.   *Source: CME Group; Chicago Mercantile Exchange (CME)*

Average Open Interest of Lumber[1] Futures in Chicago   In Contracts

Year	Jan.	Feb.	Mar.	Apr.	May	June	July	Aug.	Sept.	Oct.	Nov.	Dec.
2014	3,945	4,602	4,618	5,020	4,422	5,013	4,080	4,419	3,751	3,698	4,610	4,289
2015	4,831	5,256	6,336	6,860	6,379	4,660	4,389	6,151	6,104	5,553	3,974	4,158
2016	4,619	5,292	4,478	4,561	5,050	4,782	4,692	5,167	3,479	4,323	3,818	4,005
2017	3,786	4,992	5,353	6,044	5,180	4,378	4,158	4,510	5,489	6,494	6,800	6,278
2018	6,775	7,290	6,406	6,964	6,827	6,550	5,649	4,714	3,986	4,078	4,120	3,984
2019	3,657	3,334	2,510	3,357	3,913	3,497	2,541	2,593	2,052	2,554	3,108	3,240
2020	3,302	4,078	2,990	2,761	2,602	2,509	3,672	4,520	3,642	3,300	2,829	3,026
2021	2,745	3,042	3,088	2,830	2,264	2,228	2,190	2,463	1,818	1,910	1,661	2,266
2022	2,446	2,595	2,548	2,760	2,381	2,351	1,991	2,510	2,540	2,720	2,473	3,316
2023	3,187	3,133	3,397	4,565	5,937	7,146	5,962	7,365	7,221	8,429	6,711	6,933

Contract size = 110,000 board feet.   [1]Data through March 1996, Lumber and Random Lumber; August 2022 through May 2023, Random Lumber and Physical Lumber.   *Source: CME Group; Chicago Mercantile Exchange (CME)*

LUMBER AND PLYWOOD

Production of Plywood by Selected Countries   In Thousands of Cubic Meters

Year	Austria	Canada	Finland	France	Germany	Italy	Japan	Poland	Romania	Russia	Spain	Sweden	United States
2013	311	1,792	1,090	255	135	225	2,761	430	665	3,303	275	87	9,680
2014	306	1,810	1,160	245	148	266	2,813	406	623	3,540	284	82	11,151
2015	241	1,929	1,150	246	108	244	2,756	390	316	3,607	371	60	10,972
2016	291	2,205	1,140	250	114	280	3,063	462	285	3,759	379	60	11,239
2017	291	2,253	1,240	254	100	236	3,287	546	277	3,729	509	85	11,600
2018	290	1,742	1,230	258	118	320	3,298	583	73	4,013	541	85	10,104
2019	157	1,922	1,090	253	111	320	3,337	519	260	4,061	565	85	9,925
2020	168	1,672	990	234	100	265	2,999	483	239	3,999	508	90	9,500
2021[1]	184	1,698	1,130	270	103	265	3,172	543	279	4,550	578	90	9,705
2022[2]	131	1,604	1,110	253	85	265	3,059	525	227	3,241	578	90	9,254

[1] Preliminary.   [2] Estimate.   *Source: Food and Agricultural Organization of the United Nations (FAO)*

Imports of Plywood by Selected Countries   In Thousands of Cubic Meters

Year	Austria	Belgium	Canada	Denmark	France	Germany	Italy	Japan	Netherlands	Sweden	Switzerland	United Kingdom	United States
2013	145	537	1,469	266	368	1,338	428	3,644	399	155	99	1,370	2,829
2014	160	554	1,587	266	429	1,369	453	3,491	468	163	184	1,399	2,872
2015	190	525	1,492	211	420	1,412	448	2,886	552	150	182	1,466	4,253
2016	181	575	1,228	242	478	1,458	458	2,770	536	175	192	1,479	4,877
2017	231	589	1,744	242	529	1,528	539	3,017	632	206	203	1,215	4,934
2018	242	589	1,562	281	539	1,620	527	2,934	640	222	200	1,598	5,466
2019	217	501	1,406	276	533	1,486	602	2,558	605	248	197	1,453	4,664
2020	234	422	1,174	276	649	1,437	413	2,227	635	235	197	1,362	6,461
2021[1]	267	565	1,406	276	541	1,483	612	2,648	695	203	203	1,541	8,086
2022[2]	181	374	1,220	276	476	1,319	731	2,745	577	236	203	1,117	6,259

[1] Preliminary.   [2] Estimate.   *Source: Food and Agricultural Organization of the United Nations (FAO)*

Exports of Plywood by Selected Countries   In Thousands of Cubic Meters

Year	Austria	Baltic States	Belgium	Canada	Finland	France	Germany	Italy	Netherlands	Poland	Russia	Spain	United States
2013	339	312	369	426	920	141	297	192	71	181	1,758	166	888
2014	346	302	403	482	998	145	310	210	75	203	1,969	189	828
2015	298	345	381	647	981	156	334	215	68	250	2,206	224	643
2016	340	439	437	625	940	153	349	240	73	257	2,458	252	697
2017	348	454	404	670	1,039	171	381	279	83	307	2,483	274	936
2018	307	474	395	733	1,012	174	393	211	102	336	2,696	291	700
2019	309	493	352	655	918	160	376	217	84	286	2,748	326	556
2020	299	544	213	543	828	225	373	204	89	309	2,904	249	528
2021[1]	357	560	425	634	955	164	388	230	95	374	3,039	333	759
2022[2]	295	552	212	654	900	140	330	288	95	369	2,130	363	771

[1] Preliminary.   [2] Estimate.   *Source: Food and Agricultural Organization of the United Nations (FAO)*

Magnesium

Magnesium (atomic symbol Mg) is a silvery-white, light, and fairly tough, metallic element and is relatively stable. Magnesium is one of the alkaline earth metals. Magnesium is the eighth-most abundant element in the earth's crust and the third most plentiful element found in seawater. Magnesium is ductile and malleable when heated, and except for beryllium, is the lightest metal that remains stable under ordinary conditions. First isolated by the British chemist Sir Humphrey Davy in 1808, magnesium today is obtained mainly by electrolysis of fused magnesium chloride.

Magnesium compounds, primarily magnesium oxide, are used in the refractory material that line the furnaces used to produce iron and steel, nonferrous metals, glass, and cement. Magnesium oxide and other compounds are also used in the chemical, agricultural, and construction industries. Magnesium's principal use is as an alloying addition for aluminum. These aluminum-magnesium alloys are used primarily in beverage cans. Due to their lightness and considerable tensile strength, the alloys are also used in structural components in airplanes and automobiles.

Prices – The average monthly price of ferromanganese (high carbon, FOB plant) in 2021 surged +69.1% yr/yr to $2,038.93 per gross ton, below the 2008 record high of $2,953.84 per gross ton.

Supply – World primary production of magnesium in 2022 fell by -10.5% yr/yr to 940 million metric tons. The world's largest primary producer of magnesium in 2023 was China, with 830,000 metric tons, which is 88.3% of the world's total production. Kazakhstan produced 25,000 metric tons, and both Brazil and Israel produced 22,000 metric tons.

Demand – Total US consumption of magnesium for all structural products in 2021 rose by +5.5% yr/yr to 30,855 metric tons. In 2021, for structural products, 96.5% of magnesium was used for castings, and the remaining 3.5% was used for wrought product. US consumption of magnesium for aluminum alloys in 2021 fell by -32.2% yr/yr to 10.300 metric tons. The consumption of magnesium for other uses in 2021 rose by +4.9% yr/yr to 40.7 metric tons. Total US consumption of primary magnesium in 2023 rose by +10.0% at 55,000 metric tons.

Trade – US exports of magnesium in 2023 fell by -55.6% yr/yr to a record low of 4,000 metric tons. US imports of magnesium in 2023 rose by +6.7% yr/yr to 95,000 metric tons.

World Production of Magnesium (Primary)   In Metric Tons

Year	Brazil	Canada	China	Israel	Kazakhstan	Russia	Serbia	Ukraine	United States	Total
2014	16,000	874,000	25,993	9,500	----	62,000	----	7,200	W	995,000
2015	15,000	859,000	19,307	8,100	----	60,000	200	7,700	W	970,000
2016	16,000	872,800	22,548	10,000	----	58,900	3,750	6,770	W	993,000
2017	20,000	904,600	23,000	12,000	----	65,000	14,000	7,300	W	1,050,000
2018	21,000	863,000	21,000	17,000	----	67,000	4,000	7,000	W	1,000,000
2019	22,000	970,000	21,000	25,000	----	67,000	7,000	8,000	W	1,120,000
2020	18,000	886,000	19,000	16,000	----	48,000	12,000	6,000	W	1,000,000
2021	20,000	930,000	18,000	16,000	----	58,000	13,000	10,000	W	1,070,000
2022[1]	22,000	933,000	22,000	27,000	----	21,000	14,000	2,000	W	1,050,000
2023[2]	22,000	830,000	22,000	25,000	----	20,000	15,000	----	W	940,000

[1] Preliminary. [2] Estimate. W = Withheld. *Source: U.S. Geological Survey (USGS)*

Salient Statistics of Magnesium in the United States   In Metric Tons

Year	Production Primary (Ingot)	Secondary New Scrap	Secondary Old Scrap	Total	Total Exports[3]	Imports for Consumption	Stocks Dec. 31[4]	Price $ Per Pound[5]	Castings	Wrought	Total Structural Products	Aluminum Alloys	Other Uses	Total
2014	W	55,200	25,000	81,100	17,000	51,900	W	2.15	9,638	2,340	11,978	22,600	41,100	63,700
2015	W	65,600	22,900	88,500	15,200	49,200	W	2.15	9,361	1,040	10,401	21,400	42,400	63,800
2016	W	72,700	29,400	102,000	19,300	45,500	W	2.15	29,739	1,870	31,609	13,000	56,000	69,000
2017	W	85,400	29,000	114,000	13,700	41,900	W	2.15	28,372	892	29,264	15,300	49,700	65,000
2018	W	80,400	28,700	109,000	12,000	47,000	W	2.17	25,093	206	25,299	15,100	40,900	56,000
2019	W	74,500	26,100	103,000	10,000	59,000	W	2.47	24,990	206	25,196	16,400	40,600	57,000
2020	W	70,300	24,500	95,000	15,000	61,000	W	2.48	29,050	206	29,256	15,200	38,800	54,000
2021	W	79,300	23,900	103,000	10,000	54,000	W	3.73	29,785	1,070	30,855	10,300	40,700	51,000
2022[1]	W			107,000	9,000	89,000	W	7.59						50,000
2023[2]	W			100,000	4,000	95,000	W	5.00						55,000

[1] Preliminary.   [2] Estimate.   [3] Metal & alloys in crude form & scrap.   [4] Estimate of Industry Stocks, metal.   [5] Magnesium ingots (99.8%), f.o.b. Valasco, Texas.   [6] Distributive or sacrificial purposes.   W = Withheld proprietary data.   *Source: U.S. Geological Survey (USGS)*

Manganese

Manganese (atomic symbol Mn) is a silvery-white, very brittle, metallic element used primarily in making alloys. Manganese was first distinguished as an element and isolated in 1774 by Johan Gottlieb Gahn. Manganese dissolves in acid and corrodes in moist air.

Manganese is found in the earth's crust in the form of ores such as rhodochrosite, franklinite, psilomelane, and manganite. Pyrolusite is the principal ore of manganese. Pure manganese is produced by igniting pyrolusite with aluminum powder or by electrolyzing manganese sulfate.

Manganese is used primarily in the steel industry for creating alloys, such as ferromanganese and spiegeleisen. In steel, manganese improves forging and rolling qualities, strength, toughness, stiffness, wear resistance, and hardness. Manganese is also used in plant fertilizers, animal feed, pigments, and dry cell batteries.

Prices – The average monthly price of ferromanganese (high carbon, FOB plant) in 2023 fell by -43.2% yr/yr to $1,441.294 per gross ton, below the 2008 record high of $2,953.84 per gross ton.

Supply – World production of manganese ore in 2021 rose by +1.1% yr/yr to 56.900 million metric tons. The world's largest producers of manganese ore in 2021 were South Africa with 33.2% of world production, Gabon with 16.9%, Australia with 13.9%, and China with 13.7%.

Demand – US consumption of manganese ore in 2023 fell by -2.0% yr/yr to 350,000 metric tons. US consumption of ferromanganese in 2023 rose by +0.3% yr/yr to 340,000 metric tons, below the 2012 record high of 382,000 metric tons.

Trade – The US still relies on imports for 100% of its manganese consumption, as it has since 1985. US imports of manganese ore for consumption in 2023 fell by -11.7% yr/yr to 500,000 metric tons. US imports of ferromanganese for consumption in 2023 fell by -9.1% yr/yr to 300,000 metric tons. US imports of silico-manganese in 2023 fell by -40.5% yr/yr to 250,000 metric tons.

World Production of Manganese Ore   In Thousands of Metric Tons (Gross Weight)

Year	Australia[2] (37%-53%)	Brazil (37%)	China (20%-30%)	Gabon (45%-53%)	Ghana (32%-34%)	India (10%-54%)	Kazakh-stan (29%-30%)	Malaysia (32%-45%)	Mexico (27%-50%)	South Africa (30%-48%+)	Ukraine (30%-35%)	Other	World Total
2013	7,447	2,883	17,478	3,997	1,812	3,112	1,121	1,125	580	10,958	1,525	1,670	54,500
2014	7,505	2,723	19,590	3,781	1,497	2,200	1,092	835	652	14,051	1,526	----	57,600
2015	7,400	2,868	10,566	4,112	1,478	2,300	616	502	600	11,033	1,203	----	44,500
2016	5,164	2,811	14,117	3,379	1,967	3,365	510	701	600	10,806	1,250	----	46,200
2017	6,473	3,334	19,032	4,717	3,004	1,957	464	1,226	590	14,653	1,425	----	59,100
2018	8,193	3,189	10,403	5,071	4,552	3,924	434	1,263	560	14,920	1,521	----	57,000
2019	7,545	3,726	10,325	6,169	5,383	3,134	460	1,131	576	17,002	1,687	----	60,900
2020	7,976	2,469	12,856	7,916	2,358	1,809	276	870	575	16,199	1,888	----	58,600
2021	7,900	1,426	8,000	9,643	3,336	1,759	371	913	580	19,156	1,760	----	57,800
2022[1]	7,169	1,691	6,500	10,375	3,103	2,543	390	916	582	18,967	950	----	56,400

[1] Preliminary.   [2] Metallurgical Ore.   [3] Concentrate.   [4] Ranges of percentage of manganese.   *Source: U.S. Geological Survey (USGS)*

Salient Statistics of Manganese in the United States   In Thousands of Metric Tons (Gross Weight)

Year	Net Import Reliance As a % of Apparent Consump	Manganese Ore (35% or More Manganese) Imports for Con-sumption	Exports	Con-sumption	Stocks Dec. 31[3]	Ferromanganese Imports for Con-sumption	Exports	Con-sumption	Avg Price Mn. Metal-lurgical Ore $/Metric Ton Unit[4]	Silicomanganese Exports	Imports
2014	100	387	1	508	189	365	6	360	4.49	3.0	448.0
2015	100	441	1	451	187	292	5	344	3.53	1.0	301.0
2016	100	282	1	410	207	229	7	342	3.41	2.0	264.0
2017	100	297	1	378	141	331	9	345	6.43	8.0	351.0
2018	100	440	3	369	139	427	10	348	7.17	4.0	412.0
2019	100	434	1	442	143	332	5	336	6.60	2.0	351.0
2020	100	367	1	378	229	223	5	325	----	2.0	269.0
2021	100	497	1	399	237	329	9	335	----	5.0	313.0
2022[1]	100	566	1	357	234	330	3	339	----	3.0	420.0
2023[2]	100	500	1	350	230	300	2	340	----	3.0	250.0

[1] Preliminary.   [2] Estimate.   [3] Including bonded warehouses; excludes Gov't stocks; also excludes small tonnages of dealers' stocks.
[4] 46-48% Mn, C.I.F. U.S. Ports.   *Source: U.S. Geological Survey (USGS)*

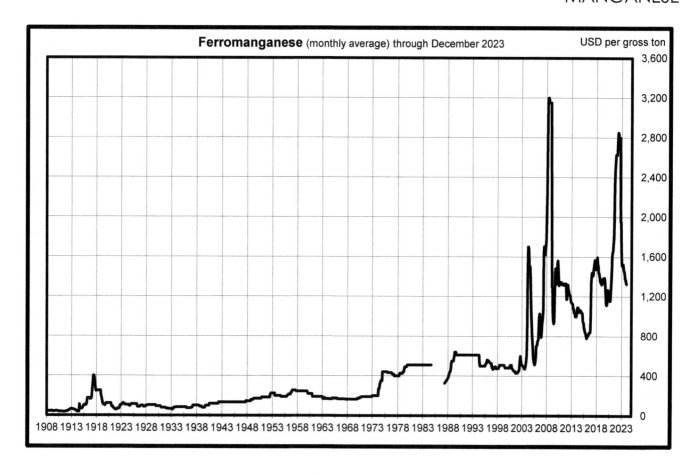

Ferromanganese (monthly average) through December 2023   USD per gross ton

Imports[3] of Manganese Ore (20% or More Mn) in the United States   In Metric Tons (Mn Content)

Year	Australia	Brazil	Gabon	Mexico	Morocco	South Africa	Total	Customs Value ($1,000)
2013	29,200	3,850	192,000	4,810	3,800	12,900	263,000	126,000
2014	17,500	1,690	143,000	3,440	954	17,200	186,000	88,300
2015	16,700	2,210	171,000	2,100	128	23,800	232,000	92,500
2016	3,510	290	106,530	8,820	87	14,968	135,200	40,700
2017	9,770	340	134,640	10,690	135	14,400	170,100	73,300
2018	13,500	3,890	141,130	15,290	66	38,170	204,800	122,000
2019	----	9,070	187,000	21,400	165	22,540	241,000	126,000
2020	----	273	123,000	30,000	762	31,500	186,000	86,700
2021[1]	----	97	202,000	21,300	1,210	36,600	261,000	99,800
2022[2]	----	106	173,000	29,400	9	85,000	287,000	126,000

[1] Preliminary.   [2] Estimate.   [3] Imports for consumption.   *Source: U.S. Geological Survey (USGS)*

Average Price of Ferromanganese[1]   In Dollars Per Gross Ton -- Carloads

Year	Jan.	Feb.	Mar.	Apr.	May	June	July	Aug.	Sept.	Oct.	Nov.	Dec.	Average
2014	1,006.19	1,066.50	1,088.58	1,090.00	1,080.00	1,078.22	1,041.25	1,060.00	1,053.34	1,055.22	1,060.00	1,039.53	1,059.90
2015	1,042.00	1,036.06	1,029.09	944.66	939.75	929.77	876.82	875.00	841.67	836.36	825.00	797.73	914.49
2016	779.34	792.00	797.50	805.00	813.57	821.59	836.25	835.00	836.67	845.00	1,012.12	1,320.24	874.52
2017	1,410.00	1,438.42	1,430.87	1,406.50	1,418.64	1,470.68	1,509.00	1,547.39	1,568.50	1,552.84	1,540.00	1,473.12	1,480.50
2018	1,500.60	1,564.21	1,595.45	1,527.62	1,509.32	1,438.57	1,433.57	1,404.57	1,375.00	1,345.65	1,337.50	1,327.12	1,446.60
2019	1,321.90	1,324.34	1,346.67	1,379.76	1,374.55	1,374.00	1,358.18	1,386.36	1,344.50	1,296.09	1,193.42	1,115.63	1,317.95
2020	1,112.50	1,125.63	1,167.50	1,265.00	1,247.50	1,220.00	1,220.00	1,191.25	1,155.00	1,172.50	1,247.50	1,343.00	1,205.62
2021	1,464.00	1,605.00	1,644.38	1,665.00	1,717.50	1,783.75	1,975.00	2,325.00	2,475.00	2,562.50	2,625.00	2,625.00	2,038.93
2022	2,625.00	2,625.00	2,750.00	2,850.00	2,837.50	2,800.00	2,800.00	2,800.00	2,790.00	1,950.00	1,950.00	1,669.00	2,537.21
2023	1,512.50	1,525.00	1,525.00	1,525.00	1,487.50	1,455.00	1,450.00	1,409.00	1,376.25	1,370.00	1,343.00	1,325.00	1,441.94

[1] Domestic standard, high carbon, FOB plant, carloads.   *Source: American Metal Market (AMM)*

Meats

U.S. commercial red meat includes beef, veal, lamb, and pork. Red meat is a good source of iron, vitamin B12, and protein, and eliminating it from the diet can lead to iron and zinc deficiencies. Today, red meat is far leaner than it was 30 years ago due to newer breeds of livestock that carry less fat. The leanest cuts of beef include tenderloin, sirloin, and flank. The leanest cuts of pork include pork tenderloin, loin chops, and rib chops.

The USDA (United States Department of Agriculture) grades various cuts of meat. "Prime" is the highest USDA grade for beef, veal, and lamb. "Choice" is the grade designation below Prime for beef, veal, and lamb. "Commercial" and "Cutter" grades are two of the lower designations for beef, usually sold as ground meat, sausage, and canned meat. "Canner" is the lowest USDA grade designation for beef and is used primarily in canned meats not sold at retail.

Supply – World total meat production in 2023 rose +0.4% to 174.589 million metric tons. China was the world's largest meat producer in 2023, with 64.400 million metric tons of production (up +2.9% yr/yr), accounting for 36.9% of world production. US production of red meats in 2022 fell by -0.6% yr/yr to 55.561 billion pounds. US production of beef in 2022 rose by +1.2% yr/yr to 28.358

billion pounds. Beef accounted for 51.0% of all US meat production in 2022. US production of pork in 2022 fell by -2.5% yr/yr to 27.009 billion pounds, below the record high of 28.318 billion pounds in 2020. Pork accounted for 48.6% of US meat production. Based on 2022 data, veal accounted for only 0.1% of US meat production, and lamb and mutton accounted for only 0.2% of US meat production.

Demand – US per-capita meat consumption in 2022 rose by +0.1% yr/yr to 111.6 pounds per person per year, above the 2014 record low of 101.7 pounds per person. Meat consumption has fallen sharply from 192 pounds per person back in 1970, reflecting the trend towards eating more chicken and fish and the availability of meat substitutes. Per-capita beef consumption in 2022 rose by +0.3% from 2021's 58.9 pounds, about half the record high of 127.5 pounds seen in 1976. Per capita pork consumption in 2022 remained unchanged yr/yr to 51.1 pounds per person per year, well above the 2011 record low of 45.7 pounds.

Trade – World red meat exports in 2023 fell by -4.5% to 21.939 million metric tons. The world's largest red meat exporters in 2023 were the US with 20.2% of world exports, Brazil with 19.7%, the European Union with 16.9%, Canada with 8.5%, Australia with 7.4%, and India with 6.5%.

World Total Meat Production[4]   In Thousands of Metric Tons

Year	Argentina	Australia	Brazil	Canada	China[4]	European Union	India	Mexico	New Zealand	Russia	South Africa	United States	World Total
2014	3,142	2,957	13,123	2,906	64,365	29,983	4,000	2,962	705	3,846	1,207	21,443	168,891
2015	3,204	2,921	12,944	2,946	62,623	30,933	4,080	3,014	734	3,953	1,271	21,938	169,501
2016	3,152	2,511	13,100	3,044	60,424	29,886	4,170	3,090	693	4,159	1,334	22,827	165,987
2017	3,394	2,557	13,475	3,159	60,864	29,709	4,230	3,192	700	4,284	1,278	23,554	167,979
2018	3,638	2,733	13,738	3,220	60,480	30,223	4,240	3,301	718	4,512	1,275	24,199	170,153
2019	3,735	2,830	14,025	3,342	49,220	29,960	4,270	3,435	757	4,698	1,281	24,928	159,914
2020	3,825	2,542	14,100	3,429	43,060	30,122	3,760	3,530	772	4,989	1,280	25,234	153,718
2021	3,696	2,338	14,115	3,486	54,480	30,498	4,195	3,613	799	5,080	1,290	25,294	166,315
2022[1]	3,863	2,314	14,700	3,494	62,590	28,999	4,350	3,707	773	5,230	1,305	25,142	173,814
2023[2]	4,062	2,685	15,035	3,405	64,400	27,280	4,435	3,790	790	5,270	1,270	24,678	174,589

[1] Preliminary.   [2] Forecast.   [4] Predominately pork production.   *Source: Foreign Agricultural Service, U.S. Department of Agriculture (FAS-USDA)*

Production and Consumption of Red Meats in The United States

	Beef			Veal			Lamb & Mutton			Pork (Excluding Lard)			All Meats		
	Commercial Production	Consumption		Commercial Production	Consumption		Commercial Production	Consumption		Commercial Production	Consumption		Commercial Production	Consumption	
Year	- Million Pounds -	Total	Per Capita Lbs.	- Million Pounds -	Total	Per Capita Lbs.	- Million Pounds -	Total	Per Capita Lbs.	- Million Pounds -	Total	Per Capita Lbs.	- Million Pounds -	Total	Per Capita Lbs.
2014	24,250	24,687	54.2	100	98	0.3	161	340	0.9	22,858	18,836	45.9	47,435	43,955	101.3
2015	23,698	24,773	54.0	88	88	0.2	155	357	1.0	24,517	20,592	49.8	48,520	45,806	105.0
2016	25,288	25,673	55.6	81	73	0.2	155	381	1.0	24,957	20,892	50.2	50,481	47,015	107.0
2017	26,250	26,492	57.0	80	78	0.2	150	396	1.1	25,598	21,034	50.2	52,078	48,000	108.5
2018	26,938	26,763	57.3	81	89	0.2	158	415	1.1	26,329	21,490	51.0	53,507	48,758	109.7
2019	27,155	27,276	57.8	75	81	0.2	153	422	1.1	27,652	22,189	52.1	55,108	49,968	111.9
2020	27,174	27,559	58.2	64	66	0.2	138	451	1.4	28,303	22,122	51.8	55,680	50,198	111.4
2021[1]	27,948	27,973	58.9	53	64	0.2	138	506	1.5	27,675	21,868	51.1	55,815	50,410	111.5
2022[2]	28,291	28,157	59.1	54	61	0.2	131	484	1.5	26,996	21,951	51.1	55,471	50,653	111.6
2023[3]	26,963	27,807	58.1	48	53	0.2	130	420	1.3	27,301	21,674	50.2	54,442	49,954	109.5

[1] Preliminary.   [2] Estimate.   [3] Forecast.   *Source: Economic Research Service, U.S. Department of Agriculture (ERS-USDA)*

Total Red Meat Imports (Carcass Weight Equivalent) of Principal Countries   In Thousands of Metric Tons

Year	Brazil	Canada	Egypt	European Union	Hong Kong	Japan	Korea, South	Mexico	Philip-pines	Russia	Taiwan	United States	World Total
2014	80	485	270	377	989	2,049	823	879	357	1,375	196	1,796	13,173
2015	59	482	360	365	727	1,955	963	982	313	954	237	2,034	13,441
2016	65	456	340	560	851	2,058	1,065	1,024	350	809	226	1,861	15,921
2017	56	447	250	548	971	2,266	1,113	1,073	401	836	264	1,864	16,013
2018	48	464	300	591	932	2,320	1,268	1,166	470	533	279	1,833	16,787
2019	45	446	340	599	687	2,346	1,244	1,174	407	516	291	1,816	18,351
2020	52	523	230	510	891	2,244	1,103	1,107	358	376	269	1,925	21,297
2021	65	475	300	419	735	2,227	1,158	1,327	683	314	266	2,052	21,447
2022[1]	74	448	270	493	377	2,300	1,308	1,465	816	302	311	2,148	20,034
2023[2]	57	505	245	465	373	2,155	1,260	1,540	610	295	335	2,212	19,524

[1] Preliminary.   [2] Forecast.   Source: Foreign Agricultural Service, U.S. Department of Agriculture (FAS-USDA)

Total Red Meat Exports (Carcass Weight Equivalent) of Principal Countries   In Thousands of Metric Tons

Year	Argen-tina	Australia	Brazil	Canada	China	European Union	India	New Zealand	Russia	Ukraine	United States	Uruguay	World Total
2014	193	1,795	2,398	1,528	312	2,375	2,022	552	14	35	3,477	331	16,423
2015	181	1,802	2,277	1,561	257	2,585	1,754	609	18	65	3,300	352	16,200
2016	211	1,445	2,472	1,684	217	4,577	1,709	560	33	44	3,536	396	18,744
2017	286	1,454	2,579	1,734	228	4,378	1,786	565	44	56	3,852	409	19,282
2018	508	1,623	2,743	1,754	223	4,407	1,511	603	53	53	4,099	436	19,995
2019	772	1,772	3,175	1,811	156	4,967	1,494	624	85	51	4,240	436	21,759
2020	846	1,507	3,717	2,057	116	5,889	1,284	635	189	36	4,640	411	23,798
2021	755	1,329	3,641	2,076	121	5,668	1,397	686	208	41	4,741	557	23,660
2022[1]	824	1,273	4,217	1,999	121	4,801	1,442	644	215	22	4,486	513	22,973
2023[2]	880	1,615	4,312	1,860	110	3,710	1,420	676	245	31	4,437	450	21,939

[1] Preliminary.   [2] Forecast.   Source: Foreign Agricultural Service, U.S. Department of Agriculture (FAS-USDA)

Exports and Imports of Meats in the United States (Carcass Weight Equivalent)[3]

| | ------- Exports ------- | | | | ------- Imports ------- | | | |
Year	Beef and Veal	Lamb and Mutton	Pork[3]	All Meat	Beef and Veal	Lamb and Mutton	Pork[3]	All Meat
2014	2,574	7	5,092	7,673	2,947	195	1,011	4,153
2015	2,267	4	5,010	7,281	3,368	214	1,116	4,698
2016	2,557	5	5,239	7,801	3,012	216	1,091	4,319
2017	2,859	6	5,632	8,497	2,993	252	1,116	4,361
2018	3,160	6	5,877	9,043	2,998	273	1,042	4,313
2019	3,026	6	6,321	9,353	3,058	272	945	4,275
2020	2,951	3	7,280	10,234	3,339	302	904	4,545
2021	3,428	3	7,024	10,455	3,345	364	1,180	4,889
2022[1]	3,544	6	6,345	9,895	3,390	358	1,344	5,092
2023[2]	3,038	5	6,818	9,861	3,727	284	1,143	5,154

[1] Preliminary.   [2] Estimate.   [3] Includes meat content of minor meats and of mixed products.
Source: Economic Research Service, U.S. Department of Agriculture (FAS-USDA)

Average Wholesale Prices of Meats in the United States   In Cent Per Pound

Year	Composite Retail Price of Beef, Choice, Grade 3	of Pork[3]	Wholesale Value[4] Beef	Wholesale Value[4] Pork	Net Farm Value[5] of Pork	Cow Beef Canner & Cutter, Central US	Boxed Beef Cut-out, Choice 1-3, Central US 550-700 Lb.	Pork Carcass Cut-out, U.S., No. 2	Lamb Carcass, Choice-Prime, E. Coast, 55-65 lbs.	Pork[6] Loins, Central US 14-18 lbs.	Skinned Ham, Central US 17-20 lbs.	Pork Bellies, Central US 12-14 lbs.
2014	597.03	401.88	364.71	187.66	131.80	----	238.94	110.10	339.65	141.93	107.00	144.90
2015	628.89	385.25	362.78	145.72	87.39	----	237.48	78.96	343.07	103.77	65.11	121.07
2016	596.38	374.67	316.78	150.12	80.05	----	207.00	78.36	332.90	96.95	66.73	123.94
2017	590.86	378.42	321.47	155.37	87.41	----	209.74	84.02	339.16	97.28	64.63	148.76
2018	592.33	374.45	328.55	140.14	79.16	----	214.06	76.09	----	92.91	56.80	133.73
2019	604.37	384.33	341.48	145.38	82.95	----	222.86	77.14	----	88.88	67.66	131.84
2020	653.55	402.93	365.51	148.09	74.51	----	236.36	77.31	----	99.22	54.66	95.86
2021	724.52	450.31	423.19	200.96	116.03	----	280.30	104.11	----	103.03	70.18	190.83
2022[1]	758.59	489.71	397.88	199.53	121.52	----	263.94	103.72	----	116.08	85.54	172.81
2023[2]	798.36	480.88	452.92	166.80	99.30	----	299.02	89.78	----	106.75	83.03	130.43

[1] Preliminary.   [2] Estimate.   [3] Sold as retail cuts (ham, bacon, loin, etc.).   [4] Quantity equivalent to 1 pound of retail cuts.
[5] Portion of gross farm value minus farm by-product allowance.   Source: Economic Research Service, U.S. Department of Agriculture (ERS-USDA)

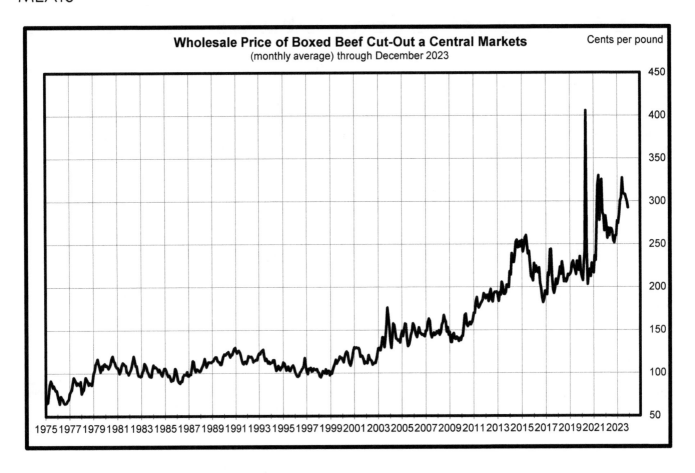

Wholesale Price of Boxed Beef Cut-Out a Central Markets Cents per pound
(monthly average) through December 2023

Average Wholesale Price of Boxed Beef Cut-Out[2], Choice 1-3, at Central US In Cents Per Pound

Year	Jan.	Feb.	Mar.	Apr.	May	June	July	Aug.	Sept.	Oct.	Nov.	Dec.	Average
2014	218.00	214.43	239.03	229.14	228.96	236.60	252.87	254.83	246.14	246.80	253.18	247.35	238.94
2015	254.45	241.30	247.62	257.44	260.25	250.06	238.91	241.81	227.68	212.10	210.63	207.46	237.48
2016	227.76	217.46	224.61	218.88	216.91	222.59	204.88	199.30	187.77	182.29	186.27	195.23	207.00
2017	194.40	191.42	216.36	213.78	243.43	244.16	212.22	197.48	192.79	198.65	209.08	203.09	209.74
2018	207.94	213.66	223.50	215.29	229.34	221.03	206.32	209.15	206.07	208.18	214.59	213.60	214.06
2019	215.03	217.81	227.45	230.30	223.61	221.28	214.81	230.17	221.35	219.70	235.53	217.24	222.86
2020	211.87	207.60	228.05	241.94	405.80	242.31	203.24	216.71	220.56	212.41	228.00	217.82	236.36
2021	216.73	236.49	231.23	271.67	317.59	329.70	278.00	321.67	325.24	285.97	283.46	265.82	280.30
2022	282.54	272.77	256.95	268.39	260.08	268.16	267.86	264.90	254.11	251.58	259.56	260.37	263.94
2023[1]	277.04	274.00	284.21	300.54	304.30	327.27	309.83	308.21	307.91	303.10	299.30	292.52	299.02

[1] Preliminary. [2] 600-900 pounds. *Source: Economic Research Service, U.S. Department of Agriculture (ERS-USDA)*

Production (Commercial) of All Red Meats in the United States In Millions of Pounds (Carcass Weight)

Year	Jan.	Feb.	Mar.	Apr.	May	June	July	Aug.	Sept.	Oct.	Nov.	Dec.	Total
2014	4,248.9	3,653.1	3,814.8	3,976.9	3,952.8	3,824.0	3,906.9	3,795.3	3,958.8	4,319.3	3,759.3	4,136.2	47,346
2015	4,087.0	3,731.8	4,064.3	4,015.5	3,805.3	4,017.4	4,038.5	3,901.4	4,140.2	4,313.4	4,033.2	4,274.0	48,422
2016	4,055.6	3,904.2	4,261.8	3,982.9	3,997.1	4,225.9	3,866.0	4,432.2	4,323.1	4,426.5	4,498.4	4,402.2	50,376
2017	4,291.4	3,937.9	4,535.1	3,968.1	4,276.0	4,350.8	3,988.9	4,630.5	4,403.8	4,635.3	4,553.2	4,402.4	51,973
2018	4,588.4	4,059.5	4,520.5	4,278.2	4,501.5	4,327.7	4,235.3	4,765.9	4,187.8	4,901.4	4,682.7	4,367.8	53,417
2019	4,701.6	4,172.4	4,433.7	4,551.5	4,566.2	4,369.3	4,588.8	4,650.2	4,443.5	5,064.0	4,743.1	4,726.6	55,011
2020	4,959.2	4,452.7	4,995.3	3,862.1	3,762.5	4,792.1	4,810.8	4,691.6	4,706.2	5,085.9	4,683.8	4,852.6	55,655
2021	4,801.4	4,386.3	5,047.9	4,707.8	4,295.6	4,669.0	4,383.1	4,588.2	4,580.1	4,755.0	4,804.8	4,782.9	55,802
2022	4,561.0	4,431.8	4,978.9	4,545.5	4,484.9	4,724.6	4,233.5	4,826.2	4,665.4	4,757.1	4,790.6	4,470.9	55,470
2023[1]	4,764.6	4,263.1	4,909.9	4,203.4	4,592.7	4,551.4	4,128.0	4,673.2	4,349.4	4,774.9	4,684.6	4,546.5	54,442

[1] Preliminary. *Source: Economic Research Service, U.S. Department of Agriculture (ERS-USDA)*

Production (Commercial) of Beef in the United States   In Millions of Pounds (Carcass Weight)

Year	Jan.	Feb.	Mar.	Apr.	May	June	July	Aug.	Sept.	Oct.	Nov.	Dec.	Total
2014	2,141.1	1,788.9	1,938.4	2,042.8	2,071.6	2,068.7	2,085.9	2,024.4	2,067.4	2,171.5	1,850.6	2,000.7	24,252
2015	1,963.8	1,768.7	1,931.6	1,928.5	1,924.9	2,001.2	2,046.1	1,934.1	2,085.7	2,125.3	1,934.1	2,045.9	23,690
2016	1,953.5	1,885.0	2,096.0	1,964.0	2,029.5	2,193.0	2,024.4	2,264.4	2,179.2	2,210.1	2,239.3	2,173.3	25,212
2017	2,118.3	1,933.7	2,247.7	1,962.7	2,162.1	2,279.1	2,107.5	2,401.2	2,222.3	2,300.7	2,289.6	2,148.0	26,173
2018	2,279.0	1,983.9	2,203.5	2,117.7	2,307.0	2,300.9	2,231.6	2,429.6	2,157.5	2,430.6	2,315.1	2,116.0	26,872
2019	2,308.9	1,987.6	2,117.7	2,261.5	2,327.9	2,224.6	2,359.9	2,373.5	2,189.3	2,438.1	2,297.0	2,265.0	27,151
2020	2,387.6	2,130.7	2,410.8	1,815.4	1,865.1	2,373.6	2,421.2	2,334.6	2,354.5	2,471.5	2,262.9	2,324.8	27,153
2021	2,309.0	2,105.5	2,480.6	2,346.3	2,210.9	2,399.3	2,318.8	2,360.0	2,299.2	2,366.4	2,379.4	2,362.0	27,937
2022	2,266.2	2,250.4	2,505.8	2,327.1	2,287.7	2,453.7	2,249.0	2,506.5	2,391.0	2,404.0	2,424.3	2,225.6	28,291
2023[1]	2,324.6	2,092.2	2,404.8	2,069.4	2,305.8	2,335.0	2,107.9	2,363.5	2,149.4	2,340.9	2,280.9	2,189.9	26,964

[1] Preliminary.   *Source: Economic Research Service, U.S. Department of Agriculture (ERS-USDA)*

Production (Commercial) of Pork in the United States   In Millions of Pounds (Carcass Weight)

Year	Jan.	Feb.	Mar.	Apr.	May	June	July	Aug.	Sept.	Oct.	Nov.	Dec.	Total
2014	2,086.1	1,844.4	1,854.5	1,910.5	1,859.5	1,734.3	1,799.3	1,752.1	1,871.9	2,126.7	1,890.7	2,114.5	22,845
2015	2,104.7	1,945.2	2,111.5	2,066.8	1,861.9	1,995.8	1,972.6	1,949.1	2,035.5	2,168.9	2,080.2	2,207.1	24,499
2016	2,084.2	2,000.6	2,145.1	2,000.1	1,948.6	2,013.3	1,824.6	2,149.1	2,125.7	2,198.1	2,240.3	2,209.0	24,939
2017	2,154.5	1,987.4	2,267.3	1,988.1	2,095.8	2,053.0	1,864.7	2,210.1	2,164.2	2,316.3	2,244.8	2,235.0	25,581
2018	2,290.1	2,058.1	2,296.8	2,141.9	2,174.4	2,008.6	1,985.5	2,316.3	2,012.9	2,450.5	2,348.0	2,232.1	26,315
2019	2,373.6	2,167.5	2,297.2	2,268.8	2,218.6	2,127.6	2,210.7	2,258.1	2,237.2	2,606.2	2,428.8	2,443.0	27,637
2020	2,553.3	2,306.2	2,566.5	2,030.8	1,879.6	2,400.4	2,371.7	2,341.2	2,335.9	2,598.5	2,405.5	2,510.2	28,300
2021	2,477.4	2,265.3	2,548.5	2,343.6	2,070.0	2,254.3	2,049.7	2,213.6	2,265.8	2,372.6	2,408.8	2,404.0	27,674
2022	2,280.3	2,168.0	2,455.9	2,201.6	2,182.0	2,254.9	1,970.1	2,303.3	2,259.4	2,338.2	2,350.8	2,229.9	26,994
2023[1]	2,425.4	2,157.0	2,488.2	2,119.4	2,271.3	2,201.6	2,006.8	2,295.0	2,186.2	2,418.5	2,388.2	2,342.0	27,300

[1] Preliminary.   *Source: Economic Research Service, U.S. Department of Agriculture (ERS-USDA)*

Cold Storage Holdings of All[2] Meats in the United States, on First of Month   In Millions of Pounds

Year	Jan.	Feb.	Mar.	Apr.	May	June	July	Aug.	Sept.	Oct.	Nov.	Dec.
2014	1,022.2	1,077.0	1,093.6	1,012.3	1,015.9	981.4	930.1	939.1	934.0	970.8	956.5	930.3
2015	988.5	1,131.2	1,224.3	1,196.3	1,229.0	1,172.9	1,147.6	1,136.2	1,170.0	1,202.1	1,159.5	1,122.8
2016	1,105.9	1,213.4	1,182.7	1,142.9	1,151.1	1,129.1	1,099.2	1,118.1	1,130.5	1,205.1	1,173.3	1,079.2
2017	1,083.8	1,101.3	1,112.9	1,051.4	1,092.7	1,042.4	1,012.8	1,029.8	1,100.0	1,159.7	1,149.4	1,032.3
2018	1,021.2	1,129.2	1,118.6	1,124.4	1,159.9	1,142.2	1,064.1	1,096.5	1,136.4	1,150.8	1,135.7	1,069.3
2019	1,045.6	1,119.9	1,134.5	1,095.9	1,098.1	1,077.8	1,069.4	1,113.9	1,128.7	1,115.1	1,121.6	1,092.6
2020	1,101.5	1,157.3	1,185.8	1,162.0	1,136.9	936.2	939.5	950.9	960.7	968.6	981.7	966.2
2021	986.1	1,010.5	1,031.7	967.9	937.6	907.5	870.7	868.9	897.2	940.3	947.8	920.4
2022	929.3	986.4	1,035.1	1,048.5	1,092.8	1,097.2	1,081.4	1,066.8	1,088.5	1,097.9	1,051.2	1,006.7
2023[1]	1,028.2	1,081.4	1,053.7	1,039.1	1,045.6	983.5	923.3	909.8	892.0	910.0	910.6	896.4

[1] Preliminary.   [2] Includes beef and veal, mutton and lamb, pork and products, rendered pork fat, and miscellaneous meats. Excludes lard.
Source: Economic Research Service, U.S. Department of Agriculture (ERS-USDA)

Cold Storage Holdings of Frozen Beef in the United States, on First of Month   In Millions of Pounds

Year	Jan.	Feb.	Mar.	Apr.	May	June	July	Aug.	Sept.	Oct.	Nov.	Dec.
2014	439.4	429.3	409.5	405.8	402.3	377.6	358.2	367.9	346.6	378.2	380.9	400.8
2015	444.4	492.0	491.9	481.5	484.3	474.6	474.3	460.1	470.3	498.3	509.1	510.6
2016	512.5	534.1	506.4	481.8	467.8	461.7	464.5	469.7	476.6	519.0	533.1	531.0
2017	567.9	538.2	502.4	464.0	458.4	411.5	415.3	431.8	476.6	496.0	507.0	485.2
2018	488.1	501.7	459.3	464.0	471.2	464.7	448.6	484.2	501.3	507.2	515.6	514.7
2019	495.6	510.2	474.0	451.9	430.2	405.2	405.6	454.5	469.9	469.0	466.3	478.3
2020	480.1	488.2	494.6	502.3	479.5	417.4	429.3	440.2	449.3	463.0	500.2	511.4
2021	535.9	519.4	512.5	483.0	448.9	416.7	401.5	400.8	414.9	439.6	473.8	490.4
2022	507.1	525.7	531.6	535.8	532.2	526.1	516.8	511.8	513.8	526.1	510.3	523.2
2023[1]	544.0	535.2	500.8	477.8	452.1	425.7	410.7	410.5	395.4	420.8	445.7	457.4

[1] Preliminary.   *Source: Economic Research Service, U.S. Department of Agriculture (ERS-USDA)*

Mercury

Mercury (atomic symbol Hg) was known to the ancient Hindus and Chinese and was also found in Egyptian tombs dating back to 1500 BC. The ancient Greeks used mercury in ointments, and the Romans used it in cosmetics. Alchemists thought mercury turned into gold when it hardened.

Mercury, also called quicksilver, is a heavy, silvery, toxic, transitional metal. Mercury is the only common metal that is liquid at room temperatures. When subjected to a pressure of 7,640 atmospheres (7.7 million millibars), mercury becomes a solid. Mercury dissolves in nitric or concentrated sulfuric acid but is resistant to alkalis. It is a poor conductor of heat. Mercury has superconductivity when cooled to sufficiently low temperatures. It has a freezing point of about −39 degrees Celsius and a boiling point of about 357 degrees Celsius.

Mercury is found in its pure form or combined in small amounts with silvers, but is found most often in the ore cinnabar, a mineral consisting of mercuric sulfide. Pure mercury is produced by heating the cinnabar ore in the air until the mercuric sulfide breaks down. Mercury forms alloys called amalgams with all common metals except iron and platinum. Most mercury is used for the manufacture of industrial chemicals and electrical and electronic applications. Other uses for mercury include its use in gold recovery from ores, barometers, diffusion pumps, laboratory instruments, mercury-vapor lamps, pesticides, batteries, and catalysts. A decline in mercury production and usage since the 1970s reflects a trend for using mercury substitutes due to its toxicity.

Supply – World mine production of mercury in 2023 rose by +3.4% yr/yr to 1,200 metric tons. The world's largest miners of mercury in 2023 were China, which had 83.0% of world production, and Tajikistan, which had 8.0%.

Trade – US imports of mercury in 2023 rose by +89.6% yr/yr to 4.0 metric tons. US imports were mostly from Chile and Peru.

World Mine Production of Mercury   In Metric Tons (1 tonne = 29.008216 flasks)

Year	Chile (byproduct)	China	Finland	Kyrgyzstan	Mexico (Exports)	Morocco	Peru (Exports)	Russia	Tajikistan	United States	World Total
2014	18	2,260	----	48	301	8	40	NA	35	NA	2,770
2015	14	2,801	----	46	306	5	35	NA	30	NA	3,300
2016	2	3,482	----	20	262	5	40	----	30	----	4,000
2017	11	3,573	----	20	225	14	40	----	100	----	4,060
2018	3	2,317	----	20	230	32	35	----	100	----	2,780
2019	----	2,232	----	15	50	2	35	----	91	----	2,500
2020	----	1,993	----	7	70	2	30	----	178	----	2,300
2021	----	1,280	----	6	20	2	30	----	117	----	1,480
2022[1]	----	1,000	----	6	----	2	30	----	100	----	1,160
2023[2]	----	1,000	----	6	----	2	30	----	100	----	1,200

[1] Preliminary.   [2] Estimate.   NA = Not available   W = Withheld.   *Source: U.S. Geological Survey (USGS)*

Salient Statistics of Mercury in the United States   In Metric Tons

Year	Producing Mines	Secondary Production — Industrial	Secondary Production — Government[3]	NDS[4] Shipments	Consumer & Dealer Stocks, Dec. 31	Industrial Demand	Exports	Imports
2014	NA	NA	----	----	NA	NA	----	50
2015	NA	NA	----	----	NA	NA	0	26
2016	NA	NA	----	----	NA	NA	----	24
2017	NA	NA	----	----	NA	NA	----	20
2018	NA	NA	----	----	NA	NA	----	3
2019	NA	NA	----	----	NA	NA	----	9
2020	NA	NA	----	----	NA	NA	----	3
2021	NA	NA	----	----	NA	NA	----	1
2022[1]	NA	NA	----	----	NA	NA	----	2
2023[2]	NA	NA	----	----	NA	NA	----	4

[1] Preliminary.   [2] Estimate.   [3] Secondary mercury shipped from the Department of Energy.   [4] National Defense Stockpile.   [5] Less than 1/2 unit.   NA = Not available.   *Source: U.S. Geological Survey (USGS)*

Milk

Evidence of human consumption of animal milk was discovered in a temple in the Euphrates Valley near Babylon, dating back to 3,000 BC. Humans drink the milk produced from a variety of domesticated mammals, including cows, goats, sheep, camels, reindeer, buffaloes, and llama. In India, half of all milk consumed is from water buffalo. Camels' milk spoils slower than other types of milk in the hot desert, but virtually all milk used for commercial production and consumption comes from cows.

Milk directly from a cow in its natural form is called raw milk. Raw milk is processed by spinning it in a centrifuge, homogenizing it to create a consistent texture (i.e., by forcing hot milk under high pressure through small nozzles), and then sterilizing it through pasteurization (i.e., heating to a high temperature for a specified length of time to destroy pathogenic bacteria). Condensed, powdered, and evaporated milk are produced by evaporating some or all of the water content. Whole milk contains 3.5% milk fat. Lower-fat milks include 2% low-fat milk, 1% low-fat milk, and skim milk, which has only 1/2 gram of milk fat per serving.

The CME Group has three different milk futures contracts: Milk Class III which is milk used in the manufacturing of cheese, Milk Class IV which is milk used in the production of butter and all dried milk products, and Nonfat Dry Milk which is used in commercial or consumer cooking or to reconstitute nonfat milk by the consumer. The Milk Class III contract has the largest volume and open interest.

Prices – The average monthly price received by farmers for all milk sold to plants in 2023 fell by -19.5% yr/yr to $20.48 per hundred pounds.

Supply – World milk production in 2023 rose +1.1% to 666.595 million metric tons. The biggest producers were India with 31.1% of world production, the European Union with 22.4%, and the US with 15.4%. US 2023 milk production remained unchanged yr/yr to 226.551 billion pounds, setting a record high.

The number of dairy cows on US farms has fallen sharply in the past three decades from the 12 million level seen in 1970. In 2023, there were 9.395 million dairy cows on US farms, down by -0.1% yr/yr. Dairy farmers have been able to increase milk production even with fewer cows because of a dramatic increase in milk yield per cow. In 2023, the average cow produced a record 24,113 pounds of milk per year, a +0.1% yr/yr increase, more than double the 9,751 pounds seen in 1970.

Trade – US imports of milk in 2023 were up by +1.0% yr/yr at 7.130 billion pounds, still well below the record high of 7.500 billion pounds posted in 2005-06.

World Fluid Milk Production (Cow's Milk)   In Thousands of Metric Tons

Year	Argentina	Australia	Brazil	Canada	China	European Union	India	Mexico	New Zealand	Russia	Ukraine	United States	World Total
2015	11,552	10,091	25,650	8,773	33,298	154,550	155,481	11,900	21,587	29,688	10,864	94,579	585,047
2016	10,191	9,486	25,857	9,081	32,240	142,507	165,118	12,122	21,224	29,587	10,625	96,367	595,997
2017	10,090	9,462	26,766	9,675	31,886	144,794	176,061	12,288	21,530	29,972	10,520	97,762	613,081
2018	10,837	9,451	26,745	9,944	32,250	146,305	187,700	12,537	22,017	30,398	10,300	98,688	629,489
2019	10,640	8,832	27,292	9,903	32,976	147,106	191,000	12,820	21,896	31,154	9,866	99,084	635,219
2020	11,445	9,099	28,015	10,035	35,500	149,732	194,800	12,921	21,980	32,010	9,466	101,292	649,540
2021	11,900	9,067	27,825	10,157	37,950	148,978	199,000	13,022	21,995	32,020	9,000	102,646	656,881
2022	11,904	8,450	26,630	10,178	40,350	148,528	202,500	13,152	21,051	32,150	7,957	102,722	659,127
2023[1]	11,700	8,400	27,685	10,265	42,200	149,000	207,100	13,420	21,300	32,300	7,015	102,921	666,595
2024[2]	11,500	8,500	28,200	10,310	42,700	148,795	210,200	13,672	21,200	32,500	6,605	103,874	671,460

[1] Preliminary.   [2] Forecast.   Source: Foreign Agricultural Service, U.S. Department of Agriculture (FAS-USDA)

Salient Statistics of Milk in the United States   In Millions of Pounds

Year	Number of Milk Cows on Farms3 (Thousands)	Production Per Cow[4] (Pounds)	Production Total[4]	Beginning Stocks[5]	Imports	Total Supply	Exports[5]	Domestic Fed to Calves	Domestic Humans	Total Use	All Milk, Wholesale	Milk, Eligible for Fluid Market	Milk, Manufacturing Grade	Per Capita Consumption[6] (Fluid Milk in Lbs)
2014	9,257	22,259	206,046	10,344	4,372	220,762	12,159	872	196,308	209,340	23.98	----	----	
2015	9,314	22,396	208,633	10,487	5,759	224,879	8,500	879	202,260	211,639	17.11	----	----	
2016	9,328	22,775	212,436	12,335	6,937	231,708	8,395	898	211,412	220,705	16.30	----	----	
2017	9,392	22,941	215,466	12,722	5,977	234,165	9,223	901	214,535	224,659	17.66	----	----	
2018	9,399	23,149	217,575	13,397	6,347	237,319	10,458	928	216,551	227,937	16.26	----	----	
2019	9,336	23,391	218,382	13,790	6,500	238,672	10,700	932	217,362	228,994	18.63	----	----	
2020	9,388	23,778	223,220	13,623	6,775	243,618	10,200	993	222,230	233,423	18.25	----	----	
2021	9,447	23,947	226,258	14,337	6,537	247,132	11,541	947	225,262	237,750	18.61	----	----	
2022[1]	9,402	24,087	226,462	14,386	7,058	247,906	13,366	914	225,468	239,748	25.43	----	----	
2023[2]	9,386	24,117	226,364	14,386	7,130	247,880					20.48	----	----	

[1] Preliminary.   [2] Estimate.   [3] Average number on farms during year including dry cows, excluding heifers not yet fresh.   [4] Excludes milk sucked by calves.   [5] Government and commercial.   [6] Product pounds of commercial sales and on farm consumption.
Source: Economic Research Service, U.S. Department of Agriculture (ERS-USDA)

MILK

Milk-Feed Price Ratio[1] in the United States   In Pounds

Year	Jan.	Feb.	Mar.	Apr.	May	June	July	Aug.	Sept.	Oct.	Nov.	Dec.	Average
2014	2.46	2.59	2.54	2.42	2.24	2.20	2.36	2.63	2.96	2.92	2.75	2.40	2.54
2015	2.11	2.05	2.01	1.95	1.97	2.07	2.01	2.10	2.23	2.30	2.45	2.29	2.13
2016	2.18	2.18	2.12	1.99	1.89	1.91	2.16	2.44	2.49	2.38	2.59	2.73	2.26
2017	2.71	2.62	2.40	2.22	2.20	2.31	2.27	2.51	2.46	2.47	2.54	2.38	2.42
2018	2.18	2.03	1.99	1.89	1.90	1.98	1.93	2.06	2.13	2.22	2.21	2.07	2.05
2019	2.06	2.07	2.14	2.11	2.10	2.08	2.16	2.26	2.34	2.42	2.65	2.57	2.25
2020	2.42	2.35	2.24	1.85	1.78	2.38	2.72	2.48	2.27	2.49	2.58	2.17	2.31
2021	2.00	1.80	1.76	1.75	1.69	1.59	1.52	1.48	1.66	1.84	1.92	1.96	1.75
2022	2.16	2.06	2.02	1.95	1.98	1.92	1.77	1.69	1.71	1.90	1.92	1.83	1.91
2023[1]	1.73	1.59	1.56	1.48	1.42	1.36	1.38	1.67	1.89	2.03	2.12	2.00	1.69

[1] Pounds of 16% protein mixed dairy feed equal in value to one pound of whole milk.   [2] Preliminary.   *Source: Economic Research Service, U.S. Department of Agriculture (ERS-USDA)*

Milk Production[2] in the United States   In Millions of Pounds

Year	Jan.	Feb.	Mar.	Apr.	May	June	July	Aug.	Sept.	Oct.	Nov.	Dec.	Total
2014	17,284	15,907	17,829	17,480	18,094	17,323	17,435	17,224	16,514	17,071	16,551	17,334	206,046
2015	17,685	16,166	18,085	17,788	18,428	17,504	17,665	17,403	16,617	17,130	16,689	17,473	208,633
2016	17,693	16,904	18,401	17,947	18,613	17,771	17,908	17,692	16,990	17,565	17,100	17,852	212,436
2017	18,128	16,694	18,740	18,332	18,952	18,060	18,268	18,049	17,156	17,769	17,260	18,058	215,466
2018	18,437	16,973	18,989	18,412	19,131	18,288	18,329	18,245	17,395	17,873	17,348	18,155	217,575
2019	18,612	16,966	18,845	18,433	19,058	18,225	18,375	18,267	17,595	18,135	17,506	18,365	218,382
2020	18,877	17,895	19,402	18,684	18,972	18,414	18,756	18,632	18,031	18,603	18,103	18,851	223,220
2021	19,365	17,685	19,797	19,350	19,855	18,942	19,097	18,721	18,018	18,623	18,015	18,790	226,258
2022	19,050	17,540	19,715	19,147	19,755	18,920	19,180	19,016	18,242	18,809	18,184	18,904	226,462
2023[1]	19,308	17,718	19,811	19,204	19,852	18,948	18,985	18,828	18,181	18,645	18,051	18,833	226,364

[1] Preliminary.   [2] Excludes milk sucked by calves.   *Source: Economic Research Service, U.S. Department of Agriculture (ERS-USDA)*

Milk Cows[2] in the United States   In Thousands of Head

Year	Jan.	Feb.	Mar.	Apr.	May	June	July	Aug.	Sept.	Oct.	Nov.	Dec.	Total
2014	9,212	9,212	9,223	9,240	9,252	9,267	9,268	9,268	9,274	9,277	9,284	9,299	9,257
2015	9,308	9,308	9,311	9,316	9,324	9,323	9,314	9,315	9,317	9,320	9,322	9,320	9,314
2016	9,304	9,311	9,321	9,321	9,322	9,326	9,329	9,334	9,331	9,335	9,344	9,354	9,328
2017	9,359	9,365	9,383	9,392	9,401	9,404	9,404	9,404	9,399	9,395	9,398	9,400	9,392
2018	9,438	9,436	9,430	9,418	9,422	9,414	9,392	9,389	9,368	9,367	9,358	9,353	9,399
2019	9,354	9,352	9,333	9,332	9,333	9,327	9,315	9,318	9,333	9,347	9,345	9,343	9,336
2020	9,365	9,377	9,391	9,377	9,360	9,355	9,372	9,374	9,395	9,414	9,432	9,442	9,388
2021	9,450	9,456	9,482	9,500	9,507	9,501	9,483	9,438	9,405	9,387	9,382	9,373	9,447
2022	9,367	9,380	9,404	9,404	9,417	9,413	9,413	9,406	9,406	9,412	9,404	9,396	9,402
2023[1]	9,401	9,419	9,433	9,414	9,418	9,397	9,368	9,365	9,366	9,355	9,345	9,348	9,386

[1] Preliminary.   [2] Includes dry cows, excludes heifers not yet fresh.   *Source: Economic Research Service, U.S. Department of Agriculture (ERS-USDA)*

Milk Per Cow[2] in the United States   In Pounds

Year	Jan.	Feb.	Mar.	Apr.	May	June	July	Aug.	Sept.	Oct.	Nov.	Dec.	Total
2014	1,876	1,727	1,933	1,892	1,956	1,869	1,881	1,858	1,781	1,840	1,783	1,864	22,259
2015	1,900	1,737	1,942	1,909	1,976	1,878	1,897	1,868	1,784	1,838	1,790	1,875	22,396
2016	1,902	1,815	1,974	1,925	1,997	1,906	1,920	1,895	1,821	1,882	1,830	1,908	22,775
2017	1,937	1,783	1,997	1,952	2,016	1,920	1,943	1,919	1,825	1,891	1,837	1,921	22,941
2018	1,953	1,799	2,014	1,955	2,030	1,943	1,952	1,943	1,857	1,908	1,854	1,941	23,149
2019	1,990	1,814	2,019	1,975	2,042	1,954	1,973	1,960	1,885	1,940	1,873	1,966	23,391
2020	2,016	1,908	2,066	1,993	2,027	1,968	2,001	1,988	1,919	1,976	1,919	1,997	23,778
2021	2,049	1,868	2,088	2,037	2,088	1,994	2,014	1,984	1,916	1,984	1,920	2,005	23,947
2022	2,034	1,870	2,096	2,036	2,098	2,010	2,038	2,022	1,939	1,998	1,934	2,012	24,087
2023[1]	2,054	1,881	2,100	2,040	2,108	2,016	2,027	2,010	1,941	1,993	1,932	2,015	24,117

[1] Preliminary.   [2] Excludes milk sucked by calves.   *Source: Economic Research Service, U.S. Department of Agriculture (ERS-USDA)*

Average Price Received by Farmers for All Milk (Sold to Plants)   In Dollars Per Hundred Pounds (Cwt.)

Year	Jan.	Feb.	Mar.	Apr.	May	June	July	Aug.	Sept.	Oct.	Nov.	Dec.	Average
2014	23.50	24.90	25.10	25.30	24.20	23.20	23.30	24.20	25.70	24.90	23.00	20.40	23.98
2015	17.60	16.80	16.60	16.50	16.80	17.00	16.70	16.70	17.50	17.70	18.20	17.20	17.11
2016	16.10	15.70	15.30	15.10	14.50	14.80	16.10	17.20	17.40	16.70	17.80	18.90	16.30
2017	18.90	18.50	17.30	16.50	16.70	17.30	17.20	18.10	17.90	18.10	18.20	17.20	17.66
2018	16.10	15.30	15.70	15.70	16.20	16.30	15.50	16.10	16.90	17.50	17.20	16.60	16.26
2019	16.60	16.80	17.60	17.70	18.00	18.10	18.70	18.90	19.30	20.00	21.10	20.70	18.63
2020	19.60	18.90	17.90	14.40	13.70	18.20	20.60	18.60	17.70	20.00	21.10	18.30	18.25
2021	17.50	17.10	17.30	18.30	19.10	18.20	17.90	17.60	18.30	19.60	20.70	21.70	18.61
2022	24.20	24.70	25.90	27.00	27.30	26.70	25.50	24.30	24.10	25.60	25.40	24.50	25.43
2023[1]	23.10	21.60	21.10	20.70	19.30	17.90	17.40	19.70	21.00	21.60	21.70	20.60	20.48

[1] Preliminary.   Source: Economic Research Service, U.S. Department of Agriculture (ERS-USDA)

Production of Nonfat Dry Milk in the United States   In Thousands of Pounds

Year	Jan.	Feb.	Mar.	Apr.	May	June	July	Aug.	Sept.	Oct.	Nov.	Dec.	Total
2014	138,661	141,187	167,853	160,342	162,139	148,648	166,602	116,134	112,467	134,973	151,402	164,224	1,764,632
2015	167,705	150,960	180,878	180,771	180,013	165,441	155,265	123,892	119,974	118,360	127,939	151,150	1,822,348
2016	137,463	142,978	172,003	170,796	165,837	146,643	150,787	117,550	125,486	140,051	128,105	154,935	1,752,634
2017	153,868	143,252	160,931	172,840	167,912	162,827	151,831	136,767	134,587	145,008	141,440	164,014	1,835,277
2018	159,272	157,105	177,980	169,428	165,670	152,244	150,193	129,077	114,030	121,595	134,424	142,522	1,773,540
2019	172,690	153,806	161,829	167,758	173,666	157,948	172,329	132,525	117,806	132,716	138,880	164,869	1,846,822
2020	176,259	159,128	173,665	202,632	127,236	154,033	166,138	147,194	126,249	141,255	155,435	208,252	1,937,476
2021	198,025	183,614	198,254	193,792	205,470	185,604	137,789	121,559	139,384	120,721	161,011	167,804	2,013,027
2022	170,306	170,815	191,815	195,821	192,677	168,971	165,726	133,625	122,804	129,037	160,743	167,711	1,970,051
2023[1]	174,953	182,528	199,448	198,595	208,766	178,017	135,135	110,809	100,666	127,425	115,702	147,701	1,879,745

[1] Preliminary.   Source: Economic Research Service, U.S. Department of Agriculture (ERS-USDA)

Production of Dry Whey in the United States   In Thousands of Pounds

Year	Jan.	Feb.	Mar.	Apr.	May	June	July	Aug.	Sept.	Oct.	Nov.	Dec.	Total
2014	70,011	65,603	71,504	71,629	82,480	79,309	73,475	71,192	69,537	68,684	70,994	75,283	869,701
2015	75,342	76,630	86,409	76,512	80,778	85,506	81,225	83,585	78,823	75,576	82,959	94,223	977,568
2016	83,459	74,891	82,762	82,075	81,836	80,002	82,354	76,505	75,864	83,966	72,893	78,534	955,141
2017	82,255	77,548	87,602	85,218	83,545	87,886	99,652	94,248	90,561	79,749	81,237	85,913	1,035,414
2018	90,569	89,431	91,368	85,731	85,904	86,603	90,171	78,814	69,951	84,003	72,306	74,505	999,356
2019	81,202	74,948	77,378	74,998	79,090	82,976	82,906	84,897	90,627	90,843	75,111	79,821	974,797
2020	84,272	76,490	83,482	75,824	84,109	81,713	82,616	78,720	76,954	75,148	68,652	81,301	949,281
2021	83,988	75,323	76,909	77,435	77,277	76,350	81,016	82,302	75,185	74,882	75,856	76,044	932,567
2022	80,406	70,288	77,764	79,446	79,205	80,062	84,287	75,314	75,792	75,348	72,041	74,930	924,883
2023[1]	76,713	66,824	77,542	79,592	81,777	84,544	87,861	82,826	76,792	74,316	67,356	72,550	928,693

[1] Preliminary.   Excludes all modified dry whey products.   Source: Economic Research Service, U.S. Department of Agriculture (ERS-USDA)

Production of Whey Protein Concentrate in the United States   In Thousands of Pounds

Year	Jan.	Feb.	Mar.	Apr.	May	June	July	Aug.	Sept.	Oct.	Nov.	Dec.	Total
2014	44,325	42,165	45,076	46,127	46,630	43,871	44,876	44,945	41,621	46,971	46,066	47,428	540,101
2015	44,061	38,365	42,234	42,375	43,812	39,307	41,736	39,380	37,474	41,302	40,137	42,766	492,949
2016	42,602	39,780	41,851	39,027	39,349	38,037	38,437	35,665	36,745	38,060	39,419	39,457	468,429
2017	40,714	36,457	42,736	42,469	41,993	40,669	41,587	38,737	39,109	41,203	40,935	42,313	488,922
2018	44,257	41,182	50,463	41,887	42,424	41,001	40,877	42,856	41,991	42,392	40,919	43,722	513,971
2019	43,170	39,295	42,026	40,639	41,911	38,840	39,802	39,903	40,068	40,672	40,696	43,106	490,128
2020	41,935	35,600	40,094	37,341	39,074	40,189	39,655	40,061	40,988	40,971	39,311	43,137	478,356
2021	43,800	37,512	40,832	49,956	40,450	38,515	68,689	41,587	44,812	46,622	43,440	46,935	543,150
2022	47,226	40,718	36,764	36,914	36,329	36,215	36,463	35,120	38,654	39,326	39,907	41,708	465,344
2023[1]	41,517	37,173	42,501	41,663	43,829	42,401	42,053	39,932	39,688	39,548	40,443	4,419	455,167

[1] Preliminary.   Source: Economic Research Service, U.S. Department of Agriculture (ERS-USDA)

MILK

Production of Cottage Cheese, Creamed[2] in the United States   In Thousands of Pounds

Year	Jan.	Feb.	Mar.	Apr.	May	June	July	Aug.	Sept.	Oct.	Nov.	Dec.	Total
2014	25,477	22,723	25,455	26,364	26,281	26,174	26,226	25,656	26,631	25,318	21,499	25,309	303,113
2015	24,103	25,188	26,991	25,811	26,284	27,179	28,791	27,810	27,369	27,130	24,212	26,663	317,531
2016	25,636	26,945	29,154	27,052	28,946	28,335	27,163	29,684	27,782	26,901	26,041	25,805	329,444
2017	26,122	25,698	29,010	25,942	29,538	27,626	28,007	30,434	27,146	28,829	26,066	26,066	330,484
2018	27,933	27,261	32,655	29,410	32,320	31,006	30,114	31,920	27,141	29,828	27,051	26,146	352,785
2019	28,322	26,094	29,846	30,945	29,312	28,265	32,350	31,495	29,488	31,956	27,025	28,427	353,525
2020	27,622	26,172	31,391	31,530	31,032	29,649	31,016	30,517	33,831	32,294	27,508	29,258	361,820
2021	26,622	27,470	31,597	27,116	28,165	28,624	39,474	29,527	28,604	27,437	26,136	27,472	348,244
2022	27,422	28,452	29,527	26,629	27,362	29,366	28,727	31,436	29,634	27,832	28,464	29,136	343,987
2023[1]	28,894	29,357	33,090	28,368	33,021	32,271	32,233	34,401	32,330	33,413	31,288	29,463	378,129

[1] Preliminary.   [2] Fat content 4 percent or more.   *Source: Economic Research Service, U.S. Department of Agriculture (ERS-USDA)*

Production of Cottage Cheese, Lowfat[2] in the United States   In Thousands of Pounds

Year	Jan.	Feb.	Mar.	Apr.	May	June	July	Aug.	Sept.	Oct.	Nov.	Dec.	Total
2014	29,755	28,227	31,134	32,698	31,304	32,664	31,289	30,662	31,799	31,225	25,088	28,769	364,614
2015	28,993	28,913	32,157	29,848	29,919	32,113	31,483	31,377	31,918	29,543	26,652	30,088	363,004
2016	30,270	30,311	34,486	30,326	32,490	30,751	30,359	32,260	30,566	29,954	28,456	27,586	367,815
2017	28,655	28,142	30,711	29,610	31,746	27,924	28,450	31,370	27,396	29,205	26,060	25,152	344,421
2018	29,299	27,577	31,340	29,982	31,476	28,321	29,296	29,342	26,943	28,706	25,181	24,621	342,084
2019	28,134	25,374	27,765	29,039	27,512	25,433	29,611	29,747	26,427	27,922	24,008	23,879	324,851
2020	26,333	24,434	27,979	26,753	24,688	24,951	27,393	25,885	26,719	27,540	22,228	23,495	308,398
2021	24,428	24,271	29,719	25,862	24,753	25,730	26,481	26,252	25,745	24,129	22,085	23,028	302,483
2022	24,313	24,832	26,571	24,821	23,930	24,359	24,826	27,427	25,420	23,911	22,035	21,858	294,303
2023[1]	26,110	24,320	25,899	24,605	28,066	27,307	29,280	32,495	31,564	29,659	25,996	26,489	331,790

[1] Preliminary.   [2] Fat content less than 4 percent.   *Source: Economic Research Service, U.S. Department of Agriculture (ERS-USDA)*

Production of Cottage Cheese, Curd in the United States   In Thousands of Pounds

Year	Jan.	Feb.	Mar.	Apr.	May	June	July	Aug.	Sept.	Oct.	Nov.	Dec.	Total
2014	32,401	27,764	32,362	33,612	32,119	32,656	33,684	32,565	33,149	32,647	26,851	31,336	381,146
2015	31,334	31,903	34,171	33,099	33,498	34,206	35,767	35,753	34,670	33,065	30,026	33,142	400,634
2016	32,489	33,018	36,339	33,039	35,043	33,896	33,004	35,510	39,670	32,558	30,965	30,897	406,428
2017	32,063	31,222	34,803	32,599	35,558	32,374	33,267	35,563	30,998	33,444	29,668	28,850	390,409
2018	32,660	31,545	36,016	33,353	36,368	34,349	34,706	36,300	33,010	33,463	31,073	29,519	402,362
2019	32,575	30,242	33,388	34,505	32,004	31,947	36,978	34,227	31,108	33,497	28,701	28,837	388,009
2020	30,838	28,990	33,225	33,349	30,987	30,864	32,906	31,733	34,376	33,867	27,989	29,688	378,812
2021	29,551	29,790	34,363	28,853	28,192	30,328	31,629	30,533	30,042	29,015	26,924	29,212	358,432
2022	29,080	29,912	31,853	29,363	29,226	30,076	30,751	33,424	31,809	29,255	38,464	29,036	372,249
2023[1]	31,115	30,400	32,820	30,198	34,665	34,172	33,637	40,134	34,292	33,413	30,938	31,079	396,863

[1] Preliminary.   [2] Fat content less than 4 percent.   *Source: Economic Research Service, U.S. Department of Agriculture (ERS-USDA)*

Production of Sour Cream in the United States   In Thousands of Pounds

Year	Jan.	Feb.	Mar.	Apr.	May	June	July	Aug.	Sept.	Oct.	Nov.	Dec.	Total
2014	107,452	94,174	107,114	107,177	105,491	106,167	106,911	105,603	103,548	117,465	120,244	121,564	1,302,900
2015	109,701	96,386	110,972	103,654	104,424	110,833	105,239	107,407	108,576	121,581	126,165	120,691	1,325,629
2016	106,584	106,240	115,534	100,532	113,834	118,015	103,622	114,645	108,701	123,534	133,364	129,454	1,374,059
2017	113,967	99,700	115,648	109,615	118,884	117,764	107,401	118,709	108,314	126,023	129,312	121,812	1,387,149
2018	120,265	98,965	116,365	111,335	119,221	114,106	109,820	119,327	107,914	128,883	130,767	126,443	1,403,411
2019	120,975	100,923	108,617	117,973	120,332	111,416	118,403	119,252	111,282	133,320	129,785	130,139	1,422,417
2020	121,591	101,869	115,545	110,956	135,931	121,733	112,681	117,149	120,885	138,408	130,353	132,789	1,459,890
2021	115,248	113,749	133,781	119,051	120,142	126,500	121,174	122,915	118,932	132,583	133,456	136,439	1,493,970
2022	121,358	117,010	126,440	116,700	125,804	123,165	115,623	127,030	121,170	131,035	133,978	133,622	1,492,935
2023[1]	126,074	113,600	125,905	117,517	127,349	127,333	117,830	123,536	116,079	139,526	141,618	131,736	1,508,103

[1] Preliminary.   *Source: Economic Research Service, U.S. Department of Agriculture (ERS-USDA)*

Production of Ice Cream, Regular, Hard in the United States   In Thousands of Gallons

Year	Jan.	Feb.	Mar.	Apr.	May	June	July	Aug.	Sept.	Oct.	Nov.	Dec.	Total
2014	56,393	56,987	68,176	70,217	70,554	74,048	73,797	67,794	62,494	60,880	53,604	52,138	767,082
2015	57,146	59,915	71,944	68,966	65,730	72,674	72,497	69,632	65,485	63,399	54,998	52,826	775,212
2016	58,997	61,075	72,610	72,627	72,194	76,456	71,210	72,745	63,055	59,325	51,477	49,392	781,163
2017	53,262	55,868	70,879	66,450	69,130	70,987	66,406	70,143	57,909	55,392	48,794	45,942	731,162
2018	53,684	55,447	63,553	62,821	64,551	70,263	68,966	70,111	56,601	60,610	48,070	43,855	718,532
2019	53,551	52,120	65,957	64,681	67,414	64,920	64,846	64,242	58,155	58,581	46,927	47,039	708,433
2020	52,157	52,484	64,287	63,439	64,598	72,777	73,592	70,473	38,194	63,264	54,826	53,441	723,532
2021	56,990	55,630	68,982	68,856	61,168	66,028	64,257	63,201	55,511	54,598	52,137	52,283	719,641
2022	51,240	54,872	66,216	65,427	62,248	66,973	61,063	65,493	63,076	59,468	54,126	53,665	723,867
2023[1]	52,963	58,382	66,245	61,008	63,592	67,211	61,962	66,453	62,527	57,432	49,837	47,304	714,916

[1] Preliminary.   Source: Economic Research Service, U.S. Department of Agriculture (ERS-USDA)

Production of Ice Cream, Lowfat Total in the United States   In Thousands of Gallons

Year	Jan.	Feb.	Mar.	Apr.	May	June	July	Aug.	Sept.	Oct.	Nov.	Dec.	Total
2014	29,551	30,222	35,523	40,702	39,490	42,314	39,978	35,453	33,149	31,617	26,229	27,473	411,701
2015	30,422	32,283	38,429	40,473	40,067	46,059	43,039	43,451	36,576	32,920	27,531	27,741	438,991
2016	30,247	31,851	40,659	40,323	39,399	44,492	40,516	43,295	35,503	32,383	28,692	28,508	435,868
2017	31,700	38,803	45,145	41,629	46,354	46,392	42,695	43,891	34,944	34,414	27,499	27,948	461,414
2018	32,568	34,823	41,108	40,800	42,471	45,471	42,333	41,742	34,907	36,607	30,121	28,152	451,103
2019	31,559	32,235	42,538	44,505	47,873	44,364	43,582	42,021	37,206	36,315	29,068	28,110	459,376
2020	30,886	33,278	42,867	39,368	45,133	47,269	45,547	45,371	41,756	38,173	33,279	32,167	475,094
2021	30,737	33,507	47,296	42,986	43,855	43,004	42,723	40,724	36,106	35,214	29,451	28,727	454,330
2022	27,545	30,891	42,726	40,423	41,179	43,257	40,620	42,693	37,344	35,656	29,075	27,182	438,591
2023[1]	29,018	31,897	39,634	37,670	40,755	41,917	42,214	40,681	33,374	32,293	26,969	23,896	420,318

[1] Preliminary.   Source: Economic Research Service, U.S. Department of Agriculture (ERS-USDA)

Production of Sherbet, Hard in the United States   In Thousands of Gallons

Year	Jan.	Feb.	Mar.	Apr.	May	June	July	Aug.	Sept.	Oct.	Nov.	Dec.	Total
2014	3,181	3,339	3,988	3,986	3,791	4,109	3,923	3,201	3,438	2,752	2,688	2,528	40,924
2015	2,982	3,224	3,873	3,527	3,743	3,876	3,769	3,554	3,407	2,927	2,535	2,080	39,497
2016	2,731	3,369	4,014	3,953	3,768	3,892	3,376	3,351	3,585	2,848	2,166	2,360	39,413
2017	3,291	3,005	3,764	3,779	3,574	3,815	3,308	3,681	3,274	2,542	2,346	2,182	38,561
2018	2,858	3,112	3,368	3,578	3,513	3,563	3,151	3,255	3,084	2,978	2,341	2,100	36,901
2019	2,551	2,653	3,225	3,067	3,191	3,166	2,795	2,382	2,703	2,445	2,053	2,056	32,287
2020	2,577	3,021	2,721	2,425	2,328	3,246	3,210	3,416	2,962	2,882	2,300	2,816	33,904
2021	2,666	2,605	2,497	2,823	2,364	2,617	2,793	2,336	2,148	1,957	1,773	1,833	28,412
2022	2,303	2,519	2,614	1,991	2,040	2,065	2,224	2,003	1,981	2,161	1,671	1,678	25,250
2023[1]	1,971	2,308	1,969	2,047	2,007	1,914	1,639	1,869	1,637	1,702	1,454	1,261	21,778

[1] Preliminary.   Source: Economic Research Service, U.S. Department of Agriculture (ERS-USDA)

Production of Yogurt, Plain and Flavored in the United States   In Thousands of Pounds

Year	Jan.	Feb.	Mar.	Apr.	May	June	July	Aug.	Sept.	Oct.	Nov.	Dec.	Total
2014	392,831	403,679	436,674	392,677	389,082	400,769	388,147	405,926	463,704	381,177	319,921	381,975	4,756,562
2015	372,687	420,942	435,314	385,454	397,051	390,556	382,686	385,322	421,638	371,200	334,443	348,301	4,645,594
2016	379,455	377,179	400,818	373,280	364,390	378,786	341,896	399,633	411,235	361,347	311,210	359,170	4,458,399
2017	381,760	369,737	411,605	375,287	385,257	376,339	349,476	396,288	393,702	368,553	317,597	352,603	4,478,204
2018	372,015	376,710	389,848	358,160	373,431	373,079	360,886	396,296	369,989	363,128	310,848	343,698	4,388,088
2019	360,050	365,389	399,699	379,341	354,516	364,013	348,614	377,322	381,495	357,443	319,612	348,979	4,356,473
2020	347,758	375,155	438,213	361,848	373,099	398,683	365,149	382,228	391,449	386,630	326,611	358,291	4,505,114
2021	385,594	381,121	443,374	414,884	393,724	389,530	401,106	411,210	409,977	386,014	355,335	370,532	4,742,401
2022	372,943	373,445	429,558	373,945	399,140	391,060	379,818	402,223	398,067	391,563	337,045	371,368	4,620,175
2023[1]	391,637	400,599	440,775	382,713	404,050	401,095	400,464	409,566	417,544	390,148	352,983	357,336	4,748,910

[1] Preliminary.   Source: Economic Research Service, U.S. Department of Agriculture (ERS-USDA)

MILK

MILK (CLASS III) - CME
Weekly Nearest Futures as of 03/28/2024

WEEKLY NEAREST FUTURES
As of 03/28/2024

Chart High 25.20   on 05/31/2022
Chart Low   11.21   on 05/04/2020

Cents / lb.

Nearby Futures through Last Trading Day.

Volume of Trading of Class III Milk Futures in Chicago   In Contracts

Year	Jan.	Feb.	Mar.	Apr.	May	June	July	Aug.	Sept.	Oct.	Nov.	Dec.	Total
2014	37,317	27,468	31,390	23,084	22,764	21,118	26,702	28,532	38,651	33,233	25,464	42,936	358,659
2015	30,448	29,457	23,844	22,999	21,087	21,649	23,920	16,422	19,958	18,049	22,488	25,218	275,539
2016	20,769	20,574	19,533	22,613	27,322	44,457	18,030	30,654	28,089	24,141	28,134	37,643	321,959
2017	27,439	28,001	33,774	20,263	30,371	25,574	25,564	31,494	22,438	22,205	27,303	25,402	319,828
2018	23,610	18,682	17,419	19,020	21,425	33,116	23,538	27,829	22,004	35,993	30,999	28,617	302,252
2019	27,638	25,049	23,083	26,149	24,669	22,034	26,154	24,635	35,003	36,380	31,377	33,676	335,847
2020	29,402	29,816	35,523	41,515	38,908	40,852	38,242	37,938	27,094	36,808	33,363	39,179	428,640
2021	31,111	20,329	21,789	24,751	22,622	21,903	24,560	25,672	22,299	30,414	32,169	31,501	309,120
2022	34,866	26,791	36,614	27,800	27,238	29,126	28,648	27,857	25,869	21,666	25,144	27,903	339,522
2023	27,460	21,625	30,507	25,402	36,644	39,402	42,426	31,258	33,635	38,801	33,415	36,688	397,263

Contract size = 200,000 lbs.   *Source: CME Group; Chicago Mercantile Exchange (CME)*

Average Open Interest of Class III Milk Futures in Chicago   In Contracts

Year	Jan.	Feb.	Mar.	Apr.	May	June	July	Aug.	Sept.	Oct.	Nov.	Dec.
2014	26,264	28,094	29,393	28,695	27,114	26,298	26,128	29,218	32,844	36,731	39,197	43,959
2015	46,134	44,918	42,292	37,710	34,509	31,725	28,890	28,792	26,554	25,839	27,821	29,784
2016	32,267	33,051	31,996	31,881	32,970	30,976	30,323	29,969	31,548	31,845	31,605	33,695
2017	31,058	31,194	34,015	34,006	31,200	28,498	28,226	25,863	25,933	23,510	24,940	25,949
2018	24,834	23,883	23,021	22,280	22,375	22,572	23,397	22,391	22,843	25,498	29,760	28,206
2019	26,355	25,593	23,301	21,497	22,591	22,221	20,718	19,169	20,918	21,182	22,763	20,166
2020	17,223	17,888	18,801	23,000	23,875	24,576	26,035	23,371	19,973	21,649	22,465	20,318
2021	21,022	21,665	22,925	25,416	25,925	24,870	26,145	25,126	23,727	23,445	25,508	27,655
2022	30,313	30,813	31,801	32,978	32,901	30,806	30,725	30,274	28,593	26,196	23,555	23,337
2023	24,782	24,686	23,409	21,868	24,494	27,758	27,005	20,687	18,859	21,277	22,104	25,595

Contract size = 200,000 lbs.   *Source: CME Group; Chicago Mercantile Exchange (CME)*

Molybdenum

Molybdenum (atomic symbol Mo) is a silvery-white, hard, malleable, metallic element. Molybdenum melts at about 2610 degrees Celsius and boils at about 4640 degrees Celsius. Swedish chemist Carl Wilhelm Scheele discovered molybdenum in 1778.

Molybdenum occurs in nature in the form of molybdenite and wulfenite. Contributing to the growth of plants, it is an important trace element in soils. Approximately 70% of the world supply of molybdenum is obtained as a by-product of copper mining. Molybdenum is chiefly used as an alloy to strengthen steel and resist corrosion. It is used for structural work, aircraft parts, and forged automobile parts because it withstands high temperatures and pressures and adds strength. Other uses include lubricants, a refractory metal in chemical applications, electron tubing, and as a catalyst.

Prices – The average monthly US merchant price of molybdic oxide in 2023 rose by +29.3% yr/yr to $24.87 per pound.

Supply – World mine production of molybdenum in 2023 rose by +2.8% yr/yr to 260,000 metric tons. The major producers in 2023 were China with 42.3% of world production, Chile with 17.7%, Peru with 14.2%, and the US with 13.1%. US mine production of molybdenum in 2023 fell by -1.7% yr/yr to 34,000 metric tons.

Demand – US consumption of molybdenum products in 2022 rose by +0.6% yr/yr to 16,000 metric tons.

Trade – US imports of molybdenum concentrate for consumption in 2023 rose by +7.6% yr/yr to 31,000 metric tons.

World Mine Production of Molybdenum   In Metric Tons (Contained Molybdenum)

Year	Armenia	Canada[3]	Chile	China	Iran	Kazak-hstan	Mexico	Mongolia	Peru	Russia	United States	Uzbek-isten	World Total
2014	7,162	9,358	48,770	129,000	3,494	----	14,370	1,999	17,018	3,114	68,200	450	306,000
2015	6,300	2,505	52,579	135,000	3,500	----	12,279	2,557	20,153	3,000	47,400	450	288,000
2016	6,300	2,708	55,647	129,000	3,500	----	11,896	2,444	25,757	3,000	36,200	450	278,000
2017	5,800	5,290	62,500	130,000	3,500	----	14,000	1,800	28,100	3,100	40,700	450	297,000
2018	5,000	4,680	60,200	133,000	3,500	----	15,100	1,800	28,000	2,800	41,400	200	297,000
2019	5,000	3,900	56,000	130,000	3,500	----	16,600	1,800	30,400	2,800	43,600	200	294,000
2020	8,700	2,530	59,400	120,000	1,400	----	16,600	2,890	32,200	2,700	51,100	200	298,000
2021	7,760	1,390	49,400	95,300	3,100	----	16,300	2,970	34,100	1,700	41,100	1,600	255,000
2022[1]	7,800	952	45,600	106,000	3,700	----	15,500	3,000	31,600	1,700	34,600	1,700	253,000
2023[2]	7,800	1,000	46,000	110,000	3,700	----	15,000	3,100	37,000	1,700	34,000	1,700	260,000

[1] Preliminary.   [2] Estimate.   [3] Shipments.   *Source: U.S. Geological Survey (USGS)*

Salient Statistics of Molybdenum in the United States   In Metric Tons (Contained Molybdenum)

Year	Concentrate - Production	Concentrate - Total (Including Exports) Shipments	Value Million $	For Exports	Con-sumption	Imports For Con-sumption	Stocks Dec. 31[3]	Net Production Grand Total	Net Production Molybolic Oxide[5]	Molyb-denum Metal Powder	Avg Price Value $ / Kg.[6]	To Oxide for Domestic Dest-inations	Exports, Gross Weight	Con-sumption	Producer Stocks, Dec. 31
2014	68,200	71,900	----	----	W	15,800	W	----	----	----	25.84	W	1,740	19,500	W
2015	47,400	50,500	----	----	W	12,900	W	----	----	----	15.01	W	1,300	17,600	W
2016	36,200	38,600	----	----	W	14,900	W	----	----	----	14.40	W	853	15,800	W
2017	40,700	43,200	----	----	W	36,000	W	----	----	----	18.06	W	534	17,400	W
2018	41,400	48,400	----	----	W	37,500	W	----	----	----	27.04	W	874	16,700	W
2019	43,600	67,200	----	----	W	34,200	W	----	----	----	26.50	W	524	16,400	W
2020	51,100	62,600	----	----	W	24,700	W	----	----	----	19.90	W	1,110	16,000	W
2021	41,100	59,900	----	----	W	30,200	W	----	----	----	35.30	W	839	16,100	W
2022[1]	34,600	51,100	----	----	W	28,800	W	----	----	----	41.35	W		15,900	W
2023[2]	34,000	51,000	----	----	W	31,000	W	----	----	----	55.60	W		16,000	W

[1] Preliminary.   [2] Estimate.   [3] At mines & at plants making molybdenum products.   [4] Comprises ferromolybdenum, molybdic oxide, & molybdenum salts & metal.   [5] Includes molybdic oxide briquets, molybdic acid, molybdenum trioxide, all other.   [6] U.S. producer price per kilogram of molybdenum oxide contained in technical-grade molybdic oxide.   W = Withheld proprietary data.   E = Net exporter.   *Source: U.S. Geological Survey (USGS)*

US Merchant Price of Molybdic Oxide   In Dollars Per Pound

Year	Jan.	Feb.	Mar.	Apr.	May	June	July	Aug.	Sept.	Oct.	Nov.	Dec.	Average
2016	5.32	5.45	5.45	5.55	6.87	7.95	6.91	7.11	7.13	6.88	6.82	6.71	6.51
2017	7.22	7.75	8.38	9.03	8.56	7.49	7.41	8.22	8.76	8.53	8.53	9.33	8.27
2018	11.42	12.33	12.96	12.48	11.95	11.43	11.28	12.15	12.16	12.06	12.01	12.22	12.04
2019	11.59	11.64	12.50	12.14	12.33	12.32	12.10	11.99	11.91	11.28	9.41	9.53	11.56
2020	9.89	10.34	9.14	8.31	8.66	8.18	7.27	7.73	8.35	8.55	9.20	9.31	8.74
2021	10.29	11.85	12.19	11.25	13.04	17.63	18.90	19.83	19.69	19.31	19.31	19.16	16.04
2022	19.24	19.18	19.68	19.80	19.23	18.48	17.37	16.41	17.44	19.43	19.65	24.79	19.23
2023	30.79	37.13	32.85	23.88	21.50	22.03	22.48	25.09	24.33	21.38	18.40	18.53	24.87

Source: American Metal Market (AMM)

Nickel

Nickel (atomic symbol Ni) is a hard, malleable, ductile metal that has a silvery tinge that can take on a high polish. Nickel is somewhat ferromagnetic and is a fair conductor of heat and electricity. Nickel is primarily used in the production of stainless steel and other corrosion-resistant alloys. Nickel is used in coins to replace silver, in rechargeable batteries, and in electronic circuitry. Nickel plating techniques, like electro-less coating or single-slurry coating, are employed in such applications as turbine blades, helicopter rotors, extrusion dies, and rolled steel strip.

Nickel futures and options trade at the London Metal Exchange (LME). The nickel futures contract calls for the delivery of 6 metric tons of primary nickel with at least 99.80% purity in the form of full plate, cut cathodes, pellets or briquettes. The contract is priced in terms of U.S. dollars per metric ton.

Supply – World mine production of nickel in 2023 rose by +10.1% yr/yr to a record 3.600 million metric tons.

The world's largest mine producers of nickel in 2023 were Indonesia with 50.0% of world production, the Philippines with 11.1%, New Caledonia with 6.4%, and Russia with 5.6%.

Demand – US consumption of nickel in 2023 fell by -9.5% yr/yr to 190,000 metric tons. In 2019, the primary US nickel consumption use was for stainless and heat-resisting steels, which accounted for 67.7% of US consumption. Other consumption uses in 2019 were superalloys at 14.6%, nickel alloys at 9.0% electroplating anodes at 3.5%, alloy steels at 3.4%, and chemicals at 1.1%.

Trade – The US relied on imports for 57% of its nickel consumption in 2023. US imports of primary and secondary nickel in 2023 fell by -3.2% yr/yr to 159,000 metric tons, well above the 2009 record low of 117,600 metric tons. US exports of primary and secondary nickel in 2023 rose by +24.5% yr/yr to 69,000 metric tons.

World Mine Production of Nickel   In Metric Tons (Contained Nickel)

Year	Australia[3]	Botswana	Brazil	Canada	China	Dominican Republic	Greece	Indonesia	New Caledonia	Philippines	Russia	South Africa	World Total
2015	225,227	16,789	94,800	225,351	101,400	4,000	19,610	129,600	193,199	415,021	276,710	56,689	2,110,000
2016	203,135	16,878	86,400	230,210	100,200	19,900	19,431	204,000	204,207	300,506	258,840	48,994	2,010,000
2017	185,466	----	76,800	206,354	102,300	28,300	19,073	355,000	215,382	339,377	267,300	48,383	2,200,000
2018	160,022	----	74,400	177,867	110,000	34,700	17,925	606,000	216,225	344,966	272,300	43,236	2,400,000
2019	158,751	----	60,600	181,410	120,000	56,900	13,655	853,000	208,185	323,325	278,700	42,936	2,610,000
2020	169,000	----	77,100	167,000	120,000	47,000		771,000	200,000	334,000	283,000		2,510,000
2021	151,000	----	76,000	134,000	109,000			1,040,000	18,600	387,000	205,000		2,730,000
2022[1]	155,000	----	88,500	143,000	114,000			1,580,000	200,000	345,000	222,000		3,270,000
2023[2]	160,000	----	89,000	180,000	110,000			1,800,000	230,000	400,000	200,000		3,600,000

[1] Preliminary. [2] Estimate. [3] Content of nickel sulfate and concentrates. *Source: U.S. Geological Survey (USGS)*

Salient Statistics of Nickel in the United States   In Metric Tons (Contained Nickel)

Year	Net Import Reliance As a % of Apparent Consumption	Production Plant[4]	Production Secondary[5]	Alloy Sheets	Cast Iron	Copper Base Alloys	Electro-plating Anodes	Nickel Alloys	Stainless & Heat Resisting Steels	Super Alloys	Chemicals	Apparent Consumption	Stocks, Dec. 31 At Consumer Plants	Stocks, Dec. 31 At Producer Plants	Primary & Secondary Exports	Primary & Secondary Imports	Avg. Price LME $/Lb.
2015	50	----	115,590	3,330	205	2,240	7,490	W	127,000	26,900	252	234,000	8,570	10,600	61,510	157,100	5.37
2016	44	----	130,790	5,380	160	2,780	7,370	14,700	153,000	24,400	1,750	235,000	8,690	6,370	74,000	143,300	4.35
2017	51	----	132,740	6,810	----	----	7,350	16,500	169,000	27,300	1,550	273,000	8,040	6,550	62,500	188,100	4.72
2018	52	----	122,690	8,510	----	----	7,240	20,600	159,000	27,300	2,830	259,000	9,570	6,780	69,180	189,100	5.95
2019	49	----	110,820	7,340	----	----	7,590	19,600	147,000	31,600	2,460	217,000	6,500	6,860	60,600	156,700	6.31
2020	48	----										210,000			57,600	136,800	6.25
2021	49	----										200,000			40,800	142,400	8.38
2022[1]	54	----										210,000			55,400	164,300	11.71
2023[2]	57	----										190,000			69,000	159,000	9.80

[1] Exclusive of scrap. [2] Preliminary. [3] Estimate. [4] Smelter & refinery. [5] From purchased scrap (ferrous & nonferrous).
W = Withheld proprietary data.   NA = Not available.   *Source: U.S. Geological Survey (USGS)*

Average Price of Nickel (Cash) in London   In U.S. Dollars per Metric Ton

Year	Jan.	Feb.	Mar.	Apr.	May	June	July	Aug.	Sept.	Oct.	Nov.	Dec.	Average
2017	9,971.5	10,643.3	10,204.7	9,609.3	9,155.1	8,931.8	9,491.4	10,890.0	11,215.8	11,335.8	11,972.1	11,499.4	10,410.0
2018	12,840.1	13,566.4	13,416.6	13,938.1	14,366.5	15,105.7	13,793.9	13,411.4	12,510.4	12,314.9	11,239.7	10,835.1	13,111.5
2019	11,523.1	12,685.2	13,026.3	12,772.8	12,016.3	11,943.9	13,546.3	15,748.6	17,656.9	17,046.2	15,171.8	13,829.4	13,913.9
2020	13,506.9	12,715.6	11,846.2	11,804.0	12,179.6	12,727.2	13,402.3	14,537.8	14,857.5	15,239.4	15,807.7	16,283.0	13,742.3
2021	17,863.2	18,584.4	16,406.7	16,521.3	17,577.1	17,979.6	18,818.5	19,141.3	19,376.9	19,362.4	19,932.9	20,015.6	18,465.0
2022	22,355.4	24,015.6	37,652.0	33,132.7	28,102.2	25,658.6	21,481.9	22,057.4	22,689.1	22,032.9	25,562.7	28,946.8	26,140.6
2023	28,194.6	26,728.0	23,288.6	23,894.6	21,970.4	21,233.3	21,091.3	20,438.7	19,644.6	18,264.0	17,027.4	16,460.8	21,519.7

Contract Size = 6 Metric Tons   *Source: London Metal Exchange (LME)*

Oats

Oats are seeds or grains of a genus of plants that thrive in cool, moist climates. There are about 25 species of oats that grow worldwide in the cooler temperate regions. The oldest known cultivated oats were found inside caves in Switzerland and are believed to be from the Bronze Age. Oats are usually sown in early spring and harvested in mid to late summer, but in southern regions of the northern hemisphere, they may be sown in the fall. Oats are used in many processed foods such as flour, livestock feed, and furfural, a chemical used as a solvent in various refining industries. The oat crop year begins in June and ends in May. Oat futures and options are traded at the CME Group.

Prices – CME oat futures prices (Barchart.com symbol ZO) on the nearest-futures chart in 2023 closed the year up +5.0% at $3.8575 per bushel.

Supply – World oat production in 2023/24 is expected to fall by -22.7% yr/yr to 19.424 million metric tons, remaining above the record low of 19.340 million metric tons posted in 2010/11. World annual oat production in the past three decades has dropped very sharply from levels above 50 million metric tons in the early 1970s. The world's largest oat producers in 2023/24 are expected to be the European Union with 30.4% of world production, Russia with 17.0%, Canada with 13.6%, and Brazil with 5.7%.

US oat production in the 2023/24 marketing year is expected to fall by -1.1% yr/yr to 57.045 million bushels. US oat production has fallen sharply from levels mostly above 1 billion bushels seen from the early 1900s into the early 1960s. US farmers are expected to harvest 831,000 acres of oats in 2023/24, down -1.1% yr/yr. That is far below the almost 40 million acres harvested back in the 1950s. The oat yield in 2023/24 is expected to rise by +5.9% yr/yr to 68.6 bushels per acre. Oat stocks in the US as of December 2023 were up by +16.5% yr/yr at 62.576 million bushels. The largest US oat-producing states in 2023 were the states of North Dakota with 14.0% of US production, Iowa with 13.3%, Minnesota with 11.7%, South Dakota with 9.0%, Wisconsin with 8.0%, and Texas with 6.6%.

Demand – US usage of oats in 2023/24 is expected to fall by -1.2% yr/yr to 136.000 million bushels. US usage of oats in 2023/24 is expected to be 54.6% for food, alcohol, and industrial, 40.4% for feed and residual, 5.0% for seed, and the rest for export.

Trade – US exports of oats in 2023/24 are expected to rise by +4.3% yr/yr to 2.000 million bushels. US imports of oats in 2023/24 are expected to rise by +1.1% yr/yr to 85.000 million bushels.

World Production of Oats   In Thousands of Metric Tons

Crop Year	Argentina	Australia	Belarus	Brazil	Canada	Chile	China	European Union	Kazakstan	Russia	Ukraine	United States	World Total
2014-15	525	1,198	522	307	2,977	421	310	7,821	226	5,267	610	1,019	22,123
2015-16	553	1,300	492	351	3,425	533	340	7,524	244	4,527	498	1,298	22,082
2016-17	785	2,266	390	828	3,231	713	500	7,228	335	4,750	510	938	24,346
2017-18	492	1,227	460	634	3,733	571	550	7,183	285	5,448	481	720	23,628
2018-19	572	1,135	342	795	3,436	385	560	6,946	336	4,715	423	815	22,222
2019-20	600	1,143	368	879	4,227	477	600	6,965	267	4,420	427	773	23,206
2020-21	510	1,898	445	853	4,576	525	600	8,473	240	4,127	515	954	25,711
2021-22[1]	725	1,735	350	1,143	2,899	578	600	7,471	182	3,733	478	578	22,685
2022-23[2]	429	1,587	375	1,190	5,226	315	600	7,409	229	4,500	380	837	25,126
2023-24[3]	610	1,100	350	1,220	2,636	450	600	5,900	220	3,300	350	828	19,424

[1] Preliminary.   [2] Estimate.   [3] Forecast.   *Source: Foreign Agricultural Service, U.S. Department of Agriculture (FAS-USDA)*

World Consumption of Oats   In Thousands of Metric Tons

Crop Year	Argentina	Australia	Belarus	Brazil	Canada	Chile	China	European Union	Norway	Russia	Ukraine	United States	World Total
2014-15	525	950	500	305	1,682	355	400	7,730	295	5,200	600	2,447	22,227
2015-16	550	1,025	500	345	1,600	495	500	7,400	296	4,600	450	2,700	21,806
2016-17	760	1,500	400	775	1,874	655	730	7,150	315	4,800	450	2,537	24,143
2017-18	525	900	460	675	2,041	570	850	7,050	320	5,400	480	2,358	23,869
2018-19	550	900	375	775	2,083	390	870	7,000	250	4,700	450	2,326	23,037
2019-20	600	970	370	845	2,419	520	870	6,900	345	4,200	420	2,344	23,147
2020-21	525	1,200	440	845	2,340	615	900	8,250	320	4,050	475	2,362	24,684
2021-22[1]	710	1,200	350	1,125	1,920	570	925	7,475	322	3,650	465	2,015	23,160
2022-23[2]	450	1,100	375	1,175	2,565	405	1,050	7,400	320	4,300	405	2,227	24,116
2023-24[3]	600	850	350	1,200	1,950	525	950	6,275	315	3,150	350	2,205	20,904

[1] Preliminary.   [2] Estimate.   [3] Forecast.   *Source: Foreign Agricultural Service, U.S. Department of Agriculture (FAS-USDA)*

OATS

Oat Stocks in the United States   In Thousands of Bushels

Year	On Farms Mar. 1	On Farms June 1	On Farms Sept. 1	On Farms Dec. 1	Off Farms Mar. 1	Off Farms June 1	Off Farms Sept. 1	Off Farms Dec. 1	Total Stocks Mar. 1	Total Stocks June 1	Total Stocks Sept. 1	Total Stocks Dec. 1
2014	19,800	9,710	41,400	31,300	15,323	15,029	32,910	35,670	35,123	24,739	74,310	66,970
2015	20,810	15,120	47,800	36,750	38,609	38,625	46,066	45,981	59,419	53,745	93,866	82,731
2016	26,800	18,350	37,400	30,430	48,429	38,452	41,190	45,003	75,229	56,802	78,590	75,433
2017	22,320	13,540	33,950	23,300	40,885	36,790	38,039	43,166	63,205	50,330	71,989	66,466
2018	17,240	11,410	39,200	25,410	37,699	29,606	35,573	41,864	54,939	41,016	74,773	67,274
2019	18,050	10,500	37,900	24,770	32,232	27,314	22,153	29,139	50,282	37,814	60,053	53,909
2020	16,970	10,070	39,850	28,830	30,722	26,693	27,017	33,712	47,692	36,763	66,867	62,542
2021	16,880	12,540	32,150	18,530	34,585	25,513	29,912	36,871	51,465	38,053	62,062	55,401
2022	13,560	9,890	41,650	24,180	29,444	22,763	20,897	29,515	43,004	32,653	62,547	53,695
2023[1]	17,130	13,840	35,450	24,030	25,779	20,967	39,874	38,194	42,909	34,807	75,324	62,224

[1] Preliminary.   Source: National Agricultural Statistics Service, U.S. Department of Agriculture (NASS-USDA)

Supply and Utilization of Oats in the United States   In Millions of Bushels

Crop Year Beginning June 1	Acreage Planted (1,000 Acres)	Acreage Harvested (1,000 Acres)	Yield Per Acre (Bushels)	Production	Imports	Total Supply	Feed & Residual	Food, Alcohol & Industrial	Seed	Exports	Total Use	Ending Stocks	Farm Price	Findley Loan Rate	Target Price
						In Millions of Bushels							Dollars Per Bushel		
2014-15	2,753	1,035	67.9	70.2	108.9	203.8	71.2	69.0	8.0	148.2	1.8	53.7	3.21	1.39	2.40
2015-16	3,088	1,276	70.2	89.5	85.6	228.8	93.5	69.4	7.1	170.1	2.0	56.8	2.12	1.39	2.40
2016-17	2,829	981	66.0	64.8	90.2	211.7	81.6	69.9	6.4	157.9	3.4	50.3	2.06	1.39	2.40
2017-18	2,589	804	61.7	49.6	89.2	189.1	68.3	70.6	6.8	145.7	2.4	41.0	2.59	1.39	2.40
2018-19	2,746	865	64.9	56.1	86.5	183.6	66.2	70.9	7.0	144.1	1.7	37.8	2.66	1.39	2.40
2019-20	2,830	828	64.3	53.3	92.0	183.1	62.7	74.0	7.5	144.2	2.1	36.8	2.82	2.00	2.40
2020-21	3,009	1,009	65.1	65.4	85.4	187.9	68.3	72.2	6.1	146.6	3.2	38.1	2.77	2.00	
2021-22	2,550	650	61.3	39.8	81.0	158.9	44.3	73.0	6.4	123.7	2.5	32.7	4.55	2.00	
2022-23[1]	2,582	880	65.5	57.7	84.1	174.4	56.7	74.2	6.8	137.7	1.9	34.8	4.75	2.00	
2023-24[2]	2,555	831	68.6	57.0	85.0	176.9	55.0	74.2	6.8	136.0	2.0	38.9			

[1] Preliminary.   [2] Forecast.   [3] Less than 500,000 bushels.   NA = Not available.
Source: Economic Research Service, U.S. Department of Agiculture (ERS-USDA)

Production of Oats in the United States, by States   In Thousands of Bushels

Year	Illinois	Iowa	Michigan	Minnesota	Nebraska	New York	North Dakota	Ohio	Pennsylvania	South Dakota	Texas	Wisconsin	Total
2014	2,000	3,520	2,760	7,875	2,400	2,520	7,665	2,205	3,480	9,300	1,710	8,680	70,232
2015	1,925	4,161	3,350	12,480	2,680	2,320	10,360	2,520	3,575	12,615	2,640	14,040	89,535
2016	1,620	3,268	1,740	8,160	1,500	3,300	7,260	1,850	3,350	9,020	3,000	6,600	64,770
2017	1,580	3,234	2,160	7,125	1,715	1,925	4,640	1,400	2,320	4,200	2,700	5,015	49,585
2018	2,075	2,079	3,150	6,195	1,518	2,322	8,610	1,950	1,610	7,790	2,500	5,490	56,130
2019	650	4,002	1,425	6,200	1,134	2,340	9,890	1,150	2,650	6,150	2,000	6,480	53,258
2020	870	5,694	1,650	10,560	1,827	1,696	8,190	900	2,750	10,780	2,700	8,253	65,355
2021	1,245	4,004	1,260	4,389	1,456	1,972	3,984	1,340	2,340	3,752	1,575	3,782	39,836
2022	830	3,280	1,586	8,540	918	2,695	13,680	1,050	3,599	6,000	1,760	4,810	57,669
2023[1]	1,530	7,600	1,650	6,699	1,272	2,640	7,980	1,140	2,867	5,106	3,780	4,575	57,045

[1] Preliminary.   Source: National Agricultural Statistics Service, U.S. Department of Agriculture (NASS-USDA)

Official Oats Crop Production Reports in the United States   In Thousands of Bushels

Year	July 1	Aug. 1	Sept. 1	Oct. 1	Dec. 1	Final	Year	July 1	Aug. 1	Sept. 1	Oct. 1	Dec. 1	Final
2012	65,276	66,519	----	----	----	61,486	2018	66,384	65,668	----	----	----	56,130
2013	74,459	75,210	----	----	----	64,642	2019	61,628	60,385	----	----	----	53,258
2014	75,507	77,267	----	----	----	70,232	2020	65,024	64,907	----	----	----	65,355
2015	83,640	85,456	----	----	----	89,535	2021	41,309	41,431	----	----	----	39,836
2016	76,609	76,854	----	----	----	64,770	2022	52,613	52,576	----	----	----	57,669
2017	53,674	53,719	----	----	----	49,585	2023[1]	49,883	49,454	----	----	----	57,045

[1] Preliminary.   Source: National Agricultural Statistics Service, U.S. Department of Agriculture (NASS-USDA)

OATS - CBOT
Weekly Nearest Futures as of 03/28/2024

WEEKLY NEAREST FUTURES
As of 03/28/2024

Chart High 811.00 on 04/12/2022
Chart Low 157.00 on 08/30/2016

Nearby Futures through Last Trading Day.

Volume of Trading in Oats Futures in Chicago   In Contracts

Year	Jan.	Feb.	Mar.	Apr.	May	June	July	Aug.	Sept.	Oct.	Nov.	Dec.	Total
2014	18,860	30,902	18,786	18,113	11,938	19,491	11,446	13,556	11,300	16,754	21,903	7,482	200,531
2015	14,618	19,923	12,461	25,243	15,152	21,734	11,399	13,953	9,614	13,216	24,979	12,283	194,575
2016	15,634	25,543	14,663	26,235	14,762	34,447	11,971	19,094	9,399	21,957	21,435	10,090	225,230
2017	15,129	16,691	13,180	17,122	10,845	24,381	10,292	11,920	8,370	11,522	19,561	10,239	169,252
2018	15,633	14,913	14,719	21,901	10,995	16,616	7,060	16,254	9,029	17,965	20,659	7,195	172,939
2019	10,494	16,765	10,206	19,410	14,000	22,122	9,460	9,034	9,145	12,466	19,901	9,548	162,551
2020	10,088	17,749	13,193	9,646	10,702	18,060	6,579	9,703	10,037	10,124	15,829	8,962	140,672
2021	7,568	11,486	7,479	12,665	9,657	15,397	11,563	9,872	11,009	14,010	20,154	10,043	140,903
2022	10,480	13,898	7,366	8,564	6,991	9,820	5,102	7,648	7,471	9,780	12,155	8,303	107,578
2023	8,477	12,482	12,634	16,122	12,697	19,637	13,679	15,341	10,239	12,318	16,224	7,878	157,728

Contract size = 5,000 bu.   *Source: CME Group; Chicago Board of Trade (CBT)*

Average Open Interest of Oats in Chicago   In Contracts

Year	Jan.	Feb.	Mar.	Apr.	May	June	July	Aug.	Sept.	Oct.	Nov.	Dec.
2014	10,414	11,168	9,529	8,350	7,356	7,793	7,292	8,382	8,987	9,787	9,813	8,151
2015	7,684	8,794	8,965	8,729	8,375	8,570	7,926	8,408	8,902	10,129	10,793	8,789
2016	9,457	10,452	10,883	10,418	9,947	10,282	9,969	10,511	10,755	9,261	8,304	6,946
2017	7,314	7,952	6,597	6,656	6,104	6,764	6,687	6,369	5,902	6,674	7,795	6,561
2018	6,491	5,995	5,740	6,470	5,468	5,232	4,898	4,723	3,990	6,113	6,608	5,712
2019	5,686	5,322	4,562	5,973	6,623	6,305	4,809	4,560	5,178	6,016	6,991	5,585
2020	5,004	5,405	4,391	3,450	4,211	4,809	4,420	4,677	5,238	5,491	5,783	4,519
2021	4,754	4,509	4,347	4,501	4,602	3,907	4,135	4,651	4,676	5,184	5,456	4,625
2022	3,944	3,745	3,005	3,210	3,024	2,992	2,530	2,919	3,718	4,113	4,171	3,968
2023	3,536	3,598	4,444	4,753	4,719	4,242	4,219	4,354	4,271	3,985	4,558	3,305

Contract size = 5,000 bu.   *Source: CME Group; Chicago Board of Trade (CBT)*

OATS

OATS
Quarterly Cash as of 03/28/2024

QUARTERLY CASH
As of 03/28/2024
Chart High 801.00   on 11/18/2021
Chart Low   25.63   on 08/30/1940

#2 White, Mpls: to 12/1974; #2 White, Mpls: 01/02/1975 to date

Average Cash Price of No. 2 Heavy White Oats in Minneapolis   In U.S. Dollars Per Bushel

Crop Year	June	July	Aug.	Sept.	Oct.	Nov.	Dec.	Jan.	Feb.	Mar.	Apr.	May	Average
2014-15	3.88	3.85	3.83	3.86	3.68	3.53	3.49	3.26	3.11	3.14	2.94	2.75	3.44
2015-16	2.89	2.82	2.63	2.70	2.58	2.67	2.60	2.64	2.60	2.43	2.49	2.49	2.63
2016-17	2.58	2.61	2.34	2.29	2.67	2.84	2.97	2.92	3.07	2.90	2.86	2.88	2.74
2017-18	2.95	3.17	2.98	2.87	2.97	2.94	2.90	2.73	2.96	2.79	2.72	2.89	2.90
2018-19	2.88	2.84	2.91	2.91	3.18	3.22	3.28	3.31	3.23	3.18	3.25	3.25	3.12
2019-20	3.15	3.10	3.01	3.03	3.15	3.22	3.21	3.43	3.37	3.21	3.21	3.40	3.21
2020-21	3.43	3.35	2.94	2.97	3.07	3.17	3.59	3.71	3.68	3.85	3.92	3.88	3.46
2021-22	3.89	4.17	4.68	5.47	6.26	7.47	7.66	7.02	7.38	7.06	7.33	7.10	6.29
2022-23	7.01	5.54	4.57	4.34	4.23	4.29	4.17	4.12	4.10	4.04	3.64	3.80	4.49
2023-24[1]	4.14	4.34	4.50	4.43	4.42	4.25	4.32	4.44	4.37				4.36

[1] Preliminary.   Source: Economic Research Service, U.S. Department of Agriculture (ERS-USDA)

Average Price Received by Farmers for Oats in the United States   In U.S. Dollars Per Bushel

Crop Year	June	July	Aug.	Sept.	Oct.	Nov.	Dec.	Jan.	Feb.	Mar.	Apr.	May	Average
2014-15	3.73	3.49	3.24	3.20	3.16	2.95	3.21	3.02	3.08	2.96	2.82	2.90	3.15
2015-16	2.83	2.33	2.07	2.04	2.20	2.11	2.12	1.93	2.21	2.20	1.97	2.26	2.19
2016-17	1.98	1.89	1.84	1.97	2.03	2.23	2.35	2.31	2.39	2.39	2.32	2.63	2.19
2017-18	2.74	2.33	2.32	2.56	2.55	2.68	2.94	3.29	2.63	2.80	2.93	3.14	2.74
2018-19	3.04	2.61	2.47	2.62	2.71	2.55	2.67	2.67	2.84	2.67	3.01	3.11	2.75
2019-20	3.31	3.09	2.72	2.67	2.83	2.95	3.02	2.84	2.73	2.79	2.97	3.10	2.92
2020-21	3.16	2.97	2.54	2.47	2.72	2.97	2.69	3.00	3.11	3.07	3.41	3.42	2.96
2021-22	3.42	3.60	3.63	3.73	4.30	4.81	5.65	5.68	6.05	5.89	6.48	6.35	4.97
2022-23	6.61	5.68	4.62	4.43	4.38	4.36	4.54	4.34	4.01	4.22	4.04	4.31	4.63
2023-24[1]	4.15	3.91	3.70	3.86	3.77	3.92	3.98	4.07	4.10				3.94

[1] Preliminary.   Source: National Agricultural Statistics Service, U.S. Department of Agriculture (NASS-USDA)

Olive Oil

Olive oil is derived from the fruit of the olive tree and originated in the Mediterranean area. Olives designated for oil are picked before ripening in the fall. Olive picking is usually done by hand. The olives are then weighed and washed in cold water. The olives, along with their oil-rich pits, are then crushed and kneaded until a homogeneous paste is formed. The paste is spread by hand onto metal plates, which are then stacked and pressed hydraulically to yield a liquid. The liquid is then centrifuged to separate the oil. It takes 1,300 to 2,000 olives to produce 1 quart of olive oil. The best olive oil is still produced from the first pressing, which is usually performed within 24 to 72 hours after harvest and is called *extra virgin* olive oil.

Supply – World production of olive oil (pressed oil) in the marketing year 2022/23 fell -24.2% to 2.770 million metric tons, below the 2011/12 record high of 3.629 million metric tons. The world's largest producers of olive oil in 2022/23 were Spain with 27.8% of world production,

Türkiye with 14.3%, Greece with 14.1%, Italy with 8.2%, Tunisia with 7.0%, Syria with 5.5%, and Morocco with 5.4%.

Demand – World consumption of olive oil in the 2022/23 marketing year fell by -10.2% yr/yr to 3.179 million metric tons. The US consumption of olive oil in 2022/23 fell -4.6% yr/yr to 386,600 metric tons, representing 12.1% of world consumption.

Trade – World olive oil imports in 2022/23 fell by -4.1% to 1.308 million metric tons. The US was the world's largest importer in 2022/23, with 380,000 metric tons, representing 29.1% of world imports. World olive oil exports in 2022/23 fell by -4.2% to 1.312 million metric tons. The world's largest exporters in 2022/23 were Spain with 22.9% of world exports, Türkiye with 17.9%, and Tunisia with 16.7%.

World Production of Olive Oil (Pressed Oil)   In Thousands of Metric Tons

Crop Year	Algeria	Argentina	Greece	Italy	Jordan	Libya	Morocco	Portugal	Spain	Syria	Tunisia	Türkiye	World Total
2014-15	69.5	15.0	333.0	235.3	23.0	15.5	132.0	69.0	959.3	113.0	374.0	174.0	2,685.0
2015-16	82.0	24.0	354.0	498.3	29.5	18.0	142.0	123.0	1,518.0	127.0	154.0	164.0	3,419.8
2016-17	63.0	24.0	219.0	193.3	20.0	16.0	122.0	78.0	1,398.0	121.0	114.0	192.0	2,768.8
2017-18	82.5	45.0	388.0	446.1	21.0	18.0	156.0	149.7	1,340.7	106.0	340.0	278.0	3,584.8
2018-19	97.0	28.0	207.0	180.6	21.0	16.0	225.0	105.7	1,935.1	121.0	153.0	207.0	3,509.6
2019-20	125.5	30.0	313.5	381.2	34.5	17.0	157.0	150.5	1,247.1	132.0	455.0	245.0	3,507.5
2020-21[1]	70.5	30.0	311.0	295.5	23.5	16.5	180.0	105.0	1,501.7	161.5	155.0	208.5	3,264.4
2021-22[2]	91.0	33.0	263.0	345.5	25.5	16.5	225.0	216.2	1,619.4	123.5	255.0	250.0	3,656.2
2022-23[3]	81.0	28.0	390.0	226.5	27.5	15.5	150.0	132.5	770.0	153.5	195.0	395.0	2,770.0

[1] Preliminary.   [2] Estimate.   [3] Forecast.   *Source: The Oil World*

World Imports and Exports of Olive Oil (Pressed Oil)   In Thousands of Metric Tons

	Imports							Exports					
Crop Year	Australia	Brazil	Italy	Japan	Spain	United States	World Total	Greece	Italy	Spain	Tunisia	Türkiye	World Total
2014-15	22.8	67.8	98.2	61.9	119.8	312.1	1,049.7	18.8	220.5	282.5	313.1	16.9	1,056.1
2015-16	26.9	50.6	42.6	56.7	58.7	331.5	1,023.6	23.0	244.5	395.7	114.3	12.8	994.3
2016-17	29.6	58.5	37.1	56.9	60.7	316.6	1,027.5	22.0	231.3	389.0	99.3	34.7	1,008.2
2017-18	31.7	78.6	64.5	57.0	124.1	322.2	1,163.6	22.1	216.9	389.1	217.5	70.0	1,171.8
2018-19	32.3	86.4	49.2	71.0	117.4	356.5	1,245.0	24.1	228.7	452.4	184.6	59.8	1,225.6
2019-20	36.6	104.2	81.8	72.0	170.6	398.0	1,455.9	25.2	247.3	531.3	351.9	49.3	1,490.6
2020-21[1]	36.6	106.8	51.2	61.1	125.9	390.5	1,382.8	26.7	244.4	535.0	236.6	45.3	1,374.9
2021-22[2]	34.4	103.5	51.6	64.6	115.9	412.2	1,364.2	26.2	255.2	539.1	198.0	62.5	1,369.4
2022-23[3]	30.0	100.0	63.0	56.8	147.0	380.0	1,308.0	52.0	190.0	300.0	210.0	235.0	1,312.4

[1] Preliminary.   [2] Estimate.   [3] Forecast.   *Source: The Oil World*

World Consumption and Ending Stocks of Olive Oil (Pressed Oil)   In Thousands of Metric Tons

	Consumption							Ending Stocks					
Crop Year	Brazil	Morocco	Syria	Tunisia	Türkiye	United States	World Total	European Union	Morocco	Tunisia	Türkiye	United States	World Total
2014-15	67.8	130.7	119.8	45.5	149.7	310.0	3,070.6	330.0	60.0	43.0	40.0	40.0	601.9
2015-16	50.6	132.5	111.2	44.0	157.7	321.0	3,145.8	590.0	55.0	69.0	35.0	52.0	918.2
2016-17	58.5	134.9	99.9	40.2	162.3	323.9	3,071.5	387.2	26.0	52.0	30.0	43.0	639.8
2017-18	78.6	140.3	89.7	40.4	183.1	326.3	3,203.9	655.4	26.0	137.0	55.0	39.0	1,012.5
2018-19	86.4	148.2	87.0	39.4	189.9	347.3	3,356.9	863.8	61.0	68.0	34.0	52.0	1,184.6
2019-20	104.2	150.2	90.0	38.7	199.2	381.8	3,457.9	719.0	58.0	134.0	65.0	70.0	1,199.5
2020-21[1]	106.8	152.9	95.0	26.2	203.3	395.0	3,520.5	586.0	66.0	28.0	52.0	63.0	951.3
2021-22[2]	103.5	160.2	104.9	28.1	202.8	404.6	3,538.9	653.0	90.0	58.0	45.0	70.0	1,063.4
2022-23[3]	100.0	156.0	93.0	26.0	170.0	386.0	3,179.0	348.0	44.0	18.0	64.0	63.0	650.0

[1] Preliminary.   [2] Estimate.   [3] Forecast.   *Source: The Oil World*

Onions

Onions are the bulbs of plants in the lily family. Onions can be eaten raw, cooked, pickled, used as a flavoring or seasoning, or dehydrated. Onions rank in the top 10 vegetables produced in the U.S. in terms of dollar value. Since 1629, onions have been cultivated in the U.S., but are believed to be indigenous to Asia.

The two main types of onions produced in the U.S. are yellow and white onions. Yellow varieties comprise approximately 75% of all onions grown for bulb production in the U.S. Onions that are planted as a winter crop in warm areas are milder in taste and odor than onions planted during the summer in cooler regions.

Prices – Onion prices in 2023 averaged $32.31 per hundred pounds, down -24.8% yr/yr.

Supply –The farm value of the US production crop in 2022 rose by +31.0% to $1.633 billion. In 2022, US farmers harvested 127,200 acres of onions, down -6.3% yr/yr. The onion yield in 2022 was down by +1.2% at 505.9 pounds per acre.

Salient Statistics of Onions in the United States

Crop Year	Harvested Acres	Yield Per Acre	Production 1,000 Cwt.	Price Per Cwt.	Farm Value $1,000	Jan. 1 Pack Frozen	Anual Pack Frozen	Imports Canned	Exports (Fresh)	Imports (Fresh)	Per Capita[3] Utilization -- Lbs., Farm Weight -- All	Fresh
						------------------------- In Millions of Pounds -------------------------						
2014	139,150	523	72,806	13.60	933,630	49.8	----		656.2	1,134.7	19.8	18.4
2015	132,900	507	67,380	17.60	993,360	45.0	----		605.5	1,109.7	20.3	18.3
2016	147,900	567	83,791	13.70	1,059,318	45.0	----		671.6	1,191.4	20.8	22.7
2017	151,500	544	82,389	12.90	1,042,090	62.1	----		682.2	1,257.9	22.4	25.0
2018	129,600	559	72,438	12.50	886,941	69.8	----		713.5	1,300.9		20.6
2019	129,400	540	69,893	14.60	1,001,986	68.8	----		823.7	1,253.4		19.9
2020	131,300	563	73,932	13.30	958,393	65.9	----		760.5	1,302.5		20.8
2021	143,700	506	72,645	18.40	1,324,944	74.7	----		704.6	1,557.3		20.8
2022[1]	135,000	519	70,071	26.60	1,842,922	50.9	----		202.8	1,252.4		19.2
2023[2]	133,700	547	73,093	20.90	1,510,071	65.2	----					

[1] Preliminary. [2] Forecast. [3] Includes fresh and processing. *Source: Economic Research Service, U.S. Department of Agiculture (ERS-USDA)*

Cold Storage Stocks of Frozen Onions in the United States, on First of Month   In Thousands of Pounds

Year	Jan.	Feb.	Mar.	Apr.	May	June	July	Aug.	Sept.	Oct.	Nov.	Dec.
2014	49,806	50,425	47,054	46,423	46,175	50,046	55,773	64,252	60,862	52,736	50,282	45,791
2015	45,001	43,865	48,055	48,960	52,702	56,379	56,673	53,467	53,428	48,106	48,935	46,921
2016	45,024	46,533	48,136	50,950	58,093	57,549	57,806	54,588	61,991	58,574	59,158	59,871
2017	62,106	61,514	63,908	66,174	72,770	76,063	71,368	68,219	73,667	70,900	64,044	67,319
2018	69,847	68,858	73,548	77,794	80,907	78,747	78,136	74,810	76,314	72,265	64,402	65,232
2019	68,823	69,721	71,636	75,066	82,588	89,921	87,458	77,280	78,543	76,481	67,368	68,541
2020	65,942	67,871	74,223	84,038	92,375	87,078	87,703	77,129	80,875	78,285	73,373	73,626
2021	74,651	75,867	74,888	70,476	74,722	74,524	71,915	66,844	64,683	58,904	54,307	52,979
2022	50,945	50,246	49,500	50,087	57,639	58,660	53,082	51,681	56,660	62,271	55,661	60,496
2023[1]	65,240	67,940	70,540	69,948	70,989	72,518	63,705	67,282	62,507	57,324	51,773	55,876

[1] Preliminary. *Source: National Agricultural Statistics Service, U.S. Department of Agiculture (NASS-USDA)*

Average Price Received by Growers for Onions in the United States   In Dollars Per Hundred Pounds (Cwt.)

Year	Jan.	Feb.	Mar.	Apr.	May	June	July	Aug.	Sept.	Oct.	Nov.	Dec.	Season Average
2014	NQ	NQ	NQ	25.10	27.20	17.30	23.50	14.50	11.90	10.30	9.12	9.56	13.60
2015	8.39	7.67	7.89	18.90	19.30	30.20	31.90	15.60	11.80	12.50	12.00	12.20	17.60
2016	14.40	15.30	14.90	21.10	25.80	27.70	26.70	12.70	9.78	7.58	6.76	6.43	13.70
2017	11.10	8.82	7.77	14.00	14.00	20.90	22.30	13.60	16.40	16.30	15.60	17.00	12.90
2018	15.00	13.20	11.60	14.80	17.10	18.20	21.40	15.20	11.20	11.20	11.30	10.90	12.50
2019	14.20	12.30	17.90	23.60	24.30	32.40	39.80	30.30	11.90	13.70	10.90	11.20	14.60
2020	14.10	19.30	20.60	24.80	27.90	30.40	30.80	23.30	19.40	20.00	20.50	19.50	13.30
2021	19.50	19.20	20.40	22.20	25.70	28.20	31.30	27.90	29.30	33.80	34.70	35.10	27.28
2022	39.80	46.50	51.50	48.30	50.50	46.80	47.90	43.40	42.10	34.00	32.70	32.30	42.98
2023[1]	30.50	27.60	24.40	28.00	36.90	48.00	41.30	31.60	29.20	25.80	26.00	38.60	32.33

[1] Preliminary.   NQ = Not quoted.   *Source: Economic Research Service, U.S. Department of Agiculture (ERS-USDA)*

Oranges and Orange Juice

The orange tree is a semi-tropical, non-deciduous tree, and the fruit is technically a hesperidium, a kind of berry. The three major varieties of oranges include the sweet orange, the sour orange, and the mandarin orange (or tangerine). In the U.S., only sweet oranges are grown commercially. These include Hamlin, Jaffa, navel, Pineapple, blood orange, and Valencia. Sour oranges are mainly used in marmalade and in liqueurs such as triple sec and curacao.

Frozen Concentrated Orange Juice (FCOJ) was developed in 1945, which led to oranges becoming the main fruit crop in the U.S. Two to four medium-sized oranges will produce about 1 cup of juice, and modern mechanical extractors can remove the juice from 400 to 700 oranges per minute. Before juice extraction, orange oil is recovered from the peel. Approximately 50% of the orange weight is juice, with the remainder being peel, pulp, and seeds, which are dried to produce nutritious cattle feed.

The U.S. marketing year for oranges begins December 1 of the first year shown (e.g., the 2020-21 marketing year extends from December 1, 2020, to November 30, 2021). Orange juice futures prices are subject to upward spikes during the U.S. hurricane season (officially June 1 to November 30), and the Florida freeze season (late-November through March).

Frozen concentrate orange juice futures and options are traded at the ICE Futures US Exchange. The ICE orange juice futures contract calls for the delivery of 15,000 pounds of orange solids and is priced in terms of cents per pound.

Prices – ICE frozen concentrate orange juice (FCOJ) futures prices (Barchart.com symbol OJ) posted their low for 2023 of 202.20 cents in January. FCOJ prices rallied sharply throughout 2023 as hurricane damage, frost, and citrus greening disease decimated Florida's 2022/23 orange crop. In April, the USDA estimated the 2022/23 Florida orange crop at 16.1 million boxes, down -61% yr/yr and the smallest since 1936. The total 2023 US orange crop of 62.25 million boxes was the lowest output in 86 years. With limited US supplies, demand for FCOJ from Brazil, the world's largest orange juice exporter, soared and Brazil's 2023 orange juice inventory fell -41% yr/yr to a record low of 84,745 MT. FCOJ prices surged to a record high of 431.95 cents in October as orange juice supplies continued to tighten. US stockpiles of orange juice in cold storage sank to a 54-year low in December of 181.13 billion pounds. Record high orange juice prices began to curb demand as the USDA reported US orange juice consumption in 2023 fell to a 5-year low. FCOJ prices fell moderately toward the year-end on the weaker demand but still finished 2023 up sharply by +55% yr/yr at 320.20 cents.

Supply – World production of oranges in the 2023/24 marketing year is expected to rise by +1.8% yr/yr to 48.819 million metric tons. The world's largest producers of oranges in the 2023/24 marketing year are expected to be Brazil with 33.8% of world production, followed by China with 15.6%, the European Union with 11.2%, Mexico with 10.0%, and Egypt with 7.6%.

US production of oranges in 2022/23 fell by -25.3% yr/yr to 60.130 million boxes (1 box equals 90 lbs). Florida's production in 2022/23 fell by -61.7% yr/yr to 15.800 million boxes, and California's production rose by +10.5% yr/yr to 43.200 million boxes.

World Production of Oranges   In Thousands of Metric Tons

Crop Year	Argentina	Australia	Brazil	China	Egypt	European Union	Mexico	Morocco	South Africa	Türkiye	United States	Vietnam	World Total
2014-15	800	504	16,714	6,600	2,635	5,954	4,515	868	1,645	1,650	5,763	566	48,971
2015-16	800	506	14,414	6,900	2,930	6,038	4,603	925	1,275	1,800	5,523	637	47,242
2016-17	700	526	20,890	7,000	3,000	6,739	4,630	1,037	1,363	1,850	4,616	768	53,995
2017-18	750	528	15,953	7,300	3,120	6,270	4,737	1,021	1,586	1,905	3,515	855	48,412
2018-19	800	515	19,298	7,200	3,600	6,800	4,716	1,183	1,590	1,900	4,923	855	54,219
2019-20	700	485	14,870	7,400	3,200	6,268	2,530	806	1,414	1,700	4,766	1,017	46,035
2020-21	750	505	14,676	7,500	3,570	6,531	4,649	1,039	1,511	1,300	3,980	1,161	48,126
2021-22[1]	726	535	16,932	7,550	3,000	6,728	4,595	1,150	1,609	1,750	3,108	1,583	50,248
2022-23[2]	580	505	16,673	7,600	3,600	5,564	4,854	783	1,630	1,320	2,256	1,583	47,955
2023-24[3]	900	530	16,500	7,630	3,700	5,475	4,870	820	1,620	1,731	2,536	1,583	48,819

[1] Preliminary.   [2] Estimate.   [3] Forecast.   NA = Not available.   *Source: Foreign Agricultural Service, U.S. Department of Agriculture (FAS-USDA)*

Salient Statistics of Oranges & Orange Juice in the United States

	Production[4]					Florida Crop Processed				Frozen Concentrated Orange Juice - Florida			
	California	Florida	Total U.S.	Farm Price $ Per Box	Farm Value Million $	Frozen Concentrates	Chilled Products	Total Processed	Yield Per Box Gallons[5]	Carry-in	Pack	Total Supply	Total Season Movement
Crop Year	Million Boxes					Million Boxes				In Millions of Gallons (42 Deg. Brix)			
2013-14	49.5	104.7	156.0	14.29	2,254.3	22.7	76.0	99.2	1.6	76.9	85.4	162.3	97.3
2014-15	48.2	97.0	146.6	13.29	1,963.4	19.2	71.9	92.0	1.5	66.0	72.6	138.5	86.2
2015-16	58.5	81.7	141.9	13.55	1,927.3	15.8	61.8	77.8	1.4	70.8	63.7	134.5	88.2
2016-17	48.3	68.9	118.5	16.30	1,943.7	12.6	53.2	66.0	1.4	52.7	55.9	108.6	87.5
2017-18	44.2	45.1	91.1	19.82	1,830.4	7.7	34.4	42.3		46.2	38.4	84.7	73.1
2018-19	52.2	71.9	126.6	14.43	1,765.3	15.2	53.8	69.1		58.5	51.1	109.6	76.3
2019-20	54.1	67.4	122.8	13.93	1,711.6	14.1	49.8	64.2		76.5	47.9	124.3	75.9
2020-21[1]	49.0	53.0	103.0	15.65	1,611.8	5.8	43.6	49.7		62.5	32.4	94.8	68.4
2021-22[2]	39.1	41.2	80.5	19.00	1,529.4	4.2	34.4	38.6		56.0	35.8	91.8	78.6
2022-23[3]	43.2	15.8	60.1	16.38	984.8								

[1] Preliminary.   [2] Estimate.   [3] Forecast.   [4] Fruit ripened on trees, but destroyed prior to picking not included.   [5] 42 deg. Brix equivalent.
Source: Economic Research Service, U.S. Department of Agriculture (ERS-USDA); Florida Department of Citrus

ORANGES AND ORANGE JUICE

WEEKLY NEAREST FUTURES
As of 03/28/2024

Chart High 431.95   on 10/31/2023
Chart Low   90.30   on 05/01/2019

Cents / lb.

Nearby Futures through Last Trading Day.

Volume of Trading of Frozen Concentrated Orange Juice Futures in New York   In Contracts

Year	Jan.	Feb.	Mar.	Apr.	May	June	July	Aug.	Sept.	Oct.	Nov.	Dec.	Total
2014	27,695	39,560	29,605	51,337	24,033	51,811	21,141	36,438	18,068	35,974	27,182	35,685	398,529
2015	21,377	37,435	34,855	39,065	23,789	42,032	18,914	42,607	24,694	48,774	28,965	36,060	398,567
2016	28,008	34,218	25,553	40,101	20,743	50,207	24,414	47,704	24,848	49,991	22,202	45,915	413,904
2017	30,883	37,187	35,311	33,218	25,193	34,836	18,627	36,316	34,697	25,936	16,504	34,791	363,499
2018	23,671	29,581	16,795	36,685	27,571	36,726	16,771	40,982	18,075	46,573	25,131	38,293	356,854
2019	23,436	50,269	30,857	55,326	27,698	43,007	17,848	51,082	18,589	47,780	14,462	53,282	433,636
2020	21,096	55,057	43,596	23,691	18,093	29,550	16,520	27,567	21,867	28,658	20,472	28,289	334,456
2021	19,272	36,891	20,474	33,674	22,776	38,150	22,018	35,756	16,070	36,477	23,241	38,503	343,302
2022	26,044	37,281	23,007	37,893	18,926	33,453	19,857	31,241	19,688	32,612	15,834	32,405	328,241
2023	20,315	42,373	15,468	28,868	18,626	24,932	17,715	28,877	12,342	30,609	21,046	34,784	295,955

Contract size = 15,000 lbs.   *Source: ICE Futures U.S. (ICE)*

Average Open Interest of Frozen Concentrated Orange Juice Futures in New York   In Contracts

Year	Jan.	Feb.	Mar.	Apr.	May	June	July	Aug.	Sept.	Oct.	Nov.	Dec.
2014	15,542	15,905	16,793	18,372	18,487	17,605	13,552	13,068	12,175	13,385	13,798	12,089
2015	10,973	12,605	15,506	15,799	14,630	14,192	12,421	13,196	13,358	15,172	14,651	14,759
2016	12,887	12,224	12,408	13,452	13,239	17,154	18,182	16,433	16,312	15,940	16,285	14,857
2017	12,528	11,357	10,887	11,104	11,212	11,929	11,277	11,441	8,972	8,741	9,378	9,882
2018	10,670	10,703	12,349	13,460	14,934	15,644	15,041	14,133	13,370	16,227	17,994	16,807
2019	19,118	21,665	20,689	20,601	21,261	19,818	19,459	19,413	17,375	17,719	17,325	18,687
2020	18,961	19,374	15,961	11,510	10,593	11,095	10,244	9,590	9,214	10,873	10,713	10,877
2021	10,181	12,474	11,929	12,737	13,472	12,030	11,580	12,052	11,612	11,895	11,730	11,152
2022	12,017	12,645	12,348	13,270	12,223	12,811	10,847	10,627	10,094	11,145	11,180	11,278
2023	11,914	12,169	10,118	9,624	8,829	8,900	9,499	9,769	9,385	9,804	9,209	9,176

Contract size = 15,000 lbs.   *Source: ICE Futures U.S. (ICE)*

Cold Storage Stocks of Orange Juice Concentrate[2] in the U.S., on First of Month   In Millions of Pounds

Year	Jan.	Feb.	Mar.	Apr.	May	June	July	Aug.	Sept.	Oct.	Nov.	Dec.
2014	739.5	750.5	799.3	813.0	877.8	872.9	853.7	815.9	773.0	712.0	721.9	676.8
2015	734.8	720.7	728.4	832.3	857.5	947.9	943.8	868.1	807.8	757.1	695.9	641.7
2016	639.3	623.0	633.4	702.0	751.4	772.5	766.5	711.0	653.1	603.1	579.9	519.6
2017	516.6	503.4	506.3	517.1	542.2	575.4	544.4	505.5	471.5	495.6	493.5	468.1
2018	505.1	517.1	501.0	563.1	632.6	730.9	733.8	691.1	633.4	609.0	566.4	528.9
2019	547.9	604.7	633.5	704.4	795.4	884.2	859.8	822.3	808.0	809.6	757.8	725.6
2020	766.2	772.9	784.9	802.4	838.5	852.7	830.4	777.8	723.9	677.1	653.1	620.3
2021	626.9	635.7	662.6	664.5	754.9	737.1	698.6	695.1	630.9	614.5	551.0	527.7
2022	496.6	447.0	457.7	479.6	488.6	530.5	520.6	493.8	396.2	353.2	307.7	309.3
2023[1]	290.3	288.5	272.9	327.4	353.7	341.9	327.8	325.1	235.4	189.2	211.4	185.4

[1] Preliminary.   [2] Adjusted to 42.0 degrees Brix equivalent (9.896 pounds per gallon).   Source: Agricultural Statistics Board, U.S. Department of Agriculture (ASB-USDA)

Producer Price Index of Frozen Orange Juice Concentrate   1982 = 100

Year	Jan.	Feb.	Mar.	Apr.	May	June	July	Aug.	Sept.	Oct.	Nov.	Dec.	Average
2014	2.414	2.430	2.457	2.426	2.571	2.510	2.547	2.547	2.566	2.605	2.646	2.651	2.531
2015	2.732	2.734	2.678	2.662	2.709	2.680	2.658	2.739	2.732	2.753	2.715	2.733	2.710
2016	2.731	2.752	2.758	2.747	2.796	2.772	2.768	2.774	2.810	2.550	2.530	2.571	2.713
2017	2.608	2.653	2.661	2.645	2.579	2.582	2.827	2.868	2.619	2.619	2.573	2.615	2.654
2018	2.521	2.538	2.513	2.481	2.481	2.469	2.504	2.440	2.493	2.478	2.475	2.434	2.486
2019	2.407	2.427	2.450	2.448	2.454	2.486	2.404	2.416	2.414	2.369	2.264	2.336	2.406
2020	2.321	2.319	2.277	2.398	2.375	2.360	2.339	2.339	2.257	2.307	2.285	2.333	2.326
2021	2.341	2.359	2.285	2.364	2.387	2.594	2.612	2.580	2.544	2.631	2.651	2.654	2.500
2022	2.621	2.754	2.696	2.770	2.856	2.887	2.889	2.751	2.777	2.744	2.672	2.718	2.761
2023[1]	2.823	2.982	2.893	3.010	3.175	3.270	3.336	3.415	3.427	3.669	3.638	3.717	3.280

[1] Preliminary.   Source: Bureau of Labor Statistics, U.S. Department of Labor (BLS)

Average Price Received by Farmers for Oranges (Equivalent On-Tree) in the U.S.   In Dollars Per Box

Year	Jan.	Feb.	Mar.	Apr.	May	June	July	Aug.	Sept.	Oct.	Nov.	Dec.	Average
2014	8.24	10.71	10.90	9.68	10.27	11.12	14.60	14.78	15.84	13.82	16.26	9.43	12.14
2015	9.35	9.85	11.32	10.78	10.74	10.53	10.79	12.01	15.25	17.73	17.35	9.59	12.11
2016	8.96	9.78	9.30	9.08	9.47	8.21	8.19	8.62	8.66	10.11	16.57	9.64	9.72
2017	9.63	11.62	12.35	11.81	12.46	18.53	20.33	18.18	20.52	25.61	16.47	12.55	15.84
2018	15.06	21.28	15.05	13.93	16.32	23.08	20.29	17.73	20.17	19.60	15.61	10.46	17.38
2019	10.10	9.95	11.70	11.23	11.06	7.56	7.26	7.31	7.70	11.95	15.18	10.20	10.10
2020	9.40	9.68	10.06	11.03	12.82	16.15	15.53	15.56	15.62	23.96	19.03	11.30	14.18
2021	10.95	12.88	11.58	11.36	12.83	11.05	13.79	12.14	12.49	18.00	18.21	11.95	13.10
2022	12.51	15.37	14.47	14.87	17.80	21.66	19.36	19.04	31.38	27.34	17.77	12.91	18.71
2023[1]	14.88	13.90	11.46	12.88	17.31	14.61	14.03	14.05	16.13	17.31	20.33	9.58	14.71

[1] Preliminary.   Source: Economic Research Service, U.S. Department of Agriculture (ERS-USDA)

Oranges (monthly average) through December 2023   USD per box

Palm Oil

Palm oil is an edible vegetable oil produced from the flesh of the fruit of the oil palm tree. The oil palm tree is a tropical palm tree native to Africa's west coast and is different from the coconut palm tree. The fruit of the oil palm tree is reddish, about the size of a large plum, and grows in large bunches. A single seed, the palm kernel, is contained in each fruit. Oil is extracted from the fruit's pulp (becoming palm oil) and the kernel (palm kernel oil). About one metric ton of palm kernel oil is obtained for every ten metric tons of palm oil.

Palm oil is commercially used in soap, ointments, cosmetics, detergents, and machinery lubricants. It is also used worldwide as cooking oil, shortening, and margarine. Palm kernel oil is a lighter oil and is used exclusively for food use. Crude palm oil and crude palm kernel oil are traded on the Kuala Lumpur Commodity Exchange.

Prices – The monthly average wholesale price of palm oil (CIF, bulk, US ports) in 2022 rose by +11.7% yr/yr to 63.14 cents per pound.

Supply – World production of palm oil in the 2023/24 marketing year rose by +1.8% to 79.464 million metric tons, a new record high. World palm oil production has grown sharply from the production level of 1.922 million metric tons seen back in 1970. Indonesia and Malaysia are the world's two major global producers of palm oil. Indonesian production in 2023/24 rose by +1.1% yr/yr to a record high of 47.000 million metric tons, and Indonesian production accounted for 59.1% of world production. Malaysian production in 2023/24 rose by +3.3% to 19.000 million metric tons, and Malaysian production accounted for 23.9% of world production. Other smaller global producers include Thailand with 4.3% of world production, Columbia with 2.4%, and Nigeria with 1.9%.

Trade – The world's largest exporters of palm oil in 2023/24 were Indonesia, with a 56.0% share of world exports, and Malaysia, with a share of 32.2%. World palm oil imports in 2023/24 rose by +2.5% to 48.216 million metric tons. The world's largest importers were India with a 19.3% share of world imports, and China with a 13.3% share.

World Production of Palm Oil In Thousands of Metric Tons

Crop Year	Brazil	Colom-bia	Costa Rica	Cote d'Ivoire	Ecuador	Guate-mala	Hon-duras	Indo-nesia	Malaysia	Nigeria	Papua New Guinea	Thailand	World Total
2014-15	400	1,203	188	415	694	510	470	33,000	19,879	940	537	2,068	62,090
2015-16	415	1,167	251	415	535	625	490	32,000	17,700	955	560	1,804	58,746
2016-17	485	1,537	247	486	587	740	620	36,000	18,858	990	650	2,500	65,571
2017-18	500	1,574	245	483	604	852	580	39,500	19,683	1,025	680	2,778	70,511
2018-19	525	1,626	243	514	584	862	580	41,500	20,800	1,130	705	3,034	74,165
2019-20	540	1,598	260	525	509	862	580	42,500	19,255	1,140	575	2,652	73,111
2020-21	545	1,628	266	550	465	865	450	43,500	17,854	1,275	720	2,963	73,277
2021-22[1]	550	1,762	265	575	380	880	600	42,000	18,152	1,400	720	3,376	72,964
2022-23[2]	570	1,800	270	600	470	910	600	46,500	18,387	1,400	780	3,415	78,063
2023-24[3]	585	1,900	275	600	480	920	595	47,000	19,000	1,500	800	3,450	79,464

[1] Preliminary. [2] Estimate. [3] Forecast. *Source: Foreign Agricultural Service, U.S. Department of Agriculture (FAS-USDA)*

World Trade of Palm Oil In Thousands of Metric Tons

	Imports						Exports						
Crop Year	China	European Union	India	Pakistan	Other	World Total	Benin	European Union	Indonesia	Malaysia	Papua/ New Guinea	United Arab Emirates	World Total
2013-14	5,573	6,969	7,820	2,725	18,631	41,718	600	162	21,719	17,344	556	250	43,190
2014-15	5,696	6,935	9,139	2,826	19,888	44,484	500	116	25,964	17,403	607	250	47,397
2015-16	4,689	6,717	8,857	2,720	19,397	42,380	450	148	22,906	16,667	580	210	43,895
2016-17	4,881	6,964	9,341	3,285	21,913	46,384	500	259	27,633	16,313	622	270	49,030
2017-18	5,320	6,834	8,608	3,285	22,746	46,793	476	261	26,967	16,472	615	180	48,759
2018-19	6,795	7,070	9,710	3,482	23,484	50,541	275	214	28,279	18,362	571	170	51,746
2019-20	6,719	7,112	7,398	3,416	22,832	47,477	200	152	26,249	17,212	598	170	48,491
2020-21[1]	6,818	5,970	8,411	3,500	22,827	47,526	190	159	26,874	15,878	645	200	48,188
2021-22[2]	4,387	4,970	8,004	2,824	22,554	42,739	170	185	22,321	15,527	634	225	43,821
2022-23[3]	7,200	5,300	9,030	3,600	24,733	49,863	150	150	28,450	16,900	664	190	51,218

[1] Preliminary. [2] Estimate. [3] Forecast. *Source: Foreign Agricultural Service, U.S. Department of Agriculture (FAS-USDA)*

Palm Oil (monthly average) through December 2023 — Cents per pound

Supply and Distribution of Palm Oil in the United States   In Thousands of Metric Tons

Crop Year Beginning Oct. 1	Stocks Oct. 1	Imports	Total Supply	Consumption Edible Products	Inedible Products	Total End Products	Total Disap-pearance	Exports	U.S. Import Value[4]	Malaysia, F.O.B., RBD	Palm Kernel Oil, Malaysia, C.I.F Rotterdam
				-------- In Millions of Pounds ---------						-------- U.S. $ Per Metric Ton ---------	
2014-15	136.0	1,143.0	1,279.0	----	----	----	1,279.0	22.0	----	659	941
2015-16	165.0	1,307.0	1,472.0	----	----	----	1,472.0	14.0	----	655	1,126
2016-17	189.0	1,367.0	1,556.0	----	----	----	1,556.0	17.0	----	727	1,307
2017-18	184.0	1,527.0	1,711.0	----	----	----	1,711.0	16.0	----	649	1,082
2018-19	132.0	1,526.0	1,658.0	----	----	----	1,658.0	6.0	----	522	662
2019-20	156.0	1,503.0	1,659.0	----	----	----	1,659.0	5.0	----	669	756
2020-21	171.0	1,576.0	1,747.0	----	----	----	1,747.0	7.0	----	1,073	1,305
2021-22[1]	142.0	1,588.0	1,730.0	----	----	----	1,730.0	9.0	----	1,494	2,101
2022-23[2]	160.0	1,887.0	2,047.0	----	----	----	2,047.0	11.0	----		
2023-24[3]	161.0	1,900.0	2,061.0	----	----	----	2,061.0	12.0	----		

[1] Preliminary.   [2] Estimate.   [3] Forecast.   [4] Market value in the foreign country, excluding import duties, ocean freight and marine insurance.
W = Withheld.   *Sources: The Oil World; Economic Research Service, U.S. Department of Agriculture (ERS-USDA)*

Average Wholesale Palm Oil Prices, CIF, Bulk, U.S. Ports   In Cents Per Pound

Year	Jan.	Feb.	Mar.	Apr.	May	June	July	Aug.	Sept.	Oct.	Nov.	Dec.	Average
2014	40.90	42.50	45.00	43.44	42.40	40.38	40.63	38.35	36.56	37.00	36.94	34.19	39.86
2015	36.05	34.88	34.50	32.38	33.05	33.19	32.15	29.88	29.25	30.75	29.50	29.60	32.10
2016	30.06	31.44	32.80	35.35	34.94	33.00	31.45	35.25	36.85	36.44	37.13	37.95	34.39
2017	37.75	37.38	35.90	34.06	36.31	35.05	35.19	35.06	36.44	36.19	35.44	33.25	35.67
2018	34.13	33.69	34.10	33.81	32.88	32.35	30.38	30.10	29.94	29.63	27.00	27.13	31.26
2019	28.94	30.00	28.40	28.63	28.00	27.75	27.19	28.90	28.63	28.94	32.95	37.25	29.63
2020	39.40	35.31	31.38	30.81	29.20	32.38	34.00	37.00	38.56	39.35	44.44	47.45	36.61
2021	49.81	52.13	52.13	54.25	57.75	50.63	53.30	56.69	58.31	64.35	66.31	62.55	56.52
2022	65.75	73.44	85.06	82.80	82.31	74.59	55.10	51.44	46.33	45.75	47.50	47.60	63.14
2023	47.44	47.94	48.30	49.44	44.89	41.65	44.81	43.50	42.30	41.13	42.38	41.70	44.62

Source: Economic Research Service, U.S. Department of Agriculture (ERS-USDA)

Paper

The earliest known paper that is still in existence was made from cotton rags around 150 AD. Around 800 AD, paper made its appearance in Egypt but was not manufactured there until 900 AD. The Moors introduced the use of paper to Europe, and around 1150, the first papermaking mill was established in Spain, followed by England in 1495, and the U.S. in 1690.

During the 17th and 18th centuries, the increased usage of paper created a shortage of cotton rags, which were then the only source for papermaking. The solution to this problem led to the introduction of the ground-wood process of pulp-making in 1840 and the first chemical pulp process ten years later.

Today, the paper and paperboard industries, including newsprint, are sensitive to the economic cycle. As the economy strengthens, paper use increases, and vice versa.

Prices – The average monthly index price (1982 = 100) for paperboard in 2023 fell by -2.5% yr/yr to 338.7, below the 347.4 record high posted in 2022. The average monthly producer price index of standard newsprint paper in 2023 fell by -2.4% to 160.8, below the 164.7 record high posted in 2022.

Supply – US production of paper and paperboard in 2022 fell by -3.3% yr/yr to 65.257 million metric tons. The US is the world's largest producer of paper and paperboard by far with 15.8% of the world's supply, followed by Germany with 5.2%, Russia and Canada with 2.2%, and Italy and Sweden with 2.1%.

Production of Paper and Paperboard by Selected Countries   In Thousands of Metric Tons

Year	Austria	Canada	Finland	France	Germany	Italy	Nether-lands	Norway	Russia	Spain	Sweden	United Kingdom	United States
2013	4,837	11,174	10,592	8,043	22,401	8,652	2,792	1,079	7,747	6,685	10,792	4,561	71,732
2014	4,865	10,775	10,408	8,096	22,540	8,648	2,767	1,023	8,023	6,036	10,419	4,397	73,093
2015	4,965	10,300	10,320	7,984	22,601	8,840	2,643	979	8,068	6,195	10,255	3,970	72,397
2016	4,995	9,911	10,140	7,984	22,629	8,888	2,671	1,099	8,547	6,219	10,102	3,677	71,902
2017	4,860	9,958	10,276	8,021	22,925	9,071	2,983	1,097	8,717	6,218	10,261	3,857	72,045
2018	5,055	10,142	10,540	7,864	22,682	9,081	2,980	1,134	9,048	6,157	10,141	3,895	70,891
2019	4,985	9,473	9,720	7,325	22,080	8,909	2,895	1,155	9,150	6,437	9,616	3,851	68,157
2020	4,719	8,665	8,190	6,873	21,348	8,514	2,869	933	9,527	6,268	9,280	3,634	66,239
2021	5,065	9,195	8,660	7,359	23,127	9,489	2,942	1,010	9,512	6,773	8,924	3,642	67,475
2022[1]	4,633	8,994	7,935	7,092	21,612	8,696	2,884	1,036	9,293	6,773	8,531	3,462	65,257

[1] Preliminary.   Source: Food and Agriculture Organization of the United Nations (FAO)

Index Price of Paperboard   (1982 = 100)

Year	Jan.	Feb.	Mar.	Apr.	May	June	July	Aug.	Sept.	Oct.	Nov.	Dec.	Average
2014	249.0	249.6	249.7	249.2	249.3	249.3	249.2	248.8	247.7	247.3	247.0	246.9	248.6
2015	246.9	245.2	244.5	242.6	243.6	242.6	241.9	241.4	242.2	242.1	242.2	242.0	243.1
2016	241.2	236.0	232.2	230.6	230.9	230.5	230.6	230.0	230.0	232.3	236.2	240.7	233.4
2017	244.7	244.1	244.2	249.3	252.5	262.7	264.0	264.5	265.5	266.3	266.1	266.6	257.5
2018	265.5	265.9	264.8	266.6	275.6	276.8	278.3	278.1	277.9	278.0	276.9	277.3	273.5
2019	276.9	274.6	273.9	273.1	272.9	270.4	264.8	262.3	262.2	262.4	261.9	260.9	268.0
2020	259.0	256.5	256.0	255.0	255.7	254.7	256.1	256.3	255.3	256.3	256.3	261.7	256.6
2021	270.6	274.6	275.4	280.5	289.3	293.6	298.8	304.7	308.4	320.4	321.0	323.4	296.7
2022	325.2	329.6	333.9	340.3	343.9	354.0	356.4	356.4	356.7	357.6	358.5	356.7	347.4
2023[1]	354.8	351.1	348.1	345.1	336.3	339.5	332.2	331.2	332.8	332.8	332.5	327.4	338.7

[1] Preliminary.   Source: Bureau of Labor Statistics, U.S. Department of Commerce (BLS) (0914)

Producer Price Index of Standard Newsprint   (1982 = 100)

Year	Jan.	Feb.	Mar.	Apr.	May	June	July	Aug.	Sept.	Oct.	Nov.	Dec.	Average
2014	130.7	130.5	130.2	129.2	128.3	129.2	129.1	129.0	128.7	128.4	128.1	127.2	129.1
2015	126.3	123.3	121.4	119.1	116.1	114.4	112.9	106.5	106.3	105.6	105.4	105.4	113.6
2016	106.7	109.6	111.9	112.3	113.3	114.9	116.4	117.8	118.3	118.4	118.1	118.3	114.7
2017	118.8	118.3	117.4	117.0	117.3	118.1	118.0	117.5	118.0	118.1	120.8	122.9	118.5
2018	124.8	127.0	128.1	130.4	136.0	141.2	143.5	146.0	146.3	146.2	146.0	146.2	138.5
2019	146.2	146.0	147.5	145.9	137.9	137.4	136.4	136.8	136.0	134.3	130.8	129.9	138.8
2020	125.8	123.0	119.8	118.8	116.6	116.6	115.3	111.6	110.4	110.7	109.7	109.4	115.6
2021	110.3	114.3	115.8	117.9	123.1	125.7	128.2	134.7	136.6	138.1	140.0	140.0	127.1
2022	144.6	147.5	152.0	156.9	160.4	168.3	169.5	171.1	176.0	179.2	177.5	173.4	164.7
2023[1]	174.2	176.5	172.3	172.1	168.9	166.1	156.8	152.1	155.4	148.0	143.4	143.4	160.8

[1] Preliminary.   Source: Bureau of Labor Statistics, U.S. Department of Commerce (BLS) (0913-02)

Peanuts and Peanut Oil

Peanuts are the edible seeds of a plant from the pea family. Although called a nut, the peanut is actually a legume. Ancient South American Inca Indians were the first to grind peanuts to make peanut butter. Peanuts originated in Brazil and were later brought to the U.S. via Africa. The first major use of peanuts was as feed for pigs. It wasn't until the Civil War that peanuts were used as human food when both Northern and Southern troops used the peanut as a food source during hard times. In 1903, Dr. George Washington Carver, a talented botanist who is considered the "father of commercial peanuts," introduced peanuts as a rotation crop in cotton-growing areas. Carver discovered over 300 uses for the peanut, including shaving cream, leather dye, coffee, ink, cheese, and shampoo.

Peanuts come in many varieties, but there are four basic types grown in the U.S.: Runner, Spanish, Valencia, and Virginia. Over half of Runner peanuts are used to make peanut butter. Spanish peanuts are primarily used to make candies and peanut oil. Valencia peanuts are the sweetest of the four types. Virginia peanuts are mainly roasted and sold in and out of the shell.

Peanut oil is extracted from shelled and crushed peanuts through hydraulic pressing, expelled pressing, or solvent extraction. Crude peanut oil is used as a flavoring agent, salad oil, and cooking oil. Refined, bleached and deodorized peanut oil is used for cooking and in margarines and shortenings. The by-product called press cake is used for cattle feed along with the tops of the plants after the pods are removed. The dry shells can be burned as fuel.

Prices – The average monthly price received by farmers for peanuts (in the shell) in the first five months of the 2023/24 marketing year (Aug/July) fell by -0.2% to 26.9 cents per pound. The record high is 34.7 cents, posted in 1990/91. The average monthly price of peanut oil in the first three months of the 2023/24 marketing year fell by -13.6% yr/yr to 80.85 cents per pound, falling back from the 2021/22 record high of 107.22 cents per pound.

Supply – World peanut production in 2023/24 is forecasted to rise by +2.2% to 50.459 million metric tons. The world's largest peanut producers are expected to be China with 36.9% of world production, India with 12.7%, Nigeria with 8.5%, the U. S. with 5.3%, and Sudan with 5.0%.

US peanut production in the 2023/24 marketing year is expected to rise by +7.9% yr/yr to 5.983 billion pounds, below the 2017/18 record high of 7.115. US farmers are expected to harvest 1.599 million acres of peanuts in 2023/24, up +15.5% yr/yr. The US peanut yield in 2023/24 is expected to fall by -6.7% yr/yr to 3,740 pounds per acre, remaining below the 2012/13 record high of 4,211 pounds per acre. The largest peanut-producing states in the US in 2023 were Georgia with 52.8% of US production, Texas with 11.0%, North Carolina with 8.4%, Florida with 7.6%, Alabama with 7.5%, and South Carolina with 5.0%. US shelled peanut oil production in 2022/23 remained unchanged yr/yr at 353.366 million pounds.

Demand – US disposition of peanuts in 2023/24 is expected to rise by +2.1% yr/yr to 6.097 billion pounds. Of that disposition, 54.4% of the peanuts will go for food, 21.3% for exports, 12.3% for crushing into peanut oil, and 12.0% for seed, loss, and residual. The most popular type of peanut grown in the US is the Runner peanut, with 89.2% of US production in 2022/23. The next most popular peanut is the Virginia peanut, with a 9.4% production share. Peanut butter is a primary use for Runner and Virginia peanuts. Peanut butter accounts for 61.8% of Runner peanut usage. Snack peanuts are also a key usage category and account for 31.9% of Virginia peanut usage.

Trade – US exports of peanuts in 2023/24 are expected to rise by +8.7% yr/yr to 1.300 billion pounds. US imports of peanuts are expected to rise by +11.7% yr/yr to 115 million pounds.

World Production of Peanuts (in the Shell) In Thousands of Metric Tons

Crop Year	Argentina	Burma	Cameroon	China	India	Indonesia	Nigeria	Senegal	Sudan	Tanzania	United States	Vietnam	World Total
2014-15	1,188	1,465	579	15,901	4,855	1,150	3,399	669	1,871	1,635	2,354	452	41,776
2015-16	930	1,502	609	15,961	4,470	1,130	3,467	1,050	1,042	1,836	2,722	441	41,261
2016-17	1,288	1,518	748	16,361	6,924	1,120	4,361	991	1,826	1,100	2,532	462	45,878
2017-18	867	1,572	600	17,092	6,665	1,075	4,521	1,405	1,648	1,100	3,228	450	46,925
2018-19	1,419	1,583	600	17,333	4,685	1,025	4,422	1,502	2,884	1,100	2,491	439	46,676
2019-20	1,285	1,375	600	17,520	6,255	990	4,441	1,421	2,828	1,100	2,479	425	47,747
2020-21	1,270	1,562	600	17,993	7,300	970	4,231	1,797	2,773	1,100	2,795	413	50,487
2021-22	1,340	1,600	600	18,308	8,700	960	4,228	1,678	2,355	1,100	2,885	410	51,967
2022-23[1]	963	1,650	600	18,330	6,300	930	4,284	1,502	2,500	1,100	2,514	400	49,383
2023-24[2]	1,375	1,700	600	18,600	6,400	880	4,300	1,715	2,500	1,100	2,672	390	50,459

[1] Preliminary. [2] Estimate. *Source: Foreign Agricultural Service, U.S. Department of Agriculture (FAS-USDA)*

PEANUTS AND PEANUT OIL

World Exports of Peanuts (in the Shell)   In Thousands of Metric Tons

Crop Year	Argen-tina	Brazil	China	Egypt	European Union	Gambia, The	India	Malawi	Nica-ragua	Senegal	South Africa	United States	World Total
2014-15	848	141	501	28	31	18	875	10	130	113	33	490	3,419
2015-16	883	163	483	28	32	15	773	7	102	193	16	700	3,633
2016-17	735	220	646	82	62	8	932	7	115	135	21	602	3,927
2017-18	588	296	651	49	61	8	743	5	131	97	23	577	3,524
2018-19	798	271	646	45	57	3	615	23	125	312	22	544	3,888
2019-20	983	350	554	39	52	1	974	24	101	430	26	730	5,014
2020-21	940	351	456	44	48	1	881	36	132	497	20	648	5,059
2021-22	936	389	455	66	48	1	718	39	151	241	23	537	4,424
2022-23[1]	750	415	458	45	45	1	1,028	35	143	172	20	542	4,660
2023-24[2]	950	425	500	45	55	1	800	40	150	325	20	590	4,848

[1] Preliminary.   [2] Estimate.   *Source: Foreign Agricultural Service, U.S. Department of Agriculture (FAS-USDA)*

Salient Statistics of Peanuts in the United States

Crop Year Beginning Aug. 1	Acreage Planted	Acreage Harvested for Nuts	Average Yield Per Acre In Lbs.	Pro-duction (1,000 Lbs)	Season Farm Price (Cents Lb.)	Farm Value (Million Dollars)	Exports Unshelled	Exports Shelled	Imports Unshelled	Imports Shelled
	----- 1,000 Acres -----						In Thousands of Pounds			
2014-15	1,353.5	1,322.5	3,923	5,188,665	22.0	1,158.3	1,080,000	676,509	90,000	64,345
2015-16	1,625.0	1,560.9	3,845	6,001,357	19.3	1,160.6	1,544,000		94,000	
2016-17	1,671.0	1,536.0	3,634	5,581,570	19.7	1,088.2	1,328,000		162,000	
2017-18	1,871.6	1,775.6	4,007	7,115,410	22.9	1,634.0	1,271,000		171,000	
2018-19	1,425.5	1,373.5	4,001	5,461,600	21.5	1,170.0	1,200,000		117,000	
2019-20	1,432.7	1,389.7	3,934	5,466,487	20.5	1,131.4	1,610,000		114,000	
2020-21	1,662.5	1,615.2	3,813	6,158,350	21.0	1,294.5	1,429,000		121,000	
2021-22	1,578.3	1,538.0	4,135	6,359,190	24.3	1,562.0	1,184,140		107,030	
2022-23[1]	1,448.5	1,381.4	4,012	5,541,772	26.8	1,501.2	1,195,930		102,910	
2023-24[2]	1,645.0	1,574.0	3,742	5,890,020	27.0	1,613.8	1,300,000		115,000	

[1] Preliminary.   [2] Estimate.   *Source: Economic Research Service, U.S. Department of Agriculture (ERS-USDA)*

Supply and Disposition of Peanuts (Farmer's Stock Basis) in the United States

Crop Year Beginning Aug. 1	Production	Imports	Stocks Aug. 1	Total	Exports	Crushed for Oil	Seed, Loss & Residual	Food	Total Disap-pearance
		Supply					Disposition		
					In Millions of Pounds				
2014-15	1,858	5,189	90	7,136	2,982	675	298	1,080	5,035
2015-16	2,101	6,001	94	8,197	3,053	709	1,100	1,544	6,406
2016-17	1,791	5,582	162	7,534	3,086	880	799	1,328	6,093
2017-18	1,442	7,115	171	8,728	3,149	705	887	1,271	6,011
2018-19	2,717	5,462	117	8,330	3,099	648	962	1,200	5,909
2019-20	2,421	5,466	114	8,001	3,221	774	287	1,610	5,883
2020-21	2,118	6,158	121	8,398	3,357	873	771	1,429	6,429
2021-22	1,968	6,359	107	8,434	3,313	842	735	1,184	6,074
2022-23[1]	2,360	5,542	103	8,005	3,201	795	781	1,196	5,973
2023-24[2]	2,032	5,890	115	8,037	3,319	750	729	1,300	6,097

[1] Preliminary.   [2] Estimate.   *Source: Economic Research Service, U.S. Department of Agriculture (ERS-USDA)*

Production of Peanuts (Harvested for Nuts) in the United States, by States   In Thousands of Pounds

Crop Year	Alabama	Florida	Georgia	Mississippi	New Mexico	North Carolina	Oklahoma	South Carolina	Texas	Virgina	Total
2014	544,950	668,000	2,435,515	124,000	15,750	401,760	44,000	410,400	459,740	84,550	5,188,665
2015	637,000	648,000	3,364,410	143,500	15,337	302,760	30,600	262,400	528,000	69,350	6,001,357
2016	619,200	554,800	2,753,400	152,000	22,400	349,470	44,400	339,200	559,650	76,650	5,581,570
2017	704,450	638,250	3,572,250	172,000	26,600	479,700	79,380	472,000	697,200	119,880	7,115,410
2018	571,550	564,850	2,875,450	93,600	15,675	379,260	46,050	272,000	464,000	100,800	5,461,600
2019	522,600	589,000	2,752,200	76,000	15,087	448,800	56,000	235,600	488,000	111,600	5,466,487
2020	622,200	564,400	3,316,600	96,800	14,820	409,500	59,080	296,000	484,500	112,050	6,158,350
2021	609,700	585,100	3,337,500	69,700	25,740	495,900	66,750	277,200	575,580	141,000	6,359,190
2022	554,200	574,560	2,862,800	63,000	15,552	506,920	63,240	282,200	327,180	125,720	5,541,772
2023[1]	480,510	504,640	3,133,900	57,600	21,000	528,900	58,500	299,700	468,000	140,070	5,890,020

[1] Preliminary.   *Source: Agricultural Statistics Board, U.S. Department of Agriculture (ASB-USDA)*

Supply and Reported Uses of Shelled Peanuts and Products in the United States   In Thousands of Pounds

Crop Year Beginning Aug. 1	Shelled Peanuts -- Stocks, Aug. 1 -- Edible	Oil Stock[2]	Shelled Peanuts ----- Production ----- Edible	Oil Stock[2]	Candy[3]	Snack[4]	Butter[5]	Other Products	Total	Shelled Peanuts Crushed[6]	Crude Oil Pro- duction	Cake & Meal Production
2013-14	519,824	25,364	3,098,392	373,008	395,726	429,796	1,218,170	29,103	2,072,795	497,272	209,808	268,554
2014-15	431,674	31,012	2,997,078	391,728	375,856	428,477	1,303,755	53,179	2,161,267	506,677	214,041	278,380
2015-16	467,139	65,350	3,141,099	442,650	377,505	505,692	1,299,634	61,388	2,244,219	531,770	226,219	291,193
2016-17	482,010	26,372	2,944,760	448,377	407,701	470,292	1,338,195	56,769	2,272,957	659,966	283,689	357,751
2017-18	535,730	24,232	2,853,147	358,282	379,504	524,845	1,314,567	95,943	2,314,859	528,750	231,748	282,346
2018-19	540,802	23,498	2,932,229	368,168	380,936	467,676	1,342,437	112,651	2,303,700	486,398	219,334	255,683
2019-20	510,369	29,092	2,908,778	405,622	395,647	481,430	1,410,264	91,567	2,378,908	580,628	254,109	304,718
2020-21	466,158	27,227	2,975,072	378,693	433,206	505,548	1,448,852	72,676	2,460,282	654,699	282,503	337,127
2021-22	521,131	25,843	3,292,875	353,341	490,132	485,359	1,409,120	60,173	2,444,784	631,840	283,736	330,684
2022-23[1]	453,602	17,972	3,132,911	353,366	441,779	455,623	1,480,173	45,352	2,422,927	596,042	264,875	320,301

[1] Preliminary.   [2] Includes straight run oil stock peanuts.   [3] Includes peanut butter made by manufacturers for own use in candy.   [4] Formerly titled "Salted Peanuts."   [5] Includes peanut butter made by manufacturers for own use in cookies and sandwiches, but excludes peanut butter used in candy.
[6] All crushings regardless of grade.   *Source: National Agricultural Statistics Service, U.S. Department of Agriculture (NASS-USDA)*

Shelled Peanuts (Raw Basis) Used in Primary Products, by Type   In Thousands of Pounds

Crop Year Beginning Aug. 1	Virginia Candy[2]	Peanuts	Butter[3]	Total	Runner Candy[2]	Peanuts	Butter[3]	Total	Spanish Candy[2]	Peanuts	Butter[3]	Total
2013-14	17,109	85,298	86,759	202,536	W	337,934	1,128,206	1,844,490	15,996	6,564	W	W
2014-15	12,079	91,909	102,340	232,768	348,367	329,930	1,196,277	1,901,311	15,410	6,638	W	27,188
2015-16	14,319	89,766	108,156	238,494	346,831	408,726	1,186,810	1,977,495	16,355	7,200	W	28,225
2016-17	13,427	92,331	118,109	247,473	379,549	370,766	1,215,212	1,998,683	14,725	7,195	W	26,801
2017-18	15,455	84,479	129,823	258,754	346,985	434,139	1,179,186	2,027,253	17,064	6,227	W	28,851
2018-19	15,589	81,418	120,939	236,696	349,081	380,165	1,213,018	2,036,161	16,266	6,093	W	30,840
2019-20	9,145	94,614	140,527	264,121	372,153	W	1,259,768	2,084,164	14,349	W	W	30,622
2020-21	W	68,725	W	249,240	408,607	W	1,285,959	2,166,988	W	W	W	44,058
2021-22	W	66,873	W	234,844	463,268	W	1,256,040	2,177,468	W	W	W	32,474
2022-23[1]	W	72,605	W	227,931	412,443	W	1,335,633	2,161,129	W	W	W	33,864

[1] Preliminary.   [2] Includes peanut butter made by manufacturers for own use in candy.   [3] Includes peanut butter made by manufacturers for own use in cookies and sandwiches, but excludes peanut butter used in candy.
Source: National Agricultural Statistics Service, U.S. Department of Agriculture (NASS-USDA)

Farmer Stock Equivalent Total[2/3] Stocks of Peanuts in the United States at End of Month   In Million Pounds

Crop Year	Aug.	Sept.	Oct.	Nov.	Dec.	Jan.	Feb.	Mar.	Apr.	May.	June	July
2014-15	1,426.7	1,330.5	4,246.1	4,717.3	4,573.2	4,297.1	3,893.3	3,487.2	3,105.8	2,717.9	2,401.4	2,101.0
2015-16	1,455.3	1,846.4	4,496.2	5,317.9	5,360.6	4,863.2	4,347.8	3,798.7	3,279.7	2,656.4	2,108.6	1,790.9
2016-17	1,239.1	1,509.3	4,156.1	4,701.6	4,389.9	3,992.8	3,550.0	3,087.8	2,668.3	2,241.0	1,806.7	1,441.6
2017-18	1,013.5	1,806.4	4,739.2	5,587.7	5,379.1	5,032.3	4,585.7	4,225.5	3,787.6	3,357.5	2,982.1	2,717.1
2018-19	2,309.8	2,594.7	4,195.3	5,002.8	5,056.8	4,727.8	4,326.0	3,976.9	3,490.6	3,075.9	2,765.4	2,421.1
2019-20	2,045.2	2,442.1	4,106.7	4,637.5	4,610.5	4,322.4	4,001.2	3,636.6	3,214.2	2,744.7	2,379.4	2,118.2
2020-21	1,557.9	1,465.0	3,493.8	4,496.8	4,386.8	4,142.3	4,337.6	3,834.8	3,323.8	2,900.3	2,377.9	1,968.2
2021-22	1,596.1	1,451.8	4,493.1	5,484.6	5,301.1	4,960.7	4,554.6	4,086.9	3,643.4	3,219.2	2,774.7	2,360.3
2022-23	1,913.2	2,599.1	4,870.5	5,457.3	5,051.3	4,634.9	4,247.0	3,768.9	3,215.6	2,788.0	2,354.4	2,033.1
2023-24[1]	1,796.8	1,679.6	3,796.3	4,780.6	4,805.9	4,498.1	4,176.0					

[1] Preliminary.   [2] Excludes stocks on farms. Includes stocks owned by or held for account of peanut producers and CCC in commercial storage facilities. Farmer stock on net weight basis.   [3] Actual farmer stock, plus roasting stock, plus shelled peanuts.   W = Withheld.   *Source: Agricultural Marketing Service, U.S. Department of Agriculture (AMS-USDA)*

Farmer Stock Peanuts[2], Total All Types, in the United States at End of Month   In Millions of Pounds

Crop Year	Aug.	Sept.	Oct.	Nov.	Dec.	Jan.	Feb.	Mar.	Apr.	May.	June	July
2014-15	661.8	573.0	3,517.7	4,046.4	3,947.9	3,622.6	3,224.0	2,789.6	2,394.6	2,056.4	1,697.5	1,445.3
2015-16	874.6	1,305.6	3,883.8	4,690.3	4,733.5	4,207.8	3,621.4	3,058.7	2,584.2	1,948.7	1,413.6	1,051.1
2016-17	648.2	960.2	3,594.2	4,093.3	3,747.5	3,317.9	2,828.0	2,342.8	1,919.8	1,465.8	1,050.4	733.0
2017-18	373.9	1,252.0	4,131.7	4,977.2	4,679.2	4,283.4	3,831.6	3,351.3	2,906.0	2,508.7	2,192.0	1,916.8
2018-19	1,568.9	1,811.5	3,426.7	4,286.5	4,301.9	3,976.5	3,576.0	3,144.1	2,703.0	2,334.7	1,964.9	1,627.9
2019-20	1,312.9	1,702.2	3,350.0	3,905.2	3,865.2	3,577.5	3,247.9	2,951.6	2,442.2	2,048.5	1,685.8	1,363.4
2020-21	839.0	792.9	2,878.8	3,858.8	3,713.5	3,418.6	3,578.2	3,006.2	2,514.8	2,063.9	1,641.6	1,280.3
2021-22	914.4	798.1	3,842.2	4,839.1	4,644.5	4,249.1	3,786.9	3,253.4	2,805.9	2,419.0	1,957.7	1,589.1
2022-23	1,185.9	1,885.3	4,176.0	4,783.1	4,395.3	3,961.7	3,501.3	3,043.0	2,553.2	2,116.1	1,708.4	1,375.3
2023-24[1]	1,125.5	1,041.4	3,186.2	4,168.5	4,091.4	3,832.7	3,506.8					

[1] Preliminary.   [2] Excludes stocks on farms. Includes stocks owned by or held for account of peanut producers and CCC in commercial storage facilities. Farmer stock on net weight basis.   *Source: Agricultural Marketing Service, U.S. Department of Agriculture (AMS-USDA)*

Peanuts (monthly average) through December 2023 — Cents per pound

Average Price[2] Received by Farmers for Peanuts (in the Shell) in the United States — In Cents Per Pound

Crop Year	Aug.	Sept.	Oct.	Nov.	Dec.	Jan.	Feb.	Mar.	Apr.	May.	June	July	Average[1]
2014-15	22.1	21.5	21.0	21.4	20.9	22.5	22.2	22.5	22.1	22.5	21.8	23.0	22.0
2015-16	20.7	19.6	18.8	18.5	17.8	19.3	19.8	19.5	19.8	19.6	19.5	19.0	19.3
2016-17	19.0	19.1	19.5	19.0	18.6	19.8	20.1	20.6	19.8	19.4	19.7	20.5	19.6
2017-18	19.7	23.0	23.2	22.7	23.0	22.9	22.7	24.4	23.3	22.7	22.7	22.4	22.7
2018-19	22.0	22.3	21.8	21.6	20.5	22.7	22.3	19.8	20.3	20.5	21.5	20.6	21.3
2019-20	20.5	19.8	20.4	19.2	19.6	20.9	20.5	20.6	20.6	21.1	20.7	20.7	20.4
2020-21	20.6	20.5	20.9	21.2	20.4	20.5	20.5	21.2	21.4	21.3	21.3	21.6	21.0
2021-22	21.3	22.2	23.9	25.4	24.1	25.9	24.8	25.0	24.8	25.3	25.2	25.3	24.4
2022-23	25.0	25.6	26.4	28.8	24.5	27.7	27.0	26.9	27.3	27.9	27.9	27.7	26.9
2023-24[1]	27.1	26.7	26.7	29.5	24.3	27.1	26.4						26.8

[1] Preliminarily. [2] Weighted average by sales. *Source: National Agricultural Statistics Service, U.S. Department of Agriculture (NASS-USDA)*

Average Price of Domestic Crude Peanut Oil (in Tanks) F.O.B. Southeast Mills — In Cents Per Pound

Crop Year	Oct.	Nov.	Dec.	Jan.	Feb.	Mar.	Apr.	May	June	July	Aug.	Sept.	Average
2014-15	59.95	60.63	60.13	56.15	55.56	54.69	54.81	54.65	56.31	58.15	58.63	58.69	57.36
2015-16	57.70	58.06	58.50	56.19	55.00	55.55	56.20	61.38	61.10	62.10	61.00	61.60	58.70
2016-17	64.88	66.00	63.10	62.88	63.13	65.80	69.69	70.75	76.20	75.75	69.63	66.60	67.87
2017-18	65.44	65.00	65.20	66.13	66.63	67.00	66.88	66.50	67.70	68.00	68.00	67.63	66.68
2018-19	66.63	64.80	62.25	61.88	61.13	61.00	65.25	66.00	66.00	66.13	66.00	67.00	64.51
2019-20	61.50	63.10	60.13	59.00	59.00	59.75	59.50	62.10	84.75	85.00	90.00	90.00	69.49
2020-21	93.00	98.75	100.00	90.00	93.00	105.25	109.20	110.00	108.19	106.00	108.75	105.00	102.26
2021-22	101.50	100.00	100.00	103.13	105.00	107.50	115.00	116.25	116.25	103.20	107.25	111.60	107.22
2022-23	107.75	111.00	101.00	95.38	88.00	84.40	81.75	85.50	89.60	94.25	95.25	88.40	93.52
2023-24[1]	83.25	81.50	77.80	76.50									79.76

[1] Preliminary. *Source: Agricultural Marketing Service, U.S. Department of Agriculture (AMS-USDA)*

Pepper

The pepper plant is a perennial climbing shrub that originated in India and Sri Lanka. Pepper is considered the world's most important spice and has been used to flavor foods for over 3,000 years. Pepper was once considered so valuable that it was used to ransom Rome from Attila the Hun. Black pepper alone accounts for nearly 35% of the world's spice trade. Unlike many other popular herbs and spices, pepper can only be cultivated in tropical climates. The pepper plant produces a berry called a peppercorn. Both black and white pepper are obtained from the same plant. The colors of pepper are determined by the maturity of the berry at harvest and by different processing methods.

Black pepper is picked when the berries are still green and immature. The peppercorns are then dried in the sun until they turn black. White pepper is picked when the berries are fully ripe and bright red. The red peppercorns are then soaked, washed to remove the skin of the berry, and dried to produce a white to yellowish-white peppercorn. Black pepper has a slightly hotter flavor and stronger aroma than white pepper. Piperine, an alkaloid of pyridine, is the active ingredient in pepper that makes it hot.

Black pepper oil is obtained from crushed berries using solvent extraction. Black pepper oil is used in the treatment of pain, chills, flu, muscular aches, and in some perfumes. It is also helpful in promoting digestion in the colon.

The world's key pepper varieties are known by their place of origin. Popular types of pepper include Lampong Black and Muntok White from Indonesia, Brazilian Black, and Malabar Black and Tellicherry from India.

Production – World production of pepper in 2022 rose by +3.1% yr/yr to 812,674 metric tons. The world's largest pepper producer in 2022 was Vietnam with a 33.5% share of world production, followed by Brazil with a 15.8% share, Indonesia with a 10.1% share, and India with a 7.9% share. Pepper production in 2022 in Vietnam fell by -1.3% yr/yr to 272,235 metric tons. In 2022, Brazil production rose by +8.7% yr/yr to 128,331 metric tons.

Trade – The world's largest exporters of pepper in 2022 were Vietnam with a 41.5% share of 195,978 metric tons of exports, Brazil with a 18.3% share of 86,385 metric tons, the European Union with a 10.3% share of 48,375 metric tons, Indonesia with a 6.3% share of 29,580 metric tons, India with a 4.2% share of 19,968 metric tons, the Netherlands with a 2.8% share of 13,423 metric tons, and Germany with a 2.8% share of 13,110 metric tons.

World Production of Pepper   In Metric Tons

Year	Brazil	Cambodia	China	India	Indonesia	Madagascar	Malaysia	Mexico	Philippines	Sri Lanka	Thailand	Vietnam	World Total
2015	51,739	2,503	34,224	65,000	81,501	6,881	28,300	3,567	1,847	31,226	1,405	176,789	547,124
2016	54,430	2,500	32,859	55,000	86,334	6,183	29,245	5,206	1,436	32,145	1,409	216,432	592,321
2017	79,106	2,499	33,340	72,000	87,991	5,559	30,433	7,951	1,369	35,142	2,536	252,576	668,724
2018	101,624	2,497	35,062	66,000	88,949	5,000	32,292	9,141	1,308	48,253	2,005	262,658	788,343
2019	109,401	2,507	33,758	66,000	87,619	4,500	33,940	9,384	1,132	41,429	2,219	264,854	786,496
2020	114,749	2,499	34,057	66,000	86,083	4,508	30,804	10,399	1,028	43,557	1,031	261,981	811,170
2021[1]	118,057	2,503	34,296	64,524	83,316	5,095	31,636	9,841	965	42,485	1,034	275,745	788,032
2022[2]	128,331	2,507	34,039	64,205	81,962	4,994	38,169	10,815	1,005	44,090	742	272,235	812,674

[1] Preliminary.   [2] Estimate.   *Source: Food and Agricultural Organization of the United Nations (FAO-UN)*

World Imports of Pepper   In Metric Tons

Year	European Union	France	Germany	India	Japan	Netherlands	Pakistan	Russia	Singapore	United Arab Em.	United Kingdom	United States	World Total
2015	112,962	10,203	29,239	21,460	9,068	13,630	7,119	6,922	20,177	18,363	12,038	80,357	392,340
2016	116,203	11,505	29,452	23,484	8,741	12,450	10,160	7,699	6,452	14,969	14,270	75,178	386,250
2017	119,500	10,814	32,630	30,431	8,193	13,063	8,932	8,204	5,583	19,361	12,963	78,287	422,994
2018	120,408	11,372	30,765	26,009	9,485	14,219	8,240	8,047	5,784	17,257	11,771	74,923	419,783
2019	128,984	11,264	33,955	29,357	9,714	15,215	11,187	10,306	2,753	27,003	12,722	84,312	476,716
2020	127,820	12,044	32,862	27,441	9,428	12,388	13,302	9,867	3,568	35,359	13,609	86,550	493,078
2021[1]	134,143	13,311	32,812	38,059	9,079	15,809	18,272	9,270	2,864	46,664	13,454	94,174	515,727
2022[2]	116,360	11,162	26,780	43,475	11,050	17,235	9,754	1,960	2,474	27,614	12,221	87,619	466,350

[1] Preliminary.   [2] Estimate.   *Source: Food and Agricultural Organization of the United Nations (FAO-UN)*

World Exports of Pepper   In Metric Tons

Year	Brazil	European Union	Germany	India	Indonesia	Malaysia	Mexico	Netherlands	Singapore	Sri Lanka	United States	Vietnam	World Total
2015	38,034	42,161	14,067	34,801	58,075	13,910	8,216	10,115	19,088	16,657	15,933	131,544	421,058
2016	31,085	44,199	14,841	23,863	53,100	12,549	8,556	9,283	5,485	7,876	14,129	178,134	419,093
2017	59,501	46,486	15,482	18,269	45,780	12,184	6,478	9,916	3,859	13,312	12,947	215,049	484,369
2018	72,580	44,234	15,304	16,726	47,614	11,777	8,415	8,582	4,807	12,706	9,292	186,202	462,610
2019	84,676	43,600	13,964	19,642	64,177	9,860	3,525	8,500	2,023	7,813	9,292	262,917	561,217
2020	89,756	43,547	13,724	17,489	58,378	8,518	3,104	8,005	1,731	9,761	7,891	259,300	555,017
2021[1]	92,065	49,237	15,726	21,971	37,738	7,451	2,367	10,482	1,529	17,959	7,959	249,342	554,062
2022[2]	86,385	48,375	13,110	19,968	29,580	6,795	1,764	13,423	1,244	11,416	8,927	195,978	471,715

[1] Preliminary.   [2] Estimate.   *Source: Food and Agricultural Organization of the United Nations (FAO-UN)*

Petroleum

Crude oil is petroleum that is acquired directly from the ground. Crude oil was formed millions of years ago from the remains of tiny aquatic plants and animals that lived in ancient seas. Ancient societies such as the Persians, 10th century Sumatrans, and pre-Columbian Indians believed that crude oil had medicinal benefits. Around 4,000 BC in Mesopotamia, bitumen, a tarry crude, was used as caulking for ships, as a setting for jewels and mosaics, and as an adhesive to secure weapon handles. The walls of Babylon and the famed pyramids were held together with bitumen, and Egyptians used it for embalming. During the 19th century in America, an oil find was often met with dismay. Pioneers, who dug wells to find water or brine, were disappointed when they struck oil. It wasn't until 1854, with the invention of the kerosene lamp, that the first large-scale demand for petroleum emerged. Crude oil is a relatively abundant commodity. The world has produced approximately 650 billion barrels of oil, but another trillion barrels of proved reserves have yet to be extracted. Crude oil was the world's first trillion-dollar industry and accounts for the single largest product in world trade.

Futures and options on crude oil trade at the CME Group and at the ICE Futures Europe exchange in London. The CME trades two main types of crude oil: light sweet crude oil and Brent crude oil. The light sweet futures contract calls for the delivery of 1,000 barrels of crude oil in Cushing, Oklahoma. Light sweet crude is preferred by refiners because of its low sulfur content and relatively high yield of high-value products such as gasoline, diesel fuel, heating oil, and jet fuel. The Brent blend crude is based on a light, sweet North Sea crude oil. Brent blend crude production is approximately 500,000 barrels per day and is shipped from Sullom Voe in the Shetland Islands.

Prices – CME West-Texas Intermediate (WTI) crude oil prices (Barchart.com symbol CL) traded sideways to lower the first half 2023 and posted a 2-year low in May of $63.57 a barrel. The Federal Reserve's tightening campaign in 2023 raised concerns about a recession in the US, which weighed on crude prices. Also, China's recovery from the pandemic was weaker than expected,

undercutting its energy demand. Crude oil prices ratcheted higher into Q3 and posted a 1-1/2 year high in September at $95.02 a barrel. Dollar weakness boosted crude prices when the dollar index fell to a 1-1/2 year low in July. Also, US crude supplies tightened after crude stockpiles at Cushing, the delivery point for WTI futures, fell to a 9-year low of 21 million barrels in October. In addition, crude garnered support from geopolitical tensions after a war began between Israel and Hamas in October, stoking worries that an escalation of the war could jeopardize crude shipments from the Middle East, a region that accounts for about a third of the world's oil output. Also, Houthi rebels in Yemen began attacks on commercial shipping in the Red Sea, disrupting oil supplies since shippers were forced to divert shipments around the southern tip of Africa instead of going through the Red Sea. Crude prices found support after OPEC+ in November agreed to cut crude production by -1.0 million bpd through June 2024, and Saudi Arabia maintained its unilateral crude production cut of 1.0 million bpd at a 3-year low of 9 million bpd. However, crude prices retreated into year-end as global energy demand remained tepid and as US crude oil production rose to a record high of 13.3 million bpd. Crude oil finished 2023 down by -10.7% yr/yr at $71.65 a barrel.

Supply – World crude oil production in 2022 rose by +4.7% yr/yr to 97.862 million bpd. US crude oil production in 2023 rose by +8.5% yr/yr to 12.925 million barrels per day. Alaskan oil production in 2023 fell by -2.7% yr/yr to 425,701 barrels per day, far below the peak level of 2.017 million barrels per day seen in 1988.

Demand –US demand for crude oil in 2023 fell by -0.1% yr/yr to 15.959 million barrels per day. Most of that demand was for US refinery production of petroleum products such as gasoline fuel, diesel fuel, aviation fuel, heating oil, kerosene, asphalt, and lubricants.

Trade – US imports of crude oil in 2023 rose by +3.3% yr/yr to 6.491 million barrels per day, down sharply from the 2005 record high of 10.126 million barrels. US exports of crude oil in 2023 rose by +12.6% yr/yr to 4.028 million barrels per day.

World Production of Crude Petroleum   In Thousands of Barrels Per Day

Year	Canada	China	Iran	Iraq	Kuwait	Mexico	Nigeria	Russia	Saudi Arabia	United Arab Em	United States	Vene-zuela	World Total
2013	4,001	4,609	3,354	3,095	2,900	2,882	2,357	10,748	11,267	3,429	11,309	2,675	89,114
2014	4,322	4,737	3,482	3,440	2,892	2,789	2,402	10,836	11,324	3,531	13,077	2,675	91,672
2015	4,434	4,838	3,549	4,135	3,064	2,592	2,231	11,010	11,745	3,660	14,093	2,569	94,383
2016	4,516	4,569	4,432	4,542	3,184	2,459	1,934	11,220	12,152	3,753	13,732	2,322	94,844
2017	4,881	4,457	4,773	4,531	3,028	2,229	2,016	11,205	11,814	3,708	14,562	2,057	95,479
2018	5,286	4,469	4,552	4,693	3,062	2,059	1,974	11,359	12,095	3,770	16,772	1,531	98,102
2019	5,409	4,574	3,275	4,795	3,021	1,901	2,006	11,447	11,448	4,114	18,402	919	97,877
2020	5,170	4,611	2,984	4,163	2,738	1,930	1,851	10,471	10,828	3,765	17,687	545	91,750
2021[1]	5,467	4,712	3,450	4,162	2,720	1,951	1,598	10,749	10,816	3,769	18,040	605	93,471
2022[2]	5,624	4,848	3,653	4,566	3,026	2,012	1,366	10,947	12,124	4,220	19,269	714	97,863

Includes lease condensate.   [1] Preliminary.   [2] Estimate.   *Source: Energy Information Administration, U.S. Department of Energy (EIA-DOE)*

World Imports of Crude Petroleum   In Thousands of Barrels Per Day

Year	China	France	Germany	India	Italy	Japan	Korea, South	Nether-lands	Singa-pore	Spain	United Kingdom	United States	World Total
2011	5,096	1,296	1,828	3,366	1,449	3,398	996	25	2,528	1,053	1,003	8,935	42,909
2012	5,428	1,139	1,881	3,746	1,377	3,429	1,008	28	2,583	1,184	1,083	8,527	43,509
2013	5,658	1,120	1,829	3,857	1,154	3,393	953	37	2,475	1,169	1,016	7,730	42,344
2014	6,193	1,082	1,805	3,785	1,059	3,205	959	25	2,525	1,192	940	7,344	42,072
2015	6,737	1,160	1,843	3,927	1,261	3,187	1,055	24	2,802	1,307	864	7,363	44,034
2016	7,599	1,105	1,837	4,267	1,226	3,138	1,094	10	2,931	1,292	794	7,850	45,275
2017	8,389	1,152	1,832	4,409	1,340	3,145	1,067	36	3,041	1,332	888	7,969	47,140
2018[1]	9,238	1,065	1,721	4,530	1,253	3,013	1,097	66	3,034	1,365	892	7,768	47,536
2019[2]		986	1,742		1,284	3,007	1,157	62	2,934	1,336	920	6,801	
2020[2]		663	1,663		1,009	2,419	994	62	2,646	1,099	705	5,877	

Includes lease condensate.   [1] Preliminary.   [2] Estimate.   *Source: Energy Information Administration, U.S. Department of Energy (EIA-DOE)*

World Exports of Crude Petroleum   In Thousands of Barrels Per Day

Year	Angola	Canada	Iran	Iraq	Kuwait	Mexico	Nigeria	Norway	Russia	Saudi Arabia	United Arab Em	Vene-zuela	World Total
2011	1,585	1,808	2,328	2,163	1,816	1,421	2,222	1,455	4,943	7,077	2,487	1,785	41,822
2012	1,663	1,933	1,455	2,414	2,070	1,333	2,288	1,314	4,759	7,397	2,571	1,741	41,930
2013	1,677	2,218	1,086	2,363	2,058	1,270	2,028	1,226	4,700	7,553	2,654	1,857	41,168
2014	1,632	2,382	1,084	2,518	1,995	1,208	2,120	1,294	4,500	7,120	2,651	1,729	40,640
2015	1,746	2,487	1,113	2,990	1,964	1,210	2,114	1,311	4,937	7,242	2,593	1,872	42,275
2016	1,658	2,907	2,313	3,916	1,859	1,277	1,847	1,398	5,080	7,599	2,457	1,645	45,376
2017	1,518	2,922	2,531	3,914	1,734	1,264	1,906	1,354	5,040	7,120	2,428	1,510	45,691
2018[1]	1,367	3,177	2,231	3,976	1,838	1,283	1,889	1,243	5,196	7,341	2,427	1,003	46,656
2019[2]		3,195				1,151		1,254					
2020[2]		3,017				1,192		1,494					

Includes lease condensate.   [1] Preliminary.   [2] Estimate.   *Source: Energy Information Administration, U.S. Department of Energy (EIA-DOE)*

World Production of Petroleum Products   In Thousands of Barrels Per Day

Year	Brazil	Canada	China	Germany	India	Italy	Japan	Korea, South	Russia	Saudi Arabia	United Kingdom	United States	World Total
2005	2,180	2,102	6,354	2,617	2,745	2,116	4,360	2,502	4,361	2,088	1,823	17,800	82,535
2006	2,167	2,069	6,495	2,580	2,896	2,050	4,262	2,559	4,548	2,289	1,757	17,975	82,611
2007	2,184	2,117	7,018	2,539	3,122	2,112	4,215	2,552	4,568	2,146	1,719	17,994	81,606
2008	2,007	2,029	7,069	2,484	3,226	1,971	4,136	2,535	4,803	2,103	1,678	18,146	81,772
2009	2,237	1,962	8,209	2,333	3,836	1,823	3,863	2,476	4,935	1,935	1,570	17,882	82,410
2010	2,467	2,015	8,737	2,197	4,220	1,886	3,857	2,537	5,299	1,935	1,532	18,453	84,163
2011	2,472	1,905	9,298	2,183	4,356	1,791	3,658	2,686	5,390	1,901	1,578	18,673	84,687
2012	2,555	1,926	9,880	2,207	4,506	1,693	3,645	2,789	5,516	1,971	1,436	18,564	85,182
2013[1]	2,810	1,893	10,345	2,151	4,776	1,506	3,689	2,697	5,770	1,884	1,380	19,106	86,426
2014[2]	2,899	1,877	10,852	2,126	4,793	1,418	3,536	2,772	6,174	2,221	1,301	19,654	87,766

Includes lease condensate.   [1] Preliminary.   [2] Estimate.   *Source: Energy Information Administration, U.S. Department of Energy (EIA-DOE)*

Supply and Disposition of Crude Oil in the United States   In Thousands of Barrels Per Day

Year	-- Field Production -- Total Domestic	Alaskan	Imports Total	Imports SPR[2]	Imports Other	Unaccounted for Crude Oil	Stock Withdrawal[3] SPR[2]	Stock Withdrawal[3] Other	Refinery Inputs	Exports	Ending Stocks Total	Ending Stocks SPR[2]	Ending Stocks Other Primary
2014	8,791	496	7,344	----	----	----	----	----	15,848	351	1,052	691	361
2015	9,439	483	7,363	----	----	----	----	----	16,188	465	1,144	695	449
2016	8,846	490	7,850	----	----	----	----	----	16,187	591	1,180	695	485
2017	9,357	495	7,969	----	----	----	----	----	16,590	1,158	1,084	663	422
2018	10,951	479	7,768	----	----	----	----	----	16,969	2,048	1,092	649	443
2019	12,311	466	6,801	----	----	----	----	----	16,563	2,982	1,068	635	433
2020	11,318	448	5,875	----	----	----	----	----	14,212	3,206	1,124	638	485
2021	11,268	437	6,114	----	----	----	----	----	15,147	2,963	1,015	594	421
2022	11,911	437	6,281	----	----	----	----	----	15,977	3,576	802	372	430
2023[1]	12,925	426	6,491	----	----	----	----	----	15,960	4,028	786	355	432

Field Production, Imports, Disposition: In Thousands of Barrels Per Day. Ending Stocks: In Millions of Barrels.

[1] Preliminary.   [2] Strategic Petroleum Reserve.   [3] A negative number indicates a decrease in stocks and a positive number indicates an increase.
Source: Energy Information Administration, U.S. Department of Energy (EIA-DOE)

PETROLEUM

Crude Petroleum Refinery Operations Ratio[2] in the United States   In Percent of Capacity

Year	Jan.	Feb.	Mar.	Apr.	May	June	July	Aug.	Sept.	Oct.	Nov.	Dec.	Average
2014	87.2	86.6	85.8	90.7	90.2	90.3	94.6	93.7	91.8	87.7	92.0	94.2	90.4
2015	88.4	87.6	88.7	92.0	92.5	94.0	95.1	93.9	90.5	86.6	91.8	92.6	91.1
2016	89.4	88.3	88.8	88.6	89.9	91.1	92.2	92.1	90.4	85.4	89.6	91.3	89.8
2017	88.4	85.0	88.0	92.7	94.3	94.3	95.0	92.8	85.3	88.3	92.5	94.7	90.9
2018	91.1	88.1	91.3	92.0	93.3	97.0	95.1	96.6	93.5	90.0	94.1	95.4	93.1
2019	91.1	85.8	86.1	88.8	90.6	94.2	94.1	94.9	89.0	85.8	90.7	92.5	90.3
2020	88.8	86.7	83.1	70.2	72.0	76.3	79.6	78.8	76.9	75.3	79.3	79.1	78.8
2021	82.6	70.6	81.9	86.3	89.0	92.4	90.9	90.4	87.2	86.1	89.1	91.2	86.5
2022	89.0	88.9	91.5	89.9	93.3	95.4	94.1	94.1	92.5	90.3	94.1	88.0	91.8
2023[1]	86.5	87.0	87.7	90.1	91.7	93.2	93.8	94.2	91.5	86.7	89.9	93.1	90.5

[1] Preliminary.   [2] Based on the ration of the daily average crude runs to stills to the rated capacity of refineries per day.   *Source: Energy Information Administration, U.S. Department of Energy (EIA-DOE)*

Crude Oil Refinery Inputs in the United States   In Thousands of Barrels Per Day

Year	Jan.	Feb.	Mar.	Apr.	May	June	July	Aug.	Sept.	Oct.	Nov.	Dec.	Average
2014	15,311	15,128	15,116	15,864	15,946	15,817	16,534	16,460	16,074	15,361	16,043	16,469	15,844
2015	15,456	15,342	15,640	16,273	16,402	16,701	16,879	16,700	16,168	15,440	16,458	16,742	16,183
2016	15,951	15,843	16,082	15,920	16,237	16,433	16,621	16,593	16,340	15,454	16,235	16,516	16,186
2017	16,118	15,493	16,048	16,954	17,222	17,204	17,317	16,981	15,460	16,061	16,840	17,274	16,581
2018	16,599	15,936	16,665	16,766	16,969	17,666	17,357	17,623	16,991	16,412	17,162	17,409	16,963
2019	16,783	15,846	15,935	16,341	16,719	17,236	17,175	17,297	16,403	15,681	16,482	16,793	16,558
2020	16,229	15,865	15,230	12,772	12,968	13,734	14,334	14,152	13,573	13,445	14,124	14,140	14,214
2021	14,542	12,371	14,387	15,162	15,596	16,190	15,852	15,726	15,232	15,045	15,684	15,757	15,129
2022	15,468	15,397	15,847	15,648	16,239	16,571	16,358	16,428	16,141	15,776	16,450	15,377	15,975
2023[1]	15,086	15,128	15,513	15,840	16,207	16,395	16,598	16,689	16,239	15,357	15,937	16,464	15,954

[1] Preliminary.   *Source: Energy Information Administration, U.S. Department of Energy (EIA-DOE)*

Production of Major Refined Petroleum Products in Continental United States   In Millions of Barrels

Year	Asphalt	Aviation Gasoline	Fuel Oil Distillate	Fuel Oil Residual	Gasoline	Jet Fuel	Kero-sene	Natural Gas Plant Liquids	Lubri-cants	Liquified Gasses Total	at L.P.G.[2]	AT L.P.G.[3]
2014	118.7	4.3	1,463.7	93.9	3,257	536.6	3.2	940.7	45.2	1,322.3	1,081.9	240.3
2015	125.4	4.2	1,451.1	94.7	3,344	561.6	2.4	1,038.1	49.4	1,418.1	1,194.6	223.4
2016	128.8	4.1	1,419.1	130.6	3,414	587.9	2.6	1,114.4	47.4	1,501.5	1,272.9	228.6
2017	128.7	4.1	1,437.3	130.9	3,401	613.8	1.6	1,363.7	39.7	1,593.1	1,363.7	229.4
2018	120.1	4.4	1,508.8	117.4	3,402	624.5	1.9	1,090.2	41.0	1,818.8	1,587.4	231.4
2019	116.7	4.5	1,875.0	131.8	3,685	655.7	3.7	1,145.7	60.9	1,982.1	1,760.9	221.1
2020	117.5	3.7	1,734.9	69.8	3,199	372.6	4.4	1,170.0	55.6	2,088.8	1,889.0	199.8
2021	135.2	4.3	1,439.2	114.1	3,210	500.5	1.9	1,134.1	37.8	2,090.8	1,970.0	120.8
2022	136.0	4.4	1,446.3	125.3	3,204	568.8	1.4	1,209.1	40.8	2,275.5	2,147.2	128.3
2023[1]	134.6	4.2	1,435.5	100.3	3,264	602.9	4.1	1,163.7	30.3	2,476.8	2,347.3	129.5

[1] Preliminary.   [2] Gas processing plants.   [3] Refineries.   *Source: Energy Information Administration, U.S. Department of Energy (EIA-DOE)*

Stocks of Petroleum and Products in the United States on January 1   In Millions of Barrels

Year	Crude Petroleum	Strategic Reserve	Refined Products Total	Asphalt	Aviation Gasoline	Fuel Oil Distillate	Fuel Oil Residual	Finished Gasoline	Jet Fuel	Kero-sene	Gases[2]	Lubri-cants	Motor Gasoline Total	Motor Gasoline Finished[3]
2015	1,051.8	691.0	286.9	21.2	1.1	136.3	33.7	30.6	38.3	2.1	154.8	11.2	240	31
2016	1,144.3	695.1	325.1	24.6	0.9	161.3	42.1	28.5	40.4	2.6	176.7	13.5	235	28
2017	1,179.7	695.1	329.7	22.9	1.0	166.1	41.5	28.6	43.0	2.3	178.4	12.4	239	29
2018	1,084.5	662.8	291.6	21.5	1.0	145.6	29.4	24.6	41.3	2.1	184.8	12.0	237	25
2019	1,091.6	649.1	294.3	27.0	1.0	140.0	28.3	25.7	41.6	2.6	188.5	14.0	221	26
2020	1,067.9	635.0	291.9	23.1	1.1	140.0	30.9	26.0	40.5	2.9	208.8	12.7	228	26
2021	1,123.3	638.1	303.9	23.0	1.1	160.4	30.2	25.3	38.6	2.7	226.9	9.7	218	25
2022	1,015.1	593.7	260.6	23.9	1.3	129.9	25.4	17.7	35.8	2.2	186.3	12.8	214	18
2023	801.6	372.0	256.2	25.7	1.3	118.8	30.7	17.4	35.0	2.1	209.2	13.3	207	17
2024[1]	781.1	354.6	262.0	22.8	1.2	130.7	24.1	18.1	39.8	1.9	222.0	12.1	262	18

[1] Preliminary.   [2] Includes ethane & ethylene at plants and refineries.   [3] Includes oxygenated.
Source: Energy Information Administration, U.S. Department of Energy (EIA-DOE)

Stocks of Crude Petroleum in the United States, on First of Month   In Millions of Barrels

Year	Jan.	Feb.	Mar.	Apr.	May	June	July	Aug.	Sept.	Oct.	Nov.	Dec.
2014	1,059.7	1,069.3	1,079.7	1,086.5	1,085.0	1,074.9	1,059.7	1,051.6	1,051.9	1,073.0	1,078.5	1,084.7
2015	1,112.4	1,139.0	1,165.8	1,174.3	1,171.7	1,163.4	1,150.6	1,152.9	1,155.9	1,181.8	1,182.5	1,176.5
2016	1,166.9	1,187.3	1,199.9	1,204.4	1,207.0	1,196.0	1,188.6	1,181.8	1,166.6	1,186.3	1,185.8	1,179.7
2017	1,201.9	1,220.2	1,230.1	1,213.1	1,201.3	1,180.7	1,162.3	1,138.8	1,143.2	1,128.7	1,114.3	1,084.5
2018	1,085.0	1,089.3	1,090.4	1,100.5	1,094.4	1,075.2	1,069.7	1,067.6	1,076.7	1,088.6	1,098.9	1,091.6
2019	1,098.1	1,100.8	1,108.0	1,118.4	1,125.9	1,108.3	1,086.4	1,074.9	1,070.4	1,084.5	1,080.9	1,067.7
2020	1,075.2	1,087.5	1,118.3	1,166.9	1,169.9	1,188.7	1,176.3	1,151.9	1,139.9	1,132.5	1,138.8	1,123.6
2021	1,114.4	1,131.6	1,140.2	1,122.6	1,104.6	1,069.4	1,060.0	1,042.8	1,038.1	1,047.2	1,034.9	1,014.9
2022	1,002.0	987.4	980.3	965.2	938.2	911.1	892.1	864.8	845.4	838.2	805.0	802.1
2023[1]	831.4	843.9	836.6	823.6	815.2	801.9	787.2	767.6	768.7	777.3	794.0	786.3

[1] Preliminary.   Source: Energy Information Administration; U.S. Department of Energy

Production of Crude Petroleum in the United States   In Thousands of Barrels Per Day

Year	Jan.	Feb.	Mar.	Apr.	May	June	July	Aug.	Sept.	Oct.	Nov.	Dec.	Average
2014	8,051	8,136	8,274	8,573	8,612	8,718	8,782	8,886	9,041	9,221	9,303	9,467	8,755
2015	9,385	9,511	9,578	9,650	9,464	9,344	9,430	9,400	9,460	9,388	9,318	9,251	9,431
2016	9,197	9,055	9,081	8,866	8,824	8,671	8,635	8,670	8,519	8,787	8,888	8,778	8,831
2017	8,861	9,101	9,162	9,100	9,183	9,108	9,235	9,248	9,512	9,653	10,071	9,973	9,351
2018	10,018	10,281	10,504	10,510	10,460	10,649	10,891	11,361	11,498	11,631	11,999	12,038	10,987
2019	11,848	11,653	11,899	12,125	12,141	12,179	11,896	12,475	12,572	12,771	12,966	12,910	12,286
2020	12,850	12,844	12,795	11,911	9,714	10,446	11,004	10,579	10,926	10,456	11,196	11,172	11,324
2021	11,137	9,916	11,351	11,318	11,390	11,366	11,392	11,276	10,921	11,564	11,782	11,678	11,258
2022	11,480	11,258	11,806	11,770	11,734	11,800	11,834	11,985	12,325	12,378	12,376	12,138	11,907
2023[1]	12,568	12,532	12,770	12,650	12,694	12,894	12,925	13,041	13,247	13,224	13,308	13,223	12,923

[1] Preliminary.   Source: Energy Information Administration, U.S. Department of Energy (EIA-DOE)

U.S. Foreign Trade of Petroleum and Products   In Thousands of Barrels Per Day

Year	Exports Total[2]	Petroleum Products	Crude	Imports Petroleum Products	Distillate Fuel Oil	Residual Fuel Oil	Net Imports[3]
2014	4,176	4,247	7,344	1,529	195	173	5,065
2015	4,738	4,888	7,363	1,694	200	192	4,711
2016	5,261	5,469	7,850	1,854	147	205	4,795
2017	6,376	6,132	7,969	1,836	151	189	3,768
2018	7,601	6,502	7,768	1,788	175	211	2,341
2019	8,471	6,587	6,801	1,989	202	149	670
2020	8,498	6,554	5,875	1,604	218	166	-635
2021	8,536	6,900	6,114	1,885	288	186	-62
2022	9,520		6,281	1,658	188	202	-1,191
2023[1]	10,086		6,491	1,751	168	110	-1,567

[1] Preliminary.   [2] Includes crude oil.   [3] Equals imports minus exports.
Source: Energy Information Administration, U.S. Department of Energy (EIA-DOE)

Domestic First Purchase Price of Crude Petroleum at Wells[2]   In U.S. Dollars Per Barrel

Year	Jan.	Feb.	Mar.	Apr.	May	June	July	Aug.	Sept.	Oct.	Nov.	Dec.	Average
2014	89.57	96.86	96.17	96.49	95.74	98.68	96.70	90.72	86.87	78.84	71.07	54.86	87.71
2015	43.06	44.35	42.66	49.30	54.38	55.88	47.70	39.98	41.60	42.33	38.19	32.26	44.31
2016	27.02	25.51	31.87	35.59	41.02	43.96	40.70	40.46	40.54	45.00	41.65	47.12	38.37
2017	48.19	49.41	46.39	47.23	45.19	42.19	43.42	44.96	47.17	49.13	55.19	56.98	47.95
2018	62.25	61.20	60.68	63.50	66.16	62.80	67.00	62.64	63.55	65.18	55.65	47.72	61.53
2019	47.85	52.51	57.47	63.01	59.68	54.22	56.47	53.63	55.07	53.14	54.96	58.41	55.54
2020	56.55	49.66	31.01	15.18	18.02	33.81	37.44	39.37	36.82	36.39	38.25	43.92	36.37
2021	49.47	56.44	60.43	59.87	62.80	68.58	70.12	65.68	69.09	78.51	76.45	70.56	65.67
2022	80.33	89.41	107.07	103.34	108.29	113.77	100.84	93.76	84.62	86.61	84.43	76.45	94.08
2023[1]	75.71	74.32	72.09	77.22	70.14	68.58	74.05	79.78	87.96	84.65	77.46		76.54

[1] Preliminary.   [2] Buyers posted prices.   Source: Energy Information Administration, U.S. Department of Energy (EIA-DOE)

PETROLEUM

Refiner Sales Prices of Residual Fuel Oil   In U.S. Dollars Per Gallon

Year	Jan.	Feb.	Mar.	Apr.	May	June	July	Aug.	Sept.	Oct.	Nov.	Dec.	Average
2015	0.936	1.150	1.093	1.124	1.198	1.175	1.080	0.797	0.819	0.812	0.766	0.552	0.959
2016	0.477	0.475	0.582	0.633	0.729	0.850	0.876	0.842	0.846	0.961	0.920	1.024	0.768
2017	1.099	1.174	1.103	1.038	0.986	0.937	1.026	1.042	1.150	1.153	1.302	1.254	1.105
2018	1.301	1.221	1.227	1.311	1.462	1.487	1.543	1.499	1.520	1.620	1.360	1.252	1.400
2019	1.626	1.808	W	W	W	W	1.455	1.331	W	1.535	1.681	1.758	1.599
2020	1.788	1.673	1.188	0.796	0.792	1.018	1.153	1.189	1.098	1.078	1.164	1.351	1.191
2021	1.491	1.583	1.780	1.780	1.828	1.909	1.852	1.842	1.913	2.124	2.065	1.940	1.842
2022[1]	2.210	2.415	2.932										2.519

Sulfur 1% or less, excluding taxes.   [1] Preliminary.   *Source: Energy Information Administration, U.S. Department of Energy (EIA-DOE)*

Refiner Sales Prices of No. 2 Fuel Oil   In U.S. Dollars Per Gallon

Year	Jan.	Feb.	Mar.	Apr.	May	June	July	Aug.	Sept.	Oct.	Nov.	Dec.	Average
2015	1.669	1.850	1.847	1.740	1.852	1.813	1.654	1.461	1.438	1.411	1.356	1.126	1.601
2016	0.976	0.948	1.070	1.113	1.291	1.404	1.305	1.307	1.341	1.443	1.386	1.507	1.258
2017	1.560	1.553	1.495	1.499	1.447	1.375	1.392	1.522	1.668	1.695	1.781	1.841	1.569
2018	1.990	1.889	1.848	1.982	2.143	2.089	2.079	2.114	2.214	2.281	2.098	1.796	2.044
2019	1.813	1.907	1.958	1.993	1.989	1.824	1.847	1.795	1.901	1.926	1.884	1.919	1.896
2020	1.863	1.627	1.238	0.872	0.795	1.002	1.152	1.179	1.091	1.089	1.156	1.341	1.200
2021	1.481	1.667	1.726	1.700	1.806	1.927	1.931	1.885	2.041	2.356	2.267	2.111	1.908
2022[1]	2.438	2.742	3.479										2.886

Excluding taxes.   [1] Preliminary.   *Source: Energy Information Administration, U.S. Department of Energy (EIA-DOE)*

Refiner Sales Prices of No. 2 Diesel Fuel   In U.S. Dollars Per Gallon

Year	Jan.	Feb.	Mar.	Apr.	May	June	July	Aug.	Sept.	Oct.	Nov.	Dec.	Average
2015	1.616	1.861	1.815	1.805	1.973	1.881	1.729	1.562	1.551	1.572	1.456	1.176	1.666
2016	1.015	1.043	1.189	1.251	1.432	1.531	1.426	1.440	1.471	1.592	1.469	1.606	1.372
2017	1.636	1.641	1.581	1.627	1.552	1.465	1.533	1.681	1.847	1.852	1.936	1.918	1.689
2018	2.042	1.972	1.952	2.099	2.258	2.203	2.192	2.203	2.282	2.379	2.130	1.794	2.126
2019	1.789	1.950	2.020	2.100	2.106	1.874	1.938	1.865	1.955	1.984	1.974	1.943	1.958
2020	1.858	1.671	1.278	0.908	0.878	1.135	1.254	1.275	1.195	1.215	1.315	1.475	1.288
2021	1.580	1.806	1.956	1.911	2.072	2.147	2.182	2.146	2.240	2.504	2.454	2.273	2.106
2022[1]	2.550	2.830	3.582										2.987

Excluding taxes.   [1] Preliminary.   *Source: Energy Information Administration, U.S. Department of Energy (EIA-DOE)*

Refiner Sales Prices of Kerosine-Type Jet Fuel   In U.S. Dollars Per Gallon

Year	Jan.	Feb.	Mar.	Apr.	May	June	July	Aug.	Sept.	Oct.	Nov.	Dec.	Average
2015	1.612	1.722	1.731	1.709	1.933	1.813	1.655	1.479	1.443	1.451	1.400	1.207	1.596
2016	1.022	1.017	1.100	1.155	1.311	1.428	1.354	1.313	1.366	1.471	1.406	1.511	1.288
2017	1.561	1.592	1.520	1.545	1.459	1.378	1.436	1.587	1.771	1.704	1.795	1.846	1.600
2018	1.969	1.911	1.893	2.032	2.175	2.152	2.140	2.148	2.214	2.296	2.100	1.811	2.070
2019	1.822	1.925	1.960	2.022	2.061	1.879	1.938	1.864	1.898	1.931	1.922	1.932	1.930
2020	1.891	1.613	1.189	0.703	0.690	1.002	1.144	1.162	1.076	1.107	1.180	1.353	1.176
2021	1.456	1.599	1.720	1.688	1.790	1.871	1.946	1.922	2.008	2.281	2.283	2.145	1.892
2022[1]	2.422	2.655	3.285										2.787

Excluding taxes.   [1] Preliminary.   *Source: Energy Information Administration, U.S. Department of Energy (EIA-DOE)*

Refiner Sales Prices of Propane[2]   In U.S. Dollars Per Gallon

Year	Jan.	Feb.	Mar.	Apr.	May	June	July	Aug.	Sept.	Oct.	Nov.	Dec.	Average
2015	0.713	0.748	0.689	0.566	0.475	0.404	0.405	0.402	0.469	0.524	0.505	0.499	0.533
2016	0.460	0.470	0.497	0.458	0.511	0.497	0.476	0.453	0.494	0.608	0.588	0.703	0.518
2017	0.788	0.792	0.671	0.641	0.631	0.585	0.634	0.742	0.864	0.942	0.997	0.991	0.773
2018	0.990	0.889	0.827	0.792	0.867	0.807	0.854	0.907	0.951	0.948	0.826	0.798	0.871
2019	0.775	0.772	0.754	0.660	0.595	0.493	0.478	0.458	0.477	0.544	0.655	0.632	0.608
2020	0.557	0.530	0.410	0.378	0.454	0.514	0.507	0.536	0.516	0.597	0.630	0.725	0.530
2021	0.922	1.032	0.985	0.849	0.824	0.950	1.075	1.110	1.280	1.460	1.329	1.140	1.080
2022[1]	1.249	1.376	1.483										1.369

[1] Preliminary.   [2] Consumer Grade, Excluding taxes.   *Source: Energy Information Administration, U.S. Department of Energy (EIA-DOE)*

WTI CRUDE OIL - NYMEX
Weekly Nearest Futures as of 03/28/2024

WEEKLY NEAREST FUTURES
As of 03/28/2024
Chart High 130.50 on 03/07/2022
Chart Low -40.32 on 04/20/2020

Nearby Futures through Last Trading Day.

Volume of Trading of Crude Oil Futures in New York   In Thousands of Contracts

Year	Jan.	Feb.	Mar.	Apr.	May	June	July	Aug.	Sept.	Oct.	Nov.	Dec.	Total
2014	11,162	9,862	11,700	11,467	10,283	11,398	13,174	11,016	12,824	15,939	12,204	14,119	145,147
2015	16,514	20,263	17,884	17,638	13,553	13,995	14,863	19,197	16,605	17,484	16,145	18,064	202,202
2016	21,710	25,607	22,954	23,614	21,494	20,790	18,841	23,051	24,332	23,019	27,375	23,981	276,768
2017	22,430	20,528	26,417	21,225	27,527	29,141	27,618	34,725	27,571	25,031	27,636	20,205	310,053
2018	28,504	26,784	25,003	27,977	30,951	28,578	23,056	19,661	21,113	24,507	27,571	22,909	306,613
2019	25,965	22,698	23,824	27,629	28,524	23,436	22,825	27,902	26,970	23,298	19,066	19,327	291,465
2020	26,079	28,131	40,910	39,351	21,325	19,172	16,204	15,728	17,103	17,063	17,680	15,434	274,180
2021	18,924	22,104	26,039	18,813	19,084	20,264	20,471	18,842	18,938	24,524	22,982	17,330	248,314
2022	20,272	23,349	23,658	14,055	13,854	16,135	16,082	17,553	15,268	14,319	16,388	14,786	205,718
2023	16,208	14,553	19,719	15,151	17,101	17,973	16,358	18,819	19,500	18,851	16,326	13,661	204,220

Contract size = 1,000 bbl.   *Source: CME Group; New York Mercantile Exchange (NYMEX)*

Average Open Interest of Crude Oil Futures in New York   In Thousands of Contracts

Year	Jan.	Feb.	Mar.	Apr.	May	June	July	Aug.	Sept.	Oct.	Nov.	Dec.
2014	1,607.4	1,628.5	1,653.4	1,654.8	1,633.4	1,703.8	1,687.6	1,572.7	1,518.4	1,495.4	1,464.1	1,450.3
2015	1,699.2	1,713.6	1,725.0	1,734.5	1,683.7	1,648.2	1,693.9	1,702.7	1,661.4	1,652.0	1,666.0	1,674.5
2016	1,741.4	1,821.0	1,774.8	1,751.3	1,708.3	1,737.3	1,727.7	1,810.2	1,842.7	1,851.9	1,982.7	2,063.4
2017	2,143.1	2,148.1	2,181.9	2,190.6	2,241.2	2,168.4	2,158.7	2,259.7	2,379.9	2,446.4	2,550.6	2,513.1
2018	2,589.4	2,509.2	2,444.7	2,567.8	2,662.5	2,501.2	2,425.1	2,292.2	2,246.9	2,182.7	2,044.7	2,065.2
2019	2,082.0	2,044.0	2,000.5	2,077.4	2,121.6	2,039.0	2,049.8	2,033.4	2,071.4	2,094.0	2,141.0	2,170.0
2020	2,193.9	2,195.2	2,199.0	2,321.5	2,200.6	2,073.0	1,984.7	2,049.4	2,065.0	2,047.8	2,070.4	2,135.4
2021	2,253.1	2,464.2	2,436.5	2,341.3	2,446.7	2,444.5	2,341.2	2,154.2	2,138.5	2,199.9	2,065.3	1,926.7
2022	2,013.9	2,117.7	1,851.8	1,769.5	1,742.6	1,714.4	1,607.3	1,539.9	1,492.9	1,467.5	1,442.1	1,424.2
2023	1,603.8	1,778.9	1,785.6	1,877.1	1,875.1	1,880.9	1,766.1	1,682.5	1,737.9	1,695.8	1,622.1	1,609.2

Contract size = 1,000 bbl.   *Source: CME Group; New York Mercantile Exchange (NYMEX)*

Platinum-Group Metals

Platinum (atomic symbol Pt) is a relatively rare, chemically inert metallic element that is more valuable than gold. Platinum is a grayish-white metal that has a high fusing point, is malleable and ductile, and has a high electrical resistance. Chemically, platinum is relatively inert and resists attack by air, water, single acids, and ordinary reagents. Platinum is the most important of the six-metal group, which also includes ruthenium, rhodium, palladium, osmium, and iridium. The word "platinum" is derived from the Spanish word *platina* meaning silver.

Platinum is one of the world's rarest metals with new mine production totaling only about 5 million troy ounces a year. All the platinum mined to date would fit in the average-size living room. Platinum is mined all over the world with supplies concentrated in South Africa. South Africa accounts for nearly 80% of world supply, followed by Russia, and North America.

Because platinum will never tarnish, lose its rich white luster, or even wear down after many years, it is prized by the jewelry industry. The international jewelry industry is the largest consumer sector for platinum, accounting for 51% of total platinum demand. In Europe and the U.S., the normal purity of platinum is 95%. Ten tons of ore must be mined, and a five-month process is needed, to produce one ounce of pure platinum.

The second major consumer sector for platinum is for auto catalysts, with 21% of total platinum demand. Catalysts in autos are used to convert most of vehicle emissions into less harmful carbon dioxide, nitrogen, and water vapor. Platinum is also used in the production of hard disk drive coatings, fiber optic cables, infra-red detectors, fertilizers, explosives, petrol additives, platinum-tipped spark plugs, glassmaking equipment, biodegradable elements for household detergents, dental restorations, and in anti-cancer drugs.

Palladium (atomic symbol Pd) is very similar to platinum and is part of the same general metals group. Palladium is mined with platinum, but it is somewhat more common because it is also a by-product of nickel mining. The primary use for palladium is in the use of automotive catalysts, with that sector accounting for about 63% of total palladium demand. Other uses for palladium include electronic equipment (21%), dental alloys (12%), and jewelry (4%).

Rhodium (atomic symbol Rh), another member of the platinum group, is also used in the automotive industry in pollution control devices. To some extent, palladium has replaced rhodium. Iridium (atomic symbol Ir) is used to process catalysts, and it has also found use in some auto catalysts. Iridium and ruthenium (atomic symbol Ru) are used in the production of polyvinyl chloride. As the prices of these metals change, there is some substitution. Therefore, strength of platinum prices relative to palladium should lead to the substitution of palladium for platinum in catalytic converters.

Platinum futures and options and palladium futures are traded at the CME Group. Platinum and palladium futures are traded on the Tokyo Commodity Exchange (TOCOM). The CME platinum futures contract calls for the delivery of 50 troy ounces of platinum (0.9995 fineness) and the contract trades in terms of dollars and cents per troy ounce. The CME palladium futures contract calls for the delivery of 50 troy ounces of palladium (0.9995 fineness), and the contract is priced in terms of dollars and cents per troy ounce.

Prices – CME platinum futures prices (Barchart.com symbol PL) on the nearest-futures chart in 2023 closed the year down -7.3% at $995.0 per troy ounce. CME palladium futures prices (Barchart.com symbol PA) on the nearest-futures chart in 2023 closed the year down by -38.3% at $1,104.0 per troy ounce.

Supply – World mine production of platinum in 2023 rose by +3.4% yr/yr to 180,000 kilograms and remained well below the 2006 record high of 218,000 kilograms. South Africa is the world's largest producer of platinum by far, with 66.7% of world production in 2023, followed by Russia with 12.8%, Zimbabwe with 10.6%, and Canada with 3.1%. World mine production of palladium in 2023 was up +3.4% at 210,000 kilograms. The world's largest palladium producers were Russia with 43.8% of world production in 2023, South Africa with 33.8%, Canada with 7.6%, Zimbabwe with 7.1%, and the US with 4.7%. World production of platinum group metals other than platinum and palladium in 2022 fell by -10.2% yr/yr to 58,700 kilograms, below the 2005 record high of 77,700 kilograms.

US mine production of platinum in 2023 fell by -3.3% yr/yr to 2,900 kilograms, below the record high of 4,390 kilograms posted in 2002. US mine production of palladium in 2023 fell by -3.0% yr/yr to 9,800 kilograms, below the record high of 14,800 kilograms posted in 2002.

Trade – US imports of refined platinum and palladium in 2022 fell by -45.4% yr/yr to 197,700 kilograms. US exports of refined platinum and palladium in 2022 fell by -0.6% yr/yr to 111,720 kilograms. The US relied on imports for 83% of its platinum and palladium consumption in 2023.

World Mine Production of Platinum   In Kilograms

Year	Australia	Canada	Colombia[3]	Finland	Japan	Russia	Serbia/ Montenegro	Africa	United States	Zimbabwe	World Total
2014	170	7,200	1,142	1,060	1,124	23,000	3	93,991	3,660	12,483	145,000
2015	120	8,600	861	992	1,379	23,000	4	139,125	3,670	12,564	191,000
2016	170	8,400	917	1,178	1,485	22,000	4	133,241	3,890	15,110	188,000
2017	170	7,600	567	1,418	1,747	22,000	2	132,500	4,000	14,257	185,000
2018	120	7,600	270	1,576	----	22,000	5	137,053	4,160	14,703	190,000
2019	110	8,600	178	953	----	24,000	10	132,989	4,150	13,857	187,000
2020	110	4,600	414	1,277	----	23,000	20	111,993	4,200	15,005	163,000
2021	100	5,000	672	1,447	----	21,000	20	141,625	4,020	14,732	191,000
2022[1]	90	5,400	400	1,243	----	20,000	15	124,401	3,000	17,000	174,000
2023[2]		5,500			----	23,000		120,000	2,900	19,000	180,000

[1] Preliminary.   [2] Estimate.   [3] Placer platinum.   W = Withheld.   *Source: U.S. Geological Survey (USGS)*

World Mine Production of Palladium and Other Group Metals   In Kilograms

Year	Australia	Canada	Finland	Japan	Russia	Serbia/ Montenegro	South Africa	United States	Zimbabwe	Total	Russia	South Africa	World Total
2014	600	23,000	808	6,969	86,000	23	58,410	12,400	10,138	193,000	8,200	36,043	48,000
2015	420	24,000	784	7,073	85,000	31	82,691	12,500	10,055	218,000	7,600	53,699	65,100
2016	590	22,000	901	7,172	83,000	31	76,273	13,100	12,222	209,000	7,700	54,139	66,000
2017	600	19,000	1,021	7,715	88,000	38	80,713	14,000	11,822	217,000	3,415	49,543	56,680
2018	420	21,000	1,157	----	90,000	55	80,629	14,300	12,094	221,000	2,928	52,964	60,440
2019	380	21,928	699	----	97,000	100	80,684	14,300	11,640	228,000	3,326	54,395	62,310
2020	410	10,897	858	----	93,000	100	66,264	14,600	12,890	200,000	2,454	48,211	54,570
2021	370	15,433	1,036	----	86,000	150	84,334	13,700	12,398	215,000	2,778	59,034	65,380
2022[1]	330	16,099	960	----	87,000	110	73,104	10,100	14,337	203,000	2,300	52,741	58,700
2023[2]		16,000		----	92,000		71,000	9,800	15,000	210,000			

[1] Preliminary.   [2] Estimate.   *Source: U.S. Geological Survey (USGS)*

Salient Statistics of Platinum and Allied Metals[3] in the United States   In Kilograms

Year	Net Import Reliance as a % of Apparent Consump	Mine Production Platinum	Mine Production Palladium	Refinery Production (Secondary)	Total Refined	Stocks as of Dec. 31 Platinum	Stocks as of Dec. 31 Palladium	Stocks as of Dec. 31 Other[4]	Total	Imports Refined	Imports Total	Exports Refined	Exports Total	Apparent Consumptio
2014	69	3,660	12,400	69,400	69,400	261	----	15	276	274,682	----	292,234	----	----
2015	66	3,670	12,500	65,100	65,100	261	----	15	276	270,848	----	284,940	----	----
2016	66	3,890	13,100	69,900	69,900	261	----	15	276	297,137	----	81,130	----	----
2017	71	4,000	14,000	80,900	80,900	261	----	15	276	521,676	----	107,544	----	----
2018	74	4,160	14,300	144,800	144,800	261	----	15	276	225,545	----	105,510	----	----
2019	67	4,150	14,300	143,500	143,500	261	----	15	276	188,875	----	94,910	----	----
2020	76	4,200	14,600	111,800	111,800	261	----	15	276	362,420	----	112,180	----	----
2021	75	4,020	13,700	139,600	139,600	261	----	15	276	362,310	----	112,450	----	----
2022[1]	77	3,000	10,100	150,200	150,200	----				197,700	----	111,720	----	----
2023[2]	83	2,900	9,800			----				----		----		----

[1] Preliminary.   [2] Estimate.   [3] Includes platinum, palladium, iridium, osmium, rhodium, and ruthenium.   [4] Includes iridium, osmium, rhodium, and ruthenium.   W = Withheld.   *Source: U.S. Geological Survey (USGS)*

Average Producer Price of Rhodium in the United States   In Dollars Per Troy Ounce

Year	Jan.	Feb.	Mar.	Apr.	May	June	July	Aug.	Sept.	Oct.	Nov.	Dec.	Average
2014	1,047.7	1,068.0	1,092.1	1,134.5	1,071.7	1,118.8	1,187.3	1,375.2	1,310.5	1,228.7	1,224.4	1,206.4	1,172.1
2015	1,196.0	1,184.5	1,166.6	1,146.9	1,105.8	976.1	857.1	847.9	772.4	768.0	741.9	678.7	953.5
2016	650.0	654.3	711.5	740.0	690.9	657.3	647.4	640.2	675.0	692.1	786.1	783.0	694.0
2017	833.4	874.1	959.6	1,023.5	955.7	982.1	1,023.8	1,052.8	1,160.2	1,401.1	1,443.9	1,607.6	1,109.8
2018	1,709.6	1,848.8	1,932.3	2,070.7	2,137.2	2,255.2	2,296.4	2,360.2	2,468.3	2,511.5	2,515.7	2,533.3	2,219.9
2019	2,473.3	2,624.8	3,152.6	2,992.3	2,896.1	3,173.8	3,493.5	3,960.7	5,008.6	5,364.1	5,744.1	6,048.0	3,911.0
2020	8,863.6	11,851.3	10,511.4	8,266.7	7,682.5	8,406.8	8,645.5	11,348.8	13,790.5	14,004.6	15,138.2	16,485.7	11,249.6
2021	19,744.7	22,755.3	27,452.2	28,742.9	27,267.5	21,588.6	18,723.8	18,377.3	14,459.5	13,947.6	14,195.0	14,034.1	20,107.4
2022	16,737.5	18,265.8	19,567.4	18,810.0	16,133.3	14,154.6	14,452.2	14,361.0	14,361.9	13,990.5	13,507.5	12,582.5	15,577.0
2023	12,290.0	11,639.5	9,041.3	7,968.4	7,484.1	5,940.5	4,172.5	4,126.1	4,200.0	4,556.8	4,401.3	4,500.0	6,693.4

Source: American Metal Market (AMM)

PLATINUM-GROUP METALS

PLATINUM
Quarterly Cash as of 03/28/2024

QUARTERLY CASH
As of 03/28/2024
Chart High 2275.00 on 03/04/2008
Chart Low 35.00 on 10/31/1940

USD / troy oz.

Producer: to 03/2006; Ind Engelhard: 04/2006 to 06/2009; Composite: 07/2009 to date.

Average Merchant's Price of Platinum in the United States   In Dollars Per Troy Ounce

Year	Jan.	Feb.	Mar.	Apr.	May	June	July	Aug.	Sept.	Oct.	Nov.	Dec. Average
2014	1,423.73	1,411.30	1,457.52	1,435.38	1,461.07	1,457.81	1,497.05	1,449.90	1,362.10	1,263.61	1,213.00	1,222.48	1,387.91
2015	1,247.38	1,200.79	1,140.00	1,154.33	1,143.25	1,091.77	1,011.23	985.86	966.38	978.95	885.10	863.30	1,055.70
2016	857.19	924.14	971.78	997.19	1,036.73	986.50	1,087.29	1,123.91	1,047.36	961.10	955.91	919.27	989.03
2017	970.55	1,009.75	965.22	963.35	934.35	933.64	921.52	975.65	968.76	924.00	937.73	912.52	951.42
2018	991.35	991.20	956.82	927.05	907.78	887.90	835.27	807.91	807.20	833.57	849.45	793.62	882.43
2019	808.91	820.45	847.05	890.32	834.96	811.20	846.48	861.86	947.70	900.78	905.10	929.00	866.98
2020	990.41	963.79	764.18	756.86	795.35	823.77	867.64	943.57	911.95	879.95	912.58	1,032.81	886.91
2021	1,095.58	1,206.79	1,187.48	1,212.19	1,219.30	1,128.00	1,090.43	1,012.55	977.05	1,020.86	1,046.30	947.90	1,095.37
2022	993.21	1,046.41	1,041.63	962.98	957.70	952.36	871.81	906.38	877.12	915.12	1,000.50	1,021.10	962.19
2023	1,061.20	967.95	981.43	1,056.79	1,069.77	975.29	953.80	930.57	926.60	897.18	911.10	949.95	973.47

Source: American Metal Market (AMM)

Average Dealer Price[1] of Palladium in the United States   In Dollars Per Troy Ounce

Year	Jan.	Feb.	Mar.	Apr.	May	June	July	Aug.	Sept.	Oct.	Nov.	Dec. Average
2014	738.59	733.90	783.19	804.62	829.67	841.19	880.95	884.10	844.57	784.30	783.78	810.71	809.96
2015	788.29	789.95	789.55	771.86	787.00	729.77	643.64	598.24	612.76	693.82	575.57	555.96	694.70
2016	505.67	510.48	572.78	578.81	582.64	557.27	649.19	703.57	686.32	652.62	700.68	706.20	617.19
2017	749.09	780.35	780.65	803.90	797.04	867.68	859.29	917.26	937.52	963.91	1,005.45	1,028.48	874.22
2018	1,097.74	1,027.60	990.91	974.81	984.70	990.00	936.41	924.17	1,017.90	1,089.52	1,147.50	1,254.14	1,036.28
2019	1,333.96	1,448.70	1,541.14	1,396.95	1,336.96	1,449.65	1,551.39	1,460.73	1,611.00	1,735.22	1,771.14	1,910.85	1,545.64
2020	2,247.77	2,535.42	2,136.64	2,097.05	1,910.40	1,930.77	2,056.55	2,181.90	2,313.71	2,363.41	2,367.21	2,369.10	2,209.16
2021	2,397.11	2,368.26	2,508.83	2,796.76	2,896.10	2,741.27	2,749.86	2,561.09	2,114.76	2,018.33	2,033.90	1,811.14	2,416.45
2022	2,021.38	2,328.56	2,574.08	2,302.22	2,045.86	1,898.42	1,973.95	2,121.40	2,112.97	2,060.83	1,948.30	1,839.50	2,102.29
2023	1,741.50	1,559.63	1,447.61	1,522.89	1,501.18	1,359.57	1,278.30	1,262.22	1,252.40	1,155.45	1,063.15	1,084.95	1,352.40

[1] Based on wholesale quantities, prompt delivery.   Source: American Metal Market (AMM)

PLATINUM - NYMEX
Weekly Selected Futures as of 03/28/2024

WEEKLY SELECTED FUTURES
As of 03/28/2024
Chart High 1516.00 on 07/10/2014
Chart Low 562.00 on 03/16/2020

Nearby Futures through Last Trading Day.

Volume of Trading of Platinum Futures in Chicago   In Contracts

Year	Jan.	Feb.	Mar.	Apr.	May	June	July	Aug.	Sept.	Oct.	Nov.	Dec.	Total
2014	217,465	194,296	389,315	182,628	239,397	379,860	210,163	179,938	399,265	271,921	211,151	360,542	3,235,941
2015	243,017	200,204	408,528	217,744	211,710	434,374	262,007	268,391	443,850	281,094	261,514	408,711	3,641,144
2016	284,203	262,873	413,082	248,758	249,861	435,018	279,689	278,246	456,092	302,621	360,457	423,172	3,994,072
2017	345,619	286,893	515,593	280,575	354,263	529,562	321,062	394,884	528,953	344,217	381,004	569,535	4,852,160
2018	444,074	346,507	562,720	423,705	392,326	652,863	393,517	412,710	580,643	383,720	372,849	498,165	5,463,799
2019	362,449	384,444	633,174	398,312	414,824	593,552	444,188	496,003	739,168	408,309	399,670	588,197	5,862,290
2020	468,298	473,531	738,101	218,691	242,913	350,424	316,024	301,382	453,351	271,140	277,596	466,080	4,577,531
2021	287,469	375,176	512,365	275,683	300,637	493,395	294,112	302,530	500,154	299,521	364,392	445,429	4,450,863
2022	359,631	402,774	592,236	325,352	335,096	527,835	312,283	373,986	556,416	415,982	433,587	541,880	5,177,058
2023	388,036	471,190	599,072	374,319	413,837	621,654	358,031	492,256	700,156	501,375	568,411	698,741	6,187,078

Contract size = 50 oz.   *Source: CME Group; New York Mercantile Exchange (NYMEX)*

Average Open Interest of Platinum Futures in Chicago   In Contracts

Year	Jan.	Feb.	Mar.	Apr.	May	June	July	Aug.	Sept.	Oct.	Nov.	Dec.
2014	59,980	63,324	69,278	65,308	68,150	68,004	71,271	64,416	64,103	59,701	61,768	65,647
2015	66,436	66,642	70,775	69,165	71,645	79,378	79,326	76,953	73,817	72,160	72,938	73,105
2016	68,301	65,306	62,884	59,152	64,862	63,825	72,441	80,327	74,296	70,022	66,480	65,869
2017	62,849	66,421	66,618	65,191	72,742	73,137	72,273	72,013	76,162	75,280	78,273	85,097
2018	86,391	87,064	78,963	76,759	80,900	86,235	81,652	83,049	86,436	74,712	72,385	81,227
2019	84,646	82,418	74,956	73,945	78,080	87,406	77,906	77,789	93,443	86,189	90,358	96,111
2020	104,485	99,383	69,178	62,027	50,911	49,719	50,513	57,638	59,353	52,240	53,169	62,949
2021	61,411	71,241	71,866	65,309	66,412	64,205	57,303	63,857	70,049	59,490	60,009	53,793
2022	56,525	59,917	65,982	63,707	66,397	66,333	73,668	63,748	66,521	54,622	62,157	69,331
2023	71,408	67,325	63,751	64,600	72,819	68,478	67,394	78,531	79,229	82,749	76,565	73,564

Contract size = 50 oz.   *Source: CME Group; New York Mercantile Exchange (NYMEX)*

PLATINUM-GROUP METALS

PALLADIUM - NYMEX
Weekly Selected Futures as of 03/28/2024

WEEKLY SELECTED FUTURES
As of 03/28/2024
Chart High 3380.50 on 03/07/2022
Chart Low 451.50 on 01/12/2016

USD / troy oz.

Nearby Futures through Last Trading Day.

Volume of Trading of Palladium Futures in Chicago   In Contracts

Year	Jan.	Feb.	Mar.	Apr.	May	June	July	Aug.	Sept.	Oct.	Nov.	Dec.	Total
2014	87,502	158,760	136,126	111,648	195,880	101,610	97,809	208,474	126,132	115,708	161,947	72,376	1,573,972
2015	99,787	146,928	100,748	78,232	131,105	91,044	102,665	185,094	87,201	92,284	162,382	66,956	1,344,426
2016	90,129	151,159	96,917	93,887	142,585	94,937	104,219	169,852	88,440	113,977	198,537	91,224	1,435,863
2017	111,959	141,648	98,308	97,861	191,603	120,488	82,725	164,153	80,618	87,270	153,217	72,890	1,402,740
2018	98,800	164,476	101,277	145,138	127,272	93,661	98,611	176,108	89,368	116,003	148,110	74,888	1,433,712
2019	107,039	147,433	113,193	96,677	129,839	74,368	79,652	133,300	80,152	90,724	131,275	83,049	1,266,701
2020	148,896	127,560	76,650	23,544	39,796	23,542	41,067	51,521	29,227	34,644	59,389	34,951	690,787
2021	38,520	68,969	45,404	33,356	65,204	31,687	35,785	71,896	48,616	42,972	84,800	37,373	604,582
2022	44,742	82,539	51,573	27,933	53,027	29,050	32,801	55,490	33,013	40,121	77,831	42,915	571,035
2023	44,246	102,284	44,924	44,387	91,821	47,515	48,300	122,939	52,886	82,202	161,316	74,896	917,716

Contract size = 100 oz.   *Source: CME Group; New York Mercantile Exchange (NYMEX)*

Average Open Interest of Palladium Futures in Chicago   In Contracts

Year	Jan.	Feb.	Mar.	Apr.	May	June	July	Aug.	Sept.	Oct.	Nov.	Dec.
2014	39,059	40,226	41,494	42,071	43,466	39,964	43,791	44,286	38,776	33,587	34,170	32,060
2015	33,813	33,807	31,897	32,138	31,396	33,426	36,629	34,717	27,329	25,978	27,440	25,030
2016	26,200	27,339	22,964	23,573	23,912	23,048	24,043	28,475	25,272	23,968	24,431	26,124
2017	27,919	29,500	29,601	34,312	35,204	35,544	33,508	35,549	32,465	32,910	35,411	35,320
2018	38,468	29,987	24,894	23,645	23,008	23,045	21,676	22,511	19,056	26,129	27,046	26,158
2019	27,723	28,365	26,618	22,825	20,757	20,861	25,138	22,436	22,028	26,569	25,844	25,338
2020	25,122	19,937	10,294	7,754	7,209	6,698	8,719	9,970	9,523	10,030	10,608	9,322
2021	9,604	9,811	9,788	11,167	11,544	10,086	10,130	10,011	8,827	9,619	11,024	9,569
2022	9,002	7,831	7,102	6,663	8,255	7,396	6,982	7,349	6,091	7,090	8,520	8,012
2023	9,138	12,202	11,876	12,073	12,399	12,771	16,217	19,488	17,629	21,201	24,487	18,970

Contract size = 100 oz.   *Source: CME Group; New York Mercantile Exchange (NYMEX)*

Potatoes

The potato is a member of the nightshade family. The leaves of the potato plant are poisonous, and a potato will begin to turn green if left too long in the light. This green skin contains solanine, a substance that can cause the potato to taste bitter and even cause illness in humans.

In Peru, the Inca Indians were the first to cultivate potatoes around 200 BC. The Indians developed potato crops because their staple diet of corn would not grow above an altitude of 3,350 meters. In 1536, after conquering the Incas, the Spanish Conquistadors brought potatoes back to Europe. At first, Europeans did not accept the potato because it was not mentioned in the Bible and was therefore considered an "evil" food. But after Marie Antoinette wore a crown of potato flowers, it finally became a popular food. In 1897, during the Alaskan Klondike gold rush, potatoes were so valued for their vitamin C content that miners traded gold for potatoes. The potato became the first vegetable to be grown in outer space in October 1995.

The potato is a highly nutritious, fat-free, cholesterol-free, and sodium-free food. The potato is an important dietary staple in over 130 countries. A medium-sized potato contains only 100 calories. Potatoes are an excellent source of vitamin C and provide B vitamins as well as potassium, copper, magnesium, and iron. According to the U.S. Department of Agriculture, "a diet of whole milk and potatoes would supply almost all of the food elements necessary for the maintenance of the human body."

Potatoes are one of the largest vegetable crops grown in the U.S. and are grown in all fifty states. The U.S. ranks about 4th in world potato production. The top three types of potatoes grown extensively in the U.S. are white, red, and Russets (Russets account for about two-thirds the U.S. crop). Potatoes in the U.S. are harvested in all four seasons, but the vast majority of the crop is harvested in fall. Potatoes harvested in the winter, spring, and summer are used mainly to supplement fresh supplies of fall-harvested potatoes and are also important to the processing industries. The four principal categories for U.S. potato exports are frozen, potato chips, fresh, and dehydrated. Fries account for approximately 95% of U.S. frozen potato exports.

Prices – The average monthly price received for potatoes by US farmers in 2023 fell by -0.6% yr/yr to $18.96 per hundred pounds.

Supply –The total US potato crop in 2022 fell by -3.9% yr/yr to 39.689 billion pounds, well below the record high of 50.358 billion pounds posted in 2000.

The largest producing states for the 2022 fall potato crop were Idaho with 30.4% of the crop, Washington with 23.9%, Wisconsin with 7.0%, Oregon with 6.4%, North Dakota with 5.6%, and Colorado with 5.3%. Farmers harvested 895.6 acres of potatoes in 2022, down -4.3% yr/yr. The potato yield in 2022 was unchanged at 43.8 pounds per acre.

Demand – Total utilization of potatoes in 2021 was down by -2.4% yr/yr at 40.982 billion pounds, but still above the 2010 record low of 40.427 billion pounds. The breakdown shows that the largest consumption category for potatoes is frozen French fries with 39.0% of total consumption, followed closely by table stock with 23.0%, chips-shoestrings with 14.7%, and dehydration with 9.9%. US per capita consumption of potatoes in 2021 fell by -2.6% to 112.07 pounds, below the record high of 145.0 pounds per capita seen in 1996.

Salient Statistics of Potatoes in the United States

Crop Year	Acreage Planted --- 1,000 Acres ---	Acreage Harvested	Yield Per Harvested Acre Cwt.	Total Production	Seed & Feed	Shrinkage & Loss	Sold[2]	Farm Price ($ Cwt.)	Pro-duction[3]	Sales	Stocks Jan. 1 (1,000 Cwt)	Exports (Fresh)	Imports	Consumption[4] Per Capita Fresh	Total
2014	1,063	1,051	421	442,170	4,192	26,762	411,216	8.88	3,928	3,658	NA	922,152	1,036,452	33.6	112.1
2015	1,066	1,054	418	441,205	4,631	26,509	410,065	8.76	3,866	3,597	NA	904,783	882,276	34.2	113.7
2016	1,057	1,038	434	450,324	4,437	26,883	419,004	9.08	4,091	3,812	----	1,077,958	1,093,271	33.7	
2017	1,053	1,045	432	450,921	4,410	25,139	421,372	9.17	4,133	3,875	----	1,204,437	1,106,264	34.9	
2018	1,027	1,015	443	450,020	4,047	25,526	420,447	8.48	4,006	3,747	----	1,060,545	1,072,508	33.1	
2019	963	937	453	424,419	4,608	25,016	394,795	12.36	4,217	3,935	----	1,203,916	909,070	30.1	
2020	919	912	761	420,020	4,550	23,453	392,017	13.23	3,907	3,654	----	1,107,932	1,105,447	30.3	
2021	939	930	444	412,639	3,579	23,367	382,883	12.17	4,204	3,912	----	1,315,845	1,030,635	28.6	
2022	923	918	438	402,054	3,528	21,945	373,271	19.08	5,166	4,801	----	1,214,039	1,337,376	28.4	
2023[1]	965	960	459	440,750				18.96	5,647		----				

[1] Preliminary. [2] For all purposes, including food, seed processing & livestock feed. [3] Farm weight basis, excluding canned and frozen potatoes. [4] Calendar year. *Source: Economic Research Service, U.S. Department of Agriculture (ERS-USDA)*

POTATOES

Potato Crop Production Estimates, Stocks and Disappearance in the United States   In Millions of Cwt.

	------ Crop Production Estimates ------			------------ Total Storage Stocks[2] ------------							----------------- Fall Crop -----------------				
												----------- 1,000 Cwt. -----------			
	------ Total Crop ------			------ Fall Crop ------		----------- Following Year -----------				Pro-	Disap-pearance	Stocks	Average Price	Value of Sales
Year	Oct. 1	Nov. 1	Dec. 1	Oct. 1	Nov. 1	Dec. 1	Jan. 1	Feb. 1	Mar. 1	Apr. 1	May 1	duction	(Sold)	Dec. 1	($/Cwt.)	($1,000)
2014	----	442.8	----	----	406.2	267.5	----	206.6	----	139.2	----	406,080	411,216	265,700	8.35	3,113,990
2015	----	441.2	----	----	404.7	267.9	----	205.9	----	137.2	----	409,281	410,667	262,700	8.27	3,094,832
2016	----	439.6	----	----	405.2	275.8	----	213.0	----	142.6	----	412,688	382,471	272,900	8.46	3,231,305
2017	----	439.0	----	----	398.9	277.9	----	210.6	----	138.8	----	406,800	377,994	274,900	8.28	3,135,521
2018	----	452.6	----	----	417.5	279.3	----	212.8	----	144.7	----	414,499	385,794	283,600	8.48	3,269,884
2019	----	424.4	----	----	----	268.3	----	202.4	----	126.6	----	----	----	----	----	----
2020	----	415.5	----	----	----	269.4	----	204.8	----	124.7	----	----	----	----	----	----
2021	----	413.2	----	----	----	267.1	----	199.7	----	127.7	----	----	----	----	----	----
2022	----	396.9	----	----	----	257.6	----	191.9	----	121.3	----	----	----	----	----	----
2023[1]	----	434.2	----	----	----	283.7	----	215.7	----		----	----	----	----	----	----

[1] Preliminary.   [2] Held by growers and local dealers in the fall producing areas.
Source: Agricultural Statistics Board, U.S. Department of Agriculture (ASB-USDA)

Production of Potatoes in the United States   In Thousands of Cwt.

Year	California	Colorado	Idaho	Maine	Michigan	Minne-sota	Nebraska	New York	North Dakota	Oregon	Wash-ington	Wisconsin	U.S. Total
2014	3,901	23,196	132,880	14,645	15,725	16,400	7,943	4,345	23,870	22,562	101,475	26,240	406,080
2015	3,528	22,575	130,400	16,160	17,550	16,200	6,885	4,144	27,600	21,784	100,300	27,813	409,281
2016	3,516	22,236	139,320	15,113	17,390	17,200	7,380	3,552	21,600	22,951	105,625	27,840	412,688
2017	3,321	21,220	134,850	15,200	18,315	18,428	9,025	4,032	24,420	25,245	99,220	29,750	406,800
2018	3,212	21,722	141,750	15,035	18,240	18,705	9,264	3,886	23,725	27,000	100,800	27,135	414,499
2019	16,842	19,666	130,900	16,738	20,370	17,845	9,595	----	19,430	25,311	104,960	28,700	424,419
2020	12,861	22,596	134,775	13,462	17,550	17,922	9,212	----	23,800	27,000	99,653	28,770	420,020
2021	11,049	21,484	132,090	18,389	21,070	17,553	9,261	----	22,500	26,880	91,928	28,595	412,639
2022	8,465	21,425	120,745	18,425	20,958	19,147	9,652	----	21,750	26,400	95,410	26,200	402,054
2023[1]	10,534	21,098	144,980	17,884	21,533	18,240	10,950	----	26,250	27,450	99,688	29,363	440,750

[1] Preliminary.   *Source: Agricultural Statistics Board, U.S. Department of Agriculture (ASB-USDA)*

Utilization of Potatoes in the United States   In Thousands of Cwt.

	-- Sales --											------------- Non-Sales -------------			
	------------------------------- For Processing -------------------------------								-------- Other Sales --------			Used on			
Crop Year	Table Stock	Chips, Shoe-strings	Dehyd-ration	Frozen French Fries	Other Frozen Products	Canned Potatoes	Other Canned Products[2]	Starch & Flour	Live-stock Feed	Seed	Total Sales	Farms Where Grown	Shrink-age & Loss	Total Non-Sales	Total
2013	106,930	60,485	47,411	134,966	18,451	188	1,089	8,579	1,251	22,431	404,118	3,215	26,211	30,534	434,652
2014	107,344	73,960	48,707	152,832	9,208	435	886	6,907	768	22,774	411,216	3,343	26,762	30,954	442,170
2015	110,960	56,807	48,016	152,329	13,573	985	730	6,420	919	25,648	410,065	3,765	26,509	31,140	441,205
2016	114,227	60,266	48,015	156,985	12,695	1,234	698	6,000	1,150	26,811	419,004	3,758	26,883	31,320	450,324
2017	109,824	58,751	45,761	155,798	13,803	1,152	703	6,160	1,913	25,224	421,372	3,526	25,139	29,549	450,921
2018	106,462	62,700	49,066	163,140	15,956	1,113	758	5,550	697	24,079	420,447	3,491	25,526	29,573	450,020
2019	97,865	59,639	41,621	162,394	11,848	898	836	6,031	1,528	19,677	394,795	3,995	25,016	29,624	424,419
2020	101,195	59,217	44,893	155,623	10,968	1,429	1,172	6,490	1,173	19,399	392,017	3,949	23,453	28,003	420,020
2021	94,399	60,289	40,553	159,637	11,118	1,314	862	7,200	1,236	19,149	382,883	3,027	23,367	26,946	409,829
2022[1]	91,569	62,076	37,853	156,730	12,133	1,142	611	8,226	934	18,314	373,271	3,006	21,945	25,473	398,744

[1] Preliminary.   [2] Hash, stews and soups.   *Source: Agricultural Statistics Board, U.S. Department of Agriculture (ASB-USDA)*

Cold Storage Stocks of All Frozen Potatoes in the United States, on First of Month   In Millions of Pounds

Year	Jan.	Feb.	Mar.	Apr.	May	June	July	Aug.	Sept.	Oct.	Nov.	Dec.
2014	1,095.3	1,104.8	1,124.1	1,044.3	1,009.2	983.4	1,012.8	924.2	936.6	1,039.7	1,099.5	1,105.6
2015	1,030.4	1,091.7	1,132.9	1,146.4	1,127.2	1,135.6	1,151.7	1,065.4	1,047.0	1,058.0	1,093.0	1,055.6
2016	1,006.9	1,021.7	1,046.0	1,072.2	1,095.0	1,122.2	1,175.8	1,149.0	1,160.5	1,217.2	1,253.5	1,180.5
2017	1,124.6	1,195.7	1,210.6	1,212.3	1,219.7	1,209.3	1,230.6	1,201.7	1,190.2	1,237.0	1,273.5	1,274.1
2018	1,183.0	1,258.3	1,265.2	1,225.8	1,192.8	1,156.7	1,212.0	1,096.7	1,140.8	1,185.0	1,250.2	1,198.4
2019	1,174.6	1,265.2	1,299.0	1,291.8	1,211.2	1,172.9	1,184.5	1,134.3	1,162.3	1,160.7	1,170.7	1,180.9
2020	1,155.9	1,201.2	1,249.5	1,309.5	1,192.8	1,099.4	1,085.1	1,087.7	1,139.7	1,175.4	1,241.4	1,176.5
2021	1,122.1	1,162.4	1,159.5	1,146.6	1,117.5	1,132.8	1,114.3	1,080.5	1,079.8	1,090.9	1,163.0	1,113.2
2022	1,064.0	1,150.1	1,211.9	1,178.0	1,173.6	1,189.9	1,238.3	1,214.0	1,214.2	1,200.0	1,258.2	1,180.8
2023[1]	1,219.4	1,256.7	1,278.1	1,274.5	1,240.0	1,191.4	1,235.3	1,209.6	1,174.5	1,183.9	1,216.9	1,168.5

[1] Preliminary.   *Source: Agricultural Statistics Board, U.S. Department of Agriculture (ASB-USDA)*

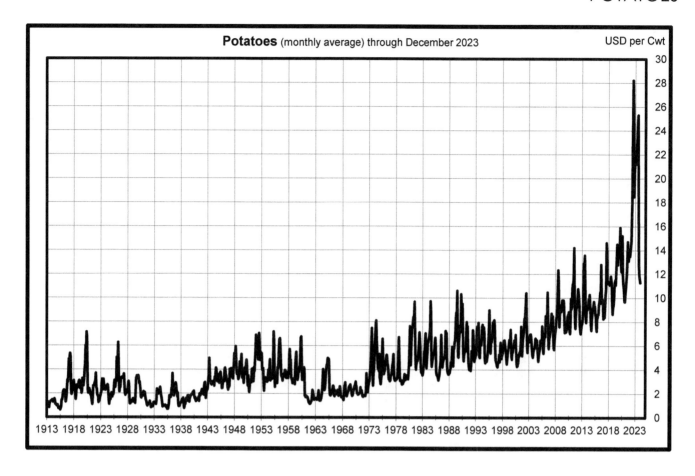

Potatoes (monthly average) through December 2023 — USD per Cwt

Average Price Received by Farmers for Potatoes in the U.S. In Dollars Per Hundred Pounds (Cwt.)

Year	Jan.	Feb.	Mar.	Apr.	May	June	July	Aug.	Sept.	Oct.	Nov.	Dec.	Season Average
2014	9.02	9.22	9.47	9.92	9.53	10.28	9.72	8.88	7.76	7.30	8.19	8.63	8.88
2015	9.12	9.14	9.38	9.69	9.26	9.27	8.62	8.45	7.58	7.24	8.23	8.38	8.76
2016	8.63	8.64	9.41	9.61	9.98	10.52	9.58	12.80	10.48	9.59	9.91	9.59	9.08
2017	8.27	8.42	8.65	8.40	9.40	10.25	10.79	14.61	13.86	11.33	11.22	11.39	9.17
2018	11.30	11.20	11.10	11.20	11.40	11.80	11.50	11.20	9.44	8.65	9.22	9.37	8.48
2019	9.88	10.70	11.30	11.50	11.10	12.10	13.30	14.50	13.30	12.80	13.90	13.90	12.36
2020	14.30	14.50	15.90	14.60	12.80	12.20	14.80	15.20	12.00	11.20	10.90	10.30	13.23
2021	9.70	9.70	10.40	10.80	11.40	12.00	13.20	14.70	14.00	13.10	13.50	13.50	12.17
2022	13.50	13.90	14.30	14.80	16.30	18.10	23.70	28.20	25.90	18.50	20.40	21.30	19.08
2023[1]	21.20	21.20	22.00	22.80	23.00	24.70	25.30	19.70	12.80	11.90	11.60	11.30	18.96

[1] Preliminary.   Source: Agricultural Statistics Board, U.S. Department of Agriculture (ASB-USDA)

Per Capita Utilization of Potatoes in the United States In Pounds (Farm Weight)

Year	Total	Fresh	Freezing	Chips & Shoe-string	Dehy-drating	Canning	Total Processing
2013	113.6	34.6	47.7	17.8	12.9	0.6	79.0
2014	113.1	33.6	47.1	20.0	12.1	0.3	79.5
2015	113.4	34.2	49.7	19.6	11.6	0.4	79.2
2016	110.2	33.7	47.4	16.6	12.0	0.4	76.5
2017	117.8	34.9	51.8	17.8	12.9	0.5	82.9
2018	117.6	33.1	53.4	17.8	12.9	0.4	84.5
2019	112.6	30.1	52.4	17.9	11.9	0.4	82.5
2020	115.0	30.3	54.6	17.6	12.1	0.5	84.8
2021[1]	112.1	28.6	53.8	17.5	12.4	0.6	82.8
2022[2]		28.4	53.3	16.9	11.6	0.5	

[1] Preliminary.   [2] Forecast.   Source: Agricultural Statistics Board, U.S. Department of Agriculture (ASB-USDA)

POTATOES

Potatoes Processed[1] in the United States, Eight States   In Thousands of Cwt.

States	Storage Season	to Dec. 1	to Jan. 1	to Feb. 1	to Mar. 1	to Apr. 1	to May 1	to June 1	Entire Season
Idaho and Oregon- Malheur Co.	2015-16	26,850	33,115	39,655	46,455	53,710	61,050	68,435	86,250
	2016-17	25,720	32,650	39,475	46,880	54,625	61,950	70,110	92,760
	2017-18	24,840	31,920	38,950	46,610	54,060	61,285	69,840	87,379
	2018-19	25,325	32,020	39,495	47,395	55,250	63,225	71,340	95,974
	2019-20	26,655	33,170	39,840	47,980	55,775	61,640	69,395	86,863
	2020-21	27,195	34,360	41,695	49,565	57,390	64,815	73,065	90,755
	2021-22	27,070	34,300	41,530	48,715	56,370	63,875	71,680	83,070
	2022-23	25,800	33,145	40,455	47,915	55,545	62,610	70,575	86,633
	2023-24	29,630	36,560	44,070					
Maine[2]	2015-16	1,170	1,590	2,050	2,490	2,980	3,495	4,065	5,724
	2016-17	1,260	1,665	2,175	2,660	3,080	3,470	3,825	5,059
	2017-18	1,510	1,880	2,370	2,880	3,460	4,010	4,560	4,829
	2018-19	1,470	1,890	2,400	2,870	3,450	3,870	4,290	5,050
	2019-20	1,585	2,050	2,610	2,875	3,285	3,590	4,040	5,050
	2020-21	1,475	1,750	2,095	2,400	2,720	3,055	3,375	4,307
	2021-22	1,735	2,250	2,890	3,475	4,065	4,590	5,050	5,399
	2022-23	W	W	W	W	W	W	W	W
	2023-24	W	W	W					
Washing- ton & Oregon- Other	2015-16	33,955	39,970	46,320	54,455	60,985	67,560	74,285	91,720
	2016-17	36,700	42,180	47,835	55,365	62,125	68,705	76,635	90,785
	2017-18	32,885	39,925	46,515	54,355	61,780	68,555	76,495	91,160
	2018-19	36,405	43,420	50,400	57,720	65,095	71,405	79,130	97,176
	2019-20	34,755	42,045	49,685	59,535	67,325	71,280	78,895	94,700
	2020-21	31,930	38,235	45,085	53,300	60,990	68,955	78,055	89,406
	2021-22	34,920	42,380	49,870	59,620	67,870	76,105	84,965	94,882
	2022-23	36,630	43,550	50,160	57,680	65,220	72,480	80,225	89,648
	2023-24	36,325	42,255	49,490					
Other States[3]	2015-16	8,995	12,515	16,380	20,720	24,550	28,665	33,020	38,742
	2016-17	10,035	13,570	17,140	21,005	25,085	28,505	32,385	38,631
	2017-18	10,030	14,181	18,075	22,740	26,535	30,425	34,740	42,856
	2018-19	10,643	15,048	18,836	23,479	27,079	30,423	34,392	40,470
	2019-20	13,315	17,485	21,170	24,940	28,430	31,263	34,565	39,346
	2020-21	11,380	14,854	18,134	21,545	25,200	28,587	32,302	38,101
	2021-22	11,882	16,011	19,773	22,981	26,364	29,486	33,035	39,642
	2022-23	12,208	16,894	19,725	23,284	27,273	30,935	34,503	40,775
	2023-24	12,791	16,286	19,976					
Total	2015-16	70,970	87,190	104,405	124,120	142,225	160,770	179,805	222,436
	2016-17	73,715	90,065	106,625	125,910	144,915	162,630	182,955	227,235
	2017-18	69,265	87,906	105,910	126,585	145,835	164,275	185,635	226,224
	2018-19	73,843	92,378	111,131	131,464	150,874	168,923	189,152	238,670
	2019-20	76,310	94,750	113,305	135,330	154,815	167,773	186,895	225,959
	2020-21	71,980	89,199	107,009	124,810	146,300	165,412	186,797	222,569
	2021-22	75,607	94,941	114,063	134,791	154,669	174,056	194,730	222,993
	2022-23	75,378	93,589	111,615	130,344	149,733	167,900	187,378	219,669
	2023-24	79,571	96,156	114,851					
Dehy- drated[4]	2015-16	12,155	15,885	19,620	23,560	27,605	31,585	35,645	45,735
	2016-17	11,560	15,305	19,085	22,675	26,565	30,545	34,890	46,317
	2017-18	10,595	14,304	18,085	21,680	25,775	29,800	34,410	44,263
	2018-19	13,810	17,065	20,775	24,420	28,315	32,620	36,660	47,648
	2019-20	11,850	15,075	18,620	21,865	25,510	28,780	32,080	40,285
	2020-21	13,140	16,435	19,715	23,245	27,090	30,780	34,430	43,735
	2021-22	11,855	15,715	19,495	22,335	26,080	29,360	32,415	40,406
	2022-23	11,095	14,560	17,680	20,765	24,220	27,510	31,130	37,663
	2023-24	11,445	14,990	18,615					

[1] Total quantity received and used for processing regardless of the State in which the potatoes were produced. Amount excludes quantities used for potato chips in Maine, Michigan and Wisconsin.   [2] Includes Maine grown potatoes only.   [3] Colorado, Minnesota, , Nevada, North Dakota and Wisconsin.
[4] Dehydrated products except starch and flour. Included in above totals. Includes CO, ID, NV, ND, OR, WA, and WI.
Source: National Agricultural Statistics Service, U.S. Department of Agriculture (NASS-USDA)

Rice

Rice is a grain that is cultivated on every continent except Antarctica and is the primary food for half the people in the world. Rice cultivation probably originated as early as 10,000 BC in Asia. Rice is grown at varying altitudes (sea level to about 3,000 meters), in varying climates (tropical to temperate), and on dry to flooded land. The growth duration of rice plants is 3-6 months, depending on variety and growing conditions. Rice is harvested by hand in developing countries or by combines in industrialized countries. Asian countries produce about 90% of rice grown worldwide. Rough rice futures and options are traded at the CME Group.

Prices – CME rough rice futures price (Barchart.com symbol ZR) on the monthly nearest-futures chart in 2023 closed the year down -4.1% yr/yr at $17.305 per hundredweight (cwt).

Supply – World rice production in the 2023/24 marketing year is expected to rise by +0.1% to 767.016 million metric tons. The world's largest rice producers

are expected to be China with 26.9% of world production in 2023/24, India with 25.8%, Indonesia with 7.3%, Bangladesh with 7.1%, Vietnam with 5.6%, and Thailand with 4.0%. US production of rice in 2023/24 is expected to rise by +36.4% yr/yr to 9.901 million metric tons.

Demand – World consumption of rice in 2023/24 is expected to fall by -0.1% yr/yr to 520.289 million metric tons. US rice consumption in 2023/24 is expected to rise by +11.7% yr/yr to 5.144 million metric tons.

Trade – World exports of rice in 2023/24 is expected to fall by -5.3% yr/yr to 51.497 million metric tons. The world's largest rice exporters will be India with 31.1% of world exports, Thailand with 15.9%, Vietnam with 14.8%, Pakistan with 9.7%, the US with 5.2%, and Cambodia with 3.8%. US rice imports in 2023/24 are expected to rise by +5.3% yr/yr to a new record high of 1.334 million metric tons. US rice exports in 2022/23 are expected to fall by -19.7% yr/yr to 2.096 million metric tons.

World Production of Rough Rice   In Thousands of Metric Tons

Crop Year	Bangla-desh	Brazil	Burma	China	India	Indo-nesia	Japan	Pakistan	Philip-pines	Thailand	United States	Vietnam	World Total
2014-15	51,755	12,449	19,688	209,609	158,239	56,000	11,098	10,506	18,911	28,409	10,079	45,066	720,349
2015-16	51,755	10,603	19,000	212,141	156,628	57,008	10,819	10,204	17,473	23,939	8,759	44,134	711,137
2016-17	51,872	12,328	19,766	211,094	164,563	58,505	10,891	10,275	18,549	29,091	10,167	43,840	734,922
2017-18	48,980	12,065	20,625	212,676	169,154	58,268	10,696	11,176	19,421	31,177	8,084	44,251	738,650
2018-19	52,369	10,500	20,625	212,129	174,743	53,858	10,518	10,804	18,622	30,818	10,150	43,750	743,811
2019-20	53,780	11,179	19,766	209,614	178,323	54,646	10,455	10,810	18,932	26,750	8,390	43,360	743,849
2020-21	51,905	11,766	19,688	211,857	186,571	54,331	10,398	12,631	19,708	28,580	10,293	43,810	759,676
2021-22[1]	53,780	10,790	19,375	212,843	194,226	54,173	10,489	13,986	19,905	30,118	8,666	42,672	766,083
2022-23[2]	54,530	10,300	18,438	208,494	203,653	53,543	10,275	8,251	20,040	31,680	7,260	43,104	766,197
2023-24[3]	54,455	11,000	18,672	206,600	198,020	52,756	10,027	13,501	20,000	30,303	9,901	43,200	767,016

[1] Preliminary.   [2] Estimate.   [3] Forecast.   Source: Foreign Agricultural Service, U.S. Department of Agriculture (FAS-USDA)

World Imports of Rice (Milled Basis)   In Thousands of Metric Tons

Crop Year	China	Cote d'Ivoire	European Union	Indo-nesia	Iran	Iraq	Malaysia	Nigeria	Philip-pines	Saudi Arabia	Senegal	South Africa	World Total
2014-15	4,700	1,300	1,706	1,350	1,350	1,205	1,051	2,600	1,800	1,601	1,200	980	41,710
2015-16	4,800	1,250	1,804	1,050	1,100	912	823	2,100	1,600	1,260	1,020	950	38,690
2016-17	5,300	1,300	1,505	350	1,250	1,191	900	2,500	1,100	1,195	1,100	1,006	41,664
2017-18	5,500	1,370	1,652	2,350	1,000	1,170	800	2,000	1,300	1,290	1,100	1,074	47,263
2018-19	3,200	1,350	1,803	600	1,300	1,209	1,000	1,900	3,600	1,425	1,100	1,010	44,265
2019-20	2,600	980	2,009	550	1,200	1,154	1,220	1,400	2,450	1,613	1,050	960	42,577
2020-21	4,215	1,350	1,784	650	850	1,227	1,160	2,200	2,200	1,157	1,100	1,021	46,437
2021-22[1]	5,949	1,665	2,408	740	1,270	1,754	1,240	2,450	3,600	1,324	1,500	1,054	54,482
2022-23[2]	4,384	1,456	2,303	3,100	775	2,194	1,300	2,275	3,750	1,400	1,400	1,087	54,500
2023-24[3]	2,700	1,450	2,400	2,500	1,150	2,000	1,200	2,100	3,800	1,400	1,400	1,150	49,686

[1] Preliminary.   [2] Estimate.   [3] Forecast.   Source: Foreign Agricultural Service, U.S. Department of Agriculture (FAS-USDA)

World Exports of Rice (Milled Basis)   In Thousands of Metric Tons

Crop Year	Argen-tina	Brazil	Burma	Cam-bodia	Guyana	India	Pakistan	Para-guay	Thailand	United States	Uruguay	Vietnam	World Total
2014-15	312	930	1,735	1,150	446	12,238	3,800	371	9,779	3,078	766	6,606	43,867
2015-16	526	546	1,300	1,050	513	10,357	4,200	556	9,891	3,384	972	5,088	40,735
2016-17	343	830	3,350	1,150	478	11,710	3,548	538	11,658	3,645	947	6,488	47,892
2017-18	426	1,122	2,750	1,300	516	12,041	4,011	653	11,213	2,763	773	6,590	47,885
2018-19	350	878	2,700	1,350	448	10,420	4,493	689	7,565	2,959	846	6,581	44,184
2019-20	361	1,219	2,300	1,350	511	12,520	3,820	803	5,715	2,991	865	6,167	43,448
2020-21	385	950	1,900	1,850	552	20,216	3,879	640	6,283	2,969	785	6,272	51,240
2021-22[1]	422	1,392	2,335	1,700	406	22,025	4,817	752	7,682	2,650	986	7,054	56,901
2022-23[2]	350	1,200	1,500	1,900	358	20,245	3,764	880	8,700	2,042	925	8,400	54,375
2023-24[3]	375	1,300	1,800	1,950	440	16,000	5,000	780	8,200	2,699	950	7,600	51,497

[1] Preliminary.   [2] Estimate.   [3] Forecast.   Source: Foreign Agricultural Service, U.S. Department of Agriculture (FAS-USDA)

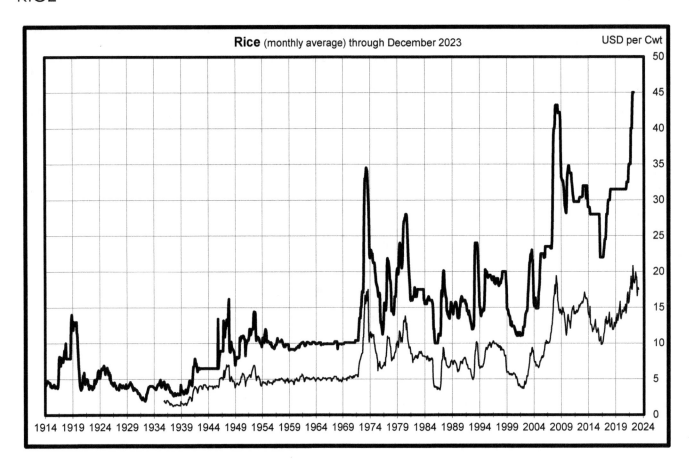

Rice (monthly average) through December 2023 — USD per Cwt

Average Wholesale Price of Rice No. 2 (Medium)[2] Southwest Louisiana   In Dollars Per Cwt. Bagged

Crop Year	Aug.	Sept.	Oct.	Nov.	Dec.	Jan.	Feb.	Mar.	Apr.	May	June	July	Average
2014-15	30.50	29.00	29.00	29.00	29.00	28.75	28.00	28.00	28.00	28.00	28.00	28.00	28.60
2015-16	28.00	28.00	28.00	28.00	28.00	28.00	28.00	28.00	28.00	28.00	28.00	28.00	28.00
2016-17	28.00	28.00	28.00	26.00	22.00	22.00	22.00	22.00	22.00	22.00	22.00	22.20	23.85
2017-18	23.00	23.60	24.50	24.50	24.50	25.63	28.00	28.00	28.00	29.50	30.00	30.00	26.60
2018-19	30.00	30.00	31.13	31.50	31.50	31.50	31.50	31.50	31.50	31.50	31.50	31.50	31.22
2019-20	31.50	31.50	31.50	31.50	31.50	31.50	31.50	31.50	31.50	31.50	31.50	31.50	31.50
2020-21	31.50	31.50	31.50	31.50	31.50	31.50	31.50	31.50	31.50	31.50	31.50	31.50	31.50
2021-22	31.50	31.50	31.83	32.50	32.50	32.50	32.50	34.50	35.00	35.00	35.00	35.00	33.28
2022-23	40.00	40.00	40.00	42.50	45.00	45.00	45.00	46.10	50.50	50.50	50.50	50.50	45.47
2023-24[1]	50.50	50.50	42.63	40.00	40.00	40.00	40.00						43.38

[1] Preliminary.   [2] U.S. No. 2 -- broken not to exceed 4%.   *Source: Economic Research Service, U.S. Department of Agriculture (ERS-USDA)*

Average Price Received by Farmers for Rice (Rough) in the United States   In Dollars Per Hundred Pounds (Cwt.)

Crop Year	Aug.	Sept.	Oct.	Nov.	Dec.	Jan.	Feb.	Mar.	Apr.	May	June	July	Average[2]
2014-15	15.60	14.40	14.00	14.30	13.60	15.10	12.80	12.60	12.60	12.50	12.00	11.60	13.43
2015-16	12.00	11.90	12.20	12.50	12.80	13.30	12.10	11.80	11.50	11.70	11.70	12.10	12.13
2016-17	11.80	10.60	10.30	10.40	10.50	10.90	10.10	10.10	10.10	10.20	10.20	10.70	10.49
2017-18	11.30	11.50	12.20	13.30	12.90	13.70	12.70	12.70	13.10	12.80	13.10	13.70	12.75
2018-19	14.30	12.40	12.30	12.60	12.70	13.50	12.40	11.90	12.00	11.90	12.20	12.90	12.59
2019-20	12.70	12.30	12.80	13.60	12.80	14.10	13.70	13.80	14.10	14.50	14.90	14.70	13.67
2020-21	15.80	13.70	13.40	13.90	14.10	14.60	14.40	14.40	14.40	15.00	15.00	14.60	14.44
2021-22	15.40	14.20	14.80	15.70	16.80	17.10	15.60	15.70	16.20	16.90	17.80	17.70	16.16
2022-23	19.30	17.70	17.50	18.30	20.80	20.30	19.60	18.40	18.80	18.90	19.90	19.20	19.06
2023-24[1]	19.20	16.60	17.60	17.70	17.50	19.60	17.80						18.00

[1] Preliminary.   [2] Weighted average by sales.   *Source: Economic Research Service, U.S. Department of Agriculture (ERS-USDA)*

Salient Statistics of Rice, Rough & Milled (Rough Equivalent) in the United States   In Millions of Cwt.

Crop Year Beginning Aug. 1	Supply				Disappearance							Government Support Program					
					Domestic						Total Disap-pearance	CCC Stocks July 31	Put Under Price Support	Loan Rate ($ Per Cwt.)			
	Stocks Aug. 1	Pro-duction	Imports	Total Supply	Food	Brewers	Seed	Total	Resi-dual	Exports				Rough[3]			Milled Long
														Long	Med-ium	All Classes	
2014-15	31.8	222.2	24.7	278.7	131.2	4	3.2	133.9	4	96.3	230.2	0	42.3	6.50	6.50	6.50	10.25
2015-16	48.5	193.1	24.1	264.9	107.7	4	3.9	112.7	4	106.6	219.3	0		6.50	6.50	6.50	10.22
2016-17	46.5	224.1	23.5	294.1	NA	4	NA	133.2	4	114.8	248.0	0		6.50	6.50	6.50	9.98
2017-18	46.0	178.2	26.9	251.8	----	4	----	135.4	4	87.1	222.4			6.50	6.50	6.50	10.01
2018-19	29.4	224.2	29.0	282.1	----	4	----	144.1	4	93.6	237.3			6.50	6.50	6.50	10.08
2019-20	44.9	184.7	37.3	267.2	----	4	----	144.3	4	94.2	238.5			7.00	7.00	7.00	11.09
2020-21	28.7	227.6	34.1	289.7	----	4	----	152.5	4	93.5	246.0			7.00	7.00	7.00	11.10
2021-22	43.7	191.1	37.8	272.5	----	4	----	149.3	4	83.5	232.8			7.00	7.00	7.00	11.06
2022-23[1]	39.7	160.0	39.9	239.7	----	4	----	145.1	4	64.3	209.4			7.00	7.00	7.00	
2023-24[2]	30.3	218.3	43.0	291.5	----	4	----	162.0	4	87.0	249.0						

[1] Preliminary.   [2] Forecast.   [3] Loan rate for each class of rice is the sum of the whole kernels' loan rate weighted by its milling yield (average 56%) and the broken kernels' loan rate weighted by its milling yield (average 12%).   [4] Included in Food.
Source: Economic Research Service, U.S. Department of Agriculture (ERS-USDA)

Acreage, Yield, Production and Prices of Rice in the United States

Crop Year Beginning Aug. 1	Acreage Harvested 1,000 Acres			Yield Per Harvested Acre (In Lbs.)		Production 1,000 Cwt.			Value of Pro-duction ($1,000)	Wholesale Prices $ Per Cwt.		Milled Rice, Average C.I.F. Rotterdam		
	Southern States	Cali-fornia	United States	Cali-fornia	United States	Southern States	Cali-fornia	United States		Arkan-sas[2]	Hous-ton[2]	U.S. No. 2[4]	Thai "A"[5]	Thai "B"[5]
												$ Per Metric Ton		
2014-15	2,491	442	2,933	8,580	7,576	184,279	37,936	222,215	3,075,618	29.87	26.52	----	----	----
2015-16	2,159	426	2,585	8,890	7,472	155,271	37,877	193,148	2,421,955	24.23	24.72	----	----	----
2016-17	2,561	536	3,097	8,840	7,237	176,751	47,394	224,145	2,384,690	22.51	22.51	----	----	----
2017-18	1,931	443	2,374	8,410	7,507	140,951	37,277	178,228	2,360,439	27.86	25.31	----	----	----
2018-19	2,411	504	2,915	8,620	7,692	180,786	43,425	224,211	2,898,996	30.69	26.56	----	----	----
2019-20	1,976	501	2,477	8,460	7,473	142,313	42,362	184,675	2,631,955	31.82	27.89	----	----	----
2020-21	2,472	514	2,986	8,720	7,619	182,773	44,810	227,583	3,314,161	32.37	30.21	----	----	----
2021-22	2,073	405	2,478	9,050	7,710	154,399	36,653	191,052	3,273,164	35.09	28.63	----	----	----
2022-23	1,915	252	2,167	8,770	7,385	137,938	22,103	160,041	3,210,556	46.80	35.08	----	----	----
2023-24[1]	2,342	512	2,854	8,590	7,649	174,320	43,971	218,291	4,248,445			----	----	----

[1] Preliminary.   [2] F.O.B. mills, Arkansas, medium.   [3] Houston, Texas (long grain).   [4] Milled, 4%, container, FAS.
[5] SWR, 100%, bulk.   NA = Not available.   *Source: Economic Research Service, U.S. Department of Agriculture (ERS-USDA)*

U.S. Exports of Milled Rice, by Country of Destination   In Thousands of Metric Tons

Trade Year Beginning October	Canada	Haiti	Iran	Ivory Coast	Jamaica	Mexico	Nether-lands	Peru	Saudi Arabia	South Africa	Switzer-land	United Kingdom	Total
2013-14	242.6	346.0	.2	13.5	2.3	741.2	5.4	6.8	106.1	2.3	.6	23.6	3,355
2014-15	219.2	392.1	----	.1	2.6	837.4	5.3	9.0	111.9	1.6	.6	30.6	3,971
2015-16	207.1	413.5	61.4	16.0	2.5	769.6	6.7	6.6	115.7	.9	.7	28.0	3,789
2016-17	212.6	478.0	----	17.2	3.1	962.0	6.0	8.7	130.1	.8	.6	34.0	3,986
2017-18	211.3	450.0	----	19.0	3.8	730.5	7.4	.2	88.5	.3	.5	22.3	3,052
2018-19	238.4	459.0	----	1.2	4.0	861.4	5.8	.2	110.4	.6	.6	18.7	3,600
2019-20	239.0	397.3	----	38.2	5.4	609.9	5.3	.1	120.3	.3	.5	28.5	3,106
2020-21	226.4	437.0	----	51.7	5.8	856.1	7.4	.1	102.6	.5	.7	29.6	3,730
2021-22	249.4	445.6	----	15.4	5.0	513.0	11.6	.1	86.1	.4	.2	23.1	2,815
2022-23[1]	221.0	349.9	----	1.3	5.6	322.4	4.4	.2	81.8	.3	.1	19.6	2,292

[1] Preliminary.   *Source: Economic Research Service, U.S. Department of Agriculture (ERS-USDA)*

Production of Rice (Rough) in the United States, by Type and Variety   In Thousands of Cwt.

Year	Long Grain	Medium Grain	Short Grain	Total	Year	Long Grain	Medium Grain	Short Grain	Total
2014	162,665	57,222	2,328	222,215	2019	125,610	57,098	2,396	184,675
2015	133,401	57,041	2,706	193,148	2020	170,784	53,920	2,810	227,583
2016	166,465	54,533	3,147	224,145	2021	143,961	44,428	2,663	191,052
2017	127,850	47,867	2,511	178,228	2022	128,461	29,532	2,048	160,041
2018	163,956	57,339	2,916	224,211	2023[1]	153,871	63,217	1,203	218,291

[1] Preliminary.   *Source: National Agricultural Statistics Service, U.S. Department of Agriculture (NASS-USDA)*

Rubber

Rubber is a natural or synthetic substance characterized by elasticity, water repellence, and electrical resistance. Pre-Columbian Native South Americans discovered many uses for rubber, such as containers, balls, shoes, and waterproofing for fabrics such as coats and capes. The Spaniards tried to duplicate these products for many years but were unsuccessful. The first commercial application of rubber began in 1791 when Samuel Peal patented a waterproofing cloth method by treating it with a rubber and turpentine solution. In 1839, Charles Goodyear revolutionized the rubber industry by discovering a process called vulcanization, which involved combining rubber and sulfur and heating the mixture.

Natural rubber is obtained from latex, a milky white fluid, from the Hevea Brasiliensis tree. The latex is gathered by cutting a chevron shape through the bark of the rubber tree. The latex is collected in a small cup, with approximately one fluid ounce per cutting. The cuttings are usually done every other day until the cuttings reach the ground. The tree is then allowed to renew itself before a new tapping is started. The collected latex is strained, diluted with water, and treated with acid to bind the rubber particles together. The rubber is then pressed between rollers to consolidate the rubber into slabs or thin sheets and is air-dried or smoke-dried for shipment.

During World War II, natural rubber supplies from the Far East were cut off, and the rubber shortage accelerated the development of synthetic rubber in the U.S. Synthetic rubber is produced by chemical reactions, condensation, or polymerization, of certain unsaturated hydrocarbons. Synthetic rubber is made of raw material derived from petroleum, coal, oil, natural gas, and acetylene and is almost identical to natural rubber in chemical and physical properties.

Natural rubber and Rubber Index futures are traded on the Osaka Mercantile Exchange (OME). The OME's natural rubber contract is based on the RSS3 ribbed smoked sheet No. 3. The OME's Rubber Index Futures Contract is based on a composite of 8 component grades from 6 rubber markets in the world. Rubber futures are also traded on the Shanghai Futures Exchange (SHFE), the Singapore Exchange (SGX), and the Tokyo Commodity Exchange (TOCOM).

Prices – Singapore SGX Rubber futures prices (Barchart.com symbol U6) on the nearest-futures chart in 2023 closed the year up +13.9% yr/yr at $173.10 per metric ton.

Supply – World production of natural rubber in 2021 rose by +0.1% yr/yr to 14.022 million metric tons, below the 2019 record high of 14.536 million metric tons. The world's largest producers of natural rubber in 2021 were Thailand with 33.1% of world production, Indonesia with 22.3%, Vietnam with 9.1%, India with 5.3%, China with 5.3%, and Ivory Coast with 5.2%.

Trade – World exports of natural rubber in 2021 rose by +1.4% yr/yr to 1.877 million metric tons. The world's largest exporter of natural rubber in 2021 was Thailand, with 63.2% of world exports. US imports of natural dry rubber in 2021 rose by +23.3% yr/yr to 946,234 metric tons.

World Production of Natural Rubber   In Thousands of Metric Tons

Year	Brazil	China	Côte d'Ivoire	India	Indonesia	Liberia	Malaysia	Nigeria	Philip-pines	Sri Lanka	Thailand	Vietnam	World Total
2013	185.7	864.8	289.6	900.0	3,107.5	74.6	826.4	150.1	444.8	130.4	4,305.1	946.9	13,126.4
2014	192.4	840.2	316.1	940.0	3,153.2	47.5	668.6	148.9	453.1	109.2	4,566.3	961.1	13,385.0
2015	191.5	816.1	350.0	944.5	3,145.4	58.6	722.1	146.9	398.1	91.0	4,466.1	1,012.7	13,361.5
2016	189.8	815.9	453.0	950.6	3,307.1	60.5	673.5	146.3	362.6	79.1	4,519.0	1,035.3	13,613.3
2017	190.5	817.4	580.0	713.0	3,680.4	63.0	740.1	146.8	407.0	83.1	4,503.1	1,094.5	13,906.8
2018	199.7	824.1	624.1	660.0	3,630.4	75.4	603.3	147.5	423.4	82.6	4,813.5	1,137.7	14,233.3
2019	217.4	839.9	780.1	702.0	3,448.5	89.4	639.8	148.5	431.7	74.8	4,840.0	1,182.5	14,522.7
2020	225.6	687.6	936.1	687.6	3,037.3	86.5	514.7	148.5	422.4	78.2	4,859.7	1,226.1	14,184.9
2021[1]	239.9	749.0	1,100.4	749.0	3,045.3	101.4	469.7	149.0	430.6	76.9	4,892.5	1,272.0	14,629.3
2022[2]	250.2	843.0	1,286.0	843.0	3,135.3	107.1	377.0	149.4	415.7	70.9	4,825.9	1,339.5	15,125.4

[1] Preliminary.   [2] Estimate.   *Source: Food and Agricultural Organization of the United Nations (FAO-UN)*

World Imports of Natural Rubber   In Metric Tons

Year	Brazil	Canada	China	European Union	Germany	Italy	Korea, South	Malaysia	Mexico	Pakistan	United Kingdom	United States	World Total
2013	17,849	22,309	345,330	164,192	32,169	20,894	20,130	344,581	19,318	14,023	28,656	45,939	1,094,300
2014	29,603	18,870	375,538	218,822	26,123	21,481	33,719	315,711	21,582	20,086	45,644	49,914	1,268,199
2015	28,048	18,802	386,157	145,989	18,092	21,065	34,398	318,300	21,796	14,223	38,546	50,278	1,196,131
2016	27,832	3,088	432,273	129,251	21,089	22,518	34,302	318,419	22,967	6,722	19,313	48,619	1,172,683
2017	28,549	2,768	501,350	134,852	18,580	21,556	32,686	323,121	24,000	10,095	14,388	54,724	1,267,024
2018	29,700	2,205	597,640	142,203	17,086	21,600	26,268	333,427	25,606	10,551	14,332	47,795	1,381,809
2019	30,088	1,293	560,345	132,472	14,837	20,008	24,172	312,006	31,483	8,755	13,341	47,384	1,292,159
2020	31,470	838	576,027	141,556	12,085	16,917	20,864	348,311	51,165	11,386	11,871	36,756	1,374,758
2021[1]	36,184	1,997	555,696	175,868	16,876	21,445	21,018	337,255	62,021	18,211	16,662	54,597	1,426,176
2022[2]	33,398	910	663,046	156,792	15,064	25,419	18,877	286,943	104,304	15,164	14,572	40,046	1,472,054

[1] Preliminary.   [2] Estimate.   *Source: Food and Agricultural Organization of the United Nations (FAO-UN)*

World Exports of Natural Rubber In Metric Tons

Year	Belgium	Came-roon	Hong Kong	Germany	Guate-mala	India	Indonesia	Malaysia	Myanmar	Nether-lands	Thailand	United States	World Total
2013	54,754	9,866	1,414	8,209	24,068	4,635	5,907	33,538	80	3,328	1,038,421	5,398	1,253,098
2014	80,932	7,169	1,802	5,982	42,899	815	5,410	32,370	----	12,967	1,057,520	6,470	1,348,083
2015	19,981	5,596	2,346	5,136	41,910	653	6,410	31,904	----	17,834	1,072,710	7,119	1,303,512
2016	37,912	6,241	1,692	6,070	40,242	2,148	6,067	30,375	410	20,240	1,240,189	6,045	1,522,245
2017	24,628	6,918	1,888	9,598	51,286	15,580	6,213	32,920	2,798	30,436	1,185,942	5,753	1,553,472
2018	20,076	10,849	1,970	11,030	52,390	535	5,154	27,019	12,859	30,667	1,298,800	5,176	1,784,597
2019	27,711	12,897	768	8,726	54,842	1,093	4,864	23,188	16,586	19,035	1,155,887	3,327	1,757,985
2020	21,819	11,355	239	6,487	60,126	6,550	5,208	19,644	8,170	17,342	1,147,585	3,518	1,854,560
2021[1]	30,522	15,055	320	3,636	76,079	3,322	2,395	21,106	3,188	25,332	1,187,302	6,482	1,829,305
2022[2]	24,591	17,931	354	2,052	65,643	1,089	3,386	16,874	3,575	22,768	1,104,458	5,671	2,033,389

[1] Preliminary. [2] Estimate. *Source: Food and Agricultural Organization of the United Nations (FAO-UN)*

World Imports of Natural Dry Rubber In Metric Tons

Year	Brazil	Canada	China	European Union	France	Germany	Italy	Japan	Korea, South	Malaysia	Spain	United States	World Total
2013	205,903	109,375	2,241,937	1,440,785	159,935	342,548	97,455	711,490	376,217	660,136	143,491	881,396	7,494,684
2014	211,843	110,737	2,352,994	1,534,502	154,533	361,112	107,044	678,945	383,051	589,328	164,149	897,012	7,873,239
2015	191,039	113,698	2,460,397	1,588,344	161,967	353,750	115,197	677,837	367,806	639,001	169,108	899,721	8,169,952
2016	206,383	118,204	2,178,575	1,619,850	160,774	315,651	116,682	655,337	361,975	611,916	162,043	897,493	7,868,585
2017	196,052	125,100	2,409,917	1,663,256	167,182	292,603	122,666	477,288	364,758	789,885	183,887	917,585	8,204,930
2018	195,665	139,483	2,105,367	1,711,504	168,438	282,150	119,539	705,747	352,674	681,357	175,553	949,536	8,353,274
2019	195,287	141,174	1,998,757	1,672,325	156,893	247,256	115,854	727,558	341,110	770,694	183,639	962,455	8,259,967
2020	141,173	103,815	1,825,358	1,375,349	104,846	215,170	98,047	554,382	286,818	873,582	157,084	767,174	7,545,908
2021[1]	197,817	133,319	1,928,931	1,718,598	139,116	262,563	118,813	692,090	327,688	870,047	186,860	946,234	9,762,778
2022[2]	218,040	135,490	2,058,922	1,718,853	130,706	267,230	122,731	762,596	384,963	878,647	207,672	1,033,345	9,219,047

[1] Preliminary. [2] Estimate. *Source: Food and Agricultural Organization of the United Nations (FAO-UN)*

World Exports of Natural Dry Rubber In Metric Tons

Year	Côte d'Ivoire	Germany	Guate-mala	India	Indonesia	Liberia	Malaysia	Nigeria	Philip-pines	Sri Lanka	Thailand	Vietnam	World Total
2013	259,860	110,488	64,182	22,134	2,696,087	58,946	813,714	51,332	66,930	23,007	2,398,556	674,342	7,648,372
2014	352,543	148,976	65,355	2,171	2,618,061	67,688	689,352	38,760	87,162	15,415	2,351,795	918,574	7,930,414
2015	409,815	142,222	60,862	4,685	2,623,903	55,819	674,589	37,115	78,604	12,050	2,579,309	709,029	8,066,183
2016	492,322	98,908	57,302	5,882	2,572,097	66,393	611,588	33,292	68,788	15,529	2,356,971	585,250	7,656,891
2017	644,446	60,326	64,269	9,584	3,188,798	65,025	583,120	42,738	133,745	13,290	2,482,824	473,634	8,600,302
2018	557,764	53,822	66,110	5,516	2,806,801	76,148	611,896	40,775	111,178	15,983	2,226,029	559,636	7,969,487
2019	691,056	44,444	62,079	8,872	2,651,554	89,089	608,116	42,828	122,946	12,146	2,136,048	590,750	8,011,485
2020	847,427	40,533	60,779	5,919	2,274,882	74,190	544,907	32,992	144,608	13,693	1,506,110	382,771	6,943,523
2021[1]	1,079,463	59,900	69,129	2,414	2,332,339	106,894	632,139	42,986	203,204	12,539	2,229,982	514,095	8,583,977
2022[2]	1,055,380	61,310	67,076	1,445	2,034,518	121,028	605,210	42,853	187,866	14,067	2,176,699	465,239	8,215,338

[1] Preliminary. [2] Estimate. *Source: Food and Agricultural Organization of the United Nations (FAO-UN)*

U.S. Imports of Natural Rubber (Includes Latex & Guayule) In Metric Tons

Year	Jan.	Feb.	Mar.	Apr.	May	June	July	Aug.	Sept.	Oct.	Nov.	Dec.	Total
2011	82,559	83,695	100,449	94,540	104,094	82,569	92,187	95,040	68,872	90,280	79,167	75,984	1,049,435
2012	80,134	87,794	93,327	95,541	75,109	62,804	68,098	83,118	88,059	75,963	80,187	78,828	968,960
2013	75,848	66,517	84,667	80,380	72,054	82,234	77,067	72,617	76,176	76,111	88,195	76,234	928,100
2014	80,647	75,094	87,363	95,293	70,447	72,062	79,663	82,402	71,885	77,073	74,484	80,532	946,946
2015	84,504	57,323	86,017	81,059	102,381	78,643	83,734	79,336	83,083	77,489	73,360	65,115	952,042
2016	77,751	72,275	77,523	85,225	88,091	79,224	86,991	80,035	70,754	83,342	72,110	72,826	946,147
2017	78,217	71,901	88,085	85,883	64,955	97,920	82,746	79,584	82,898	80,086	71,825	88,396	972,495
2018	82,600	75,326	96,446	75,441	101,791	86,553	65,733	84,977	87,418	97,657	73,051	70,410	997,403
2019	103,581	64,889	102,213	91,161	84,602	88,177	64,568	93,991	78,237	72,177	96,745	69,546	1,009,887
2020[1]	70,468	80,501	83,060	94,526	87,448	45,332	43,862	51,601	58,419	48,980	66,297		796,900

[1] Preliminary. *Source: Economic Research Service, U.S. Department of Agriculture (ERS-USDA)*

Rye

Rye is a cereal grain and a member of the grass family. Hardy varieties of rye have been developed for winter planting. Rye is most widely grown in northern Europe and Asia. In the U.S., rye is used as an animal feed and as an ingredient in bread and some whiskeys. Bread using rye was developed in northern Europe in the Middle Ages, where bakers developed dark, hearty bread consisting of rye, oat, and barley flours. Those were crops that grew more readily in the wet and damp climate of northern Europe, as opposed to wheat, which fares better in the warmer and drier climates in central Europe. Modern rye bread is made with a mixture of white and rye flours. Coarsely ground rye flour is also used in pumpernickel bread and helps provide the dark color and coarse texture, along with molasses. The major producing states are North and South Dakota, Oklahoma, and Georgia. The crop year runs from June to May.

Supply – World rye production in 2023/24 marketing year is forecasted to fall by -5.5% yr/yr to 11.596 million metric tons.

The world's largest producers of rye in 2023/24 are expected to be the European Union with 65.4% of world production, followed by Russia with 14.7%, Belarus with 6.7%, and Canada with 3.1%. US production of rye accounts for only 2.3% of world production.

US production of rye in 2023 fell by -16.7% to 10.375 million bushels, far below the production levels of over 20 million bushels seen from the late 1800s through the 1960s. US production of rye posted a record low of 6.051 million bushels in 2011. US acreage harvested with rye in 2023/24 is expected to fall by -6.7% yr/yr to 322,000 acres. US farmers in the late 1800s through the 1960s typically harvested more than 1 million acres of rye, showing how domestic planting of rye has dropped off sharply in recent decades. Rye yield in 2023/24 is expected to fall by -10.8% yr/yr to 32.2 bushels per acre.

Demand – Total US domestic usage of rye in 2023/24 is expected to fall by -6.3% yr/yr to 22.405 million bushels. The breakdown of 2023/24 domestic usage is expected to show that 18.3% of rye will be used for feed and residual, 44.6% for industry, 20.8% for seed, and 16.3% for food.

Trade – World exports of rye in the 2023/24 marketing year are expected to fall by -4.6% yr/yr to 457,000 metric tons, above the record low of 225,000 metric tons in 2008/09. The largest exporters will be Canada, with 39.4% of the world total at 180,000 metric tons, and the European Union with 38.3% at 175,000 metric tons. World imports of rye in 2023/24 are expected to rise by +11.8% to 510,000 metric tons. US imports of rye in 2023/24 are expected to fall by -0.7% yr/yr to 305,000 metric tons.

World Production of Rye   In Thousands of Metric Tons

Crop Year	Argentina	Australia	Belarus	Canada	Chile	European Union	Kazakhstan	Norway	Russia	Türkiye	Ukraine	United States	World Total
2014-15	97	30	867	218	5	8,864	61	38	3,279	300	475	183	14,469
2015-16	61	30	753	226	5	7,833	37	66	2,084	330	394	295	12,162
2016-17	79	30	651	436	5	7,405	41	23	2,538	300	394	339	12,333
2017-18	86	30	670	341	5	7,366	39	50	2,540	320	510	260	12,304
2018-19	87	31	503	236	5	6,176	23	9	1,914	320	396	215	10,005
2019-20	220	32	756	333	5	8,395	23	50	1,424	320	339	271	12,261
2020-21	135	32	1,051	488	5	8,968	30	50	2,376	320	459	294	14,305
2021-22[1]	225	32	800	372	5	8,011	40	50	1,716	330	600	249	12,515
2022-23[2]	179	32	750	520	5	7,610	60	50	2,000	320	315	316	12,271
2023-24[3]	165	32	780	358		7,580	30	50	1,700	320	230	264	11,596

[1] Preliminary.   [2] Estimate.   [3] Forecast.   *Source: Foreign Agricultural Service, U.S. Department of Agriculture (FAS-USDA)*

World Imports and Exports of Rye   In Thousands of Metric Tons

Crop Year	European Union	Japan	Korea, South	Norway	Russia	United States	World Total	Belarus	Canada	European Union	Russia	United States	World Total
	Imports							Exports					
2014-15	102	22	4	8	5	237	409	----	86	184	114	6	413
2015-16	51	16	5	1	8	222	335	20	98	161	48	5	353
2016-17	16	24	4	3	4	167	232	11	142	79	9	4	257
2017-18	65	21	3	4	----	224	363	----	193	91	71	4	398
2018-19	297	23	3	18	----	304	693	----	144	198	283	4	718
2019-20	4	19	4	9	90	302	447	----	163	262	1	5	439
2020-21	87	22	4	8	4	244	408	17	150	156	83	5	429
2021-22[1]	258	13	4	6	1	262	614	10	149	159	125	5	616
2022-23[2]	109	11	4	4	1	307	456	10	196	141	65	2	479
2023-24[3]	150	15	5	5	----	305	510	5	180	175	80	6	457

[1] Preliminary.   [2] Estimate.   [3] Forecast.   *Source: Foreign Agricultural Service, U.S. Department of Agriculture (FAS-USDA)*

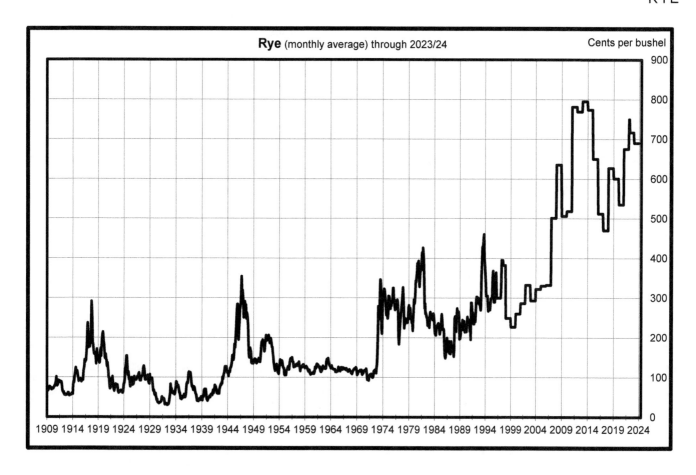

Rye (monthly average) through 2023/24 — Cents per bushel

Production of Rye in the United States   In Thousands of Bushels

Year	Georgia	Minnesota	North Dakota	Oklahoma	Pennsylvania	Other States[2]	Total
2014	540	----	----	495	----	6,154	7,189
2015	420	----	----	2,040	----	9,156	11,616
2016	630	----	----	1,875	----	10,832	13,337
2017	475	W	W	1,080	W	8,697	10,252
2018	390	W	W	1,100	W	6,942	8,454
2019	W	702	2,565	1,485	364	4,826	10,668
2020	W	570	2,200	728	1,872	5,362	11,582
2021	----	484	1,152	1,250	600	5,502	9,808
2022	----	1,456	2,760	1,000	798	5,279	12,453
2023[1]	----	968	2,583	765	612	4,832	10,375

[1] Preliminary.   [2] Includes IL, KS, ME, MD, MI, MN, NE, NJ, NY, NC, ND, PA, SC, SD, TX, VA, and WI.   *Source: Agricultural Statistics Board, U.S. Department of Agriculture (ASB-USDA)*

Salient Statistics of Rye in the United States   In Thousands of Bushels

Crop Year Beginning June 1	Supply Stocks June 1	Supply Pro-duction	Supply Imports	Supply Total Supply	Domestic Use Food	Domestic Use Industry	Domestic Use Seed	Domestic Use Feed & Residual	Domestic Use Total	Exports	Total Disap-pearance	Acreage Planted	Acreage Harvested for Grain	Yield Per Harvested Acre (Bushels)
2014-15	285	7,189	9,319	16,793	3,450	3,173	3,200	6,141	15,964	240	16,204	1,434	258	27.9
2015-16	589	11,616	8,757	20,962	3,480	5,321	3,840	7,685	20,326	181	20,507	1,584	365	31.8
2016-17	455	13,337	6,586	20,378	3,500	5,727	4,110	6,168	19,505	175	19,680	1,891	411	32.5
2017-18	698	10,252	8,825	19,775	3,530	6,326	4,270	4,899	19,025	157	19,182	1,961	300	34.2
2018-19	593	8,454	11,964	21,011	3,550	7,054	3,910	5,929	20,443	149	20,592	2,021	274	30.9
2019-20	419	10,668	11,908	22,995	3,570	9,947	4,110	4,063	21,690	205	21,895	1,875	312	34.2
2020-21	1,100	11,582	9,615	22,297	3,590	10,000	4,510	2,756	20,856	188	21,044	1,975	332	34.9
2021-22[1]	1,253	9,808	10,331	21,392	3,610	10,000	4,550	2,403	20,563	197	20,760	2,133	294	33.4
2022-23[2]	632	12,453	12,102	25,187	3,630	10,000	4,840	5,430	23,900	82	23,982	2,175	345	36.1
2023-24[3]	1,205	10,375	12,000	23,580	3,650	10,000	4,650	4,105	22,405	235	22,640	2,293	322	32.2

[1] Preliminary.   [2] Estimate.   [3] Forecast   *Source: Economic Research Service, U.S. Department of Agriculture (ERS-USDA)*

Salt

Salt, also known as sodium chloride, is a chemical compound that is an essential element in the diet of humans, animals, and even many plants. Since prehistoric times, salt has been used to preserve foods and was commonly used in the religious rites of the Greeks, Romans, Hebrews, and Christians. Salt, in the form of salt cakes, served as money in ancient Ethiopia and Tibet. As long ago as 1450 BC, Egyptian art shows records of salt production.

The simplest method of obtaining salt is through the evaporation of saltwater from areas near oceans or seas. In most regions, rock salt is obtained from underground mining or by wells sunk into deposits. Salt is soluble in water, is slightly soluble in alcohol, but is insoluble in concentrated hydrochloric acid. In its crystalline form, salt is transparent and colorless, shining with an ice-like luster.

Prices – The price of salt in 2023 (FOB mine, vacuum, and open pan) rose by +4.8% yr/yr to $220.00 per metric ton.

Supply – World production of salt in 2023 was unchanged yr/yr at 270.000 million metric tons. The world's largest salt producers were China with 19.6% and the US with 15.6% of world production. US salt production in 2023 rose by +2.4% to 42.000 million metric tons.

Demand – US consumption of salt in 2023 fell -3.5% yr/yr at 55.000 million metric tons, well below the 2014 record high of 65.300 million.

Trade – US imports of salt for consumption in 2023 fell by -10.1% yr/yr to 16.000 million metric tons, below the 2015 record high of 21.600. The US relied on imports for 29.1% of its salt consumption in 2023. US exports of salt in 2023 rose by +158.4% yr/yr to 2.300 metric tons.

World Production of All Salt   In Thousands of Metric Tons

Year	Australia	Canada	China	France	Germany	India	Italy	Mexico	Poland	Spain	United Kingdom	United States	World Total
2016	10,410	10,252	66,201	5,463	14,477	27,500	3,035	8,907	4,321	4,453	3,899	41,796	278,000
2017	11,675	11,424	66,542	5,003	15,568	28,000	3,047	9,000	4,598	4,038	2,362	39,975	280,000
2018	12,894	10,713	63,640	5,653	16,248	40,000	3,000	9,000	4,411	4,395	3,430	44,055	300,000
2019	11,474	11,936	67,014	5,439	16,628	45,000	4,200	9,000	4,440	4,218	2,254	44,845	308,000
2020	11,000	10,000	63,000	5,400	15,300	29,000	1,540	9,000	3,780	4,200	4,700	41,000	280,000
2021	12,200	11,800	64,000	5,400	15,000	45,000	1,900	9,000	4,000	4,200	2,400	42,000	294,000
2022[1]	13,000	12,000	54,000	5,500	15,000	30,000	1,900	8,700	4,300	3,900	2,400	41,000	270,000
2023[2]	14,000	12,000	53,000	5,600	15,000	30,000	2,000	9,000	4,200	4,000	2,300	42,000	270,000

[1] Preliminary.   [2] Estimate.   *Source: U.S. Geological Survey (USGS)*

Salient Statistics of the Salt Industry in the United States   In Thousands of Metric Tons

Year	Net Import Reliance As a % of Apparent Consumption	Average Value FOB Mine Vacuum & Open Pan ($ Per Ton)	Production Total	Open & Vacuum Pan	Solar	Rock	Brine	Sold or Used, Producers — Open & Vacuum Pan	Rock	Brine	Total Salt	Imports for Consumption Value[3] Million $	Imports for Consumption	Exports Total	Exports To Canada	Apparent Consumption
2016	22	197.78	41,700	4,050	2,900	17,900	16,900	4,040	16,100	16,400	39,900	$2,190	12,100	729	594	51,300
2017	23	211.71	39,900	4,490	3,340	16,500	15,600	4,500	15,500	15,500	38,700	$2,390	12,600	1,130	971	50,200
2018	28	220.00	43,900	4,260	2,950	18,900	17,900	4,210	19,400	17,900	44,200	$2,570	17,900	986	811	61,100
2019	28	211.57	44,800	4,280	3,520	19,100	17,900	4,420	19,200	17,900	44,900	$2,650	18,700	1,020	886	62,500
2020	27	212.21	42,600								39,600		15,800	1,250		54,200
2021	30	203.72	39,300								39,800		17,700	1,010		56,400
2022[1]	30	210.00	41,000								40,000		17,800	890		57,000
2023[2]	25	220.00	42,000								41,000		16,000	2,300		55,000

[1] Preliminary.   [2] Estimate.   [3] Values are f.o.b. mine or refinery & do not include cost of cooperage or containers.   *Source: U.S. Geological Survey (USGS)*

Salt Sold or Used by Producers in the U.S. by Classes & Consumers or Uses   In Thousands of Metric Tons

Year	Chemical[2]	Tanning Leather	Textile & Dyeing[3]	Meat Packers	Canning	Baking	Agricultural Distribution	Feed Dealers	Feed Manufacturers	Rubber	Oil & Pulp	Paper Processing	Metal Processing	Water Treatment	Grocery Stores	Water Conditioning Distrib.	Ice Control and/or Stabilization
2012	16,824	36	41	248	182	160	253	1,010	392	7	441	61	53	446	591	472	11,100
2013	17,990	38	39	258	179	162	351	913	516	5	409	66	42	472	665	627	20,340
2014	20,360	39	38	240	171	158	389	939	514	6	400	71	56	603	708	504	24,490
2015	19,430	38	39	275	175	181	306	849	336	3	302	69	46	723	707	440	22,760
2016	18,350	36	64	283	181	171	428	660	377	4	316	63	41	469	669	437	20,300
2017	17,050	33	30	257	177	177	470	708	458	3	275	62	34	471	537	447	19,520
2018	20,820	44	37	310	203	215	526	761	363	4	313	76	38	566	570	520	22,880
2019[1]	20,040	46	37	284	181	192	413	742	303	8	301	72	45	650	701	510	21,760

[1] Preliminary.   [2] Chloralkali producers and other chemical.   *Source: U.S. Geological Survey (USGS)*

Sheep and Lambs

Sheep and lambs are raised for both their wool and meat. In countries that have high wool production, there is also demand for sheep and lamb meat due to the easy availability. Production levels have declined in New Zealand and Australia, but that has been counteracted by a substantial increase in China.

Prices – The average monthly wholesale price of slaughter lambs (choice) at San Angelo, Texas, in 2023 fell by -3.5% to 170.72 cents per pound.

Supply – World sheep and goat numbers in 2022 rose by +2.1% to 2.471 billion head, a new record high. The world's largest producers of sheep and goats are China with 13.2% of world production in 2022, India with 9.1%, Australia with 3.0%, Türkiye with 2.3%, and the United Kingdom with 1.3%.

The number of sheep and lambs on US farms in 2023 (Jan 1) was down by -0.9% yr/yr at 5.020 million head. US states with the most sheep and lambs are Texas with 13.4% of the US total, California with 11.0%, Colorado with 8.3%, Wyoming with 6.7%, and Utah with 5.6%.

World Sheep and Goat Numbers in Specified Countries on January 1   In Thousands of Head

Year	Argentina	Australia	China	India	Kazakhstan	New Zealand	Romania	Russia	South Africa	Spain	Türkiye	United Kingdom	World Total
2013	18,950	79,098	289,777	197,800	17,633	30,867	10,100	24,180	30,556	18,729	35,783	32,954	2,127,193
2014	18,934	76,182	289,770	196,000	17,561	29,901	10,449	24,337	30,094	18,136	38,510	33,843	2,137,123
2015	19,580	74,510	304,238	204,694	18,016	29,196	10,935	24,683	29,810	19,533	41,485	33,438	2,191,641
2016	19,576	71,193	311,668	211,464	18,184	27,696	11,250	24,606	28,906	19,051	41,924	34,047	2,226,391
2017	19,610	75,725	302,079	216,207	18,329	27,625	11,359	24,717	28,164	19,023	41,329	34,936	2,256,068
2018	18,907	73,828	297,388	219,733	18,699	27,384	11,716	24,389	27,905	18,617	46,117	33,885	2,281,064
2019	19,413	69,663	300,490	223,261	19,156	26,915	11,954	23,129	27,336	18,138	48,481	33,691	2,339,587
2020	19,268	67,424	307,096	226,736	20,058	26,146	11,893	22,618	26,775	18,090	54,113	32,809	2,392,644
2021[1]	17,629	71,999	319,377	223,842	20,877	25,850	11,580	21,660	26,615	17,671	57,519	33,068	2,421,557
2022[2]	16,589	74,242	326,030	225,346	21,786	25,422	11,731	20,959	26,571	16,916	56,266	33,177	2,471,536

[1] Preliminary.   [2] Forecast.   *Source: Food and Agricultural Organization of the United Nations (FAO-UN)*

Salient Statistics of Sheep & Lambs in the United States (Average Live Weight)   In Thousands of Head

| | - Inventory, Jan. 1 - | | | | --- Marketings[3] --- | | -------- Slaughter -------- | | | | | Production (Live Weight) | Farm Value ------ Jan. 1 ------- |
Year	Without New Crop Lambs	With New Crop Lambs	Lamb Crop	Total Supply	Sheep	Lambs	Farm	Commercial	Total[4]	Net Exports	Total Disappearance	(Mil. Lbs.)	Total
2014	5,245	5,356	3,440	8,796	----	----	95	2,310	2,404	----	----	----	----
2015	5,280	5,385	3,290	8,675	----	----	95	2,224	2,319	----	----	----	----
2016	5,300	5,405	3,265	8,670	----	----	95	2,238	2,333	----	----	----	----
2017	5,250	5,356	3,230	8,586	----	----	96	2,178	2,274	----	----	----	----
2018	5,265	5,372	3,235	8,607	----	----	92	2,261	2,353	----	----	----	----
2019	5,230	5,338	3,230	8,568	----	----	92	2,322	2,413	----	----	----	----
2020	5,200	5,308	3,210	8,518	----	----	93	2,225	2,318	----	----	----	----
2021	5,170	5,277	3,160	8,437	----	----	92	2,263	2,355	----	----	----	----
2022[1]	5,065	5,170	3,099	8,269	----	----	95	2,071	2,166	----	----	----	----
2023[2]	5,130	5,233	3,030	8,263	----	----	96	2,149	2,245	----	----	----	----

[1] Preliminary.   [2] Estimate.   [3] Excludes interfarm sales.   [4] Includes all commercial and farm.
Source: Economic Research Service, U.S. Department of Agriculture (ERS-USDA)

Sheep and Lambs[3] on Farms in the United States on January 1   In Thousands of Head

Year	California	Colorado	Idaho	Iowa	Minnesota	Montana	New Mexico	Ohio	Dakota	Texas	Utah	Wyoming	Total
2016	575	435	255	175	125	230	90	120	265	725	285	355	5,300
2017	600	420	250	175	130	230	97	117	250	710	275	360	5,250
2018	570	445	235	165	130	225	96	119	250	750	275	345	5,265
2019	550	420	220	153	125	215	100	121	255	750	290	350	5,230
2020	570	425	230	151	115	200	95	126	250	735	285	340	5,200
2021	555	445	230	160	113	200	85	126	245	730	285	340	5,170
2022	575	430	230	160	112	190	90	127	235	700	270	330	5,065
2023	530	415	235	162	115	190	85	136	230	680	280	335	5,130
2024[1]	500	400	235	155	111	180	75	143	210	655	270	320	5,030

[1] Preliminary.   [2] Includes sheep & lambs on feed for market and stock sheep & lambs.   *Source: Economic Research Service, U.S. Department of Agriculture (ERS-USDA)*

SHEEP AND LAMBS

Average Wholesale Price of Slaughter Lambs (Choice[2]) at San Angelo Texas   In Dollars Per Hundred Pounds (Cwt.)

Year	Jan.	Feb.	Mar.	Apr.	May	June	July	Aug.	Sept.	Oct.	Nov.	Dec.	Average
2015	155.25	148.75	137.75	137.38	147.25	147.88	140.50	148.00	150.20	139.00	148.67	139.88	145.04
2016	139.00	134.07	127.45	136.56	136.40	135.50	130.66	139.90	142.00	130.50	126.13	139.00	134.76
2017	138.10	139.25	139.38	140.50	159.00	160.88	146.00	147.00	138.88	127.50	130.17	136.00	141.89
2018	130.88	133.75	135.50	149.05	155.63	159.91	157.29	145.58	140.98	136.58	134.35	131.98	142.62
2019	132.45	134.63	141.61	152.39	156.15	159.93	160.22	153.47	151.10	150.12	151.64	151.69	149.62
2020	153.52	161.27	163.15	----	----	----	----	----	----	----	167.50	159.78	161.04
2021	158.24	163.77	172.49	184.64	202.60	238.36	264.00	258.93	247.09	239.61	231.22	230.71	215.97
2022	234.84	228.78	225.00	219.25	213.76	210.33	167.54	132.81	117.20	119.29	124.23	129.28	176.86
2023[1]	131.56	130.75	139.15	157.61	153.07	174.19	190.27	194.10	199.74	200.97	191.20	186.08	170.72

[1] Preliminary.   *Source: Economic Research Service, U.S. Department of Agriculture (ERS-USDA)*

Federally Inspected Slaughter of Sheep & Lambs in the United States   In Thousands of Head

Year	Jan.	Feb.	Mar.	Apr.	May	June	July	Aug.	Sept.	Oct.	Nov.	Dec.	Total
2015	153.0	149.9	190.0	179.1	152.7	172.8	166.8	155.5	167.4	166.3	162.6	182.3	1,998.4
2016	144.4	159.9	187.5	169.7	166.7	174.0	152.4	173.3	170.1	163.0	169.6	178.9	2,009.5
2017	161.6	144.8	177.3	156.1	157.1	165.5	146.3	171.9	153.9	165.1	167.3	170.1	1,937.0
2018	161.9	146.0	185.2	163.3	177.8	158.8	158.0	174.1	148.1	176.1	174.1	176.2	1,999.6
2019	165.7	146.1	170.3	204.5	182.0	151.6	162.6	171.3	154.7	179.8	158.9	172.9	2,020.4
2020	161.3	142.6	165.0	154.1	166.6	166.7	163.9	148.6	154.4	151.0	152.2	168.5	1,894.9
2021	140.7	142.8	188.5	189.8	153.4	158.9	153.5	147.5	153.7	162.0	171.3	165.2	1,927.3
2022	133.3	121.5	163.2	167.5	138.3	147.4	132.9	155.3	146.8	142.5	155.6	154.4	1,758.7
2023[1]	144.3	138.3	179.1	156.7	154.6	148.8	130.9	150.9	143.8	163.3	168.4	159.7	1,838.8

[1] Preliminary.   *Source: Economic Research Service, U.S. Department of Agriculture (ERS-USDA)*

Average Live Weight of Sheep & Lambs Slaughtered in the United States   In Pounds per Head

Year	Jan.	Feb.	Mar.	Apr.	May	June	July	Aug.	Sept.	Oct.	Nov.	Dec.	Average
2015	144	144	142	142	145	142	141	137	132	131	134	135	139
2016	142	145	141	138	144	138	138	132	128	130	133	135	137
2017	141	144	143	133	134	136	135	134	131	131	136	138	136
2018	144	148	142	141	140	141	138	136	137	134	136	134	139
2019	138	138	142	134	132	135	131	129	125	127	128	127	132
2020	134	136	136	128	135	135	129	127	121	121	122	126	129
2021	134	136	135	126	125	125	119	119	119	124	126	127	126
2022	132	132	135	128	137	137	132	132	129	125	126	126	131
2023[1]	126	132	129	122	126	127	122	117	118	118	118	117	123

[1] Preliminary.   *Source: Economic Research Service, U.S. Department of Agriculture (ERS-USDA)*

Federally Inspected Slaughter of Goats in the United States   In Thousands of Head

Year	Jan.	Feb.	Mar.	Apr.	May	June	July	Aug.	Sept.	Oct.	Nov.	Dec.	Total
2015	34.9	28.3	38.2	35.5	33.8	40.1	38.5	37.2	40.4	36.5	36.2	41.7	441.3
2016	31.1	32.5	38.1	32.0	35.5	39.9	35.4	41.8	40.8	38.1	38.8	44.9	448.9
2017	36.9	32.2	36.8	38.1	45.1	42.9	38.9	43.9	41.7	43.2	42.4	46.7	488.8
2018	39.4	35.3	42.4	38.6	45.8	42.6	43.0	47.7	36.8	46.0	46.4	50.1	514.1
2019	42.9	36.6	41.0	48.1	49.3	40.0	47.7	48.2	44.4	48.9	46.3	52.2	545.6
2020	43.2	37.6	44.4	36.1	39.9	43.4	44.9	41.7	44.3	46.0	45.2	51.1	517.8
2021	38.0	31.4	41.9	38.9	36.4	39.8	41.8	43.8	42.3	44.4	45.8	49.1	493.6
2022	39.9	36.1	44.0	43.8	39.0	39.6	36.4	43.0	41.9	44.2	44.1	47.0	499.0
2023[1]	41.0	38.2	47.7	41.8	44.2	43.7	39.6	44.4	41.6	47.1	47.5	51.2	528.0

[1] Preliminary.   *Source: Economic Research Service, U.S. Department of Agriculture (ERS-USDA)*

Cold Storage Holdings of Lamb and Mutton in the United States, on First of Month   In Thousands of Pounds

Year	Jan.	Feb.	Mar.	Apr.	May	June	July	Aug.	Sept.	Oct.	Nov.	Dec.
2015	33,942	35,206	36,771	34,250	37,004	38,360	35,470	39,064	41,883	41,921	40,742	44,693
2016	41,452	47,111	40,051	40,648	39,787	44,816	39,518	40,979	36,563	32,736	29,439	21,876
2017	26,140	20,361	25,694	25,792	28,603	29,859	26,177	26,770	32,383	31,415	31,594	28,977
2018	26,714	26,790	28,280	28,615	33,992	35,591	38,678	42,129	39,386	40,466	39,321	37,859
2019	36,454	38,376	35,503	31,026	40,949	38,484	40,025	43,052	46,642	41,648	37,805	34,022
2020	34,752	36,856	37,379	37,575	40,790	48,023	46,524	44,712	39,466	30,668	25,731	25,917
2021	24,911	24,470	26,833	25,342	24,753	21,896	21,489	21,010	22,051	25,607	27,155	23,487
2022	22,124	21,856	22,224	24,006	24,414	22,185	22,807	25,626	29,198	30,823	28,651	29,674
2023[1]	26,505	25,312	29,658	25,772	24,519	25,111	24,834	27,398	26,174	26,155	26,127	22,430

[1] Preliminary.   *Source: Economic Research Service, U.S. Department of Agriculture (ERS-USDA)*

Silk

Silk is a fine, tough, elastic fiber produced by caterpillars, commonly called silkworms. Silk is one of the oldest known textile fibers. Chinese tradition credits Lady Hsi-Ling-Shih, wife of the Emperor Huang Ti, with the discovery of the silkworm and the invention of the first silk reel. A group of ribbons, threads, and woven silk fragments were found in China dating back to 3000 BC. Also found, along the lower Yangzi River, were 7,000-year-old spinning tools, silk thread, and fabric fragments.

Silk filament was first woven into cloth in Ancient China. The Chinese successfully guarded this secret until 300AD, when Japan, and later India, learned the secret. In 550 AD, two Nestorian monks were sent to China to steal mulberry seeds and silkworm eggs, which they hid in their walking staffs, and then brought them back to Rome. By the 17th century, France was the silk center of the West. Unfortunately, the silkworm did not flourish in the English climate, nor has it ever flourished in the U.S.

Sericulture is the term for the raising of silkworms. The blind, flightless moth, Bombyx mori, lays more than 500 tiny eggs. After hatching, the tiny worms eat chopped mulberry leaves continuously until they are ready to spin their cocoons. After gathering the complete cocoons, the first step in silk manufacturing is to kill the insects inside the cocoons with heat. The cocoons are then placed in boiling water to loosen the gummy substance, sericin, holding the filament together. The filament is unwound, and then rewound in a process called reeling. Each cocoon's silk filament is between 600 and 900 meters long. Four different types of silk thread may be produced: organzine, crepe, tram, and thrown singles. During the last 30 years, despite the use of man-made fibers, world silk production has doubled.

Supply – World production of raw silk in 2021 fell by -9.2% yr/y to 85,415 metric tons. China is the world's largest silk producer by far, with a 54.7% share of world production in 2021. Another key producer is India, which accounts for 39.5% of the world's production.

Trade – In 2022, the world's largest exporter of silk was China, with 53.8 % of world exports. In 2022, the world's largest importers of silk were India, with 44.0% of world imports, Italy with 6.0%, and Japan with 2.5%.

World Production of Raw Silk   In Metric Tons

Year	Brazil	China	India	Iran	Japan	Korea, North	Korea, South	Kyrgyzstan	Thailand	Turkmenistan	Uzbekistan	Vietnam	World Total
2012	437	126,000	23,060	123	30	400	1	50	655	4,500	940	1,128	155,176
2013	433	130,001	23,679	123	30	400	1	50	680	4,500	980	954	159,680
2014	429	158,400	26,480	110	30	----	1	50	692	4,500	1,100	1,014	191,067
2015	600	170,000	28,708	120	30	----	1	50	698	----	1,200	450	204,643
2016	650	158,400	28,523	125	30	----	1	50	712	----	1,256	523	193,047
2017	600	142,000	30,348	120	20	----	1	50	680	----	1,200	520	178,315
2018	650	120,000	31,906	110	20	----	1	50	680	----	1,800	680	156,544
2019	469	68,600	35,261	227	16	----	1	50	700	----	2,037	795	108,806
2020[1]	377	53,359	35,820	270	16	----	1	50	520	----	2,037	969	94,081
2021[2]	373	46,700	33,770	272	10	----	1	50	503	----	2,037	1,067	85,415

[1] Preliminary.   [2] Estimate.   NA = Not avaliable.   *Source: Food and Agricultural Organization of the United Nations (FAO-UN)*

World Trade of Silk by Selected Countries   In Metric Tons

| | ------- Imports ------- | | | | | | | ------- Exports ------- | | | | | |
Year	France	Hong Kong	India	Italy	Japan	Korea, South	World Total	Brazil	China	Hong Kong	Japan	Korea, South	World Total
2013	248	----	3,609	676	570	410	24,917	----	6,690	----	18	118	8,454
2014	230	----	3,403	785	497	346	8,169	----	6,359	----	1	73	8,654
2015	185	----	3,454	733	391	313	7,644	----	6,695	----	----	17	9,193
2016	156	----	3,757	710	395	310	8,848	----	6,927	----	----	97	9,981
2017	185	----	4,003	607	456	271	8,128	----	5,936	----	----	----	10,612
2018	236	----	2,728	660	303	184	7,036	----	4,581	----	----	----	7,668
2019	131	----	3,264	911	292	138	7,701	----	4,305	----	----	----	9,121
2020	138	----	1,920	495	147	112	4,838	----	2,354	----	----	----	6,083
2021	115	----	2,031	520	185	94	5,082	----	1,863	----	----	----	6,909
2022[1]	173	----	3,866	527	219	85	8,777	----	4,535	----	----	----	8,425

[1] Preliminary.   *Source: Food and Agricultural Organization of the United Nations (FAO-UN)*

Silver

Silver is a white, lustrous metallic element that conducts heat and electricity better than any other metal. In ancient times, many silver deposits were near the earth's surface. Before 2,500 BC, silver mines were worked in Asia Minor. Around 700 BC, ancient Greeks stamped a turtle on their first silver coins. Silver assumed a key role in the U.S. monetary system in 1792 when Congress based the currency on the silver dollar. However, the U.S. discontinued the use of silver in coinage in 1965. Today Mexico is the only country that uses silver in its circulating coinage.

Silver is the most malleable and ductile of all metals, apart from gold. Silver melts at about 962 degrees Celsius and boils at about 2212 degrees Celsius. Silver is not very chemically active, although tarnishing occurs when sulfur and sulfides attack silver, forming silver sulfide on the surface of the metal. Because silver is too soft in its pure form, a hardening agent, usually copper, is mixed into the silver. Copper is usually used as the hardening agent because it does not discolor the silver. The term "sterling silver" refers to silver that contains at least 925 parts of silver per thousand (92.5%) to 75 parts of copper (7.5%).

Silver is usually found combined with other elements in minerals and ores. In the U.S., silver is mined in conjunction with lead, copper, and zinc. In the U.S., Nevada, Idaho, Alaska, and Arizona are the leading silver-producing states. For industrial purposes, silver is used for photography, electrical appliances, glass, and as an antibacterial agent for the health industry.

Silver futures and options are traded at the CME Group and the London Metal Exchange (LME). Silver futures are traded on the Tokyo Commodity Exchange (TOCOM). The CME silver futures contract calls for the delivery of 5,000 troy ounces of silver (0.999 fineness) and is priced in terms of dollars and cents per troy ounce.

Prices – CME silver futures prices (Barchart.com symbol SI) moved lower in early 2023 and posted a 1-year low of $19.83 per troy ounce in March. Silver prices were undercut when Federal Reserve Chairman Jerome Powell told Congress in March that the Fed might speed up the pace of its rate hikes due to persistent inflation. Silver prices then reversed and rallied into May when they posted a 2-year high of $26.20 per troy ounce. Silver prices rallied after the FOMC at its May meeting hinted its tightening campaign might be nearing an end. However, silver then retreated into October as the 10-year T-note yield rose to a 16-year high and the dollar index rose to a 1-year high. Also, China's economy was underperforming due to its long-standing property crisis, which curbed demand for industrial metals. Silver prices then pushed higher into year-end after Fed Chair Powell signaled in December that the Fed was done with its tightening cycle and would pivot toward cutting interest rates in 2024. Silver prices finished 2023 little changed yr/yr at $23.85 per troy ounce.

Supply – World mine production of silver in 2023 remained unchanged yr/yr at 26,000 metric tons, below the 2016 record high of 28,600. The world's largest mine producers in 2023 were Mexico with 24.6% of world production, China with 13.1%, Peru with 11.9%, Chile with 5.4%, Poland with 5.0%, Russia as well as Australia and Bolivia with 4.6%, and the US with 4.2%. US production of refined silver in 2022 fell by -23.1% yr/yr to 4,803 metric tons.

Trade – US imports of silver bullion in 2022 fell by -27.8% yr/yr to 3,782 metric tons. The bulk of US silver imports come from Mexico and Canada.

World Mine Production of Silver   In Thousands of Kilograms (Metric Ton)

Year	Australia	Bolivia	Canada[3]	Chile	China	Kazak-hstan	Mexico	Peru	Poland	Russia	Sweden	United States	World Total[2]
2014	1,847	1,398	472	1,572	3,568	475	5,766	3,768	1,384	2,360	383	1,180	27,800
2015	1,430	1,306	371	1,504	3,568	370	5,592	4,102	1,407	2,297	480	1,090	27,400
2016	1,418	1,353	385	1,501	3,754	587	5,409	4,375	1,482	2,261	515	1,150	28,600
2017	1,120	1,196	368	1,319	3,601	461	6,109	4,304	1,290	1,373	488	1,030	26,500
2018	1,254	1,191	392	1,370	3,422	369	6,049	4,160	1,264	1,400	471	934	25,900
2019	1,325	1,153	350	1,309	3,443	422	5,840	3,860	1,249	1,407	424	981	25,800
2020	1,343	1,153	325	1,576	3,405	435	5,541	2,772	1,218	1,380	401	1,080	24,100
2021	1,363	1,292	325	1,282	3,501	420	6,108	3,310	1,303	1,322	468	1,020	25,000
2022[1]	1,167	1,214		1,274	3,480	1,053	6,195	3,079	1,316	1,280		1,100	26,000
2023[2]	1,200	1,200		1,400	3,400	990	6,400	3,100	1,300	1,200		1,000	26,000

[1] Preliminary.   [2] Estimate.   [3] Shipments.   *Source: U.S. Geological Survey (USGS)*

Handy and Harman: to 05/1990; Composite: 06/1990 to date.

Average Price of Silver in New York (Handy & Harman)   In Cents Per Troy Ounce (.999 Fine)

Year	Jan.	Feb.	Mar.	Apr.	May	June	July	Aug.	Sept.	Oct.	Nov.	Dec.	Average
2014	1,988	2,087	2,072	1,974	1,934	1,989	2,092	1,974	1,837	1,716	1,597	1,629	1,907
2015	1,724	1,679	1,624	1,634	1,683	1,607	1,505	1,494	1,475	1,581	1,445	1,409	1,572
2016	1,411	1,517	1,546	1,636	1,695	1,729	1,999	1,959	1,933	1,764	1,741	1,645	1,715
2017	1,690	1,793	1,762	1,803	1,674	1,693	1,615	1,695	1,743	1,694	1,698	1,617	1,707
2018	1,713	1,658	1,647	1,665	1,649	1,654	1,572	1,499	1,427	1,460	1,435	1,477	1,571
2019	1,562	1,581	1,530	1,506	1,466	1,504	1,579	1,722	1,816	1,765	1,716	1,714	1,622
2020	1,797	1,788	1,489	1,506	1,630	1,771	2,065	2,700	2,574	2,423	2,408	2,497	2,054
2021	2,593	2,728	2,565	2,569	2,750	2,700	2,569	2,399	2,323	2,341	2,423	2,253	2,518
2022	2,313	2,352	2,528	2,452	2,187	2,151	1,910	1,968	1,889	1,943	2,102	2,333	2,177
2023	2,374	2,192	2,198	2,501	2,427	2,342	2,426	2,347	2,310	2,235	2,349	2,388	2,341

Source: American Metal Market (AMM)

Average Price of Silver in London (Spot Fix)   In Pence Per Troy Ounce (.999 Fine)

Year	Jan.	Feb.	Mar.	Apr.	May	June	July	Aug.	Sept.	Oct.	Nov.	Dec.	Average
2014	1,207	1,260	1,247	1,178	1,148	1,176	1,225	1,182	1,127	1,068	1,012	1,042	1,156
2015	1,138	1,095	1,085	1,092	1,089	1,031	968	959	962	1,031	951	940	1,028
2016	981	1,060	1,085	1,143	1,167	1,216	1,521	1,495	1,470	1,430	1,399	1,319	1,274
2017	1,368	1,436	1,427	1,426	1,296	1,322	1,243	1,308	1,309	1,283	1,283	1,206	1,326
2018	1,239	1,188	1,179	1,183	1,225	1,245	1,194	1,164	1,093	1,122	1,113	1,167	1,176
2019	1,211	1,215	1,161	1,156	1,142	1,186	1,267	1,418	1,470	1,394	1,332	1,308	1,272
2020	1,374	1,381	1,205	1,213	1,326	1,414	1,628	2,056	1,987	1,868	1,822	1,857	1,594
2021	1,901	1,967	1,851	1,856	1,953	1,926	1,860	1,739	1,693	1,711	1,802	1,693	1,829
2022	1,707	1,738	1,921	1,898	1,757	1,747	1,592	1,644	1,669	1,719	1,788	1,916	1,758
2023	1,940	1,815	1,810	2,009	1,945	1,853	1,883	1,847	1,865	1,836	1,889	1,886	1,882

Source: American Metal Market (AMM)

SILVER

Nearby Futures through Last Trading Day.

Volume of Trading of Silver Futures in Chicago   In Thousands of Contracts

Year	Jan.	Feb.	Mar.	Apr.	May	June	July	Aug.	Sept.	Oct.	Nov.	Dec.	Total
2014	915.0	1,498.8	973.7	1,388.9	883.1	1,459.4	957.2	1,216.7	990.8	1,013.7	1,435.1	964.7	13,697.2
2015	979.5	1,196.0	875.8	1,431.4	886.3	1,499.6	988.4	1,511.0	822.3	1,107.5	1,291.7	864.9	13,454.4
2016	960.5	1,694.2	1,212.5	1,974.1	1,183.6	1,828.3	1,458.7	1,939.3	1,290.1	1,327.6	2,214.4	1,135.5	18,218.7
2017	1,414.0	1,809.3	1,495.9	2,120.9	1,904.5	2,371.5	1,829.7	2,604.7	1,730.4	1,826.4	2,539.5	1,388.1	23,035.0
2018	2,186.6	2,155.7	1,842.3	2,625.8	1,702.2	2,486.3	1,582.4	2,364.1	1,648.3	1,793.5	2,299.1	1,300.6	23,987.1
2019	1,526.3	1,783.6	1,418.5	1,920.3	1,476.3	2,651.2	2,087.0	3,018.6	2,579.9	1,810.5	2,334.3	1,542.7	24,149.1
2020	2,012.7	2,515.3	2,275.1	1,357.8	1,210.9	1,846.7	2,623.6	4,633.8	2,183.5	1,645.6	2,139.7	1,682.0	26,126.8
2021	2,028.4	2,595.9	1,580.5	1,762.6	1,515.7	2,003.3	1,272.4	1,693.7	1,143.6	1,184.3	1,880.8	1,008.1	19,669.5
2022	1,289.2	1,601.7	1,440.7	1,488.9	1,204.0	1,596.9	1,206.2	1,570.9	1,358.8	1,346.7	1,849.0	1,123.7	17,076.5
2023	1,366.0	1,632.1	1,518.8	1,655.3	1,438.8	1,699.8	1,189.9	1,869.4	1,293.4	1,439.0	1,787.7	1,257.2	18,147.4

Contract size = 5,000 oz.   *Source: CME Group; Commodity Exchange (COMEX)*

Average Open Interest of Silver Futures in Chicago   In Contracts

Year	Jan.	Feb.	Mar.	Apr.	May	June	July	Aug.	Sept.	Oct.	Nov.	Dec.
2014	137,682	145,743	141,847	157,064	152,154	161,079	161,447	161,613	168,883	172,012	169,706	148,854
2015	158,200	167,554	171,411	177,026	176,403	190,678	190,121	173,457	155,598	164,457	167,660	164,215
2016	161,725	167,337	170,875	190,935	203,017	203,311	217,206	207,634	197,360	192,183	177,922	161,707
2017	172,215	198,811	194,560	220,791	202,476	203,230	207,098	192,201	187,569	190,554	198,941	199,229
2018	197,597	198,883	207,295	218,714	199,496	220,429	212,471	233,201	206,398	201,730	211,615	175,572
2019	189,481	213,207	191,157	210,647	206,496	226,614	227,668	234,590	215,936	214,545	220,824	211,176
2020	233,640	228,860	169,311	140,127	145,645	175,076	179,905	192,625	159,633	157,366	157,744	161,855
2021	171,024	177,706	157,192	165,421	177,605	181,280	152,970	150,282	142,312	141,546	147,733	139,752
2022	146,589	154,885	158,420	153,584	143,515	145,143	144,032	141,012	133,857	133,475	135,170	125,910
2023	133,240	130,734	121,785	146,282	140,648	139,277	136,532	137,333	126,455	125,728	133,995	133,982

Contract size = 5,000 oz.   *Source: CME Group; Commodity Exchange (COMEX)*

Mine Production of Recoverable Silver in the United States   In Metric Tons

Year	Arizona	Idaho	Montana	Nevada	New Mexico	Other States	Total
2014	W	W	W	326	W	858	1,180
2015	W	W	W	296	W	777	1,070
2016	87	W	W	276	W	264	1,150
2017	79	W	W	265	W	173	1,030
2018	58	W	W	247	W	164	934
2019	65	W	W	190	W	186	981
2020	71	140	W	189	W	217	1,080
2021	80	142	W	167	W	841	1,008
2022	W	W	W	184	W	838	1,022
2023[1]	W	W	W	157	W	841	998

[1] Preliminary.   W = Withheld proprietary data; included in "Other States".   *Source: U.S. Geological Survey (USGS)*

Production[2] of Refined Silver in the United States, from All Sources   In Metric Tons

Year	Jan.	Feb.	Mar.	Apr.	May	June	July	Aug.	Sept.	Oct.	Nov.	Dec.	Total
2014	431	334	348	399	450	418	458	386	506	456	430	474	5,080
2015	515	507	473	505	434	479	467	498	453	480	390	547	5,750
2016	496	476	581	507	496	429	455	575	545	503	475	481	6,020
2017	507	497	398	461	390	426	485	348	326	374	425	345	4,980
2018	480	380	317	357	458	304	395	424	383	392	382	412	4,684
2019	415	356	419	426	375	301	377	488	425	417	375	390	4,764
2020	398	322	380	470	444	606	1,076	543	746	578	643	590	6,796
2021	457	475	607	483	697	560	671	608	381	453	479	370	6,243
2022	373	303	374	477	462	430	421	356	362	354	387	505	4,804
2023[1]	408	346	410	416	558	397	401	364	411	386	421	603	5,119

[1] Preliminary.   [2] Includes U.S. mine production of recoverable silver plus imports of refined silver.   *Source: U.S. Geological Survey (USGS)*

Mine Production of Recoverable Silver in the United States   In Metric Tons

Year	Jan.	Feb.	Mar.	Apr.	May	June	July	Aug.	Sept.	Oct.	Nov.	Dec.	Total
2014	95.5	86.2	95.5	94.2	102.0	90.8	106.0	101.0	103.0	103.0	105.0	110.0	1,180.0
2015	94.2	90.1	99.5	89.8	90.6	87.5	88.0	90.8	83.6	93.9	89.2	94.2	1,090.0
2016	94.0	95.4	98.0	92.2	93.8	90.6	91.0	104.0	98.5	100.0	94.6	96.1	1,150.0
2017	98.4	84.1	94.3	87.5	82.9	85.4	84.7	83.6	74.5	82.4	87.6	82.4	1,030.0
2018	75.1	67.6	69.7	73.7	76.5	79.4	73.6	80.1	78.7	87.2	80.0	88.3	934.0
2019	80.7	71.2	75.6	84.3	84.1	84.2	86.7	83.2	85.2	75.1	87.0	77.8	975.1
2020	80.1	77.1	77.1	70.5	75.9	75.3	88.2	87.3	86.2	88.5	86.1	93.5	985.8
2021	85.4	83.2	86.1	84.2	86.8	90.2	83.3	83.0	79.0	83.4	76.9	86.2	1,007.7
2022	82.7	85.1	89.9	88.0	85.6	82.2	86.4	85.9	80.7	83.9	81.2	90.0	1,021.6
2023[1]	90.7	84.8	93.8	87.7	89.0	86.6	86.5	77.9	70.9	78.2	70.8	81.1	998.0

[1] Preliminary.   *Source: U.S. Geological Survey (USGS)*

Mine Production of Recoverable Silver in Nevada   In Metric Tons

Year	Jan.	Feb.	Mar.	Apr.	May	June	July	Aug.	Sept.	Oct.	Nov.	Dec.	Total
2014	25.0	23.9	26.5	24.9	29.2	28.3	29.1	29.1	28.3	29.9	29.6	31.1	326.0
2015	25.1	23.7	25.6	26.0	26.2	25.3	24.8	24.2	22.5	22.8	21.5	22.9	290.0
2016	22.1	20.7	21.6	22.6	22.9	22.0	23.5	24.3	23.6	23.9	24.5	25.8	276.0
2017	23.1	22.1	22.1	22.2	22.8	23.1	20.7	19.4	19.2	21.5	22.6	23.2	265.0
2018	18.8	18.4	19.6	19.4	18.9	19.2	19.9	20.3	20.4	22.8	21.7	23.7	247.0
2019	16.2	14.6	15.7	14.9	16.0	15.9	16.2	16.1	15.8	15.5	15.8	15.7	190.0
2020	12.2	12.4	12.5	12.3	12.5	12.8	12.2	12.3	12.5	12.0	12.6	12.7	165.0
2021	12.8	12.8	12.7	12.5	12.5	12.5	12.4	15.5	15.4	15.6	15.8	16.2	166.7
2022	15.4	14.6	15.8	15.4	15.9	15.8	13.7	14.2	13.9	16.1	16.2	16.6	183.6
2023[1]	14.0	13.6	14.4	13.0	13.5	13.4	12.4	12.9	12.6	12.2	12.6	12.6	157.2

[1] Preliminary.   *Source: U.S. Geological Survey (USGS)*

SILVER

U.S. Imports of Silver Bullion   In Metric Tons

Year	Jan.	Feb.	Mar.	Apr.	May	June	July	Aug.	Sept.	Oct.	Nov.	Dec.	Total
2014	335.0	248.0	252.0	305.0	348.0	327.0	352.0	285.0	403.0	353.0	325.0	364.0	3,900.0
2015	421.0	417.0	373.0	415.0	343.0	391.0	379.0	407.0	369.0	386.0	301.0	453.0	4,660.0
2016	402.0	381.0	483.0	415.0	402.0	338.0	364.0	471.0	446.0	403.0	380.0	385.0	4,870.0
2017	409.0	413.0	304.0	373.0	307.0	341.0	400.0	264.0	251.0	292.0	337.0	263.0	3,950.0
2018	405.0	312.0	247.0	283.0	381.0	225.0	321.0	344.0	304.0	305.0	302.0	324.0	3,750.0
2019	334.0	285.0	343.0	342.0	291.0	217.0	290.0	405.0	340.0	342.0	288.0	312.0	3,789.0
2020	318.0	245.0	303.0	399.0	368.0	531.0	988.0	456.0	660.0	489.0	557.0	496.0	5,810.0
2021	372.0	392.0	521.0	399.0	610.0	470.0	588.0	525.0	302.0	370.0	402.0	284.0	5,235.0
2022	290.0	218.0	284.0	389.0	376.0	348.0	335.0	270.0	281.0	270.0	306.0	415.0	3,782.0
2023[1]	317.0	261.0	316.0	328.0	469.0	310.0	314.0	286.0	340.0	308.0	350.0	522.0	4,121.0

[1] Preliminary.   Source: U.S. Geological Survey (USGS)

Commodity Exchange Warehouse of Stocks of Silver, on First of Month   In Thousands of Troy Ounces

Year	Jan. 1	Feb. 1	Mar. 1	Apr. 1	May 1	June 1	July 1	Aug. 1	Sept. 1	Oct. 1	Nov. 1	Dec. 1
2014	173,927	179,297	182,831	179,791	174,483	175,267	175,517	175,317	179,292	182,194	181,185	177,008
2015	174,359	178,053	177,163	176,650	176,310	179,287	182,384	175,671	170,562	165,009	162,813	158,954
2016	160,671	158,266	154,261	154,999	151,780	153,898	151,481	154,090	162,921	173,354	173,583	178,616
2017	183,006	180,805	186,606	190,223	196,524	201,367	208,937	215,512	217,741	218,121	225,904	235,906
2018	244,724	246,977	251,320	260,510	262,948	270,519	275,911	286,599	295,357	289,725	290,258	295,015
2019	293,901	298,005	298,844	305,542	306,750	304,961	305,683	310,364	311,900	313,603	315,503	314,008
2020	317,166	321,312	324,302	321,002	316,635	311,570	321,179	334,509	344,970	375,203	381,797	388,052
2021	396,542	397,323	393,063	370,157	361,318	353,573	350,695	355,823	362,072	361,010	353,278	352,644
2022	355,704	354,059	346,810	340,970	333,532	337,178	336,855	336,774	327,803	313,060	301,160	297,539
2023	298,992	292,082	287,247	278,264	270,974	274,068	276,513	281,696	277,734	272,832	267,930	266,191

Source: CME Group; Commodity Exchange (COMEX)

U.S. Exports of Refined Silver   In Kilograms

Year	Australia	Canada	Germany	Hong Kong	India	Italy	Japan	Mexico	Singapore	Switzerland	United Arab Emirates	United Kingdom	Total
2012	27,900	79,200	48,200	6,470	19,100	115	86,200	5,280	250,000	7,480	13,500	360,000	946,000
2013	125,000	77,300	10,900	5,930	39,300	302	18,700	2,950	76,300	16,200	2,900	7,780	409,000
2014	57,000	200,000	4,240	1,380	2,160	3,570	----	96	66,900	14,600	3,970	6,860	383,000
2015	24,100	430,000	11,900	2,810	287,000	5,880	----	1,910	15,400	15,100	5,580	4,280	818,000
2016	19,000	137,000	18,800	1,430	41,500	1,460	----	10,300	7,360	12,500	10,200	7,630	289,000
2017	8,060	56,000	8,450	569	13,100	4,880	169	7,110	6,720	8,870	13,600	6,310	157,000
2018	3,180	19,000	11,400	885	401,000	6,890	25,700	881	20,000	11,600	13,600	67,200	602,000
2019	4,240	25,500	7,220	139	130,000	4,520	16	----	13,400	3,070	16,300	1,220	220,000
2020	2,650	99,800	4,520	123	653	731	----	560	11,700	6,020	5,140	1,370	141,000
2021[1]	1,760	94,400	256	16,000	448	----	2,290	----	3,640	3,310	9,790	1,430	137,000

[1] Preliminary.   Source: U.S. Geological Survey (USGS)

U.S. Imports of Silver From Selected Countries   In Kilograms

	Ores and Concentrates				Refined Bullion						
Year	Canada	Mexico	Other Countries	Total	Canada	Korea, South	Mexico	Peru	Poland	United Kingdom	Total
2012	73,800	7,770	----	82,700	1,330,000	55,600	2,390,000	44,100	36,700	330	4,030,000
2013	26	10,700	----	10,700	1,600,000	36,300	2,010,000	38,300	55,500	20,700	3,830,000
2014	----	----	59	59	1,120,000	333,000	2,140,000	77,800	77,000	41,000	3,900,000
2015	----	----	----	253	1,920,000	159,000	1,980,000	90,300	234,000	3,000	4,660,000
2016	4,430	203	[3]	4,630	1,720,000	188,000	2,030,000	128,000	250,000	21,200	4,870,000
2017	5,940	803	90	6,840	1,170,000	126,000	1,780,000	136,000	175,000	54,600	3,950,000
2018	1,700	517	----	2,260	1,430,000	53,900	1,650,000	86,000	112,000	175	3,750,000
2019	5,460	1,750	77	7,290	1,160,000	18,900	1,980,000	31,900	186,000	1,070	3,790,000
2020	7,720	1,210	[3]	8,930	1,180,000	487,000	1,830,000	9,920	330,000	613,000	5,830,000
2021[1]	14,500	321	----	14,800	838,000	250,000	1,640,000	52,700	460,000	190,000	5,240,000

[1] Preliminary.   [3] Less than 1/2 unit..   Source: U.S. Geological Survey (USGS)

Soybean Meal

Soybean meal is produced through processing and separating soybeans into oil and meal components. If the soybeans are of particularly good quality, then the processor can get more meal weight by including more hulls in the meal while still meeting a 48% protein minimum. Soybean meal can be further processed into soy flour and isolated soy protein, but the bulk of soybean meal is used as animal feed for poultry, hogs, and cattle. Soybean meal accounts for about two-thirds of the world's high-protein animal feed, followed by cottonseed and rapeseed meal, which together account for less than 20%. Soybean meal consumption has been moving to record highs in recent years. The soybean meal marketing year begins in October and ends in September. Soybean meal futures and options are traded at the CME Group. The CME soybean meal futures contract calls for the delivery of 100 tons of soybean meal produced by conditioning ground soybeans and reducing the oil content of the conditioned product and having a minimum of 48.0% protein, minimum of 0.5% fat, maximum of 3.5% fiber, and maximum of 12.0% moisture.

Soybean crush – The term soybean "crush" refers to both to the physical processing of soybeans and to the dollar-value premium received for processing soybeans into their component products of meal and oil. The conventional model says that processing 60 pounds (one bushel) of soybeans produces 11 pounds of soybean oil, 44 pounds of 48% protein soybean meal, 3 pounds of hulls, and 1 pound of waste. The Gross Processing Margin (GPM) or crush equals (0.22 times Soybean Meal Prices in dollars per ton) + (11 times Soybean Oil prices in cents/pound) – Soybean prices in $/bushel. A higher crush value will occur when the price of the meal and oil products are strong relative to soybeans, e.g., because of supply disruptions or because of an increase in demand for the products. When the crush value is high, companies will have a strong incentive to buy raw soybeans and boost the output of the products. That supply increase should eventually bring the crush value

back into line with the long-term equilibrium.

Prices – CME soybean meal futures prices (Barchart.com symbol ZM) on the nearest-futures chart in 2022 closed the year down -19.3% yr/yr at $386 per short ton.

Supply – World soybean meal production in 2023/24 is expected to rise by +4.8% yr/yr to a new record high of 258.592 million metric tons. The world's largest soybean meal producers are expected to be China, with 30.0% of world production in 2023/24, the US with 19.0%, Brazil with 16.1%, and Argentina with 10.7%.

US production of soybean meal in 2023/24 is expected to rise by +3.2% yr/yr to 54.154 million short tons, a new record high. US soybean meal ending stocks in 2023/24 are expected to rise by +7.8% yr/yr to 400,000 short tons.

Demand – World consumption of soybean meal in 2023/24 is expected to rise by +3.2% yr/yr to 253.732 million metric tons, a new record high. China is expected to account for 30.2% of that consumption, the US for 14.1%, and the European Union for 10.6%. US consumption of soybean meal in 2022/23 is expected to rise by +2.7% yr/yr to 35.765 million metric tons, a new record high.

Trade – World exports of soybean meal in 2023/24 are expected to rise by +4.3% yr/yr to a new record high at 69.836 million metric tons. Argentina is expected to account for 34.9% of total world exports, Brazil for 29.4%, and the US for 19.9%. World imports of soybean meal in 2023/24 are expected to rise by +6.0% yr/yr to 66.697 million metric tons, below the record high of 67.153 million metric tons in 2021/22. US exports of soybean meal in 2023/24 are expected to rise by +4.3% yr/yr to 15.300 million short tons, a record high. US imports of soybean meal in 2023/24 are expected to fall by -5.1% yr/yr to 600,000 short tons.

Supply and Distribution of Soybean Meal in the United States   In Thousands of Short Tons

Crop Year Beginning Oct. 1	For Stocks Oct. 1	Pro-duction	Total Supply	Domestic	Exports	Total	Decatur 48% Protein Solvent	Decatur 44% Protein Solvent	Brazil FOB 45-46% Protein	Rotter-dam CIF
2014-15	250	45,062	45,645	32,277	13,108	45,384	368.49	406	376	403
2015-16	260	44,672	45,336	33,118	11,954	45,072	324.56	358	335	351
2016-17	264	44,787	45,400	33,420	11,580	45,000	316.88	349	322	336
2017-18	401	49,226	50,121	35,497	14,057	49,554	345.02	380	368	382
2018-19	555	48,814	50,053	36,212	13,438	49,651	308.28	340	325	329
2019-20	402	51,100	52,142	37,967	13,834	51,801	299.50	330	328	338
2020-21	341	50,565	51,691	37,674	13,675	51,350	392.31	432	447	463
2021-22[1]	341	51,814	52,810	38,959	13,540	52,499	439.81	484	476	520
2022-23[2]	311	52,493	53,436	38,402	14,664	53,065	410.00	503	500	537
2023-24[3]	371	54,154	55,125	39,425	15,300	54,725				

[1] Preliminary.   [2] Estimate.   [3] Forecast.   *Source: Economic Research Service, U.S. Department of Agriculture (ERS-USDA)*

SOYBEAN MEAL

World Production of Soybean Meal   In Thousands of Metric Tons

Crop Year	Argentina	Bolivia	Brazil	China	European Union	India	Japan	Mexico	Para-guay	Russia	Taiwan	United States	World Total
2014-15	15,700	57,400	2,600	30,142	4,500	4,000	2,850	3,365	5,050	4,100	29,282	4,750	202,067
2015-16	16,450	62,620	2,950	30,567	4,460	4,150	3,125	3,440	5,700	4,180	30,037	5,565	213,958
2016-17	17,000	68,575	3,100	27,792	4,674	4,250	3,125	3,485	5,870	4,200	30,314	5,540	222,472
2017-18	17,311	69,900	3,200	27,717	4,739	4,450	3,235	3,544	6,150	4,250	32,237	5,680	229,182
2018-19	17,645	66,685	3,300	27,867	5,530	4,625	3,325	3,450	6,625	4,450	32,901	5,780	230,860
2019-20	18,200	71,145	3,450	28,292	5,780	4,900	3,400	3,655	6,650	4,795	34,444	6,130	240,601
2020-21	19,000	72,875	3,600	28,342	5,850	5,200	3,430	3,615	6,725	4,745	34,179	6,330	244,725
2021-22[1]	19,700	69,630	3,650	27,842	6,273	5,550	3,500	3,610	6,875	4,900	35,343	6,385	244,792
2022-23[2]	20,300	73,950	2,800	26,792	6,650	5,580	2,950	3,550	6,930	4,750	34,837	6,185	245,919
2023-24[2]	20,700	76,750	3,050	26,892	6,975	5,630	3,100	3,560	7,125	4,980	35,765	6,390	253,732

Crop year beginning October 1.   [1] Preliminary.   [2] Forecast.   *Source: Foreign Agricultural Service, U.S. Department of Agriculture (FAS-USDA)*

World Exports of Soybean Meal   In Thousands of Metric Tons

Crop Year	Argen-tina	Bolivia	Brazil	Canada	China	European Union	India	Korea, South	Norway	Para-guay	Russia	United States	World Total
2014-15	28,575	1,674	14,290	212	1,595	362	1,521	112	175	2,569	505	11,891	64,638
2015-16	30,333	1,726	15,407	335	1,909	304	409	76	198	2,561	480	10,843	65,851
2016-17	31,323	1,289	13,762	291	1,111	734	2,019	100	181	2,370	323	10,505	65,405
2017-18	26,265	1,653	16,033	357	1,198	770	1,863	41	182	2,625	384	12,717	65,795
2018-19	28,833	1,638	16,095	425	932	753	2,185	71	157	2,332	374	12,141	68,052
2019-20	27,461	1,723	17,499	329	1,012	874	1,166	44	202	2,138	557	12,549	67,942
2020-21	28,325	2,117	16,577	363	1,052	847	2,395	43	196	1,916	640	12,406	69,434
2021-22[1]	26,589	2,153	20,207	406	484	762	940	51	164	1,270	700	12,283	68,830
2022-23[2]	20,751	2,100	21,342	379	795	732	1,871	61	200	1,875	750	13,303	66,960
2023-24[2]	24,400	1,800	20,500	350	1,000	700	1,000	55	210	2,000	800	13,880	69,836

Crop year beginning October 1.   [1] Preliminary.   [2] Forecast.   *Source: Foreign Agricultural Service, U.S. Department of Agriculture (FAS-USDA)*

World Imports of Soybean Meal   In Thousands of Metric Tons

Crop Year	Algeria	European Union	Indo-nesia	Iran	Japan	Korea, South	Malaysia	Mexico	Peru	Philip-pines	Thailand	Vietnam	World Total
2014-15	1,132	19,623	3,844	1,948	1,699	1,751	1,465	1,795	1,145	2,204	3,068	4,311	61,339
2015-16	1,488	19,213	4,203	1,420	1,721	2,118	1,291	2,367	1,277	2,617	2,433	5,093	63,346
2016-17	1,242	17,353	4,255	1,623	1,621	1,764	1,427	2,064	1,327	2,660	2,782	4,583	61,834
2017-18	1,511	16,992	4,486	1,544	1,728	1,846	1,609	1,875	1,353	2,886	3,191	4,847	63,693
2018-19	1,405	17,197	4,449	2,542	1,596	1,855	1,278	1,887	1,345	2,935	2,889	5,127	64,226
2019-20	1,136	16,329	5,043	618	1,858	1,992	1,414	1,818	1,414	2,906	2,854	5,336	63,323
2020-21	422	16,504	5,356	2,018	1,839	1,727	1,263	1,854	1,560	2,839	2,687	5,200	65,360
2021-22[1]	116	16,536	5,535	1,406	1,699	1,726	1,292	1,827	1,483	2,895	3,077	5,531	67,153
2022-23[2]	500	16,014	5,434	500	1,540	1,492	1,346	1,668	1,500	2,600	3,141	5,000	62,916
2023-24[2]	175	15,800	5,725	900	1,600	1,650	1,400	2,050	1,600	2,925	3,150	5,200	66,697

Crop year beginning October 1.   [1] Preliminary.   [2] Forecast.   *Source: Foreign Agricultural Service, U.S. Department of Agriculture (FAS-USDA)*

U.S. Exports of Soybean Cake & Meal by Country of Destination   In Thousands of Metric Tons

Year	Algeria	Australia	Canada	Dominican Republic	Italy	Japan	Mexico	Nether-lands	Philip-pines	Russia	Spain	Vene-zuela	Total
2014	3.0	0.1	971.6	374.4	253.0	211.0	1,593.3	1.6	1,104.3	15.0	267.0	842.6	10,281
2015	30.6	0.2	805.4	472.8	75.2	174.4	2,001.4	10.3	1,509.2	----	315.5	540.9	11,394
2016	27.3	0.5	755.9	506.2	0.4	158.4	2,130.3	1.1	1,847.2	----	0.0	311.9	10,539
2017	15.1	0.7	894.6	489.4	2.0	250.0	1,598.3	2.5	2,041.1	----	114.3	301.8	10,585
2018	----	0.6	979.9	491.5	125.1	330.7	1,760.3	4.5	2,156.7	----	354.7	182.8	12,852
2019	----	0.4	961.1	543.4	106.1	335.7	1,758.5	4.4	2,136.0	----	70.0	150.3	12,030
2020	----	30.5	1,121.2	456.5	----	226.3	1,770.4	3.0	2,429.9	----	224.3	244.4	12,748
2021	36.0	12.8	1,228.3	473.8	46.6	260.9	1,783.7	21.6	2,169.8	----	165.6	353.5	12,167
2022	----	0.5	1,229.9	481.4	0.2	288.1	1,691.1	51.0	1,977.7	----	1.6	458.6	11,776
2023[1]	34.0	0.3	1,194.4	497.0	----	209.8	1,599.7	24.9	2,448.5	----	85.9	635.7	14,101

[1] Preliminary.   *Source: Foreign Agricultural Service, U.S. Department of Agriculture (FAS-USDA)*

SOYBEAN MEAL - CBOT
Weekly Nearest Futures as of 03/28/2024

WEEKLY NEAREST FUTURES
As of 03/28/2024

Chart High 531.20 on 08/10/2022
Chart Low 255.70 on 02/26/2016

Nearby Futures through Last Trading Day.

Volume of Trading of Soybean Meal Futures in Chicago   In Thousands of Contracts

Year	Jan.	Feb.	Mar.	Apr.	May	June	July	Aug.	Sept.	Oct.	Nov.	Dec.	Total
2014	1,519.1	1,918.1	1,409.7	1,711.2	1,138.3	1,811.9	1,703.3	1,664.5	1,613.9	2,456.8	2,070.8	1,619.9	20,637.4
2015	1,558.6	1,863.0	1,627.7	2,118.1	1,655.7	2,861.9	2,181.3	2,145.4	1,942.1	2,106.6	2,147.4	2,107.4	24,315.3
2016	1,547.6	2,055.5	1,696.5	3,289.2	2,564.1	2,971.6	2,027.7	1,880.0	1,738.5	1,967.8	2,156.9	2,058.7	25,953.9
2017	1,858.5	2,157.2	1,854.4	2,379.1	1,812.1	2,591.4	2,356.1	2,184.0	1,940.2	1,781.8	2,591.0	2,490.8	25,996.4
2018	2,482.4	3,466.9	2,294.9	3,361.6	2,275.4	3,268.2	2,417.4	2,725.2	2,329.5	2,641.3	2,470.2	2,105.7	31,838.9
2019	1,838.0	2,688.8	1,871.1	2,796.4	2,667.8	2,811.9	1,992.6	2,270.8	2,086.4	2,372.2	3,009.2	2,998.4	29,403.5
2020	2,241.9	3,323.9	2,982.5	2,240.4	1,489.6	2,759.8	2,252.5	2,244.2	2,847.2	2,570.3	2,454.8	2,507.8	29,914.8
2021	1,927.9	2,111.5	1,985.1	2,619.6	1,912.4	2,775.5	1,815.0	1,835.3	1,863.9	2,487.7	3,045.5	2,396.8	26,776.2
2022	2,273.1	2,792.1	1,850.2	2,095.5	1,733.7	2,590.0	2,179.7	2,450.5	2,438.0	2,267.8	2,633.3	2,787.5	28,091.6
2023	2,245.4	2,679.0	2,975.6	2,745.3	2,865.0	3,973.5	2,778.9	3,162.2	2,700.4	4,178.8	3,867.8	2,985.2	37,157.3

Contract size = 100 tons.   Source: CME Group; Chicago Board of Trade (CBT)

Average Open Interest of Soybean Meal Futures in Chicago   In Contracts

Year	Jan.	Feb.	Mar.	Apr.	May	June	July	Aug.	Sept.	Oct.	Nov.	Dec.
2014	272,424	307,186	312,283	321,497	310,358	320,237	309,536	319,263	340,910	362,209	382,227	353,605
2015	347,095	363,919	341,479	342,428	352,507	402,421	400,309	385,239	379,936	401,497	422,294	415,217
2016	411,932	416,103	376,318	369,967	367,597	389,845	373,020	359,333	362,886	375,331	373,239	350,214
2017	356,312	382,823	366,137	377,335	379,196	399,940	353,194	370,584	381,819	380,034	403,480	409,863
2018	401,624	465,945	454,202	506,093	522,647	510,772	518,013	507,407	524,092	525,893	503,197	448,462
2019	449,026	460,468	453,985	454,723	493,991	477,710	441,846	445,260	442,094	419,844	429,417	446,866
2020	467,470	500,452	426,318	406,124	435,722	451,089	430,972	445,888	453,829	443,089	440,686	425,125
2021	412,016	412,107	410,079	412,143	410,456	399,884	370,032	361,063	362,051	426,818	443,775	388,644
2022	403,211	431,048	388,836	394,769	362,978	388,199	397,860	407,524	384,266	374,103	396,856	396,335
2023	414,465	443,461	432,165	442,218	462,632	500,843	485,655	478,600	462,905	482,999	544,472	476,900

Contract size = 100 tons.   Source: CME Group; Chicago Board of Trade (CBT)

SOYBEAN MEAL

Central IL, 44% Protein: to 10/1992; Central IL, 48% Protein: 11/1992 to date.

Average Price of Soybean Meal (48% Solvent) in Decatur Illinois   In Dollars Per Short Ton -- Bulk

Crop Year	Oct.	Nov.	Dec.	Jan.	Feb.	Mar.	Apr.	May.	June	July	Aug.	Sept.	Average
2014-15	381.50	441.39	431.73	380.03	370.38	357.83	336.61	320.23	335.03	375.71	357.85	333.62	368.49
2015-16	327.97	308.60	289.78	279.56	273.61	276.22	303.81	376.35	408.57	371.49	340.80	337.95	324.56
2016-17	323.37	322.41	321.02	332.34	334.42	320.34	305.67	307.63	300.72	326.04	301.05	307.70	316.89
2017-18	315.23	313.52	319.22	322.60	362.85	379.85	385.84	393.55	355.71	341.08	332.50	318.32	345.02
2018-19	319.15	310.62	311.70	314.92	306.83	306.38	304.26	297.52	324.75	310.77	296.92	295.57	308.28
2019-20	309.48	303.13	299.59	300.11	295.28	312.38	295.40	288.56	288.66	291.25	290.18	319.99	299.50
2020-21	367.11	387.83	396.68	439.20	427.28	410.02	413.36	421.03	378.18	365.23	358.21	343.55	392.31
2021-22	325.43	358.73	399.53	421.21	460.45	493.98	475.36	441.28	445.93	467.87	510.90	473.94	439.55
2022-23	468.68	436.75	462.85	482.40	500.53	484.40	457.25	423.58	413.46	443.15	438.80	411.07	451.91
2023-24	416.16	464.27	440.60	378.40	363.63								440.34

Source: Economic Research Service, U.S. Department of Agriculture (ERS-USDA)

Average Price of Soybean Meal (44% Solvent) in Decatur Illinois   In Dollars Per Short Ton -- Bulk

Crop Year	Oct.	Nov.	Dec.	Jan.	Feb.	Mar.	Apr.	May.	June	July	Aug.	Sept.	Average
1992-93	168.6	170.9	176.4	175.6	167.5	172.4	175.6	181.7	181.3	217.6	206.9	186.5	181.8
1993-94	180.6	195.7	192.5	185.9	184.4	182.0	176.4	191.1	183.0	168.1	165.6	162.5	180.7
1994-95	156.4	150.9	145.4	145.1	149.4	145.7	151.0	148.1	149.1	160.1	157.5	171.8	152.5
1995-96	183.4	194.1	213.6	220.5	216.7	215.7	237.9	232.3	227.9	242.3	251.1	265.5	225.1
1996-97	238.0	242.7	240.9	240.7	253.6	270.4	277.7	296.0	275.9	261.5	261.6	265.7	260.4
1997-98	216.0	231.6	214.9	193.1	182.1	165.3	152.8	150.3	157.8	173.3	135.7	126.9	175.0
1998-99	129.4	139.3	139.6	131.0	124.4	127.2	128.6	127.0	131.7	125.7	135.9	144.1	132.0
1999-00	147.2	148.1	145.4	155.0	163.6	166.6	168.1	180.1	170.2	156.8	151.4	166.9	160.0
2000-01	166.0	173.7	187.9	175.6	158.3	149.1	149.7	155.6	163.1	183.9	170.6	163.5	166.4
2001-02	157.7	157.2	146.6	Discontinued									153.8

Source: Economic Research Service, U.S. Department of Agriculture (ERS-USDA)

Soybean Oil

Soybean oil is the natural oil extracted from whole soybeans. Typically, about 19% of a soybean's weight can be extracted as crude soybean oil. The oil content of U.S. soybeans correlates directly with the temperatures and amount of sunshine during the soybean pod-filling stages. Edible products produced with soybean oil include cooking and salad oils, shortening, and margarine. Soybean oil is the most widely used cooking oil in the U.S. It accounts for 80% of margarine production and for more than 75% of total U.S. consumer vegetable fat and oil consumption. Soy oil is cholesterol-free and high in polyunsaturated fat. Soy oil is also used to produce inedible products such as paints, varnish, resins, and plastics. Of the edible vegetable oils, soy oil is the world's largest at about 32%, followed by palm oil and rapeseed oil. Soybean oil futures and options are traded at the CME Group.

Prices – CME soybean oil futures prices (Barchart.com symbol ZL) on the nearest-futures chart in 2023 closed the year down -25.0% yr/yr at 47.84 cents per pound.

Supply – World production of soybean oil in 2023/24 is expected to rise by +4.7% yr/yr to a new record high of 61.912 million metric tons. China will account for 27.7% of world soybean oil production, while the US will account for 19.4%, Brazil for 16.4%, and Argentina for 12.2%. US production of soybean oil in 2023/24 is expected to rise by +3.0% yr/yr to 12.258 million metric tons, a new record high.

Demand – World consumption of soybean oil in 2023/24 is expected to rise by +4.6% yr/yr to a new record high of 60.775 million metric tons. In 2023/24, China will account for 29.1% of world consumption, while the US will account for 20.3%, and Brazil for 13.9%. US consumption of soybean oil in 2023/24 is expected to rise by +2.2% yr/yr to 12.338 million metric tons, a new record high.

Trade – World exports of soybean oil in 2023/24 are expected to remain unchanged yr/yr to 11.525 million metric tons. US exports of soybean oil in 2023/24 are expected to fall by -20.5% yr/yr to 136,000 metric tons, a new record low.

World Production of Soybean Oil   In Thousands of Metric Tons

Crop Year	Argentina	Bolivia	Brazil	China	European Union	India	Japan	Mexico	Paraguay	Russia	Taiwan	United States	World Total
2014-15	7,687	450	7,759	13,350	2,746	1,386	414	745	725	645	352	9,706	49,362
2015-16	8,433	470	7,627	14,605	2,841	990	445	785	725	717	352	9,956	51,654
2016-17	8,395	406	7,755	15,770	2,660	1,620	467	885	725	788	360	10,035	53,947
2017-18	7,236	490	8,485	16,128	2,755	1,386	468	1,005	746	824	355	10,783	55,294
2018-19	8,044	500	8,180	15,232	2,850	1,728	485	1,135	725	834	375	10,976	56,145
2019-20	7,700	482	8,998	16,397	2,964	1,550	467	1,110	665	834	370	11,299	58,551
2020-21	7,930	575	8,951	16,666	3,002	1,800	462	1,145	630	809	365	11,350	59,314
2021-22[1]	7,664	584	9,762	15,752	2,926	1,530	519	1,171	418	862	370	11,864	59,271
2022-23[2]	5,991	575	10,226	17,024	2,717	1,854	511	1,227	627	968	366	11,897	59,121
2023-24[3]	7,011	528	10,350	17,562	2,850	1,800	516	1,196	665	1,057	375	12,258	61,912

Crop year beginning October 1.   [1] Preliminary.   [2] Forecast.   *Source: Foreign Agricultural Service, U.S. Department of Agriculture (FAS-USDA)*

World Consumption of Soybean Oil   In Thousands of Metric Tons

Crop Year	Algeria	Argentina	Bangladesh	Brazil	China	Egypt	European Union	India	Iran	Korea, South	Mexico	United States	World Total
2014-15	640	2,401	673	6,215	14,200	752	2,040	4,100	660	435	961	8,599	47,790
2015-16	690	2,840	749	6,288	15,350	885	2,285	5,250	660	440	1,050	9,145	52,113
2016-17	715	3,085	935	6,570	16,350	660	1,955	5,150	650	450	1,140	9,010	53,536
2017-18	725	2,981	1,090	6,940	16,500	735	1,935	4,670	600	470	1,180	9,698	54,412
2018-19	755	2,624	1,254	7,165	15,850	910	2,255	4,750	615	505	1,240	10,376	55,303
2019-20	785	2,175	1,264	7,750	17,000	915	2,380	5,125	650	535	1,285	10,122	57,094
2020-21	825	2,042	1,205	7,950	17,600	1,075	2,430	4,950	725	580	1,290	10,574	58,486
2021-22[1]	860	2,660	1,100	7,450	16,700	980	2,305	5,825	800	590	1,300	11,262	59,224
2022-23[2]	820	2,050	960	7,675	16,750	660	2,355	5,400	775	545	1,305	12,072	58,084
2023-24[3]	865	2,250	990	8,425	17,700	785	2,505	5,100	800	540	1,335	12,338	60,775

Crop year beginning October 1.   [1] Preliminary.   [2] Forecast.   *Source: Foreign Agricultural Service, U.S. Department of Agriculture (FAS-USDA)*

SOYBEAN OIL

World Exports of Soybean Oil   In Thousands of Metric Tons

Crop Year	Argentina	Bolivia	Brazil	Canada	European Union	Malaysia	Para-guay	Russia	South Africa	Ukraine	United States	Vietnam	World Total
2014-15	5,094	392	1,510	118	1,010	170	699	423	86	136	914	104	11,191
2015-16	5,698	444	1,550	151	915	148	709	431	66	152	1,017	17	11,834
2016-17	5,387	249	1,241	175	973	137	680	529	52	177	1,159	35	11,452
2017-18	4,164	380	1,511	157	1,074	124	691	568	56	192	1,108	41	10,780
2018-19	5,268	393	1,085	169	977	120	652	572	40	334	880	10	11,473
2019-20	5,404	408	1,156	144	909	118	631	641	61	338	1,287	10	12,384
2020-21	6,137	525	1,262	119	1,065	108	562	561	74	232	786	76	12,611
2021-22[1]	4,873	523	2,409	153	970	120	371	550	62	235	803	59	12,322
2022-23[2]	4,137	500	2,686	138	914	106	510	720	75	277	171	75	11,525
2023-24[3]	4,750	430	1,850	170	900	115	600	750	80	345	136	100	11,525

Crop year beginning October 1.   [1] Preliminary.   [2] Forecast.   *Source: Foreign Agricultural Service, U.S. Department of Agriculture (FAS-USDA)*

World Imports of Soybean Oil   In Thousands of Metric Tons

Crop Year	Algeria	Bangla-desh	China	Colom-bia	Egypt	European Union	India	Iran	Korea, South	Peru	Morocco	Vene-zuela	World Total
2014-15	631	508	773	304	498	253	2,815	421	257	432	395	461	10,147
2015-16	720	647	586	372	688	325	4,269	299	250	465	382	206	11,740
2016-17	674	826	711	352	246	306	3,534	291	306	497	449	268	11,254
2017-18	776	859	481	344	227	288	2,984	127	276	502	503	205	9,965
2018-19	899	1,036	783	343	299	419	3,000	346	328	536	539	116	11,119
2019-20	693	696	998	387	375	483	3,626	79	402	573	521	160	11,543
2020-21	632	676	1,221	285	428	493	3,251	570	407	507	594	193	11,794
2021-22[1]	604	689	291	317	215	459	4,231	372	392	529	471	209	11,537
2022-23[2]	500	681	409	242	198	621	3,968	75	353	525	525	135	10,653
2023-24[3]	580	725	400	350	235	400	3,300	275	350	550	575	160	10,773

Crop year beginning October 1.   [1] Preliminary.   [2] Forecast.   *Source: Foreign Agricultural Service, U.S. Department of Agriculture (FAS-USDA)*

Supply and Distribution of Soybean Oil in the United States   In Millions of Pounds

Crop Year	Beginning Stocks Oct. 1	Pro-duction	Imports	Exports	Domestic Total	Biodiesel	Food & Other	Exports	Total Disap-pearance	Ending Stocks
2014-15	1,165	21,399	264	22,828	18,959	5,039	13,922	2,014	20,973	1,855
2015-16	1,855	21,950	288	24,093	20,163	5,670	14,493	2,243	22,406	1,687
2016-17	1,687	22,123	319	24,129	19,862	6,200	13,662	2,556	22,418	1,711
2017-18	1,711	23,772	335	25,819	21,380	7,134	14,247	2,443	23,823	1,995
2018-19	1,995	24,197	398	26,590	22,873	7,863	15,010	1,941	24,814	1,775
2019-20	1,775	24,911	320	27,007	22,317	8,658	13,660	2,837	25,154	1,853
2020-21	1,853	25,023	302	27,177	23,314	8,920	14,394	1,731	25,046	2,131
2021-22	2,131	26,155	303	28,589	24,827	10,379	14,449	1,771	26,598	1,991
2022-23[1]	1,991	26,227	376	28,594	26,614	12,491	14,123	378	26,992	1,602
2023-24[2]	1,602	27,025	450	29,077	27,200	13,000	14,200	300	27,500	1,577

Crop year beginning October 1.   [1] Preliminary .   [2] Forecast.   *Source: Economic Research Service, U.S. Department of Agriculture (ERS-USDA)*

U.S. Exports of Soybean Oil[2], by Country of Destination   In Metric Tons

Crop Year	Canada	Ecuador	Ethiopia	Haiti	India	Mexico	Morocco	Pakistan	Panama	Peru	Türkiye	Vene-zuela	Total
2013-14	31,755	13	390	1,576	22	189,759	29,702	0	4,139	42,121	----	18,988	852,074
2014-15	28,755	11	450	649	39	245,163	64,658	9,190	5,434	104,743	----	61,920	913,704
2015-16	15,647	6	----	2,687	51	235,554	50,521	11,165	6,054	75,355	----	50,055	1,017,200
2016-17	22,658	8	----	1,307	139	265,028	30,432	7,137	7,055	2	75	32,437	1,159,229
2017-18	21,213	9	----	----	105	166,657	11,798	----	7,723	93,051	17	48,345	1,108,143
2018-19	21,805	47	----	28	118	125,570	----	10,893	3,157	11,959	----	1,007	880,161
2019-20	31,613	31	----	2,645	103	128,945	82,900	12,975	2,304	26,437	----	59,037	1,286,703
2020-21	40,162	40	----	1,758	36,090	64,051	----	----	2,204	50,856	----	60,021	785,941
2021-22	72,237	----	----	5,536	192,637	91,764	----	----	2,067	18	----	59,118	803,276
2022-23[1]	53,960	2	----	16	36	47,672	----	----	2,002	51	----	5,259	171,492

Crop year beginning October 1.   [1] Preliminary.   [2] Crude & Refined oil combined as such.   *Source: Foreign Agricultural Service, U.S. Department of Agriculture (FAS-USDA)*

CORN OIL
Quarterly Cash as of 03/20/2024

QUARTERLY CASH
As of 03/20/2024
Chart High 88.50 on 05/07/2008
Chart Low 5.10 on 10/31/1940

Cents / lb.

Crude Wet Milling: Decatur: to 06/1985; Chicago: 07/1985 to date.

Production of Soybean Oil in the United States   In Millions of Pounds

Crop Year	Oct.	Nov.	Dec.	Jan.	Feb.	Mar.	Apr.	May	June	July	Aug.	Sept.	Total
2014-15	----	----	----	----	----	----	----	----	----	----	----	----	21,399
2015-16	1,962.9	1,901.9	1,929.0	1,864.9	1,795.9	1,943.5	1,840.3	1,876.2	1,787.2	1,789.4	1,642.5	1,616.6	21,950
2016-17	2,028.5	1,961.3	1,950.2	1,977.2	1,752.5	1,857.1	1,731.7	1,839.3	1,735.6	1,801.4	1,762.2	1,701.8	22,099
2017-18	2,016.9	1,977.0	2,015.3	1,995.6	1,889.8	2,079.1	1,964.9	1,966.5	1,936.9	2,043.3	1,945.0	1,936.9	23,767
2018-19	2,134.6	2,060.6	2,135.4	2,115.8	1,899.2	2,094.4	1,989.1	1,916.0	1,811.5	2,090.2	2,048.2	1,900.7	24,196
2019-20	2,150.0	1,999.6	2,110.9	2,154.4	1,999.5	2,201.1	2,099.5	2,057.6	2,035.3	2,123.2	2,012.8	1,967.6	24,912
2020-21	2,282.5	2,206.8	2,233.5	2,308.8	1,924.7	2,222.1	1,991.9	2,043.1	1,908.6	1,972.7	1,989.7	1,938.2	25,023
2021-22	2,347.6	2,235.4	2,324.2	2,277.4	2,064.2	2,277.5	2,143.1	2,158.8	2,068.6	2,158.0	2,095.6	1,993.0	26,143
2022-23	2,338.1	2,200.0	2,195.4	2,252.3	2,091.2	2,339.6	2,236.3	2,228.4	2,074.9	2,180.0	2,014.2	2,077.1	26,227
2023-24[1]	2,375.7	2,324.7	2,376.2	2,288.6									28,095

[1] Preliminary.   Source: Economic Research Service, U.S. Department of Agriculture (ERS-USDA)

U.S. Exports of Soybean Oil (Crude and Refined)   In Millions of Pounds

Year	Jan.	Feb.	Mar.	Apr.	May	June	July	Aug.	Sept.	Oct.	Nov.	Dec.	Total
2014	267.2	277.5	195.5	92.6	45.8	79.7	198.0	119.0	75.6	159.2	231.4	236.2	1,978
2015	256.7	220.5	233.5	125.7	72.5	157.4	64.6	154.6	101.9	179.6	233.0	320.7	2,121
2016	168.0	114.6	233.1	126.2	103.8	158.4	281.8	93.1	227.2	241.0	236.7	235.5	2,219
2017	259.4	238.7	294.5	258.3	161.2	138.2	199.4	163.1	130.2	212.8	132.0	173.0	2,361
2018	180.7	181.1	201.5	212.3	431.4	228.3	174.7	197.6	121.7	146.1	215.8	170.5	2,462
2019	221.1	91.7	271.8	148.2	205.7	95.4	174.3	165.6	48.5	252.5	247.4	184.3	2,106
2020	125.1	396.2	320.8	230.2	357.8	167.7	164.6	201.7	180.1	184.0	177.2	235.0	2,740
2021	327.8	256.0	155.8	129.6	71.2	91.6	35.7	24.6	33.9	57.2	253.6	182.7	1,620
2022	284.4	235.6	266.4	168.1	73.9	73.2	118.2	57.1	45.1	23.1	23.4	34.7	1,403
2023[1]	15.4	26.0	12.8	60.6	50.2	39.9	37.2	26.1	28.0	13.0	13.8	12.7	336

[1] Preliminary.   Source: Bureau of the Census, U.S. Department of Commerce

SOYBEAN OIL

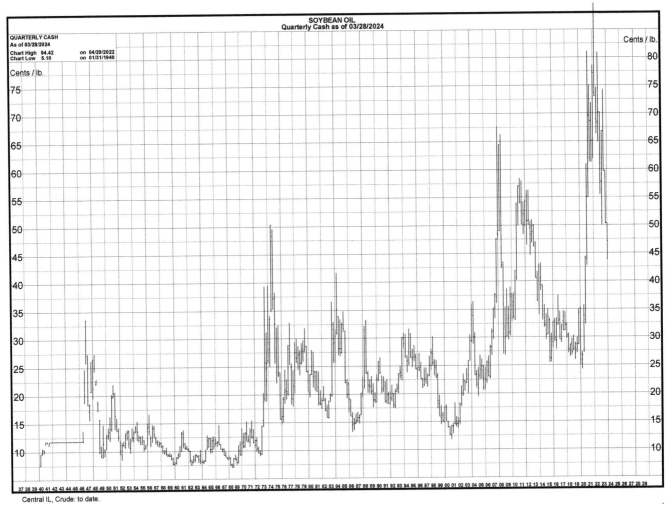

Stocks of Soybean Oil (Crude and Refined) at Factories and Warehouses in the U.S.   In Millions of Pounds

Crop Year	Oct. 1	Nov. 1	Dec. 1	Jan. 1	Feb. 1	Mar. 1	Apr. 1	May 1	June 1	July 1	Aug. 1	Sept. 1
2014-15	1,165.0	----	----	----	----	----	----	----	----	----	----	----
2015-16	1,854.8	1,940.4	1,965.9	1,972.5	2,110.8	2,280.2	2,324.9	2,420.0	2,466.1	2,424.1	2,214.3	1,985.7
2016-17	1,686.8	1,795.3	1,780.7	1,872.3	2,112.6	2,205.9	2,353.4	2,233.8	2,269.3	2,142.9	2,000.6	1,810.3
2017-18	1,711.0	1,626.2	1,690.6	1,950.7	2,239.8	2,425.4	2,444.5	2,688.8	2,374.1	2,304.8	2,383.6	2,214.8
2018-19	1,995.4	2,047.6	1,900.3	1,945.8	2,004.7	2,149.1	2,232.9	2,257.6	2,018.9	2,014.4	2,039.5	1,805.6
2019-20	1,775.3	1,821.0	1,880.4	2,134.1	2,355.9	2,376.8	2,326.6	2,600.6	2,445.4	2,270.8	2,123.2	1,945.1
2020-21	1,852.7	1,968.0	2,117.1	2,110.8	2,306.0	2,306.0	2,245.3	2,177.6	2,147.0	2,100.7	2,070.1	2,183.4
2021-22	2,131.2	2,386.3	2,406.0	2,465.9	2,499.9	2,566.1	2,433.7	2,424.2	2,384.4	2,315.5	2,228.2	2,103.7
2022-23	1,991.1	2,093.6	2,112.3	2,306.1	2,356.4	2,363.8	2,387.5	2,539.7	2,386.2	2,203.0	2,136.2	1,772.4
2023-24[1]	1,607.1	1,501.6	1,599.1	1,823.8								

On First of Month.   [1] Preliminary.   *Source: Economic Research Service, U.S. Department of Agriculture (ERS-USDA)*

Average Price of Crude Domestic Soybean Oil (in Tank Cars) F.O.B. Decatur   In Cents Per Pound

Crop Year	Oct.	Nov.	Dec.	Jan.	Feb.	Mar.	Apr.	May	June	July	Aug.	Sept.	Average
2014-15	34.10	33.45	32.56	32.33	31.57	30.89	31.13	32.65	33.73	31.54	28.87	26.43	31.60
2015-16	27.14	26.42	29.72	28.89	29.79	30.86	32.45	30.76	30.35	28.75	31.21	31.99	29.86
2016-17	33.86	34.52	35.57	33.58	32.00	30.86	29.57	30.60	30.74	32.82	33.17	33.28	32.55
2017-18	32.35	33.43	32.27	31.61	30.63	30.28	29.70	29.40	28.30	27.21	27.60	27.73	30.04
2018-19	28.89	27.49	28.14	28.44	29.58	28.62	27.86	26.93	28.24	27.68	28.41	28.81	28.26
2019-20	30.14	30.62	32.27	33.04	30.26	27.04	25.69	25.27	26.61	28.71	32.13	34.20	29.67
2020-21	33.91	37.79	40.85	44.31	48.37	56.00	62.88	74.75	74.75	72.93	70.01	65.93	56.87
2021-22	70.42	66.46	63.69	65.70	70.91	76.41	83.85	87.39	80.30	67.75	72.34	70.63	72.99
2022-23	72.67	79.18	68.14	66.00	63.24	58.83	55.48	52.49	60.01	70.89	70.97	65.23	65.26
2023-24[1]	56.60	53.39	52.33	49.10	47.33								52.86

[1] Preliminary.   *Source: Economic Research Service, U.S. Department of Agriculture (ERS-USDA)*

SOYBEAN OIL - CBOT
Weekly Nearest Futures as of 03/28/2024

WEEKLY NEAREST FUTURES
As of 03/28/2024
Chart High 91.40 on 04/29/2022
Chart Low 24.64 on 04/27/2020

Nearby Futures through Last Trading Day.

Volume of Trading of Soybean Oil Futures in Chicago   In Thousands of Contracts

Year	Jan.	Feb.	Mar.	Apr.	May	June	July	Aug.	Sept.	Oct.	Nov.	Dec.	Total
2014	1,752.1	2,531.9	1,657.5	2,058.5	1,450.2	2,199.9	1,869.4	1,775.4	1,768.9	2,199.9	2,386.3	2,119.2	23,769
2015	1,985.3	2,348.9	1,683.5	2,527.2	2,042.6	3,236.5	2,358.9	2,412.7	2,190.7	2,519.5	2,667.4	2,924.0	28,897
2016	1,713.2	2,310.9	1,866.0	3,407.3	2,476.6	2,822.7	2,165.3	2,385.6	2,143.2	2,393.9	3,144.7	2,599.8	29,429
2017	2,001.6	2,737.6	2,421.6	2,639.6	1,882.5	2,952.5	2,467.6	2,721.7	2,451.3	2,125.4	3,128.1	2,702.9	30,232
2018	2,127.2	3,503.1	2,185.3	3,210.2	2,097.3	3,481.7	2,175.5	2,203.0	2,375.4	2,312.2	3,139.3	2,455.6	31,266
2019	1,975.0	2,890.1	2,023.1	3,012.6	2,405.6	2,762.6	2,231.8	2,651.3	2,527.4	2,759.0	3,242.7	3,213.2	31,694
2020	2,779.1	3,334.0	3,258.7	2,946.4	1,772.2	2,785.2	2,494.8	2,316.3	2,775.4	2,674.1	2,927.0	2,898.7	32,962
2021	2,635.6	2,586.4	3,100.9	3,056.4	2,282.9	3,949.3	2,278.4	2,464.7	2,472.5	2,437.2	2,813.6	2,597.6	32,675
2022	2,261.2	2,618.7	2,036.8	2,258.5	1,770.1	2,796.9	2,343.0	2,638.3	2,663.6	2,429.1	3,003.4	3,232.4	30,052
2023	2,310.0	2,941.5	3,218.7	2,690.6	3,294.1	4,279.5	3,076.9	2,859.9	3,009.8	3,230.0	3,776.2	2,812.7	37,500

Contract size = 60,000 lbs.   Source: CME Group; Chicago Board of Trade (CBT)

Average Open Interest of Soybean Oil Futures in Chicago   In Contracts

Year	Jan.	Feb.	Mar.	Apr.	May	June	July	Aug.	Sept.	Oct.	Nov.	Dec.
2014	364,056	339,211	302,398	326,545	313,757	333,690	325,337	347,395	373,086	391,486	395,330	365,382
2015	370,576	385,819	367,203	383,502	394,773	410,233	372,932	390,494	413,151	420,227	448,872	412,621
2016	404,388	411,898	415,026	457,557	404,143	389,896	361,443	378,813	399,625	443,699	446,001	407,110
2017	391,377	386,979	385,217	423,805	412,142	414,657	398,719	416,321	438,439	440,831	469,775	467,647
2018	480,781	499,421	496,026	519,883	514,763	505,702	512,638	534,033	575,527	539,882	556,831	497,905
2019	492,981	507,871	480,036	483,650	535,026	472,080	435,429	466,176	498,072	496,430	536,756	521,342
2020	537,082	509,621	460,552	460,731	468,485	464,880	440,128	448,159	473,386	469,071	484,466	482,763
2021	469,161	490,193	491,039	501,302	501,643	523,176	468,859	431,637	389,345	408,042	425,305	391,390
2022	398,767	419,837	350,206	371,203	370,679	385,154	369,909	395,214	400,811	409,532	448,350	406,558
2023	389,193	449,805	455,510	478,317	513,388	513,151	488,644	477,044	455,176	442,780	505,432	476,988

Contract size = 60,000 lbs.   Source: CME Group; Chicago Board of Trade (CBT)

Soybeans

Soybean is the common name for the annual leguminous plant and its seed. The soybean is a member of the oilseed family and is not considered a grain. The soybean seeds are contained in pods, and are nearly spherical. The seeds are usually light yellow. The seeds contain 20% oil and 40% protein. Soybeans were an ancient food crop in China, Japan, and Korea and were only introduced to the U.S. in the early 1800s. Today, soybeans are the second-largest crop produced in the U.S. behind corn. Soybean production in the U.S. is concentrated in the Midwest and the lower Mississippi Valley. Soybean crops in the U.S. are planted in May or June and are harvested in autumn. Soybean plants usually reach maturity 100-150 days after planting, depending on growing conditions.

Soybeans are used to produce a wide variety of food products. The key value of soybeans lies in the relatively high protein content, which makes it an excellent source of protein without many of the negative factors of animal meat. Popular soy-based food products include whole soybeans (roasted for snacks or used in sauces, stews and soups), soy oil for cooking and baking, soy flour, protein concentrates, isolated soy protein (which contains up to 92% protein), soy milk and baby formula (as an alternative to dairy products), soy yogurt, soy cheese, soy nut butter, soy sprouts, tofu and tofu products (soybean curd), soy sauce (which is produced by a fermentation process), and meat alternatives (hamburgers, breakfast sausage, etc.).

The primary market for soybean futures is at the CME Group. The CME's soybean contract calls for the delivery of 5,000 bushels of No. 2 yellow soybeans (at contract par), No. 1 yellow soybeans (at 6 cents per bushel above the contract price), or No. 3 yellow soybeans (at 6 cents under the contract price). Soybean futures are also traded at exchanges in Brazil, Argentina, China, and Tokyo.

Prices – CME soybean futures prices (Barchart. com symbol ZS) traded sideways to lower into Q2 of 2023 and posted a 2-year low of $12.71 per bushel in May. A decline in soybean demand from China, the world's largest soybean importer, undercut prices as it switched to wheat-based hog feed in an effort to reduce its reliance on soybean imports. Also, China's post-pandemic economic recovery stalled in the first half of 2023, curbing its demand for commodities, including soybeans. Ramped-up soybean production in Brazil, the world's largest soybean producer, weighed on prices after Conab, Brazil's national crop forecasting agency, raised its 2022/23 soybean production estimate in May to a record 155.66 MMT, up +21% yr/yr. In the May WASDE report, the USDA signaled ample global soybean supplies as it projected stronger-than-expected global 2023/24 soybean production and larger-than-expected global 2023/24 soybean ending stocks. Soybeans then reversed and rallied more than $3 a bushel to a 1-1/2 year high of $16.16 per bushel in July. The USDA in June reported in its 2023 acreage report that US farmers planted 83.5 million acres of soybeans, well below estimates of 87.7 million acres and the fewest in 3 years. Soybean prices tumbled into October when they fell to a 2-year low of $12.50 per bushel. Soybean prices fell on ample US soybean supplies and a jump in soybean exports from Brazil. The USDA's Q3 Grain stocks report in September showed U.S soybean stocks as of September 1 at 268 million bushels, above estimates of 244 million bushels. Also, Brazil's September soybean exports soared +60% yr/yr to 6.398 MMT. Soybean prices recovered slightly toward the year's end as dry weather in Brazil threatened its 2023/24 soybean crop as an El Nino weather pattern limited rainfall in its soybean growing areas. Also, the USDA, in the December WASDE report, cut its 2023/24 global soybean production and ending stock estimates. The recovery in soybean prices was limited after Conab forecasted a record 2023/24 Brazil soybean crop of 160.2 MMT in December. Soybean prices finished 2023 down sharply by -14.8% yr/yr at $12.94 per bushel.

Supply – World soybean production during the 2023/24 marketing year (Sep-Aug) is expected to rise by +6.3% yr/yr to a record 398.976 million metric tons. World soybean production has risen sharply from only 80 million metric tons back in the 1980s. The world's largest soybean producers in 2023/24 are expected to be Brazil with 39.4% of world production, the US with 28.4%, Argentina with 12.5%, China with 5.2%, and India with 2.8%.

The US soybean production in 2023/24 is expected to fall by -2.5% yr/yr to 113.344 million metric tons. US farmers are expected to harvest 82.791 million acres of soybeans in 2023/24, down -4.1% yr/yr. The average yield in 2023/24 is expected to rise by +0.6% yr/yr to 49.9 bushels per acre, below the 2016/17 record high of 51.9 bushels per acre. US ending stocks for the 2023/24 marketing year are expected to rise by +6.0% yr/yr to 280.0 million bushels.

Demand – Total US soybean distribution in 2023/24 is expected to fall by -2.9% yr/yr to 4.178 billion bushels. The distribution tables for US soybeans for the 2023/24 marketing year show that 55.0% of US soybean usage will go for crushed oil and meal products, 42.0% for exports, and 3.0% for seed, feed, and residual. The quantity of US soybeans that will go for crushing is expected to rise by +4.0% yr/yr in 2023/24 to 2.300 billion bushels. The world soybean crush in 2023/24 is expected to rise by +4.9% yr/yr to a new record high of 329.396 million metric tons.

Trade – World exports of soybeans in 2023/24 are expected to fall by -0.4% to 170.941 million metric tons. The world's largest soybean exporters in 2023/24 are expected to be Brazil with 58.2% of world exports, the US with 27.9%, Paraguay with 3.7%, and both Argentina and Canada with 2.7%. Brazil's soybean exports have more than doubled in the past decade. US soybean exports in 2022/23 fell by -2.6% yr/yr to 1.995 billion bushels.

World soybean imports in 2023/24 are expected to rise by +2.1% yr/yr to 168.348 million metric tons. The world's largest importers of soybeans in 2023/24 are expected to be China with 60.6% of world imports, the European Union with 8.2%, Mexico with 3.8%, and Thailand with 2.3%. China's imports in 2023/24 are expected to rise by +1.1% yr/yr to 102.000 million metric tons.

World Production of Soybeans   In Thousands of Metric Tons

Crop Year[4]	Argen- tina	Bolivia	Brazil	Canada	China	European Union	India	Para- guay	Russia	Ukraine	United States	Uruguay	World Total
2014-15	61,450	3,106	97,100	6,045	12,686	1,839	8,711	8,404	2,362	3,900	106,905	3,394	321,514
2015-16	58,800	3,205	95,700	6,456	12,367	2,332	6,929	9,295	2,707	3,932	106,869	2,256	316,137
2016-17	55,000	2,671	114,900	6,597	13,596	2,465	10,992	10,032	3,134	4,286	116,931	3,688	350,878
2017-18	37,800	2,942	123,400	7,717	15,283	2,619	8,350	9,906	3,621	3,985	120,065	1,427	343,822
2018-19	55,300	2,991	120,500	7,417	15,967	2,737	10,930	8,844	4,027	4,831	120,515	3,045	363,513
2019-20	48,800	2,829	128,500	6,145	18,092	2,711	9,300	10,553	4,359	4,499	96,644	2,330	341,430
2020-21	46,200	3,318	139,500	6,359	19,602	2,600	10,456	9,642	4,307	3,000	114,749	1,997	369,222
2021-22[1]	43,900	3,457	130,500	6,224	16,395	2,833	11,889	4,183	4,760	3,800	121,504	3,233	360,410
2022-23[2]	25,000	3,650	160,000	6,543	20,284	2,549	12,411	9,750	5,996	4,100	116,221	700	375,397
2023-24[3]	50,000	3,400	157,000	6,981	20,840	3,060	11,000	10,300	6,800	5,200	113,344	2,900	398,976

[1] Preliminary.   [2] Estimate.   [3] Forecast.   [4] Spilt year includes Northern Hemisphere crops harvested in the late months of the first year shown combined with Southern Hemisphere crops harvested in the early months of the following year.   *Sources: Foreign Agricultural Service, U.S. Department of Agriculture (FAS-USDA)*

World Crushings of Soybeans   In Thousands of Metric Tons

Crop Year	Argen- tina	Bolivia	Brazil	China	European Union	India	Japan	Mexico	Para- guay	Russia	Taiwan	United States	World Total
2014-15	40,235	2,450	40,435	74,500	14,450	7,700	2,150	4,175	3,900	3,600	1,980	50,975	265,279
2015-16	43,267	2,550	39,747	81,500	14,950	5,500	2,283	4,400	3,900	4,000	1,980	51,335	275,825
2016-17	43,309	2,150	40,411	88,000	14,000	9,000	2,392	4,800	3,900	4,400	1,995	51,742	288,463
2017-18	36,933	2,600	44,205	90,000	14,500	7,700	2,430	5,450	3,950	4,600	2,000	55,926	295,660
2018-19	40,567	2,650	42,527	85,000	15,000	9,600	2,470	6,150	3,820	4,650	2,100	56,935	299,194
2019-20	38,770	2,550	46,742	91,500	15,600	8,600	2,385	6,000	3,500	4,650	2,080	58,910	312,656
2020-21	40,162	3,050	46,500	93,000	15,800	10,000	2,300	6,200	3,325	4,500	2,050	58,257	316,036
2021-22[1]	38,825	3,100	50,712	87,900	15,400	8,500	2,640	6,350	2,200	4,800	2,075	59,980	314,503
2022-23[2]	30,318	3,050	53,096	95,000	14,300	10,300	2,600	6,650	3,300	5,400	2,050	60,199	313,912
2023-24[3]	35,500	2,800	53,750	98,000	15,000	10,000	2,625	6,480	3,500	5,900	2,100	62,596	329,396

[1] Preliminary.   [2] Estimate.   [3] Forecast.   *Sources: Foreign Agricultural Service, U.S. Department of Agriculture (FAS-USDA)*

World Exports of Soybeans   In Thousands of Metric Tons

Crop Year	Argen- tina	Bolivia	Brazil	Canada	China	India	Para- guay	Russia	Serbia	Ukraine	United States	Uruguay	World Total
2014-15	10,575	8	50,612	3,855	143	234	4,576	313	136	2,422	50,136	3,113	126,442
2015-16	9,922	91	54,383	4,236	114	134	5,400	456	68	2,369	52,869	2,221	132,837
2016-17	7,025	13	63,137	4,592	114	268	6,124	375	186	2,904	58,964	3,199	147,736
2017-18	2,132	8	76,136	4,925	134	217	6,029	891	28	2,757	58,071	1,354	153,403
2018-19	9,104	13	74,887	5,239	116	165	4,901	797	143	2,531	47,721	2,967	149,222
2019-20	10,004	17	92,135	3,909	90	80	6,619	1,298	252	2,633	45,800	2,148	165,821
2020-21	5,195	111	81,650	4,554	70	32	6,330	1,355	143	1,466	61,664	1,774	165,182
2021-22[1]	2,861	588	79,063	4,284	102	61	2,273	700	15	1,385	58,571	3,049	154,218
2022-23[2]	4,185	445	95,505	4,240	90	22	6,300	1,450	10	3,097	54,208	800	171,663
2023-24[3]	4,600	100	99,500	4,550	100	50	6,300	1,250	225	2,900	47,763	2,400	170,941

[1] Preliminary.   [2] Estimate.   [3] Forecast.   *Sources: Foreign Agricultural Service, U.S. Department of Agriculture (FAS-USDA)*

World Imports of Soybeans   In Thousands of Metric Tons

Crop Year	China	Egypt	European Union	Indo- nesia	Japan	Korea, South	Mexico	Russia	Taiwan	Thailand	Türkiye	Vietnam	World Total
2014-15	78,350	1,947	13,914	2,006	3,004	1,246	3,819	1,986	2,520	2,411	2,256	1,707	124,283
2015-16	83,230	1,575	15,120	2,274	3,186	1,249	4,126	2,336	2,476	2,798	2,376	1,362	133,904
2016-17	93,495	2,114	12,742	2,649	3,175	1,286	4,479	2,221	2,566	3,078	2,273	1,646	145,215
2017-18	94,093	3,255	13,915	2,484	3,256	1,256	5,134	2,237	2,666	2,482	2,872	1,806	154,154
2018-19	82,537	3,657	14,346	2,623	3,314	1,373	5,933	2,162	2,614	3,155	2,411	1,644	145,966
2019-20	98,532	4,956	15,017	2,636	3,325	1,291	5,743	2,047	2,708	3,831	3,148	1,903	165,294
2020-21	99,740	3,687	14,786	2,617	3,085	1,336	6,101	2,042	2,615	4,157	2,745	1,951	165,495
2021-22[1]	90,501	4,566	14,548	2,307	3,455	1,268	5,956	1,850	2,622	3,243	2,949	1,839	155,517
2022-23[2]	100,846	1,992	13,199	2,308	3,332	1,337	6,442	1,620	2,700	3,238	2,888	2,050	164,841
2023-24[3]	102,000	3,100	13,800	2,650	3,500	1,400	6,400	1,100	2,750	3,900	3,100	2,600	168,348

[1] Preliminary.   [2] Estimate.   [3] Forecast.   *Sources: Foreign Agricultural Service, U.S. Department of Agriculture (FAS-USDA)*

SOYBEANS

World Ending Stocks of Soybeans   In Thousands of Metric Tons

Crop Year	Argentina	Bolivia	Brazil	Canada	China	European Union	India	Japan	Paraguay	Türkiye	Ukraine	United States	World Total
2014-15	27,069	433	24,498	458	17,060	857	200	212	463	401	166	5,188	79,305
2015-16	27,156	635	23,803	380	16,643	1,559	338	255	389	328	113	5,354	79,550
2016-17	26,996	783	32,632	355	20,120	974	880	212	334	314	151	8,208	95,703
2017-18	23,734	745	33,031	651	22,562	1,111	339	200	192	515	76	11,923	99,995
2018-19	28,890	751	33,342	700	18,350	1,387	428	177	253	255	223	25,176	114,621
2019-20	26,650	717	20,419	621	24,484	1,721	338	239	572	428	92	14,657	95,528
2020-21	25,060	526	29,579	294	30,856	1,560	120	166	477	247	102	6,994	100,263
2021-22[1]	23,903	121	27,598	428	29,250	1,680	1,493	243	177	222	967	7,468	98,028
2022-23[2]	17,209	103	35,351	646	33,790	1,317	1,584	178	212	235	221	7,190	101,870
2023-24[3]	25,959	280	35,801	677	36,030	1,287	634	226	582	275	353	7,621	114,596

[1] Preliminary.   [2] Estimate.   [3] Forecast.   *Sources: Foreign Agricultural Service, U.S. Department of Agriculture (FAS-USDA)*

Supply and Distribution of Soybeans in the United States   In Millions of Bushels

Crop Year Beginning Sept. 1	Stocks, Sept. 1 Farms	Stocks, Sept. 1 Mills, Elevators[3]	Total Stocks	Production	Imports	Total Supply	Crushings	Seed, Feed & Residual Use	Exports	Total Distribution	Ending Stocks
2014-15	21.3	70.7	92.0	3,927	33	4,052	1,873	146	1,842	3,862	191
2015-16	49.7	140.9	190.6	3,926	24	4,140	1,886	115	1,942	3,944	197
2016-17	41.6	155.2	196.7	4,296	22	4,515	1,901	146	2,166	4,214	302
2017-18	87.9	213.7	301.6	4,412	22	4,735	2,055	108	2,134	4,297	438
2018-19	101.0	337.1	438.1	4,428	14	4,880	2,092	127	1,752	3,971	909
2019-20	265.0	644.1	909.1	3,552	15	4,476	2,165	108	1,679	3,952	525
2020-21	141.2	383.3	524.5	4,216	20	4,761	2,141	97	2,266	4,504	257
2021-22	68.1	188.9	257.0	4,464	16	4,737	2,204	107	2,152	4,463	274
2022-23[1]	62.9	211.5	274.4	4,270	25	4,569	2,212	101	1,992	4,305	264
2023-24[2]	72.0	192.2	264.2	4,165	30	4,459	2,300	124	1,755	4,179	280

[1] Preliminary.   [2] Estimate.   [3] Also warehouses.   *Source: Economic Research Service, U.S. Department of Agriculture (ERS-USDA)*

Salient Statistics & Official Crop Production Reports of Soybeans in the United States   In Millions of Bushels

Crop Year	Planted 1,000 Acres	Acreage Harvested 1,000 Acres	Yield Per Acre (Bu.)	Farm Price ($/Bu.)	Farm Value (Million Dollars)	Yield of Oil (Lbs. Per Bushel Crushed)	Yield of Meal (Lbs. Per Bushel Crushed)	Crop Production Reports In Thousands of Bushels Aug. 1	Sept. 1	Oct. 1	Nov. 1	Dec. 1	Final
2014-15	83,276	82,591	47.5	10.00	39,475	----	----	3,815,679	3,913,079	3,926,812	3,958,272	----	3,927,090
2015-16	82,650	81,732	48.0	9.18	35,192	----	----	3,916,448	3,935,277	3,887,721	3,981,337	----	3,926,339
2016-17	83,453	82,706	51.9	9.46	40,695	----	----	4,060,188	4,200,985	4,268,884	4,361,023	----	4,296,496
2017-18	90,162	89,542	49.3	9.38	41,309	----	----	4,381,053	4,431,043	4,430,621	4,425,279	----	4,411,633
2018-19	89,167	87,594	50.6	8.43	37,558	----	----	4,585,916	4,693,135	4,689,628	4,599,530	----	4,428,150
2019-20	76,100	74,939	47.4	8.52	30,526	----	----	3,680,217	3,632,651	3,550,281	3,549,977	----	3,551,908
2020-21	83,354	82,603	51.0	12.30	45,732	----	----	4,424,800	4,312,819	4,267,890	4,170,262	----	4,216,302
2021-22	87,195	86,292	51.4	14.23	59,140	----	----	4,338,853	4,373,927	4,448,043	4,424,942	----	4,464,492
2022-23[1]	87,450	86,174	49.6	14.41	60,696	----	----	4,530,561	4,378,194	4,312,949	4,345,524	----	4,270,381
2023-24[2]	83,600	82,356	50.6	12.78	52,815	----	----	4,205,450	4,146,036	4,104,379	4,129,449	----	4,164,677

[1] Preliminary.   [2] Forecast.   NA = Not available.   *Source: National Agricultural Statistics Service, U.S. Department of Agriculture (NASS-USDA)*

Stocks of Soybeans in the United States   In Thousands of Bushels

Year	On Farms Mar. 1	On Farms June 1	On Farms Sept. 1	On Farms Dec. 1	Off Farms Mar. 1	Off Farms June 1	Off Farms Sept. 1	Off Farms Dec. 1	Total Stocks Mar. 1	Total Stocks June 1	Total Stocks Sept. 1	Total Stocks Dec. 1
2014	381,900	109,100	21,325	1,218,000	611,928	295,945	70,666	1,309,744	993,828	405,045	91,991	2,527,744
2015	609,200	246,300	49,700	1,308,500	717,399	380,768	140,910	1,405,577	1,326,599	627,068	190,610	2,714,077
2016	727,500	281,300	41,560	1,335,000	803,406	590,481	155,169	1,563,379	1,530,906	871,781	196,729	2,898,379
2017	668,500	332,500	87,900	1,485,000	1,070,433	633,356	213,695	1,675,679	1,738,933	965,856	301,595	3,160,679
2018	855,000	377,000	101,000	1,935,000	1,254,303	842,329	337,105	1,810,824	2,109,303	1,219,329	438,105	3,745,824
2019	1,270,000	730,000	265,000	1,519,500	1,457,069	1,053,080	644,052	1,732,988	2,727,069	1,783,080	909,052	3,252,488
2020	1,011,500	633,000	141,200	1,308,500	1,243,382	748,394	383,341	1,638,240	2,254,882	1,381,394	524,541	2,946,740
2021	594,000	219,900	68,100	1,522,000	967,684	549,140	188,879	1,614,524	1,561,684	769,040	256,979	3,136,524
2022	750,000	331,400	62,930	1,477,000	1,181,817	636,125	211,464	1,544,152	1,931,817	967,525	274,394	3,021,152
2023[1]	749,500	322,800	72,000	1,453,000	937,132	473,588	192,184	1,547,719	1,686,632	796,388	264,184	3,000,719

[1] Preliminary.   *Source: National Agricultural Statistics Service, U.S. Department of Agriculture (NASS-USDA)*

Commercial Stocks of Soybeans in the United States, on First of Month   In Millions of Bushels

Year	Jan.	Feb.	Mar.	Apr.	May	June	July	Aug.	Sept.	Oct.	Nov.	Dec.
2005	26.5	21.5	19.5	16.0	14.8	12.1	11.5	8.8	5.4	17.0	36.7	36.1
2006	36.8	30.2	26.1	25.7	17.6	20.5	14.6	14.5	14.5	19.0	40.1	43.7
2007	42.0	36.5	37.3	34.3	29.7	27.4	26.6	24.6	25.5	32.0	54.0	61.3
2008	51.1	45.5	41.8	36.3	28.2	25.6	19.2	14.8	11.4	19.6	40.5	46.1
2009	44.6	36.8	27.0	15.6	13.9	11.8	10.0	5.8	5.9	24.7	40.5	44.3
2010	30.0	28.5	20.1	22.3	10.8	8.0	8.2	4.5	3.3	19.2	45.0	32.0
2011	32.6	23.2	16.0	11.3	10.2	5.9	6.2	5.7	4.6	9.8	49.4	50.7
2012	42.7	34.8	29.9	28.5	27.1	23.8	16.6	10.4	5.2	18.8	41.6	33.8
2013	25.2	20.3	16.1	10.0	6.4	6.6	4.1	2.9	2.1	27.2	36.9	35.5
2014	30.7	20.4	15.5	12.2	7.0	5.1	5.2	2.3	----	----	----	----

This report was discontinued as of August 26, 2014.   *Source: Livestock Division, U.S. Department of Agriculture (LD-USDA)*

Production of Soybeans for Beans in the United States, by State   In Millions of Bushels

Crop Year	Arkansas	Illinois	Indiana	Iowa	Kentucky	Michigan	Minnesota	Mississippi	Missouri	Nebraska	Ohio	Tennessee	Total
2014-15	158.4	547.1	301.9	498.3	83.1	86.7	301.7	113.9	259.9	287.8	246.2	74.1	3,927.1
2015-16	155.3	544.3	275.0	553.7	88.7	99.0	377.5	104.4	181.0	305.7	237.0	79.1	3,926.3
2016-17	145.2	593.0	323.7	566.4	89.0	104.0	389.5	97.0	271.5	314.2	263.8	73.4	4,296.5
2017-18	178.5	611.9	320.8	566.6	102.8	96.5	384.3	115.0	292.5	326.0	252.0	83.0	4,411.6
2018-19	162.1	666.8	342.7	550.5	98.4	109.7	374.9	118.3	257.2	324.2	281.1	76.0	4,428.2
2019-20	127.9	532.4	273.4	501.6	77.7	69.7	297.9	81.5	230.5	283.1	209.2	64.4	3,551.9
2020-21	144.2	615.0	338.1	506.0	101.2	105.1	369.0	111.2	296.3	299.3	270.6	81.0	4,216.3
2021-22	156.0	683.2	338.4	631.9	103.0	109.1	356.3	117.2	276.9	350.9	278.2	76.0	4,464.5
2022-23	163.3	677.3	335.2	586.8	98.9	105.3	369.5	123.7	274.8	276.9	281.9	77.8	4,270.4
2023-24[1]	159.3	648.9	334.3	573.0	100.1	93.4	349.4	119.3	265.0	266.8	274.3	80.1	4,164.7

[1] Preliminary.   *Source: Agricultural Statistics Board, U.S. Department of Agriculture (ASB-USDA)*

U. S. Exports of Soybeans   In Millions of Bushels

Crop Year	Sept.	Oct.	Nov.	Dec.	Jan.	Feb.	Mar.	Apr.	May	June	July	Aug.	Total
2014-15	77.9	329.9	405.3	301.7	257.5	166.6	94.1	49.7	44.0	34.4	39.7	42.6	1,843.5
2015-16	86.4	369.0	336.3	250.1	218.1	207.5	95.8	52.3	33.8	36.8	98.5	152.6	1,937.1
2016-17	138.5	415.9	378.6	291.2	272.9	162.4	114.7	89.4	53.3	66.0	83.2	113.1	2,179.3
2017-18	170.6	347.1	332.1	237.2	211.9	154.9	119.1	79.7	110.0	119.7	126.0	123.8	2,131.9
2018-19	119.0	205.2	186.3	150.9	177.5	168.3	136.3	88.2	94.1	117.4	135.3	181.3	1,759.8
2019-20	143.4	216.7	250.9	208.0	195.6	101.4	94.5	79.5	72.3	66.1	81.5	173.1	1,683.0
2020-21	263.9	425.5	408.0	397.7	324.6	167.6	84.4	50.9	46.6	34.0	34.8	48.1	2,286.0
2021-22	77.2	395.2	389.0	291.9	235.0	139.4	117.1	134.5	88.7	83.5	85.4	12.2	2,049.1
2022-23	78.0	359.6	355.4	304.9	314.7	197.6	115.3	93.9	36.3	30.6	46.9	62.6	1,995.8
2023-24[1]	90.8	348.4	274.4	177.4									

[1] Preliminary.   *Source: Economic Research Service, U.S. Department of Agriculture (ERS-USDA)*

Soybean Crushed (Factory Consumption) in the United States   In Millions of Bushels

Crop Year	Sept.	Oct.	Nov.	Dec.	Jan.	Feb.	Mar.	Apr.	May	June	July	Aug.	Total
2014-15	----	687.3	----	----	480.2	----	----	522.7	----	151.6	155.8	144.6	1,873.5
2015-16	134.6	170.1	165.8	167.0	160.5	154.6	166.4	158.2	160.9	154.1	153.5	140.6	1,886.3
2016-17	138.3	175.9	170.7	169.0	170.4	151.0	160.0	149.8	158.0	148.2	155.6	151.6	1,898.5
2017-18	145.4	175.9	173.3	176.3	174.7	165.0	182.2	171.6	172.5	169.6	178.9	169.9	2,055.3
2018-19	169.3	183.6	178.1	183.8	183.1	162.8	179.4	171.5	165.4	157.6	179.5	177.3	2,091.4
2019-20	162.3	187.2	174.6	184.7	188.8	175.3	192.2	183.4	179.6	177.3	184.5	174.7	2,164.6
2020-21	171.1	196.6	191.0	193.1	196.5	164.4	188.2	169.9	173.5	161.7	166.3	168.3	2,140.6
2021-22	164.2	196.9	190.6	198.2	194.3	174.4	192.9	180.9	180.9	174.1	181.3	175.1	2,203.8
2022-23	167.6	196.7	189.6	187.4	191.1	176.9	198.0	187.0	189.3	174.6	184.8	169.0	2,212.0
2023-24[1]	174.8	201.4	200.1										2,305.2

[1] Preliminary.   *Source: Economic Research Service, U.S. Department of Agriculture (ERS-USDA)*

SOYBEANS

SOYBEANS - CBOT
Weekly Nearest Futures as of 03/28/2024

WEEKLY NEAREST FUTURES
As of 03/28/2024
Chart High 1784.00 on 06/09/2022
Chart Low   780.50   on 05/13/2019

Nearby Futures through Last Trading Day.

Volume of Trading of Soybean Futures in Chicago   In Thousands of Contracts

Year	Jan.	Feb.	Mar.	Apr.	May	June	July	Aug.	Sept.	Oct.	Nov.	Dec.	Total
2014	3,692.7	5,090.5	3,613.9	4,191.9	2,914.6	3,929.4	3,765.7	2,967.5	3,672.1	7,261.6	3,661.2	4,408.2	49,169
2015	3,570.3	4,867.3	4,011.2	5,029.8	3,422.5	6,284.1	4,425.8	4,256.8	3,693.6	6,251.6	3,314.6	4,967.4	54,095
2016	3,846.1	5,203.8	4,455.3	8,380.0	6,211.8	7,135.0	4,779.8	3,432.5	3,373.1	5,936.7	4,085.1	4,891.6	61,731
2017	3,760.7	5,197.1	3,837.0	4,612.5	3,781.0	5,251.6	5,287.5	4,132.3	3,629.0	6,075.2	3,726.4	5,213.9	54,504
2018	4,066.9	6,799.5	5,116.2	6,789.1	4,592.8	6,603.2	3,794.3	4,088.9	3,151.9	5,831.5	3,439.6	4,264.6	58,539
2019	3,245.1	4,692.8	3,351.5	4,801.5	5,096.2	5,784.5	3,820.6	3,771.8	3,445.3	6,913.2	3,416.5	4,994.4	53,333
2020	3,719.9	5,513.0	5,500.2	4,709.2	3,341.8	5,562.8	4,115.7	4,432.9	5,669.6	7,545.1	4,910.5	6,102.4	61,123
2021	5,400.5	5,117.7	4,344.1	5,529.0	3,784.8	5,600.8	3,301.1	3,328.9	3,105.6	5,388.3	3,633.7	4,790.0	53,324
2022	4,262.6	6,391.4	3,777.9	4,230.3	3,328.8	4,914.0	3,395.2	3,567.3	4,123.4	5,495.6	3,523.4	4,707.7	51,718
2023	4,138.8	5,391.4	5,317.4	5,280.9	4,816.4	6,880.9	4,534.1	4,358.1	4,649.7	6,985.5	4,965.8	5,108.1	62,427

Contract size = 5,000 bu.   Source: CME Group; Chicago Board of Trade (CBT)

Average Open Interest of Soybean Futures in Chicago   In Contracts

Year	Jan.	Feb.	Mar.	Apr.	May	June	July	Aug.	Sept.	Oct.	Nov.	Dec.
2014	589,906	675,981	649,898	645,604	601,103	616,406	622,020	642,043	724,924	766,218	664,485	668,492
2015	644,320	698,627	708,314	746,322	698,151	722,449	663,522	653,707	675,762	701,419	673,127	681,902
2016	674,273	721,934	723,375	824,649	840,893	859,598	747,309	668,100	636,957	657,062	642,826	709,587
2017	681,161	736,942	691,919	729,828	654,509	695,963	648,861	645,305	666,063	723,614	712,476	747,181
2018	762,139	781,574	846,901	923,139	879,489	893,661	838,433	797,279	846,361	839,514	743,667	723,335
2019	683,830	706,877	693,239	767,901	763,593	734,373	658,702	636,025	675,040	736,987	753,829	807,431
2020	767,124	846,942	790,798	826,659	849,949	865,514	830,455	839,763	938,439	1,010,657	928,015	935,198
2021	935,234	905,458	857,961	873,376	806,462	773,210	680,714	667,051	667,573	712,214	658,746	654,705
2022	701,786	823,877	75,114	746,268	714,941	731,705	606,032	593,948	650,416	670,484	614,213	623,336
2023	644,070	712,743	702,942	682,484	635,815	649,389	647,444	657,182	755,199	807,209	732,613	688,756

Contract size = 5,000 bu.   Source: CME Group; Chicago Board of Trade (CBT)

SOYBEANS
Quarterly Cash as of 03/28/2024

QUARTERLY CASH
As of 03/28/2024
Chart High 1790.00 on 07/20/2012
Chart Low 74.25 on 10/07/1940

Cents / Bushel

Cents / Bushel

Chicago #2 yellow: to 12/1956; Chicago #1 yellow: 01/1957 to date.

Average Price Received by Farmers for Soybeans in the United States   In Dollars Per Bushel

Crop Year	Sept.	Oct.	Nov.	Dec.	Jan.	Feb.	Mar.	Apr.	May	June	July	Aug.	Average
2014-15	10.90	9.97	10.20	10.30	10.30	9.91	9.85	9.69	9.58	9.58	9.95	9.71	10.00
2015-16	9.05	8.81	8.68	8.76	8.71	8.51	8.56	9.01	9.76	10.20	10.20	9.93	9.18
2016-17	9.41	9.30	9.47	9.64	9.71	9.86	9.69	9.33	9.29	9.10	9.42	9.24	9.46
2017-18	9.35	9.18	9.22	9.30	9.30	9.50	9.81	9.85	9.84	9.55	9.08	8.59	9.38
2018-19	8.78	8.59	8.36	8.56	8.64	8.52	8.52	8.28	8.02	8.31	8.38	8.22	8.43
2019-20	8.35	8.60	8.59	8.70	8.84	8.60	8.47	8.35	8.28	8.34	8.50	8.66	8.52
2020-21	9.24	9.63	10.30	10.60	10.90	12.70	13.20	13.90	14.80	14.50	14.10	13.70	12.30
2021-22	12.20	11.90	12.10	12.50	12.90	14.70	15.40	15.80	16.10	16.40	15.50	15.30	14.23
2022-23	14.20	13.50	14.00	14.40	14.50	15.10	14.90	14.90	14.40	14.20	14.70	14.10	14.41
2023-24[1]	13.20	12.70	13.00	13.10	12.80	11.90							12.78

[1] Preliminary.   *Source: Economic Research Service, U.S. Department of Agriculture (ERS-USDA)*

Average Cash Price of No. 1 Yellow Soybeans at Illinois Processor   In Cents Per Bushel

Crop Year	Sept.	Oct.	Nov.	Dec.	Jan.	Feb.	Mar.	Apr.	May	June	July	Aug.	Average
2001-02	469	430	441	438	437	440	464	471	492	519	575	567	479
2002-03	579	541	575	566	570	590	580	611	640	635	601	589	590
2003-04	639	729	763	772	823	872	975	992	958	890	809	641	822
2004-05	562	519	534	545	539	544	628	622	644	701	703	639	598
2005-06	565	553	574	592	576	575	569	562	581	576	577	542	570
2006-07	535	580	661	657	683	735	730	718	749	792	801	804	704
2007-08	907	944	1,032	1,123	1,216	1,335	1,312	1,292	1,324	1,499	1,516	1,288	1,232
2008-09	1,140	903	893	868	991	938	917	1,025	1,166	1,237	1,096	1,136	1,026
2009-10	1,012	978	1,009	1,033	984	944	949	975	955	955	1,030	1,066	991
2010-11[1]	1,065	1,148	1,252	1,311	1,378	1,386	1,350	1,364	1,368	1,382	1,384	1,381	1,314

[1] Preliminary.   *Source: Economic Research Service, U.S. Department of Agriculture (ERS-USDA)*

SOYBEANS

Weekly Outstanding Export Sales and Cumulative Exports of U.S. Soybeans In Thousands of Metric Tons

Marketing Year 2022/2023 Week Ending	Weekly Exports	Accumulated Exports	Net Sales	Outstanding Sales	Marketing Year 2023/2024 Week Ending	Weekly Exports	Accumulated Exports	Net Sales	Outstanding Sales
Sep 01, 2022	46,592	46,592	3,947,846	24,391,430	Sep 07, 2023	408,378	408,378	703,862	16,236,512
Sep 08, 2022	375,918	422,510	842,989	24,858,501	Sep 14, 2023	488,549	896,927	377,728	16,125,691
Sep 15, 2022	522,535	945,045	446,364	24,782,330	Sep 21, 2023	492,094	1,389,021	621,043	16,254,640
Sep 22, 2022	269,208	1,214,253	1,003,017	25,516,139	Sep 28, 2023	671,463	2,060,484	808,486	16,391,663
Sep 29, 2022	574,130	1,788,383	733,706	25,675,715	Oct 05, 2023	1,351,103	3,411,587	972,001	16,012,561
Oct 06, 2022	887,954	2,676,337	724,405	25,512,166	Oct 12, 2023	1,990,481	5,402,068	1,371,875	15,393,955
Oct 13, 2022	1,813,956	4,490,293	2,252,726	25,950,936	Oct 19, 2023	2,361,294	7,763,362	1,354,858	14,387,519
Oct 20, 2022	2,748,615	7,238,908	1,026,381	24,228,702	Oct 26, 2023	1,991,366	9,754,728	1,010,009	13,406,162
Oct 27, 2022	2,582,254	9,821,162	760,621	22,407,069	Nov 02, 2023	2,236,528	11,991,256	1,079,531	12,249,165
Nov 03, 2022	2,612,700	12,433,862	655,229	20,449,598	Nov 09, 2023	1,926,189	13,917,445	3,853,236	14,176,212
Nov 10, 2022	2,012,048	14,445,910	2,960,367	21,397,917	Nov 16, 2023	1,592,337	15,509,782	893,261	13,477,136
Nov 17, 2022	2,352,673	16,798,583	610,215	19,655,459	Nov 23, 2023	1,477,736	16,987,518	1,895,319	13,894,719
Nov 24, 2022	2,046,570	18,845,153	623,363	18,232,252	Nov 30, 2023	1,222,129	18,209,647	1,404,386	14,076,976
Dec 01, 2022	2,247,641	21,092,794	1,716,221	17,700,832	Dec 07, 2023	1,074,729	19,284,376	999,003	14,001,250
Dec 08, 2022	1,846,026	22,938,820	2,943,405	18,798,211	Dec 14, 2023	1,329,059	20,613,435	1,989,428	14,661,619
Dec 15, 2022	1,918,361	24,857,181	664,844	17,544,694	Dec 21, 2023	1,081,669	21,695,104	849,585	14,429,535
Dec 22, 2022	1,705,947	26,563,128	563,257	16,402,004	Dec 28, 2023	1,000,620	22,695,724	201,646	13,630,561
Dec 29, 2022	1,478,296	28,041,424	720,997	15,644,705	Jan 04, 2024	862,277	23,558,001	280,398	13,048,682
Jan 05, 2023	1,620,720	29,662,144	717,415	14,741,400	Jan 11, 2024	1,670,720	25,228,721	781,277	12,159,239
Jan 12, 2023	2,066,189	31,728,333	986,196	13,661,407	Jan 18, 2024	1,117,528	26,346,249	560,869	11,602,580
Jan 19, 2023	1,900,328	33,628,661	1,145,723	12,906,802	Jan 25, 2024	949,899	27,296,148	164,475	10,817,156
Jan 26, 2023	1,891,607	35,520,268	667,954	11,683,149	Feb 01, 2024	1,520,302	28,816,450	206,314	9,503,168
Feb 02, 2023	1,743,076	37,194,948	373,892	10,313,965	Feb 08, 2024	1,383,688	30,200,138	283,977	8,403,457
Feb 09, 2023	1,846,566	39,041,514	456,124	8,923,523	Feb 15, 2024	1,197,121	31,397,259	55,919	7,262,255
Feb 16, 2023	1,614,468	40,655,982	419,672	7,728,727	Feb 22, 2024	958,949	32,356,208	16,989	6,320,295
Feb 23, 2023	828,577	41,484,559	308,407	7,208,557	Feb 29, 2024	1,418,034	33,774,242	613,534	5,515,795
Mar 02, 2023	580,955	42,065,514	-23,234	6,604,368	Mar 07, 2024	947,858	34,722,100	375,980	4,943,917
Mar 09, 2023	763,872	42,829,386	655,424	6,495,920	Mar 14, 2024	773,126	35,495,226	494,028	4,664,819
Mar 16, 2023	639,261	43,468,647	87,459	5,944,118	Mar 21, 2024				
Mar 23, 2023	1,038,967	44,507,614	348,177	5,253,328	Mar 28, 2024				
Mar 30, 2023	558,688	45,066,302	155,292	4,849,932	Apr 04, 2024				
Apr 06, 2023	533,909	45,600,211	214,472	4,530,495	Apr 11, 2024				
Apr 13, 2023	454,479	46,054,690	-28,190	4,047,826	Apr 18, 2024				
Apr 20, 2023	453,708	46,508,398	311,252	3,905,370	Apr 25, 2024				
Apr 27, 2023	561,235	47,069,633	289,730	3,633,865	May 02, 2024				
May 04, 2023	353,296	47,422,929	4,447	3,285,016	May 09, 2024				
May 11, 2023	189,143	47,612,072	16,950	3,112,823	May 16, 2024				
May 18, 2023	287,327	47,899,399	115,042	2,940,538	May 23, 2024				
May 25, 2023	230,813	48,130,212	123,396	2,833,121	May 30, 2024				
Jun 01, 2023	247,583	48,377,795	207,236	2,792,774	Jun 06, 2024				
Jun 08, 2023	141,312	48,519,107	478,368	3,129,830	Jun 13, 2024				
Jun 15, 2023	387,766	48,906,873	457,543	3,199,607	Jun 20, 2024				
Jun 22, 2023	191,027	49,097,900	227,375	3,235,955	Jun 27, 2024				
Jun 29, 2023	209,424	49,307,324	131,156	3,157,687	Jul 04, 2024				
Jul 06, 2023	297,643	49,604,967	39,616	2,899,660	Jul 11, 2024				
Jul 13, 2023	174,777	49,779,744	61,660	2,786,543	Jul 18, 2024				
Jul 20, 2023	326,513	50,106,257	145,402	2,605,432	Jul 25, 2024				
Jul 27, 2023	288,397	50,394,654	34,106	2,351,141	Aug 01, 2024				
Aug 03, 2023	322,972	50,717,626	348,393	2,376,562	Aug 08, 2024				
Aug 10, 2023	292,071	51,009,697	-48,540	2,035,951	Aug 15, 2024				
Aug 17, 2023	363,895	51,373,592	279,686	1,951,742	Aug 22, 2024				
Aug 24, 2023	319,738	51,693,330	-50,665	1,581,339	Aug 29, 2024				
Aug 31, 2023	514,196	52,207,526	155,603	1,222,746	Aug 31, 2023				

Source: Foreign Agricultural Service, U.S. Department of Agriculture (FAS-USDA)

Stock Index Futures - U.S.

A stock index simply represents a basket of underlying stocks. Indexes can be either price-weighted or capitalization-weighted. In a price-weighted index, such as the Dow Jones Industrial Average, the individual stock prices are simply added up and then divided by a divisor, meaning that stocks with higher prices have a higher weighting in the index value. In a capitalization-weighted index, such as the Standard and Poor's 500 index, the weighting of each stock corresponds to the size of the company as determined by its capitalization (i.e., the total dollar value of its stock). Stock indexes cover a variety of different sectors. For example, the Dow Jones Industrial Average contains 30 blue-chip stocks that represent the industrial sector. The S&P 500 index includes 500 of the largest blue-chip U.S. companies. The NYSE index includes all the stocks that are traded at the New York Stock Exchange. The Nasdaq 100 includes the largest 100 companies that are traded on the Nasdaq Exchange. The most popular U.S. stock index futures contract is the E-mini S&P 500 futures contract, which is traded at the CME Group.

Prices – The S&P 500 index (Barchart.com symbol $SPX) posted its low for 2023 of 4682.11 in January on concerns that a strong labor market and sticky inflation pressures would force the Federal Reserve to keep interest rates "higher for longer." The US January unemployment rate fell to a 54-year low of 3.4%, and January CPI rose +6.4% yr/yr, well above the Fed's 2% target. However, stocks trended higher for the remainder of the year as expectations for easier Fed policy bolstered the outlook for an economic soft landing. As a result, the S&P 500 finished 2023 up by +24% yr/yr at 4769.83.

Stocks found support from the February FOMC meeting, even after the FOMC raised the federal funds target range by +25 basis points to 4.50%-4.75%, because Fed Chair Powell said the "disinflation process has

started," suggesting the Fed's aggressive tightening cycle was nearing an end.

Stocks came under brief pressure in March on US banking concerns after the collapse of Silicon Valley Bank, the largest US banking failure since the 2008 financial crisis. However, the crisis was short-lived because contagion was limited to a few regional banks with large commercial property market exposure and because the US government stepped in to provide broader deposit insurance coverage to protect bank customers.

Stocks continued higher into July as the FOMC paused raising interest rates at the June policy meeting. Also, the US economy remained strong and inflation pressures eased. Specifically, May nonfarm payrolls showed a large increase of +303,000, and the June CPI eased to a 3-year low of +3.0% yr/yr.

Stocks ratcheted lower into late October because of concern that US economic strength would prompt the Fed to keep interest rates higher for longer. The FOMC, at its September meeting, indicated it might tighten monetary policy further and scaled back its estimates for interest rate cuts in 2024. Bond yields soared and undercut stocks as the 10-year T-note yield posted a 16-year high of 5.02% in October.

However, stock prices stabilized in early November and continued higher into year-end as the US economy remained resilient, boosting corporate earnings. Q3 GDP expanded at a 4.9% (q/q annualized) pace, the strongest in 2 years.

Stocks rallied late in the year when the FOMC, at its December meeting, signaled an end to its rate hike cycle and pivoted toward an easing of policy when it projected 75 basis points of interest rate cuts for 2024.

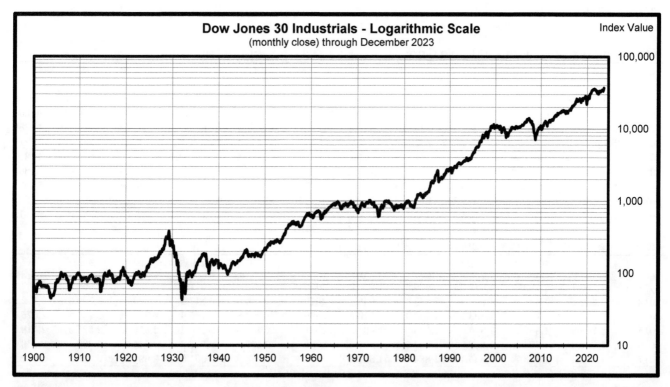

Dow Jones 30 Industrials - Logarithmic Scale
(monthly close) through December 2023

STOCK INDEX FUTURES - U.S.

Composite Index of Leading Indicators   (1992 = 100)

Year	Jan.	Feb.	Mar.	Apr.	May	June	July	Aug.	Sept.	Oct.	Nov.	Dec.	Average
2006	104.7	104.4	104.6	104.4	103.7	103.9	103.7	103.3	103.7	103.9	103.8	104.4	104.0
2007	104.0	103.7	104.1	103.9	104.0	103.9	104.6	103.6	103.7	103.2	102.8	102.6	103.7
2008	102.1	101.9	101.9	102.0	101.9	101.9	101.2	100.3	100.3	99.4	99.0	98.8	100.9
2009	98.8	98.3	98.1	99.2	100.6	101.3	102.5	103.1	104.2	104.7	105.8	106.2	101.9
2010	106.7	107.2	108.6	108.6	109.0	108.8	109.0	109.1	109.9	110.1	111.4	112.3	109.2
2011	91.8	92.7	93.7	93.7	94.2	94.2	94.4	93.7	93.2	93.8	94.1	92.2	93.5
2012	92.2	92.9	93.1	92.9	93.3	92.7	93.1	92.7	93.2	93.4	93.4	94.3	93.1
2013	94.8	95.3	95.1	95.8	96.0	96.1	96.5	97.2	98.2	98.5	99.4	113.8	98.1
2014	113.7	114.3	115.4	115.8	116.5	117.2	118.4	118.5	119.2	119.9	120.5	121.0	117.5
2015[1]	121.2	120.9	121.2	121.9	122.9	123.6	Discontinued						122.0

[1] Preliminary.   *Source: The Conference Board*

Consumer Confidence, The Conference Board   (2004 = 100)

Year	Jan.	Feb.	Mar.	Apr.	May	June	July	Aug.	Sept.	Oct.	Nov.	Dec.	Average
2006	106.8	102.7	107.5	109.8	104.7	105.4	107.0	100.2	105.9	105.1	105.3	110.0	105.9
2007	110.2	111.2	108.2	106.3	108.5	105.3	111.9	105.6	99.5	95.2	87.8	90.6	103.4
2008	87.3	76.4	65.9	62.8	58.1	51.0	51.9	58.5	61.4	38.8	44.7	38.6	58.0
2009	37.4	25.3	26.9	40.8	54.8	49.3	47.4	54.5	53.4	48.7	50.6	53.6	45.2
2010	56.5	46.4	52.3	57.7	62.7	54.3	51.0	53.2	48.6	49.9	57.8	63.4	54.5
2011	64.8	72.0	63.8	66.0	61.7	57.6	59.2	45.2	46.4	40.9	55.2	64.8	58.1
2012	61.5	71.6	69.5	68.7	64.4	62.7	65.4	61.3	68.4	73.1	71.5	66.7	67.1
2013	58.4	68.0	61.9	69.0	74.3	82.1	81.0	81.8	80.2	72.4	72.0	77.5	73.2
2014	79.4	78.3	83.9	81.7	82.2	86.4	90.3	93.4	89.0	94.1	91.0	93.1	86.9
2015[1]	103.8	98.8	101.4	94.3	94.6	101.4	Discontinued						99.1

[1] Preliminary.   *Source: The Conference Board (TCB) Copyrighted.*

Capacity Utilization Rates (Total Industry)   In Percent

Year	Jan.	Feb.	Mar.	Apr.	May	June	July	Aug.	Sept.	Oct.	Nov.	Dec.	Average
2014	77.2	77.8	78.5	78.5	78.7	78.9	79.0	78.8	79.0	78.9	79.4	79.3	78.7
2015	78.6	78.1	77.8	77.3	77.0	76.7	77.2	77.1	76.9	76.6	76.0	75.6	77.1
2016	76.0	75.6	75.1	75.3	75.1	75.4	75.5	75.4	75.3	75.3	75.0	75.5	75.4
2017	75.4	75.1	75.6	76.4	76.6	76.8	76.7	76.4	76.6	77.7	77.9	78.2	76.6
2018	78.2	78.6	79.0	79.9	79.2	79.8	79.9	80.4	80.4	80.3	80.3	80.2	79.7
2019	79.7	79.2	79.1	78.6	78.7	78.7	78.2	78.7	78.5	77.7	78.1	77.8	78.6
2020	77.4	77.6	74.5	64.6	65.6	70.0	72.7	73.4	73.5	74.1	74.6	75.6	72.8
2021	76.4	73.9	76.2	76.5	77.4	77.8	78.4	78.5	77.8	78.8	79.5	79.3	77.6
2022	79.4	79.9	80.5	80.7	80.6	80.5	80.7	80.7	80.8	80.6	80.3	78.9	80.3
2023[1]	79.6	79.5	79.5	79.8	79.5	78.9	79.5	79.4	79.4	78.6	78.8	78.7	79.3

[1] Preliminary.   *Source: Bureau of Economic Analysis, U.S. Department of Commerce (BEA)*

Manufacturers New Orders, Durable Goods   In Millions of Constant Dollars

Year	Jan.	Feb.	Mar.	Apr.	May	June	July	Aug.	Sept.	Oct.	Nov.	Dec.	Average
2014	224,720	232,400	234,867	237,974	233,821	238,175	297,311	238,130	236,971	232,753	227,919	225,328	238,364
2015	225,583	219,261	228,929	226,400	217,773	229,862	225,207	223,617	218,286	226,002	224,273	218,351	223,629
2016	228,376	218,324	217,946	230,089	222,343	207,317	214,614	218,193	216,736	233,161	217,757	219,506	220,364
2017	218,959	222,710	222,381	223,956	223,013	236,306	216,917	222,157	228,374	227,767	231,932	240,990	226,289
2018	227,031	234,407	242,104	240,986	242,260	241,144	232,691	242,703	245,115	237,105	233,504	239,527	238,215
2019	234,212	226,038	234,890	227,712	221,561	220,513	225,425	225,092	222,770	222,598	214,077	216,195	224,257
2020	230,043	233,666	199,092	160,657	181,645	198,944	218,392	221,125	226,373	231,003	230,692	234,659	213,858
2021	244,935	244,658	246,475	245,453	250,043	253,573	252,955	258,736	254,759	257,816	261,651	267,750	253,234
2022	273,151	269,191	268,835	271,541	273,368	277,698	275,455	275,063	275,857	278,512	269,783	281,966	274,202
2023[1]	278,372	270,825	279,837	283,311	288,857	301,262	284,282	283,917	295,365	280,217	295,403	295,383	286,419

[1] Preliminary.   *Source: Bureau of Economic Analysis, U.S. Department of Commerce (BEA)*

Corporate Profits After Tax -- Quarterly   In Billions of Dollars

Year	First Quarter	Second Quarter	Third Quarter	Fourth Quarter	Total	Year	First Quarter	Second Quarter	Third Quarter	Fourth Quarter	Total
2012	1,705.7	1,672.7	1,643.7	1,629.2	1,662.8	2018	2,028.4	2,071.0	2,072.0	2,099.6	2,067.7
2013	1,622.8	1,643.1	1,646.4	1,680.0	1,648.1	2019	2,124.5	2,147.2	2,220.3	2,199.6	2,172.9
2014	1,563.7	1,712.5	1,793.1	1,783.3	1,713.1	2020	1,993.8	1,785.0	2,386.8	2,137.6	2,075.8
2015	1,706.9	1,689.2	1,675.6	1,585.2	1,664.2	2021	2,401.0	2,596.3	2,553.3	2,521.9	2,518.1
2016	1,664.9	1,624.2	1,649.9	1,707.0	1,661.5	2022	2,497.9	2,712.6	2,754.6	2,700.1	2,666.3
2017	1,791.4	1,803.7	1,845.1	1,884.6	1,831.2	2023[1]	2,588.6	2,601.8	2,697.9	2,803.2	2,672.9

[1] Preliminary.   *Source: Bureau of Economic Analysis, U.S. Department of Commerce (BEA)*

Change in Manufacturing and Trade Inventories   In Billions of Dollars

Year	Jan.	Feb.	Mar.	Apr.	May	June	July	Aug.	Sept.	Oct.	Nov.	Dec.	Average
2006	85.9	-49.7	129.5	82.7	169.3	169.3	92.2	93.2	65.9	22.9	28.3	4.2	85.2
2007	37.8	43.6	-17.0	59.5	68.1	55.0	75.6	62.7	87.7	23.8	53.3	96.3	53.4
2008	169.4	78.5	35.6	81.4	66.2	133.3	202.6	34.8	-64.9	-99.6		-250.0	35.2
2009	-170.2	-188.5	-232.1	-197.4	-196.7	-218.1	-159.1	-232.5	-46.8	59.8	75.6	-14.9	-126.7
2010	27.9	104.4	95.5	95.3	54.9	136.3	173.2	139.3	179.6	190.5	63.3	173.4	119.5
2011	167.1	129.1	226.8	154.7	184.1	50.0	75.1	114.0	-26.5	158.7	69.4	79.7	115.2
2012	139.9	118.4	47.8	46.5	56.8	27.0	128.1	85.0	118.2	60.8	37.4	33.6	75.0
2013	205.4	30.2	-18.8	66.4	-1.8	17.5	62.3	71.5	117.8	137.2	95.7	82.0	72.1
2014	65.6	74.8	82.9	124.5	104.5	64.6	70.8	32.9	54.1	52.7	20.9	15.3	63.6
2015[1]	-29.5	57.0	25.4	83.8	59.8	Discontinued							39.3

[1] Preliminary.   *Source: Bureau of Economic Analysis, U.S. Department of Commerce (BEA)*

Productivity: Index of Output per Hour, All Persons, Nonfarm Business -- Quarterly   (2017 = 100)

Year	First Quarter	Second Quarter	Third Quarter	Fourth Quarter	Total	Year	First Quarter	Second Quarter	Third Quarter	Fourth Quarter	Total
2012	95.1	95.6	95.3	94.9	95.2	2018	101.4	101.4	101.7	101.5	101.5
2013	95.4	95.2	95.9	96.8	95.8	2019	102.7	103.3	104.4	105.4	104.0
2014	96.0	96.6	97.4	97.1	96.8	2020	105.3	111.1	111.9	110.8	109.8
2015	97.6	98.1	98.4	97.8	98.0	2021	111.5	111.4	110.7	111.4	111.2
2016	98.2	98.3	98.6	99.3	98.6	2022	109.8	108.7	108.7	109.3	109.1
2017	99.4	99.5	100.3	101.0	100.1	2023[1]	109.1	109.9	111.2	112.1	110.6

[1] Preliminary.   *Source: Bureau of Economic Analysis, U.S. Department of Commerce (BEA)*

Civilian Unemployment Rate - U3

Year	Jan.	Feb.	Mar.	Apr.	May	June	July	Aug.	Sept.	Oct.	Nov.	Dec.	Average
2014	6.6	6.7	6.6	6.2	6.3	6.1	6.2	6.1	5.9	5.7	5.8	5.6	6.2
2015	5.7	5.5	5.4	5.4	5.5	5.3	5.2	5.1	5.0	5.0	5.0	5.0	5.3
2016	4.9	4.9	5.0	5.0	4.7	4.9	4.9	4.9	4.9	4.8	4.6	4.7	4.9
2017	4.8	4.7	4.5	4.4	4.3	4.4	4.3	4.4	4.2	4.1	4.1	4.1	4.4
2018	4.1	4.1	4.1	3.9	3.8	4.0	3.9	3.8	3.7	3.8	3.7	3.9	3.9
2019	4.0	3.8	3.8	3.6	3.6	3.7	3.7	3.7	3.5	3.6	3.5	3.5	3.7
2020	3.5	3.6	4.4	14.7	13.3	11.1	10.2	8.4	7.9	6.9	6.7	6.7	8.1
2021	6.3	6.2	6.0	6.1	5.8	5.9	5.4	5.2	4.7	4.6	4.2	3.9	5.4
2022	4.0	3.8	3.6	3.6	3.6	3.6	3.5	3.7	3.5	3.7	3.6	3.5	3.6
2023[1]	3.4	3.6	3.5	3.4	3.7	3.6	3.5	3.8	3.8	3.8	3.7	3.7	3.6

[1] Preliminary.   *Source: Bureau of Economic Analysis, U.S. Department of Commerce (BEA)*

S&P 500 Index - Logarithmic Scale
(monthly close) through December 2023

Index Value

STOCK INDEX FUTURES - U.S.

DOW JONES INDUSTRIALS
Weekly Cash as of 03/28/2024

WEEKLY CASH
As of 03/28/2024
Chart High 39889.05 on 03/21/2024
Chart Low 13622.96 on 01/22/2013

"Dow Jones", "The Dow", "Dow Jones Industrial Average" and "DJIA" are service marks of Dow Jones & Company, Inc.   Shaded areas indicate US recessions.

Average Value of Dow Jones Industrials Index (30 Stocks)

Year	Jan.	Feb.	Mar.	Apr.	May	June	July	Aug.	Sept.	Oct.	Nov.	Dec.	Average
2014	16,243.6	15,958.4	16,308.6	16,399.5	16,567.3	16,843.8	16,988.3	16,775.2	17,098.1	16,701.9	17,649.0	17,754.2	16,774.0
2015	17,542.3	17,945.4	17,931.7	17,970.5	18,124.7	17,927.2	17,795.0	17,061.6	16,340.0	17,182.3	17,723.8	17,542.9	17,590.6
2016	16,305.3	16,299.9	17,302.1	17,844.4	17,692.3	17,754.9	18,341.2	18,495.2	18,267.4	18,184.6	18,697.3	19,712.4	17,908.1
2017	19,908.2	20,424.1	20,823.1	20,684.7	20,936.8	21,317.8	21,581.3	21,914.1	22,173.4	23,036.2	23,557.9	24,545.4	21,741.9
2018	25,804.0	24,981.5	24,582.2	24,304.2	24,572.5	24,790.1	24,978.2	25,630.0	26,232.7	25,609.3	25,258.7	23,805.5	25,045.8
2019	24,157.8	25,605.5	25,722.6	26,401.6	25,744.8	26,160.1	27,089.2	26,057.8	26,900.2	26,736.8	27,797.1	28,167.0	26,378.4
2020	28,880.0	28,519.7	22,637.4	23,293.9	24,271.0	26,062.3	26,385.8	27,821.4	27,733.4	28,005.1	29,124.0	30,148.6	26,906.9
2021	30,821.4	31,283.9	32,373.3	33,803.3	34,270.3	34,289.9	34,798.8	35,244.0	34,688.4	35,055.5	35,848.6	35,641.3	34,009.9
2022	35,456.2	34,648.5	34,029.7	34,315.0	32,379.5	31,446.7	31,535.3	33,009.6	30,649.6	30,570.7	33,418.0	33,482.3	32,911.7
2023	33,656.0	33,648.3	32,483.5	33,731.3	33,316.8	33,905.0	34,777.2	34,880.7	34,318.9	33,319.5	34,704.5	36,947.9	34,140.8

Source: New York Stock Exchange (NYSE)

Volume of Trading of Mini Dow Jones Industrials Index Futures in Chicago   In Thousands of Contracts

Year	Jan.	Feb.	Mar.	Apr.	May	June	July	Aug.	Sept.	Oct.	Nov.	Dec.	Total
2014	3,180.8	3,115.6	3,965.0	3,351.6	2,637.7	2,641.1	3,028.9	2,683.7	3,476.0	5,444.0	1,954.8	3,574.5	39,053.7
2015	4,146.7	2,343.8	3,126.0	2,988.1	2,558.3	3,546.6	3,063.7	4,651.2	4,649.7	3,226.2	2,566.1	3,734.5	40,601.1
2016	5,169.8	4,307.1	3,300.6	3,164.9	3,083.4	4,152.0	2,600.0	2,641.6	4,047.4	3,274.0	3,887.6	2,927.5	42,555.9
2017	2,515.6	2,343.6	3,891.9	2,722.0	2,564.0	3,465.6	2,132.3	2,858.2	2,672.1	2,144.2	2,707.7	2,849.1	32,866.3
2018	3,623.3	6,592.1	6,939.8	5,479.4	4,405.7	4,558.5	3,310.8	2,989.4	3,521.3	7,088.2	4,886.0	6,929.7	60,324.2
2019	4,900.8	3,651.9	4,927.9	3,353.4	5,889.6	4,224.5	3,566.3	5,763.7	3,868.9	3,924.5	2,713.2	3,593.0	50,377.7
2020	5,015.6	6,334.8	8,432.1	4,349.6	4,357.1	6,025.1	4,459.1	3,451.9	5,188.2	4,656.0	3,681.5	3,420.6	59,371.7
2021	3,761.1	3,493.0	5,203.9	2,927.1	3,438.6	3,440.8	3,244.2	2,973.8	4,520.8	3,651.7	3,527.1	4,222.6	44,404.7
2022	5,436.3	4,892.6	4,627.7	3,706.9	4,270.1	4,374.1	3,318.9	3,780.1	4,309.0	4,207.3	4,221.5	3,872.4	51,016.8
2023	3,432.3	3,576.6	5,052.9	2,794.0	3,643.8	3,732.4	2,804.9	3,585.7	3,667.9	4,616.1	2,791.9	2,791.6	42,490.3

Contract value = $5.   Source: Chicago Board of Trade (CBT)

Average Open Interest of Mini Dow Jones Industrials Index Futures in Chicago   In Contracts

Year	Jan.	Feb.	Mar.	Apr.	May	June	July	Aug.	Sept.	Oct.	Nov.	Dec.
2014	127,534	114,491	134,383	119,028	127,150	131,818	124,601	115,822	140,265	119,716	139,521	135,980
2015	106,993	111,350	109,677	104,565	112,992	110,880	92,351	93,151	77,209	75,595	100,777	98,535
2016	65,416	62,194	83,643	117,857	119,596	122,482	120,095	144,885	135,208	120,288	127,896	140,802
2017	131,853	130,492	145,630	130,214	121,956	129,328	131,569	149,149	159,249	157,990	155,973	154,854
2018	153,793	126,347	118,343	100,414	102,356	96,326	87,601	100,558	112,896	95,850	80,908	80,929
2019	77,165	83,432	85,168	80,534	79,824	80,412	91,970	90,051	100,267	105,282	112,609	108,479
2020	102,791	102,595	75,348	60,895	71,735	79,524	78,506	90,866	76,430	91,547	94,005	94,361
2021	88,108	95,365	94,672	92,836	97,114	109,248	106,382	110,073	106,144	103,990	104,634	102,108
2022	94,070	81,108	74,789	74,225	83,020	77,368	69,484	77,446	72,973	69,519	76,463	83,216
2023	79,129	86,762	87,497	92,909	95,263	96,727	102,555	102,130	92,841	100,570	99,460	100,807

Contract value = $5.   Source: Chicago Board of Trade (CBT)

WEEKLY CASH
As of 03/28/2024

Chart High 5264.85 on 03/28/2024
Chart Low 1481.16 on 01/22/2013

S&P 500 INDEX
Weekly Cash as of 03/28/2024

The S&P 500® Index is a trademark of The McGraw-Hill Companies, Inc.   Shaded areas indicate US recessions.

Average Value of Standard & Poor's 500 Index

Year	Jan.	Feb.	Mar.	Apr.	May	June	July	Aug.	Sept.	Oct.	Nov.	Dec.	Average
2014	1,822.4	1,817.0	1,863.5	1,864.3	1,889.8	1,947.1	1,973.1	1,961.5	1,993.2	1,937.3	2,044.6	2,054.3	1,930.7
2015	2,028.2	2,082.2	2,080.0	2,094.9	2,111.9	2,099.3	2,094.1	2,039.9	1,944.4	2,024.8	2,080.6	2,054.1	2,061.2
2016	1,918.6	1,904.4	2,022.0	2,075.5	2,065.6	2,083.9	2,148.9	2,177.5	2,157.7	2,143.0	2,165.0	2,246.6	2,092.4
2017	2,275.1	2,329.9	2,366.8	2,359.3	2,395.4	2,434.0	2,454.1	2,456.2	2,492.8	2,557.0	2,593.6	2,664.3	2,448.2
2018	2,789.8	2,705.2	2,702.8	2,653.6	2,701.5	2,754.4	2,793.6	2,857.8	2,901.5	2,785.5	2,723.2	2,567.3	2,744.7
2019	2,607.4	2,754.9	2,804.0	2,903.8	2,854.7	2,890.2	2,996.1	2,897.5	2,982.2	2,977.7	3,104.9	3,176.8	2,912.5
2020	3,278.2	3,277.3	2,652.4	2,762.0	2,919.6	3,104.7	3,207.6	3,391.7	3,365.5	3,418.7	3,549.0	3,695.3	3,218.5
2021	3,793.8	3,883.4	3,910.5	4,141.2	4,167.9	4,238.5	4,363.7	4,454.2	4,445.5	4,460.7	4,667.4	4,674.8	4,266.8
2022	4,573.8	4,436.0	4,391.3	4,391.3	4,040.4	3,899.0	3,911.7	4,158.6	3,850.5	3,726.1	3,917.5	3,912.4	4,100.7
2023	3,960.7	4,079.7	3,968.6	4,121.5	4,146.2	4,345.4	4,508.1	4,457.4	4,409.1	4,269.4	4,460.1	4,685.1	4,284.2

Source: Index and Option Market (IOM), division of the Chicago Mercantile Exchange (CME)

Volume of Trading of E-mini S&P 500 Stock Index Futures in Chicago   In Thousands of Contracts

Year	Jan.	Feb.	Mar.	Apr.	May	June	July	Aug.	Sept.	Oct.	Nov.	Dec.	Total
2014	33,770	33,265	43,038	34,460	27,653	33,330	33,263	28,020	40,843	54,465	22,223	40,690	425,020
2015	38,362	25,643	38,949	26,801	24,516	39,037	32,990	46,325	48,962	36,264	28,643	43,312	429,803
2016	47,987	42,532	44,628	34,639	33,049	48,583	31,172	33,429	49,729	32,532	38,250	36,148	472,679
2017	28,663	26,871	43,248	27,397	28,105	40,315	22,213	32,605	33,473	24,444	27,662	30,604	365,602
2018	29,153	42,946	47,450	35,694	28,915	35,955	23,295	25,086	33,325	53,156	37,153	53,071	445,199
2019	33,983	25,491	38,615	23,894	41,914	36,451	25,475	44,708	35,370	31,055	23,059	35,129	395,144
2020	37,026	46,041	78,873	38,201	35,313	52,930	35,600	26,785	50,101	36,020	31,134	34,203	502,227
2021	30,235	29,958	50,906	28,565	32,577	32,498	28,690	25,059	41,991	29,063	29,498	44,600	403,640
2022	41,943	36,439	43,282	32,288	42,556	48,010	34,151	38,653	59,775	48,152	36,343	42,202	503,794
2023	34,077	36,593	55,639	29,228	35,703	43,686	27,789	36,379	39,281	43,989	31,697	38,482	452,543

Contract value = $50.   *Source: Index and Option Market (IOM), division of the Chicago Mercantile Exchange (CME)*

Average Open Interest of E-mini S&P 500 Stock Index Futures in Chicago   In Thousands of Contracts

Year	Jan.	Feb.	Mar.	Apr.	May	June	July	Aug.	Sept.	Oct.	Nov.	Dec.
2014	2,865.8	3,123.2	3,283.5	2,800.4	2,949.6	3,160.0	2,946.3	2,985.7	3,153.2	2,821.8	2,990.2	3,025.6
2015	2,724.4	2,820.5	3,000.4	2,707.2	2,776.2	2,863.5	2,672.8	2,893.6	3,179.8	2,921.9	2,889.2	2,801.6
2016	2,792.2	3,072.3	3,109.5	2,863.7	2,884.5	3,056.9	2,971.7	2,971.2	3,115.3	2,960.2	2,985.0	2,989.9
2017	2,833.2	2,991.5	3,112.3	2,905.0	3,049.8	3,062.1	2,924.0	3,192.3	3,279.6	3,104.8	3,293.9	3,348.8
2018	3,310.8	3,366.2	3,200.3	3,017.3	3,081.8	2,985.4	2,745.8	2,833.8	2,950.5	2,887.7	2,993.6	3,024.4
2019	2,669.4	2,643.7	2,620.1	2,604.3	2,667.3	2,721.3	2,617.6	2,585.9	2,677.3	2,532.7	2,772.7	2,940.4
2020	2,737.3	2,820.8	3,584.9	3,415.4	3,232.2	3,077.7	2,637.2	2,720.0	2,664.9	2,452.8	2,492.2	2,666.4
2021	2,598.9	2,648.0	2,742.6	2,663.0	2,692.8	2,774.1	2,645.6	2,724.6	2,701.4	2,411.4	2,447.6	2,455.4
2022	2,331.1	2,298.7	2,320.7	2,157.0	2,252.6	2,358.4	2,322.8	2,333.5	2,319.2	2,310.4	2,322.0	2,181.2
2023	2,034.9	2,075.9	2,224.1	2,254.7	2,349.8	2,440.2	2,234.3	2,238.9	2,245.7	2,127.5	2,221.3	2,318.2

Contract value = $50.   *Source: Index and Option Market (IOM), division of the Chicago Mercantile Exchange (CME)*

STOCK INDEX FUTURES - U.S.

The NASDAQ 100® Index is a trademark of The Nasdaq Stock Market, Inc.   Shaded areas indicate US recessions.

Average Value of NASDAQ 100 Index

Year	Jan.	Feb.	Mar.	Apr.	May	June	July	Aug.	Sept.	Oct.	Nov.	Dec.	Average
2014	3,557.9	3,615.0	3,661.1	3,554.5	3,621.1	3,792.1	3,926.7	3,979.4	4,070.3	3,964.6	4,221.1	4,260.8	3,852.0
2015	4,182.6	4,343.5	4,389.2	4,418.9	4,476.4	4,481.7	4,528.3	4,422.3	4,261.6	4,445.5	4,653.2	4,628.0	4,435.9
2016	4,259.3	4,129.6	4,377.1	4,491.9	4,379.4	4,427.0	4,592.6	4,785.7	4,813.3	4,845.3	4,791.8	4,886.3	4,564.9
2017	5,056.8	5,261.2	5,386.2	5,447.9	5,687.4	5,767.0	5,816.1	5,874.4	5,954.9	6,088.5	6,328.2	6,398.0	5,755.5
2018	6,790.5	6,704.4	6,844.9	6,606.9	6,875.9	7,159.6	7,296.6	7,453.1	7,528.0	7,171.6	6,855.0	6,498.0	6,982.0
2019	6,619.8	7,021.1	7,254.2	7,660.6	7,481.0	7,505.2	7,897.8	7,619.8	7,814.0	7,859.7	8,284.4	8,527.4	7,628.7
2020	9,031.2	9,297.5	7,835.4	8,437.0	9,208.0	9,898.7	10,658.3	11,406.5	11,330.8	11,605.0	11,893.3	12,622.1	10,268.6
2021	13,048.1	13,473.8	12,900.2	13,832.3	13,470.8	14,064.5	14,849.7	15,173.0	15,315.1	15,143.7	16,237.2	16,135.4	14,470.3
2022	15,207.2	14,428.7	14,151.3	13,964.7	12,375.0	11,916.7	12,140.2	13,090.4	11,841.0	11,212.4	11,458.1	11,365.2	12,762.6
2023	11,496.3	12,372.2	12,429.9	13,026.0	13,555.8	14,808.1	15,445.1	15,144.9	15,089.0	14,763.2	15,609.6	16,452.5	14,182.7

Source: Index and Option Market (IOM), division of the Chicago Mercantile Exchange (CME)

Volume of Trading of E-mini NASDAQ 100 Index Futures in Chicago   In Thousands of Contracts

Year	Jan.	Feb.	Mar.	Apr.	May	June	July	Aug.	Sept.	Oct.	Nov.	Dec.	Total
2014	5,641.0	5,236.1	7,514.0	7,765.8	5,541.1	5,252.7	5,305.9	4,774.4	7,103.7	10,105.5	4,013.9	7,229.6	75,483.7
2015	6,833.3	3,985.2	6,094.0	4,617.1	3,880.7	5,542.4	5,100.7	7,432.1	7,310.1	5,782.1	4,431.2	6,301.3	67,310.3
2016	8,223.6	6,818.4	5,768.6	5,007.9	4,813.8	6,045.0	3,857.8	4,059.2	6,567.4	4,716.0	5,396.7	4,476.2	65,750.5
2017	3,626.6	3,403.0	5,698.7	4,376.9	5,129.1	9,012.5	5,528.7	7,491.5	6,785.4	5,498.9	6,481.7	6,526.1	69,559.1
2018	7,000.4	10,100.0	12,243.8	10,030.7	7,692.8	8,400.0	7,283.8	7,592.7	9,416.3	16,684.0	13,094.0	14,657.0	124,195.5
2019	10,846.1	7,708.1	10,799.4	8,157.1	12,812.9	9,468.0	7,921.1	13,397.1	9,556.8	9,475.4	6,734.3	8,204.2	115,080.5
2020	12,102.9	15,474.5	17,447.9	9,248.0	9,155.6	11,842.5	12,107.8	9,570.3	16,216.4	13,214.9	10,349.1	9,987.2	146,717.1
2021	10,203.8	10,836.7	15,925.4	10,569.4	10,578.8	10,625.7	10,561.6	10,480.8	13,332.1	11,194.4	11,829.1	14,268.4	140,406.3
2022	16,376.2	13,920.8	15,190.8	12,884.5	15,730.9	15,520.8	12,307.7	14,022.5	17,684.3	16,051.8	13,225.9	13,916.6	176,832.7
2023	12,343.4	12,247.5	17,964.3	11,689.4	14,351.3	14,718.7	12,165.1	15,206.6	13,999.5	16,893.7	12,635.4	12,720.3	166,935.1

Contract value = $20.   *Source: Index and Option Market (IOM), division of the Chicago Mercantile Exchange (CME)*

Average Open Interest of E-mini NASDAQ 100 Index Futures in Chicago   In Contracts

Year	Jan.	Feb.	Mar.	Apr.	May	June	July	Aug.	Sept.	Oct.	Nov.	Dec.
2014	427,403	428,404	452,936	352,802	355,239	383,300	365,320	359,978	399,636	349,013	357,410	376,694
2015	314,070	325,766	352,413	335,425	322,640	342,629	327,815	337,292	287,155	285,539	348,170	334,859
2016	287,540	269,926	244,045	227,743	227,844	237,463	242,541	295,495	301,601	303,400	269,558	247,601
2017	224,988	233,695	249,237	256,682	273,541	324,978	286,106	295,726	292,471	278,159	286,310	306,756
2018	264,915	239,065	250,925	242,489	243,195	251,523	243,189	244,958	268,030	250,113	245,902	240,458
2019	212,112	217,827	217,867	206,137	217,691	222,946	218,856	200,522	213,935	214,090	228,363	224,543
2020	213,795	208,540	226,372	181,126	199,383	206,398	220,553	233,772	300,472	238,614	235,732	237,238
2021	230,761	237,554	243,141	216,397	233,224	243,498	229,947	229,064	238,682	235,924	258,832	236,222
2022	231,103	243,997	238,907	233,598	249,365	265,397	258,178	262,812	286,551	279,588	265,951	260,538
2023	264,240	272,478	250,618	243,257	270,315	280,768	259,608	266,407	259,910	256,632	275,966	288,182

Contract value = $20.   *Source: Index and Option Market (IOM), division of the Chicago Mercantile Exchange (CME)*

DOW JONES TRANSPORTS
Weekly Cash as of 03/28/2024

WEEKLY CASH
As of 03/28/2024
Chart High 18246.51 on 11/02/2021
Chart Low 5691.23 on 01/22/2013

"Dow Jones", "The Dow", "Dow Jones Industrial Average" and "DJIA" are service marks of Dow Jones & Company, Inc.   Shaded areas indicate US recessions.

Average Value of Dow Jones Transportation Index (20 Stocks)

Year	Jan.	Feb.	Mar.	Apr.	May	June	July	Aug.	Sept.	Oct.	Nov.	Dec.	Average
2014	7,361.9	7,235.3	7,512.0	7,587.8	7,854.6	8,135.4	8,308.7	8,272.8	8,534.2	8,308.9	9,033.8	9,025.7	8,097.6
2015	8,853.6	9,005.2	8,942.9	8,725.1	8,592.8	8,361.0	8,214.8	8,134.2	7,929.8	8,117.2	8,174.0	7,658.2	8,392.4
2016	6,871.7	7,133.1	7,771.2	7,919.7	7,700.9	7,615.7	7,817.1	7,845.3	7,913.3	8,054.3	8,622.5	9,207.6	7,872.7
2017	9,192.9	9,368.9	9,184.5	9,096.5	9,058.9	9,382.3	9,542.7	9,208.8	9,573.3	9,901.8	9,665.7	10,463.4	9,470.0
2018	11,106.0	10,471.7	10,477.7	10,427.8	10,631.9	10,795.0	10,663.5	11,220.3	11,443.3	10,604.3	10,507.1	9,544.1	10,657.7
2019	9,657.2	10,426.4	10,262.2	10,816.6	10,427.1	10,222.2	10,581.9	10,053.4	10,474.0	10,376.8	10,907.5	10,779.3	10,415.4
2020	10,994.0	10,617.1	7,941.0	8,002.8	8,307.7	9,249.4	9,600.0	10,829.0	11,292.7	11,603.4	12,095.7	12,568.9	10,258.5
2021	12,735.8	13,023.0	14,038.4	14,990.1	15,663.7	15,157.5	14,670.0	14,669.2	14,387.2	15,122.8	16,619.9	16,140.2	14,768.1
2022	15,726.6	15,199.7	15,843.7	14,977.0	14,343.4	13,546.7	13,553.1	14,658.3	13,081.5	12,877.0	14,079.7	13,802.1	14,307.4
2023	14,174.2	15,109.4	14,220.5	14,157.4	13,907.9	14,656.9	16,043.5	15,994.3	15,198.3	14,515.6	14,689.2	15,713.1	14,865.0

Source: New York Stock Exchange (NYSE)

DOW JONES UTILITIES
Weekly Cash as of 03/28/2024

WEEKLY CASH
As of 03/28/2024
Chart High 1077.08 on 04/20/2022
Chart Low 462.10 on 01/22/2013

"Dow Jones", "The Dow", "Dow Jones Industrial Average" and "DJIA" are service marks of Dow Jones & Company, Inc.   Shaded areas indicate US recessions.

Average Value of Dow Jones Utilities Index (15 Stocks)

Year	Jan.	Feb.	Mar.	Apr.	May	June	July	Aug.	Sept.	Oct.	Nov.	Dec.	Average
2014	491.9	513.0	519.8	540.7	540.0	556.0	557.5	547.2	555.3	569.2	596.5	609.7	549.7
2015	634.5	610.4	582.6	589.7	584.5	564.1	570.8	587.1	558.1	588.0	566.9	567.7	583.7
2016	585.1	621.9	649.2	655.4	657.7	682.6	712.9	686.2	676.4	654.6	642.6	650.1	656.2
2017	658.2	674.0	696.8	703.8	705.4	726.4	712.0	738.2	736.9	740.9	760.2	742.3	716.3
2018	694.2	671.0	679.0	693.4	687.0	683.9	719.6	729.3	729.1	734.2	730.9	734.5	707.2
2019	708.6	741.2	773.2	776.7	784.7	810.1	820.1	829.5	859.4	867.4	848.0	863.5	806.9
2020	901.5	929.8	776.3	784.2	764.6	796.7	806.9	820.2	804.7	870.5	888.6	856.6	833.4
2021	853.3	850.3	844.0	907.2	904.6	896.8	900.3	932.9	913.7	899.7	914.1	945.8	896.9
2022	950.4	929.1	991.7	1,049.9	1,001.9	961.5	969.7	1,032.7	999.3	880.6	932.0	975.8	972.9
2023	973.9	944.4	912.3	962.8	932.5	910.1	926.4	885.9	866.0	813.4	854.5	879.2	905.1

Source: New York Stock Exchange (NYSE)

STOCK INDEX FUTURES - U.S.

"Dow Jones", "The Dow", "Dow Jones Industrial Average" and "DJIA" are service marks of Dow Jones & Company, Inc.   Shaded areas indicate US recessions.

Average Value of Standard & Poor's MidCap 400 Index

Year	Jan.	Feb.	Mar.	Apr.	May	June	July	Aug.	Sept.	Oct.	Nov.	Dec.	Average
2014	1,333.5	1,333.4	1,373.9	1,355.0	1,361.6	1,410.5	1,413.6	1,402.5	1,415.2	1,351.5	1,435.2	1,438.2	1,385.3
2015	1,440.1	1,493.5	1,509.4	1,527.7	1,525.0	1,528.8	1,499.9	1,463.3	1,399.8	1,427.8	1,449.2	1,413.6	1,473.2
2016	1,299.3	1,296.5	1,408.0	1,456.5	1,458.3	1,489.2	1,534.0	1,559.7	1,546.7	1,526.0	1,571.6	1,668.8	1,484.5
2017	1,684.1	1,720.7	1,715.5	1,715.7	1,724.7	1,749.1	1,763.1	1,722.3	1,754.8	1,822.3	1,845.6	1,892.9	1,759.2
2018	1,959.7	1,876.7	1,902.7	1,886.0	1,930.2	1,981.1	1,988.5	2,016.0	2,032.4	1,892.6	1,859.1	1,715.6	1,920.0
2019	1,765.3	1,892.3	1,888.8	1,951.4	1,898.0	1,902.8	1,956.5	1,876.9	1,935.3	1,923.8	1,997.6	2,035.0	1,918.6
2020	2,062.5	2,034.1	1,520.6	1,523.4	1,656.9	1,804.9	1,820.0	1,931.5	1,867.7	1,963.4	2,108.2	2,265.3	1,879.9
2021	2,409.4	2,501.1	2,580.6	2,700.1	2,709.4	2,708.2	2,670.8	2,714.3	2,697.9	2,737.2	2,867.5	2,770.5	2,672.3
2022	2,714.1	2,646.6	2,649.9	2,618.4	2,449.0	2,364.7	2,354.1	23,536.6	2,356.3	2,322.6	2,486.0	2,463.3	4,246.8
2023	2,546.0	2,654.6	2,481.0	2,483.9	2,444.7	2,551.2	2,681.0	2,635.8	2,552.7	2,425.8	2,497.0	2,715.0	2,555.7

Source: Index and Option Market (IOM), division of the Chicago Mercantile Exchange (CME)

Volume of Trading of E-mini S&P 400 Index Futures in Chicago   In Contracts

Year	Jan.	Feb.	Mar.	Apr.	May	June	July	Aug.	Sept.	Oct.	Nov.	Dec.	Total
2014	369,537	360,548	604,474	385,135	334,222	500,963	343,309	283,606	618,774	648,830	242,848	593,469	5,285,715
2015	414,909	332,866	599,168	325,498	293,658	554,697	369,498	498,662	649,465	402,087	332,728	607,797	5,381,033
2016	529,519	442,219	633,841	325,445	347,829	654,024	305,479	313,218	626,528	336,632	352,772	538,251	5,405,757
2017	356,153	255,217	592,956	327,303	308,302	537,053	246,470	308,005	431,674	229,221	282,517	457,169	4,332,040
2018	316,880	430,453	590,759	332,663	294,698	498,591	268,791	227,276	481,588	531,815	363,033	614,553	4,951,100
2019	300,487	282,789	506,895	226,763	307,568	431,823	276,230	328,178	448,052	278,563	214,891	505,898	4,108,137
2020	331,980	370,629	776,538	235,431	224,250	549,761	278,221	239,926	497,873	286,787	252,149	488,901	4,532,446
2021	275,491	187,703	358,524	193,589	213,736	343,645	216,569	192,521	377,878	252,718	285,053	431,447	3,328,874
2022	383,829	276,798	483,893	277,688	278,614	452,469	237,655	251,129	432,479	293,057	264,797	343,449	3,975,857
2023	226,895	215,527	484,189	193,076	260,498	353,262	198,198	240,914	330,870	280,493	304,765	371,529	3,460,216

Contract value = $20.   *Source: Index and Option Market (IOM), division of the Chicago Mercantile Exchange (CME)*

Civilian Unemployment Rate - U6

Year	Jan.	Feb.	Mar.	Apr.	May	June	July	Aug.	Sept.	Oct.	Nov.	Dec.	Average
2014	12.7	12.6	12.7	12.3	12.2	12.1	12.2	12.0	11.7	11.5	11.4	11.2	12.1
2015	11.3	11.0	10.9	10.8	10.8	10.5	10.4	10.3	10.0	9.8	9.9	9.9	10.5
2016	9.9	9.7	9.8	9.7	9.7	9.6	9.7	9.7	9.7	9.5	9.3	9.2	9.6
2017	9.4	9.2	8.9	8.6	8.4	8.6	8.6	8.6	8.3	7.9	8.0	8.1	8.6
2018	8.2	8.2	8.0	7.8	7.6	7.8	7.5	7.4	7.5	7.4	7.6	7.6	7.7
2019	8.1	7.3	7.3	7.3	7.1	7.2	7.0	7.2	6.9	7.0	6.9	6.7	7.2
2020	6.9	7.0	8.7	22.8	21.2	18.0	16.5	14.2	12.8	12.1	12.0	11.7	13.7
2021	11.1	11.1	10.7	10.4	10.2	9.8	9.2	8.8	8.5	8.3	7.8	7.3	9.4
2022	7.1	7.2	6.9	7.0	7.1	6.7	6.7	7.0	6.7	6.8	6.7	6.5	6.9
2023[1]	6.6	6.8	6.7	6.6	6.7	6.9	6.7	7.1	7.0	7.2	7.0	7.1	6.9

The U6 unemployment rate counts not only people without work seeking full-time employment (the more familiar U-3 rate), but also counts "marginally attached workers and those working part-time for economic reasons." Note that some of these part-time workers counted as employed by U-3 could be working as little as an hour a week. And the "marginally attached workers" include those who have gotten discouraged and stopped looking, but still want to work. The age considered for this calculation is 16 years and over.

[1] Preliminary.   *Source: Bureau of Economic Analysis, U.S. Department of Commerce (BEA)*

Stock Index Futures - WorldWide

World stocks – World stock markets in 2023 closed higher as the world's key central banks stopped raising interest rates, leading to market hopes for interest rate cuts in 2024. The markets were also pleased with the resiliency of the world economy to the US interest rate hikes seen from early 2022 through mid-2023. The MSCI World Index, a benchmark for large companies based in 23 developed countries, rose by +21.8% in 2023, reversing the -19.5% decline seen in 2022.

Small-Capitalization Stocks – The MSCI World Small-Cap Index, which tracks companies with market caps between $200 million and $1.5 billion, rose by +13.8% in 2023, reversing part of the -20.1% decline in 2022. The MSCI World Small-Cap Index in 2023 underperformed the +21.8% gain in the large-cap MSCI World Index. Small caps in 2023 under-performed the large-caps for the third consecutive year and have now underperformed large-caps in five of the last six years.

World Industry Groups – All but two of the ten MSCI industry groups rose in 2023. The two sectors that fell were the Utilities and Energy sectors. The ranked returns of the sectors in 2023 were as follows: Information Technology (+52.3%), Telecom (+44.0%), Consumer Discretionary (+33.6%), Industrials (+21.2%), Financials (+13.1%), Materials (+11.7%), Health Care (+2.4%), Consumer Staples (+0.1%), Energy (-0.7%), and Utilities (-2.5%).

Emerging markets – The MSCI Emerging Markets Free Index, which tracks companies based in 26 emerging countries, rose by +7.0% in 2023, reversing part of the declines of -4.6% in 2021 and -22.4% in 2022. The +7.0% gain in emerging market stocks in 2023 was much less than the +21.8% gain seen in the MSCI World Index.

G7 – The G7 stock markets in 2023 all closed higher. Japan's Nikkei Index showed the largest gain, while the UK FTSE 100 index showed the smallest gain. The ranked returns of the G-7 countries were as follows: Japan's Nikkei Index (+28.2%), Italy's MIB index (+28.0%), US S&P 500 index (+24.2%), German Dax index (+20.3%), French CAC-40 (+16.5%), Canada's Toronto Composite index (+8.1%), and UK FTSE 100 index (+3.8%).

North America – In North America, the US S&P 500 index in 2023 showed the largest gain by rising +24.2%, followed by Mexico's Bolsa index with a +18.4% gain, and Canada's Toronto Composite index with a +8.1% gain.

STOCK INDEX FUTURES - WORLDWIDE

Comparison of International Indices   (2010=100)

Year	Jan.	Feb.	Mar.	Apr.	May	June	July	Aug.	Sept.	Oct.	Nov.	Dec.	Average
United States													
2016	164.8	164.7	174.8	180.3	178.8	179.4	185.3	186.9	184.6	183.7	188.9	199.2	180.9
2017	201.2	206.4	210.4	209.0	211.6	215.4	218.1	221.4	224.0	232.8	238.0	248.0	219.7
2018	260.7	252.4	248.4	245.6	248.3	250.5	252.4	259.0	265.1	258.8	255.2	240.5	253.1
2019	244.1	258.7	259.9	266.8	260.1	264.3	273.7	263.3	271.8	270.2	280.9	284.6	266.5
2020	291.8	288.2	228.7	235.4	245.2	263.3	266.6	281.1	280.2	283.0	294.3	304.6	271.9
2021	311.4	316.1	327.1	341.6	346.3	346.5	351.6	356.1	350.5	354.2	362.2	360.1	343.6
2022	358.3	350.1	343.8	346.7	327.2	317.7	318.6	333.5	309.7	308.9	337.7	338.3	332.6
2023	340.1	340.0	328.2	340.8	336.6	342.6	351.4	352.4	346.8	336.7	350.7	373.3	345.0
Canada													
2015	119.8	125.5	123.6	126.7	125.3	122.9	119.6	116.1	111.6	113.9	111.2	108.6	118.7
2016	102.4	104.6	110.9	113.1	114.7	116.3	119.7	121.6	121.2	121.9	122.8	126.4	116.3
2017	128.3	129.6	128.5	129.6	128.3	126.8	125.5	125.2	126.6	131.1	132.8	133.3	128.8
2018	134.8	127.8	128.3	127.4	132.2	134.6	136.1	135.3	133.6	127.9	125.4	120.5	130.3
2019	124.5	131.0	133.5	136.4	135.2	135.2	136.8	134.6	138.2	135.9	140.2	141.0	135.2
2020	144.0	145.3	114.0	116.6	123.5	128.2	132.1	137.4	134.5	134.4	138.7	145.1	132.8
2021	147.7	151.2	154.6	158.8	161.1	166.6	167.0	169.5	169.9	172.1	177.6	173.3	164.1
2022	174.2	175.9	179.1	178.8	Discontinued		----	----	----	----	----	----	----
France													
2016	115.8	111.7	118.1	118.6	116.7	114.6	115.2	118.1	118.7	120.0	120.2	127.1	117.9
2017	129.8	129.3	133.6	137.0	142.8	140.5	138.1	136.7	139.0	143.8	144.0	143.4	138.2
2018	146.3	140.3	138.8	142.6	147.8	144.3	144.3	145.1	143.6	138.0	134.3	128.0	141.1
2019	128.7	136.6	141.8	147.1	143.0	144.6	148.9	142.8	135.2	150.1	157.2	157.8	144.5
2020	160.1	158.0	119.6	118.1	119.9	132.3	133.4	132.4	131.7	129.2	142.4	148.0	135.4
2021	149.1	152.0	159.1	166.0	169.6	175.4	173.9	180.0	177.1	177.5	187.1	186.7	171.1
2022	190.1	184.7	172.2	175.0	169.2	163.8	162.7	171.7	160.6	160.9	174.9	176.1	171.8
2023	185.5	193.0	191.2	199.2	196.5	193.6	195.7	194.6	192.8	186.0	191.0	200.5	193.3
Germany													
2016	158.8	150.2	159.4	162.0	161.8	159.3	161.0	170.2	169.8	171.7	171.2	181.3	164.7
2017	187.8	189.8	194.7	197.7	204.6	205.4	200.4	196.4	201.7	210.3	212.7	211.4	201.1
2018	214.5	201.4	196.6	200.6	208.7	204.7	203.3	201.4	196.9	188.4	183.6	175.1	197.9
2019	177.3	182.3	186.6	195.0	195.2	196.6	200.5	189.4	198.6	202.6	213.4	213.2	195.9
2020	216.1	215.5	162.2	167.7	177.7	199.0	205.9	208.2	209.5	203.7	209.5	217.0	199.3
2021	223.4	225.5	234.5	246.3	247.4	252.4	251.7	255.6	251.9	248.9	257.6	251.9	245.6
2022	254.2	244.0	226.5	229.0	226.1	219.8	209.8	217.4	205.1	204.8	227.4	229.0	224.4
2023	240.8	249.0	246.7	254.7	257.5	259.3	259.7	255.8	252.7	243.4	252.6	269.6	253.5
Italy													
2013	82.6	77.9	75.1	75.3	81.8	76.1	75.5	80.8	83.1	89.4	89.9	86.9	81.2
2014	92.8	95.1	98.9	102.8	100.4	103.9	99.4	94.4	99.1	91.7	92.1	91.2	96.8
2015	92.0	101.1	107.9	111.5	110.8	109.1	109.2	108.3	102.2	105.3	105.6	10.2	97.8
2016	91.9	81.1	87.3	85.9	84.8	80.4	78.0	79.0	79.0	79.8	78.7	88.2	82.8
2017	92.0	89.7	94.3	95.9	101.0	99.1	101.1	103.1	105.4	106.8	106.7	105.8	100.1
2018	110.5	107.4	106.6	111.2	111.0	103.7	103.6	99.6	99.7	92.5	90.5	89.1	102.1
2019	91.6	95.0	99.5	103.3	98.4	98.5	103.7	98.4	103.9	105.0	111.1	110.8	101.6
2020	113.0	115.0	83.5	81.2	82.6	92.2	94.8	94.3	92.2	Discontinued		----	94.3
Japan													
2016	172.9	163.3	168.8	165.3	166.0	160.5	161.5	165.7	167.2	170.3	176.7	190.5	169.1
2017	191.8	191.7	193.2	187.2	197.1	200.3	200.3	196.5	199.1	212.5	225.0	227.5	201.8
2018	236.9	219.7	213.7	218.5	225.7	225.4	222.9	224.7	231.4	226.7	219.5	210.1	222.9
2019	204.4	211.0	213.9	219.4	212.0	210.4	215.7	206.1	215.6	221.8	232.6	236.4	216.6
2020	236.2	231.6	189.6	191.9	205.2	224.7	225.1	228.8	232.8	234.4	253.6	267.5	226.8
2021	281.5	294.2	292.9	294.0	284.9	289.2	280.9	276.7	298.6	285.6	293.4	284.9	288.1
2022	278.8	270.4	265.6	270.2	266.3	269.3	269.6	283.2	273.9	269.6	278.8	271.9	272.3
2023	265.8	274.8	276.7	282.5	301.2	327.2	326.6	321.4	326.9	313.5	329.3	330.9	306.4

Not Seasonally Adjusted.   *Source: Economic and Statistics Administration, U.S. Department of Commerce (ESA)*

DAX® is Deutsche Börse's blue chip index for the German stock market. It comprises the 30 largest and most actively traded German companies.   Shaded areas indicate German recessions.

Average Value of Deutscher Aktienindex (DAX)

Year	Jan.	Feb.	Mar.	Apr.	May	June	July	Aug.	Sept.	Oct.	Nov.	Dec.	Average
2014	9,516.8	9,509.5	9,339.9	9,490.0	9,709.5	9,927.4	9,751.8	9,273.1	9,638.7	8,971.9	9,490.3	9,812.3	9,535.9
2015	10,133.6	10,977.1	11,784.9	11,956.3	11,599.1	11,236.3	11,288.1	10,818.0	9,953.3	10,222.3	10,986.3	10,673.0	10,969.0
2016	9,827.1	9,291.4	9,859.9	10,023.2	10,010.6	9,859.2	9,960.5	10,530.3	10,504.5	10,624.2	10,595.5	11,214.9	10,191.8
2017	11,620.1	11,745.4	12,047.6	12,232.6	12,661.1	12,710.6	12,397.5	12,153.8	12,479.5	13,012.1	13,159.4	13,079.9	12,441.6
2018	13,270.7	12,459.4	12,165.9	12,411.6	12,911.2	12,667.6	12,581.7	12,458.9	12,185.2	11,659.1	11,359.6	10,834.5	12,247.1
2019	10,968.9	11,280.8	11,542.6	12,068.0	12,079.6	12,164.2	12,406.9	11,719.8	12,285.3	12,538.2	13,200.8	13,193.3	12,120.7
2020	13,370.5	13,330.6	10,034.3	10,374.5	10,993.7	12,313.7	12,741.0	12,882.4	12,960.9	12,603.1	12,960.7	13,426.0	12,332.6
2021	13,823.3	13,951.2	14,508.1	15,236.4	15,305.8	15,619.0	15,573.5	15,816.1	15,584.5	15,401.9	15,938.8	15,587.8	15,195.5
2022	15,726.9	15,094.5	14,012.7	14,167.0	13,991.9	13,601.0	12,981.4	13,449.6	12,692.6	12,673.5	14,068.9	14,168.9	13,885.7
2023	14,896.4	15,404.2	15,262.7	15,761.0	15,932.6	16,041.2	16,069.7	15,829.5	15,638.0	15,059.2	15,631.8	16,681.7	15,684.0

Source: EUREX

The FTSE 100 Index covers 100 of the largest companies traded on the LSE.   Shaded areas indicate United Kingdom recessions.

Average Value of FTSE 100 Stock Index

Year	Jan.	Feb.	Mar.	Apr.	May	June	July	Aug.	Sept.	Oct.	Nov.	Dec.	Average
2009	4,281.85	4,074.38	3,760.23	4,046.33	4,393.78	4,349.25	4,374.50	4,755.63	5,033.13	5,161.18	5,242.29	5,309.54	4,565.17
2010	5,411.65	5,231.92	5,621.03	5,720.73	5,238.81	5,139.26	5,158.39	5,276.00	5,514.67	5,687.17	5,735.84	5,874.87	5,467.53
2011	5,971.31	6,021.12	5,858.24	6,007.85	5,937.95	5,792.18	5,909.81	5,271.31	5,228.50	5,408.62	5,402.52	5,480.08	5,690.79
2012	5,694.45	5,893.35	5,875.40	5,725.58	5,461.45	5,480.44	5,636.47	5,796.96	5,805.45	5,831.81	5,787.52	5,922.72	5,742.63
2013	6,161.87	6,316.35	6,435.58	6,361.01	6,647.35	6,299.43	6,517.86	6,521.48	6,552.36	6,571.95	6,694.32	6,572.98	6,471.05
2014	6,714.51	6,690.79	6,631.69	6,651.96	6,834.80	6,804.31	6,772.02	6,712.21	6,777.75	6,408.63	6,644.12	6,542.62	6,682.12
2015	6,612.63	6,878.54	6,884.51	7,012.39	6,981.68	6,783.17	6,646.60	6,455.96	6,087.34	6,340.81	6,306.91	6,162.31	6,596.07
2016	5,922.67	5,881.74	6,155.24	6,271.90	6,164.88	6,175.30	6,655.88	6,821.69	6,813.75	7,011.20	6,803.33	6,961.04	6,469.89
2017	7,211.36	7,240.42	7,359.53	7,263.60	7,422.66	7,463.97	7,395.85	7,409.18	7,334.65	7,508.18	7,441.23	7,481.74	7,377.70
2018	7,695.65	7,255.90	7,090.09	7,288.22	7,690.22	7,656.93	Discontinued		----	----	----	----	7,446.17

Source: Euronext LIFFE

STOCK INDEX FUTURES - WORLDWIDE

Average Value of S&P TSX Index

Year	Jan.	Feb.	Mar.	Apr.	May	June	July	Aug.	Sept.	Oct.	Nov.	Dec.	Average
2013	12,668.8	12,737.0	12,777.3	12,299.2	12,585.1	12,221.4	12,479.7	12,622.7	12,818.9	13,057.7	13,396.1	13,339.2	12,750.3
2014	13,728.1	13,964.5	14,281.4	14,440.5	14,635.7	14,960.5	15,268.3	15,389.4	15,353.5	14,460.8	14,824.8	14,330.5	14,636.5
2015	14,460.9	15,155.0	14,921.6	15,299.3	15,127.2	14,835.9	14,436.4	14,010.4	13,477.6	13,751.9	13,424.2	13,115.1	14,334.6
2016	12,361.0	12,632.4	13,382.1	13,650.4	13,851.9	14,042.4	14,445.8	14,680.8	14,634.0	14,718.2	14,821.9	15,254.5	14,039.6
2017	15,486.6	15,639.7	15,515.3	15,642.3	15,486.8	15,308.8	15,153.5	15,108.9	15,284.5	15,826.0	16,032.6	16,092.8	15,548.2
2018	16,272.5	15,430.6	15,490.4	15,380.4	15,964.4	16,253.3	16,432.6	16,332.4	16,125.6	15,441.2	15,144.0	14,546.8	15,734.5
2019	15,031.9	15,811.2	16,119.6	16,470.4	16,316.8	16,322.6	16,515.0	16,243.1	16,683.3	16,403.2	16,926.0	17,020.0	16,321.9
2020	17,382.0	17,542.7	13,757.1	14,071.5	14,903.8	15,480.9	15,942.5	16,584.3	16,234.7	16,226.7	16,743.6	17,521.0	16,032.6
2021	17,830.7	18,250.1	18,658.1	19,168.9	19,442.9	20,110.1	20,165.3	20,462.6	20,510.9	20,777.6	21,439.1	20,917.4	19,811.1
2022	21,033.2	21,232.4	21,626.3	21,586.5	Discontinued		----	----	----	----	----	----	21,369.6

Source: Toronto Stock Exchange

The CAC 40® is a free float market capitalization weighted index that reflects the performance of the 40 largest and most actively traded shares listed on Euronext Paris, and is the most widely used indicator of the Paris stock market.   Shaded areas indicate French recessions.

Average Value of CAC 40 Index

Year	Jan.	Feb.	Mar.	Apr.	May	June	July	Aug.	Sept.	Oct.	Nov.	Dec.	Average
2014	4,248.4	4,301.1	4,338.1	4,437.3	4,484.8	4,522.0	4,362.0	4,249.6	4,425.3	4,129.8	4,261.0	4,262.2	4,335.1
2015	4,384.2	4,768.5	5,000.7	5,173.4	5,058.2	4,927.9	4,956.2	4,887.1	4,526.6	4,715.6	4,910.3	4,665.7	4,831.2
2016	4,340.1	4,184.8	4,427.5	4,445.2	4,373.5	4,293.9	4,317.6	4,425.4	4,448.6	4,497.6	4,504.3	4,764.5	4,418.6
2017	4,863.6	4,846.7	5,008.4	5,134.6	5,352.0	5,263.8	5,175.0	5,122.7	5,208.8	5,389.8	5,398.0	5,373.0	5,178.0
2018	5,483.0	5,257.8	5,200.6	5,345.3	5,537.6	5,408.3	5,409.4	5,438.3	5,381.7	5,170.1	5,035.1	4,798.2	5,288.8
2019	4,822.7	5,118.2	5,315.3	5,511.4	5,360.8	5,420.3	5,578.7	5,351.9	5,067.5	5,623.6	5,892.8	5,915.3	5,414.9
2020	6,001.1	5,923.3	4,481.8	4,425.2	4,492.5	4,958.3	4,999.9	4,962.6	4,937.4	4,843.4	5,335.7	5,546.8	5,075.7
2021	5,589.5	5,697.5	5,962.0	6,220.1	6,358.0	6,574.4	6,517.7	6,746.1	6,637.7	6,651.9	7,012.9	6,998.9	6,413.9
2022	7,125.2	6,920.8	6,452.0	6,558.0	6,341.9	6,139.3	6,096.0	6,435.9	6,017.4	6,030.4	6,556.7	6,600.2	6,439.5
2023	6,952.4	7,231.7	7,164.4	7,464.7	7,363.2	7,256.4	7,336.0	7,292.2	7,224.4	6,970.6	7,160.0	7,514.4	7,244.2

Source: Euronext Paris

HANG SENG INDEX
Weekly Cash as of 03/28/2024

WEEKLY CASH
As of 03/28/2024
Chart High 33484.1 on 01/29/2018
Chart Low 14597.3 on 10/31/2022

The Hang Seng Index is a freefloat-adjusted market capitalization-weighted stock market index in Hong Kong. The Index was created by Hong Kong banker Stanley Kwan in 1969.

Average Value of Hang Seng Index

Year	Jan.	Feb.	Mar.	Apr.	May	June	July	Aug.	Sept.	Oct.	Nov.	Dec.	Average
2014	22,725.2	22,188.3	21,980.8	22,598.5	22,584.9	23,144.9	23,760.0	24,812.1	24,341.8	23,301.2	23,779.1	23,386.2	23,216.9
2015	24,209.9	24,670.4	24,306.8	27,451.5	27,656.2	27,009.0	25,032.2	23,223.2	21,365.1	22,649.3	22,509.5	21,910.2	24,332.8
2016	19,733.6	19,134.5	20,299.8	20,986.5	20,174.0	20,646.4	21,497.8	22,663.9	23,543.0	23,406.1	22,618.9	22,229.6	21,411.2
2017	22,814.5	23,725.3	24,029.6	24,262.7	25,189.4	25,828.2	26,326.0	27,532.4	27,790.9	28,394.4	29,213.7	29,109.6	26,184.7
2018	31,831.9	30,969.3	30,898.1	30,376.0	30,698.7	30,070.3	28,466.1	27,925.8	27,275.6	25,705.4	26,081.0	26,075.6	28,864.5
2019	26,711.6	28,392.4	28,900.0	29,882.0	28,132.3	27,718.0	28,465.3	25,987.1	26,474.3	26,458.2	26,979.0	27,264.3	27,613.7
2020	28,214.4	27,214.7	24,107.0	24,008.8	23,807.6	24,478.4	25,316.2	25,100.2	24,253.2	24,440.4	26,119.8	26,524.8	25,298.8
2021	28,662.9	29,869.8	28,836.3	28,875.1	28,537.1	28,850.2	27,252.4	25,928.8	25,223.4	25,304.4	24,912.9	23,481.2	27,144.5
2022	23,974.5	24,154.5	21,338.2	21,118.5	20,382.3	21,516.5	20,947.7	19,901.8	18,563.5	16,390.9	17,177.2	19,419.6	20,407.1
2023	21,569.8	20,952.0	19,883.8	20,231.6	19,522.4	19,243.5	19,128.5	18,680.5	17,991.2	17,450.4	17,533.5	16,545.9	19,061.1

Source: Hong Kong Futures Exchange

NIKKEI 225 Index
Weekly Cash as of 03/29/2024

WEEKLY CASH
As of 03/29/2024
Chart High 41087.75 on 03/22/2024
Chart Low 10441.11 on 01/24/2013

The Nikkei Stock Average is owned by and proprietary to Nihon Keisai Shimbun.   Shaded areas indicate Japan recessions.

Average Value of Nikkei 225 Index

Year	Jan.	Feb.	Mar.	Apr.	May	June	July	Aug.	Sept.	Oct.	Nov.	Dec.	Average
2014	15,578.3	14,617.6	14,694.8	14,475.3	14,343.2	15,131.8	15,379.3	15,358.7	15,948.5	15,394.1	17,179.0	17,541.7	15,470.2
2015	17,274.4	18,053.2	19,197.6	19,767.9	19,974.2	20,403.8	20,372.6	19,919.1	17,944.2	18,374.1	19,581.8	19,202.6	19,172.1
2016	17,302.3	16,347.0	16,897.3	16,543.5	16,612.7	16,068.8	16,168.3	16,586.1	16,737.0	17,044.5	17,689.5	19,066.0	16,921.9
2017	19,194.1	19,188.7	19,340.2	18,736.4	19,726.8	20,045.6	20,044.9	19,670.2	19,924.4	21,267.5	22,525.2	22,769.9	20,202.8
2018	23,712.2	21,991.7	21,395.5	21,868.8	22,590.1	22,562.9	22,309.1	22,494.1	23,159.3	22,690.8	21,967.9	21,032.4	22,314.6
2019	20,460.5	21,123.6	21,414.9	21,964.9	21,218.4	21,060.2	21,593.7	20,629.7	21,585.5	22,197.5	23,278.1	23,660.4	21,682.3
2020	23,642.9	23,181.9	18,974.0	19,208.4	20,543.3	22,486.9	22,529.5	22,901.5	23,307.0	23,464.1	25,384.9	26,773.0	22,699.8
2021	28,175.4	29,443.6	29,315.3	29,426.8	28,517.1	28,943.2	28,118.8	27,692.7	29,893.6	28,586.2	29,370.6	28,514.2	28,833.1
2022	27,904.0	27,066.5	26,584.1	27,043.3	26,653.8	26,958.4	26,986.7	28,351.7	27,419.0	26,983.2	27,903.3	27,214.7	27,255.7
2023	26,606.3	27,509.1	27,692.1	28,275.8	30,147.5	32,754.5	32,694.1	32,167.4	32,725.6	31,381.0	32,960.3	33,118.0	30,669.3

Source: Singapore Exchange

Sugar

The white crystalline substance called "sugar" is the organic chemical compound sucrose, one of several related compounds, all known as sugars. These include glucose, dextrose, fructose, and lactose. All sugars are members of the larger group of compounds called carbohydrates and are characterized by a sweet taste. Sucrose is considered a double sugar because it is composed of one molecule of glucose and one molecule of fructose. While sucrose is common in many plants, it occurs in the highest concentration in sugarcane (Saccharum officinarum) and sugar beets (Beta vulgaris). Sugarcane is about 7 to 18 percent sugar by weight, while sugar beets are 8 to 22 percent.

Sugarcane is a member of the grass family and is a perennial. Sugarcane is cultivated in tropical and subtropical regions around the world roughly between the Tropics of Cancer and Capricorn. It grows best in hot, wet climates where there is heavy rainfall followed by a dry season. The largest cane producers are Florida, Louisiana, Texas, and Hawaii. On a commercial basis, sugarcane is not grown from seeds but from cuttings or pieces of the stalk.

Sugar beets, which are produced in temperate or colder climates, are annuals grown from seeds. Sugar beets do best with moderate temperatures and evenly distributed rainfall. The beets are planted in the spring and harvested in the fall. The sugar is contained in the root of the beet, but the sugars from beets and cane are identical. Sugar beet production takes place mostly in Europe, the U.S., China, and Japan. The largest sugar beet producing states are Minnesota, Idaho, North Dakota, and Michigan. Sugar beets are refined to yield white sugar, and very little raw sugar is produced.

Sugar beets and sugarcane are produced in over 100 countries around the world. Of all the sugar produced, about 25% is processed from sugar beets, and the remaining 75% is from sugar cane. The trend has been that the production of sugar from cane is increasing relative to that produced from beets. The significance of this in that sugarcane is a perennial plant while the sugar beet is an annual, and due to the longer production cycle, sugarcane production and the sugar processed from that cane, may not be quite as responsive to changes in price.

Sugar futures are traded at the ICE Futures U.S. exchange , the Bolsa de Mercadorias & Futuros (BM&F), Kansai Commodities Exchange (KANEX), the Tokyo Grain Exchange (TGE), and the ICE Futures Europe exchange.

Raw sugar is traded on the ICE Futures U.S. exchange, while white sugar is traded on the ICE Futures Europe exchange. The most actively traded contract is the No. 11 (World) sugar contract at the ICE exchange. The No. 11 contract calls for the delivery of 112,000 pounds (50 long tons) of raw cane centrifugal sugar from any of 28 foreign countries of origin and the United States. The ICE exchange also trades the No. 14 sugar contract (Domestic), which calls for the delivery of raw centrifugal cane sugar in the United States. Futures on white sugar are traded on the London International Financial Futures Exchange and call for the delivery of 50 metric tons of white beet sugar, cane crystal sugar, or refined sugar of any origin from the crop current at the time of delivery.

Prices – ICE World No. 11 sugar futures prices (Barchart.com symbol SB) posted their low for 2023 in January at 18.92 cents per pound. Sugar then soared to a 12-year high in April at 27.41 cents per pound on concern about global sugar production as an El Nino weather pattern disrupted global sugar production. An El Nino weather pattern typically brings heavy rain to Brazil and drought to India, negatively impacting sugar crop production. The Indian Sugar Mills Association (ISMA) in April cut its 2022/23 India sugar production estimate to 32.8 MMT, down -8.6% yr/yr. The lower production forecast caused India to cap its sugar exports at 6.1 MMT during the 2022/23 season (ending September 30), down from the record exports of 11.1 MMT seen in the previous season. India is the second-largest sugar producer in the world. A poor sugar crop in Thailand, the world's third-largest sugar producer and the second-largest sugar exporter, also boosted prices after the Thai Sugar Millers Corp cut its 2022/23 Thailand sugar production estimate to 11.4 MMT from a previous estimate of 13 MMT. Sugar prices retreated into June on larger production in Brazil after Unica reported that Brazil's 2023/24 sugar production through mid-June surged +32.1% to 9.528 MMT. However, prices ratcheted higher and posted a 12-year high in November of 28.14 cents per pound as India extended restrictions on sugar exports after October 31 to maintain adequate domestic supplies. India's Weather Department said the 2023 monsoon rain (June-September) was 6% below average and the lowest monsoon rainfall in 5 years. However, sugar prices retreated into year-end as the supply outlook improved. The USDA, in its bi-annual report released on November 23, projected that global 2023/24 sugar production would climb +4.7% y/y to a record 183.461 MMT. Sugar prices finished 2023 up +2.7% yr/yr at 20.58 cents per pound.

Supply – World production of centrifugal (raw) sugar in the 2023/24 marketing year (Oct 1 to Sep 30) is expected to rise by +4.7% yr/yr to 183.461 million metric tons. The world's largest sugar producers in 2023/24 are expected to be Brazil with 22.3% of world production, India with 19.6%, and the European Union with 8.5%. US sugar production in 2023/24 is expected to fall by -0.2% yr/yr to 8.372 million metric tons. US production of cane sugar in 2023/24 is expected to fall by -1.9% yr/yr to 3.985 million short tons, and beet sugar production is expected to rise by +4.2% yr/yr to 5.407 million short tons. World ending stocks in 2021/22 fell by -5.5% yr/yr to 47.531 million metric tons, below the 2018/19 record high of 52.827 million metric tons.

Demand – World domestic consumption of centrifugal (raw) sugar in 2021/22 remained unchanged from 2020/21 at 174.477 million metric tons. US domestic disappearance (consumption) of sugar in 2023/24 is expected to be down by -0.5% yr/yr at 12.790 million short tons.

Trade – World exports of centrifugal sugar in 2023/24 are expected to rise by +4.8% yr/yr to 67.409 million metric tons. The world's largest sugar exporters in 2023/24 are expected to be Brazil with 48.2% of total world exports, Thailand with 14.8%, and India with 9.6%.

US sugar exports in 2023/24 are expected to rise by +94.0% yr/yr at 160,000 short tons. US sugar imports in 2023/24 are expected to fall by -9.9% yr/yr to 2.840 million metric tons.

World Production, Supply & Stocks/Consumption Ratio of Sugar   In 1000's of Metric Tons (Raw Value)

Marketing Year	Beginning Stocks	Production	Imports	Total Supply	Exports	Domestic Consumption	Ending Stocks	Stocks As a % of Consumption
2014-15	44,798	177,582	50,248	272,648	55,033	168,037	48,756	29.0
2015-16	48,756	164,972	54,629	268,310	54,187	168,976	44,422	26.3
2016-17	44,422	172,143	55,418	272,643	60,047	169,148	42,012	24.8
2017-18	42,012	194,222	55,621	291,855	65,868	173,287	51,574	29.8
2018-19	51,574	179,158	53,161	283,893	58,271	171,994	52,827	30.7
2019-20	52,827	166,559	53,735	273,121	53,536	171,252	47,652	27.8
2020-21	47,652	180,114	59,096	286,862	63,858	171,883	50,313	29.3
2021-22[1]	50,313	180,663	55,933	286,909	64,803	173,636	47,531	27.4
2022-23[2]	47,531	175,307	57,409	280,247	64,316	176,380	38,862	22.0
2023-24[3]	38,862	183,461	57,872	280,195	67,409	178,431		

[1] Preliminary.   [2] Estimate.   [3] Forecast.   *Source: Foreign Agricultural Service, U.S. Department of Agriculture (FAS-USDA)*

World Production of Sugar (Centrifugal Sugar-Raw Value)   In Thousands of Metric Tons

Year	Australia	Brazil	China	Cuba	European Union	India	Indonesia	Mexico	Pakistan	Thailand	United States	Ukraine	World Total
2014-15	4,700	35,950	11,000	1,850	18,449	30,460	2,100	6,344	5,164	10,793	1,728	7,853	177,582
2015-16	4,900	34,650	9,050	1,625	14,283	27,385	2,025	6,484	5,265	9,743	1,638	8,155	164,972
2016-17	5,100	39,150	9,300	1,800	15,505	22,200	2,050	6,314	6,825	10,033	2,156	8,137	172,143
2017-18	4,480	38,870	10,300	1,100	19,508	34,309	2,100	6,371	7,225	14,710	2,180	8,430	194,222
2018-19	4,725	29,500	10,760	1,300	16,750	34,300	2,200	6,812	5,270	14,581	1,753	8,164	179,158
2019-20	4,285	30,300	10,400	1,200	17,040	28,900	2,250	5,596	5,340	8,294	1,638	7,392	166,559
2020-21	4,335	42,050	10,600	850	15,216	33,760	2,130	6,058	6,505	7,587	1,240	8,376	180,114
2021-22[1]	4,120	35,450	9,600	475	16,577	36,880	2,300	6,556	7,560	10,157	1,450	8,307	180,663
2022-23[2]	4,200	38,050	8,960	400	14,710	32,000	2,400	5,537	6,860	11,059	1,330	8,391	175,307
2023-24[3]	4,100	41,000	10,000	410	15,532	36,000	2,600	5,650	6,260	9,400	1,510	8,372	183,461

[1] Preliminary.   [2] Estimate.   [3] Forecast.   *Source: Foreign Agricultural Service, U.S. Department of Agriculture (FAS-USDA)*

World Stocks of Centrifugal Sugar at Beginning of Marketing Year   In Thousands of Metric Tons (Raw Value)

Year	Australia	Brazil	China	Cuba	European Union	India	Indonesia	Iran	Mexico	Philippines	Russia	United States	World Total
2014-15	111	350	9,977	140	3,066	8,227	1,299	700	881	1,032	370	1,642	44,798
2015-16	140	950	10,390	180	4,151	10,607	949	400	860	997	100	1,647	48,756
2016-17	230	750	9,591	115	791	9,294	1,098	460	1,099	1,168	150	1,863	44,422
2017-18	220	850	7,811	125	1,776	6,570	1,743	535	1,062	1,167	350	1,702	42,012
2018-19	130	920	6,567	110	1,547	14,214	1,793	480	1,479	1,067	440	1,822	51,574
2019-20	137	220	5,408	127	1,260	17,614	2,300	485	1,239	1,234	550	1,618	52,827
2020-21	38	590	4,027	120	2,076	14,614	1,941	430	910	1,289	609	1,468	47,652
2021-22[1]	135	340	5,374	100	1,106	13,213	2,653	565	1,116	1,196	565	1,547	50,313
2022-23[2]	294	340	5,014	70	1,464	9,506	2,370	545	1,022	931	624	1,652	47,531
2023-24[3]	384	690	2,091	76	1,269	5,306	2,330	520	885	1,465	580	1,701	38,862

[1] Preliminary.   [2] Estimate.   [3] Forecast.   *Source: Foreign Agricultural Service, U.S. Department of Agriculture (FAS-USDA)*

Centrifugal Sugar (Raw Value) Imported into Selected Countries   In Thousands of Metric Tons

Year	Algeria	Canada	China	European Union	Indonesia	Iran	Japan	Korea, South	Malaysia	Nigeria	Russia	United States	World Total
2014-15	1,844	1,184	5,058	2,918	2,950	266	1,360	1,882	2,063	1,465	1,100	3,223	50,248
2015-16	1,921	1,229	6,116	3,055	3,724	822	1,275	1,900	2,009	1,470	750	3,031	54,629
2016-17	2,135	1,139	4,600	2,908	4,781	962	1,232	1,757	1,893	1,820	327	2,943	55,418
2017-18	2,261	1,238	4,350	1,612	4,325	203	1,240	1,864	2,002	1,870	274	2,972	55,621
2018-19	2,328	1,268	4,086	2,374	5,362	935	1,187	1,999	2,139	1,870	562	2,785	53,161
2019-20	2,468	1,245	3,808	2,235	4,758	1,111	1,142	1,926	1,966	1,890	604	3,778	53,735
2020-21	2,258	1,389	6,379	1,792	6,124	1,421	1,051	1,934	2,142	1,880	584	2,922	59,096
2021-22[1]	2,245	1,319	5,000	1,998	5,466	1,081	1,004	1,983	1,961	1,930	860	3,308	55,933
2022-23[2]	1,985	1,380	3,800	3,000	5,800	1,074	1,034	1,819	2,127	1,950	305	3,152	57,409
2023-24[3]	2,000	1,385	4,600	2,500	5,630	1,000	1,127	1,775	1,975	1,930	250	2,840	57,872

[1] Preliminary.   [2] Estimate.   [3] Forecast.   *Source: Foreign Agricultural Service, U.S. Department of Agriculture (FAS-USDA)*

SUGAR

SUGAR
Quarterly Cash as of 03/28/2024

QUARTERLY CASH
As of 03/28/2024
Chart High 65.50 on 11/20/1974
Chart Low 1.23 on 01/06/1967

Spot raw, NY: to 02/1961; World raw #8, NY: 02/1961 to 12/1970; World raw #11, NY: to date.

Centrifugal Sugar (Raw Value) Exported From Selected Countries   In Thousands of Metric Tons

Year	Australia	Brazil	Colom-bia	Cuba	Dominican Republic	European Union	Guate-mala	India	Mauritius	South Africa	Swazi-land	Thailand	World Total
2014-15	3,561	23,950	835	915	186	641	1,582	2,340	2,580	457	772	8,252	55,033
2015-16	3,700	24,350	584	1,112	186	665	1,548	2,029	3,800	463	305	7,055	54,187
2016-17	4,000	28,500	695	1,160	185	587	1,987	1,978	2,125	474	218	7,016	60,047
2017-18	3,600	28,200	732	557	184	519	4,349	1,881	2,236	390	768	10,907	65,868
2018-19	3,735	19,600	801	636	185	582	2,411	2,125	4,700	347	1,041	10,612	58,271
2019-20	3,600	19,280	778	600	212	778	1,459	1,858	5,800	396	1,451	6,695	53,536
2020-21	3,400	32,150	669	378	215	634	1,278	1,395	8,406	369	1,007	3,739	63,858
2021-22[1]	3,120	25,950	663	156	250	524	1,217	1,651	11,927	320	548	7,012	64,803
2022-23[2]	3,250	28,200	670	110	190	545	905	1,657	7,433	240	722	9,500	64,316
2023-24[3]	3,300	32,500	680	110	190	581	905	1,662	6,500	240	770	10,000	67,409

[1] Preliminary.   [2] Estimate.   [3] Forecast.   *Source: Foreign Agricultural Service, U.S. Department of Agriculture (FAS-USDA)*

Average Wholesale Price of Refined Beet Sugar[2]--Midwest Market   In Cents Per Pound

Year	Jan.	Feb.	Mar.	Apr.	May	June	July	Aug.	Sept.	Oct.	Nov.	Dec.	Average
2014	26.50	26.25	26.50	29.75	31.60	35.00	36.00	36.60	37.50	36.60	36.00	36.00	32.86
2015	36.00	35.25	35.13	35.50	34.30	34.00	33.80	33.13	33.00	32.40	32.00	32.00	33.88
2016	32.00	31.00	31.00	30.50	30.00	29.75	29.00	28.50	28.50	28.50	28.50	28.50	29.65
2017	28.50	28.63	29.10	29.50	29.50	30.70	31.88	32.13	32.90	33.50	34.63	35.00	31.33
2018	35.25	36.00	36.00	36.00	36.00	36.00	36.00	36.00	36.00	33.38	34.90	35.00	35.54
2019	35.00	35.00	35.00	35.00	35.00	35.00	35.00	35.00	35.00	35.00	40.40	43.25	36.14
2020	44.00	44.00	44.00	44.00	44.00	44.00	44.00	44.00	44.00	36.50	36.50	36.50	42.13
2021	36.50	36.50	36.50	36.50	36.50	36.50	37.20	39.00	39.00	39.00	39.00	39.00	37.60
2022	39.00	41.00	42.00	42.00	NQ	NQ	70.00	70.00	70.00	55.25	58.00	NQ	54.14
2023[1]	NQ	60.00	60.00	60.00	62.00	62.00	62.00	62.00	62.00	57.00	57.00	57.00	60.09

[1] Preliminary.   [2] These are f.o.b. basis prices in bulk, not delivered prices.   *Source: Economic Research Service, U.S. Department of Agriculture (ERS)*

Average Price of World Raw Sugar[1]   In Cents Per Pound

Year	Jan.	Feb.	Mar.	Apr.	May	June	July	Aug.	Sept.	Oct.	Nov.	Dec.	Average
2014	15.42	16.28	17.58	17.01	17.50	17.22	17.18	15.89	14.60	16.48	15.89	14.99	16.34
2015	15.06	14.52	12.84	12.93	12.70	11.75	11.88	10.67	11.32	14.14	14.89	15.00	13.14
2016	14.29	13.31	15.43	15.00	16.68	19.34	19.69	20.01	21.30	22.92	20.81	18.83	18.13
2017	20.54	20.40	18.06	16.32	15.66	13.53	14.11	13.80	13.92	14.23	14.66	14.43	15.81
2018	13.99	13.56	12.83	11.82	11.85	12.06	11.17	10.46	10.78	13.18	12.78	12.55	12.25
2019	12.70	12.94	12.47	12.55	11.82	12.44	12.15	11.56	11.16	12.46	12.69	13.34	12.36
2020	14.18	15.07	11.81	10.07	10.65	11.83	11.92	12.81	12.42	14.29	14.93	14.67	12.89
2021	15.94	16.97	15.81	16.17	17.20	17.21	17.73	19.38	19.28	19.62	19.75	19.17	17.85
2022	18.46	18.20	19.11	19.68	19.27	18.80	18.35	18.06	18.19	18.30	19.40	20.02	18.82
2023[1]	19.95	21.40	20.96	24.63	25.75	24.68	24.04	24.19	26.60	26.90	27.31	22.22	24.05

[1] Contract No. 11, f.o.b. stowed Caribbean port, including Brazil, bulk spot price.   [2] Preliminary.   *Source: Economic Research Service, U.S. Department of Agriculture (ERS-USDA)*

Average Price of Raw Sugar in New York (C.I.F., Duty/Free Paid, Contract #12 & #14)   In Cents Per Pound

Year	Jan.	Feb.	Mar.	Apr.	May	June	July	Aug.	Sept.	Oct.	Nov.	Dec.	Average
2014	20.27	21.65	22.03	24.33	24.66	25.65	24.78	25.64	25.36	26.41	24.26	24.81	24.15
2015	25.24	24.62	24.07	24.39	24.61	24.76	24.67	24.50	24.21	25.04	26.63	25.83	24.88
2016	25.76	25.50	26.32	27.90	27.26	27.68	28.15	28.54	28.16	28.57	28.76	29.24	27.65
2017	29.44	30.59	29.95	28.72	28.41	27.83	26.77	25.11	26.90	27.09	27.28	26.93	27.92
2018	26.60	25.83	24.73	24.92	24.59	25.72	25.56	25.60	25.40	25.21	25.04	25.23	25.37
2019	25.57	25.90	26.23	26.95	26.33	26.49	25.66	25.80	25.65	26.07	27.21	26.01	26.16
2020	25.90	26.71	27.09	26.02	25.85	25.95	26.59	27.39	26.85	27.55	29.33	28.42	26.97
2021	28.79	29.72	30.48	31.24	32.42	33.05	35.77	34.50	35.72	37.06	37.12	36.71	33.55
2022	35.48	35.43	36.33	36.66	36.38	36.15	34.83	35.63	34.97	34.70	35.94	36.51	35.75
2023[1]	36.50	36.98	37.88	41.27	42.56	41.05	38.61	40.83	42.66	44.44	44.72	40.36	40.66

[1] Preliminary.   *Source: Economic Research Service, U.S. Department of Agriculture (ERS-USDA)*

Supply and Utilization of Sugar (Cane and Beet) in the United States   In Thousands of Short Tons (Raw Value)

	Supply								Utilization						
	Production			Offshore Receipts							Net		- Domestic Disappearance -		
Year	Cane	Beet	Total	Foreign	Terri-tories	Total	Beginning Stocks	Total Supply	Total Use	Exports	Changes in Invisible Stocks	Refining Loss Ad-justment	In Poly-hydric Alcohol[4]	Total	Per Capita Pounds
2014-15	3,763	4,893	8,656	3,553	0	3,553	1,810	14,019	12,204	185		0	28	11,888	68.2
2015-16	3,870	5,119	8,989	3,341	0	3,341	1,815	14,145	12,091	74	-33	0	22	11,881	69.3
2016-17	3,867	5,103	8,970	3,244	0	3,244	2,054	14,267	12,391	95	38	0	29	12,102	69.8
2017-18	4,014	5,279	9,293	3,277	0	3,277	1,876	14,445	12,438	170	82	0	28	12,048	69.3
2018-19	4,060	4,939	8,999	3,070	0	3,070	2,008	14,077	12,294	35	28	0	27	12,106	68.7
2019-20	3,798	4,351	8,149	4,165	0	4,165	1,783	14,097	12,479	61	74	0	20	12,246	68.4
2020-21	4,142	5,092	9,233	3,221	0	3,221	1,618	14,072	12,367	49	40	0	27	12,161	69.0
2021-22[1]	4,002	5,155	9,157	3,646	0	3,646	1,705	14,508	12,688	29	81	0	27	12,470	
2022-23[2]	4,063	5,187	9,250	3,614	0	3,614	1,820	14,685	12,842	82	171	0	22	12,473	
2023-24[3]	3,985	5,407	9,391	3,310	0	3,310	1,843	14,544	12,790	160		0	25	12,525	

[1] Preliminary.   [2] Estimate.   [3] Forecast.   [4] Includes feed use.   *Source: Economic Research Service, U.S. Department of Agriculture (ERS-USDA)*

Sugarcane for Sugar & Seed and Production of Cane Sugar and Molasses in the United States

Year	Acreage Harvested (1,000 Acres)	Yield of Cane Per Havested Acre Net Tons	Production for Sugar (1,000 Tons)	Production for Seed (1,000 Tons)	Total (1,000 Tons)	Sugar Yield Per Acre (Short Tons)	Farm Price ($ Per Ton)	Farm Value of Cane Used for Sugar (1,000 Dollars)	Farm Value of Cane Used for Sugar & Seed (1,000 Dollars)	Total Raw Value (1,000 Tons)	Per Ton of Cane (In Lbs.)	Refined Basis (1,000 Tons)	Molasses Made Edible (1,000 Gallons)	Molasses Made Total[3] (1,000 Gallons)
2014	868.5	35.0	28,895	1,529	30,424	4.57	34.7	1,002,138	1,054,657	3,764	----	----	----	----
2015	874.7	36.7	30,555	1,567	32,122	4.64	31.2	953,328	1,000,620	3,857	----	----	----	----
2016	903.1	35.6	30,371	1,747	32,118	4.52	32.6	990,209	1,043,953	3,856	----	----	----	----
2017	904.1	36.8	31,182	2,056	33,238	4.72	31.0	1,025,524		4,017	----	----	----	----
2018	899.7	38.4	32,934	1,608	34,542	4.69	33.4	1,154,907		4,029	----	----	----	----
2019	913.2	35.0	30,287	1,650	31,937	4.36	38.3	1,223,686		3,790	----	----	----	----
2020	947.6	38.1	34,338	1,762	36,100	4.65	40.9	1,476,508		4,199	----	----	----	----
2021	935.2	35.1	32,838	1,797	32,838	4.43	46.9	1,540,497		3,940	----	----	----	----
2022[1]	930.2	37.3	34,671		34,671	4.74	52.1	1,807,418		4,116	----	----	----	----
2023[2]	931.5	35.4	32,956		32,956					3,931	----	----	----	----

[1] Preliminary.   [2] Estimate.   [3] Excludes edible molasses.   *Source: Economic Research Service, U.S. Department of Agriculture (ERS-USDA)*

SUGAR

U.S. Sugar Beets, Beet Sugar, Pulp & Molasses Produced from Sugar Beets and Raw Sugar Spot Prices

	Acreage		Yield Per Harvested Acre (Sh. Tons)	Pro-duction (1,000 Tons)	Sugar Yield Per Acre (Sh. Tons)	Price[3] (Dollars)	Farm Value (1,000 $)	Sugar Production		Raw Sugar Prices			Wholesale List Price
								Equiv-alent Raw Value[4]	Refined Basis	World[5] Refined #5	CSCE		HFCS (42%)
Year of Harvest	Planted	Harvested						1,000 Short Tons		In Cents Per Pound	#11 World	N.Y. Duty Paid	Midwest
	1,000 Acres												
2014	1,163	1,146	27.3	31,285	4.27	46.00	1,440,068	4,893	----	20.05	16.34	24.15	29.96
2015	1,160	1,145	30.9	35,359	4.47	47.20	1,669,310	5,119	----	16.94	13.14	24.88	32.75
2016	1,163	1,126	32.8	36,920	4.53	35.70	1,318,267	5,103	----	22.63	18.13	27.65	37.68
2017	1,132	1,114	31.7	35,317	4.74	41.20	1,456,165	5,279	----	19.62	15.81	27.92	39.79
2018	1,113	1,095	30.3	33,145	4.50	35.60	1,183,562	4,939	----	15.56	12.25	25.37	39.32
2019	1,133	980	29.2	28,650	4.44	38.30	1,098,421	4,351	----	15.18	12.36	26.16	41.23
2020	1,162	1,142	29.4	33,610	4.46	50.50	1,696,742	5,092	----	17.02	12.89	26.97	42.53
2021	1,161	1,109	33.2	36,772	4.65	53.00	1,948,573	5,155	----	21.40	17.85	33.55	42.53
2022[1]	1,160	1,138	28.7	32,644	4.44	65.20	2,129,629	5,187	----	24.17	18.82	35.75	43.67
2023[2]	1,137	1,127	31.2	35,226				5,407	----	30.05	24.05	40.66	49.35

[1] Preliminary. [2] Estimate. [3] Includes support payments, but excludes Gov't. sugar beet payments. [4] Refined sugar multiplied by factor of 1.07.
[5] F.O.B. Europe. *Source: Economic Research Service, U.S. Department of Agriculture (ERS-USDA)*

Sugar Deliveries and Stocks in the United States   In Thousands of Short Tons (Raw Value)

			Deliveries by Primary Distributors						Stocks, Jan. 1					
Year	Quota Allocation	Actual Imports	Cane Sugar Refineries Deliveries	Beet Sugar Factories Deliveries	Importers of Direct Con-sumption Sugar	Mainland Cane Sugar Mills[3]	Total Deliveries	Total Domestic Con-sumption	Cane Sugar Re-fineries	Beet Sugar Factories	CCC	Refiners' Raw	Mainland Cane Mills	Total
2014	----	----	6,069	4,875	760	----	11,704	11,831	572	1,603	0	592	1,714	4,481
2015	----	----	6,285	4,614	1,034	----	11,933	12,067	351	1,589	0	556	1,634	4,130
2016	----	----	6,386	4,809	921	----	12,115	12,287	413	1,889	0	322	1,336	3,960
2017	----	----	5,976	5,425	682	----	12,083	12,232	325	2,041	0	362	1,623	4,351
2018	----	----	6,219	5,121	705	----	12,045	12,183	316	1,716	0	538	1,529	4,099
2019	----	----	6,317	5,099	645	----	12,062	12,185	288	1,889	0	528	1,673	4,378
2020	----	----	6,593	4,387	1,201	----	12,182	12,276	326	1,454	0	565	1,510	3,855
2021	----	----	6,235	5,043	1,147	----	12,424	12,546	339	1,760	0	560	1,422	4,081
2022[1]	----	----	6,458	5,286	679	----	12,423	12,526	327	1,744	0	483	1,524	4,077
2023[2]	----	----	6,526	4,992	821	----	12,338	12,458	348	1,624	0	590	1,591	4,153

[1] Preliminary. [2] Estimate. [3] Sugar for direct consumption only. [4] Refined. *Source: Economic Research Service, U.S. Department of Agriculture (ERS-USDA)*

Sugar, Refined--Deliveries to End User in the United States   In Thousands of Short Tons

Year	Bakery & Cereal Products	Bev-erages	Confec-tionery[2]	Hotels, Restar. & Insti-tutions	Ice Cream & Dairy Products	Canned, Bottled & Frozen Foods	All Other Food Uses	Retail Grocers[3]	Wholesale Grocers[4]	Non-food Uses	Non-Industrial Uses	Industrial Uses	Total Deliveries
2014	2,435	598	1,142	118	756	434	853	1,193	2,151	118	3,965	6,336	10,300
2015	2,391	755	1,172	103	764	473	791	1,230	2,086	162	3,832	6,509	10,341
2016	2,517	695	1,156	92	764	433	880	1,303	2,248	179	4,100	6,625	10,725
2017	2,519	680	1,171	105	753	420	1,048	1,250	2,206	137	4,055	6,729	10,784
2018	2,468	725	1,222	91	812	375	1,147	1,224	2,175	138	3,825	6,887	10,713
2019	2,526	725	1,189	83	760	409	1,160	1,237	2,264	127	3,875	6,896	10,771
2020	2,421	620	993	90	766	430	1,016	1,311	2,244	143	3,951	6,389	10,340
2021	2,476	746	1,039	132	822	399	1,076	1,227	2,271	126	3,943	6,683	10,627
2022	2,592	837	1,189	94	835	394	963	2,434	1,283	119	4,120	6,929	11,049
2023[1]	2,483	804	1,187	92	846	358	1,054	2,256	1,313	104	4,020	6,835	10,855

[1] Preliminary. [2] And related products. [3] Chain stores, supermarkets. [4] Jobbers, sugar dealers.
Source: Economic Research Service, U.S. Department of Agriculture (ERS-USDA)

Deliveries[1] of All Sugar by Primary Distributors in the United States, by Quarters   In Thousands of Short Tons

Year	First Quarter	Second Quarter	Third Quarter	Fourth Quarter	Total	Year	First Quarter	Second Quarter	Third Quarter	Fourth Quarter	Total
2012	2,663	2,915	2,954	2,873	11,405	2018	2,926	2,964	3,223	3,071	12,183
2013	2,720	2,954	3,222	3,229	12,124	2019	2,935	3,059	3,166	3,024	12,185
2014	2,742	3,053	3,225	2,847	11,867	2020	3,119	2,964	3,241	2,951	12,276
2015	2,861	3,070	3,274	2,862	12,067	2021	2,958	3,185	3,184	3,220	12,546
2016	2,992	2,946	3,250	3,098	12,287	2022	3,016	3,181	3,160	3,168	12,526
2017	2,869	3,130	3,161	3,073	12,232	2023[2]	3,131	3,107	3,183	3,037	12,458

[1] Includes for domestic consumption and for export. [2] Preliminary. *Source: Economic Research Service, U.S. Department of Agriculture (ERS-USDA)*

SUGAR #11 - ICE-US
Weekly Selected Futures as of 03/28/2024

WEEKLY SELECTED FUTURES
As of 03/28/2024
Chart High 28.14 on 11/07/2023
Chart Low 9.05 on 04/28/2020

Nearby Futures through Last Trading Day using selected contract months: March, May, July and October.

Volume of Trading of World Sugar #11 Futures in New York   In Thousands of Contracts

Year	Jan.	Feb.	Mar.	Apr.	May	June	July	Aug.	Sept.	Oct.	Nov.	Dec.	Total
2014	2,461.6	4,157.3	2,477.4	2,857.3	1,906.5	3,370.3	1,981.4	1,853.3	3,657.9	1,651.3	1,574.3	1,448.0	29,397
2015	2,547.7	3,635.6	2,790.0	3,850.9	2,274.2	3,789.2	2,260.8	2,315.0	4,329.7	2,600.5	2,303.8	1,697.0	34,394
2016	3,182.7	3,772.8	2,652.9	3,517.9	2,596.7	4,210.0	1,738.1	2,008.6	3,963.5	1,721.8	1,964.4	1,786.0	33,115
2017	2,494.1	3,269.3	2,773.6	3,294.8	2,484.6	3,515.7	1,859.0	2,291.5	3,359.1	1,665.9	2,055.1	1,898.4	30,961
2018	3,212.7	3,692.3	2,839.4	4,157.9	3,195.2	3,984.1	2,003.6	2,836.6	4,144.2	3,216.5	2,129.3	1,599.2	37,011
2019	3,371.9	3,497.8	3,015.9	4,319.7	3,170.8	4,020.9	2,198.2	2,495.6	4,812.1	2,059.5	2,308.6	2,417.1	37,688
2020	4,764.5	5,033.4	4,650.2	3,940.6	2,903.6	3,812.2	2,238.7	2,418.5	3,936.7	2,522.3	2,033.8	1,694.8	39,949
2021	2,570.6	3,512.8	2,629.1	3,537.5	2,092.9	3,337.2	2,070.3	2,307.4	3,439.3	1,815.9	1,900.6	1,789.1	31,003
2022	2,360.9	3,011.4	2,788.3	3,305.4	2,088.8	3,260.4	2,071.4	2,084.2	3,562.5	2,118.0	2,595.5	2,028.4	31,275
2023	2,769.0	3,730.8	3,159.4	4,337.0	3,018.2	4,678.9	1,807.2	2,688.4	3,566.4	2,052.7	1,963.7	3,459.1	37,231

Contract size = 112,000 lbs.   Source: ICE Futures U.S. (ICE)

Average Open Interest of World Sugar #11 Futures in New York   In Contracts

Year	Jan.	Feb.	Mar.	Apr.	May	June	July	Aug.	Sept.	Oct.	Nov.	Dec.
2014	834,655	838,471	787,473	792,420	809,219	870,191	842,551	885,193	851,724	766,320	811,959	828,791
2015	824,778	848,192	862,965	876,247	853,458	885,602	805,457	837,922	790,609	766,704	838,992	861,944
2016	870,944	830,246	795,043	820,305	841,639	894,893	837,385	880,629	885,571	841,889	837,131	818,873
2017	828,436	824,169	778,676	791,551	790,116	833,483	768,669	812,524	773,437	700,720	709,575	752,794
2018	844,185	891,797	915,120	1,003,293	1,012,957	977,622	973,446	1,041,981	871,673	774,976	791,152	840,548
2019	905,607	889,863	889,788	890,306	997,302	947,567	903,584	1,036,573	1,012,939	913,104	968,649	1,002,550
2020	1,084,021	1,222,255	1,073,698	991,547	960,551	970,496	942,507	1,026,601	1,009,797	992,075	1,065,231	1,059,590
2021	1,099,067	1,102,368	1,040,251	1,030,890	1,019,569	978,263	936,320	1,027,094	979,906	881,092	902,347	867,312
2022	880,822	887,549	822,512	883,294	824,490	795,711	711,378	752,195	739,528	706,106	819,550	911,523
2023	924,494	961,005	934,684	976,833	963,554	966,240	888,379	932,294	952,197	839,481	869,663	803,058

Contract size = 112,000 lbs.   Source: ICE Futures U.S. (ICE)

Sulfur

Sulfur (atomic symbol S) is an odorless, tasteless, light yellow, nonmetallic element. As early as 2000 BC, Egyptians used sulfur compounds to bleach fabric. The Chinese used sulfur as an essential component when they developed gunpowder in the 13th century.

Sulfur is widely found in both its free and combined states. Free sulfur is found mixed with gypsum and pumice stone in volcanic regions. Sulfur dioxide is an air pollutant that is released by the burning of fossil fuels. The most important use of sulfur is for the production of sulfur compounds. Sulfur is used in skin ointments, matches, dyes, gunpowder, and phosphoric acid.

Supply – World production of all forms of sulfur in 2022 rose by +0.7% yr/yr to 82.000 million metric tons.

The world's largest producers of sulfur in 2022 were China with 22.0% of the world's production, the US with 10.5%, Russia with 8.9%, Saudi Arabia with 8.5%, and Canada with 6.0%. US production of sulfur in 2022 rose by +6.6% yr/yr to 8.600 million metric tons.

Demand – US consumption of all forms of sulfur in 2022 was up by +3.5% at 9.800 million metric tons. US consumption of elemental sulfur in 2021 fell by -3.4% yr/yr to 7.940 million metric tons. US consumption of sulfuric acid in 2021 fell -2.3% yr/yr to 6.860 million metric tons.

Trade – US exports of recovered sulfur in 2021 rose by +42.9% yr/yr to 1.900 million metric tons. US imports of recovered sulfur in 2021 rose by +6.3% yr/yr to 2.370 million metric tons.

World Production of Sulfur (All Forms) In Thousands of Metric Tons

Year	Canada	China	France	Germany	Kazakh-stan	Japan	Mexico	Poland	Russia	Saudi Arabia	Spain	United States	World Total
2016	5,381	17,000	400	930	3,518	3,151	673	1,196	7,072	6,000	----	9,740	80,200
2017	5,327	17,440	400	866	3,372	3,514	551	1,236	7,297	6,500	----	9,628	80,400
2018	5,333	17,690	400	674	3,408	3,510	443	1,191	7,561	6,500	----	9,669	81,900
2019	4,933	19,060	400	741	3,259	4,636	365	1,130	7,538	6,500	----	8,707	83,800
2020	5,074	18,850	400	566	3,141	4,476	264	992	7,526	6,500	----	7,886	80,700
2021	4,879	18,800	400	592	3,150	4,603	176	995	7,530	7,000	----	8,068	81,400
2022[1]	4,900	18,800		610	3,140	4,300		1,050	7,530	7,500	----	8,640	82,000
2023[2]	4,900	19,000		610	3,100	4,300		1,100	7,000	8,000	----	8,600	82,000

[1] Preliminary. [2] Estimate. *Source: U.S. Geological Survey (USGS)*

Salient Statistics of Sulfur in the United States In Thousands of Metric Tons (Sulfur Content)

Year	Native Sulfur[3] Frasch	Recovered Petroleum & Cole	Natural Gas	Total	Total Elemental Sulfur	By-product Sulfuric Acid[4]	Other Sulf. Acid Com-pounds	Imports Sulfuric Acid[4]	Exports Sulfuric Acid[4]	Producer Stocks, Dec. 31[5]	Apparent Con-sumption (All Forms)	Frasch	Recovered	Average Total
2016	----	8,290	781	9,070	673	----	9,740	3,220	180	142	10,500	----	----	37.88
2017	----	8,410	662	9,070	560	----	9,630	2,920	246	124	10,100	----	----	46.39
2018	----	8,378	626	9,005	672	----	9,670	3,050	342	118	10,400	----	----	81.16
2019	----	7,788	341	8,128	596	----	8,710	2,970	220	124	9,250	----	----	51.10
2020	----	7,029	276	7,303	581	----	7,890	3,650	349	109	9,940	----	----	24.60
2021	----	6,915	551	7,464	600	----	8,060	3,260	395	113	9,460	----	----	90.90
2022[1]	----	7,500	503	8,004	636	----	8,640	3,230	376	126	9,480	----	----	178.50
2023[2]	----	7,596	422	8,016	600	----	8,600	3,320	199	100	9,400	----	----	100.00

[1] Preliminary. [2] Estimate. [3] Or sulfur ore; Withheld included in natural gas. [4] Basis 100% H2SO4, sulfur equivalent. [5] Frasch & recovered.
W = Withheld proprietary data. Source: U.S. Geological Survey (USGS)

Sulfur Consumption & Foreign Trade of the United States In Thousands of Metric Tons (Sulfur Content)

Year	Native Sulfur (Frasch)	Rec-overed Sulfur	Total Elemental Form	Pulpmills & Paper Products	Inorganic Chem-icals[3]	Synthetic Rubber & Plastic	Phosph-atic Fertilizers	Petro-leum Refining[4]	Frasch	Re-Frasch	Exports covered	Value $1,000	Re-Frasch	Imports covered	Value $1,000
2014	----	----	9,450	6,410	129	74	6	4,810	410	----	2,010	315,000	----	2,370	134,000
2015	----	----	9,310	6,320	124	128	6	4,610	428	----	1,850	284,000	----	2,240	136,000
2016	----	----	8,840	7,550	119	79	6	5,820	387	----	2,060	214,000	----	1,820	79,800
2017	----	----	8,630	6,650	125	90	7	5,010	347	----	2,340	251,000	----	1,850	110,000
2018	----	----	8,860	6,790	139	107	12	5,070	338	----	2,390	299,000	----	2,230	205,000
2019	----	----	7,750	6,470	133	70	11	4,850	337	----	2,200	173,000	----	1,840	137,000
2020	----	----	8,220	7,020	129	66	9	5,440	336	----	1,330	94,600	----	2,230	121,000
2021[1]	----	----	7,940	6,860	129	66	9	5,440	336	----	1,900	215,000	----	2,370	272,000

[1] Preliminary. [2] Sulfur equivalent. [3] Including inorganic pigments, paints & allied products, and other inorganic chemicals & products.
[4] Including other petroleum and coal products. W = Withheld proprietary data. NA = Not available. *Source: U.S. Geological Survey (USGS)*

Sunflowerseed, Meal and Oil

Sunflowers are native to South and North America but are now grown almost worldwide. Sunflower oil accounts for approximately 14% of the world's production of seed oils. Sunflower varieties that are commercially grown contain from 39% to 49% oil in the seed. Sunflower crops produce about 50 bushels of seed per acre on average, which yields approximately 50 gallons of oil.

Sunflower oil accounts for around 80% of the value of the sunflower crop. Refined sunflower oil is edible and used primarily as a salad and cooking oil and in margarine. Crude sunflower oil is used industrially for making soaps, candles, varnishes, and detergents. Sunflower oil contains 93% of the energy of U.S. No. 2 diesel fuel and is being explored as a potential alternate fuel source in diesel engines. Sunflower meal is used in livestock feed, and when fed to poultry, increases the yield of eggs. Sunflower seeds are also used for birdfeed and as a snack for humans.

Prices – The average monthly price received by US farmers for sunflower seeds in the first four months of the 2023/24 marketing year (Sep/Aug) fell by -16.7% to $22.73 per hundred pounds.

Supply – World sunflower seed production in 2023/24 is expected to rise by +6.0% yr/yr to 55.544 million metric tons. The world's largest sunflower seed producers are forecasted to be Russia with 30.8% of world production, Ukraine with 26.1%, the European Union with 18.4%, Argentina with 7.4%, China with 4.1%, Türkiye with 2.8%, Kazakhstan with 2.2%, and the US with 1.8%.

US production of sunflower seeds in 2023/24 is expected to fall by -19.4% yr/yr to 1.027 million metric tons. US farmers are expected to harvest 1.262 million acres of sunflowers in 2023/24, down -21.4% yr/yr. US sunflower seed yield in 2023/24 is expected to be 17.38 hundred pounds per acre, down -0.7% yr/yr.

Demand – Total US disappearance of sunflower seeds in 2023/24 is expected to fall by -12.0% yr/yr to 1.363 million metric tons, of which 48.5% will go to non-oil and seed use, 38.2% to exports, and 3.8% to crushing for oil and meal.

Trade – World sunflower seed exports in 2023/24 are expected to fall by -27.1% yr/yr to 2.944 million metric tons. The world's largest exporters will be Ukraine, accounting for 17.0% of world exports, and the European Union, Russia and China, each accounting for 15.3% of world exports. World sunflower seed imports in 2023/24 are expected to fall by -27.9% yr/yr to 2.781 million metric tons. The world's largest importers will be Türkiye with 28.8% of world imports and the European Union with 18.0%.

World Production of Sunflowerseed In Thousands of Metric Tons

Crop Year	Argen- tina	China	European Union	India	Kazakh- stan	Pakistan	Russia	Serbia	South Africa	Türkiye	Ukraine	United States	World Total
2014-15	3,160	2,582	8,974	383	513	169	8,374	525	663	1,200	10,200	1,004	39,249
2015-16	3,000	2,872	7,721	323	534	86	9,173	450	755	1,100	11,900	1,327	40,699
2016-17	3,547	3,201	8,651	318	755	106	10,858	650	874	1,320	15,200	1,203	48,330
2017-18	3,538	3,149	10,128	230	903	147	10,362	540	862	1,550	13,700	970	47,935
2018-19	3,530	2,494	9,505	172	848	133	12,710	734	678	1,800	15,000	953	50,324
2019-20	2,857	2,664	9,474	140	839	147	15,305	729	789	1,750	16,500	884	53,796
2020-21	3,247	2,570	8,898	150	844	92	13,269	637	678	1,560	14,100	1,351	48,833
2021-22	4,050	2,154	10,328	140	1,032	84	15,572	608	846	1,750	17,500	862	56,856
2022-23[1]	5,019	1,900	9,181	215	1,304	148	16,254	643	724	1,900	12,200	1,274	52,388
2023-24[2]	4,100	2,250	10,200	112	1,200	135	17,100	725	935	1,550	14,500	1,027	55,544

[1] Preliminary.   [2] Forecast.   Source: Economic Research Service, U.S. Department of Agriculture (ERS-USDA)

World Exports of Sunflowerseed In Thousands of Metric Tons

Crop Year	Argen- tina	Canada	China	European Union	Israel	Kazakh- stan	Moldova	Russia	Serbia	Türkiye	Ukraine	United States	World Total
2014-15	63	34	244	518	3	118	339	61	77	41	45	116	1,675
2015-16	308	29	286	424	3	168	369	107	134	109	83	99	2,132
2016-17	77	18	365	421	2	275	604	368	127	126	191	90	2,683
2017-18	63	17	480	705	1	321	674	98	112	148	39	79	2,756
2018-19	148	27	452	680	1	451	629	363	162	116	105	64	3,213
2019-20	212	38	500	528	1	318	479	1,253	140	99	53	45	3,687
2020-21	176	51	475	624	1	266	273	554	82	123	191	59	2,900
2021-22	156	43	438	397	1	224	524	275	84	118	1,622	50	3,952
2022-23[1]	96	31	380	585	1	310	275	260	80	102	1,856	50	4,041
2023-24[2]	150	50	450	450	1	275	300	450	125	75	500	52	2,944

[1] Preliminary.   [2] Forecast.   Source: Economic Research Service, U.S. Department of Agriculture (ERS-USDA)

SUNFLOWERSEED, MEAL AND OIL

World Imports of Sunflowerseed   In Thousands of Metric Tons

Crop Year	Belarus	Canada	Egypt	European Union	Iran	Mexico	Moldova	Morocco	Pakistan	Russia	Türkiye	United States	World Total
2014-15	19	30	57	266	69	19	3	3	38	178	88	462	75	1,626
2015-16	25	22	63	622	120	21	6	15	94	121	483	72	2,111
2016-17	53	29	62	699	160	28	4	8	40	107	656	80	2,455
2017-18	27	22	102	521	66	27	3	19	45	47	770	97	2,383
2018-19	56	24	91	555	47	25	5	2	4	52	1,116	115	2,891
2019-20	58	26	76	976	31	20	4	11	5	56	1,178	181	3,343
2020-21	19	36	66	779	42	22	5	40	5	70	907	170	2,735
2021-22	50	37	44	1,795	59	30	88	4	4	75	669	174	3,795
2022-23[1]	135	40	15	1,460	40	34	10	15	2	75	941	140	3,857
2023-24[2]	140	35	40	500	50	30	20	4	5	50	800	170	2,781

[1] Preliminary.   [2] Forecast.   *Source: Economic Research Service, U.S. Department of Agriculture (ERS-USDA)*

World Production of Sunflowerseed Oil   In Thousands of Metric Tons

Crop Year	Argentina	Burma	China	European Union	India	Pakistan	Russia	Serbia	South Africa	Türkiye	Ukraine	United States	World Total
2014-15	1,153	131	466	3,232	121	132	3,428	161	308	677	4,429	146	14,968
2015-16	1,170	131	502	3,042	105	68	3,552	153	291	587	5,010	205	15,403
2016-17	1,335	131	609	3,335	105	38	4,171	191	367	761	6,351	211	18,293
2017-18	1,385	131	645	3,755	75	44	4,192	212	373	881	5,913	197	18,569
2018-19	1,425	131	466	3,671	58	48	4,935	230	274	1,066	6,364	204	19,588
2019-20	1,160	131	430	3,645	45	52	5,699	234	358	1,086	7,390	163	21,149
2020-21	1,350	131	430	3,460	49	30	5,121	225	293	1,044	5,913	212	18,967
2021-22	1,503	131	448	4,394	41	52	5,782	217	335	923	4,644	183	19,620
2022-23[1]	1,695	131	287	4,014	71	52	6,484	222	321	1,064	6,020	252	21,681
2023-24[2]	1,630	131	394	3,845	36	48	6,815	238	356	928	6,065	218	21,804

[1] Preliminary.   [2] Forecast.   *Source: Economic Research Service, U.S. Department of Agriculture (ERS-USDA)*

World Production of Sunflowerseed Meal   In Thousands of Metric Tons

Crop Year	Argentina	Burma	China	European Union	India	Kazakhstan	Pakistan	Russia	South Africa	Türkiye	Ukraine	United States	World Total
2014-15	1,147	128	709	4,131	156	135	137	3,407	313	866	4,254	179	16,173
2015-16	1,180	128	763	3,888	135	135	71	3,530	295	743	4,811	252	16,537
2016-17	1,350	128	927	4,263	135	176	40	4,146	372	963	6,030	259	19,491
2017-18	1,400	128	981	4,801	97	217	46	4,167	378	1,114	5,679	242	20,007
2018-19	1,435	128	709	4,696	75	155	50	4,911	277	1,348	6,112	247	20,933
2019-20	1,170	128	654	4,663	58	215	55	5,672	363	1,361	6,455	198	21,766
2020-21	1,335	128	654	4,432	63	225	32	5,096	298	1,306	5,679	257	20,200
2021-22	1,514	128	681	5,621	53	369	55	5,754	340	1,156	4,460	222	21,157
2022-23[1]	1,705	128	436	5,135	92	445	55	6,453	326	1,334	5,782	306	23,053
2023-24[2]	1,643	128	600	4,919	46	415	51	6,780	361	1,166	5,825	265	23,122

[1] Preliminary.   [2] Forecast.   *Source: Economic Research Service, U.S. Department of Agriculture (ERS-USDA)*

Sunflowerseed Statistics in the United States   In Thousands of Metric Tons

Crop Year Beginning Sept. 1	Acres Harvested (1,000)	Harvested Yield Per CWT	Farm Price ($/Metric Ton)	Value of Production (Million $)	Stocks, Sept. 1	Supply — Production	Supply — Imports	Supply — Total Supply	Crush	Disappearance — Exports	Disappearance — Non-Oil Use & Seed	Disappearance — Total Disappearance
2014-15	1,510	14.69	478	497.8	91	1,004	75	1,170	116	366	580	1,170
2015-16	1,799	16.25	432	574.2	108	1,327	72	1,507	99	495	726	1,507
2016-17	1,532	17.31	384	464.0	187	1,203	80	1,470	90	508	605	1,470
2017-18	1,334	16.03	379	375.1	267	970	97	1,334	79	475	605	1,334
2018-19	1,217	17.31	384	370.4	175	953	115	1,243	64	485	564	1,243
2019-20	1,254	15.60	430	386.3	130	884	181	1,195	45	389	673	1,195
2020-21	1,666	17.90	470	632.0	88	1,351	170	1,609	59	504	867	1,609
2021-22[1]	1,244	15.30	725	616.4	179	862	174	1,215	50	435	596	1,215
2022-23[2]	1,606	17.51	613	763.1	134	1,274	140	1,548	50	600	732	1,548
2023-24[2]	1,262	17.38	437	418.7	166	1,027	170	1,363	52	520	661	1,363

[1] Preliminary.   [2] Forecast.   *Source: Economic Research Service, U.S. Department of Agriculture (ERS-USDA)*

Sunflower Oil Statistics in the United States   In Thousands of Metric Tons

Crop Year Beginning Sept. 1	Supply				Disappearance			Price $ Per Metric Ton (Crude Mpls.)
	Stocks, Oct. 1	Production	Imports	Total Supply	Exports	Domestic Use	Total Disap-pearance	
2014-15	23	146	80	249	29	197	226	1,449
2015-16	23	205	42	270	39	197	236	1,309
2016-17	34	211	54	299	32	226	258	1,182
2017-18	41	197	73	311	40	238	278	1,205
2018-19	33	204	60	297	55	223	278	1,173
2019-20	19	163	169	351	40	289	329	1,430
2020-21	22	212	134	368	45	297	342	1,543
2021-22	26	183	204	413	56	328	384	2,530
2022-23[1]	29	252	152	433	33	361	394	1,798
2023-24[2]	39	218	159	416	39	348	387	1,368

[1] Preliminary.   [2] Forecast.   *Source: Economic Research Service, U.S. Department of Agriculture (ERS-USDA)*

Sunflower Meal Statistics in the United States   In Thousands of Metric Tons

Crop Year Beginning Sept. 1	Supply				Disappearance			Price USD Per Metric Ton 28% Protein
	Stocks, Oct. 1	Production	Imports	Total Supply	Exports	Domestic Use	Total Disap-pearance	
2014-15	5	179	20	204	7	192	204	224
2015-16	5	252	21	278	12	261	278	175
2016-17	5	259	11	275	5	265	275	161
2017-18	5	242	1	248	6	237	248	190
2018-19	5	247	2	254	15	234	254	182
2019-20	5	198	2	205	20	180	205	201
2020-21	5	257	4	266	28	233	266	270
2021-22	5	222	14	241	28	208	241	308
2022-23[1]	5	306	13	324	17	302	324	272
2023-24[2]	5	265	14	284	18	261	284	266

[1] Preliminary.   [2] Forecast.   *Source: Economic Research Service, U.S. Department of Agriculture (ERS-USDA)*

Average Price Received by Farmers for Sunflower[2] in the United States   In Dollars Per Hundred Pounds (Cwt.)

Crop Year	Sept.	Oct.	Nov.	Dec.	Jan.	Feb.	Mar.	Apr.	May	June	July	Aug.	Average
2014-15	20.20	21.70	20.30	19.70	19.10	21.50	22.50	23.20	26.40	25.40	26.40	24.20	22.55
2015-16	25.20	18.40	18.30	19.30	20.10	20.40	21.10	20.90	19.50	20.10	19.00	19.60	20.16
2016-17	17.90	17.00	16.40	17.20	17.20	17.60	17.40	17.90	17.30	17.60	17.90	19.10	17.54
2017-18	17.40	16.80	16.60	17.00	17.60	17.70	17.30	18.00	17.90	17.70	17.40	16.90	17.36
2018-19	16.70	16.70	17.00	16.90	17.30	18.00	17.80	17.60	18.30	17.90	18.00	17.80	17.50
2019-20	18.50	17.50	17.70	17.80	19.50	20.40	20.90	20.30	20.50	21.70	23.70	25.80	20.36
2020-21	23.70	19.10	18.90	19.20	19.50	21.40	21.50	23.70	26.40	28.40	28.00	29.40	23.27
2021-22	30.70	30.50	30.30	31.60	31.00	32.20	33.90	37.10	40.10	40.20	36.20	37.80	34.30
2022-23	32.90	29.30	28.40	29.50	29.00	29.90	26.90	26.90	25.00	20.70	25.00	23.60	27.26
2023-24[1]	24.00	20.10	22.60	24.20	21.30	22.40							22.43

[1] Preliminary.   [2] KS, MN, ND and SD average.   *Source: Economic Research Service, U.S. Department of Agriculture (ERS-USDA)*

Average Price of Crude Sunflower Oil at Minneapolis   In Cents Per Pound

Crop Year	Sept.	Oct.	Nov.	Dec.	Jan.	Feb.	Mar.	Apr.	May	June	July	Aug.	Average
2014-15	63.00	63.00	61.75	58.00	63.00	65.63	65.56	65.50	65.00	69.75	73.40	75.00	65.72
2015-16	75.00	72.00	64.50	62.00	58.00	54.25	53.80	53.80	54.00	54.20	55.20	56.00	59.40
2016-17	56.00	56.00	56.00	56.00	56.00	55.00	52.00	51.00	50.50	50.80	51.25	52.75	53.61
2017-18	55.20	56.00	55.50	54.80	55.50	55.00	54.00	54.00	54.00	54.00	54.00	54.00	54.67
2018-19	54.00	54.00	52.80	53.50	53.50	53.00	53.20	54.00	53.40	51.00	52.50	53.40	53.19
2019-20	55.00	56.00	56.00	76.00	70.00	70.00	76.00	76.00	74.00	56.00	56.40	57.00	64.87
2020-21	57.00	57.00	NA	NA	NA	NA	NA	83.00	83.00	NA	NA	NA	70.00
2021-22	129.00	129.00	125.00	125.00	123.13	115.33	129.00	120.40	113.50	97.75	78.20	92.00	114.78
2022-23	88.40	93.75	106.00	92.30	85.75	81.25	76.60	73.00	68.63	67.00	73.25	72.69	81.55
2023-24[1]	71.10	64.75	62.25	58.60	58.13	57.38							62.04

[1] Preliminary.   *Source: Economic Research Service, U.S. Department of Agriculture (ERS-USDA)*

SUNFLOWERSEED, MEAL AND OIL

Average Price of Sunflower Meal (26% protein) in the United States — In Cents Per Pound

Crop Year	Sept.	Oct.	Nov.	Dec.	Jan.	Feb.	Mar.	Apr.	May	June	July	Aug.	Average
2014-15	139.50	162.50	208.13	245.00	247.50	225.63	202.50	202.50	192.50	180.50	214.38	222.50	203.60
2015-16	216.00	212.50	187.50	163.13	156.88	131.88	120.00	109.38	149.50	165.63	151.88	141.00	158.77
2016-17	148.75	148.75	140.50	145.00	159.00	161.88	155.00	147.50	144.00	140.00	130.63	134.50	146.29
2017-18	134.38	153.00	165.00	185.00	178.00	185.63	187.50	191.88	201.50	175.63	155.50	153.13	172.18
2018-19	150.63	164.00	171.25	187.50	190.50	187.50	189.38	166.50	141.25	143.13	142.00	144.38	164.84
2019-20	142.50	169.00	166.88	180.00	185.00	188.13	180.00	183.75	180.63	187.50	202.50	217.50	181.95
2020-21	211.50	211.25	213.13	252.50	280.63	291.88	279.50	258.13	265.00	252.50	206.25	219.50	245.15
2021-22	221.25	222.50	256.50	289.17	301.25	320.00	333.33	321.00	285.63	281.88	268.50	255.00	279.67
2022-23	225.00	NA	NA	200.00	355.00	336.25	308.00	252.50	237.50	208.00	159.17	185.00	246.64
2023-24[1]	202.00	229.17	266.67	270.00	270.00	210.00							241.31

[1] Preliminary.   Source: Economic Research Service, U.S. Department of Agriculture (ERS-USDA)

Production of Sunflower in the United States — In Thousands of Pounds

Crop Year	California	Colorado	Kansas	Minnesota	Nebraska	North Dakota	Oklahoma	South Dakota	Texas	Total
2014	61,925	95,700	91,540	87,870	47,375	847,420	3,200	876,620	137,400	2,219,050
2015	44,720	85,200	135,560	166,050	79,410	1,068,800	6,600	1,230,040	107,350	2,923,730
2016	61,875	90,500	82,660	113,550	58,150	1,137,450	----	1,057,050	50,400	2,651,635
2017	51,305	86,200	84,520	68,475	61,800	704,250	----	1,020,000	61,200	2,137,750
2018	76,500	61,950	74,250	113,835	47,380	739,400	----	966,150	27,580	2,107,045
2019	70,680	59,400	53,925	102,630	44,850	740,700	----	831,600	39,650	1,943,435
2020	57,170	46,110	120,540	137,640	54,180	1,338,250	----	1,167,020	79,980	2,982,890
2021	49,850	46,265	51,200	90,860	34,550	761,900	----	817,800	46,970	1,899,395
2022	33,250	30,775	44,450	171,650	45,720	1,340,510	----	1,082,400	59,800	2,808,555
2023[1]	29,425	28,060	28,430	132,000	44,175	1,122,980	----	817,200	61,250	2,263,520

[1] Preliminary.   Source: Economic Research Service, U.S. Department of Agriculture (ERS-USDA)

Production of Sunflower Oil in the United States — In Thousands of Pounds

Crop Year	California	Colorado	Kansas	Minnesota	Nebraska	North Dakota	Oklahoma	South Dakota	Texas	Total
2014	57,200	44,800	57,540	65,250	29,000	683,400	2,100	668,000	56,800	1,664,090
2015	42,900	68,400	80,560	123,750	42,660	889,350	4,800	1,048,000	82,650	2,383,870
2016	60,075	68,400	57,540	96,000	37,800	1,055,300	----	960,300	33,600	2,369,015
2017	49,875	73,000	65,000	64,350	37,050	628,650	----	848,000	45,600	1,847,525
2018	74,100	53,900	61,500	99,000	34,080	665,000	----	878,400	21,280	1,887,260
2019	68,600	44,000	49,000	94,350	33,800	660,000	----	782,000	33,800	1,765,550
2020	55,250	26,560	76,440	128,640	40,950	1,184,400	----	1,064,000	41,100	2,617,340
2021	48,950	35,340	36,800	85,680	28,050	715,500	----	744,000	37,950	1,732,270
2022	32,550	22,000	35,100	154,050	40,500	1,225,500	----	1,009,200	47,500	2,566,400
2023[1]	28,875	22,560	24,180	110,400	35,400	965,300	----	726,000	54,000	1,966,715

[1] Preliminary.   Source: Economic Research Service, U.S. Department of Agriculture (ERS-USDA)

Production of Sunflower Oil in the United States — In Thousands of Pounds

Crop Year	California	Colorado	Kansas	Minnesota	Nebraska	North Dakota	Oklahoma	South Dakota	Texas	Total
2014	4,725	20,900	34,000	22,620	18,375	164,020	1,100	208,620	80,600	554,960
2015	1,820	16,800	55,000	42,300	36,750	179,450	1,800	181,240	24,700	539,860
2016	1,800	22,100	25,120	17,550	20,350	82,150	----	96,750	16,800	282,620
2017	1,430	13,200	19,520	4,125	24,750	75,600	----	136,000	15,600	290,225
2018	2,400	8,050	12,750	14,835	13,300	74,400	----	87,750	6,300	219,785
2019	2,080	15,400	9,125	8,280	11,050	89,100	----	49,600	5,850	190,485
2020	1,920	19,550	26,100	9,000	13,230	153,850	----	103,020	38,880	365,550
2021	900	10,925	14,400	5,180	6,500	46,400	----	73,800	9,020	167,125
2022	700	8,775	9,350	17,600	5,220	115,010	----	73,200	12,300	242,155
2023[1]	550	5,500	4,250	21,600	8,775	157,680	----	91,200	7,250	296,805

[1] Preliminary.   Source: Economic Research Service, U.S. Department of Agriculture (ERS-USDA)

Tallow and Greases

Tallow and grease are derived from processing (rendering) the fat of cattle. Tallow is used to produce both edible and inedible products. Edible tallow products include margarine, cooking oil, and baking products. Inedible tallow products include soap, candles, and lubricants. Production of tallow and greases is directly related to the number of cattle produced. Those countries that are the leading cattle producers are also the largest producers of tallow. The American Fats and Oils Association provides specifications for a variety of different types of tallow and grease, including edible tallow, lard (edible), top white tallow, all beef packer tallow, extra fancy tallow, fancy tallow, bleachable fancy tallow, prime tallow, choice white grease, and yellow grease. The specifications include such characteristics as the melting point, color, density, moisture content, insoluble impurities, and others.

Prices– The monthly average wholesale price of tallow (inedible, No. 1 Packers-Prime, delivered to Chicago) in 2023 fell by -21.0% yr/yr to 59.51 cents per pound.

Supply – World production of tallow and greases (edible and inedible) in 2022 rose by +0.8% yr/yr to 11.402 million metric tons. The world's largest producer of tallow and greases by far is the US, with 40.4% of world production, followed by Brazil with 9.6%, Australia with 4.4%, and Canada with 2.8%. US production of edible tallow in 2022 fell by -3.1% yr/yr to 2.292 billion pounds.

Demand – US consumption of edible tallow in 2022 rose by +3.5% yr/yr to 2.209 billion, a new record high.

Trade – US exports of edible tallow in 2022 fell by -38.8% yr/yr to 153 million pounds.

World Production of Tallow and Greases (Edible and Inedible)   In Thousands of Metric Tons

Year	Argentina	Australia	Brazil	Canada	France	Germany	Korea, South	Nether-lands	New Zealand	Russia	United Kingdom	United States	World Total
2013	175	548	654	241	191	130	21	103	169	207	138	4,457	9,319
2014	167	601	635	248	192	131	20	101	167	213	142	4,225	9,189
2015	171	605	707	238	196	132	20	105	176	219	145	4,205	9,298
2016	167	507	717	248	198	132	19	108	165	226	147	4,432	9,451
2017	212	543	941	296	234	161	30	116	172	243	180	4,652	10,995
2018	224	581	1,081	308	238	160	31	103	177	250	181	4,670	11,287
2019	231	564	1,094	317	235	160	31	104	177	255	185	4,722	11,300
2020	234	511	1,103	312	235	157	32	106	177	260	188	4,552	11,106
2021[1]	224	496	1,068	325	234	152	33	108	184	260	183	4,613	11,315
2022[2]	234	501	1,100	325	223	141	33	106	177	260	185	4,601	11,402

[1] Preliminary.   [2] Forecast.   *Source: Foreign Agricultural Service, U.S. Department of Agriculture (FAS-USDA)*

Salient Statistics of Tallow and Greases (Inedible) in the United States   In Millions of Pounds

Year	Production	Stocks, Jan. 1	Total	Exports	Soap	Feed	Total	Edible, (Loose) Chicago	Inedible, Chicago No. 1
	-------------------- Supply --------------------				--------------- Consumption ---------------			Wholesale Prices, Cents Per Lb. ------	
2006	6,460	309	6,769	730	W	2,585	2,585	18.6	16.9
2007	6,369	291	6,661	795	W	2,385	2,385	30.7	27.8
2008	6,224	350	6,573	703	W	2,095	2,095	38.0	34.2
2009	5,878	315	6,193	727	W	1,770	1,770	27.5	25.2
2010	5,887	286	6,174	778	W	1,574	1,574	35.1	33.3
2011	3,654	281	3,934	753	W	1,560	1,560	53.2	49.6
2012[1]	NA	NA	NA	NA	NA	NA	NA	47.8	43.8
2013[2]	NA	NA	NA	NA	NA	NA	NA	42.6	40.4
2014[2]	----	----	----	----	----	----	----	38.7	36.7
2015[2]	----	----	----	----	----	----	----	28.4	26.9

[1] Preliminary.   [2] Forecast.   *Source: Foreign Agricultural Service, U.S. Department of Agriculture (FAS-USDA)*

TALLOW AND GREASES

TALLOW
Quarterly Cash as of 03/28/2024

QUARTERLY CASH
As of 03/28/2024
Chart High 82.00 on 06/28/2022
Chart Low 3.52 on 08/30/1940

Cents / lb.

Spot raw, NY: to 02/1961; World raw #8, NY: 02/1961 to 12/1970; World raw #11, NY: to date.

Supply and Disappearance of Edible Tallow in the United States   In Millions of Pounds, Rendered Basis

	Supply			Disappearance					
Year	Stocks, Jan. 1	Production	Total Supply	Domestic Disap-pearance	Exports	Total Disap-pearance	Direct Use	Baking or Frying Fats	Per Capita (Lbs.)
2014	30	1,922	2,004	1,884	90	1,974	----	----	----
2015	30	1,928	2,003	1,830	143	1,973	----	----	----
2016	30	2,143	2,235	1,929	265	2,194	----	----	----
2017	41	2,053	2,158	1,954	171	2,125	----	----	----
2018	33	2,233	2,302	2,010	260	2,270	----	----	----
2019	32	2,252	2,298	2,012	268	2,280	----	----	----
2020	18	2,202	2,244	2,007	227	2,234	----	----	----
2021	10	2,365	2,406	2,135	250	2,385	----	----	----
2022[1]	21	2,292	2,385	2,211	152	2,362	----	----	----
2023[2]	23	2,346	2,402	2,290	101	2,391	----	----	----

[1] Preliminary.   [2] Forecast.   W = Withheld.   *Sources: Economic Research Service, U.S. Department of Agriculture (ERS-USDA); Bureau of the Census, U.S. Department of Commerce*

Average Wholesale Price of Tallow, Inedible, No. 1 Packers (Prime), Delivered, Chicago   In Cents Per Pound

Year	Jan.	Feb.	Mar.	Apr.	May	June	July	Aug.	Sept.	Oct.	Nov.	Dec.	Average
2014	31.95	31.61	38.52	42.60	44.57	42.04	39.96	39.85	34.90	29.51	32.47	32.09	36.67
2015	28.77	28.84	30.42	28.22	28.64	29.72	28.50	29.21	28.71	22.41	19.48	19.50	26.87
2016	23.14	26.50	29.64	32.93	32.67	31.34	29.04	27.50	27.50	27.90	31.49	31.64	29.27
2017	31.35	31.11	30.11	30.33	33.49	35.40	35.50	35.37	33.96	27.83	26.36	26.50	31.44
2018	26.38	25.00	25.59	24.61	24.20	26.35	28.05	27.88	25.20	23.76	25.85	26.50	25.78
2019	26.50	26.50	26.52	28.14	28.69	29.63	30.65	31.32	28.26	26.29	23.77	25.56	27.65
2020	30.57	34.67	31.57	30.95	33.94	25.14	23.50	30.33	31.58	32.10	32.50	35.80	31.05
2021	40.45	44.22	51.04	54.02	55.05	58.92	61.95	66.77	65.51	69.08	67.05	57.69	57.65
2022	66.65	71.08	74.11	74.94	80.50	81.33	80.32	81.00	77.40	74.00	74.00	68.93	75.36
2023[1]	67.45	60.21	54.91	52.75	56.66	58.98	65.78	68.67	69.68	61.08	51.82	46.10	59.51

[1] Preliminary.   *Sources: Economic Research Service, U.S. Department of Agriculture (ERS-USDA)*

Tea

Tea is the common name for a family of mostly woody flowering plants. The tea family contains about 600 species placed in 28 genera and they are distributed throughout the tropical and subtropical areas, with most species occurring in eastern Asia and South America. The tea plant is native to Southeast Asia. There are more than 3,000 varieties of tea, each with its own distinct character, and each is generally named for the area in which it is grown. Tea may have been consumed in China as long ago as 2700 BC and certainly since 1000 BC. In 2737 BC, the Chinese Emperor Shen Nung, according to Chinese mythology, was a scholar and herbalist. While his servant boiled drinking water, a leaf from the wild tea tree he was sitting under dropped into the water, and Shen Nung decided to try the brew. Today, half the world's population drinks tea. Tea is the world's most popular beverage next to water.

Tea is a healthful drink and contains antioxidants, fluoride, niacin, folic acid, and as much vitamin C as a lemon. The average 5 ounce cup of brewed tea contains approximately 40 to 60 milligrams of caffeine (compared to 80 to 115 mg in brewed coffee). Decaffeinated tea has been available since the 1980s. Herbal tea contains no true tea leaves but is actually brewed from a collection of herbs and spices.

Tea grows mainly between the tropic of Cancer and the tropic of Capricorn, requiring 40 to 50 inches of rain per year and a temperature ideally between 50 to 86 degrees Fahrenheit. The bushes must be pruned every four to five years to rejuvenate the bush and keep it at a convenient height for the pickers to access. A tea bush can produce tea for 50 to 70 years, but after 50 years, the yield declines.

The two key factors in determining different varieties of tea are the production process (sorting, withering, rolling, fermentation, and drying methods) and the growing conditions (geographical region, growing altitude, and soil type). Black tea, often referred to as fully fermented tea, is produced by allowing picked tea leaves to wither and ferment for up to 24 hours. After fermenting, the leaves are fired, which stops oxidation. Green tea, or unfermented tea, is produced by immediately and completely drying the leaves and omitting the oxidization process, thus allowing the tea to remain green in color.

Supply – World production of tea in 2021 rose by +5.4% to 6.807 million metric tons, a new record high. The world's largest producers of tea in 2021 were China with 46.5% of world production, India with 19.8%, Kenya with 7.9%, Sri Lanka with 4.4%, Türkiye with 4.3%, and Vietnam with 3.7%.

Trade – US tea imports in 2023 rose by +8.0% to 201,600 metric tons. World tea imports in 2022 rose by +2.1% to 1.976 million metric tons. The world's largest tea importers in 2022 were Pakistan with 12.8% of total world imports, Russia with 7.0%, the US with 6.1%, and the United Kingdom with 5.9%. World exports of tea in 2022 fell by -4.5% yr/yr to 2.054 million metric tons. The world's largest exporters of tea in 2022 were Kenya with 26.9% of world exports, China with 18.8%, Sri Lanka with 12.0%, and India with 11.3%.

World Tea Production, in Major Producing Countries — In Metric Tons

Year	Argentina	Bang-ladesh	China	India	Indo-nesia	Iran	Japan	Kenya	Malawi	Sri Lanka	Türkiye	Ex-USSR[2]	World Total
2015	82,492	66,101	2,277,000	1,233,140	132,615	26,500	79,500	399,100	39,447	332,090	265,600	235,500	5,384,475
2016	85,015	64,500	2,313,000	1,250,490	144,015	31,500	80,200	473,000	43,127	292,574	270,000	240,400	5,496,419
2017	81,476	81,850	2,460,400	1,325,050	146,251	33,123	82,000	439,857	45,582	307,720	260,000	260,600	5,735,224
2018	82,781	78,150	2,610,400	1,338,630	140,237	34,200	86,300	492,990	50,588	303,840	296,100	251,400	6,009,296
2019	83,241	90,685	2,777,200	1,390,080	128,724	35,000	81,700	458,850	48,193	300,120	281,500	236,600	6,142,012
2020	73,890	89,931	2,931,800	1,261,545	144,064	34,000	69,800	569,500	45,173	278,489	283,500	243,100	6,461,607
2021[1]	81,872	90,329	3,164,000	1,348,748	137,837	32,000	78,100	537,800	50,600	299,488	290,000	253,700	6,807,377

[1] Preliminary. [2] Mostly Georgia and Azerbaijan. *Sources: Foreign Agricultural Service, U.S. Department of Agriculture (FAS-USDA); Food and Agriculture Organization of the United Nations (FAO-UN)*

World Exports of Tea from Producing Countries — In Metric Tons

Year	Argentina	Bang-ladesh	Brazil	China	India	Indonesia	Kenya	Malawi	Papua New Guinea	Sri Lanka	Vietnam	Zim-babwe	World Total
2016	78,177	721	367	336,618	230,456	51,317	481,076	43,656	896	286,760	136,362	11,083	2,040,835
2017	74,921	2,149	297	367,550	261,419	51,357	467,024	41,273	938	286,863	146,441	13,396	2,133,983
2018	72,619	949	227	380,860	262,423	49,030	500,591	47,625	711	164,709	77,234	14,229	2,028,119
2019	75,322	880	305	385,783	258,050	42,008	475,997	46,944	345	289,586	134,931	14,534	2,170,322
2020	65,978	2,225	235	361,799	210,486	45,265	575,509	46,923	308	285,087	126,458	12,138	2,173,153
2021[1]	64,201	881	182	384,097	197,240	42,640	556,552	36,158	327	282,986	122,086	11,569	2,151,435
2022[2]	68,917	851	213	386,871	231,395	44,979	552,014	49,395	224	246,767	61,276	12,633	2,054,465

[1] Preliminary. [2] Estimate. *Source: Food and Agriculture Organization of the United Nations (FAO-UN)*

Imports of Tea in the United States — In Metric Tons

Year	Jan.	Feb.	Mar.	Apr.	May	June	July	Aug.	Sept.	Oct.	Nov.	Dec.	Total
2018	15,231	11,716	11,611	17,712	20,164	18,202	17,370	18,866	17,850	13,205	13,993	12,314	188,234
2019	14,523	14,128	16,810	18,058	19,626	17,829	20,574	18,243	15,784	15,231	15,738	14,250	200,796
2020	16,085	11,457	17,037	17,600	18,745	16,861	15,970	17,250	17,458	15,650	15,075	14,861	194,048
2021	15,114	14,923	16,339	16,174	20,623	16,345	19,321	18,667	7,080	13,502	16,140	16,514	190,741
2022	14,660	14,130	19,271	20,913	21,339	17,806	22,263	19,965	23,101	15,008	16,742	13,914	219,112
2023[1]	14,193	15,823	14,256	15,001	17,425	19,656	18,031	20,130	17,840	16,599	17,681	14,965	201,601

[1] Preliminary. *Source: Foreign Agricultural Service, U.S. Department of Agriculture (FAS-USDA)*

Thorium

World Production of Monazite Concentrate   In Metric Tons (gross weight)

Year	Brazil	India	Madagascar	Malaysia	Nigeria	Thailand	United States	Vietnam	World Total
2011	290	3,000	----	571	----	5,100	----	360	9,320
2012	2,700	3,000	----	113	----	200	----	370	6,380
2013	600	3,000	----	261	----	210	----	180	4,250
2014	----	3,000	----	372	104	3,200	----	----	6,680
2015	1,625	3,000	----	499	80	1,300	----	460	6,960
2016	4,525	2,500	----	220	----	2,600	----	400	10,200
2017	2,900	3,000	----	380	55	2,200	----	360	8,900
2018	2,000	5,000	16,000	50	50	1,700	500	1,500	26,800
2019[1]	1,200	5,000	21,000	90	54	3,200	1,700	2,200	34,400
2020[2]	1,200	5,000	25,000	160	210	6,000	960	1,200	83,700

[1] Preliminary.   [2] Estimate.   *Source: U.S. Geological Survey (USGS)*

Salient U.S. Thorium Statistics   In Metric Tons (gross weight)

Year	Exports: Thorium Ore, including Monazite	Exports: Metal, Waste and Scrap	Exports: Compounds	Imports for Consumption: Thorium Ore, including Monazite	Imports for Consumption: Compounds	Shipments from Gov't stockpile excesses	Consumption: Reported Non-energy applications	Prices, yearend ($/kg): Nitrate/3	Prices, yearend ($/kg): Oxide, 99.9% purity/3	Prices, yearend ($/kg): Compounds: France	Prices, yearend ($/kg): Compounds: India	Net Import Reliance as a % of Apparent Consumption
2014	----	----	14.800	----	11.000	----	----	----	----	----	$65.00	100
2015	----	----	2.700	----	2.740	----	----	----	----	----	$63.00	100
2016	----	----	64.000	16.000	3.120	----	----	----	----	----	$65.00	100
2017	----	----	89.000	----	8.510	----	----	----	----	----	$73.00	100
2018	521.000	----	21.000	1.000	9.000	----	----	----	----	----	$72.00	100
2019	1,680.000	----	154.000	----	3.970	----	----	----	----	$29.00	$72.00	100
2020	958.000	----	60.300	3.000	1.920	----	----	----	----	$29.00	NA	100
2021	----	----	45.600	16.000	5.790	----	----	----	----	$29.00	NA	100
2022[1]	22.000	----	25.900	----	1.930	----	----	----	----	$26.00	NA	100
2023[2]	----	----	67.000	----	13.000	----	----	----	----	$29.00	$74.00	100

[1] Preliminary.   [2] Estimate.   [3] Free on board port of entry, duty paid, thorium oxide basis.   *Source: U.S. Geological Survey (USGS)*

U.S. Foreign Trade in Thorium and Thorium-Bearing Materials   In Metric Tons (gross weight)

Year	Exports: Thorium Ore, including Monazite	Exports: Metals	Exports: Compounds	Exports: Thorium Ore, including Monazite: Value (USD)	Exports: Metals: Value (USD)	Exports: Compounds: Value (USD)	Imports for Consumption: Thorium Ore, including Monazite	Imports for Consumption: Compounds	Imports for Consumption: Thorium Ore, including Monazite: Value (USD)	Imports for Consumption: Compounds: Value (USD)
2014	----	----	14.800	----	----	1,970,000	----	11.000	----	761,000
2015	----	----	2.700	----	----	779,000	----	2.740	----	216,000
2016	----	----	64.000	----	----	1,790,000	16.000	3.120	----	284,000
2017	----	----	89.000	----	----	1,340,000	----	8.510	----	731,000
2018	521.000	----	21.000	----	----	1,150,000	1.000	9.000	----	567,000
2019	1,680.000	----	154.000	----	----	9,380,000	----	3.970	----	213,000
2020	958.000	----	60.300	----	----	817,000	3.000	1.920	----	55,400
2021	----	----	45.600	----	----		16.000	5.790	----	
2022	22.000	----	25.900	----	----		----	1.930	----	
2023[1]	----	----	67.000	----	----		----	13.000	----	

[1] Preliminary.   [2] Based on manufacture of 2,205 gas mantles per kilogram ThO2.   *Source: U.S. Geological Survey (USGS)*

Tin

Tin (atomic symbol Sn) is a silvery-white, lustrous gray metallic element. Tin is soft, pliable and has a highly crystalline structure. When a tin bar is bent or broken, a crackling sound called a "tin cry" is produced due to the breaking of the tin crystals. People have been using tin for at least 5,500 years. Tin has been found in the tombs of ancient Egyptians. In ancient times, tin and lead were considered different forms of the same metal. Tin was exported to Europe in large quantities from Cornwall, England, during the Roman period, from approximately 2100 BC to 1500 BC. Cornwall was one of the world's leading sources of tin for much of its known history and into the late 1800s.

The principal ore of tin is the mineral cassiterite, which is found in Malaya, Bolivia, Indonesia, Thailand, and Nigeria. About 80% of the world's tin deposits occur in unconsolidated placer deposits in riverbeds and valleys, or on the seafloor, with only about 20% occurring as primary hard-rock lodes. Tin deposits are generally small and are usually allied with granite. Tin is also recovered as a by-product of mining tungsten, tantalum, and lead. After extraction, tin ore is ground and washed to remove impurities, roasted to oxidize the sulfides of iron and copper, washed a second time, and then reduced by carbon in a reverberatory furnace. Electrolysis may also be used to purify tin.

Pure tin, rarely used by itself, was used as currency in the form of tin blocks and was considered legal tender for taxes in Phuket, Thailand, until 1932. Tin is used in the manufacture of coatings for steel containers used to preserve food and beverages. Tin is also used in solder alloys, electroplating, ceramics, and in plastic. The world's major tin research and development laboratory, ITRI Ltd, is funded by companies that produce and consume tin. The research efforts have focused on possible new uses for tin that would take advantage of tin's relative non-toxicity to replace other metals in various products. Some of the replacements could be lead-free solders, antimony-free flame-retardant chemicals, and lead-free shotgun pellets. No tin is currently mined in the U.S.

Tin futures and options trade on the London Metal Exchange (LME). Tin has traded on the LME since 1877, and the standard tin contract began in 1912. The futures contract calls for the delivery of 5 metric tons of tin ingots of at least 99.85% purity. The contract trades in terms of U.S. dollars per metric ton.

Prices – The average monthly price of tin (straights) in New York in 2023 fell by -17.3% yr/yr to $16.07 per pound. The average monthly price of ex-dock tin in New York in 2022 fell by -4.1% yr/yr to $15.26 per pound.

Supply – World mine production of tin in 2022 rose by +1.6% yr/yr to 310,000 metric tons, below the 2018 record high of 318,000 metric tons. The world's largest mine producers of tin in 2022 were China with 30.6% of world production, Indonesia with 23.9%, Burma with 10.0%, Peru with 9.4%, and Congo with 6.5%. World smelter production of tin in 2019 fell by -6.7% yr/yr to 349,000 metric tons. The world's largest producers of smelted tin are China, with 47.6% of world production in 2019, Indonesia with 21.9%, and Malaysia with 7.0%. The US does not mine tin, and therefore its supply consists only of scrap and imports. US tin recovery in 2022 fell by -4.7% yr/yr to 5,100 metric tons.

Demand – US consumption of tin (pig) in 2023 fell by -0.6% yr/yr to 18,249 metric tons. The breakdown of US consumption of tin by finished products in 2020 showed that the largest consuming industry of tin is chemicals with 24.8% of consumption, followed by tin plate with 22.4%, solder with 8.8%, and bronze and brass with 6.3%.

Trade – US imports of unwrought tin metal in 2022 fell by -10.8% yr/yr to 34,000 metric tons.

World Mine Production of Tin   In Metric Tons (Contained Tin)

Year	Australia	Bolivia	Brazil	Burma	China	Congo	Indonesia	Malaysia	Nigeria	Peru	Rwanda	Vietnam	World Total
2014	6,900	19,802	25,534	30,000	104,000	6,500	51,801	3,777	2,800	23,105	4,200	5,400	285,000
2015	7,000	20,000	25,000	34,271	110,156	6,400	52,000	3,800	2,500	19,511	2,000	5,400	289,000
2016	6,640	17,000	25,000	54,000	92,000	5,500	52,000	4,000	2,290	18,800	2,200	5,500	288,000
2017	7,200	18,500	18,000	47,000	93,000	9,500	83,000	3,810	5,960	17,800	2,860	4,560	313,000
2018	6,870	16,900	17,100	54,600	90,000	7,400	85,000	4,300	7,800	18,600	2,400	4,560	318,000
2019	7,740	17,000	14,000	42,000	84,500	12,200	77,500	3,610	5,800	19,900	2,300	5,500	296,000
2020	8,120	14,700	16,900	29,000	84,000	17,300	53,000	2,960	5,000	20,600	1,800	5,400	264,000
2021	8,772	19,628	15,517	36,900	90,000	16,700	70,000	5,000	1,600	26,995	2,000	5,400	305,000
2022[1]	9,000	17,600	17,000	47,000	71,000	18,600	70,000	5,000	7,000	28,200	3,300	5,900	307,000
2023[2]	9,100	18,000	18,000	54,000	68,000	19,000	52,000	6,100	8,100	23,000	3,800	5,300	290,000

[1] Preliminary.   [2] Estimate.   *Source: U.S. Geological Survey (USGS)*

TIN

World Smelter Production of Primary Tin   In Metric Tons

Year	Australia	Belgium	Bolivia	Brazil	China	Indo-nesia	Japan	Malaysia	Peru	Russia	Thailand	United States	World Total
2011	400	10,000	14,295	9,632	156,000	43,832	947	40,281	32,290	726	20,000	11,000	344,000
2012	400	11,400	14,626	12,205	148,000	51,400	1,133	37,823	24,811	700	19,996	11,200	342,000
2013	400	12,000	14,862	14,721	159,000	54,800	1,786	32,699	24,181	550	19,088	10,600	353,000
2014	400	9,810	15,439	22,334	187,000	69,800	1,746	34,971	24,462	550	16,494	10,100	401,000
2015	400	8,860	15,464	16,531	167,200	67,400	1,688	30,209	20,396	550	10,616	10,100	357,000
2016	400	8,540	16,810	12,542	182,500	66,900	1,620	26,758	19,390	----	10,807	9,960	365,000
2017	----	9,700	16,648	13,796	178,400	80,000	1,624	27,200	17,906	----	10,588	10,000	373,000
2018	----	9,330	15,611	12,900	182,000	81,427	1,650	27,197	18,255	----	10,721	9,900	374,000
2019	----	9,300	15,111	11,927	166,000	76,389	1,547	24,320	19,555	----	10,956	10,500	351,000
2020[1]	----	8,980	10,414	11,810	168,000	58,790	1,558	22,360	19,585	----	11,270	10,300	328,000

[1] Preliminary.   Source: U.S. Geological Survey (USGS)

United States Foreign Trade of Tin   In Metric Tons

| | | Concentrates[2] (Ore) | | | Imports for Consumption | | | | | | | | |
| | | | | | | | | Unwruoght Tin Metal | | | | | |
Year	Exports (Metal)	Total All Ore	Bolivia	Peru	Total All Metal	Bolivia	Brazil	China	Indo-nesia	Malaysia	Singa-pore	Thailand	United Kingdom
2014	5,700	----	----	----	35,600	4,570	3,030	3,470	8,140	6,050	375	291	----
2015	3,350	----	----	----	33,600	6,260	2,950	1,230	5,210	9,990	225	20	2
2016	1,150	----	----	----	32,200	6,170	2,120	229	8,580	7,560	176	392	----
2017	1,560	----	----	----	34,300	6,450	1,720	510	9,910	7,050	40	449	----
2018	941	----	----	----	36,800	6,310	2,740	1,310	10,500	7,590	50	422	----
2019	1,300	----	----	----	34,100	5,940	3,020	1,340	5,230	7,120	----	600	----
2020	519	----	----	----	31,600	5,060	3,080	[4]	9,170	3,740	----	174	----
2021	1,290	----	----	----	38,100								
2022	1,310	----	----	----	33,200								
2023[1]	1,100	----	----	----	30,000								

[1] Preliminary.   [2] Tin content.   [4] Less than 1/2 unit.   Source: U.S. Geological Survey (USGS)

Consumption (Total) of Tin (Pig) in the United States   In Metric Tons

Year	Jan.	Feb.	Mar.	Apr.	May	June	July	Aug.	Sept.	Oct.	Nov.	Dec.	Total
2014	1,819	1,818	1,878	1,938	2,164	2,212	2,202	2,202	2,212	2,182	2,193	2,143	24,963
2015	2,183	2,181	2,211	2,241	2,211	2,271	2,251	2,261	2,261	2,231	2,161	2,191	26,590
2016	2,239	2,239	2,179	2,179	2,189	2,209	2,189	2,239	2,209	2,197	2,165	2,127	26,360
2017	2,137	2,127	2,155	2,165	2,194	2,176	2,166	2,195	2,158	2,187	2,061	1,804	25,525
2018	1,870	1,832	1,835	1,874	1,856	1,843	1,823	1,859	1,838	1,809	1,827	1,949	22,215
2019	1,874	1,884	1,857	1,834	1,875	1,947	1,854	1,908	1,826	1,875	1,855	1,805	22,394
2020	1,880	1,910	1,937	1,951	1,925	1,921	1,913	1,932	1,920	1,972	1,924	1,904	23,089
2021	1,878	1,859	1,541	1,564	1,539	1,491	1,560	1,495	1,529	1,560	1,508	1,518	19,042
2022	1,551	1,542	1,548	1,539	1,556	1,544	1,525	1,526	1,565	1,522	1,471	1,472	18,361
2023[1]	1,548	1,560	1,545	1,506	1,510	1,517	1,502	1,495	1,504	1,499	1,484	1,393	18,063

[1] Preliminary.   Source: U.S. Geological Survey (USGS)

Tin Stocks (Pig-Industrial) in the United States, on First of Month   In Metric Tons

Year	Jan.	Feb.	Mar.	Apr.	May	June	July	Aug.	Sept.	Oct.	Nov.	Dec.
2014	6,520	6,540	6,560	6,570	6,490	6,800	6,800	6,770	6,740	7,360	7,060	6,970
2015	7,010	6,860	6,910	6,960	6,910	6,910	7,360	6,970	6,900	7,510	6,930	6,940
2016	6,420	6,420	6,400	6,350	6,380	6,310	6,220	6,220	6,210	6,320	6,480	6,510
2017	6,490	6,550	6,570	6,580	6,480	6,540	6,520	6,580	6,590	6,560	6,550	6,570
2018	6,300	6,330	6,300	6,430	6,280	6,360	6,400	6,310	6,400	5,180	5,610	5,610
2019	5,140	5,350	4,700	5,880	5,540	5,390	5,350	4,790	5,910	4,840	4,820	5,940
2020	6,540	6,560	5,110	5,110	5,090	5,080	5,070	5,090	5,100	5,060	5,100	5,150
2021	5,240	5,150	4,540	4,550	4,540	4,500	4,460	4,440	4,530	4,510	4,530	4,550
2022	5,040	5,060	4,940	4,750	4,710	4,770	4,740	4,700	4,740	4,770	4,710	5,020
2023[1]	4,910	4,910	4,800	4,740	4,800	4,890	5,140	5,200	5,080	5,180	6,310	5,840

[1] Preliminary.   Source: U.S. Geological Survey (USGS)

QUARTERLY CASH
As of 03/28/2024
Chart High 3029.63 on 03/08/2022
Chart Low 45.94 on 02/29/1940

TIN
Quarterly Cash as of 03/28/2024

Straights, Composite: to date.

Average Price of Ex-Dock Tin in New York[1] In Cents Per Pound

Year	Jan.	Feb.	Mar.	Apr.	May	June	July	Aug.	Sept.	Oct.	Nov.	Dec.	Average
2014	1,026.81	1,061.00	1,074.64	1,088.65	1,083.18	1,059.89	1,041.12	1,037.98	983.57	929.95	931.02	925.65	1,020.29
2015	910.45	857.51	818.81	754.37	745.34	721.70	NQ	NQ	NQ	733.84	694.41	693.59	770.00
2016	653.01	737.23	797.61	798.88	786.39	796.12	834.14	861.60	913.95	940.57	987.73	990.44	841.47
2017	965.02	907.96	925.11	931.47	943.03	920.97	946.70	959.93	971.40	953.69	913.47	907.11	937.15
2018	965.23	1,009.51	987.72	993.12	974.52	962.92	918.93	900.01	887.62	891.53	893.21	898.89	940.27
2019	955.87	993.47	1,001.46	964.84	910.96	893.74	838.94	773.46	786.32	777.06	767.10	799.46	871.89
2020	795.91	769.10	719.07	709.11	724.63	785.65	815.13	824.32	836.15	846.26	864.00	923.79	801.09
2021	1,033.85	1,257.16	1,312.26	1,373.28	1,569.40	1,624.10	1,717.85	1,773.89	1,762.79	1,867.24	1,904.74	1,902.07	1,591.55
2022	1,999.52	2,106.62	2,121.54	2,062.23	1,751.30	1,559.91	1,232.29	1,203.14	1,059.67	980.36	1,048.41	1,187.81	1,526.07
2023	1,366.87	1,323.43	1,183.00	1,260.04	1,244.51	1,304.15	1,373.24	1,246.78	1,224.77	1,178.85			1,270.56

Source: American Metal Market (AMM)

Average Price of Tin (Straights) in New York In Cents Per Pound

Year	Jan.	Feb.	Mar.	Apr.	May	June	July	Aug.	Sept.	Oct.	Nov.	Dec.	Average
2014	1,345.40	1,388.75	1,406.24	1,423.40	1,416.15	1,388.17	1,365.31	1,362.21	1,289.78	1,219.57	1,223.03	1,211.06	1,336.59
2015	1,193.00	1,125.26	1,076.19	989.76	978.73	930.77	924.68	933.28	945.21	973.65	908.21	909.01	990.65
2016	854.30	965.15	1,050.78	1,056.03	1,037.46	1,051.94	1,105.23	1,143.75	1,208.97	1,246.19	1,309.82	1,314.74	1,112.03
2017	1,282.89	1,205.68	1,232.26	1,233.41	1,251.83	1,218.85	1,253.86	1,272.12	1,289.49	1,263.32	1,212.57	1,207.57	1,243.65
2018	1,282.77	1,342.47	1,316.42	1,321.32	1,294.62	1,280.95	1,223.25	1,191.67	1,175.96	1,185.53	1,182.02	1,194.59	1,249.30
2019	1,268.38	1,318.36	1,326.39	1,276.72	1,210.19	1,189.98	1,114.63	1,027.78	1,043.50	1,029.41	1,012.80	1,062.75	1,156.74
2020	1,055.81	1,021.78	948.04	927.43	954.67	1,043.95	1,083.14	1,094.94	1,112.98	1,126.95	1,148.39	1,225.20	1,061.94
2021	1,359.06	1,631.58	1,677.78	1,751.49	1,997.51	2,015.16	2,109.25	2,169.18	2,163.01	2,338.82	2,427.84	2,446.77	2,007.29
2022	2,583.94	2,726.97	2,724.88	2,666.46	2,231.75	1,977.19	1,574.54	1,528.93	1,310.29	1,202.25	1,317.47	1,497.94	1,945.22
2023	1,745.56	1,665.50	1,488.00	1,594.32	1,587.91	1,687.43	1,782.08	1,614.50	1,585.58	1,519.09	1,498.41	1,525.31	1,607.81

Source: U.S. Geological Survey (USGS)

Tin Plate Production & Tin Recovered in the United States   In Metric Tons

| | Tin Content of Tinplate Produced | | | | Tin Recovered from Scrap by Form of Recovery | | | | | | | | |
| | Tinplate Waste | Tinplate (All Forms) | Tin Content (Met. Ton) | Tin per Tonne of Plate (Kilograms) | Tin Metal | Bronze & Brass | Solder | Type Metal | Babbitt | Anti-monial Lead | Chemical Com-pounds | Misc.[2] | Grand Total |
Year	----- Gross Weight -----												
2014	32,900	1,030,000	5,680	5.5	----	----	----	----	----	----	----	----	----
2015	43,800	812,000	4,650	5.7	----	----	----	----	----	----	----	----	----
2016	29,800	623,000	7,840	12.6	----	----	----	----	----	----	----	----	----
2017	27,700	496,000	5,340	10.8	----	----	----	----	----	----	----	----	----
2018	NA	487,000	4,600	9.3	----	----	----	----	----	----	----	----	----
2019	NA	437,000	4,690	10.7	----	----	----	----	----	----	----	----	----
2020	----	518,000	5,550	10.8	----	----	----	----	----	----	----	----	----
2021	----	470,000	5,350	11.4	----	----	----	----	----	----	----	----	----
2022	----	633,000	5,330	8.2	----	----	----	----	----	----	----	----	----
2023[1]	----	505,000	4,610	9.2	----	----	----	----	----	----	----	----	----

[1] Preliminary.   [2] Includes foil, terne metal, cable lead, and items indicated by symbol "W".   W = Withheld.   NA = Not available.
Source: U.S. Geological Survey (USGS)

Consumption of Primary and Secondary Tin in the United States   In Metric Tons

| Year | Net Import Reliance as a % of Apparent Consump | Stocks, Jan. 1[2] | Net Receipts | | | | Available Supply | Stocks, Dec. 31 (Total Available Less Total Processed) | Total Pro-cessed | Consumed in Manu-facturing Products |
			Primary	Secondary	Scrap	Total				
2014	76	5,530	24,000	1,250	2,450	27,700	33,200	5,350	27,800	27,500
2015	76	5,330	24,200	1,180	2,140	27,500	32,800	5,700	27,100	26,800
2016	76	7,090	22,600	1,140	2,040	25,800	31,200	5,480	25,700	25,400
2017	76	6,370	23,100	1,230	2,210	26,500	32,100	5,320	26,800	26,400
2018	77	6,660	28,100	2,890	2,210	33,200	42,300	9,230	33,000	32,700
2019	76	10,100	28,400	2,460	2,150	33,000	41,700	8,590	33,100	32,700
2020	76	10,200	28,000	2,460	972	31,400	40,000	9,010	31,000	30,400
2021	81	10,400								
2022[1]	77	9,010								
2023[1]	74	8,930								

[1] Preliminary.   [2] Includes tin in transit in the U.S.   NA = Not available.   *Source: U.S. Geological Survey (USGS)*

Consumption of Tin in the United States, by Finished Products   In Metric Tons (Contained Tin)

Year	Tin-plate[2]	Solder	Babbitt	Bronze & Brass	Tinning	Chem-icals[3]	Tin Powder	Bar Tin & Anodes	White Metal	Other	Total
2011	6,230	4,100	315	3,810	552	9,990	W	W	W	757	28,500
2012	6,090	4,930	281	2,460	467	9,860	W	W	W	726	27,800
2013	6,030	5,940	820	2,380	511	6,790	W	W	W	807	30,400
2014	5,940	4,860	282	1,720	514	5,420	W	W	W	4,780	27,500
2015	5,880	4,400	312	1,750	463	5,410	W	W	W	6,090	26,800
2016	4,660	4,220	289	1,720	405	5,320	W	W	W	6,190	25,400
2017	5,440	2,520	265	1,880	337	5,450	W	W	W	7,440	26,400
2018	5,760	4,170	403	2,260	427	7,150	W	W	W	8,740	32,700
2019	5,820	3,740	318	1,840	423	7,290	W	W	W	8,540	32,700
2020[1]	6,810	2,660	227	1,910	314	7,540	W	W	W	6,650	30,400

[1] Preliminary.   [2] Includes small quantity of secondary pig tin and tin acquired in chemicals.   [3] Including tin oxide.
W = Withheld proprietary data.   *Source: U.S. Geological Survey (USGS)*

Salient Statistics of Recycling Tin in the United States

| Year | New Scrap[1] | Old Scrap[2] | Recycled Metal[3] | Apparent Supply | Percent Recycled | New Scrap[1] | Old Scrap[2] | Recycled Metal[3] | Apparent Supply |
	--------------------- In Metric Tons ---------------------					---------------- Value in Thousands of Dollars ----------------			
2014	2,060	10,600	12,600	44,900	27.0	46,400	238,000	285,000	1,040,000
2015	1,120	10,100	11,200	43,800	25.0	18,700	168,000	186,000	722,000
2016	8,770	9,960	18,700	50,900	37.0	162,000	184,000	346,000	942,000
2017	8,080	10,000	18,100	52,400	35.0	167,000	207,000	374,000	1,080,000
2018	8,110	9,890	18,000	54,800	33.0	167,000	204,000	371,000	1,130,000
2019	8,120	10,100	18,600	52,800	35.0	155,000	201,000	356,000	1,010,000
2020	7,990	9,550	17,500	49,200	36.0	141,000	168,000	309,000	866,000
2021	7,570	9,030	16,600	54,700	30.0	264,000	315,000	578,000	1,910,000

[1] Scrap that results from the manufacturing process.   [2] Scrap that results from consumer products.   [3] Metal recovered from new plus old scrap.
Source: U.S. Geological Survey (USGS)

Titanium

Titanium (atomic symbol Ti) is a silver-white, metallic element used primarily to make light, strong alloys. It ranks ninth in abundance among the elements in the crust of the earth, but it is never found in its pure state. It occurs as an oxide in various minerals. It was first discovered in 1791 by Rev. William Gregor and was first isolated as a basic element in 1910. Titanium was named after the mythological Greek god Titan for its strength.

Titanium is extremely brittle when cold but is malleable and ductile at low heat, making it easy to fabricate. Due to its strength, low weight, and resistance to corrosion, titanium is used in metallic alloys and as a substitute for aluminum. It is used extensively in the aerospace industry, in desalinization plants, construction, medical implants, paints, pigments, and lacquers.

Supply – World production of titanium ilmenite concentrates in 2022 remained unchanged yr/yr at 8.900 million metric tons. The world's largest producers of titanium ilmenite concentrates are China with 38.2% of world production in 2022, Australia with 7.4%, Norway with 4.8%, and both Ukraine and India with 2.2%. World production of titanium rutile concentrates in 2022 fell by -4.5% yr/yr to 590,000 metric tons. The world's largest producers of titanium rutile concentrates are Australia with 32.2% of world production in 2022, followed by Sierra Leone with 22.0%, South Africa with 16.1, and Ukraine with 9.7%.

Demand – US consumption of titanium dioxide pigment in 2022 rose by +9.7% yr/yr to 940,000 metric tons, below 2004 record high of 1.170 million metric tons.

Trade – US imports of titanium dioxide pigment in 2022 rose by +3.6% yr/yr to 260,000 metric tons. US imports of ilmenite in 2020 fell by -33.7% yr/yr to 481,000 metric tons.

World Produciton of Titanium Illmenite Concentrates   In Thousands of Metric Tons

Year	Australia[2]	Brazil	China	Egypt	India	Malaysia	Norway	Ukraine	United States	Vietnam	World Total	-- Titaniferous Slag[4] --- Canada	Africa
2014	1,250	136	4,240	----	663	8	864	450	200	558	10,400	900	1,100
2015	1,156	133	3,910	----	552	6	630	350	300	238	9,440	700	94
2016	1,400	106	3,800	----	618	4	590	350	100	211	9,800	700	800
2017	1,500	67	3,830	----	517	6	670	392	100	226	10,100	880	1,000
2018	1,400	110	4,200	----	172	14	590	745	100	235	10,300	700	950
2019	1,000	41	4,600	----	291	2	640	819	100	217	10,600	800	903
2020	800	57	5,100	----	290	3	740	773	100	230	11,100	700	820
2021	600	33	3,400	----	204	----	468	316	100	122	8,900	430	900
2022	400	28	3,140	----	210	----	410	190	200	170	8,800	520	1,100
2023[1]	400	54	3,100	----	210	----	430	60	200	140	8,600	500	1,000

[1] Preliminary.   [2] Includes leucoxene.   [3] Approximately 10% of total production is ilmenite. Beginning in 1988, 25% of Norway's ilmenite production was used to produce slag containing 75% TiO2.   NA = Not available.   *Source: U.S. Geological Survey (USGS)*

Salient Statistics of Titanium in the United States   In Metric Tons

Year	--- Titanium Dioxide Pigment --- Production	Imports[3]	Apparent Consumption	------ Ilmenite ------ Imports[3]	Consumption	-- Titanium Slag --- Imports[3]	Consumption	------- Rutile[4] -------- Imports[3]	Consumption	----- Exports of Titanium Products ------ Ores & Concentrates	Scrap	Dioxide & Pigments	Ingots, Billets, Etc.
2014	1,260,000	224,000	802,000	355,000	----	678,000	----	342,500	----	2,240	4,610	685,000	11,500
2015	1,220,000	221,000	792,000	649,000	----	399,000	----	394,000	----	2,040	6,860	649,000	10,400
2016	1,240,000	247,000	840,000	592,000	----	402,000	----	349,700	----	7,330	9,720	651,000	10,100
2017	1,260,000	240,000	870,000	748,000	----	479,000	----	334,100	----	8,940	9,450	634,000	10,900
2018	1,150,000	268,000	890,000	706,000	----	500,000	----	260,100	----	51,400	11,900	528,000	11,300
2019	1,000,000	226,000	825,000	726,000	----	473,000	----	342,300	----	12,200	15,000	401,000	12,100
2020	1,000,000	262,000	880,000	481,000	----	435,000	----	158,128	----	28,800	14,100	386,000	8,040
2021	1,150,000	251,000	906,000	----		----		----				494,000	
2022[1]	1,150,000	265,000	1,040,000	----		----		----				378,000	
2023[2]	920,000	240,000	880,000	----		----		----				280,000	

[1] Preliminary.   [2] Estimate.   [3] For consumption.   [4] Natural and synthetic.   W = Withheld.   *Source: U.S. Geological Survey (USGS)*

TITANIUM

World Production of Titanium Rutile Concentrates   In Metric Tons

Year	Australia	Brazil	India	Mada-gascar	Malaysia	Mozam-bique	Sierra Leone	South Africa	Sri Lanka	Ukraine	United States	World Total
2016	300,000	270	16,200	5,400	3,810	7,781	143,000	120,000	2,237	100,000	W	799,000
2017	300,000	1,000	14,100	8,100	5,266	9,137	168,000	110,000	2,174	100,000	W	818,000
2018	200,000	2,000	11,000	5,070	5,070	8,830	121,500	110,000	2,319	106,858	W	679,000
2019	200,000	600	12,000	5,947	5,947	8,264	137,200	105,000	1,959	100,000	W	667,000
2020	190,000	226	12,000	8,000	5,136	5,958	120,200	95,000	1,311	100,000	W	632,000
2021	190,000	----	12,000	10,000	----	8,000	123,000	95,000	----	95,000	W	618,000
2022	200,000	----	13,000	----	----	8,000	130,000	100,000	----	95,000	W	640,000
2023[1]	200,000[2]	----	13,000	----	----	9,000	110,000	100,000	----	50,000	W	560,000

[1] Preliminary.   Source: U.S. Geological Survey (USGS)

World Production of Titanium Sponge Metal & U.S. Consumption of Titanium Concentrates

| | Production of Titanium (In Metric Tons) | | | | | | --- U.S. Consumption of Titanium Concentrates, by Products (In Metric Tons) --- | | | | | | |
| | ------------------------- Sponge Metal[2] -------------------- | | | | | | ------ Ilmenite (TiO$_2$ Content) ------ | | | ------------ Rutile (TiO$_2$ Content) ------------ | | | |
Year	China	Japan	Russia	United Kingdom	United States	Total	Pigments	Misc.	Total	Welding Rod Coatings	Pigments	Misc.	Total
2014	110,000	25,000	42,000	----	W	194,000	NA	NA	1,430,000	----	----	----	----
2015	62,000	42,000	40,000	----	W	160,000	NA	NA	1,390,000	----	----	----	----
2016	60,000	54,000	38,000	----	W	170,000	NA	NA	1,390,000	----	----	----	----
2017	72,000	51,000	40,000	----	W	181,000	NA	NA	1,410,000	----	----	----	----
2018	70,000	52,000	40,000	----	W	180,000	NA	NA	1,290,000	----	----	----	----
2019	85,000	49,000	44,000	----	W	200,000	NA	NA	1,250,000	----	----	----	----
2020	123,000	49,200	31,000	----	W	230,000				----	----	----	----
2021[1]	120,000	35,000	27,000	----	W	210,000				----	----	----	----

[1] Preliminary.   [2] Unconsolidated metal in various forms.   [4] Included in Pigments.   NA = Not available.   W = Withheld.
Source: U.S. Geological Survey (USGS)

Average Prices of Titanium in the United States

	Ilmenite FOB Australian Ports[2]	Slag, 85% TiO2 FOB Richards Bay, South Africa	Rutile Large Lots Bulk, FOB U.S. East Coast[3]	Rutile Bagged FOB Australian Ports	Avg. Price of Grade A Titanium Sponge, FOB Shipping Point	Titanium Metal Sponge	Titanium Dioxide Pigments FOB US Plants Anatase	Titanium Dioxide Pigments FOB US Plants Rutile
Year	------------------------ Dollars Per Metric Ton -------------------				------------------------------ Dollars Per Pound -------------------------			
2013	$230 - $300	$405 - $455	$1,100-$1,400	$1,200-$1,500	----	$3.20 - $6.23	----	----
2014	$150 - $165	$690 - $835	$820 - $950	$840 - $1,000	----	$4.07 - $5.96	----	----
2015	$100 - $120	$630 - $751	$790 - $890	$800 - $840	----	$3.32 - $5.36	----	----
2016	$100 - $110	$674 - $676	$710 - $770	$770 - $850	----	$5.03 - $5.42	----	----
2017	$160 - $185	$600 - $690	$710 - $770	$770 - $850	----	$6.88 - $11.26	----	----
2018	----	$770 - $790	$1,000 - $1,050	$1,045 - $1,350	----	$9.50 - $10.81	----	----
2019	----	$805 - $955	$1,100 - $1,200	$1,250 - $1,300	----	$10.60	----	----
2020[1]	----	$540-$1,010	$1,150 - $1,200	$1,300 - $1,350	----	$11.50	----	----

[1] Preliminary.   NA = Not available.   Source: U.S. Geological Survey (USGS)

Average Price of Titanium[1] in United States   In Dollars Per Pound

Year	Jan.	Feb.	Mar.	Apr.	May	June	July	Aug.	Sept.	Oct.	Nov.	Dec.	Average
2018	8.02	8.02	8.02	8.10	8.12	8.12	8.12	8.12	8.12	8.30	8.38	8.38	8.15
2019	9.11	9.40	9.40	9.38	9.38	9.38	9.92	10.12	10.12	10.12	10.13	10.13	9.72
2020	10.13	10.13	10.13	10.13	10.13	9.53	9.25	9.25	9.25	9.25	9.25	9.25	9.64
2021	8.38	8.38	8.38	8.00	8.00	8.00	8.25	8.25	8.25	8.25	8.25	8.25	8.22
2022	8.25	8.25	8.25	11.50	11.50	11.50	13.25	13.25	13.25	15.75	15.75	15.75	12.19
2023	15.75	15.75	15.75	15.75	15.75	15.75	13.00	13.00	13.00	13.00	13.00	13.00	14.38

[1] Ingot, 6Al - 4V.   Source: American Metal Market (AMM)

Average Price of Titanium[1] in United States   In Dollars Per Pound

Year	Jan.	Feb.	Mar.	Apr.	May	June	July	Aug.	Sept.	Oct.	Nov.	Dec.	Average
2018	29.00	29.00	29.00	30.43	31.00	31.00	29.48	29.00	29.00	29.70	30.00	30.00	29.72
2019	32.50	33.50	33.50	33.50	33.50	33.50	33.50	33.50	33.50	32.80	32.50	32.50	33.19
2020	32.50	32.50	32.50	32.50	32.50	29.09	27.50	27.50	27.50	27.50	27.50	27.50	29.72
2021	27.50	27.50	27.50	27.50	27.50	27.50	27.50	27.50	27.50	27.50	27.50	27.50	27.50
2022	27.50	27.50	27.50	30.50	30.50	30.50	31.00	31.00	31.00	31.00	31.00	31.00	30.00
2023	31.00	31.00	31.00	31.00	31.00	31.00	----	----	----	----	----	----	31.00

[1] Plate, Alloy.   Source: American Metal Market (AMM)

Tobacco

Tobacco is a member of the nightshade family. It is commercially grown for its leaves and stems, which are rolled into cigars, shredded for use in cigarettes and pipes, processed for chewing, or ground into snuff. Christopher Columbus introduced tobacco cultivation and use to Spain after observing natives from the Americas smoking loosely rolled tobacco-stuffed tobacco leaves.

Tobacco is cured, or dried, after harvesting and then aged to improve its flavor. The four common methods of curing are: air cured, fire cured, sun cured, and flue cured. Flue curing is the fastest method of curing and requires only about a week compared with up to 10 weeks for other methods. Cured tobacco is tied into small bundles of about 20 leaves and aged one to three years.

Virginia tobacco is by far the most popular type used in pipe tobacco since it is the mildest of all blending tobaccos. Approximately 60% of the U.S. tobacco crop is Virginia-type tobacco. Burley tobacco is the next most popular tobacco. It is air-cured, burns slowly and provides a relatively cool smoke. Other tobacco varieties include Perique, Kentucky, Oriental, and Latakia.

Prices – US tobacco farm prices in 2023 rose by +2.1% to 231.3 cents per pound.

Supply – World production of leaf tobacco in 2022 fell by -1.7% yr/yr to 5.780 million metric tons, the smallest production since 1980. The world's largest producers of tobacco in 2022 were China, with 37.9% of world production, followed by India with 13.4%, Brazil with 11.5%, Indonesia with 3.9%, the US with 3.5%, and Zimbabwe with 3.0%.

US production in 2022 fell by -2.3% yr/yr to 202,920 metric tons. Tobacco in the US is grown primarily in the mid-Atlantic States. In 2023, the largest tobacco-producing states in the US were North Carolina with 60.1% of US production, Kentucky with 19.8%, Virginia with 7.1%, Tennessee with 5.4%, Georgia with 3.1%, South Carolina with 2.7%, and Pennsylvania with 1.8%.

US production of flue-cured tobacco (type 11-14), the most popular tobacco type grown in the US, rose by +4.9% yr/yr to 315.030 million pounds in 2023. The second most popular type is Class A light air-cured (type 31-32), which saw US production in 2023 rose by 10.2% yr/yr to 64.727 million pounds. Total US production of tobacco in 2023 fell by -1.2% yr/yr to 432.452 million pounds.

In 2023, US harvested tobacco acreage fell by -5.4% yr/yr to 187.630 acres. The US tobacco yield in 2023 rose by +4.4% to 2,305 pounds per acre. The farm value of the US tobacco crop in 2023 rose by +0.8% yr/yr to $1.000 billion.

Trade – US tobacco exports in 2023 rose by +2.7% yr/yr to 230.8 million pounds.

World Production of Leaf Tobacco   In Metric Tons

Year	Brazil	Canada	China	Greece	India	Indo-nesia	Italy	Japan	Pakistan	Türkiye	United States	Zim-babwe	World Total
2013	850,673	28,620	3,375,400	26,690	765,154	260,200	49,770	19,800	108,307	93,158	328,210	147,068	7,508,485
2014	862,396	27,744	2,997,050	40,940	719,420	196,300	53,925	20,000	129,878	74,696	397,533	184,003	7,212,855
2015	867,355	27,525	2,678,604	37,031	738,029	193,790	51,406	18,700	120,022	75,000	326,210	171,083	6,715,277
2016	677,472	27,963	2,575,371	37,865	747,977	126,728	48,470	17,900	115,574	74,238	285,180	168,974	6,341,651
2017	865,620	27,744	2,392,335	32,712	744,410	181,142	56,398	19,000	100,015	93,666	322,120	110,816	6,265,241
2018	756,232	27,744	2,242,437	22,730	744,046	195,482	49,530	16,998	106,727	75,276	241,870	239,906	6,042,915
2019	769,801	27,817	2,612,991	22,530	747,895	269,803	41,860	16,798	104,355	70,000	212,260	184,584	6,498,844
2020	702,728	27,768	2,135,384	20,870	757,846	261,017	37,830	13,748	132,872	76,540	169,130	203,488	5,816,136
2021[1]	744,173	27,776	2,129,001	19,370	764,999	245,338	41,010	14,237	168,165	73,000	207,800	162,370	5,882,621
2022[2]	667,293	27,787	2,189,489	13,910	772,152	225,579	30,850	8,782	133,562	82,250	202,920	166,919	5,780,940

[1] Preliminary.   [2] Estimate.   *Source: Food and Agriculture Organization of the United Nations (FAO-UN)*

World Imports of Leaf Tobacco   In Metric Tons

Year	Belgium	China	Egypt	France	Germany	Indo-nesia	Nether-lands	Poland	Republic of Korea	Russia	Türkiye	United States	World Total
2013	104,165	174,593	16,915	113,865	165,412	121,218	127,185	88,299	59,503	241,616	61,099	199,731	2,502,941
2014	167,586	199,041	63,508	97,874	164,534	95,732	90,466	96,119	48,910	210,741	66,252	164,221	2,444,884
2015	181,372	179,371	71,704	75,251	183,277	75,353	104,020	115,230	44,110	202,614	67,445	152,614	2,356,763
2016	185,399	162,383	40,939	64,425	159,119	81,502	87,847	111,011	60,826	194,190	73,459	153,766	2,303,344
2017	233,557	171,942	29,654	59,710	181,922	168,060	78,685	126,939	60,092	154,313	74,577	134,908	2,451,453
2018	264,024	156,281	57,418	57,708	158,168	121,390	81,550	137,084	52,611	151,503	83,178	135,647	2,457,795
2019	236,242	184,244	86,491	46,758	150,392	103,561	94,192	137,901	47,230	158,403	87,316	132,855	2,363,481
2020	204,883	108,708	68,993	45,896	136,327	110,275	83,464	143,039	52,772	150,787	93,829	108,315	2,143,818
2021[1]	184,595	173,737	16,345	55,559	153,297	116,931	86,957	135,412	44,145	143,807	74,418	129,829	2,167,877
2022[2]	187,045	184,511	12,781	58,877	170,891	140,920	86,240	139,495	47,390	87,834	89,788	125,008	2,258,563

[1] Preliminary.   [2] Estimate.   *Source: Food and Agriculture Organization of the United Nations (FAO-UN)*

TOBACCO

World Exports of Leaf Tobacco   In Metric Tons

Year	Argentina	Belgium	Brazil	China	India	Italy	Malawi	Mozambique	Tanzania	Turkey	United States	Zimbabwe	World Total
2013	70,053	73,348	609,927	199,967	253,934	69,083	135,676	60,708	69,449	57,512	171,844	147,873	2,597,396
2014	54,607	105,205	460,525	159,760	215,656	61,500	154,708	58,607	76,525	67,895	158,767	141,559	2,385,145
2015	44,232	164,509	497,956	154,708	205,610	58,601	126,235	67,671	65,682	54,153	110,127	148,268	2,333,294
2016	90,948	161,656	466,300	173,582	217,859	64,521	150,104	82,559	74,341	50,742	173,908	155,191	2,496,396
2017	83,656	186,540	442,921	206,710	191,006	68,059	150,533	69,555	48,280	48,899	159,276	157,337	2,460,431
2018	61,804	223,938	440,755	187,114	194,280	74,136	139,844	66,326	72,236	60,625	151,479	171,281	2,442,708
2019	52,674	229,522	530,168	194,641	185,946	67,478	136,411	90,463	42,581	46,665	104,696	173,559	2,437,294
2020	56,431	219,956	485,115	186,066	176,700	59,254	112,439	60,936	42,558	48,243	97,785	177,606	2,246,355
2021[1]	32,709	204,736	434,178	192,154	190,184	59,822	118,481	53,322	37,705	51,689	105,453	177,171	2,242,055
2022[2]	71,662	176,697	552,723	221,530	260,090	71,085	100,353	49,452	49,260	56,409	104,845	188,369	2,535,456

[1] Preliminary.   [2] Estimate.   *Source: Food and Agriculture Organization of the United Nations (FAO-UN)*

Production of Tobacco in the United States, by States   In Thousands of Pounds

Year	Georgia	Kentucky	North Carolina	Ohio	Pennsylvania	South Carolina	Tennessee	Virginia	Total
2014	34,500	214,280	453,860	4,300	22,250	33,180	52,155	57,651	876,415
2015	32,400	149,830	380,250	3,610	18,090	26,000	48,770	55,655	719,171
2016	28,350	136,280	331,800	----	20,460	24,700	35,690	51,440	628,720
2017	26,250	183,300	360,040	----	18,990	25,200	43,000	53,381	710,161
2018	23,750	134,370	251,925	----	17,400	22,140	39,610	44,046	533,241
2019	18,900	123,390	234,700	----	14,300	15,770	30,490	30,406	467,956
2020	19,355	102,395	178,727	----	13,440	6,600	27,940	24,420	372,877
2021	13,090	108,160	248,120	----	10,530	12,045	29,390	35,088	456,423
2022	11,700	94,425	247,522	----	8,780	11,600	33,445	30,303	437,775
2023[1]	13,545	85,645	260,098	----	7,830	11,505	23,205	30,624	432,452

[1] Preliminary.   *Source: Agricultural Statistics Board, U.S. Department of Agriculture (ASB-USDA)*

Salient Statistics of Tobacco in the United States

Year	Acres Harvested 1,000 Acres	Yield Per Acre Pounds	Production Million Pounds	Farm Price cents Lb.	Farm Value Million $	Tobacco (June - July) Exports[2] - Million Pounds -	Imports[3] - Million Pounds -	U.S. Exports of Cigarettes ---- In Millions -----	Cigars & Cheroots In Millions	All Tobacco In Millions of Pounds	Smoking Tobacco[4] In Millions of Pounds	Stocks of Tobacco[5] Various Types All Tobacco In Millions of Pounds	Fire Cured[6] In Millions of Pounds	Cigar Filler[7] In Millions of Pounds	Maryland In Millions of Pounds
2014	378.4	2,316	876	209.4	1,835	----	----	----	-----	----	----	----	----	----	----
2015	328.7	2,188	719	200.3	1,441	----	----	----	-----	----	----	----	----	----	----
2016	319.7	1,967	629	200.7	1,262	----	----	----	-----	----	----	----	----	----	----
2017	321.5	2,209	710	205.8	1,462	----	----	----	-----	----	----	----	----	----	----
2018	291.4	1,830	533	205.1	1,093	----	----	----	-----	----	----	----	----	----	----
2019	227.1	2,060	468	200.9	940	----	----	----	-----	----	----	----	----	----	----
2020	191.1	1,951	373	210.5	785	----	----	----	-----	----	----	----	----	----	----
2021	209.4	2,179	456	213.9	976	----	----	----	-----	----	----	----	----	----	----
2022	198.3	2,208	438	226.5	992	----	----	----	-----	----	----	----	----	----	----
2023[1]	187.6	2,305	432	231.3	1,000	----	----	----	-----	----	----	----	----	----	----

[1] Preliminary.   [2] Domestic.   [3] For consumption.   [4] In bulk.   [5] Flue-cured and cigar wrapper, year beginning July 1; for all other types, October 1.
[6] Kentucky-Tennessee types 22-23.   [7] Types 41-46.   *Source: Economic Research Service, U.S. Department of Agriculture (ERS-USDA)*

Tobacco Production in the United States, by Types   In Thousands of Pounds (Farm-Sale Weight)

Year	Class 1, Flue-cured (11-14)	Class 2, Fire-cured (21-23)	Class 3A, Light air-cured (31-32)	Class 3B, Dark air-cured (35-37)	Total Cigar types (41-61)	US Total
2014	572,880	59,146	217,860	17,490	9,039	876,415
2015	489,475	56,125	148,195	17,050	8,326	719,171
2016	431,450	39,520	143,890	10,020	3,840	628,720
2017	460,650	59,531	165,460	20,200	4,320	710,161
2018	338,690	58,926	103,515	26,590	5,520	533,241
2019	297,170	45,766	92,830	24,390	5,500	467,956
2020	227,555	37,335	80,332	21,215	5,520	372,877
2021	307,015	46,325	75,493	22,490	5,100	456,423
2022	300,195	49,868	58,737	23,675	5,300	437,775
2023[1]	315,030	35,595	64,727	12,100	5,000	432,452

[1] Preliminary.   *Source: Agricultural Statistics Board, U.S. Department of Agriculture (ASB-USDA)*

U.S. Exports of Unmanufactured Tobacco   In Millions of Pounds (Declared Weight)

Year	Australia	Belgium-Luxem.	Denmark	France	Germany	Italy	Japan	Nether-lands	Sweden	Switzer-land	Thailand	United Kingdom	Total U.S. Exports
2014	.1	9.8	1.2	9.8	14.4	.5	.0	14.3	.4	63.5	3.2	3.2	330.2
2015	.1	10.9	1.1	5.2	15.2	.6	.0	7.9	.4	89.7	1.8	1.0	343.0
2016	.0	20.5	.9	2.0	11.9	6.3	.2	8.5	.3	79.5	.6	1.1	362.2
2017	----	14.6	.9	1.2	6.6	7.2	.3	7.5	.4	76.6	----	1.0	317.8
2018	----	13.8	.9	2.9	5.5	8.6	.2	9.4	.1	70.4	----	1.2	326.9
2019	.1	12.2	.7	.9	2.2	12.2	.1	2.6	.1	58.2	----	1.4	222.5
2020	.0	11.1	.7	1.3	2.6	4.6	.1	3.9	.3	34.2	----	----	206.3
2021	----	7.0	.7	2.7	1.1	1.1	.9	2.4	.4	39.2	----	.0	226.5
2022	.0	21.3	.7	3.3	1.0	1.6	.0	2.7	.1	31.3	.0	.0	224.7
2023[1]	----	48.9	.6	.5	1.1	3.8	.0	2.3	.2	4.8	.0	----	230.8

[1] Preliminary.   Source: Economic Research Service, U.S. Department of Agriculture (ERS-USDA)

U.S. Salient Statistics for Flue-Cured Tobacco (Types 11-14) in the United States   In Millions of Pounds

Crop Year	Acres Harvested 1,000	Yield Per Acre Pounds	Mar-ketings	Stocks Oct. 1	Total Supply	Exports	Domestic Disap-pearance	Total Disap-pearance	Farm Price cents/Lb.	Placed Under Gov't Loan (Mil. Lb.)	Price Support Level (cents/) Lb.	Loan Stocks Nov. 30	Uncom-mitted
2014-15	245.3	2,335	----	----	----	----	----	----	----	----	----	----	----
2015-16	220.0	2,225	----	----	----	----	----	----	----	----	----	----	----
2016-17	213.5	2,021	----	----	----	----	----	----	----	----	----	----	----
2017-18	209.5	2,199	----	----	----	----	----	----	----	----	----	----	----
2018-19	197.8	1,712	----	----	----	----	----	----	----	----	----	----	----
2019-20	149.3	1,990	----	----	----	----	----	----	----	----	----	----	----
2020-21	124.1	1,834	----	----	----	----	----	----	----	----	----	----	----
2021-22	147.2	2,086	----	----	----	----	----	----	----	----	----	----	----
2022-23[1]	138.9	2,161	----	----	----	----	----	----	----	----	----	----	----
2023-24[2]	138.0	2,283	----	----	----	----	----	----	----	----	----	----	----

[1] Preliminary.   [2] Estimate.   NA = Not available.   Source: Economic Research Service, U.S. Department of Agriculture (ERS-USDA)

Salient Statistics for Burley Tobacco (Type 31) in the United States   In Millions of Pounds

Crop Year	Acres Harvested 1,000	Yield Per Acre Pounds	Mar-ketings	Stocks Oct. 1	Total Supply	Exports	Domestic Disap-pearance	Total Disap-pearance	Farm Price cents/Lb.	Gross Sales[3]	Price Support Level cents/Lb.	Loan Stocks Nov. 30	Uncom-mitted
2014-15	101.5	2,100	----	----	----	----	----	----	----	----	----	----	----
2015-16	78.9	1,834	----	----	----	----	----	----	----	----	----	----	----
2016-17	80.0	1,747	----	----	----	----	----	----	----	----	----	----	----
2017-18	81.5	1,977	----	----	----	----	----	----	----	----	----	----	----
2018-19	61.1	1,645	----	----	----	----	----	----	----	----	----	----	----
2019-20	48.6	1,910	----	----	----	----	----	----	----	----	----	----	----
2020-21	41.0	1,959	----	----	----	----	----	----	----	----	----	----	----
2021-22	36.6	2,053	----	----	----	----	----	----	----	----	----	----	----
2022-23[1]	32.4	1,808	----	----	----	----	----	----	----	----	----	----	----
2023-24[2]	31.4	2,059	----	----	----	----	----	----	----	----	----	----	----

[1] Preliminary.   [2] Estimate.   [3] Before Christmas holidays.   NA = Not available.
Source: Economic Research Service, U.S. Department of Agriculture (ERS-USDA)

Exports of Tobacco from the United States (Quantity and Value)   In Metric Tons

Year	Unmanufactured Flue-Cured	Value 1,000 USD	Burley	Value 1,000 USD	Total	Value 1,000 USD	Manu-factured	Value 1,000 USD
2014	76,239	645,462	25,441	217,329	149,758	1,085,958	18,111	426,981
2015	77,942	657,188	26,100	226,807	155,578	1,108,756	21,880	423,179
2016	88,283	707,889	20,202	166,246	164,276	1,085,439	18,620	408,341
2017	77,830	643,791	16,335	139,327	144,136	1,010,325	16,321	197,428
2018	81,873	670,927	19,888	165,051	148,259	1,049,085	14,540	184,761
2019	52,250	427,691	10,098	85,776	100,924	732,495	12,711	210,520
2020	36,848	290,318	9,602	78,211	93,595	665,805	14,216	213,011
2021	53,282	442,388	3,202	28,223	102,729	827,318	15,454	201,883
2022[1]	57,536	492,667	3,835	33,408	101,936	844,996	13,729	208,054
2023[2]	64,630	574,857	4,396	45,009	104,671	927,618	12,286	217,919

[1] Preliminary.   [2] Forecast.   Source: Foreign Agricultural Service, U.S. Department of Agriculture (FAS-USDA)

Tungsten

Tungsten (atomic symbol W) is a grayish-white, lustrous, metallic element. The atomic symbol for tungsten is W because of its former name of Wolfram. Tungsten has the highest melting point of any metal at about 3410 degrees Celsius and boils at about 5660 degrees Celsius. In 1781, the Swedish chemist Carl Wilhelm Scheele discovered tungsten.

Tungsten is never found in nature but is instead found in the minerals wolframite, scheelite, huebnertite, and ferberite. Tungsten has excellent corrosion resistance qualities and is resistant to most mineral acids. Tungsten is used as filaments in incandescent lamps, electron and television tubes, alloys of steel, spark plugs, electrical contact points, cutting tools, and in the chemical and tanning industries.

Prices – The average monthly price of tungsten at US ports in 2023 fell by -5.0% yr/yr to $324.62 per short ton, below the 2012 record high of $375.16.

Supply – World concentrate production of tungsten in 2023 fell by -2.3% yr/yr to 78,000 metric tons. The world's largest producer of tungsten by far is China, with 63,000 metric tons of production in 2022, which was 80.8% of total world production. Russia is the next largest producer at 2.6%, with a small production level of 2,000 metric tons.

Trade – The US in 2023 relied on imports for more than 50% of its tungsten consumption. US imports for consumption in 2023 fell by -29.6% yr/yr to 1,500 metric tons. US exports in 2023 fell by -10.4% yr/yr to 550 metric tons.

World Concentrate Production of Tungsten   In Metric Tons (Contained Tungsten[3])

Year	Austria	Bolivia	Brazil	Burma	Canada	China	Korea, North	Mongolia	Portugal	Russia	Rwanda	Thailand	Total
2014	819	1,252	510	247	2,344	65,000	70	557	671	3,775	1,000	99	82,600
2015	861	1,460	432	144	1,600	67,000	70	351	474	3,262	850	35	83,700
2016	954	1,110	323	182	----	64,000	50	732	549	2,707	820	33	78,400
2017	975	994	411	216	----	67,000	310	284	669	2,144	720	65	81,200
2018	936	1,365	400	77	----	65,000	1,410	386	715	2,234	920	69	80,700
2019	892	1,064	400	82	----	69,000	1,130	166	518	2,433	900	40	82,000
2020	890	1,347	400	80	----	66,000	410	70	550	2,400	860	40	78,400
2021	900	1,563			----	71,000	400		502	2,300	1,340		83,800
2022[1]	910	1,360			----	66,000	1,520		500	2,000	1,400		79,800
2023[2]	910	1,500			----	63,000	1,700		500	2,000	1,400		78,000

[1] Preliminary.   [2] Estimate.   [3] Conversion Factors: WO$_3$ to W, multiply by 0.7931; 60% WO$_3$ to W, multiply by 0.4758.
Source: U.S. Geological Survey (USGS)

Salient Statistics of Tungsten in the United States   In Metric Tons (Contained Tungsten)

Year	Net Import Reliance as a % Apparent Consump	Total Con- sumption	Steel — Tool	Steel — Stainless & Heat Assisting	Alloy Steel[3]	Super- alloys	Cutting & Wear Resistant Materials	Products Made From Metal Powder	Miscel- laneous	Chemical and Ceramic	Exports	Imports for Con- sumption	Stocks, Dec. 31 — Concentrates — Con- sumers	Stocks, Dec. 31 — Concentrates — Pro- ducers
2014	>25	W	W	82	W	W	6,880	W	----	88	1,230	4,080	W	W
2015	>25	W	W	205	W	W	6,310	W	----	88	398	3,970	W	W
2016	>25	W	W	94	W	W	5,760	W	----	88	183	3,580	W	W
2017	>50	W	W	87	W	W	6,550	W	----	88	531	3,920	W	W
2018	>50	W	W	84	W	W	6,950	W	----	88	284	4,050	W	W
2019	>50	W	W	82	W	W	6,940	W	----	88	583	2,760	W	W
2020	>50	W	W	82	W	W	5,500	W	----	88	480	2,020	W	W
2021	>50	W	W		W	W		W	----		441	1,600	W	W
2022[1]	>50	W	W		W	W		W	----		614	2,130	W	W
2023[2]	>50	W	W		W	W		W	----		550	1,500	W	W

[1] Preliminary.   [2] Estimate.   [3] Other than tool.   [4] Included with stainless & heat assisting.   W = Withheld.
Source: U.S. Geological Survey (USGS)

Average Price of Tungsten at U.S. Ports (Including Duty)   In Dollars Per Short Ton

Year	Jan.	Feb.	Mar.	Apr.	May	June	July	Aug.	Sept.	Oct.	Nov.	Dec.	Average
2016	171.79	167.74	175.43	189.52	217.82	212.75	188.69	191.74	190.00	192.45	198.89	191.39	190.68
2017	194.33	200.30	211.83	211.18	217.80	221.68	222.76	252.28	310.60	286.02	280.68	296.79	242.19
2018	311.96	321.62	327.93	327.55	338.02	349.36	341.50	307.52	282.50	283.48	285.00	281.31	313.15
2019	268.80	266.25	276.14	275.95	273.00	257.50	222.13	205.50	202.50	228.75	235.00	239.38	245.91
2020	240.00	242.50	242.50	236.88	219.00	215.00	208.50	208.75	220.88	219.90	222.50	228.13	225.38
2021	239.50	255.00	270.88	274.00	274.00	276.50	291.60	312.25	313.75	319.50	322.50	322.50	289.33
2022	330.63	339.75	348.75	351.70	347.88	347.00	343.50	342.50	339.50	337.50	336.25	334.80	341.65
2023	336.38	343.00	338.58	327.50	327.50	327.50	320.63	318.13	315.00	315.00	313.75	312.50	324.62

U.S. Spot Quotations, 65% WO$_3$, Basis C.I.F.   *Source: U.S. Geological Survey (USGS)*

Turkeys

During the past three decades, the turkey industry has experienced tremendous growth in the U.S. Turkey production has more than tripled since 1970, with a current value of over $7 billion. Turkey was not a popular dish in Europe until a roast turkey was eaten on June 27, 1570, at the wedding feast of Charles XI of France and Elizabeth of Austria. The King was so impressed with the birds that the turkey subsequently became a popular dish at banquets held by French nobility.

The most popular turkey product continues to be the whole bird, with strong demand at Thanksgiving and Christmas. The primary breeders maintain and develop the quality stock, concentrating on growth and conformation in males and fecundity in females, as well as characteristics important to general health and welfare. Turkey producers include large companies that produce turkeys all year round, and relatively small companies and farmers who produce turkeys primarily for the seasonal Thanksgiving market.

Prices – The average monthly price received by farmers for turkeys in the US in 2023 fell by -12.0% yr/yr to 94.0 cents per pound, below the record high of 106.8 cents per pound posted in 2022.

Supply – World production of turkeys in 2022 fell by -5.4% yr/yr to 5.081 million metric tons. World production of turkeys has grown by more than 2.5 times since 1980, when production was 2.090 million metric tons. The US is the world's largest producer of turkeys by far, with 2.368 million metric tons of production in 2022, accounting for a hefty 46.6% of world production. The value of US turkey production in the US in 2021 was $5.891 billion.

Demand – US per-capita consumption of turkeys in 2023 rose by +4.1% to 15.2 pounds per person per year.

World Production of Turkey Meat — In Thousands of Metric Tons (Ready-to-Cook-Equivalents)

Year	Brazil	Canada	Chile	France	Germany	Italy	Morocco	Poland	Spain	Tunisia	United Kingdom	United States	World Total
2013	363.5	168.2	3.5	340.4	458.1	310.6	75.0	128.5	156.9	63.8	187.0	2,633.3	5,502.6
2014	326.5	167.9	3.4	377.9	469.1	309.9	78.0	145.0	158.5	70.9	172.0	2,610.7	5,509.6
2015	327.2	171.6	3.1	352.6	464.8	313.0	90.0	162.4	170.7	69.6	181.0	2,552.2	5,531.7
2016	368.0	183.4	2.9	394.0	483.3	331.9	90.0	179.1	191.7	73.5	166.0	2,713.0	5,850.0
2017	390.5	171.2	2.9	374.8	465.6	308.6	90.0	172.2	197.9	79.0	147.0	2,712.7	5,728.5
2018	181.3	168.6	2.8	331.0	467.0	300.1	100.0	376.6	210.4	81.8	157.0	2,666.3	5,664.6
2019	172.3	165.0	2.5	317.0	471.0	300.7	107.0	385.6	212.8	84.7	175.1	2,638.8	5,634.1
2020	159.7	158.3	3.1	321.0	476.0	313.3	100.0	406.8	226.0	83.8	174.0	2,605.1	5,618.4
2021[1]	157.1	150.4	2.7	295.0	441.0	297.8	115.0	363.2	224.8	86.6	125.0	2,521.3	5,371.5
2022[2]	162.3	150.2	2.2	244.9	406.0	211.1	120.0	409.2	231.6	89.3	117.0	2,368.8	5,081.5

[1] Preliminary. [2] Forecast. *Source: Food and Agriculture Organization of the United Nations (FAO-UN)*

World Exports of Turkey Meat — In Thousands of Metric Tons (Ready-to-Cook-Equivalents)

Year	Brazil	Canada	Chile	France	Germany	Hungary	Italy	Netherlands	Poland	Spain	United Kingdom	United States	World Total
2013	92.1	23.6	19.1	75.2	102.7	36.3	58.3	41.1	108.9	30.5	54.3	310.2	1,032.5
2014	79.6	23.3	24.7	76.2	106.5	38.5	59.2	37.9	119.7	33.9	41.9	329.0	1,057.9
2015	83.5	21.2	35.9	69.8	98.7	36.9	60.7	34.3	146.6	37.6	29.8	201.7	942.0
2016	93.4	25.8	37.1	72.1	102.7	39.9	68.5	25.0	153.0	44.9	28.7	216.5	1,002.4
2017	72.4	22.8	13.2	77.6	109.2	33.8	65.3	21.6	140.7	50.6	27.0	231.4	962.0
2018	62.7	19.2	25.8	67.9	101.0	34.2	64.6	23.6	153.3	48.2	23.7	219.3	935.6
2019	35.0	20.3	25.3	58.4	100.7	33.2	57.8	23.4	169.6	47.7	22.2	242.4	927.2
2020	38.2	24.7	24.5	53.0	95.5	27.7	58.6	19.5	168.2	46.8	15.7	213.8	872.2
2021[1]	41.8	26.6	22.5	50.3	96.6	34.3	58.9	27.4	153.8	52.8	11.5	216.2	891.0
2022[2]	56.9	24.0	28.2	46.8	89.8	28.5	37.7	20.0	168.0	44.6	9.1	133.7	778.3

[1] Preliminary. [2] Forecast. *Source: Food and Agriculture Organization of the United Nations (FAO-UN)*

World Imports of Turkey Meat — In Thousands of Metric Tons (Ready-to-Cook-Equivalents)

Year	Austria	Belgium	Benin	China	France	Germany	Mexico	Netherlands	Portugal	South Africa	Spain	United Kingdom	World Total
2013	38.3	38.6	67.8	54.0	33.2	108.9	154.1	26.4	20.2	35.2	24.9	28.4	908.0
2014	38.9	34.7	61.6	34.6	29.8	110.1	153.7	26.2	24.7	24.3	30.2	31.8	1,000.8
2015	35.4	31.7	57.8	20.3	29.8	116.7	126.4	18.8	27.9	10.6	33.2	32.8	948.8
2016	34.6	40.1	47.0	50.3	29.7	114.8	156.9	20.3	29.6	31.4	42.8	35.4	1,031.2
2017	31.5	35.5	41.8	12.3	28.6	117.8	161.8	22.3	25.4	32.2	37.3	41.1	937.6
2018	29.2	32.3	42.0	13.2	29.3	121.1	156.3	21.8	23.3	26.3	37.4	41.0	916.2
2019	25.6	39.7	42.9	22.7	28.6	113.6	150.2	22.7	25.0	27.8	46.0	33.2	918.2
2020	25.4	37.7	40.0	30.9	28.9	106.1	131.2	23.7	24.0	24.6	43.5	25.3	884.7
2021[1]	26.2	31.4	50.7	19.6	31.6	95.9	154.6	27.4	22.8	25.3	34.5	23.7	890.6
2022[2]	25.7	32.4	47.4	19.0	31.7	89.6	102.6	22.2	20.8	12.6	29.9	24.0	797.8

[1] Preliminary. [2] Forecast. *Source: Food and Agriculture Organization of the United Nations (FAO-UN)*

TURKEYS

Salient Statistics of Turkeys in the United States

Year	Poults Placed[3] --- In Thousands ----	Number Raised[4]	Liveweight Pro-duced Mil Lbs	Liveweight Price cents Per Lb.	Value of Pro-duction Million $	Ready-to-Cook Basis Pro-duction	Ready-to-Cook Basis Be-ginning Stocks	Ready-to-Cook Basis Exports	Consumption Total	Consumption Per Capita Lbs.	Production Costs Feed - Liveweight Basis -	Production Costs Total	Wholesale Ready-to-Cook Pro-duction Costs	Wholesale Ready-to-Cook 3-Region Weighted Avg Price[5]
2013	260,571	240,000	7,277.5	66.4	4,839.6	5,806	296,479	741	5,068	16.0	----	----	----	----
2014	267,153	237,500	7,217.0	73.2	5,304.5	5,756	237,407	775	5,052	15.8	----	----	----	----
2015	257,999	233,100	7,038.1	81.1	5,707.9	5,627	193,429	529	5,136	16.0	----	----	----	----
2016	270,711	241,418	7,487.0	82.5	6,184.2	5,981	201,011	569	5,386	16.6	----	----	----	----
2017	270,561	245,200	7,544.4	64.5	4,873.7	5,981	278,741	622		16.5	----	----	----	----
2018	267,489	238,000	7,422.9	51.0	3,785.7	5,878	309,625	611		16.2	----	----	----	----
2019	261,185	228,500	7,468.0	57.9	4,324.0	5,818	302,763	639		15.9	----	----	----	----
2020	252,024	223,000	7,292.8	70.9	5,170.6	5,743	232,652	571		15.7	----	----	----	----
2021[1]	247,644	216,500	7,177.3	82.4	5,892.6	5,592	223,024	561		15.3	----	----	----	----
2022[2]	254,016	210,000	6,655.4	106.8	7,101.3	5,222	165,754	407		14.6	----	----	----	----

[1] Preliminary.   [2] Estimate.   [3] Poults placed for slaughter by hatcheries.   [4] Turkeys place August 1-July 31.   [5] Regions include central, eastern and western. Central region receives twice the weight of the other regions in calculating the average.
Source: Economic Research Service, U.S. Department of Agriculture (ERS-USDA)

Turkey-Feed Price Ratio in the United States   In Pounds[2]

Year	Jan.	Feb.	Mar.	Apr.	May	June	July	Aug.	Sept.	Oct.	Nov.	Dec.	Average
2014	5.2	5.4	5.3	5.1	5.4	5.6	6.2	6.8	7.6	8.3	8.1	7.1	6.3
2015	6.3	6.6	6.8	7.1	7.9	8.4	8.5	9.4	10.0	10.6	10.2	9.8	8.5
2016	8.7	9.0	9.0	9.2	8.8	8.9	9.3	9.5	10.3	9.9	9.3	8.4	9.2
2017	7.6	7.3	7.5	7.5	7.7	7.4	7.3	7.2	6.9	7.1	6.5	6.0	7.2
2018	5.7	5.5	5.2	5.2	5.1	5.3	5.7	5.8	5.9	5.7	6.0	5.5	5.6
2019	5.6	5.8	5.3	6.3	6.1	6.1	6.2	6.6	7.0	7.0	7.5	6.9	6.4
2020	6.7	7.0	7.4	7.9	8.3	8.5	8.7	8.7	8.6	8.2	7.3	6.9	7.9
2021	6.7	6.0	5.8	5.7	5.5	5.8	5.8	6.0	7.2	7.3	6.3	6.1	6.2
2022	6.2	5.8	5.5	5.4	5.5	5.9	6.5	6.6	7.4	8.2	8.1	7.7	6.6
2023[1]	7.6	7.2	7.4	7.3	6.8	6.7	6.3	5.8	6.1	5.8	5.2	3.7	6.3

[1] Preliminary.   [2] Pounds of feed equal in value to one pound of turkey, liveweight.   *Source: Economic Research Service, U.S. Department of Agriculture (ERS-USDA)*

Average Price Received by Farmers for Turkeys in the United States (Liveweight)   In Cents Per Pound

Year	Jan.	Feb.	Mar.	Apr.	May	June	July	Aug.	Sept.	Oct.	Nov.	Dec.	Average
2014	64.5	66.4	68.3	68.7	72.6	72.8	74.0	75.6	77.5	82.2	82.1	73.4	73.2
2015	66.2	66.9	68.3	70.2	75.9	81.2	84.8	89.7	92.5	97.2	92.2	88.6	81.1
2016	78.9	79.4	78.9	83.2	83.1	86.5	86.6	84.3	87.8	85.2	81.5	74.4	82.5
2017	68.9	67.2	69.0	66.6	68.6	65.8	67.8	64.7	62.3	62.7	57.7	52.9	64.5
2018	50.8	50.6	49.9	50.0	49.8	50.8	51.9	51.7	53.1	51.1	53.0	49.8	51.0
2019	50.9	52.8	53.2	55.6	53.3	56.1	57.6	59.2	62.2	63.9	67.1	62.4	57.9
2020	62.5	64.4	66.4	67.7	70.1	71.4	73.7	73.5	77.6	78.4	73.4	72.1	70.9
2021	72.3	73.7	73.9	76.8	80.1	83.1	83.3	87.8	96.1	94.0	83.9	83.9	82.4
2022	86.7	89.8	92.0	94.5	98.6	105.0	109.0	110.0	120.0	127.0	127.0	122.0	106.8
2023[1]	120.0	117.0	118.0	116.0	106.0	102.0	96.0	84.0	82.0	75.0	65.2	47.1	94.0

[1] Preliminary.   *Source: Economic Research Service, U.S. Department of Agriculture (ERS-USDA)*

Average Wholesale Price of Turkeys[1] (Hens, 8-16 Lbs.) in New York   In Cents Per Pound

Year	Jan.	Feb.	Mar.	Apr.	May	June	July	Aug.	Sept.	Oct.	Nov.	Dec.	Average
2014	99.78	99.88	102.34	103.52	106.15	107.18	108.56	109.15	112.79	116.20	118.78	106.79	107.59
2015	99.12	99.12	100.57	104.06	108.82	112.53	120.86	126.62	131.65	135.68	130.63	123.96	116.14
2016	114.71	114.77	114.73	116.17	116.00	117.21	119.45	118.95	123.57	121.84	122.54	105.33	117.11
2017	99.81	100.56	100.90	99.25	99.44	98.54	97.61	96.38	96.59	94.97	88.76	80.16	96.08
2018	79.10	79.64	79.31	79.50	79.31	79.98	79.11	80.03	82.09	82.00	82.24	79.85	80.18
2019	80.96	83.50	83.90	84.31	84.74	87.38	88.26	90.43	93.76	96.88	99.24	97.17	89.21
2020	95.45	97.25	99.63	101.78	103.92	105.39	109.56	110.90	113.48	115.74	112.97	112.20	106.52
2021	108.76	109.66	111.99	113.55	118.15	121.40	122.00	129.33	136.30	135.13	135.32	129.87	122.62
2022	129.47	129.84	134.88	137.08	141.48	153.22	164.00	163.64	168.57	179.38	178.11	175.00	154.56
2023[1]	172.00	168.92	171.50	169.93	154.14	152.15	144.76	127.49	125.36	115.51	104.60	82.14	140.71

[1] Ready-to-cook.   [2] Preliminary.   *Source: Economic Research Service, U.S. Department of Agriculture (ERS-USDA)*

Per Capita Consumption of Turkeys in the United States   In Pounds

Year	First Quarter	Second Quarter	Third Quarter	Fourth Quarter	Total	Year	First Quarter	Second Quarter	Third Quarter	Fourth Quarter	Total
2013	3.7	3.6	4.0	4.8	16.0	2019	3.4	3.7	4.0	4.8	15.9
2014	3.4	3.5	3.9	5.0	15.8	2020	3.6	3.5	3.9	4.7	15.7
2015	3.5	3.6	3.9	4.9	16.0	2021	3.4	3.6	3.8	4.5	15.3
2016	3.6	3.9	4.2	4.9	16.6	2022	3.4	3.2	3.6	4.3	14.6
2017	3.7	3.7	4.0	5.0	16.5	2023[1]	3.4	3.6	3.7	4.1	14.8
2018	3.5	3.8	3.9	4.9	16.2	2024[2]	3.3	3.3	3.6	4.4	14.6

[1] Preliminary.   [2] Estimate.   Source: Economic Research Service, U.S. Department of Agriculture (ERS-USDA)

Certified Federally Inspected Turkey Slaughter in the U.S. (Ready-to-Cook Weights)   In Thousands of Pounds

Year	Jan.	Feb.	Mar.	Apr.	May	June	July	Aug.	Sept.	Oct.	Nov.	Dec.	Total
2014	451,344	419,636	454,990	468,525	469,331	484,245	497,961	480,569	490,385	558,196	478,421	472,065	5,725,668
2015	489,634	431,503	498,992	493,905	432,442	455,913	446,207	447,301	450,088	522,359	466,917	458,298	5,593,559
2016	472,415	451,760	500,407	482,346	496,204	532,226	476,204	535,290	492,914	514,928	511,897	475,553	5,942,144
2017	495,763	454,965	526,631	433,274	520,061	519,205	581,127	673,714	581,261	686,143	642,370	573,273	6,687,787
2018	633,654	571,596	598,038	597,493	633,247	603,743	604,483	644,881	531,593	710,416	619,092	558,969	7,307,205
2019	637,240	570,119	596,483	601,863	611,273	590,011	610,283	622,416	573,499	681,966	583,138	557,236	7,235,527
2020	641,354	556,414	631,105	548,888	531,730	622,960	630,187	590,712	587,725	647,572	569,190	584,075	7,141,912
2021	556,549	522,972	649,318	571,606	561,687	605,013	571,231	588,402	585,139	601,443	564,684	530,205	6,908,249
2022	550,324	526,903	629,785	520,697	512,320	548,829	488,099	556,488	518,659	577,085	532,304	512,111	6,473,604
2023[1]	519,110	519,506	600,366	529,335	605,788	613,606	541,053	608,542	538,063	621,189	562,530		6,828,096

[1] Preliminary.   Source: Economic Research Service, U.S. Department of Agriculture (ERS-USDA)

Storage Stocks of Turkeys (Frozen) in the United States on First of Month   In Thousands of Pounds

Year	Jan.	Feb.	Mar.	Apr.	May	June	July	Aug.	Sept.	Oct.	Nov.	Dec.
2014	237,407	275,787	310,756	336,383	375,013	422,502	462,586	489,758	494,786	484,547	390,654	187,563
2015	193,429	280,400	321,337	345,578	394,415	441,388	462,020	494,037	477,579	449,622	351,828	190,268
2016	201,011	289,746	341,094	368,073	398,719	454,147	504,385	530,278	532,579	511,199	400,355	236,862
2017	278,741	339,493	378,370	428,752	471,484	529,904	565,123	595,623	600,013	569,963	460,856	288,536
2018	309,625	375,188	427,618	462,985	493,844	536,026	561,858	594,927	606,359	564,746	445,059	274,166
2019	302,763	390,972	452,174	470,335	471,592	494,439	538,714	557,031	563,076	528,394	393,008	221,996
2020	232,652	301,623	340,709	387,503	417,981	420,129	474,786	522,325	533,285	501,131	376,347	192,559
2021	223,024	301,409	320,144	350,589	362,510	390,655	405,996	435,483	428,055	414,128	301,999	139,670
2022	165,754	243,749	292,897	308,087	332,513	377,588	411,855	425,848	438,257	391,538	283,581	140,260
2023[1]	189,715	289,596	317,477	338,731	367,965	402,186	437,904	439,794	446,884	421,231	319,650	203,101

[1] Preliminary.   Source: Economic Research Service, U.S. Department of Agriculture (ERS-USDA)

Average Retail Price of Turkeys (Whole frozen) in the United States   In U.S. Dollars Per Pound

Year	Jan.	Feb.	Mar.	Apr.	May	June	July	Aug.	Sept.	Oct.	Nov.	Dec.	Average
2011	1.459	1.526	1.572	1.562	1.596	1.581	1.603	1.641	1.676	1.673	1.541	1.574	1.584
2012	1.671	1.671	1.812	1.791	1.608	1.557	1.561	1.586	1.621	1.661	1.488	1.433	1.622
2013	1.579	1.591	1.593	1.649	1.654	1.595	1.624	1.663	1.819	NA	1.721	1.650	1.649
2014	1.713	1.699	1.733	1.610	1.602	1.606	1.641	1.604	1.584	1.667	1.425	1.331	1.601
2015	1.445	1.480	1.503	1.487	1.527	1.541	1.568	1.546	1.538	1.558	1.424	1.448	1.505
2016	1.528	1.494	1.509	1.488	1.527	1.515	1.586	1.622	1.649	1.692	1.527	1.495	1.553
2017	1.581	1.570	1.585	1.567	1.532	1.576	1.622	1.615	1.623	1.656	1.556	1.502	1.582
2018	1.399	1.435	1.512	1.483	1.526	1.529	1.585	1.567	1.578	1.582	1.400	1.413	1.501
2019	1.455	1.488	1.521	1.543	1.560	1.574	1.531	1.562	1.604	1.601	1.412	1.389	1.520
2020[1]	1.580	1.639	----	----	----	----	----	----	----	----	----	----	1.610

[1] Preliminary.   Source: Economic Research Service, U.S. Department of Agriculture (ERS-USDA)

Uranium

Uranium (atomic symbol U) is a chemically reactive, radioactive, steel-gray, metallic element and is the main fuel used in nuclear reactors. Uranium is the heaviest of all the natural elements. Traces of uranium have been found in archeological artifacts dating back to 79 AD. Uranium was discovered in pitchblende by German chemist Martin Heinrich Klaproth in 1789. Klaproth named it uranium after the recently discovered planet Uranus. French physicist Antoine Henri Becquerel discovered the radioactive properties of uranium in 1896 when he produced an image on a photographic plate covered with a light-absorbing substance. Following Becquerel's experiments, investigations of radioactivity led to the discovery of radium (atomic symbol Ra) and to new concepts of atomic organization.

Uranium is mainly used as fuel in nuclear power plants. Demand for uranium concentrates is directly linked to the level of electricity generated by nuclear power plants. Uranium ores are widely distributed throughout the world and are primarily found in Canada, DRC (formerly Zaire), and the U.S. Uranium is obtained from primary mine production and secondary sources. Two Canadian companies, Cameco and Cogema Resources, are the primary producers of uranium from deposits in the Athabasca Basin of northern Saskatchewan. Secondary sources of uranium include excess inventories from utilities and other fuel cycle participants, used reactor fuel, and dismantled Russian nuclear weapons.

Supply – World production of uranium oxide (U308) concentrate in 2022 fell by -18.7% yr/yr to 35,961 metric tons, below the record high of 59,934 metric tons in 2016. The world's largest uranium producers in 2022 were Kazakhstan with 61.2% of world production, Namibia with 15.6%, Australia with 12.7%, Uzbekistan with 9.2%, and Niger with 5.6%.

Trade – US imports of uranium in 2021 rose by +4.3% yr/yr to 41.300 million pounds. The record high of 66.100 million pounds was posted in 2004. The US has been forced to import more uranium due to declining domestic production. US exports of uranium in 2021 fell by -24.2% yr/yr to 7.500 million pounds.

Uranium Industry Statistics in the United States   In Millions of Pounds U_3O_8

	----- Production -----		Concentrate Shipments	----------- Employment - Person Years ----------					Deliveries to U.S. Utilities[2]	Avg Price Delivered Uranium $/lb U_3O_8	Imports	Avg Price Delivered Uranium Imports $/lb U_3O_8	Exports
Year	Mine	Concentrate		Exploration	Mining	Milling	Processing	Total[1]					
2013	W	50.44	W	51.93	56.37	51.13	43.83	54.00	57.5	54.99	56.2	51.44	18.0
2014	W	42.90	W	47.62	48.11	46.03	36.64	49.73	57.4	51.99	57.4	48.27	18.9
2015	52.35	44.67	W	44.66	43.86	44.14	36.80	46.04	53.3	46.16	56.5	44.03	20.0
2016	48.86	50.56	W	44.85	43.92	42.26	29.62	46.11	56.5	44.13	64.2	42.95	25.7
2017	48.77	51.80	20.02	41.16	35.55	39.04	22.36	41.58	50.6	42.43	50.7	40.45	17.2
2018	46.59	52.51	W	39.82	45.26	38.11	27.51	40.99	43.0	38.80	42.1	37.09	14.0
2019	W	48.16	W	36.28	W	W	27.89	37.73	40.3	38.81	41.5	35.73	13.9
2020	36.01	30.09	W	35.27	W	W	28.70	34.74	48.3	35.59	42.9	34.77	11.7
2021	32.32	39.67	W	33.35	43.04	33.40	30.56	34.71	48.9	33.27	39.6	33.79	9.9
2022	W	W	W	39.78	W	W	40.70	38.81	46.7	33.91	41.3	33.26	7.5

[1] From suppliers under domestic purchases.   *Source: Energy Information Administration, U.S. Department of Energy (EIA-DOE)*

Commercial and U.S. Government Stocks of Uranium, End of Year   In Millions of Pounds U_3O_8 Equivalent

	---------------- Utility ----------------		---------- Domestic Supplier -----------		Total Commercial Stocks	DOE Owned & USEC Held	
Year	Natural Uranium	Enriched Uranium[1]	Natural Uranium	Enriched Uranium[1]		Natural Uranium	Enriched Uranium[1]
2013	56.5	56.6	W	21.3	134.4	W	W
2014	59.9	54.2	W	18.7	132.7	W	W
2015	68.8	52.4	W	14.3	135.5	W	W
2016	74.4	53.6	W	16.7	144.6	W	W
2017	71.2	52.6	W	17.8	141.7	W	W
2018	62.6	48.6	W	19.3	130.5	W	W
2019	64.7	48.4	W	17.5	130.7	W	W
2020	59.7	47.2	W	24.2	131.0	W	W
2021	56.1	52.4	W	33.2	141.7	W	W
2022	49.9	53.8	W	36.2	140.0	W	W

[1] Includes amount reported as UF_6 at enrichment suppliers.   DOE = Department of Energy   USEC = U.S. Energy Commission
Source: Energy Information Administration, U.S. Department of Energy (EIA-DOE)

World Production of Uranium Oxide (U3O8) Concentrate In Metric Tons (Uranium Content)

Year	Australia	Canada	China	Czech Republic	Kazakh- stan	Namibia	Niger	Russia	South Africa	United States	Ukraine	Uzbeki- stan	World Total
2014	5,001	9,134	1,500	193	23,127	3,255	4,156	2,990	393	926	1,919	2,400	54,282
2015	5,654	11,709	1,616	155	23,800	2,993	4,115	3,055	322	1,200	1,256	2,385	56,451
2016	6,315	14,039	1,616	138	24,575	3,654	3,478	3,004	490	1,005	1,125	2,404	59,934
2017	5,882	13,116	1,885	70	23,391	4,224	3,485	2,917	308	550	940	2,404	57,225
2018	6,517	7,001	1,885	----	21,705	5,525	2,910	2,904	346	1,180	582	2,404	50,978
2019	6,613	6,938	1,885	----	22,808	5,476	2,982	2,911	346	801	58	2,404	51,158
2020[1]	6,203	3,885	1,885	----	19,477	5,413	2,992	2,846	250	744	6	3,500	44,101
2021[2]	4,192	4,693	1,885			5,753			385	455	8	3,500	17,986

[1] Preliminary. [2] Estimate. *Source: Food and Agriculture Organization of the United Nations (FAO-UN)*

Total Production of Uranium Concentrate in the United States, by Quarters In Pounds U3O8

Year	First Quarter	Second Quarter	Third Quarter	Fourth Quarter	Total	Year	First Quarter	Second Quarter	Third Quarter	Fourth Quarter	Total
2012	1,078,404	1,061,289	1,048,018	957,936	4,145,647	2018	226,780	365,421	528,870	345,425	1,466,496
2013	1,147,031	1,394,232	1,171,278	946,301	4,658,842	2019	58,481	44,569	32,211	38,614	173,875
2014	1,242,179	1,095,011	1,468,608	1,085,534	4,891,332	2020	8,098	W	W	W	8,098
2015	1,154,408	789,980	774,541	624,278	3,343,207	2021	W	W	5,297	9,978	15,275
2016	626,522	745,306	818,783	725,947	2,916,558	2022[1]	9,946	6,042	3,245	174,712	193,945
2017	450,215	726,375	643,212	622,987	2,442,789	2023[2]	2,511	7,443	27,012	12,653	49,619

[1] Preliminary. [2] Estimate. *Source: Energy Information Administration, U.S. Department of Energy (EIA-DOE)*

URANIUM - NYMEX
Weekly Nearest Futures as of 03/28/2024

WEEKLY NEAREST FUTURES
As of 03/28/2024
Chart High 106.55 on 01/22/2024
Chart Low 17.50 on 11/29/2016

Nearby Futures through Last Trading Day.

Volume of Trading of Uranium Futures In Contracts

Year	Jan.	Feb.	Mar.	Apr.	May	June	July	Aug.	Sept.	Oct.	Nov.	Dec.	Total
2017	370	1,180	744	200	915	530	286	232	17	----	978	941	6,393
2018	650	35	200	27	100	431	521	190	1,298	827	2,169	714	7,162
2019	1,558	1,000	3,117	1,000	1,175	1,234	300	----	1,217	----	----	20	10,621
2020	9	1,200	621	5	1	18	----	----	----	1	----	----	1,855
2021	----	----	400	----	460	5	120	120	25	53	----	----	1,183
2022	6	----	----	----	----	----	----	----	----	----	----	----	6
2023	----	----	----	----	----	----	----	----	4	1	----	----	5

Contract size = 250 pounds of U3O8. *Source: CME Group; New York Mercantile Exchange (NYMEX)*

Average Open Interest of Uranium Futures In Contracts

Year	Jan.	Feb.	Mar.	Apr.	May	June	July	Aug.	Sept.	Oct.	Nov.	Dec.
2017	4,100	4,447	4,768	4,348	4,565	4,808	4,447	4,288	4,236	4,191	3,785	3,810
2018	3,707	2,952	2,926	2,764	2,719	2,628	2,499	3,026	3,420	4,636	4,619	4,097
2019	3,854	3,322	3,218	3,611	3,003	2,688	2,699	2,718	2,406	2,406	2,403	2,343
2020	1,809	1,702	1,281	344	333	320	318	310	302	303	303	302
2021	300	300	683	700	907	1,160	1,222	1,211	930	800	800	800
2022	800	800	800	800	800	800	800	800	800	800	800	800
2023	800	737	200	----	----	----	----	----	2	1	1	1

Contract size = 250 pounds of U3O8. *Source: CME Group; New York Mercantile Exchange (NYMEX)*

URANIUM

Uranium Industry Statistics in the United States   In Millions of Pounds U₃O₈

Year	Total Operable Units[2/3] Number	Net Summer Capacity of Operable Units[3/4] Million Kilowatts	Nuclear Electricity Net Generation Million Kilowatthours	Nuclear Share of Electricity Net Gen. Percent	Capacity Factor Percent	Year	Total Operable Units[2/3] Number	Net Summer Capacity of Operable Units[3/4] Million Kilowatts	Nuclear Electricity Net Generation Million Kilowatthours	Nuclear Share of Electricity Net Gen. Percent	Capacity Factor Percent
2010	104.0	101.2	806,968	19.6	91.1	2017	99.0	99.6	804,950	20.0	92.2
2011	104.0	101.4	790,204	19.3	89.1	2018	98.0	99.5	807,078	19.4	92.5
2012	104.0	101.9	769,331	19.0	86.1	2019	96.0	98.8	809,412	19.7	93.4
2013	100.0	99.2	789,016	19.4	89.9	2020	94.0	97.2	789,878	19.8	92.4
2014	99.0	99.1	797,167	19.5	91.7	2021	93.0	95.8	778,187	19.1	92.7
2015	99.0	98.6	797,177	19.6	92.3	2022	92.0	95.0	771,537	18.3	92.8
2016	99.0	99.5	805,325	19.9	92.3	2023[1]	93.0	95.2	770,673	18.6	92.7

[1] Preliminary.   [2] Total of nuclear generating units holding full-power licenses, or equivalent permission to operate, at end of period. [3] At end of period.   [4] Beginning in 2011, monthly capacity values are estimated in two steps: 1) uprates and derates reported on Form EIA-860M are added to specific months; and 2) the difference between the resulting year-end capacity and final capacity is allocated to the month of January. purchases.   *Source: Energy Information Administration, U.S. Department of Energy (EIA-DOE)*

Nuclear Electricity Net Generation   In Million Kilowatthours

Year	Jan.	Feb.	Mar.	Apr.	May	June	July	Aug.	Sept.	Oct.	Nov.	Dec.	Total
2014	73,163	62,639	62,397	56,385	62,947	68,138	71,940	71,129	67,535	62,391	65,140	73,363	797,167
2015	74,270	63,462	64,547	59,757	65,833	68,546	71,412	72,415	66,466	60,571	60,264	69,634	797,177
2016	72,525	65,638	66,149	62,365	66,576	67,175	70,349	71,526	65,448	60,733	65,179	71,662	805,325
2017	73,121	63,560	65,093	56,743	61,313	67,011	71,314	72,384	68,098	65,995	66,618	73,700	804,950
2018	74,649	64,790	67,033	59,133	67,320	69,688	72,456	72,282	64,725	59,397	63,948	71,657	807,078
2019	73,701	64,715	65,080	60,581	67,124	68,805	72,199	71,911	66,064	62,033	64,125	73,074	809,412
2020	74,170	65,911	63,997	59,170	64,338	67,205	69,385	68,982	65,727	59,362	61,760	69,871	789,878
2021	71,732	62,954	63,708	57,092	63,394	66,070	68,832	69,471	64,520	56,945	62,749	70,720	778,187
2022	70,577	61,852	63,154	55,290	63,382	65,715	68,857	68,897	63,733	58,945	62,041	69,094	771,537
2023[1]	70,870	60,807	62,820	56,662	61,473	64,965	69,888	69,744	65,560	61,403	62,258		770,673

[1] Preliminary.   Source: Energy Information Administration, U.S. Department of Energy (EIA-DOE)

Nuclear Share of Electricity Net Generation   In Percent

Year	Jan.	Feb.	Mar.	Apr.	May	June	July	Aug.	Sept.	Oct.	Nov.	Dec.	Average
2014	19.4	19.3	18.8	18.9	19.4	19.0	18.6	18.5	19.9	19.8	20.5	21.7	19.5
2015	20.6	19.0	19.9	20.3	20.4	18.9	17.8	18.5	19.0	19.4	20.0	21.5	19.6
2016	20.6	20.9	21.7	21.3	21.0	18.2	17.1	17.4	18.6	19.4	21.9	20.8	19.9
2017	21.3	21.9	20.5	19.3	19.0	18.7	17.6	18.8	20.3	20.6	21.5	20.9	20.0
2018	19.9	21.2	20.9	19.6	19.8	18.7	17.6	17.7	18.1	18.2	19.8	21.2	19.4
2019	20.5	20.5	19.9	20.4	20.3	19.5	17.6	17.9	18.3	19.4	20.3	21.6	19.7
2020	21.7	20.6	20.7	21.2	21.1	19.1	16.9	17.3	19.7	18.9	20.5	20.3	19.8
2021	20.5	19.4	20.5	19.5	19.8	17.7	17.0	16.8	18.6	17.9	20.0	21.0	19.1
2022	18.9	19.1	19.5	18.2	18.5	17.3	16.3	16.7	18.1	18.8	19.3	19.2	18.3
2023[1]	20.4	19.7	19.0	18.9	18.8	18.2	16.4	16.5	18.3	18.6	19.3		18.6

[1] Preliminary.   Source: Energy Information Administration, U.S. Department of Energy (EIA-DOE)

Capacity Factor   In Percent

Year	Jan.	Feb.	Mar.	Apr.	May	June	July	Aug.	Sept.	Oct.	Nov.	Dec.	Average
2014	99.1	94.0	84.5	78.8	85.2	95.4	97.5	96.4	94.6	84.5	91.3	99.6	91.7
2015	101.3	95.8	88.0	84.3	89.8	96.4	97.3	98.6	93.6	82.5	84.8	94.9	92.3
2016	98.5	95.3	89.9	88.1	90.5	94.2	94.5	96.1	90.9	81.7	90.9	96.7	92.2
2017	98.7	94.9	87.8	79.1	82.7	93.4	96.2	97.6	94.9	89.0	92.9	99.4	92.2
2018	100.7	96.7	90.4	82.4	90.8	97.1	97.7	97.5	90.4	80.5	89.4	96.9	92.5
2019	99.6	96.8	88.0	84.5	90.8	96.6	98.1	97.7	93.1	85.0	90.8	100.1	93.4
2020	101.6	96.5	87.7	83.9	89.1	96.2	96.1	95.5	94.0	82.2	88.9	97.3	92.4
2021	99.9	97.0	88.7	82.1	89.2	96.0	96.8	97.7	93.8	80.1	91.2	99.5	92.7
2022	99.4	96.5	89.0	80.5	89.3	96.4	97.8	97.8	93.5	83.7	91.0	98.1	92.8
2023[1]	100.6	95.6	89.2	83.1	87.3	95.3	99.1	97.9	95.1	86.2	90.3		92.7

[1] Preliminary.   [2] Beginning in 2008, capacity factor data are calculated using a new methodology.   Source: Energy Information Administration, U.S. Department of Energy (EIA-DOE)

Vanadium

Vanadium (atomic symbol V) is a silvery-white, soft, ductile, metallic element. Discovered in 1801, but mistaken for chromium, vanadium was rediscovered in 1830 by Swedish chemist Nils Sefstrom, who named the element in honor of the Scandinavian goddess Vanadis.

Never found in the pure state, vanadium is found in about 65 different minerals such as carnotite, roscoelite, vanadinite, and patronite, as well as in phosphate rock, certain iron ores, some crude oils, and meteorites. Vanadium is one of the hardest of all metals. It melts at about 1890 degrees Celsius and boils at about 3380 degrees Celsius.

Vanadium has good structural strength and is used as an alloying agent with iron, steel, and titanium. It is used in aerospace applications, transmission gears, photography as a reducing agent, and as a drying agent in various paints.

Prices – The price of vanadium in 2022 rose by +13.2% yr/yr to $9.25 per pound, below the record high of $16.28 per pound posted in 2018.

Supply – Virtually all (99%) vanadium is produced from ores, concentrates, and slag, with the remainder coming from petroleum residues, ash, and spent catalysts. World vanadium production in 2023 from ore, concentrates, and slag fell by -2.0% yr/yr to 100,000 metric tons. The world's largest producer of vanadium from ores, concentrates, and slag in 2023 was China, with 68,000 metric tons of production, which was 68.0% of total world production. The two other major producers were Russia, with 20,000 metric tons of production and 20.0% of world production, and South Africa, with 9,100 metric tons of production and 9.1% of world production.

Trade – US exports of vanadium in 2021 were in the forms of vanadium pent-oxide and anhydride at 17 metric tons (down -66.0% yr/yr), ferro-vanadium at 173 metric tons (down -17.6% yr/yr), and oxides and hydroxides at 235 metric tons (up +360.8% yr/yr). US imports of vanadium in 2021 were in the forms of ferro-vanadium at 2,170 metric tons (up +59.6% yr/yr), vanadium pent-oxide at 1,710 metric tons (up +2.4% yr/yr), ore, slag, and residues at 1,680 metric tons (up +8.4% yr/yr), and oxides and hydroxides at 69 metric tons (up +3.0% yr/yr).

World Production of Vanadium   In Metric Tons (Contained Vanadium)

| | ------------------------- From Ores, Concentrates and Slag ------------------------- | | | | | | From Petroleum Residues Ash, Spent Catalysts ------------ | | | |
Year	Australia	China[3]	Kazak-hstan	Russia	South Africa	Total[4]	Japan[5]	United States[6]	Total	World Total
2014	578	48,000	15,100	21,600	----	85,300	580	----	580	82,700
2015	3,250	45,000	16,000	17,788	----	82,000	600	----	600	79,400
2016	4,460	41,000	16,000	8,160	----	69,600	----	----	----	----
2017	5,206	55,900	18,636	7,959	----	87,700	----	----	----	----
2018	5,500	59,500	17,052	7,700	----	89,800	----	----	----	----
2019	5,923	60,000	18,380	8,030	460	92,800	----	----	----	----
2020	6,622	70,200	19,533	8,584	17	105,000	----	----	----	----
2021	5,780	70,300	20,100	8,800	----	105,000	----	----	----	----
2022[1]	5,840	66,900	20,000	8,870	----	102,000	----	----	----	----
2023[2]	6,400	68,000	20,000	9,100	----	100,000	----	----	----	----

[1] Preliminary.   [2] Estimate.   [3] In vanadiferous slag product.   [4] Excludes U.S. production.   [5] In vanadium pentoxide product.
[6] In vanadium pentoxide and ferrovanadium products.   Source: U.S. Geological Survey (USGS)

Salient Statistics of Vanadium in the United States   In Metric Tons (Contained Vanadium)

| | Con-sumer & Producer Stocks, Dec. 31 | -------- Vanadium Consumption by Uses in the U.S. -------- | | | | | | | | | -------- Exports --------- | | | ------------- Imports --------------- | | | |
Year		Tool Steel	Cast Irons	High Strength, Low Alloy	Stainless & Heat Resisting	Super-alloys	Carbon	Full Alloy	Total	Average $ Per Lb. V₂O₅	Vanadium Pent-oxide & Anhydride	Oxides & Hydr-oxides	Ferro-Vana-dium	Ores, Slag, Residues	Vanadium Pent-oxide & Anhydride	Oxides & Hydr-oxides	Ferro-Vana-dium
2014	225	W	W	W	61	8	710	1,540	4,070	5.61	171	231	253	3,450	3,410	104	3,230
2015	W	W	W	W	61	9	743	1,460	3,930	4.16	303	66	122	4,600	2,870	94	1,980
2016	W	W	W	W	61	10	718	1,460	3,830	3.38	5	81	394	5,030	2,460	660	1,590
2017	W	W	W	W	62	9	755	1,260	3,880	7.61	126	148	229	4,530	3,400	148	2,810
2018	W	W	W	W	63	W	798	1,270	5,640	16.40	563	53	575	2,810	4,600	98	2,970
2019	W	W	W	W	63	W	763	1,260	4,840	12.17	423	750	295	2,120	3,620	105	2,280
2020	W	W	W	W	88	W	1,100	1,760	7,920	6.68	50	51	210	1,550	1,670	67	1,360
2021	W	W	W	W	88	W	1,460	1,770	8,030	8.17	17	235	173	1,680	1,710	69	2,170
2022[1]	W	W	W	W		W				9.25	143	309	172	2,240	1,980	222	2,650
2023[2]										9.25	5	200	200	3,100	2,100	100	2,400

[1] Preliminary.   [2] Estimate.   W = Withheld.   *Source: U.S. Geological Survey (USGS)*

Vegetables

Vegetables are the edible products of herbaceous plants, which are plants with soft stems. Vegetables are grouped according to the edible part of each plant, including leaves (e.g., lettuce), stalks (celery), roots (carrot), tubers (potato), bulbs (onion), fruits (tomato), seeds (pea), and flowers (broccoli). Each of these groups contributes to the human diet in its own way. Fleshy roots are high in energy value and good sources of the vitamin B group, seeds are relatively high in carbohydrates and proteins, while leaves, stalks, and fruits are excellent sources of minerals, vitamins, water, and roughage. Vegetables are an important food for the maintenance of health and prevention of disease. Higher intakes of vegetables have been shown to lower the risks of cancer and coronary heart disease.

Vegetables are best consumed fresh in their raw state to derive the maximum benefits from their nutrients. While canned and frozen vegetables are often thought to be inferior to fresh vegetables, they are sometimes nutritionally superior to fresh produce because they are usually processed immediately after harvest when nutrient content is at its peak. When cooking vegetables, aluminum utensils should not be used, because aluminum is a soft metal that is affected by food acids and alkalis. Scientific evidence shows that tiny particles of aluminum from foods cooked in aluminum utensils enter the stomach and can injure the sensitive lining of the stomach.

Prices – The monthly average index of fresh vegetable prices received by growers in the US in 2023 fell by -20.4% yr/yr to 291.1.

Demand – The leading vegetable in terms of US per capita consumption in 2019 was the potato with 118.8 pounds of consumption, followed by tomatoes with 88.3 pounds, lettuce with 25.0 pounds, onions with 22.1 pounds, and sweet corn with 18.9 pounds. Total US per capita vegetable consumption in 2019 was 409.2 pounds.

Index of Prices Received by Growers for Fresh Vegetables in the United States   (1990-92=100)

Year	Jan.	Feb.	Mar.	Apr.	May	June	July	Aug.	Sept.	Oct.	Nov.	Dec.	Average
2014	197.0	193.3	197.1	200.2	195.9	214.6	197.3	184.7	191.0	219.6	249.1	229.0	205.7
2015	253.2	197.1	200.5	211.0	230.2	213.5	209.9	206.2	235.1	229.4	228.3	284.0	224.9
2016	343.7	266.3	222.6	209.1	240.2	226.3	225.4	184.8	217.0	205.8	179.7	182.3	225.3
2017	185.1	223.6	244.6	332.3	266.8	228.1	211.8	185.4	209.9	262.3	268.3	239.8	238.2
2018	252.3	160.8	247.0	183.7	235.5	189.5	173.9	197.7	190.2	221.6	317.8	432.9	233.6
2019	295.9	238.4	289.4	242.7	262.1	272.2	277.6	205.5	191.6	287.8	296.1	265.2	260.4
2020	350.0	208.0	203.3	200.8	220.9	256.9	220.3	213.4	276.9	381.3	342.6	254.0	260.7
2021	283.8	218.8	197.5	172.4	188.0	184.5	175.8	191.7	251.1	323.5	366.7	291.6	237.1
2022	275.7	237.5	394.0	251.1	262.4	249.0	277.4	226.8	336.2	509.7	729.6	640.6	365.8
2023[1]	352.9	277.5	239.7	384.2	284.6	274.9	292.7	265.7	256.4	265.4	309.7	289.3	291.1

[1] Preliminary.   Not seasonally adjusted.   *Source: National Agricultural Statistics Service, U.S. Department of Agriculture (NASS-USDA)*

Producer Price Index of Canned[2] Processed Vegetables in the United States   (1982 = 100)

Year	Jan.	Feb.	Mar.	Apr.	May	June	July	Aug.	Sept.	Oct.	Nov.	Dec.	Average
2014	173.2	173.4	173.0	172.4	172.3	172.9	173.0	173.7	174.2	174.6	174.7	174.8	173.5
2015	175.7	176.3	179.4	175.0	174.9	177.0	176.2	172.6	172.1	172.3	172.6	168.8	174.4
2016	166.7	168.4	165.4	166.6	167.3	166.0	165.9	166.2	165.9	165.4	165.4	165.5	166.2
2017	164.2	164.6	163.6	165.4	166.4	165.7	165.6	166.4	165.5	165.8	167.6	167.4	165.7
2018	167.4	170.2	168.8	169.1	168.6	169.5	168.5	170.8	171.5	173.4	175.7	177.4	170.9
2019	176.5	176.5	176.8	176.0	175.2	175.7	175.9	177.2	178.0	178.8	180.4	181.8	177.4
2020	183.3	182.7	183.3	184.4	185.0	183.8	183.3	182.0	184.2	184.3	185.4	185.4	183.9
2021	185.9	186.0	186.6	186.6	187.1	185.3	186.8	188.0	190.8	194.0	193.9	195.6	188.9
2022	197.7	199.5	203.8	206.6	214.4	217.2	223.2	227.1	233.2	234.6	240.8	241.8	220.0
2023[1]	239.9	241.1	244.6	243.2	248.7	247.9	249.9	251.2	254.7	255.5	255.5	255.6	249.0

[1] Preliminary.   [2] Includes canned vegetables and juices, including hominy and mushrooms.   Not seasonally adjusted.   *Source: Bureau of Labor Statistics, U.S. Department of Labor (BLS)*

Producer Price Index of Frozen Processed Vegetables in the United States   (1982 = 100)

Year	Jan.	Feb.	Mar.	Apr.	May	June	July	Aug.	Sept.	Oct.	Nov.	Dec.	Average
2014	192.2	192.3	192.3	192.4	192.4	192.3	192.3	192.9	193.2	193.5	193.5	193.5	192.7
2015	193.8	193.1	193.2	193.3	193.5	193.3	193.3	193.1	195.9	195.8	195.3	195.3	194.1
2016	195.2	195.2	195.2	195.2	195.3	195.4	195.5	195.3	195.3	195.6	196.0	196.0	195.4
2017	198.6	199.5	199.6	199.5	199.6	199.6	202.7	202.7	204.3	205.7	205.7	206.8	202.0
2018	208.0	208.1	209.3	209.5	209.6	210.3	211.5	211.5	213.6	213.9	213.5	211.5	210.9
2019	211.6	211.9	212.1	212.1	212.1	212.2	212.2	214.7	214.4	215.2	215.2	215.9	213.3
2020	216.4	216.1	216.2	216.4	216.3	216.3	216.4	216.8	218.8	219.0	219.0	220.0	217.3
2021	220.0	220.1	218.6	219.0	220.1	220.3	220.3	220.4	222.3	222.8	223.7	224.2	221.0
2022	227.4	229.0	231.1	234.0	246.2	249.1	249.3	254.3	271.7	274.3	280.1	279.3	252.1
2023[1]	281.8	289.1	289.4	290.2	291.4	304.5	305.1	307.1	316.7	316.7	314.4	315.1	301.8

[1] Preliminary.   Not seasonally adjusted.   *Source: Bureau of Labor Statistics, U.S. Department of Labor (BLS)*

Per Capita Use of Selected Commercially Produced Fresh and Processing Vegetables and Melons in the United States   In Pounds, farm weight basis

Crop	2010	2011	2012	2013	2014	2015	2016	2017	2018[10]	2019[11]
Asparagus, All	1.6	1.6	1.7	1.6	1.8	1.6	1.8	1.8	1.9	1.9
Fresh	1.4	1.4	1.4	1.4	1.7	1.5	1.6	1.6	1.8	1.8
Canning	0.1	0.1	0.1	0.1	0.1	0.1	0.1	0.1	0.1	0.1
Freezing	0.1	0.1	0.1	0.1	0.1	0.1	0.2	0.1	0.1	0.1
Snap beans, All	7.5	6.4	6.5	6.6	6.0	6.4	6.9	6.6	6.3	6.6
Fresh	1.9	1.7	1.6	1.6	1.5	1.6	1.7	1.6	1.6	1.8
Canning	3.7	3.2	2.9	2.9	2.8	3.0	3.2	3.1	2.9	2.9
Freezing	2.0	1.5	1.9	2.1	1.8	1.9	2.0	1.9	1.8	1.9
Broccoli, All [1]	8.4	8.6	8.9	9.4	9.2	10.0	10.1	9.5	8.4	8.8
Fresh	6.0	6.0	6.3	6.9	6.7	7.4	7.5	7.1	5.9	6.1
Freezing	2.5	2.7	2.6	2.5	2.6	2.6	2.6	2.4	2.5	2.6
Cabbage, All	8.5	7.6	7.4	7.9	7.6	7.2	7.0	7.5	6.4	7.1
Fresh	7.5	6.6	6.3	6.9	6.7	6.3	5.9	6.2	5.7	6.5
Canning (kraut)	1.0	1.0	1.2	1.0	0.9	0.9	1.0	1.3	0.8	0.7
Carrots, All [2]	10.0	9.9	9.9	10.5	10.4	10.9	10.8	10.9	15.6	16.6
Fresh	7.8	7.5	8.0	8.0	8.5	8.8	7.8	7.4	12.2	13.6
Canning	0.8	0.8	0.8	0.8	0.7	0.7	1.1	1.1	1.0	1.2
Freezing	1.5	1.6	1.2	1.7	1.2	1.4	1.9	2.4	2.4	1.8
Cauliflower, All [1]	1.7	1.7	1.5	1.7	1.6	1.9	2.1	2.9	3.1	3.7
Fresh	1.3	1.2	1.2	1.3	1.3	1.6	1.7	2.4	2.5	3.0
Freezing	0.4	0.4	0.3	0.3	0.4	0.3	0.4	0.5	0.6	0.7
Celery	6.1	6.0	6.0	5.5	5.5	5.1	5.0	4.7	4.9	5.3
Sweet Corn, All [3]	24.7	23.8	24.3	21.7	21.1	22.0	19.6	20.3	19.9	18.9
Fresh	9.3	8.2	8.7	8.9	7.7	8.6	7.1	7.2	6.8	6.8
Canning	6.9	5.8	5.9	5.8	5.8	5.3	5.0	5.1	5.2	5.3
Freezing	8.6	9.8	9.8	7.0	7.7	8.0	7.5	8.1	7.9	6.9
Cucumbers, All	10.5	9.2	10.1	10.6	11.3	11.0	11.1	11.1	11.3	11.4
Fresh	6.7	6.4	7.1	7.3	7.4	7.6	8.1	7.4	8.0	8.0
Pickling	3.7	2.8	3.0	3.2	3.9	3.4	3.0	3.7	3.3	3.4
Melons	26.4	25.5	----	----	----	----	----	----	----	----
Watermelon	15.7	14.8	----	----	----	----	----	----	----	----
Cantaloupe	8.6	8.7	----	----	----	----	----	----	----	----
Honeydew	1.5	1.5	----	----	----	----	----	----	----	----
Other	0.6	0.5	----	----	----	----	----	----	----	----
Lettuce, All	27.9	27.6	27.9	25.5	25.3	25.5	31.4	30.4	24.5	25.0
Head lettuce	15.9	15.8	16.0	14.1	14.5	13.6	16.9	15.3	12.3	12.7
Romaine & Leaf	12.0	11.7	11.9	11.4	10.8	11.9	14.5	15.1	12.1	12.3
Onions, All	20.9	20.4	20.7	19.6	19.4	19.7	24.5	26.5	21.1	22.1
Fresh	19.6	19.1	19.3	18.5	18.4	18.3	22.8	25.1	20.5	20.4
Dehydrating	1.3	1.2	1.4	1.1	1.1	1.4	1.7	1.4	0.6	1.7
Green Peas, All [4]	2.6	2.4	2.7	2.4	2.3	2.3	1.8	2.0	1.9	1.9
Canning	1.1	0.8	0.8	0.9	0.7	0.8	0.8	0.7	0.6	0.7
Freezing	1.5	1.6	1.9	1.5	1.6	1.5	1.0	1.3	1.3	1.3
Peppers, All	11.2	11.4	11.7	10.9	11.6	11.6	12.0	12.2	12.0	12.2
Bell Peppers, All	10.3	10.6	10.8	10.0	10.7	10.7	11.1	11.3	11.2	11.3
Chile Peppers, All	0.8	0.8	0.9	0.9	0.9	0.9	1.0	0.9	0.9	0.9
Tomatoes, All	91.3	86.8	87.4	86.3	88.0	76.9	81.5	78.0	85.9	88.3
Fresh	20.6	21.0	20.8	20.3	20.6	20.6	20.3	20.1	20.3	20.3
Canning	70.8	65.8	66.6	66.0	67.4	56.3	61.2	57.9	65.6	68.0
Other, Fresh [5]	18.3	18.8	19.3	18.8	20.5	18.3	23.9	24.5	23.4	23.4
Other, Canning [6]	2.5	2.6	2.7	2.7	2.6	2.9	3.0	3.0	3.3	3.2
Other, Freezing [7]	4.5	4.3	4.5	4.3	4.6	4.7	4.6	4.7	6.1	6.4
Subtotal, All [8]	262.7	253.8	258.2	251.1	254.5	242.9	262.0	261.8	261.4	267.6
Fresh	144.7	142.2	144.8	141.2	142.6	141.9	155.9	157.1	149.2	153.3
Canning	97.1	89.6	91.1	90.3	92.1	80.6	86.0	83.3	89.6	92.6
Freezing	20.9	22.0	22.3	19.6	19.9	20.5	20.2	21.4	22.6	21.6
Potatoes, All	113.8	110.5	114.9	113.6	113.1	115.4	110.2	117.8	116.0	118.8
Fresh	36.8	34.1	34.6	34.6	33.6	34.2	33.7	34.9	33.0	34.1
Processing	77.0	76.4	80.3	79.0	79.5	81.2	76.5	82.9	83.0	84.7
Sweet Potatoes	6.3	7.1	6.9	6.3	7.5	7.6	7.2	8.0	5.6	7.9
Mushrooms	3.7	3.8	4.0	3.8	3.8	3.9	4.0	4.0	3.9	3.8
Dry Peas & Lentils [9]	1.6	1.1	0.9	1.0	0.8	1.2	4.0	3.4	4.8	4.2
Dry Edible Beans	6.7	5.1	5.9	5.5	5.6	7.2	6.7	7.7	8.9	6.9
Total, All Items	394.9	381.4	390.8	381.3	385.3	378.2	394.1	402.7	400.6	409.2

[1] All production for processing broccoli and cauliflower is for freezing.   [2] Industry allocation suggests that 27 percent of processing carrot production is for canning and 73 percent is for freezing.   [3] On-cob basis.   [4] In-shell basis.   [5] Includes artichokes, brussels sprouts, eggplant, endive/escarole, garlic, radishes, green limas, squash, and spinach. In 2000, okra, pumpkins, kale, collards, turnip greens and mustard greens added.   [6] Includes beets, green limas (1992-2003), spinach, and miscellaneous imports (1990-2001).   [7] Includes green limas, spinach, and miscellaneous freezing vegetables.   [8] Fresh, canning, and freezing data do not sum to the total because onions for dehydrating are included in the total.   [9] Production from new areas in upper midwest added in 1998. A portion of this is likely for feed use.   [10] Preliminary.   [11] Forecast.   NA = Not available.   *Source: Economic Research Service, U.S. Department of Agriculture (ERS-USDA)*

VEGETABLES

Average Price Received by Growers for Broccoli in the United States   In Dollars per Cwt

Year	Jan.	Feb.	Mar.	Apr.	May	June	July	Aug.	Sept.	Oct.	Nov.	Dec.	Season Average
2014	NA	NA	NA	40.10	48.00	49.60	31.80	47.10	53.40	34.60	45.00	33.10	40.70
2015	67.30	29.90	47.80	50.60	54.50	34.70	38.20	49.90	57.10	58.10	65.10	84.70	49.10
2016	50.80	26.80	30.90	39.30	48.10	49.30	41.60	28.00	36.60	37.70	35.90	34.80	37.70
2017	55.70	54.10	70.90	95.60	82.60	50.50	51.00	62.10	82.10	66.60	54.80	40.30	45.40
2018	45.00	28.50	46.80	39.70	56.90	46.80	37.60	53.90	51.40	56.50	70.70	85.50	42.80
2019	56.20	50.60	62.40	50.00	77.90	51.10	40.20	43.60	71.60	77.40	57.50	38.10	56.38
2020	99.00	41.00	79.60	53.80	46.00	118.00	54.20	48.10	102.00	64.50	106.00	71.60	73.65
2021	56.10	36.90	52.10	41.70	37.90	39.90	49.40	50.10	99.70	128.00	116.00	90.70	66.54
2022	91.00	61.00	58.00	59.00	50.60	58.20	70.30	51.40	98.80	137.00	181.00	205.00	93.44
2023[1]	87.60	69.20	86.60	168.00	74.00	96.70	81.60	92.40	102.00	85.00	91.00	71.60	92.14

[1]Preliminary.   NA = Not available.   *Source: National Agricultural Statistics Service, U.S. Department of Agriculture (NASS-USDA)*

Average Price Received by Growers for Carrots in the United States   In Dollars per Cwt

Year	Jan.	Feb.	Mar.	Apr.	May	June	July	Aug.	Sept.	Oct.	Nov.	Dec.	Season Average
2014	NA	NA	NA	28.20	27.20	25.50	25.10	23.00	21.50	26.90	28.00	33.40	27.10
2015	33.80	33.00	32.20	31.80	31.40	30.60	29.90	30.20	30.40	31.30	31.00	32.90	30.50
2016	34.40	35.80	34.90	38.60	39.30	31.80	29.90	29.30	28.90	28.90	28.90	27.90	24.80
2017	28.60	28.40	28.00	27.80	27.80	25.70	25.90	28.90	30.80	24.20	31.30	31.30	22.50
2018	31.40	31.00	27.90	27.30	27.70	26.70	27.10	25.80	26.30	26.60	26.50	26.40	22.20
2019	26.50	26.30	29.00	28.10	28.10	28.20	28.60	28.50	28.80	29.30	29.70	29.90	28.42
2020	50.90	49.70	57.50	47.50	47.00	48.30	49.30	48.30	46.10	45.10	42.30	42.60	47.88
2021	43.10	42.90	42.00	44.60	46.10	46.00	45.30	42.10	45.10	40.50	40.50	40.50	43.23
2022	44.50	50.70	50.20	50.20	50.20	45.50	42.60	38.70	40.20	48.30	49.70	50.00	46.73
2023[1]	52.90	52.20	51.60	46.50	46.50	46.50	47.00	59.40	50.80	56.00	57.10	57.10	51.97

[1]Preliminary.   NA = Not available.   *Source: National Agricultural Statistics Service, U.S. Department of Agriculture (NASS-USDA)*

Average Price Received by Growers for Cauliflower in the United States   In Dollars per Cwt

Year	Jan.	Feb.	Mar.	Apr.	May	June	July	Aug.	Sept.	Oct.	Nov.	Dec.	Season Average
2014	NA	NA	NA	65.80	79.10	66.30	43.10	31.80	64.70	43.20	67.60	84.80	50.10
2015	58.40	40.10	85.10	87.80	108.00	49.60	31.10	42.80	55.50	68.60	121.00	184.00	61.50
2016	59.10	45.30	39.80	53.70	82.00	62.20	41.00	39.10	42.70	42.80	42.40	81.10	55.70
2017	56.70	65.00	134.00	136.00	70.60	55.60	44.90	35.60	49.90	56.00	73.20	90.10	45.90
2018	47.80	42.90	87.60	60.80	78.60	35.50	38.40	39.80	45.30	46.40	95.50	74.80	45.80
2019	79.00	105.00	99.70	67.00	112.00	47.50	65.40	57.70	65.20	111.00	92.20	41.90	78.63
2020	97.00	70.40	102.00	72.00	43.30	79.90	40.90	32.00	40.30	45.80	95.90	101.00	68.38
2021	43.20	46.30	69.60	52.60	48.80	35.00	42.30	38.10	51.30	78.80	52.70	50.80	50.79
2022	99.10	60.50	94.20	59.80	50.40	42.70	42.60	39.90	83.60	101.00	263.00	200.00	94.73
2023[1]	69.40	143.00	113.00	230.00	90.00	47.90	49.50	50.70	60.20	78.00	61.20	72.00	88.74

[1]Preliminary.   NA = Not available.   *Source: National Agricultural Statistics Service, U.S. Department of Agriculture (NASS-USDA)*

Average Price Received by Growers for Celery in the United States   In Dollars per Cwt

Year	Jan.	Feb.	Mar.	Apr.	May	June	July	Aug.	Sept.	Oct.	Nov.	Dec.	Season Average
2014	NA	NA	NA	15.50	15.80	14.50	20.60	18.70	17.90	16.90	26.60	28.70	17.10
2015	19.40	14.60	14.00	18.60	26.80	17.60	17.10	23.50	22.70	28.00	40.60	59.80	24.80
2016	67.20	29.90	18.80	20.00	26.20	18.80	17.70	16.40	15.80	18.60	26.60	17.30	18.10
2017	17.50	15.60	24.50	39.30	79.90	42.40	27.70	17.70	17.30	19.20	29.60	23.60	20.10
2018	20.80	19.20	25.20	30.70	27.10	24.70	21.10	16.80	18.60	20.20	30.50	46.60	25.00
2019	52.10	70.90	96.00	113.00	109.00	88.80	26.60	23.30	26.30	29.90	35.60	27.40	58.24
2020	45.90	33.90	55.70	49.60	45.10	46.80	58.70	40.50	35.00	36.90	49.80	55.10	46.08
2021	112.00	47.80	31.10	28.70	31.70	35.70	36.60	33.10	35.20	43.70	54.50	44.30	44.53
2022	51.70	49.90	64.90	46.90	97.50	61.40	52.60	40.60	40.60	50.70	97.40	191.00	70.43
2023[1]	162.00	67.00	65.20	47.80	142.00	158.00	141.00	56.50	62.30	55.70	65.80	73.10	91.37

[1]Preliminary.   NA = Not available.   *Source: National Agricultural Statistics Service, U.S. Department of Agriculture (NASS-USDA)*

Average Price Received by Growers for Sweet Corn in the United States   In Dollars per Cwt

Year	Jan.	Feb.	Mar.	Apr.	May	June	July	Aug.	Sept.	Oct.	Nov.	Dec.	Season Average
2014	NA	NA	NA	26.00	25.40	32.00	37.70	29.00	23.10	42.20	40.70	41.40	23.90
2015	39.80	40.00	31.70	29.60	26.80	27.70	33.70	29.50	32.30	47.90	24.40	26.00	21.80
2016	43.80	58.70	67.50	34.30	26.20	25.40	29.50	23.60	28.20	33.60	37.40	37.50	20.70
2017	30.90	35.70	26.20	30.80	29.80	34.30	30.70	26.80	21.30	32.50	54.70	34.10	29.10
2018	35.40	24.70	26.90	32.60	28.30	27.10	26.20	24.40	30.50	30.50	45.80	31.70	30.34
2019	35.70	47.90	26.60	34.80	30.50	31.20	35.90	51.80	NA	NA	34.30	30.50	35.92
2020	52.70	38.20	28.60	28.20	33.20	75.90	54.30	33.30	49.60	61.20	35.60	72.90	46.98
2021	97.40	77.40	47.00	34.40	28.40	26.30	25.80	21.90	24.30	52.10	66.50	48.20	45.81
2022	43.50	48.60	45.60	40.50	37.70	31.10	64.70	48.60	44.20	42.60	55.00	56.30	46.53
2023[1]	61.50	71.20	38.50	33.60	37.90	43.30	48.60	40.50	40.60	42.90	48.40	60.50	47.29

[1]Preliminary.   NA = Not available.   *Source: National Agricultural Statistics Service, U.S. Department of Agriculture (NASS-USDA)*

Average Price Received by Growers for Head Lettuce in the United States   In Dollars per Cwt

Year	Jan.	Feb.	Mar.	Apr.	May	June	July	Aug.	Sept.	Oct.	Nov.	Dec.	Season Average
2014	NA	NA	NA	18.20	26.10	35.30	29.00	29.60	32.90	33.40	49.10	15.90	24.40
2015	38.20	15.20	19.10	23.10	25.10	30.30	18.80	35.70	48.90	34.40	60.10	51.90	29.10
2016	42.00	20.90	15.40	20.80	32.50	25.90	26.00	20.70	20.80	20.60	26.60	30.20	26.70
2017	29.10	51.40	49.60	82.50	26.10	22.80	25.60	24.70	31.70	42.20	23.00	30.50	35.90
2018	26.00	27.00	46.70	25.50	28.90	25.90	20.90	27.80	25.90	28.60	76.70	74.80	30.10
2019	33.80	37.60	52.40	28.10	19.70	41.00	41.50	22.70	22.90	39.20	65.30	49.00	37.77
2020	80.50	20.60	27.40	22.30	20.80	24.50	25.00	18.60	38.60	48.60	58.30	21.20	33.87
2021	21.80	15.80	21.40	16.10	14.70	17.60	19.90	19.30	31.90	74.90	63.00	22.50	28.24
2022	21.10	22.10	68.70	28.70	22.10	23.30	24.80	37.90	50.30	126.00	181.00	142.00	62.33
2023[1]	34.00	30.90	26.30	76.10	39.20	20.80	33.50	35.50	24.20	23.20	33.30	21.10	33.18

[1]Preliminary.   NA = Not available.   *Source: National Agricultural Statistics Service, U.S. Department of Agriculture (NASS-USDA)*

Average Price Received by Growers for Tomatoes in the United States   In Dollars per Cwt

Year	Jan.	Feb.	Mar.	Apr.	May	June	July	Aug.	Sept.	Oct.	Nov.	Dec.	Season Average
2014	NA	NA	NA	45.20	39.10	57.60	27.00	33.20	34.70	54.60	71.80	66.70	41.50
2015	34.80	49.40	44.20	45.20	24.00	33.50	41.30	36.30	35.80	41.80	39.30	42.50	46.30
2016	108.00	88.30	70.90	38.60	30.40	32.00	30.40	28.10	34.50	37.50	42.80	29.40	42.50
2017	28.40	28.50	30.20	32.90	62.80	43.90	28.20	30.10	37.20	42.40	62.40	80.20	37.30
2018	47.90	34.40	40.00	25.70	35.40	28.30	15.30	29.90	29.00	39.60	55.50	57.20	36.52
2019	53.30	45.40	52.20	43.40	36.20	36.10	32.10	34.20	33.00	40.90	54.40	112.00	47.77
2020	130.00	84.70	57.60	65.00	87.00	57.10	47.70	44.60	48.00	86.50	82.60	73.50	72.03
2021	95.40	46.20	47.20	37.10	58.30	41.80	35.30	42.60	55.40	94.60	70.70	48.60	56.10
2022	52.20	51.40	45.70	53.80	68.90	45.80	40.40	55.40	60.00	107.00	131.00	92.30	66.99
2023[1]	66.80	53.40	47.50	41.60	61.90	67.20	46.40	42.90	56.40	50.90	72.00	108.00	59.58

[1]Preliminary.   NA = Not available.   *Source: National Agricultural Statistics Service, U.S. Department of Agriculture (NASS-USDA)*

Average Price Received by Growers for Asparagus in the United States   In Dollars per Cwt

Year	Jan.	Feb.	Mar.	Apr.	May	June	July	Aug.	Sept.	Oct.	Nov.	Dec.	Season Average
2014	NA	NA	NA	116.00	131.00	115.00	NA	NA	NA	NA	NA	NA	106.00
2015	NA	NA	113.00	143.00	133.00	71.30	NA	NA	NA	NA	NA	NA	116.00
2016	NA	115.00	103.00	125.00	122.00	134.00	NA	NA	NA	NA	NA	NA	110.00
2017	NA	NA	96.60	126.00	119.00	90.50	NA	NA	NA	NA	NA	NA	120.00
2018	NA	NA	165.00	105.00	107.00	87.60	NA	NA	NA	NA	NA	NA	113.00
2019	NA	NA	NA	119.00	121.00	96.40	NA	NA	NA	NA	NA	NA	112.13
2020	NA	NA	NA	284.00	262.00	211.00	NA	NA	NA	NA	NA	NA	252.33
2021	NA	NA	NA	226.00	206.00	201.00	NA	NA	NA	NA	NA	NA	211.00
2022	NA	NA	NA	NA	225.00	219.00	NA	NA	NA	NA	NA	NA	222.00
2023[1]	NA	NA	NA	NA	232.00	220.00	NA	NA	NA	NA	NA	NA	226.00

[1]Preliminary.   NA = Not available.   *Source: National Agricultural Statistics Service, U.S. Department of Agriculture (NASS-USDA)*

VEGETABLES

Average Price Received by Growers for Cantaloupes in the United States   In Dollars per Cwt

Year	Jan.	Feb.	Mar.	Apr.	May	June	July	Aug.	Sept.	Oct.	Nov.	Dec.	Season Average
2014	NA	NA	NA	NA	20.50	24.70	19.20	21.70	21.40	36.10	31.90	21.30	22.10
2015	NA	NA	NA	NA	17.30	17.70	26.20	25.70	27.70	22.30	NQ	NQ	19.50
2016	NA	NA	NA	NA	23.80	17.50	20.60	16.30	18.50	22.70	21.50	NQ	17.20
2017	NA	NA	NA	NA	22.80	26.80	34.90	23.30	24.10	29.50	29.60	NQ	19.20
2018	NA	NA	NA	NA	23.20	20.40	16.60	16.90	20.00	27.60	35.00	39.00	22.70
2019	NA	NA	NA	NA	12.80	21.40	21.80	21.80	25.90	26.00	24.30	NQ	22.00
2020	NA	NA	NA	NA	31.90	26.90	29.70	20.00	27.10	26.30	22.60	NQ	26.36
2021	NA	NA	NA	32.60	26.90	29.00	22.30	24.10	22.90	32.20	51.40	NQ	30.18
2022	NA	NA	NA	37.30	34.20	25.70	35.70	24.60	30.50	37.60	50.00	NQ	34.45
2023[1]	NA	NA	NA	NA	28.00	31.80	23.00	24.50	30.50	37.80	27.80	NQ	29.06

[1]Preliminary.   NA = Not available.   *Source: National Agricultural Statistics Service, U.S. Department of Agriculture (NASS-USDA)*

Average Price Received by Growers for Cucumbers in the United States   In Dollars per Cwt

Year	Jan.	Feb.	Mar.	Apr.	May	June	July	Aug.	Sept.	Oct.	Nov.	Dec.	Season Average
2014	NA	NA	NA	26.20	40.00	25.50	21.30	29.90	24.10	37.00	24.80	34.20	24.40
2015	30.60	27.60	40.80	24.00	23.40	36.30	25.30	28.90	33.00	W	29.30	38.40	26.10
2016	35.00	NA	48.70	26.20	36.10	24.40	21.00	19.90	20.60	W	25.90	18.70	25.90
2017	39.20	NA	37.80	34.30	33.40	36.70	20.30	16.00	17.50	41.90	34.50	29.90	29.50
2018	41.10	NA	33.40	32.70	43.50	35.40	20.50	17.80	19.10	42.60	37.50	36.70	32.75
2019	37.40	NA	33.30	29.20	26.30	30.40	23.60	18.80	24.00	39.60	31.10	41.50	30.47
2020	NA	NA	NA	23.40	27.20	29.60	25.30	33.50	37.70	25.00	31.80	26.70	28.91
2021	NA	NA	27.70	39.50	28.60	20.30	27.40	23.20	24.50	30.80	27.90	21.80	27.17
2022	NA	NA	43.30	45.40	28.30	22.00	29.30	27.00	24.30	49.80	43.00	28.00	34.04
2023[1]	NA	36.40	22.40	32.20	30.40	23.30	33.90	28.80	32.70	28.90	31.40	35.90	30.57

[1]Preliminary.   NA = Not available.   *Source: National Agricultural Statistics Service, U.S. Department of Agriculture (NASS-USDA)*

Average Price Received by Growers for Celery in the United States   In Dollars per Cwt

Year	Jan.	Feb.	Mar.	Apr.	May	June	July	Aug.	Sept.	Oct.	Nov.	Dec.	Season Average
2014	NA	NA	NA	52.30	74.20	48.60	83.50	77.20	85.70	63.10	62.00	68.10	60.20
2015	40.80	53.90	60.50	54.80	85.30	W	W	W	W	W	72.80	118.00	59.40
2016	95.90	125.00	95.20	42.80	46.40	W	107.00	75.00	85.30	89.90	78.40	50.60	60.20
2017	36.50	54.90	59.90	67.10	74.10	W	W	93.80	64.70	W	72.30	69.50	55.60
2018	101.00	61.50	45.90	66.50	64.50	W	W	W	W	W	99.00	62.80	71.60
2019	57.90	55.90	30.40	60.00	58.50	W	60.60	W	W	W	99.10	89.30	63.96
2020	62.80	48.40	43.20	45.30	49.50	84.10	W	58.70	46.70	78.40	77.70	86.80	61.96
2021	75.70	54.00	36.50	56.10	43.80	42.10	51.20	47.80	65.10	75.10	80.40	43.40	55.93
2022	70.00	74.80	50.10	48.80	65.40	63.60	51.10	55.30	57.90	112.00	125.00	79.10	71.09
2023[1]	106.00	80.60	42.40	64.40	78.30	53.60	45.00	54.10	62.50	121.00	105.00	116.00	77.41

[1]Preliminary.   NA = Not available.   W = Withheld.   *Source: National Agricultural Statistics Service, U.S. Department of Agriculture (NASS-USDA)*

Cold Storage Stocks of Frozen Asparagus in the United States, on First of Month   In Thousands of Pounds

Year	Jan.	Feb.	Mar.	Apr.	May	June	July	Aug.	Sept.	Oct.	Nov.	Dec.
2014	9,758	9,701	9,497	9,038	7,946	10,252	15,185	15,656	16,324	16,916	14,873	14,572
2015	13,603	12,620	11,115	10,608	10,084	13,037	14,457	14,209	14,270	13,283	12,579	12,883
2016	11,926	12,144	11,225	10,877	10,290	12,246	14,490	13,429	12,697	12,328	12,089	12,133
2017	11,395	10,780	10,273	9,243	9,012	9,781	11,137	11,395	12,102	11,928	10,893	9,914
2018	10,188	9,690	8,119	6,989	6,036	7,767	10,855	10,971	10,120	9,358	8,933	8,364
2019	8,106	7,694	7,136	6,419	5,714	5,807	7,220	7,297	6,454	6,372	6,344	6,257
2020	6,002	5,936	4,893	4,610	4,298	5,090	8,393	7,666	7,179	6,435	5,933	5,591
2021	5,293	4,531	4,151	4,192	3,928	5,420	9,778	8,470	7,553	7,093	6,412	6,316
2022	5,451	4,831	4,807	4,505	4,196	7,629	11,689	10,803	10,305	9,254	8,821	8,348
2023[1]	7,668	6,917	6,145	5,591	5,341	5,814	6,890	6,226	6,243	6,048	5,311	4,828

[1] Preliminary.   *Source: Economic Research Service, U.S. Department of Agriculture (ERS-USDA)*

Frozen Vegetables: January 1 and July 1 Cold Storage Holdings in the United States   In Thousands of Pounds

Crop	2020 Jan. 1	July 1	2021 Jan. 1	July 1	2022 Jan. 1	July 1	2023 Jan. 1	July 1	2024[1] Jan. 1
Asparagus	6,002	8,393	5,293	9,778	5,451	11,689	7,668	6,890	4,902
Lima Beans	33,509	14,576	21,497	7,107	28,305	13,751	22,228	13,071	19,989
Green Beans, Reg. Cut	155,713	68,409	204,173	90,561	182,212	84,671	197,366	95,420	215,989
Green Beans, Fr. Style	14,887	9,697	13,061	7,610	14,285	9,100	16,921	11,324	14,866
Broccoli, Spears	41,991	47,273	34,491	42,749	36,795	50,925	30,310	40,542	45,191
Broccoli, Chopped & Cut	34,048	31,362	36,427	35,964	25,773	22,519	21,670	23,008	16,914
Brussels sprouts	13,254	9,613	8,016	12,709	11,881	12,466	13,967	10,256	10,321
Carrots, Diced	173,673	100,000	152,684	88,092	174,895	106,780	168,251	100,256	169,088
Carrots, Other	98,720	59,108	112,189	80,049	85,334	69,031	80,509	67,436	80,863
Cauliflower	24,382	27,252	30,408	31,042	24,638	22,305	24,090	26,280	23,956
Corn, Cut	567,306	270,432	597,036	264,952	612,730	282,762	593,790	313,925	568,772
Corn, Cob	275,612	106,869	272,573	78,876	300,426	161,719	316,250	142,090	318,512
Mixed vegetables	41,323	45,371	50,758	61,610	47,821	53,742	44,316	55,756	46,811
Okra	48,906	33,460	33,817	19,240	34,970	19,222	30,463	21,112	31,100
Onion Rings	14,918	14,144	14,203	11,103	12,859	17,570	23,522	17,754	18,740
Onions, Other	51,024	73,559	60,448	60,812	38,086	35,512	41,718	45,951	40,135
Blackeye Peas	1,227	2,168	1,779	2,645	2,497	1,397	1,891	2,294	992
Green Peas	212,684	232,490	243,072	231,790	207,468	167,215	232,097	233,026	236,174
Peas and Carrots Mixed	9,058	8,779	7,809	7,890	6,605	5,662	6,850	7,555	8,822
Spinach	33,492	58,434	53,278	64,854	49,212	57,986	39,805	49,248	32,067
Squash, Summer/Zucchini	56,884	37,204	56,841	40,641	57,436	40,318	53,927	41,244	51,913
Southern greens	10,908	11,380	15,577	15,559	17,082	13,788	15,787	14,143	15,453
Other Vegetables	435,111	373,489	460,079	323,050	401,496	302,061	392,617	288,130	355,531
Total	2,354,632	1,643,462	2,485,509	1,588,683	2,378,257	1,562,191	2,376,013	1,626,711	2,327,101
Potatoes, French Fries	948,850	868,583	917,398	912,824	864,148	990,097	999,180	991,866	874,356
Potatoes, Other Frozen	207,080	216,545	204,660	201,477	199,872	248,179	220,267	243,471	232,804
Potatoes, Total	1,155,930	1,085,128	1,122,058	1,114,301	1,064,020	1,238,276	1,219,447	1,235,337	1,107,160
Grand Total	3,510,562	2,728,590	3,607,567	2,702,984	3,442,277	2,800,467	3,595,460	2,862,048	3,434,261

Cold Storage Stocks of Frozen Limas in the United States, on First of Month   In Thousands of Pounds

Year	Jan.	Feb.	Mar.	Apr.	May	June	July	Aug.	Sept.	Oct.	Nov.	Dec.
2014	60,262	58,462	54,696	51,382	43,074	39,818	34,333	31,632	35,991	52,979	73,497	69,543
2015	64,530	58,804	53,249	51,849	47,874	42,782	41,133	37,376	44,819	62,195	66,999	59,313
2016	57,841	53,533	50,432	47,576	46,603	42,577	40,193	37,743	45,577	61,184	66,795	59,516
2017	55,895	51,451	48,414	44,371	40,852	39,116	36,817	33,753	33,807	48,322	63,786	56,226
2018	54,024	49,217	45,506	42,318	37,826	36,355	33,421	29,161	33,072	44,301	47,691	42,601
2019	38,647	34,443	29,861	26,059	18,879	17,010	14,441	11,091	15,153	31,086	39,771	35,701
2020	33,509	30,762	27,080	24,133	21,005	18,479	14,576	11,083	15,256	24,571	27,107	25,544
2021	21,497	19,938	16,728	12,506	9,807	8,062	7,107	5,626	8,734	28,637	33,454	32,965
2022	28,305	24,657	22,524	18,570	17,853	16,192	13,751	11,704	13,258	20,637	28,050	26,335
2023[1]	22,228	20,425	18,737	17,031	15,115	13,897	13,071	10,988	12,641	22,894	24,880	23,478

[1] Preliminary.   Source: Economic Research Service, U.S. Department of Agriculture (ERS-USDA)

Cold Storage Stocks of Frozen Green Beans[2] in the United States, on First of Month   In Thousands of Pounds

Year	Jan.	Feb.	Mar.	Apr.	May	June	July	Aug.	Sept.	Oct.	Nov.	Dec.
2014	181,073	162,305	149,444	139,195	125,882	109,855	96,376	147,470	225,135	253,066	235,830	205,861
2015	182,136	161,510	153,916	135,211	123,221	119,151	113,449	155,410	226,850	255,661	243,986	225,001
2016	199,994	180,082	158,534	142,228	136,727	131,014	122,127	169,238	242,529	265,200	263,320	233,980
2017	209,496	190,073	174,009	159,278	144,992	132,483	115,498	138,593	196,016	238,830	230,850	216,052
2018	191,291	172,503	155,853	128,304	109,337	93,324	81,164	115,005	173,836	202,123	190,921	173,687
2019	152,495	143,960	130,780	117,427	110,140	87,598	82,556	125,225	163,225	203,481	185,412	173,403
2020	155,713	142,537	126,346	107,604	91,905	76,783	68,409	125,541	197,217	252,835	240,075	219,751
2021	204,173	176,731	156,314	139,827	120,531	100,787	90,561	128,013	178,850	230,704	214,727	200,020
2022	182,212	166,098	145,802	131,115	111,740	97,077	84,671	112,993	177,435	232,588	243,962	222,146
2023[1]	197,366	172,161	165,629	135,955	121,210	105,583	95,420	129,113	201,311	247,084	252,935	242,242

[1] Preliminary.   [2] Regular cut.   Source: Economic Research Service, U.S. Department of Agriculture (ERS-USDA)

VEGETABLES

Cold Storage Stocks of Frozen Green Beans[2] in the United States, on First of Month — In Thousands of Pounds

Year	Jan.	Feb.	Mar.	Apr.	May	June	July	Aug.	Sept.	Oct.	Nov.	Dec.
2014	14,248	13,479	11,607	11,680	10,675	8,790	8,194	15,306	18,840	20,852	18,439	16,975
2015	14,754	13,214	10,323	10,177	8,250	7,246	8,025	12,653	12,695	19,787	19,142	16,305
2016	15,279	14,378	14,121	13,331	12,092	10,477	9,912	13,009	18,951	20,521	18,876	16,312
2017	14,482	14,324	13,321	12,838	11,522	9,874	8,923	12,355	16,478	18,836	18,222	16,302
2018	15,187	14,738	13,923	13,402	12,230	10,651	11,184	12,886	14,413	15,847	15,328	13,793
2019	13,747	12,622	12,025	11,534	11,471	10,112	9,879	16,571	21,160	20,285	19,950	17,134
2020	14,887	14,569	13,264	12,967	11,788	10,857	9,697	11,301	14,283	16,864	15,253	14,809
2021	13,061	13,044	11,790	10,384	9,310	8,696	7,610	11,259	14,740	19,400	22,686	20,254
2022	14,285	12,214	11,619	11,049	9,620	8,928	9,100	11,912	17,281	20,345	19,300	17,710
2023[1]	16,921	15,471	14,368	14,197	13,750	12,999	11,324	13,394	17,611	20,963	19,214	16,920

[1] Preliminary.   [2] French style.   *Source: Economic Research Service, U.S. Department of Agriculture (ERS-USDA)*

Cold Storage Stocks of Frozen Broccoli[2] in the United States, on First of Month — In Thousands of Pounds

Year	Jan.	Feb.	Mar.	Apr.	May	June	July	Aug.	Sept.	Oct.	Nov.	Dec.
2014	21,705	19,728	20,956	23,558	30,509	34,882	34,093	34,054	32,216	30,285	30,697	29,339
2015	27,108	25,796	27,826	29,124	29,731	29,475	27,821	26,272	27,564	28,387	26,873	27,317
2016	25,023	24,480	26,498	26,783	33,170	29,783	27,727	28,986	27,355	25,951	25,119	24,068
2017	21,870	24,405	26,382	32,156	31,070	30,890	30,877	28,038	27,541	24,817	26,515	22,921
2018	23,877	25,814	29,513	31,806	34,494	38,616	45,339	44,166	44,250	37,705	35,174	30,802
2019	26,691	26,337	28,628	34,710	40,829	39,849	43,927	45,936	48,278	47,694	46,109	43,369
2020	41,991	41,480	45,744	49,290	50,584	51,904	47,273	46,002	40,460	39,828	39,271	33,879
2021	34,491	30,236	31,453	31,548	39,376	43,656	42,749	45,550	43,612	41,671	41,144	38,682
2022	36,795	34,637	40,873	46,173	48,863	45,821	50,925	45,454	44,894	42,332	39,107	31,660
2023[1]	30,310	31,884	35,831	39,494	42,938	42,358	40,542	46,039	50,604	50,074	48,163	43,980

[1] Preliminary.   [2] Spears.   *Source: Economic Research Service, U.S. Department of Agriculture (ERS-USDA)*

Cold Storage Stocks of Frozen Broccoli[2] in the United States, on First of Month — In Thousands of Pounds

Year	Jan.	Feb.	Mar.	Apr.	May	June	July	Aug.	Sept.	Oct.	Nov.	Dec.
2014	34,836	34,253	33,570	31,421	30,447	32,993	33,394	38,547	41,970	41,131	43,775	37,347
2015	36,143	34,751	38,107	37,416	39,532	39,932	42,211	41,556	50,159	50,323	44,935	41,373
2016	39,398	38,275	35,525	34,633	35,389	34,273	37,574	40,191	44,837	41,996	41,969	41,462
2017	42,915	46,006	43,333	40,864	39,286	36,102	31,521	34,386	39,995	37,178	34,739	33,388
2018	32,738	30,206	31,302	33,530	36,759	35,108	34,532	38,981	41,735	43,080	41,796	39,422
2019	37,761	36,913	39,476	37,688	35,876	32,798	32,061	36,520	43,555	45,550	39,750	37,303
2020	34,048	34,106	33,750	32,692	31,544	32,163	31,362	29,903	29,956	32,250	37,907	35,867
2021	36,427	33,513	33,034	31,411	36,950	34,205	35,964	32,986	32,830	28,362	27,209	24,422
2022	25,773	22,924	22,154	22,571	22,377	22,217	22,519	21,727	20,724	23,630	23,030	22,352
2023[1]	21,670	19,585	21,677	20,931	22,150	23,131	23,008	23,103	21,944	21,732	19,347	18,165

[1] Preliminary.   [2] Chopped & cut.   *Source: Economic Research Service, U.S. Department of Agriculture (ERS-USDA)*

Cold Storage Stocks of Frozen Brussel Sprouts in the United States, on First of Month — In Thousands of Pounds

Year	Jan.	Feb.	Mar.	Apr.	May	June	July	Aug.	Sept.	Oct.	Nov.	Dec.
2014	13,612	15,327	15,343	14,071	14,283	13,452	12,480	10,911	10,142	9,798	12,149	13,585
2015	15,960	15,090	14,120	13,448	13,170	13,658	14,691	13,401	12,241	12,352	14,338	16,636
2016	19,843	18,028	16,367	14,363	13,801	13,785	13,061	13,569	12,265	11,564	15,110	18,241
2017	22,021	23,187	22,721	20,508	19,588	18,428	16,253	14,379	14,101	13,415	16,126	17,219
2018	21,878	21,121	20,636	20,900	20,736	19,317	17,361	17,102	15,536	13,257	13,410	13,940
2019	15,680	15,728	13,164	12,916	13,341	12,501	12,774	12,930	12,823	12,237	12,982	12,505
2020	13,254	13,256	11,691	9,494	9,172	10,074	9,613	10,118	10,037	9,947	9,355	8,640
2021	8,016	9,276	11,028	12,199	12,726	12,672	12,709	12,879	12,781	12,368	11,711	12,336
2022	11,881	12,709	11,743	12,629	11,620	11,876	12,466	12,902	14,323	15,334	14,632	13,184
2023[1]	13,967	13,462	11,715	11,256	11,272	11,038	10,256	10,768	11,271	10,692	9,822	9,988

[1] Preliminary.   *Source: Economic Research Service, U.S. Department of Agriculture (ERS-USDA)*

Cold Storage Stocks of Frozen Carrots[2] in the United States, on First of Month   In Thousands of Pounds

Year	Jan.	Feb.	Mar.	Apr.	May	June	July	Aug.	Sept.	Oct.	Nov.	Dec.
2014	157,220	153,372	143,648	130,512	114,796	109,991	97,279	81,749	74,944	71,990	130,075	173,870
2015	168,289	155,485	144,853	134,587	121,669	115,221	99,334	87,345	84,143	83,391	148,160	172,525
2016	161,755	159,472	148,175	142,072	129,994	116,769	99,573	95,109	83,701	85,034	125,903	173,404
2017	161,641	145,245	127,999	119,945	114,784	107,957	97,296	86,068	79,758	75,024	109,489	152,316
2018	142,941	128,815	121,470	114,872	108,053	98,881	84,708	65,564	53,967	48,927	86,070	129,184
2019	125,994	120,219	116,148	109,514	105,619	110,909	100,442	84,444	72,505	62,579	113,835	171,712
2020	173,673	169,269	156,725	139,078	129,593	118,912	100,000	84,686	69,085	57,589	103,313	142,673
2021	152,684	137,414	132,324	115,552	107,679	97,098	88,092	72,849	60,728	55,855	101,665	160,063
2022	174,895	166,403	157,744	148,310	137,032	126,488	106,780	89,137	78,133	67,319	115,722	158,821
2023[1]	168,251	147,922	146,282	136,264	129,907	117,246	100,256	85,522	77,420	72,336	129,301	167,360

[1] Preliminary.   [2] Diced.   *Source: Economic Research Service, U.S. Department of Agriculture (ERS-USDA)*

Cold Storage Stocks of Frozen Carrots[2] in the United States, on First of Month   In Thousands of Pounds

Year	Jan.	Feb.	Mar.	Apr.	May	June	July	Aug.	Sept.	Oct.	Nov.	Dec.
2014	160,585	146,956	134,187	121,009	118,973	114,263	102,942	97,360	103,813	130,307	171,014	195,425
2015	180,493	155,156	138,003	120,999	117,545	102,967	88,645	83,838	79,673	106,742	157,115	173,385
2016	166,317	163,079	154,349	144,494	141,373	132,722	119,896	109,006	113,894	117,326	163,522	197,013
2017	191,102	171,689	157,377	152,193	143,200	129,246	112,691	100,623	106,683	118,442	144,425	160,556
2018	164,466	149,233	136,166	125,914	119,288	104,184	94,449	87,118	84,641	96,342	105,654	113,794
2019	110,822	100,107	93,262	87,761	77,125	73,787	64,844	57,293	53,727	67,712	86,019	105,246
2020	98,720	93,213	81,789	72,680	69,704	67,242	59,108	55,115	54,034	76,293	97,060	115,016
2021	112,189	103,845	97,456	96,316	95,033	93,905	80,049	73,240	64,594	58,234	81,048	93,261
2022	85,334	81,678	75,903	75,476	77,886	76,253	69,031	65,757	58,003	52,283	65,854	81,790
2023[1]	80,509	77,968	72,154	73,512	70,335	70,855	67,436	62,607	56,024	61,408	77,727	89,579

[1] Preliminary.   [2] Other.   *Source: Economic Research Service, U.S. Department of Agriculture (ERS-USDA)*

Cold Storage Stocks of Frozen Cauliflower in the United States, on First of Month   In Thousands of Pounds

Year	Jan.	Feb.	Mar.	Apr.	May	June	July	Aug.	Sept.	Oct.	Nov.	Dec.
2014	23,139	21,680	21,139	18,386	17,768	18,035	16,497	15,461	14,427	15,581	22,014	21,897
2015	20,567	20,172	18,289	17,903	17,761	17,424	18,203	16,963	15,146	14,226	24,622	24,833
2016	26,448	25,971	24,669	23,833	23,236	23,443	22,634	21,690	18,853	19,651	26,266	26,986
2017	27,325	28,913	28,826	29,002	27,679	27,497	28,013	28,703	26,193	25,043	33,584	32,655
2018	34,083	34,901	36,257	35,212	32,896	30,354	25,340	24,701	24,088	23,258	30,422	28,645
2019	29,760	28,000	26,134	24,059	23,981	18,478	18,926	19,682	18,565	19,684	21,973	23,324
2020	24,382	26,212	29,012	29,567	28,132	30,131	27,252	28,570	28,218	28,301	32,386	31,667
2021	30,408	30,165	28,788	27,276	29,590	29,136	31,042	29,242	25,502	25,035	25,854	23,925
2022	24,638	23,079	21,810	19,531	20,094	22,289	22,305	22,399	22,011	21,338	22,233	23,246
2023[1]	24,090	25,676	28,273	26,430	27,717	25,098	26,280	26,317	25,200	24,501	23,851	24,162

[1] Preliminary.   *Source: Economic Research Service, U.S. Department of Agriculture (ERS-USDA)*

Cold Storage Stocks of Frozen Sweet Corn[2] in the United States, on First of Month   In Thousands of Pounds

Year	Jan.	Feb.	Mar.	Apr.	May	June	July	Aug.	Sept.	Oct.	Nov.	Dec.
2014	550,708	492,643	460,752	397,092	345,504	296,765	250,726	273,738	462,352	596,616	631,669	576,419
2015	529,586	464,026	431,593	395,330	348,564	313,388	262,028	287,729	446,215	621,237	640,668	582,672
2016	520,804	488,940	479,571	412,766	381,312	339,900	289,897	301,633	464,716	587,865	600,062	552,697
2017	522,396	463,549	414,754	371,774	316,608	275,307	220,012	216,938	377,400	519,847	568,117	521,589
2018	479,654	446,194	403,945	356,223	312,151	276,599	240,908	257,797	443,885	558,378	592,617	530,696
2019	475,712	433,018	394,400	351,796	295,948	259,917	240,636	250,720	461,516	662,567	674,400	637,174
2020	567,306	510,508	451,650	418,608	372,483	316,418	270,432	261,628	428,745	648,159	694,618	644,835
2021	597,036	564,162	511,718	449,689	389,300	325,593	264,952	275,274	452,627	675,517	722,281	666,265
2022	612,730	568,673	515,530	435,572	414,658	355,656	282,762	260,025	408,005	654,726	688,598	651,363
2023[1]	593,790	560,040	512,207	473,003	443,320	366,094	313,925	334,194	499,929	659,935	708,292	649,171

[1] Preliminary.   [2] Cut.   *Source: Economic Research Service, U.S. Department of Agriculture (ERS-USDA)*

VEGETABLES

Cold Storage Stocks of Frozen Sweet Corn[2] in the United States, on First of Month   In Thousands of Pounds

Year	Jan.	Feb.	Mar.	Apr.	May	June	July	Aug.	Sept.	Oct.	Nov.	Dec.
2014	238,575	225,426	200,562	174,569	156,311	121,262	101,087	108,477	175,199	258,604	268,087	240,784
2015	223,053	206,000	175,910	156,425	132,387	110,912	88,817	112,873	165,657	239,922	244,687	229,113
2016	220,295	216,834	198,513	164,351	135,956	112,977	91,597	97,354	177,551	223,337	250,261	227,305
2017	207,064	197,123	177,461	150,107	128,032	101,904	73,922	74,754	181,921	278,137	297,466	286,139
2018	257,185	231,840	207,582	176,477	142,645	107,713	79,134	105,145	208,224	276,776	307,075	288,300
2019	269,689	242,621	226,032	202,924	169,151	149,776	137,539	137,583	246,139	332,852	345,723	307,982
2020	275,612	246,556	216,990	191,158	177,364	133,697	106,869	128,561	207,408	290,645	317,958	306,616
2021	272,573	234,201	207,331	169,892	132,944	112,487	78,876	91,040	194,189	307,591	357,651	327,096
2022	300,426	272,063	239,377	220,008	193,655	172,037	161,719	164,793	280,245	334,701	367,932	332,755
2023[1]	316,250	295,061	249,695	227,869	199,215	171,159	142,090	152,465	295,808	346,075	370,835	345,944

[1] Preliminary .   [2] Cob.   *Source: Economic Research Service, U.S. Department of Agriculture (ERS-USDA)*

Cold Storage Stocks of Mixed Vegetables in the United States, on First of Month   In Thousands of Pounds

Year	Jan.	Feb.	Mar.	Apr.	May	June	July	Aug.	Sept.	Oct.	Nov.	Dec.
2014	50,977	56,257	54,208	47,594	48,023	47,670	49,422	52,108	58,514	60,248	62,359	59,702
2015	53,082	55,851	56,039	57,851	59,040	58,132	58,099	56,960	60,109	62,186	58,359	55,274
2016	55,067	56,725	55,364	57,650	59,996	61,403	60,593	66,007	65,596	65,498	62,944	61,384
2017	62,424	68,538	68,978	72,412	73,221	69,127	69,734	67,369	72,540	74,115	71,407	68,516
2018	57,762	59,410	60,105	53,310	52,886	54,013	56,417	60,139	66,995	63,700	60,301	56,423
2019	53,845	52,405	54,958	53,253	55,753	48,189	47,214	52,260	50,131	47,185	50,241	41,737
2020	41,323	42,714	45,978	41,802	44,271	44,150	45,371	46,385	51,430	55,198	52,011	48,504
2021	50,758	51,609	55,592	52,793	56,307	56,589	61,610	59,752	64,928	66,635	57,398	51,599
2022	47,821	45,533	44,307	42,537	47,473	50,868	53,742	48,908	48,795	60,713	52,232	45,326
2023[1]	44,316	44,245	50,325	51,145	53,205	53,241	55,756	55,734	63,307	60,945	55,155	47,780

[1] Preliminary.   *Source: Economic Research Service, U.S. Department of Agriculture (ERS-USDA)*

Cold Storage Stocks of Frozen Okra in the United States, on First of Month   In Thousands of Pounds

Year	Jan.	Feb.	Mar.	Apr.	May	June	July	Aug.	Sept.	Oct.	Nov.	Dec.
2014	21,405	14,964	10,651	7,129	7,353	7,670	14,800	26,511	36,605	46,743	48,448	44,192
2015	39,375	34,631	29,153	23,998	19,361	16,410	16,337	31,938	48,184	66,862	70,851	63,695
2016	56,080	46,590	38,266	27,614	18,995	15,574	27,167	40,280	46,536	51,893	45,379	38,372
2017	33,964	27,901	22,677	15,482	12,582	13,608	24,246	35,802	38,821	41,607	35,675	30,451
2018	27,190	20,870	16,743	14,666	13,443	12,632	30,181	41,318	50,058	54,779	55,093	48,631
2019	44,156	37,915	31,855	21,396	16,652	17,388	28,658	43,014	56,509	58,883	57,568	52,782
2020	48,906	43,036	35,209	27,603	25,797	26,520	33,460	39,287	41,001	41,934	40,734	38,120
2021	33,817	28,637	25,641	20,088	15,071	13,626	19,240	29,431	35,977	39,183	39,815	39,424
2022	34,970	31,655	28,607	21,228	18,517	13,545	19,222	28,371	33,950	37,250	38,050	35,990
2023[1]	30,463	25,832	22,242	20,079	18,730	18,090	21,112	26,070	31,669	33,727	36,553	34,094

[1] Preliminary.   *Source: Economic Research Service, U.S. Department of Agriculture (ERS-USDA)*

Cold Storage Stocks of Frozen Blackeye Peas in the United States, on First of Month   In Thousands of Pounds

Year	Jan.	Feb.	Mar.	Apr.	May	June	July	Aug.	Sept.	Oct.	Nov.	Dec.
2014	1,386	1,925	1,620	2,072	1,684	2,145	1,655	1,830	1,484	1,784	1,870	1,929
2015	1,565	1,969	1,846	1,822	2,364	2,816	2,869	2,975	2,121	2,330	2,159	2,493
2016	2,434	2,245	2,249	2,222	1,740	1,674	1,377	1,511	1,332	1,650	1,243	1,629
2017	1,600	1,806	1,758	1,440	1,477	1,308	1,804	1,728	1,900	2,048	2,015	1,564
2018	1,484	1,606	1,655	1,512	1,357	1,407	1,293	2,089	2,009	2,000	2,037	1,790
2019	1,479	1,497	1,394	1,712	1,495	1,373	1,413	1,615	1,655	1,930	1,904	1,332
2020	1,227	1,187	1,135	1,338	1,499	1,749	2,168	1,589	1,759	1,723	1,261	1,623
2021	1,779	1,345	1,375	2,623	3,253	2,909	2,645	2,318	2,692	2,300	2,118	3,512
2022	2,497	2,076	1,830	1,518	1,465	1,411	1,397	1,498	1,855	1,401	1,275	1,400
2023[1]	1,891	2,653	3,012	2,268	2,638	2,494	2,294	2,100	1,921	1,825	1,482	1,256

[1] Preliminary.   *Source: Economic Research Service, U.S. Department of Agriculture (ERS-USDA)*

Cold Storage Stocks of Frozen Green Peas in the United States, on First of Month   In Thousands of Pounds

Year	Jan.	Feb.	Mar.	Apr.	May	June	July	Aug.	Sept.	Oct.	Nov.	Dec.
2014	228,586	192,134	168,608	136,081	111,179	95,529	284,293	427,634	395,401	354,716	314,577	285,406
2015	243,251	205,887	189,997	154,385	127,621	127,985	314,155	414,632	397,020	372,987	335,536	308,934
2016	274,778	251,096	225,590	195,128	166,005	173,146	360,749	455,262	437,827	401,126	361,786	343,397
2017	323,820	294,248	267,497	238,263	205,494	191,203	322,460	428,002	410,645	381,666	342,202	305,457
2018	277,206	247,040	223,679	198,966	190,125	177,152	284,008	341,193	319,549	303,905	268,892	244,288
2019	207,808	188,769	174,792	147,662	132,510	121,763	233,194	385,001	352,447	309,511	277,596	250,797
2020	212,684	185,946	154,812	135,690	112,569	90,073	232,490	341,429	342,432	309,867	279,854	259,458
2021	243,072	206,560	180,490	156,380	138,486	125,457	231,790	320,166	309,734	282,403	263,263	240,454
2022	207,468	181,801	165,529	130,013	115,849	99,425	167,215	334,539	303,787	289,483	260,744	251,800
2023[1]	232,097	216,779	194,147	182,378	147,719	131,735	233,026	343,126	339,633	318,124	284,688	258,989

[1] Preliminary.   *Source: Economic Research Service, U.S. Department of Agriculture (ERS-USDA)*

Cold Storage Stocks of Frozen Peas & Carrots in the United States, on First of Month   In Thousands of Pounds

Year	Jan.	Feb.	Mar.	Apr.	May	June	July	Aug.	Sept.	Oct.	Nov.	Dec.
2014	6,250	6,051	7,608	7,234	7,106	6,494	7,274	7,813	7,840	7,703	7,483	7,525
2015	7,671	7,299	7,326	7,315	6,964	7,459	7,580	7,637	8,292	8,225	8,135	7,751
2016	7,052	7,409	7,783	8,168	8,970	8,308	8,348	8,125	8,462	8,570	8,046	6,640
2017	6,884	7,052	7,082	7,843	8,829	8,820	8,989	8,965	8,685	8,985	9,184	8,819
2018	7,914	7,454	8,135	7,410	8,083	7,758	6,754	7,424	7,605	6,947	7,457	6,928
2019	7,262	7,826	7,391	8,001	7,954	8,436	9,098	9,953	9,545	8,515	8,423	8,567
2020	9,058	10,076	10,364	9,479	10,361	9,129	8,779	8,490	8,965	7,877	7,778	7,420
2021	7,809	9,101	8,613	9,350	9,409	8,253	7,890	8,659	8,190	7,173	6,324	6,356
2022	6,605	6,462	6,036	5,387	5,935	6,575	5,662	6,440	6,198	6,465	7,093	6,685
2023[1]	6,850	7,940	7,280	6,536	7,315	6,599	7,555	8,127	8,957	7,868	7,825	8,080

[1] Preliminary.   *Source: Economic Research Service, U.S. Department of Agriculture (ERS-USDA)*

Cold Storage Stocks of Other Frozen Vegetables in the United States, on First of Month   In Thousands of lbs

Year	Jan.	Feb.	Mar.	Apr.	May	June	July	Aug.	Sept.	Oct.	Nov.	Dec.
2014	425,010	371,053	366,772	359,294	311,776	285,450	281,639	310,021	348,093	402,271	415,446	392,454
2015	381,070	357,718	335,823	327,915	319,475	307,475	302,891	321,753	364,047	397,496	407,400	391,876
2016	391,886	368,774	346,407	326,102	322,249	328,465	331,768	340,474	405,041	441,482	476,689	463,852
2017	453,978	447,244	447,065	451,698	416,977	385,932	397,044	418,221	518,807	618,682	660,094	646,967
2018	626,616	563,016	504,878	461,985	406,018	376,945	377,555	422,205	502,853	569,778	623,597	603,165
2019	582,039	535,862	510,354	476,131	440,646	377,702	355,236	354,953	384,582	423,955	458,115	455,499
2020	435,111	406,680	402,718	386,470	381,515	366,163	373,489	363,933	686,604	449,473	499,198	477,272
2021	460,079	434,674	400,757	372,563	357,090	342,259	323,050	323,858	338,441	376,810	419,162	424,223
2022	401,496	358,563	337,398	320,872	315,329	310,075	302,061	306,956	329,977	364,602	390,779	395,983
2023[1]	392,617	359,246	333,758	318,310	311,432	301,993	288,130	299,544	314,301	338,234	359,391	365,278

[1] Preliminary.   *Source: Economic Research Service, U.S. Department of Agriculture (ERS-USDA)*

Cold Storage Stocks of Total Frozen Vegetables in the United States, on First of Month   In Millions of Pounds

Year	Jan.	Feb.	Mar.	Apr.	May	June	July	Aug.	Sept.	Oct.	Nov.	Dec.
2014	2,360.4	2,157.4	2,025.0	1,842.1	1,660.2	1,519.9	1,607.9	1,863.8	2,232.8	2,530.6	2,663.6	2,546.8
2015	2,359.3	2,144.9	1,995.5	1,850.1	1,714.1	1,620.7	1,697.1	1,889.1	2,222.9	2,570.1	2,688.7	2,580.2
2016	2,423.8	2,302.3	2,169.7	1,973.7	1,861.4	1,769.2	1,855.6	2,028.6	2,413.9	2,626.6	2,757.7	2,695.1
2017	2,570.3	2,407.5	2,256.6	2,125.7	1,954.2	1,803.6	1,814.2	1,938.1	2,366.1	2,731.8	2,866.1	2,788.6
2018	2,626.0	2,412.9	2,221.9	2,018.1	1,838.3	1,682.5	1,706.5	1,867.7	2,276.2	2,544.6	2,669.9	2,548.1
2019	2,374.2	2,193.7	2,064.7	1,902.1	1,738.6	1,575.7	1,621.9	1,821.9	2,191.6	2,530.1	2,615.7	2,555.2
2020	2,354.6	2,184.6	2,018.9	1,869.7	1,759.6	1,598.3	1,643.5	1,781.1	2,122.9	2,531.8	2,693.5	2,616.5
2021	2,485.5	2,283.8	2,102.0	1,889.7	1,750.9	1,610.8	1,588.7	1,716.8	2,039.4	2,437.8	2,613.5	2,554.0
2022	2,378.3	2,183.0	2,011.9	1,821.3	1,738.9	1,614.2	1,562.2	1,711.4	2,032.7	2,429.9	2,552.0	2,491.9
2023[1]	2,376.0	2,210.3	2,059.5	1,917.9	1,802.2	1,652.2	1,626.7	1,803.9	2,195.7	2,463.4	2,592.8	2,513.9

[1] Preliminary.   *Source: Economic Research Service, U.S. Department of Agriculture (ERS-USDA)*

Wheat

Wheat is a cereal grass. Wheat was a wild grass before humans started to cultivate it for larger-scale food production. It has been grown in temperate regions and cultivated for food since prehistoric times. Wheat is believed to have originated in southwestern Asia. Archeological research indicates that wheat was grown as a crop in the Nile Valley about 5,000 BC. Wheat is not native to the U.S. and was first grown here in 1602 near the Massachusetts coast. The common types of wheat grown in the U.S. are spring and winter wheat. Wheat planted in the spring for summer or autumn harvest is mostly red wheat. Wheat planted in the fall or winter for spring harvest is mostly white wheat. Winter wheat accounts for nearly three-fourths of total U.S. production. Wheat is used mainly for human consumption and supplies about 20% of the food calories for the world's population. The primary use for wheat is flour, but it is also used for brewing and distilling, and for making oil, gluten, straw for livestock bedding, livestock feed, hay or silage, newsprint, and other products.

Wheat futures and options are traded at the CME Group, ICE Futures US Exchange, the MatbaRofex exchange (Argentina), Sydney Futures Exchange (SFE), Euronext (Paris), Zhengzhou Commodity Exchange, and the South Africa Futures Exchange. The CME's wheat futures contract calls for the delivery of soft red wheat (No. 1 and 2), hard red winter wheat (No. 1 and 2), dark northern spring wheat (No. 1 and 2), No.1 northern spring at 3 cents/bushel premium, or No. 2 northern spring at par.

Prices – CME wheat futures prices (Barchart.com symbol ZW) posted their high for 2023 in February of $7.98 per bushel. Wheat prices then retreated and posted a 3-year low of $5.73 per bushel in May on the outlook for bumper wheat crops in Russia and the EU. Russian wheat exports were estimated to climb to a record 44.4 MMT in 2022/23. Also, an extension of the Black Sea grain export deal in May kept Ukrainian wheat supplies flowing, adding to a supply glut. Ukraine and Russia together account for about one-quarter of the global wheat trade. Wheat prices jumped more than $2 per bushel into July on concerns about disruption to global supplies after Russia pulled out of an agreement that allowed Ukraine to ship grain through the Black Sea. Also, Russian missiles damaged port infrastructure in Ukraine's Odesa region, curbing its ability to export wheat. However, the gains were short-lived as bigger US wheat supplies weighed on prices. In September, the USDA projected that US 2023 all-wheat production would climb to a 3-year high of 1.812 billion bushels. Also, the USDA said that Q3 US wheat stocks of 1.78 million bushels were above market estimates. Wheat prices sank to a 3-1/2 year low in November of $5.28 per bushel. Ramped-up exports of cheaper Russian wheat reduced demand for more expensive US wheat and weighed on wheat prices. In 2023, US wheat exports fell to a 51-year low of 20.647 MMT. Abundant wheat supplies undercut prices as the USDA, in the November WASDE report, projected higher-than-expected 2023/24 US and global wheat ending stocks. Wheat prices recovered slightly into year-end on disruption of wheat supplies with the ongoing Russian-Ukraine war and after Houthi rebels from Yemen began attacking commercial ships transiting the Red Sea, forcing nearly half the container fleet to divert shipments around the southern tip of Africa instead of going through the Red Sea. Wheat prices finished 2023 down sharply by -20.7% yr/yr at $6.28 per bushel.

Supply – World wheat production in the 2023/24 marketing year is forecasted to fall by -0.5% yr/yr to 784.908 million metric tons, below the record high of 789.166 in 2022/23. The world's largest wheat producers in 2023/24 are expected to be China with 17.4% of world production, the European Union with 17.1%, India with 14.1%, Russia with 11.6%, and the US with 6.3%. China's wheat production in 2023/24 is expected to fall by -0.8% yr/yr to a record 136.590 million metric tons. India's wheat production in 2023/24 is expected to rise by +6.3% yr/yr to 110.55 million metric tons. The world land area harvested with wheat in 2023/24 is expected to rise +1.4% yr/yr to 223.0 million hectares (1 hectare equals 10,000 square meters or 2.471 acres). The world wheat yield in 2023/24 is expected to fall by -1.9% yr/yr to 3.52 million metric tons, below the 2022/23 record high of 3.59 million metric tons.

US wheat production in 2023/24 is expected to rise by +5.2% yr/yr to 1.734 billion bushels. The US winter wheat crop in 2023 rose by +11.2% yr/yr to 1.227 billion bushels, which was well below the record winter wheat crop of 2.097 billion bushels seen in 1981. US production of durum wheat in 2023 fell by -10.3% yr/yr to 57.377 million bushels. US production of other spring wheat in 2023 fell by -6.8% yr/yr to 449.575 million bushels. The US states producing the largest amount of winter wheat in 2023 were Kansas, with 16.9% of US production, Washington with 7.7%, Montana with 6.5%, Colorado with 6.0%, and Texas with 5.7%. US farmers planted 49.808 million acres of wheat in 2023, up by +8.9% yr/yr. The US wheat yield in 2023/24 is expected to be down by -1.5% yr/yr at 45.8 bushels per acre.

Demand – World wheat utilization in 2023/24 is forecasted to rise by +0.7% yr/yr to 796.4 million metric tons. US consumption of wheat in 2023/24 is expected to rise by +3.2% yr/yr to 1.154 billion bushels, below the 2012/13 record high of 1.389 billion bushels. The wheat usage breakdown in 2023/24 is expected to be 84.1% for food, 10.4% for feed and residuals, and 5.5% for seed.

Trade – World trade in wheat in 2023/24 is expected to fall by -4.8% yr/yr to 209.5 million metric tons. US exports of wheat in 2023/24 are expected to fall by -4.5% yr/yr to 725.0 million bushels. US imports of wheat in 2023/24 are expected to rise by +18.9% yr/yr to 145.0 million bushels.

World Production of Wheat   In Thousands of Metric Tons

Crop Year	Australia	Canada	China	European Union	India	Iran	Kazakh-stan	Pakistan	Russia	Türkiye	Ukraine	United States	World Total
2014-15	23,743	29,442	128,235	156,912	95,850	13,000	12,996	25,979	59,080	15,250	24,750	55,147	731,580
2015-16	22,275	27,647	132,555	160,480	86,527	14,500	13,748	25,086	61,044	19,500	27,274	56,117	739,079
2016-17	31,819	32,140	133,188	130,986	87,000	14,500	14,985	25,633	72,529	17,250	26,791	62,832	756,832
2017-18	20,941	30,377	134,241	136,681	98,510	12,700	14,802	26,674	85,167	21,000	26,981	47,380	760,285
2018-19	17,598	32,352	131,441	123,124	99,870	14,500	13,947	25,076	71,685	19,000	25,057	51,311	729,782
2019-20	14,480	32,670	133,600	138,799	103,600	15,550	11,452	24,349	73,610	17,500	29,171	52,581	759,391
2020-21	31,923	35,437	134,250	126,684	107,860	15,000	14,256	25,248	85,352	18,250	25,420	49,523	773,094
2021-22[1]	36,237	22,422	136,946	138,160	109,586	12,000	11,814	27,464	75,158	16,000	33,007	44,804	780,049
2022-23[2]	40,545	34,335	137,723	134,185	104,000	13,200	16,404	26,400	92,000	17,250	21,500	44,898	789,166
2023-24[3]	25,500	31,954	136,590	134,300	110,554	14,000	12,000	28,000	91,000	19,500	23,400	49,314	784,908

[1] Preliminary.   [2] Estimate.   [3] Forecast.   *Source: Foreign Agricultural Service, U.S. Department of Agriculture (FAS-USDA)*

World Consumption of Wheat   In Thousands of Metric Tons

Crop Year	Australia	Brazil	China	Egypt	European Union	India	Iran	Pakistan	Russia	Türkiye	Ukraine	United States	World Total
2014-15	7,200	10,700	118,000	20,000	124,677	93,102	16,400	24,500	35,500	17,500	11,500	31,328	702,266
2015-16	7,125	11,100	117,500	20,800	129,850	88,548	16,100	24,400	37,000	17,700	12,200	31,943	713,929
2016-17	7,450	11,800	119,000	20,800	112,100	97,234	16,250	24,500	40,000	17,000	10,300	31,865	734,214
2017-18	8,475	11,800	121,000	19,800	113,500	95,677	15,900	25,000	43,000	18,300	9,800	29,245	739,516
2018-19	9,200	11,900	125,000	20,100	106,300	95,629	16,100	25,400	40,500	18,800	8,800	29,991	731,240
2019-20	8,000	11,900	126,000	20,300	107,250	95,403	17,200	25,500	40,000	20,000	8,300	30,437	739,581
2020-21	8,025	11,800	155,000	20,500	104,750	102,217	17,400	26,300	42,500	20,600	8,700	30,185	777,570
2021-22[1]	8,500	11,750	148,000	20,500	108,250	109,882	18,200	27,700	41,750	20,200	9,000	30,411	788,320
2022-23[2]	8,000	11,950	148,000	20,550	108,000	108,676	18,100	29,200	42,250	20,600	7,700	30,422	782,232
2023-24[3]	7,500	12,200	153,500	20,600	110,000	109,904	17,800	29,600	43,000	21,300	8,600	31,407	796,048

[1] Preliminary.   [2] Estimate.   [3] Forecast.   *Source: Foreign Agricultural Service, U.S. Department of Agriculture (FAS-USDA)*

World Exports of Wheat   In Thousands of Metric Tons

Crop Year	Argentina	Australia	Brazil	Canada	European Union	Kazakh-stan	Mexico	Russia	Türkiye	Ukraine	United States	Uruguay	World Total
2014-15	5,301	16,591	1,691	24,170	35,455	5,539	1,104	22,800	4,090	11,269	23,523	624	164,253
2015-16	9,600	16,119	1,059	22,091	34,760	7,414	1,568	25,546	5,878	17,431	21,168	692	172,972
2016-17	13,825	22,639	619	20,218	28,366	7,409	1,119	27,815	6,699	18,107	28,600	246	186,778
2017-18	12,730	13,849	230	22,000	24,895	9,000	1,147	41,447	6,698	17,775	24,658	44	185,449
2018-19	12,188	9,002	602	24,427	24,686	8,296	526	35,863	6,814	16,019	25,503	325	176,209
2019-20	12,785	9,136	425	24,139	39,788	6,986	1,168	34,485	6,534	21,016	26,373	279	194,558
2020-21	11,531	23,773	925	26,429	29,736	8,194	612	39,100	6,469	16,851	27,048	542	203,453
2021-22[1]	16,000	27,511	3,070	15,116	31,927	8,098	924	33,000	6,714	18,844	21,656	706	202,767
2022-23[2]	3,662	31,823	2,687	25,591	35,079	10,874	800	47,500	6,875	17,122	20,647	766	220,171
2023-24[3]	10,000	19,000	2,500	24,000	36,500	10,000	1,000	51,000	8,500	14,000	19,731	650	209,540

[1] Preliminary.   [2] Estimate.   [3] Forecast.   *Source: Foreign Agricultural Service, U.S. Department of Agriculture (FAS-USDA)*

World Imports of Wheat   In Thousands of Metric Tons

Crop Year	Algeria	Brazil	Egypt	European Union	Indonesia	Iran	Japan	Korea, South	Mexico	Nigeria	Philip-pines	Türkiye	World Total
2014-15	7,257	5,374	11,300	5,977	7,477	6,315	5,878	3,942	4,471	4,244	5,054	5,841	159,410
2015-16	8,153	6,745	11,925	6,928	10,045	3,500	5,715	4,420	4,805	4,410	4,919	4,087	170,106
2016-17	8,414	7,349	11,181	6,287	10,190	1,200	5,911	4,667	5,370	4,972	5,708	4,732	183,660
2017-18	8,172	7,021	12,407	6,060	10,763	200	5,876	4,269	5,245	5,162	6,059	6,222	184,221
2018-19	7,515	7,020	12,354	5,763	10,934	180	5,726	3,908	4,861	4,659	7,570	6,395	174,098
2019-20	7,145	7,029	12,811	5,551	10,586	2,000	5,683	3,941	5,080	5,338	7,065	10,851	188,429
2020-21	7,680	6,395	12,149	5,390	9,995	2,200	5,493	3,889	4,724	6,586	6,105	8,081	194,451
2021-22[1]	8,286	6,392	11,256	4,629	11,229	7,300	5,605	5,099	5,326	6,187	6,886	9,421	199,927
2022-23[2]	8,141	4,678	11,221	12,103	9,446	4,500	5,452	4,533	5,221	4,732	5,743	12,072	211,475
2023-24[3]	8,300	5,600	11,000	11,000	10,500	3,800	5,500	4,500	5,400	4,800	5,900	10,000	209,149

[1] Preliminary.   [2] Estimate.   [3] Forecast.   *Source: Foreign Agricultural Service, U.S. Department of Agriculture (FAS-USDA)*

WHEAT

World Ending Stocks of Wheat   In Thousands of Metric Tons

Crop Year	Australia	Canada	China	Egypt	European Union	India	Iran	Kazakh-stan	Morocco	Russia	Ukraine	United States	World Total
2014-15	4,665	7,101	77,682	5,611	16,733	17,220	9,466	3,284	4,417	6,287	5,678	20,477	226,475
2015-16	3,858	5,178	95,484	5,875	19,531	14,540	11,166	2,790	6,974	5,604	3,348	26,552	248,759
2016-17	5,757	6,931	113,334	5,134	13,551	9,800	10,416	3,537	4,926	10,823	1,773	32,131	268,259
2017-18	4,557	6,732	129,508	5,381	17,897	13,230	6,766	2,581	5,133	12,010	1,238	29,907	287,800
2018-19	4,454	6,041	138,088	4,894	15,798	16,992	4,936	1,713	5,423	7,778	1,555	29,386	284,231
2019-20	2,695	5,499	150,015	4,986	13,110	24,700	4,786	663	3,611	7,228	1,504	27,985	297,912
2020-21	3,018	5,953	139,120	5,032	10,698	27,800	4,336	1,475	1,457	11,380	1,505	23,001	284,434
2021-22[1]	3,454	3,663	136,759	5,330	13,310	19,500	5,086	1,491	2,385	12,088	6,765	18,355	273,323
2022-23[2]	4,373	3,641	138,818	4,840	16,519	9,500	4,486	3,271	1,533	14,638	3,502	15,501	271,561
2023-24[3]	3,573	3,495	133,508	3,510	15,319	10,000	4,286	1,321	1,818	11,938	4,382	17,623	260,030

[1] Preliminary.   [2] Estimate.   [3] Forecast.   *Source: Foreign Agricultural Service, U.S. Department of Agriculture (FAS-USDA)*

World Supply and Demand of Wheat   In Millions of Metric Tons/Hectares

Crop Year	Area Harvested	Yield	Production	World Trade	Utilization Total	Ending Stocks	Stocks as a % of Utilization
2014-15	221.5	3.30	731.6	164.3	707.1	226.5	32.0
2015-16	223.7	3.30	739.1	173.0	716.8	248.8	34.7
2016-17	222.4	3.40	756.8	186.8	737.3	268.3	36.4
2017-18	218.0	3.49	760.3	185.4	740.7	287.8	38.9
2018-19	214.9	3.40	729.8	176.2	733.4	284.2	38.8
2019-20	215.4	3.53	759.4	194.6	745.7	297.9	40.0
2020-21	220.5	3.51	773.1	203.5	786.6	284.4	36.2
2021-22[1]	221.9	3.51	780.0	202.8	791.2	273.3	34.5
2022-23[2]	220.0	3.59	789.2	220.2	790.9	271.6	34.3
2023-24[3]	223.0	3.52	784.9	209.5	796.4	260.0	32.6

[1] Preliminary.   [2] Estimate.   [3] Forecast.   *Source: Foreign Agricultural Service, U.S. Department of Agriculture (FAS-USDA)*

Salient Statistics of Wheat in the United States

Crop Year	Planting Intentions	Winter	Spring	All	Average All Yield Per Acre in Bushels	Value of Production $1,000	Domestic Exports[2]	Imports[3]	Flour	Cereal
		Acreage Harvested — 1,000 Acres					Foreign Trade[5] — In Millions of Bushels		Per Capita[4] Consumption — In Pounds	
2014-15	56,841	32,299	14,086	46,385	43.7	11,914,954	864.3	151.2	----	----
2015-16	54,999	32,346	14,972	47,318	43.6	10,018,323	777.8	112.8	----	----
2016-17	50,116	20,235	13,613	43,848	52.7	9,179,190	1,050.9	118.0	----	----
2017-18	46,052	25,301	12,254	37,555	46.3	8,255,119	905.9	158.0	----	----
2018-19	47,815	24,742	14,870	39,612	47.6	9,661,916	937.1	134.6	----	----
2019-20	45,485	24,592	12,802	37,394	51.7	8,919,117	969.0	104.0	----	----
2020-21	44,450	23,029	13,760	36,789	49.7	9,389,104	994.0	100.0	----	----
2021-22	46,740	25,464	11,681	37,145	44.3	12,208,186	796.0	96.0	----	----
2022-23	45,769	23,454	12,031	35,485	46.5	14,213,326	759.0	122.0	----	----
2023-24[1]	49,575	24,683	12,589	37,272	48.6	12,741,229	725.0	145.0	----	----

[1] Preliminary.   [2] Includes flour milled from imported wheat.   [3] Total wheat, flour & other products.   [4] Civilian only.   [5] Year beginning June.
Source: Economic Research Service, U.S. Department of Agriculture (ERS-USDA)

Supply and Distribution of Wheat in the United States   In Millions of Bushels

Crop Year Beginning June 1	On Farms	Mills, Elevators[3]	Total Stocks	Pro-duction	Imports[4]	Total Supply	Food	Seed	Feed & Residual[5]	Total	Exports[4]	Total Disap-pearance
	Supply — Stocks, June 1						Domestic Disappearance					
2014-15	97.0	493.3	590.3	2,026.3	151.2	2,767.8	958.3	79.4	113.4	1,151.1	864.3	2,015.4
2015-16	155.2	597.2	752.4	2,061.9	112.8	2,927.1	957.2	67.2	149.4	1,173.8	777.8	1,951.5
2016-17	197.2	778.4	975.6	2,308.7	118.0	3,402.3	948.9	61.3	160.7	1,170.8	1,050.9	2,221.7
2017-18	191.8	988.8	1,180.6	1,739.6	158.0	3,079.5	964.2	63.4	47.2	1,074.7	905.9	1,980.7
2018-19	130.5	968.4	1,098.9	1,885.2	134.6	3,118.6	954.4	59.5	87.9	1,101.8	937.1	2,038.9
2019-20	206.5	873.2	1,079.8	1,932.0	104.0	3,116.0	962.0	62.0	95.0	1,118.0	969.0	2,087.0
2020-21	228.6	799.7	1,028.3	1,828.0	100.0	2,948.0	961.0	64.0	85.0	1,109.0	994.0	2,103.0
2021-22	141.7	703.5	845.2	1,646.3	96.0	2,588.0	971.0	58.0	88.0	1,117.0	796.0	1,913.0
2022-23[1]	93.0	605.5	698.4	1,649.9	122.0	2,446.0	973.0	68.0	77.0	1,118.0	759.0	1,876.0
2023-24[2]	124.4	445.1	569.6	1,734.2	145.0	2,527.0	970.0	64.0	120.0	1,154.0	725.0	1,879.0

[1] Preliminary.   [2] Estimate.   [3] Also warehouses and all off-farm storage not otherwise designated, including flour mills.   [4] Imports & exports are for wheat, including flour & other products in terms of wheat.   [5] Mostly feed use.
Source: Economic Research Service, U.S. Department of Agriculture (ERS-USDA)

Stocks, Production and Exports of Wheat in the United States, by Class — In Millions of Bushels

Crop Year	Hard Spring Stocks June 1	Hard Spring Pro- duction	Hard Spring Exports[3]	Durum[2] Stocks June 1	Durum[2] Pro- duction	Durum[2] Exports[3]	Hard Winter Stocks June 1	Hard Winter Pro- duction	Hard Winter Exports[3]	Soft Red Winter Stocks June 1	Soft Red Winter Pro- duction	Soft Red Winter Exports[3]	White Stocks June 1	White Pro- duction	White Exports[3]
2014-15	169	556	274	22	54	37	237	739	272	113	455	134	50	224	147
2015-16	212	568	254	26	84	29	294	830	227	154	359	120	67	221	147
2016-17	272	491	319	28	104	25	446	1,082	453	157	345	91	74	286	163
2017-18	235	384	229	36	55	18	589	750	373	215	293	91	105	259	195
2018-19	191	587	259	35	78	22	581	662	332	205	286	128	87	272	197
2019-20	263	520	269	55	54	42	516	845	378	158	240	92	88	273	188
2020-21	280	531	286	42	69	28	506	654	340	105	264	69	95	302	270
2021-22	235	297	208	27	38	14	428	750	315	85	361	111	70	201	147
2022-23	142	446	214	24	64	23	356	531	224	99	336	107	54	272	190
2023-24[1]	155	468	225	28	59	25	223	601	145	90	449	175	74	235	155

[1] Preliminary. [2] Includes "Red Durum." [3] Includes four made from U.S. wheat & shipments to territories.
Source: Economic Research Service, U.S. Department of Agriculture (ERS-USDA)

Seeded Acreage, Yield and Production of all Wheat in the United States

Year	Seed Acreage - 1,000 Acres Winter	Seed Acreage - 1,000 Acres Other Spring	Seed Acreage - 1,000 Acres Durum	Seed Acreage - 1,000 Acres All	Yield Per Harvested Acre (Bushels) Winter	Yield Per Harvested Acre (Bushels) Other Spring	Yield Per Harvested Acre (Bushels) Durum	Yield Per Harvested Acre (Bushels) All	Production (Million Bushels) Winter	Production (Million Bushels) Other Spring	Production (Million Bushels) Durum	Production (Million Bushels) All
2014	42,409	13,025	1,407	56,841	42.6	46.7	40.2	43.7	1,377.2	595.0	54.1	2,026.3
2015	39,681	13,367	1,951	54,999	42.5	46.3	43.5	43.6	1,374.7	603.2	84.0	2,061.9
2016	36,149	11,555	2,412	50,116	55.3	47.3	44.0	52.7	1,672.6	532.2	103.9	2,308.7
2017	32,726	11,019	2,307	46,052	50.2	41.0	26.0	46.3	1,270.3	415.9	54.8	1,739.6
2018	32,542	13,200	2,073	47,815	47.9	48.3	39.5	47.6	1,183.9	623.2	78.0	1,885.2
2019	31,474	12,670	1,341	45,485	53.6	48.3	45.8	51.7	1,317.0	561.1	54.0	1,932.0
2020	30,450	12,310	1,690	44,450	50.9	48.6	41.5	49.7	1,171.4	587.5	69.1	1,828.0
2021	33,678	11,420	1,642	46,740	50.2	32.6	24.7	44.3	1,277.8	330.9	37.6	1,646.3
2022	33,281	10,835	1,632	45,769	47.0	46.2	40.5	46.5	1,103.7	482.7	64.0	1,649.9
2023[1]	36,699	11,200	1,676	49,575	50.6	46.0	37.0	48.6	1,227.2	504.9	59.3	1,734.2

[1] Preliminary. *Source: Economic Research Service, U.S. Department of Agriculture (ERS-USDA)*

Production of Winter Wheat in the United States, by State — In Thousands of Bushels

Year	Colorado	Idaho	Illinois	Kansas	Missouri	Montana	Nebraska	Ohio	Okla-homa	Oregon	Texas	Wash-ington	Total
2014	89,300	58,400	44,890	246,400	42,920	91,840	71,050	40,330	47,600	40,700	67,500	85,280	1,377,216
2015	81,030	58,220	33,800	321,900	32,330	91,020	45,980	32,160	98,800	34,545	106,500	89,040	1,374,690
2016	105,120	66,740	34,780	467,400	39,900	105,350	70,740	44,800	136,500	35,500	89,600	130,260	1,672,582
2017	86,860	53,600	35,720	333,600	36,720	66,780	46,920	34,040	98,600	43,470	68,150	120,450	1,270,282
2018	70,200	61,200	36,960	277,400	30,680	78,500	49,490	33,750	70,000	46,565	56,000	125,400	1,183,939
2019	98,000	59,160	36,850	348,400	24,570	95,000	55,290	21,560	110,000	49,640	71,400	119,000	1,316,963
2020	41,040	66,660	35,360	281,250	22,940	75,990	34,030	34,790	104,000	46,400	61,500	133,000	1,171,397
2021	69,560	45,440	48,190	364,000	31,850	53,630	41,160	43,775	115,050	31,725	74,000	70,980	1,277,755
2022	35,750	63,900	44,240	244,200	24,600	59,400	26,240	36,735	68,600	48,620	39,000	122,400	1,103,707
2023[1]	74,620	56,070	67,860	201,250	42,000	85,680	36,960	53,100	68,600	40,600	77,700	94,500	1,227,235

[1] Preliminary. *Source: Crop Reporting Board, U.S. Department of Agriculture (CRB-USDA)*

Official Winter Wheat Crop Production Reports in the United States — In Thousands of Bushels

Crop Year	May 1	June 1	July 1	August 1	September 1	Current December	Final
2014-15	1,402,505	1,381,060	1,367,432	1,396,742	----	----	1,377,216
2015-16	1,471,802	1,505,072	1,455,516	1,438,278	----	----	1,374,690
2016-17	1,427,084	1,506,626	1,627,664	1,657,440	----	----	1,672,582
2017-18	1,246,392	1,250,192	1,279,363	1,287,133	----	----	1,270,282
2018-19	1,191,542	1,197,716	1,192,585	1,189,199	----	----	1,183,939
2019-20	1,268,461	1,274,451	1,290,626	1,326,223	----	----	1,316,963
2020-21	1,254,600	1,265,700	1,217,784	1,198,362	----	----	1,171,397
2021-22	1,282,925	1,309,000	1,364,205	1,318,735	----	----	1,277,755
2022-23	1,173,547	1,181,632	1,200,691	1,197,650	----	----	1,103,707
2023-24[1]	1,130,415	1,136,465	1,206,435	1,227,235	----	----	1,227,235

[1] Preliminary. *Source: Crop Reporting Board, U.S. Department of Agriculture (CRB-USDA)*

WHEAT

Production of All Spring Wheat in the United States, by State   In Thousands of Bushels

			Durum Wheat						Other Spring Wheat					
Year	Arizona	Cali-fornia	Idaho	Mon-tana	North Dakota	Total	Idaho	Minne-sota	Montana	North Dakota	Oregon	South Dakota	Wash-ington	Total
2014	8,436	3,150	737	13,330	28,223	54,056	34,580	64,900	104,300	291,650	3,744	71,680	23,180	595,038
2015	15,150	6,695	700	18,755	42,463	84,009	30,450	85,800	78,740	319,200	4,650	60,480	22,860	603,240
2016	9,408	4,042	750	31,365	58,118	103,914	34,365	74,340	75,960	269,100	4,437	47,250	27,030	532,227
2017	8,989	2,484	1,848	12,560	28,920	54,777	35,275	75,710	48,090	270,050	4,599	20,770	22,050	415,851
2018	7,738	3,515	935	23,250	42,463	77,985	42,275	92,630	95,880	318,010	5,025	40,530	27,810	623,232
2019	3,640	2,244	435	21,715	25,925	53,959	39,160	79,800	101,010	291,550	----	25,370	24,205	561,095
2020	4,851	1,479	801	26,910	35,100	69,141	45,045	72,080	125,780	275,870	----	35,485	33,245	587,505
2021	5,310	2,200	539	9,920	19,680	37,649	30,555	55,680	37,060	174,535	----	16,820	16,200	330,850
2022	9,576	3,850	455	18,900	31,200	63,981	29,160	73,810	61,000	263,000	----	34,080	21,620	482,670
2023[1]	3,811	1,938	650	20,925	32,005	59,329	32,390	78,120	80,100	267,720	----	27,950	18,620	504,900

[1] Preliminary.   Source: Crop Reporting Board, U.S. Department of Agriculture (CRB-USDA)

Stocks of All Wheat in the United States   In Thousands of Bushels

		On Farms				Off Farms				Total Stocks		
Year	Mar. 1	June 1	Sept. 1	Dec. 1	Mar. 1	June 1	Sept. 1	Dec. 1	Mar. 1	June 1	Sept. 1	Dec. 1
2014	237,530	96,995	713,450	472,800	819,435	493,288	1,193,770	1,056,830	1,056,965	590,283	1,907,220	1,529,630
2015	278,710	155,170	650,200	503,450	861,697	597,224	1,446,889	1,242,457	1,140,407	752,394	2,097,089	1,745,907
2016	319,800	197,210	728,200	571,280	1,051,862	778,393	1,816,830	1,506,042	1,371,662	975,603	2,545,030	2,077,322
2017	349,500	191,755	491,800	394,080	1,309,175	988,847	1,774,275	1,479,335	1,658,675	1,180,602	2,266,075	1,873,415
2018	259,310	130,475	632,700	504,280	1,236,131	968,414	1,757,071	1,505,205	1,495,441	1,098,889	2,389,771	2,009,485
2019	367,870	206,545	734,500	519,470	1,225,201	873,216	1,611,025	1,321,305	1,593,071	1,079,761	2,345,525	1,840,775
2020	338,690	228,585	705,050	483,470	1,076,724	799,699	1,452,775	1,219,220	1,415,414	1,028,284	2,157,825	1,702,690
2021	283,920	141,655	419,190	273,290	1,026,870	703,496	1,354,347	1,103,873	1,310,790	845,151	1,773,537	1,377,163
2022	174,410	92,965	591,130	361,900	854,758	605,466	1,185,709	949,930	1,029,168	698,431	1,776,839	1,311,830
2023[1]	227,485	124,420	598,140	401,060	713,733	445,148	1,168,981	1,020,019	941,218	569,568	1,767,121	1,421,079

[1] Preliminary.   Source: National Agricultural Statistics Service, U.S. Department of Agriculture (NASS-USDA)

Stocks of Durum Wheat in the United States   In Thousands of Bushels

		On Farms				Off Farms				Total Stocks		
Year	Mar. 1	June 1	Sept. 1	Dec. 1	Mar. 1	June 1	Sept. 1	Dec. 1	Mar. 1	June 1	Sept. 1	Dec. 1
2014	20,700	12,800	38,700	23,900	17,430	8,724	19,121	20,147	38,130	21,524	57,821	44,047
2015	16,200	10,250	44,900	35,700	21,454	15,406	29,146	24,787	37,654	25,656	74,046	60,487
2016	17,700	12,190	65,500	49,200	24,785	15,609	26,386	23,696	42,485	27,799	91,886	72,896
2017	32,400	18,350	33,400	30,700	20,584	17,953	32,756	25,351	52,984	36,303	66,156	56,051
2018	25,800	14,950	51,800	46,700	23,740	19,996	38,260	36,830	49,540	34,946	90,060	83,530
2019	40,600	26,050	49,600	33,200	33,789	28,920	38,773	31,187	74,389	54,970	88,373	64,387
2020	23,500	17,700	43,500	39,000	27,898	24,230	27,517	22,639	51,398	41,930	71,017	61,639
2021	22,600	13,500	21,000	16,900	19,592	13,843	25,010	25,086	42,192	27,343	46,010	41,986
2022	12,600	9,290	31,500	25,900	17,713	14,449	22,259	22,166	30,313	23,739	53,759	48,066
2023[1]	17,100	12,780	33,200	20,600	18,704	14,965	24,079	22,674	35,804	27,745	57,279	45,274

[1] Preliminary.   Source: National Agricultural Statistics Service, U.S. Department of Agriculture (NASS-USDA)

Wheat Supply and Distribution in Canada, Australia and Argentina   In Millions of Metric Tons

	Canada (Year Beginning Aug. 1)					Australia (Year Beginning Oct. 1)					Argentina (Year Beginning Dec. 1)				
	Supply			Disappearance		Supply			Disappearance		Supply			Disappearance	
Crop Year	Stocks Aug. 1	New Crop	Total Supply	Domestic	Exports[3]	Stocks Oct. 1	New Crop	Total Supply	Domestic	Exports[3]	Stocks Dec. 1	New Crop	Total Supply	Domestic	Exports[3]
2013-14	5.1	37.6	42.7	9.5	23.3	4.7	25.3	30.0	7.0	18.6	0.3	10.5	10.8	6.1	2.3
2014-15	10.4	29.4	39.8	9.1	24.2	4.6	23.7	28.3	7.2	16.6	2.5	13.9	16.4	6.4	5.3
2015-16	7.1	27.6	34.7	8.0	22.1	4.7	22.3	26.9	7.1	16.1	4.8	11.3	16.1	5.7	9.6
2016-17	5.2	32.1	37.3	10.7	20.2	3.9	31.8	35.7	7.5	22.6	0.8	18.4	19.2	5.2	13.8
2017-18	6.9	30.4	37.3	9.0	22.0	5.8	20.9	26.7	8.5	13.8	0.2	18.5	18.7	5.6	12.7
2018-19	6.7	32.4	39.1	9.1	24.4	4.5	17.6	22.1	9.2	9.0	0.5	19.5	20.0	6.1	12.2
2019-20	6.0	32.7	38.7	9.8	24.1	4.4	14.5	18.9	8.0	9.1	1.7	19.8	21.5	6.3	12.8
2020-21	5.5	35.4	40.9	9.1	26.4	2.7	31.9	34.6	8.0	23.8	2.5	17.6	20.1	6.3	11.5
2021-22[1]	6.0	22.3	28.2	10.0	15.1	3.0	36.3	39.3	8.5	27.5	2.3	22.2	24.5	6.2	16.0
2022-23[2]	3.7	33.8	37.5	8.6	26.0	3.5	36.6	40.1	8.6	27.5	2.4	12.5	14.9	6.2	7.5

[1] Preliminary.   [2] Forecast.   [3] Including flour.   Source: Foreign Agricultural Service, U.S. Department of Agriculture (FAS-USDA)

Quarterly Supply and Disappearance of Wheat in the United States   In Millions of Bushels

Crop Year Beginning June 1	Supply				Disapperance						Ending Stocks		
	Beginning Stocks	Pro-duction	Imports[3]	Total Supply	Domestic Use				Exports[3]	Total Disap-pearance	Total Stocks	Gov't Owned[4]	Privately Owned[5]
					Food	Seed	Feed & Residual	Total					
2013-14	717.9	2,135.0	172.5	3,025.3	955.1	75.6	228.2	1,258.8	1,176.2	2,435.1	590.3	----	----
June-Aug.	717.9	2,135.0	35.7	2,888.5	234.8	4.1	422.4	661.4	357.5	1,018.9	1,869.6	----	----
Sept.-Nov.	1,869.6	----	48.0	1,917.7	249.3	52.7	-168.0	134.0	308.8	442.8	1,474.9	----	----
Dec.-Feb.	1,474.9	----	42.0	1,516.9	231.1	1.9	-0.8	232.2	227.7	459.9	1,057.0	----	----
Mar.-May	1,057.0	----	46.7	1,103.7	239.9	16.8	-25.4	231.3	282.1	513.4	590.3	----	----
2014-15	590.3	2,026.3	151.2	2,767.8	958.3	79.4	113.4	1,151.1	864.3	2,015.4	752.4	----	----
June-Aug.	590.3	2,026.3	44.2	2,660.8	238.9	6.4	255.7	501.0	252.5	753.5	1,907.2	----	----
Sept.-Nov.	1,907.2	----	34.6	1,941.8	248.2	48.8	-92.6	204.4	207.7	412.1	1,529.6	----	----
Dec.-Feb.	1,529.6	----	36.7	1,566.4	230.8	2.1	7.9	240.9	185.1	426.0	1,140.4	----	----
Mar.-May	1,140.4	----	35.8	1,176.2	240.3	22.1	-57.6	204.8	219.0	423.8	752.4	----	----
2015-16	752.4	2,061.9	112.8	2,927.1	957.1	67.2	149.5	1,173.8	777.8	1,951.5	975.6	----	----
June-Aug.	752.4	2,061.9	26.5	2,840.9	240.2	1.0	297.8	539.0	204.8	743.8	2,097.1	----	----
Sept.-Nov.	2,097.1	----	27.0	2,124.1	248.7	44.2	-107.2	185.8	192.4	378.2	1,745.9	----	----
Dec.-Feb.	1,745.9	----	34.4	1,780.3	229.5	1.7	2.2	233.5	175.2	408.6	1,371.7	----	----
Mar.-May	1,371.7	----	24.9	1,396.5	238.6	20.3	-43.4	215.5	205.5	420.9	975.6	----	----
2016-17	975.6	2,308.7	118.0	3,402.3	948.9	61.3	160.7	1,170.8	1,050.9	2,221.7	1,180.6	----	----
June-Aug.	975.6	2,308.7	32.6	3,316.9	237.6	0.6	265.7	504.0	267.9	771.9	2,545.0	----	----
Sept.-Nov.	2,545.0	----	29.5	2,574.5	245.5	40.6	-30.2	255.8	239.3	495.2	2,079.4	----	----
Dec.-Feb.	2,079.4	----	24.6	2,104.0	227.9	1.3	-13.0	216.2	229.1	445.3	1,658.7	----	----
Mar.-May	1,658.7	----	31.3	1,689.9	237.9	18.7	-61.8	194.8	314.5	509.3	1,180.6	----	----
2017-18	1,180.6	1,740.9	158.0	3,079.5	964.2	63.4	47.2	1,074.7	905.9	1,980.7	1,098.9	----	----
June-Aug.	1,180.6	1,740.9	42.0	2,963.6	238.8	0.9	164.8	404.4	292.4	696.8	2,266.8	----	----
Sept.-Nov.	2,266.8	----	35.9	2,302.7	250.6	40.1	-54.7	235.9	193.3	429.2	1,873.5	----	----
Dec.-Feb.	1,873.5	----	37.8	1,911.3	232.9	1.8	-19.5	215.1	200.8	415.9	1,495.4	----	----
Mar.-May	1,495.4	----	42.2	1,537.7	242.0	20.6	-43.3	219.3	219.5	438.8	1,098.9	----	----
2018-19	1,098.9	1,885.2	134.6	3,118.6	954.4	59.5	87.9	1,101.8	937.1	2,038.9	1,079.8	----	----
June-Aug.	1,098.9	1,885.2	40.9	3,024.9	239.2	2.1	189.2	430.5	204.6	635.2	2,389.8	----	----
Sept.-Nov.	2,389.8	----	31.2	2,421.0	246.5	37.6	-75.1	209.0	202.5	411.5	2,009.5	----	----
Dec.-Feb.	2,009.5	----	32.1	2,041.5	229.1	2.8	-27.4	204.6	243.9	448.5	1,593.1	----	----
Mar.-May	1,593.1	----	30.4	1,623.4	239.5	17.0	1.1	257.7	286.0	543.7	1,079.8	----	----
2019-20	1,079.8	1,932.0	103.8	3,115.6	961.6	60.0	96.7	1,118.3	969.0	2,087.3	1,028.3	----	----
June-Aug.	1,079.8	1,932.0	23.2	3,035.0	238.2	3.6	195.7	437.5	251.9	689.4	2,345.5	----	----
Sept.-Nov.	2,345.5	----	22.5	2,368.0	247.0	37.3	9.6	293.8	233.4	527.2	1,840.8	----	----
Dec.-Feb.	1,840.8	----	28.3	1,869.1	236.1	2.0	-21.2	216.9	236.8	453.7	1,415.4	----	----
Mar.-May	1,415.4	----	29.9	1,445.3	240.4	17.1	-87.3	170.1	246.9	417.0	1,028.3	----	----
2020-21	1,028.0	1,820.0	100.0	2,948.0	961.0	64.0	85.0	1,109.0	994.0	2,103.0	845.0	----	----
June-Aug.	1,028.0	1,820.0	30.0	2,878.0	241.0	2.0	205.0	448.0	272.0	720.0	2,158.0	----	----
Sept.-Nov.	2,158.0	----	28.0	2,186.0	249.0	42.0	-46.0	246.0	237.0	483.0	1,703.0	----	----
Dec.-Feb.	1,703.0	----	22.0	1,725.0	232.0	1.0	-30.0	202.0	212.0	414.0	1,311.0	----	----
Mar.-May	1,311.0	----	21.0	1,332.0	239.0	19.0	-44.0	213.0	273.0	486.0	845.0	----	----
2021-22	845.0	1,646.0	96.0	2,588.0	971.0	58.0	88.0	1,117.0	796.0	1,913.0	674.0	----	----
June-Aug.	845.0	1,646.0	25.0	2,517.0	237.0	1.0	255.0	493.0	250.0	743.0	1,774.0	----	----
Sept.-Nov.	1,774.0	----	24.0	1,798.0	249.0	40.0	-55.0	234.0	187.0	421.0	1,377.0	----	----
Dec.-Feb.	1,377.0	----	22.0	1,399.0	237.0	3.0	-50.0	189.0	181.0	370.0	1,029.0	----	----
Mar.-May	1,029.0	----	25.0	1,054.0	249.0	14.0	-61.0	202.0	178.0	380.0	674.0	----	----
2022-23[1]	674.0	1,650.0	122.0	2,446.0	973.0	68.0	77.0	1,118.0	759.0	1,876.0	570.0	----	----
June-Aug.	674.0	1,650.0	33.0	2,357.0	248.0	5.0	119.0	372.0	209.0	580.0	1,777.0	----	----
Sept.-Nov.	1,777.0	----	27.0	1,804.0	250.0	47.0	-13.0	283.0	210.0	492.0	1,312.0	----	----
Dec.-Feb.	1,312.0	----	32.0	1,344.0	234.0	1.0	-11.0	223.0	179.0	403.0	941.0	----	----
Mar.-May	941.0	----	29.0	971.0	242.0	16.0	-18.0	240.0	161.0	401.0	570.0	----	----
2023-24[2]	570.0	1,812.0	145.0	2,527.0	970.0	64.0	120.0	1,154.0	725.0	1,879.0	648.0	----	----
June-Aug.	570.0	1,812.0	36.0	2,418.0	239.0	3.0	245.0	487.0	164.0	650.0	1,767.0	----	----
Sept.-Nov.	1,767.0	----	37.0	1,804.0	252.0	43.0	-56.0	239.0	155.0	394.0	1,410.0	----	----

[1] Preliminary.   [2] Forecast.   [3] Imports & exports include flour and other products expressed in wheat equivalent.   [4] Uncommitted, Government only.
[5] Includes total loans.   [6] Includes alcoholic beverages.   *Source: Economic Research Service, U.S. Department of Agriculture (ERS-USDA)*

WHEAT

Exports of Wheat (Only)[2] from the United States   In Thousands of Bushels

Crop Year	June	July	Aug.	Sept.	Oct.	Nov.	Dec.	Jan.	Feb.	Mar.	Apr.	May	Total
2014-15	77,912	73,314	95,989	97,967	58,258	45,692	59,967	51,471	68,363	74,564	74,102	64,539	842,136
2015-16	59,531	60,229	79,422	90,351	44,850	50,968	62,994	51,899	54,281	70,087	65,495	63,676	753,784
2016-17	83,009	75,485	103,642	103,742	63,389	65,452	80,095	60,537	82,555	98,116	98,509	112,397	1,026,928
2017-18	109,687	87,501	89,362	86,496	48,308	54,448	72,945	64,994	58,101	76,469	72,031	66,140	886,482
2018-19	57,363	65,546	76,856	66,047	70,998	60,225	84,023	72,254	82,437	74,980	101,249	104,930	916,907
2019-20	83,335	68,853	94,857	79,901	83,641	64,645	80,808	70,543	80,660	66,051	91,275	84,125	948,693
2020-21	83,699	88,446	94,222	98,699	63,899	69,498	69,076	73,081	64,838	83,106	93,696	91,289	973,550
2021-22	68,781	80,972	95,627	85,740	45,835	50,380	45,465	61,626	69,420	59,739	63,718	49,833	777,136
2022-23	57,469	53,729	92,548	112,607	50,855	41,845	41,576	65,309	68,770	50,027	55,322	52,142	742,199
2023-24[1]	42,244	64,037	53,544	67,953	39,237	42,256	54,968	53,307					618,542

[1] Preliminary.   [2] Grains.   *Source: Economic Research Service, U.S. Department of Agriculture (ERS-USDA)*

Wheat Government Loan Program Data in the United States   Loan Rates--Cents Per Bushel

| | | | ---------- Farm Loan Prices ---------- | | | | | | | ---------------- Stocks, May 31 ---------------- | | | | |
| | | | | Central & | | | | | Acquired | | | Total --- Outstanding --- | | | |
Crop Year Beginning June 1	National Average[3]	Target Rate[4]	Corn Belt (Soft Red Winter)	Southern Plains (Hard Winter)	Northern Plains (Spring & Durum)	Pacific Northwest (White)	Placed Under Loan	% of Pro- duction	by CCC Under Program	Total Stocks May 31	CCC Stocks May 31	CCC Loans	Farmer- Owned Reserve	"Free"
										In Millions of Bushels				
2010-11	294	417	----	----	----	----	67	3.0	0	862	0	----	----	----
2011-12	294	417	----	----	----	----	36	1.8	0	743	0	----	----	----
2012-13	294	417	----	----	----	----	28	1.2	0	718	0	----	----	----
2013-14	294	417	----	----	----	----	25	1.2	0	590	0	----	----	----
2014-15	294	550	----	----	----	----	43	2.1	0	752	0	----	----	----
2015-16	294	550	----	----	----	----	81	3.9	0	976	0	----	----	----
2016-17	294	550	----	----	----	----	151	6.5	0.25	1,181	0	----	----	----
2017-18	294	550	----	----	----	----	45	2.6	0	1,099	0	----	----	----
2018-19[1]	294	550	----	----	----	----	65	5.9	0	1,080	0	----	----	----
2019-20[2]	338	550	----	----	----	----	69	3.6	0	1,028	0	----	----	----

[1] Preliminary.   [2] Estimate.   [3] The national average loan rate at the farm as a percentage of the parity-priced wheat at the beginning of the marketing year.   [4] 1996-97 through 2001-02 marketing year, target prices not applicable.   NA = Not avaliable.
Source: Agricultural Marketing Service, U.S. Department of Agriculture (AMS-USDA)

United States Wheat and Wheat Flour Imports and Exports   In Thousands of Bushels

	--------------------------- Imports ---------------------------					-------------------------------------- Exports --------------------------------------						
	------- Wheat --------										Export	
		Wheat					Foreign			CCC	Enhance-	Total
Crop Year Beginning June 1	Suitable for Milling	Unfit for Human Consump.	Grain	Flour & Products[2]	Total	P.L. 480	Donations Sec. 416	Aid[3]	Total con- cessional	Export Credit	ment Program	U.S. Wheat
			-- Wheat Equivalent --					In Thousands of Metric Tons				
2013-14	141,665	----	141,665	30,802	172,467	----	----	----	----	----	----	----
2014-15	116,973	----	116,973	34,276	151,249	----	----	----	----	----	----	----
2015-16	76,433	----	76,433	36,292	112,725	----	----	----	----	----	----	----
2016-17	83,849	----	83,849	34,291	118,140	----	----	----	----	----	----	----
2017-18	120,746	----	120,746	37,238	157,984	----	----	----	----	----	----	----
2018-19	97,657	----	97,657	36,975	134,633	----	----	----	----	----	----	----
2019-20[1]	65,345	----	65,345	39,664	105,009	----	----	----	----	----	----	----

[1] Preliminary.   [2] Includes macaroni, semolina & similar products.   [3] Shipment mostly under the Commodity Import Program, financed with foreign aid funds.   NA = Not available.   *Source: Economic Research Service, U.S. Department of Agriculture (ERS-USDA)*

Comparative Average Cash Wheat Prices   In Dollars Per Bushel

			No 1		-- Minneapolis --					------ Export Prices[2] (U.S. $ Per Metric Ton) --------				
			Hard Red		No 1		No 1	No 2			Canada			Rotterdam
		No. 2	Ordinary	No 2	Dark	No 1	Soft	Western	No 2	Aust-	Vancouver	Argen-	U.S. Gulf	C.I.F.
Crop Year June to May	Received by U.S. Farmers	Soft Red Winter, Chicago	Protein, Kansas City	Soft Red Winter, St. Louis	Northern Spring 14%	Hard Amber Durum	White , Portland, Oregon	White Pacific Northwest	Soft White, Toledo	ralian Standard White	No 1 CWRS 13 1/2 %	tina F.O.B. B.A.	No 2 Hard Winter	U.S. No 2 Hard Winter
2016-17	3.89	4.06	4.60	4.14	6.28	----	4.79	----	4.09	195	216	191	157	----
2017-18	4.72	4.46	5.58	4.58	7.62	----	5.35	----	4.49	227	260	198	188	----
2018-19	5.16	4.90	6.10	5.12	6.79	----	6.09	----	4.96	278	253	235	212	----
2019-20	4.58	5.28	5.66	5.46	6.39	----	5.99	----	5.34	247	240	231	205	----
2020-21	5.05	6.01	6.55	6.24	7.09	----	6.44	----	5.96	250	272	260	245	----
2021-22	7.63	8.18	10.00	8.36	11.36	----	10.40	----	8.18	329	406	332	339	----
2022-23	9.10	7.66	10.56	7.65	11.01	----	8.73	----	7.54	337	375	396	363	----
2023-24[1]	7.02	5.96	8.17	5.95	9.32	----	6.99	----	5.64	288	325	305	303	----

[1] Preliminary.   [2] Calendar year.   NA = Not available.   *Source: Economic Research Service, U.S. Department of Agriculture (ERS-USDA)*

WHEAT
Quarterly Cash as of 03/28/2024

QUARTERLY CASH
As of 03/28/2024
Chart High 1278.75 on 05/17/2022
Chart Low 73.00 on 08/12/1940

Chicago #2 red: to 04/1982; St. Louis #2 red: to date.

Average Price of No. 2 Soft Red Winter (30 Days) Wheat in Chicago   In Dollars Per Bushel

Crop Year	June	July	Aug.	Sept.	Oct.	Nov.	Dec.	Jan.	Feb.	Mar.	Apr.	May	Average
2014-15	5.87	5.30	5.34	4.82	5.04	5.43	6.21	5.56	5.19	5.07	5.02	4.87	5.31
2015-16	5.17	5.40	5.00	4.86	5.02	4.98	4.83	4.75	4.69	4.70	4.71	4.65	4.90
2016-17	4.70	4.12	3.99	3.76	3.82	3.88	3.94	4.16	4.26	4.06	3.93	4.08	4.06
2017-18	4.41	4.96	4.12	4.23	4.22	4.13	4.12	4.27	4.55	4.69	4.74	5.08	4.46
2018-19	4.92	4.98	5.32	4.81	4.88	5.01	5.24	5.20	4.97	4.46	4.43	4.57	4.90
2019-20	5.27	5.12	4.78	4.76	5.05	5.15	5.42	5.86	5.76	5.47	5.51	5.22	5.28
2020-21	5.08	5.25	5.12	5.37	5.94	5.89	5.93	6.57	6.54	6.41	6.84	7.21	6.01
2021-22	6.79	6.67	7.05	6.78	7.35	7.97	7.83	7.69	8.02	10.91	10.15	10.99	8.18
2022-23	9.69	7.71	7.63	8.31	8.34	7.95	7.58	----	7.49	6.87	6.60	6.07	7.66
2023-24[1]	6.51	6.56	5.84	5.35	5.62	5.78	6.05						5.96

[1] Preliminary.   Source: Economic Research Service, U.S. Department of Agriculture (ERS-USDA)

Average Price of No. 1 Hard Red Winter (Ordinary Protein) Wheat in Kansas City   In Dollars Per Bushel

Crop Year	June	July	Aug.	Sept.	Oct.	Nov.	Dec.	Jan.	Feb.	Mar.	Apr.	May	Average
2014-15	8.23	7.61	7.33	7.11	7.35	7.20	7.54	6.75	6.44	6.46	6.22	6.18	7.04
2015-16	6.40	6.27	5.70	5.44	5.62	5.55	5.60	5.46	5.28	5.34	5.22	5.08	5.58
2016-17	5.04	4.24	4.15	4.24	4.40	4.64	4.56	4.91	5.04	4.80	4.37	4.80	4.60
2017-18	5.24	5.65	4.80	5.07	5.11	5.30	5.38	5.73	5.93	6.05	6.09	6.56	5.58
2018-19	6.35	6.20	6.61	6.03	6.11	6.18	6.36	6.26	6.02	5.94	5.61	5.50	6.10
2019-20	6.06	5.56	5.11	5.00	5.24	5.54	5.72	5.92	6.59	5.74	5.83	5.63	5.66
2020-21	5.44	5.45	5.24	5.70	6.34	6.48	6.61	7.33	7.37	6.94	7.52	8.12	6.55
2021-22	7.42	7.20	8.07	8.05	8.56	9.56	10.52	10.03	9.91	12.35	13.81	14.50	10.00
2022-23	12.50	10.11	10.18	10.75	11.41	11.73	10.40	9.99	10.29	9.68	9.92	9.72	10.56
2023-24[1]	9.71	9.46	8.25	7.96	7.32	7.14	7.36						8.17

[1] Preliminary.   Source: Economic Research Service, U.S. Department of Agriculture (ERS-USDA)

WHEAT

Average Price Received by Farmers for All Wheat in the United States   In Dollars Per Bushel

Crop Year	June	July	Aug.	Sept.	Oct.	Nov.	Dec.	Jan.	Feb.	Mar.	Apr.	May	Average
2014-15	6.49	6.15	5.97	5.71	5.71	6.04	6.14	6.15	5.89	5.70	5.56	5.33	5.90
2015-16	5.42	5.23	4.84	4.72	4.86	4.86	4.75	4.82	4.61	4.40	4.46	4.45	4.79
2016-17	4.20	3.75	3.68	3.48	3.68	3.88	3.90	4.01	4.16	4.37	4.16	4.05	3.94
2017-18	4.37	4.77	4.84	4.65	4.64	4.72	4.50	4.65	4.92	5.10	5.28	5.39	4.82
2018-19	5.17	5.00	5.31	5.15	5.22	5.23	5.28	5.28	5.33	5.19	4.93	4.78	5.16
2019-20	4.81	4.52	4.34	4.26	4.45	4.39	4.64	4.88	4.88	4.86	4.85	4.76	4.64
2020-21	4.57	4.54	4.54	4.73	4.98	5.24	5.46	5.48	5.83	5.86	6.04	6.46	5.31
2021-22	6.23	6.26	7.14	7.75	7.92	8.52	8.59	8.48	9.16	9.93	10.20	10.90	8.42
2022-23	9.61	8.69	8.55	8.78	9.18	9.15	8.97	8.81	8.54	8.34	8.31	8.07	8.75
2023-24[1]	7.67	7.61	7.35	7.07	6.98	6.53	6.79	6.79	6.36				7.02

[1] Preliminary.   *Source: Economic Research Service, U.S. Department of Agriculture (ERS-USDA)*

Average Farm Prices of Winter Wheat in the United States   In Dollars Per Bushel

Crop Year	June	July	Aug.	Sept.	Oct.	Nov.	Dec.	Jan.	Feb.	Mar.	Apr.	May	Average
2014-15	6.34	5.99	5.90	5.69	5.65	5.87	6.14	6.02	5.70	5.55	5.50	5.19	5.80
2015-16	5.20	5.15	4.80	4.64	4.76	4.66	4.57	4.63	4.47	4.28	4.31	4.28	4.65
2016-17	3.97	3.56	3.41	3.25	3.37	3.41	3.40	3.53	3.77	3.82	3.70	3.77	3.58
2017-18	4.11	4.56	4.27	4.11	4.17	4.07	3.89	4.15	4.63	4.73	4.90	5.05	4.39
2018-19	5.05	4.92	5.24	5.14	5.22	5.20	5.24	5.25	5.40	5.16	4.86	4.74	5.12
2019-20	4.77	4.48	4.28	4.19	4.35	4.35	4.58	4.86	4.98	4.84	4.88	4.83	4.62
2020-21	4.44	4.53	4.51	4.68	4.97	5.33	5.60	5.55	5.96	6.05	6.20	6.55	5.36
2021-22	6.10	6.10	6.78	7.18	7.23	7.78	7.79	7.70	8.51	9.50	9.84	10.50	7.92
2022-23	9.16	8.34	8.43	8.72	9.09	8.91	8.47	8.33	8.37	8.25	8.07	7.67	8.48
2023-24[1]	7.32	7.46	7.09	6.71	6.43	6.10	6.20	6.29	5.80				6.60

[1] Preliminary.   *Source: Economic Research Service, U.S. Department of Agriculture (ERS-USDA)*

Average Farm Prices of Durum Wheat in the United States   In Dollars Per Bushel

Crop Year	June	July	Aug.	Sept.	Oct.	Nov.	Dec.	Jan.	Feb.	Mar.	Apr.	May	Average
2014-15	7.96	8.13	8.03	8.25	8.48	11.00	10.70	9.89	10.10	9.50	7.79	8.02	8.99
2015-16	9.16	8.74	7.28	6.36	6.57	6.97	6.93	6.60	6.08	6.03	6.24	6.57	6.96
2016-17	6.50	6.47	5.66	5.61	5.51	6.00	6.07	5.90	5.71	5.72	5.90	5.82	5.91
2017-18	6.69	6.30	6.89	6.31	6.41	6.55	6.25	6.05	6.19	5.66	5.41	6.02	6.23
2018-19	6.33	5.79	5.05	5.00	4.99	4.72	4.83	4.86	4.72	5.05	4.85	4.92	5.09
2019-20	5.58	5.53	4.67	4.64	4.54	4.17	4.44	4.72	4.96	5.46	5.26	5.27	4.94
2020-21	6.52	6.01	5.59	5.66	5.66	5.83	5.87	5.88	6.37	6.00	6.46	7.15	6.08
2021-22	7.14	7.69	9.98	13.80	14.00	14.00	12.70	14.90	15.90	15.30	15.50	14.30	12.93
2022-23	12.00	12.70	10.80	9.92	10.20	10.40	11.20	10.60	9.34	9.13	9.06	10.30	10.47
2023-24[1]	10.70	9.10	10.20	10.40	10.10	9.53	9.66	9.36	9.26				9.81

[1] Preliminary.   *Source: Economic Research Service, U.S. Department of Agriculture (ERS-USDA)*

Average Farm Prices of Other Spring Wheat in the United States   In Dollars Per Bushel

Crop Year	June	July	Aug.	Sept.	Oct.	Nov.	Dec.	Jan.	Feb.	Mar.	Apr.	May	Average
2014-15	6.60	6.23	5.93	5.51	5.57	5.73	5.80	5.84	5.55	5.53	5.51	5.29	5.76
2015-16	5.20	5.15	4.71	4.68	4.78	4.91	4.80	4.81	4.56	4.47	4.55	4.64	4.77
2016-17	4.61	4.48	4.26	4.22	4.38	4.48	4.66	4.74	4.83	4.86	4.83	4.81	4.60
2017-18	5.35	6.09	5.86	5.62	5.56	5.78	5.62	5.72	5.66	5.74	5.78	5.84	5.72
2018-19	5.66	5.41	5.41	5.16	5.26	5.33	5.36	5.37	5.30	5.23	5.03	4.86	5.28
2019-20	4.79	4.64	4.43	4.35	4.70	4.53	4.79	4.92	4.74	4.82	4.72	4.51	4.66
2020-21	4.47	4.36	4.51	4.73	4.91	5.03	5.17	5.34	5.62	5.64	5.86	6.31	5.16
2021-22	6.63	7.35	7.88	7.93	8.73	8.84	8.75	8.53	9.16	9.86	10.20	11.00	8.74
2022-23	10.90	9.96	8.72	8.80	9.13	9.24	9.11	9.05	8.69	8.33	8.40	8.24	9.05
2023-24[1]	7.97	8.21	7.62	7.02	7.22	6.85	7.10	7.04	6.66				7.30

[1] Preliminary.   *Source: Economic Research Service, U.S. Department of Agriculture (ERS-USDA)*

WHEAT, CHICAGO - CBOT
Weekly Nearest Futures as of 03/28/2024

WEEKLY NEAREST FUTURES
As of 03/28/2024
Chart High 1426.25   on 03/07/2022
Chart Low   369.50   on 08/31/2016

Nearby Futures through Last Trading Day.

Volume of Trading of Wheat Futures in Chicago   In Thousands of Contracts

Year	Jan.	Feb.	Mar.	Apr.	May	June	July	Aug.	Sept.	Oct.	Nov.	Dec.	Total
2014	1,888.8	2,681.9	2,375.1	2,605.2	2,389.1	3,028.9	2,210.8	3,064.6	1,804.6	1,793.2	2,387.5	1,962.5	28,192.3
2015	1,787.2	2,612.3	2,394.8	3,074.8	2,433.3	4,087.8	2,753.5	2,961.6	1,919.4	2,322.0	3,144.4	1,611.0	31,102.0
2016	1,820.7	3,224.7	2,084.5	3,611.5	2,355.1	3,693.2	2,353.2	3,410.3	1,457.6	2,200.7	3,270.0	1,578.1	31,059.7
2017	2,384.5	3,190.9	2,293.9	3,293.2	2,515.3	4,132.5	3,121.2	3,381.6	1,891.5	2,200.8	3,692.9	1,619.4	33,717.8
2018	2,699.7	3,731.2	3,045.3	3,473.5	3,416.5	4,219.7	2,990.5	4,177.6	2,082.6	2,407.8	3,073.7	1,486.9	36,805.2
2019	1,924.5	3,438.2	2,584.2	3,062.6	2,879.6	3,497.9	2,271.6	2,877.3	1,539.8	1,952.4	2,614.6	1,764.3	30,407.1
2020	2,524.0	3,404.0	3,342.7	2,699.6	1,870.2	3,369.4	2,600.7	3,292.5	2,253.8	2,749.4	3,199.5	2,059.6	33,365.3
2021	2,440.7	2,906.9	2,091.4	3,652.5	2,182.5	3,304.4	2,284.4	3,153.6	1,656.9	1,725.1	2,997.8	1,580.8	29,977.0
2022	1,946.1	3,141.5	2,930.8	1,788.5	1,826.2	2,581.7	1,811.1	2,374.2	1,842.9	1,797.4	2,543.6	1,371.4	25,955.4
2023	1,584.1	2,665.4	2,479.7	2,801.3	2,482.8	3,689.3	2,789.1	2,956.7	1,849.0	2,508.9	3,124.5	1,990.0	30,920.8

Contract size = 5,000 bu.   *Source: CME Group; Chicago Board of Trade (CBT)*

Average Open Interest of Wheat Futures in Chicago   In Contracts

Year	Jan.	Feb.	Mar.	Apr.	May	June	July	Aug.	Sept.	Oct.	Nov.	Dec.
2014	429,507	413,808	350,290	371,767	371,689	389,610	407,989	417,932	400,815	419,886	403,348	372,284
2015	382,618	415,559	426,147	453,404	444,906	432,352	402,961	406,381	372,538	377,775	381,822	351,546
2016	396,301	436,358	430,193	437,750	404,026	411,893	457,192	456,866	460,023	483,899	494,269	445,295
2017	473,794	458,494	463,099	508,045	445,294	441,396	430,971	452,301	433,612	486,843	551,386	521,674
2018	546,304	499,112	481,428	477,365	489,652	514,394	472,514	483,532	460,995	500,521	493,664	435,278
2019	450,353	467,963	494,051	479,684	469,294	412,885	371,636	380,149	358,914	396,981	392,793	385,505
2020	476,950	499,412	397,950	364,502	368,140	405,629	387,116	380,385	380,499	430,462	434,387	388,969
2021	434,655	438,308	419,004	430,490	411,472	394,468	341,669	385,714	361,253	391,152	412,390	358,848
2022	377,141	389,613	344,266	335,989	321,534	321,360	294,737	313,672	289,571	310,501	342,221	332,531
2023	341,377	355,992	369,617	378,246	376,438	358,558	305,098	361,840	399,848	436,634	437,818	364,904

Contract size = 5,000 bu.   *Source: CME Group; Chicago Board of Trade (CBT)*

WHEAT

Average Price of No. 1 Dark Northern Spring (13% Protein) Wheat in Minneapolis   In Dollars Per Bushel

Crop Year	June	July	Aug.	Sept.	Oct.	Nov.	Dec.	Jan.	Feb.	Mar.	Apr.	May	Average
2014-15	8.32	8.04	7.57	7.02	7.14	7.52	7.41	6.82	6.78	6.79	6.40	6.44	7.19
2015-16	6.50	6.33	5.72	5.88	6.23	6.30	5.94	5.82	5.69	5.66	5.98	5.85	5.99
2016-17	5.86	5.50	5.61	5.40	6.28	6.26	6.28	6.47	6.22	6.08	5.86	6.38	6.02
2017-18	7.26	8.24	7.43	6.84	7.07	7.16	6.94	7.10	6.91	7.24	7.28	7.35	7.24
2018-19	6.84	6.62	6.70	6.52	6.76	6.94	6.60	6.72	7.14	7.26	6.34	6.27	6.73
2019-20	6.63	6.18	5.76	6.12	6.36	6.84	6.60	6.57	6.36	6.54	6.33	5.29	6.30
2020-21	6.47	6.18	5.80	6.37	6.74	----	----	7.37	7.32	7.33	8.10	8.80	7.05
2021-22	8.59	9.65	10.47	----	11.65	11.96	11.44	----	----	----	12.60	----	10.91
2022-23	11.49	10.55	10.51	----	----	----	10.82	----	10.33	----	9.87	9.75	10.47
2023-24[1]	9.70	9.59	8.80	8.69	8.39	8.40	8.66						8.89

[1] Preliminary.   *Source: Economic Research Service, U.S. Department of Agriculture (ERS-USDA)*

Average Price of No. 1 Dark Northern Spring (14% Protein) Wheat in Minneapolis   In Dollars Per Bushel

Crop Year	June	July	Aug.	Sept.	Oct.	Nov.	Dec.	Jan.	Feb.	Mar.	Apr.	May	Average
2014-15	9.00	8.66	8.18	8.48	8.12	8.50	8.22	7.37	7.51	7.91	7.39	7.62	8.08
2015-16	7.56	7.12	6.16	6.15	6.44	6.49	6.25	6.05	5.93	5.84	6.11	6.02	6.34
2016-17	6.11	5.74	5.87	5.62	6.48	6.32	6.64	6.75	6.58	6.33	6.34	6.60	6.28
2017-18	7.66	8.64	7.64	7.18	7.36	7.66	7.40	7.41	7.68	7.58	7.57	7.66	7.62
2018-19	7.14	6.86	6.72	6.48	6.76	7.02	6.77	6.79	7.17	7.19	6.33	6.23	6.79
2019-20	6.59	6.22	5.90	6.24	6.54	6.98	6.76	5.82	6.54	6.58	6.22	6.32	6.39
2020-21	6.66	6.16	6.20	6.73	6.82	6.87	6.84	7.40	7.41	7.40	8.00	8.61	7.09
2021-22	9.01	10.16	10.40	10.20	11.09	11.55	11.78	11.08	11.20	12.23	13.23	14.40	11.36
2022-23	13.21	10.85	10.56	10.67	11.36	11.90	11.37	11.13	10.69	10.23	10.15	10.04	11.01
2023-24[1]	10.09	10.15	8.99	8.79	8.80	9.02	9.41						9.32

[1] Preliminary.   *Source: Economic Research Service, U.S. Department of Agriculture (ERS-USDA)*

Average Price of No. 2 Soft Red Winter Wheat in Toledo, OH   In Dollars Per Bushel

Crop Year	June	July	Aug.	Sept.	Oct.	Nov.	Dec.	Jan.	Feb.	Mar.	Apr.	May	Average
2014-15	5.89	5.41	4.65	3.65	5.13	5.44	6.19	5.54	4.45	5.17	5.08	4.92	5.13
2015-16	5.22	5.58	5.20	5.04	5.25	5.16	4.97	4.93	4.69	4.61	4.63	4.61	4.99
2016-17	4.69	4.22	4.03	3.72	3.90	3.92	3.80	4.09	4.28	4.14	4.08	4.19	4.09
2017-18	4.44	4.94	4.20	4.27	4.24	4.18	4.04	4.22	4.54	4.75	4.85	5.24	4.49
2018-19	5.15	5.20	5.48	5.04	5.04	5.00	5.14	5.12	4.95	4.48	4.43	4.50	4.96
2019-20	5.42	5.28	4.99	4.99	5.26	5.31	5.54	5.78	5.62	5.41	5.35	5.07	5.34
2020-21	4.95	5.28	5.14	5.43	5.93	5.79	5.95	6.50	6.47	6.32	6.71	7.09	5.96
2021-22	6.74	6.70	7.27	6.89	7.30	7.89	7.74	7.56	7.83	10.73	10.37	11.18	8.18
2022-23	9.94	7.88	7.63	8.29	8.36	7.86	7.19	7.16	7.23	6.60	6.41	5.98	7.54
2023-24[1]	6.34	6.53	5.73	5.23	5.12	5.02	5.48						5.64

[1] Preliminary.   *Source: Economic Research Service, U.S. Department of Agriculture (ERS-USDA)*

Average Price of No. 1 Soft White Wheat in Portland, OR   In Dollars Per Bushel

Crop Year	June	July	Aug.	Sept.	Oct.	Nov.	Dec.	Jan.	Feb.	Mar.	Apr.	May	Average
2013-14	----	7.23	7.32	7.17	7.27	7.04	6.97	6.78	7.20	7.55	7.65	7.65	7.26
2014-15	6.99	6.69	6.88	6.75	6.79	7.00	7.19	6.52	6.49	6.36	6.23	5.94	6.65
2015-16	----	----	5.55	5.38	5.49	5.37	----	5.31	5.30	----	5.33	5.34	5.38
2016-17	5.46	5.07	4.89	4.77	4.65	4.64	4.57	4.63	4.74	4.70	4.61	4.77	4.79
2017-18	4.91	5.40	5.13	5.19	5.30	5.26	5.22	5.30	5.39	5.64	5.63	5.79	5.35
2018-19	5.92	5.88	6.18	5.98	6.11	6.25	6.23	6.29	6.36	6.10	5.94	5.83	6.09
2019-20	5.94	5.96	5.76	5.83	5.99	5.96	5.96	6.22	6.24	6.02	6.06	5.94	5.99
2020-21	5.87	5.79	5.39	5.26	----	6.21	6.26	6.60	7.28	7.35	----	8.40	6.44
2021-22	8.44	8.36	9.90	10.69	10.43	10.83	10.79	10.78	10.88	11.44	11.00	11.26	10.40
2022-23[1]	11.09	9.29	8.85	9.37	9.11	9.01	8.63	8.36	8.47				9.13

[1] Preliminary.   *Source: Economic Research Service, U.S. Department of Agriculture (ERS-USDA)*

338

Average Producer Price Index of Wheat Flour (Spring[2])   June 1983 = 100

Crop Year	Jan.	Feb.	Mar.	Apr.	May	June	July	Aug.	Sept.	Oct.	Nov.	Dec.	Average
2014	223.3	224.9	235.6	229.5	234.8	225.5	225.7	218.8	231.5	225.3	225.6	230.5	227.6
2015	213.4	214.5	214.5	210.5	212.2	216.1	214.3	193.5	189.1	192.6	191.2	196.3	204.9
2016	194.3	192.1	193.5	193.4	195.2	195.1	186.3	183.8	183.8	187.9	186.4	186.2	189.8
2017	188.9	189.2	184.5	181.1	187.4	194.5	215.4	197.9	194.0	193.1	197.1	193.1	193.0
2018	194.8	193.0	196.0	196.4	197.0	197.9	193.3	196.5	191.8	193.1	193.8	193.5	194.8
2019	192.4	193.5	191.8	190.4	188.1	194.3	192.4	185.2	182.9	191.0	192.1	192.3	190.5
2020	195.6	193.3	192.7	193.4	191.3	192.4	192.2	189.5	191.8	193.7	196.8	196.3	193.3
2021	204.9	203.7	208.0	206.0	219.8	219.0	230.6	246.7	246.7	256.7	261.8	263.2	230.6
2022	259.5	262.7	282.6	288.9	304.2	302.8	283.5	274.4	283.4	290.7	294.2	286.0	284.4
2023[1]	283.3	285.4	269.9	274.7	278.1	265.0	265.3	258.9	260.6	256.7	255.9	260.2	267.8

[1] Preliminary.   [2] Standard patent.   *Source: Bureau of Labor Statistics, U.S. Department of Commerce (BLS) (0212-0301)*

United States Wheat Flour Exports (Grain Equivalent[2])   In Thousands of Bushels

Crop Year	June	July	Aug.	Sept.	Oct.	Nov.	Dec.	Jan.	Feb.	Mar.	Apr.	May	Total
2014-15	955	1,214	1,067	1,301	1,182	1,430	1,096	1,057	1,283	1,524	1,062	1,315	14,486
2015-16	1,222	1,225	1,208	1,431	1,466	1,491	1,521	1,457	1,085	1,685	1,303	1,467	16,562
2016-17	1,711	1,338	1,399	1,672	1,872	1,774	1,469	1,624	1,430	1,288	1,191	1,574	18,344
2017-18	1,463	1,438	1,664	915	716	873	1,072	935	1,136	1,162	1,094	1,367	13,833
2018-19	1,371	945	1,097	1,016	1,624	1,191	1,250	1,282	1,267	1,172	1,167	1,105	14,485
2019-20	1,057	1,198	1,284	1,227	1,327	1,141	993	1,142	1,163	1,265	1,291	1,168	14,255
2020-21	1,214	1,128	1,220	1,110	1,116	1,228	1,084	983	879	1,259	1,188	1,100	13,510
2021-22	1,000	959	1,055	1,054	927	1,031	1,031	933	945	1,062	1,060	1,003	12,060
2022-23	951	983	1,057	910	872	790	688	627	647	812	742	720	9,799
2023-24[1]	791	619	817	1,047	1,295	1,034	959	915					11,217

[1] Preliminary.   [2] Includes meal, groats and durum.   *Source: Economic Research Service, U.S. Department of Agriculture (ERS-USDA)*

Supply and Distribution of Wheat Flour in the United States

Year	Wheat Ground -- 1,000 Bu. --	Milfeed Production - 1,000 Tons -	Flour Production[3]	Flour & Product Imports[2]	Total Supply In 1,000 Cwt.	Exports Flour	Exports Products	Domestic Disappearance	Total Population July 1 -- Millions --	Per Capita Disappearance -- Pounds --
2014	921,264	6,423	424,949	13,859	438,808	5,303	3,664	429,841	318.5	134.9
2015	923,641	6,641	424,910	14,753	439,663	6,376	3,567	429,720	320.8	133.9
2016	914,635	6,559	423,846	15,038	438,884	7,368	2,973	428,543	323.1	132.6
2017	917,816	6,447	426,399	14,843	441,242	6,212	2,777	432,253	325.1	132.9
2018	918,373	6,458	426,871	15,552	442,423	5,693	2,723	434,008	326.9	132.8
2019	912,609	6,485	422,277	15,692	437,969	5,867	2,600	429,502	328.5	130.8
2020	917,978	6,547	425,797	19,068	444,865	5,791	3,183	435,890	331.2	131.6
2021	913,380	6,639	421,176	16,208	437,384	5,097	3,073	429,215	332.3	129.2
2022	928,615	6,732	430,284	19,653	449,937	4,486	2,963	442,488	333.5	132.7
2023[1]	677,812	4,913	314,651	18,741	438,498	3,790	2,905	431,803	335.1	128.8

[1] Preliminary.   [2] Commercial production of wheat flour, whole wheat, industrial and durum flour and farina reported by Bureau of Census.
Source: Economic Research Service, U.S. Department of Agriculture (ERS-USDA)

Wheat and Flour Price Relationships at Milling Centers in the United States   In Dollars

Crop Year	At Kansas City — Cost of Wheat to Produce 100 lb. Flour[1]	At Kansas City — Wholesale Price of Bakery Flour 100 lb. Flour[2]	At Kansas City — Wholesale Price of By-Products Obtained 100 lb. Flour[3]	At Kansas City — Total Products Actual	At Kansas City — Total Products Over Cost of Wheat	At Minneapolis — Cost of Wheat to Produce 100 lb. Flour[1]	At Minneapolis — Wholesale Price of Bakery Flour 100 lb. Flour[2]	At Minneapolis — Wholesale Price of By-Products Obtained 100 lb. Flour[3]	At Minneapolis — Total Products Actual	At Minneapolis — Total Products Over Cost of Wheat
2015-16	13.16	14.00	1.61	15.61	2.45	14.00	14.34	1.28	15.62	1.17
2016-17	12.74	13.14	1.35	14.49	1.75	14.32	14.51	.65	15.16	.84
2017-18	15.33	15.51	1.79	17.31	1.97	17.38	17.24	.73	17.96	.59
2018-19	14.41	15.40	1.96	17.37	2.96	15.57	15.28	.79	16.06	.48
2019-20	14.11	14.31	2.07	16.38	2.26	14.58	14.63	.91	15.55	.96
2020-21	15.76	15.78	2.69	18.47	2.71	16.17	15.40	1.08	16.48	.31
2021-22	24.41	23.63	3.28	26.91	2.50	24.42	23.22	1.38	24.60	.18
2022-23	24.09	22.96	3.90	26.85	2.77	25.11	23.54	3.71	27.25	2.14
2023-24	19.49	19.46	2.90	22.36	2.87	21.22	20.35	2.95	23.30	2.09
June-Aug.	20.94	21.00	2.88	23.88	2.94	22.21	21.55	2.96	24.51	2.30
Sept.-Nov.	18.03	17.92	2.91	20.83	2.80	20.22	19.15	2.94	22.09	1.87

[1] Based on 73% extraction rate, cost of 2.28 bushels: At Kansas City, No. 1 hard winter 13% protein; and at Minneapolis, No. 1 dark northern spring, 14% protein.   [2] quoted as mid-month bakers' standard patent at Kansas City and spring standard patent at Minneapolis, bulk basis.   [3] Assumed 50-50 millfeed distribution between bran and shorts or middlings, bulk basis.   *Source: Agricultural Marketing Service, U.S. Department of Agriculture*

WHEAT

Weekly Outstanding Export Sales and Cumulative Exports of U.S. Wheat   In Thousands of Metric Tons

Marketing Year 2022/2023 Week Ending	Weekly Exports	Accumu- lated Exports	Net Sales	Out- standing Sales	Marketing Year 2023/2024 Week Ending	Weekly Exports	Accumu- lated Exports	Net Sales	Out- standing Sales
Jun 02, 2022	212,022	212,022	450,955	4,346,835	Jun 01, 2023	190,122	190,122	1,112,147	3,596,086
Jun 09, 2022	370,137	582,159	236,857	4,213,555	Jun 08, 2023	249,736	439,858	164,978	3,511,328
Jun 16, 2022	336,344	918,503	477,776	4,354,987	Jun 15, 2023	155,913	595,771	109,664	3,465,079
Jun 23, 2022	241,395	1,159,898	496,719	4,610,311	Jun 22, 2023	157,591	753,362	155,167	3,462,655
Jun 30, 2022	287,056	1,446,954	286,385	4,609,640	Jun 29, 2023	306,182	1,059,544	405,763	3,562,236
Jul 07, 2022	269,985	1,716,939	1,017,156	5,356,811	Jul 06, 2023	384,871	1,444,415	395,713	3,573,078
Jul 14, 2022	141,803	1,858,742	511,086	5,726,094	Jul 13, 2023	236,232	1,680,647	170,658	3,507,504
Jul 21, 2022	345,842	2,204,584	411,989	5,792,241	Jul 20, 2023	395,132	2,075,779	233,203	3,345,575
Jul 28, 2022	288,415	2,492,999	249,923	5,753,749	Jul 27, 2023	507,403	2,583,182	421,282	3,259,454
Aug 04, 2022	615,250	3,108,249	359,165	5,497,664	Aug 03, 2023	351,804	2,934,986	567,574	3,475,224
Aug 11, 2022	349,630	3,457,879	207,152	5,355,186	Aug 10, 2023	229,410	3,164,396	359,539	3,605,353
Aug 18, 2022		3,457,879		5,355,186	Aug 17, 2023	345,141	3,509,537	405,986	3,666,198
Aug 25, 2022	1,147,211	4,605,090	999,538	5,207,513	Aug 24, 2023	353,922	3,863,459	329,141	3,641,417
Sep 01, 2022	546,611	5,151,701	192,625	4,853,527	Aug 31, 2023	316,606	4,180,065	370,341	3,695,152
Sep 08, 2022	676,767	5,828,468	217,336	4,394,096	Sep 07, 2023	411,302	4,591,367	437,850	3,721,700
Sep 15, 2022	678,196	6,506,664	183,467	3,899,367	Sep 14, 2023	296,047	4,887,414	307,704	3,733,357
Sep 22, 2022	620,679	7,127,343	279,793	3,558,481	Sep 21, 2023	584,590	5,472,004	544,539	3,693,306
Sep 29, 2022	629,766	7,757,109	229,400	3,158,115	Sep 28, 2023	387,954	5,859,958	273,139	3,578,491
Oct 06, 2022	560,497	8,317,606	211,823	2,809,441	Oct 05, 2023	342,500	6,202,458	651,964	3,887,955
Oct 13, 2022	242,584	8,560,190	163,128	2,729,985	Oct 12, 2023	385,085	6,587,543	632,759	4,135,629
Oct 20, 2022	136,762	8,696,952	533,220	3,126,443	Oct 19, 2023	131,587	6,719,130	363,696	4,367,738
Oct 27, 2022	118,125	8,815,077	348,054	3,356,372	Oct 26, 2023	100,461	6,819,591	275,556	4,542,833
Nov 03, 2022	151,524	8,966,601	322,501	3,527,349	Nov 02, 2023	134,312	6,953,903	354,298	4,762,819
Nov 10, 2022	118,572	9,085,173	290,299	3,699,076	Nov 09, 2023	310,509	7,264,412	176,296	4,628,606
Nov 17, 2022	138,382	9,223,555	511,769	4,072,463	Nov 16, 2023	298,616	7,563,028	171,753	4,501,743
Nov 24, 2022	271,230	9,494,785	155,534	3,956,767	Nov 23, 2023	340,412	7,903,440	622,803	4,784,134
Dec 01, 2022	257,445	9,752,230	189,858	3,889,180	Nov 30, 2023	198,864	8,102,304	356,412	4,941,682
Dec 08, 2022	255,918	10,008,148	468,962	4,102,224	Dec 07, 2023	289,627	8,391,931	1,490,470	6,142,525
Dec 15, 2022	235,346	10,243,494	334,207	4,201,085	Dec 14, 2023	337,379	8,729,310	322,702	6,127,848
Dec 22, 2022	337,074	10,580,568	478,122	4,342,133	Dec 21, 2023	341,982	9,071,292	276,406	6,062,272
Dec 29, 2022	81,488	10,662,056	47,142	4,307,787	Dec 28, 2023	285,877	9,357,169	131,601	5,907,996
Jan 05, 2023	193,620	10,855,676	90,803	4,204,970	Jan 04, 2024	585,638	9,942,807	128,058	5,450,416
Jan 12, 2023	308,908	11,164,584	473,124	4,369,186	Jan 11, 2024	244,889	10,187,696	707,632	5,913,159
Jan 19, 2023	264,248	11,428,832	500,429	4,605,367	Jan 18, 2024	323,097	10,510,793	451,368	6,041,430
Jan 26, 2023	496,170	11,925,002	136,383	4,245,580	Jan 25, 2024	267,126	10,777,919	322,516	6,096,820
Feb 02, 2023	538,149	12,463,151	131,389	3,838,820	Feb 01, 2024	314,729	11,092,648	378,399	6,160,490
Feb 09, 2023	500,140	12,963,291	209,847	3,548,527	Feb 08, 2024	388,769	11,481,417	332,780	6,104,501
Feb 16, 2023	338,033	13,301,324	338,828	3,549,322	Feb 15, 2024	373,056	11,854,473	233,521	5,964,966
Feb 23, 2023	610,016	13,911,340	284,115	3,223,421	Feb 22, 2024	538,728	12,393,201	327,279	5,753,517
Mar 02, 2023	377,135	14,288,475	266,685	3,112,971	Feb 29, 2024	368,272	12,761,473	271,130	5,656,375
Mar 09, 2023	250,698	14,539,173	336,672	3,198,945	Mar 07, 2024	453,502	13,214,975	83,804	5,286,677
Mar 16, 2023	361,552	14,900,725	125,568	2,962,961	Mar 14, 2024	395,885	13,610,860	-109,629	4,781,163
Mar 23, 2023	309,269	15,209,994	83,499	2,737,191	Mar 21, 2024				
Mar 30, 2023	197,739	15,407,733	193,645	2,733,097	Mar 28, 2024				
Apr 06, 2023	280,247	15,687,980	135,680	2,588,530	Apr 04, 2024				
Apr 13, 2023	202,761	15,890,741	259,039	2,644,808	Apr 11, 2024				
Apr 20, 2023	303,567	16,194,308	155,733	2,496,974	Apr 18, 2024				
Apr 27, 2023	288,903	16,483,211	211,053	2,419,124	Apr 25, 2024				
May 04, 2023	204,038	16,687,249	26,263	2,241,349	May 02, 2024				
May 11, 2023	216,622	16,903,871	-42,136	1,982,591	May 09, 2024				
May 18, 2023	386,317	17,290,188	-45,083	1,551,191	May 16, 2024				
May 25, 2023	381,052	17,671,240	-210,472	959,667	May 23, 2024				
Jun 01, 2023	87,289	17,758,529	4,981	877,359	May 30, 2024				

Source: Foreign Agricultural Service, U.S. Department of Agriculture (FAS-USDA)

Wool

Wool is light, warm, absorbs moisture, and is resistant to fire. Wool is also used for insulation in houses, for carpets and furnishing, and for bedding. Sheep are sheared once a year and produce about 4.3 kg of "greasy" wool per year.

Greasy wool is wool that has not been washed or cleaned. Wool fineness is determined by fiber diameter, which is measured in microns (one-millionth of a meter). Fine wool is softer, lightweight, and produces fine clothing. Merino sheep produce the finest wool.

Prices – Average monthly wool prices at US mills in 2023 rose by +4.2% yr/yr to $3.62 per pound. The value of US wool production in 2022 fell by -11.2% yr/yr to $33.907

million, well below the 2011 record high of $48.925 million.

Supply – World production of wool has been falling in the past decade due to the increased use of polyester fabrics. Greasy wool world production in 2022 fell by -3.0% yr/yr to 1.759 million metric tons. The world's largest producers of greasy wool in 2022 were China with 20.2% of world production, followed by Australia with 18.6%, and New Zealand with 7.2%. US wool production of 10.081 metric tons in 2022 accounted for only 0.6% of world production.

Trade – US exports of domestic wool in 2021 rose by +31.5% yr/yr to 4.970 million pounds. US imports in 2021 fell by -2.7% to 2.996 million pounds, a record low.

World Production of Wool, Greasy   In Metric Tons

Year	Argen-tina	Australia	China	Kazak-hstan	New Zealand	Pakistan	Romania	Russia	South Africa	United Kingdom	United States	Uruguay	World Total
2013	44,000	358,854	471,111	37,638	159,548	43,600	20,719	54,651	43,902	68,000	12,247	36,224	2,051,126
2014	45,988	350,546	459,564	37,779	152,480	44,100	----	56,409	45,200	67,426	12,111	35,755	2,026,704
2015	46,000	363,824	413,134	38,025	147,731	44,600	----	55,644	49,788	68,390	12,270	31,000	1,983,479
2016	42,700	354,991	411,642	38,518	153,253	45,100	----	56,006	46,297	68,791	11,816	25,672	1,977,223
2017	42,400	376,967	410,523	38,980	150,680	45,700	----	56,733	45,524	68,904	11,204	25,497	1,993,022
2018	40,424	385,945	356,608	39,166	148,467	45,043	----	55,471	45,344	69,282	11,068	26,634	1,855,867
2019	42,000	328,608	341,120	39,492	144,401	43,520	----	50,211	46,223	70,154	10,891	26,557	1,767,789
2020	40,677	283,794	333,624	40,210	140,131	43,555	----	51,660	44,870	70,939	10,489	24,720	1,732,103
2021[1]	39,742	348,608	356,216	41,199	133,752	43,490	----	47,838	44,966	71,471	10,184	23,376	1,813,492
2022[2]	37,995	328,000	356,193	41,582	126,880	43,510	----	46,037	45,063	72,010	10,081	25,600	1,759,760

[1] Preliminary.   [2] Estimate.   NA = Not avaliable.   *Source: Food and Agriculture Organization of the United Nations (FAO-UN)*

Salient Statistics of Wool in the United States

| | | | | | | | | | | ---------- Raw Wool (Clean Content) ---------- | | | | |
Year	Sheep & Lambs Shorn[4] -1,000's-	Weight per Fleece -In Lbs.-	Shorn Wool Pro-duction 1,000 Lbs.	Price per Lb.	Value of Pro-duction Support -$1,000-	Shorn Wool Payment -- Cents	Shorn Payment Rate Per Lb. --	Total Wool Pro-duction	Domestic Pro-duction	Domestic Wool Exports	Dutiable Imports for Consump-tion[3] (48's & Finer)	Total New Supply[2]	Duty Free Raw Imports (Not Finer than 46's)	Mill Consumption Apparel	Carpet
								------------------------------- In Thousands of Pounds -------------------------------							
2016	3,585	7.30	26,050	145.0	37,721	115	40.0	26,050	13,754	7,826	3,909	12,015	2,178	----	----
2017	3,435	7.20	24,810	148.0	36,774	115	40.0	24,810	13,100	11,002	3,396	7,779	2,285	----	----
2018	3,372	7.20	24,400	175.0	42,772	115	40.0	24,400	12,883	10,421	3,116	6,033	2,348	----	----
2019	3,320	7.20	24,010	189.0	45,364	115	40.0	24,010	11,294	6,895	4,790	5,439	2,714	----	----
2020	3,275	7.10	23,124	166.0	38,387	115	40.0			3,781	3,079		2,857	----	----
2021	3,195	7.00	22,451	170.0	38,177					4,970	2,996		3,683	----	----
2022	3,303	7.00	23,269	153.0	35,527									----	----
2023[1]	3,222	7.00	22,700	156.0	35,323									----	----

[1] Preliminary.   [2] Production minus exports plus imports; stocks not taken into consideration.   [3] Apparel wool includes all dutiable wool; carpet wool includes all duty-free wool.   [4] Includes sheep shorn at commercial feeding yards.
Source: Economic Research Service, U.S. Department of Agriculture (ERS-USDA)

Shorn Wool Prices   In Dollars Per Pound

	US Farm Price Shorn Wool Greasy Basis[1]	---------------- Australian Offering Price, Clean[2] ----------------						-------- Graded Territory Shorn Wool, Clean Basis[4] --------				
Year		Grade 70's type 61	Grade 64's type 63	Grade 62's type 64	Grade 60/62's type 64A	Grade 58's-56's 433-34	Market Indicator[3]	62's Staple 3"& up	60's Staple 3"& up	58's Staple 3 1/4"& up	56's Staple 3 1/4"& up	54's Staple 3 1/2"& up
	-- cents/Lb --	------------------ In Dollars Per Pound ------------------					Cents/Kg. -	------------------ In Dollars Per Pound ------------------				
2015	145.0	4.71	4.50	4.54	4.38	3.58	1,198	3.58	3.15	3.04	2.63	2.39
2016	145.0	5.19	4.89	4.98	4.79	3.69	1,293	3.94	3.22	3.21	2.43	2.36
2017	148.0	6.67	5.50	5.84	5.13	3.80	1,540	4.36	3.57	3.24	2.36	NA
2018	175.0	7.70	7.23	7.37	7.04	4.62	1,908	6.04	4.85	4.43	4.18	NA
2019	189.0	6.60	6.50	6.47	6.53	4.29	1,740	5.75	5.04	3.90	3.54	NA
2020	166.0	4.59	4.35	4.28	3.39	2.83	1,227	3.08	2.30	1.83	1.45	NA
2021	170.0	5.73	4.80	4.51	NA	2.82	1,334	3.85	3.16	NA	NA	NA
2022	153.0	5.42	4.65	4.65	4.05	2.30	1,360	3.48	2.42	2.38	NA	NA

[1] Annual weighted average.   [2] F.O.B. Australian Wool Corporation South Carolina warehouse in bond.   [3] Index of prices of all wool sold in Australia for the crop year July-June.   [4] Wool principally produced in Texas and the Rocky Mountain States.
Source: Economic Research Service, U.S. Department of Agriculture (ERS-USDA)

WOOL

WOOL
Quarterly Cash as of 03/29/2024

QUARTERLY CASH
As of 03/29/2024
Chart High 630.00 on 04/27/2018
Chart Low 58.00 on 06/25/1971

Wool, 64's, Staple, Terr. Del: to date.

Average Wool Prices¹ of Australian 64's, Type 62, Duty Paid at U.S. Mills   In Dollars Per Pound

Year	Jan.	Feb.	Mar.	Apr.	May	June	July	Aug.	Sept.	Oct.	Nov.	Dec.	Average
2014	5.18	5.06	4.86	4.92	5.04	4.98	5.02	4.86	4.79	4.71	4.68	4.56	4.89
2015	4.34	4.27	4.21	4.34	4.90	5.17	4.64	4.62	4.30	4.28	4.43	4.55	4.50
2016	4.53	4.65	4.72	4.89	4.80	4.86	5.17	5.23	5.06	4.99	4.90	4.94	4.90
2017	5.14	5.16	5.28	5.10	5.23	5.40	5.48	5.97	5.77	5.70	5.81	5.96	5.50
2018	6.60	6.86	6.85	6.92	7.26	7.95	7.67	7.70	7.47	7.23	7.08	7.17	7.23
2019	7.38	7.72	7.54	7.45	7.11	6.82	6.60	5.34	5.36	5.44	5.53	5.50	6.48
2020	5.66	5.88	4.88	4.32	4.00	4.06	3.98	3.52	3.30	3.74	4.10	4.19	4.30
2021	4.36	4.61	4.68	4.57	4.62	4.76	4.61	4.35	4.37	4.32	4.48	4.42	4.51
2022	4.57	4.60	4.54	4.50	4.47	4.70	4.53	4.31	4.14	4.01	4.04	4.40	4.40
2023	4.71	4.84	4.51	4.50	4.43	4.06	4.25	4.05	3.90	3.91	3.99	4.19	4.28

¹ Raw, clean basis.   *Source: Economic Research Service, U.S. Department of Agriculture (ERS-USDA)*

United States Imports² of Unmanufactured Wool (Clean Yield)   In Thousands of Pounds

Year	Jan.	Feb.	Mar.	Apr.	May	June	July	Aug.	Sept.	Oct.	Nov.	Dec.	Total
2014	597.6	379.1	348.3	583.8	868.5	553.2	707.7	718.8	544.0	967.5	403.5	420.5	7,092.5
2015	504.8	800.1	420.0	657.0	765.2	585.8	681.5	619.8	404.9	664.2	527.1	655.5	7,285.9
2016	564.6	321.8	600.5	942.4	514.6	746.8	419.2	229.9	330.1	300.3	488.1	568.8	6,027.1
2017	488.1	490.8	747.9	706.3	427.9	552.7	341.0	627.6	486.6	357.7	283.0	171.7	5,681.3
2018	279.8	281.0	485.3	624.8	416.8	383.4	629.0	591.4	550.5	443.1	449.3	328.9	5,463.3
2019	271.8	784.0	1,158.3	787.8	1,241.1	590.6	380.1	497.4	254.9	622.1	667.5	248.0	7,503.6
2020	623.4	299.1	933.0	650.5	281.2	291.1	296.1	368.7	963.7	483.9	397.0	348.8	5,936.5
2021	547.3	289.9	486.0	795.3	307.9	1,025.5	550.2	286.6	821.0	457.0	814.8	296.6	6,678.1
2022	444.5	325.9	424.0	590.1	609.0	860.9	521.3	514.6	335.9	491.8	473.8	613.4	6,205.2
2023¹	538.6	268.5	423.6	344.4	518.9	324.6	487.5	526.5	92.4	337.0	353.6	151.8	4,367.4

¹ Preliminary.   ² Data are imports for consumption.   *Source: Economic Research Service, U.S. Department of Agriculture (ERS-USDA)*

Zinc

Zinc (atomic symbol Zn) is a bluish-white metallic element that is the 24th most abundant element in the earth's crust. Zinc is never found in its pure state but rather in zinc oxide, zinc silicate, zinc carbonate, zinc sulfide, and also in minerals such as zincite, hemimorphite, smithsonite, franklinite, and sphalerite. Zinc is used as a protective coating for other metals, such as iron and steel, in a process known as galvanizing. Zinc is used as an alloy with copper to make brass, and also as an alloy with aluminum and magnesium. There are, however, a number of substitutes for zinc in chemicals, electronics, and pigments. For example, for aluminum, steel and plastics can substitute for galvanized aluminum sheets. Aluminum alloys can also replace brass. Zinc is used as the negative electrode in dry cell (flashlight) batteries and also in the zinc-mercuric-oxide battery cell, which is the round, flat battery typically used in watches, cameras, and other electronic devices. Zinc is also used in medicine as an antiseptic ointment.

Zinc futures and options are traded on the London Metals Exchange (LME). The LME zinc futures contract calls for the delivery of 25 metric tons of at least 99.995% purity zinc ingots (slabs and plates). The contract trades in terms of U.S. dollars per metric ton. Zinc first started trading on the LME in 1915.

Prices – Zinc prices in 2022 rose by +30.7% yr/yr to a monthly average of 191.06 cents per pound, a new record high.

Supply – World smelter production of zinc in 2021 fell by -2.9% yr/yr to 13.400 million metric tons. The world's largest producer of zinc in 2021 was China, with 47.8% of world smelter production, followed by Canada with 4.8%,

Japan with 3.9%, Spain with 3.8%, and Australia with 3.5%. China's record-high production of 6.408 million metric tons in 2021 was more than ten times its production level of 550,000 metric tons seen in 1990.

US smelter production in 2021 rose by +22.2% yr/yr to 220,000 metric tons. US mine production of recoverable zinc in 2022 rose by +4.2% yr/yr to 744,800 metric tons. US production in 2021 of slab zinc on a primary remained unchanged yr/yr at 110,000 metric tons, while secondary production rose by +57.1% yr/yr to 110,000 metric tons.

Demand – US consumption of slab zinc in 2023 fell by -0.5% yr/yr to 970,000 metric tons. US consumption of refined zinc in 2022 rose by +7.1% yr/yr to 968,800 metric tons. The breakdown of consumption by industries for 2021 showed that 86.5% of slab zinc consumption was for galvanizers, 8.4% for brass products, and the rest for other miscellaneous industries. The consumption breakdown by grades for 2021 showed that 47.7% was for re-melt and other, 31.4% was for special high grade, 18.0% was for high grade, and 2.9% was for prime western.

Trade – The US in 2023 relied on imports for 77% of its consumption of zinc, up sharply from the 35% average seen in the 1990s. US imports for consumption of slab zinc fell by -1.6% yr/yr at 750,000 metric tons in 2023. The breakdown of imports in 2022 shows that zinc is imported as blocks, pigs and slabs (762,300 metric tons); ores (4.868 metric tons); dust, powder, and flakes (208 metric tons); dross, ashes, and fume (272 metric tons); and sheets, plates, other (26,600 metric tons).

Salient Statistics of Zinc in the United States   In Metric Tons

| | Slab Zinc Production | | Mine | Imports for Consumption | | Exports | | Consumption | | | Net Import Reliance | High- |
| | ---- Production ----- | | Production | Slab | Ore (Zinc | Slab | Ore (Zinc | Slab Consumed | | | As a % of Apparent | Grade, Price |
Year	Primary	Secondary	Recovered	Zinc	Content)	Zinc	Content)	Zinc	as Ore	All Classes[3]	Consump	-Cents/Lb.-
2014	110,000	70,000	831,000	805,000	2	19,800	644,000	965,000	----	----	81	107.10
2015	124,000	48,000	825,000	771,000	----	13,000	708,000	931,000	----	----	81	95.50
2016	111,000	15,000	805,000	713,000	----	47,000	597,000	792,000	----	----	84	101.40
2017	117,000	15,000	774,000	729,000	----	33,000	682,000	829,000	----	----	84	139.30
2018	101,000	15,000	824,000	775,000	----	23,000	806,000	868,000	----	----	87	141.00
2019	99,900	15,000	753,000	830,000	----	5,000	792,000	939,000	----	----	88	124.10
2020	110,000	70,000	723,000	700,000	----	2,000	546,000	878,000	----	----	79	110.80
2021	110,000	110,000	704,000	701,000	----	13,000	644,000	908,000	----	----	76	145.80
2022[1]			761,000	762,000	----	8,000	644,000	975,000	----	----	77	190.20
2023[2]			750,000	750,000	----	5,000	730,000	970,000	----	----	77	152.00

[1] Preliminary.   [2] Estimate.   [3] Based on apparent consumption of slab zinc plus zinc content of ores and concentrates and secondary materials used to make zinc dust and chemicals.   *Source: U.S. Geological Survey (USGS)*

ZINC

World Smelter Production of Zinc[3]   In Thousands of Metric Tons

Year	Australia	Belgium	Canada	China	France	Germany	Italy	Japan	Kazak-hstan	Mexico	Spain	United States	World Total
2012	498.3	250.0	648.6	4,890.0	161.0	169.4	100.0	571.0	319.8	323.6	489.5	261.0	12,600
2013	498.3	252.0	651.6	5,310.0	152.0	166.0	267.6	587.3	320.2	322.8	490.5	233.0	13,200
2014	481.6	262.0	649.2	5,610.0	171.0	168.0	155.0	583.0	324.9	320.9	491.3	180.0	13,500
2015	489.0	260.0	683.1	5,910.0	169.0	169.0	158.2	566.6	323.8	326.6	493.8	172.0	13,700
2016	464.0	236.0	691.0	6,196.0	149.0	168.0	189.0	534.0	326.0	321.0	495.0	126.0	13,800
2017	462.0	249.0	598.0	6,144.0	166.0	174.0	186.0	524.0	331.0	327.0	500.0	132.0	13,700
2018	490.0	275.0	620.0	5,607.0	155.0	180.0	195.0	521.0	318.0	336.0	505.0	116.0	13,200
2019	436.0	270.0	655.0	6,162.0	150.0	180.0	188.0	527.0	318.0	389.0	508.0	115.0	13,600
2020[1]	447.0	270.0	682.0	6,342.0	166.0	161.0	181.0	501.0	311.0	363.0	511.0	180.0	13,800
2021[2]	463.0	270.0	641.0	6,408.0	168.0	160.0	181.0	517.0	327.0	357.0	510.0	220.0	13,400

[1] Preliminary.   [2] Estimate.   [3] Secondary metal included.   *Source: U.S. Geological Survey (USGS)*

Consumption (Reported) of Slab Zinc in the United States, by Industries and Grades   In Metric Tons

Year	Total	--- By Industries --- Galvanizers	Brass Products	Zinc-Base Alloy[3]	Zinc Oxide	Other	--- By Grades --- Special High Grade	High Grade	Remelt and Other	Prime Western
2012	806,000	685,000	49,700	44,700	----	26,500	255,000	138,000	357,455	55,300
2013	428,000	369,000	24,900	24,200	----	9,660	105,000	85,200	208,038	30,300
2014	403,000	340,000	25,600	33,000	----	4,460	101,000	97,900	182,185	21,200
2015	433,000	367,000	27,400	34,300	----	4,710	126,000	78,200	210,260	18,800
2016	462,000	397,000	26,900	34,000	----	4,190	136,000	78,200	227,337	21,100
2017	536,000	469,000	29,000	33,900	----	4,540	189,000	89,200	238,328	20,200
2018	509,000	450,000	21,100	34,000	----	4,490	187,000	93,100	210,161	19,100
2019	562,000	477,000	30,400	49,800	----	4,830	206,000	107,000	231,175	17,100
2020[1]	535,000	472,000	40,300	19,900	----	2,560	17,000	97,200	205,000	62,600
2021[2]	430,000	372,000	36,300	19,400	----	2,840	135,000	77,500	205,000	12,300

[1] Preliminary.   [2] Estimated.   [3] Die casters.   [4] Included in other.   W = Withheld.   NA = Not applicable.   *Source: U.S. Geological Survey (USGS)*

United States Foreign Trade of Zinc   In Metric Tons

Year	---- Imports for Consumption ---- Ores[3]	Blocks, Pigs, Slabs	Sheets, Plates, Other	Waste & Scrap	Dross, Ashes, Fume	Dust, Powder & Flakes	Zinc Ore & Manufactures Exported --- Blocks, Pigs, Anodes, etc. --- Un-wrought	Wrought & Alloys --- Un-wrought Alloys	Sheets, Plates & Strips	Angles, Bars, Rods, etc.	Waste & Scrap	Dust (Blue Powder)	Zinc Ore & Con-centrates
2013	2,550	713,000	3,570	21,000	13,000	24,500	11,500	23,200	6,500	8,580	87,500	10,700	670,000
2014	2	805,000	4,090	24,900	8,590	31,700	19,800	27,100	6,710	10,000	71,400	10,400	644,000
2015	22	771,000	3,680	18,000	5,610	29,100	12,700	19,700	8,010	15,400	55,200	12,300	708,000
2016	60	713,000	3,650	11,300	3,770	27,800	49,792	16,194	6,960	8,101	30,091	12,753	604,000
2017	6,780	730,000	3,690	11,100	6,350	27,100	32,700	14,500	7,670	9,110	33,600	12,800	688,000
2018	31,000	774,700	5,410	12,900	4,300	26,600	23,300	21,800	7,170	10,600	40,400	13,500	789,790
2019	10,000	829,500	19	272	1,250	12,900	21,800	10,600	8,300	7,170	179	40,400	868,500
2020	3,171,000	700,400	4,300	115,000	26,600	272	10,600	7,170	23,900	8,300	60,200	179	548,190
2021[1]	13,426,000	701,700	1,250	208	12,900	115,000	7,170	8,300	13,500	23,900	281	60,200	701,700
2022[2]	4,868,000	762,300	26,600	98,800	272	208	8,300	23,900	40,400	13,500	1,000	281	762,300

[1] Preliminary.   [2] Estimate.   [3] Zinc content.   *Source: U.S. Geological Survey (USGS)*

Mine Production of Recoverable Zinc in the United States   In Thousands of Metric Tons

Year	Jan.	Feb.	Mar.	Apr.	May	June	July	Aug.	Sept.	Oct.	Nov.	Dec.	Total
2014	67.9	67.8	70.6	69.5	63.3	61.2	64.6	65.6	66.4	63.2	71.3	75.0	803.0
2015	67.3	63.6	72.4	68.5	74.5	70.4	62.5	65.9	58.4	58.9	59.6	56.9	781.0
2016	54.3	55.9	68.6	66.8	67.1	68.9	59.0	67.1	66.0	68.6	54.2	52.6	777.0
2017	58.2	50.5	60.0	62.3	53.7	53.4	64.9	71.3	62.9	73.7	72.2	62.5	748.0
2018	63.9	55.5	51.9	65.7	69.5	74.9	74.7	68.3	70.5	79.1	56.5	77.0	807.5
2019	71.6	43.3	46.1	73.2	67.7	70.3	70.4	65.1	66.1	57.8	50.3	57.2	739.1
2020	56.0	58.8	60.1	38.2	47.0	47.6	57.9	75.0	59.9	59.9	59.5	71.5	691.4
2021	71.6	51.2	61.3	56.1	65.8	69.1	56.9	65.7	50.3	56.3	46.7	63.5	714.5
2022	49.7	60.9	69.7	65.4	63.0	64.4	71.1	75.0	62.7	54.0	45.4	63.5	744.8
2023[1]	6.6	54.1	58.1	54.5	64.1	69.1	69.4	50.1	57.5	74.0	55.1	79.7	692.3

[1] Preliminary.   *Source: U.S. Geological Survey (USGS)*

Mine Production of Zinc Content of Concentrate in the United States   In Thousands of Metric Tons

Year	Jan.	Feb.	Mar.	Apr.	May	June	July	Aug.	Sept.	Oct.	Nov.	Dec.	Total
2014	70.2	70.2	73.0	71.9	65.5	63.4	66.9	67.9	68.7	65.5	73.7	77.5	832.0
2015	69.5	65.8	74.9	70.9	76.9	72.8	64.7	68.2	60.5	60.9	61.7	58.9	808.0
2016	58.9	57.8	71.0	69.1	69.4	71.3	61.0	69.3	68.3	71.0	56.0	54.4	803.0
2017	60.1	52.2	62.1	64.3	55.6	55.2	67.0	73.8	65.0	76.2	74.7	64.6	774.0
2018	66.0	57.4	53.7	68.0	71.9	77.5	77.3	70.7	71.7	81.9	58.4	79.6	834.1
2019	74.0	44.9	47.6	75.5	69.7	71.8	72.5	67.1	68.1	59.6	51.7	58.9	761.4
2020	57.7	60.6	61.9	39.4	48.5	49.1	59.7	77.3	61.7	61.7	61.2	73.6	712.4
2021	73.8	52.3	62.6	57.3	57.3	70.6	58.2	67.2	51.5	57.6	47.7	64.9	721.0
2022	50.8	62.3	71.2	66.8	64.4	65.9	72.7	76.7	64.1	55.3	46.4	64.9	761.5
2023[1]	67.7	55.3	59.5	55.8	65.6	70.7	71.5	51.3	58.9	75.7	56.4	81.4	769.8

[1] Preliminary.   *Source: U.S. Geological Survey (USGS)*

Smelter Production of Refined Zinc in the United States   In Thousands of Metric Tons

Year	Jan.	Feb.	Mar.	Apr.	May	June	July	Aug.	Sept.	Oct.	Nov.	Dec.	Total
2014	18.3	18.0	18.0	18.0	17.1	17.1	12.1	11.0	10.5	13.6	13.8	15.7	180.0
2015	15.0	14.6	14.6	14.0	15.2	14.8	15.1	13.7	13.5	12.7	14.4	13.5	172.0
2016	----	10.6	10.6	10.6	10.6	10.6	10.6	9.6	9.6	9.6	11.3	11.3	126.0
2017	10.6	10.9	10.9	10.9	11.3	11.3	11.3	9.9	9.9	9.9	9.9	9.9	132.0
2018	11.3	6.1	11.3	10.9	10.6	10.6	11.5	9.3	8.9	9.9	9.9	9.9	120.2
2019	8.4	8.6	8.6	8.6	8.6	8.6	8.6	9.9	9.9	9.9	9.9	9.9	109.5
2020	9.9	9.9	9.9	9.9	9.9	12.0	14.0	14.0	15.0	15.0	15.0	18.0	152.5
2021	18.0	18.0	18.0	18.0	18.0	18.0	18.0	18.0	18.0	18.0	18.0	18.0	216.0
2022	18.0	18.0	18.0	18.0	18.0	18.0	8.0	18.0	18.0	18.0	18.0	18.0	206.0
2023[1]	18.0	18.0	18.0	18.0	18.0	18.0	18.0	18.0	18.0	18.0	18.0	18.0	216.0

[1] Preliminary.   Reported zinc content in both zinc and lead concentrates. Includes zinc metal used to manufacture zinc oxide.
Source: U.S. Geological Survey (USGS)

Imports of Refined Zinc in the United States   In Thousands of Metric Tons

Year	Jan.	Feb.	Mar.	Apr.	May	June	July	Aug.	Sept.	Oct.	Nov.	Dec.	Total
2014	88.7	48.5	52.1	70.4	99.9	52.4	58.7	81.8	64.1	57.6	66.3	65.8	805.0
2015	58.9	47.5	60.8	60.0	103.0	78.9	52.3	84.7	56.2	56.1	56.3	56.2	771.0
2016	54.1	52.0	54.8	53.1	85.5	51.8	61.3	58.8	64.2	60.7	62.7	53.8	713.0
2017	97.0	52.2	89.3	68.4	54.6	56.9	45.1	47.9	49.6	58.0	44.2	66.6	730.0
2018	57.4	57.2	67.2	79.9	64.5	62.6	58.6	69.0	64.4	77.4	57.2	59.3	774.7
2019	74.4	60.2	69.2	66.4	68.2	67.5	71.4	63.1	81.5	68.2	61.1	78.3	829.5
2020	69.5	50.9	73.4	64.7	61.8	46.8	66.0	56.4	46.7	59.0	54.3	50.9	700.4
2021	57.5	55.8	57.2	54.9	50.9	62.5	53.8	77.2	62.0	64.6	55.9	49.4	701.7
2022	57.5	46.7	56.0	62.8	57.6	82.6	48.3	67.7	45.4	65.9	65.8	106.0	762.3
2023[1]	99.5	74.9	69.6	61.0	49.2	4.1	63.3	49.3	48.1	46.7	42.9	46.2	654.8

[1] Preliminary.   *Source: U.S. Geological Survey (USGS)*

Exports of Refined Zinc in the United States   In Thousands of Metric Tons

Year	Jan.	Feb.	Mar.	Apr.	May	June	July	Aug.	Sept.	Oct.	Nov.	Dec.	Total
2014	1.1	4.0	0.9	1.7	1.5	0.3	0.2	0.5	2.4	8.8	0.8	2.3	19.8
2015	0.7	1.2	1.7	0.1	2.1	1.3	1.2	0.2	0.2	2.6	0.3	1.1	12.7
2016	10.5	21.4	2.3	7.1	0.5	2.0	2.1	1.0	1.1	1.3	0.4	0.2	49.8
2017	2.1	5.4	4.1	2.6	1.6	2.9	4.2	1.1	2.0	1.5	3.6	1.8	32.7
2018	1.7	0.5	0.4	0.3	3.3	4.3	1.9	2.2	1.8	1.4	2.1	3.6	23.2
2019	1.4	0.3	0.3	0.3	0.4	0.2	0.2	0.3	0.3	0.3	0.3	0.3	4.6
2020	0.5	0.2	0.4	0.2	0.1	0.1	0.2	0.1	0.1	0.3	0.2	0.2	2.5
2021	0.3	0.2	1.8	0.2	0.1	0.6	0.2	0.3	0.3	0.8	4.9	3.7	13.4
2022	2.0	2.8	0.4	0.2	0.2	0.2	0.3	1.0	0.3	0.3	0.3	0.6	8.6
2023[1]	0.3	0.4	0.1	0.1	0.6	0.1	1.9	0.1	0.2	0.1	0.1	0.1	4.0

[1] Preliminary.   *Source: U.S. Geological Survey (USGS)*

ZINC

ZINC
Quarterly Cash as of 03/28/2024

QUARTERLY CASH
As of 03/28/2024
Chart High 236.35 on 04/19/2022
Chart Low 5.54 on 02/29/1940

Special High Grade: to date.

Average Price of Zinc, Prime Western Slab (Delivered U.S. Basis)   In Cents Per Pound

Year	Jan.	Feb.	Mar.	Apr.	May	June	July	Aug.	Sept.	Oct.	Nov.	Dec.	Average
2014	101.35	101.41	100.58	101.54	102.75	105.78	113.91	114.56	112.82	112.02	111.17	107.09	107.08
2015	104.08	103.48	100.33	108.09	112.42	102.59	98.49	89.77	85.54	86.07	79.26	76.02	95.51
2016	75.65	84.61	88.64	90.59	91.48	98.21	105.64	110.08	110.30	111.42	122.23	127.26	101.34
2017	129.14	135.58	134.68	128.04	126.96	125.45	135.06	144.21	150.02	157.19	155.18	153.34	139.57
2018	164.74	169.02	157.64	153.85	147.33	149.04	129.11	122.68	119.08	129.99	126.18	127.68	141.36
2019	124.85	131.63	138.27	142.02	133.68	126.46	119.18	111.66	113.84	119.36	119.36	111.58	124.32
2020	115.12	104.53	94.90	94.38	97.53	99.89	106.60	117.67	119.37	118.98	129.02	134.63	111.05
2021	131.28	132.62	134.98	136.38	143.11	142.29	141.98	144.28	147.63	164.78	164.25	171.16	146.23
2022	183.79	187.33	204.60	228.46	205.14	206.62	178.44	201.35	179.40	171.19	169.55	176.80	191.06
2023	183.89	176.99	167.62	158.83	144.20	136.07	136.50	136.29	140.23	137.35			151.80

Source: American Metal Market (AMM)

Consumption of Refined Zinc in the United States   In Thousands of Metric Tons

Year	Jan.	Feb.	Mar.	Apr.	May	June	July	Aug.	Sept.	Oct.	Nov.	Dec.	Total
2014	106.0	62.4	69.2	86.7	116.0	69.3	70.6	92.3	72.2	62.4	79.3	79.2	965.0
2015	73.2	60.9	73.8	73.9	116.0	92.5	66.2	98.2	69.5	66.3	70.4	68.5	931.0
2016	----	41.2	63.2	56.7	95.5	60.3	69.8	67.4	72.7	68.9	73.5	64.8	789.0
2017	106.0	57.8	96.1	76.7	64.3	65.3	52.1	56.7	57.6	66.5	50.5	74.8	829.0
2018	66.9	62.9	78.0	90.5	71.8	68.9	68.3	76.1	71.6	86.0	65.1	65.6	871.7
2019	81.5	67.9	77.5	74.7	76.4	75.8	79.8	72.8	91.1	77.8	70.7	88.0	934.0
2020	79.0	60.6	82.9	74.4	71.6	58.7	79.7	70.3	61.6	73.7	69.1	68.7	850.3
2021	75.2	73.5	73.4	72.7	68.8	79.9	71.6	94.9	79.7	81.8	69.0	63.7	904.2
2022	73.5	61.9	73.6	80.5	75.4	100.0	66.0	84.8	63.1	83.6	83.4	123.0	968.8
2023[1]	117.0	92.5	87.5	78.9	66.7	62.1	79.4	67.2	65.9	64.6	60.8	64.0	906.6

[1] Preliminary.   Source: U.S. Geological Survey (USGS)